www.whitman**books**.com

© **2005 by Whitman Publishing, LLC**
3101 Clairmont Road • Suite C • Atlanta, GA 30329

THE OFFICIAL RED BOOK® and THE OFFICIAL RED BOOK OF
UNITED STATES COINS™ are trademarks of Whitman Publishing, LLC.

ISBN: 079481920-6
Printed in Canada

Q. David Bowers, of American Numismatic Rarities, LLC, in Wolfeboro, New Hampshire, has been in the rare coin business since he was a teenager in 1953. He currently serves as numismatic director of, and a writer for, Whitman Publications, LLC.

Bowers is a recipient of the Pennsylvania State University College of Business Administration's Alumni Achievement Award (1976), and has served as president of the American Numismatic Association (1983–1985) and president of the Professional Numismatists Guild (1977–1979). He is a recipient of the highest honor bestowed by the ANA (the Farran Zerbe Award); he was the first ANA member to be named Numismatist of the Year (1995); and he has been inducted into the ANA Numismatic Hall of Fame.

Bowers is also a recipient of the highest honor given by the Professional Numismatists Guild (the Founders' Award) and has received more "Book of the Year Award" and "Best Columnist" honors given by the Numismatic Literary Guild than has any other writer. In 2000, he was the first annual recipient of the Burnett Anderson Memorial Award for writing. In July 1999, Bowers was recognized as one of only 18 "Numismatists of the Century" in a poll by Ed Reiter published in *COINage*.

He is the author of more than 40 books, hundreds of auction and other catalogs, and several thousand articles, including columns in *Coin World* (now the longest-running column by any author in numismatic history), *Paper Money*, and, in past years, *The Numismatist*. Among his books on the subject at hand are *Collecting Rare Coins for Profit, High Profits From Rare Coin Investment,* and *A Buyer's Guide to the Rare Coin Market.* His past commercial affiliations have included Empire Coin Co., Bowers and Ruddy Galleries, and Bowers and Merena, as well as American International Galleries and the Mekanisk Musik Museum (in Copenhagen, Denmark).

Despite having handled a large share of major collections and just about every rarity in the book, Bowers claims, "I have never worked a day in my life. I love what I do." His prime enjoyments in numismatics are knowing "coin people," from newcomers to old-timers, and studying the endless lore and history of coins, tokens, medals, and paper money.

Credits and Acknowledgments

The author expresses appreciation to the following for help in the ways indicated:

John W. Adams made several contributions to the text and illustrations. **ANACS** provided illustrations. **Harold Anderson** encouraged the project from its inception and provided ideas and suggestions.

Dr. Richard Bagg provided proofreading and copyediting and shared his expertise and experience concerning the sale of coins at auction. **Remy Bourne** loaned catalogs for research. The **Harry W. Bass, Jr., Foundation** assisted in various ways, including granting permission to use photographs, through **David Calhoun. Andrew V. Bowers** provided proofreading and copyediting. **Wynn D. Bowers** provided proofreading and copyediting. **Kenneth E. Bressett** wrote the foreword, helped with proofreading, and made many suggestions.

Frank Campbell, librarian of the American Numismatic Society Library, helped with research requests. **Jane Colvard**, of the American Numismatic Association Library, helped with research requests and assisted in other ways.

Beth Deisher, editor of *Coin World,* has made the pages of that publication a sounding board for me for many years, through reader feedback from my column. **Thomas M. Denly** provided information concerning Confederate notes and the market for federal paper money.

Roger H. Durand furnished suggestions concerning obsolete currency and reviewed the chapter on obsolete bank notes.

John Feigenbaum of David Lawrence Rare Coins supplied illustrations. **Roberta French** assisted with correspondence, the gathering of information, and other matters during the research for and writing of the book.

David L. Ganz helped with coin-market history. **David Gladfelter** made suggestions concerning early paper money. **Rusty Goe** supplied illustrations. **Thomas S. Gordon, Sr.,** contributed a reminiscence about his uncle, Philip Gutman Straus. **Nancy Green**, of the American Numismatic Association Library, helped with research. **Barbara Gregory**, editor of *Numismatist*, provided illustrations.

Bruce Roland Hagen shared his thoughts concerning obsolete bank notes. **Heritage Galleries** provided illustrations. **Charles A. Hilton** furnished an image of a Confederate note. **Wayne Hilton** furnished images of several Confederate notes and made suggestions. **Wayne Homren** provided suggestions for the text and contributed an illustration. **Peter Huntoon** provided suggestions regarding currency and helped with several avenues of research.

Independent Coin Grading Co. provided illustrations.

Katherine Jaeger shared her enthusiasm for historical research into tokens and medals and provided suggestions for many topics throughout the book.

Christine Karstedt provided proofreading and suggestions. **Melissa Karstedt** helped with proofreading and copyediting. **Don C. Kelly** reviewed information on federal currency, including National Bank Notes, and made suggestions. **George F. Kolbe** provided suggestions regarding numismatic books and contributed a commentary. **John Kraljevich** helped with proofreading, suggestions, and historical information.

Dana Linett supplied illustrations of certain colonial currency.

Jennifer Meers provided proofreading, copyediting, and suggestions. **Cliff Mishler** contributed a recollection of his life in numismatics and also made suggestions for the general text. **Col. Bill Murray** contributed a commentary on building a numismatic library.

Eric P. Newman made suggestions and provided illustrations. **Susan Novak** was important in project coordination, correspondence, and research during the first stages of the project. **Numismatic Guaranty Corporation** provided illustrations.

Dr. Joel J. Orosz helped with proofreading and copyediting of selected chapters.

John Pack provided comments on auction consignment procedures. **Vernon R. Padgett** reviewed the text and made copyediting and proofreading suggestions. **Donn Pearlman** supplied photographs. **Doug Plasencia** provided an archive of thousands of photographs taken on behalf of American Numismatic Rarities, from which many selections were made. **Brent Pogue** helped in several ways. **Professional Coin Grading Service** provided illustrations.

Rare Coin Wholesalers provided photographs. **Fred L. Reed III** made suggestions relating to currency. **Kenneth W. Rendell** made suggestions. **P. Scott Rubin** provided proofreading and research information. **Russ Rulau** assisted with tokens and medals.

Amanda Sheheen provided information about the market for Confederate States of America paper money and provided multiple illustrations. **David E. Schenkman** provided suggestions for chapter 25. **R.M. Smythe & Co.** provided illustrations. **Lawrence Stack**, of Stack's, contributed valuations and suggestions. **Stack's** provided illustrations. **David Sundman**, of Littleton Coin Co., provided proofreading, suggestions, and many photographs.

Saul Teichman contributed suggestions and research information.

Frank Van Valen was key to proofreading and copyediting.

Robin M. Wells provided proofreading, copyediting, suggestions, and a recollection contributed to the book. **Stephanie Westover**, of Littleton Coin Co., provided photographs. **Crutch Williams** provided photographs of currency. **Wendell Wilson** of *Mineralogical Record* provided an illustration.

William Youngerman provided illustrations.

FOREWORD

by Kenneth E. Bressett
Editor,
A Guide Book of United States Coins

Interview any of the millions of people who collect coins, and every one will probably give a different reason why he or she buys them. Throughout the past 50 years I have asked hundreds of people what motivated them to buy or collect coins, and while their reasons vary, common themes emerge. In this mix of motives, many extol the beauty of coin designs, the historical aspects, the thrill of completing a particular set, pride of ownership, and the profit that sometimes comes from insightful purchases.

Coins touch every life in one way or another—they are familiar to everyone. The mystique of old coins unites us with the past in a tangible way—a nostalgic link to people, places, and events. Collecting interesting coins has been a popular pastime throughout recorded history. The challenge of acquiring something others understand and respect, but that few people actually own, is a point of pride that drives many collectors to strive to own the best, the rarest, the most unusual, or the most expensive coins available.

Collectors, however, are not the only buyers of coins—many others buy coins as gifts, as objects of art, or as investments. The motives for acquisition are diverse, but just as compelling. Each year, two to three million people regularly buy Uncirculated and Proof coins from the United States Mint. They may be serious collectors who want to fill their sets with complete runs of dates and mintmark pieces of each year, people who buy on speculation with the knowledge that future demand could lead to increased resale values for their purchases, or those who buy coins as gifts for relatives and friends. Untold numbers of modern coins have been given as gifts for decades. Some have been saved by budding collectors, many have been sold and have reentered the numismatic market, and some have very likely been spent or misplaced. Many people also save coins found in circulation, and enjoy the hobby in a rather elementary way, and will perhaps eventually become serious numismatists as they explore the many other interesting facets of the hobby.

Serious collectors who make numismatics a lifetime interest appreciate coins for their beauty, historical importance, and educational aspects. They see coins as a part of their enjoyment of the finer things in life, and have an urge to preserve these objects for future generations. They are often the educators who display, explain, teach, and pass on their knowledge for others to enjoy through books and their involvement in the hobby. For many in this group, owning coins is not their primary concern, and whether the value of their coins goes up or down is not a burning question.

Some coin buyers are investors or speculators, but they also may have some interest in both casual collecting and the serious side of numismatics. Their primary concern, however, is in buying coins that will someday rise in value and show a profit when eventually sold. They may not be professional coin dealers, but they enjoy speculating in the investment potential of coins. By far the most successful of these are the ones who understand the coin market, and who are willing to spend time selecting coins that have potential for a profitable turnover or for retention for many years in a fine collection.

Within this mix of interests, everyone wants to buy coins at an advantageous price, knowing that sometime in the future they will be worth what was paid, or perhaps show a profit. It is human nature to hope that you have made a careful and prudent investment of your time and money. Author Q. David Bowers has written this book detailing his experiences and observations in the rare coin field, sharing his views about buying coins with the purpose of achieving the best value for the money spent. But along with that, Dave adds a fullness to the collecting process by encouraging the reader to acquire a knowledge of the history, art, and economic events surrounding each series of coins, and to become knowledgeable about the life and times of the people who may have used a coin.

Whatever your particular interest in coins, there is no question that drawing on Dave Bowers's professional experience will help you become a more successful coin buyer. Even if you read no further than his "Quick Guide to Getting Started" in chapter 2, you will enhance your opportunities for success and avoid costly mistakes. But I doubt that anyone will stop reading at that point. This book, like the many others that Dave has written, is akin to spending an evening chatting with him and listening to his stories and sage advice. His style is entertaining, informative, and motivating. The profits you will accrue from reading this book will extend far beyond the monetary.

Are there really "secrets" to successful coin buying? You bet! And Dave Bowers reveals them in the pages to follow, in a way that will be helpful to everyone from the beginner to the most advanced collector or professional dealer. Not only does this book tell what to buy, it emphasizes what to avoid. The advice is not simply textbook wordage; it comes from a professional with a half century of experience as one of the most successful coin dealers and auctioneers of our time. Beyond that, Dave not only presents his personal formula for success, but recounts the stories of some of the most successful collectors he has known throughout the years, and of some of the most exceptional collections.

Among the many absorbing "firsts" presented in this book's secrets for success is a discussion about market fads, trends, and cycles in chapter 9. The coverage is exceptionally thorough and is something that I have never seen touched upon by any other author in the numismatic field. The information brought back memories of the past, and prompted thoughts about the future. Will history repeat itself? Probably so, and armed with this analysis we should all be better prepared for future trends in the coin market.

You will also enjoy reading about the trends—present, past, and future—in coin rarity, condition, demand, and grading concerns. Population reports, certification, and unsettled pricing all have their mysteries stripped away when they are fully explained herein.

This book is far more than a manual on investing in U.S. coins. The reader cannot help but benefit from the depth of Bowers's knowledge and his explanations about each of the various coin types. The information contained in this book will add immensely to the knowledge and confidence of any coin buyer and will help in forming a quality collection, as well as providing assurance that the money invested in coins is well spent.

In a thorough reading of this text I could not help but transpose Dave's principles of Optimal Collecting Grade (OCG) to my own personal interest in ancient Greek coins. Remarkably, the same principles apply. One can extend his concepts of seeking optimal condition, eye appeal, historical value, and aesthetic appreciation to any numismatic item and thus be better equipped to make wise purchases.

This is a textbook on investing in, collecting, and simply enjoying U.S. coins and related items—essentially what American numismatics is all about. To be cliché, it tells you everything you ever wanted to know about the subject, and does it in easy-to-understand language. Beyond that, it leaves the reader with a sense of empowerment for success in a field where knowledge is king.

Even a cursory reading of this book will make you a more confident buyer. A more thorough reading will surely make you an expert investor while at the same time giving you knowledge that is equal to that of some of the most experienced numismatists in our field. If I could add only one personal bit of advice, I would recommend that in selecting coins for purchase, you buy from the heart, and not simply from grading numbers or someone else's advice. If a coin appeals to you emotionally, it will likely please others when you want to sell it.

Do not close this book until you have read, absorbed, and memorized the most important words that Dave has offered: "Along the way, have a good time."

Kenneth E. Bressett
Colorado Springs, Colorado

INTRODUCTION

by the author

In a word, coins are *fun*. Some coins are rare and valuable, others are common and inexpensive. To me, all are *interesting*. Rare coins have been an integral and enjoyable part of my life. I am one of the relatively few people who embarked on a career at age 14 and, now in my 60s, enjoy it as much as ever!

Coins, tokens, medals, and paper money are fascinating to own and contemplate. There are myriad aspects of art, history, and romance to consider and enjoy, plus the pride of possession.

In this book I share my experiences and opinions on these and other aspects of numismatics. I hope to give you the inside track on techniques for successful buying, selling, and investing in rare coins, paper money, and other numismatic items. Along the way, if I were to inspire you to enjoy and profit from numismatics—called by many the world's greatest hobby—my greatest ambition will have been realized.

•

I have bought and sold some of the most legendary rarities in the rare coin field, including several examples of "the King of American Coins," the 1804 silver dollar, of which the finest known is the Childs Collection specimen, auctioned in 1999 for the then–world record price of $4,100,000. I have also written about the 1804 dollars, complete with details of how they were minted and distributed and with the biographies of nearly 200 people who have owned examples over the years as they passed from one collection to another.

I have been involved in the sale or transfer of four of the five 1913 Liberty Head nickels, rarities that have captured the public imagination. I cataloged all of the gold and most of the copper, nickel, and silver coins in the Louis E. Eliasberg Collection, and wrote a book about the man who did the impossible: acquired one of each date and mint of U.S. coins from the 1793 half cent to the 1933 double eagle. Yes, one of everything! This will never be done again, and, as a professional numismatist, my experience in handling the collection will forever remain unique. (I'll say more about Eliasberg in chapter 1.)

While great rarities are the stuff of which numismatic dreams are made, I have also cataloged my share of obscure, fascinating, and sometimes valuable (but often not) items for which information is scarce. A few years back I spent several *days* cataloging a single lot in the Virgil M. Brand Collection: a small display case containing the three different designs of the large and beautiful Washington "Seasons" medals, which were struck in England in the late 1790s (the United States Mint did not have a press large enough to make them), sent to America, and given to western agents and explorers to present to Indian chiefs. A nice supply of them went with the Lewis and Clark expedition of 1804 to 1806. By looking in out-of-print reference works, old auction catalogs, government records, and elsewhere, I pieced together the story of how and why they were made, how they were distributed, and their rarity today, presenting it as a little essay in the auction catalog.

I have spent a lot of enjoyable time immersing myself in the lore and lure of statehood quarter dollars, starting with the 1999 Delaware and continuing to the present. There has been no single place to find everything that interested me about these coins—including the identities of who designed each piece, how the coins were distributed, and more. By poking around, I have learned that some of the 2003 Maine quarters were made in *chocolate* (not officially, but on hand at the launching ceremony), and that the "Charter Oak" shown on the 1999 Connecticut quarter is the wrong tree and does not even slightly resemble the Charter Oak as recorded by history! Concerning another variety, Jay Johnson, director of the Mint when the 2003 Missouri quarter motif was completed, said, "I still remember the remark that the design looked like three men in a tub rowing between two clumps of broccoli!" I am gathering information for a book on these interesting and affordable coins of our era. Relevant to the words you are reading now is this: a complete collection of each and every date, mintmark, and special striking (Proofs in silver) of these quarters from 1999 to date, comprising dozens of different pieces, all in superb gem Mint State and Proof finish, costs just a few hundred dollars. Or at least this was the case until January 2005, when two intriguing varieties of 2004-D Wisconsin quarters—"extra leaf high" and "extra leaf low"—were publicized. How these curious pieces were made—a bit of mischief by someone at the Mint with access to dies?—is a question unanswered as this book goes to press. In the meantime, the varieties have captured a lot of ink in the numismatic press. In numismatics, there is always something new—the fascination is never-ending.

The hobby and pastime of numismatics—some call it an *industry*—is one of contrasts. I suppose in my own life it is interesting that I wrote a book about the legendary 1804 dollar worth millions, but that now I am every bit as excited as I continue research on modern state quarters, most of which can be found in pocket change!

•

Every once in a while a reader of one of my books or my "Joys of Collecting" column in *Coin World* will suggest that I stop discussing coins, tokens, medals, and paper money in general, and concentrate on the memorable experiences I have had as a rare coin dealer. "If Ted Williams had been a writer, he would have featured the Red Sox, the players, and managers, and competitors in the sport, and he would not have told readers how to enjoy watching or playing the game!"

I responded that my *Coin World* column simply represented what I found interesting and significant about rare coins and related items and was not an "infomercial" for my business interests. Similarly, in this book I have emphasized the *collecting* aspect of numismatics as being the key to *successful investing*—how to play and, hopefully, win the numismatic game. However, I also discuss my professional activities, for they are closely intertwined, including my position with American Numismatic Rarities and the fine people there. In the past, eminent dealers Abe Kosoff and Hans M.F. Schulman, to mention just two, devoted the vast majority of their writing to their own businesses and their relationships with buyers and sellers.

I guess I am a collector first and foremost, although being a professional has paid my way through numismatic life and has introduced me to many wonderful people and experiences. In the 1970s I wrote a monograph for *Coin World* under the title *How to Be a Successful Rare Coin Dealer*, which went through three editions. Today the information would be about as current as the Dead Sea scrolls—for back then we had no numerical grading (except for early copper cents), no "slabs," no Internet, and none of the many other "improvements" that are now part of the hobby. Perhaps I should write a new version sometime! In the present book you will see that numismatics is ever-changing. The hobby today is far different from what it was a few decades ago. Probably, years from now it will have still other aspects.

•

It is never too early or too late to discover coins and the other delights that make up the world of collecting. If you are a preteen, welcome! Similarly, if you are in retirement, welcome! Numismatics knows no restrictions of age, race, religion, politics, or anything else.

Clarence S. Bement, of Philadelphia, was not introduced to the joys of numismatics until he was more than 70 years old. He still had ample time to read about coins, carefully acquire pieces in the fashion of a true connoisseur, and enjoy what he owned. Later, in May 1916, his holdings were auctioned by Henry Chapman via the *Catalogue of the Collection of American Colonial and State Coins and Foreign*

Crowns, the Property of Clarence Bement, Esq. Today, in the pantheon of American numismatics Bement is remembered as a great figure.

While septuagenarian Clarence S. Bement enjoyed his coins, it could well be that a typical third-grader at the Carpenter School here in Wolfeboro finds it just as thrilling when Frank Van Valen in one of his talks to school kids shows them a strange Mercury dime or Indian Head cent.

More than a few youngsters have been bitten by the "coin bug" (more about this insect later, in chapter 3!) and have spent all of their lives immersed in the hobby. It seems that once bitten, at age 7 or age 70, there is no cure!

•

How should I start collecting? Ask five people this question, and you'll get five different answers. There is no right or wrong way. However, no matter what you choose to do, if you are a smart buyer you will do better than if you are not informed. Helping you to be a smart buyer is the main thrust of this book.

To best savor all that numismatics has to offer, take your time and enjoy the experience. Buy your coins carefully, contemplating each one. Some pieces you can buy rather quickly—such as those statehood quarters in Proof or Mint State. Others will take some time, such as early copper cents or Capped Bust half dollars—fields in which grading interpretations, eye appeal, and market prices can vary widely. The same care is needed to buy tokens, medals, and paper money. Enjoy the challenge, the stimulation. These are great advantages. Without them, a generous measure of enjoyment would be lost.

Perhaps it is like a person who one day buys a pound of salmon at the grocery store, but another time spends a day among mosquitoes, in wading boots in a cold mountain stream, fly fishing for trout. Both fish weigh the same and both end up on the dinner table, but how they got there is vastly different.

As I write these words I have in front of me some copy I wrote a few years ago for my "Joys of Collecting" column in *Coin World:*

> I recall that a few years ago a wealthy man from the Midwest had begun collecting, and within a week or two he subscribed to our catalogs. He then telephoned to say that, for starters, he wanted to build a complete set of Proof $20 gold coins from 1858 to 1915, and what did we have in stock?
>
> I replied that we either had none or perhaps one or two at most, and that it would take 10 to 20 years to put together such a set. At least that is what it took Harry W. Bass, Jr., and Ed Trompeter, and even then they did not achieve absolute completion. The man expressed some mild displeasure at the inadequacy of our inventory, and said that there were plenty of other dealers who would fill his set if we could not!
>
> A month later we obtained a lovely gem Proof 1884 double eagle, one of the most prized dates from its era, and we contacted him about it.
>
> "I am no longer collecting coins," he said. "No one had what I wanted."

In the same article I went on to say:

> Just stop and think of this: if when you played golf you could get a perfect score of 18 each time, or when you worked a crossword puzzle you could perfect it in 10 minutes, or when you were dealt a hand of cards you always got four aces, *you would leave these pursuits immediately.* There would be no challenge!

If anything can be gained from the preceding it is this: start slowly, and look forward to a *challenge.* This will keep you interested and stimulated—perhaps from now through the rest of your life!

You may or may not be a crossword puzzle fan. If you are, you will understand that the greater the challenge, *up to a point,* the more interesting a puzzle can be. Ever since I was in high school I've tried to work the Sunday crossword in the *New York Times,* currently edited by Will Shortz (who loves the game, and who is also prominent on National Public Radio). The *Times* also has a daily puzzle, Monday through Saturday. Shortz has scaled these in terms of difficulty, with Monday being easy and Saturday being, well, the puzzle from hell (as someone has said). I love the Saturday puzzle, and, with my wife Christie, complete it about half to two-thirds of the time, and come close on the remainder.

Esoteric clues can be delightful, especially if "punny," such as the following (paraphrased, as I did not write down the exact words):

Clue: Royal challenge.
Answer: PEA (from the princess and the pea story)

Clue: Vendor recognized animal in basement.
Answer: SELLER KNEW CELLAR GNU

Clue: It turns into a different story.
Answer: SPIRAL STAIRCASE

You get the idea!

At the same time, it is nice to have some easy clues among the obscure ones. Similarly, in numismatics you can easily collect Susan B. Anthony dollars ("Susies") or state quarters, but get set for a challenge if you try colonials and early federal issues. Each is a part of the coin-collecting game.

•

Does it take a large budget to be a coin collector? This is, as they say on the Internet, an FAQ, or frequently asked question.

Although it is nice to have a large budget for buying, a well-endowed banking account is not at all necessary to enjoy numismatics. I have had just as much fun collecting the aforementioned state quarters—total budget a few hundred dollars—as if I had been the buyer of the $4,140,000 Childs Collection 1804 silver dollar that I auctioned in 1999. Actually, I could not have bought it for that, for

the winner might have kept going and going—to an even higher amount. The buyer, by the way, enjoys his coin immensely, but by necessity must keep it in a bank vault. He is also a fine friend. In my home is a pet cat, given to us when she was a kitten, from this collector's ranch out West. Why do I mention this? Simply because while coins are coins, *people* are always involved, and part of numismatics is getting to know and enjoy others in the hobby.

Over a long period of time, most of my customers have had modest to medium budgets—from a thousand or so dollars per year to, perhaps, a few tens of thousands. There have been many exceptions both ways. The numismatist with a modest budget but a generous measure of enthusiasm is the foundation of the hobby.

•

Will I ever become an expert on all coins? Another FAQ.

In theory, it would be nice to know *everything* about collecting coins, tokens, medals, and paper money. However, no one has ever achieved this. This is the way it should be. Probably, no one on earth knows everything about banking in the 19th century, or insects native to Trinidad, or the evolution of the automobile, or the life of Elvis Presley. So there!

For starters, certain aspects of numismatics defy definition and are largely a matter of opinion. These include even such important things as grade, rarity, and price!

Books have been written on each of these subjects, and yet not everyone shares the same conclusions. The situation is not unlike that of reading case studies in law, the annals of psychiatry, or journals of economics, foreign policy, or ecology: highly educated people have contributed to the body of literature, and yet the state of the art and interpretations change, sometimes rapidly. I've enjoyed studying American financial and economic history. If there is one rule I have learned, it is this: there are no rules. Each situation is different, as is each era, each market.

There are, of course, many *facts* to go along with the subjective and quintessential appeals of numismatics. We know that 625 Proof quarter dollars were minted in 1867. A fact. We know that W. Elliot Woodward, who quickly grew in prominence and respect as a cataloger and dealer of rare coins, had his first auction sale on June 27, 1860. Another fact. We know that Glenna Goodacre designed the 2000 Sacagawea "golden dollar." More facts: 1932 was the first year that Washington quarter dollars were made. Mintages were as follows: 5,404,000 (Philadelphia Mint), 436,000 (Denver Mint), and 408,000 (San Francisco Mint).

For every fact in numismatics, there are lots of estimates, guesses, and conjectures. Even when facts are known, they do not intuitively relate to coin price, rarity, or availability. As an example: although by all reasoning a Mint State or nice-as-new 1932-D Washington quarter, with its mintage of 436,000, should today be slightly more readily available than a similar 1932-S, of which 408,000 were coined, this is not so. In my professional experience, the higher-mintage 1932-D is at least 5 to 10 times rarer!

More: although at the Philadelphia Mint more than 1,000 varieties of pattern coins were made in the 19th century, precise information as to mintage, present-day rarity, and the reason they were made is absent for at least half of these varieties—leaving numismatists to come up with theories and estimates.

In a more popular vein, pick any year from the late 19th or early 20th century. 1880? 1900? 1916? Today, no one knows what the distribution of coins and paper money was in a typical cash drawer of a bank or department store! What was once everyone's knowledge is now no one's. If, in 1900, in Wanamaker's department store in Philadelphia, someone surveyed $100 in a cash register, that person may or may not have seen some gold coins. How many Indian Head cents might have been on hand? Among paper money, how many Silver Certificates or Coin Notes were there? If there were National Bank Notes, where were they from? Were there 20 silver dollars, or 6, or none?

As you approach numismatics, you can be thankful for so many unknowns. There are enough to keep you stimulated for a long time, perhaps forever!

•

In this book I relate my own thoughts, opinions, and experiences about different aspects of numismatics. I leave it up to you to come to your own conclusions, drawing upon other sources as well. This book may serve in a way as your coin-collecting "university," but after you get your degree (by reading it all the way through), you will learn more from your subsequent real-life experiences.

Reading is far and away the best avenue to knowledge. In 1979, I wrote a book, *The History of United States Coinage*, for The Johns Hopkins University. I endeavored to describe how coins were made and also how they were collected. One reviewer called reading it "equal to a university course in numismatics." Jim Halperin, who at that time headed the New England Rare Coin Co. (now, he is a principal in the highly successful Heritage firm), gave new employees a copy of that book and said, "Read it!" There was no better way, he told me, to have would-be coin dealers learn about the field they were about to enter. Col. Bill Murray, perhaps the most prolific book reviewer in the hobby, picked this as an ideal companion on the proverbial desert island.

No two numismatists have ever collected exactly the same things, nor have they had the same experiences. The field is so vast, so interesting, and with so many things subject to opinion, that the challenges are never ending, and there is always something else stimulating to learn about or aspire to own, or even to catch in your collecting net.

After leaving the White House in 1909, President Theodore Roosevelt took a hunting trip into the African jungle. His exciting adventures were captured on film and shown in "nickelodeon" theaters around the country. Decades later, Ernest Hemingway went into Africa to seek trophy animals, then wrote about his experiences, thrilling readers all over the world. Neither person ever saw more than a fraction of Africa, and for every lion or elephant shot, thousands of others were unseen.

Today, if the president of the United States shot and killed an elephant, there would probably be great protests, not at all what Roosevelt experienced. The sport of hunting has changed over the years, as has most everything else—including numismatics. In the pages to follow you will read of constant evolution in our hobby. The scenario today, early in the 21st century, is not at all like it was in the 1980s, an era that in turn was dramatically different from when I first started collecting, in the 1950s. We can only imagine the excitement that W. Elliot Woodward experienced when he had his first sale in 1860. Whatever it was, a momentum was established, and for the rest of his life, into the 1890s, his life was richer for his involvement.

In 1860, in the 1950s, in the 1980s, and today—numismatics equals enjoyment!

•

This book is not theoretical, not even slightly. Instead, it is based upon my experience, dating back to my early teenage years when I first called myself a rare coin dealer. I have "been there, done that," and along the way I have helped form some of the finest collections in American numismatics. I have also sold many of them. To my knowledge, each and every one of my customers who bought carefully and with a plan in mind, and who held the coins for 10 years or more, has done very well on the investment.

This statement has never been challenged: collectors who buy carefully always realize better long-term profits than do investors who simply buy what they are told is "hot," but do not learn about coins.

Whether you build a landmark collection or gather selected interesting sets and series, I hope these pages will inspire and enlighten you. Read every chapter, and I believe you will be as informed on the ins and outs of the market as are many leading rare-coin professionals.

I would like for you, *as a collector*, to become a smart buyer, to evaluate coins in the marketplace and to recognize features and potential often overlooked by others. Make your purchases carefully and with a plan in mind, think of the long term, and if numismatics continues the course it has followed for many generations, your rare coin collection may prove to be one of the most profitable investments you've ever made! The wide world of numismatics beckons to you.

The icing on the cake is that while smart buying of coins is a worthy challenge, and the potential of their being a great financial investment is an incentive, you will also have a great investment in the pleasure of being a numismatist.

Enjoy!

Q. David Bowers
Wolfeboro, New Hampshire

LIST OF ABBREVIATIONS

ABNCo	American Bank Note Co.
AG	About Good
AJN	*American Journal of Numismatics*
ANACS	Formerly stood for "American Numismatic Association Certification Service"
ANR	American Numismatic Rarities
AU	About Uncirculated
BG	Breen-Gillio
BN	brown
C	Charlotte, North Carolina (mintmark)
C4	Colonial Coin Collectors Club
CAA	Currency Auctions of America
CC	Carson City (mintmark)
CGC	Comics Guaranty, LLC
CSNS	Central States Numismatic Society
D	Dahlonega, Georgia (mintmark; gold coins only, 1838–1861)
D	Denver, Colorado (mintmark; 1906 to date)
DLRC	David Lawrence Rare Coins
EAC	Early American Coppers Club
EF	Extremely Fine
EG	Elisha Gallaudet (most likely)
ESNA	Empire State Numismatic Association
FB	Full Bands
FBL	Full Bell Lines
FD	Full Details
FH	Full Head
FT	Full Torch
FUN	Florida United Numismatists
G	Good
IAPN	International Association of Professional Numismatists
ICG	Independent Coin Grading Company

MACO	Medallic Art Company
MANA	Middle Atlantic Numismatic Association
MPC	military payment certificate
MS	Mint State
NASC	Numismatic Association of Southern California
NCS	Numismatic Conservation Services
NE	New England
NENA	New England Numismatic Association
NGC	Numismatic Guaranty Corporation
O	New Orleans (mintmark)
OCG	Optimal Collecting Grade
P	Philadelphia (mintmark)
PCDA	Professional Currency Dealers Association
PCGS	Professional Coin Grading Service
PMG	Paper Money Guaranty
PNG	Professional Numismatists Guild
PSSP	Patent Stereotype Steel Plate
RARCOA	Rare Coin Company of America
RB	red and brown
RD	red
S	San Francisco (mintmark)
SPMC	Society of Paper Money Collectors
SUSCC	Society for U.S. Commemorative Coins
TNA	Texas Numismatic Association
Unc	Uncirculated
V.D.B.	Victor David Brenner
VF	Very Fine
VG	Very Good
W	West Point, New York (mintmark)

Discover the World of Money

As a Member of the AMERICAN NUMISMATIC ASSOCIATION

The American Numismatic Association — a non-profit, educational organization — encourages people to study and collect money and related items. From beginner to expert, celebrity to financier, individuals with common interests and unique resources **connect** at the ANA.

1 YEAR OF MEMBERSHIP MEANS BIG REWARDS.

- **12** issues of *Numismatist* magazine delivered to your door.
- Mediation and consumer advocate **assistance**.
- Members-only **discounts**.

MEMBERSHIP

- ○ One-Year Regular, $36
- ○ Two-Year Regular, $70
- ○ One-Year Senior, $31 *(65 and older)*
- ○ Two-Year Senior, $60 *(65 and older)*

Yes! Please make me a member of America's premiere numismatic association.

NAME: _____ DATE OF BIRTH: _____
(For senior discount)

ADDRESS: _____ CITY: _____ STATE: ___ ZIP: ___

PHONE: _____ E-MAIL: _____

Please accept my application for membership in the ANA, subject to the bylaws of the Association. I also agree to abide by the Code of Ethics adopted by the Association.
○ Periodically, the ANA's mailing list is sold or provided to third parties. If you do not want your information provided for non-ANA-related mailings, please check here.

PLEASE CHARGE MY: ○ Visa ○ Mastercard ○ AmEx ○ Discover

Card Number: _____ Exp. Date: _____

Cardholder Signature: _____

OR Send Check, payable to:
American Numismatic Association
818 N. Cascade Ave.
Colorado Springs, CO 80903

800-367-9723 • www.money.org

Join online at www.money.org!

WHB

CHAPTER ONE

RARE COINS:
A Great Investment

The majority of coin collectors commence their cabinets with the single thought of finding amusement, and view collecting merely as a pastime, interesting and fascinating, but with no more substantial value than to employ agreeably a few idle hours. The acquisition accidentally or otherwise, of one or more coins or medals, which are at the time unknown and strange to them and therefore arouse their curiosity, engenders a desire to possess other specimens with similar attributes—and thus they become collectors.

—Virgil M. Brand, May 1905

Do It for the Money

Investment Success

Quite a few coin collectors are in it for the money—pun intended. While they enjoy buying rare coins and related items, their primary interest (another pun) is a financial return on their investment. Indeed, over the years many buyers have done exceedingly well in this regard. Accordingly, this is the ideal topic to begin this book. Hopefully, it will capture your interest and attention, so that *later* you will become fascinated with some of the less obvious, but equally worthwhile, aspects of numismatics.

I had the pleasure of knowing Louis E. Eliasberg, Sr., the Baltimore numismatist who, from 1925 to 1950, set about building a fine collection, eventually changing his goal to the ultimate: to obtain one of each date and mint and major type of United States coin ever struck—as I mentioned in the introduction. By 1950 he had accomplished what many thought was impossible—and owned everything from a 1793 copper half cent to a 1933 gold double eagle.

In the summer of 1975, I was Eliasberg's guest for a week in Baltimore, reviewing his collection and discussing aspects of it with him. Later, after his passing (in 1976), his two sons, Louis, Jr., and Richard, who had inherited the incredible collection, asked me to make proposals to present the coins at auction. I did, and the rest is numismatic history. The collection that had cost Eliasberg less than $400,000 realized more than $40,000,000! The latter figure does not even include the extra millions realized when the Eliasberg gold coins of the world (other than the United States) were auctioned by American Numismatic Rarities (ANR) in 2005. I was as proud as can be to see the sale cataloged mostly by staffers John Kraljevich, Frank Van Valen, and John Pack, world-recognized experts today who were not even born in 1953, when I first started in the coin profession. Again, the hobby evolves, and this is part of what makes it dynamic.

Although Louis E. Eliasberg was best known for the collection he built, and often shared his love of the hobby with others (exhibiting it in many places, including at banks and even at the Philadelphia Mint), he was also a consummate student of American financial history. If asked, he could have stood on a proverbial soapbox and regaled his listeners with stories of coins and paper money and how they were used over the years. I must mention that one of the venues for the coin exhibit was the Smithsonian Institution, where it was shown for just four months and attracted 1,500,000 viewers! That's right: one and a half million! Pardon a slight digression, but more recently, in 2003, Dwight Manley and his partners set up a display in California of the gold coins and ingots recovered from the fabulous *S.S. Central America* treasure (lost at sea in 1857 and recovered in the late 20th century), and an estimated 700,000 people came to see it. Coins can attract a lot of attention!

On November 9, 1975, Louis E. Eliasberg, Sr., addressed a group of numismatists and others at the Evergreen House, a mansion on North Charles Street, Baltimore. Now the property of The Johns Hopkins University, generations earlier it had been the home of T. Harrison Garrett and, later, his son John Work Garrett and his wife. The Garretts formed the greatest of all early coin collections—and by 1888, that of T. Harrison Garrett (which I and staff members had the opportunity to catalog and present at auction from 1979 to 1981) was the finest in private hands in America. It is interesting how persons, places, and things can weave together.

Eliasberg's 1975 talk was titled "Why, When, and How I Assembled the Most Complete Collection of United States Coins." Excerpts:[1]

> If you are a numismatist or coin collector, I hope you will derive the degree of pleasure and happiness I have in assembling *my* collection.
>
> In making your purchases you should buy them through reputable dealers. If you invest any significant portion of your assets in rare coins, be sure that you are thoroughly familiar with all aspects of such an operation.

Aha! Mr. Eliasberg's comment, "be sure that you are thoroughly familiar with all aspects of such an operation," is exactly what the present book is all about!

More from 1975:

> The profitability of collecting coins can be measured in part by my own experience.... Based on our recent [1975] appraisal I find that I have averaged a minimum return of over 11.9% a year on the original cost.

Koshkarian, Bareford, and Pittman

Lest you think that the Eliasberg investment success is unique, I hasten to say that among old-time collections it isn't even *unusual!* Handsome returns have been the rule, not the exception. So far as I know, each and every old-time collection for which my associates and I have prepared catalogs, sold at auction, or purchased outright has shown a great profit. This experience ranges from years ago, when I had the Bowers Coin Company and, with Jim Ruddy, the Empire Coin Company, evolving down to the present—as with the relatively recent ANR sale of the Dr. Haig Koshkarian Collection. A fine collection does not necessarily have to be "old time" to do well at auction in a strong market— witness the spectacular sale by ANR of the Oliver Jung Collection in 2004, a cabinet formed beginning in 1997.

The highlight in the Koshkarian holding was a superb gem 1797 half dollar that I had enjoyed cataloging in 1988 as part of the Norweb Collection (another great American holding). At the Norweb sale, Dr. Koshkarian was present and bought this coin, and I congratulated him on his purchase—which cost $220,000, a world record at the time. In 2004, I had the privilege cataloging it again, for ANR, and of seeing it sell for a new record of $966,000. There was an enthusiastic round of applause at the sale as it went to the Southern gentleman who was its next owner.

While I have had my share, or even more than my share, of great collections and rarities over the years, many other professional numismatists have also achieved success for their clients. As I write these words I am reminded of Harold S. Bareford, who began collecting coins in 1947 and who continued until 1954, spending exactly $13,832 in the process. In the meantime he practiced law and, among other activities in his profession, was general counsel for Warner Bros., the entertainment company. His collection was later sold by Stack's in a series of four sales, 1978 to 1985, and realized $1,207,215, or nearly 100 times its cost! Today, if the same coins were sold you could probably move the decimal point one space to the right and get $12 million. John J. Ford, Jr., a longtime coin dealer but never a wealthy man in terms of conspicuous expenditures, devoted much of his life to his collection of coins, tokens, medals, and paper money. In a series of sales not yet complete, Stack's has garnered tens of millions of dollars from the items offered.

John J. Pittman, an employee (not an executive) of the Eastman Kodak Company in Rochester, New York, collected coins from the 1940s until his death in 1996. He was not a wealthy man, either, and in one instance he took a second mortgage on his modest home to pay for some coins at a major auction sale. His financial investment over a long period of years was likely in the hundreds of thousands of dollars, not the millions, and some of that amount was gained by selling and trading duplicates. When his collection was cataloged and auctioned by David W. Akers, the realization was about $30,000,000.

More often, that scenario is repeated on a lesser scale. A collector spends several tens of thousands of dollars building a collection and realizes several hundreds of thousands of dollars when it is sold.

The Case of the 1895 Morgan Dollar

Today, Morgan silver dollars of the 1878 to 1921 era are the most widely collected coins of the late 19th and early 20th centuries. Over a long span of years, such coins have been excellent investments for thousands of collectors who have enjoyed putting sets together.

Although it is not the most valuable Morgan dollar in higher grades, the rarest is the 1895 Philadelphia issue, of which just 880 were made, all in mirror-field Proof format, from specially polished dies. These were sold to collectors at the time. Today, perhaps 600 to 700 or so exist. It is a nice example of rare-coin investment success.

My first encounter with a Proof 1895, or actually the specter of one, was in 1953, when an early mentor of mine in the hobby, George P. Williams, sold me a few coins, but stated that he no longer had an 1895 dollar. "Joe Stack came through town, stopped by, and offered me $200 for it—and I took it," he said. Today a superb gem is worth $65,000!

1895 Proof Morgan Silver Dollar

In 1989 I updated my popular 1974 work, *High Profits From Rare Coin Investment* (now out of print). I gave the market prices of this coin at five-year intervals, to 1989 (to that data I've added the aforementioned $65,000 for a gem today):

The gem 1797 half dollar, in superb Mint State, was a highlight in the collection of Ambassador and Mrs. R. Henry Norweb. In 1988, when the Norweb Collection crossed the auction block, the buyer was Dr. Haig A. Koshkarian, at $220,000. In 2004, when the Koshkarian Collection was sold, the same coin realized $996,000. At present it resides in a fine southern cabinet.

Among Morgan-design silver dollars (minted from 1878 to 1921) the 1895 is an icon. At the Philadelphia Mint that year, only 880 Proofs were struck, with no accompanying pieces for circulation. Today it is estimated that 600 to 700 survive.

1948: $80 • 1953: $200 (which is what George Williams sold his coin for—full market price at the time) •1958: $650 • 1963: $2,500 • 1968: $4,750 • 1973: $6,000 • 1978: $9,000 • 1983: $25,000 • 1989: $20,000 (a six-year jump to coincide with the date of the book; notice the price had slipped slightly from 1983, reflecting that coins do not always go up; sometimes they go down) • 2005: $65,000 (*Coin Values*, published by *Coin World*).

By calculation, this coin had increased in price by 24,900% from 1948 to 1989! Today the return, valuing the coin at $65,000, is far more than double that.

In the case of the 1895 dollar, or any other coin I mention in this book, the opportunities have been available to one and all. You did not have to have special knowledge or be an "insider" to buy them. Over the years I've probably bought and sold Proof 1895 dollars on several hundred occasions, including quite a few reofferings of the same coins. Anyone could have bought one from me in the 1950s or the 1960s, or can buy one now. The inventories and auction offerings of other firms have included many gem Proof 1895 Morgan dollars as well.

One more thing is worth mentioning: The above is what a connoisseur would realize if he or she had bought a gem 1895. However, if a buyer had been hunting bargains back in 1948, no doubt a scuffed-up Proof could have been bought at a discount, say just $50 instead of $80. Today, such a coin would not command the $65,000 market price of a gem, but would be worth about half that price.

The Case of the 1833 Half Dollar

The 1895 Morgan silver dollar is quite rare. Contrasting this is a choice (MS-63 or so) half dollar of 1833, one of the most common dates of the 1807 to 1836 Capped Bust design. Historical market prices were given in my 1989 book, by which time this coin showed an investment return of

20,567%. Today, the *Guide Book of United States Coins* (in print since 1946, and America's best-selling book on prices) lists such a coin at $1,400, nearly doubling this spectacular figure!

Years ago, most collectors were not concerned with quality, and it was often the case that choice and gem coins could be acquired for little (if any) more than a typical example would cost.

However, a connoisseur who in 1949 bought a *gem* half dollar with good eye appeal (which today would grade MS-65 or finer) would have a coin worth on the long side of $4,000! Think of it—if, in 1983, you had bought 10 gem coins of this and other common Capped Bust half dollar dates, perhaps a small collection of 10 different for $500 each, today your investment of $5,000 would cost $40,000 to replace!

Capped Bust half dollars of the type minted from 1807 to 1836 in grades from MS-63 to MS-65 are plentiful, and over the years I have bought, sold, and auctioned thousands of them. Again, you did not have to have special connections or an inside track to buy them.

This lovely 1833 Capped Bust half dollar, die variety Overton-109, was auctioned in 2005 in the Jewell Collection sale and described as "MS-63 (NGC). Lustrous deep golden gray with a wealth of rose, gold, and blue iridescent highlights. Nicely struck." Among Capped Bust half dollars of the 1807 to 1836 design, the 1833 is one of the dates most often encountered. Over a long period of time, such coins have steadily increased in value.

1948 value: $4 • 1953: $5 • 1958: $10 • 1963: $20 • 1968: $60 • 1973: $200 • 1978: $450 • 1983: $500 • 1989: $775 • 2005: $1,400 (from the current *Guide Book*).

Of course, the performance of the past is not a guarantee or even necessarily an indicator of the future. Coin prices can and do fluctuate, various items wax and wane in popularity, and market cycles have an influence—all to be discussed in later pages.

Indices and Statistics
Coins vs. the Stock Market

There are some parallels between the rare-coin market and the market for securities (stocks and bonds), but there also are many differences. Sometimes a newcomer in the coin-collecting field will ask, "Should I sell all my stocks and buy coins?" This may be especially true after he or she reads about coin investment profits after, perhaps, suffering a bad year in the stock market.

In truth, the stock market has had good times and the coin market has had good times. And, both have had times we would all like to forget.

Fads and cycles are a part of both markets. In the year 2000, I was fascinated to see leading stock brokerages make space available to Tom, Dick, and Harry, off the street with little training or expertise, who wanted to make profits in day trading, perhaps using money from their savings accounts or retirement funds. Helping matters along, certain news networks, ever eager for interesting stories (especially those concerning unusual behavior), were happy to showcase John Doe, who bought Super-Profit Dot.Com (remember all of the "dot-com" stocks?) for $21 last Monday and sold it for $33 on Friday. (When the stock later went down to $4, then became utterly worthless, John Doe was no longer an interesting interviewee for the media.)

Not much different from this scenario is the coin market of the early 1960s, when bank-wrapped 40-coin rolls of 1950-D nickels were hot as firecrackers. Only 2,630,000 were minted, which for the Jefferson nickel was not many. (For the 1949-D, 36,498,000 were minted.) Obviously, the 1950-D nickel, which seemed to be for sale everywhere around the market, was the rarity of the future. "You gotta get some!" was the theme.

The 1950-D nickel caused a lot of excitement in the 1960s, when it was the most talked-about investment in the rare coin market. This numismatic supernova faded quickly in 1965, the price dropped, and buyers turned to other things.

It so happened that a few years earlier *most of the mintage* had been bought up by coin dealers and investors, with A.J. Mitula, a Texas dealer, being especially active. With his profits Mitula constructed a vacation home in the Rockies, at Cascade, Colorado, calling it "the house that 1950-D nickels built." In the late 1950s such rolls were selling for $15 or so each. Later, the price was about $200, but the real action had yet to begin.

A non-collecting friend of numismatist Ken Bressett heard about all of the investment action, wanted to buy some, and had Ken locate a couple of rolls, which he then tossed into a desk drawer and forgot.

In 1964, when the price of a roll crossed the $1,200 mark and challenged $1,400, Ken called his friend, reminded him of the two rolls, and encouraged him to sell—which he did, for $1,200 each! Other smart sellers did the same, not all at $1,200—some for a bit less and others for a bit more, but over the $1,000 mark. Later, the price crashed to below $400 per roll. Today, it still hasn't recovered, but as of early 2005 it was making a good try! (I have more to say about the 1950-D nickel excitement in chapter 12.) However, unlike stocks, most coins *do* regain much if not all of their market price. Coins do not "liquidate," "go bankrupt," or "get delisted." On the other hand, coins do not pay cash dividends.

Bulls and Bears

At the risk of being facetious, I mention that in numismatics, bears are more popular than bulls. In the stock market, bears can be found hiding behind hedges (in hedge funds) and here and there, but are not a good omen. Not so in coins. Bears are common, and out in plain view—such as a 1925-S California Diamond Jubilee half dollar or a 1936 Oakland–San Francisco Bay Bridge half dollar. "Panda" coins issued by China depict bears, as does a rare Civil War token issued by a Mr. *Behr*, and so on.[2] Coin bears are very desirable—the more the better! In fact, Theodore Roosevelt, the all-time greatest numismatically interested president of the United States, inspired the teddy *bear*.

In numismatics, a bull can be found on the face of a popular Hard Times token bearing the inscription A FRIEND TO THE CONSTITUTION, and another is on Cincinnati restaurateur Lew Boman's 1862 and 1863 tokens. The 2004 Wisconsin quarter dollar shows a cow (female), but she doesn't count (though perhaps she has had a bull friend or two). The Old Spanish Trail commemorative half dollar shows the skull of a bovine creature, *Cabeza*

A nice numismatic "bear" in the market is found on the reverse of the 1925-S California Diamond Jubilee commemorative half dollar.

Wall Street, a center of banking and finance, in the mid-1850s.

Railroads were the great growth industry in the 1850s, and shares of the various lines were a sensation in the stock market. Perhaps it was only logical that the Bank of Canandaigua, in upstate New York, selected a train motif, implying progress, for use on a $10 bill of this era. (Courtesy of Tom Denly)

de Vaca, said to be the head of a cow. So much for whimsy.

Watching Stock Market Bears

Relating selected bear markets (down-markets) for stocks to the rare-coin markets at the time shows this:

Bear Stock Market	*Coin Market*
1930s (Depression)	Great growth.
5/1946–5/1947	Boom.
12/1961–6/1962	Boom (all of those 1950-D nickels rising in price).
2/1966–10/1966	Bears in both markets; gloom prevailed.
1/1973–12/1974	Boom.
9/1976–9/1978	Boom.
4/1981–8/1982	Bears everywhere.
8/1987–10/1987	Boom.
7/1990–10/1990	So many bears around, only Bayer aspirin could relieve the headaches!
3/2000–2003*	Afire with interest in ultra-high-grade certified modern coins.

NASDAQ peaked at 5048.62 on March 10, 2000, and fell to a bear-market low of 1114.11 on October 9, 2002.[3] The Dow Jones Industrial Average fell, but not nearly as much, as it was/is composed of more seasoned stocks.

I discuss separate movements of the rare-coin market later in this book. The coin market has had its share of knocks, such as 1947 to 1950, when stocks were doing very well but buyers for coins, even rarities, were scarcely seen. A fair summary is to say that while both the coin and stock markets have their own cycles, hardly ever do the twain meet.

It is also fair to say that choice rare coins have been a great *passive* investment, when bought carefully and held. In contrast, successful investing in stocks would seem to require constant management. The darlings of a generation ago can be dead today.

Food for Thought

Not so long ago, in connection with some research I have been doing on early paper money, I thought it interesting to take note of the New York Stock Market and what was active—this from *Banker's Magazine*, October 1854, showing the leading shares on the exchange as of September 22, 1854:

Panama Railroad: 85 • New York and Erie Railroad: 44 3/4 • New York Central Railroad: 96 1/4 • Michigan Central Railroad: 89 3/4 • Michigan Southern Railroad: 90 • Nor. and Wor. Railroad: 46 • Hudson River Railroad: 42 3/4 • Reading Railroad: 74 • Long Island Railroad: 27 1/4 • Illinois Central Railroad: 99 3/4 • Pennsylvania Coal Company: 101 3/4 • Delaware and Hudson Canal Co.: 116 • Cumberland Coal Company: 30 1/2 • New Jersey Zinc Co.: 5 3/4 • Canton Co.: 20 1/4 • Nicaragua Transit: 23 1/2 • Crystal Palace: 3 • New York & Harlem Railroad: 33 1/2

I cannot help but wonder how $1,000 invested in 1854 in a "basket" of such stocks, dominated by railroads, would have done, dividends included, if held in a family until the present day. The same amount of money invested in a face-value mix of current 1854 copper, silver, and gold coins from a bank would be worth millions of dollars today.

I do know that the New York & Harlem Railroad issued tokens during this era, good for one fare, valued at 6¢ to 12 1/2¢. If, in 1854, your great-great-grandfather had bought a share of this railroad's stock for $33.50, it might or might not be worth a lot now (I don't know). However, if he had spent the same amount on tokens for, say, 10¢ each, and had acquired 335 pieces, today his collection would be worth a total of $603,000 ($1,800 apiece)![4]

A Commentary From David L. Ganz

In a recent article in *Numismatic News*, David L. Ganz, popular columnist and a past president of the ANA, had this to say (excerpt):

> The rare coin market is roaring ahead of inflation, the price of gold and the

Consumer Price Index, but not the stock market this year. Over a 66-year period of time, 1938 to 2004, however, rare coins increased an average of 13.647%, compared to 8.38% for the Dow Jones Industrial Average.

Both the Dow Jones and the index compilation for rare coins use a market basket approach, measuring selected coins designed to represent the whole marketplace, and selected stocks that are broadly representative of the industrial sector of the American economy. The components of the Dow Jones have changed during the period (though the results have not); the coins are static.

Dow Jones statistics are calculated daily and based on actual components; the coin list was compiled by Salomon Brothers going back to 1978, and carried through 1990. The back pricing and forward pricing are independently examined....

Coin grading changes over the years are taken into account. Annual review of the rare coin market, contrasting it with the rate of inflation, the price of gold and other precious metals as well as specific rare coins has been a feature of this column for more than 15 years.[5]

The Ganz database, too lengthy to give in detail here, contains:

A total of 20 different individual coin types...none of them gold, most of them subsidiary coinage (dimes, quarters and half dollars), some of them minor coinage (half cent through nickel three cents) and a couple of silver dollars and commemoratives. Each is broadly representative of a class of coins or a type that is widely collected and hence easy to value....

As just one example of an "ordinary" coin—not a rarity, not in gem grade, but the kind of coin a serious collector would enjoy owning, Ganz cites this:

The 1794 half cent in Extremely Fine condition. The mintage is

about 82,000 pieces and *Guide Book* pricing runs from About Good to About Uncirculated.

In 1938, the data sources that I used valued it at $8; in 2004, Dennis Baker's *Numismedia*, which has provided data since 1998 for my annual survey, quotes it at $4,310. Its price does not go up every year, some years it is flat, others down but over 66 years the coin has an average price gain of about 13.81%. It has been flat in 11 of the years (i.e., about 16% of the time no gain or loss); it has gone up in at least 41 of 66 years (or about two-thirds of the time). The rest it has declined.

Adding to the Ganz commentary, I note that the latest (59th) of the *Guide Book* gives these grades and prices for the coin:

1794 half cent—About Good–3: $250 • Good-4: $450 • Very Good–8: $650 • Fine-12: $1,200 • Very Fine–20: $2,000 • Extremely Fine–40: $4,500 • About Uncirculated–50: $8,500.

In the 1940 (1941 cover date) *Standard Catalogue*, Wayte Raymond listed the 1794 half cent in just two grades: Good: $4, and Fine: $7.50.

Of course, the fluctuations in grading interpretations over the years complicate the interpretation of old data in comparison to current market figures.

The Salomon Brothers Coin Index

For many years Salomon Brothers, a leading Wall Street brokerage house, published an index of rare coin prices. The cachet of the Salomon name attracted much publicity. To prevent investors from simply buying the 20-coin content of the "market basket," the dates and grades of specific coins were kept confidential. The numbers were compiled yearly for Salomon by the staff of Stack's. Secrecy had the intended benefit, but, *per contra*, it was not possible for observers to make objective critiques.

Then, surprise! The April 1986 issue of *The Numismatist* printed this:

Ever wonder just what coins are used by Salomon Brothers, Incorporated, to determine the firm's investment performance index of rare coins, which shows a 15% annual rate of return and often is quoted by those promoting coins as an investment? Author Neil Berman did and found all he had to do was ask.

While researching a new book, *The Investor's Guide to United States Coins*, Berman asked Salomon Brothers for a list of the 20 coins used to determine its rate of appreciation of rare coin investment. The actual pieces considered in the index had been top secret—until Berman's request mistakenly was filled by a Salomon Brothers employee.

The cat—er, the *coin*—was out of the bag, and the list was revealed as including:[6]

This 1794 half cent did its duty in circulation, and today it is graded Fine-15 (Professional Coin Grading Service [PCGS]). These coins are collected by die varieties, this one classified as Breen-6 and Cohen-4, from reference books written by Walter H. Breen and Roger S. Cohen, Jr. In any and all grades, from well worn to Mint State, the 1794 half cent has always been a numismatic favorite. Most in existence range from Good to Fine in their grades.

1. 1794 Liberty Cap half cent, Extremely Fine;
2. 1873 two-cent piece, brilliant Proof;
3. 1866 Shield nickel with rays, brilliant Proof;
4. 1862 silver three-cent piece, brilliant Uncirculated;
5. 1862 half dime, brilliant Uncirculated;
6. 1807 Draped Bust dime, brilliant Uncirculated;
7. 1866 Liberty Seated dime, brilliant Uncirculated;
8. 1876 Liberty Seated 20 cents, brilliant Uncirculated;
9. 1873 Liberty Seated quarter dollar, with arrows, brilliant Uncirculated;
10. 1886 Liberty Seated quarter dollar, brilliant Uncirculated;
11. 1916 Standing Liberty quarter dollar, brilliant Uncirculated;
12. 1815 Capped Bust half dollar (key) Uncirculated;
13. 1834 Capped Bust half dollar (common date), brilliant Uncirculated;
14. 1855-O Liberty Seated half dollar, brilliant Uncirculated;
15. 1921 Liberty Walking half dollar, brilliant Uncirculated;
16. 1795 Draped Bust dollar, brilliant Uncirculated;
17. 1847 Liberty Seated dollar, brilliant Uncirculated;
18. 1884-S Morgan dollar, brilliant Uncirculated;
19. 1881 Trade dollar, brilliant Proof; and
20. 1928 Hawaiian commemorative half dollar, Uncirculated.

My Rare Coin Index

In 1974, I wrote *High Profits From Rare Coin Investment*. This book, one of many foundation stones for the present text, had on the title page, "The basic premise of this book: Successful rare coin investment requires knowledge." Today, this still holds true.

The 12th edition of that book, published in 1989, included a chart (p. 342) relating that $1,000 in cash, if deposited in a savings account yielding 5% interest in 1948, would have increased in value to $7,040 by 1989. The same $1,000 invested in the Dow Jones Industrial Average would have yielded $11,801 (including stock splits, but not dividends). A thousand dollars invested in my index of 129 selected rare coins would have had a replacement cost of $121,983.

If I were to calculate the same index today I would have to make some assumptions. Unlike years ago, today there are wide differences in price among *categories* of what were once simple grades.

As an example, I listed the 1934-S Peace silver dollar as being worth $12.50 in 1948 (the first year studied), increasing to $2,300 in 1989. Today, using 59th-edition *Guide Book* prices, the 1934-S is listed this way:

AU-50: $550 • MS-60 (lowest Mint State category): $1,800 • MS-63: $3,500 • MS-64: $4,750 • MS-65 (gem Mint State): $7,250.

In 1989, it was still possible for a connoisseur to buy gem coins for "regular" prices, but this was changing with the increasing popularity of Numismatic Guaranty Corporation of America (NGC), PCGS, and other grading services, not to overlook ANACS (formerly American Numismatic Association Certification Service), which had been in operation since the 1970s (but not with coins sealed in plastic). In my investment writings from day one I have always recommended buying quality coins. I suppose it might be fair to say that if you were a smart buyer back in the 1980s you would have acquired an MS-65 1934-S worth $6,500 today. On the other hand, if you were a bargain hunter examining all of those discount ads emphasizing low price, you would have probably ended up with an AU-50 (worth $550 in the *Guide Book* today) or an MS-60 ($1,800).

Further, although my "market basket" has stood the test of time and has not been altered or revised to take out any poor performers, investors in stocks do not have the same, level playing field for comparison. Witness all of those railroads that dominated the New York Stock Exchange trading in 1854. Where are they now? The Dow Jones Industrial Average, devised in later times, is regularly pruned. The stocks included in the DJIA of 1948 are mostly different from those in use today. I suppose that if, today, seeking to have only good performers and "growth" coins in my index, I were to change its content, then figure backward to 1948, I could make coin performance seem even more spectacular!

While not all DJIA stocks pay dividends, many do, and an index of stock performance should factor these in. It would be interesting to take the DJIA for the last trading day in 1948, freeze the same stocks, and calculate the prices of these same stocks today, plus dividends, and compare them to coins. I have talked to several Wall Street friends about doing this, but, seemingly, such information is not easily available, due to mergers, acquisitions, bankruptcies, and other factors. If a present reader comes up with this information, let me know, and I will revisit the situation.

As to my recommendations of coins versus stocks: I believe that selected stocks of good companies, in a good market, are a fine investment, with the advice of a trustworthy financial analyst. Stocks can yield dividends and, further, can be instantly liquidated at current market price. I have a portfolio of stocks myself (although it has not kept pace with my numismatic holdings).

I believe that selected rare coins have been a steadier, more reliable, and higher-yielding investment over a long period of time than have securities, but they cannot be instantly liquidated at current

The 1934-S Peace silver dollar is distinguished by a tiny S (for San Francisco) mintmark at the lower left of the reverse, below the O in ONE. Although the mintage quantity was a generous 1,011,000, most were probably paid out or melted. Today the 1934-S is the key issue in the 1921 to 1935 Peace dollar series. Mint State coins are rare in proportion to the demand for them.

A Gallery of Coins and Prices, 1950–2005

For collectors, coins from the early years of the United States Mint are among the most challenging of regular federal issues—those of the 1790s in particular, with later dates becoming more readily available. With some patience, the diligent collector can put together a representative selection. Here are some early silver coinage designs. Prices listed are their values over the years (taken from the 1956, 1986, 1996, and 2006 editions of the *Guide Book of United States Coins*), and what a lower-grade example of each would cost today.

Most of these coins are found in lower grades of VG to VF. Today, an example in VG-8 condition is worth $1,200.

1797 Draped Bust, Small Eagle
half dime (in Mint State)
1956: **$120** • 1986: **$7,500** • 1996: **$6,000** • 2006: **$12,500**

Almost all examples of this series are lightly struck, so don't expect crisp, sharp details, even on an Uncirculated coin. Today, a VG-8 specimen is worth about $550.

1805 Draped Bust, Heraldic Eagle
dime (in Mint State)
1956: **$45** • 1986: **$5,000** • 1996: **$4,000** • 2006: **$4,500**

Today's collector will pay about $200 for a G-4 specimen.

1806 Draped Bust, Heraldic Eagle
quarter dollar (in Mint State)
1956: **$65** • 1986: **$6,750**
1996: **$4,500** • 2006: **$5,000**

Only 200 to 300 are believed to exist today, with perhaps two dozen in Mint State. An example in G-4 condition will cost about $20,000.

1796 Draped Bust, Small Eagle
half dollar (in Fine condition)
1956: **$375** • 1986: **$15,000**
1996: **$15,000** • 2006: **$35,000**

Those that are available are typically found in grades ranging from VF to the lower end of Mint State. A VF-20 example can be had for about $2,200.

1802 Draped Bust,
Heraldic Eagle
silver dollar (in Mint State)
1956: **$110** • 1986: **$8,000**
1996: **$8,500** • 2006: **$17,000**

market price, and there can be diverse opinions as to the grades and market prices of given pieces. Successful rare coin investment requires knowledge, as I have mentioned. If you spend some enjoyable time to gain knowledge, you should do well. Selling coins is an art in itself, but on the other hand, so is the selling of closely held profitable companies, or key pieces of real estate, or a fine collection of Old Masters paintings.

It seems to me that the more expertise that is required in the buying and selling of investment items—securities as well as rare coins—the greater are the returns to the owners.

Interest Rates and Rare Coins

Classic economic theory has it that when interest rates on money, including yields on certificates of deposit, Treasury bills, and so on, are high, cash will fly to those investment areas. In practice, this has often been true, but not always. During the Jimmy Carter administration of the 1970s, we had the curious situation of double-digit interest rates coinciding with one of the most intense periods of coin market activity ever recorded. This was a special situation involving great speculation in silver and gold.

However, as a general rule, when yields of money market funds, certificates of deposit, and related instruments are low, many people turn their eyes toward other areas. It becomes more enticing to buy rare coins, real estate, and other properties. Moreover, if those other properties are bought on time payments or otherwise financed, the interest rates can be attractively low.

While, historically, the coin market has not marched in lock-step with interest rates, and in some instances has diverged greatly, there is no doubt that when interest rates are low, investing in rare coins can be a more attractive prospect than when rates are high.

CHAPTER TWO

QUICK GUIDE TO GETTING STARTED

Collectors who bought their coins 10 to 30 years since, and who bought any very considerable number of fine specimens, have had the satisfaction of seeing a handsome fortune go around the objects of their amusement. Many a gold piece that then sold at little more than face value now finds an eager purchaser at hundreds or even thousands of dollars. The increase in the value of great collections of historical coins within the last two or three decades has reached into the millions and very far into the millions, too. In comparison, the enormous increment to the holdings of United States Steel stock brought about through recent gyrations in its market value is but a bagatelle.

—Dr. T. Louis Comparette, Mint Collection curator, February 1910

Get Ready, Get Set, Go!
Time is Money

One of my favorite numismatic items is a copper token issued in 1837 by Smith's Clock Establishment, located in lower New York City at 7 1/2 Bowery. On the obverse it displays the face of a clock and the inscription TIME IS MONEY.

Today, in the early 21st century, most of us are in a hurry. Of course, we have the same number of hours in a day as our forebears did back in 1837, but there are a lot more things to do. Indeed, time *is* money.

Recently I bought a new laptop computer. With it was a small book detailing how to do just about everything with the various keys and buttons, plus instructions to connect to the Internet for still more information.

Also included with the computer was a simple fold-out sheet with a few basic instructions for getting started. I looked at the sheet, followed the steps, and within a few minutes had it up and running. Soon, I transferred a bunch of files from another laptop, to be sure that the word processing program ran properly. It did, and I spent the rest of the day writing.

A few days later I started reading the instruction book. Even now, as I write these words, I have not absorbed every page, and probably never will. There are entire programs on the computer that I do not plan to explore. However, I have learned enough to keep me content.

Similarly, this chapter is a quick guide to coin investment—the highlights. Each of these elements will be discussed in detail in following chapters. In those later chapters you can immerse yourself in grading, market history, and other things. I do *not* want you to be content with the quick steps given here. To learn more, read as much of the rest of the book as you want to. The more the better. However, this is a quick start.

By way of analogy: in 1960, John J. Ford, Jr., upon learning that I was going on a trip to England, France, and Switzerland to hunt for coins, said, "Buy a copy of *Fielding's Travel Guide to Europe*, and it will tell you all you need to know." I did, and I felt like an experienced traveler when I visited London, Paris, and Zurich for the first time.

In 1978, I went on a tour of the Greek mainland and a cruise to the nearby islands. I had never been there before and had only a vague idea of the history, culture, appearance, and importance of that part of the world. A month before I departed I bought a half dozen guides and read or skimmed them. When I actually visited the different locations, from Crete to Ephesus, I believe I enjoyed myself and appreciated the experience much more than did others on the trip. I even took a photo, numismatically related, of the ancient treasury building at Delphi, while others in the tour paid scant attention to this pile of stone.

With some pleasant reading and learning, numismatics offers a wonderful world of pleasure and potential profit. Almost all of the people I know who have become deeply involved have remained in the hobby for the rest of their lives.

Four Steps to Success in Coin Buying
Be a Smart Buyer

What are the secrets of being a smart buyer? Some time ago, in the course of another project for Whitman Publishing, LLC (*A Guide Book of United States Type Coins*), I had many ideas on the subject, but only a small space in which to discuss them. I devised the following steps. Since that time I have shared the concept with others, and buyers have found the steps to be useful.

Expanded information will be found in later pages, but here are the basics—part of the "let's get started, and quickly!" theme of the present chapter. I make the assumption that you have your eye on acquiring a coin of interest—a Morgan silver dollar, a double eagle, a commemorative—and that you have reviewed a price guide and have in mind a grade level. So many coins. So many opportunities. Now, to find one that is just right!

Step 1: Observe the Numerical Grade on the Holder

Your first step is to look at the grade of a coin offered in response to your inquiry, or, if you are familiar with grading, to assign your own number. If you are just entering numismatics, you would do well to only consider coins that have been certified by the four leading grading services, alphabetically: ANACS, Independent Grading Service (IGS), Numismatic Guaranty Corporation of America (NGC), and the Professional Coin Grading Service (PCGS). NGC and PCGS are the two largest by far, and ANACS, NGC, and PCGS each publish population reports delineating the

coins that have passed through their hands. There are other grading services; however, at present the above seem to be the most widely used by advanced collectors. Familiarize yourself with these, before checking out the other worthwhile services. Price information for many commercially graded coins can be found in many places, in particular the *Certified Coin Dealer Newsletter* (the "Greysheet").

Numismatic Guaranty Corporation of America has paid licensing fees to become the "official" grading service of both the American Numismatic Association (ANA) and the Professional Numismatists Guild (PNG), but before a 2004 renegotiation of contracts, PCGS was the official service for the PNG. At one time, ANACS was known as the American Numismatic Association Certification Service and was operated by the ANA as its official arbiter of grading interpretations. Today it is owned by Anderson Press, but is separately operated in Ohio. Neither the ANA nor the PNG guarantees any grading service, or participates in the grading of coins by any service. Similarly, the books of Whitman Publishing, headquartered in Atlanta and with a connection to Anderson Press, endeavor to present objective information, as do *Coin World*, *Numismatic News*, and other leading publications. If anything, NGC and PCGS get more ink in this book than ANACS, simply because more of their coins are in numismatic circulation.

In my opinion, the grade listed on a certified coin holder (popularly called a *slab*) is simply the starting point in the buying process. *This is one of the most important concepts for success in rare coin investment.* Probably 90% or more of the other buyers in the rare coin market are happy with certified coin holders and their grading labels and do not look further. This will be a wonderful advantage for you as you gain knowledge—a great inside edge!

When you visit a coin shop or a convention, or contemplate a catalog or Internet offering, have an approximate grade in mind for each coin you are seeking. If, by consulting a price guide, you find that a certain Morgan silver dollar is priced at about $50 in Extremely Fine–40 (EF-40) grade, $200 in Mint State–60 (MS-60), and $1,250 in MS-65, and you have just a couple hundred dollars budgeted for that coin, then consider pieces graded MS-60, more or less—perhaps down to About Uncirculated–58 (AU-58). There is no sense asking to see MS-65 coins, or EF-40 coins, either, unless the seller has time available and you simply want to see what those grades look like.

Within any given grade, reject any coins that seem to you to be overgraded. This will come with some experience. If, at a convention, you look through 100 Morgan dollars classified as MS-65, you'll soon enough see which ones seem to be on target and which seem to be below par. In fact, you will quickly learn about what to expect for an MS-65 coin and that some are better or worse than others. You are on your way to becoming a sophisticated buyer. Meanwhile, most others will simply see the MS-65 label on a coin and write a check.

In the beginning, however, you may not be able to tell an overgraded coin from one that is right on target. If you are not yet familiar with grading, continue through the next three steps; then, if a coin is still in consideration and has passed step 4, ask a couple other collectors, or a dealer or two, for their opinions. Most in the hobby are very willing to help anyone with an enthusiastic beginning interest in numismatics. Chapter 7 will tell you more about grading.

Step 2: Assess Eye Appeal at First Glance

At this point, take a quick glance at the coin. Is it "pretty"? Is the toning (if present) attractive, or is it dark or blotchy? Is the coin stained? If it is brilliant, is it attractively lustrous, or is it dull and lifeless?

For nearly all coins you will be considering, there are many opportunities in the marketplace. It is unnecessary in *any* instance to compromise on eye appeal!

This lovely 1810 over 09 overdate cent, attributed as the Sheldon-281 variety, was purchased in the 1940s. It remained off the market until 2005, at which time it was certified by PCGS as MS-64 Brown. While such grading numbers alone suffice for most coin buyers, I consider it desirable to examine a coin closely to determine its overall quality and eye appeal. Is it barely MS-64 and unattractive? Or is it a choice example within this grade? John Kraljevich described this particular coin as follows, for an auction presentation in the Jewell Collection sale (ANR). Read these words and see if you get a better picture of the coin, beyond a simple grading number:

"An exceptional specimen of this overdate variety, one of the very finest known. Rich medium brown surfaces show golden color near the peripheries, where mint color was last to subside, and exemplary cartwheel luster is evident. While only traces of mint color survive on the obverse, mostly around the bust tip and within the protected areas around LIBERTY, the reverse shows halos of mint color around the wreath and ONE CENT, in addition to traces elsewhere.

"Importantly, for a variety that so often comes bluntly struck, this piece is exceptionally well struck from the earliest die state—indeed the 'faint crack or guide line through tops of TED' mentioned by Breen is barely even visible here!

"Full dentils remain around both sides, though the alignment of the dies makes only the tips of some visible; in a later state, the dentils are nearly completely gone. This early die state also allows far greater remains of the 09 at the date visible than usually seen, an interesting aspect to study.

"There are few contact marks, spots noted beneath the date and below star 1, another in the dentils below the reverse, and a thin hairline connects the base of D in UNITED with the base of the first S in STATES. A few other little specks are only discernible under magnification. The visual appeal is superb, especially so for a top grade survivor of this rarity."

If it is not attractive, then reject it and go on to look at another. Even if the price seems to be a super-bargain, cast the coin aside. Stop right here, and go back to step 1 with another coin. An ugly coin graded as MS-65 is still ugly, and if it were my decision I would not buy it for *half* of the current market price! Do not be tempted by overgraded and/or ugly coins offered at "below wholesale" prices. Keep your wallet in your pocket.

If the coin is attractive to your eye, then in some distant future year when time comes to sell it, the piece will be attractive to the eyes of other buyers—an important consideration.

Now, with an attractive coin in hand, you have a candidate *for your further consideration.*

Step 3: Evaluate Sharpness and Related Features

At this point you have a coin that you believe to be more or less in the numerical grade assigned on the ANACS, IGS, NGC, or PCGS holder, and one with excellent eye appeal. The next step is to take out a magnifying glass and evaluate its sharpness. Here, one rule does not fit all. It will be useful if you consult other references as to what to expect. I realize that this will take a bit of effort, but I suggest that you do it. Recall my earlier comment that 90% of the other buyers will not investigate the details of what they contemplate purchasing—but I suggest that you do.

As an example, among certified Morgan silver dollars of the 1891-O (New Orleans Mint) variety, most are flatly struck at the centers. However, some are fairly sharp. Certified coin holders are simply marked MS-60, MS-63, or whatever, giving no clue as to the sharpness. If you know what to look for, you may be able buy a rare sharp strike for a "regular" price. Knowledge is king, and reference books (e.g., my *Guide Book of Morgan Silver Dollars*) are the source for information on aspects of sharpness and eye appeal.

For 1881-S (San Francisco Mint) Morgan silver dollars, nearly all are very sharply struck. For some date and mint-mark varieties you can expect to find a sharp specimen. For some others, this will range from difficult to nearly impossible. In the beginning I suggest that you stay only with sharply struck coins—until you learn more. If Morgan silver dollars, made in nearly 100 different date and mintmark varieties from 1878 to 1921, interest you, start by buying only pieces that are sharp. Later, you may have to make some compromises, but in the meantime each coin you acquire will be an excellent example of its variety. Buffalo (Indian head) nickels of the 1920s are sometimes seen struck as flat as a pancake, and other times they're sharp. Anyone simply reading the grades on commercial holders will be clueless as to this aspect. To determine sharpness, you must examine the coin!

If you are seeking Liberty Walking half dollars, minted from 1916 to 1947, buy only sharply struck ones. You won't be able to buy many of them (sharpness across the series is much harder to find than for Morgan silver dollars), but the ones you do acquire will be first class in every respect. In this way, as you become more sophisticated, you will not have to retrace your steps. The coins you have already bought will do just fine.

In chapter 8, I discuss "Full Details" (abbreviated FD), a notation that, if adopted by the commercial grading services, would serve to identify Buffalo nickels, Morgan silver dollars, and other coins with sharp features. At present, you are on your own!

As a further part of step 3, look at the coin's planchet (the blank disk of metal that is struck to make the coin) and surface quality. This is of concern mainly with early coins, say, those from the 1790s through about 1810. Mint-caused *adjustment marks* are common. (During the planchet preparation process, those found to be slightly overweight were filed down to the legal requirement. At the Mint, dozens of employees were kept busy in a special room doing this task. It was easier to make a planchet slightly overweight and to adjust it, than to make it under-weight and have to return it to the melting pot for recycling.) Also, as you begin your education in rare coins you should avoid all early and unusual issues. Later, as you gain knowledge, you can be a smart buyer of these, too.

In other instances, coins were struck from "tired" dies that had been used in some instances to strike more than 100,000 pieces. Such dies often became grainy or streaked—common on Morgan silver dollars (1878–1921). Bulged and uneven dies caused irregularities that are common on the reverse of many Lincoln cents, especially of the years from 1916 to 1958. Many other examples could be mentioned. These details are completely absent from the information on the slabs of commercially graded coins.

Beyond this, some planchets were made from imperfect strips of metal, with gran-ularity, or the inclusion of carbon or dark spots and flecks, or bits of copper (causing copper stains on gold coins). In other instances, bits of thread, human hair, or debris clung to the surface of a die, caus-ing recessed lintmarks on the finished coins, this being quite common on some Proofs. Again, these flaws are not men-tioned on certified coin slabs.

Examine your prospective coin care-fully, and reject it if there are *any* problems with the surface or planchet. No compro-mise need be made. As certified coin labels make no mention of these prob-lems, and few buyers even know about the possibilities, this translates into a great advantage for you! Already, you are on your way to becoming one of the smartest buyers in the hobby.

If the coin you are considering buying has passed the preceding tests, it is ready *for your further consideration*. Chances are good that you are holding a very nice coin in your hand!

Step 4: Establish a Fair Market Price

At this point, if you are not sure as to whether its numerical grade is correct, show the coin to one or several other numismatists and ask their opinions (as I recommended in step 1). This is especially important if the coin you're considering is expensive.

If you've done everything right, you have a coin that is correctly graded, of superb eye appeal, and very well struck. Such leg-endary connoisseurs from the past as Louis Eliasberg, Emery May Holden Norweb, and John Jay Pittman would be very proud

This lustrous 1925-S Buffalo nickel, commercially graded as MS-64, is flatly struck in many areas, including the hair above the braid on the obverse, and, on the reverse, the bison's head (no fur details) and shoul-der. David Lange, a student of this spe-cialty, called the 1925-S "one of the most poorly struck dates in the series." To make a good purchase decision, the smart buyer must carefully examine examples of this date and mint. More about Buffalo nickels and their striking will be found in chapter 17.

What is a sharply struck Buffalo nickel supposed to look like? This 1916 Philadelphia Mint coin answers the question—note the hair detail on the obverse, the head and shoulder of the bison, and so on. For some varieties, such as most Philadelphia Mint coins early in the series, one can find sharp pieces without difficulty. For others, such as 1919-D, 1919-S, 1920-S, 1925-D, 1925-S, 1926-D, and 1926-S, finding a sharp coin can take a long time, but when success is achieved, it is worth it! Such coins are really worth sharp premiums over market prices, but as most of your competitors in the marketplace are unaware of differences in striking, you can have an inside advan-tage with knowledge.

of you if they were living today! And I will be proud of you, too!

Next comes the evaluation of its price.

For starters, use one or several handy market guides for a ballpark estimate. More details will be provided in later chapters.

Now comes the fun part: if the coin is common enough in a given grade, with sharp strike, with fine planchet quality, and with good eye appeal, then the market price is very relevant, as you can shop around. If a coin is common in the grade you want, and with all other desired features, and you have ascertained that the market price level is about $300, then there is no sense paying $400 or $500. Wait until you find one at or near $300. On the other hand, chances are good that you will not find a problem-free coin for, say, $200 or $250. The fact that something is being offered to you for below wholesale simply means that any dealer wanting to buy a choice coin would not buy *this* one—and, accordingly, it is available for less!

For many of the varieties you will find interesting to own, high-quality coins are no problem at all. Stay with these at the outset. Later, as you gain knowledge, explore early issues. This can be a lot of fun. You will learn that there are quite a few American coins that are always weakly struck and usually come on low-quality planchets, but these are interesting as can be, just as a folk art painting can be more interesting to own than a crisply detailed photograph. For the specialist in Vermont copper coins of the 1785 to 1788 years, for which there are 39 different varieties, many if not most coins in an advanced collection will be in grades from Fine (F-12) to Extremely Fine (EF-40), with not a single Mint State coin in sight! This is just the opposite of what a specialist in Morgan silver dollars (1878–1921) will achieve—for even a low-budget collection of these dollars is apt to have at least half of them in Mint State. If you do as I do and get a complete set of gem Mint State and Proof quarters of the statehood series (1999 to date), you will find that nearly all meet the first three tests given above (though there are

scattered exceptions, such as weakly struck 2004-D Michigan pieces, so don't close your eyes when buying).

There is a very good possibility—another beautiful part of this process—that when you do find a sharply struck coin of a variety not often encountered this way, it will simply be certified in a given grade, and you can buy it for little more than you might pay for an ordinary example. Here, knowledge is king. As you gain knowledge and branch out into different older series, many opportunities will present themselves.

Consider what I also call the "Optimal Collecting Grade," abbreviated OCG, introduced in my *Guide Book of Morgan Silver Dollars: A Complete History and Price Guide*. In instances in which a very small difference in grade makes a very large difference in price, opt for the lower grade. As a dramatic example in another series, the current Red Book lists the price of an MS-64 1927-D Peace silver dollar at $700, and an MS-65 coin for $5,200. If I were spending my money I would rather have an MS-64, and use the extra $4,500 to buy other coins for my collection! On the other hand, if MS-64 were listed at $600 and MS-65 at $900, I would probably opt for the better grade.

At the moment, if you are a beginner, limit yourself to less expensive issues in popular series. Using the laptop-computer analogy, in numismatics at this point you've just read the leaflet—not the instruction book!

However, as you progress in your involvement and enjoyment of numismatics, you will want to read the instruction book—for the *actions* (buying, selling, grading, etc.) you contemplate, plus for *selected programs* (numismatic specialties) of interest.

Keys to Enjoying Numismatics

Appreciate What You Have

After you buy a few coins you have a choice. You can tuck them away in a drawer or safe deposit box and not look at them for a long while, or you can study and appreciate each piece carefully and contemplate its characteristics. Today, with an inexpensive digital camera you may be able to do both—put your coins in a safe place and enjoy their images on your computer screen (I do this with my collection, and it works well).

No two coin types are the same. A modern 2000-P Sacagawea dollar has a rich story to tell, although it is not very old. It is the first so-called "golden dollar," made of a special manganese-brass exterior that yields a distinct appearance. The obverse, with Indian guide Sacagawea holding her infant, evokes images of the Lewis and Clark expedition of 1804 to 1806 through the newly acquired lands of the Louisiana Purchase.

A few years after the first Sacagawea dollar was struck, the Lewis and Clark theme was expanded by the United States Mint (the name used by a Treasury-Department division that includes several mints) to create a series of new designs for the nickel five-cent piece, the first two of which were minted in 2004. The "buffalo" rides again on the 2005 nickel. Who knows what the future will hold?

Beyond this little sketch, the Lewis and Clark subject can be explored by learning about certain commemorative gold dollars—the first such in American history—minted in 1903, in two different varieties. One bears the image of William McKinley (assassinated in 1901), and the other depicts Thomas Jefferson.

The distribution of these particular gold dollars was through Farran Zerbe, a numismatist and entrepreneur. Having the right connections, he secured the franchise to set the retail price and control their sale. With high hopes, he arranged for 125,000 of each variety to be struck. News releases, advertisements, and assorted hype promoted these as great investments—rarities of the future—for just $3 each. However, $3 was three times the face value, and there were few buyers. When all was said and done, only 17,500 of each variety were

sold, and 90,000 coins were returned to the Mint and melted! However, today a selected gem example of either variety is worth more than $3,000!

Like the above, a common, inexpensive 2000-P Sacagawea dollar is a coin either to be bought and stored, or to be contemplated for its truly marvelous associations. I am sure that a worthwhile *book* could be written on all of the diverse numismatic aspects of the Lewis and Clark expedition! To me, learning a coin's history makes it come alive.

Also, this illustrates that coins do not have to be expensive to be interesting. I have mentioned my fascination with the current statehood series of Washington quarters. On the other hand, there are some modern-era coins I don't particularly care for. I am not a fan of the Eisenhower dollar design (1971–1978), although my fine friend, the late Frank Gasparro, chief engraver at the Mint, designed it. I do like his Susan B. Anthony dollars, or "Susies," made from 1979 to 1981, and I have a full set—inexpensive enough. Surprising to me, in 1999 three more varieties of Susies were made, but I haven't picked these up yet.

I find some modern commemoratives to be as ugly as sin, and I wouldn't want them even as a gift, unless I decided to build a full set and was *forced*, for example, to acquire a bull-necked Jefferson dollar of 1993 or a 1991 United Services Organization dollar (the bottom of the artistic barrel?). Of course, beauty is in the eye of the beholder, and this has been true for a long time. In 1793, a newspaper writer viewing what I consider to be the wonderful, desirable, and otherwise excellent Chain AMERI. copper cent (a classic now but then newly released) sniffed that "the American *cents* do not answer our expectations. The chain on the reverse is but a bad omen for liberty, and Liberty herself appears to be in a fright." [7]

The point is that you have lots of choices in numismatics; there are modern as well as older series that are inexpensive and fun to collect; and we all have our favorites and preferences.

A high-grade example of the 1793 Chain AMER-ICA cent, Sheldon-2 variety. While such coins are eminently desirable to numismatists of the present era, in its day the design was criticized.

Learn More About History

Coins, tokens, medals, and paper money are interwoven with American history. Money was and still is the link between people and most of their material possessions as well as the services they need and many of the pleasures they experience.

In 1776, a soldier in the Continental Army might have had in his pocket a pewter coin, worth a dollar, with a sundial design on one side and, on the other, abbreviations for the various colonies (soon to become states), expressed as PENNSILV, MASSACHS, N. HAMPS, and so on—perhaps not the way we would abbreviate them today, but in that era such coins were made from hastily manufactured dies. Among the several varieties of Continental dollars, most have the inscription CONTINENTAL CURRENCY on the obverse, but one has a misspelled word: CURRENCEY. Again, contemplating such a coin makes it come *alive*. One can almost shiver from the snow at Valley Forge!

In 1837, the earlier-mentioned TIME IS MONEY copper token issued by Smith's Clock Establishment not only was an advertisement for that business, but also served in circulation at the value of one cent. This was the Hard Times era, in which government-issued coins were widely hoarded. Filling the gap and facilitating purchases—of newspapers, crackers from a barrel in a country store, or a plate of oysters—were all sorts of privately issued tokens, these in addition to paper currency issued by various banks. Some tokens satirized Andrew Jackson, and by showing a turtle (a diamondback terrapin,

to be exact) illustrated the slowness with which federal funds were moving to banks. Other tokens showed such things as an umbrella, a hair comb, boots, or even a coffee pot. Each has its story to tell.

During the Civil War (1861–1865), silver and gold coins were hoarded by the public, as no one knew which side would be victorious. When the conflict commenced, in April 1861, most Northerners viewed it as an easy win. Parades and parties were staged to send soldiers off to war, to serve the three-month enlistment term directed by President Lincoln. Soon, the thinking went, they would all be back home for more celebrations. After all, the Confederacy did not have much in the way of industrial strength, and many envisioned the typical white citizen of that area to be busy managing cotton fields, or sipping drinks on the porch of a plantation house.

However, on July 21, 1861, things went wrong for the Union forces—terribly wrong. The Confederate troops were victorious. Later, in his *Recollections*, John Sherman wrote:

> The Battle of Bull Run was an important event. It dispelled the illusion of the people of the North as to the duration and gravity of the war. It demonstrated the folly of ninety days' enlistments. It brought also, to every intelligent mind, the dangers that would inevitably result from disunion. On the 22nd of July, the day after the battle, the bill to authorize the employment of 500,000 volunteers became a law.

As months went on, the war evolved into an epic struggle. In January 1862, gold coins disappeared from circulation, into the hands of hoarders, soon followed by silver, then by copper-nickel one-cent pieces. By the second week of July in 1862, no coins at all were to be seen in New York City or Boston, or, in the South, in Charleston or Atlanta. All sorts of tokens and paper money issues took their place. Among these were privately issued tokens showing everything from a mythical hippocampus, to George Washington, to a mansion on a hill, to an elephant wearing boots (the last an advertising token for a shoe store in Albany).

Although cents soon returned to circulation, silver and gold coins were absent from the channels of commerce until the late 1870s. This situation spawned several new types of coins in copper and nickel, including the two-cent piece (introduced in 1864), the nickel three-cent piece (1865), and the nickel five-cent piece (1866). In the meantime, silver and gold coins were available from brokers, banks, and exchange offices, but a premium had to be paid for them in terms of paper money, such as in Legal Tender bills issued by the Treasury.

In 1863, it took $1.04 in silver bullion, at the price at that time, to make a silver dollar—yet, 27,200 were struck. Today in numismatics, most collectors simply look at market listings for the 1863 dollar and see such prices as, per the 59th edition of the *Guide Book:*

VG-8: $350 • F-12: $400 • VF-20: $475 • EF-40: $650 • AU-50: $1,200 • MS-60: $2,700 • MS-63 (the highest grade listed): $5,400.

Why were such coins struck, if it cost more than their face value to make them? And, as 27,200 were made, why is an MS-63 coin worth as much as $5,000 today?

I could leave you dangling—and not give the answers. However, there are so many similar, interesting situations in numismatics for you to consider that I'll save you the pleasurable effort of researching this coin, and tell you why:

In 1863, U.S. merchants like those involved in the large import-export trade between American ports and Canton, China, paid with coins struck in precious metals. Merchants, banks, and governments in distant lands did not want Uncle Sam's paper Legal Tender bills. They wanted "hard money" in the form of silver and gold. In that year, certain depositors of silver bullion at the Philadelphia Mint

requested silver dollars in exchange for their bullion, received them, and sent them off to distant places, such as Canton, Rio de Janeiro, Liverpool, or LeHavre—where no attention was paid to the value inscribed on such coins. Instead, they were valued at $1.04 each, this being their worth in silver.

As to the second question—why are 1863 silver dollars rare today?—in 1863, just about any numismatist desiring a current silver dollar of the Liberty Seated design would order a Proof, with mirror finish, made for collectors and sold by the Mint for a sharp premium. Circulation strikes were desired not at all by collectors—only by businessmen. Years later, research by numismatic scholars revealed that most 1863 silver dollars were shipped to China, and from there sent by the Chinese to Calcutta, India, where they were melted. Accordingly, most were destroyed within a few years of their creation. As no silver dollars of 1863 or any other date were in circulation during that Civil War year, citizens did not have the opportunity to hoard them.

Now, if you contemplate a rare 1863 silver dollar, you will know not only its value, but, even more interesting, its history!

While you might not be able to afford such a rarity as this particular silver dollar, just about any budget will accommodate a 1943 Lincoln cent made of steel, zinc coated, with a current *Guide Book* price of just $2 in MS-63 grade. This cent has its own history, and a few paragraphs could be expended to give you just the high points—what was happening in 1943? why was steel used for only one year?

The point is that, upon looking into the matter, you find that just about every coin ever made has a fascinating background. American history comes to life when coins are contemplated in connection with it. Accordingly, if this suits your turn of mind, I highly recommend that you become involved in the historical aspect of numismatics—another one of my rules for success, although in this instance, not *absolutely* necessary.

A lustrous Mint State 1863 Liberty Seated silver dollar. At the time it was struck, such a coin required $1.04 in silver to produce. Virtually all were shipped overseas as "trade" coins, where they were valued for their silver content, and their face value made no difference.

Appreciate Tradition

American numismatics has a rich tradition, with widespread popularity dating back to 1857, the year the old copper "large" cents were discontinued in favor of small copper-nickel coins. A wave of nostalgia swept the country—a desire for the "pennies" of yesteryear, the coins of childhood. Many people endeavored to find in circulation one of each of as many different dates as possible, all the way back to the first year they were issued, 1793. The 1815 proved impossible, as this was the one year in which no cents were coined, and the 1793, 1799, 1804, and 1823 were elusive, but most of the others could be found. In chapters 10, 11, and 12 you will read about this as part of market and coinage history.

In 1859, the first large-size book intended for coin collectors was published: the *American Numismatical Manual*, by Dr. Montroville W. Dickeson (a fascinating man who was a medical doctor, but who spent much time in the West digging into Indian burial mounds, gaining fame among archaeologists for this endeavor). In the same year, teenager Augustus B. Sage, who with friends had founded the American Numismatic Society in 1858, was the most important auction cataloger on the scene and created descriptions for four notable sales.

As the years went on, the hobby expanded and evolved. In 1866, the *American Journal of Numismatics* was launched as the first regularly issued coin magazine, followed by others, including *The Numismatist* in 1888. In 1891, the American Numismatic Association was founded.

In the next several decades many auctions were conducted, books were published, and conventions took place. However, it was not until the 1930s that the first regularly issued guide to coin prices (the *Standard Catalogue*, by Wayte Raymond) appeared and convenient album pages and folders were available to store and display coins.

Today, the field of numismatics is dynamic, building on the tradition and experience of our forebears. Learning about past great events, ranging from popularity fads and market cycles to the actions of notable personalities such as the Chapman brothers and B. Max Mehl, to the development of grading systems, is a fascinating pursuit. This information, too, awaits you in the pages to follow.

Participate in the Numismatic World Around You

While I suppose you could collect coins all by yourself, hidden away in a room somewhere, most numismatists enjoy the world around them. Such weekly magazines as *Coin World* (founded in 1960) and *Numismatic News* (1952) are filled with the latest information—auction sales, new products of the U.S. Mint, convention coverage, market notes, and more.

Sold on newsstands to a wider and perhaps less sophisticated audience are the monthlies *COINage* and *Coins*, each packed with interesting articles and information. The *Coin Dealer Newsletter* and the *Certified Coin Dealer Newsletter* each contain "bid" and "ask" figures for many different coins, these usually intended for the so-called "investment market" (more for those who buy looking only at grading numbers, not at the sharpness of strike, eye appeal, etc.), although the information is useful to all.

Enjoy the Learning Process

Part of the enjoyment of numismatics is learning about the minting process. Producing a coin involves many steps, several of which are shown here. These scenes are from the Philadelphia Mint in the 1880s.

Exterior of the Philadelphia Mint. The cornerstone for this building was laid on July 4, 1829, and the building was occupied in 1833. It served until autumn 1902, when it was replaced by a modern facility.

Visitors to the Philadelphia Mint were allowed to watch a coining press in operation. The operator fed planchets or blank discs into the machine, two dies came together with force, and a finished coin was ejected out the back of the press. In the 1880s it was common to buy a souvenir before leaving, two popular choices being a freshly minted Indian Head cent or gold dollar.

Steel dies such as these were fitted into the coining press, one die for the obverse and the other for the reverse.

Metal ingots were rolled into long strips to make planchets.

Cutting circular blanks from a planchet strip.

The blanks were fed into a milling machine, which made a raised rim on each; the planchets were then softened by annealing, cleaned, and used in a coining press.

The Internet, the great innovation that sprang to life in the hobby in the late 1990s and now includes pages and web sites for many dealers, organizations, and collectors, is a rich resource for information and for buying and selling coins. Time was when nearly everyone communicated with me by U.S. postal mail. Today, probably 95% of the comments I receive when I write a book, auction catalog, or article arrive by email—handy and very effective for all concerned.

The ANA, headquartered in Colorado Springs, publishes the *Numismatist* each month, conducts coin shows, and gives educational symposiums, most notably the two-week Summer Seminar held annually. The ANA is the world's most popular such organization, with about 32,000 members.

The American Numismatic Society (ANS; web site www.amnumsoc.org), based in New York City, has several thousand members and is oriented toward advanced collectors. At its headquarters on Fulton Street is a fine museum and America's largest numismatic library.

Special-interest groups' memberships usually range from a few hundred to perhaps more than a thousand, and cater to those who specialize in large copper cents, Liberty Seated silver coins, Civil War tokens, paper money, early half dollars, colonials, or one or another of the many interesting numismatic byways.

Coin stores around the country, conventions, and club meetings offer the chance to meet others, to "talk coins," and to

Montroville W. Dickeson, M.D., was the author of the 1859 book *American Numismatical Manual*, the first comprehensive study of coins published in the United States. The book was a great success and was published in later editions in 1860 and 1865, slightly retitled as *American Numismatic Manual*.

buy items of interest. Sharing your enthusiasm with others is a great way to gain knowledge and to get different perspectives on grading, the market, and other topics of the day.

While you or anyone else could simply buy coins for investment and nothing more, the world of numismatics is rich with history, tradition, and fellowship, all beckoning you to participate. Coin people can become good friends, as well.

With these comments as a beginning, on to the details....

CHAPTER THREE

DYNAMICS OF THE RARE COIN MARKET

The science of coins and medals is as old as antiquity itself. There is probably no other branch of collecting so ancient and honorable, or that has received the attention of the students of all ages, as that of coin collecting.... If there are "sermons in stones," etc., what eloquence and learning must be stored up in these bits of metal? If they could only talk, what strange stories would they tell?

—Dr. Geo. F. Heath, November 1889

Measuring the Market

Counting the Participants

What is the nature of the rare coin market today? How many people are involved? How many of them are casual collectors? How many are serious? How many dealers are there?

Precise figures are elusive. In April 1986, *The Numismatist* carried this:

> On the average, Americans have nearly a thousand pennies around their homes, according to the latest Epcot Poll, a special survey conducted by Walt Disney World on behalf of the United States Mint. The poll revealed that of approximately 12,000 visitors to the popular Florida attraction, 33% of adults and nearly 50% of children collect coins in general. More than 33% of adults reported having more than $10 worth of pennies at home; 50% of adults use pennies daily; and 40% of adults and 60% of children save pennies. Of all U.S. coins, quarter dollars are most used and half dollars are least used.
>
> Regarding coin collecting among adults, 21% said they collect as a hobby, 12% as an investment; of the juniors surveyed, 27% collect as a hobby, 19% as an investment. The Epcot Poll is a daily activity at Epcot's Center's Electronic Forum and is conducted in association with the market research firm of ASK Associates, Inc. The January 14–February 10 coin survey sampled 10,532 U.S. adults and 1,462 youngsters.

While visitors to Walt Disney World no doubt have more disposable income than do 12,000 people selected at random from all across the American population, these figures are nonetheless impressive.

Jay Johnson, who served as director of the Mint at the turn of the 21st century, including when the Sacagawea "golden dollars" were making news headlines, said in the year 2000 that 130,000,000 people collected coins. This number included citizens who might casually save a newly minted 1999 quarter of the Delaware motif with horse and rider on the reverse, or the 2000 New Hampshire quarter with the Old Man of the Mountain and the motto "Live Free or Die," as well as those who might set aside one of the Sacagawea dollars. Billions of Kennedy half dollars have been struck in our generation, and yet I can go shopping for a year without receiving one in change. Where have they all gone? Probably to some of those 130 million collectors.

Coins are interesting to just about everyone. Time was when Mint directors stayed in their office in Washington, DC. That changed in the 1960s when Director Eva Adams became a frequently seen figure at coin conventions and was even a participant in skits put on by the Numismatic Literary Guild. Her successors have followed suit, and recently retired Director Henrietta Holsman Fore was a much appreciated visitor to coin shows and other events, always willing to listen to collectors and to share ideas.

The "Ship of Gold" exhibit at the Tucson Gem and Mineral Show, the largest event of its kind in the world. Featured in 2004 were gold coins and ingots from the treasure recovered from the wreck of the *S.S. Central America*. On hand to greet visitors was Bob Evans, a principal in the treasure-finding team. (Courtesy of Wendell Wilson, the *Mineralogical Record*)

According to *Coin World* editor Beth Deisher, in 2002 the total paid circulation for the seven major national numismatic periodicals (*Coin World; COINage; Coins; Coin Prices; Numismatic News; World Coin News;* and *The Numismatist*) was just under 250,000. She extrapolated, taking into account such factors as duplication (one person subscribing to multiple periodicals) and pass-along (subscribers sharing their periodicals with friends) to arrive at a "coin hobby core" of about 445,000 people who read these publications on a regular basis. "Radiating out from the core are probably two to three times as many people who spend serious time and money on coins, but who for whatever reason do not obtain information regularly from hobby publications. Many, based on the activity we see on the Internet and cable television, are no doubt depending on the electronic world for information."[8] This would suggest a population of about 1.3 to 1.8 million serious collectors.

Figures can be bandied about with reckless abandon, and in the everyday news there is no lack of charts, tallies, estimates, surveys, and the like, relating to business, political favorites, consumer preferences, and more. However, as one wag said, 37% of all estimates are just made up!

Anyway, the numismatic numbers mentioned here are a combination of my guesses and those of people I have consulted.

At the California State Fair some time ago, Dwight Manley and others in the California Gold Marketing Group set up the "Ship of Gold" exhibit for the public to see, and an estimated 700,000 people came to appreciate and to gawk and wonder at the gold coins and ingots on display—all found in the wreck of the *S.S. Central America* lost at sea on September 12, 1857. My own involvement in this exhibit will forever remain one of my fondest memories. Still, it might not be correct to say that all 700,000 people who spent time seeing these coins had a numismatic interest or were potential collectors.

More recently, at the Tucson Gem and Mineral Show (an annual event that draws worldwide attendance), thousands of people waited in line over a period of several days to view the treasures. For the first time in this event's 50-year history, crowd control procedures had to be put in place—not necessary at earlier shows, even when the Hope Diamond and Fabergé eggs were featured! How many viewers became numismatists?

What about the 1,500,000 people who waited their turn at the Smithsonian Institution a generation ago to view the gem coins of the Eliasberg Collection? How many were collectors then? How many became numismatists after they were inspired by the exhibit? Who knows?

A Closer View

Narrowing the focus somewhat, we find that there have been upward of 2,000,000 buyers on the U.S. Mint mailing list in recent years. Such people have laid out their hard-earned dollars to acquire Proof sets, commemoratives, and other modern Mint products.

It is likely that many hobbyists have walked into local or regional coin show publicized in newspapers, radio, and television, and, perhaps, have bought a coin or two, perhaps an old silver dollar or a Proof set from the year they were born, but may never buy anything else.

This happens even with truly rare coins. In the 1970s, a Chicago resident read something I wrote about the famous 1894-S Barber dime, of which only 24 were struck and of which fewer than a dozen are known today. He simply had to have one, never mind that it cost the best part of $100,000. This was the only coin in his "collection." In another instance, a couple years ago a real estate broker saw me on one of the documentaries about the *S.S. Central America* treasure (produced for the History Channel, or perhaps it was the Discovery Channel or a network news feature)—the finding of the coins attracted wide attention and was widely covered by most networks. He determined that owning a brilliant Mint State 1857-S double eagle, one of about 5,400 such coins found in the shipwreck, would be very satisfying. He bought one, at which time I mentioned that he might enjoy the magazines and catalogs that would be coming his way from our company. At that point he said that he was not a coin collector and did not intend to become one, and that this single coin was all he wanted. I suppose that it is fair to

include the buyer of the 1894-S dime and also the owner of the 1857-S $20 as part of the community of collectors, whether they want to be or not.

On the other end of the scale, I read of a tavern-keeper who found Buffalo nickels (minted 1913–1938) to be interesting. In the 1940s and 1950s many were still in circulation. Each time he took one in payment he tossed it behind the back bar, eventually "collecting" thousands of them. I suppose he was a collector, too.

Although not all active collectors buy a copy of *A Guide Book of United States Coins* every year, and some who do buy the book are not collectors at all, it is worth noting that today this is among the 10 best-selling nonfiction titles of all time. In one record year more than a million copies were sold!

Putting all of this together, it may be fair to estimate that at least 2,000,000 people in the United States are interested enough to buy an occasional book on the subject, or to order coins now and then from the U.S. Mint—in other words, to pay a premium for coins and information, or to seriously and systematically extract interesting pieces from circulation.

Core Collectors

Narrowing the focus a bit further, I estimate that upward of 250,000 people subscribe to one or another of the numismatic publications (*Coin World, Numismatic News, Coinage, COINS* magazine, the *Coin Dealer Newsletter*, etc.), belong to coin clubs, are customers of established rare coin dealers, and attend local, regional, and national coin shows at least on an occasional basis, buying from several to many old coins (opposed to modern Mint products) for their collections. Actually, as the annual sales of the *Guide Book* are considerably higher than 250,000, I believe that there are 250,000 to 500,000 core collectors.

Offhand, one might think that just about every truly serious advanced collector belongs to the American Numismatic Association (membership currently greater than 32,000), but this is not the case. When

I was president of the ANA (1983–1985), I occasionally gave talks to various clubs. Once in New Britain, Connecticut, I met with a very active group, a roomful of enthusiasts, and asked a few questions. Seeking a show of hands to see how many belonged to the ANA, I found that, of the more than 100 people present, fewer than 10 indicated their membership. Then I asked how many people subscribed to *Coin World*, saw perhaps a couple dozen hands, then to *Numismatic News*, and saw about 10 or so. I then asked how many people subscribed to both *Coin World* and *Numismatic News* and scarcely any collectors indicated they doubled up.

At the 2004 summer convention of the ANA, generally thought to be the biggest show of the year, nearly 14,000 people registered, including more than 1,000 dealers and their assistants who staffed more than 500 tables, plus many dealers who did not set up. Perhaps the count was about 2,000 to 3,000 dealers plus 11,000 to 12,000 col-

lectors and potential collectors. Among these visitors were many with just a casual interest, or with no interest at all yet, but eager to learn (such as a troop of Boy Scouts I saw come into the room). Others came armed with checking account balances sufficient to buy Proof double eagles or $20 Demand Notes of 1861, among other notable rarities.

The Professional Numismatists Guild (PNG) has about 300 members, these generally representing the larger-volume dealers in *rare* coins. There are other important dealers who do not belong to the PNG for one reason or another, or who have never applied, including quite a few leading specialists in numismatic items other than coins—such as tokens, medals, paper money, and books. At a regional coin show I saw more than 50 dealers set up, and only one belonged to the PNG. A few years ago Chet Krause, founder of *Numismatic News*, told me it was his estimate that there were 6,000 rare-coin dealers in the

View of the bourse area at the 2004 American Numismatic Association convention, with hundreds of dealers set up. (David M. Sundman photograph)

Ronald Gillio, a past president of the Professional Numismatists Guild, at a convention, with a box full of coins, mostly in certified holders. Ron conducts the Long Beach Collectibles Expo, held several times a year.

The store of Harlan J. Berk, Ltd., in Chicago is one of many examples of a large rare-coin dealership with a staff of specialists tending to sales in many venues, from walk-in retail to mail order to the Internet. (David M. Sundman photograph)

United States, many of them dealing on a casual or part-time basis.

By the way, I like to think of numismatics as a hobby, a pleasant pastime, and rare-coin dealing as a combined art and profession. However, quite a few in the field insist on calling it an *industry*, probably because *hobby* sounds casual, and *industry* sounds like a big deal. Perhaps one of these days, neurologists and sculptors will want to call themselves industrialists. Who knows?

Small Numbers That Count!

Cutting to an even tighter number, how many people actually registered to bid on the two most valuable rare coins ever auctioned? One was the finest-known 1804 silver dollar (of which 15 exist, some in museums), which I cataloged for the Childs family and auctioned in 1999 for more than $4 million. The other was the 1933 $20 double eagle cataloged by David E. Tripp and sold by Sotheby's and Stack's in the summer of 2002 for $7.6 million. In each instance, about a dozen people were registered and had their credit approved to bid into the millions. At both events there were many others who attended and simply watched—adding to the excitement.

For these two rarities it did not matter whether there were 130,000,000 collectors in America (Director Johnson's earlier quoted estimate), or 500,000 advanced or serious collectors, or any other number. All it took in each instance was *two* people who desired the coin and were able to pay the price!

This reminds me of a sale we held back in 1974 of the Stanislas Herstal Collection, the finest offering of coins of Poland to cross the auction block in many years. The cataloging was done by Karl Stephens (who later went on to conduct his own business), and it fell to me to write some of the background and introduction as well as the publicity and advertising. In the same catalog, many superb U.S. coins from other consignors were also featured.

The American coins did very well and played to a full house of enthusiastic bidders. Lots of excitement, many bidder hands in the air, many different buyers. Then came the Herstal Collection part of the sale, and the gallery emptied. Only a handful of bidders remained! *Woe is me*, I thought. Bravely, I carried on with feigned enthusiasm.

The auctioneer began to cry out the numbers from the podium. Immediately, all bets were off, presale estimates became meaningless, and excitement prevailed! The several active bidders, scattered here and there in the otherwise vacant room, must have been the world's most enthusiastic buyers of Polish coins, long starving for such an opportunity. When the dust settled, the entire collection brought nearly *five times* what we had anticipated!

Not long ago, American Numismatic Rarities and Stack's conducted a joint auction at the MidAmerica Coin Expo in Chicago, via shared space in the same catalog (in addition, Stack's had a separate catalog for the Ford Collection items). Staffers from both organizations worked very hard for several days, and each company did very well. When all was over we all enjoyed a memorable dinner at Carlucci's Restaurant nearby.

We had every good reason to celebrate, as many records had been set. However, one part of the event was rather lightly attended—the offering of Hard Times tokens (privately issued in the 1830s and early 1840s) formed over a long period of time by John J. Ford, Jr. Such tokens are a rather arcane specialty, and not many people know about them at all (too bad, as they are very interesting!). However, despite the empty chairs, at that part of the sale, tokens expected to bring $1,000 often sold for several times that figure, and more than a million dollars was realized! It was a replay of the Herstal Collection scenario—large numbers of bidders are not nearly as important as a small group of really serious buyers.

Collecting Quietly

After becoming involved in the hobby, many if not most serious collectors concentrate on doing business with just one or two dealers. Although some numismatists are gregarious, attend conventions and auctions, and enjoy socializing, others do not.

I recall a father-and-son team who bought coins from me for a long time, then in 1965 auctioned them under the name of the Century Collection. They tapped Jim Ruddy (my partner at that time) and me to be their eyes and ears, and, so far as I know, never attended a coin show or auction in person. They did read extensively and had a library with all of the basics. However, from a distance they were very active bidders at most of the important auctions of the era. For example, in the March 1961 sale of the Edwin M. Hydeman Collection, conducted by Abe Kosoff, I bought for them the 1894-S dime, paying $29,000. Today, the same coin would be worth in the $500,000 to $1,000,000 range, but a few years earlier, in 1957, I had bought another one for just $5,750. It is tempting to pause and just talk about prices, but I will continue on track. I believe my company was the sole supplier of rare coins to this marvelous collection.

This desire for remaining in the background reminds me of another incident. On December 10, 1960, at Stack's, the Fairbanks Collection crossed the block. Lot 576 was a nice example of the rare 1804 silver dollar, and presale estimates suggested it would bring $15,000 to $20,000. Ambassador R. Henry Norweb accompanied me to the sale, having instructed me to bid on his behalf to and beyond $25,000, as he wanted to purchase it as a birthday present for his wife, Emery May, one of the most dedicated collectors of all time. The ambassador wanted to remain anonymous. And he did. From the back of the room he watched as I bid the coin up to close to $30,000, then yielded to a representative of Samuel Wolfson, who later told me he would have paid *any* price to get it.

Buying items through trusted dealers is a common practice in other areas of pursuit. My fine friend since childhood, Ken Rendell, was given the commission to build a personal library of historical and literary volumes for Bill Gates, founder of Microsoft. Gates commissioned Rendell alone to accomplish this, as he was assured of expertise, good coverage of the market, and a wide selection of opportunities.

Counting the Money

In contemplating the dynamics of the rare coin market, there is no public accounting required of rare coin dealers, auctioneers, and others involved in numismatics. We do know that the United States Mint has sold hundreds of millions of dollars' worth of Proof coins, commemoratives, sets, bullion "eagles," and other coins in recent years. However, beyond that, much is conjecture. No statistics are kept by collectors' or dealers' organizations (or by any government agency) on their activities.

Coin sales can be divided into auctions and outright sales, the latter being wholesale or retail.

In the auction area, ranging from important collections and rarities offered by a half dozen or so leading firms, to everyday action on eBay and elsewhere, sales are greater than $100,000,000 annually and may exceed $200,000,000. Factor in the many coins sold by dealers, coin offerings on television, telemarketing firms, dealers in bulk gold coins for investment, and others, and that figure may double or triple, probably topping $500,000,000. To this can be added the yearly sales of current coins by the Mint. Some years have higher volume than do others, but these sales estimates are probably on target as an average.

In the rare coin market there is no dealer monopoly or oligopoly, no cartel. Prices float freely depending upon supply and demand. The business is conducted by dealers who began business yesterday along with people who have been in the profession for decades.

While there are numerous large companies, particularly in the auction and investment sales fields, there are also many one-person and modest-size operations that enjoy excellent business and fine reputations. At a recent convention I had nice conversations with Tony Terranova, Julian Leidman, and Ken Goldman, each individual proprietors. These professionals have done a large amount of business with me for a long time, and with good results for all concerned. I rather imagine that if I were to ask Tony, Julian, or Ken if they would like to add a staff of a dozen people to help them, they would say no. They like it the way it is. On the other hand, David M. Sundman, a personal friend for a long time, is the main owner of Littleton Coin Company, which employs more than 300 people and conducts business from a 65,000-square-foot building—the largest such operation in the world. Littleton's trade is mainly in lower-value coins and

supplies, just as important to the market as are the activities of, for example, Laura Sperber, who recently sold a 1913 Liberty Head nickel for well over a million dollars. Tom Denly, a well-known currency dealer, is essentially a one-*man* operation, but his personable assistants, Martha and Jennifer, provide a lot of help. Indeed, in paper money, the field is dominated by sole proprietorships, with great success. The same can be said for some of the finest dealerships in rare books and autographs.

A review of the roster of the PNG or the Professional Currency Dealers Association (PCDA) will quickly confirm this. The majority of members are on their own or work with just a small staff. Such dealers go about their business quietly and add to the

Dealers dealing. At a recent show, Laura Sperber shows a Proof Liberty Seated half dollar to Stu Levine. Often, coin conventions are dominated by dealer-to-dealer activity, as professionals seek to build their inventories and fill "want lists" for customers.

Ken Goldman, a long-time professional from Massachusetts, checks some certified coins at a Baltimore coin show. Ken is an avid collector of music boxes and related items, also interests of the author.

Visiting a coin shop is a great way to learn about coins. Shown here is Rusty Goe, owner of Southgate Coins in Reno, Nevada, with staffers (left to right) Heather Wirtz, Sharleen Flansaas, and Sarah DeArman. Cases are filled with coins for sale, while against the back wall are numismatic books, albums, and supplies.

On a warm day in the summer, most of Littleton Coin Company's 320 employees were on the front lawn of the firm's building in Littleton, New Hampshire, posing for this group photograph. This multifaceted operation conducts a worldwide business and reflects the other end of the scale, quite different from a single-proprietor concern.

overall sales numbers of the numismatic field, but the extent of their activity cannot be measured.

In addition to established professionals, there are many part-timers in that group of 6,000 dealers estimated by Chet Krause. Once, I received a letter from a seller whose stationery included the notation "A.F.D." after his name. I asked what this meant, and the explanation was "After-Five Dealer." When he returned home from work at five in the afternoon, he then started selling coins to mail-order customers!

Many dealers specialize in a narrow area, such as tokens, obsolete paper money, Morgan silver dollars, or modern Proof coins with frosted cameo contrast. Other dealers reach out to the investment community, attend "hard money" seminars and the like, and reach those who enjoy owning gold and silver (the two most popular metals), but do not want to become numismatists. Still others sell modern coin books and supplies, while some deal only in out-of-print numismatic literature.

While most rare coin dealers concentrate on numismatics, either generally or in a specialty, some art auction houses such as Christie's and Sotheby's occasionally sell coins and paper money. Some other firms, well known in numismatics, also sell sports memorabilia, posters, autographs, comic books, and the like. In the latter category, Early American History Auctions (Dana Linett), Larry and Ira Goldberg, and Heritage (Jim Halperin and Steve Ivy) come to mind, but there are others. Steve Hayden specializes in auctioning tokens, while Currency Auctions of America (CAA, now a division of Heritage), Lyn Knight, and Smythe & Co. concentrate on paper money. Early copper coins are the specialty of the McCawley-Grellman auction duo.

Investment Money

Every so often there is a big influx of investment money into numismatics, as in 1988 and 1989 when many Wall Streeters decided buying coins instead of stocks was a great thing to do. Several brokerage firms, including Merrill Lynch and Kidder

Peabody, got into the act. A big hoopla resulted, "Wall Street money" poured into the hobby, and prices of so-called investment-grade coins (being mostly silver and gold in grades of MS-65 and higher, and in certified holders) skyrocketed. Limited partnerships and rare-coin funds were set up and took in millions of dollars. The bubble burst (no surprise at all to me, and you will understand it too when you read about coin market cycles in chapter 9). After a while most investors disappeared, headed for greener pastures, perhaps including the dot-com stocks that were all the rage in the 1990s—until they, too, crashed in 2000.

I can only speculate, but coin market sales rose to perhaps $1 billion or more during the Wall Street fever. When the newcomers exited, prices of certain "investment-quality" coins plummeted, but the rest of the market—comprising the majority of trading activity—did just fine.

Perhaps coin market sales figures, not knowable, are not as important as the knowledge that year after year, decade after decade, many people have enjoyed the hobby of coin collecting. Today, it is a well-established field, with many buyers and sellers, ample available information, and a good track record of long-term price performance.

A superb gem 1897 Barber half dollar graded Proof-68. Only 731 such Proofs were minted in this year, and few are of this quality. Such coins are usually of attractive appearance, and their aspects are easy to understand. Accordingly, specimens of this general type are very popular with investors. Market and demand conditions change, and even a first-class item such as this should be considered carefully before you make a purchase.

Old and rare coins, evocative of early America, offer a way to hold history in your hands. A collection of coins is a personal museum, each piece reflecting the art, commerce, and society of its era—a nostalgia trip. Shown here are coins from earlier times, each a prized collector's item today. Historical values (of circulated examples) are taken from past editions of the ***Guide Book of United States Coins*** (at 21 million copies, the best-selling coin price guide on the market).

From the *Mayflower* to Pine Trees...

Massachusetts Pine Tree shillings, dated 1652, were made in large quantities. These silver coins circulated widely through the colonies in the Northeast. Today they are numismatic favorites.

1652 Pine Tree shilling (in Fine condition)
1956: **$60** • 1976: **$475** • 1996: **$1,400** • 2006: **$2,000**

The new nation's first dollar-size coin

Although no records have been located concerning their issuance, it is believed that 1776 Continental dollars were produced under authority of the Continental Congress. The motto "Mind Your Business" was inspired by Benjamin Franklin. This example, struck in pewter, has a word on the obverse misspelled as CURENCY.

1776 Continental dollar, pewter (in Fine condition)
1956: **$65** • 1976: **$3,000** • 1996: **$3,200** • 2006: **$8,000**

The original American dollar

Spanish 8-*reales* coins were valued at a dollar and were a staple in American commerce into the late 1850s, by which time the United States had been producing its own coins for decades. This 1739 example was struck in Mexico City (note the Mo mintmark). It features the famous "Pillar dollar" design, depicting the Pillars of Hercules (symbolizing the Straits of Gibraltar). Some say today's dollar sign ($) originated from this design.

"Weighing six pennyweight and six grains apiece..."

New Jersey issued copper coins from 1786 to 1788, minted by private contractors in several cities in the state. After the legislature granted contractors authority to make these coins, their profit was limited only by the difference between expenses and face value. With their weight established by contract, and the entire operation given official status, the copper pieces were trusted by the public and achieved wide circulation. Many varieties exist.

**1787 New Jersey cent, common variety
(in Fine condition)**
1956: **$3.50** • 1976: **$45** • 1996: **$175** • 2006: **$200**

The United States' first mint building (in Philadelphia), used from 1792 until 1833, is shown

HISTORY IN YOUR HANDS

The memories and associations continue with this selection of coins through the early 19th century. In 1838, the first branch mints opened—at Charlotte (North Carolina), Dahlonega (Georgia), and New Orleans, with the last facility being by far the largest.

From five cents to five dollars in a few minutes

In 1883, the Mint launched the Liberty Head design for the five-cent nickel coin. Its denomination was expressed simply by the Roman numeral V. Miscreants gold-plated these coins and passed them as similar-sized $5 gold pieces. The Mint realized its mistake and soon added the word CENTS. Word spread that the CENTS-less pieces, as shown here, would become very rare and valuable. However, so many were saved that this, one of the most romantic of all 19th-century coins, is relatively inexpensive today.

1883 nickel, without CENTS (in Mint State)
1956: **$1.50** • 1976: **$40** • 1996: **$30** • 2006: **$45**

enlarged

A record-breaking investment

In contrast to the first nickel in the Liberty Head series, the last date, 1913, is a great rarity. The Eliasberg specimen, the finest of five known examples, was auctioned in 1996 for $1,485,000—the first coin to cross the million-dollar mark. In 2005, the same coin traded hands privately for about $4 million.

enlarged

One of the new "small cents"

Designed by Chief Engraver James B. Longacre, the Flying Eagle cent, made of copper-nickel alloy, entered circulation on May 25, 1857. The design proved difficult to strike, and many coins showed weakness in areas (the one shown here is an exception). After 1858, the motif was discontinued in favor of the new Indian Head cent.

1858 Flying Eagle cent (in Mint State)
1956: **$22.50** • 1976: **$485** • 1996: **$250** • 2006: **$600**

enlarged

"Eureka!"

Principals of Norris, Gregg & Norris, a New York plumbing and hardware firm, joined the Forty Niners in the Gold Rush, taking with them equipment to strike coins. $5 gold pieces such as this were made in Benicia City, on San Francisco Bay. These were in circulation by May 1849, possibly the very first of the Gold Rush issues.

1849 N.G. & N. gold half eagle (in Mint State)
1956: **$225** • 1976: **$4,000** • 1996: **$20,000** • 2006: **$25,000**

A grand new mint for the South

The New Orleans Mint opened for business in 1838 and continued through early 1861. It was closed during the Civil War, and reopened for coinage in 1879, minting silver and gold coins through 1909. The O mintmark on this $5 gold piece tells us it was struck in New Orleans.

1842-O gold half eagle (in Mint State)
enlarged 1956: **$40** • 1976: **$775** • 1996: **$12,000** • 2006: **$24,000**

Many artistic motifs have been used on United States coins over a long period of time. In the 18th and 19th centuries these were mostly the work of the chief engraver at the Mint or his assistants. In the early 20th century, artists and sculptors in the private sector were tapped to create designs. A selection of such issues is given here.

The Lincoln cent, by sculptor and numismatist Victor D. Brenner, was first minted in 1909.

1934 Lincoln cent (in gem Mint State)
1956: **$0.30** • 1976: **$2.25** • 1996: **$6** • 2006: **$10**

Sculptor Hermon A. MacNeil designed the Standing Liberty quarter dollar, first struck in 1916.

1917 Standing Liberty quarter, Type I (in Mint State)
1956: **$5.50** • 1976: **$175** • 1996: **$300** 2006: **$300**

enlarged

James Earle Fraser, a famous artist and sculptor of Midwestern themes, created the Indian Head (or Buffalo) design, first struck in 1913, for the nickel five-cent piece.

1913 Buffalo nickel, variety 1 (in Mint State)
1956: **$1.50** • 1976: **$25** • 1996: **$40** • 2006: **$55**

enlarged

In 1916, sculptor Adolph A. Weinman created the "Mercury" or Winged Liberty Head dime.

1929 Mercury dime (in Mint State)
1956: **$2.25** • 1976: **$15** • 1996: **$30** • 2006: **$75**

Weinman's other 1916 design, the Liberty Walking half dollar, was made until 1947.

1935-D Walking Liberty half dollar (in Mint State)
1956: **$10** • 1976: **$100** • 1996: **$100** • 2006: **$220**

Augustus Saint-Gaudens, America's most acclaimed sculptor, was commissioned by President Theodore Roosevelt in 1905 to redesign all coinage denominations, including the $20 gold piece.

MCMVII (1907) gold double eagle (in Mint State)
1956: **$145** • 1976: **$4,400** • 1996: **$6,750** 2006: **$26,500**

A Panorama of Silver Dollars

Silver dollars, first minted in 1794, were produced intermittently over a long span of years to 1935. While many early issues range from scarce to rare, Morgan (1878–1921) and Peace (1921–1935) dollars exist by the millions; many can be obtained in Mint State for less than $50 per coin. After the era of silver, dollars of other metals were made, including the Eisenhower dollars of 1971 to 1978, the Susan B. Anthony dollars of 1979 to 1999, and the Sacagawea dollars of 2000 to date.

1794 dollar (in Mint State)

1956: **$2,250** • 1976: **$90,000**
1996: **$175,000** • 2006: **$375,000**

This choice and lustrous Mint State dollar of 1794 from the Martin Logies Collection sold for more than a million dollars in 2005. Only 1,758 dollars of this date were distributed, from which an estimated 135 or so survive today, mostly in lower grades. The Mint experienced great difficulty in striking these pieces. All known examples have lightness of details, typically at the lower left of the obverse and corresponding part of the reverse. Most show adjustment or file marks on the planchet, sometimes severe, but on this coin they are minimal.

1800 dollar (in Mint State)

1956: **$100** • 1976: **$5,000**
1996: **$8,500** • 2006: **$16,500**

The Draped Bust design was introduced in late 1795. This 1800 example displays the Heraldic Eagle reverse, instituted in 1798. Dollars of this design combination were made from 1798 through 1803, then in 1834, on coins from dies antedated 1804. Many different die varieties exist.

1836 Gobrecht dollar (Proof)

1956: **$350** • 1976: **$4,250**
1996: **$7,500** • 2006: **$18,000**

In December 1836, the Philadelphia Mint coined 1,000 silver dollars of a new design, with dies by Christian Gobrecht, after sketches by Titian Peale and Thomas Sully. An additional 600 coins from the same dies were made in 1837. These were struck in Proof format and with a plain edge. Most were placed into circulation. Later, beginning in spring 1859, many restrikes were made. Proofs in higher grades sell for strong premiums.

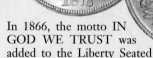

In 1866, the motto IN GOD WE TRUST was added to the Liberty Seated dollar, above the eagle on the reverse. This type was made through 1873. Shown is a particularly nice Mint State example of the rare 1872-S dollar.

1872-S Liberty Seated dollar
(in Mint State)
1956: **$90** • 1976: **$950**
1996: **$7,500** • 2006: **$30,000**

Morgan silver dollars, minted from 1878 to 1904 and again in 1921, are among the most enthusiastically collected series today. There are nearly 100 different dates and mintmarks, the majority of which are inexpensive in Mint State (although there are exceptions, including the rare Carson City dollar of 1889, shown here).

1889-CC Morgan dollar
(in Mint State)
1956: **$45** • 1976: **$3,100**
1996: **$13,000** • 2006: **$30,000**

Peace dollars were made from 1921 through 1935, except from 1929 to 1933. There are just 24 basic date and mintmark varieties today, all of which are highly collectible. Illustrated is a 1934 dollar struck in Denver.

1934-D Peace dollar
(in Mint State)
1956: **$5** • 1976: **$80**
1996: **$165** • 2006: **$325**

Trade dollars, of the special weight of 420 grains and heavier than a silver dollar, were made for use in the export trade to the Orient. Circulation strikes were produced from 1873 to 1878, while Proofs for collectors were made from 1873 to 1885. Shown here is an 1878 Proof.

1878 trade dollar (Proof)
1956: **$32.50** • 1976: **$1,200**
1996: **$2,100** • 2006: **$2,500**

GOING FOR THE GOLD

The Philadelphia Mint struck its first gold coins in the summer of 1795. From then until 1933, a cascade of gold pieces came from Philadelphia, added to by production from mints in Charlotte (North Carolina), Dahlonega (Georgia), New Orleans, San Francisco, Carson City (Nevada), and Denver. Denominations included $1, $2.50, $3, $5, $10, and $20, with most of the total value (over 75%) in the $20 coins or double eagles.

The dollar, the smallest denomination struck in gold, was made in three different design types. Shown here is a Proof striking of the 1855 Indian Princess design—a rarity valued at $185,000+.

enlarged

1855 gold dollar (in Mint State)
1956: **$20** • 1976: **$2,000** • 1996: **$2,300** • 2006: **$14,000**

The Philadelphia Mint delivered its first gold coins, $5 half eagles, in July 1795. The denomination proved popular, and many were made in ensuing years.

enlarged

1795 gold half eagle (in Mint State)
1956: **$250** • 1976: **$8,500**
1996: **$25,000** • 2006: **$140,000**

Boston sculptor Bela Lyon Pratt designed the $2.50 and $5 Indian Head coins used from 1908 to 1929. A departure from regular coinage, these featured the motifs and lettering incuse, or recessed in the field. 1909 is a common date in this series.

1909 gold half eagle (in Mint State)
1956: **$12** • 1976: **$225** • 1996: **$350** • 2006: **$1,750**

enlarged

Counting freshly minted $20 gold double eagles at the Philadelphia Mint in 1894. This denomination, made in especially large quantities, was in great demand for the export trade and settling international balances. Today, most double eagles from the late 19th and early 20th centuries are

GOLDEN SHIPWRECK COINS FROM THE SEA

One of the earliest widely published color maps showing the Gold Rush area of California as depicted in Hinton's *History of the United States*, 1850. Privately minted and federal gold coins from this era are enthusiastically collected today.

A stunning display of gold coins, mostly 1857-S double eagles. Today, all of these have been sold and are highly prized by collectors and museums. Now and again, examples reappear on the market.

On September 12, 1857, the *S.S. Central America* was lost at sea off the coast of North Carolina, on its way to New York City, taking with it $1,600,000 face value of gold coins and ingots from California. In the late 1980s, much of the treasure was recovered by the Columbus-America Discovery Group, yielding items with a market value approaching $100 million. Beginning in 2000, the California Gold Marketing Group (Dwight Manley, president) offered the treasure for sale.

A "garden" of gold ingots and coins recovered from the *S.S. Central America*.

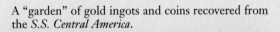

A gem Mint State 1857-S $20 double eagle from the *S.S. Central America*, one of about 5,400 such coins recovered. Today, most examples are valued in the $5,000 to $20,000 range, depending on grade.

COMMEMORATIVE COINS

The World's Columbian Exposition, scheduled to open in 1892 to observe the 400th anniversary of Columbus's "discovery" of America, but delayed until 1893, furnished the venue for an extensive issue of commemorative half dollars and a commemorative quarter dollar.

The World's Columbian Exposition opened its gates to the public in 1893. There was a rush to buy commemorative half dollars of the 1892 and 1893 dates for $1 each, but less interest in the 1893 Isabella quarter, also priced at $1, as it was perceived as being less of a value for the price paid. The fair was known as the White City from the color of its buildings.

(coins shown enlarged)

The gigantic Ferris Wheel—a main attraction—drew thousands of eager riders. Years later, in 1904, it was moved to the St. Louis World's Fair, where it entertained countless more. Later, it was scrapped. (Benjamin Kilburn photograph from stereo view)

From the World's Columbian Exposition in 1892 to the present day, many different commemorative coins have been made, in silver, gold, and clad metal.

NUMISMATICS: A KEY TO STATE HISTORY

Coins are a key to the history of America. Today the 50 State Quarters® Program showcases each state with a reverse design selected by its citizens or representatives. The Vermont quarter features a maple-sapping scene, with Camel's Hump Mountain in the background. Some other Vermont connections to numismatics are shown here.

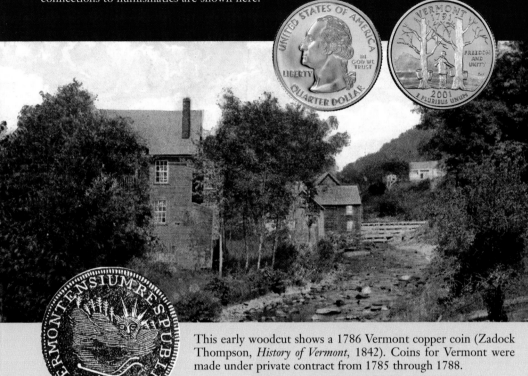

This early woodcut shows a 1786 Vermont copper coin (Zadock Thompson, *History of Vermont*, 1842). Coins for Vermont were made under private contract from 1785 through 1788.

1786 Vermont copper (in Fine condition)
1956: **$12.50** • 1986: **$375** • 1996: **$550** • 2006: **$825**

The 1927 Vermont Sesquicentennial commemorative half dollar observed the 150th anniversary of the Battle of Bennington and the independence of Vermont. The district remained its own "country" or entity until it was admitted to the Union in 1791.

1927 Vermont half dollar (in Mint State)
1956: **$16** • 1986: **$250** • 1996: **$190** • 2006: **$850**

This About Uncirculated $5 bill (Series of 1882) was issued by the First National Bank of Montpelier. It was purchased at auction in 2005 for $5,100. Many different National Banks in the state issued federal paper money with their imprints, circa 1865 to 1935.

TOKENS AND MEDALS

Tokens and medals have formed a prime focus of collecting interest for many years. Most are scarce or rare in comparison to coins. While the market is mainly limited to specialists and is quiet, over a span of time many choice pieces have appreciated handsomely in value.

This brass Hard Times token of the 1830s features William H. Seward, candidate for governor of New York. This variety (HT-28) is valued in the *Standard Catalog of U.S. Tokens* at $600 in Extremely Fine and $1,500 in MS-60.

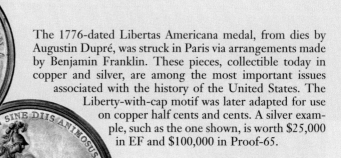

The 1776-dated Libertas Americana medal, from dies by Augustin Dupré, was struck in Paris via arrangements made by Benjamin Franklin. These pieces, collectible today in copper and silver, are among the most important issues associated with the history of the United States. The Liberty-with-cap motif was later adapted for use on copper half cents and cents. A silver example, such as the one shown, is worth $25,000 in EF and $100,000 in Proof-65.

This well-worn 1840 copper cent was counterstamped USE GOODWIN'S GRAND GREASE JUICE FOR THE HAIR. This 1850s tonsorial product, sold by Charles H. Goodwin of Exeter, New Hampshire, was also known as G.G.G. The counterstamped cent is worth $300 to $500.

This is a common variety of Civil War token, issued in 1863 when federal cents were being hoarded. Such tokens were made in thousands of varieties, usually with patriotic inscriptions (as here) or with advertisements. Common patriotic pieces are worth $8 in Fine condition, $18 in EF, and $40 in MS-60.

American paper money dates back to early colonial times. Its rich history continues through the Revolutionary War, and evolves into a panorama of thousands of different issues of the 19th century.

The bills shown here do not trade often on the numismatic market, so values are subject to wide variation. The prices reflect transactions involving the particular bills illustrated.

Continental Currency notes were issued from 1775 through 1780, in face values up to $80. The $20 issue of May 10, 1775, printed on special paper with colored marbling at the left end, is one of the most valuable today. The paper was obtained in France by Benjamin Franklin. (Extremely Fine; sold for $4,000 in 2004)

Obsolete bank notes furnish vignettes of American life at the time. This $2 bill of the Nemaha Valley Bank, Brownville, Nebraska, was issued in 1857. (Extremely Fine; sold for $215 in 2004)

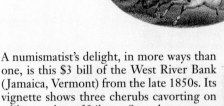

A numismatist's delight, in more ways than one, is this $3 bill of the West River Bank (Jamaica, Vermont) from the late 1850s. Its vignette shows three cherubs cavorting on a like number of Liberty Seated silver dollars. Such notes are readily available today from undistributed remainders. (Value in Uncirculated grade, about $150)

THE BEAUTY OF U.S. PAPER MONEY

The federal government issued relatively small quantities of paper money in its early years, with the Continental Currency series. Starting in the 1860s, federal bills were distributed in great quantity in many different series and styles. Prices below are from *A Guide Book of United States Paper Money* (2005).

The famous and beautiful $5 "Educational Note," Silver Certificate, Series of 1896, features an allegorical scene of *Electricity Presenting Light to the World*. This exciting new energy source was showcased widely, including at the recent World's Columbian Exposition in 1893. (VF-20: **$2,000** • EF-40: **$2,800** • Unc-63: **$7,500**)

This Series of 1890 Coin Note or Treasury Note has a face value of $1—the lowest denomination in a group of designs that culminated with the $1,000 "Grand Watermelon Note." Coin Notes were redeemable in gold and silver coins. (VF-20: **$900** • EF-40: **$1,350** • Unc-63: **$4,000**)

This $1 note, series of 1875, is from the Brandon (Vermont) National Bank—chartered in 1864 as the Second National Bank of Brandon, successor to the state-chartered Brandon Bank. The bank's directors did not like the word *Second*, so they changed the title to the Brandon National Bank. This note is printed on paper tinged blue at the left, a style used for a short time on various series of federal notes. (Purchased at auction in 2005 for $3,100 plus 15% buyer's fee plus 5% to the dealer who did the bidding)

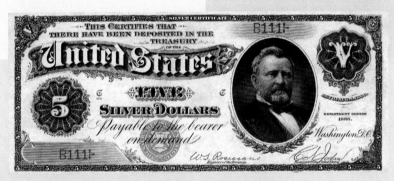

Known as the "Silver Dollar Note," the Series of 1886 $5 Silver Certificate displays five Morgan dollars across its back. As might be expected, this motif has been popular with numismatists for a long time. (VF-20: **$1,650** • EF-40: **$2,500** • Unc-63: **$5,000**)

WHAT MIGHT HAVE BEEN

Patterns tell the story of coin designs that were created at the Mint but never used, strikings in metals other than those eventually adopted, and experiments with edges, weights, and sizes. The pattern, trial, and experimental pieces below, from the ninth edition of J. Hewitt Judd's *United States Pattern Coins*, illustrate the beautiful diversity of America's coins that "might have been."

In 1850, the Mint experimented with ideas to replace the large copper cents then in circulation, as these had become too expensive to produce. Many different patterns were created during the decade, in various proportions of copper and nickel, called *German silver*. This pattern was created in haste, by combining a regular *quarter eagle* obverse with a quickly made reverse lettered ONE CENT. The dies were not polished.

1853 one-cent pattern (J-151), in German silver
MS-60: **$1,750** • MS-63: **$2,750** • MS-65: **$4,500**

enlarged

This pattern dime of 1870 (J-866, struck in aluminum) is one of hundreds of different Standard Silver issues created in 1869 and 1870 to provide items for Mint insiders to sell into the numismatic market for their private profit. Denominations ranged from three cents to one dollar.

1870 dime pattern (J-866), in aluminum
Proof-60: **$1,700** • Proof-63: **$2,350** • Proof-65: **$4,000**

This 1871 pattern dollar (J-1150) combines an Indian Princess design (by the late James B. Longacre, who died on January 1, 1869) with a regular silver dollar reverse. Strikings were made in aluminum (as shown here), copper, and silver, with reeded and plain edges. Mint officials sold the coins to friends and associates in the numismatic community for their own personal gain.

1871 dollar pattern (J-1150), in aluminum
Proof-60: **$9,500** • Proof-63: **$19,000** • Proof-65: **$29,000**

Chief Engraver William Barber created a beautiful set of pattern designs in 1872. The impressive figure of Miss Liberty (on the obverse) inspired the nickname for these "Amazonian" patterns. Silver pieces were struck in quarter dollar, half dollar, and dollar denominations, to the tune of perhaps two dozen sets. A similar set in gold, with a bust of Liberty wearing a Phrygian cap, contains a dollar, quarter eagle, $3 piece, half eagle, eagle, and double eagle. The gold set is unique—only one of each coin was struck—and is one of the great masterpieces of American coinage. The double eagle is valued at $1.5 million.

Among 19th-century pattern coins, the half dollars of 1877 combine different obverse and reverse dies by William Barber, George T. Morgan, and Anthony C. Paquet, with copper and silver versions, to create a dazzling panorama of great rarities. This reeded-edge copper example, J-1502, is by Barber. No more than a dozen are believed to exist today.

1877 half dollar pattern (J-1502)
Proof-60: **$15,000** • Proof-63: **$22,500**
Proof-65: **$32,000**

This silver 1916 pattern (J-1992) preceded the Liberty Walking half dollar. Note the subtle differences between this pattern, of which 7 to 12 are believed to exist, and the coin eventually minted in the tens of millions for circulation. The history of this and other silver-series 1916 pattern coins (dime, quarter, and half dollar) is just beginning to be studied in depth, through the efforts of Saul Teichman, Roger W. Burdette, John Dannreuther, and others. All patterns of this year are very rare.

1916 half dollar pattern (J-1992), in silver
Proof-60: **$40,000** • Proof-63: **$71,500**
Proof-65: **$125,000**

NUMISMATIC PEOPLE AND EVENTS

Some of the biggest dividends paid from numismatics are in the forms of friendship and memories. In that sense—whether you think of coin and currency collecting as a hobby or as an "industry"—your investment is guaranteed.

This scene shows action at the Eliasberg Collection sale (2005), with auctioneer Christine Karstedt at the podium. This was the final presentation of a series of sales featuring the most valuable numismatic collection ever to cross the auction block.

John Mercanti, long-time sculptor-engraver at the United States Mint, was happy to share his thoughts at the 2005 American Numismatic Association convention in San Francisco. Here he explains changes to be made to the nickel five-cent reverse design in 2006. Standing to his left is Gloria Eskridge, deputy director of the Mint. (Photograph courtesy of Donn Pearlman)

Jay Johnson (former Mint director), Garrett Burke (designer of the 2005 California state quarter) and his wife Michelle, and, to the right, Dennis Tucker (publisher) and Mary Counts (president) of Whitman Publishing, all enjoyed a fine dinner and camaraderie at the ANA banquet and reception (July 2005).

Numismatists on a field trip. The time is October 2003, and the place is the long-abandoned Gold Coin Mine in Victor, Colorado, high in the Rockies. Left to right: Wynn Bowers, Larry Goldberg, Dwight Manley, and his daughter, Victoria Manley.

Newcomers and Old Timers

The Coin Bug

As to the length of time the typical collector remains involved with the hobby, I recently asked several dealers and publishers about this, and three years was about average. This is for someone who comes in, discovers coins, becomes serious about the hobby, buys intensely, then runs out of money, or interest, or both. The late R.W. McLachlan called such a collector a *comet*—appearing from nowhere, blazing brightly, then disappearing.[9]

A lot of day-trippers come into the hobby, and first-year nonrenewals and drop-out rates often exceed 50% with publications and coin clubs. Perhaps this is a natural weeding-out. However, once people collect for a few years, chances are good they will remain in the hobby for the rest of their lives.

As I mentioned in the introduction, once you are bitten by the "coin bug," as it used to be called, there is no cure! You may well have this marvelous affliction for the rest of your life. Years ago at every ANA convention it was customary to sing the *Coin Bug Song*, with new lyrics each time around, to the tune of *It Ain't Gonna Rain No More*. Sometimes verses would run into the dozens, often made up on the spot, about particular dealers and collectors. This was before my time, and I have only read about it in back issues of *The Numismatist*. This might be a nice tradition to revive.

A Lifetime Pursuit

I can think of no better example of longevity in the hobby than the Rittenhouse Society. In the 1950s, while in high school, and, later, at Pennsylvania State University, I spent a great deal of time studying the history of United States coins, checking into die varieties of state and colonial coins, trying to find out about the enigmatic Machin's Mills (a private coining facility in Newburgh, New York), and otherwise tracking down obscure information.

At the time, relatively few others were interested in numismatic research.

A bunch of us concerned with such matters got together, had informal meetings and discussions, and called ourselves the Rittenhouse Society, after the first director of the Mint, David Rittenhouse, a scholar, artist, and philosopher. A few years later, in 1960, we wrote something on paper, not a charter or anything so formal, but at least a listing of names and addresses. The original or founding members included D. Wayne ("Dick") Johnson, Kenneth W. Rendell, Grover Criswell, Kenneth E. Bressett, George Fuld, Walter Breen, Eric P. Newman, and me. Today, as I write these words in 2005, each and every member is still very active in numismatics—collecting, reading, and enjoying the hobby—except for two who have passed away, Grover Criswell and Walter Breen. I wonder if any other group has commanded such attention from its original membership for such a long time?

This was among the first special-interest groups in American numismatics. Not long afterward other niche groups were formed, including the Society of Paper Money Collectors (SPMC) and the Token and Medal Society (TAMS). Today, there are at least a couple dozen such societies, and I belong to perhaps half of them.

Apparently, the Rittenhouse Society example of sustained interest is hardly

Eric P. Newman, a founding member of the Rittenhouse Society, with a rarity from his collection, *Uncurrent Bank Bills, Minnesota, Vol. 1*. The author of several books and many articles, Newman is one of the prime figures in numismatic study and research.

unique. Recently, in *Numismatic News*, editor Dave Harper reported survey findings showing that 43% of his readers have been collecting for 40 years or more.[10]

Newcomers Important

While old-time collectors are enjoyable to talk with, much of the dynamics in the marketplace comes from newcomers with fresh-faced enthusiasm and excitement. No doubt newcomers spend more money on average each year than old-timers do, a boon to the economics of our hobby.

My favorite type of new collector is someone—anyone—who has a sincere interest in numismatics. Of course, eventually spending significant sums on rare coins is desirable for the bottom line of my business, but it is true that quite a few collectors who keep in touch with me spend very little. However, they contribute a great deal to my enjoyment of the business, by communicating on research and sharing experiences.

I could tell quite a few stories about people who began in a modest way, then went on to become highly important in the field. Robert A. ("Bob") Vlack commenced in the 1950s by ordering from me a "starter collection" of old Connecticut copper cents, 1785 to 1788, became enthralled with the purchase, learned more, and the rest is history. Not long afterward, he jumped feet-first into research, and within a year or two he wrote a *book* on colonial coins. At the summer 2004 ANA convention, Bob showed me his *latest* book, one on French colonial issues.

For a number of years I taught the "All About Coins" class at Colorado College in Colorado Springs, part of the ANA Summer Seminar. Usually, most of my students were newcomers. At least two of them, both teenagers when they attended, found the week-long immersion in rare coins sufficiently interesting that they decided then and there to become professional numismatists! One was Dwight Manley, who a few years ago headed the sale of the *S.S. Central America* treasure and, among other things, has owned such rarities as the finest known 1913 Liberty Head nickel (the Eliasberg specimen) and an 1804 silver dollar. The other was Kerry Wetterstrom, who today is one of the leading dealers in ancient Greek and Roman coins and is editor of the *Celator*, a highly acclaimed magazine.

One of my favorite Summer Seminar stories involves Mrs. M.W., a lady who enrolled in my class but warned me at the beginning of the first day, "I do not collect coins and am not interested in them. I came on the trip just to keep my husband company. Do not call on me or ask any questions. I will be in the back row, reading and knitting." What happened probably surprised her, and it certainly surprised me: I don't think a page was turned or a piece of yarn was handled. At the end of the week she said, "I enjoyed every minute. Now I know why my husband is so excited about coin collecting."

"Bert" Bressett, wife of Ken (writer of the foreword to this book), came to my "All About Coins" class one year, liked it a lot, and the next year came back to take it all over again. This was fine, as each year I changed the course somewhat, and there were always new things to talk about.

Another newcomer in the early 1980s was Liz Arlin, who had just graduated from secretarial school and landed her very first job with me. This was during the time I was president of the ANA, giving her first-hand experience at dealing with everything from convention planning, to budgets, to growth of the collecting hobby, to resolving disputes—you name it, and it probably crossed Liz's desk! She became so interested that she learned about coin grading, market values, and other skills, after which she decided to become a professional dealer in her own right. Today, with her husband Miles Coggan (a distant relative of the late dealer B. Max Mehl, by the way), she operates the Boston firm of J.J. Teaparty & Co., with notable success.

Newcomers are indeed important—especially those who are bitten by the coin bug and stay with the hobby. May more keep coming, and may the bug keep biting!

Easy Come, Easy Go— or Perhaps Stay!

In contrast with newcomers who develop a deep interest, some are here today and gone tomorrow. Frequently, a big spender will come onto the scene with a flash, determined to build a fine collection quickly. Some who can afford it will even go after "trophy coins," such as an 1879 Flowing Hair $4 gold Stella, an MCMVII High Relief $20, or even an 1804 silver dollar. Most such coins have done well for their uneducated but wealthy buyers, simply because as the market rises, classic issues rise with it. However, with knowledge, even trophy coins can be bought to better advantage. While I always give this advice, and the reminder that one should learn about coins before jumping into the field too deeply, not everyone wants to hear it.

Some such buyers prove to be a flash in the pan, easy come and easy go. Others decide to stay.

I recall a bidder, previously unknown to me, who spent several hundred thousand dollars on a trophy coin in one of our sales. *Afterward*, he bought his first book on coins. Soon, he learned how to pronounce *numismatist*, and became one!

In another instance, a gentleman bought a spectacular collection of pattern coins from me, then asked me to track down a book on the subject (by Edgar H. Adams and William H. Woodin; this was in the 1950s, before the popular book on the same subject by Dr. J. Hewitt Judd was published). This man was in the financial accounting business. He liked coins so much that he decided to become a dealer, which he did, with some success.

Getting Comfortable

I am not suggesting that when you discover coins you sit down in an armchair and do nothing but read before making any purchases. Indeed, it is normal to get your feet wet, and even to jump into the numismatic water. This is true in many other fields as well. I bought my first music box and *then* decided to learn about

Miles Coggan (right), president of J.J. Teaparty, Inc., discusses a lovely 1869 Indian Head cent with collector Gary Sjostedt. The firm was founded in 1957 by Ed Leventhal, and today is owned by Miles and his wife, Liz, née Arlin (who discovered numismatics as a teenager in the early 1980s, when she was hired as the personal secretary to the author).

what I had bought (eventually making this one of my collecting specialties). Ditto when I bought my first Currier & Ives print, *The Clipper Ship Dreadnought off Tuskar Light*, although, unlike with music boxes, my interest in these prints has remained at the casual level.

Probably most collectors begin by buying an interesting silver dollar through a television marketing program, or by ordering items from the U.S. Mint, or perhaps by visiting a coin dealer. A California man bought a large and expensive group of 100 bullion-type gold coins from a telemarketer, turned a nice profit in a rising market, then got acquainted with dealers in rare coins and set about collecting $20 gold double eagles by date and mintmark. Eventually, his collection was of such importance that several auctioneers each did headstands trying to land his consignment.

Fascination with coins is generated quickly—choice and beautiful specimens can have that effect! If you spend a few thousand dollars or even more to get started, you are in good company. See the second chapter of this book, about how to get started right away, *before* gaining knowledge!

With a bunch of interesting coins at your elbow, *then* there may be time for you to read, to snuggle into an overstuffed chair and get comfortable. The *Guide Book of United States Coins* beckons with all of its information, and beyond that, *Walter Breen's Complete Encyclopedia of U.S. and Colonial Coins* is a gold mine of information, if a bit more technical. Acquire both of these books and read them, and you will have as much knowledge as most experts.

When I was a teenager I loved coins, but could not afford most of those that I desired. I could afford books, and much of my budget was spent in that direction. Since then I have said many times that if I could not replace it, I would not trade my library for its weight in gold! I consider books to be so important that I've devoted chapter 31 to this subject.

It is likely that if you begin your interest in coins by buying a few pieces that catch your eye, then along the way browse through some books, attend a coin show or two, sign up for some dealers' catalogs, and subscribe to a numismatic newspaper—all the while conserving your budget—the coin bug will take a nip. Then, in the sunset years of your life, you will have a wonderful asset: the rare coin hobby. With some good planning, careful buying, and good fortune, your favorite pastime may well be your most profitable investment as well. Other treasures are those that money cannot buy—the memories of nice experiences and many fine friends.

Such are the dynamics of the numismatic market—a hobby or an industry if you prefer—with many collectors and dealers buying, selling, and appreciating the pleasures and possibilities of coins, tokens, medals, and paper money.

CHAPTER FOUR

INVESTING IN AND ENJOYING RARE COINS

Numismatics, while no doubt an expensive hobby, is the most harmless and the most educating and refining in its influences, that one could pursue. Ennobling, by leading one to pursue his investigations into history and the arts, it is engrossing and all pervading. The numismatist thinks of nothing but rare coins, muses on them, dreams of them. His enjoyment involves all species of pleasure and mental excitement. He is a sportsman, a gamester, an artist, a detective, a critic, an expert. He follows the scent of a rare coin as a hound does that of a rabbit, and is never satisfied till he has traced it to its burrow. The passions excited are ambition, hope, desire and envy, but never to any extent to be injurious.

Your true numismatist is usually a man of gentlemanly instincts and scholarly attainments. His associations are with men who think, reason, compare, sift evidence, and judge. He is little likely to be gulled, being always on the lookout for counterfeits; still less likely to deceive others, having a wholesome contempt for base fabrication. On the whole, this hobby is one which should be encouraged, because it leads the workings of the mind into proper channels, trains the faculties, and educates and encourages a sound, healthful taste for the aesthetic.

—E.L. Mason, Jr., June 1867

In the Beginning

Getting Started

What should I collect? What is the right thing to collect in today's market? Where can I get the best value for my money? Where do I start?

These are the usual questions collectors and dealers hear all the time. In the beginning, so many possibilities exist and so many opinions are given, one can be easily overwhelmed.

Generally, newcomers are more comfortable if they collect a popular series.

Morgan dollars are a great starting point. There are a lot of these coins around, hundreds of thousands of people collect them casually, and tens of thousands of numismatists are serious about them. There are many books and articles in print—including a Whitman book I authored (*Morgan Silver Dollars: A Complete History and Price Guide*), not to overlook a dozen worthwhile titles by others, plus offerings and information about Morgan dollars in magazines, at shows, and on the Internet. Of course, you don't want to *drown* in Morgan silver dollar information—but if you select this series, there are a lot of people and lots of coins available to help you begin.

A friend once suggested, "If you want to give someone an interesting old coin to get them started, give them an 1881-S dollar."

Good advice. The 1881-S Morgan silver dollar is common in Mint State (well over a million exist), old enough to be historical and fascinating (120+ years of age and counting), and inexpensive—significantly less than $50 for a fairly decent Mint State coin, not much over $100 for a gem.

Another suggestion, this from a highly successful dealer friend, Dave Sundman: "Give a worn Liberty Head nickel, Buffalo nickel, and Indian cent. Each is a strange design to most people, and they cost only a few dollars."

I have found that if someone gives a friend or relative two or three interesting coins, a *Guide Book*, and an album or two (such as for statehood quarters—easily collectible), this can be a great catalyst to spark their interest in collecting. Sometimes this can be done on a grand scale, as in this event, chronicled by Michele Orzano in the pages of *Coin World:*

> Bill Himmelwright had folks crawling on the floor at the Minneapolis Institute of Arts recently. No, they weren't looking for a missing artifact;

they were looking for Lincoln cents. Himmelwright, a coin dealer and owner of Premium Quality Coins in Minneapolis, gave away 155 "penny boards" to children and their families to fill while searching through 45,000 Lincoln cents as part of the October 10th Ford Free Sunday Family Day event at the museum.

Himmelwright provided 20,000 Lincoln, Wheat reverse cents and 25,000 Lincoln, Memorial cents for a "Penny Frenzy" treasure hunt–type of activity. The Ford Motor Co. sponsored the family day.... Children and their parents were also able to learn about the history and value of money as well as the importance of saving money.[11]

While scrambling around the floor of a hall is a great way to get started, perhaps a more popular method is to go to a coin shop or visit a coin show and simply browse around. If you see something of interest, ask about it. When was this type of coin made? Why? In what different grades is this variety available, and for what price? Is this particular piece a nice example of its grade? How did you determine its price?

Then, if you go through steps 1 through 4 outlined in chapter 2, you'll take home a dandy example of an 1881-S dollar, or a 1938-D/S overmintmark Buffalo nickel, or a chocolate-brown 1854 copper cent, or a 1968-S Proof set, or whatever you fancy. (Actually, if you're typical you won't have bought this book yet! No matter, buying first and learning afterward is the usual procedure. Hopefully, your first steps have been small ones. Every beginner makes mistakes. I've made plenty of them myself. That's part of the learning process.)

Now, with some knowledge, it's onward and upward!

Changing Preferences

Very few people decide at the beginning, or even in the first few months, what they would like to collect in a serious manner.

Once they do make a choice, they seldom stay in this niche for the rest of their lives. It's normal to switch from one interest to another. When a series nears completion and interesting items are not acquired often, or are out of reach, it's time for a new vista, a new challenge.

Many numismatists of my acquaintance have explored several areas of the hobby. The late Ray Byrne, of Pittsburgh, an undertaker by profession, specialized in Barber-design silver coins (1892–1916) for a time, then went on to other things. His reason for leaving Barber coins was interesting. He was thoroughly confused with grading, as one dealer would sell something as "brilliant Uncirculated," but to Ray's eye there would be some wear or rubbing, or perhaps it had been polished, while a coin from another source would be lustrous and frosty. These were the days before commercial grading services. He then turned to tokens of Pennsylvania, then to counterstamped coins used in the West Indies.

Armand Champa, operator of several roller-skating rinks in and around Louisville, Kentucky, built a fantastic collection of United States pattern coins, which, when I cataloged it in 1972, was one of the finest such offerings of its era. Without skipping a beat he turned to another area: out-of-print numismatic books and catalogs. Curiously, Armand rarely *read* any of his books—he just collected them, often had them expertly rebound (by Alan Grace), and enjoyed discussing them with other numismatic bibliophiles.

John Whitney Walter formed a beautiful collection of Roman coins, then went on to build an award-winning display of United States coinage of the year 1796 (a year especially laden with formidable rarities), and then continued to form a memorable collection of American paper money (auctioned in 2004 by Lyn F. Knight).

Herman Halpern became an icon in the world of collecting large copper cents, then went on to assemble a truly great collection of paper money, after which he took up United States coins by design types.

Denis Loring achieved prominence as a collector of large copper cents and, among other activities, was a major buyer from the 1982 catalog of 1794-dated cents from the John W. Adams collection—one of my favorite publications (created with the help of Adams and my associate, Rick Bagg). While Loring still maintains his interest in that area, he has explored other channels as well. At a recent national convention he gave a talk on California gold coins, an interest ignited by purchasing from me an 1848 CAL. quarter eagle (made at the Philadelphia Mint in late 1848 from gold received from California, and given a special CAL. stamp on the reverse) and reading my book, *A California Gold Rush History*.

If I were to introduce you to 100 long-time numismatists, you would find that at least 90 of them are now excited about one or more *new* specialties! Probably only a few will have any trophy rarities, but all will be immersed in new discoveries among commemoratives, Liberty Seated silver coins, half cents, patterns, or something else.

There is no right thing to collect first—or last. You can follow your heart!

My Own Experience

Over the years, I've enjoyed collecting many things, often selling a set of one specialty to provide money for the next. In the 1950s, my funds were very limited, so that was the natural thing to do. I enjoyed gathering a type set of gem commemorative silver coins from 1892 to 1954, with 48 different half dollars plus the 1893 Isabella quarter and the 1900 Lafayette dollar, cherrypicking for high quality. (The *cherrypicking* term, popular in the hobby, refers to closely examining coins and selecting those of special quality or with interesting characteristics.) At that time, dealers simply called commemoratives *Uncirculated* or a lower grade such as About Uncirculated or Extremely Fine. There were no gradations of Uncirculated (Mint State) such as the MS-60, MS-61, MS-62, and so on, that we know today. However, at the out-

set I had an eye for quality, and found it curious that not many others did.

I recall that in the 1950s Ken Rendell and I visited the coin office of Arthur Conn, one of America's leading specialists in commemoratives. He did business from a room in his fine home in Melrose, Massachusetts, and each month had a double-spread advertisement in the *Numismatic Scrapbook Magazine*. I found it quite interesting that all of his Uncirculated 1900-dated Lafayette dollars were priced at precisely the same amount, no matter whether they showed some nicking or scuffing, or whether they were flawless gems! If you are at all skeptical about this, just get a few copies of *The Numismatist* or the *Numismatic Scrapbook* from the 1950s, or, for that matter, some of my old catalogs, and you will see such listings. It was usual to advertise a commemorative simply as "brilliant Uncirculated," no numbers, no other adjectives. I tried to emphasize quality, and charged a premium for what I considered to be coins from a carefully selected inventory. Aubrey and Adeline Bebee, in Omaha, emphasized quality. In the field of paper money, Texas banker, collector, and dealer William A. Philpott, Jr., felt a gem note was worth more than an ordinary one. However, we were all exceptions. Then as now, most buyers were mainly concerned about *price*. Probably not one in 10 emphasizes *quality*.

I have always tried to buy high quality, as the coins were nicer and, often, they did not cost any more! Actually, they did cost more in terms of time, for often it took great effort to track down pieces with good eye appeal.

At a slightly earlier time—this was in 1952 and 1953—I collected Indian Head cents. I bought for $11 a gem 1859 from the Copley Coin Co., my first mail-order purchase. The co-owner of Copley (with Frank Washburn) was Maurice M. Gould. We later became fine professional friends, and still later he sold me his personal collection of counterstamped copper cents. I bought most of my Indian cents at the Wilkes-Barre Coin Club, not far from my hometown of Forty Fort, Pennsylvania. A gem Mint State cent of the early 1900s was worth about a dollar. Once, I telephoned Harvey Stack, in New York City, about an 1856 Flying Eagle cent—I simply had to own one! He apologized that as the market was so active, and as his recent Anderson-Dupont sale had done so well, he would have to get a very high price—$300—for a gem he had just bought. Today, that $11 Indian cent of 1859 would be worth $2,000 or more, and the 1856 Flying Eagle cent would sell in the $30,000 range! I didn't keep them, but, presumably, they have made later owners happy!

I decided to collect Proof half dollars from the first Liberty Seated year, 1839, through the end of the Barber series, 1915. I completed all years 1854 to 1915 and obtained about half of the earlier years, including 1839. Such coins were inexpensive, with gem Barber halves of the 1890s costing about $7 to $9 each. At the time, there wasn't much of a market for the very early pre-1858 Proofs, as they were not listed in the *Guide Book*, and just about everybody used that familiar red-covered reference as the arbiter on what to collect. I also enjoyed buying and selling pre-1858 Proofs in various series. As amazing as it may seem to you to read this today, if I had a Proof 1846 half dollar for sale back then, not many people would have wanted it, for it was not listed in the *Guide Book*. However, if I had a Proof 1914 or 1915 for sale, at a higher price, I would get a dozen orders for each!

I became excited about pattern coins, and bought all I could afford, usually for resale, as the series was too expensive for me to collect. At the time I started dealing in coins (in 1953), patterns were not at all popular in the marketplace. However, Sol Kaplan (of Cincinnati) and Abe Kosoff (partner with Abner Kreisberg in the Numismatic Gallery in Beverly Hills) had large quantities—hundreds of different examples. I eagerly bought them, usually through Sol (who then reported sales to Abe and Abner), and became his best customer. Meanwhile, I was busy selling patterns to my own select list of private buyers, including Dr. J. Hewitt Judd, who would later write a definitive book on the subject, and to Lester Merkin, a professional musician who went on to become a prominent dealer.

In 1953, it was announced that the Palace Collections, so called, of ousted King Farouk of Egypt would be auctioned in Cairo. Kaplan offered to be my agent at the auction, presuming that I would be a big buyer, not knowing that I was literally living from coin to coin, and that in order to afford 20 new ones I had to sell 15 or so from my inventory. When the sale was held, Abe Kosoff, Sol Kaplan, Ambassador and Mrs. R. Henry Norweb, Hans M.F. Schulman, Robert Schermerhorn, John J. Pittman, James P. Randall, Paul Wittlin, Gaston DiBello, and Maurice Storck were the American contingent. I didn't go, but I bought many of the patterns afterward. I knew all of these people, most of whom are gone now (but not so long ago I ran into Maurice Storck at a coin show).

A few more things could be added to the list of coins I have collected, studied, and then sold, such as Vermont copper cents of 1785 to 1788, Connecticut coppers of the same years, and Hard Times tokens of the 1830s, but you get the idea.

One of my pet collections, and one that is still going strong, was started in 1955 and consisted of large copper cents of 1793 to 1857 stamped with advertisements for merchants, political slogans, and the like, such as VOTE THE LAND FREE or DR. G.G. WILKINS. These used to be nearly free, or cost a dollar or two. By the time I bought Maurice Gould's collection, in the 1960s, $3 to $6 was about the going price. No longer. In 2004, I spent several thousand dollars buying just two copper cents with Washington/Lafayette counterstamps, from one of Stack's sales of the Ford Collection—to go with a bunch of others I have, some of which cost me just a few dollars years ago. If I were to suggest today that worn copper cents with counterstamps might be good investments, I would be laughed at—but the truth of the matter is that the pieces I bought back then have multiplied in price 50 to 100 times. The same goes for obsolete paper money, another pet series. Recently I glanced at a $1 bill from the Peterborough (New Hampshire) Bank, issued in the 1850s, that cost me $1.50. Today, if I wanted to sell it (which I do not), I could easily get $500 or more.

Very early on I fell in love with old numismatic publications. Among my first purchases were sets of the *American Journal of Numismatics* from 1866 onward, all issues of *The Numismatist* from 1894 onward (later, I bought reprints of the earlier years back to 1888), and a set of the *Numismatic Scrapbook* from 1935 onward. Auction catalogs were usually free for the asking at coin club meetings, except that a nice copy of B. Max Mehl's 1941 Dunham Collection might cost $3 to $5. I bought all of the reference books I could find; most of them were cheap. I have never lost my passion for these things, and today I still have all of the old books and catalogs that were so interesting and useful to me.

In more recent times, I helped build a "company collection." In connection with one of my books, *Commemorative Coins of the United States: A Complete Encyclopedia*, Ray Merena and I decided to test our own long-time recommendation that there are a lot of really nice coins in the market that are not necessarily graded on the high side of MS-65. We selected MS-63 as a nice combination of fairly high grade and fairly low market price (investors wanted only MS-65 or better, freeing up the supply of lesser-grade pieces, which were sometimes just as nice). We assembled the collection, had Capital Plastics make for us some display holders, and mounted the impressive display as a noncompetitive exhibit at several coin conventions. Accompanying the coins were historical descriptions, postcards and pictures of fairs and exhibitions, original sales literature for the coins, and more.

As to my latest personal coin collection, I've already mentioned the fascinating state quarter dollars. From the outset, with

The Numismatic Scrapbook Magazine, published by Lee F. Hewitt, January 1940. This standard cover design was used for most of the run of this magazine. Today, a file of this publication, 1935 to 1976, is a valuable resource for anyone interested in the history of the hobby.

the launch of the first design in 1999, these have interested me. I casually picked them up here and there, but did not keep pace with all of the new releases. At the launch for the 2000 New Hampshire quarter, I was the reporter on the spot for *Coin World*, this after having participated (in an unusual way) in the selection of the design. In 2004, I asked my friend Dave Sundman at Littleton Coin Company to send me a complete collection of state quarters, Mint State and Proof, in albums, with an invoice—which he did. Since then I have kept fairly current with new releases.

In the meantime, in addition to collecting in a few specialties and enjoying numismatic books, I have been deeply and enjoyably immersed in the world of coin dealing, auctioneering, writing, and research.

Ways to Collect
Selecting a Specialty

Probably the best way to embark on a specialty is to look at the pictures and read the prices and descriptions in the *Guide Book of United States Coins*. I have used this reference ever since I was a teenager, and it is still the classic coin text.

Your budget may be limited. By reviewing the prices and grade headings you can determine what coins are available and how much they cost. If you envision spending a few thousand dollars per year, there is no use considering Proof $20 gold coins. On the other hand, Proof nickel three-cent pieces of 1865 to 1889 might be in the realm of possibility, or perhaps a nicely matched set of Indian Head cents in, say, EF or AU grade.

The 1921 Peace silver dollar has the motifs in high relief. The center would not strike up properly, creating weakness on Miss Liberty's hair details. Accordingly, in the following year the design was modified to shallow contrast.

No matter how much money you have, there are certain series that cannot be completed in certain grades or, for that matter, completed at all.

As an example, no one has ever assembled a full collection in Mint State of Liberty Head $10 gold coins from the first year of issue, 1838, to the last, 1907, although getting 80% of them in that state is a possibility. For the other varieties, EF and AU coins will have to do, which is perfectly satisfactory. Not even Louis E. Eliasberg, Sr., or Harry W. Bass, Jr., both of whom had full date and mintmark sets, had everything in Mint State.

As another example, the Carson City Mint struck gold coins of the $5, $10, and $20 denominations from 1870 to 1885 and again from 1889 to 1893. No one has ever put together a Mint State set.

As to series that no one has ever completed in *any* grade, there are many, including Hard Times tokens, Washington medals, patterns, National Bank notes, Civil War tokens, and varieties of Massachusetts silver coins—and this is just a short list!

I have picked two specialties for you to explore—one being a popular series, readily obtainable in Mint State, yet having its own challenges—the series of Peace silver dollars 1921 to 1935. The other specialty, Vermont copper coins, is a bit esoteric, but lovable as such. My purpose is to share

views of the methods involved. You can then go on your own to check out dozens of other areas that call for investigation.

My goal is not to pique your interest in either Peace silver dollars or Vermont coppers, but to illustrate the methodology of going beyond simple date, grade, and price listings that you may find in a basic reference book.

Peace Silver Dollars (1921–1935)

Although the *Guide Book* lists grades of VF-20, EF-40, AU-50, MS-60, MS-63, MS-64, and MS-65, for purposes of illustration and commentary, I will discuss only the Mint State categories:

1921—MS-60: $225 • MS-63: $400 • MS-64: $725 • MS-65: $2,500. All are in high relief, which caused problems in striking (in the next year the design was modified to be shallow). All have areas of light striking at the center of the obverse and, often, the center of the reverse. Luster is usually good.

1922—MS-60: $18 • MS-63: $30 • MS-64: $42 • MS-65: $150. Very common in all grades. First year of the modified design with shallow relief.

1922-D—MS-60: $28 • MS-63: $50 • MS-64: $80 • MS-65: $450. Some have a bright surface, possibly from wire-brushed dies. The reverse is often flat or weak at the center. Sharply struck MS-65 coins are finds for the cherrypicker, and MS-64 coins of similar sharpness are an even greater prize (from a monetary viewpoint).

1922-S—MS-60: $24 • MS-63: $60 • MS-64: $290 • MS-65: $2,200. Here is what I had to say in my 1993 study, *Silver Dollars and Trade Dollars of the United States: A Complete Encyclopedia:*

> 1922-S dollars do not win any awards for striking. The typical piece is rather shabby in appearance, with incomplete luster and/or raised lines in the field from abrasions acquired by the die during the surfacing process. In the left obverse field IN GOD WE is often weakly struck. The center of the reverse is usually poorly struck and is often dull on the higher points of the eagle, where marks acquired by the original planchet can often be seen. As if this were not enough, the rims are often indistinct in areas; what Wayne Miller and John Highfill call "fadeaway rims." Bagmarks are a problem with 1922-S dollars, and the usually-seen coin is well endowed with them. Is there anything good to be said about the 1922-S Peace dollar? Yes. It is this: All of the problems that beset the usual coin can be turned into an advantage for the careful buyer who may have to look through many dozens of pieces, but a *very few* sharply struck coins do exist, and can be bought at prices little if any higher than regular (i.e., aesthetically inferior) pieces. *[My philosophy for seeking* added value *by carefully inspection remains unchanged today. The point of quoting this lengthy description is simply that, to sophisticated buyers and to those (like you) who want to become such, characteristics like those described in the quote are important but are not found in standard price guides.—QDB]*

1923—MS-60: $18 • MS-63: $30 • MS-64: $42 • MS-65: $150. Common as can be. Usually attractive, but some are spotty.

1923-D—MS-60: $60 • MS-63: $130 • MS-64: $275 • MS-65: $1,200. Fairly plentiful, and with many attractive coins around. Mostly well struck on the obverse, often weak at the reverse. Cherrypicking advised!

1923-S—MS-60: $30 • MS-63: $75 • MS-64: $300 • MS-65: $6,000. Often extensively bagmarked on both sides and weak at the reverse center. Most lack eye appeal. Let those who buy coins "sight unseen" revel in all they can find—thus sopping up a lot of pigs, while *you* look for the best of the litter!

1924—MS-60: $18 • MS-63: $32 • MS-64: $50 • MS-65: $175. Very common and usually quite attractive, although some are spotted or pebbly.

1924-S—MS-60: $225 • MS-63: $450 • MS-64: $1,100 • MS-65: $7,750. Most are lightly struck on the reverse, often in combination with general dullness of surface. However, for 1924-S there are some happy exceptions waiting for you to find.

1925—MS-60: $18 • MS-63: $32 • MS-64: $50 • MS-65: $150. Very common and usually pretty, although some are stained. No problem in landing a gem.

1925-S—MS-60: $75 • MS-63: $150 • MS-64: $700 • MS-65: $22,000. Often extensively bagmarked on both sides and usually weak at the reverse center. A true gem is as rare as can be, a landmark coin if you find one sharply struck and with good eye appeal. I would rather have a well-struck and attractive MS-64 for $500 than a "bargain priced" MS-65 at half catalog—or, for that matter, for a quarter of the catalog price! However, I am not likely to find such bargains, due to the sight-unseen market from buyers who, perhaps, are truly without sight (*blind* to quality, anyway).

1926—MS-60: $35 • MS-63: $70 • MS-64: $100 • MS-65: $350. Nearly always attractive.

1926-D—MS-60: $65 • MS-63: $140 • MS-64: $275 • MS-65: $600. Common and usually with good eye appeal. Some are lightly struck at the reverse center.

1926-S—MS-60: $45 • MS-63: $80 • MS-64: $225 • MS-65: $850. Usually seen with satiny, lustrous surfaces with great eye appeal.

1927—MS-60: $75 • MS-63: $150 • MS-64: $300 • MS-65: $2,200. Usually attractive.

1927-D—MS-60: $150 • MS-63: $300 • MS-64: $700 • MS-65: $5,200. Usually bright and attractive.

1927-S—MS-60: $150 • MS-63: $350 • MS-64: $750 • MS-65: $11,000. Often lightly struck on the reverse and generally unattractive, although not as heavily bagmarked as some other S-Mint issues.

1928—MS-60: $525 • MS-63: $650 • MS-64: $950 • MS-65: $5,000. Usually with gorgeous "creamy" luster. Nearly all are very nice. (Contrast this with the situation for the 1922-S!)

1928-S—MS-60: $150 • MS-63: $550 • MS-64: $2,000 • MS-65: $21,000. Usually lacks eye appeal, not sharp in areas, and with many bagmarks. This may be the greatest challenge among MS-65 dollars.

1934—MS-60: $100 • MS-63: $200 • MS-64: $300 • MS-65: $1,000. Usually satiny surfaces (instead of deeply frosty) and attractive. Bagmarks not a problem. Some are softly struck.

1934-D—MS-60: $100 • MS-63: $325 • MS-64: $600 • MS-65: $1,700. Usually nice when found, but somewhat elusive and perhaps unappreciated as such.

1934-S—MS-60: $1,800 • MS-63: $3,500 • MS-64: $4,750 • MS-65: $7,250. The key to the series. Usually bright and lustrous with good eye appeal and a nice strike.

1935—MS-60: $75 • MS-63: $110 • MS-64: $170 • MS-65: $650. Usually with satiny luster and attractive. Typically well struck.

1935-S—MS-60: $240 • MS-63: $350 • MS-64: $550 • MS-65: $1,200. Usually attractive. If you simply *have* to buy a certified Peace dollar sight unseen, the 1935-S usually comes nice and problem free.

Total prices for collection—MS-60: $3,954 • MS-63: $7,674 • MS-64: $14,187 • MS-65: $95,325.

If you've read the comments for each issue, you are already light-years ahead of most buyers for Peace silver dollars—nearly all standard reference guides as well as certified holders simply list the grade. MS-65, and that's it. Period!

As you may already know, grading is not a science. It is an art and a matter of opinion. Accordingly, a coin might be graded MS-64 by a certification service in one instance, and upon resubmission might grade MS-63 or MS-65. Such resubmissions are a profit center for the grading services.

If you check the 1925-S and 1928-S in the list above, you will see that in MS-64 grade they are listed at $700 and $2,000 each, respectively, then at $22,000 and 21,000 in MS-65. If, in the course of cherrypicking for quality (the first of the four steps I outlined in chapter 2), you encounter a very nice, certified MS-64, you'll have very good odds of getting a higher grade if you submit it dozens of times in an attempt to get MS-65. Your cost will still be very low if you "score" and get an MS-65. Several dealer acquaintances have no stores or shops, issue no catalogs, and make most of their money on resubmissions. They do not have any more basic intelligence than you—they just have market savvy.

Returning to budgetary considerations while contemplating what collection to form: to my way of thinking, the prices for MS-64 Peace dollars fairly shout out "Value!" If I had $100,000 in the bank to buy coins, I would spend $14,187 on a hand-picked MS-64 set and use the remaining $85,813 to start a few other collections. In this instance, I call MS-64 the

Illustration of the 1785 Vermont copper with IMMUNE COLUMBIA reverse. This illogical combination of dies—a crudely lettered Vermont-related obverse with the reverse of a 1785 copper cent of unknown history—was made at Machin's Mills, a private mint near Newburgh, New York. In reality, all examples of this issue known today are irregularly struck, lack details in some areas, and have incomplete borders. This "ideal" depiction is from S.S. Crosby's *Early Coins of America*, 1875.

A 1785 Vermont copper of the "landscape" design, Ryder-2 variety, one of several varieties of this motif issued in 1785 and 1786. Vermont appears as VERMONTS, one of several styles on the coinage. These were struck in a small wooden building located on Millbrook, in Pawlet, Vermont. Reuben Harmon, Jr., operated the mint. There was great difficulty in the preparation of copper strips from which planchets could be cut for coins, and nearly all known coins from this mint have rough defects or flaws of one sort or another. This example is from the famed Eliasberg Collection.

Optimal Collecting Grade (OCG)—a really good value for the money paid.

On the other hand, the typical investor coming into the market will be clueless regarding such subtleties and will think, or be told, "MS-65 is the only way to go. These are the premium coins that lead the market," and so on.

Vermont Copper Coins (1785–1788)

To me, Vermont copper coins are fascinating, and at one time or another I have owned nearly all of the 39 known die varieties (as attributed by Ryder numbers, according to Hillyer C. Ryder in *State Coinages of New England*). However, no one has ever assembled a complete set. This compact, interesting series furnishes a good illustration.

Today, on pages 68 and 69 of the *Guide Book*, 13 different basic dates and types are listed, together with prices. If you were contemplating collecting Vermont coins, the prices below would confront you (I give just the Good and EF listings, and omit VG, F, and VF). To each I have added some personal commentary of the type you might want to seek out for *any* specialty that you find interesting.

1785, IMMUNE COLUMBIA—*Good: $5,000 • VF (the highest grade listed*

for this variety): $25,000. Curious combination of unrelated dies made at Machin's Mills, Newburgh, New York, by marrying a crudely lettered Vermont obverse with an IMMUNE COLUMBIA reverse, the second die apparently acquired by Machin from earlier use by others. Always found on a narrow-diameter planchet with parts of the letter tops missing. Usually indistinct at the centers. Dated 1785, but probably struck circa 1788. A classic "must-have" Vermont rarity due to its unusual appearance.

1785, VERMONTS—*Good: $250 • EF: $6,800.* The design shows a typical Vermont landscape on the obverse—a rocky ridge, pine trees, and a plow. The reverse has STELLA QUARTA DECIMA ("Fourteenth Star"), reflecting Vermont's ambition to join the Union. It is among the earliest of Vermont coppers, struck in a small wooden building set up as a mint on Millbrook, a stream in Pawlet, Vermont, and operated by Reuben Harmon, Jr., who had a contract from Vermont to produce the coinage on a private basis. The circumstances of minting were primitive and the equipment crude. As a result, nearly all the finished coins show planchet flaws and/or areas of light striking.

1785, VERMONTIS—*Good: $275 •
EF: $8,500.* Essentially the same as
the preceding.

1786, VERMONTENSIUM—*Good:
$200 • EF: $3,700.* This variety, also
made in Pawlet by Harmon, is at least 10
times more plentiful than either of the
preceding two. Harmon was trying to
figure out how to Latinize the word *Vermont*, and this is another version. Later,
VERMON was used on different coins.

1786, Baby Head—*Good: $300 • EF:
$7,500.* It is likely that the landscape
motif, unfamiliar to regional citizens,
may have restricted the circulation of
Vermont coppers. This piece represents
a change to an obverse portrait (a child-
ish image of no one in particular), in
combination with a seated figure on the
reverse. In total, the new 1786 Vermont
copper was somewhat similar to the
plentiful and widely accepted British
halfpennies in circulation. Most are on
crude planchets with lightness of detail.
A favorite with Vermont specialists.

1786, Bust Left—*Good: $150 • EF:
$4,000.* Going one step further to pro-
mote circulation of their coinage (this is
my opinion; no contemporaneous comment has been located), the Vermont
coiners changed the design to appear as
a virtually exact copy of a contemporary
British halfpenny, with King George II

on the obverse and the seated figure of
Britannia on the reverse, but with lettering relating to Vermont. Always on
rough, porous planchets.

1787, Bust Left—*Good: $3,800 • VF
(highest grade listed): $35,000.* Design
similar to the preceding, but dated
1787. This die broke at an early stage
(the break is visible at the date), and
only a few were made. A prime rarity. I
have handled fewer than five examples
in my career.

1787, BRITANNIA—*Good: $100 • EF:
$1,600.* An odd combination of dies,
made at Machin's Mills (as are all the
rest of the varieties from here to
the end of this listing), with a Vermont
obverse combined with a die intended
for a counterfeit British halfpenny. This
is one of the issues most often seen.

1787, Mailed Bust Right—*Good: $135 •
EF: $2,500.* A new design featuring King
George III—the detested monarch of
the Revolution!—on the obverse. Somewhat scarce. Usually seen on a high-
quality planchet. Striking details are
usually light or indistinct at the center.

1788, Mailed Bust Right—*Good: $100 •
EF: $1,500.* Same as above.

1788, Backward C in AUCTORI—
*Good: $3,500 • Fine (highest grade listed):
$9,000.* A crude obverse die with the

A 1786 Vermont "landscape" copper, this of the
Ryder-8 variety. Note the VERMONTENSIUM
spelling. The reverse inscription, STELLA
QUARTA DECIMA, or "fourteenth star,"
reflected Vermont's aspiration to become the 14th
state in the Union, which it accomplished a few
years later, in 1792. This specimen is of an extraor-
dinarily smooth planchet. Not one in two dozen is
of this quality. (Pevehouse and Davis Collections)

Illustration of the 1786 Baby Head Vermont
copper from S.S. Crosby, *Early Coins of America*, 1875. Years later, this was designated by
Hillyer C. Ryder, in *State Coinages of New
England*, as die variety Ryder-9.

lettering irregular and one letter punched backward.

1788 **ET* **LIB* **INDE*—*Good: $325 • EF: $10,000.* Listed in the *Guide Book* to reflect the transposed inscription on the back, usually INDE ET LIB (an abbreviation for "independence and liberty"), but here as ET LIB INDE, which makes no sense.

1788, GEORGIVS III REX—*Good: $425 • EF: $10,000.* A die for a counterfeit British halfpenny is combined with a reverse die intended for a Vermont copper coin.

Total price in Good—$14,560.

Total price in EF (or lower, if EF not listed)—$125,100.

In this illustration, if you have a fairly modest budget (in the context of a collector of early American coins), then Good grade coins beckon for $14,560. However, even if you have this amount in your checking account right now, there is no way you can buy all of these coins at once. You may have to wait a year or more for some, such as the 1787, Bust Left, which might not even come on the market until a fine collection is auctioned.

At the same time, if you can afford the EF grade, it may take several years to spend your $106,250, with no assurance that even this amount will suffice. Due to the wide variations of striking and quality, prices can similarly vary. In any event, the rarity of certain of the pieces make *opportunity* more important than the price paid.

Due to the unusual circumstances I mentioned in each commentary, it seems apparent that Vermont copper coins invite further study—as to how those curious dies were made, why the designs changed, and more. You may even want to join the Colonial Coin Collectors Club (C4) and attend a meeting or two, so you can talk shop about the challenge you are having assembling a set even in Good grade. You'll find lots of enthusiastic company. This year I was a featured speaker at their annual convention, and the room was packed.

A 1788 Vermont copper of the Mailed Bust Right type, Ryder-16 variety. The designs closely follow those of contemporary British halfpennies, with the portrait of King George III on the obverse and the seated figure of Britannia on the reverse, but here with different lettering. This and all other 1788-dated varieties were struck at Machin's Mills at the outlet of Orange Pond, near Newburgh, New York.

All known specimens are lightly struck at the centers, as seen here. There was not enough metal in the planchet to flow into the deepest recesses of the obverse die and, at its opposite in the coining press, into the motif of the seated figure. How to grade a coin such as this can be perplexing. This one was designated as VF-35 by American Numismatic Rarities. (Classics Sale of July 2003)

And for Good Measure...

As a final example of figuring out a budget and contemplating what to collect, here is a scenario involving Susan B. Anthony dollars, one of each date and mint that was struck in Proof finish. The figures are from a recent issue of *Coin Values* (March 7, 2005), compiled by Mark Ferguson and published by *Coin World.*

Although *Coin Values* lists all Proofs as DC (Deep Cameo, meaning frosted designs and letters) and in continuous divisions from Proof-65 DC to Proof-70 DC, including some subvarieties, I give just the Proof-65, -67, and -70 figures for illustration, one for each date and mint. (None were minted from 1982 to 1998.)

1979-S—Proof-65 DC: $10 • Proof-67 DC: $20 • Proof-70 DC: $325.

1980-S—Proof-65 DC: $10 • Proof-67 DC: $20 • Proof-70 DC: $350.

1981-S—Proof-65 DC: $10 • Proof-67 DC: $20 • Proof-70 DC: $425.

1999-P—Proof-65 DC: $10 • Proof-67 DC: $30 • Proof-70 DC: $175.

In recent years, the Mint has turned out Proofs of exceptional quality. Granted, now and then there may be one with some marks or a blemish, but by and large the *millions* of Proofs minted of these four issues are beautiful gems.

A set of one each costs $40 in Proof-65 DC, $90 in Proof-67 DC, and $1,275 in Proof-70 DC. If I were assembling a set, and this type of price differential existed when I was buying, I would not touch the Proof-70 set with a 10-foot pole. (This doesn't necessarily mean that *you* should not; it just means that *I* would not.)

Be Careful

Although it would be inappropriate for me to do any more than make suggestions, I do have a vested interest, as a dealer and as a member of the numismatic community, in your satisfaction with coin collecting. If you have a bad experience, you might leave coins and take up something else. This would be a loss for our hobby.

Recently, Anthony Swiatek, a collector and dealer for many years and a popular writer on coin investment, told of a financially well-heeled buyer who was attracted by low population figures for certified coins.[12] At an earlier time, in 1989, he was offered a 1922 Grant with-star variety commemorative gold dollar for $32,750 and the 1922 variety without star for $65,000. Both were enticingly rare *according to certified coin figures*. Most dealers in commemoratives know that 1922 Grant gold dollars are usually seen in gem grade, often in super-gem preservation. Swiatek knew this and warned the investor, who paid no heed, but elected to rely on certification data to make his decision. After all, these seemed very rare in such super-gem condition.

In December 2003, these two coins came back on the market, by which time quite a few others had been certified in ultra-high grades. One of the coins was resold for $8,000 and the other for $4,000—a loss of $85,350. The investor paid dearly for his lack of knowledge.

As it is hard to find a single rule to fit all occasions, I hasten to add that for many, if not most, issues, certification-service figures are very useful—a great place to find out how many times a given Liberty Seated quarter or Liberty Head nickel has been certified in a given grade. However, for coins that are *usually* found in gem Mint State or gem Proof and are not rare to begin with, the population figures reflect only how rare a coin is in a particular holder, not how rare it really is!

Optimal Collecting Grade (OCG)

In planning your budget, be very careful when there is a huge difference in price for the same coin in two slightly different grades. The earlier contemplation of Peace silver dollars indicates to me an MS-64 Optimal Collecting Grade (a term I introduced in the *Guide Book of Morgan Silver Dollars*, and that reflects a combination of high grade and *good value for the money paid*). For Susan B. Anthony dollars I suggest Proof-65 DC or, if you must, Proof-67 DC.

For each coin, the OCG—about which I will say more later—can be figured out at a glance—just look for big differences in price for small differences in grade in various catalogs and sale listings.

Investigate the Seller

Buying a coin is easy enough, or so it might seem. You see one offered and you buy it. Or, you see a listing in an auction sale, and you keep bidding until you are the owner. While there is always a market for choice and rare coins, if you buy a coin for $1,000 today and decide to sell it tomorrow morning, you will probably lose money. If it is choice, and the market is strong and rising, then a few years later a profit may await you. Buying one day and selling the next makes money for dealers but not for you. Ditto, if you pay a long price for a coin that is common, especially in some ultra-grade hyped as investment (see the Swiatek anecdote above).

A gem 1922 Grant commemorative gold dollar (enlarged), variety without star in the obverse field. Although just 5,000 were struck, most of them were carefully preserved by collectors, with the result that gems are fairly plentiful today— although an unstudied investor would have no way of knowing this. As a reader of this book, you will become aware of such things!

In contrast, the 1905 Lewis and Clark commemorative gold dollar (enlarged), of which 10,041 were struck, was not at all popular with collectors at the time of the coins' distribution. Most went to the ordinary public—attendees of the Lewis and Clark Centennial Exposition held in Seattle—and few were saved in high grades. Today, a gem 1905 Lewis and Clark dollar is at least 10 to 20 times rarer than a gem 1922 Grant gold dollar of half the mintage!

It is wise to check a dealer's credentials. There is no education requirement, no ethics test, no permission, no registration with any regulatory agency for some to call themselves professional numismatists or to state that they are important, the best, and so on. Does the dealer have deep knowledge of rare coins, how they were struck, their market history, and more? Or is the dealer simply a salesperson? Moreover, numismatic periodicals do not check the quality of the coins that advertisers list for sale—any more than your local paper checks the quality of the used cars or Labrador retriever pups offered in its columns. Many people do not realize this, and assume that if a dealer advertises a coin for sale, then it must be a nice example, in order to be "accepted" for listing. Not so.

Membership in a dealers' organization is often a good credential, but even then there are dealers who engage in less than satisfactory practices. My suggestion is to ask others who have been buying and selling coins. You will probably get good information, and quickly. This is not much different from asking around town who the best doctor at the local hospital is, if you are contemplating surgery. Often, such things cannot be found at all in print, but a few conversations will reveal much.

Further, your buying should be *outward directed* and come from you. Decide what you want, then seek it. To me it makes no sense at all when a buyer has a lot of money but is clueless as to what to buy, if he or she simply takes what is presented as a "good deal" or a "hot" item and writes a check. Hot items can burn! Remember Anthony Swiatek's anecdote about the buyer of the special high-grade 1922 Grant commemorative dollars. No doubt, the buyer thought it was a sure-fire investment—low-mintage coin, very high grade, popular series, low certified population, and so on—who could ask for more? Chances are excellent that the buyer knew nothing about these coins, or about grading, or anything else, but did not want to miss out on an opportunity! The two coins were indeed nice to have, but proved to be worth just tiny fractions of what he paid.

If you believe you have been cheated or defrauded, getting your money back may be difficult, expensive, or, most likely, impossible. A few years ago I was enlisted by the Federal Trade Commission to help them prosecute an allegedly fraudulent rare-coin company with a high-sounding title, which enlisted a corps of telemarketers to sell "rare coins" to investors. Upon examination by real experts, the coins were found to be vastly overpriced and, in many instances, overgraded. The FTC won the case, the business was shut down, and the FTC asked me if they could refer all of the defrauded people to my firm, so we could help them sell their coins for what they were really worth— which was, of course, just a fraction of what they paid. I accepted, but after hearing so many horror stories from victims, and meeting so many sad people, I asked them to stop the referrals. It was just too hard to take. In this case, although the FTC won, the coin buyers still lost.

The Professional Numismatists Guild has an arbitration system in place, free of charge, if you feel a PNG dealer has done something incorrect. However, using this system is time consuming, and if you simply overpaid for a coin, it will probably be your problem, not the dealer's. You can hire a lawyer, and prosecute a seller, but it is highly unlikely that when all is said and done you will get all of your money back.

It is far simpler to, per the old saying, "investigate before you invest." This comment is simply a reality check for you. Read and absorb the text of this book, and it is highly unlikely that anyone will be able to take advantage of you!

Putting It All Together

In contemplating which series of coins to collect, do some reading. The *Guide Book of United States Coins* is a good start, and to it can be added other sources and price guides, some of which have more grade categories. Certification-service figures are useful, but be exceedingly wary of paying a huge price for any modern coin that is common in MS-65 grade, but is "rare" if slabbed at MS-67, -68, -69, and -70.

Some series invite or even require a bit of immersion in numismatic lore and study. You will probably agree that collecting Vermont copper coins of 1785 to 1788 should not be done casually. Even Peace silver dollars can be bought more effectively if you have some "inside" knowledge, such as I have just given you. On the other hand, you could probably buy a set of Proof-65 DC Susan B. Anthony dollars, certified, without even looking at the coins, and have a good chance at getting a nice set (not that I would advise keeping your eyes closed).

A pleasant aspect of all of this is that with some knowledge at your fingertips you can go to a coin show or scan other offerings and make superb buys under the noses of most others in the market. It is also fun to identify a treasure that no one else recognizes!

Although there are exceptions, the chances are quite good that for most U.S. coins struck in the past 150 years, if you don't buy a coin offered today, there will be other opportunities tomorrow or next week.

Apart from the desirability of buying coins that are sharply struck and have good eye appeal, there is much to be said for getting *good value* for the money you spend. If appropriate, tap the concept of OCG, especially among Mint State and Proof coins. If a coin is priced at $1,000 in MS-64 grade and $7,000 in MS-65, the MS-64 piece would seem to be the better buy. In fact, a really gorgeous MS-64 at twice catalog price, or $2,000, to me would be more desirable than an unattractive MS-65 coin deeply discounted to $4,000. However, such deep discounts are not found, especially for coins certified by the leading services, as sight-unseen investment buyers eagerly acquire them. Put it this way: if at a vending machine a can of Coke or Pepsi were to cost $1.50 and was convenient to buy, I would make a purchase. However, if a machine charged $20 for such a can, even though I could afford the $20, I would reject it as overpriced, not a good value, and would find one somewhere else.

Take your time, plan ahead, and seek high quality and good value for everything you acquire. Along the way, have a good time!

Ideas for Collecting
Form a Type Set

A type set contains one of each basic design within a series. Today, few people can afford to collect a full set of Barber dimes from 1892 to 1916, because of the sheer number (75) of dates and mintmarks—never mind the rarity of the 1894-S (in the *Guide Book* for $1.4 million in Proof-63 grade). On the other hand, a recent issue of *Coin Values* suggests that an MS-65 example of one of the more plentiful dates can be bought for about $750, and a Proof-65 for $700.[13] Either one of these coins showcases Charles E. Barber's design. Under magnification each has the same essential details, save for date and mintmark, as the 1894-S.

Similarly, not many buyers can build a complete set of Liberty Head nickels of the regular issues of 1883 to 1912, in gem Mint State or gem Proof, but just two are needed for the type, and both are quite affordable: the 1883 without CENTS on the reverse, and your pick of a favorite date from 1883 to 1912 of the second type, with CENTS.

Peace silver dollars of 1921 to 1935 need just two for the type: the 1921 in high relief, and your choice of any other, 1922 to 1935, in shallow relief.

Counting the new statehood quarters as single types (as they are regular issues, not commemoratives), we find that there have been more than 200 major design changes and evolutions since the Philadelphia Mint opened for business in 1792. This includes copper, nickel, silver, and gold.

While it is challenging to try to get one each of those 200+ types, and quite a few people have done it, many collectors opt to have a type set of a particular denomination or era. A beautiful part of collecting a type set in one area is that you can always expand your horizons without losing anything. Accordingly, a type set of the six major $20 designs from 1850 to 1933 can be an essential part of a full type set with other denominations, if you broaden your goals. Such a $20 set includes the following:

- *Type 1 (1850–1866), Liberty Head, no motto*—Readily available in grades from VF to AU. Mint State coins are rare except for some interesting recoveries from shipwrecks, the latter including some marvelous gems.

- *Type 2 (1866–1876), Liberty Head, with IN GOD WE TRUST, denomina-tion spelled as TWENTY D.*—Readily available VF to lower Mint State ranges, scarce in gem preservation.

- *Type 3 (1877–1907), Liberty Head, with IN GOD WE TRUST, denomination spelled as TWENTY DOLLARS*—So many Mint State coins are available that MS-63 or higher is the level usually sought.

- *Type 4 (MCMVII [1907]), Saint-Gaudens, High Relief*—Scarcest of the types. About 6,000 exist, mostly Mint State. Considered by many to be America's most beautiful coin made for circulation.

- *Type 5 (1907–1908), Saint-Gaudens, no motto*—So many Mint State coins are available that MS-63 or higher is the level usually sought.

- *Type 6 (1908–1933), Saint-Gaudens, with IN GOD WE TRUST*—Ditto.

A type set of nickel five-cent pieces, including the earlier-mentioned Liberty Head types, includes the following (prices are from MS-63 listings for the commonest date or variety of the type, per the 2006 *Guide Book*):

- *Type 1 (1866–1867), Shield obverse, reverse With Rays*—MS-63: $400. Easy enough to find in MS-63, but sharply struck coins are in the minority (check the horizontal shield stripes on the obverse, the star points on the reverse), and sharply struck coins with excellent eye appeal are rarer yet. Cherrypicking is advised!

- *Type 2 (1867–1883), Shield obverse, reverse Without Rays*—MS-63: $170. Usually with good eye appeal, especially for such dates as 1882 and 1883. Check for sharpness of details.

- *Type 3, (1883), Liberty Head, without CENTS*—MS-63: $45. Common as can be, but sometimes weakly struck (check the obverse stars and, on the reverse, the wreath details). A great "story coin."

- *Type 4 (1883–1912), Liberty Head, with CENTS—MS-63: $110.* Dates in the 1900s are plentiful. Check for sharpness and eye appeal.

- *Type 5 (1913), Indian or Buffalo type, raised mound on reverse—MS-63: $55.* Usually seen well struck and with excellent eye appeal.

- *Type 6 (1913–1938), Indian or Buffalo type, flat ground on reverse—MS-63: $30.* Generally, early Philadelphia Mint coins are well struck, as are selected varieties from all three mints in the mid-1930s. Common.

- *Type 7 (1938–1965), Jefferson, without designer's initials—MS-63: $0.50.* Common and inexpensive. Some specialists check to see whether all of the steps in the Monticello building are defined (they usually aren't).

- *Type 8 (1942–1945), Jefferson, special "wartime" alloy with silver content—MS-63: $7.* Usually well struck and with superb eye appeal.

- *Type 9 (1966–2004), Jefferson, with designer's initials FS (for Felix Schlag)—MS-63: $0.50.* Current issue. No problem finding gems.

- *Types 10 (Jefferson, with peace medal reverse) and 11 (Jefferson, keelboat reverse; both 2004)—MS-63: $0.25.* Kudos to the U.S. Mint for making these!

- *Types 12 (Jefferson, bison reverse) and 13 (Jefferson, Ocean in View reverse; both 2005)—MS-63: $0.25.* See Types 9 and 10.

In choice Mint State, MS-63 (retail value: $819.00) or finer, a full set is affordable for most collectors, and MS-65 is nicer yet. Types from 7 to 13 are very inexpensive in gem preservation. The U.S. Mint plans to issue more special reverse types, so you can watch this set grow. To my way of thinking, a 13-piece type set in choice MS-63 grade, each coin selected for quality, is a great thing to own.

Apart from coins in the federal series, collecting by types is very popular for early American coins. My *Guide Book of United States Type Coins* (Whitman, 2005) lists such basic types and will give you some ideas. Commemorative silver coins of the classic era, 1892 to 1954, are most often collected by type. A full set including the 1893 Isabella quarter, the 1900 Lafayette silver dollar, and all the half dollar dates and mints comprises 144 pieces, but a type set narrows down to just 50, with 48 different types of halves in addition to the quarter and dollar.

Tokens, medals, and paper money are often collected by type, and for some series collecting by type is more popular than trying to get one of each variety.

Not only is building a type set affordable in many instances, but as each coin is of a different design, it will enable you to maximize your enjoyment of coinage history.

Specialize

On the other hand, selecting a specialty can be very stimulating. It is a challenge to try to get one of each date and mintmark in the Liberty Walking half dollar series from 1916 to 1947, or a full set of Morgan silver dollars, 1878 to 1921, or one of each Indian Head cent, 1859 to 1909.

By specializing you can observe the changes within a series. Among Indian Head cents the 1877 is rare, while the 1907 is common. The 1871 has a large date with the numerals arranged in an arc along the bottom border, while the 1872 has a small, compact date in a straight line. I find such comparisons to be fascinating.

The usual way to specialize is to collect one of each date and mintmark. For some series, especially those minted in the first century of federal coinage, die varieties can be a challenge—if you enjoy studying coins under magnification and making out the differences, often trivial, with regard to the placement of the letters in relation to each other, or the date, or the number of berries in the wreath.

For the specialist there are many excellent texts, such as Dr. William H. Sheldon's on cents of 1793 to 1814, Howard R. Newcomb's on cents of 1816 to 1857, Richard Snow's on Flying Eagle cents of 1856 to 1858 and Indian Head cents of 1859 to 1909, and David Lange's on Lincoln cents from 1909 onward. The bibliographies in the chapters referring to specific series include selected titles.

For some series there are special-interest groups, such as the Liberty Seated Collectors Club, the Early American Coppers Club, the John Reich Society (for silver coinage 1792 to about 1838), the Civil War Token Society, and the Society of Paper Money Collectors, among many others. Membership usually ranges from a few hundred to more than a thousand people, and most societies issue bulletins and newsletters.

While dates and mintmarks of coins are well known and have been studied for many years, and relatively few new discoveries are being made, among die varieties just about every specialist I know has found either great rarities posing as common coins or, less often, entirely new die varieties—sort of like astronomers being the first to find and report a new comet.

Most collectors begin with the more popular series of the past 150 or so years, then explore die varieties and other specialized situations.

Trophy Coins

If you can afford it, a trophy coin can be fun to own. Such a piece is a classic in its series—a coin that is collected all by itself and not as part of a type set or specialized series. Moreover, my view of a trophy coin is one that is basically *rare*—a key date, an icon in its own series.

More than a few people have acquired examples of the 1804 silver dollar, the "King of American Coins," simply for the achievement and honor—just as a moun-

taineer might like to climb Mount Everest, even though he or she might not have climbed Katahdin, Shasta, Mauna Kea, or Chimborazo. These buyers acquire just an 1804 and not the other dollars of 1794 to 1803 to accompany it.

On several occasions in my career, customers have asked me to get for them a set of the four different 1879 and 1880 $4 gold Stellas, of the Flowing Hair and Coiled Hair designs, each a trophy, but even more spectacular as a group of four.

"Show and tell," numismatic style, is often fun. From January 17 to February 18, 1914, the American Numismatic Society, New York City, staged a spectacular loan and reference display of colonial and American coins that included four specimens of the 1804 dollar. Contributors included F.C.C. Boyd, Henry Chapman, S. Hudson Chapman, James W. Ellsworth, George French, H.O. Granberg, Waldo C. Newcomer, Wayte Raymond, Hillyer Ryder, Howland Wood, William H. Woodin, Carl Wurtzbach, and other numismatic luminaries of the era.

The Numismatist carried this report:

> Through the energetic efforts of the director, Mr. Bauman L. Belden, many of the most important collectors of the United States were induced to place on exhibition either their entire collections or such portions as were deemed essential to avoid duplication. This general cooperation on the part of the collectors resulted in placing before the general public a number of coin rarities that had never before been shown, at a public exhibition, and which a great many collectors had never seen.
>
> Among [the coins on exhibit] may be mentioned the 1783 Nova Constellatio set in silver; 1804 dollars, including the ... Stickney specimen; the gold Brasher doubloon; the California $5 pieces of Schultz & Co. and Dunbar & Co., the $5 and $10 gold

pieces of Templeton Reid; the only known specimen of the Confederate half dollar; and many other rarities.

In addition to these, for the first time, the pattern collection of Mr. William H. Woodin was exhibited, together with his almost complete series of half eagles; Mr. Charles C. Gregory exhibited nearly his entire collection of private gold pieces. New Yorkers were privileged to see a majority of the rarities of the great collection which has been brought together by Mr. H.O. Granberg; also the unequaled cent collection of Dr. George P. French; a part of the magnificent collection of colonial coins which is owned by Mr. Hillyer Ryder; also the very fine collection of colonial pieces of Mr. Carl Wurtzbach, including his unsurpassed series of Washington coins.

Also the entire collection of minor pattern coins of Mr. Judson Brenner, by far the most complete known, and not even approached by that of any other collector. Also the rarities of the mintmark collection of Mr. Howard Newcomb. Also the very complete set of encased postage stamps of the late Ben G. Green.[14]

At the summer 2003 convention of the American Numismatic Association, held that year in Baltimore, all five of the known 1913 Liberty Head nickels were on display, including examples loaned by the ANA Museum and the Smithsonian Institution.

The fascination with trophy coins often leads to interesting situations in the marketplace. In the 1950s there were so few appearances of 1804 silver dollars that the opportunity to see one sell at auction, or to notice a private sale offering, was remarkable, something that might happen once every few years, if indeed that often. Now, the situation has changed dramatically, and in the past 20 years there have been *dozens* of transactions of 1804 silver

dollars—often the same specimen selling again and again.

Somewhat similarly, the 1873-CC Liberty Seated dime without arrows at date, unique, and cataloged by me for the Louis E. Eliasberg, Sr., Collection in 1996, later went to a buyer in Illinois, who sold it not long afterward. The coin appeared on the market several other times, apparently without finding a solid spot on which to settle, before it alighted in 2004 in the collection of Rusty Goe. However, by year's end it had been sold again. The unique 1870-S half dime, which I cataloged in the early 1980s and offered for sale for the first time, has had a somewhat similar experience—it has gone from one owner to another. In contrast, decades ago collectors such as John J. Pittman, Louis E. Eliasberg, Sr., Emery May Holden Norweb, Harry W. Bass, Jr., and others bought coins and held them for a long time, often for all of their lives. More often, in their twilight years, dedicated numismatists have enjoyed seeing their coins cataloged and showcased in fine auction catalogs, tributes to what they have accomplished.

The beauty of trophy coins and the way they frequently come up for resale after the novelty of owning them has passed, is that serious collectors (when they do want such things) have more opportunities to buy them than ever before. Accordingly, if tomorrow someone were to develop a deep interest in collecting early silver dollars (1794–1804) by date and die variety, he or she would not have to wait many years for the opportunity to acquire a prized 1804. In the meantime, trophy holders of such a coin will have enjoyed the experience.

Now and again I've bought for resale trophy coins in the federal coin series. I can appreciate the philosophy of not only numismatic trophies, but those in other areas of collectibles as well. My Currier & Ives print collection contains about a dozen trophy items, such as steamboats racing at night on the Mississippi River, and clipper ships, but has very little in the way of ordinary prints. I am not a serious stamp collector, but I have always wanted to own the great American trophy, the 1918 24¢ airmail with the "Jenny" airplane flying upside down. I probably never will, but I can appreciate someone who has one.

From an investment point, trophy coins have done well over the years. All you need to do to verify and understand this is to look at what key rarities brought in famous sales of the past (often world-record prices at the time) and see what great values they would be at the same prices today.

The first trophy coin I ever bought was the 1894-S Barber dime from Stack's Empire sale in 1957, paying a record $4,750 at the time, and later selling it to Emery May Holden Norweb for $6,000. Today, to find its value you could move the decimal point over a couple of places to, say, $600,000, then perhaps double it!

Registry Sets

Many have been interested in the concept of buying coins in Numismatic Guaranty Corporation (NGC) and/or Professional Coin Grading Service (PCGS) holders and submitting them to set registry databases conducted by these two services. The name of the game is to get as many points as possible for the coins in your collection, including for rarity, completion, and high grades. ANACS issues population reports, but to date has not established a set-registry system.

Very often, someone will put together a registry set of Buffalo nickels of 1913 to 1938, or Indian Head $10 gold pieces of 1907 to 1933, or Franklin halves of 1948 to 1963, simply for the challenge of doing so. Even though there is the market danger of paying a lot of money for ultra-high grades, the excitement of the competition often outweighs it. In recent times, the popularity of such sets has been growing. Once a set achieves a given level it is often sold—a boon to auction firms and also to buyers who scramble to get high-grade pieces that have been off the market.

It has been my experience that those who joined in this competition early have done quite well in the forming and resale of their sets. As to the future, the usual caveats apply, but in the meantime such sets have provided fodder for a lot of chatting and enthusiastic comments on the Internet and in other places.

Generally, registry sets emphasize numbers and not striking quality. Thus, for purposes of such competition, a common flat-strike 1925-S Buffalo nickel in MS-65 grade would outrace an exceedingly rare, needle-sharp strike 1925-S in "only" MS-64. Connoisseurs might feel differently, but those are the rules. You already know what I would prefer: the sharply struck MS-64! However, I might not win any contests with it.

Collecting "Experiences" and Appreciating Tradition

Experiences and pleasures can also be "collected" in numismatics. Although I have never personally owned a rare 1822 $5 gold half eagle, of which just one is in private hands today, I certainly have "collected" the memory of cataloging it and offering it for sale in 1982 as part of the Eliasberg Collection. The buyer, who still owns this rarity today and is as proud of it as ever, has remained a fine friend and, in fact, recently went sky-diving with my son Andrew (no one asked *my* permission!). In a way, I have collected not only a coin experience, but also a friend.

I no longer have the extensive set of Vermont copper coins I put together over a long period of time beginning in the 1950s, but the experience remains with me—and today I could close my eyes and recite Vermont numismatic lore to you for an hour without repeating any anecdote or item! When Tony Carlotto put together the latest reference on the series, *The Copper Coins of Vermont*, he asked me to write the introduction, which I did—largely from memory and experience.

A simple pleasure is reading certain books with interesting content. Sylvester

S. Crosby's *Early Coins of America*, published in 1875, is still the standard in the field. Although I have read most of the text and skimmed through the rest of it many times, it is always interesting to reread Crosby and to "collect" the enjoyment he offers. Similarly, the introductory chapters of Dr. William H. Sheldon's 1949 book, *Early American Cents*, are fascinating to read. The latest addition to books with a good story line is David Tripp's *Illegal Tender: Gold, Greed, and the Mystery of the Lost 1933 Double Eagle*, 2004.

In the 1950s, Jim Ruddy and I, each with a copy of the *Guide Book* at hand, would try to stump each other with numismatic trivia. Along the way, we both learned a lot. Probably from this enjoyment I came up with the idea of adding a coin quiz to the coin magazines for which I've written, beginning with *Empire Topics* in the 1950s, continuing to include a long run of the *Rare Coin Review* through 2002, and the *Numismatic Sun* today.

In time, as you pursue numismatics you will automatically acquire a large "collection" of memories, experiences, and knowledge that will always stay with you.

CHAPTER FIVE

DETERMINING COIN PRICES AND VALUES

The science of numismatics is a paying investment if a collection be formed with some judgment. An important and scientific collection of anything cannot be formed unless the collector is intensely interested in the subject and willing to devote much time to the study of all matters closely connected to the line he has selected. He must be an enthusiast....

... I do want to thoroughly impress the fact on everyone that the time to form collections of things is when no one is collecting that particular series. I have made all kinds of mistakes in collecting.... but I did manage to form a collection of United States gold when not many were interested in it....

—William H. Woodin, May 1911

Determinants of Value

The market price of a rare coin, token, medal, or currency note is dependent upon several factors, no one of which can stand alone. It is appropriate to say that price can be one thing and value another. I'll discuss market prices, and along the way suggest that some prices can represent better values than others. Of course, if a coin sells at auction for $20,000, it is also correct to say that at that moment it was valued at that sum. In the marketplace a comment such as "this coin has a market price of $20,000" is interchangeable with "this coin has a market value of $20,000."

A coin can be a great rarity, but have a low market price. A coin can be common,

but have a relatively high price. Some gem Mint State coins have low prices, and some well-worn pieces have high prices.

The factors I give in this chapter are basic. Your knowledge of each of them can be vastly expanded by reading the succeeding chapters. However, for starters, here are the fundamentals.

Rarity

The rarity of a coin, discussed in detail in chapter 6, is an important element of value. Rarity refers to the specific number of coins known to exist in numismatic hands. As new discoveries are made and as some coins become lost, a rating of rarity can

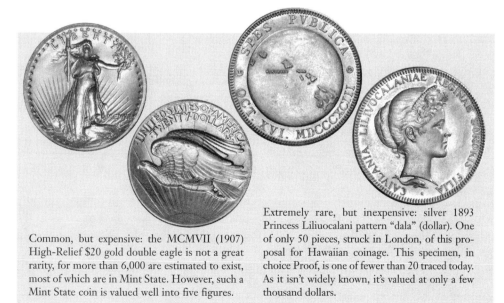

Common, but expensive: the MCMVII (1907) High-Relief $20 gold double eagle is not a great rarity, for more than 6,000 are estimated to exist, most of which are in Mint State. However, such a Mint State coin is valued well into five figures.

Extremely rare, but inexpensive: silver 1893 Princess Liliuocalani pattern "dala" (dollar). One of only 50 pieces, struck in London, of this proposal for Hawaiian coinage. This specimen, in choice Proof, is one of fewer than 20 traced today. As it isn't widely known, it's valued at only a few thousand dollars.

change. However, for most United States coins, estimates of rarity are well established. Shorthand notations for rarity, such as "Rarity-2" and "URS-12," are delineated in chapter 6.

Of the 1838-O (New Orleans Mint) half dollar, only about 12 to 15 are known today.

Of the 1970-D Kennedy half dollar, 2,150,000 were struck, all of which were sold in special sets to collectors. Accordingly, its rarity can be estimated at 2,000,000 or so Mint State coins in existence today, assuming that 150,000 may have strayed or been lost or spent.

Of the 1776–1976 Bicentennial half dollar, 234,308,000 were made for circulation. Most of these were issued, but half dollars were not often seen in circulation then, nor are they now. How many survive today is anyone's guess. In the absence of having any figures as to the government melting or destroying of such pieces, an estimate of 200,000,000 or so is reasonable.

The estimates reiterated, plus prices in the *Guide Book*, for each of the three preceding examples, are as follows:[15]

1838-O half dollar (estimated 20 known)— EF-40: $125,000 • AU-50: $150,000 • MS-60: $200,000 • MS-63: $325,000.

1970-D half dollar (estimated 2,150,000 known)—MS-63: $16.

1776–1976 half dollar (estimated 234,308,000 known)—MS-63: $1.50.

So within the half dollar series, a coin of which fewer than 20 are known can be worth hundreds of thousands of dollars, while one of which a couple hundred million are known is worth about face value (plus a slight premium for the effort in handling), never mind that the latter coin is more than a quarter century old and is in Mint State.

The 2006 *Guide Book* (page 374) also lists values for certain Civil War tokens of common varieties, in each of several metals. Most of these were struck in copper, and many were made in brass. Tokens in other metals are scarcer. Within this series, a common die variety, such as a Dix, Not

One Cent, or Monitor issue, typically exists to the extent of an estimated 1,000 to 5,000 or so examples. On the other hand, many if not most silver Civil War tokens are one of a kind for their die variety, or one of just a handful.

Adapting the *Guide Book* prices to die varieties (descriptions and estimates added by me, and assuming "Unc." to be MS-63) for certain metal listings, we get this:

1863 Civil War token, copper or brass (estimated 1,000 to 5,000 known of a given common die variety)—F-12: $12 • VF-20: $15 • EF-40: $18 • MS-63: $40.

1863 Civil War token, silver (estimated 1–5 known of a given die variety)—F-12: $125 • VF-20: $175 • EF-40: $230 • MS-63: $460.

Unlike the situation for popular United States series, prices for Civil War tokens often require a lot of digging to find. Accordingly, here are some actual market prices I have paid for certain Civil War tokens:

• *1863 Civil War token, copper; cloaked head on obverse; flag, liberty cap, etc., on reverse; die variety Fuld-36/340a (estimated 500–1,000 known)*—MS-65 red and brown: Common, but not among the most common. I paid $45 on September 29, 1997. Formerly from the Cindy Grellman Collection.

• *1863 Civil War token, silver; cloaked head on obverse; flag, liberty cap, etc., on reverse; Fuld-36/340f (estimated 2–4 known)*—MS-64, planchet lamination on obverse: Bought for $600 on August 8, 1998, from Rich Hartzog. Pedigreed to an auction held by George Fuld, June 1979, Lot 2715, where it sold for $24.

The foregoing illustrates that relative rarity is important *within the context of a given series*, but that if a series is not widely collected, extremely rare coins can be inexpensive. Conversely, in a very popular series, coins that exist in quantity can be expensive—and worth the cost—

as the market is broad and there is a strong demand.

Stated another way, an 1838-O half dollar, of which an estimated 12 to 15 are known, is valued at $250,000 in MS-63 grade, because it is rare and also part of a very popular and widely collected series. A silver Civil War token, of greater rarity (only 2–4 known) and in higher grade, is worth $600, because it is in a specialty niche, with relatively few collectors seeking it.

Another set of prices, these involving numismatic items that are believed to be unique (just one known) in collectors' hands, demonstrates the same thing—that well-known rarities bring far better prices than do pieces known only to specialists:

- *1822 $5 gold half eagle (unique in collectors' hands)*—EF-40: $3,500,000+ (2006 *Guide Book* price, p. 238).
- *1792 pattern Birch cent, white metal (unique in collectors' hands)*—EF: $450,000 (2006 *Guide Book* price, p. 85; actually, the coin is Mint State).
- *1776 Massachusetts "Janus copper" (unique in collectors' hands)*—No grade stated: $42,000 (2006 *Guide Book* price, p. 56).
- *1737 Higley "The Wheele Goes Round" copper (unique in collectors'*

hands)—Fine: $100,000 (2006 *Guide Book* price, p. 47).
- *$1 Original Series bill from the First National Bank of Skaneateles, New York (unique in collectors' hands)*—VF: $19,200 (sold for this price in the CAA sale of May 2003, ex–Bill Sabis Collection).
- *1837 Feuchtwanger token in silver, Rulau HT-268-A, Low-120, in silver rather than Feuchtwanger's composition (unique in collectors' hands)*—MS-60: $5,000 (actual transaction, 2001; related pieces, but not in rare silver, are listed in the *Guide Book*, p. 373).
- *$20 Saginaw Valley Bank note, East Saginaw, Michigan, unissued bill from the 1860s, with orange overprint design (unique in collectors' hands)*—EF: $895 (actual transaction by Larry Falater, 2004).
- *1863 Civil War token issued by Roswell Barnes, Brighton, Michigan; Fuld-MS-085A-03d; copper-nickel (unique in collectors' hands)*—MS-65: $550 (actual transaction by Rossa & Tanenbaum, 1997).

By way of explanation, the 1822 $5 gold piece is one of three extant, the other two being held by the Smithsonian Institution.

Unique! An American rarity extraordinaire—the only 1822 $5 presently in private hands, a coin the writer cataloged for the Eliasberg Collection of United States Gold Coins, 1982, and off the market since that time. (Tom Mulvaney photograph, courtesy of the coin's owner)

Unique! Although 3,000 of these Original Charter $1 bills were distributed by the First National Bank of Skaneateles, New York, only one is known to exist—as shown here. (From the Bill Sabis Collection)

Although the *Guide Book* lists it at $3,500,000, a check for twice this amount would not buy the coin if the owner did not want to sell. This prompts me to state that *the rarer the coin, the less fixed or standard are the market values.* Those with great rarities can name their own prices, and if a buyer is at hand, they might be successful.

The 1792 Birch cent was sold years ago; there are no modern prices. Although the *Guide Book* gives $450,000 as a current estimate, if auctioned it would likely bring far more. The 1776 Janus copper is in the same category. I cataloged this in the late 1970s as part of the Garrett Collection for The Johns Hopkins University, and it has not been seen on the market since. Ditto for the 1737 Higley copper, in recent years a prized possession of an eastern specialist.

The $19,200 paid for the $1 bill from the First National Bank of Skaneateles, New York, represents a treasure in the context of federal currency (which tends to sell for more, often much more, than private bank bills), and was a highlight of the Sabis Collection, one of the finest ever formed. It went to a Massachusetts buyer.

The 1837 Feuchtwanger token in silver sold for the high price of $5,000 a few years ago. However, because the Ford Collection of Hard Times tokens (Stack's 2004) did not have an example, and because many pieces of which two to four are known sold for much more than $10,000 each (some for more than $50,000) at that event, the silver Feuchtwanger would probably bring more if offered today.

The last two on the list, the Michigan bank note and the Civil War token, are classics and could be called priceless, but each is in a niche market without many players. In such specialized markets, rarities tend to be inexpensive.

As will be explained in chapter 6, a coin can be common in one grade, such as Good-4, but rare in MS-65. A coin that is rare in a certain high grade, but not in lower ranges, is

sometimes called a *condition rarity.* One cannot say that a 1901 Morgan silver dollar is rare, for 6,912,183 were minted, and well over 50,000 well-worn coins exist today. In VF-20 the *Guide Book* prices the 1901 for $40. However, in gem MS-65 only a handful exist, and the listed price is $150,000. Accordingly, as a date the 1901 is common, but in MS-65 it is a condition rarity.

Rarity is important, but only in connection with other factors.

Grade

Generally, for a given *coin*, the higher the grade, the higher the value. The 1901 Morgan dollar discussed above, worth $40 in VF-20 grade but $200,000 in MS-65, is an example. This is not always true for certain other numismatic items, as I shall explain. Most numismatic rules have exceptions.

Often, a very small difference in a grading number can mean a very big difference in market price. Consider another Morgan dollar:

1896-O Morgan silver dollar—VF-20: $18 • EF-40: $20 • AU-50: $200 • MS-60: $900 • MS-63: $7,500 • MS-64: $42,500 • MS-65: $165,000.

For some other coins, such differences are not as important to price. Here is the 1936 Elgin (Illinois) Centennial com-

The 1896-O Morgan silver dollar is common and inexpensive in lower grades, but emerges as an expensive rarity in MS-65 preservation. As the price differentials between grades are so great, much care must be taken to determine what grade is suitable for you, and, later, to assure proper quality, grade, and eye appeal when you select a coin.

memorative half dollar, these being the only prices listed in the *Guide Book:*

1936 Elgin Centennial commemorative half dollar—AU-50: $190 • MS-60: $220 • MS-63: $240 • MS-65: $265.

These illustrations also invite a reprise of the Optimal Collecting Grade (OCG) technique. No matter how much money you may have to spend, if you are seeking a Mint State 1896-O dollar, you will want to be very careful—for a tiny difference in grade can make a huge difference in market price. On the other hand, for the 1936 Elgin half dollar, go ahead and buy an MS-65. You don't have to do much thinking about it. To buy an MS-60 1896-O dollar might be quite worthwhile, in view of much higher prices for grades beyond that. However, buying an MS-60 1936 Elgin half dollar would seem to make no sense at all! (Perhaps without realizing it, if you've progressed this far in this book, you are already well on your way to becoming a smart buyer!)

Grading is discussed in detail in chapter 7. If you read everything, you will probably be as conversant with the ins and outs of grading as 95% of those who have been in numismatics for 10 years or more. As it is one of the most important determinants of value, your careful attention to the subject is encouraged. Don't let others make your decisions!

As to those exceptions I mentioned, in some instances the evidence that a numismatic item has been actually used for its intended purpose can make it far more valuable than one that was preserved in Mint State. For example:

- An Indian peace medal known to have been awarded to an Indian chief is more valuable than one made from the same dies but for a collector's cabinet.

- A silver award medal given as an exposition or competition prize may be worth, say, $50, if blank and not awarded, but in Mint State. However, if it is engraved with the name of a recipient, such as to Samuel F.B.

Most of the 20,000 Elgin commemorative half dollars struck in 1936 still exist today, and nearly all are in Mint State. Gems are common. Selecting a gem MS-65 for your collection is, as they say, a "no-brainer."

Morse for improvements in the telegraph, it might be worth hundreds or thousands of dollars.

- A $100 bill of the Piscataqua Exchange Bank of Portsmouth, New Hampshire, circa the 1850s, in crisp, Uncirculated, like-new condition, might sell for $50 to $75. Hundreds exist. However, the same bill, if hand-signed by the cashier and president of the bank, serially numbered and dated in ink, and used in circulation, is so rare that I've never seen one— and would gladly pay a few hundred dollars for one in VF grade.

In the *Guide Book of Double Eagle Gold Coins,* I included the following, and cannot resist restating it here:

The most exciting recent example of a used (in this case, *very well used to the point of being damaged*) item being worth more than a Mint State one involves an otherwise ordinary $20 gold coin recovered in 2000 from the wreck of the Confederate submarine *Hunley,* which had sunk in 1864.

The piece was dated 1860 and was disfigured from being hit by a bullet that might otherwise have killed its owner, George Dixon, who later carried it as a good luck piece while commanding the *Hunley.* Salvagers said that this coin, worth, say, a few hundred dollars if in VF grade, was worth $500,000 because of how it was used!

Examples of Indian peace medals, old bank notes, and the *Hunley* artifact are exceptions to the rule that higher grades are the most valuable. Such exceptions will probably not be relevant to what you collect, but it is worth knowing about such things. Besides, you can keep such situations in mind in case you want to stump someone in a quiz at a coin-club meeting!

Popularity

Popularity is probably the single most important determinant of value. I could devote a chapter or two to the subject, but as it isn't particularly abstruse, these few paragraphs should suffice.

Basically, if rarities and grades are comparable, a numismatic item in a widely collected series will bring a much higher price than will one in a narrow, specialized series with few adherents. Thousands of Mint State 1889-CC Morgan silver dollars exist, and yet the *Guide Book* prices an example in minimum MS-60 grade for $18,000. In contrast, not more than a few hundred 1935 Alaska Rural Rehabilitation Corporation twenty-five-cent tokens (*Guide Book*, page 385) exist, but a Mint State coin is priced at just $100.

The difference is due to popularity. Well over 100,000 enthusiasts, perhaps far more, aspire to collect Morgan silver dollars by date and mint. Although thousands of Mint State 1889-CC dollars exist, they are expensive because they are rare in relation to the demand for them. On the other hand, probably not more than a few hundred collectors aspire to gather the Alaska tokens, and a year or two can elapse before my company receives "want-list" requests for them.

This aspect also appeared under "Rarity" earlier—the unique 1822 $5 half eagle is listed at $3,500,000, while unique items in series that are not popular can be bought for very modest sums.

This general rule is true all across numismatics.

Popularity can be adjusted, manipulated, and revised. While rarity tends to remain constant, popularity can change over a period of time. Even entire collecting *fields* can change, sometimes dramatically. Birds' eggs and tobacco tags, widely collected in the 19th century, are hardly ever heard of in this context today. A friend in the stamp business mused the other day about the future of that hobby, what with memberships in societies declining and stamps seeing less use over the years.

However, as I see it, this negative thinking does not apply to numismatics—money is not going to go out of style anytime soon. Many new statehood quarters, Jefferson nickel modifications, and commemoratives are coming down the pike—enough to keep us all busy for a long time—and membership in the American Numismatic Association (ANA) has increased significantly in the past decade.

What makes a coin or an entire series popular? The following sections contain some of my thoughts on the subject.

Listings in the *Guide Book*

If a particular variety is listed in a frequently used or cited reference, its value will be enhanced. Years ago, beginning in 1934, *The Standard Catalogue of United States Coins* was the arbiter of what to collect. Many used the various editions of this text to compile lists of what they needed. If a coin was listed in the *Standard Catalogue*, it was desired. If it was rare, desirable, interesting, or anything else, but was not listed, it was not added to "want lists."

Today, the *Standard Catalogue* has lapsed into history, with the last (18th) edition being published in 1958. In the meantime, the *Guide Book of United States Coins* has become far and away the most widely used book on prices. Hence, a coin listed there becomes more popular. Of course, basic dates and mintmarks are necessarily listed in the interest of completeness. However, the addition of repunched dates, curious mintmarks, doubled dies, and so on is not at all consistent, and some are listed while others are not.

Here are some examples of curious varieties listed in the *Guide Book*, and their prices, together with a related regular issue:

1936 Lincoln cent, Doubled Die obverse— MS-60: $1,000.

1936 Lincoln cent, regular—MS-60: $8.

1892-O Barber half dollar, "micro O" mintmark—MS-60: $14,000.

1892-O Barber half dollar, regular— MS-60: $900.

Although a super-dedicated collector could search out these varieties by reading specialized texts, they would not be generally known if it were not for their inclusion in the *Guide Book*.

The most spectacular doubled-die variety in American numismatics is the 1876-CC trade dollar, with doubled-die reverse—this being the opinion of Bill Fivaz, the nation's leading authority on curious varieties. I agree with him. However, this variety is completely absent from the *Guide Book*. It will probably be listed some day, and I will recommend this. In the meantime, examples that come on the market are much less expensive than they would be if they were included in the *Guide Book*! Of the couple dozen or so known to be in collectors' hands, most have been purchased for low prices as "regular"

1876-CC trade dollars, from clueless sellers. If the variety is listed in the *Guide Book*, such opportunities will be lost!

Focus on "Numismatic Delicacies"

There are some famous American rarities that were made after a regular series ended. These were created as delicacies for collectors. Included are the 1913 Liberty Head nickel (the series otherwise ended in 1912), the 1866 without-motto silver quarter, half dollar, and dollar (that type ended in 1865), and the 1884 and 1885 trade dollars (the series ended in 1883).

Each of these is worth a lot of money, at least hundreds of thousands of dollars apiece, and for some, more than a million dollars. There is another post-issue rarity of equal importance, in my opinion: the 1868-dated large copper cent, the exact type as last regularly minted in 1857, but made in 1868 as a rarity for collectors. About a dozen exist. However, although the 1868 cent is noted in passing on page 108 of the *Guide Book*, it does not have a separate listing and price. An 1868 large copper cent in Proof-64 sold for close to $40,000 recently. If it had been a staple among *Guide Book* listings over the years,

Overall view of an 1876-CC trade dollar. On a few of these coins the reverse is seen to be the Doubled Die variety, with doubling of certain features, such as the branch at the lower right. Bill Fivaz, co-author (with J.T. Stanton) of the *Cherrypickers' Guide to Rare Die Varieties*, considers this to be the most spectacular doubled die in the American series.

This 1868 large copper cent is identical in design and appearance to a regular-issue copper cent of the 1843 to 1857 Braided Hair style, except for the date. Made as a delicacy for the numismatic trade, only about a dozen or so pieces are believed to exist today. However, as it does not have a separate entry and price in the *Guide Book*, it is not widely known, and the market price is but a fraction of those of comparable numismatic delicacies that are listed. (Hogan Pond Collection)

the demand for it would be intense now, and one might be worth as much as an 1884 trade dollar (*Guide Book* value: $300,000 in Proof-63 grade).

The pattern $4 gold pieces ("Stellas") of 1879 and 1880 are just that: patterns. They are not regular issues, but are strictly a part of the series of more than 1,800 patterns described in the ninth edition of *United States Pattern Coins*, by Dr. J. Hewitt Judd. However, as they are listed in the *Guide Book*, the demand for them is multiples of what it would be if it were listed only in the Judd book.

There are other strictly pattern coins that are listed among regular issues in the *Guide Book*, and, accordingly, they have gained great popularity. The 1856 Flying Eagle cent and the 1838 Gobrecht silver dollar are just two examples.

Listing a variety in the *Guide Book* is the equivalent of listing a common stock on the New York Stock Exchange. It (the variety or stock) becomes important and widely known.

To a lesser extent, listings in other places, such as the value guides published by *Coin World*, *Numismatic News*, the *Coin Dealer Newsletter*, and the *Certified Coin Dealer Newsletter*, help as well.

Other Aspects of Popularity

The inclusion of a variety in a Whitman, Littleton, Dansco, or other widely sold coin holder or folder can increase its pop-

The 1879 pattern $4 gold Stella (enlarged), the variety with Flowing Hair listed as J-1635 in the Judd book on patterns, is known to the extent of hundreds of specimens, from a mintage of somewhat more than 700 pieces. As a pattern coin it is one of the most plentiful of all varieties. However, because it is listed in the *Guide Book* it plays to a much wider audience and, accordingly, is in strong demand and very expensive.

ularity and hence the demand for it. In the 1930s, Wayte Raymond published his "National" album pages for many series. For large copper cents of 1793 to 1857 he included openings for the basic dates and overdates, then a selection of other varieties such as letter sizes. Those varieties he chose became desired by a generation of numismatists, and important varieties for which there were no gaping holes to be filled were ignored by most.

News coverage can influence popularity. The demand for the 2004-D Wisconsin statehood quarters with Extra Leaf High and Extra Leaf Low is very strong, as these have been given wide play in *Numismatic News*, *Coin World*, and dealer advertisements since their discovery in December 2004. As these words are being written, in 2005, news coverage is the only thing going for these varieties—listings in reference books, holes for them in albums, and so on have yet to come. However, the commercial grading services have added these varieties to their listings of significant issues.

Over the years, certain current issues have been darlings of the press, and nationwide demand arose for them—such as the Liberty Head nickel without CENTS made and publicized in 1883, and the Small Date cent of 1960. Another example is the 1979-S Anthony dollar, with "Filled S" mintmark and "Clear S." The *Guide Book* lists the former for $10 in Proof-65 grade and the latter for $100. In contrast, a Filled S vis-à-vis a Clear S on a Morgan silver dollar would attract little attention, and certainly not a tenfold differential in market price!

Auction appearances generate publicity and increase desire. Every time my company has a nice MCMVII (1907) High Relief double eagle in a sale, something is said about its history, romance, and beauty in addition to its rarity and grade. When a spectacular rarity comes up for sale, its availability and publicity combine to draw potential buyers out of the woodwork—and someone who is not an active coin collector might jump in with both feet and buy it. I have seen this happen many times. The same is true for the 1879 $4 Flowing Hair Stella mentioned above.

In other times, a collector of one series will jump ship and through a catalog description decide to plunge into another specialty entirely—based on an auction presentation. I recall spending quite some time researching and describing the early American medals in Part I of the Harry W. Bass, Jr., Collection in 1999. A North Carolina numismatist who did not specialize in medals and had not a single one in his collection—in fact, his main interest was *banjos* (the musical instruments)—became enchanted with the history of the Libertas Americana medal in silver. Although he was going on a trip to New Zealand, he kept in touch while away so as to participate in the bidding for it. (He tried, but lost in the competition.) I could mention dozens, probably even hundreds, of instances in which a nice "spread" in an auction catalog on the gold coins of the Charlotte and Dahlonega mints, or a beautiful 1879 Schoolgirl pattern silver dollar, or an obscure colonial, served as

the launchpad for a collector entering a completely new series.

The earlier-mentioned concept of "registry sets," initiated a few years ago by David Hall of Professional Coin Grading Service (PCGS) and soon joined by Numismatic Guaranty Corporation of America (NGC), has increased the demand for certain high-grade coins in these sets—with points being awarded to coins that are among the highest certified of their variety.

Market fads, trends, and cycles, explored in chapter 9 and discussed in detail in chapters 10 through 12, are exceedingly important aspects of a coin's popularity and, in consequence, of a coin's price. And yet, relatively few buyers know about these things.

Here are some vignettes from coin-market history, including the most popular items or series at the time—coins that everyone was talking about and that were leading the market. You may be surprised at some of the listings:

- *1860:* Medals with the portrait of George Washington. Even the Mint collected them!

The famous Libertas Americana medal dated July 1776, produced in Paris in 1782 through arrangements perfected by Benjamin Franklin. The dies, by Augustin Dupré, feature Miss Liberty with a liberty cap and pole—the first depiction of a motif that years later would be used on certain United States coins, commencing with copper half cents and cents in 1793. The reverse shows America in the form of a goddess, fighting off the British lion with the help of the French (France being represented by fleur de lis emblems on the shield)—an allegory illustrating the Revolutionary War.

Several hundred copper impressions of the Libertas Americana medal exist today, as do a few dozen silver Proofs. While the collecting of early American medals is a specialized pursuit, and no single book is available to yield rarity and market-price information, there is a strong demand for such pieces, and bidding competition is intense when they are offered at auction. More information about medals is found in chapter 26.

- *1899:* Hard Times tokens of the 1830s. More popular at the time than were Morgan dollars!

- *1935:* 1935-D and -S Boone half dollars with small "1934." The price skyrocketed in a matter of weeks.

- *1956:* Proof sets of 1936 to 1942, and 1950 to 1955. Prices sometimes rose hourly, as posted on "bid and ask" boards at coin shows.

- *1960:* Small Date Philadelphia cent of this year. A media event par excellence. A \$50 sack of freshly minted cents sold for more than \$12,000!

- *1962:* 1903-O Morgan dollar, a market sensation when a long-hidden cache was found.

- *1963:* 1950-D Jefferson nickels, the dazzling sensation of a great bull market in coins.

- *1975:* Franklin Mint medals sold to the general public, who could not buy them fast enough.

- *1989:* Certified MS-65 or finer silver and gold coins for investors. Prices went up and up and up some more.

- *2000s:* High-grade certified coins for registry sets. Never mind whether a similar coin that is a grade-notch or so lower is as common as can be.

Each one of these hot spots in the market was riding a popularity crest and drew many new players into numismatics.

Fame

Many coins have significant value based on their *fame*. I am not quite sure you could call the 1804 silver dollar (the "King of American Coins") *popular*, as only 15 exist, and few people have the financial wherewithal to buy an example. Certainly, reading about this coin is a popular pursuit—more ink, including that in two books, is devoted to this particular variety than to any other single rarity in the U.S. series. However, the coin itself is not a popular item in the context of widespread acquisition. Most known examples show signs of wear, and, accordingly, grade and scarcity alone do not determine its price. Its value rests on its *fame*.

There are many other famous coins in American numismatics, their fame resting on a combination of historical importance, beauty, market price, rarity, and press agentry over the years.

If a coin hits the headlines with a value of a million dollars, as a rare 1866 no-motto Liberty Seated silver dollar did in 2004 when John Kraljevich and John Pack located the coin, long missing, in the hands of a non-collector, and returned it to its rightful owner, the coin will become famous. This particular coin, not well known previously (only two are known to exist), was showcased on television programs, in newspaper articles, and elsewhere. The ANA, whose museum was the coin's destination, featured it in publicity. For a time it was the talk of the hobby. Had it been for sale (it was not), chances are good it would have fetched a record price, due to its massive exposure in the media. In January 2005, the *other* specimen of this variety, the only one in private hands, was consigned by a Texas estate and was sold by American Numismatic Rarities (ANR) for more than \$1 million.

A list of famous American coins with interesting stories would be a long one, but, for starters, would surely include the 1652 Massachusetts Pine Tree shilling, 1799 copper cent, 1856 Flying Eagle cent, 1943 error cent (struck in copper instead of the steel otherwise used this year), 1913 Liberty Head nickel, 1792 half disme, and 1851 Augustus Humbert \$50 gold "slug."

As a professional numismatist, I know well that if someone consigned an 1851 Humbert \$50 "slug," direct from the height of the California Gold Rush, it could be sold in a wink to just about anyone who could afford it—no matter whether they collected gold coins. All it takes is for someone to write about or tell of its romantic history!

The only 1866 No Motto silver dollar in private hands, this coin crossed the auction block in January 2005 for more than a million dollars.

Similarly, the *Mona Lisa*, in the Louvre in Paris, may or may not be the most beautiful of all paintings, and certainly *any* painting shares its one-of-a-kind status. Nonetheless, the *Mona Lisa* is the most famous of all paintings in the world and, consequently, probably the most valuable. If it should come on the market (theoretically, of course, as it is a French national treasure), I imagine the bidding audience would include many people who didn't own any other classic art, but wanted this icon.

Provenance

The provenance, or identities of previous owners, can contribute to a coin's value. Often a common coin, if offered as part of a famous collection, will bring a very high price, simply because it affords the opportunity to own a coin with an illustrious background. I recall that in the Garrett Collection series of sales, 1979 to 1981, a common, worn 1913 Buffalo nickel, worth perhaps $10, brought several hundred dollars because it was from this collection.

Famous collectors of the past are many, and such names as McCoy, Maris, Randall, Parmelee, Mills, Stickney, Ten Eyck, and dozens more from generations ago add value to coins attributed to these collections today. Since 1950, dozens of other famous collectors have joined the Hall of Fame, including, in no particular order, and mentioning just a few (and deliberately excluding those who formed collections that I've helped sell), Farouk, Anderson-Dupont (agents), Robinson, Wolfson, Trompeter,

Donlon, Gilhousen, Hydeman, Halpern, Gaskill, Wilkison, Hydeman, Buss, Miles, Black, Miller, Carter, Bloomfield, Benson, Browning, Naftzger, Bloomfield, Ryder, Ford, Kern, Robison, Judd, Price, Pittman, Starr, and Hawn. As to my own involvement, you can add Garrett, Norweb, Eliasberg, Bass, and a string of others.

Provenance listings for specific coins can be fascinating. The following is a listing for one of the 15 known 1804 silver dollars.

Adams Specimen of the 1804 Dollar

John W. Haseltine was the first person to exhibit this specimen, a Class-III or restrike variety, early in 1876, with the story that it had been located by a private English source.[16] This coin was purchased by Phinehas Adams of Manchester, New Hampshire. For a long time it was known as the "Lyman" dollar, after a later owner.

The following provenance is conjectural before circa 1875:

- *1858–1872:* Believed to have been struck at the Philadelphia Mint during this period.

- *1875–1876:* Captain John W. Haseltine, Philadelphia dealer.

- *1876:* Phinehas Adams, Manchester, New Hampshire.

- *1880 (circa):* Henry Ahlborn, Boston coin dealer and publisher of coin-premium lists; the handling of this coin was a bright feather in his publicity cap.

- *1880:* John P. Lyman, Boston, Massachusetts, who bought this as part of a "full set of dollars."[17] Consigned with the rest of his collection to the following.

- *1913 (November 7):* S. Hudson Chapman, Lyman Collection, Lot 16.

- *1913:* Waldo C. Newcomer, Baltimore, Maryland. Displayed at the American Numismatic Society, 1914, and illustrated on Plate 17 of the catalog titled *Exhibition of United States and Colonial Coins, January 17th to February 18, 1914.*

- *1932:* B. Max Mehl, on consignment from Newcomer.

- *1932:* Col. Edward H.R. Green.

- *1936–1943 (circa):* Col. Green estate. As of March 1943, the 1804 dollar was still in the Green estate, which was being administered by the Chase National Bank, New York City.

- *1943 (circa):* A.J. Allen, Plainfield, New Jersey; the coin changed hands for a reported $3,200.

- *1946 (circa):* Frederick C.C. Boyd, East Orange, New Jersey. Boyd must have acquired it for the satisfaction of having owned this famous rarity, holding it but briefly, after which he put it up for sale. By this time his main collection of U.S. silver coins had already been sold (by Numismatic Gallery, under the title of "The World's Greatest Collection," 1945).

- *1946:* Numismatic Gallery (Abe Kosoff and Abner Kreisberg), on consignment from Boyd.

- *1946:* Percy A. Smith, Portland, Oregon. Displayed by Smith on September 14, 1946, at the Oregon Numismatic Society meeting. Sold privately to the following.

- *1949–1950:* B. Max Mehl, who had it in his inventory by October 1949.

- *1950 (May 23):* B. Max Mehl, Golden Jubilee Sale (Jerome Kern and other collections), Lot 804.

- *1950:* Amon G. Carter, Sr., Fort Worth, Texas.

- *1955:* Amon G. Carter, Jr.; descended to him after the passing of his father.

- *1982–1984:* Amon G. Carter, Jr., estate, to his family.

- *1984 (January 18–21):* Stack's, Carter Collection, Lot 241.

- *1984:* John Nelson Rowe III, agent for the following.

- *1984–1989:* L.R. French, Jr., Texas numismatist.

- *1989 (January 18):* Stack's, L.R. French, Jr., Family Collection, Lot 15.

- *1989:* Rarities Group, Inc. (Martin B. Paul).

- *1989:* National Gold Exchange (Mark Yaffe), Tampa, Florida.

- *1989:* Heritage Rare Coin Galleries (Jim Halperin and Steve Ivy), Dallas, Texas.

- *1989–November 1993:* Indianapolis collection. In May 1992, the owner commissioned Farmington Valley Rare Coin Co., New Hartford, Connecticut (Tony Scirpo, owner), to find a buyer. At this time the coin was certified as EF-45 by PCGS.[18]

- *1993 (November):* Acquired by a private buyer located by Farmington Valley Rare Coin Co. Subsequently sold to the following.

- *1994:* David Liljestrand.

- *1994–1998:* Midwest collection.

- *1998:* David Liljestrand.

- *1998:* National Gold Exchange and Kenneth Goldman.

- *1998:* Legend Numismatics, Inc. (Laura Sperber).

- *1998:* Private collection. Now certified as AU-58.

The compilation of provenance involves some guesswork in instances in which coins were not illustrated in catalogs, or when they were sold privately without announcement. Generally, any extensive provenance is subject to updating and revision by modern scholars as more information becomes available. Until recently, the first name of Adams, in the above provenance, was spelled as "Phineas," in the style of Phineas T. Barnum. However, in reviewing some biographical information about Adams, who was also prominent in New Hampshire banking, I learned that the correct spelling is *Phinehas*.

In recent years, members of the Numismatic Bibliomania Society and others have done a great deal of provenance research, Saul Teichman and P. Scott Rubin (both contributors to the present text) prominent among them. The late Carl W.A. Carlson enjoyed compiling provenance lists, and in 1991 contributed "Tracker: An Introduction to Pedigree Research in the Field of Rare American Coins" to the *American Numismatic Association Centennial Anthology*.

Metal

Precious metals have a special appeal and are often attractive to buyers. A newcomer to the market will find it easier to be enticed by a sparkling Mint State gold $20 coin of a common date (e.g., 1901) than by a well-worn but very rare copper cent of 1799.

In some series within such specialties as tokens, pattern coins, and medals, the same dies were used to strike coins in different metals. For example, certain Stan-

dard Silver pattern coins of 1869 and 1870 were made in copper, aluminum, and silver. Generally, in such instances, copper is the least valuable striking, followed by aluminum, then silver. An 1879 pattern Schoolgirl silver dollar can be found in copper and silver, with silver being the more valuable.

Exceptions abound, and for strikings of off-metal coins from regular-issue Proof dies (not pattern designs), a half dollar struck in aluminum or copper is worth more than one in silver, and an Indian Head cent struck in aluminum (such as in 1872) is worth more than a bronze impression.

Civil War tokens were struck in various metals, some of the same die pairs in copper, brass, German silver (a nickel composition), and silver—with this also being the order of value. In all instances, a silver impression of such a token is worth more than a copper one. For 19th century medals, it is generally true that a gold impression is worth more than a silver one, and a silver medal commands a higher market price than does one in copper.

Investment Demand

Every now and then the coin market comes into sharp focus outside of the numismatic community. Investors in stocks and bonds learn about the historically excellent (mostly) returns shown by rare coins, and

An 1872 Indian Head cent (enlarged) struck from regular Proof dies, but in aluminum instead of the normal bronze—a numismatic delicacy listed in the Judd pattern text as J-1181, although it is not a pattern, strictly speaking.

For the numismatic specialist in gold double eagles the 1904-S is considered to be very common, and hundreds of thousands exist in Mint State. Of course, every specialized collection needs an example, but beyond this most of the demand for such plentiful issues is with investors. More than just a few people have bought a 1904-S or related common date as an investment item, have become piqued with its design and history, have investigated further, and have gone on to become serious collectors.

want to get into the action. Focus is usually on series in silver and gold, and in higher grades. Sometimes the values of precious metals plays a part in investment demand. A run-up in the price of gold bullion nearly always increases the demand for gold coins.

A large influx of investor money results in a sharp rise in price for the series affected. After the passion fades, as it usually does, prices subside—but usually settle at figures somewhat higher than when the action began. I discuss this in detail in chapter 9, under "The Anatomy of a Coin Market Cycle."

Sometimes the advent of large numbers of investors lifts the spirit of the market across many series. Dealers who make large profits selling bulk double eagles might spend their earnings on other series of personal interest, or to acquire a trophy rarity for the pride of possession. Conversely, a mass exodus of investors can dampen the spirit of a market, as dealers scramble to get cash to pay their obligations and are forced to cut back on overhead expenses.

Die Variety

Concluding my comment on basic aspects determining a coin's value I mention die varieties. These are examples of a regular date or mintmark issue, but with some subtle difference from the ordinary. While major varieties are listed in the *Guide Book*, most minor varieties are not. To learn about minute differences between the dies used to strike dozens of varieties of copper cents dated 1794, you must consult Sheldon's *Early American Cents* and its revision, *Penny Whimsy*. To distinguish die varieties among half cents of 1804, you need a copy of either the Cohen or the Breen text on this denomination.

Interesting and rare die varieties offer a fertile field once you gain experience as a numismatist. Valuable finds are constantly being made. The September 13, 2004, issue of *Coin World*, page 3, told of an entirely new die variety of 1807 Draped Bust silver half dollar, unknown to Haseltine, Beistle, or Overton—each of whom

wrote a book on the subject. It was discovered in June 2004, and given the new listing of "Overton-115," added on to the end of already known varieties. Then, voila! In August a *second* specimen of O-115 was found, in VF-20 grade, reported by Sheridan Downey and Dr. Glenn Peterson! At the time a "regular" (not rare die variety) 1807 Draped Bust half dollar listed for $400 in the *Guide Book*. Although the market value of each of the two newly discovered O-115 halves was not stated, I am probably safe in saying that each is worth quite a few thousand dollars.

In the very same issue of *Coin World*, page 8, Rick Snow, dealer specialist in Flying Eagle and Indian Head cents, reported cherrypicking a rare die variety of the 1856 Flying Eagle cent. The coin was misattributed and offered as a common issue, in an auction held by a Midwest firm. "His winning bid, including 15% buyer's fee, was $9,200, for what he said could easily have been a $20,000 coin."

In December 2004, one of the most famous of all die varieties of large copper cents, the 1793 Strawberry Leaf, Sheldon NC-3 ("Non-Collectible" No. 3), crossed the auction block. Although it was only in Fine-12 grade, this was far higher than any of the other three known specimens, which hover in the Fair to G-4 range. Had it been an ordinary die variety of a 1793

The collector of die varieties can appreciate this well-worn example, certified as Fine-12, of the 1793 Strawberry Leaf large copper cent. Although it is in low grade, the other three pieces, one of which is in the American Numismatic Society collection, are in far lower preservation. This particular coin appeared in the 1890 sale of the Lorin G. Parmelee Collection, and years later, in the early 1940s, was sold to a New England numismatist. In 2004, it crossed the auction block at $412,000, setting the all-time record for any United States one-cent piece of any variety in any grade.

cent, a rare date, it might have squeaked past the $1,000 mark. However, this rare variety soared to a remarkable $412,000!

A die variety, if rare, can add considerably to the value of a coin. Of course, while good fortune strikes now and then, most such things are already identified by the time you buy them. However, hope springs eternal!

Sources for Pricing Information

Introduction

In the field of stocks, if you want to learn the current price of a share of Intel, or General Motors, or Compudyne, all you need to do is know its abbreviation and your Internet stock broker's URL, and push a button. There is no single source for pricing information on all coins. If there were, then we could all refer to a given book, Internet listing, or other location and save a lot of time!

This is the case with rare coins (and stamps, and old cars, and paintings, and real estate, and unrestored "warbird" airplanes). To most enthusiasts, the seeking of price information adds to the excitement.

As a professional numismatist, *experience* is my main source—but that does not do *you* much good, unless you ask me and I want to share my ideas. Even with a great deal of experience, I have to constantly look up prices, as they are always changing. Then I have to determine which price listings are useful and which are not. Every once in a while a *book* is written as a guide to prices, but proves to be unreliable. Some years ago a volume on what are termed *so-called dollars* (medals of dollar size) offered prices that for many issues were wildly unrealistic, and the same happened with a book on small-denomination California gold. Still other books may have prices on the low side. Generally, for most rare coins needed for customers' "want lists" I will pay more than the prices listed in the popular *Handbook of United States Coins* (the wholesale price guide known as the Blue Book) published annually by Whitman. (However, the book remains generally useful as to what typical buyers will pay for average quality coins.)

A few years ago I had an 1878-CC silver trade dollar I graded as MS-65. Try as I might, I could not find any information for a recent sale at that level. Then I encountered a market-value listing for $150,000 in a popular coin periodical. Seeking the basis for the figure, I telephoned the compiler, only to be told that he could not find a price either, and guessed that $150,000 was about right. I did some more checking, some thinking, some extrapolations beyond the prices that MS-63 coins had sold for, and figured it was worth $35,000. I mentioned my methodology to several specialists in the field, and they agreed that was about right (but none offered to buy it for $35,000!). I did price it for $35,000, and it sold right away. The new owner was quite happy.

The opposite situation might be true for a 1787 Bust Left Vermont copper, a coin I mentioned earlier. I have not handled more than five examples of this coin in my career. It is not listed in many places at all. In Good-4 grade the *Guide Book* suggests $3,500. Based on my experience I would pay $5,000, perhaps more, if one were offered to me this minute!

These instances demonstrate that prices published in well-known locations are not always indicative of what I might buy or sell a coin for. However, most standard sources are at least in the ballpark.

Just as a real estate agent might investigate several sources to put a price on 100 acres of land in Vermont, bordering on Lake Champlain, and the sources might be different from those used to evaluate a cottage three blocks in from the sea at Wildwood Crest, New Jersey, and still different from a resale condominium in Trump Tower in Manhattan. No single price guide fits all numismatic situations.

In the course of business I use many sources and then add my own thoughts based on experience. In brief, published listings are usually just fine for actively traded coins in popular series, in grades in which many are known, and for which there are not many problems relating to strike, eye appeal, or other aspects of quality. For coins requiring a degree of connoisseurship to buy, published guides are only a part of the story—as a case study of the 1857-C gold dollar given in chapter 8 demonstrates. Also, recall my earlier comments on lightly struck 1925-S Buffalo nickels.

Published Guides

The *Guide Book*, issued yearly, has served as my basic reference for many years. Amos Press and Krause Publications also issue market guides that contain much valuable information. *Coin World* and *Numismatic News* each publish magazine-style listings, often including a wider range of grades than can be found in the *Guide Book*.

Ever since 1963, the *Coin Dealer Newsletter* has published "bid" prices on selected coins, expanding the coverage in recent years through the *Certified Coin Dealer Newsletter*. Prices in these two newsletters are generally for generic coins, and it is carefully noted that high-quality examples within a given grade often bring much more money.

ANACS, NGC, and PCGS publish reports showing the numbers of coins each has certified in various grades, a very valuable resource in determining the number of *submission events* (prices are not listed) of certain certified coins in certain grades. The number of *different coins* involved is often far different from the number of *submission events* for such pieces. To look at population reports, you might get the (wrong) idea that a Proof 1879 $4 gold Stella is fairly common, for there are hundreds of listings, while a VF-20 1916 cent is extremely rare, as listings are few (more about certified coin populations later).

Specialized series often have their own price guides, sometimes updated infrequently. Russell Rulau's *Standard Catalog of United States Tokens* is a foundation reference for that field, while *Paper Money of the United States*, created by the Friedberg family, is essential to the valuation of its title subject (as is the related new Whitman title, *A Guide Book of United States Paper Money*, using Friedberg numbers). The ninth edition of Dr. J. Hewitt Judd's *United States Pattern Coins* covers that series with values in several grades plus auction records. Many other examples could be given.

Electronic Media

Numismedia, a service conducted by Dennis Baker, combines data from the two titles in the *Coin Dealer Newsletter* series, plus population data, as well as other information. It is available to online users for a subscription fee. Many dealers use this as a handy source for actively traded coins and for up-to-the-minute prices—a valuable resource as, in areas such as in the trading of gold bullion coins, prices can change rapidly, sometimes several times within a single day.

Beyond standard sources, browsing the Internet will reveal many listings of prices, sometimes for coins

A special launch ceremony for a recent edition of *A Guide Book of United States Coins* was held at the Whitman Coin and Collectibles Expo Atlanta. In the foreground are Mary Counts, president of Whitman Publishing, and Ken Bressett, editor of the *Guide Book*. In the background are Harold Anderson, Charles Anderson, and John McDowell.

GOLD DOLLARS

Type 1

	Fine	Unc.
1849 Open wreath...	$6.00	$10.00
1849 Closed wreath...	8.50	15.00
1849C Closed wreath...	20.00	
1849C Open wreath—Unique		
1849D Open wreath...	20.00	
1849O Open wreath...	9.00	15.00
1850...	5.50	7.50
1850C...	50.00	150.00
1850D...	45.00	
1850O...	15.00	
1851...	5.50	7.50
1851C...	15.00	22.50
1851D...	22.50	50.00
1851O...	8.00	12.50
1852...	6.00	7.50
1852C...	17.50	30.00
1852D...	30.00	50.00
1852O...	10.00	17.50
1853...	5.00	7.50
1853C...	25.00	35.00
1853D...	30.00	45.00
1853O...	7.50	13.50
1854...	5.00	7.50
1854D...	60.00	80.00
1854S...	22.50	37.50

Type 2

	Fine	Unc.	Proof
1854...	$7.50	$12.50	
1854C (Unknown)			
1855...	7.50	12.50	$100.00
1855C...	25.00	37.50	
1855D...	175.00	250.00	
1855O...	20.00	30.00	
1856S...	20.00	30.00	

Type 3

	Fine	Unc.	Proof
1856 Slanting 5	$5.50	$9.00	$75.00
1856 Upright 5...	5.50	9.00	
1856 Upright 5...	150.00	225.00	
1857...	6.00	9.00	60.00
1857C...	30.00	45.00	
1857D...	40.00	65.00	
1857S...	25.00	40.00	
1858...	6.00	9.00	85.00
1858D...	50.00	75.00	
1858S...	27.50	42.50	
1859...	6.00	10.00	27.50
1859C...	37.50	52.50	
1859D...	42.50	75.00	
1859S...	25.00	37.50	
1860...	10.00	15.00	35.00
1860D...	200.00	300.00	
1860S...	25.00	35.00	
1861...	5.50	8.00	45.00
1861D...	250.00	350.00	
1862...	5.00	7.00	30.00
1863...	60.00	85.00	150.00
1864...	35.00	50.00	100.00
1865...	70.00	90.00	125.00
1866...	25.00	40.00	80.00
1867...	25.00	40.00	75.00
1868...	17.50	25.00	45.00
1869...	20.00	35.00	55.00
1870...	15.00	20.00	35.00
1870S...	110.00	175.00	
1871...	17.50	25.00	35.00
1872...	17.50	25.00	37.50
1873...	5.00	8.00	30.00
1874...	5.00	8.00	30.00
1875...			300.00
1876...	10.00	15.00	22.50
1877...	10.00	15.00	27.50
1878...	11.00	17.50	35.00
1879...	8.50	15.00	27.50
1880...			
1881...			
1882...			
1883...			
1884...			
1885...			
1886...			
1887...			
1888...			
1889...			

[139]

GOLD DOLLARS

INDIAN PRINCESS HEAD, LARGE HEAD (1856-1889)

VF-20 VERY FINE—Slight detail in curled feathers in headdress. Details worn smooth at eyebrow, hair below headdress, and behind ear and bottom curl.
EF-40 EXTREMELY FINE—Slight wear above and to right of eye and on top of curled feathers.
AU-50 ABOUT UNCIRCULATED—Trace of wear on feathers, nearly full luster.
AU-55 CHOICE ABOUT UNCIRCULATED—Evidence of friction on design high points. Most of original mint luster present.
MS-60 UNCIRCULATED—No trace of wear. Light marks and blemishes.
MS-63 CHOICE UNCIRCULATED—Some distracting contact marks or blemishes in prime focal areas. Impaired luster possible.
PF-63 CHOICE PROOF—Reflective surfaces with only a few blemishes in secondary focal places. No major flaws.

Indian Princess Head, Large Head (Type 3)

	Mintage	VF-20	EF-40	AU-50	AU-55	MS-60	MS-63	PF-63
1856, Upright 5	1,762,936	$150	$195	$235	$300	$525	$1,100	
1856, Slant 5		135	175	210	235	300	1,000	$25,000
1856D	1,460	3,850	6,000	8,250	12,000	32,500	75,000	
1857	774,789	135	175	210	235	300	1,000	15,000
1857C	13,280	1,000	1,500	3,500	5,500	12,500	29,000	
1857D	3,533	1,150	2,100	4,200	5,500	10,500	32,000	
1857S	10,000	500	600	1,100	1,850	6,250	20,000	
1858	117,995	135	175	210	235	300	1,000	10,000
1858D	3,477	1,200	1,650	3,000	4,750	10,500	25,000	
1858S	10,000	350	550	1,350	1,750	5,750	16,500	
1859 (80)	168,244	135	175	210	235	325	1,100	8,500
1859C	5,235	1,250	1,800	3,750	6,750	15,000	32,500	
1859D	4,952	1,250	1,800	3,000	5,500	11,000	25,000	
1859S	15,000	250	600	1,600	2,250	5,800	16,000	
1860 (154)	36,514	145	200	225	250	450	1,100	6,000
1860D	1,566	2,850	4,250	7,500	12,500	22,500	55,000	
1860S	13,000	285	450	750	1,100	2,500	7,000	
1861 (349)	527,150	135	200	225	250	450	1,100	5,500
1861D	7,500	12,000	21,500	26,500	37,500	75,000		
1862 (35)	1,361,355	145	200	225	400	450	1,100	5,500
1863 (50)	6,200	300	1,100	2,300	3,250	4,500	6,500	
1864 (50)	5,900	350	475	750	950	1,250	3,000	7,500
1865	3,725	375	600	850	1,050	1,750	3,750	7,500
1866 (30)	7,100	350	525	725	850	1,150	2,250	6,000
1867 (50)	5,200	400	500	750	900	1,200	2,250	6,000
1868 (25)	10,500	275	400	600	800	1,100	2,250	6,500
1869 (25)	5,900	350	475	650	850	1,250	2,250	6,500
1870 (35)	6,300	300	400	650	750	1,150	2,250	6,250
1870S	3,000	475	800	1,250	1,600	2,850	7,500	
1871 (30)	3,900	300	400	650	750	1,150	2,250	6,250
1872 (30)	3,500	300	400	650	750	1,150	2,250	6,500
1873, Cl 3 (25)	1,800	400	750	1,100	1,350	1,850		14,500
1873, Open 3	123,300	145	200	225	250	450	1,100	
1874 (20)	198,800	145	200	225	250	450	1,100	8,500
1875	400	2,250	3,850	5,250	5,750	9,500	15,500	
1876 (45)	3,200	275	325	500	575	750	1,350	5,000
1877 (20)	3,900	275	325	500	575	750	1,350	5,000
1878 (20)	3,000	275	325	500	575	750	1,350	6,000
1879 (30)	3,000	175	275	375	425	600	1,300	5,000
1880 (36)	1,600	175	275	375	425	600	1,250	5,000
1881 (87)	7,620	175	275	375	425	600	1,250	4,500
1882 (125)	5,000	175	275	375	425	600	1,250	4,500
1883 (207)	10,800	175	275	375	425	600	1,250	4,500
1884 (1,006)	5,230	175	275	375	425	600	1,250	4,500
1885 (1,105)	11,156	175	275	375	425	600	1,250	4,500
1886 (1,016)	5,000	175	275	375	425	600	1,250	4,500
1887 (1,043)	7,500	175	275	375	425	600	1,250	4,500
1888 (1,079)	15,501	275	275	375	425	600	1,250	4,500
1889 (1,779)	28,950	165	265	350	400	575	1,200	4,500

* Included in number above.

223

What a difference 59 editions make! Shown above is the listing for gold dollars in the first edition of the *Guide Book of United States Coins*, copyright 1946, with a cover date of 1947. Shown to the right is the same series in the latest (59th) edition, 2006. Today, the *Guide Book* stands as the longest continuously published retail price guide in the hobby, with no close competition.

being offered for sale, sometimes estimated auction values.

Auction Data

Years ago, lists of auction "prices realized" often included items that were bought back or otherwise did not find buyers. Today, most (but not all) auction houses omit prices for lots that did not sell. Sometimes a coin will "sell" back to its owner, or someone connected with the owner, in order to establish a price—perhaps through a special arrangement with the auction house. In other instances a coin may have been bid on by mistake, or found to be wrongly listed, or have a defect in its title, and the sale rescinded after the list of prices was published.

For Whitman Publishing, Jeff Garrett and John Dannreuther have prepared tabulations of prices (*The Official RED BOOK® of Auction Records 1994–2004: U.S. Gold Coinage* being a sample title).

Auction prices are useful only to a limited extent, as they often represent certified coins for which not much information is available other than the grades on the holders. For this reason a quick glance at one of the Garrett-Dannreuther studies will show that often the same company can sell two coins, certified in the same grade, in the same auction, for two significantly varying prices. However, some outside knowledge (perhaps gained by a study of the photographs in the catalogs) can help you gather more information as to why the prices were so different. In the instance of significant rarities or other expensive coins, recent auction records are particularly useful in combination with other data.

Offers and Availability

Published price lists, "Buy It Now" offers on eBay, Internet inventory listings, and catalogs are all rich sources of prices, as are advertisements in the leading numismatic periodicals. In many instances these are more valuable than listings of market values in a book, or of auction prices realized—for if you like the price, and the quality checks out (through steps 1 to 4 detailed in chapter 2), you can own the coin right away. In contrast, while reading the *Guide Book of United States Coins* or another reference source you can contemplate all of those interesting listings and prices for colonial coins, or gold dollars, or commemoratives, but you cannot reach out and buy them.

One caveat is that some dealers emphasize price but sacrifice quality. If a choice specimen of a gold coin or a silver dollar has a standard value of, say, $1,000, the chances are that a coin advertised at a bargain $700 will be below par. Many buyers specialize in "bargains," but when they sell their collections they often find that few people want to buy or bid on them, and then only at low prices.

In my opinion it is better to pay more for a high-quality coin (per steps 1 to 4 in chapter 2) than to buy an average or subpar piece at a discount. In coins, as in the rest of life, you get what you pay for.

Just Ask—The Personal Touch

Most dealers are willing to discuss the derivation of prices in their inventories. If a coin is priced at $15,000 and the *Guide Book* suggests $11,000, and listings by *Coin World* and *Numismatic News* suggest $10,500 and $12,000, ask the seller how he or she figured the $15,000 number. In the course of buying obscure things such as Civil War tokens and obsolete paper money, where no current price guides are available, I often ask questions if I cannot figure out the answer myself.

It is okay to discuss price levels of a dealer's own stock offerings, but it is *not* cricket to go to Dealer A at a convention and ask him or her to go over a string of asking prices from Dealer B. If you are a beginner and say so, and you seek information (as in step 4 in chapter 2), a dealer may or may not be willing to help (but collectors usually are). Also, if at a coin show you ask a lot of questions about a lot of coins, it is good form to buy a few! Although most in the trade are willing to assist well-meaning newcomers with information, they are not in the business of giving extensive free appraisals—any more than an attorney would welcome you into his office and give you free legal opinions, or a doctor would make an appointment to see you for a free medical checkup. I don't mean to sound overly commercial here, but dealers do have expenses (employees, travel, rent, insurance, interest on loans, etc.), and they do need to show a profit to remain in business.

Also, if a dealer is busy at a coin show, stop by later at a quiet moment and ask questions then. Most shows have their slow moments, and that is a good time to pull up a chair and chat.

By human nature, some dealers are willing to share, to help others, to educate, to give talks, to serve as club officers, and more, while others are strictly merchants and are not the slightest bit interested in doing anything that does not result in a sale. Accept this—it is true in all hobbies and businesses—and, as you learn about buying and collecting coins, find someone who will share information and time.

Surprise Endings

Sometimes, unexpectedly, such sharing can lead to more business for a dealer than simply trying to sell can ever do. Two instances come to mind as I write this.

In one instance, a young lad walked into the Stack's store in New York City, with a blue Whitman coin folder in his hand. He was seeking some inexpensive Lincoln "pennies" to add to those he had found in pocket change. His dad was with him. This story, related to me by Harvey Stack, played out this way:

Since it was a quiet time at the sales counter, Harvey stopped by to talk with the boy and ask him about his collection and to see what he had been able to find in circulation. Then his father joined the conversation and introduced himself. His name was Samuel Wolfson. He asked for a few catalogs, developed his own interest in coins, and went on to form one of the greatest collections ever—including such rarities as an 1804 dollar. Years later, Stack's auctioned his magnificent holding.

In the second situation, a friend asked me about California gold coins. He was a native of that state, knew about the Gold Rush, and had heard there were some coins associated with that memorable event in American history. Although he was not a numismatist and had no intention of becoming one, he wanted to know whether I could direct him to a museum with such items on display. He simply wanted to see what they looked like.

Not knowing of any local or regional institutions with these coins on view, I gave him a copy of the *Guide Book* so he could read about them, and said I'd let him know the next time I bought a $50 octagonal

How much is this 1854 three-dollar gold coin (enlarged) worth? Commercially graded as MS-64, the coin has excellent luster and design details. But what about the price? Determining what is just right to achieve a good buy will take some studying and, perhaps, "asking around." Although this is not a rare date, examples of this high quality are elusive.

In contrast, the 1883-CC Morgan silver dollar exists in large quantities, is usually seen in high-quality Mint State, and has a current market price easier to determine, for they are listed just about everywhere.

gold "slug" so he could stop by to see it. I found a nice 1851 Augustus Humbert $50, called him, and he came to look it over, bought it, and went on to form a marvelous collection of United States coins from half cents to double eagles—plus a specialized collection of California gold! A few years later, he consigned the collection to one of our sales, and doubled his money on his investment.

Encased postage stamps, patented by John Gault in 1862, were issued as a substitute for coins, which were scarce in circulation at the time due to hoarding. These encasements featured a regular postage stamp on the obverse, protected by a thin sheet of mica. The reverse had an embossed brass case with the imprint of a merchant.

Although prices for these can be found in several reference books, none is updated on a yearly or more frequent basis. Often, the value of rarities is uncertain and must be figured by viewing auction records and consulting with experts. The illustrated example is a good case in point. Offered in August 2005 by Early American History Auctions (EAHA), this example was described as (excerpted): "1¢, ARTHUR M. CLAFLIN, Hopkinton, MA., Choice Extremely Fine. Rated as Rarity-8 (5 to 10 known) according to Fred Reed. This is the only denomination and single example of this merchant in Dr. Gratz' collection The Claflin merchant type is considered by most to be the rarest of all 34 different major merchant types known and is a true 'key' to completing a full set.

"Therefore, owning any Claflin allows one to unlock and complete a full 34 merchants set of encased postage stamps. The example we offer here is a beautiful, problem-free example of the lowest denomination.... The overall appearance is quite outstanding, this piece having tremendous eye appeal due to the sharpness and excellent detail of the legends that only a true Choice Extremely Fine example could provide. A great opportunity for the quality conscious Encased Postage Stamp, Civil War specialists.

"We've handled only four examples of this denomination since 1995. In December 1999, we sold a similarly graded example for $9,775 and in February 2001, we sold a Choice New (possibly finest known) example for $15,525; and more recently in October 2004, we sold a 10¢ in Choice EF+ for $18,975. This specimen is ex EAHA, Inc., Lot 649, February 14, 2004. Estimate: $12,000 to $16,000."

The offering attracted great attention from bidders and was sold for $19,000 plus 15% buyer's commission, or $21,850. This illustrates at least several things. First, for a rarity such as this, past auction prices are useful, but in order to capture such a prize, often a new record has to be set. Second, although encased postage stamps are hardly in the mainstream of popularly collected items, their investment performance has been excellent. Third, although the future is unknown, likely the next time a Claflin encased postage stamp rarity crosses the block, the $21,850 price will be viewed as a *starting point*.

CHAPTER SIX

RARITY IS IMPORTANT:
A Close Focus

One of the most reliable marks of a cultured man is his active interest in the ideas and habits of other people. Another sign is a lively imagination, by the use of which he can form a complete picture from a few related facts. Indeed, a man who has the knack for it can become a world traveler without leaving his daily routine. He can live for an hour a day in any period of history which he chooses and have as his companions the most exciting people who ever lived....

Let your coins be magic carpets on which you can ride to distant lands, strange people, and different times. There is nothing wrong with being able to draw from memory the complete and accurate design of a 1909-S V.D.B. cent. You bought it for $3.25 and may be able to sell it for $8.50 in its present condition. That's profit, yes. But cannot imagination give you profit from your coins, too?

—Dr. Verner G. Rich, September 1955

How Rare Is It?

We use the word *rare* frequently when we talk about collectible coins. In this chapter I focus closely on this important aspect of a coin's value.

"I collect rare coins." "The rare coin market is active today." "Look in the *Guide Book* to find the value of rare coins." "An auction of rare coins will be held by Heritage at the Long Beach convention." "Last night the History Channel had a program on rare coins." "When I was a kid I looked for rare Lincoln cents in pocket change."

Bankers and grocery-store clerks handle coins. Numismatists handle *rare* coins. However, in an absolute sense, a coin described as rare can actually exist in large quantities.

Rarity is relative. In the context of Washington quarter dollars from 1932 to date, the 1932-D is rare, although tens of thousands still remain from the original mintage of 436,800. The 1950-D nickel is described as one of the rarest dates in the Jefferson series, and yet well over a million Mint State coins exist today.

In the context of the series of Hard Times tokens, the earlier-mentioned token issued by Smith's Clock Establishment in 1837, depicting the face of a clock, probably has a population in collectors' hands of several thousand pieces—say, 2,500 to 5,000, although there is no way of knowing the exact number. There are far fewer known than of the 1932-D quarter or the 1950-D nickel, but specialists in the Hard Times series would view the Smith's token as a rather common issue.

Morgan silver dollars, minted from 1878 to 1921, are the most widely collected early series today. The most elusive San Francisco Mint coin in that series is the 1893-S, of which just 100,000 were coined—a low figure for a Morgan dollar. It is likely that about 10,000 to 15,000 or so survive today, most being in VF-20 to VF-30 grade and showing significant wear. A dealer or collector would unhesitatingly call any 1893-S dollar rare. However, if 10,000 to 15,000 were to exist of a certain Hard Times token, it would be dismissed as very common.

Is this a rare coin? Besides the one shown here, there were 12,117,999 other 1946 Liberty Walking half dollars struck. Of these, many thousands survive today in Mint State. As will be seen in the accompanying text, rarity is relative.

How rare is rare? How many angels can dance on the head of a pin? Opinions are plentiful, but hard rules are scarce.

The key is that coins are *rare* only in the context of other coins—with relation to a given series or specialty. Beyond that, *rare* is the usual term describing the field of collectible coins, whether they exist in large numbers or only a few are around.

Of course, we all need *common* coins to go with our rare ones. No set of Lincoln cents can be complete unless it includes the prized 1909-S V.D.B., of which only 484,000 were made (low for a Lincoln cent mintage), and of which a well-worn example costs several hundred dollars and a gem Mint State piece several thousand. But neither can a set of Lincolns be complete without a 2000-D, of which 8,774,220,000 were made—a coin worth just face value (plus a handling charge). It is correct to say that a Mint State 2000-D cent has *numismatic* value, as it surely does, even though that value isn't much.

Condition Rarity

A coin can be common in certain grades and rare in others. A variety that is rare only in high grade, but that is plentiful in low grades, is a *condition rarity*. A famous example is the 1936-D Washington quarter dollar. In that year, at the three mints, the following quantities of quarter dollars were struck for circulation and are listed in the *Guide Book* at the values given for MS-65 grade:

1936 (41,300,000 minted)—MS-65: $90.

1936-D (5,374,000 minted)—MS-65: $1,600.

1936-S (3,828,000 minted)—MS-65: $400.

Without further knowledge, someone investigating the investment potential of the quarters of this year might conclude that the 1936-S, with a mintage below that of 1936-D and priced for less than a third of the value of 1936-D, is a fantastic value, a sleeper, a situation just waiting to be discovered.

In actuality, in Mint State the 1936-D is far rarer today than is the 1936-S. The rea-

son is that in 1936 there was great excitement in the market, and the focus was on more than a dozen new issues of commemorative coins that were released that year, plus older commemoratives already in collections. The series was hot, and the value of some commemoratives doubled or tripled within the year (and a few did even better than that).

Scarcely any attention was paid to currently issued Washington quarters, and most were paid out into circulation. A few years later it was realized that hardly any mint-fresh 1936-D coins could be found. Bank-wrapped rolls (40 coins per roll) were plentiful enough for 1936 and 1936-S, as some still remained in vaults here and there. However, it seemed that nearly all 1936-D quarters had slipped away unnoticed. It soon became a condition rarity—rare only if in Mint State, but common enough in worn grades.

The series of Morgan silver dollars (1878–1921) furnishes many examples of condition rarity. Some high-mintage issues, such as 1884-S, were paid out into circulation in the 19th century, with the result that well-worn pieces are plentiful today. However, relatively few were saved in Mint State, and true gem 1884-S dollars are both rare and expensive. In contrast, the 1884-CC, the lowest-mintage issue of the year, exists today by the hundreds of thousands, as most were saved in Treasury vaults and survived to the present time. The *Guide Book* shows these mintages and values (selected grades):

1884 (14,070,000 minted)—VF-20: $16 • MS-60: $30 • MS-63: $45 • MS-64: $60 • MS-65: $300.

This 1936-D quarter has been certified as MS-65. Although many were minted, few were saved. Today, the 1936-D is rare in certain grades, such as MS-65, but is common if well worn.

An 1884 Morgan dollar.

1884-CC (1,136,000 minted)—VF-20: $120 • MS-60: $200 • MS-63: $225 • MS-64: $275 • MS-65: $450.

1884-O (9,730,000 minted)—VF-20: $16 • MS-60: $30 • MS-63: $45 • MS-64: $60 • MS-65: $160.

1884-S (3,200,000 minted)—VF-20: $17 • MS-60: $5,500 • MS-63: $27,000 • MS-64: $115,000 • MS-65: $200,000.

You can see that a gem MS-65 1884-CC is relatively inexpensive, despite the variety's having far and away the lowest mintage figure of the year. A VF-20 1884-S is common and inexpensive, but is a fantastic condition rarity in MS-65 grade and worth an impressive $180,000.

Stop and think about this: an 1884-S, of which 3,200,000 were minted, is priced at $180,000 in MS-65 grade, but the far lower-mintage 1884-CC, of which only 1,136,000 were struck, is listed at $400. Such things make numismatics fascinating!

I should also mention that there are many issues in American numismatics for which most pieces in existence are Mint State or Proof, and worn pieces are very rare—condition rarities, strictly speaking. An example, one of many, is provided by the 1936 York County (Maine) Tercentenary commemorative half dollar. In that year, 25,015 coins were minted. Numismatist Walter Nichols was in charge of distribution, the price being $1.50 per coin or, if sent by mail, $1.65. Decades

later I had the pleasure of selling Nichols's personal collection for his heirs, and among the holdings were some of these half dollars. As none of the 1936 York County halves went into circulation, and all were sold at a premium to collectors and historians, today nearly all in existence are Mint State. Occasionally, a lightly worn one will turn up—perhaps carried as a pocket piece. The *Guide Book* lists these values:

1936 York County Tercentenary half dollar—AU-50: $185 • MS-60: $210 • MS-63: $230 • MS-65: $265.

An AU-50 York County half dollar is indeed a condition rarity, but who cares? I don't, and you shouldn't, either. Again, in numismatics, no one rule fits all situations. A condition rarity is of exceptional value only if it is in higher grade than others of its variety.

Sometimes a coin can be rare as a circulation strike, but not as rare in Proof format. Many numismatists rightly consider circulation issues and Proofs to be different from each other, and collect them separately (this was not always the case, and until the 1950s, many considered Proofs to be "better" than circulation strikes, and opted for Proofs). Today's desire to have one each of a Proof and a circulation strike sometimes leads to values that may be puzzling to a casual observer. Take this example from the 59th edition of the *Guide Book* (excerpts):[19]

1886 Liberty Seated quarter dollar—EF-40: $650 • AU-50: $750 • MS-60: $850 • MS-63: $1,200 • Proof-63: $700.

The explanation is that in 1886 the Proof mintage amounted to 886 coins, which went to collectors who preserved them. Of the circulation strikes, 5,000 were made, but little attention was paid to them at the time, and most slipped into circulation and were eventually lost. Today, an MS-63 coin is much rarer than a Proof-63.

An 1886 Proof quarter dollar.

This illustration is similar but even more dramatic:

1880 Shield nickel five-cent piece—EF-40: $1,100 • AU-50: $1,600 • MS-60: $3,500 • MS-63: $6,500 • Proof 63: $700.

The explanation is that in 1880, 3,955 Proofs were struck for collectors. These were sold at a premium and, for the most part, were carefully preserved and still exist today. For circulation strikes, 16,000 were made and placed into circulation, with scarce interest from collectors, who were satisfied with their Proofs.

Traditional Descriptions of Rarity

Adjectives Proliferate

Often in catalogs and elsewhere, the rarity of a coin is described by using adjectives such as *rare, very rare, exceedingly rare*, and so on. These terms do not tell much, except that the person writing about the coin believes that the coin is hard to find, or perhaps nearly impossible to find, except, of course, for the one now being offered.

All of the following descriptions are normal and are perfectly satisfactory for use in the hobby:

- 1909-S V.D.B. Lincoln cent. MS-65 RB (NGC). Lustrous original orange (popularly: "red") color now blending to rich medium brown. A very appealing example of the most famous rarity in the Lincoln cent series. *[A description from a recent price quotation]*

- 1856 Liberty Seated silver dollar. EF-40. Lavender and pale gold iridescence on silvery surfaces. A tiny obverse edge bruise is seen at 5:00. A sharp specimen of this *major rarity*, the most elusive of all Philadelphia Mint circulation strike Liberty Seated dollars after 1852. *[A description I wrote for the Childs Collection sale in 1999]*

- 1842 $2.50 gold. Minute nicks, otherwise Fine. Excessively rare. Sold for $155 in one sale. Big sales like D.S. Wilson, Zug, Smith, etc., did not have it. A great rarity. *[Thomas L. Elder's description of an example in his sale of November 1925]*

- 1815. The exceedingly rare 1815 half eagle. Practically Uncirculated, only highest portions show the slightest touch of circulation, but I believe that is only due to handling or to cabinet friction. It is well struck and centered, and fortunately free from any nicks or dents of any kind. It has an even frosty mint surface. A very satisfactory state of preservation for this great rarity. In my twenty years' numismatic experience, this is the first specimen I am offering at auction, and the second that has passed through my hands. The other specimen I handled in 1912 when I sold it at private sale for $3,500. One of the high rarities in this remarkable collection. Mr. Brown, who was closely associated with Mr. Ten Eyck informs me that this coin was prized by Mr. Ten Eyck as much as any specimen in his collection. *[B. Max Mehl's description of the James Ten Eyck Collection coin, 1922]*

While the foregoing listings indicate that certain coins are rare, the reader cannot divine the *quantity* of certain of these coins estimated to exist.

While researchers and sellers will continue to employ descriptors such as *rare*,

A 1909-S V.D.B. Lincoln cent.

An 1815 half eagle.

scarce, exceedingly rare, hard-to-find, key issue, and *famous rarity,* more specific information can be supplied through the use of rarity ratings as given later in this chapter.

A Close Look at Rarity in Coin Listings

More Information

If an estimate of quantity can be added to a coin description in a catalog, more knowledge is imparted to a prospective buyer and bidder. The following descriptions are for the same coins illustrated above, but are here modified for illustrative purposes, to indicate the numbers known:

- 1909-S V.D.B. Lincoln cent. MS-65 RB (NGC). Lustrous original orange (popularly: "red") color now blending to rich medium brown.... Although probably 5,000 to 10,000 choice and gem Mint State coins exist, plus tens of thousands of circulated examples, the demand for them is so great that offerings always meet an enthusiastic reception.

- 1856 Liberty Seated silver dollar. EF-40. Lavender and pale gold iridescence on silvery surfaces. A tiny obverse edge bruise is seen at 5:00. A sharp specimen of this *major rarity,* the most elusive of all Philadelphia Mint circulation strike Liberty Seated dollars after 1852. We estimate that just 200 to 350 circulated 1856 dollars exist, mostly in the VF and EF grade categories.

- 1842 $2.50 gold. Fine, but with many small nicks on the surface.... Generations ago the 1842 was considered to be one of the greatest rarities in the

series. Since then, additional pieces have come to light. We estimate that just 30 to 50 exist across all grades. We have never seen one in Mint State.

- 1815. The exceedingly rare 1815 half eagle. Practically Uncirculated, only highest portions show the slightest touch of circulation, but I believe that is only due to handling or to cabinet friction.... It is believed that only about a dozen exist today, including several in museums....

Estimating the Number Known

The number known to exist is a key factor in determining the value of a coin. Within the same series, type, and grade, if 1,000 exist, such a specimen is likely to sell for less than another of which just 100 exist. Accordingly, Morgan silver dollars can be compared to other Morgan silver dollars, Liberty Head nickels can be compared to other Liberty Head nickels, and commemorative half dollars can be compared to other commemorative half dollars. However, not much sense can be derived by comparing Liberty Head nickels to Morgan dollars, or Morgan dollars to commemoratives—it's the old case of comparing apples to oranges.

For some coins, such as those minted especially for collectors and sold at a premium, estimates of present-day availability are easy to make. For many others, indeed most circulation-strike issues, many variables are involved—including melting, exporting, the method of distribution, the existence of hoards, being saved as a novelty by the public, and more.

A Remarkable Half Dollar, Once Believed Unique

There are many examples of coins that are presently thought to be unique in numismatic hands (just one known to exist) or were thought to be unique in the past. Two illustrations may be of interest. First, in *The Numismatist,* October 1930, editor Frank G. Duffield inserted this comment:

An 1817/4 half dollar, close-up of overdate feature. Note traces of an earlier 4 below the 7. (Eliasberg Collection)

E.T. Wallis, of Los Angeles, Cal., writes that he has recently discovered a heretofore unknown variety of the 1817 half dollar, the last figure of the date being cut over a 4. A number of half dollars of 1817 over '13 are known, but this is the first one over '14 reported, Mr. Wallis says....

Howard R. Newcomb, of Los Angeles, and M.L. Beistle, of Shippensburg, Pa., both authorities on the half-dollar series, have examined the coin and pronounced it a hitherto unknown variety.

This was an exciting find, indeed! For a long time, many numismatists had specialized in early half dollars, and two important studies of die varieties had been written: J.W. Haseltine's *Type Table* in 1881 and M.L. Beistle's *A Register of Half Dollar Die Varieties and Sub-Varieties* in 1929. Neither of these observers had known of such a variety.[20]

Accordingly, in 1930, it would have been correct to have said, "Only one such coin *is known* to exist."

In 1934, Wallis advertised it for sale in an obscure publication (scarcely remembered today), the first edition of the *National Catalog of U.S. Coins*, page 164, pricing it at $2,500. The piece eventually landed in the Eliasberg Collection.

In time, knowledge of this remarkable rarity spread; collectors studied the "ordinary" 1817 half dollars in their collections; and several more 1817/4 half dollars were recognized. When I cataloged the Eliasberg Collection in 1997, I knew of the following examples: the Wallis/Eliasberg Specimen at EF-45; the Witham Speci-

men, F-15; the Meyer Specimen, VF-25 or finer; the Overton Specimen, G-6, repaired; the Farley Specimen, VF-20; the Burke Specimen, VF(?); and the Dosier Specimen, F-12.

In this instance, it would be correct today to say, "Only seven such coins *are known* to exist." Whether this represents the total number that actually exist, including some still in hiding or unidentified, remains to be seen. The point is that for the 1817/4, the best we can do is give an estimate based on knowledge of known pieces. In my opinion, it is likely that most have come to light by now, but I would not be shocked if in the next decade or two another appeared out of the blue.

A Remarkable Gold Dollar, Once Believed Unique

A related scenario surrounds a variety of the 1849 Charlotte Mint gold dollar, with the wreath ends on the reverse "open," rather than "close" to the top of the numeral 1. While this coin is not a distinct date and mintmark issue, it does constitute a major variety and is highly desirable. Following is an extensive description, with the progression of auction appearances reflecting not only changing estimates of rarity, but dramatic changes in grade for certain specimens, and inconsistent provenances. It is precisely such listings that arouse the sniffing instincts of a numismatic Sherlock Holmes. Perhaps in some future day the 1849-C Open Wreath gold dollar will be the subject of a research paper by someone, and certain of the inconsistencies will be straightened out.

The finest known specimen of the 1849-C Open Wreath gold dollar (enlarged), a rare variety with an interesting numismatic history. (Richmond Collection, courtesy DLRC)

For many years, numismatists thought all 1849-C gold dollars to be of the Close Wreath style, as these had appeared in many collections. Apparently, few had thought to look for an Open Wreath variation.

The earliest publication of the 1849-C Open Wreath seems to have been in B. Max Mehl's February 1944 sale of the Belden Roach Collection, although auction descriptions indicate that Waldo C. Newcomer, a Baltimore collector who died in 1934, may have had one.

In *The Numismatist*, March 1951, this letter from Robert F. Schermerhorn, Dallas collector and rare coin dealer, was published:

> About eight years ago I acquired an 1849-C mint gold dollar which I believe to be unique, for unlike all the others I have been able to locate, this one has an open wreath. It is the same weight and size as other gold dollars of 1849. I would very much appreciate hearing from other collectors who have seen or who own a similar specimen.

In this instance, the matching of photographs identifies this as the Roach coin sold by Mehl (in Fort Worth, close to Dallas) in 1944, but it is quite curious that Schermerhorn did not mention Mehl in this regard. Here is Mehl's description:

> *[1944: Belden E. Roach Collection, (B. Max Mehl) Lot 1083]* 1849-C Mint letter C below wreath, as all are. This specimen seems to be of an entirely new variety. It is open wreath and the stars on obverse are smaller; the borders are raised making the coin appear somewhat thicker than the regular issue. Uncirculated with brilliant luster. Almost equal to a Proof. Struck in light yellow gold. I unhesitatingly say that this coin is of excessive rarity, if not unique. (Not listed in the new 1944 *Standard Catalogue*.)

This is the earliest mention I have located in print for this variety. Note that it is graded as "Uncirculated." Possibly it was sold to Charles M. Williams, a Cincinnati numismatist and insurance executive, and one of the major buyers of the era. Williams may have obtained this coin in some manner and kept it until late in 1950, when he sold his collection *en bloc* to the Numismatic Gallery, operated by Abe Kosoff and Abner Kreisberg. Alternatively, it may have been sold to Schermerhorn as mentioned above.

The same specimen popped up in 1956, with no mention of its connection to the Roach sale. Now, the coin has dropped in grade to just EF-AU:

> *[1956: Chi-ANA Convention Sale (James F. Kelly) • Lot 1571]* 1849 Charlotte Mint with Open Wreath. Extremely Fine to About Uncirculated. From the Newcomer and later the Williams Collection, but discovered and first published by Mr. Schermerhorn. The above picture, which is double size, shows the distinctiveness of this type. Certainly no collection could be called complete without it. It is very difficult to set a valuation on this unique coin. Mr. Schermerhorn values it at $7,500. This seems justified when we compare it to what numerous rare coins, not unique, have brought at recent sales. This coin is mounted in a large plastic holder, approximately fifteen by ten inches, with blown up photos of the 1849 Philadelphia Open and Closed Wreaths, and 1849 Charlotte Open and Closed Wreaths for comparison. Certainly a prized possession for some fortunate collector.

Years later, the same coin was reoffered:

> *[1979: Auction '79 (Stack's) • Lot 749]* 1849-C Open Wreath. Extremely Fine.... David Akers in his book on U.S. gold dollars has clearly traced all of the known specimens, including prior ownership. In addition, since the publication of that book, one other specimen has come to light. The known specimens are as follows: 1.

Waldo C. Newcomer–Belden Roach, Charles M. Williams–Robert Schermerhorn. Last sold in the 1956 A.N.A. Auction. This coin. 2. The specimen in the G.E.N.A. Auction, 1974. 3. Sale by private treaty to New Netherlands Coin Co. 4. Sale by private treaty by NERCG recently, reportedly at a figure in the high five-figure area. It is interesting to note that there were three auction appearances representing only two coins.... It is our opinion that this specimen, the "finest known" and which also has the best pedigree of all, should realize a bid close to the six-figure mark.

Note that the grade of the coin has slid further, down to EF. Now the provenance is given as Newcomer to Roach to Williams to Schermerhorn. However, Williams did not sell his collection until 1950, and in 1951 Schermerhorn stated in *The Numismatist* that he had owned this coin for about eight years.

By 1982, the grade of this piece had revived to a low-AU category, now with hairlines and a mark carefully noted:

[1982: Orchard Hill Collection, FUN Convention Sale (New England Rare Coin Auctions) • Lot 1350] 1849-C $1 Type One, Open Wreath, AU-53, lightly circulated, with a few minor hairlines and tiny lintmark near the chin, a characteristic that may be used to identify this piece in the future. This is the Newcomer-Roach-Williams-Schermerhorn specimen, the finest of the three known examples.... Truly this coin ranks as one of the "aristocrats" of all U.S. coinage, and fully deserves being labeled as "The King" of all Charlotte gold coins.

A few years ago it reappeared in a Heritage sale, now graded AU-58 and with an especially detailed description of the dies. The "lightly circulated" aspect of the preceding description was viewed as incorrect, it seems—in the new description the coin had "no real wear visible on either side":

[1999–2001: North Georgia Collection, FUN Sale (Heritage) • Lot 7722] 1849-C Open Wreath AU-58 (PCGS). One of just four known.... As on the other relatively high grade 1849-C Open Wreath gold dollar, this piece has a distinctive quality of strike. The obverse is slightly concave, giving the portrait an almost three-dimensional appearance. At the same time, there is some weakness on the dentils and the star at 9 o'clock shows pronounced weakness. The reverse is not as sharp as the obverse but the leaves and lettering are bold; the 4 and the bottom of the 8 are a bit weak while the mintmark is very sharp. There are some obvious diagnostic features that are seen on all genuine examples. The star opposite the tip of Liberty's nose, in addition to being weak, has a short right point. The leaf below the 1 in the date is hollow while the tip of the leaf below the 9 is partly detached. The ribbons are incomplete due to die lapping and there is a tiny die file mark above RI in AMERICA. In terms of its overall appearance, this is a pleasing coin. It has light green-gold color and original surfaces with no real wear visible on either side....

The preceding illustration is informative on several levels. First, it shows how the interpretations of grades can differ among experts, as these descriptions are from some of the best-known names in the business. As to whether the coin is Very Fine (as described in an article by Walter Breen, not quoted here), Extremely Fine (as Stack's listed it in 1979), or Uncirculated (per the Mehl offering of 1944) is a matter of opinion.

To add to the narrative on the 1849-C Open Wreath, here is a listing of known specimens, as it would have been if compiled a few years ago:

1. *Newcomer specimen (so called).* Discussed above. Variously described all the way from Mint State down to VF, currently AU-58.

2. *New Netherlands specimen.* Variously graded from EF to AU-58 (PCGS).

3. *McReynolds specimen.* Pine Tree Auction Company's Great Eastern Numismatic Association sale, 1974, Lot 1952, VF, mounted at one time and used as jewelry. Currently graded Fine-15 (NGC; Douglas Winter, *Gold Coins of the Charlotte Mint, 1838–1861*, p. 40).

4. *Lumadue specimen.* Discovered by Connecticut coin dealer Donald Lumadue and offered for sale to the dealer community, including me. EF.

5. *"Private Collection" specimen.* Another specimen discovered in 1988 (Breen, *Encyclopedia*, 1988). Grade not stated.

At a coin convention early in 2004, John Feigenbaum showed me another 1849-C Open Wreath, new to the market, to be added to the coins in the Richmond Collection that DLRC Auctions was scheduled to sell. With an attractive and somewhat prooflike surface, this is the nicest I have seen. At the same convention a dealer specialist in gold told me that *still another* 1849-C Open Wreath dollar had been found, within recent months.

Accordingly, the list can be extended:

6. *Richmond Collection specimen.* MS-63. First publicized in 2004. Described as "the finest of only four (possibly five) specimens known." This sold for a record $690,000.

7. *Another specimen.* Grade not known. Reported to me in 2004. Not examined.

The 1849-C Open Wreath gold dollar situation is similar to that for the 1817/4 half dollar, in that a coin once thought to be unique in collectors' hands is now known to exist in numbers of half a dozen or so pieces. However, in the instance of the 1849-C, two reported coins have not been examined in recent times by students of the series.

A Remarkable Buffalo Nickel

In early 1962, C.G. Langworthy and Robert Kerr found a very strange 1938-D Buffalo nickel. Under magnification there clearly appeared an S mintmark peeking out from beneath the D! This was truly one of a kind. They had never heard of such a coin before. Later they found a second one.

Not believing their eyes, the two gentlemen contacted Margo Russell, editor of *Coin World*. In those days, that weekly newspaper, which had begun in 1960, lacked extensive research files. Margo called upon me to examine and verify the nickel, as she had done with other coins before.

I, too, could not believe my eyes, at least at first! The two mintmarks were each clear. The whole story was written up in the September 14, 1962, issue of *Coin World*. No one knew whether the 1938-D/S overmintmark, as it came to be known, was an extreme rarity worth a small fortune, or whether others would be found.

As to why such a coin was made, the story is likely this:

In 1938 the Buffalo/Indian Head nickel design had been in use since 1913. The Mint decided to change the motif, and a nationwide competition was held to create what became the Jefferson nickel. In the meantime, only at the Denver Mint were Buffalo nickels coined that year, these with a D mintmark.

On hand at the Philadelphia Mint, where all coinage dies were made—including those used at Denver and San Francisco—there were some perfectly good, unused reverses with S mintmarks. With the coming of the Jefferson nickel these would be useless, so rather than waste them it was decided to overpunch the S with a D. This created the 1938-D/S.

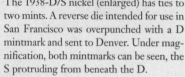

The 1888/7 Indian Head cent (enlarged) does not have an obvious overdate feature. However, under magnification, traces of a 7 can be seen extending beyond the heavier, final 8, including the tip of the base of the 7 at the lower left of the bottom of the 8. An easier, quick identifier is the small "cud" die break on the rim opposite the E of UNITED. This coin is one of only a few found after publicity concerning Jim Ruddy's discovery of the 1888/7 excited the numismatic community in 1970.

The 1938-D/S nickel (enlarged) has ties to two mints. A reverse die intended for use in San Francisco was overpunched with a D mintmark and sent to Denver. Under magnification, both mintmarks can be seen, the S protruding from beneath the D.

Within a short time of the publicizing of the 1938-D/S, everybody and his brother and sister looked through their 1938-D Buffalo nickels—it is an extremely common coin—to see if any were 1938-D/S. Many thousands were found, from three reverse dies, each with D/S but with very slight differences. Today, the 1938-D/S is considered common.

In slightly more than 40 years, the rarity estimate of this coin has gone from just two pieces known to an estimated 5,000 to 10,000 or more.

Jim Ruddy's Remarkable Find

A situation almost identical to the two discovery specimens of the 1938-D/S nickel is illustrated by a scenario from nearly 10 years later, in 1969. Jim Ruddy had purchased a small cache of Indian Head cents found in an attic of a mansion in Virginia. These had never been examined by a numismatist. Jim had been interested in die varieties for a long time, and over a span of years had discovered several remarkable items, one of which was a new die for the 1786 Date Under Plow Beam New Jersey copper, a classic in that series.

Studying his newly acquired group of Indian cents by examining them under low-power magnification, Jim noticed that one bearing the date 1888 seemed to have traces of a 7 under the last digit. Could this be? No one had ever heard of such a thing!

Jim placed the coin under a microscope, and the small 7 became even clearer—and unequivocal. Although Indian Head cents had been a popular series for many years, no one had ever identified an 1888/7 overdate! He noticed that on the left obverse rim at the 9:00 position there was a "cud" break, caused by a piece falling out of the die. Likely, this die had been retired quickly, accounting for the coin's rarity. Marvelously, his coin was in Mint State.

Lo and behold, a few coins later, Jim came across *another* 1888/7, also in Mint State! Keeping his discovery secret, Jim looked at every other 1888 cent he could find, at coin shows and in several dealers' inventories. Not another piece came to light. The announcement of the discovery was made in early 1970, and *Numismatic News, Coin World, The Numismatist,* and other periodicals described this amazing addition to the Indian cent series.

Jim watched and waited to see whether other coins, perhaps thousands (as in the case of the 1938-D/S nickel), would be discovered. Few were. Now, more than

30 years later, there are four Mint State coins known, including the two that Jim discovered, plus fewer than a dozen worn examples. The discovery coins went to collector Robert Marks and dealer Julian Leidman and, since then, have changed hands several times. Should another Mint State coin come to light, its value would probably be well into the tens of thousands of dollars!

Seeing Is Believing

First, if a coin is actually seen, then it does exist. If it is not seen, it still might exist. Today, there are many valuable coins that exist but are not known to numismatists. Some of these will be discovered, to delight future generations.

In *Penny Whimsy*, 1958, Dr. William H. Sheldon put it this way:

> Competent students in the field have always been hesitant to express an opinion on the rarity of a die because they were aware of how easy it is to be mistaken. No one can ever know *for certain* just how many examples of a particular variety exist, since there is no way of canvassing the entire supply of cents in one lifetime.
>
> Also, there is always the possibility of a new "find," in which a whole kegful of a particular variety may turn up. This has happened.
>
> There is another good reason for caution. Some of the die varieties of which few examples are known resemble common varieties so closely that the difference is for years passed over without detection, then when someone "puts his neck out" that only three or four of the rare ones are believed to exist, along comes a nice old lady with half a dozen.

The "kegful" of copper cents is a reference to the fabulous Randall Hoard, believed to have contained slightly more than 10,000 large copper cents, mostly dated 1818 and 1820, found in the 1860s located, it is said, beneath a railway platform in Georgia.

The earlier-mentioned 1817/4 half dollar, 1849-C Open Wreath gold dollar, 1938-D/S Buffalo nickel, and 1888/7 Indian Head cent are varieties that nicely fit Dr. Sheldon's comment about pieces that are passed over for years without detection. Most of the known examples of these three issues were simply collected or held as regular issues, with no note being taken of their unusual status.

Seeing is believing, but it may not tell the whole story. If I attend a symphony and do not see Sam Smith, he still might have been there. It is just that he did not catch my eye. If in my yard a visitor sees no wild deer, he cannot conclude that none are around, for the next morning I may see five of them nibbling on the grass.

Now, an Assurance of Comfort

Although many discoveries have been made in recent years, and more will continue to be made in the future, the appearance of hoards, "kegful" quantities, and the like are isolated instances. Often when such quantities appear, prices *rise* rather than drop! There is no better example than what happened in November 1962, when millions of previously rare Morgan dollars were emptied from Treasury vaults—the prices of many Morgans fell. However, within a few years the availability of such coins spawned an even greater interest in and demand for them. Morgan dollars became one of the hottest series in numismatics, and today the prices of nearly all of them are far higher than they were before they were released!

Moreover, the once-believed-unique 1817/4 half dollar and the 1849-C Open Wreath gold dollar are now much more valuable, with about seven known of each, than when they were first sold—as *unique!*—in 1930 and 1944, respectively.

When long-lost Mint State double eagles of 1857-S were found in the wreck of the *S.S. Central America* (in addition to other coins), and 1865-S coins in the wreck of the *S.S. Brother Jonathan*, these events electrified the numismatic community, spurring more people to investigate the double eagle series and collect them.

For most dates and mints, no important hoards have appeared in modern times. I am unaware of any new hoards in, for example, the entire series of large copper cents of 1793 to 1857, Flying Eagle cents of 1856 to 1858, Indian Head cents of 1859 to 1909, or early Lincoln cents beginning in 1909.

For most legendary rarities, the known numbers have not increased in a long time. No new examples of the 1804 dollar have been discovered since the "King of Siam" piece came to light in the early 1960s; and the number of 1822 five-dollar half eagles (thought to have been four in 1890, when the Parmelee coin was auctioned), dropped to three and has remained there—for the Parmelee coin was proved to be a fake.

By collecting a type set of various designs, or specializing in a series by gathering a long string of date and mintmark varieties, you automatically diversify your holdings. Consider the now-rare 1872 Indian Head cents; if, perchance, a marvelous hoard of Mint State pieces (say, 5,000—far more than are known to exist today in numismatic hands) should be found, the price of the 1872 would probably drop, at least for a time. The prices of the dozens of other coins in your collection, however, would probably continue to rise significantly, far more than enough to offset the drop for your single 1872.

Easy Estimates of Rarity

For some coins it is easy to estimate the rarity today with a high level of confidence. For example:

- *1999-S Washington quarter, Georgia state reverse, silver Proof (3,713,359 minted).* All were sold for a premium to collectors. Estimated number existing today: 3,500,000 or so.

- *1794 silver dollar (1,758 distributed).* Estimated number existing today in various grades: about 125 to 135.

This estimate has not changed much in the past 50 years of scholarship and research in the early dollar series.

- *1804 silver dollar, famous rarity (unknown number minted).* Today, 15 pieces are accounted for, with no new specimens having come to light in the present generation, despite great publicity given to its value.

- *1895 Proof Morgan dollar (880 minted).* All were sold to collectors and were ever afterward regarded as a key date. Estimated number existing today in Proof: about 600 to 700, allowing for some lost pieces.

- *1915-S Panama–Pacific Octagonal $50 commemorative gold coin (645 distributed).* All were sold to collectors and others, who paid a sharp premium for them. Estimated number existing today: about 500 to 575, nearly all in Mint State.

Such "easy estimates" are mainly limited to Proofs, commemoratives, and such coins sold primarily to collectors, and to great rarities (as to basic date and mint, not die varieties within such classifications).

Most other estimates require thinking, studying, and guessing—with the result that no two estimates are likely to be the same. A little while back, at the Whitman Publishing offices in Atlanta, Jeff Garrett and I were on hand as Ken Bressett and his son Phil finessed the price listings for the 58th edition of the *Guide Book*. Many things were discussed.

Although I did not think of it at the time, I rather imagine that if I had asked the others for their estimates for any of the several coins listed above, the numbers would have been similar to mine. However, if I had taken a few coins of medium rarity, not at all in the "famous" category, and asked for estimates, those estimates would have varied widely. Such a list might have included these, to give just a few of what could be thousands of challenges:

- *1652 Massachusetts Pine Tree shilling.* Total number known, in all grades combined.

- *1907 Indian Head cent.* Total number known in all grades, well worn on up (this is the highest mintage issue in that series).

- *1960 Small Date Lincoln cent.* Total number known, in Mint State, of this popular modern issue.

- *1949-S Roosevelt dime.* Total number known, in Mint State, of this scarce (in the context of the series) issue.

- *1905 Lewis and Clark commemorative gold dollar.* Total known in Mint State.

The next time you are at a coin-club meeting or other numismatic gathering, I expect that if you pose these questions you will get widely differing estimates.

Red Herrings and Rumors

A *red herring* is a false clue or, in modern parlance, *disinformation*. In numismatics there are many red herrings, some being common rumors, others written or spoken with the appearance of grave authority, but wrong nonetheless.

In the late 1950s, my company was the leading buyer and seller of 1955 Doubled-Die Lincoln cents. I became very interested in this unusual variety, and in my first numismatic book, *Coins and Collectors* (1964), I devoted a couple pages to its background. Since then I have learned even more.

By contacting informed people at the Philadelphia Mint I learned that on one day in 1955 a die with curiously doubled features was fitted into one of the presses, the doubling having been caused by the punching of the master die into the working die once, then again, but in a slightly different alignment. On this day a row of presses was stamping out Lincoln cents, after which they were ejected into a chute, then into a storage box behind each press. Every so often a worker would dump each box into a large metal bin.

An inspector stopping at the press with the doubled die noticed the blurred obverse, and called a supervisor's notice to it. By that time about 44,000 cents had been coined from that die. Upon checking,

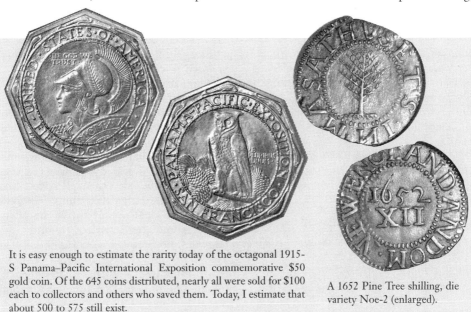

It is easy enough to estimate the rarity today of the octagonal 1915-S Panama–Pacific International Exposition commemorative $50 gold coin. Of the 645 coins distributed, nearly all were sold for $100 each to collectors and others who saved them. Today, I estimate that about 500 to 575 still exist.

A 1652 Pine Tree shilling, die variety Noe-2 (enlarged).

it was learned that about 24,000 of these had been mixed with the output from other presses and were in a large storage bin. The others were still near the press.

It was decided to destroy those at the press, but to let the others go into circulation. At the time there was no widespread numismatic interest in mint errors, usually called "freak" coins, and no one anticipated that these coins would ever be noticed.

Wrong!

Soon, they were released into circulation, primarily in the Southern Tier section of New York state (around Binghamton, Johnson City, and Endicott), in western Massachusetts (around Pittsfield), and in the Boston area. Although some Mint State coins were captured by Jim Ruddy (who was the very first to become interested) and me, most pieces found were with light evidence of circulation. In time, such "shift" cents, as they were first called (then "Doubled Dies" when the *Guide Book* listed them), came to have significant value—$5, then $10, then $50, jumping to $500, onward past the $1,000 mark. Today a gem Mint State coin with *original* brightness is worth many thousands of dollars, and a well-worn one hundreds of dollars.

Modern Lincoln cents were in 1955— and are today—often traded in 50-coin bank-wrapped rolls. Several dealers on many occasions made it their business to pooh-pooh my interest in 1955 Doubled-Die cents. "I sold a roll of them last week." "A customer of mine in Iowa has six rolls." (And so on.) Sometimes I would protest, other times not—but I was secure in the knowledge that there never was such a thing as an original bank-wrapped roll of

A 1955 Doubled-Die cent (enlarged).

fifty 1955 Doubled-Die cents, simply because when the coins left the Mint they were scrambled together with many more regular cents of the same date.

In any event, there were and still are more than just a few rare-coin dealers who enjoy one-upmanship, or bragging, with or without facts or good reason for doing so.

In the early 1990s, when I was putting the finishing touches on my two-volume study *Silver Dollars and Trade Dollars of the United States*, I had many red herrings and rumors to analyze. I endeavored, I believe successfully, to sort out and discard quite a few, and when others were questionable, but no specific information could be found, I quoted the rumors, but added my opinion.

For example, *Walter Breen's Complete Encyclopedia of U.S. and Colonial Coins*, published in 1988, states that a bag of 1,000 Mint State 1872 Liberty Seated dollars came to light in the early 1960s. I found this rather curious, as I had bought, sold, and auctioned as many Liberty Seated coins as anyone I knew, and I had never seen many of the 1872 date. I contacted Walter Breen to ask his source of information. He replied that he had heard it from Philadelphia dealer Harry Forman. I then called Harry to learn more, and he told me that over the years he had handled a few dozen *single pieces*, never a bag or anything close! What at first seemed to be fact quickly turned into nothing. Apparently, Breen had incorrectly remembered the conversation.

I mentioned the phantom bag in this book, stating that it was unverified, and told the related story. I considered this better than completely overlooking the 1,000 coins described in Breen's *Encyclopedia*, for if I had ignored them, then certainly some later writer would say, "Bowers' book states that a couple hundred Mint State 1872 dollars exist, to which must be added the 1,000-coin bag mentioned by Walter H. Breen, for a total population of 1,200."

I discussed this and other matters with Weimar W. White, a student of the series.

He commented:

> It is a terrible injustice to place a stigma on a coin such as the 1872 dollar by suggesting (as some do) that 1,000 were released, and not have concrete evidence that such a bag ever existed. This kind of stigma affects collectors' attitudes toward the coin, and it may not deserve it.[21]

Rarity Vs. Certification Reports

If you've read this chapter to this point, you will see that the evaluation of rarity is complex but understandable—and that no rule fits all situations.

Regardless, for many investors there is one, and only one, source for rarity information: population reports issued by the leading grading services, namely ANACS, NGC, and PCGS.

My opinion differs somewhat. While I and, for that matter, the numismatists on the staff of American Numismatic Rarities (ANR), consider these reports to be interesting, they constitute just one of several tools available to the coin buyer.

Generally, population reports are very useful when marketing rare and expensive coins, especially pieces in silver and gold, and in Mint State or Proof categories. Such reports can be almost useless in other areas. In any event, such numbers are best used in addition to other information, as I discussed in chapter 5.

Consider the following illustrations, and then draw your own conclusions. My commentary is given after each of the four coins studied.

Dollars of 1884: Estimated Rarity and Certified Population

The following figures reveal certain mintage, rarity, market value, and certification report statistics for the silver dollars of 1884, 1884-CC, 1884-O, and 1884-S— a wide range of such numbers within a single date in the most popularly collected classic series. The mintages and prices of these particular dollars are also discussed earlier in this chapter, in the context of grading vis-à-vis market price (under "Condition Rarity").

The following certification numbers are from the population reports of ANACS, NGC, and PCGS.[22] Although population numbers tend to inch upward (never downward) over a period of time, they should remain largely relevant for a long time, for purposes of illustration. To these I have added my own estimates of the numbers of coins known in these selected grades.[23]

Analysis of the 1884 Morgan Dollar

- *14,070,000 minted.*

- *VG-8 to AU-58—Guide Book* value in VF-20: $16. Estimated in existence today, all grades VG-8 to AU-58 combined: 1,000,000 to 2,000,000. Total certified in all grades VG-8 to AU-58 combined: 1,494.

- *MS-60 to MS-62—Guide Book* value in MS-60: $30. Estimated in existence today, all grades MS-60 to -62 combined: 150,000 to 225,000. Total certified in all grades MS-60 to -62 combined: 1,629.

- *MS-63—Guide Book* value: $45. Estimated in existence today: 50,000 to 90,000. Total certified: 5,380.

- *MS-64—Guide Book* value: $60. Estimated in existence today: 30,000 to 60,000. Total certified: 8,496.

- *MS-65—Guide Book* value: $300. Estimated in existence today: 12,500 to 20,000. Total certified: 3,214.

- *MS-66 and higher*—No *Guide Book* value listings. Estimated in existence today: 1,500 to 2,000. Total certified: 604.

- *Known hoards of Mint State coins*—Many bags were released by the Treasury Department in the decades before and up to 1962 through 1964.

- *Total number of 1884 dollars certified in all grades—17,115.*

As the 1884 Morgan dollar is priced low in most grades, relatively few have been certified. With truth, it can be said that *certified* 1884 Morgan dollars are very rare. Of course, this would be a misleading statement in connection with market value.

Taking the numbers alone, it would seem that in the MS-60 to -62 range, 1884-P dollars, of which 1,629 have been certified, are about four times rarer than the 1884-CC (see below), of which 6,003 have been certified. As both varieties are in the same series, such comparisons might seem valid, in absence of further knowledge.

However, if you observe the market price, currently $30 for the 1884 and $200 for the 1884-CC, the situation is clarified: the MS-60 1884 is "rare" in a slab simply because it is not worthwhile to pay to have it certified.

Analysis of the 1884-CC Morgan Dollar

- *1,136,000 minted.*

- *VG-8 to AU-58—Guide Book* value in VF-20: $120. Estimated in existence today, all grades VG-8 to AU-58 combined: 5,000 to 10,000. Total certified in all grades VG-8 to AU-58 combined: 41.

- *MS-60 to MS-62—Guide Book* value in MS-60: $200. Estimated in existence today, all grades MS-60 to -62 combined: 550,000 to 575,000. Total certified in all grades MS-60 to -62 combined: 6,003.

- *MS-63—Guide Book* value: $225. Estimated in existence today: 350,000 to 375,000. Total certified: 14,952.

- *MS-64—Guide Book* value: $275. Estimated in existence today: 110,000 to 120,000. Total certified: 21,962.

- *MS-65—Guide Book* value: $450. Estimated in existence today: 30,000 to 35,000. Total certified: 11,302.

- *MS-66 and higher—*No *Guide Book* listings. Estimated in existence today: 5,500 to 9,000. Total certified: 2,130.

- *Known hoards of Mint State coins—* Bags of 1,000 coins were released by the Treasury in 1938, the mid-1950s, and early in the 1960s; 962,638 were held back from 1962 to 1964 Treasury release and later sold by the General Services Administration (GSA). More than 1,000,000 Mint State coins remain.

- *Total number of 1884-CC dollars certified in all grades—*56,390.

This information is especially surprising. We know that 962,638 1884-CC dollars, nearly all in Mint State, were sold by the GSA to collectors and investors, who paid premiums to get them. Accordingly, it is highly likely that nearly all of these still exist today. Even before those were found, there were tens of thousands of Mint State coins in collectors' hands. I assume today that 1,000,000 or so—certainly a conservative estimate—exist. I also assume that of the 56,390 listed in the certification reports, at least some of the numbers include resubmissions. However, if not even a single coin was resubmitted, it is clear that as of today, only about 1 in 17 extant 1884-CC Mint State dollars has been certified. Many readers will find this to be a remarkable

An 1884-CC Morgan dollar, plentiful in Mint State.

statistic. The chief financial officer of a commercial grading service will find this to be a *heartwarming* statistic, as it reflects the great potential for coins yet to be certified.

Going one step further, most buyers in the marketplace are not particularly well informed, and given that 11,302 MS-65 coins have been certified, they might use this as an estimate of the total number known. As discussed above, this is far from being true.

Analysis of the
1884-O Morgan Dollar

- *9,730,000 minted.*

- *VG-8 to AU-58—Guide Book* value in VF-20: $16. Estimated in existence today, all grades VG-8 to AU-58 combined: 1,500,000 to 2,500,000. Total certified in all grades VG-8 to AU-58 combined: 176.

- *MS-60 to MS-62—Guide Book* value in MS-60: $30. Estimated in existence today, all grades MS-60 to -62 combined: 2,000,000 to 3,000,000. Total certified in all grades MS-60 to 62 combined: 11,885.

- *MS-63—Guide Book* value: $45. Estimated in existence today: 750,000 to 1,250,000. Total certified: 94,953.

- *MS-64—Guide Book* value: $60. Estimated in existence today: 350,000 to 500,000. Total certified: 88,820.

- *MS-65—Guide Book* value: $160. Estimated in existence today: 60,000 to 100,000. Total certified: 20,398.

- *MS-66 and higher*—No *Guide Book* listings. Estimated in existence today: 4,500 to 7,500. Total certified: 1,915.

- *Known hoards of Mint State coins*— The Treasury released bags of 1,000 coins in 1938 and in very large quantities (more than a million coins) during the great dispersal of 1962 to 1964.

- *Total number of 1884-O dollars certified in all grades*—165,754.

As with the 1884-CC, only a tiny fraction of extant 1884-O dollars have ever been certified.

Analysis of the
1884-S Morgan Dollar

- *3,200,000 minted.*

- *VG-8 to AU-58—Guide Book* value in VF-20: $17. Estimated in existence today, all grades VG-8 to AU-58 combined: 125,000 to 250,000. Total certified in all grades VG-8 to AU-58 combined: 5,909.

- *MS-60 to MS-62—Guide Book* value in MS-60: $5,500. Estimated in existence today, all grades MS-60 to -62 combined: 1,500 to 3,000. Total certified in all grades MS-60 to -62 combined: 494.

- *MS-63—Guide Book* value: $27,000. Estimated in existence today: 400 to 800. Total certified: 82.

- *MS-64—Guide Book* value: $115,000. Estimated in existence today: 80 to 150. Total certified: 26.

- *MS-65—Guide Book* value: $200,000. Estimated in existence today: 12 to 20. Total certified: 2.

- *MS-66 and higher*—No *Guide Book* listings. Estimated in existence today: 4 to 7. Total certified: 2.

- *Known hoards of Mint State coins*— None.

- *Total number of 1884-S dollars certified in all grades*—5,978.

These figures have far more meaning to me than do the numbers certified for 1884-P, 1884-CC, and 1884-O. As no hoards of the 1884-S are known to have been distributed (and the Morgan dollar series has been studied widely in this regard), and as Mint State coins are exceedingly valuable, it is likely that just about any Mint State 1884-S dollar changing hands in recent years has gone through one or another of the ANACS, NGC, or PCGS services, perhaps several times.

I can say that in Mint State the 1884-S is rare, and that in MS-64 and higher grades it is exceedingly rare. The certification numbers, in coordination with the estimated number in existence today, seem to give good guidelines for buying. If a gem MS-65 dollar comes on the market, and if it is choice, a wise buyer would do well to reach for it, perhaps paying more than standard values—for few such coins exist.

Among the shortcomings of relying *solely* upon population data for certified coins (as many buyers do) are the additional factors discussed below.

Resubmissions

Often the same coin will be sent back to a grading service for another look, a process called *resubmission*. This has become a big business for the certification companies. When coins are resubmitted, their assigned grades inch up and up, then up some more, although, of course, the coins themselves do not change.

Because of this, certification reports relate to the number of submission events, not necessarily to the number of different coins involved. Bruce Amspacher, a founder of PCGS, told me of a Mint State 1854 Liberty Seated dollar that had been submitted to that service six times, thus appearing on the population report as six events that, to unwary eyes, could be easily mistaken for six different coins. Andrew P. Harris, M.D., advised me of a single, rare, Uncirculated 1878-CC trade dollar that appears in a grading population report as four coins. In another instance a dealer told me of sending a 1916-D dime to a service more than two dozen times until it finally was certified in the grade he wanted. The value of each of these coins, in the thousands of dollars, made resubmission financially worthwhile.

A Massachusetts dealer told me of a 1796 half dollar that was graded AU-53 when he owned it, but that, a year or two later, after many resubmissions to a grading service, had "improved" to MS-62. Recently, another well-known dealer from the same state told me of a 1795 Flowing Hair silver dollar that the owner thought was Mint State, although, despite several resubmissions to a service, the best he could get was AU-55. He gave up and sold it for an AU-55 price, and the next owner promptly had it recertified as MS-62.

In autumn 2000, I "guest cataloged" a sale, "Gold Rush Treasure From the *S.S. Central America*," for the auction house Christie's. One of the rarer varieties of double eagle was certified as AU-58; after the sale, the buyer resubmitted it to the same service and it was returned as MS-62.

Resubmissions tend to exaggerate the number of expensive coins certified. A population listing of 1916-D Mercury dimes in Mint State is apt to include many more resubmissions than a listing for the rather plentiful and inexpensive 1916-S dime.

To borrow from Abbott and Costello, it is difficult to see "who's on first." The players are changing their jersey numbers in the middle of the game!

A Proposed Solution

This unreliability of rating services could be ended, and grading interpretations could be stabilized, by a recognized commercial service or respected organization's keeping a photographic record of each coin, much as law enforcement and other agencies keep fingerprints on file, or as the Gemological Institute of America (GIA) keeps diamond-identification records. In that way, the owner of a coin can learn if it was submitted earlier and, if so, what grade was assigned to it.

Grade-flation—that loosening of grading standards—might become embarrassing to those involved as, indeed, it presently is in the field of federal paper money. Each piece of currency issued from 1861 to date has a unique combination of design, plate letter, and serial number.

Accordingly, if 10 years ago it was graded "Very Fine, lightly soiled," and illustrated in a catalog, and today it reappears as "Choice Uncirculated," it is evident that the bill has been cleaned. The bill still might be very desirable, but with such information at hand, a prospective buyer can make a more informed decision.

Under a photo-registration program it could be learned that a coin now certified as, say, MS-63, had been certified as AU-55 a few years ago. Perhaps the coin was undergraded a few years ago, but in any event the information is useful to the prospective buyer. Also, if a coin is stolen, it can be identified if it comes back on the market.

More About "Grade-flation"

Over time, the grading interpretations applied to certain coins have become liberalized. This trend has been discussed at great length in the popular numismatic press. Time was when I, as a student of American gold coins (among other series), was impressed by the fact that certain early coins were nearly impossible to find in Mint State—examples being selected Charlotte and Dahlonega gold coins, and San Francisco coins of the 1850s and 1860s (except for a few varieties found in undersea treasures). I looked and looked some more, but located only a handful.

Today, "Mint State" Charlotte and Dahlonega coins are offered with frequency at conventions and auctions, never mind that many are the same pieces that were called AU years ago. In charting the market performance of many coins today, it probably would be correct to compare today's MS-65 prices to prices of coins called MS-64 a generation ago, or to compare, for certain gold coins, MS-60 to -62 prices of today to AU-58 prices of two decades ago. If this new standard were applied, the true price appreciation of coins would be significantly greater than presently stated, as now we are using weakened or depreciated grade numbers.

Notwithstanding all of this, in a *relative sense* the population data are extremely useful. If the highest grade certified by ANACS, NGC, or PCGS for Gold Coin X is MS-64, and the next highest is just MS-60, then one who is offered the MS-64 can rest assured that it is probably high enough over the Mint State border to *really* be Uncirculated, and not a recycled AU of an earlier time. Also, because it currently stands alone as MS-64, it is certainly one of the very finest in existence (allowing for the possibility that others may exist, but have not been run through the certification services).

Certification-Data Conclusions

I find that certification numbers are most useful to determine the relative rarity of expensive coins, particularly those in higher grades. When cataloging a Proof-65 Liberty Seated dollar of the 1840s, or a rare 1861-D gold dollar, or a condition rarity MS-67 1903-O dollar (common enough at lower Mint State levels), or a similar highlight, population numbers are informative and useful. To this extent they are very important.

In determining rarity of such coins, the numbers should be used in combination with other information such as relative values in different grades; the possibility of resubmissions; investment-trading activity vis-à-vis series that are held mainly by collectors; and the buyer's experience.

Also remember that the labels on the vast majority of coin holders offer no clue as to whether the coin within is poorly struck or is sharply detailed, or whether it is gorgeous to behold or ugly as a toad. You are on your own with these details. As I mention frequently in this book, such things can translate into a very powerful and profitable financial advantage for you!

Rarity Scales
Popular Modern Scales: Sheldon and Judd

Ever since the cradle days of the hobby's popularity in America, there have been efforts to create abbreviations and notations to indicate the rarity of a given coin.

Nearly all of these have dealt with absolute rarity—the number of coins estimated to exist in numismatic hands—rather than indicating scarce and rare coins within a given series.

Today, there is no agreement on a standard rarity scale. However, the most widely used is a modification of the scale proposed by Dr. William H. Sheldon in *Early American Cents* (1949) and continued in *Penny Whimsy* (1958), with intermediate steps added. In 1949, the scale was presented as follows.

Sheldon Rarity Scale:
Rarity-1: More than 1,250 estimated known today
Rarity-2: 501 to 1,250
Rarity-3: 201 to 500
Rarity-4: 76 to 200
Rarity-5: 31 to 75
Rarity-6: 13 to 30
Rarity-7: 4 to 12
Rarity-8: 2 or 3
Unique: 1

These steps were commonly abbreviated as R-1, R-2, and so on.

More than a few people felt there was a big difference in importance between a coin of which, say, four were known and one for which three times that many, or 12, were thought to exist, even though both bore the R-7 designation.

In his 1959 book, *United States Pattern Coins: Experimental and Trial Pieces*, Dr. J. Hewitt Judd proposed the following modified scale (based on the Sheldon effort).

Sheldon Rarity Scale (as modified by Judd):
Rarity-1: More than 1,250 estimated to exist
Rarity-2: 501 to 1,250
Rarity-3: 201 to 500
Rarity-4: 76 to 200
Rarity-5: 31 to 75
Low Rarity-6: 21 to 30
High Rarity-6: 13 to 20
Low Rarity-7: 7 to 12
High Rarity-7: 4 to 6
Rarity-8: 2 or 3
Unique: 1

Variations on this 11-step theme were later employed by others and remain popular today.

For some series that are laden with elusive coins, the Judd Rarity Scale serves well. For example, among the dozens of different varieties of 1794 copper cents, most have fewer than 1,250 known. Among Vermont state copper coins of 1785 to 1788 the same thing can be said, and ditto for nearly all varieties of pattern coins (Judd's specialty) from 1792 to date.

However, for many popular series the scale isn't very useful. For example, all Indian Head cent dates and mintmarks from 1859 to 1909 and all Lincoln cent issues from 1909 to date would be called R-1, because well over 1,250 are known to exist of even the scarcer varieties in those two series. To the Lincoln cent specialist, the 1909-S V.D.B., 1955 Doubled Die, and 1982 cents would all be Rarity-1—information that is about as helpful as saying that each of these coins is of round shape!

Similarly, the collector of circulation-strike Morgan silver dollars of 1878 to 1921 knows that the scarcest issues are such varieties as 1879-CC, 1889-CC, and 1893-S, while the commonest of all Morgan dollars is the 1921. And yet under the Judd Rarity Scale each is Rarity-1.

The Universal Rarity Scale

In 1993, I devised the Universal Rarity Scale (URS)—one that is mathematically sound in its progression and relationship among its divisions, and one that will be applicable to any series. Stated simply, it is a geometric progression of numbers, rounded off for convenience in use, with each category containing about twice as many members as the preceding category. The Universal Rarity Scale uses a simple geometric progression of numbers, as 1, 2, 4, 8, 16, 32, and so on.

Upon reviewing certain of the precise numbers in the higher ranges, such as URS-16 being 16,385 to 32,768, John Kroon and J. Alan Bricker suggested that the Universal Rarity Scale would be simpler if I rounded off the numbers in higher categories. I liked the idea, and changed URS-16 to start with a round number, now stated as URS-16 = 16,000 to 31,999.

Interestingly, there are 12 steps from the one-coin-known rating (URS-1) up to the 1,000-to-1,999-known rating (URS-12)—which is not much different from the Judd Rarity Scale with its 11 steps.

Universal Rarity Scale (URS):

URS-0: None known to exist today

URS-1: Unique, only one known to exist

URS-2: 2 known

URS-3: 3 or 4

URS-4: 5 to 8

URS-5: 9 to 16

URS-6: 17 to 32

URS-7: 33 to 64

URS-8: 65 to 124

URS-9: 125 to 249

URS-10: 250 to 499

URS-11: 500 to 999

URS-12: 1,000 to 1,999

URS-13: 2,000 to 3,999

URS-14: 4,000 to 7,999

URS-15: 8,000 to 15,999

URS-16: 16,000 to 31,999

URS-17: 32,000 to 64,999

URS-18: 65,000 to 124,999

URS-19: 125,000 to 249,999

URS-20: 250,000 to 499,999

URS-21: 500,000 to 999,999

URS-22: 1,000,000 to 1,999,999

URS-23: 2,000,000 to 3,999,999

URS-24: 4,000,000 to 7,999,999

URS-25: 8,000,000 to 15,999,999

URS-26: Same progression

A study in rarity ratings: Of the 1889-CC Morgan silver dollar, one of the rarest and most desired coins in the context of its series, it is estimated that about 5,000 to 8,000 exist in grades ranging from MS-60 to -62. On the Sheldon-Judd scale it would rate as Rarity-1 (more than 1,250 known), while on the more useful Universal Rarity Scale it would rate as URS-14 (4,000 to 7,999 known).

In the Peace silver dollar series, the 1923 is one of the most common dates. It is estimated that 2,500,000 to 5,000,000 exist in grades ranging from MS-60 to -62. On the Sheldon-Judd scale it would rate as Rarity-1 (more than 1,250 known), while on the Universal Rarity Scale it would rate as URS-23 (2,000,000 to 3,999,999 known).

Both the Sheldon-Judd Scale and the Universal Rarity Scale are useful for very rare coins. This 1870 pattern dime, Judd-862 (enlarged), has an estimated 4 to 6 pieces known. On the Sheldon-Judd scale it rates as High R-7, immediately indicating rarity, while the URS-4 designation (5 to 8 estimated) is similarly informative.

Whether the URS will ever catch on, I do not know. It is not copyrighted, and anyone and everyone is invited to use it without crediting the source. I suppose I could help matters along by making extensive use of it in the many things I write.

As can be seen below, the Sheldon-Judd Rarity Scale is not very useful except for coins of which very few—1 to about 1,250 or so—are known.

Rarity Scales in History

Over the years, many other rarity scales have been devised, of which the following are just a few.

In July 1858, a pamphlet titled "Dates of United States Coins, and Their Degrees of Rarity," published by Philadelphia numismatist and antiquarian Joseph J. Mickley, contained an early effort at propounding a rarity scale for U.S. coins. The scale was elementary and consisted of these letters: C = Common, R = Rare, and V.R. = Very Rare.

Dr. Montroville W. Dickeson's book, the *American Numismatical Manual*, which appeared in print in 1859, was the first widely circulated popular book on coin collecting published in America. Dickeson included a scale that was simple and con-

sisted of three dots: • = scarce, •• = rare, and ••• = very rare. Coins that were common had no designation.

In *Coins, Medals, and Seals*, published in 1861 by Harper & Brothers, New York City, W.C. Prime used a rarity scale from 1 (the most plentiful) to 6 (greatest rarity). The author advised this:

> The table of comparative rarity is based only on six orders. It is of course impossible to distinguish all coins exactly by these six numbers. Thus the dollar of 1804 might well be ranked as more rare than almost any other of the coins. But the table will serve the purposes of the collector without more minute distinctions.

In the early silver dollar series, Prime published the following ratings:

1794: Rarity-6

1795: R-2

1796: R-2

1797: R-2

1798: R-1

1799: R-1

1800: R-2

1801: R-2

1802: R-2

1803: R-1

1804: R-6

Sylvester S. Crosby's *Early Coins of America*, published in 1875, included a rarity scale ranging from C (common) through R (rare), plus R-2, R-3, R-4, R-5, and the highest degree, R-6. The ratings were not otherwise defined. The same scale was later used by Henry C. Miller and Hillyer C. Ryder in *The State Coinages of New England*, 1920.

CHAPTER SEVEN

GRADING IS IMPORTANT:
A Close Focus

During the lifetime of most coin collectors, some consideration is given the possibility of making their hobby a financial investment. This is a normal occurrence. Many coin collectors have done more than just consider the possibility, they've made investments in coins in much the same way that others have turned to stocks and bonds....

Coins are good investments. Some are better investments than others. Coins are influenced by the same economic principles as any other investment. The factors which play leading roles are, of course, supply and demand....

—Dr. Robert Bilinski, May 1956

Aspects of Grading
A Guide to Value

Up to this point I have discussed many significant aspects of being a smart buyer of coins, but *grading* is certainly the most complex and, at the same time, possibly the most important. This chapter concentrates on this vital aspect.

Grade is a term expressing the amount of wear a coin has received. Freshly coined and still in the press, a coin is gem Uncirculated, or Mint State—pristine and beautiful. Years later, after the same coin has passed from hand to hand in commerce, it may be worn down so extensively that many details can no longer be seen, perhaps what a collector might call "Very Good–8" grade, per the *Official ANA [American Numismatic Association] Grading Standards for United States Coins.*

In the field of rare coins (but not necessarily certain other fields, such as obsolete paper money), the less wear a piece has received, the more valuable it is to a collec-

tor. Accordingly, a certain Mint State half dollar of the 1890s might be worth $2,000, while the same variety, if worn nearly smooth and with its features barely discernible, might be valued at less than $10.

Price differences among grades can be dramatic. Consider my earlier example of the 1901 Morgan silver dollar, a coin of which 6,962,000 were struck. Today a worn coin in VF-20 grade is worth $40, per the *Guide Book*, while a gem MS-65 is valued at $200,000! Why the difference? Each coin variety has its own story as to why some or just a few were saved in Mint State—factors sometimes completely independent of how many were made.

By all logic, the 1901 dollar in MS-65 should be common and inexpensive. It is not, for the reason that nearly all of the 6,962,000 coins were paid out in circulation shortly after they were minted, with others melted in quantity in 1918. No col-

This well-worn 1799 cent was graded Good-4 by a commercial service. On this specimen the all-important figures in the 1799 date are very bold, perhaps offsetting the fact that the letters in the word LIBERTY at the top border are mostly gone, except for a few faint traces.

This lustrous 1916-S $10 gold coin of the Indian Head design is in sufficiently high grade that it earned the label of MS-66 on the slab in which it is encased.

This 1979-S Lincoln cent was given the ultimate grade of Proof-70 Red by a commercial service. There were 3,677,175 Proof cents struck this year, and all were carefully produced, then packaged and sold to collectors, who for the most part preserved them. While Proof-70 is a notable grade, for a modern Proof or other coin struck for sale to collectors and made in large quantities, it does not have the same significance as it would if assigned to a 19th-century Proof coin of a variety made for general circulation.

Learn to Grade Coins!

While many buyers rely upon commercial grading (loosely called "certification") services, *I strongly recommend that you learn as much as you can about grading.* Generations of numismatists have done this, giving them a great advantage in the marketplace.

Grading is learned by a combination of examining coins and reading about them. Popular references give guidelines that you can employ in the field. Try your hand at grading a Liberty Head nickel, to classify it as Very Fine-20, or Mint State-60, or whatever the case may be. Through hands-on experience you can learn quickly and effectively. After taking the week-long grading course at the ANA Summer Seminar, most students are capable of making good decisions in the marketplace. However, such total immersion is not necessary. Most collectors and dealers who are experts today learned on their own account.

You can make excellent progress simply by looking at pocket change, gazing at coins for sale at coin shows, and seeking the assistance of collectors and dealers. You will have an enjoyable time doing this, and, as you refine your skills, you will have a sense of accomplishment.

A very effective way to start is to concentrate on only one series and type, such as Morgan silver dollars, Indian Head cents, or Liberty Head nickels. You will progress faster than you think! Then, your knowledge can be adapted to other series. In fact, I daresay that if you go to a coin show and concentrate on viewing Liberty Head nickels in all grades, from worn smooth to pieces certified as MS-65 or higher, within an hour or two you will be quite conversant in grading coins of this type. Books are great sources of basic information, but as is true of many areas of learning, some "laboratory" or "field" work is needed. Another way is to visit a coin shop or two in your region, and ask if you can look through a lot of coins and ask questions. I recommend that at the outset you mention that before leaving the store, you will buy, say, $100 or more worth of

lectors are known to have saved them, since mirror-finish Proofs, made especially for numismatists, were readily available. Proofs to the extent of 813 coins were struck, nicely filling the demand at the time. Generations later, collectors desiring a lustrous, frosty Mint State coin (a finish collected separately from Proofs) came up short. Hardly any were to be found.

On the other hand, an even earlier Morgan silver dollar, the 1884-CC (analyzed in chapter 6), of which 1,136,000 were struck (a tiny fraction of the quantity of the 1901) in Mint State, is worth just a couple hundred dollars. In the 1880s there was scarcely any commercial call for these silver dollars, and they went into storage. Marvelously, they escaped the melting pot. Long afterward the government took stock of its holdings of early silver dollars in vaults, and in March 1964, found that 962,638 (84.73% of the original mintage) still remained—nearly all of the coins in brilliant Mint State! These were sold to collectors and others. Today, most of these still survive, and a beautiful Mint State coin can be purchased for just a few hundred dollars.

The point of this is that while some coins are rare in Mint State and others are not, as a general rule a Mint State specimen is worth more than a worn one—regardless of variety. Accordingly, grading is important as a key to value. How important depends on other factors, as noted above.

books or coins to take home (as a courtesy to the dealer).

Now, to the grading system that most of us use.

The Official ANA Grading Standards for United States Coins

A Quick Overview

At the moment of its creation in a press, a coin is perfect—a complete impression and reflection of the dies that created it. In the official ANA grading standards' terms, as outlined in the *Official ANA Grading Standards for United States Coins*, it is Mint State–70 (MS-70) on a scale in which the lowest number, 1, indicates a coin worn to near smoothness, and 70 indicates perfection.

These numbers serve as shorthand for longer explanations. If I mention to a customer in Spokane, "I have a rare 1893-S Morgan silver dollar in VF-20 grade," he or she will know what I mean. By definition (further discussed below) this is a coin that "shows moderate wear on the high points of the design," and on which "all major details are clear."

VF-20 is shorthand for "Very Fine–20," a specific position on the 70-point scale. Without the attached number, "Very Fine" might be misunderstood—if I were to say to my Spokane friend that I have a "Very Fine 1893-S dollar," he or she might think I have a "very nice" or "very desirable" 1893-S dollar, rather than one in a specific grade.

Similarly, such terms as *Good*, *Extremely Fine*, and *Fair* may be difficult to understand without numbers. You can imagine that if you mentioned to a cousin that you'd just purchased a "good 1799 cent," your words would not impart much meaning. However, if you said, "I purchased a 1799 cent graded as Good-4 by ANACS," this would at least invite further inquiry.

Among collectors, if not to outsiders, *G-4* (Good-4), *EF-40* (Extremely Fine–40), and *Fair-2* seem understandable enough. Even a person who just began collecting

coins yesterday will have no problem understanding that a coin in EF-40 is far finer than one in G-4 grade.

I'm not necessarily a fan of abbreviations, serial numbers, and computerese, but shortcuts for attribution have led to such in numismatics—and for those who understand the lingo, useful information can be imparted. Do you know what "1793 cent, S-NC3, F-12, High R-6" means?

What it translates to is "1793 cent, Sheldon Non-Collectible No. 3, as described in *Early American Cents*, by Dr. William H. Sheldon, 1949, and later revisions. The famous Strawberry Leaf variety. The grade is Fine-12. As a High Rarity-6 variety, only 4 to 6 are known." Of course, this information is basic, but not complete. You may want to know whether the coin is weakly struck or is sharp in its details, whether it has been cleaned, whether the surface is glossy or porous, and more.

In theory, if a coin is taken from a coining press by a gloved hand and carefully stored, without the slightest rubbing or other contact, it will remain MS-70. In practice, few coins of years past were ever cared for in this manner, and over a period of time they acquired a few marks here and there, including by counting and storing in the Mint, placing into bags, shipping, and other handling, even they might not have entered circulation.

Under the system we use, such handling before a coin reaches circulation reduces the grade to MS-69, MS-68, and on downward to the lowest level of Mint State, or MS-60, defining a coin with many abrasions, nicks, and bagmarks.

A 1795 half dollar (reduced), die variety Overton-111, presently housed in a certified holder labeled EF-40.

Once a coin enters the channels of commerce it acquires wear by friction, and soon shows rubbing and loss of mint frost or luster, placing it in the About Uncirculated category, ranging from AU-58 and downward to AU-55, AU-53, and AU-50. Below this, as a coin acquires more wear, it goes down to EF-40, VF-20, Fine-12, VG-8, G-4, and lower, to AG-3, Fair-2, and Poor-1. These distinctions and other intermediate steps are explained shortly.

Grading notations are a shorthand technique for numismatists to exchange information. Grading numbers such as MS-67, MS-63, AU-50, VG-8, and G-4 give just basic information, and nothing about the surface brilliance or toning, the sharpness of strike, or the overall eye appeal of a coin (remember steps 1, 2, 3, and 4 outlined in chapter 2). For the rare 1793 S-NC3 Strawberry Leaf cent, we still want to know about its surface characteristics and appearance. However, the numbers serve as quick identifiers, a door to further investigation.

At a coin show you might hear a dealer say, "I have an 1857-S double eagle, MS-65, NGC." This translates into a gem Mint State 1857-S $20 gold piece certified and encapsulated by the Numismatic Guaranty Corporation of America. Or, "I can offer an 1877 cent, ANACS 55," meaning it has been graded AU-55 by the ANACS grading service.

How the ANA Grading System Originated

The question is often asked, "Why is a curious system of 70 numbers used, rather than a more logical 100?" The quick answer is that it is *tradition*. Similarly, if you are a commodities trader, you might ask why the metal mercury is valued in 76-pound flask units. Again, *tradition*.

In our hobby what is now tradition was once an innovation.

The originator was Dr. William H. Sheldon, a New York psychologist, avid numismatist, and organizer of things from large cents to human body types. His later activities seem to have been checkered. Today

he is generally thought to have stolen coins from the American Numismatic Society, with which he maintained a close relationship; to have switched specimens belonging to well-known collector and past American Numismatic Association president T. James Clarke; and to have engaged in other thefts. However, it is the system, not the man, that is under discussion here.[24]

In his 1949 book, *Early American Cents*, Sheldon, then a highly respected figure in medicine as well as numismatics, attempted to devise a *market formula* in which a particular die variety of copper cent dated from 1793 through 1814 (he considered no other coins) could be reduced to numbers, enabling a numismatist to quickly calculate the market value.

As die varieties vary considerably in their value, and such issues as the 1793 Chain AMERI., 1793 Liberty Cap, and 1799 are more valuable than, say, a common variety of 1803, different basal values were set up. For purposes of illustration here, a variety that was not particularly rare might have been given a basal value of $1 in 1949, while a scarce or rare piece might have been assigned $5.

Sheldon's idea was then to determine a pricing scale by numbers, so that if the grading number was multiplied by the basal value of the variety, a market value could be obtained. Back then the emphasis on Uncirculated coins was not as strong as it is today. While, of course, collectors would rather have a coin in Uncirculated grade than one in, say, Extremely Fine, most specialists in the field of copper cents of 1793 to 1814 were content to have a "nice" example in a grade they could afford. It was often the case that an Uncirculated piece would sell for just slightly more than one in EF or AU grade. All of this changed, and dramatically so, in later years when Uncirculated coins, which Sheldon called Mint State, were avidly collected for this category alone, and prices broke away sharply from those for circulated grades. Back in 1949, though, for a typical early cent there was not a tremendous premium for Mint State pieces.

Sheldon's scale from 1 to 70, later adapted and revised as the ANA Grading Scale, was simple enough at first glance. Per his logic, a rare cent with a basal value of $5, if in VF-30 grade, would be worth $5 times 30, or $150. A coin in Mint State-60 would be worth twice as much, or $300. On the other hand, a coin with a basal value of $2, if in EF-40 grade, would be worth $80. And so it went.

The grading numbers from 1 to 70 were created in 1949 *to fit the prices then in effect.* It may have worked for a very short while. At the time, the coin market was in a slump, licking its wounds from a postwar bust, and just beginning to revive.

In the early 1950s, a new surge of interest emerged, prices rose sharply across the board, and more emphasis was placed upon Mint State coins. By 1953, the Sheldon market formula (for that is what it really was) was essentially useless.

One might ask why the numbers were not abandoned when the market-price system failed. The answer is that the numbers were convenient shorthand, and that they appeared to have a scientific or mathematical basis, implying precision.

A coin description composed of adjectives alone, like "Very Good," might indicate a satisfactory coin but not much else. Thus, a newcomer to the hobby might not necessarily know that an About Uncirculated coin was nicer than one described as Very Fine or Extremely Fine. By using Sheldon numbers such as VG-8, VF-20, EF-40, and AU-50, just about anyone could quickly figure that an EF-40 coin was not as good as an AU-50 piece, but seemingly was far finer than one in VG-8. Moreover, such numbers evoked images of a numismatic scholar situated in a laboratory, assigning a precise number based on extensive knowledge and study—perhaps as an astronomer, using scientific principles, might assign a number to a star to indicate its magnitude.

It was and is very comforting to a hobby newcomer to think that a VF-20 grade had been assigned after much care, by the numismatic equivalent of a rocket scientist. Anyone can call a coin "Very Fine," it might be thought, but to be able to precisely identify its grade as VF-20 might require years of scholarship plus experience in the field.

Under the Sheldon grading formula, explained in the 1949 book *Early American Cents*, a basal value was assigned to each large copper cent variety from 1793 to 1814. This value, multiplied by the numerical grade, was supposed to yield the current market value.

As an example, this 1814 cent, Sheldon-294, was given a basal value of 50¢ in 1949. When multiplied by the grade, say, EF-40, the market value would be revealed: $20. The system worked well in 1949, the year it was published, because the formula was constructed to match current values. However, it soon proved to be useless, as market preferences and values changed.

Considered to be more valuable by Dr. Sheldon, the S-187 cent of 1798 was assigned a basal value of 75¢. This specimen, graded as AU-50, would have been worth 75¢ x 50, or $37.50, in 1949.

Moreover, a newcomer who sees a coin graded as VF-20 and for sale for $150 in a coin shop in Boston may have every right to think that the same variety, if graded VF-20 by a dealer in Los Angeles and offered for $120, is a much better buy.

Still further, the newcomer might know of the saying "ignorance is bliss," but will not consider it to be applicable in this situation!

Increasing Use of the System

In time, these grading numbers came into wide use by collectors of early copper cents, who extended the shorthand to include later dates through 1857, and, sometimes, to include half cents, colonials, and other early copper coins. The idea of multiplying the grade by a basal value was discussed in the 1958 edition of Dr. Sheldon's book, now renamed *Penny Whimsy*, but was not widely used. In that year I was as active as anyone else in the buying and selling of large copper cents, and never did customers speak of basal values when discussing coins. Today, the term *basal value* is virtually unknown.

Beginning in 1960, there was a tremendous surge forward in the rare coin market. Information became available in increasing quantity and frequency. *Coin World* appeared and was the first numismatic periodical to be issued weekly; it was followed in 1963 by another weekly, the *Coin Dealer Newsletter*. In due course, *Numismatic News*, established as a monthly in 1952, went to a weekly format. A Teletype system was set up to provide dealers with instantaneous data.

Prices rose, and often a coin described adjectivally as a "gem," or perhaps as a "frosty brilliant gem," would bring more than a piece simply described as "Uncirculated." This was quite a contrast from earlier times, when reference books as well as dealer listings simply called coins "Uncirculated" or perhaps "Brilliant Uncirculated," but not much else.

In this rising market it was soon realized that numbers would be useful, and while Sheldon had used only three grades in

the Uncirculated or Mint State category—these being MS-60 (or minimum Mint State), MS-65 (or gem), and MS-70 (or perfect)—there were many intermediate gradations. In time, MS-63 came to be used, then other numbers, then finally the full scale of 11 numbers from MS-60 to MS-70.

Grading Designation Changes
Examples of Changing Grades and Prices

Generations ago, when only a few grading categories were used and prices were much lower than they are today, typical listings for certain coins were Fine and Uncirculated. As time went on and prices rose, such that small differences in grade could mean large differences in price, more grades were added, bringing us to the aforementioned system of 11 grades from MS-60 to MS-70.

Although many examples could be given, here are some comparisons for the same coins as listed in the 1941 edition of the *Standard Catalogue of United States Coins and Tokens* (the most popular pricing guide of that era), together with the current *Guide Book of United States Coins* (59th ed., 2006), the most widely used numismatic price-reference book today. Of course, these numbers also serve to point out the investment performances of these varieties. I have picked out some key dates:

1856 Flying Eagle Cent—*Standard Catalogue:* Fine: $25 • Uncirculated: $50 • Proof: $60. *Guide Book:* Good-4: $6,000 • VG-8: $6,700 • Fine-12: $7,300 • VF-20: $8,500 • EF-40: $9,500 • AU-50: $11,000 • MS-60: $12,000 • MS-63: $17,000 • Proof-63: $19,000.

An 1856 Flying Eagle cent (enlarged).

1926-S Buffalo Nickel—*Standard Catalogue:* Fine: $2 • Uncirculated: $10. *Guide Book:* Good-4: $18 • VG-8: $30 • Fine-12: $75 • VF-20: $450 • EF-40: $900 • AU-50: $2,800 • MS-60: $4,200 • MS-63: $7,500.

1893-CC Morgan Silver Dollar—*Standard Catalogue:* Uncirculated: $7.50. *Guide Book:* VF-20: $475 • EF-40: $1,400 • AU-50: $1,900 • MS-60: $3,200 • MS-63: $7,000 • MS-64: $12,000 • MS-65: $50,000.

MCMVII (1907) High Relief $20 Gold Piece—*Standard Catalogue:* Uncirculated: $50. *Guide Book:* VF-20: $7,500 • EF-40: $9,500 • AU-50: $10,000 • MS-60: $13,000 • MS-63: $26,500.

Even the *Guide Book*, with its expanded coverage, does not come close to listing *all* categories. For a Morgan silver dollar, a full listing of grades (prices omitted) might include the following:

1893-CC Morgan Silver Dollar—Fair-2 • AG-2 • G-4 • VG-8 • F-12 • VF-20 • VF-30 • EF-40 • EF-45 • AU-50 • AU-53 • AU-55 • AU-58 • MS-60 • MS-61 • MS-62 • MS-63 • MS-64 • MS-65 • MS-66 • MS-67 • MS-68 • MS-69 • MS-70.

Even though it would seem that these are enough numbers to boggle the mind, additional listings (such as G-6, VG-10, VF-25, etc.) are sometimes encountered.

The ANA Certification Service (ANACS)

In the early 1970s, the American Numismatic Association set up the ANA Certification Service. Charles R. Hoskins, a Philadelphia numismatist, was named director and assumed his duties in Washington, DC, on April 1, 1972. ANACS, as it came to be called (pronounced *"ă-nacks"*), had as its mission the identification of counterfeit and spurious coins. The Washington location was the home of the Smithsonian Institution and its immense reference collection of coins, and was the headquarters of the Secret Service—that branch of the Treasury Department involved in the suppression of counterfeiting. Grading coins was not part of the game plan.

At the time, there were countless fakes in the marketplace. John J. Ford, Jr., remarked at a convention that more than half of the rare 1916-D dimes he saw were phonies, most made by soldering a D mintmark onto an inexpensive Philadelphia Mint coin. Fake 1877, 1909-S V.D.B., and other cents were common, and even the rare 1792 Birch pattern cent was reproduced. Crooks used various methods, including centrifugal casting (as employed by dentists and jewelers) and making new dies by the spark-erosion process. In addition, a type of alteration known as "whizzing" was prevalent, this consisting of treating worn coins with a rapidly rotating, small-wire brush to minutely abrade the surface, giving the appearance of mint luster to the uninitiated. One operator had a factory turning out such deceptive pieces.

The ANACS office, which was later moved to ANA headquarters in Colorado Springs, did its work well, and whizzing and counterfeiting were sharply curtailed in numismatic circles. However, fake and altered coins remained abundant outside the core collecting and dealer community, as, indeed, they are today, including on the Internet (where such offerings are endemic). An investigation supported by *Coin World* in 2005 revealed that of six specimens of Chinese sycee offered on the most popular of all Internet auction sites, five were fakes. Editor Beth Deisher commented, in part:

> Many have likened the current Age of Online Auction Sites to the days of the Wild West, where lawlessness was rampant and one survived by his wits and luck. Internet auction sites such as eBay have tried mightily to create a safe harbor environment, using participant feedback and secured payment systems. While such innovations help, online sites of the eBay ilk have yet to match the

consumer protection levels offered by traditional numismatic auctioneers, who catalog [knowledgeably describe] and stand behind the authenticity of items offered in their sales, whether on the floor of a public auction room or in cyberspace or some combination thereof.

Ultimately it is the buyer's decision as to whether to believe a seller at an online auction site when the seller represents an item as "genuine." Yet, one has to question whether online auction sites could not do more to weed out those who routinely offer counterfeit items. The volume of counterfeit items being sold in some classifications of numismatic collectibles at online auction sites is startling....[25]

Today, fakes of U.S. coins are common on the Internet, and for some series, such as trade dollars dated in the 1870s, the vast majority I have seen have been fake. However, such fakes are not found in holders of the leading certification services. Clearly, rules that no uncertified coins could be sold on the Internet would help protect buyers. However, it would probably be a legal nightmare to determine which services were "good" in this regard and which were not.

In the meantime, as Beth Deisher commented, "it is the buyer's decision as to whether to believe a seller at an online auction site when the seller represents an item as 'genuine.'" The same applies, by the way, to paper money offered on the Internet. In purchases of obsolete currency I made on the Internet, offerings by dealers who were members of the Professional Currency Dealers Association (PCDA) were fine, except for one note. In contrast, two out of three I bought from private parties turned out to be photocopies! Further, many Internet offerings of tokens and medals, such as saloon and western tokens and Indian peace medals, are worthless fakes. The good news is that most leading grading services in the field of U.S.

coins guarantee the authenticity of what they put in their slabs. This is a marvelous protection that would be beneficial if it could be extended to other numismatic areas as well. However, I now return to the subject at hand, which is not authenticity, but *grading*.

The ANA Grading Book

In 1975, the ANA appointed Abe Kosoff as chairman of the ANA Grading Service Study Committee, to investigate the title subject—it was hoped with the same success that ANACS had achieved with the suppression of fakes in the main coin market.

Whether the grading of coins for a fee was a service to the collecting community, or whether it was a business venture in which the ANA should not have become involved, was a matter of strong debate at the time. However, the ANA went onward, and Kosoff began his work. The desirability of the project was publicized by Stanley Apfelbaum, a Long Island seller of investment coins who had been burned by purchasing "Uncirculated" pieces—coins that in some instances turned out to be in lower grades—from dealers. Shrugging off any need for *personal knowledge* of grading, Apfelbaum stated that he had relied upon the experts, but that the experts had been found wanting. Apfelbaum pleaded innocent and blamed his sale of overgraded coins on others. In my view, anyone conducting a large operation in the buying and selling of coins should have in-house knowledge of grading. It would be difficult for me, but apparently not for Apfelbaum, to envision a dealer in any collectible field—art, stamps, antique cars, you name it—who thinks it unnecessary to be an expert on the items he or she sells.

In recent years, the 70-point Sheldon system had been used all over the place for coins from half cents to double eagles, this far beyond the early copper cents for which the system was originally intended. Kosoff, with the blessing of the ANA board of governors, deemed it desirable to

The seal of the American Numismatic Association, with the Lamp of Knowledge, as used from the 1890s until it was discarded in the 1990s. The ANA began authenticating coins for a fee in the 1970s, followed by the establishment of ANACS, which graded coins as well.

adopt the scale, and this was done. Working from a desk in his home in Palm Springs, California, he gathered information ranging from stray comments to detailed listings, soliciting the input of collectors, dealers, and others.

Finally, Kosoff's accumulated information was sent off to Kenneth E. Bressett, editor of the *Guide Book of United States Coins*, who was in charge of seeing the data set into type and printed in book form. By that time, I had created the narrative introductory text to the book, but had not been involved in the definitions for various coin types, nor had I seen the listings. I reviewed the general concept of grading and in that text endeavored to make it understandable—a challenge I am continuing here.

In 1991, I wrote *The 1891–1991 Centennial History of the American Numismatic Association*. This commentary related to the grading project (the time is late in the year 1976):

> The manuscript of the new ANA grading guide was completed in draft form by Kenneth E. Bressett, using materials furnished by Abe Kosoff and his committee.
>
> Just as the book was scheduled to be permanently set in type, Q. David Bowers and Harvey G. Stack, prominent dealers who had followed the progress of the grading situation with great interest, examined the manuscript and found many inconsisten-

cies, apparently the result of different contributors' writing different sections, with no coordination between one section and another.

The two called for a halt in publication until the manuscript could be corrected, and Kenneth E. Bressett agreed that this should be done. Subsequently, with numerous revisions, the volume was published in 1977.

The first edition of the book illustrated coin grades by using drawings. Later, Jim Ruddy's innovative *Photograde* (launched in 1970) idea—that of illustrating actual examples of each major coin type, in different grades—was adopted.

ANACS Grades Coins

In 1979, ANACS began grading coins for a fee, using the ANA Grading System. Numismatic writer Tom DeLorey, editor of *Coin World*'s Collectors' Clearinghouse department, resigned that post and relocated to ANACS in late 1978 to take charge. In June 1979, this was reported in *The Numismatist*:

> The ANACS Grading Service is currently grading only regular issue U.S. coins. It's not grading commemoratives, patterns, colonial, territorial or any foreign coins including the Hawaiian issues of 1847 and 1883 and the Philippine coinage issued under the authority of the United States. The coins that are being graded are assigned a numerical grade on each side of the coin, obverse first then the reverse. While the majority of coins have the same grade on each side, such as EF-40/40 or MS-65/65, some have different numerical grades such as EF-40/45 or MS-65/60. In those cases where the two sides are entirely different, a notation such as VF-20/F-15 or EF-45/AU-50 will be used.
>
> The grade levels currently being used are AG-3; G-4 or G-6; VG-8 or 10; F-12 or 15; VF-20, 25, 30 or 35; EF-40 or 45; AU-50 or 55 and MS-60,

63, 65, 67 or 70. Plus and minus signs are not being used, and whizzed coins will not be graded regardless of condition. For the foreseeable future, striking characteristics such as full steps, split bands or full heads will not be included in either the description of the coin or its grading, except in the case of a coin that is unusually weakly struck. In most cases those characteristics will be discernible in the photographic certificates which will accompany the coin. Also, the term *prooflike* will not be used to describe a coin, though true Proof coins may be described as Matte Proof if applicable.

The new ANACS service caught on like wildfire, and soon a staff of more than two dozen people was busy grading, photographing, and mailing coins. Profits rolled into the ANA, bringing unprecedented prosperity to the organization.

Over time, the directorship of ANACS changed, and John Smies replaced Tom DeLorey, to be followed by Kenneth E. Bressett (editor of the *Guide Book*), Rick Montgomery, and Leonard Albrecht.

ANACS had a virtual monopoly on the coin-grading business until the Numismatic Certification Institute (Steve Ivy) and Professional Coin Grading Service (David Hall and dealer associates) were established in 1986, quickly followed by the Numismatic Guaranty Corporation of America (John Albanese) in 1987. These services and others offered encapsulation—the placing of coins in a sealed plastic "slab," labeled with the date, mintmark, and grade. Collectors and dealers found this far more convenient than the ANACS method of returning a coin to its owner, in no particular type of package, accompanied by a separate photographic certificate giving the grade opinion. In time, ANACS lost market share to the other firms.

Changes of 1990 and Beyond

In the August 1990 issue of *The Numismatist*, ANA President Kenneth Hallenbeck told of a transition:

The big news in the last few weeks has been our sale of ANACS, our certification service, to Amos Press of Sidney, Ohio…. The Board studied the options concerning the sale of ANACS for a number of months. At first there was strong sentiment not to sell, but, as more and more facts were assembled and analyzed, the picture started to change.

ANACS was originally created to fight counterfeiting and later expanded to combat the abuses of overgrading. ANA hired experts, produced certificates, and, most importantly, tried to educate our members and the numismatic public. There is no doubt that we succeeded.

The development of the encapsulated coin product, or "slab," changed numismatics dramatically. Suddenly, ANACS, instead of being first, was last. It took a long time and a large expenditure of money to produce our own encapsulated product, the ANACS Cache. Eventually we regained some of the lost market, but only about 8%....

The ANA will receive a large amount of money—$1.5 million up front and up to $3 million more over the next five years if the venture succeeds. The interest from this money can be used to fund ANA educational activities and projects. ANA can get out of a commercial activity (there had been concern that operating ANACS might affect our non-profit status) and reduce our costs dramatically by reducing staff and related expenditures....

The transaction took place, and ANACS was moved to Columbus, Ohio, with Leonard Albrecht, formerly of the ANA staff, remaining in charge of the business. Although Amos Press also owned *Coin World*, ANACS and *Coin World* were independently managed. In February 2005, Amos Press sold ANACS to Anderson Press, of Florence, Alabama.

The Book

Returning to the book created by Abe Kosoff and sent to Ken Bressett, then revised extensively at the suggestion of Harvey Stack and me, *Official Grading Standards for U.S. Coins* was published in 1977. It enjoyed significant success, although the competitive *Photograde*, by James F. Ruddy, very popular since its advent in 1970, was much easier to use. *Photograde*, however, did not detail the various levels of Mint State.

By this time, Sheldon numbers had been used with reckless abandon in the hobby. Many advertisements in popular periodicals reflected systems developed by those who had coins for sale, often without any reference to much else, with the addition of many things never dreamed of by Sheldon. It was not at all uncommon to see a coin listed as "MS-65++," "MS-65–," and so on. Moreover, especially attractive Mint State coins were often called MS-70, although they were not even close to being perfect. Anything went, and it was an interesting and confusing scene.

The original grading scheme as proposed by Sheldon in 1949 had just three levels of Mint State: 60, 65, and 70. This was also the basis for the ANA system at the beginning. Then more numbers were added, then still more. Finally, on July 4, 1986, the *Coin Dealer Newsletter* reported the following:

> This past weekend, the ANA Board of Governors met, debated, and unanimously accepted the 11 point grading scale—MS-60, 61, 62...70. Originally intended to discuss the feasibility of the MS-64 grade, the ANA Governors showed their leadership in the hobby by going the whole route and accepting all 11 grades. They felt this was a necessary action for the future as well as today.
>
> MS-64 has been used for the last couple of years in the marketplace and eventually all in-between grades will be followed. By accepting the new system, the ANA is looking to the future when grading can, at least in terminology, be standardized.

There will probably always be debates over how a coin grades, but at least now, the industry will be talking the same language—numerals.

Although the ANA book did not settle the dust completely, even with a full panorama of numbers in the Mint State category, it did put an end to the use of pluses and minuses and gave everyone the same scorecard to use. Since that time it has gone through five editions, most recently including photographs to go with the printed descriptions. In 2004, the ANA tapped Whitman Publishing as the new publisher and distributor. The sixth edition debuted at the ANA's World's Fair of Money in July 2005.

Closer Focus on the ANA Grading System

The ANA system provides for specific guidelines for most major coin types. The following section gives an example, adapted from the sixth edition of *Official Grading Standards for U.S. Coins*, for the description of Liberty Head nickels.[26]

Liberty Head Nickels (1883–1913): Mint State Grades

- *MS-70 (Uncirculated)*—A flawless coin exactly as it was minted, with no trace of wear or injury. Must have full mint luster but this may range from brilliant to frosty.

A lovely 1795 copper cent, Sheldon-74 variety, assigned the grade MS-64 in recent times. Such intermediate Mint State designations were not used by Dr. Sheldon in his 1949 market-formula grading system, which employed only MS-60, MS-65, and MS-70. Eight more grades were later added in 1986, by decree of the ANA board of governors. Since that time they have been widely employed.

SMALL CENTS

FLYING EAGLE (1856–1858)
See pages 24–27 for expanded descriptions and intermediate grades.

MINT STATE	Absolutely no trace of wear.
MS-70 Uncirculated	A flawless coin exactly as it was minted, with no trace of wear or injury. Must have full mint luster and natural color.
MS-67 Uncirculated	Virtually flawless, but with very minor imperfections.
MS-65 Uncirculated	No trace of wear; nearly as perfect as MS-67 except for some small blemish. Has full mint luster but may be unevenly toned or lightly fingermarked. A few minor nicks or marks may be present.
MS-63 Uncirculated	A Mint State coin with attractive mint luster, but noticeable detracting contact marks or minor blemishes.[1]
MS-60 Uncirculated	A strictly Uncirculated coin with no trace of wear, but with blemishes more obvious than in higher grades. May have dull mint luster; color may be uneven shades.[1]

ABOUT UNCIRCULATED	Small traces of wear are visible on highest points.[1]
AU-58 Very Choice	Has some signs of abrasion: feathers on eagle's breast; wing tips.
AU-55 Choice	OBVERSE: A trace of wear shows on the breast and left wing tip. REVERSE: A trace of wear shows on the bow. SURFACE: Considerable mint luster is still present.
AU-50 Typical	OBVERSE: Traces of wear show on the breast, left wing tip, and head. REVERSE: Traces of the wear show on the leaves and bow. SURFACE: Some of the mint luster is still present.

—88

SMALL CENTS

FLYING EAGLE (1856–1858)

EXTREMELY FINE	Very light wear on only the highest points.
EF-45 Choice	OBVERSE: Wear shows on breast, wing tips, and head. All feathers are plain. REVERSE: High points of the leaves and bow are lightly worn. SURFACE: Traces of mint luster still show.
EF-40 Typical	OBVERSE: Feathers in wings and tail are plain. Wear shows on breast, wing tips, head, and thigh. REVERSE: High points of the leaves and bow are worn.

VERY FINE	Light to moderate even wear. All major features are sharp.
VF-30 Choice	OBVERSE: Small, flat spots of wear show on breast and thigh. Feathers in wings still show bold details. Head is worn but sharp. REVERSE: Ends of leaves and bow are worn almost smooth.
VF-20 Typical	OBVERSE: Breast shows considerable flatness. Some of the details are visible in feathers of the wings. Head is worn but bold. Thigh is smooth, but feathers in tail are nearly complete. REVERSE: Ends of leaves and bow are worn smooth.

FINE	Moderate to heavy even wear. Entire design is clear and bold.
F-12	OBVERSE: Some details at breast, head, and tail show. Outlines of feathers in right wing and tail show, with no ends missing. REVERSE: Some details are visible in the wreath. Bow is very smooth.

89—

HALF DOLLARS

Notes

New Orleans issues are often softly struck. 1906-O and 1908-O exhibit a swelling appearance extending from the lower cheek area down through the jaw and neck of Liberty.

1. Coins will not always have the exact stated amount of mint luster, strike, or absence of marks. Overall eye appeal and appearance may also influence the stated grade. Weak facial hairline definition is often the result of a poor strike, and not actual wear.

LIBERTY WALKING (1916–1947)
See pages 24–27 for expanded descriptions and intermediate grades.

Prime Focal Areas
Obverse: Length of Liberty's body.
Right field.
Reverse: Breast, leg, and forward wing of eagle.

Secondary Areas
Obverse: Left field, sun and date area.
Reverse: Head, rear wing, and field above eagle. Rock on which eagle stands.

Grade	Contact Marks	Hairlines	Luster	Eye Appeal
MS-70	None show under magnification	None show under magnification	Very attractive Fully original	Outstanding
MS-69	1 or 2 minuscule; none in prime focal areas	None visible	Very attractive Fully original	Exceptional
MS-68	3 or 4 minuscule; none in prime focal areas	None visible	Attractive Fully original	Exceptional
MS-67	3 or 4 minuscule; 1 or 2 may be in prime focal areas	None visible without magnification	Above average Fully original	Exceptional
MS-66	Several small; a few may be in prime focal areas	None visible without magnification	Above average Fully original	Above average
MS-65	Light and scattered without major distracting marks in prime focal areas	May have a few scattered	Fully original	Very pleasing
MS-64	May have light, scattered marks; a few may be in prime focal areas	May have a few scattered or small patch in secondary areas	Average Fully original	Pleasing
MS-63	May have distracting marks in prime focal areas	May have a few scattered or small patch in secondary areas	May be original or slightly impaired	Rather attractive
MS-62	May have distracting marks in prime focal and/or secondary areas	May have a few scattered to a noticeable patch	May be original or impaired	Generally acceptable
MS-61	May have a few heavy (or numerous light) marks in prime focal and/or secondary areas	May have noticeable patch or continuous hairlining over surfaces	May be original or impaired	Unattractive
MS-60	May have heavy marks in all areas	May have noticeable patch or continuous hairlining throughout	May be original or impaired	Poor

—234

HALF DOLLARS

LIBERTY WALKING (1916–1947)

MINT STATE	Absolutely no trace of wear.
MS-70 Uncirculated	A flawless coin exactly as it was minted, with no trace of wear or injury. Must have full luster and brilliance or light toning.
MS-67 Uncirculated	Virtually flawless, but with very minor imperfections.
MS-65 Uncirculated	No trace of wear; nearly as perfect as MS-67 except for some small blemishes. Has full mint luster but may be unevenly toned or lightly fingermarked. May be weakly struck in one or two small spots. A few minute nicks or marks may be present.
MS-63 Uncirculated	A Mint State coin with attractive mint luster, but noticeable detracting contact marks or minor blemishes.
MS-60 Uncirculated	A strictly Uncirculated coin with no trace of wear, but with blemishes more obvious than for MS-63. May lack full mint luster, and surface may be dull, spotted, or heavily toned. A few small spots may be weakly struck.

ABOUT UNCIRCULATED	Small traces of wear are visible on highest points.
AU-58 Very Choice	Has some signs of abrasion: hair above Liberty's temple, right arm, left breast; high points of eagle's head, breast, legs and wings. Coins of this design frequently show weakly struck spots, and usually lack full head and hand details, but often lightly worn on obverse right field.
AU-55 Choice	OBVERSE: Only a trace of wear shows on highest points of head, breast, and right arm. REVERSE: A trace of wear shows below the neck and on left leg between breast and left wing. SURFACE: Much of the mint luster is still present, , but often lightly worn on obverse right field.
AU-50 Typical	OBVERSE: Traces of wear show on head, breast, arms, and left leg. REVERSE: Traces of wear show on high points of wings and at center of head. All leg feathers are visible. SURFACE: Half of the mint luster is still present.

235—

These images, from *The Official American Numismatic Association Grading Standards for United States Coins*, 6th edition, show basic grading standards plus the additional details used to differentiate Mint State grades.

- *MS-67 (Uncirculated)*—Virtually flawless but with minor imperfections.
- *MS-65 (Uncirculated)*—No trace of wear; nearly as perfect as MS-67 except for some small weakness or blemish. Has full mint luster, but may be unevenly toned, frosty, or lightly fingermarked. A few minor nicks or marks may be present.
- *MS-63 (Uncirculated)*—A Mint State coin with attractive mint luster, but noticeable detracting contact marks or minor blemishes.
- *MS-60 (Uncirculated)*—A strictly Uncirculated coin with no trace of wear, but with blemishes more obvious than for MS-63. May lack full mint luster, and surface may be dull or spotted.

Liberty Head Nickels (1883–1913): Circulated Grades

ABOUT UNCIRCULATED
Small traces of wear are visible on highest points.

- *AU-58 (Very Choice)*—Has some signs of abrasion: high points of hair left of ear and at forehead; corn ears at bottom of wreath.
- *AU-55 (Choice)*—OBVERSE: Only a trace of wear shows on the highest points of hair left of ear. REVERSE: A trace of wear shows on corn ears. SURFACE: Some mint luster is still present.
- *AU-50 (Typical)*—OBVERSE: Traces of wear show on hair left of ear and at forehead. REVERSE: Traces of wear show on the wreath and corn ears. SURFACE: Trace of mint luster is still present.

EXTREMELY FINE
Very light wear on only the highest points.

- *EF-45 (Choice)*—OBVERSE: Slight wear shows on high points of hair from forehead to the ear. REVERSE: High points of wreath are lightly worn. Many lines in corn are clearly defined. SURFACE: Traces of mint luster may still show.

- *EF-40 (Typical)*—OBVERSE: Wear shows on hair from forehead to ear, on the cheek, and on curls. REVERSE: High points of wreath are worn, but each line is clearly defined. Corn shows some wear.

VERY FINE
Light to moderate even wear. All major features are sharp.

- *VF-30 (Choice)*—OBVERSE: Three-quarters of hair details show. The coronet has full bold lettering. REVERSE: Leaves are worn but most of the ribs are visible. Some of the lines in the corn are clear, unless weakly struck.
- *VF-20 (Typical)*—OBVERSE: More than half of the details still show in hair and curls. Head is worn but bold. Every letter on coronet is plainly visible. REVERSE: Leaves are worn but some of the ribs are visible. Most details in the wreath are clear, unless weakly struck.

FINE
Moderate to heavy even wear. Entire design is clear and bold.

- *F-12*—OBVERSE: Some details show in curls and hair at top of head. All letters of LIBERTY are visible. REVERSE: Some details are visible in wreath. Letters in the motto are worn but clear.

VERY GOOD
Well worn. Design is clear but flat and lacking details.

- *VG-8*—OBVERSE: Bottom edge of coronet and most hair details are worn smooth. Some letters in LIBERTY are clear. Rim is complete. REVERSE: Wreath shows only bold outline. Some letters in the motto are very weak. Rim is complete.

GOOD
Heavily worn. Design and legend are visible, but faint in spots.

- *G-4*—OBVERSE: Entire design is well worn with very little detail remaining. Stars and date are weak but visible. REVERSE: Wreath is worn flat and not completely outlined. Legend and motto are worn nearly smooth. Rim is incomplete in spots.

About Good
Outlined design. Parts of date and legend are worn smooth.

- *AG-3*—OBVERSE: Head is outlined with nearly all details worn away. Date is readable but very weak and merging into rim. REVERSE: Entire design is partially worn away.

Grading Certification Services
In the Beginning

Revisiting the year 1986, here is how the story unfolded: in February a contingent of rare coin dealers, headed by David Hall, banded together to form PCGS. In the April issue of *The Numismatist*, Michael Fuljenz, in his "Market Forum" column, included this item:

A new dealer group, the Professional Coin Grading Service (PCGS), has

Liberty Head Nickel (1883–1913). Grade: MS-67.

Liberty Head Nickel (1883–1913). Grade: EF-40.

Liberty Head Nickel (1883–1913). Grade: MS-66.

Liberty Head Nickel (1883–1913). Grade: VF-30.

Liberty Head Nickel (1883–1913). Grade: MS-65.

Liberty Head Nickel (1883–1913). Grade: F-12.

Liberty Head Nickel (1883–1913). Grade: MS-64.

Liberty Head Nickel (1883–1913). Grade: VG-8.

Liberty Head Nickel (1883–1913). Grade: AU-50.

Liberty Head Nickel (1883–1913). Grade: G-4.

been formed, comprising more than 30 leading dealers in the United States. They pledge to buy members' coins, graded by PCGS, at their published buy prices. Only time will tell what impact this group will have on the market.

Charging a fee to grade coins was hardly new. By this time ANACS, at its Colorado Springs headquarters, had enjoyed a strong business in grading coins and returning them to customers, each coin accompanied by a certificate bearing photographs of the obverse and reverse, separate grades for both sides, a serial number, and other documentation, as earlier described.

However, PCGS operated with another plan. For a fee, coins could be submitted, viewed by several graders, verified by a "finalizer," and then sonically sealed in a clear plastic holder. This "slab" would labeled with the date, mintmark, and other basic details, plus a single numerical grade, and each would be given a serial number. Coins that were believed to have been cleaned, artificially toned, or otherwise treated in a manner to negatively affect their market value would not be encapsulated. A reference collection would be kept on hand to assure that grading interpretations would be constant.

PCGS was an instant success. By the end of the 1980s, more than 1.5 million coins had passed across its threshold. The service was a boon to investors in particular—at a glance, a coin's date, major variety, and grade could be identified. The only variable, or so it seemed, was market price. Now, some believed that, at long last, coins could be bought, sold, and traded just like stocks. A "sight-unseen" market for PCGS coins sprang up in the investment community.[27] In the meantime, traditional numismatists of the old school still wanted to hold and feel their coins.

Jumping on the Bandwagon

Inspired by the success of PCGS, and realizing the strong demand for slabs (viewed by some as the long-sought answer to the grading problem), a half dozen or more competitors joined the fray. Early on the scene, arriving at about the same time as PCGS, was the Numismatic Certification Institute (NCI) of Dallas, Texas. Operated by Steve Ivy, NCI offered a service for Mint State and Proof coins only.

> The system is based on four grading components—surface preservation, strike, luster and eye appeal—which are assigned numerical ratings from one to five. The total grade is computed as the sum of the strike, luster and eye-appeal grades plus twice the surface-preservation grade.[28]

This system didn't last long, and NCI switched to the ANA numerical scheme already being used by ANACS and PCGS, and soon to be used by others.

In 1987, John Albanese, one of the most entrepreneurial dealers of the time, started the Numismatic Guaranty Corporation of America, billed as "the sign of a new era in coin grading." Whereas the owners of PCGS were active coin dealers, NGC advertised that it was

> founded to ensure unbiased, arms-length coin grading. The principals of NGC cannot buy, sell, or trade coins commercially. NGC is creating the standard for objective, consistent, and accurate grading of higher quality, investment-graded coins.[29]

Hallmark, a grading service founded by Lee J. Bellisario and headquartered in Massachusetts, was another early startup, and there were others.[30] In time, the long-established ANACS offered what it billed as the ANA Cache, its version of a sonically sealed slab.

Slabs became more popular than anyone would have imagined. Their appeal to investors was an important, indeed essential, element of the Wall Street coin investment boom of the late 1980s. To many new buyers, a slab offered unimpeachable security that a coin was genuine and in a fixed grade, reflecting the opinions of experts in the business (which was rapidly becoming known as an *industry*).

Evolutions in Grading

The publishers of the *Coin Dealer Newsletter*, launched in 1963, added another periodical, the weekly *Certified Coin Dealer Newsletter*, which gave "bid" and "ask" prices for many popular series and types. These were "sight unseen," meaning that if a dealer offered to pay $500 for an MS-65 coin certified by NGC or another specific service, he or she stood ready to honor that price upon receiving an appropriate slab—no matter whether the coin was beautiful or ugly when examined. For the investment community this seemed to have worked, but many collectors still wanted to inspect coins for characteristics such as strike and eye appeal.

In my opinion, the coins graded by PCGS in the early years were often finer, on average, than typical unslabbed coins given the same grades, and also with "tighter" interpretations than used by certain other grading services. Of course, there were exceptions. As the years went on, it seems to me that interpretations by various leading services loosened, sometimes considerably. The result was that quite a few coins certified as, say, MS-64 in the 1980s would grade as MS-65 or higher today.

A Recent Scenario

Although quite a few people thought the "grading problem" had been neatly solved by the advent of commercial services in the late 1980s, and although euphoria prevailed for a while, questions soon arose.

The inherently subjective nature of grading is an issue that will not go away. On August 17, 2004, the Professional Numismatists Guild and the Industry Council for Tangible Assets issued a report titled "PNG & ICTA Announce Results of 2004 Grading Service Survey," noting, in part:

> The Professional Numismatists Guild (PNG) and the Industry Council For Tangible Assets (ICTA) have jointly released results of their second dealer's survey of rare coin authentication and grading services.

Survey respondents were asked for their professional opinions to evaluate eight grading services based on 12 different weighted criteria, such as grading and authentication accuracy. Each category was ranked by the respondents on a ten-point scale ranging from the lowest, Unacceptable, to the highest, Outstanding.

The final tally lists no grading service as "Outstanding."

Numismatic Guaranty Corporation of America (NGC) of Sarasota, Florida and Professional Coin Grading Service (PCGS) of Newport Beach, California were rated "Superior." ANACS of Dublin, Ohio and Independent Coin Grading Company (ICG) of Englewood, Colorado were ranked "Average."

Dealer Julian Leidman, a long-time professional who has handled many important coins, shown with his display of items for sale at the Baltimore Coin and Currency Convention, a favorite show for many. Leidman offers a wide selection of certified coins or "slabs" plus many coins that have not been encapsulated. Today, the vast majority of coins of higher values (say, $100 upward) in popular series have been certified by various services.

The report went on to list several other grading services as "Poor" or "Unacceptable." One of these services recently sued the ANA and a number of collectors and dealers, alleging defamation because certain individuals complained of the firm's operations. So far as I know, no numismatic periodical currently refuses to take the advertisements of any of these services, be they described as "Outstanding," "Poor," or whatever.

The PNG/ICTA report drew mixed reviews. Some thought it was long overdue, while others questioned the weight given to certain categories. For example, if a grading service failed the test of determining authenticity, would it matter how good its grading was? Since the survey was completed by dealers who in many instances were authorized to be agents of certain services, were they able to report in an unbiased manner?

Possible Conclusions

Where does all of this leave us?

It seems clear that quite a few dealers and others believe that certain services are better than others. Evaluating each service is difficult to do, just as rating the expertise of a doctor, a writer, or an artist might be similarly difficult to do.

To reiterate my own feelings, grading services are not at all scientific; their opinions can and do vary even when the same coins are sent back to the same service, and interpretations can change over a period of time.

Mark Ferguson, long-time collector and dealer and, in recent years, the "Coin Values" market analyst for *Coin World*, made this comment:[31]

> Each third-party grading service uses its own standards to grade coins. There are no universal standards each service must adhere to, and there is no "oversight agency" regulating coin grading. Nevertheless, coin-grading criteria are similar. However, one service's Mint State-67 may only be another's Mint State-66, where MS-70

is absolutely perfect. Although a one-point grading difference may not sound like much, in Mint State it often results in huge price differences.

While these grading certifications are professional "opinions," they give confidence to buyers who want to own high grade coins. The marketplace votes with its pocketbook on which services are most preferred, so in that sense the market is self-regulating when it comes to coin grading.

Without third-party grading, coin values probably would not have risen as high as they have during the past couple of years. And they are still rising. Grading certification has generally given buyers the needed confidence to pay the prices they're paying for coins in today's market.

Keep all of this in mind, and when it comes to buying coins for *your* collection, be sure to think for yourself—and view grading services (as well as other advice) as tools, but not as the be-all and end-all.

My own view, in a nutshell, is that coin grades from the leading certification services are simply a *starting point*. From there you can consider other factors that determine a coin's value, including strike, planchet quality, and eye appeal (part of the four steps outlined in chapter 2). To the extent that (for starters) the best-reviewed services separate a lot of chaff from wheat, reject coins determined to be fake, and check flagrant overgrading, they will save you a lot of time.

Also, remember that this "grading problem" will bother you only if you allow it to. Grading inconsistencies have been part of the numismatic hobby since day one. I have known most of the great collectors of the past 50 years, and few of them have ever complained about grading problems. Grading was never a problem for Emery May Holden Norweb, Harry W. Bass, Jr., Louis E. Eliasberg, Sr., or John Jay Pittman, simply because they viewed the learning of grading as one of the aspects of being a numismatist.

They mastered grading and thus achieved a measure of numismatic tranquility.

An Ideal Holder?

Sometimes I am an idealist in a non-ideal world. In my view, the ideal certified-coin holder would include this information:

1. The opinion of grade (EF-40, MS-66, or whatever), as established by recognized experts—still with the realization that such is largely a matter of opinion.

2. Information as to the quality of strike, such as "Full Details" (of which more will be said in chapter 8).

3. An opinion as to the quality of eye appeal as perceived by a coin critic, perhaps with the appeal rated from 1 to 10 (with 1 being ugly and 10 being gorgeous). Of course, this would be a matter of opinion, as is the assigning of a grading number. However, critics would become known for their taste, as are reviewers of books, movies, and concerts, and even wine tasters.

4. A hologram record would be kept of each coin (similar to what the GIA does now for diamonds), to prevent switching, resubmissions, and the like, and to serve as an identification of this particular specimen.

It can be argued that items 1 and 3 are a matter of opinion, but that is no different from the situation today, when we have only the first item, and it is a matter of opinion. To my mind, number 3 could become very valuable, depending upon the reviewers identified. For example, if the late Lester Merkin were alive today and were such a reviewer, a holder with his opinion given would have great meaning to me.

The above features would not eliminate the human element, but I know that if I saw a coin described as MS-65, with Full Details, and rated as a 9 or 10 in eye appeal by a critic I respected, I would have every reason to believe that this, indeed, was a worthwhile consideration for purchase.

CHAPTER EIGHT

QUALITY AND VALUE FOR THE SMART BUYER

Good coins bought intelligently will result in pleasure and, more than likely, profit. The greatest profit you derive from your collection you cannot measure in dollars and cents. Your collection will give you pleasure—and happiness is what we're all striving for.

—B. Max Mehl, November 1953

What is it worth—$225? $195? $240? $185? $200? Today there are many different places to obtain price information—perhaps too many. This is particularly true for common coins in popular series. So many choices, so little time!

For example, if you were to check the market price of a commonly traded 1882-CC Morgan dollar in Mint State (specifically discussed below), and if you were to review price guides as well as dealer offerings in print and on the Internet, you would have hundreds of different numbers at your fingertips for just about any grade category you selected. The same could be said for a 1924 or other common-date double eagle, or a 1931-S Lincoln cent (one of the lower-mintage issues, but saved in quantity), a 1949-S Franklin half dollar, or a 1968-S Proof set.

This is information overload.

An analogy can be drawn to references for words in the English language. I happen to use the *Encarta Dictionary* (a really basic listing by Microsoft, but conveniently loaded on my laptop computer) as a quick guide. Beyond that I occasionally consult the *Encyclopaedia Britannica*, also on my computer, or go to my library for something more comprehensive, such as the *Oxford English Dictionary*. If someone came to me and said, "Dave, I have a collection of 200 different dictionaries published in the past hundred years. Do you want them as a gift?" I would say no! For 99% of the information I need, the *Encarta Dictionary* on my laptop does just fine.

As to coin prices, for a long time in the rare coin business I have used the *Guide Book of United States Coins* for basic information about mintages and approximate values at a glance. For current prices, the

Coin Dealer Newsletter plus the weekly prices posted in *Numismatic News* and the magazine-style *Coin Values* (by Mark Ferguson for *Coin World*) usually fill in the gaps. Seldom do I have to look further, except for coins traded as commodities—such as low-grade common-date gold.

These standard pricing sources have served as reference points, to which is added my own experience as to how quickly an item might sell and, perhaps even more important than any other price source, my evaluation of the quality and sharpness of the coin itself (as with the 1857-C gold dollar discussed below). The population reports for certified coins published by ANACS, NGC, and PCGS are essential for the marketing of scarcer coins, but, as you already know from my previous remarks, these estimates need to be used with caution.

In instances of particularly rare or obscure coins, I will frequently search through auction catalogs or my extensive reference files. Often this is challenging and a lot of fun. I recall spending the better part of a day or two describing the rare 1787 Brasher doubloon featured in the 1979 catalog for the Garrett Collection (sold for The Johns Hopkins University). Dr. Richard ("Rick") Bagg spent even more time on this research, a week or more, including work in historical archives. When the coin crossed the auction block, it sold for an amazing $725,000—more than any other rarity of any kind had ever realized before!

For 90% or more of the federal regular-issue coins from 1793 to date that come my way, a few handy price guides suffice, plus an evaluation of each coin itself (sharpness, eye appeal, etc., in addition to grade).

However, rare die varieties in the federal series can be challenging.

Tokens, medals, and paper money require more effort, as offerings of certain issues are few and far between and quality varies. For out-of-the-way pattern coins, colonial issues, Betts medals, encased postage stamps, or perhaps a seldom-seen Civil War token from West Virginia or a $3 bill from the Exchange Bank of Shiawassee, Michigan, some real digging must be done—great fun!

It is my aim in this chapter to acquaint you with techniques and strategies of coin pricing, particularly useful in the federal series, not only so you can be cautious when offered a coin that is readily available, but so you'll know when to "stretch" and pay more than popularly published market prices. This is especially important in relation to planchet quality, surface appearance (brilliance and toning), sharpness of strike, and eye appeal. Use the "Full Details" (FD) technique when examining certified coins—while most of your competitors are unaware! More about FD later in this chapter.

No great collection was ever formed by bargain hunting. Seeking good values is always desirable, but there are times when, in order to get a prized piece, you may have to outbid all others and set a new price record. The nice part of this is that today's record price is often tomorrow's bargain. Besides, if you capture a rarity in this manner at auction, you own the coin the morning after, while everyone else is still scrambling to find one!

Surface Quality Can Affect Price

The Popular 1882-CC Silver Dollar

The 1882-CC Morgan silver dollar is an example of a coin that is plentiful in Mint State and that, when found, is usually fairly attractive and well struck. It is one of a half dozen or so Carson City dollars of this era from the fabulous Treasury hoard that came to light in quantity in the 1960s. Ear-

lier, I gave some pricing and rarity information about a related dollar, the 1884-CC. These dollars are fantastically popular and are in perennial demand. As most 1884-CC dollars have excellent surface quality, one of high quality can be found, and easily, for the standard market price.

Of the 1882-CC only 1,133,000 were minted—a rather low figure for a Morgan dollar. It was struck at the Carson City Mint, one of the most romantic of all minting locations—in the Wild West near the silver discovery of the Comstock Lode, with Wells Fargo stagecoaches rolling across the landscape!

There is a great deal of fascinating history related to the 1882-CC. Among other sources, you might want to check my 1993 two-volume study, *Silver Dollars and Trade Dollars of the United States: A Complete Encyclopedia* (now out of print), or the easily available and inexpensive *Guide Book of Morgan Silver Dollars* (published by Whitman and distributed just about everywhere).

In brief, although the mintage of the 1882-CC was small, there was little demand for such coins in circulation in the 1880s. These and other Morgan dollars were struck not for depositors of silver bullion, nor to meet any need in commerce, but as part of a political hornswoggle—the Bland-Allison Act of February 28, 1878. Silver prices were depressed, and western mining interests influenced politicians to buy millions of ounces of this metal and coin it into the highest current denomination—the dollar.

At the Carson City Mint, these freshly minted, but commercially unneeded, silver dollars were dumped into cloth bags containing 1,000 coins each, which were then tossed into vaults. The Carson City Mint ceased coining in 1893. In the early 20th century, most of the millions of coins stored there, including many 1882-CC dollars, were shipped by rail to Washington, DC, and stored in the Treasury Building, located a few steps from the White House. The dollars were largely forgotten, although now and then a few would be paid out into circulation or to those asking for

An 1882-CC Morgan silver dollar.

silver dollars at the Treasury's cash window. Many silver dollars with CC mintmarks were also shipped to the San Francisco Mint and put in vaults.

In time, the 1882-CC was viewed by numismatists as scarce. Few were aware that many hundreds of thousands remained in storage. In the 1930s several dealers (including John Zug, of Bowie, Maryland, and collector-dealer Harry X Boosel, stationed in Washington) got some Mint State coins from the Treasury and sold them for $2 to $2.25 each; they quickly sold out. These were viewed as stray coins paid out by the Treasury, and a continuing supply was not expected to be available.

By 1955, the market price for an Uncirculated 1882-CC dollar was $8 to $10. In that year, about 50 bags (50,000 coins) were released by the Treasury Department, this according to dealer Steve Ruddel, who bought many of them. The market price fell to $3 each or a bit less. However, by 1959 the market had absorbed these, and prices rose, soon surpassing their previous highs. Beginning in November 1962, and continuing until March 1964, there was a run on silver dollars held by banks, the Treasury Department, and other institutions, and most stocks were cleared out. The price of silver was rising on international markets, and silver dollars at face value seemed to be a safe investment. During this time a few bags of 1882-CC dollars were released, but the variety remained quite scarce.

In early 1964, the Treasury stopped paying out silver dollars and took stock of what it still had on hand. For the 1882-CC this amounted to 605,029 coins, or more than half of the total original mintage! Later, the General Services Administration branch of the government auctioned these. Most were in grades that today would be called MS-60 to MS-63, but some higher level examples were also found. Today, the 1882-CC dollars are widely scattered. Although there are more of them in the hands of collectors than in the days when the market price was $10, the circle of numismatists interested in such coins has expanded vastly—due to the availability of so many different Morgan dollars in high grades and the expanding popularity of coin collecting in general—so that price levels today are significantly higher than in the past.

Because of the preceding circumstances, the 1882-CC dollar is unusual in that *in worn grades* the variety is much scarcer than in Mint State. I estimate that fewer than 20,000 circulated coins exist! However, they are not worth as much as Mint State coins.

Determining Prices for the 1882-CC Dollar

In 2005, I checked a few standard printed sources for prices of an 1882-CC dollar in MS-63 grade. Because prices change, these will not be current at a later date, but they do serve to illustrate the point.

- *A Guide Book of Morgan Silver Dollars* (2nd edition): $250.
- *A Guide Book of United States Coins*, 59th edition (Whitman Publishing): $225.
- *Coin Values* (published by *Coin World*) issue of July 4, 2005: $275.
- *Coin Market* (published by *Numismatic News*) issue of July 2005: $245.
- *Certified Coin Dealer Newsletter* ("Blue Sheet"), February 5, 2005, for NGC coins: "market," $190; for PCGS coins, also "market"; $190. ("Client or sight-seen sales may command a *substantial premium* above Blue Sheet dealer-to-dealer bids."[32])

Beyond that, a check of a few dozen offerings by dealers in *Coin World* and *Numismatic News*, and on the Internet, showed prices from about $225 to $325.

Significantly, *none* of the listings stated anything about the sharpness or weakness of strike or the eye appeal, although the word "brilliant" was sometimes seen. In the instance of the 1882-CC it is likely that most coins for sale were decent strikes, for they generally come that way.

Without question, if you could gather together on a table actual specimens representing 100 different MS-63 1882-CC dollars for sale, and if you were given your choice of just one, there would be a special piece you select.

Probably, if I were buying such coins for resale, there would be no more than 50 I would pick out with a combination of good luster, not too many distracting marks, and good eye appeal. For me, 50 is a large number to select from a group of 100, and this is only because the 1882-CC usually is found in "nice" condition. In the same group of 100 I would no doubt see some coins that I would not grade even MS-62, and a few with gouges or defects that I might not want at any price.

To summarize the preceding, it seems that $275 or so was a typical retail valuation for an MS-63 1882-CC dollar when I did this study. Some casual searching would be needed to find a quality coin, but no great effort would be required. If I were seeking a really choice one for my collection and were offered a gorgeous 1882-CC for $275 or even a bit more, I would buy it. On the other hand, if I were offered a very nice coin for $400, I would not buy it, for I would be aware that there are enough others around that I could buy one for less without much difficulty.

The Curious 1857-C Gold Dollars

To the uninitiated, the methodology for determining prices of various United States coins is the same for most series—but to the informed buyer there are many differences. Again, no single rule fits all. The relative ease of finding a sharp, lustrous, and

The 1857-C gold dollar (enlarged) is one of the more interesting issues of that denomination. All examples have problems of one sort or another, such as a defective planchets, weak striking, or imperfect reeding. This is one of the finest Harry W. Bass, Jr., was able to find in more than 30 years of collecting. The coin was cataloged as EF-45, but with planchet porosity and striking weakness at the 18 of the date. (Lot 117 in the Harry W. Bass, Jr., Sale II, October 1999; earlier from Abe Kosoff's ANA Sale, August 1968, Lot 1447. Courtesy of the Harry W. Bass, Jr., Foundation)

attractive 1882-CC Morgan dollar is dramatically different from the situation confronting anyone seeking a quality 1857-C gold dollar. First of all, forget completely the idea of finding one in such grades as MS-63 or finer, as they do not exist. As to *quality*, read further.

Numismatically speaking, the 1857-C gold dollar and its story and characteristics are about as different from the 1882-CC silver dollar as is the town of Kezar Falls, Maine, from New York City. Both locations have people, cars, vending machines, pet cats, Internet connections, stores, and houses—but there are so many differences.

Both the 1857-C gold dollar and the 1882-CC dollar have a date, mintmark, portrait of Miss Liberty, and reeded edge, were struck under federal auspices, and are legal tender—but other characteristics are like night and day.

In 1857, at the Charlotte Mint, production facilities were rather primitive. A small staff, using low-capacity presses (not strong enough to strike any coins of diameter larger than a five-dollar gold coin, which was about the size of a nickel), turned out 13,280 gold dollars. The planchets used were made from roughly finished metal strip, often with flakes, irregularities, and defects. Little attention was paid to the quality of striking, either, and most 1857-C gold dollars appeared rather decrepit the moment they left the dies—with some parts of the lettering or design indistinct and with a rough planchet surface. There was absolutely no quality control, and no one cared. Moreover, there was no numismatic interest in this or any other Charlotte Mint coins, nor would there be for many years. Not even the Mint Cabinet wanted a coin for its display.

Today this might seem illogical. Yet in the November 1867 issue of *Mason's Coin and Stamp Collectors' Magazine*, E.L. Mason, Jr., pointed out the lack of knowledge and interest in mintmarks a decade after the 1857-C dollars were struck: "Our readers," he wrote, "have doubtless noticed the capital C on many U.S. gold coins, without knowing its signification. We would here state that all coins bearing the letter C are coined at Charlotte, N.C...."

It was not until many years later that Charlotte gold coins became of significant numismatic interest, beginning with the publication in 1893 of *A Treatise on Mint Marks*, by Augustus G. Heaton. By this time, the opportunity to acquire a Mint State 1857-C dollar was long gone, and those that existed were likely to be well worn—this in addition to their being poorly struck to begin with.

Fast-forward to the late 20th century, when a great interest—indeed passion—developed for collecting gold dollars by date and mintmark variety, leading to the study of the series by several scholars, including Walter Breen, David Akers, and Paul F. Taglione, Jr.

From the late 1980s onward, numerical grading alone was used by most sellers of 1857-C gold dollars, including coins certified by ANACS, NGC, and PCGS. For naïve buyers a number such as EF-40 sufficed. For this particular variety of gold dollar, though, there was *much* more to the equation.

There were some informed buyers who realized that the 1857-C gold dollar got the cellar-hole award, the booby prize, for its poor quality of striking. They came to realize that except for a few early impressions, which are slightly better than the rest, this issue is usually wretched. The striking is poor, the dentils are poorly defined, and the planchets are defective.

David W. Akers, in his 1975 study on gold dollars, stated, "The planchets used for striking 1857-C gold dollars were downright atrocious, as was the quality of minting. Even the best available specimens look terrible, and are very difficult to grade." *Walter Breen's Complete Encyclopedia of U.S. and Colonial Coins*, 1988, included this: "Planchets are virtually always defective, and striking is irregular." And Douglas Winter, in his 1998 book, *Gold Coins of the Charlotte Mint, 1838–1861*, commented that the "1857-C gold dollar generally shows a very poor strike.... This date is almost always found with severe mint-made planchet defects. The obverse fields have an irregular almost 'wavy' look, while the reverse is frequently very rough at the center...."

If the moment you read these words you pause to reflect, it will seem obvious that buying an 1857-C gold dollar requires a completely different approach from that used to buy an 1882-CC Morgan silver dollar. *You* now know this, but probably 90% of others in the numismatic community do not!

As for the number of 1857-C gold dollars known today, my estimate is 170 to 250, all but a few in circulated grades, plus two or three low-level Mint State coins. Doug Winter suggests that only about 100 to 110 are known. Either way, the 1857-C is very elusive.

Determining Prices for 1857-C Gold Dollars

The following listings are from *The Official RED BOOK® of Auction Records 1994–2003*, first edition, by Jeff Garrett and John Dannreuther. Bear in mind that these sales took place over a period of time, and that the prices should be analyzed with the auction descriptions themselves and with certification information (not given), and also the realization that some figures are not relevant to the current market. The point is simply to show that variations in price can be considerable. These are *all* of the sales recorded for 1857-C gold dollars described as Extremely Fine:

1995—EF: $770 • EF-40: $1,210 • EF-45: $1,100.

1996—Choice EF: $1,045 • EF-40: $2,090 • EF-45: $990 • EF-45: $1,100.

1997—EF: $4,950 • EF: $1,840 • EF-40: $1,265.

1998—None.

1999—EF: $4,370 • EF-40: $1,955 • EF-40: $3,450 • EF-45: $5,520.

2000—EF-40: $1,150 • EF-40: $1,725 • EF-45: $1,725.

2001—EF: $1,380.

2002—EF-40: $1,150.

As to what conclusions to draw from the preceding, it is obvious that auction offerings of EF 1857-C gold dollars are relatively infrequent. When they do appear, prices are apt to vary widely, sales of the year 1999 being particularly dramatic in this regard. The *Official RED BOOK® of Auction Records* simply lists grades and prices and gives no details concerning the actual appearance or quality of the coins.

Certainly the star performer in 1997 was the coin that brought $4,950. This was in the John Jay Pittman Collection, Part I, cataloged by David W. Akers, and offered as follows:

> Lot 878: 1857-C, Extremely Fine or better. A bit on the dull side, but with attractive light orange gold color. Very weak at the borders with considerable signs of die deterioration in the denticles. There is also evidence of significant die deterioration within the wreath at OL and 18 of that date. Purchased from Stack's 6/20/63 Walton sale, Lot 28, for $155.

The coin, not certified, brought a remarkable price among 1997 auction offerings. No doubt the Pittman provenance helped, as is often the case when old-time collections are sold. The "or better" part of the description may indicate that two or more bidders thought the coin was conservatively graded and perhaps could be certified as AU. Regardless of such variables, the authoritative description of die details no doubt served to attract advanced gold-dollar specialists who could envision exactly what they were getting. However, in 1999 that price was eclipsed by $5,520 realized by an EF-45 coin.

Although prices are not easy to find for the 1857-C gold dollar, in July 2005 these were available in standard, widely used guides, the figures representing all of the price levels listed by each:

Coin Values (published by *Coin World*)— F-12: Not listed • VF-20: $1,200 • EF-40: $1,800 • AU-50: $4,000 • AU-55: $7,000 • AU-58: $10,000 • MS-60: $15,000 • MS-63: Not listed.

Coin Market (published by *Numismatic News*)—F-12: $800 • VF-20: $950 • EF-40: $1,400 • AU-50: $2,750 • AU-55: Not listed • AU-58: Not listed • MS-60: $10,500 • MS-63: $29,000.

A Guide Book of United States Coins (59th ed., published by Whitman)— F-12: Not listed • VF-20; $1,000 • EF-40: $1,500 • AU-50: $3,500 • AU-55: $5,500 • AU-58: Not listed • MS-60: $12,500 • MS-63: $29,000.

Absent a technical knowledge of gold dollars in general and the 1857-C in particular, the casual reader of each of the above highly-regarded price sources would not be aware that the typical 1857-C is rather crude and rustic in appearance. Moreover, the prices vary from listing to listing. *Coin Values* places the worth of an AU-55 coin at $7,000, while the *Guide Book* suggests $5,500, or $1,500 less—this differential being about the price of *two* VF-20 coins. There is nothing wrong with this, as prices of other coins vary as well. If anything, the illustration shows that it is useful for you to consider multiple sources of information.

Each of the three sources prices coins at the EF-40 level, with values of $1,800, $1,400, and $1,500, respectively, or an average of $1,566.

Earlier-quoted auction prices show coins specifically graded as EF-40 (ignoring those not certified and also those listed as EF-45) as follows, narrowing the list considerably:

1995—EF-40 (NGC) $1,210.

1996—EF-40, $2,090.

1997—EF-40, $1,265.

1999—EF-40, $1,955 • EF-40 $3,450.

2000—EF-40 $1,150 • EF-40 $1,725

2002—EF-40 $1,150.

In 2002, an EF-40 coin sold for $1,150, or only a third of the $3,450 price another coin fetched in 1999. Now, the question: how does an intelligent, well-informed buyer go about acquiring an EF-40 1857-C gold dollar? How much should be paid for it?

The variables are considerable. As to what an EF coin is worth, this is hard to say. Strike and eye appeal are exceedingly important for this particular variety. If I were collecting gold dollars and were offered a scruffy coin for $1,000, I would not buy it, even though this is a nice discount from the $1,566 current average listed price. On the other hand, if I were offered a fairly sharp specimen with above-average eye appeal for $3,000, or double current value, I would be a buyer.

Someone else might feel differently, and grab the $1,000 coin as a great bargain and reject the $3,000 piece as vastly overpriced.

Among gold dollars, no single rule fits all. An 1857 *Philadelphia* Mint gold dollar, quite unlike its 1857-C cousin, is often seen with attractive surfaces and well struck—not much of a problem at all!

Most buyers of coins are clueless as to variations in striking and quality and can scarcely envision that two coins of the same denomination, made in the same year—the 1857 and the 1857-C—can be as different as night and day. To them, price is everything. To *you*, I hope that quality is also a factor—an important distinction.

A Tentative "Standard Catalog" Listing

In 1960 and 1961, I discussed with John J. Ford, Jr., and Olga Raymond (widow of Wayte Raymond) my possible editorship of a new edition of the *Standard Catalogue of United States Coins*, the previous (18th) edition of which had been published in 1958.[33] This editorship almost happened, but did not. Later, certain of the rights were sold to Western Publishing Company, and with Kenneth E. Bressett of Western I had similar, but more casual, discussions. Creating such a work is on my "to-do someday" list!

Perhaps an *excerpt* for the listings for, say, gold dollars of 1857 would look something like the following.

Gold Dollars of 1857

1857 Gold Dollar (Philadelphia Issue, No Mintmark)

Mintage. 774,789 circulation strikes; estimated 5 to 7 Proofs.

Estimated Number Known in Mint State. 400 to 600. Mint State specimens of the 1857 are scarce to rare, and represent but a tiny fraction surviving from the generous mintage. Most of these are in grades from MS-60 through MS-63, with only a few higher. Thus, the 1857 is available in Mint State, but is a *rarity* at the gem level. The usually seen 1857 has lustrous surfaces with hairlines (rather than nicks), and hovers around MS-60. A handful of gems are mentioned in auction literature. Such coins must be regarded as exceedingly rare.

Gem Mint State (MS-67) gold dollar (enlarged) from the Bass Collection. (Lot 115 in the Harry W. Bass, Jr., Sale II, October 1999; earlier from Malcolm Varner, April 21, 1979. Courtesy of the Harry W. Bass, Jr., Foundation)

Estimated Number Known in Circulated Grades. 7,000 to 12,000. Very plentiful. If only 2% existed from the original mintage, this would indicate a population of more than 15,000 coins.

Estimated Number Known in Proof. 5 to 7. Proof 1857 gold dollars were probably struck individually in one or more short press runs. These were furnished to numismatists for face value plus a small charge. So far as is known, no full Proof sets (all denominations from the cent through the $20 piece) were made. In recently checking some notes I made in 1957, I see that Walter Breen and I both agreed that about 5 to 7 Proofs were known of this date (one of which I purchased from New Netherlands Coin Co. about this time, along with an 1856). Today I find that estimate still acceptable, although David W. Akers (Pittman I sale, 1997, Lot 876) suggests 10 to 12. Of course, the exact number will never be known. I have always felt that gold and silver Proofs of 1857 are slightly scarcer than those dated 1856.

In March 1911, in his catalog of the William H. Woodin Collection, Thomas L. Elder described Lot 859 as follows: "1857. Brilliant Proof. Excessively rare. The only record I find of public sale was the Wilson specimen, which sold for $20, which would seem a low price considering its great rarity." The coin realized $25 to Virgil M. Brand. This listing is interesting and seems to suggest that Elder, one of the most important dealers of his time—a man who often emphasized numismatic study and research—must have evaluated the rarity of this coin carefully. However, he couldn't have, or he would have found quite a few earlier auction offerings, including John F. McCoy Collection (W. Elliot Woodward), May 1865, Lot 2002; Bache, Bertsch, Lightbody, Lilliendahl, Vinton, and Watson Collections (W. Elliot Woodward), March 1863, Lot 2831 (to Mendes I. Cohen, this coin later appearing in Edward D. Cogan's sale of the Cohen Collection, October 1875, Lot 243); Henry Adams Collection (Edward Cogan), June 1876, Lot 1338; Thomas Warner Collection (S.H. and Henry Chapman) June 1884, Lot 2629; John G. Mills Collection (S.H. and Henry Chapman), April 1904, Lot 636; and David S. Wilson Collection (S.H. Chapman), March 1907, Lot 290.

Die Data. 1857 four-digit date logotype: Numerals fairly widely and evenly spaced. The 1 leans slightly right. Top interior of the 8 smaller than bottom interior. The 5 is of the upright type, but not enough to be called italic or slanting. The 7 has a delicate top, the upper left serif being large and slanting right. This logotype was used on all gold-dollar dies of all mints.

Characteristics of Striking and Die Notes. Sometimes well struck, but usually not. Some show evidence of clashed dies. Dentils are fuzzy on some pieces, and a few are lightly struck on the high points of the portrait and near the center of the reverse, from the dies' being spaced slightly too far apart. Others have been cataloged as having been struck from rusted dies. Full Details (FD) coins are a possibility, but extensive cherrypicking is required to find one! Henry Chapman, in his June 1908 sale of the Taylor, Windle, and Lincoln Collections, described Lot 480 as follows: "1857 Die sunken under head. Uncirculated."

Numismatic Commentary. By most reasoning, the 1857 gold dollar, with a mintage not far short of a million coins, should be easy to find in choice Mint State preservation. However, it is not, and dealers and specialists have realized this for a long time. For example, in his June 1951 offering of duplicates from the King Farouk Collection, B. Max Mehl listed this as Lot 1794: "1857. Brilliant Uncirculated with full mint luster. Catalogs for only $10, but I think it is worth more in this beautiful condition." The coin met the cataloger's expectations and realized $12.60. For Paramount's section of Auction '81, Lot 1344, David W. Akers included this:

1857, Superb Gem Uncirculated 67. A magnificent coin with full original mint luster and very pretty natural greenish gold toning. A bit weak at some of the denticles (due to weakness in the dies, not strike) and softly struck on feathers at the top of Liberty's headdress. Both obverse and reverse show evidence of light clashing of the dies. There is one tiny mark on Liberty's cheek but the coin is otherwise absolutely perfect. Like the 1856 this is a relatively common date in circulated grades but in superb condition such as this, it is really very rare, much more so than any of the low mintage dates of the 1880s. All things considered, this coin is just about as pretty and choice as a gold dollar can be!

1857-C Gold Dollar

Mintage. 13,280 circulation strikes.

Estimated Number Known in Mint State. 2 or 3. *An extreme rarity.* It is likely that some of these would be called AU by certain observers. Thus, the 1857-C is a great *sleeper* in Mint State, but because the aesthetic appeal of high-grade pieces is very low, there has never been much excitement about them. David W. Akers (1975) wrote, "Because even Uncirculated specimens generally have such a poor appearance, they rarely bring prices that are commensurate with their true rarity."

Estimated Number Known in Circulated Grades. 170 to 250. This figure may be optimistic (Douglas Winter in his study of the series suggests that only about 100 to 110 are known). Virtually all observers agree that 1857-C is much rarer than its mintage suggests.

Die Data. Date logotype as described for the 1857 Philadelphia issue. Walter Breen (1988) states that there are "three minor varieties" of the 1857-C, while Douglas Winter (1998) states that just one pair of dies was employed. The 1857-C dollars have a significantly larger mintmark than seen on the next earlier issue from Charlotte, the 1855-C.

A duplicate 1857-C gold dollar (enlarged) from the Bass Collection. The coin was cataloged as EF-45, but with roughness in the obverse field, weak at an area of the edge reeding, and on a defective planchet. (Lot 52 in the Harry W. Bass, Jr., Sale IV, November 2000; earlier from Stack's sale of December 1972, Lot 496. Courtesy of the Harry W. Bass, Jr., Foundation)

Characteristics of Striking and Die Notes. The 1857-C gold dollar gets the cellarhole award for the poor quality of striking. Except for a few early impressions, which are slightly better than the others, this issue is usually wretched. The striking is poor, the dentils are poorly defined, and the planchets defective. Full Details (FD) coins are nonexistent. David W. Akers (1975): "The planchets used for striking 1857-C gold dollars were downright atrocious, as was the quality of minting. Even the best available specimens look terrible, and are very difficult to grade." Walter Breen (*Encyclopedia*, 1988): "Planchets are virtually always defective, and striking is irregular." Douglas Winter (1998): "The 1857-C gold dollar generally shows a very poor strike.... This date is almost always found with severe mint-made planchet defects. The obverse fields have an irregular almost 'wavy' look, while the reverse is frequently very rough at the center...." Winter noted that there are a few coins which are of better quality.

Numismatic Commentary. See pages 120–123.

1857-D Gold Dollar

Mintage. 3,533 circulation strikes. Mintage took place in April (1,896) and November (1,637). The number of additional pieces made for assay is not known.

Estimated Number Known in Mint State. 4 to 6. *Very rare* in Mint State. More Mint State examples of the famous 1860-D and

One of the finer known 1857-D gold dollars (enlarged), much sharper than normally seen, but still with some dentils weak and with some lightness on the higher-relief areas. Graded AU-58. (Lot 119 in the Harry W. Bass, Jr., Sale II, October 1999; earlier from Paramount's Auction '85 Sale, July 1985, Lot 137. Courtesy of the Harry W. Bass, Jr., Foundation)

1861-D have come on the market, by far, than have those of 1857-D. All known pieces are poorly struck—this based upon the collected observations of modern catalogers. As is true of the 1857-C, Full Details (FD) 1857-D gold dollars do not exist. Certain high-grade 1857-D coins, including Mint State, were blithely listed years ago without any information concerning striking (see citations below). It is presumed that these were also poorly struck.

Estimated Number Known in Circulated Grades. 40 to 60. The 1857-D is often compared to the 1858-D of somewhat comparable mintage. However, the 1857-D is by far the rarer of the two issues. In 1975, David W. Akers commented, "In my opinion, this date is one of the most underrated Type III gold dollars. In the 192 auction catalogs surveyed, the 1857-D was offered *10 times less* than the highly regarded 1860-D."

Die Data. Date logotype as described for the 1857 Philadelphia issue. Two obverse and two 1856-dated reverse dies were sent from Philadelphia on November 26, 1856, and arrived in Dahlonega on January 4, 1857.[34]

Characteristics of Striking and Die Notes. The 1858-D is always seen poorly struck, especially on the higher features. Miss Liberty's headdress typically lacks detail. In fact, the striking is so poor that catalogers of auction sales, who often overlook such aspects, mention this feature with frequency (of course, certification services

always overlook the strike quality and assign just a single number for grade). A number of pieces, perhaps the majority, show evidence of die clashing (the coming together of the dies without an intervening planchet, with resultant die damage), and some show a die crack above the wreath. The reverse is usually weak at the border, from 10 o'clock to 2 o'clock (moving clockwise), and at 85 (in 1857). On some, the reverse is relapped (resurfaced by grinding) with a heavy hand used by the machinist(s) at the Dahlonega Mint. In many ways the 1857-D can be compared to the 1857-C. The poor striking of the 1857-D gold dollar is not reflected in grades assigned by the certification services (nor should it be, as striking is a separate situation). In the absence of reading a specialized text, such as David W. Akers's excellent 1975 study, or Birdsall's definitive 1984 book on the Dahlonega Mint, or Breen's 1988 *Encyclopedia*, the casual collector would have no way of knowing about the characteristics of striking.

Numismatic Commentary. It was not until the 1890s that the 1858-D and other mintmarks in the gold dollar series attracted the attention of numismatists. In the early 20th century this variety appeared with some regularity in auction sales, particularly of important collections, but hardly ever with any mention of weakness or other striking characteristics. It was not until the 1950s that detailed notations were widely used, as in this description by James F. Kelly for the Chi-ANA Convention Sale, August 1956: Lot 1605: "1857 D Mint. Fine with mint luster. The reverse is weakly struck as usual though all letters and figures are readable. This is better than average." Today, in the early 21st century, the 1857-D is highly prized in all grades and is recognized as one of the keys to the series.

1857-S Gold Dollar

Mintage. 10,000 circulation strikes.

Estimated Number Known in Mint State. 3 or 4. *One of the great sleepers in the gold*

Choice MS-63 prooflike (PCGS) 1857-S gold dollar (enlarged), the finest certified by that service as of its auction offering. (Lot 121 in the Harry W. Bass, Jr., Sale II, October 1999; earlier from Mid-American's sale of August 1991, Lot 616. Courtesy of the Harry W. Bass, Jr., Foundation).

dollar series. The 1857-S is a major rarity in Mint State, although some estimates have ranged higher than the one given here. None have been seen at the gem (MS-65) level. In Mint State, the 1857-S is far and away the rarest San Francisco Mint gold dollar. The certification data probably represent multiple entries for a lesser number of actual specimens. None were found in the *S.S. Central America* treasure.

Estimated Number Known in Circulated Grades. 180 to 250. Virtually all of the famous collections over the years have had EF or AU specimens, sometimes VF, but rarely Mint State. Today, a quality AU coin is ranked as a rarity.

Die Data. Date logotype as described for the 1857 Philadelphia issue. Two minor die varieties are known, both with medium S mintmark.

Characteristics of Striking and Die Notes. Most 1857-S dollars are well struck. The luster on higher-grade coins tends to be satiny, rather than deeply frosty. Full Details (FD) coins are a possibility.

Numismatic Commentary. Today the 1857-S gold dollar is recognized as scarce in any grade and as a condition rarity in choice AU or better preservation. Among the earlier numismatic recognitions of the elusive nature of this variety is the description by Federal Brand Enterprises (Michael Kolman, Jr.), in the Empire State Numismatic Association sale of July 1966, Lot 650: "1857-S Practically Uncirculated. Very sharp. Very much underrated in standard catalogs."

To the preceding descriptions could be added market values in a range of grades as well as certified-coin populations. Although such a listing for 1857 gold dollars would not impart everything that could be said about issues of this year, buyers would be able to base their purchase decisions on much more information than just a numerical grade and price (all of which can be found in market guides today).

Prices of Brilliant Coins and Toned Coins
Surface Changes on Coins

The surface of a coin—brilliant or toned—can often affect its value. In copper, such differences can be dramatic; in nickel, silver, and gold, less so.

When an Indian Head cent of 1901 (or a Morgan silver dollar of 1878, or a double eagle of 1850) was first struck, it *usually* emerged from the coining press with a bright, brilliant surface. We can dispose of the qualifier (*usually*) by simply stating that in certain instances among very early products of the Philadelphia Mint, poor-quality copper stock was used, such as for half cents of 1794, and it may have been the case that pieces just struck were somewhat gray or irregular. We have seen that a freshly minted 1857-C gold dollar might have been dull and flaky when first struck, due to a poor planchet and rough die surfaces. However, generally, copper, nickel, silver, and gold coins were brilliant when struck.

All coinage metals are chemically reactive, and from the moment a piece left the dies it was subjected to atmospheric consideration and began to change color. Even gold coins, being made of the most inert of all metals, contain 10% copper, and the copper would tone. Nonetheless, most gold coins retain nearly all of their original gold color.

In the marketplace, some toning is considered "good" and adds value, such as for certain silver coins. Other toning, such as deep gray or even black, is viewed as "bad." To some buyers, brilliant is best. To others, coins with attractive toning are preferable. Generally, except for designations within copper coins (red, red and brown, and brown), listings of market values do not address toning. Even so, it is worthwhile for you to become acquainted with the basics of the subject.

The following are my comments, metal by metal.

Copper and Bronze Coins

When first minted, copper coins have a bright *orange* color, which somehow has been translated into "red" by the grading services, who abbreviate it as "RD," as in MS-65 RD. No copper cent was ever *red* unless it was toned in some unusual manner. Though technically inaccurate, the *red* nomenclature will likely be with us forever.

Early half cents and cents were made of pure copper, or were intended to be so. Later, beginning in 1864, bronze (95% copper, 5% tin and zinc) was used for cents and the new two-cent pieces. Generally, all freshly struck coins of copper or bronze were the same orange color.

Such pieces toned rather quickly. Even light human handling would darken the surfaces, from oils and chemicals on fingers. Also, atmospheric contaminants such as sulfur would tend to darken the copper.

In time, copper and bronze coins fade from bright orange to light brown, then to rich even brown, then to medium brown. If the coin has been touched on its surfaces (as opposed to its edge) or has acquired flecks from moisture, the toning may exhibit dark patches, corrosion spots, or traces of fingerprints. Sometimes a fingerprint can be latent, not to become visible until years later.

To my knowledge, there is no such thing today as a completely *original* full mint orange (red) large copper cent of the era 1793 to 1849. Some pieces from 1850 through 1856 that were part of hoards come fairly close to having full mint color, and perhaps a handful are of full original color. Most hoard coins are orange with light toning, usually with little flecks or specks of one sort of another. Also, their edges (as viewed edge-on) are light brown.

Today, the grading services typically use "RD" to indicate a coin that is mostly original red, "RB" to indicate one that has a mixture of red and brown in no particular proportion but with significant amounts of each, and "BN" to indicate one that is brown.

It seems that there are no hard-and-fast rules in these interpretations. I have seen coins described as MS-65 RD that have flecks and finger marks on them, and while they might be original red *except* for the marks and spots, a buyer would have no way of knowing without actually seeing the coin. Coins described as RB, or red and brown, vary all over the place. Generally it seems to be the intent of the grading services to have a balance of half red and half brown, plus or minus, ranging from, say, 40% of one color to 60% of another. Certain coins with just a small percentage of brown are often called RD. Coins that are mostly brown, but with just some tinges of red (perhaps 10% to 20%), are often called BN.

More than just a few coins marketed as RD are simply coins that naturally toned over the years, but that have been brightened by dipping or other means to make them RD. Often the dipping makes the surface unstable, and there are situations in which a coin has been certified as RD, only to change color afterward—in a sealed slab!

Purchase decisions for copper coins, more than for those of any other metal, need to take visual appeal into consideration. Also, it is very important to be careful when buying coins called "RD," particularly pieces more than a few decades old. The market structure is such that many uninformed buyers will purchase only RD coins, ignoring others, thereby creating a limited "investment market" for them. To accommodate this market, many pieces have been cleaned. As discussed in detail in chapter 16, a leading specialist in Lincoln cents made note of the surface characteristics (such as little marks and other distinguishing features) of a number of high-grade 1926-S cents, and found that some of those earlier called RB had "graduated" to being fully RD and encapsulated as such—this by virtue of cleaning. However, anyone looking only at the certified holders would not know this.

There is no rule to tell whether a copper coin has been cleaned. Experience is needed. You know for sure that a copper *Proof* coin, such as an Indian Head or Lincoln cent or a two-cent piece, has been cleaned if there are hairlines on it, as such pieces were not struck with hairlines. Without hairlines, such a piece should be called Proof-65 or finer, with appropriate color added, such as Proof-65 RD, Proof-65 RB, or Proof-65 BN.

Accordingly, if you purchase a Proof-64 RD and see under magnification that it has light hairlines, you know that it has been cleaned. There is nothing necessarily wrong with this, except that the entire subject of cleaning is often swept under a rug. Accordingly, cleaning is *implicit* in such descriptions.

For example, if you see a coin described as "1907 Indian Head cent, Proof-64 RD," it probably could be fully described as "1907 Proof-64 RD, cleaned, and now with a bright surface."

If you are searching for a fully RD coin, expect it to have delicate natural toning, with some hints of brown, unless it is of fairly modern issue. The outer edges of the coin—as viewed edge-on—may be toned brown (or at least darker) from numismatic handling. This is fine and does not affect the value. A 19th-century or early 20th-century coin that is fully brilliant, including the edge as seen edge-on, is likely a piece that has been dipped.

The formation of a set of MS-65 RD (or some higher grade) Lincoln cents from 1909 through the early 1930s, with *original* surfaces, would likely take several years to complete, and even then there might be a few pieces absent, such as the 1926-S (which seems to be the needle in the haystack). Such coins, when viewed together, will be different blends of orange, ranging from fairly bright to attractive light brown.

If such Lincoln cents appeal to you, as they do to many numismatists (including me), a good strategy is to avoid pieces with spots or flecks. If you buy through a trusted dealer, just give him or her the guideline that you want no spots, no stains, no anything unattractive.

A step down from "RD" is a set of Lincoln cents in MS-65 RB. This offers a tremendous value for the price paid, in my opinion, as the designation "RB" is anathema to investors. This is good for you, the smart buyer! Of course, more than just a few investors are happy to buy an RB piece if dipped and certified as RD.

Purchasing copper and bronze coins requires quite a bit of patience. If I were buying pieces for a fine collection, I would choose only coins that are attractive, without blotches, spots, or staining. The toning should be nicely blended, with some areas brighter red than others, and some brown areas being light brown to dark brown. The transition should be gradual, not abrupt or splotchy.

Among certain early Indian Head cents (and also for Lincoln cents of the first year of issue, 1909), the planchet-rolling process was such that the alloy components of bronze did not always mix completely, and when the strips were rolled out certain of the unmixed metals became distended or elongated. Years later, when such pieces became naturally toned, the brown was in the form of parallel streaks, difficult to describe in print, but easy enough to recognize when seen. This is called "wood-grain" toning by specialists, and is considered desirable. In fact, Rick Snow, a leading specialist in the Indian Head cent, once illustrated the cover of a book with a coin exhibiting splendid wood-grain toning.

There are other variations in the alloys of coins, and, for example, 1909-S Indian Head cents were produced in a bronze that toned a pale yellow color, rather than a darker orange—quite distinctive. Copper experts are very well aware of this, and they know that a 1909-S Indian Head cent that has been dipped and then artificially retoned is apt to be the normal orange-brown color seen on many other cents, such as 1907 Philadelphia Mint examples.

Copper coins with brown toning constitute the vast majority of examples in existence. For aficionados of early copper large cents, a rich brown coloration is often preferred to just about anything else, including red and brown. Of course, a fully *original* mint red specimen would be nicer, but as such do not exist, and as most RB early copper cents are blotched or spotted (such as those from the Randall Hoard, containing dates from 1816 to 1820), a rich brown coin becomes a satisfying goal. I expect that if a survey were to be taken of old-time collectors of early copper cents, lustrous, rich brown surfaces would be preferred to those showing original red—except in the fairly rare instances in which there is no spotting or staining. It is likely the case that there is no such thing as a fully red copper cent of *any* date from 1793 to 1814, the early range of the series. John Kraljevich, who has studied the series closely, suggests that the two closest to this goal may be a 1793 Sheldon-5 cent once in the William Cutler Atwater Collection and an 1807 S-271 formerly owned by R.E. Naftzger, Jr.[35] Lustrous brown examples are seen now and again, and these are highly prized.

Among later cents in the Indian Head and Lincoln series there are many attractive brown-toned coins, including in the MS-65 BN and Proof-65 BN categories. Often Proof Indian Head cents tone with a hint of blue. Many years ago I purchased a very large hoard of Proof Indian Head cents from the 1880s that had been acquired by dealer William L. Pukall, probably with earlier links to J. Colvin Randall or John W. Haseltine. Each and every one of these coins was unbelievably beautiful—rich brown with hints of blue. Pukall also had other coins toned brown, including quite a few Matte Proof Lincoln cents of the 1909 to 1916 era. These matte pieces were issued by the Mint in thin paper wrappers, which quickly toned the surface. While some such pieces exist today as Matte Proof RB, the vast majority of the examples I have seen called Matte Proof-65 RD have been dipped.

While RB copper and bronze coins are not particularly desired by investors, this category of buyers thinks even less of coins that are BN. This offers a rich playground of opportunity. If I were putting together a set of bronze Indian Head cents from 1864 through 1909, and wanted some good value for my money, I would pick a combination of MS-65 BN and MS-65 RB. The same goes for the Proofs of BN and RB designations.

The surfaces of copper coins can be enhanced by careful conservation. This is particularly true of early copper large cents of 1793 to 1857. A camel's hair brush, run across the surface of a coin in, say, EF grade, often removes grease and makes it more attractive. This procedure was used by most old-timers and, in fact, is mentioned rather frequently in the literature, including in the early issues of *Penny-Wise*, a journal of the Early American Coppers Club. Some mineral oil applied to a surface of a copper coin can minimize the effects of porosity, and other procedures best known to coin conservators can be employed. On process used years ago (and sometimes even today) was to take an early cent and "strip it down" to the basic copper, making it unnaturally bright orange in the process, but allowing spots and stains to be removed, then recolor it to a pleasing brown hue, sometimes using powdered sulfur. The technique for doing this is given in Dr. William H. Sheldon's 1949 book, *Early American Cents*. This is generally frowned upon now. Accordingly, those who use such a process usually keep mum.

Nickel Coins

What we call nickel coins are actually made of an alloy of 75% copper and 25% nickel. A correct nickname would be to call these *coppers*, but, of course, we don't. Nickels they are.

A nickel coin, when first struck, tends to be nearly as bright as silver, but not quite as brilliant. In time, nickel will tone to a warm mixture that can best be described as a combination of blue and yellow. In the field of antique slot machines, such as those made by Caille and Mills a century ago, restorers are careful to nickel-plate the metal parts, although *chrome* plating would make them even brighter and more brilliant. It is the subtle nickel tone that is desired.

With the passage of time, some nickel coins will take on a yellow-brown hue. Liberty, Buffalo, and early Jefferson nickels are sometimes seen with attractive, light iridescent hues, often halo-like, changing from the rims inward. A lot of this is "album toning," from storage in cardboard albums of the National, Whitman, and other brands. Shield nickels, not often stored in albums, are usually toned more evenly.

Quite a few nickels have flecks or spots, these being particularly annoying on Proofs. Avoid such pieces. Nickels that have been repeatedly dipped are sometimes dull. Avoid these as well.

A lustrous Mint State nickel should have lots of "life" to it. Finding such pieces can be a challenge, especially among Shield nickels of the earlier dates (1866–1876) and Liberty Head nickels of the 1880s and 1890s. Some Jefferson nickels have greasy- or grainy-appearing surfaces caused by worn or tired dies. This is particularly the case for issues of the late 1940s through the 1960s, although there are many exceptions.

To my eyes, the best nickels are those with original brilliance enhanced by delicate blue or gold toning. I avoid deeply toned coins, as well as any and all with spots or stains. Selecting nickel coins for quality

A particularly choice 1869 Proof Shield nickel, this one graded Proof-66. Finding examples of this quality can be a challenging but rewarding pursuit.

is easier than selecting those struck in copper, but care and patience are still required.

Silver Coins

The most valuable silver coins are those with full brilliance or with attractive toning. Except for silver dollars from old hoards, fully brilliant coins dated before about 1930 have been dipped to make them that way. So far as I know, there is no such thing as a Flowing Hair, Draped Bust, Capped Bust, or Liberty Seated silver coin with full *original* brilliance. This is okay, but it is worth mentioning here, as not everyone is aware of the situation. Often a buyer will say, "I am looking only for a brilliant Mint State Capped Bust half dollar, and I don't want a toned one," not realizing that a delicately toned coin can be dipped to instantly make it bright.

Today, a bright Liberty Seated silver coin, if encapsulated in a holder, is likely to remain that way for many years. In earlier times, such pieces would tone for a spell, then need to be redipped. After a while a silver coin that has been dipped too often will acquire a gray or hazy surface as measurable amounts of the surface of the coin dissolve with each dipping.

Among coins that are brilliant, the luster can vary considerably. To an extent this depends upon the series and even the date and variety within the series. For example, among Peace silver dollars, the 1928 Philadelphia Mint coins always have a delicate, creamy or satiny luster, while those of the San Francisco Mint (1928-S) have a rich frost. A Liberty Walking half dollar of 1916 has a grainy and somewhat matte surface, of great beauty, while a coin of the same design, but dated in the 1940s, will have a rich, flashy brilliance.

For any silver series, coins struck from long-used or tired dies will have a grainy and somewhat "shiny" or "greasy" luster. This is particularly common on Morgan and, to a lesser extent, Peace silver dollars, especially the issues with higher mintages. Avoid these.

Silver coins that have delicate, halo-like toning from the rims inward (caused by storage in cardboard albums with sulfur content) or delicately blended iridescence can often be more valuable than fully brilliant coins. Many Morgan silver dollars have brilliant iridescent hues from contact with a cloth bag, perhaps damp at times, over a long period of years in storage. These coins are toned on one side, where the coin touched the bag, and brilliant on the other side.

Coins with halo toning are often from "National" or similar albums. Coins that were once dipped or even cleaned abrasively can be very attractive if they were placed in such albums and became toned. Such halo toning can be found on silver coins of any grade, well worn and upward in condition, and this toning is considered desirable, assuming the coin has good eye appeal.

In recent years, a few "coin doctors" have used heat and chemistry to create all sorts of attractively toned Franklin half dollars, Morgan dollars, and so on, and have obtained strong prices for them. A lot of these are offered on the Internet, where pictures are often used in lieu of verbal descriptions. "Original" toning,

elusive of definition but perhaps best described as toning acquired over a period of years without deliberate intervention, is much preferred. Before paying a strong premium for any attractively toned coin, you might want to have it reviewed by a trusted dealer or collector friend. Many silver coins from old-time collections are naturally toned and "original," and are highly desired.

Circulated silver coins tend to tone a light silver-gray color, which is just fine. Unless they have been dipped, 90% or more of all Capped Bust, Liberty Seated, and other coins will have this hue.

Toning can mask the true grade of a coin. There are many instances in which well-meaning numismatists have dipped a nicely toned Draped Bust silver dollar, Liberty Seated quarter, or other such coin, believed to be choice Mint State, only to find that after dipping, considerable friction became evident.

The bottom line for silver coins is this: if a coin is Mint State or Proof it should be brilliant to medium-toned, as you prefer, but in all instances it should have good eye appeal.

This 1924 Peace silver dollar was certified as MS-67, or superb gem, by a leading grading service. From the standpoint of wear and contact marks it may be an MS-67. However, it was struck from worn, tired dies and is indistinct and grainy in many areas.

Given a choice, I would rather have an MS-64 that is sharply struck from "fresh" dies than a poorly detailed coin, no matter how high a grade might be assigned to it. At present, in a contest for entering coins in a "registry set" competition, the poor MS-67 would gain high honors, while a lustrous, sharp MS-64 would not be worthy of notice. One of the main purposes of this book is to give you an inside view of such things so you can make informed choices when building a fine collection.

Flashy, frosty mint luster is seen on the surface of this attractive 1944-S Liberty Walking half dollar, a common date.

Gold Coins

Gold coins are less likely to be affected by atmospheric exposure than are coins of copper, nickel, or silver. As noted earlier, the copper element of a gold coin, usually 10% (which may also contain traces of other metals), tends to tone. This imparts a highly desirable warm and mellow orange color over time.

I have come across at least two instances in which 19th-century coiners deliberately *roasted* their gold coins in ovens to give them a warm, orange-yellow color. The most famous instance is that of Wass, Molitor & Co., private gold coiners in San Francisco in the 1850s. The other concerned a counterfeiting operation in the early 19th century, in New York City, in which fake gold Spanish-American doubloons were made, then roasted to give them the appearance of being old and genuine.

Some gold coins are a lighter yellow than others. This is particularly true of coins made from California gold, which contained measurable amounts of silver as an "impurity." Some coins from the Charlotte and Dahlonega mints are also of a lighter yellow.

Dipping a gold coin can give it a lighter hue. The late Ed Trompeter, who formed a complete set of gold Proofs from 1858 to 1915 (except for the 1858 $20), dipped all of them in a chemical that he said made them more attractive. Happily, as no friction was involved, no hairlines were added to the surfaces, and the grades remained unchanged, although the color of each was lightened.

Many gold coins have copper spots or carbon flecks from impurities or from incomplete mixture of the gold-copper alloy. These seem to be particularly common among issues of the late 19th and early 20th centuries.

As is true of coins struck in other metals, the luster on gold coins can vary from date to date and variety to variety. Double eagles of 1901 tend to have grainy luster, while those of 1857-S have "flashy" luster,

This lovely, lustrous 1847 gold half eagle (enlarged) bears the assigned grade of MS-66.

and MCMVII (1907) coins are somewhat matte or satiny.

In my opinion, light, natural, yellow-orange toning on a gold coin is desirable. Gold coins of the early 1795 to 1834 era are often seen with deeper yellow-orange hue and can be very attractive. In all instances, eye appeal is important. Of all coins, those in gold are the easiest to find without problems.

Seeking Sharply Struck Coins

First, Exceptions to the Rule

In most instances, a sharply struck example of a given variety is more desirable than a weakly struck one. Why not in *all* instances?

The most famous exception is the 1922 "plain" (also called "no D") Lincoln cent. In this year, no cents were struck at the Philadelphia Mint, but 7,160,000 pieces were made in Denver. Several obverse dies used to make these cents at the Denver Mint became clogged and indistinct from overuse, and the D mintmark became weak, finally disappearing. Imaginatively, a later generation of collectors seized upon these D-less cents as a way to acquire a look-alike substitute for the nonexistent 1922 Philadelphia issue.

Accordingly, the *Guide Book* lists these varieties and prices and includes a notation:

1922-D Lincoln cent—G-4: $9 • VG-8: $10 • F-12: $12 • VF-20 $15 • EF-40: $27 • AU-50: $45 • MS-60: $85 • MS-63: $140.

1922 Lincoln cent, No D—G-4: $450 • VG-8: $550 • F-12: $700 • VF-20 $900 •

EF-40: $1,800 • AU-50: $3,500 • MS-60: $6,500 • MS-63: $24,000.

1922 Lincoln cent, Weak D—G-4: $35 • VG-8: $40 • F-12: $55 • VF-20 $80 • EF-40: $190 • AU-50: $225 • MS-60: $375 • MS-63: $650.

1922 cents with a weak or missing mintmark were made from extremely worn dies that, when newer, had struck normal 1922-D cents. Three different die pairs were involved. Two of them produced "weak-D" coins. One die pair is acknowledged as having struck "no-D" coins. Weak-D cents are worth considerably less. Beware of removed mintmark.

In July 1937, this letter from Maurice D. Scharlack, of Corpus Christi, Texas, was printed in *The Numismatist*:

> In the interest of throwing a little more light on the much discussed 1922 Lincoln cent, I am jotting down these notes. The United States Mint record shows a coinage of only 7,160,000 coined from the Denver Mint [alone]. This is a comparatively small issue, and the writer feels confident that these pennies will increase in value as time goes on and collectors begin to take notice of their absence from circulation. I have 25,000 of them packed away in a little wooden chest, and in all due modesty I honestly believe this is the largest collection of this one cent.
>
> There is an interesting little fact I want to bring out. I said above that the 1922 Lincolns were minted only at the Denver Mint. Yet you will occasionally find a 1922 plain Lincoln cent (which ordinarily means they were minted at the Philadelphia Mint). In this particular instance I do not believe that is the case, but the only explanation I can give is that the die might have broken or worn off and thus coined a 1922 sans the D. I have in my lot some specimens showing no signs of wear, yet no D is visible, even under a lens....

Among other exceptions is the curious 1937-D "3-Legged" Buffalo nickel. After a certain reverse die was used for a while, it developed some problem, was taken from the press, and filed down slightly—but in the process, the front right leg of the animal was removed from the die. The die was then put back in service, creating this variety. Prices from the *Guide Book* for a regular 1937-D as well as for those made from a used, filed-down die are as follows:

1937-D Buffalo nickel—G-4: $0. 75 • VG-8: $0.85 • F-12: $1.75 • VF-20 $2 • EF-40: $3 • AU-50: $10 • MS-60: $30 • MS-63: $40.

1937-D 3-Legged Buffalo nickel—G-4: $400 • VG-8: $550 • F-12: $700 • VF-20 $800 • EF-40: $950 • AU-50: $1,300 • MS-60: $2,400 • MS-63: $5,250.

What to Look For

When the dies of a coin in a coining press were spaced slightly too far apart, the metal in the planchet didn't fill the deepest recesses of the dies, and the resultant coins were lightly struck in areas, especially on the high points. Sometimes in a series, scattered varieties are usually weak, while others are sharp. Among Morgan silver dollars, those made at the New Orleans Mint are often weak at the centers of the obverse and reverse, while most struck at San Francisco are sharp. Among Buffalo nickels, many Denver Mint coins of the 1920s are weak, and the 1926-D is sometimes so weak that many features are blurred and indistinct.

It was efficient for press operators at the mints to space the dies slightly too far apart, as the dies did not wear so quickly, and planchets that were slightly overweight did not cause problems. Some improperly annealed planchets were too hard and struck up poorly.

Today, the difference between a sharply struck coin and a weakly struck one can sometimes have a profound effect on its value. In other instances, few people care or know about such variations.

To determine whether a coin is sharply or weakly struck, it is important to know the details originally present in the die used to strike that coin. On the Washington quarter dollars of 1932 to 1998, the hair on the portrait is not sharp, as the design was taken from a marble bust that lacked such details. Accordingly, even the best struck Washington quarters from this era do not have minutely defined hair strands. On the other hand, on the Draped Bust obverse design used for half dollars from 1796 to 1807, Miss Liberty's portrait has finely delineated hair strands. A high-grade 1806 half dollar with few hair details would be considered a weak strike, while a 1932 Washington quarter would not.

To determine what details are present in a design, look at photographs in catalogs and reference books.

Although there are exceptions among designs, most stars have raised centers and ridges on each ray of the star. Some stars are five-pointed, others have six points. The Morgan dollar is an exception, as its obverse stars are only in outline form, and the centers are flat. On certain Liberty Seated silver coins, the stars are some-times sharp in one area of the obverse and weak in another.

On portraits, such as those of Miss Liberty, there are usually many tiny hair strands, but this varies from design to design. When there is weakness it is usually at the area highest in relief, near the center of the coin, as this was the deepest part of the die.

On many silver and gold coins, details of the eagle on the reverse—such as the feathers on the breast or, on the Peace silver dollar (1921–1935), the high part of the wing—are apt to be lightly struck at the center. On many 19th-century coins, one or both legs of the eagle can be weak.

If a wreath is present on a coin, one or the other side of it may have some weak leaves or other features. On some coins in various series, the toothlike projections around the border, called *dentils* (or *denticles*) can be weak.

For some varieties, no sharply struck coins exist. All show some weakness, as all were struck that way. For example, there is probably no such thing as an 1807 Draped Bust dime, quarter, or half dollar with needle-sharp details in all areas. On the

This lustrous 1906 Liberty Head nickel was certified as MS-65, without further comment, by a leading grading service. Notice that while most features are sharply struck, the toothlike dentils around the border are mushy and in some places (such as below the date) indistinct.

This lustrous 1908 Liberty Head nickel was certified as MS-65, without further comment, by a leading grading service. Notice that the stars are flatly struck at their centers. On the reverse the wreath is flat to the left of the ribbon knot.

This lustrous 1896 Liberty Head nickel (enlarged) was certified as MS-65, without further comment, by a leading grading service. All design details are sharp on both sides, as are the border dentils. Grading services would do well to add a designation such as Full Details (abbreviated FD) to holders to reflect such striking quality. (More about FD is said later in the present chapter.)

You, as a reader of this book, should opt to acquire a sharply struck Liberty Head nickel if you are seeking a single example for a type set. You now know what to look for!

other hand, in the Morgan silver dollar series, nearly all 1881-S dollars are superbly detailed.

You will have to learn what to look for, by consulting specialized texts. If no sharp strikes exist, then you can be content with one having some normal weakness. However, if sharp strikes are known for a variety, then it will pay to look for such a piece.

Sharp Strikes in the Spotlight

For a *few* series, guidelines for sharpness have been publicized, and coins with such sharpness can sell for much higher prices. A few price guides and listings give separate values for these pieces, with notations identifying their sharpness. The *Certified Coin Dealer Newsletter*, for example, reflects price differences for sharp strikes in certain series. The following "bid" prices are for sight-unseen Mercury dimes certified by NGC—regular strikes and those with Full Bands (FB):[36]

1916 Dime—MS-65: $60; MS-65 FB: $65 • MS-66: $116; MS-66 FB: $167 • MS-66: $270; MS-66 FB: $580.

1945 Dime—MS-65: $14; MS-65 FB: $5,300 • MS-66: $17; MS-66 FB: $7,450 • MS-67: $24; MS-67 FB: $9,750.

Among Mercury dimes the availability of coins with Full Bands varies. As indicated above, for the 1916 dime such coins are more expensive than normal or lightly struck ones, but not extremely so. However, for the 1945, just a handful of Full Bands exist, whereas hundreds of thousands of regular strikes are known. Hence, the 1945 Full Bands is of exceptional value—indeed, dramatically so.

Other series in which such guideposts for sharpness have been featured in listings and publicized, thus generating high values for pieces that are rare if sharp, include Jefferson nickels with six Full Steps (6FS) on the Monticello building on the reverse, Standing Liberty quarters of 1916 to 1930 with Full Head (FH), and Franklin half dollars with Full Bell Lines (FBL). Recently, there have been comments about a Full Torch (FT) on Roosevelt dimes.

For certain modern Proof coins, those with deep cameo frosted surfaces can bring a great premium over what normal Proofs with lightly polished portraits sell for—such being particularly true for selected varieties from 1950 to 1964.

"Full Details" (FD) Notations Would Be Useful

While a few series have guideposts or notations for sharp striking, most do not. Therein lie many wonderful opportunities for you!

Most people are unaware of the guideposts for other series, including some of the most widely collected. If and when such are publicized, recognized by the grading services, marked on holders, and listed in popular guides, those who bought sharp coins earlier will make a lot of money!

Following are a few series and points to check, plus a suggestion for a nickname:

Indian Head cents (1859–1909): Full diamonds on the ribbon (already used by some specialists), full details on the feather tips, full leaves in the wreath.

Lincoln cents (1909 to date): Full beard details on earlier issues (on many later cents, the dies for which were made from worn hubs, beard details are indistinct, even on otherwise sharply struck coins), and no graininess on the shoulder (this is from the original planchet when it is not fully compressed into the deep part of the die). FD coins are common for 1909 V.D.B., for example, but rare for certain Denver cents of the 1916 to 1929 era.

Buffalo nickels (1913–1938): On the Indian and Buffalo, Full Details (FD), which are often missing on the areas in highest relief. Very few Buffalo nickels of certain issues, especially after 1923, can meet the FD requirement.

Liberty Walking half dollars (1916–1947): Full details to the hand of Miss Liberty and her skirt lines, plus other features. FD coins are exceedingly rare for certain varieties such as 1923-S, but are not unusual for certain others, such as some issues of 1916 and 1917.

Morgan silver dollars (1878–1921): Full hair details above Miss Liberty's ear, full feathers on the eagle's breast, full details elsewhere. FD coins vary in their availability but are discussed in the literature.

Trade dollars (1873–1885): Full details on the obverse star centers; on the reverse, full details on the eagle's leg on the right.

If the certification services would adopt the FD designation across the board (rather than FH for one series, FBL for another, etc.), and would be sure that *all* details are full, this designation would be very informative!

Right now, there is some compromising. For example, I have seen some Standing Liberty quarters (e.g., of 1921) with FH (full head) listings, but some of the rivets in the shield are weak, and there is some weakness at the date. Frank Van Valen reported seeing a 1927-S "FH" Standing Liberty quarter that did not have an ear opening for Miss Liberty, and about half the shield details were blurred or not visible at all! Such coins might qualify as FH (Full Head), but they would fail miserably the FD (Full Details) test!

Some Mercury dimes designated FB (Full Bands) have weak rims or lightly struck areas in the date numerals. Such coins would flunk the FD (Full Details) test. Many more examples could be given.

Focus on Price

The Four Steps

To reiterate the four suggested steps to use when buying a coin:

1. Observe the numerical grade on the holder.

2. Gauge eye appeal at first glance.

3. Evaluate sharpness and related features, seeking Full Details on coins.

4. Establish a fair market price.

The first part of this chapter was concerned with steps 1, 2, and 3. Now, on to step 4.

Price and Value

There are many coins in the marketplace. For common coins, frequently traded and in popular series, prices are easily enough obtained from many sources. If a coin offered to you passes steps 1, 2, and 3 of your inspection, and if the price is in the ballpark, go ahead and buy it, if it seems to be a *good value* at that price.

As to good value, I recommend that you study the different price levels of a given issue, and if a small jump in price, such as from MS-64 to MS-65, is accompanied by a huge jump in value, buy the lower grade—this being what I call the Optimal Collecting Grade (OCG), discussed earlier. At the same time, be very sure that your OCG-level coin is a high-end or choice piece within that range.

At first, buy only coins that pass all of these steps with flying colors. You will find many opportunities to spend your money.

Then, when you narrow your needs, at the same time learn more about the series and what to expect. If you are collecting gold dollars, you will not expect an 1857-C with needle-sharp features and a smooth, high-quality planchet, as discussed. Similarly, if you desire an 1860-D or 1861-D gold dollar, you will want to know that *all* authentic specimens have a weakly struck U in UNITED. One of the rarest coins in a full type set of United States issues is the 1808 quarter eagle, a design made only in this year. All known 1808 quarter eagles are weakly struck in one area or another.

Equipped with specific knowledge, you can now go further, and buy a weakly struck 1808 quarter eagle. However, if you didn't know better, and in the beginning were not aware of steps 1 through 3, you might have already acquired some other weak coins for issues that you could have found with sharp details.

If, after study, you find that a prize coin is rare, in exceptional quality, attractive, and more, and that in a given span of several years only a few come on the market, you may want to reach for it by paying more than the standard price. Nearly every great collection ever formed was assembled by paying top market price, or setting a new price, when remarkable opportunities presented themselves. To my knowledge, no great collection was ever made by concentrating on bargains. In the meantime, for most of the coins in your collection you will have carefully considered them, one by one, often paying no more than market for coins with special features—sharp strike, for example—of which few others are aware.

Aspects of Timing

Ken Rendell, who has distinguished himself in the fields of autographs, manuscripts, and rare books (but who has also been a numismatist since his teenage years), mentioned this idea to me: if someone is seeking a rarity and is 20 or 30 years old, and if such a rarity comes on the market every 5 to 10 years, he or she can afford to wait until a specimen that is just right comes along. On the other hand, if someone is 70 years old and needs such an item, it would be good to seize the opportunity at hand.

Perhaps another reason for urgency would be the desire for completion. Sup-pose you work on forming a full set of MS-65 nickel three-cent pieces, each one sharply struck and choice, and you finish, except for the 1871. This seems common enough, per the listings, but for some reason one that is just right has not come along. Months pass. Then you see one at 50% over market. Buy it!

At the same time, be aware of fads and "bubbles" in the market (see the next chapter). If a coin is not particularly rare, and it has had a recent run-up in price, or if most buyers are *investors* (not numismatists), be careful!

Summary

When considering a coin for purchase, evaluate its grade, eye appeal, sharpness, and other aspects of desirability. Then comes the time of decision. The price you pay should depend on the rarity of the coin in the quality at hand, and on the tenor of the market. For a readily available coin, the price should be in or around current market levels. For a truly exceptional coin, if necessary pay above market price. However, equipped with knowledge as to what to look for, such as Full Details, you have a distinctive advantage over many of your competitors.

See chapters 14 and 15 for buying strategies in different venues.

CHAPTER NINE

COIN MARKET FADS, TRENDS, AND CYCLES

"Don'ts" for collectors include: Don't be too anxious to buy any particular set or coin. This puts you at a disadvantage in purchasing it. Don't collect too fast. The joy of our hobby is the chase—the hobby flourishes through activity. Don't fail to pay enough to get nice specimens. Don't put coins in a gloomy warehouse. Keep and inspect them—study them. Don't spare the horses but ride your hobby hard.

—William A. Philpott, Jr., November 1953

Economics and Rare Coins

A Bit of Background

Today the market for American rare coins, tokens, medals, and paper money is widespread—with hundreds of thousands (if not more) serious players, thousands of dealers, many publications, numerous Internet sites, and other ways to buy, sell, and be informed. In addition, quite a few of those 130,000,000 casual coin collectors mentioned by Director Jay Johnson (see chapter 3) have the potential of becoming more involved. All of this makes for the dynamic market discussed throughout this book.

Although at the moment the market has many buyers and sellers, and much money is invested in numismatic items, conditions today are quite unlike they were at any other time in history. Chances are excellent that 10 years from now the market will reflect many further changes.

The market never stands still.

Nothing is constant except change.

An understanding of the coin market, its history, and changing trends has been vital to my business success. To you, such an understanding will contribute to the wise spending of your money and, possibly, the timing of when to sell.

As George Santayana said, "Those who cannot remember the past are condemned to repeat it."

I have tried to learn from history, and I am still learning. Because of this, I have rarely if ever been caught unaware by a major market or popularity change.

In this chapter, mainly about trends, fads, and cycles, and in the next, I give a deeper view of the coin market. I will share observable reality. Everything is factual. There are no theories involved.

A Red-Hot Market

Over the years, the emphasis on popularity has shifted for certain items, and series that were "hot" in one era often have faded to obscurity in another, perhaps to be revived at a still later date.

In 1975, silver medals privately struck by the Franklin Mint and depicting topical and historical motifs were the hottest numismatic items in America, building on a trend that had begun the decade before. Buyers scrambled to get the latest issues, and more than a few people spent thousands of dollars to add to their collections and keep them up to date. The Franklin Mint Collectors Society was run by the company and featured a beautiful reception center to greet members who stopped by to visit company headquarters. Franklin Mint products were of a high order of artistry, some of the finest medals ever made.

In December 1968, *The Numismatist* carried this:

> Sales and earnings of The Franklin Mint, Yeadon, PA, for the third quarter and the first nine months of 1968 reached new record levels. For the third quarter of 1968, sales were $3,771,598, an increase of 426% over the $716,723 recorded for the third quarter of 1967. Net earnings for the third quarter were $295,670, or $.91 per share, as compared to $67,953, or

$.26 per share, in the like period of last year—an increase of 250%.

For the nine months ended September 30, 1968, sales amounted to $5,999,510, up 226% from $1,842,107 recorded for the first nine months of 1967. Net earnings were $459,452, or $1.52 per share, as compared to $145,849, or $.58 per share, a year ago—an increase of 162%.

The Franklin Mint operates a large, private mint specializing in the production of commercial and collector series of commemorative medals and tokens. Its output ranges from limited-edition specimens in solid platinum to runs of millions of pieces in aluminum and bronze. It now employs close to 700 people and has plants in Yeadon and Folcroft, Pennsylvania, both suburbs of Philadelphia.

In May 1969 it was reported that ground had been broken for a 175,000-square-foot minting facility, with state-of-the-art equipment, expected to far exceed in technology and efficiency anything the federal mints had.

On December 20, 1971, *Newsweek* magazine, in "Making a Mint," told of "a new set of baubles glittering from private mints: commemoratives," with "the Franklin Mint, creator and main beneficiary of the craze."

Newsweek went on to say that more than 100 million dollars' worth of medals had been sold by the Franklin Mint in the past four years to 430,000 customers, and, currently, more than 100,000 people were signed up on a subscription basis to get new medals in one or more series as they were made—so as not to miss out. However, the best part was yet to come.

In the summer of 1973, Charles L. Andes, newly named president of the Franklin Mint, stated that sales for 1973 alone, a single year, were expected to cross the $100,000,000 mark.

Onward and upward. Nothing could go wrong.

Or could it?

By 1978 the Franklin Mint had run out of new buyers. The price of silver bullion was rising on the market, and new medals were expensive to make. *60 Minutes* ran a negative story on the Franklin Mint, suggesting that some buyers of such medals had incorrect notions as to their investment potential. In one memorable scene, a dealer said that apart from customers of the Franklin Mint itself, there was no aftermarket for such things. Viewers watched their screens as a stream of these medals dropped into a metal bucket, to be sent to a refinery to be melted down for their silver value. The price of silver bullion was rising on the market, in time making many medals of the Franklin Mint and other issuers *profitable* to melt down—at least for a short time. After early 1980, the price of silver fell precipitously.

Today, most Franklin Mint medals are still worth just their silver or melt-down value, or a modest premium—typically a fraction of what they cost more than a quarter century ago.

Many of the medals themselves are indeed beautiful, including many designed by Gilroy Roberts, who in 1964, having recently designed the obverse of the new Kennedy half dollar, left his post as chief engraver at the Mint to become an executive of the Franklin Mint. The medals remain attractive, interesting, and collectible, although at the moment there is not much numismatic demand for them. I have a complete album of "American History" medals that I bought from dealer Harry Forman a few years ago, paying only slightly above "melt" for them. I also bought several sets in bronze to give as gifts.

Few would have envisioned this back in 1975, when they were all the rage with investors. What proved to be a loss for many can be a source of collecting pleasure for you, although I don't anticipate that demand will reawaken anytime soon.

You have to think for yourself!

Curious Changes in the Coin Market

Early in my collecting and dealing career I read and skimmed through nearly all of the back issues of the three leading numismatic periodicals. The *American Journal of Numismatics*, which commenced in 1866 (and more or less petered out after 1914 when changed to a series of monographs, with little or no current news), was the earliest of these sources. *The Numismatist*, which first saw the light of day in 1888 and is still going strong, now as the official publication of the American Numismatic Association, contained a goldmine of information on the hobby, a window on conditions of the late 19th and early 20th centuries. The *Numismatic Scrapbook Magazine*, commenced in 1935 and the leader

of the market when I was a teenager in the mid-1950s, was particularly useful for its coverage of new research finds and of market trends and conditions.

I also collected and read auction catalogs issued by W. Elliot Woodward, Edward Cogan, the Chapman brothers, B. Max Mehl, and others in the early days, as well as those currently being produced by the Numismatic Gallery (which split up in 1954, after which its owners, Abe Kosoff and Abner Kreisberg, conducted separate businesses) and by French's, Stack's, Hollinbeck Coin Co., M.H. Bolender, and others.

I found it very interesting that the hot items of one era were often forgotten in another. Nowhere in any standard numismatic references had I ever found an explanation of such things, and in

An auction of long ago. In May 1864 the John F. McCoy Collection sale, cataloged by W. Elliot Woodward, was the sensation of the rare coin hobby. I have learned much from reading numismatic publications of a bygone era little remembered today. While many things have changed, today many aspects of marketing, promotion, fads, and the like are not much different from those employed back then.

Collectors from another era. Shown here are attendees at the annual convention of the American Numismatic Association, as photographed in San Francisco, August 31, 1915. The location? On the front steps of the San Francisco Mint. The Panama–Pacific International Exposition was in progress in the city. It had been anticipated that many would attend the ANA meeting, but in an era of Association politics and problems, many elected to stay away. This was the most lightly attended of any ANA convention, before or since, with just 14 people registered.

However, among them were several luminaries familiar today to anyone studying old catalogs and magazines: Mr. and Mrs. B. Max Mehl and their daughter (front, left), H.O. Granberg (of Oshkosh, Wisconsin, and one of the major collectors of the day), Edgar H. Adams (of Brooklyn, New York, and a candidate for preeminent numismatic scholar of the decade), Farran Zerbe (of Tyrone, Pennsylvania, who also had the concession at the exposition, to sell commemorative coins; front row, center), George C. Arnold (important dealer from Providence, Rhode Island), and Dr. and Mrs. J.M. Henderson (of Columbus, Ohio, he a collector and part-time dealer), among others.

endeavoring to discuss market trends of generations earlier found no one sharing my curiosity.

Economic Theories

As a student at the Pennsylvania State University, working toward my degree in finance, I took a basic course in economics and found it to be quite interesting. I did outside reading as well and was soon conversant with the classical studies by Adam Smith, Nikolay D. Kondratieff, John Maynard Keynes, and others, no two of which were alike, and each with different conclusions and theories. Sometimes along the way, economics was referred to as "the dismal science," a phrase still sometimes heard.

Equipped with a good measure of standard theories, I found it interesting to see these ideas at work in the real world. No classic writer on the subject proved correct, and years later in the 1980s, when under the Jimmy Carter administration we had double-digit inflation combined with double-digit interest rates (at one time, some banks were paying 18% on certificates of deposit!), all rules went out the window. According to conventional wisdom, one could have high interest rates or runaway inflation, but not both at the same time. Then came Ronald Reagan with his "trickle down" theory (or at least the theory of his advisors), commonly called *Reaganomics*.

Tulipomania and Such

I have always enjoyed interesting books on various subjects. Somehow or other I latched on to a reprint of what I later learned was a classic, *Extraordinary Popular Delusions and the Madness of Crowds*, by Charles Mackay, published in 1841. Among his stories, in addition to John Law and the South Sea Bubble, was a gripping account of the tulip-bulb mania of Holland, during which these bulbs became an investment vehicle, became scarce in relation to the ever-increasing demand for them (as they did not grow overnight), and created great excitement.

The lessons to be gained from this were considered so important by the editors of *Banker's Magazine* that, shortly after the journal commenced publication, it gave this overview of tulipomania, which I hope you will find to be interesting reading today.[37]

The Desirability of Tulips

We learn, from Mr. Mackay's *History of Extraordinary Popular Delusions*, that tulips were first introduced in western Europe about the year 1559, and, as rare exotics, annually increased in reputation until it was deemed a proof of bad taste in any man of fortune to be without a collection of them.

In 1634, the rage among the Dutch to possess them was so great that the ordinary industry of the country was neglected, and the population, even to its lowest dregs, embarked in the tulip trade. In the year 1634, many persons were known to invest a fortune of 100,000 florins in the purchase of 40 roots; it then became necessary to sell them by their weight in perits, a small weight, less than a grain.

A tulip, of the species called *Admiral Liefken*, weighing 400 perits, was worth 4,400 florins; an *Admiral Van der Eyck*, weighing 446 perits, was worth 1,260 florins; a shilder [*Annie Schilder*], of 106 perits, was worth 1,615 florins; a *Viceroy*, of 400 perits, 3,000 florins; and, most precious of all, a *Semper Augustus*, weighing 200 perits, was thought to be very cheap at 5,500 florins. The latter was much sought after, and even an inferior bulb might command a price of 2,000 florins. It is related, that at one time, early in 1636, there were only two roots of this description to be had in all Holland, and those not of the best: one was in the possession of a dealer in Amsterdam, and the other in Harlaem. So anxious were the speculators to obtain them, that one person offered the fee-simple of 12 acres of building ground for the

Harlaem tulip; that of Amsterdam was bought for 4,600 florins, a new carriage, two grey horses, and a complete suit of harness.

The Viceroy Tulip Species

Munting, an industrious author of that day, who wrote a folio volume of 1,000 pages upon the tulipomania, has preserved the following list of the various articles, and their value, which were delivered for one single root of the rare species called the *Viceroy:* Two lasts of wheat 448 florins, Four lasts of rye 558 florins, Four fat oxen 480 florins, Eight fat swine 240 florins, Twelve fat sheep 120 florins, Two hogsheads of wine 70 florins, Four tons of beer 32 florins, Two tons of butter 192 florins, One thousand lbs of cheese 120 florins, A complete bed 100 florins, A suit of clothes 80 florins, A silver drinking cup 60 florins, Total 2,500 florins.

Here we have a case of simple barter; so that we find it possible for the world to run mad in commercial transactions without the intervention of either gold or paper, or even the assistance of a bank; for the Bank of Amsterdam was not founded till 1659; and it is a curious fact to note, that if the legislature were, in its zeal for interference, or regard for the pockets of the public, to prohibit dealing in shares and jobbing in the funds, jobbing in *bulbs* might still be carried on with all the forms of the stock exchange, and with the same results.

Profits for Everyone

Noble citizens, farmers, mechanics, seamen, footmen, maid-servants, even chimney-sweeps and old clothes-women, dabbled in tulips. The operations of the trade became so extensive and so intricate, that it was found necessary to draw up a code of laws for the guidance of the dealers. Notaries and clerks were also appointed, who devoted themselves exclusively to the interests of the trade. The designation of public notary was hardly known in some towns, that of tulip notary usurping its place.

In the smaller towns, where there was no exchange, the principal tavern was usually selected as the show place, where high and low traded in tulips, and confirmed their bargains over sumptuous entertainments.

The Conclusion

When at last a conviction spread that somebody must lose in the end, and prices began to fall, an universal panic, of the same character as in modern times, seized upon the dealers. *A* had agreed to purchase ten *Semper Augustines* from *B*, at 4,000 florins each, at six weeks after the signing of the contract. *B* was ready with the flowers at the appointed time, but the price had fallen to 300 or 400 florins, and *A* refused either to pay the difference or receive the tulips.

Defaulters were announced day after day in all the towns of Holland. Hundreds, who a few months previously had begun to doubt that there was such a thing as poverty in the land, suddenly found themselves the possessors of a few bulbs which nobody would buy, even though they offered them at one-quarter of the sums they had paid for them. The cry of distress resounded everywhere, and each man accused his neighbor.

As I write these words now, it seems apparent that tulipomania was not much different in concept from the Franklin Mint medal mania. Or the 1950-D nickel excitement.

Today, most of us still like tulips. Every garden should have a few. And, I think Franklin Mint medals are quite attractive, or at least many of them are. There is a place for a 1950-D nickel in every collection. However, when each jumped out of its proper context in life and became a sizzling hot investment vehicle, things went wrong.

Bernard Baruch's 1957 autobiography, *My Own Story*, is another favorite text of mine. In essence, Baruch, a consummate financier, observed the market with a wry viewpoint. If everyone was scrambling to buy stocks that he thought were overpriced and had no basic value in terms of assets or earnings, he was willing to sell them his shares. Conversely, if solid stocks were selling at bargain prices because they were not exciting—and this happened regularly—he was an eager buyer. Along the way he became very wealthy.

Completing my trio of favorite books combining psychology and the market is *Rosenbach*, by Edwin Wolf 2nd, with John Fleming, published in 1960. Not any of these books have anything to do with numismatics, but *Rosenbach* does share the theme of collectibles, rarities, and auctions, for A.S.W. Rosenbach, the title subject, was the preeminent rare book dealer in America in the early 20th century.

Not long ago I was the guest of Ken Rendell at a gathering in Bohemian Grove, in the redwoods of California, where each summer men (no women) gather to cast their business and worldly concerns aside and enjoy discussions, entertainment, and camaraderie. Ken and I had ample chance to talk about rare coins (before becoming a leading dealer in autographs and books he was in the coin trade, and was a founding member of the Rittenhouse Society). We both agreed that the *Rosenbach* book was about the best thing available on the ins and outs of the market for rare collectibles and the personalities of people involved. Many precepts of the book trade are applicable to rare coins as well. There are quite a few books about collectors and dealers in paintings and other art, and which contain information that can be adapted to the psychology of numismatics, but none I have read can hold a candle to the insights given by the authors of *Rosenbach*.

Anyway, with quite a bit of outside reading, plus absorption in many numismatic books and publications, plus some watching of the economy, and with considerable experience in the coin market, by the early 1960s I was drawing some conclusions. By that time I had read about several coin investment cycles in the past and had been part of one that peaked in 1956 and 1957 (of which more will be said in the next chapter). Then, in the midst of the greatest coin-buying fever in history, I set about recording my thoughts.

My study was published in February 1964 in the *Empire Investor's Report*. The report, the first study of rare-coin cycles, created quite a bit of attention and was later widely quoted, including by the *Coin Dealer Newsletter* and by popular columnists.

Here it is, updated and revised, but with the basic elements no different from the first study of 1964. However, as coins have been such a great investment in the meantime, I've moved the decimal point over a notch, for the $110, $120, and $300 coins I used in the illustration in 1964 are mostly $1,100, $1,200, and $3,000 coins now!

The Anatomy of a Coin Market Cycle: Different Cycles, Different Darlings

While many coins, tokens, medals, and paper money issues have been subject to cycles, the market as a whole has been immune to such. Each series marches to the beat of a different drummer.

When commemorative half dollars were hot in late 1935 and for much of 1936, there was not much interest in current Washington quarters or newly released Proof sets (the first such sets since 1916). Today, it may be difficult for you to imagine that there was a wild scramble to buy 1935 Old Spanish Trail half dollars at $2 each, while gem Proof sets of 1936, available in endless quantity at $1.81 each, almost went begging!

In another market, in the mid-1940s, when common-date double eagles were as hot as a firecracker, paper money was cool, and the greatest auction of currency ever held—the Grinnell Collection—attracted only a handful of buyers.

At any given time, commemoratives, silver dollars, Proof coins and sets, or Indian

Head cents may be bustling, while Liberty Seated coins, Buffalo nickels, or gold dollars may be somnolent. When gold coins may be setting new records, silver dollars may soften in price. Never has there been a market in which all series were "hot" at the same time, and never has there been a market in which all series slumped simultaneously.

Analyzing a Cycle

The anatomy of a coin cycle can be traced. The following stages are typical of the performance of many numismatic issues over the years. Coin X might be a commemorative, it might be a roll of coins, it might be a type coin, it might be a foreign Proof set, it might be one of many different coins, groups, or sets that have commanded the attention of collectors and investors during the past. In general, the more a series is dominated by investor (rather than collector) buying, the more susceptible it is to wide cyclical fluctuations.

Specialties that require a lot of study and immersion in knowledge are generally immune. In his 1949 book *Early American Cents*, Dr. William H. Sheldon selected the 1794 copper cent as a bellwether of the coin market. In good economic times and bad, in periods of coin market quiet as well as popularity, such cents continued to play to a group of steady, long-term numismatists, and to march upward in price slowly but inexorably, indifferent to fads, market bubbles, and cycles.

Mint State and Proof silver and gold coins sought by investors have been more

In early 1936, this recently issued 1935 Hudson Sesquicentennial (150th anniversary) commemorative half dollar was one of the hottest coins on the market. Only 10,000 had been released, and most had been cornered by Julius Guttag, a New York City dealer. First offered at $1, coins were now $5 to $7 each, if you could find someone willing to sell.

The commemorative market raced ahead at full speed, and for most of the next year other series were ignored. Seven dollars invested in a choice example in 1936 would have increased in value to about $1,500 today. However, if four 1936 Proof sets (coins that were generally ignored at the time) had been ordered from the Mint for about the same investment ($1.81 each, or $7.24), the coins, if preserved in superb gem condition, would be worth more than $10,000 per set today, for a total of more than $40,000. If $7 had been spent on 28 1936-D quarters at face value, also ignored at the time, these coins would be worth $1,500 or more each today, or, say, more than $40,000.

While nearly all choice coins have performed admirably as investments, the record clearly shows that such coins have done especially well if purchased at a low point in a market cycle.

A typical Saint-Gaudens double eagle in a lower Mint State range would have cost about $65 in 1946, when common-date $20 coins were in fantastic demand by investors. Today, such a coin might sell for $650 or so, a fine increase, but not at all spectacular in terms of how a typical collection of Mint State coins across various popular series would have done—sets of Lincoln cents, Liberty Walking halves, and the like.

By 1946, the 1935 Hudson Sesquicentennial commemorative half dollar was selling for about $15. The $65 for a common-date double eagle, if spent on four Hudson half dollars, would have yielded about $2,000 today for average-quality Mint State coins and about $6,000 if gems had been selected. In 1946, Hudson halves were quiet—in a market slump.

influenced by cycles than have worn coins or coins struck in copper or nickel. There are, however, many exceptions—such as the great craze of Washington tokens and medals that began in 1860. Today, one thinks of Washingtoniana as a specialty of the dedicated numismatic scholar with a magnifying glass in one hand and a copy of the Fuld-Rulau book on the series in the other. It would be hard to imagine the investment world running amok, chasing Washington medals! Then again, I suppose it would be equally improbable to think of tulip bulbs' becoming so valuable that they would need to be kept in safe-deposit boxes (figuratively speaking).

As a general rule, with relatively few exceptions (a few more could be mentioned in addition to Washingtoniana), series for which most sales are to dedicated numis-matists tend to be much less volatile than series of coins sold mainly to investors.

I have divided a typical cycle into several stages. The time span of each stage varies. Broad cycles encompassing many different series (but never all of numismatics) may span periods of 5 to 10 years. Cycles of individual coins are apt to be much shorter, with some cycles occurring in a matter of months or even weeks. Such factors as dealer promotions, the breadth of the market, availability of pieces, the quality of demand (whether from collectors primarily, from investors, or from a combination of both), and other considerations must be evaluated.

Stage I

The market for Coin X is not particularly active. Some of the dealers price Coin X at

Dr. William H. Sheldon in 1949 called a typical 1794 cent a "bellwether of the coin market," reflecting basic numismatic demand and reflective of its value to established collectors. In the more than a half century since 1949, cents of this date have remained desirable—increasing in value each decade.

This coin, a VF-35 example of the Sheldon-65 variety, would never appeal to someone interested in coins solely as an investment, as it would not be designated as "investment quality" by investment advisors. However, like the tortoise and the hare, the 1794 cent has slowly and steadily outpaced many of the hottest, "fastest" coins in the investment market.

Large in size, made of silver, and in gem Mint State, this 1925 Peace silver dollar, actually a very common coin, is of the genre of "investment-quality" coins that fascinate market newcomers who are fixated on making fast profits.

Of course, the 1925 dollar is numismatically desirable as well—every dollar specialist needs one. However, a serious numismatist would not likely become excited about such a coin, or seek to buy dozens of duplicates for investment purposes. A darling of the up-market cycle that peaked in 1990, a gem 1925 Peace dollar sells today for less than it did then.

$1,200, some at $1,100. One dealer offers a group of 10 of Coin X for $9,900 in exchange for quick payment.

At a convention, a sharp buyer (who knows that a dealer has had trouble selling his large holding of Coin X) succeeds in buying 375 pieces for only $800 each. In various numismatic publications there are few, if any, dealers stating realistic buying prices for Coin X. In other words, there just isn't much life to Coin X at all!

Popular psychology being what it is, there isn't much support for Coin X from anyone. A dealer is apt to say: "Coin X is dead, so I'm not even interested in discussing buying any for stock." A collector might say: "Why should I bother collecting items like Coin X? There doesn't seem to be much interest in them, and apparently they would be a poor investment. I don't see any buying ads, and the last dealer I talked to said that he could not care less about Coin X. Besides, I subscribe to a coin investment sheet and am on several dealers' mailing and email lists, but none of them have recommended Coin X."

Scattered reports in *Coin World, Numismatic News,* and the *Coin Dealer Newsletter* tell of auction activity and enthusiastic buying and selling at recent coin shows, but try as you might to find some comments, there is no mention of Coin X.

Stage II

Time passes. Some alert persons note that Coin X is selling for $1,000 to $1,200 and has been selling at that price for quite some time, perhaps for several years, without any extensive market activity and without any increase in price. In fact, as time wears on, the price continues to weaken as dealers give discounts and special deals to move unwanted quantities of Coin X out of stock. Apathy is the order of the day.

In the meantime Coin Y, which is not as scarce as Coin X, but which is in a currently popular field, sells for $2,500. Dealers are publishing many advertisements offering to buy Coin Y, and many are offering to pay close to the full $2,500 retail price. Investors have been telephoning and

emailing, trying to stock up on Coin Y, but there aren't many for sale. Why would anyone want to *sell* a market leader?

Coin Y remains hard to buy in quantities, as most people who own one or several pieces are busy watching the price go up! How lucky they are to be "locked in" with some of the hottest coins on the market! Gosh, soon Coin Y will be $3,000, then $5,000! You can bet on it. Confirming this, one sells for $4,400 at auction.

In the meantime, other investors, perhaps a bit more savvy, have been watching Coin X stagnate price-wise. They quietly decide that Coin X is underpriced and start buying. After all, it is made of silver (or gold), is in Mint State, and at one time was as popular as could be. The coin itself has not changed—only the price has. Dealers are contacted by telephone, email, letter, personal visits to shops and at conventions, and by any other feasible means. The formerly unwanted supply of Coin X dries up! One particularly fortunate Midwest investor buys 550 pieces for just $600 each in a quick cash deal!

Still, to most numismatists, Coin X is dead. However, the fundamentals have changed quietly. Bulk lots have been liquidated, and if anyone would take the time to check, it would be learned that there were few to be had.

Stage III

As smart buyers have gobbled up all of the available examples of Coin X at prices from $600 to $1,000 or so, newcomers to the market, some of whom have heard Coin X is undervalued, can't find many— if, indeed, they can find any at all. A certain Midwest investor who is reputed to have bought 550 pieces (but facts are scarce, and who knows?) says he will pay $1,400 each for all he can find! This is amazing for a coin that was priced at just $1,000 or less only a few months ago. Better buy some before the price rises further!

Investors are now willing to pay $1,100 to $1,200, and say so in print and in conversation. Dealers run "wanted to buy" advertisements for Coin X offering $1,100 for all specimens submitted, knowing that a few dollars of profit await them for each Coin X acquired. However, with two or three others now willing to pay up to $1,200, they don't buy any.

These "buy" advertisements create a great deal of excitement. People who were not at all interested in Coin X now have to have one or, better yet, a group of 10! Coin X becomes hot, and a leading auction firm is amazed when one sells for a record $1,650.

The writer of a coin investment newsletter suggests that there are fewer examples of Coin X around than of Coin Y (which in the meantime has recently sold for $5,500). At a seminar held at a coin show a popular speaker tells his audience that Coin X is a favorite, and he has just bought some to put away for his kids' education.

Everyone is now thinking about Coin X. After all, why is it still listed for less than $1,500, when Coin Y has broken yet another price barrier—one just crossed the auction block for $6,600!

Stage IV

Coin X becomes a hot item! Everyone is talking about Coin X! Everyone wants to buy Coin X! There are not enough to go around! Coin X is exciting!

The price of Coin X rises to $2,000, then to $3,000, then to $4,000, still not reaching the record set by Coin Y. Wait a minute—here comes some news! A dealer at a coin show sold three of Coin X for, would you believe it, $18,000, or $6,000 each! Amazing. Meanwhile, behind the scenes and with no publicity, many investors sell their supplies of Coin Y to raise money to buy Coin X.

Coin Y is no longer very exciting, and one put up at auction brings just $4,000, while two others with reserves set too high do not sell at all.

Stage V

Those who bought Coin X at prices from $600 to $1,000 or so find the current price very attractive. In fact, one just sold for $6,500, setting a new record.

Some sell. The Midwest investor who bought 550 pieces for $600 each during Stage II of the market and three others in Stage III (paying $1,800, $3,000, and finally the record auction price of $6,000 amid a lot of excitement), sells out in a very private deal to a financial planner who has a client eager to invest in coins and with a lot of money to spend. He gets $4,625 each for the 553 pieces, or $2,557,625, and smiles all the way to the bank, for his cost was just $340,800.

Others who have come to solidly believe in Coin X hold out for still higher prices, hoping for $7,000 to $10,000 each, with no reason to expect differently.

However, the bloom is off the tulip—er, the rose—and the great activity in Coin X has lessened as investors turn to other things. Coin X attracts little attention at an important auction and goes to a dealer for $4,510. Much to his surprise, the dealer cannot turn it quickly, so he dumps it for $4,200 to another dealer, and goes on to other things.

Noting that the market is not rising as sharply as before, many investors holding supplies of Coin X stop buying and try to sell. Some cash in at the $4,000 mark, others find buyers for less. Finally, the price stabilizes at about $2,500.

Stage VI

At the new $2,500 price, very few people want to invest in Coin X. It takes fortitude to buy in a falling market, and they have just seen the price fall from $6,000 all the way down to $2,500. Other investors, who missed the opportunity to sell at a greater profit, are now willing to sell additional examples of Coin X for less than $2,500. The market is sluggish.

Coin X is available in quantity for just $2,200 each! If you are in the market for a large quantity you may be able to drive a hard bargain and buy Coin X for $2,000. The story is told of a large metropolitan convention at which an investor helped a dealer unload 243 pieces of Coin X by offering him $1,800 each, an unheard-of low price in the recent market. In other words, Stage VI brings us back to Stage I. The cycle is complete!

Cycle-Analysis Conclusions

The preceding illustration is typical of many past coin price movements, particularly those of the last 50 years. Each cycle seems to take place at a succeeding higher plateau. In the next cycle, Coin X might start out at $1,800 and might rise to a new high of $10,000 before settling back to, say, $4,000.

The previously mentioned roll of 1950-D nickels that started below $20 and, in a few years, topped out at $1,200, fell back to about $325, and since then it has been inching upward. As it went up *so* fast, whether it will break into new ground any time soon is questionable, but it seems to be on its way. In the meantime, 99% of the other coins that rose to a peak in 1964 and then fell are today selling for double their prices back then (or more), some 10 to 20 times more.

If you are aware of cycles you have an advantage that will permit you to buy "dead" coins and series at favorable prices and that will caution you to pass by "hot" coins until they settle somewhat in price.

If you are more of an investor than a collector, you may want to shun such coins completely, as the darlings of the next cycle might be different players. If you are a collector-investor combined, as most of my readers probably are, and if you are looking for quite a few things for your collection, stay away from "hot" items, but just for the time being, and take a chance on being able to pick them up more cheaply later on.

Reality Check

Since I first wrote about cycles in 1964, the coin market has held true to form and has undergone several such events. Certain of these are discussed in the next chapter. In the meantime, some of the following experiences with *Coin World* may be interesting to you.

A number of years ago the editors of the *Coin World Almanac* commissioned me to write an essay on coin investment for that

In 1976 there was not much buyer interest in Indian Head cents, and a gem, such as this lustrous 1866 (enlarged), could have been bought at a price that would yield its owner a tenfold profit by now.

publication. In subsequent issues—the fifth issue appeared in the summer of 1987—I updated my earlier thoughts, and along the way I discussed cycles in the United States coin market.

In the 1976 issue I said: "Right now gold coins are 'hot' and sell very well. At the same time, Indian cents are 'quiet' and there's no rush to buy them."

In the 1977 issue of the same publication I reported: "Gold coins are now 'quiet' and Indian cents are more active! Perhaps in 1980 this situation will reverse itself again."

In 1978 I wrote: "Gold coins have indeed picked up in activity, particularly for scarcer issues. Indian cents remain active as well. Perhaps a few years from now gold coins will become intensely active and Indian cents will become quiet once more."

After that, there was a lapse of several years before the next edition of the *Coin World Almanac* appeared. For the following issue, 1984, I wrote:

> I find that gold coins are "quiet," with very little activity among common or bullion-type issues, particularly in comparison with the activity of the recent past. Indian cents are neither active nor dormant but, rather, are somewhere in-between. Moving to other series, I note that colonial coins are very quiet. Large cents and half cents, never the scene of frenzied activity, are moderately active in keeping with interest by collectors. The same goes for Indian and Lincoln cents.
>
> United States "type" coins are fairly quiet but seem to be stirring. These

were the heroes of the 1979–1980 boom market. Commemoratives are fairly active at levels less than they were several years ago. Silver dollars are very active, down from "extremely active" a few years ago, but still a lot of buying and selling is going on.

Update for Today

Right now, the hottest market items are modern coins that are plentiful in such grades as MS-65 and Proof-65, but for which relatively few have been certified at levels such as MS-68 to MS-70 (although more are being certified every day).

At the same time—now—there are many beautiful and very collectible coins in such grades as MS-63 and MS-64 that are playing to a lackluster market, such as commemoratives of the classic era (1892–1954), Proof-63 and -64 coins of most issues from 1858 through 1916, and many other series. Part of this is the continuing thinking that coins in grade 65 or higher are of "investment quality," but that others are not and are fit only for collectors!

Matters have been complicated by "grade-flation," and some of yesterday's MS-64 coins are now certified as MS-65. This means that the need for connoisseurship is greater than ever. It also means that this present book may be especially important for you to read and understand.

Most amazing to me is the rush to buy high-grade certified coins merely by reading the labels on the slabs, without concern for sharpness of strike or eye appeal, as such factors are not listed on the holders. Pardon me for emphasizing this weird situation, but to me it defies all logic. For you, as a connoisseur, this is like finding money in the street! Good buys abound, but you need to spend some time to become educated on what to look for, and you need to be patient. Of course, by now you know that is what steps 1 through 4, my buying guidelines, are all about.

Over a long period of years as a professional numismatist I have made a lot of money simply by recognizing hidden values in coins—unusual sharpness of strike, a peculiar die variety, a copper coin in gem Mint State for which examples with *original* color are rare but few people know it, and so on.

I have also kept a weather eye on cycles in the coin market, and really love buying rare coins in a quiet or even dormant series.

In my opinion, opportunities for smart buying are as great as ever!

A Proof half dollar of 1894, if attractive, has been numismatically desirable in all market seasons. Today, regardless of the overall quality and eye appeal of such a coin, an 1894 certified as Proof-63 will attract hardly any attention and can be bought for less than $1,000, cheaper today than it was a generation ago.

On the other hand, if an example were given an ultra-grade of Proof-69 or -70, it might well sell for $25,000 or more—this being a greater sum than an entire collection of Barber Proof halves, complete from 1892 through 1915, would bring in Proof-63 grade.

It is likely that an old-timer would opt to spend $25,000 and buy the complete collection. It is also likely that many fresh-faced investors would opt to own just a single super-gem 1894, all by itself. Choices such as this are very real in today's market. A knowledge of trends and cycles of the past, plus basic elements of value, can help you make a decision that is right for you.

CHAPTER TEN

THE COIN MARKET, EARLY TIMES TO 1857

Coin collecting or numismatics as a hobby or an avocation or diverting pursuit affords the individual more unadulterated pleasure, great interest, and often enhanced values than any other collectible item or items. Of variety there is no end, nor does one ever reach a time or a period in which he can state that his collection is complete. This collecting science is forever new and yet forever old. It offers a cultured pastime from the cradle to the grave.

—Robert K. Botsford, July 1938

The use of money in America is interwoven with numismatics. I have always found it interesting and informative to learn how coins, tokens, medals, and paper money were employed and under what economic and market conditions. Today, a 1652 Pine Tree shilling, a silver dollar of 1794, or a $5 gold half eagle of 1829 is all the more interesting and numismatically significant if its background is known.

Often, pivotal events in American history caused innovations and changes in money. A paper $55 Continental Currency bill dated January 14, 1779, signed by Nicholas and Gray, is interesting to own and collect, and on the market it is inexpensive. However, the joy of owning it will be enhanced if you know why it was issued, what the imprinted motto POST NUBILA PHŒBUS means, and what happened to similar bills in later years. A common 1943 Lincoln cent is worth owning as well, but knowing why it was struck in steel instead of bronze is part of its numismatic desirability—in addition to its grade and market value.

As to the importance of blending history with numismatics, here are some scenarios based on facts:

1. The time is December 1837, and two real estate deals close for $10,000 each, payable in regional bank bills, one transaction in Detroit and the other in Portsmouth, New Hampshire. Each person takes his cash and puts it in a local safe deposit box. Several years later the boxes are opened. The Detroit seller finds his bills are absolutely worthless, while the Portsmouth man takes his bills to a local bank and exchanges them at face value for gold coins.

2. The time is January 1851, and you visit a dry goods store in Philadelphia, New York, or Charleston, and tender $10 to make a purchase, receiving several dollars' worth of silver coins in change. You look at the handful of coins, and not a single Liberty Seated silver coin is in sight. *All* are foreign coins, mostly depicting Spanish kings. And, yet, Liberty Seated coins have been made in quantity since 1837.

3. The time is the early 1930s, this per an account by Louis E. Eliasberg, Sr.: "A story which I once read that impressed me was about two men who, in 1932, walked through the

Continental Currency $55 bill dated January 14, 1779, one of a series of denominations that extended from $1 to $80. Although the bill noted that "the bearer is entitled to receive fifty-five Spanish milled dollars, or an equal sum in gold or silver," the new American government had little money in its coffers, and such bills could not be exchanged at par. Soon, currency such as this became nearly worthless.

streets of Baltimore, one carrying a pint of whisky on his hip and the other carrying in his pocket six $20 gold pieces. In 1932 the man who carried the whisky was violating the Prohibition law, and the man carrying the double eagles was within the law. Consider their plight when two years later, in 1934, the man carrying the gold pieces was violating the law, and the man with the pint of whisky was within the law."

4. The time is June 1862. You have three $10 bills issued by the United States government, a $10 note in Continental Currency from Revolutionary War days, a Demand Note from 1861, and a just-issued Legal Tender note. You go to the Treasury Department to cash them in for silver and gold coins. You are told that the government repudiated the Continental Currency notes long ago and your bill has no value at all. The Demand Note can be exchanged for a gold coin, but as there are none in circulation, the paying teller has to go into a vault to get one for you. He then informs you that the Legal Tender bill is, indeed, worth $10, as it states on its face, but that it can be exchanged only for other paper money, not for silver or gold coins.

5. The time is February 1873. Each of two people, one in San Francisco and the other in New York City, has both a freshly minted silver trade dollar (weight: 420 grains, 90% silver) and a freshly minted Liberty Seated silver dollar (412 1/2 grains, 90% silver), and each seeks to exchange these coins for dimes at a bank. The San Francisco man will get 10 dimes for each coin. However, in New York City the holder of the silver dollar and the trade dollar would be told that the bank has no dimes at all to pay out and, further, that it has not had any dimes—or quarters or halves—since 1862! The New Yorker puts the two coins away, and a few years later, in

1879, tries the same thing again. The teller at the New York bank informs him that the bank is loaded with dimes, many more than they can possibly use. An exchange is made, but while the bank will give 10 dimes for the silver dollar, the trade dollar is worth only eight dimes.

Without knowledge of American monetary and economic history, each of these scenarios seems curious. To an informed numismatist, each will make sense.

The following pages in this and the next two chapters chronicle the development of numismatics and the market in America, parallel with the ever-expanding panorama of coins, tokens, medals, and paper money issued in what is now the United States. The rare coin market as a field comprising dealers, societies, and catalogs did not develop until the late 1850s. By that time there were many colonial, state, and federal coins in existence, awaiting the attention of collectors. The early years are the focus of this chapter; the years from 1857 to date are covered in the next two chapters.

Coins and Paper Money in Early Times

1607–1776: Money in Colonial Times. Jamestown, Virginia, was settled by the English in 1607; Plymouth was established in 1620 in what became the Massachusetts Bay Colony; and over a period of time, other villages and cities were built along the Atlantic coast. Eventually there were 13 colonies with varying degrees of allegiance to England, the mother country.

Nearly all coins used in commerce in the colonies were from foreign countries, most prominently the silver 8-*real* (or "dollar") and gold eight-escudo ("doubloon") coins of Spanish America, and their fractional parts. Struck at mints in Mexico, Chile, Peru, and elsewhere, the two-*real* (25-cent) denomination, called *two bits*, was the most important coin and was a fixture in everyday commerce, along with a mixture of gold, silver, and copper issues from England, France, the German states, and elsewhere. The inscriptions on many were strange and indecipherable to the average merchant, banker, or citizen. Accordingly, such pieces were generally valued by their weight and purity (for gold coins, carefully calculated using value charts). Silver coins were treated more casually, and about anything approximating the weight of a two-bit piece was worth 25¢ or close to it.

From time to time, such diverse goods and commodities as grain, cows, corn, tobacco, and musket balls had a legal tender basis in some areas. As an example, on March 27, 1694, the Massachusetts General Court set exchange rates for corn, wheat, rye, barley malt, oaks, and peas for use as currency. Each colony also issued its own paper money, typically denominated in English values of pounds, shillings, and pence. Such bills were of reduced value or were likely not to be accepted at all in distant places. For French interests in the New World, various copper and silver coins were sent across the Atlantic, some with inscriptions relating to America.

1652–1682: Silver Coins Minted in Massachusetts. The first coins struck in what is now the United States were made in Boston in 1652. The General Court of the Massachusetts Bay Colony had passed a law authorizing the establishment of a mint; John Hull and Robert Saunderson operated the facility and received a percentage of the coins struck. Denominations, all in silver, were made in values from threepence to a shilling (a common English coin). The first issues were rather crude and bore on one side the stamp NE, for New England, and on the other a mark of the denomination expressed as a Roman numeral, such as III, VI, or XII. None were dated. Designs evolved, and in time the Willow Tree, Oak Tree, and Pine Tree silver coins were made, all with the date 1652 except for the 1662 silver twopence.

1659: Maryland Coins. Cecil Calvert (the second Lord Baltimore) had coins struck in

Pine Tree shilling of Massachusetts, die variety Noe-10. Such coins were plentiful at one time and were a staple in commerce in New England. Today, all are scarce.

London, bearing inscriptions relating to the Maryland colony. Denominations included the copper penny and the silver fourpence (or groat), sixpence, and shilling. Calvert intended to establish a mint in Maryland, but, seemingly, this was never done.

1694: Elephant Coppers. These copper halfpennies were probably made in England and circulated as tokens. They depicted an elephant on the obverse and, on the reverse, the inscription GOD PRESERVE CAROLINA AND THE LORDS PROPRIETORS, 1694, and pieces of the same date with the notation GOD PRESERVE NEW ENGLAND. Little is known of their intent, manufacture, or method of circulation. Today, such pieces range from scarce to very rare.

1722–1724: Rosa Americana and Wood's Hibernia Coinage. From 1722 through 1724, William Wood, an English entrepreneur, operated under a patent or license from King George to strike coins for use in Ireland and the Americas. Those destined for what would later become the United States bore the inscription ROSA AMERICANA, in denominations of halfpenny, penny, and twopence.

The coinage for Ireland, today known as the *Wood's Hibernia issues* (*Hibernia* being an ancient name for Ireland), were made in the farthing (quarter of a penny) and halfpenny denominations, dated 1722 through 1724. Some of these may have circulated in the United States, and today they are listed in *A Guide Book of United States Coins.*

Spanish-American "dollar," or 8-*real* piece, struck in Mexico City in 1762. With the two Pillars of Hercules depicted on the obverse, coins of this design are generally referred to as pillar dollars. Such coins were the foundation of the American monetary system in the early years.

1737–1739: Higley Copper Coins. Near Granby, Connecticut, brothers Samuel and John Higley used copper from local mines to strike coins denominated as threepence.

Pioneer Numismatists

The earliest numismatically inclined person in America for whom significant information is known was Swiss-born Pierre Eugène Du Simitière (1737–1784), who settled in Philadelphia by 1774.[38] Among his sources for specimens was John Smith, of Burlington, New Jersey, who furnished him with desired pieces by 1766, and possibly as early as 1763. Du Simitière later remembered that Smith's holdings were "considerable." In the same decade, a Major James, of Philadelphia, is also said to have had a cabinet of ancient coins as well as modern European pieces, and to be in touch with Du Simitière on matters numismatic.

A few Americans also casually acquired coins and medals of historical or curiosity interest. The Rev'd Andrew Eliot (1718–1778), pastor of the famous Old North Church in Boston, by 1767 had an extensive cabinet that included many New England silver coins.[39] In 1787, William Bentley, D.D., of Salem, Massachusetts, entered in his diary some interesting observations of coins then in circulation, creating one of the earliest records of this type known to exist.[40] His notes for September 2, 1787, included the following:

> About this time there was a great difficulty respecting the circulation of

small copper coin. Those of George III, being well executed, were of uncommon thinness, and those stamped from the face of other coppers in sand, commonly called "Birmingham," were very badly executed.[41] Beside these were the coppers bearing the authority of the states of Vermont, Connecticut and New York, etc., but no accounts how issued, regularly transmitted. The Connecticut copper has a face of general form resembling the Georges, but with [an] inscription.… A mint is said preparing for the Commonwealth of Massachusetts. It may be noted that the New York and Connecticut coin face opposite ways. To remember all the coin which passes through my hands, I note down a few coppers of foreign coins, Swedish coin, shield, three bars, lion, etc., 1763, measures one inch and 3-10; another 1747, similar; Russian, a warrior on horseback with a spear piercing a dragon, on the reverse a wreath infolding a cypher.

Other Bentley diary entries were also related to coins (also see "1790s: Early Numismatists").

Coins and Paper Money of the Revolutionary Era

1773: Virginia Halfpennies. In 1773 a special coinage of copper halfpennies was struck in London for use in the colony of Virginia. These did not arrive in America until 1775, by which time the fires of the Revolution were burning. Still, many thousands reached circulation. Decades later, a hoard of several thousand uncirculated coins was found and was acquired by Baltimore numismatist Mendes I. Cohen (who ran a banking and lottery business and who at one time owned an 1804 silver dollar).

1775–1780: Continental Currency Paper Money. The American Congress authorized the issuance of paper money. Values ranged from less than a dollar up to $80. All but the fractional denominations bore multiple signatures, including those of some men who were also signers of the Declaration of Independence. Denominated in Spanish milled dollars, such paper was intended to be exchanged at par with Spanish-American silver coins, including the 8-*real* or dollar denomination, as well as its gold counterparts, denominated in escudos (an escudo being worth $2), the largest of which was the eight-escudo (or $16) gold coin, commonly called the *doubloon*. However, such paper had no real backing, and the notes depreciated rapidly. Soldiers, merchants, and others who were paid in such currency suffered losses when they attempted to spend them in commerce. As the years went on, the situation worsened as larger quantities of paper bills were circulated in an attempt to fund the Revolution, but still without any solid backing. The young American government had very little in the way of assets. Hope and energy, yes; silver and gold, no.

The following figures illustrate the depreciation of Continental bills, in terms of the amount of such needed to exchange for $100 in silver specie dollars: January 1777, $105 (first listing); February 1777, $107; January 1778, $325; January 1779, $742; January 1780, $2,934; January 1781, $7,400; February 1781 (last listing), $7,500, or a ratio of 75 to 1. An act of Congress, passed August 4, 1790, stated that Continental Currency would be received at the Treasury until September 1, 1791, at the rate of $100 in bills to $1 in specie. The Act of May 8, 1792, extended the redemption period of March 7, 1792, after which time the bills were repudiated—the status they retain today.

1776: *Continental Currency Dollar Coins.*

It is believed that the Continental Congress produced a limited coinage, the Continental Currency dollars made in pewter. The obverse of such pieces depicts a sundial with the inscription MIND YOUR BUSINESS below, and FUGIO to

Group of Continental Currency notes. (Illustration engraved by W.L. Ormsby, New York, and used widely in popular publications in the 1850s and 1860s)

the left (the latter meaning "I fly," referring to the rapid passage of time). Around the border is CONTINENTAL CURRENCY, 1776. The reverse consists of interlocking rings with abbreviated names of the states, enclosing a band inscribed AMERICAN CONGRESS, and, at the center, WE ARE ONE.

Money of the 1780s

1782: *First Commercial Bank Chartered.*

In April the state of Pennsylvania affirmed the charter of the Bank of North America, the first such commercial institution in the country. Authorized capital was not to exceed $10 million—less than that was raised, however, and business commenced with $400,000. Soon, paper money was issued with the bank's imprint, initiating a field that today is known as *obsolete currency*, extending until such bills were discontinued in 1866.

1783: *Chalmers Coinage.*

Annapolis silversmith John Chalmers produced his own coinage—silver threepence, sixpence, and shillings—most probably in large quantities, as hundreds of pieces exist today, although some varieties are rare. These had no backing by Maryland, but were strictly a private venture. They seem to have circulated extensively, as most seen today show considerable wear. No doubt they were simply valued on their silver content, much as a British coin of similar denomination would have been.

1783: Nova Constellatio Tokens Imported. Copper tokens bearing this date (later issues were dated 1785) and the inscription NOVA CONSTELLATIO were imported from England, to be used in commerce. Other tokens were imported as well. These were generally the size of contemporary British halfpennies and the (later) federal one-cent pieces.

The government of the United States explored the possibility of producing its own coinage, and in 1783 certain Nova Constellatio patterns were struck, bearing on one side an all-seeing eye surrounded by rays, as of a sun, and 13 stars, one for each state, the devices being somewhat similar to those of the Nova Constellatio coppers. At the center of most was the denomination, expressed as a number, and intended on the decimal system, with 1,000 units to be known as a *mark*, 500 as a *quint*, and so on. These were produced only in pattern form, most in silver, after which the idea lapsed.

1785–1788: State Copper Coinage. Vermont, Connecticut, New Jersey, and Massachusetts granted contracts to individuals to strike copper coins bearing inscriptions relating to the states, usually Latinized or abbreviated, such as VERMON, CONNEC, and NOVA CAESAREA. All of these coinages commenced before these entities actually were admitted to the Union, a procedure involving state legislatures' ratifying the Constitution (Delaware, not a coin issuer, was the first to ratify, on December 7, 1787). Vermont was the

1787 New Jersey copper, die variety Maris-48g. The inscription NOVA CÆSAREA is Latin for "New Jersey." Coins of this general type were minted from 1786 to 1788, under private contract and by several different individuals.

last of the coin-issuers to achieve statehood, in 1791.

In the late 1790s, Machin's Mills, a private mint near Newburgh, New York, struck some Vermont coppers under contract, but its main activity, conducted in secrecy, was counterfeiting coppers of other states and of England.

1787: Fugio Coppers Authorized. Congress granted a contract to strike cent-sized copper coins dated 1787, with a sundial and the inscriptions FUGIO and MIND YOUR BUSINESS on the obverse, and with rings on the reverse, the motifs being related to the 1776 Continental Currency pewter dollars. The Fugio coppers were made in large quantities.

Into the 1790s

1790s: Early Numismatists. The July 20, 1791, entry in William Bentley's diary included this:

> Being Commencement at Cambridge [Harvard College], I set out for Cambridge from Deacon Ridgeway's and in a chaise went to Judge Winthrop's[42] with whom I spent the day. In the morning I entertained myself with his curious cabinet of Coins and Medals. It was large and not with any antiques, but it had a great variety of small pieces and may be deemed the best we have in this part of the country. It is improving its value by constant additions, but it requires too great an interest in this country, to have its full success.

Although in America numismatists remained few, in England there was a great passion for collecting coins, tokens, and medals. Many British numismatists saved American coins when they came to hand, and in later years these formed a source for collectors in the United States.

1791: Vermont Joins the Union. The district of Vermont, which had issued paper money (1781) and coins (1785–1788), became the 14th state.

1791–1795: Washington Tokens Popular.

The portrait of George Washington, commander of the Continental Army during the Revolution, and president of the United States since 1789, is seen on many tokens, mostly copper, issued in the United States and England. Some are predated 1783. The British pieces are part of a flood of halfpennies struck in Birmingham and elsewhere for sale to collectors in that country, although some found their way to the United States.

1791–1811: First Bank of the United States.

This institution, based in Philadelphia, was privately operated. The bank, in business from 1791 until its charter expired in 1811, was viewed as a stable institution, and its bills were good. However, its very existence was controversial, as the United States government was a stockholder in this otherwise private enterprise, and the hundreds of private banks in various states, many of which had a lot of political clout, resisted its every move. Its charter was not renewed by Congress.

1792: Kentucky Joins the Union.

Kentucky becomes the 15th state.

Federal Coinage Begins

1792: Philadelphia Mint Established.

On July 31, 1792, the cornerstone was laid for the Philadelphia Mint, the second building created by the U.S. government (the first was a lighthouse). In attendance were President George Washington, Mint Director David Rittenhouse, and others. At the time, Philadelphia was the seat of the federal government, and the president resided just a short walk away. The Mint Act of April 2, 1792, created the Mint and specified the denominations to be coined, from the copper half cent to the $10 gold eagle, and the weight and metallic content of each. Unlike the Spanish and English coins then in use, the U.S. issues were based on the decimal system. By that time there was a coining press and some other equipment on hand, stored in an old carriage house on Sixth Street, above Chestnut, and owned by John Harper, a saw maker and mechanic. On July 11, 1792, Thomas Jefferson took $75 in silver to the coach house, the metal having been supplied by President Washington. It was converted into 1,500 tiny five-cent pieces, each with the inscription HALF / DISME. By

Bank of the United States, Philadelphia, as it appeared in 1799. The First Bank of the United States operated from 1791 to 1811. In 1816 it was succeeded in certain interests by the Second Bank of the United States. (William Birch, *Views of Philadelphia*, 1799)

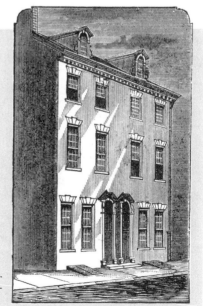

The Philadelphia Mint as it appeared in the 1790s. This was the largest of three buildings in the facility, and the structure in which coinage took place.

December, the Mint was in operation. In that month some pattern one-cent pieces and other proposals were made. Dies for some early patterns were made by an engraver named Birch, and Joseph Wright created a quarter-dollar pattern.

1792–1859. Foreign Coins Still Legal Tender. Even after the Philadelphia Mint was established in 1792, it would be many years until there was a large supply of U.S. coins in circulation. In the meantime, selected foreign silver and gold coins continued to dominate commerce. Their legal-tender status was revoked two and a half years after passage of the Act of February 21, 1857.

1793: First Copper Cents Coined. Copper one-cent pieces were first made for circulation in February 1793. The earliest versions had a head of Miss Liberty on the obverse and a chain of 15 links on the reverse, one for each state (by this time Vermont had joined the Union, in 1791, and Kentucky in 1792). Apparently, the design was less than pleasing. One newspaper account described Miss Liberty as being "in a fright," and the chain on the reverse as an ill omen for a land of freedom. The motif was changed to a different face of Miss Liberty, and, on the reverse, a wreath. That summer, copper half cents were made for the first time. Some early dies were made by Joseph Wright (who died of yellow fever that September), and possibly by Henry Voigt, an engraver on the Mint staff. In the autumn, Robert Scot, a local maker of copper plates for bank notes, maps, and illustrations, was hired as engraver.

1794: First Silver Coins Struck. In autumn 1794 the first silver coins were struck at the Philadelphia Mint, and consisted of half dollars and dollars of the Flowing Hair design. Dies dated 1794 for the half dime were made, but were not used until 1795.

1795: First Gold Coins Struck; Designs Evolve. In July of 1795 the first gold coins, $5 half eagles, were delivered, soon followed by $10 gold eagles, the largest denomination. Designs changed and evolved over the years, as discussed separately in chapters relating to the different series. It was general practice to have copper coins bear one common design, silver coins another standard motif, and gold coins still another, although sometimes there was overlapping. The Draped Bust obverse was first used on silver coins of 1795, then copper coins of 1796, while gold coins depicted Miss Liberty wearing a conical cloth cap.

1796: New Denominations. In 1796 the first silver dimes and quarter dollars were struck, as well as the first $2.50 gold quarter eagles, completing all of the denominations authorized. While half cents and cents were struck for the account and profit of the Mint, silver and gold coins were made only on the request of depositors of such precious metals (usually deposited in the form of foreign coins, but sometimes as worn-out utensils, old ornaments, etc.).

The various metals were melted and refined at the Mint, cast into ingots, and rolled into thin strips, after which round discs or planchets were cut from them. These were fed into coining presses, operated by hand, with men tugging at the ends of a weighted arm to drive the top (or hammer) die down to meet the bottom (anvil) die, and to impress a planchet in between. It was not until 1836 that steam was used to power the presses.

In the early days, dies for all denominations were cut by hand, with separate punches used to add numerals, letters, stars, and devices such as eagles and liberty heads. No two dies were ever alike, creating a wide panorama of varieties usually differing from each other slightly. However, more than just a few had interesting errors or blunders, such as having a word spelled as IINITED instead of UNITED, or having a fraction read a mathematically meaningless 1/000, instead of 1/100.

While 13 stars, or one for each of the original colonies, has been the standard count for stars on federal coins to this date, some of 1796 were given 15 stars, representing the current number of states in the Union. Tennessee joined in that year, raising the count to 16, and some coins were made with this number of stars. Soon, the idea was abandoned, and 13 became the standard. There were some exceptions, such as the erroneous 15 stars on an 1817 cent, and the use of 26 stars on the reverse of the 1836 Gobrecht dollar (26 being the roster of states in America at the time).

1799: Death of George Washington. George Washington died on December 14 at his home, Mount Vernon, on the bank of the Potomac River in Virginia. The nation went into mourning, and on February 22, 1800 (his birthday anniversary), memorial parades were held in many cities. Some in the processions wore silver funeral medals made by Jacob Perkins, of Newburyport, Massachusetts, depicting Washington on one side and, on the other, HE IS IN GLORY, THE WORLD IN TEARS. Such medals, as well as earlier tokens, would form the foundation for a later numismatic specialty.

The Early 19th Century

1800s: Lost Opportunities. As the ever-changing panorama of coin designs moved inexorably onward, there was little development in numismatic interest in America. Accordingly, countless wonderful opportunities were lost by the failure to save at least one new 1802 half dime from the 3,060 said to have been coined, or to stop by at the Mint in 1808 to get a brand-new gold $2.50 quarter eagle. Such are the vagaries and chances of preservation. Today, of the 1,500 1792 silver half dismes (half dimes) coined, more than a dozen beautiful Mint State coins are known. However, not a single 1802 in Mint State has ever appeared. The number of Uncirculated 1808 quarter eagles is so limited that they can be counted on the fingers of one hand.

1803: Louisiana Purchase. The government paid $15,000,000 to acquire the Louisiana Territory, vastly expanding the size of the nation. New Orleans, near the mouth of the Mississippi River, was the focal point of commerce. From 1804 through 1806, the Lewis and Clark expedition would explore much of the upper reaches of the Missouri River, continuing west to the Columbia River and the Pacific Ocean. Peace medals in silver and copper, some of the Washington "Seasons" issues (three designs), and others with the portrait of Thomas Jefferson, were taken along to present to Indian chiefs. The explorers also handed out silver dollars.

1806: Bank-Note Innovation. Jacob Perkins's "Patented Stereotype Steel Plate" became popular and was widely used to print bank bills. The intricate, tiny letters and designs were said to deter counterfeiting.

Washington's home as depicted decades later on a $5 note of the Mount Vernon Bank, Boston. (American Bank Note Co., circa 1860)

A $5 gold half eagle of the Capped Bust design by John Reich, introduced in 1807. A similar motif was used on half dollars the same year.

1807: *Capped Bust Design Created.* John
Reich, an assistant engraver at the Mint, created many dies from 1807 until the time he resigned, in 1817. His Capped Bust design appeared on the silver half dollars and gold half eagles in 1807, and later on other denominations in these metals. In 1808 Reich's Classic Head, another new style, was first used on the copper cent, then in 1809 on the half cent. The practice of coining gold and silver at depositors' request continued, resulting in erratic production figures. Sometimes the Mint was a beehive of activity, as in 1807, when nearly all denominations were struck, some of them in large quantities. At other times, activity was slow. In 1807 there were no half dimes, nor had there been since 1805, nor would there be until 1829.

1808–1815: *Economic Problems.* America
was prosperous from the early 1790s until 1808, when the effects of Thomas Jefferson's Embargo Act took effect. By that time, the French, then the British, had seized many American ships on the high seas, the British often kidnapping the sailors and forcing them to serve on their ships. The Embargo Act prohibited nearly all trade with foreign ports, in effect freezing the economies of most coastal cities. Many businesses failed, and other hardships were experienced. The War of 1812 created more chaos. The U.S. Navy was not strong, and to help fight the enemy, the government gave letters of marque, as they were called, to the ships' captains and owners. These individuals then engaged in privateering under the American flag, capturing whatever enemy prizes they could find, and taking the ships to ports where

they and their contents were sold at auction—with the money divided among the ship crews and owners. This was a rich undertaking for many, and more than a few family fortunes in Portsmouth, Baltimore, and other cities were augmented in this manner. The monetary situation in the United States was tumultuous. Gold and silver coins were in circulation in some periods; then one or another of these metals would rise in value, and many coins would disappear. Meanwhile, a flood of paper bills was issued by banks, merchants, and others.

1815–1816: *Scrip Notes Popular.* Small
coins become scarce in circulation in some areas, and many paper bills were issued in small denominations—scrip notes of such values as 12 1/2 cents (equal in value to the common Spanish-American one-*real*, or one-bit, coin) and 25 cents. Murray, Draper, Fairman & Co., of Philadelphia; Abner Reed, of Connecticut; and others engraved and printed notes for many stores, banks, and other customers. Times were slow at the Mint—deposits of silver and gold coins were small, and relatively few coins of these metals were struck. In 1816, only copper cents were made.

1816–1836: *Second Bank of the United States.* In 1816 the Second Bank of the
United States was formed, with a charter running until 1836. Branches were planned for Washington, Baltimore, New York City, and other locations, including small offices in the western districts. The first several years were scandal-ridden—not a good start—and the bank was called the "monster" by many. In the 1820s new management was put in place, and the bank did well—at least, it appears to have done well, from the vantage point of history. However, at the time it remained controversial. In 1828 Andrew Jackson was elected president. Amid political charges and counter-charges, he made an early statement that when the charter for the Bank of the United States came up for renewal, he would be against it.

Events of the 1820s

1820s–1830s: The Numismatic Scene.
During the early 19th century, two dozen or more historical societies, athenaeums, and libraries included coins in their holdings and exhibits. Among them were the Library Company of Philadelphia, the East India Society of Salem, Massachusetts, and the New-York Historical Society. Museums operated by Scudder, Peale, Barnum, and others, located in major cities and charging admission to the general public, often featured such items—but today little is known relating to specific coins on display. In Economy, Pennsylvania (a communal work-share settlement not far from Pittsburgh), a Cabinet of Curiosities was established circa 1827 and is said to have had coins and medals on display, although the nature of these items is no longer known.

The first professional numismatist in the United States seems to have been John Allan, born in Scotland. In 1820 he was one of just three American subscribers to Mudie's set of National Medals, published in England. The others were a Mr. Paine of New York and Thomas Lyman, whose address was given as "United States," in a leaflet distributed with the set. Philip Hone, a wealthy New Yorker who served as mayor of the city in 1826, is known to have been an active coin collector in New York City circa 1822 to 1827.[43]

The private collection of Benjamin H. Watkins, auctioned in Salem, Massachusetts, on June 12 and 13, 1828, is thought to be the first significant cataloged sale of coins in the United States, although the *cataloging* itself was poor by later standards, and consisted of grouped lots with sparse descriptions. John H. Nichols, 17-year-old son of auctioneer John Nichols, created the listing, which comprised 530 lots of coins, books, engravings, and other items, among which were several Massachusetts coins, including two New England shillings, a silver threepence, and a twopence, these being the only pieces outside of bulk lots (21 lots took care of 350 coins altogether).[44] The younger Nichols went on to pursue numismatics with a passion.

1821–1834: No U.S. Gold Coins in Circulation. The price of gold rose in relation to silver, and gold coins became worth more in melt value than face value. Large quantities were coined to the order of depositors who shipped them overseas, where they were received on the basis of weight, with the stamped value being of no importance. In the United States, anyone desiring gold coins had to pay a premium for them to a money broker or exchange office.

1824: Kneass Appointed Engraver. Robert Scot continued as chief engraver at the Mint until his death on November 3, 1823. By that time, his eyesight had been poor for many years. Today, students of Mint history are not sure who made new dies after assistant Reich resigned in 1817. William Kneass, a local engraver of copper plates for bank notes and other items, was appointed chief engraver in 1824.

Beginning about that same year, Adam Eckfeldt and perhaps one or two others working at the Philadelphia Mint

The Second Bank of the United States, Philadelphia. (Bartlett's *American Scenery*, 1840)

began saving current coinage.[45] It is said that copper cents and other items were kept on hand for sale or exchange with interested collectors. Interesting rare coins were picked out of incoming deposits and saved. Many old dies were still at the Mint, and on occasion restrikes would be made to supply needed pieces. No records were kept of such activities, and today we can only speculate as to what occurred.

1824–1825: Lafayette, "The Nation's Guest." Marquis de Lafayette, French hero of the American Revolution, visited America in 1824 and 1825 and was designated "the Nation's Guest" by Congress. He toured every state in the Union, visited with prominent officials as well as everyday citizens, and was featured in parades and ceremonies. Cents and half dollars were counterstamped with his likeness on one side and Washington's on the other (from dies by Joseph Lewis), and many medals, ribbons, and badges were made. Lafayette's portrait was subsequently used on many bank notes, along with portraits of Washington, Franklin, and other figures from history.

1829: Cornerstone Laid for New Mint. On July 4, 1829, the cornerstone was laid for a new Philadelphia Mint building. For the occasion, half dimes of the Capped Bust type were struck for the first time, there having been no coinage of this denomination since 1805.

Economic Prosperity and Related Matters

1830: Jackson's Veto of the Bank of the United States Charter Renewal. A bill to renew the charter of the second Bank of the United States went through Congress in 1830, well in advance of the 1836 expiration, but President Andrew Jackson vetoed it. From that time onward, politicians, newspapers, and others were largely divided into two groups: pro-Jackson and anti-Jackson. As if that were not enough, John C. Calhoun, senator from South Carolina, frequently suggested that South

Carolina withdraw from the Union, and that other southern states do so as well, as the commercial interests of the South (cotton, tobacco, and other agricultural products) were so different from those of the North (manufacturing, banking, etc.). In particular, high tariffs had diminished exports of cotton, to the detriment of the South, while restricting imports from Europe and thus bringing great prosperity to factories in the North.

Also in the 1820s, extensive gold strikes were made in Georgia and North Carolina. In 1830 Templeton Reid issued his own $2.50, $5, and $10 gold coins, and in Rutherfordton, North Carolina, Christopher Bechtler and his family operated a private mint that would remain in business until the early 1850s and would make $1, $2.50, and $5 coins.

1830s: Prosperous Times. Although there were many memorable political battles and controversies during this time, in the early 1830s America was generally prosperous. This was due to enthusiasm for building canals and railroads, the opening up of new lands in the West and making them easy to buy, and a general atmosphere of well-being. The age of steam was beginning in a large way and would soon revolutionize industrial America.

With the Bank of the United States on its deathbed, waiting for its charter to run out, private banks enjoyed unprece-

The steamship *Sirius* in the harbor of New York City, 1838. (From a book of vignettes issued by the Bureau of Engraving and Printing in the 1870s; this motif was used on $500 National Bank notes of the Original Series and 1875 Series)

dented business. Many of them were designated by the Jackson administration as depositories of federal money. These favored institutions were known as *pet banks.* Companies engraving and printing bills for these banks did unprecedented business, while in the meantime the designs and ornamentation of such currency evolved from rustic and simple to ornate and complex—often with fancy vignettes, illustrations of gods and goddesses, trains and buildings, farmers and mechanics at work, and countless variations of the American eagle. Railroads in particular—the growth industry of the period—were popular. Among the leading firms was Draper, Toppan, Longacre & Co. of Philadelphia. Years later, James B. Longacre would become chief engraver at the Mint.

It was often the case that a bank capitalized for $100,000 had not received $100,000 in coins for its stock. Instead, it was the usual practice for stockholders to give promissory notes or IOUs. Because of this, the annals of finance show many instances in which a bank with $100,000 in stated capital had only $10,000 to $20,000, or not even that much, paid in. Banks were allowed to issue their own paper money, usually up to the amount of their stated capital (even if not paid for in coins), and often much more. If requested, most banks would redeem their bills with coins. When a bank appeared to be stable, as most did, few bills were turned in. A bank with a published capital of $100,000, and with $250,000 in bills in circulation, might have only $5,000 to $10,000 in coins on hand for redeeming paper money, and this was considered sufficient—or at least it appeared to be.

1830s: Numismatists of the Era.
A commentary in *Norton's Literary Letter,* published years later in 1859, told of three active collectors in the 1830s:

> At a time when "coin collectors" in the United States were popularly considered little better than mono-

maniacs, two or three gentlemen—Dr. J.B. Felt, of Salem, Mass., Mr. J. Francis Fisher, of Baltimore, and Dr. Jas. Mease, of Philadelphia—were deeply interested in the subject, and communicated the results of their investigations to societies of which they were members, or published them in a separate form....[46]

By the early 1830s there were probably 50 to 100 dedicated collectors of coins in the United States, but their interests seem to have been with medals, ancient coins, and other items apart from current Philadelphia Mint products. There were scattered exceptions, such as Robert Gilmor, Jr., of Baltimore, of whom Dr. Joel Orosz has written much in recent years. Gilmor collected the American series, including gold coins by date.

1833: New Mint Opens.
Coinage equipment and activities were transferred to the new Philadelphia Mint building. While steam was used to drive the rolling mills for making planchet strips, coins continued to be struck by hand.

1834: Gold Coins Circulate Again.
The Act of June 28, 1834, reduced the amount of gold in coins, and the lightweight issues made beginning in August of that year circulated readily. Gold had not been seen in domestic commerce since 1821.

No silver dollars had been coined since 1804 (in that year, some were made from dies of earlier years). It fell to the Capped Bust half dollar to be the United States

Quarter eagle of the new Classic Head design, 1834 (enlarged), produced under the Coinage Act of June 28, 1834. Such coins, and related half eagles, were made in large quantities and circulated widely, the first time gold coins had been seen in commerce since 1821.

163

silver coin of choice, and they were made in large quantities. However, Spanish-American two-*real* and other silver coins remained dominant in commerce. In 1834 the Mint created Proof sets of current coinage for use as diplomatic gifts. For the $1 and $10 denominations, new dies were created with the 1804 date, to reflect the last time these values had been struck. The Mint did not realize that while in 1804 some $10 coins had been made, the silver dollars made in 1804 were from earlier-dated dies. Thus, 1804-dated dollars, later to become great numismatic rarities, were made for the first time in 1834.

1835: Gobrecht Hired as a Mint Engraver. In August 1835, Chief Engraver Kneass was stricken by a paralytic stroke. In the next month, Christian Gobrecht, a Philadelphia inventor and an engraver of bank notes, book plates, and other items, was hired as second engraver. A man of formidable artistic ability, Gobrecht did not want to be called "assistant," and thus the "second" in his title. As it turned out, he did most of the engraving work from that point onward, although Kneass retained the chief engravership until his death in 1840.

Changing Times of the Late 1830s

1836: Jackson's Specie Circular. Prosperity continued in America through 1836, the year that the Bank of the United States charter expired. Speculation in real estate in the prairie beyond Pennsylvania was wildly out of control. Vast tracts were purchased through credits and drafts, paper money of depreciated or uncertain value, and promissory notes. This set the scene for Andrew Jackson's Specie Circular, July 11, 1836, one of the most pivotal documents in American financial history. This decree mandated that lands be paid for in gold and silver coins instead of paper money and credits; that buyers be bona fide residents or settlers; and that the amount of acreage be restricted for each purchaser. Very few buyers of land had silver half dollars or gold half eagles, and speculation

came to an abrupt halt. Loans were called, but debtors could not pay. By early 1837 there was a chill in the American economy, and European bankers, who held many investments, were becoming concerned. Matters went from bad to worse, business slowed further, and many banks experienced difficulty.

Also in 1836, there were several changes and innovations at the Philadelphia Mint. On March 23, steam power was used for coinage for the first time, and for the rest of the year it was employed in the striking of copper cents and, in autumn, silver coins. Soon, all production was accomplished in this manner.

In the same year, the Liberty Seated design made its debut on the silver dollar, the first one coined for circulation since 1804. *Niles' Weekly Register,* December 17, 1836, printed this:

> *The new dollar.* It gives us pleasure to announce—says the *Washington Globe* of yesterday morning—that the one dollar of our own mint is soon to make its appearance. The face of the coin represents a full length figure of Liberty, seated on a rock, with the classic emblem of the *pileus* or liberty-cap surmounting a spear held in the left hand. The right hand rests on the American shield, with its thirteen stripes, crossed by a scroll, on which is the word liberty. The reverse represents the American eagle, on the wing, drawn accurately from nature; all the heraldic appendages of the old coin being discarded. Over the field are placed irregularly twenty-six stars; the entrance of Michigan into the union, having been, it seems, anticipated. The design of the face of the coin was drawn by Mr. Sully, and that of the reverse by Mr. Titian Peale; both under instructions from the director of the Mint. The dies were executed by Mr. Gobrecht, one of the engravers of the Mint. This emission of dollars is the first coined at the mint since the year [1804]. It is

intended to adopt the same design in the other coins, as soon as it is practicable to do so.

1836–1838: Many New Banks. After the charter of the second Bank of the United States expired, many banks were formed with reckless abandon. The bank-note companies in New York and Philadelphia were eager to print as many bills as they could sell, with little notice taken as to whether the banks were chartered or legitimately established.

1837: Specie Payments Suspended; Hard Times Era Begins. The system of banks' issuing large amounts of paper money worked perfectly fine in the heady days of 1835 and 1836. However, in early 1837 many people became wary of banks, and sought to redeem bills. It was quickly learned that while some banks could redeem a small percentage of their currency, no bank was able to exchange for all. On May 10, 1837, specie payments were suspended by most eastern banks, and within weeks most banks in the South and West also stopped paying out coins.

Soon, silver and gold coins disappeared completely from circulation, although copper "large" cents remained. To facilitate commerce, countless cent-sized Hard Times tokens (as we call them today) were issued, in a wide variety of designs, including advertisements for merchants, carica-tures and comments about Jackson and his veto of the Bank of the United States (Jackson's political opponents declared that if it had remained in business, America would still be prosperous), and more.

1837–1838: Many Banks Fail. With few coins in circulation and no federal currency, bank notes formed the main basis for trade. Entrepreneurs, many dishonest, set up banks to issue paper money, creating a flood of bills, most of which became worthless. In Michigan in particular, in 1837 dozens of new institutions sprang up, usually with little in the way of capital, but with grandiose pretensions to strength and size. Within a few years, more than 90% of the Michigan banks collapsed, leaving behind many distressed people holding their currency. In December 1837, after most of the abuses had already occurred, Michigan appointed several banking commissioners to make the rounds, which they did, beginning in 1838. One of them, Alpheus Felch, wrote of his experiences, including this:

> The Bank of Sandstone, for instance, never had any specie, and although its liabilities exceeded $38,000 it had no assets of any kind at the time when it was examined. The Jackson County Bank placed before the commissioners a goodly number of ponderous and well-filled boxes, but on opening

Located in Barry, Michigan, the Farmers Bank of Sandstone issued large amounts of paper money, but had virtually nothing in the way of assets. At the time it was examined by Alpheus Felch, no coins at all were on hand to redeem such notes. This $2 bill was printed in Boston by the New England Bank Note Co.

them and examining their contents the top was found covered with silver dollars,[47] but below was nothing but nails and glass. Another box said to contain silver was then brought from another room and upon inspection was found to contain coins of this metal. A director was present during the examination and attested under oath that the coins were property of the bank. However, when the bank failed, this same man brought an action against the receiver of the bank claiming the coins as his personal property! This bank, with an indebtedness of some $70,000, had no more than $5,000 of available assets.[48]

In June 1838 the Mint Cabinet was opened—a display of American coins old and new, foreign and ancient coins and medals, and mineral specimens and ores. While a few coins were purchased, the main source of supply continued to be the extraction of interesting pieces from deposits made at the Mint. Veteran Mint employee Adam Eckfeldt supplied details of Mint history to interested visitors.

Expanded commerce in the Mississippi River Valley (mainly through the port of New Orleans) and gold mining in Georgia and North Carolina prompted the opening of three branch mints in 1838—New Orleans, Dahlonega (Georgia), and Charlotte. Coins struck there were given the mintmarks O, D, and C, respectively.

Good Times Return in the 1840s

1842: Coin "Manual" Published. By the early 1840s, Jacob Reese Eckfeldt and William DuBois were curators of the pieces on display in the Mint Cabinet. In 1842 a book by these two men, *A Manual of Gold and Silver Coins of All Nations*, was published by the Mint. The text was in no way numismatic, but dealt with the weights and designations of coins in these metals. Illustrated for the first time was an 1804-dated dollar, one of the coins struck in 1834 in connection with diplomatic gift sets.

1843: Active Numismatists. A listing of active collectors made by DuBois in 1843 and sent to Matthew A. Stickney of Salem, Massachusetts, included the names of Dr. Lewis Roper, Jacob G. Morris, Richard W. Davids (a nephew of Mr. Morris), W.G. Mason, C.C. Ashmead, John Reeve, a Mr. Cooper (of Camden, New Jersey), Hon. Henry A. Muhlenberg (of Reading, Pennsylvania), Rev. Dr. Robbins (of Hartford, Connecticut, and an uncle of Matthew A. Stickney), and Edmund B. Wynn (of Hamilton, New York). Shown this roster, New York City dealer John Allan added the names of Philip Hone and Robert Gilmor, Jr. To the preceding one must add Joseph J. Mickley, a Philadelphian, born in 1799, who had been collecting coins since his teenage years. Apparently, DuBois simply forgot to include him.

By this time, several collectors sought Proof sets of current coinage. Again, no records were kept, but production must have been small. In some years, 1851 and 1853 being examples, it is believed that no full sets of Proofs were made. However, beginning in 1854, sets were issued regularly and contained coins from the copper half cent upward to the silver dollar. A few gold Proofs were also made.

1844: Hard Times End. By this time, the Hard Times era had ended, and American commerce was flourishing. Following the death of Christian Gobrecht, who had been an engraver at the Mint since 1835 and chief since 1840, James B. Longacre was appointed chief engraver. He would serve until his death on January 1, 1869. During his tenure he would create many designs for pattern and regular coinage.

1846: Booklet Describes Mint Cabinet. William DuBois's 138-page *Pledges of History* described coins and other items in the Mint Cabinet.

1848: Important Book on Medals Published. Thomas Wyatt's 315-page volume, *Memoirs of the Generals, Commodores, and Other Commanders, Who Distinguished Themselves in the American Army and Navy*

During The Wars of The Revolution, and 1812, and Who Were Presented With Medals by Congress, For Their Gallant Services. Illustrated by Eighty-Two Engravings on Steel from the Original Medals, was published in Philadelphia by Carey & Hart. The engravings were by Waterman L. Ormsby, a talented engraver of bank notes and illustrated plates.

1848–1857: The California Gold Rush. The discovery of a gleaming flake of gold in the tailrace at Sutter's Mill, on the American River, January 24, 1848, ignited the Gold Rush, the travel westward of Forty-Niners the following year, and the establishment of California as a state in 1850. This event transformed the boundaries and encouraged settlement more than any other single event in American history. Now, the country extended from sea to shining sea. The vast discoveries of precious metal engendered the establishment of several private mints in San Francisco, Sacramento, and elsewhere in 1849 and 1850, followed in time by the opening of the San Francisco Mint, March 1854, in facilities earlier used by private coiner Moffat & Co. and the United States Assay Office of Gold. Additional amounts of gold were sent to the East for coinage, usually by ship from San Francisco to Panama, then across land for about 48 miles, then connecting to another ship on the Atlantic side.

1849: Gold Dollars Introduced. The $1 gold denomination, from dies by James B. Longacre, was introduced on May 30, under the Act of March 3, 1849. In response to the large influx of gold from California, the new $1 and $20 denominations were authorized.

Numismatics and Commerce in the 1850s

1850: Double Eagles Introduced. The $20 gold piece, or double eagle, was introduced this year and was struck at the Philadelphia and New Orleans mints. These coins became exceedingly popular, and during the next 75 years, more value

was minted in this denomination than of all other United States coins combined.

Also in 1850, Jacob Reese Eckfeldt and William DuBois, assayers at the Mint and keepers of the Mint Cabinet, published a small book of 61 pages, *New Varieties of Gold and Silver Coins, Counterfeit Coins, Bullion With Mint Values.* Included was information on gold coins privately minted in California. This work was also issued in modified form in 1851 and 1852; these two later versions also included the text of DuBois's 1846 *Pledges of History* work, the latter being out of print at the time.

The influx of so much gold from California disturbed its historic ratio of value with silver, in which 15 1/2 ounces of silver equaled one ounce of gold. Gold became "common," silver increased in price, and it took less than 15 1/2 ounces to buy an ounce of gold. Beginning in 1850 nearly all silver coins disappeared from circulation, to be melted down for their bullion content, now worth more than face value.

1850s: Rare Coins on Public Display. Barnum's American Museum in New York City, the Boston Museum, Peale's Museum in Philadelphia, and other museums, all of which charged admission, often featured coins and medals as part of their advertised exhibits.

Seeking gold in a streambed in California in the 1850s. The discovery of precious metal in quantity at Sutter's Mill in 1848 set the scene for the Gold Rush, which redefined the boundaries of America.

1851: First Important Rare Coin Auction.
The first truly important American auction sale featuring rare coins was that of the late Dr. Lewis Roper, a Philadelphian who had gone west to seek his fortune in the gold fields but never returned. The coins were offered on February 20, 1851, in the salesroom of Moses Thomas & Son, Philadelphia, a popular location for the sale of antiques, books, and other items. The catalog was titled *Executors' Sale. Valuable Collection of Gold and Silver Coins and Medals, Etc., Catalogue of the Entire Collection of Rare and Valuable Coins, Medals, Autographs, Mahogany Coins Case, Etc., Late of Doctor Lewis Roper, deceased.*

That same year, the silver three-cent piece, or *trime*, was issued. Of 75% silver and 25% copper (instead of the standard 90-10 ratio), these coins were not profitable to melt, and thus they circulated in commerce at a time when other federal silver coins were being hoarded or melted.

1852: Book With Coin Illustrations Published. Benson Lossing's two-volume *Pictorial Field-Book of the Revolution* was published this year and contained many illustrations of coins and medals, and some of paper money. The book was a great success, and although it was not specifically

numismatic, the information contributed to knowledge on the subject. Waterman L. Ormsby, New York engraver of currency plates, published the large and impressive book *Bank Note Engraving*, describing various processes and methods of deterring counterfeiting, and including much history. It was illustrated by many finely engraved plates. Today it remains a standard reference.

1853: New Silver Coins Circulate. Following the Act of February 21, 1853, the authorized weights of the silver half dime, dime, quarter, and half dollar were reduced. Coins made under the new standard had arrowheads added to each side of the date to distinguish them. These lightweight coins circulated, thus ending the money problems in the market since 1850.

The first event in America with a semblance to an international exposition or fair was the opening of the Crystal Palace in New York City, which became the venue for many displays. Many of the investors in the project had seen the success of the annual fairs of the American Institute held in the city at Niblo's Garden, and felt that a permanent showcase of displays would be profitable. It was a great attraction until it burned in 1858.

Barnum's American Museum, New York City, as it appeared in 1853. Its displays included coins, tokens, medals, and paper money, the exact nature of which is not known today. At the time, the museum was New York City's single most important attraction. (*Gleason's Pictorial*, January 29, 1853)

The Crystal Palace, New York City, opened in 1853 and became a center for exhibitions. (Devens, *Our First Century*, 1881)

Many different medals were issued in connection with the building and with fairs held there (including by the American Institute, which thereafter adopted the venue). Augustus B. Sage's "All Is Vanity" medalet, from dies by George H. Lovett, is bittersweet and was produced shortly after the Crystal Palace was destroyed.

1854: San Francisco Mint Opens. The branch mint at San Francisco opened in March and commenced striking coins with S mintmarks. Commercial connections between the Atlantic and Pacific coasts were mainly by ship, interrupted by a land crossing at Panama (or, less often, Nicaragua), or were entirely by sea, around the tip of South America. Also that year, the $3 coin was introduced. It did not prove popular, mintage figures declined, and in 1889 it was discontinued.

1855–1857: Prosperity and Speculation. The American economy was enjoying a new era of prosperity brought on by the gold excitement, the continued expansion of railroads (their shares dominated the stock exchanges), and excellent business conditions everywhere. Land investment and speculation was back in vogue, and real estate agents were literally doing a land-office business in what was now known as the Midwest, the term *West* now being descriptive of the region from the Rocky Mountains to the Pacific shore.

1856: Flying Eagle Cent Patterns Made. The Mint had been experimenting since 1850 with ways to reduce the size and weight of the one-cent piece, to increase profits. The price of copper had been rising. In 1856, Chief Engraver Longacre created a cent that was proposed for adoption. The obverse featured a flying eagle (adapted from the reverse of Gobrecht's silver dollar of 1836), and the reverse used an "agricultural wreath" from the $3 gold coin of 1854. An estimated 800 to 1,000 coins were struck in late 1856 and early 1857, all dated 1856, and sent to congressmen, newspaper editors, and others to acquaint them with the new design.

1857: The Coinage and Paper Money Scene Early in the Year. The Philadelphia Mint remained the primary facility for federal coinage. The director of the Mint had his office there and supervised the operations of the branches at Charlotte, Dahlonega, New Orleans, and San Francisco. Coins in circulation or currently being minted included the copper half cent and cent; the silver three-cent piece, half dime, dime, quarter dollar, half dollar, and dollar; and the gold $1, $2.50, $3, $5, $10, and $20. Paper bills, mostly of such denominations as $1, $2, $3, $5, and $10, but also of higher values, were circulated by nearly a thousand banks. The commercial scene was stable, most banks were sound, and nearly all paper money circulated at par and was readily exchangeable in its region for other bills or coins.

Copper cents were last made in January 1857, after which the series passed into history (variety Newcomb-4). The end of the "large" cent precipitated a wave of nostalgia across America, after which the hobby of numismatics would never be the same again.

CHAPTER ELEVEN

THE COIN MARKET, 1857–1929

Lucullan Luxury: You do not know what a denarius is? Lucullus once spent 50,000 of them on a single supper in ancient Rome, so it was an $8,000 affair! What did the parrot say? "Pieces of eight. Pieces of eight!" Long John Silver taught him the byword of the Spanish Main; and you don't know what it meant! Coins, all kinds, are the very essence of history. We can show you both denarii and pieces of eight if you are intrigued.

—Spink & Son, Ltd., December 1928

The Numismatic Hobby Grows

The Act of February 21, 1857, abolished the copper half cent and cent and mandated other changes, including the planned expiration of the legal tender privilege for certain foreign silver and gold coins. New cents of the Flying Eagle design, of smaller diameter and made of copper-nickel, soon began rolling off the presses. On May 25, the first small cents were available to the public in exchange for old coppers and Spanish silver. A newspaper account told the story:

Every man and boy in the crowd had his package of coin with them. Some had their rouleaux of Spanish coin done up in bits of newspaper wrapped in handkerchiefs, while others had carpet bags, baskets and other carrying contrivances, filled with coppers....

[In the Mint yard a] temporary structure was furnished with two open windows which faced the south. Over one of these windows were inscribed the words CENTS FOR CENTS, and over the other CENTS FOR SILVER. Inside the little office were scales and other apparatus for weighing and testing coin, a goodly pile of bags containing the newly-struck compound of nickel and copper, and a detachment of weighers, clerks, etc. The bags containing the "nicks" were neat little canvas arrangements, each of which held 500 of the diminutive little strangers, and each of which bore upon the outside the pleasant inscription "$5."

Just as the State House bell had finished striking 9 o'clock the doors of the Mint were thrown open, and in rushed the eager crowd—paper parcels, well-filled handkerchiefs, carpet bags, baskets and all. But those who thought there was to be a grand scramble, and that the boldest pusher would be first served, reckoned without their host. The invading throng was arranged into lines which led to the respective windows; those who bore silver had the post of honor assigned them and went to the right, while those who bore nothing but vulgar copper [old half cents and large cents] were constrained to take the left....

We estimated that at one time there could not have been less than 1,000 persons in the zigzag lines, weighed down with small change, and waiting patiently for their turn. Those who were served rushed into the street with their moneybags, and many of them were immediately surrounded by an outside crowd, who were willing to buy out in small lots and in advance on first cost. We saw quite a number of persons on the steps of the Mint dealing out the new favorites in advance of from 30% to 100%, and some of the outside purchasers even huckstered out the coin again in smaller lots at a still heavier advance....

In a few weeks the coin will be plentiful enough at par, the Spanish coins will go out at the hands of the

Released on May 25, 1857, the new Flying Eagle cents of small size caused a lot of excitement.

brokers just as they already have disappeared from ordinary circulation, and as regard for the old cents there will be "nary red" to be seen, except such as will be found in the cabinets of coin collectors.[49]

The "cabinets of coin collectors," already recognized, would increase to numbers not before imagined. Advances "of from 30% to 100%" would become familiar to many others as old and new coins changed hands. A wave of nostalgia swept across America, and thousands of citizens looked through their pocket change and storage places, hoping to find one large copper cent of each date.

A passion for coin collecting spread rapidly, with numismatologists, as they were called, seeking rare early cents such as 1793 and 1799, while noticing other interesting old coins as well. Within several years important reference books would be published on coins, dealers would set up shop in major cities, and coin auctions would be held frequently. Thus was born an active market for rare coins, tokens, and medals. In the 1870s paper money would become a popular specialty as well—again an experience in nostalgia, as collectors sought to acquire bills of the Confederate States of America and the federal Fractional Currency issues.

Time passed, reference books were published, magazines and newspapers were issued, clubs and societies became important, and rare coins developed into a sizeable business.

The following time line traces the changes and evolutions in money and the economy, along with the progress of the ever-growing field of numismatics, from the first truly active year in the numismatic hobby until the beginning of the Depression in 1930.

The Pivotal Year of 1857

1857: Flying Eagle Cents. The Mint Act of February 21, 1857, eliminated the copper half cent and cent, and provided for a new, small cent of 88 grains' weight, made of copper-nickel alloy. The new Flying Eagle cents were struck in large quantities (amounting to 7,450,000 for the entire 1857 year), and were initially distributed on May 25.

On the same day, Mint Director James Ross Snowden wrote to Secretary of the Treasury James Guthrie: "The demand for them is enormous.… We had on hand this morning $30,000 worth, that is 3,000,000 pieces. Nearly all of this amount will be paid out today. The coinage will go forward, however, at the rate of 100,000 or more pieces per day and the demand will be met as well as we can."

In January of 1857, the *Historical Magazine* was launched; it went on to include many articles about coins, including, in August, the first installment of "The First Coinage of America," by Jeremiah Colburn, who in the same year wrote articles about old copper cents for the Boston *Evening Transcript*. In New York City, Augustus B. Sage and Charles I. Bushnell engaged in a lively debate about rare coins in the pages of the *New-York Dispatch*. In the autumn, the first issue of *Norton's Literary Letter*, mostly about books but with much information on coins, was welcomed by collectors. Still, there were no special books for the coin collector, no price lists, and the auction market was extremely quiet.

In the first part of the year, the American economy continued to enjoy prosperity, spurred by gold shipments coming from California, profitable speculations in prairie lands, excellent sales for agricultural products and manufactured goods, and the ever-growing railway system. Then, on August 24, 1857, the Ohio Life Insurance & Trust Company failed. With offices in Cincinnati and New York, it had been a big player in loans, credit, and the processing of paper relating to real estate. By then there had been some shivers in the money market, and some were apprehensive concerning seemingly unwise investments, but little was said. On the same day, the Mechanics Banking Association suspended specie payments. Fear spread, and those holding stocks and investment paper rushed to cash it in at current rates, but found few buyers. Within days, several stockbrokers and money dealers failed. This was disturbing but exciting news, and papers in major cities lost no time printing "scare" headlines, which sold more papers but also helped spread fear. In a domino effect, one failure created another, and soon the Panic of 1857 was underway. In October, all of the banks in New York City, except for the Chemical Bank, suspended specie payments.

In the meantime, on September 12, 1857, the *S.S. Central America* was lost at sea, carrying more than a million dollars in gold coins and ingots from San Francisco and several hundred unfortunate passengers to a watery fate. The loss of this bullion increased the economic uncertainty prevailing in the Eastern markets. Years later, the shipwreck would be found, and its golden treasures would electrify the coin-collecting world.

The Excitement of Coin Collecting

1858: Cent-Collecting Fever. The stage was set, and thousands of citizens cherished their sparkling new Flying Eagle cents while contemplating the disappearance of the familiar copper "pennies" of childhood days. Pocket change and cash drawers were searched, and soon quite a few collectors had strings of such coins dating all the way back to the first year of issue, 1793, but perhaps lacking the rare 1799, 1804, 1815 (which was never struck, but few were aware of this), and 1823. The earlier coins were apt to be well worn, with dates and designs barely visible. The most recent ones showed blushes of orange Mint color. Edward Cogan, an art dealer in Philadelphia, was asked to sell a friend's collection of copper cents, and sent out listings, inviting bids by mail (closing on November 1). Bids were received from 19 people. A 1793 Chain cent sold for $12.67, a 1793 Wreath cent brought $5.13, a 1793 Liberty Cap realized $7.25, a 1799 cent sold for $7, and an 1804 brought $5.50, among others. The total amount realized for the collection of cents from 1793 through 1858 was $128.68. This was exciting news; it was picked up by the local papers and was soon

A group of gold ingots lost at sea aboard the *S.S. Central America*, September 12, 1857, and recovered in the late 1980s—to the amazement and delight of the numismatic community. (*Guide Book of United States Coins*)

reprinted throughout the East. Cogan was deluged with letters from people wanting to buy and sell coins. Soon, he decided to become a professional numismatist.

On January 1, the Philadelphia Numismatic Society was formed, becoming the first such group in the United States. In March, teenager Augustus B. Sage and friends founded the American Numismatic Society in New York City. By late summer 1858 there were nearly a dozen dealers active in the United States, including, in New York City alone, the venerable John Allan, and at least three young men: Augustus Sage, Henry Bogert, and John Curtis.

Also in 1858, the first important numismatic book was published in America, *An Historical Account of American Coinage*, by John H. Hickcox. The slim volume included 151 numbered pages plus five pages of illustrations, these by John E. Gavit of Albany, a well-known engraver of bank notes. Hickcox had spent some time in research and had contacted historical societies and several numismatists as well as Mint Director James Ross Snowden. Only 200 regular copies were printed, and these were mostly sent to libraries and historical societies. For collectors there was no single, readily available source for information, and many still sought the elusive copper cent of 1815, not realizing that none were minted that year.

Proof coins became popular in 1858, and an estimated 210 sets of silver denominations were sold, plus a larger number of copper-nickel Flying Eagle cents. Proof gold coins were available singly, and the dollar was the most popular denomination in this metal, probably with a sale of a few dozen or so.

1859–1885: The Mint as a Coin Dealer.

The Mint became America's largest "coin dealer," de facto, but not officially. From 1859 until about 1885, tens of thousands of rare patterns, restrikes, and other delicacies were made for the private profit of officials holding positions there. Years later, in 1887, when a new Mint director sought to

learn details, he was amazed to find that the only records on hand were for a few 1868 Proof sets struck in aluminum. Everything else was "off the books." Today, collectors are grateful for this secret activity within the Mint walls, as otherwise most Gobrecht silver dollars of 1838 and 1839, the Flying Eagle cents of 1856, and most pattern coins would not exist!

1859: Director Snowden Seeks Washington Pieces; Mint Makes Restrikes of Rarities.

In early 1859, Director James Ross Snowden at the Mint was besieged with requests for pattern coins, Proofs, and rarities. These were supplied to the extent that examples were on hand, after which (beginning that spring) Snowden had some old dies dusted off and commenced to make restrikes of silver Gobrecht dollars of 1836 through 1839, the rare 1804 dollar, and other rarities. Snowden himself was a numismatist, and his prime interest was to secure tokens and medals of George Washington to display in the Mint Collection. Word quickly spread that anyone having such pieces could trade them at the Mint for all sorts of valuable restrikes and rarities! The pattern 1856 Flying Eagle cent became a stock-in-trade item for insiders at

Insiders at the Mint had a field day making and selling rare pattern coins to numismatists. Shown here is a pattern half dollar of 1859, variety Judd-241, with the obverse showing the "French Liberty Head" by Chief Engraver James B. Longacre, and the reverse a "cereal wreath," from an idea suggested by Philadelphia numismatist Harold P. Newlin.

the Mint, as such coins readily sold for $1 or more on the market. Newly created rare and valuable patterns, restrikes, and other delicacies were fed into the market and were eagerly purchased. There was little differentiation among collectors and dealers as to what was an original and what was a restrike. Each served equally well to fill a space in a collection and, if anything, restrikes were in higher grades and more attractive. While a later generation of numismatists would separate original and restrike half cents of the 1840s by the size of the berries in the reverse wreath, or realize that nearly all *Proof* 1856 Flying Eagle cents were restrikes and that absolutely all 1853 Proof dollars were likewise, no one cared back then.

Coin auctions became more frequent, and in 1859 dealer Sage cataloged four sales in New York City, more than any other professional. In Philadelphia, Edward Cogan and William K. Idler became important in the coin trade. Henry Cook bought and sold coins in Boston, another shop was open in Baltimore, and a few more were scattered here and there. The first really large and impressive book for coin collectors, the *American Numismatical Manual*, by Dr. Montroville W. Dickeson, was published.

The Curious Monetary Scene of the 1860s

1860–1861: Colorado Gold Coinage. In Denver the banking firm of Clark, Gruber & Co. set up a private mint and bank, and coined $2.50, $5, $10, and $20 pieces from local bullion. The district was in the middle of the "Pikes Peak or Bust" gold boom. Such coins were also made in 1861.

1860–1861: Washington Items Lead the Market. The swelling number of enthusiasts electrified the coin market. Most in demand were the old copper cents, but the hottest area in terms of rapid price appreciation was the specialty of Washington pieces. Collectors scrambled to buy them in competition with Director Snowden.

Prices multiplied, and specimens were hard to find. On February 22, 1860, the Washington Cabinet display was opened as part of the Mint Cabinet. In the same year, Snowden's name appeared on the title page of a large, handsome, and information-filled 412-page illustrated book, *A Description of Ancient and Modern Coins in the Cabinet of the Mint of the United States*. This text, primarily researched and written by William DuBois and George Bull (curator of the Mint Cabinet), stands today as an important reference. In 1861, the year that Snowden left the Mint, another book—*A Description of the Medals of Washington*, an elegantly prepared 203-page study—appeared under his name.

From the standpoint of the rare coin market and investment history, it is worth noting that this activity was fueled by several factors coming together at the same time: the gathering with much fanfare of specimens to be exhibited in the Washington Cabinet, the featuring of Washington pieces in *Historical Magazine* and other periodicals, the showcasing of items in auction sales, the striking of *new* Washington tokens and medals (including those struck by the Mint itself), and the publication of an impressive reference book. In the market circa 1860, many different Washington tokens and medals were sold for far more than the $5 to $10 commanded by choice examples of rare 1793 copper cents. Within a decade, however, the price of most Washington tokens and medals fell, while 1793 cents, never part of a speculative fever, overtook them in market price. An investment of $100 in typical Washington pieces in EF and AU grades, at the height of the market in the early 1860s, might be worth several thousand dollars today, while $100 spent on EF and AU 1793 cents at $10 each would translate into $200,000 or more now.

1861: Civil War Begins. The Civil War began on April 15, 1861, and what Yankees perceived would be an easy win soon turned into a bloody conflict lasting four years and costing more than a million lives. The monetary situation became chaotic.

Steam-powered coining press in use at the Philadelphia Mint in 1861.

"I have no pennies—would you mind taking a ticket for the Broadway Free and Easy instead?" a shopkeeper comments to a customer in this cartoon published in *Leslie's Illustrated Newspaper*, March 14, 1863. Coins had disappeared from circulation, and scrip notes, tickets, and other items served for use in exchange.

A bronze two-cent piece of 1864, the first circulating coin to bear the motto IN GOD WE TRUST.

The Charlotte, Dahlonega, and New Orleans mints fell under the control of the Confederacy in early 1861, operated for a while afterward, and then closed.

Under the Act of July 17, 1861, the Treasury Department issued $50,000,000 in Demand Notes, the first widely circulated paper money since Revolutionary times. To facilitate their acceptance, they could be exchanged at par for gold coins. Additional Demand Notes were authorized in February 1862. Meanwhile, in the Confederate States of America, coins all but disappeared. The *Richmond Enquirer*, December 31, 1861, reported that entrepreneurs were paying 30% to 50% premium in paper money to buy silver and gold coins. "The present price of specie will be hereafter quoted through all time as a damning stigma upon the character of Southern merchants." By that time, Confederate paper money circulated widely through the region.

On the West Coast, it was a different story. The California State Legislature had made the use of paper money *illegal* in commerce, beginning in 1850. When the federal government began issuing paper money in 1861, these bills were also illegal. Only "hard money" in the form of silver and gold coins was authorized.

1861–1865: Mintage Figures Low. Mintages of Proof coins fell during the Civil War, due to the difficulties of ordering them. Production of most silver and gold was low at the Philadelphia Mint, for such coins were no longer used in commerce—although an export demand continued. Many if not most dies used during the Civil War for circulating coinage at the Philadelphia Mint (but not at the San Francisco Mint) were incompletely finished, leaving minute, parallel die lines, or striae, on their faces. As a result, most coins made during this period show extensive lines in the fields, not affecting the value one way or the other.

Auctions became a regular feature, and dozens of important sales were conducted by W. Elliot Woodward, Edward D. Cogan, and others. Usually, the sales were held in commercial auction rooms and conducted by professional auctioneers, not the writers of the catalogs. Such auction firms usually sold other things as well, including books, art, furniture, and the like.

1862: Coins Hoarded. The war was not going well for either side. In the North, citizens became apprehensive and began to hoard gold and silver. By early

1862, such coins were worth a small premium in terms of paper money, the latter being in the form of bills issued by banks. Things went from bad to worse after the Act of February 25, 1862, authorized the issue of a new series of paper money, Legal Tender Notes, not redeemable in coins but exchangeable only for other paper money. Coin hoarding increased, and by summer 1862 no silver or gold coins were to be seen anywhere in circulation in the East or Midwest. Money brokers conducted a lively exchange business with investors and speculators, and daily prices were quoted for silver and gold coins. Proof coins continued to be minted for collectors, but the Philadelphia Mint would not accept Legal Tender Notes at par for them. Instead, numismatists had to go to money brokers and buy regular coins for a premium, then send these coins to the Mint, with extra coins for the proofing charge, to obtain such sets.

By the second week of July, even one-cent pieces were being hoarded. To facilitate commerce, a flood of privately issued bronze Civil War tokens (as they are called today), paper scrip notes (with 3, 5, 10, and 25 cents being the most popular denominations), and even postage stamps were used as money. John Gault patented his encased postage stamps, each displaying a regular stamp, from 1 cent to 90 cents, behind clear mica in a brass case, intended to be durable in circulation. Soon, a flood of federal Fractional Currency notes appeared, eventually swelling to many millions of dollars in 3-, 5-, 10-, 15- (scarce), 25-, and 50-cent denominations. Legal Tender notes rolled off the printing presses, and a new series of National Bank notes appeared.

1863: Civil War Tokens Abound.
To fill the need for small change, millions of bronze (mostly) tokens were issued by various private coiners, mostly in 1863, although a few have earlier dates or are dated 1864. These bore many different motifs, ranging from historical portraits to war heroes and scenes, to advertisements

of stores and services. At the very outset these became popular with numismatists and have remained so ever since.

Also in 1863, the U.S. government purchased the private mint of Clark, Gruber & Co. and designated it as the Denver Mint in its reports for the next several decades, but no coins were struck there. However, many numismatists did not know this. Cluelessly, Edward D. Cogan, in his sale of October 1875 (the Col. Mendes I. Cohen Collection), described Lot 160, a $5 gold coin, as "1839 Denver Mint. Very Fine." Of course, this was a double error, as not only was it not struck in the Denver Mint, but in 1839 there was no such town as Denver! In 1906, when federal coins were first made in the city, they were made in a new Denver Mint building.

1864: Bronze Cents and Two-Cent Pieces.
The Act of April 22, 1864, provided that bronze alloy be used for cents and the new two-cent denomination, and it made the cent legal tender up to the amount of 10 cents and the two-cent piece legal tender up to 20 cents. Thus, for the first time, coins other than silver or gold became legal tender in the United States. (It is a curious fact that the old copper half cents and cents [1793–1857] were not legal tender, and anyone had the right to refuse them in payment for debts.) IN GOD WE TRUST was employed on the two-cent piece, the first use of this motto for circulating coins. Later, it would be added to most other coins, and in 1955 to U.S. paper money.

In July in the East it took $285 in Legal Tender bills to buy $100 in gold coins from a money broker or exchange office— the all-time high for the Civil War period.[50] On the West Coast the situation was the opposite: coins were plentiful in stores, banks, and elsewhere, and paper bills brought from the East remained illegal in commerce, but could be bought or sold to money brokers at a discount deep enough to equal the premium on gold and silver coins in the East. If at a particular time it took $285 in Legal Tender Notes to buy $100 in gold coins in New York, then in San Francisco anyone with $100 in gold coins could go to an exchange dealer and buy $285 in Legal Tender Notes.

1865: Gold and Silver Coins Still Hoarded. When the Civil War ended in April 1865, it was anticipated that silver and gold coins would soon return to circulation. However, the public remained wary of all of the paper bills in commerce, and silver and gold remained at a premium. It was not until years later, in April 1876, that silver coins were again exchangeable at par with paper, and not until December 1878 that gold and paper were equal. By those times in the 1870s a generation of children had grown into adulthood without having seen a single silver or gold coin in circulation!

1866: AJN Makes Its Debut. In 1866 the first regularly issued coin magazine, the *American Journal of Numismatics*, was published by the American Numismatic and Archaeological Society ("and Archaeological" had been added to the organization's name in 1864, and was used until 1908). In the same decade, E.L. Mason, Jr., a Philadelphia dealer, issued his own combined news magazine and price list. There were no books or other guides to the market value of coins, and such determinations had to be made by reviewing auction results and consulting dealer lists. There were no grading standards, and policies varied widely. One collector's "Uncirculated" might be another's "Very Fine," and "Proof" applied to just about any coin with

a mirrorlike surface, including some that had been buffed or polished to make them that way! As the community of collectors and dealers grew increasingly close, there was extensive exchange of information.

Changes of the 1870s

1870: Carson City Mint Opens for Business. Silver and gold coins with CC mintmarks were struck in Carson City from 1870 to 1885, and again from 1889 to 1893.

1870–1879: Coin Prices Rise. Prices of most coins, tokens, and medals rose steadily, although Washington pieces, once the darlings of the market, fell from favor. For a brief time, one dealer whose identity is not known today had a "corner" in Proof sets of the year 1858, and seems to have profited from the experience.

1873: Coinage Act Important. Among many other provisions, the Coinage Act of 1873 abolished the two-cent piece and half dime, provided for the new trade-dollar denomination, and slightly increased the authorized weights of dimes, quarter dollars, and half dollars (which subsequently were made with arrowheads at the date to indicate the different standard). The standard silver dollar was not treated in the act, and this denomination therefore lapsed. Soon, there was a popular outcry that the act was unfavorable to silver-mining interests and citizens of western states, and the legislation became known as the "Crime of '73." Some politicians said that the act had

The Carson City Mint. Although pieces produced here were almost completely ignored by numismatists at the time, later they became favorites with collectors. Today, all are widely sought. (Photograph by John Calvin Scripture, 19th century; courtesy of David M. Sundman)

been rushed through passage, that they had not had time to study it, had not realized the standard dollar would be discontinued, had not liked the idea of the gold dollar becoming important by this default, would not have voted for it if they had been aware of its implications, and so on.

During the decade, the price of silver declined on world markets. In the United States, increasing production in Nevada, plus new discoveries (including in the Leadville, Colorado, district), resulted in a glut of the metal. Free Silverites, as they were called, pressured politicians to abandon gold and institute silver as the dominant coinage metal. In time this became the overwhelming political question in America, and remained so until the presidential election of 1896.

1875–1880: Boom in Collecting Paper Money.
Confederate States of America currency and federal Fractional Currency, both of the Civil War era, became very hot series on the market. Continental Currency was also popular, but to a lesser degree. At the same time, scarcely any attention was paid to federal Legal Tender, National Bank, or other bills, or to obsolete currency.

1876: Centennial Exhibition Held in Philadelphia.
In Fairmount Park many large buildings were erected for the government-sponsored world's fair in America (the privately financed Crystal Palace in 1853 had preceded it). Crowds thronged through the exhibits to see the giant Corliss steam engine (the main attraction) and other wonders. Many tokens and medals were issued in connection with the event.

Silver coins, not seen in circulation since spring 1862, returned to circulation after April 20, 1876, about which time they were exchangeable at par with paper notes. The channels of commerce and banking were slow to fill, and many banks lacked significant reserves until well into 1877.

1878: Morgan Silver Dollars Struck.
The Bland-Allison Act of February 28, 1878, directed the government to purchase millions of ounces of silver each year and coin the metal into dollars. This legislation was engineered by western mining interests in an effort to counteract the slump in silver prices. Hundreds of millions of these Morgan-designed dollars were made through 1921 and mainly stored in bank vaults. Years later, many were paid out, much to the delight of numismatists!

By 1878 the public realized that continuing to hoard older coins was purposeless, and huge quantities of long-hidden coins emerged, creating a glut on the market. As there was no need for new silver coins, mintages of dimes, quarters, and half dollars dropped sharply beginning in 1879.

1879: Gold Coins Return to Circulation.
Gold coins, not in commerce since late 1861, were once again available from banks at par, in exchange for paper money, begin-

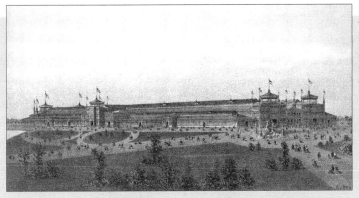

The vast Machinery Hall at the Centennial Exhibition fair held in Philadelphia in 1876. Many tokens and medals were issued in connection with this exposition, including a dollar-sized Centennial medal produced by the Mint. However, no coins were made with commemorative motifs.

A sparkling Mint State gold dollar of 1879 (enlarged)—the first year in a run of dates that became very popular with investors and speculators. While many pieces were saved from the relatively low mintage of just 3,000 coins this year, the demand today is such that examples sell for amounts well into four figures whenever offered.

ning on December 17, 1878. The Treasury Department anticipated a great "run" on gold coins and had a large stock on hand. Surprisingly, the run did not happen. By that time the public felt that since paper *could* be exchanged for gold at any time, there was no point in doing it now.

Meanwhile, a great speculation arose in gold dollars. All available supplies were bought, and the market price rose to a modest premium. New pieces produced at the Philadelphia Mint yielded instant profits for those who were lucky enough to get them. Investment interest in gold dollars continued for the rest of the decade. (Now you know why, on today's market, Mint State dollars of 1879–1889 are plentiful in relation to their low mintages, while most earlier dates are rare in this state of preservation!) At the same time, a "bubble" rose in the market for Proof silver trade dollars, a denomination that had not been made in circulation-strike form after early 1878. Investors scrambled to order 1879 Proofs from the Mint, and the production jumped up to 1,541 pieces (as compared to only 900 Proofs in 1878). The excitement continued, and in 1880 the Mint set a record of 1,987 Proofs. The passion then faded, and in 1881 just 960 Proofs were struck. While these gold dollars and Proof trade dollars were eagerly bought at the time by speculators, some of whom sold out at a loss a few years later, today gem Mint State gold dollars of this era and choice Proof trade dollars are worth thousands of dollars each.

Also in 1879, the New Orleans Mint, closed since early 1861, reopened for business. Silver and gold coins would be made there until 1909, after which time the building was used for other purposes.

The Making of the CENTS-less Nickel, and Other Events

1880–1889: Coin Market Hot. The rare coin market went into overdrive in the 1880s. Many dealers opened up shops, several issued their own magazines (Ed Frossard's *Numisma* and Scott Stamp & Coin Company's *Coin Collector's Journal* notable among them), and the field of auction catalogers grew as well. John W. Haseltine and the Chapman brothers (S. Hudson and Henry) created many memorable sales, with the 1882 Bushnell Collection by the Chapmans being the most exciting auction event of the decade. T. Harrison Garrett, of Baltimore, and Lorin G. Parmelee, of Boston, became known as super-collectors, snatching up rarities. Rare coins furnished fodder for newspapers, and metropolitan dailies carried many accounts of rare 1804 silver dollars' being sold at auction, or old Massachusetts Pine Tree shillings being found buried in the ground, and more. Throughout this scenario, the prices of scarce and rare early U.S. coins continued to rise. A 1793 cent worth $5 to $10 in 1860 was worth $20 or more by 1880, and $30 or more by 1890, part of a nonstop march that still goes on—the value is now past $10,000. Silver coins of the 1790s, any and all gold coins of 1795 through 1834, and other classics remained in steady demand.

1880s: Hobby Publications Proliferate. During the 1880s a dozen or more newspapers devoted to collecting coins, stamps, Indian relics, and other things were published, often with news on multiple fields of interest.

1883: Liberty Nickels Without CENTS. When in early 1883 the Philadelphia Mint turned out a new type of nickel five-cent piece with the denomination given as sim-

The new 1883 Liberty Head nickel without CENTS on the reverse created a nationwide sensation. It was stated in many newspaper articles that the Mint had made a terrible mistake and would be recalling all examples, after which the coins would have great value. Excitement prevailed, and thousands of newcomers entered the hobby. In the meantime, the coins never did become rare, as many were minted and large quantities were saved.

ply V, without the word CENTS, word spread that a great mistake had been made. There was a mad rush to buy up every one in sight. Of the 5,474,000 minted, it is likely that most were tracked down by the public and kept as investments. Soon, these would be of immense value, it was thought. Meanwhile, dealers with large supplies were selling them for 10¢ to 15¢ each, often as get-acquainted offers to invite other orders from price lists. The 1883 without-CENTS nickel, although it never became rare, did inch up in value over the years, and now an MS-63 coin lists for $45 in the *Guide Book*. The CENTS-less variety did its duty to boost interest in collecting, and quite a few who found them in circulation went on to become very important in the numismatic field. Interestingly, the higher-mintage 1883 with-CENTS piece, of which 16,026,200 were made, but of which relatively few were saved as there was no excitement about them, now catalogs for three times as much, or $150!

1888: The Numismatist *Published.* The *Numismatist* began publication under the auspices of Dr. George F. Heath, a Monroe, Michigan, collector.

1889–1926: *Virgil M. Brand and His Collection.* In Chicago, Virgil M. Brand, a wealthy brewer, spent most of his waking hours buying coins, including rarities in duplicate and triplicate. By the time of his death in 1926, he had amassed more than

350,000 examples, including 6 of the 10 known 1884 trade dollars, an 1822 $5 piece, a 1787 Brasher doubloon, quantities of 1793 large cents, and other treasures. The Brand Collection was subsequently disposed of over a period of more than half a century.

Economic and Numismatic Ups and Downs

1890: Dealers Active. By this time, there were dealers in most cities in the eastern part of the United States, with Boston, New York City, and Philadelphia the central points of activity. J.W. Scott, W. Elliot Woodward, the auction firm of Bangs, Merwin & Co., the Chapman brothers, John Haseltine, Lyman H. Low, Ed. Frossard, and Charles Steigerwalt were among the leading professionals of the day.

The New York Coin & Stamp Co. conducted the sale of the Lorin G. Parmelee Collection, the second finest (after T. Harrison Garrett's) cabinet in private hands in America. Results were mixed, and Parmelee, hardly a motivated seller, bought many of the rarities back. The coin market was entering a chilly period.

The Series of 1890 Coin or Treasury Notes, payable in coin, featured superbly detailed engraving on the reverse of each denomination from $1 to $1,000, with the $100 and $1,000 bills having zeros of a

Lorin G. Parmelee was active in numismatics from the 1860s through the 1890s, entering the hobby through a fascination with large copper cents. In Boston he was a leading baker of beans, which were delivered daily in pots to hotels and restaurants—a business lucrative enough that in time he acquired most major rarities. The New York Coin & Stamp Co. auctioned many of his coins in 1890.

distinctive shape, creating "Watermelon notes." However, the Treasury felt that completely filling the back of each note with engraving made the bills easy to counterfeit, and in time the Series of 1891 notes, with rather ordinary reverse designs, but with much open space, replaced them.

1891: American Numismatic Association Formed. In November in Chicago the American Numismatic Association was formed, thus providing a common meeting place for the exchange of ideas and values among collectors from all parts of the United States and elsewhere. Beginners and amateurs were encouraged to join, in contrast to the policies of some other societies that preferred numismatists with experience. Later, the ANA would adopt *The Numismatist* (which had been published since 1888) as its official journal.

1892: Barber Silver Coins Appear. Charles E. Barber's Liberty Head silver dime, quarter, and half dollar, called *Barber coins* today, were first issued this year. Dimes and quarters were produced through 1916, half dollars through 1915.

1893: World's Columbian Exposition Held in Chicago. To commemorate the 400th anniversary of Columbus's "discovery," a huge "white city" of elegant buildings, cheaply constructed for temporary use but

Selections from the Mint Collection were placed on view at the Columbian Exposition, displayed in glass-fronted wooden cabinets sent from Philadelphia. At the left side of the image, against the wall, is a coining press. (Shepp's *World's Fair Photographed*, 1893)

imposing in appearance, was built to open in 1892. The schedule ran late, and the general public did not come until 1893. Many of the Mint Cabinet coins were displayed there, and hundreds of varieties of tokens, medals, and numismatically related souvenirs were sold by private vendors.

The first commemorative half dollars, 1892 and 1893, were issued by the Mint in connection with this event and sold for $1 each. Many coins went unsold and were dumped into circulation, disappointing buyers who had hoped they would have significant value. The price dropped to about 55¢ each. *Decades later* these coins came into demand. Today, gem MS-65 1892 and 1893 halves catalog for $725 and $875, respectively, in the *Guide Book.* Commemorative Isabella quarters were also offered for $1 each, but attracted little buyer interest. Soon after the fair closed, the market value rose to $1.50, but later it dropped. Those who held on to their stocks were able to sell large quantities for $2.50 to $5 per coin in the 1920s and 1930s. Today a gem MS-65 catalogs for $2,700.

Also in 1893, J.W. Scott issued the *Standard Catalogue*, the first generally used guide to coin values in America, although it was laden with inaccuracies and was intended as a price list for the Scott firm (what would be charged for a coin *if* it was in stock). The book contained no mintage figures and was of minimal value to collectors, but was better than nothing. Several related catalogs were issued later, the last revision in 1913. More than two decades later, in 1934, Wayte Raymond created and issued a different book under the *Standard Catalogue* title.

Augustus G. Heaton, a professional artist by trade and a numismatist by avocation, published a treatise on coins from the U.S. branch mints. At the time, the presence of a "CC" (for Carson City, Nevada—a mint operated from 1870 to 1893) or an "S" (for the San Francisco Mint, which was established in 1854) on a coin attracted little interest. In fact, there was no catalog or guide listing which mintmarks were available! This seems incredible in view of the values attached today to certain rarities bearing tiny mintmarks.

Meanwhile, speculation in prairie lands, unwise loans, and, perhaps, the need for breathing space after the boom economy of the 1880s, came together in the Panic of 1893. Times were difficult, many banks failed, and there was political unrest. Participants in the Free Silver movement, a political philosophy that had been gaining adherents since the 1870s, became especially vocal. It was felt by this faction that reliance on gold was hindering national growth and prosperity, and that American coinage and international trade should be based on silver, a metal in oversupply.

The government policy of coining large amounts of silver into dollar coins was part of the "Silver Question," the pivotal political debate of the era. In this 1895 cartoon, "turtles" of silver dollars, marked "Real Value 50 Cents," are about to plunge into financial oblivion over a waterfall—suggesting what might happen to the American economy if such practice was continued. In 1896 the presidential campaign focused on this topic. (*Harper's Weekly*, September 19, 1895)

1896: Bryan-McKinley Contest. The presidential election of 1896 pitted Democrat William Jennings Bryan against Republican William McKinley. Bryan's "Cross of Gold" speech electrified the nation and gave momentum to the Free Silver movement and "easy money," making it possible for Midwesterners and others in distress to pay their debts more easily. A flood of "Bryan money"—satirical and political medals and tokens that in time became a numismatic specialty—was issued. Bryan lost, and the Free Silver movement faded out within the next decade.

The "Educational" series of $1, $2, and $5 Silver Certificates was created in 1896, and featured allegorical figures, such as *History Instructing Youth*. A later generation of paper-money collectors would admire them as among the finest products of the Bureau of Engraving and Printing. The market for United States coins at this time was slipping into the doldrums. The excitement of the 1880s had worn off, and there were fewer new collectors. The number of minor (copper and nickel) Proof sets ordered reflected this: 4,290 sets in 1886, but less than half that, or just 1,862, in 1896. The ANA was beginning to falter, and in the next two years interest was so low that it almost expired (but, luckily, it did not!).

1899: Hard Times Tokens Popular. Lyman H. Low's monograph, *Hard Times Tokens*, was published, generating further interest in an already popular series. In the next decade such pieces were among the hottest items in the market, and in auctions attracted much more attention than, for example, Indian Head cents and Liberty Head nickels.

Art in Coinage
1904: Louisiana Purchase Exposition Held in St. Louis. This was one of the largest American world's fairs. The first commemorative gold dollars, each dated 1903 (one with the portrait of Jefferson, the other of McKinley) were issued in connection with it. Heavily promoted at $3 each, their sales flopped, and of 125,000 minted of each, just 17,500 were sold. The others went back to the melting pot.

B. Max Mehl, born in 1884, had started buying and selling coins as a teenager. In 1904, while working as a shoe clerk, he ran his first advertisement in *The Numismatist*. Soon, he was well known as a professional numismatist. He achieved success on two fronts: in the serious coin trade through his direct and mail-bid catalog sales to numismatists, and in the popular sale of his *Star Rare Coin Encyclopedia*, offering large sums of money for coins that the public might find in pocket change or in a safe deposit box. Many collections and rarities came his way.

1906: New Denver Mint Opened. The Denver Mint, under construction since 1904, went into operation. Silver and gold coins were minted there at first, then cents beginning in 1911 and nickels beginning in 1912.

1907: MCMVII $20 Excitement and Speculation. The MCMVII (1907) High Relief $20 gold piece, by Augustus Saint-Gaudens, was released into circulation in December and caused great excitement. President Theodore Roosevelt had commissioned America's best-known sculptor to create these and related Indian Head $10 coins. The results were spectacular, and the coins were highly acclaimed by the public and numismatists alike. There was immediate speculation in the $20 pieces; banks and Treasury-office stocks were depleted, and the price rose to $25, then to $30, within a month or two. A few years later the interest waned, and examples were available for $21. In the late 1920s they became popular with collectors, and values have gone upward ever since.

1908: First Branch-Mint Minor Coinage. Indian Head cents were struck at the San Francisco Mint, the first branch-mint coinage of a minor (nonprecious metal) denomination. Meanwhile, in the gold series, the Sand Blast Proof finish took the place of the mirror style used in earlier years. These new Proofs were unpopular with collectors, and in the next year Satin Finish Proofs succeeded them. These also generated complaints, and in 1911 the Sand Blast Proofs were resumed, to continue in the gold series to 1915.

A 1908-S Indian Head cent.

Also in 1908, the American Numismatic Society moved into a handsome new stone building, largely financed by Archer M. Huntington (stepson of railroad magnate Collis P. Huntington), on Audubon Terrace, Morningside Heights, New York City, where it would remain until moving to 96 Fulton Street in the same city in 2004.

1909: Lincoln Cent Issued. In August the new Lincoln design for the cent, by Victor D. Brenner, a sculptor and medalist of renown, was released. The first issues had the initials V.D.B. on the reverse, but a controversy arose, and the initials were soon removed. Proofs for collectors were in the Matte style, not much different from circulation strikes upon quick glance, and were not popular.

The same year, an article in *The Numismatist* stated that $10,000 each had been paid by a private collector, William H. Woodin, for two different $50 pattern gold coins of 1877. A controversy arose, and Woodin transferred the the coins to the Mint Collection in exchange for "several crates" of various older pattern coins. Today, these coins are in the Smithsonian Institution. In 1989 I estimated their value at $1 million each. Today, closer to $10 million might be more realistic. However, the point is moot, for they are not for sale.

More Artistic Coins

1912: Wayte Raymond on Coin Investment. In this year Wayte Raymond operated the United States Coin Co. One of his advertisements began as follows:

> Coins as an Investment. Many harsh words are said about collectors who interest themselves in an actual speculation as to whether or not the coins they are buying today will have appreciated in value 10 years from now. Numismatists of the old school said the true collector is not interested in any such appreciation in the value of his collection but derives his entire profit and pleasure from the coins

while in his hands. We feel however that the average American collector, while he greatly enjoys his coins, also feels very pleased if on disposing of his collection he realizes profits....

1913: "Buffalo" Nickel Issued. The Buffalo or Indian Head five-cent piece, by sculptor James Earle Fraser, was released, replacing the Liberty Head design in use since 1883.

1914: ANS Exhibition. The American Numismatic Society mounted an impressive display from its own collections and from loans from members. Issued in connection with the event was a handsome book, *Exhibition of United States and Colonial Coins, January 17th to February 18, 1914.*

1915: Panama–Pacific International Exposition Held in San Francisco. To observe the opening of the Panama Canal (in 1914) and the rebirth of the city of San Francisco after the fire and earthquake of 1906, the exposition offered a grand "city" of elegant buildings in a world's fair similar to the Chicago event of 1893. Dealer Farran Zerbe had charge of selling commemorative coins of the half dollar, gold $1 and

$2.50 pieces, and two varieties of the $50 denominations. The ANA held its annual convention in Chicago this year, but attendance was very low.

1915–1916: End of Proof Coinage. Production of Sand Blast Proof gold coins ended in 1915, and 1916 was the last year for Matte Proof cents and nickels. These finishes were very unpopular with collectors, who preferred the older-style "brilliant" or "mirror" field type. In 1936, Proofs would again be made, of the mirror type.

1916: New Silver Coin Designs. The new "Mercury" or Winged Liberty Head dime by Adolph A. Weinman, the Standing Liberty quarter dollar by Hermon A. MacNeil, and the Liberty Walking half dollar by Weinman made their debuts this year, replacing the Barber silver coins. The new motifs, created by well-known sculptors in the private sector, were highly praised by numismatists.

1921–1923: Slow Times. The American economy took a nap following the boom years of the World War. Coin mintages slowed (except for silver dollars). The coin

B. Max Mehl in his office in Fort Worth, Texas, in 1915. By this time Mehl was well into his numismatic career and was recognized as one of America's most active dealers. Seated at his roll-top desk, he seems to be giving dictation to a secretary. On the wall to the left are photographs of attendees at ANA conventions, and, on the back wall, a Fractional Currency shield above the safe. On the table in the foreground are medals in a coin tray.

A 1917 San Francisco Mint half dollar of the Liberty Walking design by Adolph A. Weinman, who also created the "Mercury" dime of this era. The 1917-S is of the variety with the S mintmark on the obverse, below the R of TRUST. Certain others of this year have the S on the reverse.

market was in a slump. The 7,302-lot John Story Jenks Collection, described by Henry Chapman in a 653-page catalog, held from December 7 to 17, was simply too long and too much. Buyers suffered from burnout, and the sale, intended to be the apex of Chapman's career, laid an egg, although he put on a brave face. The James Ten Eyck Collection, sold via mail bids by B. Max Mehl, May 2, 1922, was also a dud, although in both sales, some coins sold well. In 1923 the James W. Ellsworth Collection was sold privately to Wayte Raymond for $100,000, with financing by John Work Garrett, who took selected pieces for his own collection. In the February 1923 issue of *The Numismatist*, dealer Thomas L. Elder lamented that the big buyers of yesteryear had no equivalents now. "With these gone the much-despised coin dealers seem to be about the best support the coin market has at the present time. Our biggest sales, without their patronage, would be fizzles and failures." By this time, William H. Woodin, H.O. Granberg, and James W. Ellsworth were no longer buyers, Virgil M. Brand and Waldo C. Newcomer were well supplied and were buying casually, and there was a lack of new buyers with a lot of money to spend. Of course, for far-seeing investors these were *good* times to buy coins!

1920–1936: The Colonel Green Collection. Colonel E.H.R. Green, a hoarder in the style of Virgil M. Brand, was an aggressive buyer from about 1915 until his death in 1936. At one time he owned all five 1913 Liberty Head nickels, and, in a related hobby, the unique sheet of one hundred 1918 24¢ airmail inverted "Jenny" stamps.

1925–1929: Investment Excitement in Other Fields; Coin Market Quiet. Florida experienced a wild boom in real estate in 1924 and 1925, but the end came soon, in 1926. In the next several years, rare books, art, and common stocks became investment sensations. The rare coin market did not participate and remained very quiet. When these other markets collapsed in 1929, coins held their values fairly well. Several wealthy people who were hurt by the economic conditions of the early 1930s found comfort in the value of their coin collections—Waldo C. Newcomer of Baltimore being one. Great numismatic rarities sold slowly, but not at significant discounts.

1929: Small-Sized Paper Money. The Series of 1929 bills were issued, of a smaller size than had been used for federal paper since 1861.

CHAPTER TWELVE

MAKING OF THE MODERN MARKET FOR RARE COINS

A great many collectors simply collect for the pleasure of collecting and possessing. However, the best part of collecting is that which comes from connecting their finds and possessions with the knowledge of the world in history, art, heraldry, geography, economics, and so forth.... In order to avail yourself of these offers I would suggest that some of the money you plan to spend for coins be spent for reference books.... Books are necessary in order to make you a numismatist instead of a collector. *Research* is the word every collector should become familiar with and practice.

—Harvey L. Hansen, February 1929

The Market as We Know It

The following pages chronicle numismatics from the 1930s to date. The span is so great, and the changes so many, that my time line emphasizes just the highlights. A more complete view can be found in my two-volume study, *The American Numismatic Association Centennial History*, and endless details are contained in contemporary issues of numismatic periodicals; these sources also tell the stories of many coin dealers and auctioneers, coin clubs, conventions, museum exhibits, new books, and so on, for which there is not room in the present text.

In the 1930s, widely issued price guides and attractive albums became available inexpensively, bringing many into the hobby and effectively changing the market, making knowledge of prices easier to obtain and changing old practices (e.g., storing coins in wooden cabinets). During the hard times of the Depression, tens of thousands of people discovered the joys of numismatics and looked for "treasures" in pocket change and, if they could afford it, bought for investment a few low-mintage 1931-S Lincoln cents.

The commemorative boom of 1935 and 1936 came next—in retrospect, a classic cycle in the coin market, but not easily predicted then. B. Max Mehl, who had been in the trade since the early days of the century, had jumped feet-first into the fray, with ever-increasing "bid" prices and excitement. Then came the cooling off in late 1936, followed by collapse. In January 1938 Mehl advertised as follows:

> Commemoratives have taken an awful spanking in recent months. And those who have large stocks (and I am one of 'em) have taken more than a mere spanking! Now, I don't intend to publicly undermine the market—

Ever since its release, the 1931-S Lincoln cent has been a numismatic favorite, with the enticingly low mintage figure of 866,000 beckoning to all comers. It is likely that most were saved. Today, the overlooked 1931-D Lincoln cent, with a mintage of 4,480,000, is much more difficult to find in Mint State.

Formerly a hot ticket in the rare-coin investment scramble of autumn 1935 and early 1936, this 1935-D Boone Bicentennial half dollar with small "1934" on the reverse was as dead as a doornail a year later. In time, the price would revive, and spectacularly; but for the short term, buyers of commemoratives had to endure a "spanking" (as B. Max Mehl put it).

but, if you are really and truly in the market for commemoratives, and will send me your want list, I will make you a price that will surprise you and one you can't resist.

World War II began in December 1941, followed by four years of domestic and worldwide sacrifices. Cash was plentiful in America and consumer goods were scarce. In 1943, the coin market went into high gear, and stayed there for the next several years, until the coin investment ice age later in the decade. Then came regeneration and a new wave of enthusiasm in the 1950s, followed by the market to end all markets from 1960 to 1964.

In the 40 years since then, changes and evolution have never stopped. Transitions have been many and have included numerical grading, "bid" and "ask" prices from electronic trading, certification, wide availability of information, and an expansion to include hundreds of thousands of serious participants nationwide.

Along the way, the hobby continues to appeal to many newcomers, while oldtimers still enjoy the hobby of a lifetime. Thus are sown the seeds for what seems to be a secure future (which I explore in the next chapter).

1930–1940: Key Coins Perform Well.
In 1930 a Mint State 1909-S V.D.B. Lincoln cent and a Proof 1885 Liberty Head nickel would have cost you 25¢ each. By 1940 the market prices were $3 and $7.50, respectively. Both of these key dates rose in prices sharply during the Depression and were not affected by the commemorative boom in 1935 and 1936 and the bust in 1937.

1931–1935: Years of Growth.
While America was enduring the Great Depression, the coin market grew measurably. The low-mintage 1931-S Lincoln cent (just 866,000 coins, the lowest since the 1909-S V.D.B.) created a lot of attention, as did albums and folders—such as those sold by Wayte Raymond in New York—that were marked to hold coins. With these convenient holders, coins could be stored, displayed, and enjoyed at the same time—

After 1933, $20 gold double eagles were no longer available to citizens, and, in fact, it became illegal to hold them unless they had recognized numismatic value. Shown here is a $20 piece of 1928, considered to be a common date.

and each empty hole beckoned to be filled. Hobbies of all kinds became popular, including jigsaw and crossword puzzles, miniature golf, and fishing. Collecting coins from pocket change was stimulating and cost very little to do. An unemployed person was not a candidate to buy a rare coin, but so many new faces came into the market that prices rose during this period. In 1935 the *Numismatic Scrapbook Magazine* was launched; it went on to be the most popular magazine in the hobby for many years, until the early 1960s.

1933–1934: The Government and Gold.
Not long after his inauguration in March 1933, President Franklin D. Roosevelt halted the paying out of gold coins from federal holdings. Soon, he issued an order for the public to turn in all they had, coins of numismatic value (not defined) being an exception. After many citizens did this, despite the uncertainties in the depth of the economic depression, Roosevelt then raised the price of gold from $20.67 per ounce to $35 per ounce, in effect stealing more than $14 an ounce from those who had patriotically surrendered their coins. Afterward followed a wholesale melting of gold coins. At the same time, many newcomers decided to

Small-sized paper currency served in the place of gold coins, this $20 bill being an example (issued in the 1930s by the Claremont National Bank in New Hampshire). Once gold coins disappeared from circulation, the American economy began unprecedented inflation and devaluation of its currency, which continues to the present day. (Swasey Collection)

collect gold, and for the first time, Liberty Head and later $5, $10, and $20 pieces were collected widely by date and mintmark variety. A review of consumer prices in America dramatically demonstrates that after gold coins left circulation, inflation raged as never before, destroying the purchasing power of the dollar. Today, federal paper money has no backing at all—except other paper money and the "good faith and credit" of the government.

1935–1936: The Commemorative Boom.

By 1935 there was a strong collector interest in buying commemorative coins, especially of low mintages. In 1928 only 10,000 examples had been made of the Hawaiian Sesquicentennial half dollar. Offered at $2 each, they sold out quickly. By 1935 they were worth $8 each. In that year, two new half dollars, one for the sesquicentennial (150th anniversary) of Hudson, New York, and the other commemorating the Old Spanish Trail, were offered at $1 and $2 each, respectively. Both sold out almost overnight, leaving many disappointed collectors. Prices quickly rose to $4 per coin, then to $6. Then in the autumn came the ultimate: Frank Dunn, distributor of the Boone Bicentennial halves, had the Denver and San Francisco mints strike just 2,000 each of a rare 1935 variety with an additional date, "1934," in small numbers in the field, to represent the actual bicentennial year. These were offered for $3.70 per pair. However, when collectors placed

their orders, most received "sold out" notices. The market value jumped to $35, then past $50, to over $80, to close to $100. The rush was on!

In the January 1936 issue of *The Numismatist*, B. Max Mehl offered a selection of other commemoratives for sale under the headline "BUY NOW—Potential $10 and $20 coins for a fraction of their near-future value!" Nothing could go wrong! In 1936 more than a dozen new commemorative designs reached the market, and most buyers turned a profit as soon as they received theirs in the mail. Others, such as those ordering 1936 Cincinnati halves (three coins, one from each mint, for $7.75 the trio), were apt to be told that all had been sold—and were left to find a set on the market for $30 or more. Isn't it amazing that all of this was going on during the Depression!

1936–1939: The Commemorative Bust.

By late 1936 the market had run out of buyers, and distributors of new issues had thousands of unsold coins on hand. Investors tried to sell out to capture profits, and some did, but by December few people were interested. Prices tanked and kept going down. By 1940 the rare pair of 1935-D and -S Boones with small 1934 could be bought for just $30, or about a third of their market high. As late as 1950 they were selling for $65. Other commemoratives suffered the same fate: they were dead in the market. With only a few excep-

A set of Cincinnati commemorative half dollars of 1936, one each from the Philadelphia, Denver, and San Francisco mints, packaged in a black leatherette holder with a clear slide on the face to permit viewing the coins. On the back of his particular set is an affidavit from the promoter of the series, Thomas Melish, attesting that this is the 110th set struck.

A set such as this was sold for $7.75 in 1936, and rode the market crest all the way to $50 within a year, only to collapse to $17 or less afterward. However, in time the value recovered and went on to new highs.

tions, time tends to heal investment wounds in the rare coin field (assuming you can wait long enough), and this happened with the 1935 Boone pair. Today, this same pair in MS-63 catalogs for $750, or $375 per coin.

The 1936 Cincinnati set, sold for $7.75 in 1936 and rising to $50 in the same year, dropped to the $15 to $17 level by 1940. Today an MS-63 set is listed at $750, equal to $250 per coin; in MS-65 the set is $2,300. This is a *slump* for the Cincinnati set, for in a market-price-cycle commentary in 1987—this being a boom period, with investors dominating the market (as they would through 1989)—an MS-63 set sold for about $1,300 and an MS-65 for about $6,500. However, a set certified in 1987 at MS-63 or MS-65 would likely be certified at a grade or two higher. As you can see, with a double set of variables—a time line plus grading interpretations—market comparisons can be difficult to make!

1936–1942: Proof Coinage Resumes. For the first time since 1916, Proof coins were

again struck for collectors in 1936. Coins were available individually or in sets of five, with the Lincoln cent, Buffalo nickel, Mercury dime, Washington quarter, and Liberty Walking half dollar. Sales were slow in the first year as buyers were busy with the commemorative boom. Afterward, production went upward, until Proof mintage was suspended in 1942, due to wartime considerations.

1943–1945: The Wartime Market for Coins. America declared war against Germany, Japan, and Italy in December 1941. By 1943 cash was plentiful, but consumer goods were scarce. Inflation was everywhere, despite federal efforts to control it. On September 10 and 11, 1943, New York City dealer Abe Kosoff conducted an auction of the Michael F. Higgy Collection. A bidding frenzy took place, and many coins sold for 5 to 10 times their pre-sale estimates! From that point, prices went onward and upward all across the market.

Among the more active players in the market were Kosoff and Abner Kreisberg (partners in the Numismatic Gallery), B. Max Mehl, Tatham Stamp & Coin Co., Stack's (which had conducted auctions since 1935), and Hollinbeck Coin Co. (A.M. and Paul Kagin). Hundreds of coin-shop operators and mail-order dealers advertised in the *Numismatic Scrapbook Magazine* and *The Numismatist*. King Farouk of Egypt and Emery May Holden Norweb were among the more aggressive buyers of the era. Stack's sales of the Flanagan and Bell collections attracted wide notice, as did several Mehl sales and the Numismatic Gallery offering of "The World's Greatest Collection" (the F.C.C. Boyd Collection, sold in two sections, 1945 and 1946), among others.

1946: The Guide Book Published. The *Guide Book of United States Coins*, written by Richard S. Yeoman with the technical assistance of Stuart Mosher, was published with a 1947 cover date. It will see its 60th edition in 2006.

Although World War II was over, consumer goods were still scarce. There was much uncertainty as to the future of the economy—would it be booming, or would it bust? The rare coin market continued to be a refuge for spare cash.

1947–1949: Coin Market Slow. Consumer goods such as appliances, automobiles, and new houses began to be available on a widespread basis, and much cash was spent in these areas. After the fast run-up of the early and mid-1940s, the coin market paused to catch its breath. Prices of common-date gold coins dropped sharply, with $20 pieces, which had sold for $65 or more earlier, shedding about a third of their value. The entire market became quiet. Investors in bulk gold coins and other items disappeared.

1949: Key-Date Coins Perform Well. The increasing popularity of numismatics, due to the coming together of many factors (including the availability of attractive albums and folders), contributed to continually rising prices for scarce and rare issues, making this a year of transition out of the slow market. In the first edition of the *Standard Catalogue*, 1934, each of the following Proof Liberty Head nickels had a market value of 50¢, and by 1949 the

rarest dates sold for more: 1884, $10; 1885, $25; 1886, $10; 1887, $4.40; and 1888, $4.50. "Key" dates such as 1885 and 1886 became more valuable than the others. In other series, 1877 Indian Head cents, 1909-S V.D.B. Lincoln cents, 1916-D dimes, 1932-D and -S quarters, and other scarcities became the varieties most in demand. Collectors started looking through millions of coins in circulation. A new price structure emerged; the prices of coins in a given series increased in direct proportion to their scarcity in circulation. All of this was helped along by the marketing of so-called penny boards—cardboard coin holders with spaces for date and mintmark varieties of Lincoln cents, Liberty nickels, Mercury dimes, and other series that could be extracted from pocket change—by Whitman and others.

Also in this year, B. Max Mehl's sale of the Dr. Charles W. Green Collection was the most sensational offering of *rare* gold coins ever, from the standpoint of unexpectedly high prices and postmarket hoopla. A new era of excitement was launched. Afterward, the collecting of gold became a passion for many newcomers. By this time, James F. Kelly and others had

The market was in the doldrums from 1947 to 1949, and even first-class numismatic rarities such as this beautiful 1795 half eagle attracted little interest. History would demonstrate that for investors this was a wonderful time to buy coins. Low prices of this era were never seen again!

In B. Max Mehl's sale of the Green Collection, 1949, a 1926-S $20 piece similar to this one caused a sensation. All of a sudden, a dozen or more numismatists decided to start collecting them by date and mint sequence. Prices rose, excitement bred more excitement, and the market slump was soon over!

tapped into huge hoards of American double eagles, plus smaller quantities of other denominations, that had been shipped overseas and tightly held there. When Roosevelt recalled gold in 1933 and 1934, foreign governments had no interest in exchanging these valuable coins for Uncle Sam's paper dollars. This set the scene for a broad and enthusiastic market in double eagles and other coins (mostly mid-19th century to date) from imports—a market that exists to the present day.

1950: Proof Coinage Resumes.

In 1950 the Philadelphia Mint produced 51,386 Proof sets, the first since 1942. In 1951, 57,500 sets were made. As production climbed year by year there began to be considerable interest in Proof sets from an investment viewpoint. I remember that James, Inc., rare coin dealers of Louisville, Kentucky, showed me a nice "thank-you letter" received from the Mint in appreciation for their particularly large 1951 Proof set order! The years when millions of sets were to be produced and when ordering quantities would be restricted were yet to come.

In 1950 the Denver Mint produced only 2,630,030 nickels—the smallest nickel five-cent-piece coinage since 1931. When the mintage figures were released, excitement prevailed! This excitement, plus the new Proofs, gave a much-needed boost to the market, which had been slow for several years. From this point it was onward and upward.

1951: Nickel Excitement Continues: The General Market.

By May 1951 a $2 face value roll of 1950-D nickels was selling for $6. One dealer in the May 1951 *Numismatic Scrapbook Magazine* said: "1950-D Nickels. Hectic! Write for prices." Still there was no widespread interest in most other modern coins, and prices remained low. A set of Mint State Lincoln cents from 1934 to 1950 cost $2.50; a set of Jefferson nickels in similar condition, 1938 (first year of issue) to date, cost $8.50; and a set of Washington quarters 1932 to date cost $77.50 (today, a gem 1932-D quarter, key to the set, is worth more than $10,000 all by itself!). Bank-wrapped rolls of Mint State coins were becoming quite popular. A roll of 40 1938-S quarters cost $35, while a roll of 1946-S cost $11, or just slightly more than face value. A recently issued roll of twenty 1949 halves cost $10.65. Among individual key-date coins in Mint State, a 1916 Standing Liberty quarter could be bought for $185; a 1917 Type I quarter cost $2.50; the ever-popular 1909-S V.D.B. cent was worth $10.50; and the low-mintage 1931-S cent cost $1.25. Increasingly, quite a few collectors thought it good practice to "put back" a few duplicates of rarities, or to go to the bank and pick up a bag filled with rolls of new coins. If things didn't work out, the rolls could always be spent.

1952: Numismatic News Begins Publication.

In Iola, Wisconsin, Chet Krause started *Numismatic News* as a monthly publication devoted to classified adver-

James F. Kelly, Dayton, Ohio, rare coin dealer, in his office in 1948. Kelly was a prolific advertiser in the *Numismatic Scrapbook Magazine* and *The Numismatist* and enjoyed a wide clientele. He was among the first Americans to import gold $20 coins in quantity from long-held reserves in Switzerland and elsewhere, adding to the active market for such issues. In 1960 Kelly was the first editor of the "Trends" section in the newly established *Coin World* newspaper. In 1965 he was president of Paramount International Coin Corporation.

tisements. In time the emphasis changed, and news articles and announcements were carried. In the early 1960s, it went to a weekly. Krause Publications, as it came to be called, included Cliff Mishler as a key executive. Today, the newspaper is highly respected and is second only to *Coin World* in terms of circulation figures. The parent company became one of America's most important publishers of magazines and reference books in many hobby and sports areas.

Beginning with the 1952 ANA Convention sale (the work of a combination of four dealers with different specialties), the New Netherlands Coin Co. of New York City, owned by Charles M. Wormser (business manager) and John J. Ford, Jr. (numismatic expert), with Walter Breen as a key employee, produced catalogs with extremely detailed descriptions. Coins came to life, the sales had an almost cult following, and the combination of salesmanship, history, market and coin-collecting gossip and remarks, and detailed descriptions of the offered pieces initiated a new trend. The combination of Ford and Breen lasted more than a decade, after which Breen was employed by others, including Lester Merkin, Harmer-Rooke, and First Coinvestors. Breen also wrote many important articles and several monographs and books. His 1988 masterwork, *Walter Breen's Encyclopedia of United States and Colonial Proof Coins 1722–1977*, is valuable. Breen died in jail in 1993, having been convicted of a non-numismatic crime.

1953: Friedberg Paper Money Book Published.
Robert Friedberg, New York rare coin dealer and the operator of leased coin boutiques in department stores, issued a handsome book, *Paper Money of the United States*, which gave "Friedberg numbers" to an otherwise confusing (to many) array of Gold Certificates, Demand Notes, Legal Tender Notes, Coin or Treasury Notes, Silver Certificates, National Bank Notes, and other series—given such designations to reflect their legislative authorization or

backing (either with nothing, as with Legal Tender Notes, or with silver dollars, as with Silver Certificates). This kindled great interest in paper money, and the market began a long rise that continues to this day.

1954–1957: Boom and Bust Market in Proof Sets.
In 1954 a Proof set of 1936 had a market value of $100, increasing to $300 in 1955, onward and upward to $500, then to $600. At several large coin shows, Cincinnati dealer Sol Kaplan posted "bid" and "ask" prices for sets from 1936 to 1942 and from 1950 to date, and prices sometimes changed hourly. A current 1956 Proof set, still available from the Mint for $2.10, was worth $2.50 to those who did not want to wait for sets to arrive in the mail. In that year, a record 669,384 sets were struck, nearly doubling the preceding year's total and exceeding by more than a dozen times the number struck six years earlier.

In 1957 the market crashed. The 1936 set dropped all the way back to $300, with scarcely a buyer in sight. Latecomers to the market racked up large losses, and many left in a hurry—perhaps muttering that coin investment was for gullible people only. In the meantime, anyone who diversified their holdings did well—as large copper cents, silver dollars, paper money, territorial gold, and Liberty Head nickels, along with just about everything else, continued to rise in price. While the market for Proof sets went bust in 1957, recovery took place in succeeding years, and today a gem 1936 Proof set is worth nearly $15,000!

1955: PNG Organized.
In 1953, Abe Kosoff and Sol Kaplan founded the Professional Numismatists Guild, an informal group with a handful of leading dealers. In 1955 it was formally organized, and a board of directors and officers were elected. The group rose to prominence and has done much to promote coin collecting and establish dealer ethics and practices. Several hundred members belong today.

The Professional Numismatists Guild, formally organized in 1955, went on to become America's leading organization of dealers in numismatic items. The guild has helped with many educational, authentication, and other matters of interest to the collecting community. Members must pledge to adhere to a code of ethics.

Coin collecting was becoming an increasingly popular pastime—conventions enjoyed record attendance (the ANA show in Omaha totaled an unprecedented 500 registrants), and dealers enjoyed excellent business as well. Proof sets, bank-wrapped rolls of Mint State coins, and commemoratives were especially popular with investors, as they were easy to understand—quite unlike esoteric colonial or pattern coins.

1958–1959: Market Growth. The years 1958 and 1959 were good ones for the collector, investor, and dealer alike. Anyone who purchased Proof sets at the reduced prices of those years would have no trouble in doubling or tripling the investment capital within the next five years, into the boom market of the early 1960s. Likely, $10,000 invested in typical key dates and high-quality coins would have been worth more than $50,000 by 1965, this being the year *after* the boom market peaked.

1960: Coin Market Vastly Expanded. 1960 was a watershed year in the coin market, leaving behind the scenario of collectors and dealers, plus a limited number of investors, participating in a relatively small market. *Coin World* was launched by the Sidney Printing and Publishing Co. (now called the Amos Press), an entrepreneurial company that sought to establish a weekly paper in a hobby field. The choice was narrowed to antiques, bowling, and coins. *Coin World* became an instant success, fueled greatly by the nationwide publicity given to the 1960 Small Date Lincoln cents. Television and newspaper coverage reported on lucky people getting $50 bags of these new cents and selling them for $10,000 to $12,000 each ($12,000 in 1960 was about twice the price of a new Cadillac, America's most popular top-of-the-line automobile). Within this year the coin market probably doubled or tripled the number of participants, launching a boom that lasted until 1964.

1960–1964: Coin Investment Market Boom. Building upon the launch of *Coin World* in 1960 and the excitement of the Small Date Lincoln cents of that year, the coin market took off like a rocket. Hundreds of thousands of new participants entered, and the circulation of *Coin World* alone crossed the 150,000 mark at one time, with D. Wayne ("Dick") Johnson as founding editor, soon followed in the post by Margo Russell (who went on to nearly 25 years of service). The *Coin World* "Trends" column, conducted by Dayton dealer James F. Kelly, gave coin market prices on a *weekly* basis—the first time ever. Teletype systems linked several hundred dealers by 1962 and 1963, and at one time PNG even had its own network. Dealers posted bid and ask prices as well as market news and lots of gossip, printed out by noisy, clacking keys on rolls of yellow paper. To many, this was like the stock exchange—instant price information from Chicago could be printed out in New York or Los Angeles. The *Coin Dealer Newsletter* was started in 1963, listing bid and ask prices for rolls, Proof sets, and other items, using Teletype data as a basis. The great silver-dollar bonanza of 1962 to 1964 added more excitement. Leading the market activity were bank-wrapped rolls of coins (the 1950-D nickel being the hottest item of all, with a 40-coin roll rising during the period from below $200 to more than $1,200), Proof sets 1936 to date, common-date gold coins (obtaining a common-date Mint State double eagle for less than $50 was very exciting), 1,000-coin bags of silver dollars, and more. The Coin and Currency

Institute featured its new "Library of Coins" albums, the most compact and attractive on the market at the time. Many interesting and attractive holders and albums were produced by others.

Many traditional market areas, such as tokens, medals, colonials, copper half cents and cents, paper money, and just about any other area requiring study and knowledge, were ignored by investors. During this era, interest in these and other specialties was growing, surely but slowly, aided by a growing interest in numismatic history, tradition, and die varieties, and with special-interest groups adding to the growing excitement. The Society of Paper Money Collectors and the Token and Medal Society, two such groups, went on to become very important to the hobby.

1962–1964: Treasury Release of Silver Dollars.

In November 1962 a long-sealed (since 1929) vault at the Philadelphia Mint was opened in order to tap reserves of silver dollars, popular for banks to pay out during the holiday season. A few hundred 1,000-coin bags of sparkling new 1903-O Morgan dollars were casually given out, this being the rarest and most famous of all coins in the series—so rare that earlier it had been estimated that no more than a dozen or two Mint State coins existed! The 1903-O listed in the *Guide Book* for $1,500, the top price level. This was like finding money in the streets; a nationwide silver rush occurred, and several hundred million silver dollars were paid out from Treasury and bank vaults. Finally, in March 1964, the supply ran out, at which time the Treasury took stock of its remaining pieces and found about 3,000,000 Carson City dollars on hand—Mint State, low-mintage issues that were later sold at a premium over a period of time. This dollar bonanza encouraged tens of thousands of people to discover numismatics and become serious collectors, while hundreds of thousands of more developed a casual interest—perhaps setting aside a few dozen dollars, or even a bag or two.

1962–1978: Investment Market for Modern Medals.

A passion for collecting and investing in modern medals began in a significant way with the success of the Presidential Art Medal Co., of Vandalia, Ohio. The firm hired sculptor Ralph Menconi to create a series of medals commemorating current as well as historical events. One depicted President John F. Kennedy, who liked the medal so much that he ordered large quantities to give as gifts to visitors to the White House. One of the founders of Presidential Art, Max J. Humbert, went on in 1965 to establish Paramount International Coin Co., which became prominent in the field of rare coins and auctions as well as the distribution of modern Proof sets. About this time, entrepreneur Joseph Segel founded the General Numismatics Corporation (name later changed to the Franklin Mint), to make medals and also dollar-sized tokens for use in casinos, at a time when silver dollars were no longer available. The Franklin Mint advertised nationally in many media, achieved incredible success, and one year was the hottest stock on the New York Stock Exchange. In the late 1970s the market for modern medals collapsed. The story of the rise and fall of Franklin Mint is told in chapter 9.

1965: Investment-Market Crash.

In 1965 the coin investment market ran out of new players. The silver-dollar excitement was history, and rolls of 1950-D nickels seemed to have stopped in their tracks at the $1,200 level or so—and holders of quantity could find few buyers at this figure. Rolls, Proof sets, 1960 Small Date Lincoln cents, and the number of subscribers to coin newspapers and magazines slumped. In the meantime, other areas that did not participate in the investment boom were doing just fine—colonials, paper money, early copper, and more. Old-time numismatists were still collecting as seriously as ever, joined by thousands of investors who discovered that collecting could be fun, never mind whether they lost some money when they came into the market.

In the coin market of the late 1960s, silver dollars remained hot—for there were many on the market, and they became easy to acquire and attractive to own. Meanwhile, much of the investment market for coins that were hot from 1960 to 1964 was in a slump.

Morgan and Peace silver dollars remained strong, once it was realized that the vaults were empty and that there would be no more "surprise" bags of rarities coming on the market. Many dealers specialized in dollars alone. Prices rose, and while the valuations of 1964 were peaking for rolls and Proof sets, the 1964 prices for silver dollars would soon prove to be incredible bargains.

1965–1980: The Silver Rush and the Coin Shortage. Several parallel coin markets existed in the 1960s. The price of silver rose on international markets, and in 1965 the Treasury Department abandoned this traditional metal for use in the dime and quarter, and created a reduced-silver version of the half dollar (until 1970). New clad-metal compositions were used instead. The price of silver continued to rise, and all silver coins in circulation became worth more than face value—and profitable to melt down, a repeat of the 1850 to 1853 situation in American history. Great investment interest arose in bulk silver coins, while another market existed in ordinary Silver Certificates—the paper notes still in circulation, which could be exchanged for their equivalent in silver metal at the Treasury Department. A large business arose in this; many bankers and others who handled quantities of silver coins and paper bills made a lot of money, and one particular dealer even bought an airplane (a used DC-3) to go here and there to pick up quanti-

ties of certificates. In the meantime, in the mid-1960s the public hoarded copper cents, and scarcely a single coin could be found anywhere. Mint Director Eva Adams blamed this on coin collectors, and "punished" them by removing mint-marks from branch-mint (Denver) coins and by discontinuing the making of Proof sets. Later, Miss Adams "got religion," realized it was really the fault of the general public, became interested in numismatics, and actually sought and was elected to the office of governor of the ANA. Interest in silver continued, and apart from the activities of the Franklin Mint and other mass marketers of modern medals, there was a large and growing interest in "art bars" and "rounds," these being ingots or medals, generally made of an ounce of silver, and bearing different designs. In the meantime, the Hunt brothers—wealthy Texas investors—sought to buy large quantities of silver bullion and silver futures. By early 1980 the price of silver rose to nearly $50 per ounce.

1968–1974: Renewed Vigor in the Coin Investment Market. In 1968, Proof sets were again made available for collectors. For the first time, they were struck at the San Francisco Mint and bore S mint-marks. Interest in collecting and investing in coins entered a new period of growth. Investors had been absent from the market for several years. In 1969 and 1970, and again in 1973 and 1974, the stock market was weak—at a period when the coin market exhibited great strength, making coins all the more attractive as an alternate investment. In particular, gold was a hot item (see below).

1971–1974: The Gold Rush. In 1933 the government had prohibited American citizens from holding gold in bulk form such as in ingots, and did not allow the importation of modern gold (1933 and later) coins, except for Proofs, krugerrands made in South Africa, and a few other specific issues. Pegged at $35 per ounce, gold remained at this level for decades, until the 1960s, when it began going upward. In the early 1970s, the price of gold bullion continued to rise steadily. In America, where investors could not buy bulk, they could and did buy quantities of modern krugerrands. In 1974 there was great excitement as the restriction was to end on December 31. The prices of common gold coins escalated. The *Los Angeles Times*, seeking to learn about this frenetic market, interviewed leading coin dealers, all of whom, except one, said that after December 31 the price of gold coins would *really* soar. When December 31 came and passed, the news was a letdown, as most interested buyers had laid in coins before then, and not many wanted modern ingots. During this frenzied activity I told interested investors and collectors to be cautious—to stick with tried, true, and traditional items and not to jump on a bandwagon that, to me, seemed to have very weak axles.

Richard Buffum, a columnist for the *Los Angeles Times*, interviewed coin dealers and others to ask for their reactions to the coming gold boom. I was a solitary voice in the wilderness, and instead of urging *Times* readers to spend their money as soon as possible on anything that was round and yellow, I urged caution. I even had the audacity to say that the gold boom would be a fizzle. I was the only one who did so! December 31, 1974, came and went, and gold bullion—which had nearly touched the $200 mark shortly before that magic date—didn't go to $400. In fact, it didn't even go to $300. In fact it did something that no one else but me had predicted: it dropped! With it dropped the value of quite a few gold coins and other items that had been artificially inflated in price earlier. Later, in the autumn of 1976, the *Los Angeles Times* published a follow-up article on the subject and I was given credit as the only person who'd correctly predicted several years earlier what would happen.

1975–1977: Coin Investment Market Slump. In 1975 there was little joy in the coin market. Many dealers had been caught up in the end of the boom market for krugerrands, double eagles, and other gold-coin investments, and to the public, *coin investment* was a bad term. Even serious collectors pulled in their horns, with the result that many fine-quality coins, including such things as Proof gold, slumped during this time. The 1776–1976 Bicentennial coins, which would have been as hot as a pistol in normal "up" periods of the investment cycle, laid an egg, and the Mint had a hard time pushing Proofs and special strikings out the door—and had a supply on hand for several years afterward. Serious collectors and alert investors with a contrarian turn of mind bought quietly during this period, and were to reap great profits later.

1978–1980: Gold and Silver Mania Fuel Coin Investment Market. In 1978 and 1979 there was a mad rush to invest in silver and gold bullion, sparked by the Hunt brothers, wealthy Texans seeking to buy all the silver and silver futures they could. Coin dealers who had shops and stores bought large quantities of worn silver coins, tableware, and other items, as well as scrap silver and gold jewelry, to make profits by selling to refiners. Many profited handsomely and used their gains to buy trophy coins and rarities in the coin market. The Johns Hopkins University, owner of the Garrett Collection when it was offered for sale by Bowers and Ruddy Galleries (of which I was chairman at the time), estimated that the collection would bring about $8 million—in fact, it brought $25 million. Although I like to think the magnificent catalogs and my book *The History of United States Coinage as Illustrated by the Garrett Collection* helped, the market itself was very active. Series that required sophistication to collect became popular—including pattern coins, colonials, territorial gold, and more. In the meantime, the price of an ounce of bullion silver approached $50, and gold went over $800,

Pattern cent of 1854 (Judd-164). During the 1970s there was an increased awareness of pattern coins and other rarities, many of which required specialized books to learn about and appreciate. In the Garrett Collection sales, patterns, territorial gold coins, colonials, medals, and other items attracted much attention—in addition to regular federal issues.

seemingly headed for $1,000 or more. "Hard-money" advocates had a field day, with predictions of $2,000 per ounce.

By 1979, coin investment was one of the hottest things going, and by early 1980 coin prices were riding a crest. The situation was caused by the coming together of several factors all at once. First, under the presidential administration of Jimmy Carter, the United States experienced so-called double-digit inflation: inflation over 10% per year. At one time the annual inflation rate actually exceeded 13%. At the same time, money in savings accounts yielded less than 6% (and even this low amount was subject to high income tax rates). Certificates of deposit, a particularly popular way for wealthy people to invest, yielded higher amounts, but these, too, were subject to taxation at high rates. A quest began for fields of investment that were taxable at the low capital gains rates then in effect and that at the same time performed sufficiently well to outpace inflation. As a result, many people with money in banks and elsewhere turned to coins. The worldwide energy crisis received great publicity, and scarcely a day passed without newspaper headlines about the ever-increasing prices of gasoline and oil. Certain Arab oil interests publicly stated they did not want to be paid in paper American dollars but instead wanted payment in gold. Paper dollars were no good, it was implied. This in turn generated much unfavorable publicity about the future of the American dollar. Its price plummeted on overseas markets, causing more dollars to be dumped. Obviously, if Arabs wanted gold rather than paper money, they knew something we didn't know—or at least, many people thought they did. Numerous editors of newsletters, "hard-money" advocates, and others proclaimed that anyone holding paper dollars was a fool, an idiot, or worse. Gold (and to a lesser extent silver) was the only way to go.

In 1980, a coin investment advisor wrote an article for *Coin World* stating that what should be considered is "the sizzle, not the steak," and that investment performance is more important than the coins themselves. By this time, most *serious numismatists* were sitting on the sidelines and not buying any of the hot coins that investors were lapping up. On the contrary, quite a few numismatists took the opportunity to *sell*—not much different from what Bernard Baruch had done with stocks a few decades earlier (successful techniques don't change much!). Then the expected (to many coin market insiders) or, to some, the unexpected (to investors) happened: the market for most "investment-grade" silver and gold coins peaked in early 1980. In the next several years many prices nose-dived to fractions of their former highs. Nearly all coin investment advisors found they had no customers.

The price of bullion gold peaked at $873 in January 1980. On January 18, 1980, Allen Harriman, editor of the *Coin Dealer Newsletter*, said this: "With both silver and gold bullion soaring into new uncharted ranges, trading in many areas of the coin market becomes more uncertain each day—if not each hour! Most strongly affected, of course, is the bullion-related material...." At the Central States Numismatic Society convention held in Lincoln, Nebraska, in March, a long-time client, Dr. C., from Michigan, told me that he had been offered $15,000 *per coin* for the set of Barber Proof half dollars of 1892 through 1915 purchased from me a few years earlier for less than $2,000 per coin. Although he was an avid collector of these, I recommended that he cash in and run—

which he did. In the same month, March 1980—some say even during the Central States convention itself—the investment market for rare coins collapsed, and the prices of many "investment-grade" coins (generally, MS-65 and Proof-65 or finer silver and gold coins) fell sharply. Many other areas of numismatics, such as copper coins, tokens, medals, and the like, were not affected. Allen Harriman said this on March 21: "This week's unprecedented drop in the price of both silver and gold bullion has as yet had little or no effect on the numismatic market. In fact, plus signs are very liberally scattered across virtually all of the various pricing charts once again this week...." Later, Dr. C. could replace his collection of gem Proofs for less than $3,000 per coin. Today, a set of gems such as his would probably be graded Proof-66 and -67 and would cost close to $5,000 per coin for hand-picked quality.

For collectors and dealers in coins of traditional numismatic value, Dr. Sheldon's "bellwether" 1794 copper cent being an example, the market remained solid. "Collector coins" continued to do well, as did tokens, medals, and paper money—these not having participated in the investment market run-up. In this as in other market cycles for series that became "hot," *very few serious numismatists bought coins for their collections once investors took over those sections of the market. The market was mainly dealers selling to investors and collectors selling out to investors.* Because of this, after the crash most collectors remained very content,

although some rued that they had not sold their duplicates or parts of their collections that were no longer their prime interest.

1980–1983: Coin Investment Market Slump. The *investment market* for coins was in a blue funk for the next several years. In the meantime, scarce and rare Capped Bust and Liberty Seated silver coins, large copper cents, colonials, Charlotte and Dahlonega mint gold, and other collector-oriented series continued to play to a solid market.

A series of sales, commencing with Auction '79, was conducted by a consortium of four dealers: Paramount, Stack's, Superior, and RARCOA. For the next decade catalogs of 2,000 lots per sale (500 for each dealer) played to an enthusiastic audience, with good results. Jim Halperin was busy in Boston with the New England Rare Coin Co., which had become a big player in the market, while in Dallas, Steve Ivy had a successful business. Years later the two merged to form Heritage. Coin conventions were successful for the most part, and traditional numismatics continued apace.

1982: New Commemoratives. In 1982 the Treasury Department resumed the issuance of commemorative coins, the first since 1954. The Washington commemorative half dollar, designed by Elizabeth Jones, accompanied by publicity and enthusiasm generated by Mint Director Donna Pope, was issued to observe the 250th anniversary of the birth of the first U.S. president. The pieces, made with Proof finish by the San Francisco Mint and with Mint State finish by the Denver Mint, were very well received, and within a year or so most of the pieces were sold. However, remainders were trickled out over several subsequent years. This set the stage for an impressive and vast program of commemorative coins, silver and gold, that continues today.

The Eliasberg Collection of United States Gold Coins, cataloged by me and auctioned by my firm in October 1982, likewise created great attention, primarily

A lustrous Mint State 1841-C half eagle struck at the Charlotte Mint and so identified by the mintmark C below the eagle on the reverse. During the coin investment market slump of the early 1980s, such gold coins, of proven rarity and collector demand, remained strong.

on the part of numismatic connoisseurs. Containing one of each date and mint-mark issue in the U.S. gold series, the auction realized $12.4 million, and in the process numerous world record prices were established. Clearly, the market was solidly in the hands of collectors.

1986–1989: Commercial Grading Services. In 1986, David Hall and a group of dealer associates formed the Professional Coin Grading Service (PCGS), which offered, for a fee, to receive coins, to give an opinion of grade via several experts, and to sonically seal each coin in a hard plastic holder, which became known as a *slab*. In 1987 John Albanese, earlier with PCGS, established the Numismatic Guaranty Corporation of America (NGC), which became spectacularly successful. Other services (more than 100 in all) were founded, and some enjoyed niches in the marketplace. (See chapter 7 for more information.)

1987–1990: The Economic Scene. The American dollar, strong overseas in 1984 and 1985, became very weak by 1987, thus creating record trade imbalances. This was an important factor in causing the record 508-point drop in the Dow Jones Industrial Average on October 19 of that year. Although investment was not in the mainstream of numismatic activity during the mid-1980s, the subject received new life through vast telemarketing organizations that were set up to promote the sale of coins by telephone solicitation. Common silver dollars, Proof sets, and the like were aggressively marketed, often at prices far above what knowledgeable collectors would pay. An investigation conducted by the Federal Trade Commission in 1986 revealed, for example, that one firm sold Liberty Walking half dollars to clients for several hundred dollars each, billing them as MS-65, when in reality they were worn pieces worth no more than $15 each! A typical group of coins sold for $10,000 was found to have a replacement value of about $2,000. Such abuses cast a shadow on all of numismatics, even though reputable firms

weren't involved. Among the collecting fraternity, quality was emphasized, and grading underwent a transition (as discussed in detail in my separate chapter on the subject). Market emphasis was put on pieces grading MS-65 and Proof-65, with the result that lesser-grade pieces appeared to be bargains by comparison. This spawned a new wave of collecting interest in such issues as Liberty Seated coins; Barber dimes, quarters, and half dollars; and other issues that were and are basically scarce but that had not participated in the great market boom of the late 1970s. Interviewed at the close of 1984, Raymond N. Merena, president of Bowers and Merena Galleries, Inc., noted that the previous 12 months had set a sales record. "If I could put the coin market on 'hold' and keep it this way forever, I would," he observed. He went on to say the market was composed primarily of experienced buyers paying reasonable prices for truly scarce and rare items. Clearly, it was a good time to engage in the formation of a meaningful collection.

By 1988 there were thousands of certified coins available from these services, plus some lesser-known services as well. Now, coins could truly be bought and sold as investment vehicles, as it was thought that the problem of one great unknown—the grade of a coin—had been neatly solved. It was a simple matter to trade in certified coins, mostly of the popular silver and gold metals, by simply looking at the grade and market price. Interest spawned more interest, and soon Wall Street firms got into the act. Merrill Lynch, for one, started a coin fund, and other brokerage houses became involved. Here, indeed, was a product that could be sold to investors and yield greater fees and commissions than could be obtained from simply buying and selling common stocks. The advent of "Wall Street money" was widely publicized, excitement prevailed, and prices of so-called "investment-quality" coins rose sharply. As to that particular quality, it was once again generally defined as MS-65 or Proof-65 or finer. These were the coins that collectors wanted most, and therefore it seemed logical that investors should buy them in anticipation of that great demand.

1990: Coin Investment Market Slumps.

The market activity of 1989 largely resulted in dealers' and collectors' selling to investors at prices often far beyond what any seasoned collector would pay. Finally, the boom ran out of steam, and in early 1990 few wanted to get into the coin investment game. In the meantime, the prices of "investment-quality" coins had ascended to such heights that collectors were not interested. The market crashed, and prices fell back to basic or foundational levels reflecting collector demand. Today, in the early 21st century, while many coins have exceeded the highs of that market, some still remain lower.

1990–2000: Growth of Numismatics.

During the decade, coin collecting became an increasingly popular hobby, and most dealers did well. There was a great growth of interest in specialties, and collector groups drew enthusiastic members to write about, share experiences of, and simply enjoy such things as Capped Bust half dollars, Civil War tokens, paper money, colonial coins, copper half cents and cents, commemoratives, Liberty Seated coins, trade tokens and store cards, out-of-print numismatic books, and more.

As time went on, writers in the popular numismatic press told of *grade-flation*, or certification services' assigning higher numbers than the same coins had received earlier. By the turn of the next century, when the Y2K or millennium calendar switch occupied the attention of news media, the coin market was in a state of transition. By this time, many if not most uncertified silver and gold coins, if priced at a few thousand dollars or more in a dealer's stock, were apt to be viewed with suspicion by new buyers, who felt that such coins might have problems (and sometimes they did). On the other hand,

A gem Proof 1878 nickel three-cent piece, a key in the series (and a coin of which only 2,350 were struck), is numismatically desirable on all counts. However, the price went up too fast and too far in the investment surge of the late 1980s, and today such a coin is less expensive than it was then.

auction houses had a different policy, and quite a few old-time collections and consignments were not certified, simply because those who gathered the coins had done so before the certification era and either did not like the thought of certified coins or were confused by it. However, like as not, choice pieces sold at such auctions were quickly certified by the new buyers.

For dealers, certification solved many problems, although I am not aware that this has ever been discussed in print before. Prior to certification, coin shops, auction houses, and others assigned their own grades, which often varied, sometimes widely. Human nature being what it is, sometimes a buyer of a rare prize at an auction sale would take it to a local dealer, who would look at it closely and then criticize its grade, appearance, or other aspects—either because the coin deserved such or, sometimes, to impress upon the buyer that the money would have been better spent with the dealer rather than at an auction. Similarly, coins sold by dealer A at a convention or store might be criticized by dealer B or C. The situation was not much different from one in which a person buys a car from one dealer and drives it over to another and asks how the second dealer likes it. Probably the flaws and shortcomings of the car would be quickly pointed out. With the certification of coins, dealers and auction houses were, in effect, absolved of all responsibility for grading interpretations and knowledge! In fact, more than just a few auction offerings stated that certified coins could not be returned for any reason. No longer did dealers have to explain or justify the grade on a coin—they simply pointed to the holder and stated matter-of-factly that XYZ Grading Service called it MS-65. This situation prevails today.

2001 to Date: Growth of Numismatics.

Chapter 3, "Dynamics of the Rare Coin Market," covers much of the hobby and business as it is today. There is a great deal of enthusiasm in the field, and the Internet brings in new faces every day—certainly a great outlook.

The early 21st century has given rise to a new investment passion, that of modern

This well-struck, lustrous, and beautiful 1795 half dollar, die variety Overton-105, is at once a "trophy" coin and a prize for the connoisseur. In the early 21st century, increasing attention is being paid to such classics. However, as with any other purchase, one should take care when evaluating such items, as there are many factors to consider.

coins that are common in grades up through and including MS-65, but for which few have thus far been certified in ultra grades such as MS-68, -69, or -70. The same situation applied to Proofs. Seemingly overlooked as not being important is the fact that among Proof sets of recent decades, or coins widely available in roll or bag quantities, there are many super gems. Earlier, it did not pay to certify them, but now the first people to certify certain common pieces have "condition rarities." Regarding the investment interest in ultra-grade coins of which relatively few have been certified at high levels, but that are available easily enough in MS-65 or -66, my advice is to be very careful. If I had a bunch of ultra-grade coins I would be a seller, not a buyer. At the same time, the hobby of numismatics is doing just fine—and there are a lot of opportunities among modern coins, 1930s to date, to fill in your Lincoln cents, Jefferson nickels, Mercury and Roosevelt dimes, several types of half dollars, and several designs of dollars, at the MS-64, -65, and -66 levels. "Trophy" items are in demand in various coin and paper money series. Such classics are always a pleasure to own. However, care must be taken to secure a good value for the price paid.

Today, more than ever, there are great opportunities for *you* as a smart buyer. Review every coin through steps 1 to 4 (see chapter 2), pay attention to the Optimal Collecting Grade (be very careful when a *little* difference in a grading number means a *huge* difference in price), read this book carefully, take your time, savor your experiences, and enjoy yourself!

CHAPTER THIRTEEN

PREDICTING THE RARE COIN MARKET

This is the age of collections, and the spirit of gathering together and classifying is abroad. It shows itself in the gigantic museums, the vast art and antiquarian collections, and the great libraries that grace the capitals and literary centers of the world, that have become the Meccas of so many pilgrims today.… There is nothing you can collect that will represent so much, if properly selected, or will cost so little, if properly bought, as a variety of fifty, one or two hundred coins.

—Dr. Geo. F. Heath, September 1888

The Past Is Prologue

Rather than gazing into a crystal ball or reading tea leaves to predict the future of numismatics and the coin market, I have always tried to rely on common sense, plus a knowledge of coin-collecting history in combination with economic trends and human psychology.

In 1964, when I wrote the first study on coin-market cycles, I drew from the past—some of it from my own experience from 1952 onward, the rest from history. Today, more than 40 years after that study, there have been several well-defined cycles in the investment market for rare coins. I say *investment* market, for, with few exceptions, niches and specialties in numismatics are immune to cycles. Such items as obsolete paper money of Maine, copper coins of Vermont from 1785 through 1788, die varieties of 1795 half dollars, copper-nickel cent patterns of 1858, and even Mint State Barber coins of 1892 through 1916, exist in relatively small numbers—there are not enough cards in the deck or pieces on the board to allow many players to participate.

Preferences have been different for each boom period in the coin investment market. Here are some of the the buyer values that defined "investment-quality" coins in the run-up of the late 1980s (the "Wall Street money" boom):

- *High grades:* MS-65, Proof-65, or finer.
- *Gold or silver:* These are "precious metals," and as such they make investment even more attractive.
- *Ease of understanding:* Or, more accurately, *apparent* ease—such as a grade on a certified holder that instantly tells you *everything* you need to know, except the price. No need even to look at the coin—just buy it, sight unseen.
- *Ease of pricing:* Prices must be easily available in sheets and elsewhere—no research needed.
- *Ready availability:* There has to be plenty of "product" so you can buy immediately—no waiting until next week or next month. (Which is no problem with common-date gold, most coins minted since 1934, most Proof coins from 1936 to date, etc.)
- *Dazzling action and hype:* Lots of enthusiastic comments in dealer ads, suggestions that this is where the action is, that the coins are gems, or rare, or just the things collectors would die for, and on and on.
- *A new definition of "rare":* It is not important that millions of a desired coin exist, so long as few have been certified. To us (we investors, that is) such coins are *rare*. Make that *Rare*, with a capital *R*. And don't you forget it!
- *Irrelevance of history:* Facts—including that a coin might be common, or that it is selling for $1,000 now but could be bought for $300 five years ago, or that only 10 have been certified in this grade now but 100 might be in the future—must at all costs be ignored or dismissed as stupid and irrelevant. Obviously, anyone who is

a naysayer is completely out of touch with market reality. Learning is for the birds. Besides, books cost money and take time to read. Why bother with such effort?

These buyer values that dictated "investment-quality" characteristics in the late 1980s enticed many newcomers to invest millions of dollars. Of course, the coins were and still are of high quality. It is just that the market for them at the time was not based upon *true numismatic demand*.

The coins themselves don't change. They are as collectible as ever. However, their market prices do change, and if you are a smart buyer, you can build a higher-quality collection and at lower cost than anyone who simply has money, but knows little.

As to coin investors who don't want to learn anything, but who have a lot of money, all serious collectors owe them a debt of gratitude—for buying all of those coins, including lots of real dogs that connoisseurs don't want! This helps sustain the general market. The headline "Baggy Generic Morgans Up" in the *Certified Coin Dealer Newsletter* (September 24, 2004) reflects this—noting that bagmarked common dollars were in strong demand. I doubt if even a *single person* who reads this book and takes my advice to heart would want a "baggy generic" dollar for his or her collection.

What has happened in the past will undoubtedly be prologue to the future, plus there will be some events and evolutions that we cannot envision. However, *numismatic common sense*, a guiding precept of this book, will not go out of style!

When Should I Start?

"The best time to plant a tree is 20 years ago. The second best time is now." So goes an old proverb.

In 1971 the coin market was so-so in activity, not in the doldrums, but not hot, either. Collectors were collecting, dealers were dealing, but not many investors were investing.

For the *Forecaster*, an investment newsletter published by John Kamin, I wrote a piece about coin investment, picking a 1902 Proof Barber half dollar as a miscellaneous but good example of a rare coin. I was quite familiar with such coins. When I first started my business, they were worth $7 to $10, this being for a gem, as you could find gems if you looked for them. All Proofs were $7 to $10—some having nicks, others being superb—it made no difference. Only 777 Proofs were made, and thus the term *rare* seemed applicable back then, as it still does.

Over the years, the price rose, and although I did not profit from this, as I simply bought and sold them (as I still do), anyone who bought a 1902 Proof in 1953 was pleased in 1963 that it had appreciated in value to become worth $80. By 1971, when I wrote my *Forecaster* article, the price had gone up further. I posed this question:

> Will the 1902 Proof half dollar, a coin which might cost $180 today, be a good investment for the future? After all, quite a bit of profit has already been made by others on the coins—by people who bought them when they were cheaper 10 years ago. This is a logical and reasonable question to ask.
>
> Perhaps the quickest way to answer would be to say that 10 years ago isn't now, and we must concern ourselves with the present, not the past. Valuable objects in any field—Rembrandt paintings, antiques, etc.—have a history of price appreciation over the years. Waiting to buy them for the prices of 10 or 20 years ago is not realistic. So long as the trend of our economy is inflationary, prices seem to be headed for an ever-upward spiral. Coins have shared in this spiral and will continue to do so.
>
> Today [remember, this was written in 1971] the number of available 1902 Proof half dollars combined with the

number of people desiring them, have set the price at approximately $180. Again we remind our readers that we have picked the 1902 Proof half dollar merely as an example. The reasoning applies to many coins in the United States series.

I have no way of knowing how many, if any, readers of the *Forecaster* rushed out to buy Proof Barber half dollars. It turned out that $180 was a great value. Today a beautiful gem would cost more than $5,000, which, for the 1902, is low in its market cycle—during the silver and gold mania of 1980, one could have been sold (and some were sold) for $15,000, as I mentioned in the last chapter.

This prompts me to mention that *collectors* seldom buy "investment-quality" coins at market peaks—it is the *investors* who do all the buying. Usually, when coins that are not basically rare experience an abnormal run-up in price or a much-hyped buying fad sets in, collectors keep their checkbooks in their pockets and collect items in other series. However, they often *sell* into market peaks—which, of course, is a good thing to do!

While investors will continue to come and go, *collectors* will be around for a long time. Such are the foundations of the art and science of collecting and enjoying coins, tokens, medals, and paper money.

Strength for the Future

As I see it, numismatics will be a dynamic hobby for a long time to come. The advantages, including the following, seem to be in place, ready for *you*.

Many Participants. The hobby has hundreds of thousands of serious participants and millions of casual dabblers. There are enough people involved that just about any specialty within numismatics, from obscure to obvious, has a sizeable contingent.

New and Exciting Coin Issues. The program of continuing coinage in the United States by the Treasury Department and the United States Mint will bring to us more statehood quarters, plus, it seems, commemoratives and other interesting issues. Some might be controversial, others might seem illogical, but they will be there to collect. As each new variety is introduced, whether it be a distinctive topic on the back of a quarter for Idaho or California, or a substitution of a Lewis and Clark motif for the Monticello building on the reverse of a Jefferson nickel, or something else, more people will take notice and become interested. At the same time, in the allied field of paper money, the continuing parade of issues by the 12 different Federal Reserve districts, plus signature combinations, plus a fascination with collecting plate numbers and serial numbers, seems to assure new faces in that area.

Eager Buyers With Money to Spend. There is a lot of money in the market (no pun intended), and when collections are bought and sold, there is a lot of activity. This denotes strength, and is far different from a field that comprises just a handful of enthusiasts. There are more dealers, more market sites (including those on the Internet), more people active in selling coins than ever before. This means more choices when you buy and more options when you sell.

Interest Added by Research and Study. Numismatic research and study, once the focal point of just a few dozen people in the hobby, has become widespread, resulting in a delightful panorama of interesting historical facts, die varieties, and other things being publicized. Such activities lend their own brand of enthusiasm.

Universal Fondness for Money. Money is a popular subject, doesn't seem to go out of style, and attracts the interest of just about everyone. I know from my own experiences in television, including on the Discovery Channel, the History Channel, and the major networks, that certain features regarding gold coins or sunken treasures or related things seem to have everlasting interest—and can be run again and again. As time goes on, new treasure ships will be

And the beat goes on.... In recent years the U.S. Mint has provided collectors with a fascinating panorama of different designs in the regular and commemorative coin series, several of which are shown here.

found on the ocean floor, a scarce piece of paper money will come to light in a bank vault in Montana, and the Mint will produce weird varieties (such as the combination Washington quarter and Sacagawea dollar that excited the nation in the year 2000). All of these factors will keep numismatics in the limelight. Societies, special-interest groups, and others will remain active and proliferate. The American Numismatic Society and American Numismatic Association are both long established and offer many services. Coin clubs and societies with interests in areas as diverse as out-of-print books and Indian Head cents will continue to attract members, and other meeting places will be developed, including connections on the Internet. Technology is always advancing.

Availability of Useful Information. Good numismatic publications, as well as information in electronic media, will be developed and will be available inexpensively, enabling numismatists to have a wonderful world of useful information at their fingertips, quickly and inexpensively. To this can be added the Internet as an information source. If you would like to know about the biography of David Rittenhouse, the first director of the Mint, a web search will probably give you about all you need for a basic speech at your local coin-club meeting. I recently purchased for $45 a CD-ROM with all the back issues of the *Colonial Newsletter,* in searchable format—a combination of low cost and versatility not dreamed of a generation ago. Soon, the entire numismatic world will be at your fingertips, or so it seems likely.

Ease of Storing and Displaying. Coins, tokens, medals, and paper money are easy to store, and a valuable collection can be housed in a bank vault. Also, their small size makes them easy to ship from place to place safely and conveniently. Moreover, the coin market is scarcely local, but is national for all American series, and international for series beyond that. If here in New Hampshire I have a VF-20 example of the curious 1794 large copper cent, variety Sheldon-48,

known as the "Starred Reverse," with 94 tiny five-pointed stars around the rim, and I offer it for sale, the chances are that it will be sold to a buyer in some distant place—perhaps someone in Seattle who will request it by air shipment and have it available for examination the next day, or perhaps someone in Salt Lake City or Fort Lauderdale. Moreover, through the use of electronic and other images, as well as a grading interpretation that we all understand (more or less), we all have the same score card. Indeed, if I tell John Doe in Seattle that I have an Sheldon-48 cent in VF-20 grade, "with medium brown surfaces, very lightly porous on the obverse, rather smooth on the reverse, well struck, with all of the 94 stars visible, and without any serious edge dings, nicks, or scrapes," a transaction can probably be made without the buyer's even seeing the coin! In many other areas of investment interest, such as paintings, antique automobiles, and real estate, such ease is not possible.

Good Times in the Offing. Coin people are enjoyable to know, and coin events are fun to attend. The pleasures of numismatics can enrich your life, whether you begin as a youngster or are in your retirement years.

Lucky *you*! To the preceding can be added the opportunity of being a "smart buyer" in the marketplace, which I hope you will become! As you already know, this is somewhat of a sport, a game—using knowledge to find sharply struck coins, or pieces of unusual quality, or items of exceptional value, while your competitors in the marketplace are unaware.

In Their Words

In the future, as in the past, the life of numismatics will be in the people who participate. Coins by themselves are not numismatics. Thousands of gold double eagles on the sea floor in the wreck of the *S.S. Central America* are not numismatics, nor are a thousand bags of 1903-O dollars stored in a Philadelphia Mint vault, nor is a 1955 Doubled-Die cent

Daniel Carr, designer of three of the statehood quarter dollars (2001 New York, 2001 Rhode Island, and 2003 Maine), and Robin Wells, who has just recently joined the hobby, are shown here while visiting with the author (and, in this instance, photographer) at the ANA convention in the summer of 2004.

Joe Wells, Robin's six-year-old son, has become a numismatist. Looking through rolls to pick out coins for his album is a favorite way to spend a rainy day. Albums beckon to be filled with statehood quarters.

resting undiscovered in a child's piggy-bank in Newark Valley, New York.

People are needed to make coins, tokens, medals, and paper money interesting, to turn them into a hobby, to make them a focus of personal enjoyment and, possibly, financial security.

In connection with this book I invited two numismatists, one of each gender, one new to the hobby and the other an old-timer, to share their thoughts on the significance of the hobby to them.

Robin Wells

Robin Wells, a lady from Texas who for the first time visited an ANA convention on August 2004 in Pittsburgh, stopped by to say hello at the American Numismatic Rarities bourse table and to have me sign a copy of my *Guide Book of Morgan Silver Dollars*. She really enjoys the hobby, she said. At the same time, Daniel Carr, designer of three of the Statehood reverse quarter dollars, was chatting with me about that coin program and how interesting it was. After Mrs. Wells returned home she sent this commentary:

As a child I enjoyed the time spent with my father poring over his coin

collection and filling holes in his albums from pocket change. Isn't that how so many of us have started out? The years progressed and my interest in this with him waxed and waned as I grew up and began a life of my own.

The launch of the 50 State Quarters® Program served to reignite that flame of interest in my father as well as in me, helping us reestablish a connection that brought back many warm memories from my youth in a small town in Wisconsin. Unfortunately he passed away last year, a loss to his family and all who knew him. I know he loved his new collection of quarters. Like many others I am diligently working on filling my state quarter album, not only for myself but as a tribute to and in memory of him, and as a thank you for opening my eyes to this great hobby.

The state quarters and other coins I have collected have brought many pleasures, indeed gifts, to my life. I have a newfound interest and appreciation of our country's history. I've been sharing the hobby with my son Joe, a first grader, and have seen his eyes light up with excitement every time he fills another hole in his album. I have also enjoyed meeting many people and making some wonderful friends along the way. "Coin people" have a special warmth and kindness, and it is very impressive that at the convention everyone was so willing to share information and give suggestions.

Being a relative newcomer to the more serious side of numismatics, I find myself doing all that I can to increase my knowledge of the hobby and the history that it so grandly represents. I subscribe to various periodicals and publications as well as adhering to the wise advice of "buying the book before the coin." However, I've found that some of the best knowledge that I've acquired has come from attending shows, both large and small. No amount of reading and researching can compare to actually studying the objects of my desire up close. The ANA convention was my first large show. I am in awe at the wealth of information available at these functions and the willingness of collectors to share it. From viewing various exhibits to attending lectures in my areas of interest, there seems to be no end to the knowledge and information available to anyone willing to take the time to pursue it. All of this is in addition to the stunning merchandise available at every turn. Anyone lucky enough to be able to attend a show of this magnitude will be faced with the same dilemma that I had: what to do first? fill my brain with knowledge or empty my wallet?

We all have our own special stories of what piqued our interest in coins and how we got started on this road of collecting, some simple, many sentimental, but all meaningful to ourselves. For me, the knowledge and excitement gained from attending the recent ANA show was truly priceless, and an experience that I will never forget. It is something that every collector from the seasoned veteran to the youngest "newbie" should experience, so as to feel more educated and excited than ever about numismatics. I look forward to learning more about coins and meeting more fine people.

Cliff Mishler

To give all of the numismatic accomplishments of Cliff Mishler would require a separate chapter, and even then it would be only a summary. During his career, which is still in progress, he has shared with Chet Krause the management of Krause Publications, publisher of *Numismatic News*, *Coins* magazine, and many reference books, some of the best of which have Cliff's name on the cover.

Here is his contribution, with his suggested title, "A Collector by Accident; an Advocate by Conviction."

> Many of the acquaintances I have made through the years, outside the hobby community, have inquired about how and why I became a coin collector, what it is about the hobby that caused me to become a lifelong collector, and why I chose to pursue the discipline as a career. The answer

Chet Krause (left) and Cliff Mishler, by now honored veterans in the hobby, at a reception held by Whitman Publishing in 2004. Chet founded *Numismatic News* in 1952, and in later years Cliff directed the operation, which came to include Krause Publications, issuer of many reference books in different fields. (David M. Sundman photograph)

is both quite simple and rather detailed. Hopefully, what follows digests a comprehensible and motivating overview of those developments into the space available.

The beginning came during the summer of 1950, as I was nearing my 11th birthday. I had moved into a new community and met a new friend, who happened to share an interest in the collecting of postally cancelled stamps with his mother, and who was eager to have me join in that interest. That idea did not take root, but in scanning the contents of a publication they were subscribing to, an advertisement offering *coins* on approval sparked an ember of inquisitiveness.

Among the coins included in the selection that reached me a few days after I sent away a dime—for 10 pieces of obsolete World War II currency promised with that first approval selection—in a 3¢ stamped envelope, was a quite worn copper coin from a faraway place, Zanzibar, that immediately captured my fascination. I had to have it, as it appeared to my uninitiated mind to be more than 750 years old—a bargain at any price, or I thought—although I learned not too long after acquiring it that what had appeared to me to be a crudely rendered Christian date of 1199 was really the Mohammedan-era date of 1299 rendered in Arabic numerals, or 1882 by Christian reckoning!

It was the mysterious connotations of that coin, I'm convinced, that caused me to become a coin collector. First came the purchase of a few more coins of various origins from similar approval selections. Then, the saving of U.S. coins culled from circulation and pressed into the die-cut holes of the then-ubiquitous Whitman blue folders became my focus. Initially, that obsolete WWII currency broadcast little appeal to me.

Rather, I discovered a hobby shop where I could buy a few coins, the two or three times a year that I got there, that eluded me in my searches of pocket change and bank-wrapped rolls of U.S. coins. By the time I graduated from high school I was even buying coins at auction.

Along the way, however, the diversity offered by the numismatic discipline was blossoming for me. I soon became actively interested in paper money, principally of foreign origins—that obsolete WWII currency that I had initially given short shrift resurfaced, along with a small olive-drab pouch of paper money and coins my father had carried home from his service time in the South Pacific theater—while the fascinating prospects offered up by pursuit of tokens and medals, now collectively known as *exonumia*, unfolded before me as well.

As my fascination and commitment grew, I was on the receiving end of much encouragement, most particularly from my parents, along with my many relatives and teachers and the kids I grew up with. This encouragement was embodied in many forms. There was the patronizing and fiscal support provided by my parents. There was the respect I was accorded by my peers for the specialized knowledge I gained. There was the deferential treatment accorded by teachers in calling upon me to share my blossoming outside world in the classroom.

Educationally, development of an ongoing interest in coin collecting was undoubtedly a godsend to me. While I had developed an abiding interest in the subjects of history, math, and spelling at an early age, I'm certain that I became a much more interested and skilled student of those subjects, along with geography, politics, economics, and English, than would have otherwise been the case as my schooling rolled into junior high and high school. And, while my personal artistic capabilities were and remain very minimal, I believe I also became more appreciative of artistic expression than would have otherwise been the case.

I have found that through the years my appreciation for each of these disciplines has been unabated, with virtual equilibrium in appeal. Invariably, when reading a news story or feature item, or becoming engaged in a discussion with anyone about anyplace in the world, I find myself unconsciously creating a tie to my knowledge of the coins or paper money of that place. Not infrequently, this causes me to seek out a numismatic reference or an encyclopedic reference to seek greater detail on some historical, geographical, or monetary fact that surfaces as a consequence of the experience.

As time passed and my inquisitiveness became a flame, I also came to recognize and appreciate the attributes of numismatic items as storehouses of wealth. I've always acquired my collectible coins and related objects, first and foremost, for what they represent and what they are: historical relics that preserve the economic and cultural histories of their issuers, gathered systematically by succeeding generations. And the beautiful thing about a collection is that its form is something the individual can control as to both scope and quality. Acquired and assembled intelligently and with long-term objectives, they provide fiscal preservation, at the same time they are providing aesthetic and acquisitional satisfactions to the dispositions of the owner.

Eventually, of course, I progressed beyond merely collecting and enjoying, to studying and learning the history and heritage of what I was collecting. That's a natural and beneficial transition experienced by most of those who are bitten by the collecting

bug, but for me, that was just the beginning. As I learned, my instincts motivated me to a predisposition to share the knowledge I'd gained. Knowledge can be gained from many sources and shared in many ways, including exhibiting, speaking, and organizational involvement, but for me the primary vehicles of both input and output became the written word.

The coin-collecting discipline had garnered my dedication to ongoing pursuit by the time I was passing from schooldays to adulthood. After casting about for a time seeking direction to my life, doing some writing about the objects of my pursuits, engaging in some self-publishing, creating a few commercial products, and becoming involved at the organizational level, the opportunity to embark upon a career in the hobby community presented itself. I jumped at that opportunity. The pursuit of my interests soon became an obsession, and I have never looked back, so to speak, as the ever-changing visage of the hobby community has bloomed before me.

Numismatics (coin collecting) is a hobby community that is multifaceted. Its pursuit can be casual or serious, inexpensively or extravagantly focused, by individuals from all age groups and stations in life. I have always found the audience mix to be most appealing, as everyone from train conductors to doctors, sanitation engineers to professors, and from innumerable other stations in life, gather to exchange their views, knowledge, and treasures. Most importantly, perhaps, while no two are cut from the same bolt of cloth, just as no two collections are the same, they blend into a seemingly seamless montage of interests and objectives.

For me, it doesn't matter if I'm admiring my latest nondescript stickered dollar acquisition, my high-quality and valuable historic 1792 silver half disme, or that well-worn, once-mysterious 1882 Zanzibar one-pysa coin—each conjures up in my mind its own distinctive and compelling heritage and history that motivated me to make the acquisition. Rather, it's the coin from Zanzibar that got me started some 54 years ago, that's perhaps worth no more in today's market than what I paid for it at the time. It is also that example of the first U.S. coin (the 1792 half disme) that I acquired nearly seven years ago, which has certainly grown appreciably in value. To these can be added the many thousands of items of varied descriptions that I have added to my accumulations over more than half a century of enjoying my immersion in the hobby community. I cherish each and every one for what they have added to my life's experience, in knowledge and value alike.

While I became a coin collector by accident many years ago, I'm proud to be an advocate for the hobby community by conviction today. I am firmly convinced that exposure enhances the individual's comprehension and appreciation of, and ongoing homage to, educational opportunities. Beyond that, it provides a degree of personal satisfaction where achievement and accomplishment are concerned. Then, there are the benefits gained from personal interaction by communication, in clubs and at shows. In addition, it can be financially beneficial. Most importantly, however, it can provide temporary liberation and refreshment of the mind from lifestyles both mundane and hectic.

It seems to me that with people who, like Robin Wells, come into the hobby with fresh-faced enthusiasm, and those who, like Cliff Mishler, have been in the hobby for decades but with "appreciation unabated" today, numismatics has a secure future!

CHAPTER FOURTEEN

TECHNIQUES OF SMART BUYING:
From Coin Shops to the Internet

Investing in rare coins can be a rewarding experience for anyone who approaches the calling armed with the right attitude and background knowledge about this exciting field. It can just as easily become a costly mistake for anyone who attempts to profit from coins without giving serious thought to the idiosyncrasies of this unique market.

The best advice given to anyone considering investing in rare coins is to use common sense. No thinking person would consider buying a diamond ring from a street peddler, or an art masterpiece at a garage sale. It is just the same with rare coins, and the more careful you are in selecting a qualified dealer and making an educated evaluation of the coins you purchase, the greater will be your chance of making a profitable investment.

—Kenneth E. Bressett, *A Guide Book of United States Coins* (59th ed.)

This and the next chapter are very meaty. In fact, they could probably make a whole separate book! Fasten your seat belt, and pay attention, please!

By the time you read these words you will have reviewed much information on how to be a smart buyer—what to look for in terms of grade, sharpness, eye appeal, and more—and have gained an awareness of past market conditions. Now, to the art and technique of buying—how to spend your money most effectively when you bid in an auction, or write a check, or otherwise actually acquire the items you desire.

It's popular to think that sellers want the highest price while buyers want to pay as little as possible. This may be true for some buyers and sellers in other venues—new and used cars, real estate, and the like. However, it seems to me that in numismatics the situation is different (not that everyone will agree with my mindset).

The reason is that the human element intervenes. Coin collecting is a hobby, or a combination of a hobby and an investment, and in most instances both the buyer and the seller want the other party to have a pleasant experience, and would like to develop a continuing relationship. If both buyer and seller enjoy the transaction, the two will meet again in the future. If the buyer feels that he or she has been pressed to the very limit of price, or if the seller is exhausted after a round of dickering, neither will look forward to a future encounter—and there might not be one.

Thus, my mindset is not to encourage you in the skill of sharp negotiating so as to triumph over the seller. Instead, it is to share my philosophy that you, the buyer, should be happy, but that the seller should be pleased as well. Both sides should have a warm feeling when all is said and done. The art of bidding and buying, in my view, is that the result should be a win-win situation. That accomplished, the buyer and seller each look forward to the next transaction. In the coin trade and elsewhere, this is called "leaving something on the table" for the other person.

Do Your Homework

Generally, money is hard to earn. It is practical, in my opinion, to use care when spending it. In numismatics, with the exception of great rarities, there are enough things available for outright purchase or at auction that you will never lack for opportunities to acquire the objects of your desire. Rarely is it necessary to act in haste.

Before entering into any purchase, do your homework regarding the specific items you seek. Review steps 1 through 4 in chapter 2. Learn as much as you can about the coins, tokens, medals, or paper money you want to add to your collection.

Here are a few hypothetical numismatic items that come to mind, as illustrations of the thought processes I would go through if they became available for bidding or immediate purchase. I am casting myself in the position of a well-financed buyer, as a *collector* (not as a dealer buying for resale) who is familiar with the coins being offered and with their characteristics and market prices. The assumption is made that each coin has been accurately graded by an expert.

1652 Massachusetts Pine Tree Shilling, Die Variety Noe-1, EF-40. Slightly porous surface. Edge clipped on one side. Dark stain on the reverse. In a dealer's stock at a coin show. Offered at a 25% discount from current listings. *My thought process:* Quality and eye appeal are exceedingly important, and several examples of this particular Noe-1 die variety, which turns up on the market with some frequency (but which is still rare), may need to be reviewed before I find one that is just right. As this particular coin has a porous surface, I'll pass it by and wait for another opportunity. If in doubt, I'll ask another dealer or two as to their opinions.

1786 Vermont Copper, Baby Head, Variety Ryder-6, EF-40. Smooth planchet. Priced at twice market value on a dealer's Internet site. *My thought process:* A very exciting coin, this! Not one in 20 of these coins has a smooth, defect-free planchet. The image looks very nice on my computer monitor. I'm a buyer. As the dealer is a member of the Professional Numismatists Guild (PNG), I don't have to worry that it might be a fake (otherwise, I would do serious checking before going further). But, oops! I call the dealer and find that six other people were ahead of me, and that the coin is long gone. The dealer simply forgot to remove the listing.

1855 Half Cent, MS-65. Red. Full original brilliance. A few flecks. Coming up for auction in a convention sale next month. *My thought process:* From the description and illustration it looks quite nice. From my research I know that 1855 is a "hoard coin"

date, so I'll bid carefully, say market plus 10% or so. No hurry to get this one. I'll ask a dealer-friend-representative to view the lot before bidding, to be sure it is okay.

1814 Large Copper Cent, VF-30. Dark and slightly grainy. On display in a local coin shop; for sale at a nice discount. *My thought process:* A quick glance, and this one is rejected. As there are quite a few around at this grade level, I'll bide my time until I find one with a smooth planchet and nice eye appeal. However, from my reading about copper cents I know that those of this date are often grainy and porous. I realize that I may have to look longer for a nice 1814 than I would for one of, say, 1812 (which usually has a smooth surface).

1936 Lincoln Cent, Proof-65. Red. In a dealer's case at a coin show. Priced right at market. *My thought process:* This coin will require close examination to be sure it is not dipped or hairlined, and that the "red" (actually orange) color is original and natural. If it passes inspection, I am a buyer, for probably not one in five coins is really choice. I check this one, and there is some staining on the reverse. Also, by using the stronger of the two magnifying glasses I carry, I see there are light hairlines in the field, meaning that it was cleaned or rubbed sometime in its career. I'll bide my time and wait for another.

1896-O Morgan Silver Dollar, MS-63. Quite well struck, and with a very attractive surface. In the display case of a coin-show dealer who specializes in Morgan dollars. Available for instant purchase if I want to buy. *My thought process:* Here, indeed, is a real find. The dealer is a high-volume seller and knows that this particular 1896-O is much nicer than usual, but tells me that most people don't care. Still, he wants a 10% premium over the price of another MS-63 dollar, graded by the same certification service, in his inventory. I strike a deal for the nicer one, recognizing at once that it is at a grade that represents excellent value and is also far above average in eye appeal. I cross the 1896-O off my want list.

1857-C Gold Dollar, AU-55. Coming up in an auction sale, described as being a key issue seldom seen at this level. *My thought process:* I see from the photograph that the coin has a rough, flaky surface and is very dull. Although I need the 1857-C and will be attending the sale, when this comes up for bidding my hands will be in my pockets, even if it sells for half of the market listing. In fact, I won't even bother to look at it during lot viewing. I'll wait, and if a high-quality coin comes along I'll be a buyer at 50% over the market, and will have a bargain.

2003-S Proof Set. Nice enough in appearance, Mint-fresh it seems, in original packaging. In a local dealer's display case. *My thought process:* A no-brainer. All such sets are nice. I am a buyer, but only at the current standard market price.

Libertas Americana Medal in Silver, Proof-60. Excellent strike and eye appeal. Quoted to me by a dealer who has my want list. Priced at 20% more than a comparably graded coin sold for two years ago, but this one is of better quality. *My thought process:* Here's my check!

You get the idea!

Most of your competitors in the marketplace will not do much checking, but will simply read labels on holders or descriptions in auction catalogs. As they will have no strategy, they may bid 90% of market price for the unappealing 1857-C gold dollar and believe they have captured a bargain. They may bid a 50% premium for the gorgeous 1881-S Morgan dollar in an Internet sale, and consider ridiculous the price of what seems to be an ordinary, worn 1786 Vermont copper coin.

Strategies for Buying Outright
About the Price

Generally, most dealers who own coins that are for sale will post an asking price on each. It has been my experience that no two dealers do this in the same way. Some simply look at the *Coin Dealer Newsletter,*

Coin Values, the *Guide Book,* "Coin Market" (*Numismatic News*), or some other handy guide, or use several of these, and go from there. The prices in the *Coin Dealer Newsletter* are sometimes wholesale, and a percentage can be added. Prices in the other listings just mentioned are intended to be retail. In all instances, such listings are for *typical coins of average quality.* The worth of a given specimen at hand may be higher or lower, depending on factors I've already discussed—including sharpness of strike, planchet quality, and eye appeal.

In most retail offerings, coins are priced generically. Accordingly, if a dealer has five examples of a 1925-S California Diamond Jubilee commemorative half dollar, all graded MS-64 (Numismatic Guaranty Corporation, or NGC), his asking price is apt to be the same for each. Ditto if he has three 1903-O dollars in MS-63 (ANACS), seven 2004-S Wisconsin quarters in Proof-65 (Professional Coin Grading Service, or PCGS), or whatever.

It would seem logical that except for modern coins there would be some differences in quality. And, unless the dealer is *very* careful in buying (most are not), there are, indeed, differences. It would also seem logical that the dealer might ask more for the coins with the best strike and eye appeal, and less for those that are not as nice. However, dealers do not often do this because it complicates their listings.

The following is a three-part case study that may be informative, although a bit technical.

Case Study 1-A

Here is a hypothetical example provided to me by Frank Van Valen, of American Numismatic Rarities (ANR). Consider a common and very popular commemorative half dollar—an early variety that is sometimes found "nice," but more often simply so-so (or downright unattractive) in appearance—but that, in this case, is certified as MS-65. Frank suggested that in the marketplace, an average-quality MS-65 example would sell retail for $750 to $800 or so, but that a choice gem with superb eye appeal would bring at least $975.

Say Dealer A wants to buy a group of 40 of these as a lot for $650 each; upon closer examination, he finds that the quality in the lot varies. They're listed in a catalog as "Commemorative X MS-65 (Certified by Z) $795." Not being stupid, Dealer A cherrypicks the group for quality, and holds back the nicer ones—say, five hand-picked coins—either to consign to an auction or to resubmit to a grading service in hopes of being upgraded to MS-66, in which instance he could ask $1,200 each. He could also simply ask a higher price for these coins and sell them directly to Dealer B, who specializes in coins of hand-picked quality (a rather rare species in the dealer world). If the latter, Dealer B might pay $850 each for all five and sell them for $975 each. Let's further suppose that in the original group of 40 coins, Dealer A has found three real dogs—dull, stained pieces that were simply horrible in appearance, despite being certified as MS-65. He wholesales these to Dealer C for $600 each, taking a slight loss on each, but getting rid of them.

Then, we see the following dealer advertisements:

Dealer A—Commemorative X, MS-65: $795.

Dealer B—Commemorative X, MS-65: $975.

Dealer C—Commemorative X, MS-65: $695.

To the uninitiated buyer it seems that Dealer C is the person to buy from, that Dealer A is a bit overpriced and Dealer B is *way* overpriced. However, *you* can now see that this is not true—Dealer B might well offer the best buy of all!

At the same time, there are instances in which Dealer A is in a hurry to move merchandise, does not look at the coins closely (the certified holder provides all the information he's interested in), and simply elects to move them all out quickly at, say, $750 each. In such an instance, you can cherrypick on your own and get a potential $975 coin.

As to why Dealer A does not price them by quality, doing so would take time and space. He would have to advertise them individually as, for example:

Coin No. 1—Commemorative X, MS-65: Lightly struck at the reverse center. Brilliant except for a blotch on the reverse. $725.

Coin No. 2—Commemorative X, MS-65: Dull with black stains on the obverse, iridescent red and green area on the reverse. Not attractive, but a bargain at $645.

Coin No. 3—Commemorative X, MS-65: Iridescent toning on both sides, artificially applied. Otherwise sharp. $745.

Coin No. 4—Commemorative X, MS-65: Superb gem, sharply struck, brilliant silver surfaces with light golden toning. A connoisseur's coin! $975.

And so on. Lots of work. Also, after spending an hour or so creating listings for 40 different gradations of coin quality and offering them for sale, there would be confusion and frustration when orders were received. A lot of people might want Coin No. 4, but there is just one coin available. No one might want Coin No. 3, so what to do with it?

Far simpler it is to revert to the earlier illustration and make one listing take care of lots of sales possibilities:

Commemorative X, MS-65: $795.

As illustrated earlier, real gems could be picked out and sold for a premium to a high-quality dealer, and doggy coins could be dumped on a wholesale basis.

The main lesson of this case study is that a listed price is not worth much in terms of making a purchase decision, unless you have additional information. The lowest price might be for a low-quality coin and not a good buy at all.

Case Study 1-B

Here is a related illustration of price, but on a different basis. We have two dealers: the Dealer B mentioned above, and a new entry, Dealer D, each of whom has a superb gem example of Commemorative X, hand picked for quality:

Dealer B—*Commemorative X, MS-65 (Certified by Z):* Superb quality in all respects. $975.

Dealer D—*Commemorative X, MS-65 (Certified by Z):* Superb quality in all respects. $1,400.

Which one is the best buy? Is one a good buy, the other not? Or are both overpriced? Or—

Published price guides are of no help, for Commemorative X is listed far below either price. Such guides reflect the selling price for typical, ordinary examples, not for coins of hand-picked quality. There is no price guide for superb-quality coins!

So, what next?

Again, knowledge comes to the forefront. Through studying and the use of current auction catalogs and other items in your library (see chapter 31), you will know that as a superb coin, sharply struck and with good eye appeal, Commemorative X is a rarity. So, you have a mindset to pay a higher price, if need be. How much higher? There is no definite answer. Auction prices realized might help if you can figure out whether the auctioned coins were of the same high quality. Asking around will help, too.

Here is what I would probably do. Realizing that ordinary examples of Commemorative X, in decent preservation, but not sharply struck gems with eye appeal, are on the market in the $800 area; and knowing that Dealer B, who has a great reputation for delivering good quality and with whom I've been doing business for quite some time, has a hand-picked gem for $975, I would buy Dealer B's coin. The price difference is not all that great, and I know that I can then cross this off my want list.

If Dealer B did not have one in stock, and the only offering I could find was that of Dealer D at $1,400, I would probably consider this to be a stretch over the $800 price for a typical coin, and would either try to buy it cheaper from Dealer D or wait until another one comes along.

Case Study 1-C

Should I "dicker" the price? Make a counteroffer when I buy? Do a bit of haggling?

As to the asking price in a direct transaction versus the price you really have to pay, sometimes you can negotiate, and sometimes not. Many buyers fall into the "price is everything" trap, even if the price is reasonable to begin with. Often heard is this: "I know your price is (blank), but what is *really* the price to me?"

Let's go back to Dealer B with Commemorative X, a hand-picked gem for $975, and Dealer D with a similar coin for $1,400.

In the real world, if Dealer B says, "Sorry, that's my best price," and Dealer D says, "My best price is $1,200," most buyers would think that Dealer D was a "nicer guy" and had the best deal. That is, if they did not know about Dealer B.

In brief, the actual price you pay for the coin is what counts—not whether it is presented as full retail, wholesale, or somewhere in between. Again, you need pricing knowledge to begin with, in order get the best value for your money.

A number of years ago I was on a tour in a Mediterranean country, and visited an emporium offering Oriental rugs. All seemed very high priced to me (compared to what I had paid for a few I had at home). I was about to walk out when my tour guide said, "These are just *asking* prices. Negotiate! Make an offer! The seller expects this." Well, I didn't do that, but another person in my tour group offered $2,000 for a rug priced at $5,000, and bought it. I don't know how much extra he had to pay in shipping and customs by the time he had it in his living room back in the United States, but to my eyes he could have bought the same rug stateside for no more than $2,000. Of course, it would not have been a "bargain" then! However, he felt had made the best buy of his life, had outwitted any dealers of Oriental rugs that might be in his hometown in America, and so on.

Negotiating Price

Having stated the preceding, I'll add that if you enjoy dickering, fine—but it is the real value of the coin that is most important. It's better to pay full asking price for a coin worth $1,000 than to get a 20% discount on a coin that's worth $1,000, but is priced at $1,500. Be *value* conscious, not *price* conscious.

Some dealers (particularly those setting up at shows) will set prices higher than the figures they really want, so they can give a discount—and thus the *appearance* of a good buy—as did the seller of Oriental rugs I mentioned. In rare coins, however, the asking prices may be set high, but not super-high. Shoppers at coin shows tend to dicker more than do mail-order clients. On the other hand, dealers who publish price lists are less apt to set elevated prices for ordinary coins, for if their listed prices are too high, they won't get many orders.

Make no mistake, however. There are many occasions for which fine dealers will allow courtesy discounts for nice coins. And, between dealers, professional courtesy is nearly always granted when items are bought for resale. Further, a retail customer who offers to spend a lot of money at one time, with little discussion, complication, or hassle with the dealer, may receive a discount when asked.

Sometimes a dealer will give a special price for a quick sale, if several items are bought at once, if a customer is a friend or long-term buyer, if a coin has remained in stock too long, or if the dealer made a mistake when purchasing it. Not all dealers have ready markets for all coins. I once bought a dandy 1861 Confederate States of America one-cent piece from a coin shop owner who had bought it and been excited about having it in stock, but a year later could find no takers. He sold it to me at his cost, and I was delighted.

There are no rules as to how sellers set their asking prices. Ten different dealers might price the same grade and variety of coin at 10 different prices. However, as I mentioned, it is the real value of the coin that counts, and nothing else.

Beyond the above, a few other considerations are worth mentioning.

Credit and Time Payments

First, some dealers take credit cards as payment, and others do not. Credit card companies charge fees to dealers. Thus, a dealer might prefer to sell you a coin for a $5,000 good check than to put it on your credit card. Ask before paying.

Time payments are sometimes available. Depending on a dealer's margin of profit, the interest might be very little if the payments are completed in a short time. It's normal to charge interest for longer periods. No one rule fits all. You can appreciate that a dealer who sells you a high-quality coin priced to be a good value for $1,000, and lets you buy it over a year, but charges interest, may be delivering a much better value to you than another dealer who prices the same coin at $1,350, and lets you pay for it over a year interest-free.

With some experience in finance and banking (including a board directorship), I have always found it curious that most people are very conscious of a list price or asking price in a deal, but are not aware of the actual cost of money on interest. If a transaction includes interest, take the time to calculate the *total real cost* of the coin. Then you need to figure out the *real value* of the coin—which means considering its quality, not just its cost.

Promoting Long-Term Relationships

Business Etiquette. My own etiquette when buying something I need for my collection is to pay the asking price if I consider it to be reasonable. If I do not, and making a counteroffer wouldn't offend the seller, I would make such an offer—but not merely to save a few dollars or to try to demonstrate that I'm a sharp buyer.

At a recent convention I paid $250, the price asked by collector Richard A., for a worn copper cent counterstamped MESCHUTT'S / METROPOLITAN / COFFEE ROOM / 433. BdWAY, and to dealer Tony Terranova I paid the $7,855 asked from all comers, dealers as well as collectors, for a rare, large, and quite impressive gold medal relating to the 1858 laying of the Atlantic cable.

I am quite sure that if I'd said to Richard, "I'll buy the counterstamp for two hundred twenty-five, but no more than that," and I'd offered Tony $7,500 for the medal, I could have bought both. However, I did not, and when either of these two gentlemen, both of whom I have known for many years, have something they think I will be interested in, chances are good I'll be offered it first, or that I'll at least be among the first. Each can reflect on many good experiences in selling to me: an instant decision, instant payment in full, and a pleasant encounter overall.

Whatever you do, play each situation as it lies. Building a fine, long-term relationship with a dealer is more important, in my opinion, than being tolerated as a semi-nuisance haggler. Dealers often talk about this sort of buyer when they get together.

It's also important to live up to your obligations. If you say that you need two weeks' time to sell some stock or raise some money in order to buy a 1799 copper cent, and will send your check for $5,000 at that time, be sure to do so on a timely basis. When you do write a check for $5,000, be sure you have money in the bank to cover it. Don't be like the fellow that Midwestern dealer Joe F. told about: "This guy argued and argued, and finally I sold the coin to him. Then his check bounced, and his replacement check also bounced. If I ever see him again I won't sell to him, even if he has a wad of hundred-dollar bills!"

Social Etiquette. In addition to the business etiquette just discussed, there are some elements of *social* etiquette that may benefit you if they're observed.[51]

When handling a dealer's coins, paper money, or anything else, do it very carefully. Coins as well as holders should be lifted and held only by their edges. Paper money, usually in a clear envelope or holder, should be handled with care. In any and all instances, but particularly with paper items that may be unprotected, be sure your hands are clean. If you've just had a hamburger, go wash your hands, then return to the dealer's table. If you're carrying a beverage around with you, be sure it isn't in a position to fall or spill on any numismatic items.

If you're looking at numismatic books and supplies for sale, and spend a lot of time doing so, make at least a courtesy purchase. Many such things are inexpensive. If a book is sealed, don't open it without the seller's permission. If books are unsealed, look through them carefully so they will still be as new when they're sold.

Even if smoking is permitted in the shop or bourse (which today would be unusual), it is best to refrain from doing it. Others nearby might be offended.

Dress neatly and always in *clean* clothes. Generally, a dealer or anyone else will pay more attention to a nicely dressed man or woman than to someone wearing a food-stained T-shirt. A few years ago the PNG set up a rule that members had to dress well at coin shows. Good plan.

If a dealer is talking with someone else, wait your turn. If the conversation seems to be interminable, in a nice way get his or her brief attention and ask when a good time would be to return to the table.

If you are well financed and can buy everything you see, keep the details of your wealth to yourself or (if credit is important) limit them to conversations with the dealer. It's probably poor form to let all others within earshot learn of your success. In fact, some of the wealthiest people I know are also the most modest.

Not everyone cares about etiquette. However, a bit of care, kindness, and thoughtfulness from parties on each side of a transaction will reap great dividends in enjoyment and, probably, better bottom-line values for you as a buyer.

Buying Coins at a Shop or Office

There are many coin shops throughout the United States. Some of these are stores, with display counters, racks of books and supplies for sale, perhaps framed items on the walls, and a proprietor—sometimes backed by a staff—ready to greet walk-in visitors. Often such businesses are located on the ground floor or somewhere else easy to access.

In contrast, many other dealers catering to a retail trade operate from office buildings and conduct their business quietly, perhaps keeping the coins in a nearby bank vault rather than on display. Such dealers may do business by appointment, rather than on a walk-in basis.

The PNG, the Professional Currency Dealers Association (PCDA), and the *Coin Dealer Newsletter* all publish dealer directories. In addition, telephone directories often give information, as do advertisements in numismatic periodicals and web sites.

Nomenclature on what to call such a retail outlet is not standard. Harlan White, a long-time San Diego, California, dealer, calls his place of business the Old Coin Shop, which certainly permits instant identification in a phone book. On the other hand, World Numismatiques, the trade style used by the late James Kelly in Dayton, Ohio, might not be deciphered by everyone. *Mint* and *bank* have been used in some store names (Jay Parrino's "The Mint," B. Max Mehl's "Numismatic Bank of Texas"). The word *collectibles* (or *collectables*) is sometimes used today, as is *exchange*. The word *office* is seldom used, even in coin businesses located in private office buildings.

Once you've located a coin shop, it's a good practice to call in advance unless you know for sure that it will be open when you arrive. The owners or expert numismatists at even the most active walk-in businesses are often away at coin shows. You might also want to ask what times tend to be less busy than others. It may be easier for a shop owner to chat on Tuesday morning than on Saturday afternoon.

Upon your arrival or in your telephone inquiry, it's perfectly okay to say something such as, "I'm a newcomer to the hobby, and I'd just like to come and look around, and perhaps buy a book or two." There is no reason at all to act like you might be a "big spender," although quite a few people will do so. In my view, you want to go where you will be welcomed, big spender, moderate spender, or just interested in a few books or supplies.

It can be said that anyone operating a coin store that is open to the public should welcome any and all comers, but in professional numismatics the situation can be a bit different. As coins and paper money of significant value are often on hand, gawkers and lookers are often discouraged from visiting, unless they have at least a potential interest in numismatics. Coin shops are not meant to be museums. However, this commentary is no doubt irrelevant to you, or you wouldn't have read this far in the present book! For this reason, it's good form to make at least a modest purchase as a courtesy when you visit, perhaps an inexpensive book, a magnifying glass, or something else of the sort.

Most proprietors and staff of coin shops are more than eager to see interested collectors, beginners as well as advanced specialists. While it's a popular notion that big spenders receive the best attention, in practice most shop owners are happy to talk to anyone. Besides, someone buying a common-date Morgan dollar today may be looking for a rare Proof double eagle a year from now! Remember the story I related in chapter 5 about how magnate Samuel Wolfson started when his son was treated nicely when buying some cheap coins at a store? No one dreamed that this would lead to Wolfson's owning a famous 1804 silver dollar!

The typical street-floor coin store has a walk-in area with multiple counters or cases. Often displayed in the cases, under glass, are popular coins such as modern Proofs and commemoratives, sets, medals, and the like. Many shops handle numismatic gifts, such as souvenir silver bars, joke or gag paper money with funny portraits, and the like. Some also stock stamps, sports cards, gems, mineral specimens, jewelry, watches, and other things not related to coin collecting.

Such stores often carry numismatic literature, furnishing an excellent opportunity for you to look through the books for sale and select the ones that promise to be of the greatest worth to you. It's also desirable to ask a store employee for recommendations—to learn which books have been the most popular, which titles have garnered the most favorable reviews by customers.

Supplies are offered for sale as well, including different types of holders, albums, and folders. The possibilities are many, and again you might ask an employee for specific recommendations. If you're buying a gift to give to a youngster, possibly an inexpensive folder or album for Jefferson nickels or statehood quarters would be a good choice—certainly not something expensive, deluxe, and in a slipcase. On the other hand, if you are an established collector and are seeking something to display your coins nicely, then something more expensive is called for. Boxes and containers for certified and slabbed coins are available, as are other accessories.

A good magnifying glass will always be an aid for you or for a gift recipient. I prefer a double magnifying glass with two lenses, my current favorite being a magnifier with two lenses of 4x each, which can be overlapped to gain 8x (more or less). You don't want to have an extremely powerful magnifying glass for casually looking at coins or buying them, as you might be able to see minute details, but overall aspects of rubbing, luster, and other characteristics will be lost in the shuffle—sort of like concentrating on one tree and ignoring the forest. However, for the detailed inspection of mintmarks, die doubling, and other characteristics, by all means, get a powerful magnifying glass to use in addition to the low-power one I just mentioned. Beyond that, there are several varieties of excellent microscopes available, the stereo or binocular microscope being best. Through these you can see a tiny S mintmark appear about

as large as an Egyptian pyramid! It is often very interesting to examine dates, mintmarks, and other minor characteristics under high magnification.

Speaking of gifts, I'm often asked questions such as, "How do I get my teenaged son to become interested in coins?"

The quick answer is to buy him a *Guide Book* and perhaps one or two others of general content (don't buy more than just a few, so as not to overwhelm him), and a couple of albums. Let him buy actual coins on his own, perhaps with a gift certificate you provide him. If you must buy him some coins, keep it simple—a beautiful but inexpensive Mint State Morgan silver dollar, a dozen different state-reverse quarters in an album with openings beckoning to be filled with others, or a Proof set of his birth year.

Coin-Shop Prices for Common Coins

Of course, the main reason to go to a coin shop is the coins themselves. Bear in mind that a degree of understanding is needed when contemplating the prices of common coins for sale at a shop. For inexpensive pieces, handling is a major consideration and can become a very important element of the price.

While a dealer might be able to buy a roll containing 50 current Lincoln cents for face value, it isn't possible to put them all in little holders, add them to inventory, and place them on sale for, say, 2¢ each. The current *Guide Book* lists a minimum price of 20¢ for a modern Lincoln cent in MS-65 grade. No doubt you can get some similar modern pieces at face value by going to a bank yourself. However, if you go to a dealer and find that one is priced at 20¢, be assured that there's little profit being made. In fact, if the dealer charged 50¢ or $1 each for a current Lincoln cent, not much profit would be made, either.

Amazingly, it's probably easier to buy 50 different MS-63 Morgan silver dollars on the Internet or through the mail than it is to buy 50 different MS-65 Lincoln cents

B. Max Mehl in his office, Fort Worth, Texas, in 1946. Mehl liked to "talk coins" with selected visitors, but didn't enjoy in-person sales. However, in mail-order sales he had no peer—that was his forte.

In 1937 the New York City firm of Stack's Rare Coins, established two years before by Joseph B. and Morton Stack, published this photograph of its new coin shop / office.

Times change, but traditions do not. View at the front of Stack's store and gallery in New York City, 2005—this on West 57th Street, a different location from the preceding.

Long-time dealer William Youngerman is shown in the front part of his store in Boca Raton, Florida. Offered for sale are rare coins, currency, precious metals, and other items, including numismatic books and supplies. As do many professionals, Bill often sets up at bourse tables around the country when time permits.

Visitors at the store in the reception area at Littleton Coin Company headquarters in New Hampshire are greeted with an array of items for sale as well as interesting historical displays.

at shows and shops! Not so long ago, in preparation for a book I'm doing for Whitman Publishing on the subject of nickel five-cent pieces, I thought it a good idea to have a full set of Mint State Jeffersons from 1938 onward. I quickly realized that this would be a daunting task if I gathered them individually, and that coin conventions would be of little help, as few people have the more-common dates—and if they do, they don't cart them to shows. So I simply called up my fine numismatic friend, Dave Sundman, at Littleton Coin Company, and asked him to make up a set and send it to me with a bill. Of course, I paid more than I would had I spent a month (at least) picking up the pieces one by one and checking them for quality, but the results were excel-

lent and instantaneous. In any event, while mail-order dealers will be of little help for modern coins on a single basis, a coin shop can be. Expect to pay a premium for the handling involved. If the vendor has sorted through common coins to pick out ones that are above average in quality, such coins are apt to cost more.

People often fail to consider the value of time, even their own. Once I mentioned to my friend Ken Rendell some annoyance I'd experienced while intending to visit about a dozen different shops and offices in New York City in the course of a day. It was very frustrating to find cabs in some places—and during this particular day, after leaving the new headquarters for the American Numismatic Society at 96 Fulton Street, I had to walk 45 minutes and several blocks to find an unoccupied cab. I ended the day by not being able to go to several places I had hoped to. "Why don't you do what I do when I go to New York?" Ken suggested. "Hire a cab for the *day* and have the driver take you around and wait for you."

Pausing to consider the idea, I realized that I'd been hiring 10 separate cabs, having to track down each one and sometimes lose a lot of time doing so. Not only was the experience frustrating, there was the value of my professional time that I'd lost during a normal eight-hour business day to consider. Since then, in New York and elsewhere, I've followed Ken's advice! You may want to do this as well, making arrangements through your hotel concierge. It's curious that many collectors, while balking at paying 20¢ or 50¢ for a modern Lincoln cent, might spend $10 or more sending this same coin off to a certification service to be graded. The result is a 5¢ coin in a $10 holder—but, somehow, they seem to think this is okay!

Big-Ticket Items

Many coin shops and stores are well stocked with big-ticket items. For such coins, prices are usually highly competitive, for sales are made not only to walk-in customers, but to distant clients by telephone, catalogs, and the Internet. Although it might not be on display, don't be surprised if a store has an 1856 Flying Eagle cent in the safe, or a Panama-Pacific commemorative set waiting in a bank vault. It will pay you to ask, once you become serious about adding scarce and rare items to your collection.

Many coin-store proprietors will also help you track down items on your "want list." Most have connections with other dealers and welcome the opportunity to do some scouting for you. Many coin-store owners also attend conventions and can find needed items there.

Policies and Technicalities

All Sales Final. Generally, most coin stores have this policy: if you've examined an item in the store and have bought it, you own it.

If you buy a coin on Monday and decide on Tuesday that you don't want it because you've noticed a scratch on the reverse, or because you've found one cheaper somewhere else, don't expect to get a full refund. If you've paid $1,000 for it, the dealer might want to buy it back wholesale, treating it as a new inventory purchase, for, say, $800.

"All sales are final" is a common sign in a coin shop. In any event, you should ask about the policy of returns and adjustments. Also ask if authenticity is guaranteed. While it might seem natural that it is, in practice some dealers say, "You had a chance to look at it carefully. Now it's your problem," or, "I don't care if Expert X thinks it's a fake, I still think it's genuine."

The PNG has a Code of Ethics and some rules about authenticity, and its members must comply. Still, authenticity can be a legitimate difference of opinion. If you are unsure about the authenticity of a coin, simply make this request before you buy it: "I respect the opinion of Expert X. May I show it to him (or her) before making a final decision?" Your request will probably be honored. Alternatively, a shop owner might put a coin on hold for you for a few days while you think about it.

In any case, the best policy is this: Be sure of all aspects of a coin—appearance, desirability, price, and everything else—before making a decision.

Sales Tax. Most states charge a sales tax, and some municipalities do, as well. Sales tax can be an important consideration—a coin bought for $2,000 plus 7% sales tax totals $2,140 cost, and is thus more expensive than a coin bought for $2,100 in a tax-free transaction.

Policies are not at all standard, however. In some states, coins and certain other numismatic items are completely exempt from tax. In certain others, they are exempt for purchases higher than a certain amount. In still others, full tax must be paid. In most venues, dealers are exempt from paying tax if they have appropriate sales-tax permits or documentation. In some venues, no tax has to be paid if the purchases are shipped out of state. Rules are in a constant state of flux. The easy way to find out is to ask the shop owner what the current rules are, if you do not already know.

The Social Side

A store is a great place to "talk coins" with the proprietor or a knowledgeable staff member. I have mentioned this several times already, and I repeat it now: there is no substitute for tapping the experience of someone else. However, as also noted, some etiquette should be observed. The owner of a coin store is in business to make a profit. Expenses are high and include, but are not limited to, salaries of staff, insurance, rent, travel, telephone, computers, accounting, taxes, and more. Accordingly, it is always good form to make some purchases when you visit, even if it's just a book or two. If you're a purchaser of rare coins, while much of your activity may be done with distant sellers and auction firms, don't forget to spend some money at home as well. Perhaps your local dealer can help you track down some pieces you need—the want list I mentioned earlier.

In fact, the cost of doing business is so high that the number of shops open to the public is fewer than years ago. Probably for every 10 shops that were doing business in the 1960s, just two or three are in operation today.

Further on the subject of etiquette, it is probably a good idea to keep your composure at all times, and not be angry if you are slighted or do not receive the attention you expect. There are other places to do business, and I would simply try another store instead. There is little to be gained from getting into arguments about price, quality, attitudes, or anything else, and it's better to walk than to wrangle. In saying this I am not making excuses, but simply being practical and endeavoring to help you maintain a high level of enjoyment.

Generally, coin-shop proprietors should not be asked to appraise coins bought elsewhere, should not be asked to give opinions of their competition, and should not otherwise be put in uncomfortable situations.

However, basic discussions of coins, grading techniques, and the like are fine. In all instances the Golden Rule applies—treat a coin shop employee as you would like to be treated yourself.

It is common for boasters to say, "I just bought an 1879 Stella from XYZ for $100,000," while at the same time, arguing the price of a $500 coin with a store owner. Generally, the owner is not particularly interested in what you bought from someone else. Similarly, if you just sold your set of Indian cents to Jones, Dealer Smith is really not interested in hearing about it.

There is also a practical side to avoiding puffery. In World War II a popular poster had an inscription to the effect that "Loose Lips Sink Ships," encouraging people not to divulge details of certain matters, lest in some later retelling the information be learned by an enemy. Sometimes those who brag about their rare coins set themselves up for burglaries or other unfortunate events. Something said may or may not be repeated by the listener, but it is certain that something *not said* will forever remain private. While most coin-shop owners are well versed in and respect the privacy and security of their customers, there is no telling what others who may hear you will do or say. Be careful.

In the antique trade they have what are called "looky-loos," some of whom are also "be-backers." Such a person comes in, looks around, asks the prices of a lot of things, perhaps tells what their grandmother used to own but sold 20 years ago, buys nothing at all, but cheerfully says upon leaving, "I'll be back!"

Don't be a looky-loo or a be-backer! Make at least a courtesy purchase before you leave.

Just as certain large bookstores can have a clubby atmosphere, what with music, coffee, and the like, certain coin shops, while perhaps not as spacious or elegant, can be very comfortable places to visit. Often, other collectors are on hand to converse with, news can be shared, and the employees of a store can become personal friends. For most collectors, this turns into the rule, not the exception—a fine local coin shop can almost be a substitute for a private club!

As a "member" of the "club" hosted by a local dealer, do your part and pay dues now and then!

Buying Coins at a Convention
Many Shows

In any given week there are apt to be a dozen or more local and regional coin shows in the United States, and in any given month or two there is an important show that attracts national interest and participation. Chances are that an event will be held within driving distance of your home within the next few weeks—unless you live in North Dakota or Maui! Even if you're in a remote place, you can probably hop on an airplane inexpensively, spend a day at a show in a major city, and return that evening.

Shows put on by societies and clubs are sometimes called *conventions*, presumably because the members *convene*. Shows or conventions, often they are one and the same.

Listings of shows are regularly published in numismatic magazines, in newspapers, and on the Internet. Now and again a show is canceled or moved, so it pays to check in advance before you travel a distance. This is particularly true for the smaller shows. For several years the American Numismatic Association (ANA) advertised that its forthcoming summer 2005 convention would be held in San Jose, California. Then, less than a year before the show, it moved the venue to San Francisco.

It is a good idea to go to shows, at least occasionally. They offer the chance to meet and greet people you've known only by mail or on the Internet, and there is the opportunity to review coin grades and offerings, and to ask questions.

What to Expect at a Coin Show

A small coin show, such as a local or regional event held on a weekend, is apt to have from a few dozen to a hundred or so dealers set up. When traveling to or from a show, be very careful. Do not leave

coins unattended at any time. It pays to be cautious.

The sales area at a typical show is nearly always referred to as a *bourse*, for reasons I do not know. It is a French term, but in France it relates to the stock exchange. I'm not sure when this was first used, but it was a long time ago. The October 1934 issue of *The Numismatist* carried an account of the ANA convention held in Cleveland from August 18 to 23, including this:

> A new feature this year, and one that was rigidly adhered to, was that no buying or selling of coins was permitted on the exhibit floor. One end of the room was arranged as a numismatic bourse, at which buying and selling was permitted, and even welcomed and encouraged. To the casual observer it was evident that many coins found new owners during the four or five days of the convention, and the pleased expressions of buyers and sellers suggested that the new feature was working satisfactorily.

At the entry of a small coin show will be a registration table where you can pay admission and get a ticket. Charges are usually nominal—a few dollars or so. In most medium-sized and large shows, registration is required in order to get a sticker or badge, but not even the ANA (which runs the largest shows) requires proof of identification. This is an alert for you to be careful. The person standing next to you when you're talking about your coins could be a seasoned criminal. It doesn't happen frequently, but the situation is not rare, either. Again, be careful! If you want to talk about your collection, or want to buy something, try do be as private as you can in your conversation with the seller. The seller and staff can be trusted, but bystanders cannot be.

Near the entrance to some shows there is a dealer directory posted, while other shows have handouts or programs listing such. At still other shows you are on your own and need to rely on signs on the tables.

Veteran dealer Ed Hipps, assisted by his son Lance, is shown at his corner bourse table doing a brisk business on a Saturday morning at the 47th Annual Texas Numismatic Association (TNA) Convention held in May 2005 at the Amon G. Carter Exhibits Hall in Fort Worth, Texas. The show had 195 bourse tables, a very creditable turnout for a regional event. (Robin Wells photograph)

The youth auction is a highlight of the TNA Convention for many budding numismatists. The dealers on the bourse floor generously donate all of the items up for "bid." At the May 2005 event, more than 40 kids participated in a heated session that would rival any big-dollar, high-profile auction house sale. The future of this hobby is bright with these youngsters on their way up! (Robin Wells photograph)

Larry Goldberg holding down the fort at the bourse table of Larry and Ira Goldberg Coins & Collectibles of Beverly Hills, California, at the 2003 ANA Convention.

Dave Bowers and John J. Ford, Jr., share reminiscences at the 2000 ANA convention held in Philadelphia.

Dealer Jonathan Kern at his bourse table at the Chicago International Coin Fair sponsored by Krause Publications, June 2004.

The bourse floor at the first Whitman Coin and Collectibles Atlanta Expo, June 2004.

Among the exhibits at the 2004 Whitman Coin and Collectibles Atlanta Expo was this display, featuring 25 of the 100 greatest U.S. coins, as described in a book by that title written by Ron Guth and Jeff Garrett.

Stu Levine (left) chats about coins with Tony Terranova at the Baltimore Coin and Currency Show (where all of the photos on this page were taken). Both professionals are familiar sights at the dealer bourses at conventions around the country.

Gail Watson, of J.J. Teaparty in Boston, visits at the bourse table of Jack and Sondra Beymer, who hail from California. Jack, a dealer of the "old school," has made many important discoveries of die varieties, has aided in pinpointing counterfeits, and has helped the hobby in many other ways.

Eddie Robinson, of Tidewater Coins, discusses the sale of coin books and supplies with Whitman Publishing representative Dawn Burbank.

Steve Hayden (left) and Steve Tanenbaum tend their bourse table filled with tokens and medals. Few such pieces have been commercially graded in the hobby, and thus displays are in the old style—in paper envelopes, cardboard holders, in coin trays.

Silvano DiGenova (seated) and Wayne Pratali discuss the merits of a 1796 $10 gold coin at the Superior Galleries table.

Jeff Garrett, a well-known Kentucky dealer and author, rests for a moment at one of the show events. Held several times a year, the Baltimore gatherings have been popular for a long time and draws many dealers and collectors, often with two or three auctions at the show or just before it.

John Yasuk and a display of paper money at Sergio Sanchez's bourse table. Shown are bills certified by PMG, some of the first to be graded by that service.

Most dealers have their coins, tokens, medals, or paper money arranged under glass in shallow cases. Sometimes the prices are clearly marked, but most often they are not. This is a matter of security, a protection against the occasional criminal out to "case" a coin bourse. Unfortunately, this is reality. A few years back, a well-known dealer in large copper cents had a nice offering of scarce and rare coins, each prominently marked with a price. Some criminals casing the show were impressed at the seemingly great value displayed by this dealer, but had no way to evaluate the perhaps even more valuable coins shown by others. When the dealer left the show, they followed his car and ultimately stole his stock.

Usually one to several dealers at a small show will have numismatic books and supplies for sale. Some others may have other collectibles such as postcards, jewelry, and trinkets for sale in their display. At a recent convention in Baltimore I bought a *fossil dinosaur*, a cute little one (measuring about six inches long), from a coin dealer from California set up next to the ANR table.

Most dealers stay with numismatic items of mainstream interest. If you're a specialist, you might want to check in advance before traveling a distance, to be sure that one or more dealers will be there with items of appeal. I enjoy Civil War cents, obsolete bank notes, and old numismatic books—and have gone to quite a few shows where none of these things have been offered. On the other hand, a show set up by a special-interest group, such as the PCDA or the Early American Coppers Club (EAC), can be virtual heaven for anyone interested in those things!

Larger conventions can offer a smorgasbord of delights, including but not limited to displays of collections and private holdings, exhibits by the U.S. Mint and/or the Bureau of Engraving and Printing, educational workshops and seminars, walk-through (as they call it) grading setups by leading certification companies, and one or more auctions of numismatic items. Some of the bigger events can have

400 to 600 or more dealers in place and eager to do business.

For a few of the larger shows, including the summer ANA convention, there is a Professional Numismatists Guild Day event immediately beforehand. Anyone can attend simply by requesting an invitation from a PNG member.

Youngsters Welcome

It is the rule, not the exception, that most coin-show hosts are delighted to have youngsters attend. Robin Wells, a collector from the Midwest (see her comments in chapter 13), sent a commentary on her experience:

> Nearly all shows I have attended are "kid-friendly." This ranges from dealers who have freebies for the youngsters to the occasional kids' auction for which all of the items are donated by dealers—out of generosity, but also to help ignite a flame of interest in the next generation of the hobby.[52]

The Young Numismatists branch of the ANA often has special programs at ANA shows. Whitman Publishing has scored a success with drawings and prizes given to young people who sign up at their exhibit at shows.

Changing Scenarios

Conventions can wax or wane in popularity over a period of time. When I was a teenager in the 1950s and first started attending shows, the ANA was the big event of the year, held each summer. The first one had been held in 1891, when the ANA was formed. My first was the Omaha show in 1955, which drew a record 500 visitors. In contrast, the aforementioned Cleveland show of 1934 (where the term *bourse* was used) drew "about 100" attendees, according to reports. The ANA show has endured and is still important. In recent decades the Mid-Winter ANA Show was started, but after a memorable freezing situation (when the bourse was set up on a thin covering over an ice rink), plus unfavorable connotations of traveling in the winter, it was renamed the ANA Money Show.

The Florida United Numismatists (FUN) convention was the new kid on the block in 1954, and I went to my first one in 1956. In the early years it moved around from city to city. Held in January, it was an attraction to northerners especially, as it was a respite from snow and cold. Later, Orlando was selected as a permanent (more or less) venue. The "more or less" reflects that for a string of consecutive years Orlando was the site, but in 2005 it was in Fort Lauderdale. Today, the FUN show rides high.

The Central States Numismatic Society (CSNS) show was around in the 1950s and still is today. This convention moves around from city to city. In some years it has been as active as can be, and in other years it has been dull.

In the 1950s and 1960s, the Numismatic Association of Southern California (NASC), New York Metropolitan, New England Numismatic Association (NENA), Empire State Numismatic Association (ESNA), Penn-Ohio, and Middle Atlantic Numismatic Association (MANA) shows ranged from medium-sized to large and important. No longer. A few decades ago, active shows were held each year in Cherry Hill, New Jersey, and Lanham, Maryland—again, no longer.

On the other hand, some shows that did not exist in the 1950s and 1960s have come into prominence, including the Long Beach Collectibles Expo (managed by Ron Gillio) and the Baltimore Coin & Currency Show (Gordon Berg and Ed Kuzmar), to mention just two of several. The Whitman Coin and Collectibles Atlanta Expo, launched by Whitman Publishing in 2004, is one of the newer entries in the line-up, perhaps to become prominent some day. The projectors have high hopes.

On several occasions the PNG has held its own shows, but results have been mixed or poor, and they are no longer regularly scheduled. On the other hand the PNG Day events just before major coin shows have always been a hot ticket.

If you are contemplating attending a coin show located at a distance, do not rely upon tradition. Instead, ask around and find out how many dealers will be there and what other attractions are part of the schedule.

Helpful Hints and Suggestions

Here are some suggestions that may facilitate your enjoyment and comfort at a coin show. These are *my* ideas, based on my experiences; you might want to ask the advice of others as well. Here are some thoughts, in no particular order:

Be an Early Bird. Be on hand the first day of the show. Generally, most action takes place the first day or two. In today's world, it's likely that you can arrange with your employer to take off for some weekdays, rather than waiting until the weekend. Of course, this is irrelevant for a one-day show held only on the weekend. If a weekend show is held on both Saturday and Sunday, come for the first day. A show that begins on a Wednesday, a Thursday, or even a Friday is apt to be deadly dull by Sunday, and many dealers will have gone home. On the other hand, some say that staying until late can result in picking up bargains from dealers whose sales have been disappointing.

Budget Your Time in Advance. Before making your hotel and travel arrangements, try to find how much time is needed to see the sights and the show and participate in

Three seasoned conventioneers: Chet Krause, standing, with Dave Bowers and Eric P. Newman—who have been meeting now and then at coin shows since the 1950s. (David Sundman photograph)

activities of interest (including any preshow events worth attending, such as auctions). Some shows that would best be conducted in just one or two days of excitement are stretched out to include dull and boring third or fourth days. And some shows are just plain dead, period. A long time ago I went to a Penn-Ohio show in Akron. Two days came and went, and I didn't sell a single thing! Holding a table next to mine was William Fox Steinberg (today his son Robert is active in the trade; "Foxy" Steinberg died a few years back). On the third day, I bought one thing from Foxy, an encased postage stamp, and he bought a British crown from me—so both of us had at least one sale! Within the past year, I went to a really sleepy show in the Midwest—you could have rolled a bowling ball down the aisles without hitting anyone. My son Andrew went to a West Coast show that was similar. Happily, these have been the exceptions. There have been many shows that were a veritable carnival midway of action!

Another tip: find out as much in advance as you can about what the *dealers* (who usually have the inside track) expect at a show, and budget your time accordingly.

Make a Beeline. If you know that a certain dealer specializes in, say, encased postage stamps, when you're seeking items in such a series, make a beeline to see that dealer first—before his or her stocks are picked over. Then, at leisure, make the rounds of other tables in the bourse.

Bring Your List. Bring with you either a list of what you already have (if it isn't too extensive) or a want list. In that way you'll know if something that attracts you is needed for your collection. Very few people can commit to memory the specific 27 Morgan dollars, 18 Mercury dimes, or 72 Lincoln cents they still need to fill their sets, or whether they have that scenic remainder note from Boston with a green ONE overprint.

Security. If you bring coins with you, put them in a "security room" (if the show has

one). In any event, don't discuss valuable coins with strangers. When you buy coins you need, offer to pay the dealer a few dollars extra to have the pieces shipped to you when the dealer gets home. I always do this, and make it a rule *never* to travel with valuable coins. This is a nuisance, but it's a good way to go. Many shows have tables operated by the U.S. Postal Service and/or FedEx, and you can use these to ship your purchases. If you do travel by automobile and carry coins, keep them in your possession at all times.

Be Aware and Learn About Dealers' Integrity. Most coin show hosts simply sell bourse table space to anyone who applies, so long as they have a dealer business card or a resale permit. Sometimes, tables are sold to collectors as well. There is no "vetting" (as a very few antique shows do) of the items being offered—as to authenticity, grade, representation, or value for the price paid. When a dealer operates at a show, this does not mean that his or her actions, ethics, or other dealings are either approved of or guaranteed by the show. Even the largest shows with the most impressive sponsors can have rascals at the bourse tables. At one ANA show 20 years ago, a well-known dealer gave me a bad check for $8,000. It didn't help me that the ANA, after learning of phony checks he gave a lot of people, denied him the privilege of having a table in the future. He still owes me the money. So, be aware. The vast majority of dealers are apt to be fair and square, but those who aren't are the ones who cause all the problems. If you're unsure of a dealer's reputation, ask around and learn what you can.

Think Carefully Before Buying. Just as is the case with purchases in coin shops, sales at shows are usually final. You buy it and you own it. There are no refunds if you later discover a problem, as you had a chance to inspect before buying. If you're unsure, either don't buy the coin or, more practically (and also agreeable to most sellers), request to have a friend or known

ANA Convention Scenes. Snapshots of this and that, here and there, from the 2004 ANA Convention held in Pittsburgh.

Sometimes an ANA convention is favored by the visit of a Mint director. In this instance we have two: the recently retired Henrietta Holsman Fore, center, and to the right, her predecessor in office, Jay Johnson. They came by to visit the Whitman Publishing exhibit; Whitman president Mary Counts is pictured at the left.

ANA education director Gail Baker, who also ran the Numismatic Theatre presentations at the show, with Bob Evans, a scientist who was instrumental in locating the long-lost *S.S. Central America* treasure.

Melissa Karstedt, of ANR, admires a rare 1927-D double eagle shown to her by dealer Bob Higgins. At coin shows, much business is done dealer to dealer as they seek to add items to their inventories and fill want lists.

David Lange, with his lunch (a slice of pizza), holding forth at the Authors' Table, a regular feature of ANA shows. Writers of books stop by at intervals and chat with readers, sign autographs, and discuss their latest projects. Dave has a nice string of titles to his credit.

After a day at the bourse, nothing is finer than a nice dinner in town, as here at the La Mont restaurant overlooking the Pittsburgh skyline. From the foreground, clockwise: Julie Abrams, Andrew Bowers, Brent Pogue, Dave Bowers, Mary Counts, Larry Stack, and Dave Sundman.

The "ANA in the News" bulletin board posted local news clippings as they were published. The event attracted much regional attention in addition to the usual ANA members from just about everywhere.

FUN Convention Scenes. Snapshots mostly taken by Fred Lake at the 2005 Florida United Numismatists (FUN) convention held in Fort Lauderdale, a departure from the usual Orlando venue.

Dealers galore wait their turn at the registration desk. As can be seen, dress at the FUN con-

A young numismatist gets a boost from his dad at the registration table at the FUN convention. Members of the younger set are always welcome at coin shows and lend a special element of enthusiasm.

vention is casual—quite a departure from shows of generations ago, where coats and ties were worn by most men.

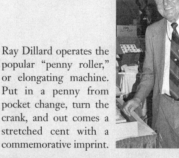

Ray Dillard operates the popular "penny roller," or elongating machine. Put in a penny from pocket change, turn the crank, and out comes a stretched cent with a commemorative imprint.

Get ready! Get set! A large crowd outside the FUN convention hall waiting for the doors to open.

A lively bourse is a traditional feature of the FUN show, usually with 500 or more tables set up, offering everything from U.S. coins to tokens, medals, and paper money, to ancient and world coins, to books and supplies. Most dealers are happy to chat and "talk coins" when they have a spare moment.

Paper-money dealer Tom Denly and his associate, Jennifer Cangeme, at the Denly's of Boston bourse table.

Heritage bourse table at the show, a partial view of a large layout.

Randy Campbell, professional grader for ANACS, in a light-hearted moment. At the show, ANACS, PCGS, NGC, Independent Coin Grading Company (ICG), and other services set up displays, often giving informal opinions as to coin grades and the procedures for determining them.

Who are these people, and why are they all wearing dark glasses? The audience, who are just beginning to be seated, are wearing special 3-D glasses, all set to view an educational presentation by David Sundman. Shown on the screen will be three-dimensional views of mints and minting procedures, adapted from century-old stereograph cards.

Chris Cipoletti, executive director of the ANA, with American Numismatic Rarities auction director John Pack following a special ceremony observing the tracking down by ANR of a long-lost rarity, an 1866 No Motto silver dollar valued at more than a million dollars and missing since 1966. The coin was returned to the Willis DuPont family, who then placed it on loan exhibit with the ANA.

expert come by the bourse table to view the coin and aid with your decision.

Taxes. Sometimes state and local taxes apply. Check on this, as such taxes add to your purchase price.

Lighting. Different types of light can make a coin look nicer than it really is. Generally, distant illumination, such as by a lamp far overhead, will mask defects, while a bright *incandescent* light, close-up, will reveal them. A fluorescent lamp is used by some, but is not as good for revealing hairlines and other minute characteristics. You should examine a coin carefully in all directions and from all angles, rotating it as you go, since lines or scratches not visible at all from one angle can be prominent when viewed as the coin is turned.

Magnification. Use a 4x or 8x glass for your first viewing of a coin, then a higher-power glass for closer inspection of the surface details, all under a strong light closely placed. *Take your time.* Do not be in a hurry.

Ask Questions. Most dealers will answer any questions you have about a coin. Chances are very good that they have studied it carefully. Ask questions, and learn.

Negotiating Price. Refer to my comments earlier in this chapter. A coin is worth what it is worth, and a coin realistically priced at $1,000 is a better buy than the same coin priced at $1,400, but for which you negotiate a 20% discount. Also, if a dealer quotes a net price, he or she is under no obligation to hold to that price if you don't buy it now, but come back later. One dealer of my acquaintance recently said, "I have a twenty-twenty policy when I make offers or quote special prices—they expire in twenty minutes or when a person walks twenty feet away from my table, whichever happens first!" Seems fair enough.

Guard Your Tongue. For all the coins, tokens, medals, and paper money items on display, you have the choice to buy or not to buy. It's poor etiquette or form to criticize dealers' offerings. "I think that Indian cent has been artificially recolored," or

"That MS-65 1902-S dollar is over-graded," or "Your price of five hundred is fifty dollars more than Jones wants for a better coin at his table"—such comments may be true, but few dealers want to hear them. Also, if you have a complaint or an issue with the dealer, talk about it off to the side, not where others can hear. It is a proven rule of management, but useful in numismatics, as well: criticize in private, praise in public.

Etiquette and good manners are always in style. Use them.

Learn by Looking at Things You Do Not Want to Buy. Once you've checked out sellers with things of interest to you, look around at other things. A show is an excellent place to view coins in other series and specialties. Often, this can lead to learning about a new series or starting a new specialty. While "looky-loos" and "be-backers" might be persona non grata in a coin shop, at a coin convention no one cares, and there are always people wandering aimlessly around the aisles. It's perfectly fine to look at as much as you care to. However, if a dealer is busy, don't interrupt him or her with idle conversation—which brings me to my next point.

Make an Appointment. If you have a matter to discuss at length, or a research question, or want to have a coin examined, or want to sell some coins, ask the bourse-table holder to suggest a good time when you can come back and attend to the matter. Or, keep an eye on his or her table, and reapproach when there is no one else there. Just about every show has busy moments as well as slow times. Pick a slow time.

Check the Show's Program Schedule. Perhaps the director of the Mint will be there at 10:00 this morning; Scott Travers will be conducting a consumer awareness seminar at noon; David Lange or Ken Bressett will be autographing books at 1:00 and 4:00 P.M.; David Sundman will be giving a show of three-dimensional pictures in a room at 2:30—these are actual things that have taken place at recent shows. Many events

have from a few to several dozen attractions. Review the schedule in advance (even before you go to the show, if it is published in *Coin World* or *Numismatic News* or on the Internet), and set aside time to attend those of interest.

Hotel Accommodations. If your trip to a show involves an overnight or multiple-night stay, do some checking as to suitable hotel accommodations. Sometimes very nice shows are held in rather poor hotels (as such hotels give attractive discount rates to exhibitors who lease ballroom or display space), and you might want to stay somewhere else. If the latter, check to see how far it is from the coin show. It's generally better to pay a bit more and stay a block from the coin show than to get a room at a discount, but stay a mile away. Taxis and transportation can be a nuisance.

Often a numismatic organization or show promoter will get a discount rate on rooms that can be passed on to those who plan to attend the show. However, it is also the case that if rooms remain unsold near the time of the event, the hotel will give even better discounts to those who ask. When I was a member of the board of governors of the ANA, the board always heard complaints about this. There was and is no easy answer. Similar to the parable of the vineyard in the Bible, if someone gets a better price, all who hear about it become upset!

Fine Dining. Although there may be exceptions (I don't know of any, however), food available at concession stands at or near coin bourses is apt to be very basic— hot dogs, pizza, sandwiches, salads, or whatever, often prepared long in advance. If you're staying in town for a couple of days, do as most dealers and savvy collectors do: minimize your food intake during the bourse hours. Then, in the evening go to a really *nice* restaurant. Don't select a place from advertising or from a guide in your hotel room. Instead, ask a couple of coin dealers. They always know the good places! In Baltimore, where I go often, my favorites include the Prime Rib, Hampton's, Kali's

Court, Ruth's Chris (one of the best links in this large chain), and Morton's (another chain)—to give a short list, to which I could add a few more. Old places sometimes deteriorate, and fine new places open up, so it's always best to check when you arrive in town. A few years ago Ray Merena and I went to a great restaurant in Indianapolis, but were surprised to find that hardly anyone else was there. We were soon dismayed to find that the service was indifferent, as was the food quality. What had been a top-notch restaurant a decade earlier had deteriorated. We should have checked.

If you join a large group of collectors or dealers at a single table in a restaurant, you should offer to help split the tab, unless someone has specifically invited you or has offered to host the event.

Enjoy the Surroundings. If you have time, do some shopping in the convention city, visit some local tourist attractions, and look around. Admittedly, this is a bit easier to do in Orlando or New York City than it is in Syracuse or Fresno (no offense meant to either of these fine places), so consider the possibilities in advance before you go. If the place is known as a tourist destination, you might want to take some family members with you.

Purchasing Coins by Mail and on the Internet

Probably, most great collections are formed over a long period of time through purchases made by mail. Orders and contacts can be originated in many ways, including through catalogs, Internet listings, telephone calls, and more. Such are usually called mail-order sales, although there are other ways to ship besides through Uncle Sam, such as by FedEx or another express company.

Selling coins by mail has a long and rich tradition, dating back to the 1850s, when John K. Curtis and others issued catalogs of things for sale. As time went on, catalogs improved and sometimes became truly impressive in size and content. The collecting of such catalogs is an interesting specialty in itself and is discussed in chapter 31.

Today, printed catalogs are becoming a rare species, as the Internet offers faster, cheaper listings, usually with better illustrations. However, not everyone uses the Internet, and there is something to be said for tradition. Printed catalogs used to arrive in my mailbox frequently. Now, they come only occasionally, and are apt to focus on a specialty such as tokens, obsolete bank notes, numismatic literature, or something similar—not on a general presentation of U.S. coins from half cents to double eagles. Sometimes, a price list is combined with a house organ or private magazine, as is the case with the *Numismatic Sun* published by American Numismatic Rarities. At one time, I could have made a fairly lengthy list, including fixed-price catalogs issued by B. Max Mehl, James F. Kelly, Stack's, Abe Kosoff, Tatham Stamp & Coin Co., New Netherlands Coin Co., R. Green, and more—all much appreciated when they arrived in the 1950s when I was in the early years of my career. Now, most are gone. Too bad, as they were always interesting to read.

What we've lost with the dwindling of printed catalogs has been more than made up for by the Internet. Today, thousands of coins are offered for fixed prices on the Internet, a panorama far more extensive than presentations in the glory years of paper catalogs.

However, the rules of engagement have not changed much. Mail-order sales—perhaps *distance sales* is a better term (much like *distance learning* for off-premises education)—are still conducted about the same way, so far as relationships between collectors and dealers are concerned.

Know Your Dealer

A fancy catalog or, more likely, a colorful and impressive web site, is no guarantee that a dealer is honest or reputable, or delivers worthwhile items. Once again, it boils down to knowing your dealer. If he or she has an established reputation and is well respected by others in the trade, you will probably be in good hands. Make inquiries of your collector and dealer acquaintances, and check the reputation of someone unknown to you, from whom you contemplate making purchases.

Years ago Lee F. Hewitt, founder and editor of the *Numismatic Scrapbook Magazine*, was fond of saying: "There is no Santa Claus in numismatics." If a coin that's priced in a certain grade at $1,000 by leading reputable dealers is offered to you at $600, chances are virtually certain that there is a problem. It might be ugly, overgraded, or posing in a certified holder with a high-sounding name issued by a no-account grading service—or it might even be fake.

It's a popular misconception that coins advertised in the leading popular numismatic newspapers and magazines have been "approved" by those publications. In reality, I unaware of *any* publication that does this. Often, dealers can continue to deliver subpar coins posing as bargains, and get away with it. How so? The formula is simple: A certain percentage of people who buy from such sources are clueless as to quality and believe the items are correctly described. Those who complain are given instant refunds to shut them up; so instead of complaining, they take future business elsewhere. If you're at all skeptical about this, the next time you're at a coin show and see a booth for a leading periodical, just ask: "Do you guarantee the grading, value, or integrity of your advertisers?"

While this situation is unfortunate with printed periodicals, it's much worse on the Internet. There, *anything* goes! There is no group or organization or anyone else regulating the offerings, descriptions, or any other aspects of coins. Counterfeits abound. If you are victimized, you can go to law enforcement officials. However, your chances of recovering your money are slight.

Avoiding such problems is really very simple:

1. Remember that there is no Santa Claus in numismatics.
2. Carefully check the reputation of anyone from whom you make a purchase.
3. If in doubt, go back to number 1.

Guarantees, Policies, and Suggestions

Most reputable dealers and others offering coins for sale via catalogs or the Internet have terms of sale. If you don't see them, be sure to ask. Policies can vary, and widely, on aspects such as the following.

Return Privilege. If, after seeing a coin, you don't like it, can you send it back for a refund? If so, what is the time limit? Some dealers permit refunds within several days, a week, or other short time, but not a month or a year later. Some dealers will not permit refunds if coins are in certified holders. Some dealers will give refunds within a specified time, less a restocking fee. A common practice is to allow no refund if a coin has been examined before buying (e.g., on an approval shipment), or if the price has been negotiated, or if it has been out of the buyer's possession (e.g., when it's been sent to a commercial grading service to see what happens to the grade evaluation).

Authenticity. Is the dealer willing to issue you an invoice stating that the coin is absolutely authentic? If not, then take your business elsewhere. A very common ploy in selling fake coins is this: "The price is so low because this is an off-the-books transaction. Pay me in cash. No records. No invoices. We both benefit." (This is a modern and often-used version of the old "green-goods game.") The scenario usually ends in one of several ways: The coin seller cannot be found, or the web site or mailing address has been discontinued. Or, the seller can be found, but denies the transaction completely, or claims the coins have been switched, or says that the transaction was for a different amount. Or, the bargain-hunter, not wanting to be caught trying to help someone evade taxes, remains quiet and absorbs the loss.

Another common claim made by fraudulent Internet sellers: "I said I didn't know what it was when I ran the picture. It was offered as-is, and I said so. Now, it's *your* problem."

Legitimacy. Does the seller have a verifiable permanent address? Can he or she furnish bank or trade references (of others in the numismatic business)? It is not unusual for someone to rent a commercial mail-drop box, say hypothetical Box 1000, then advertise as the World's Greatest Coin Company, Suite 1000, 123 Center Street, in a real city and state. Sounds impressive, but it's really nothing. Again, know your dealer.

Happiness and Tranquility

There *is* happiness on the horizon. Tranquility beckons. Enjoyment is in the offing. As I mentioned, buying through the mail—*distance buying*—is the way most collections have been built, at least in large part, including those of such legendary numismatists as T. Harrison Garrett, Louis E. Eliasberg, Sr., Mrs. R. Henry Norweb, and even King Farouk of Egypt.

In all instances of long-term satisfactory mail-order transactions, a bond is formed between collector and dealer. Mutual trust and appreciation arise naturally. Coins and other items are sent for approval inspection.

Such an experience awaits you. From the comfort and convenience of your office, or your favorite overstuffed chair at home, you can open a package from a fine dealer and view the latest purchases and selections. Here is a little saying I believe to be true: "It's always fun to get an interesting package in the mail." It's like opening a present!

Other Places to Buy Coins

There are many other places to buy coins by outright purchase. Some are good, and others are not so good. Taking a cue from the *Forbes* magazine guide to restaurants, I'll offer some of my opinions (which are just that: opinions, like those offered for good dining spots).

Go!

In the *good* or even *excellent* category is the United States Mint. This is a great source for the latest Proof set, or commemorative, or specially packaged statehood quarter, or other offering. Not everything is perfect, and sometimes commemoratives and other items sold at sharp premiums over face value can decline in value on the aftermarket. However, if you buy single pieces (not a wheelbarrow full) for your own collection, this is a great way to keep up to date. Designs might be gorgeous or unattractive, but all are interesting in one way or another. I believe that the current products of the U.S. Mint are without peer anywhere else in the world.

Banks provide a good source for acquiring current coins in quantity—say, when you want to put away a few rolls of modern Lincoln cents or statehood quarters or Sacagawea dollars.

Other collectors may have duplicate coins for sale and offer them to you. Based on your own knowledge, perhaps with the consultation of your friends, evaluate the items. At coin-club meetings and elsewhere, other collectors can be a fine source for acquiring pieces you need.

Consider!

Antique shops and flea markets require a special degree of consideration, of caution. Some "group shops" have displays of coins set up by reputable dealers or collectors and might be okay. However, any item offered by a dealer in antiques who says, "I don't know anything about coins; this came in an old estate," or similar, bears a caution flag. If you're unsure of the coin, its authenticity, or value, and if the dealer is otherwise reputable (in the field of antiques, but not knowledgeable in numismatics), ask to buy it with a one-week or other convenient return privilege, stating that you want to show the coin to some fellow numismatists. If this request is denied, walk.

Caution should also be used when buying coins from jewelers, unless they have numismatic credentials (in which case all can be fine). Counterfeit and altered coins abound in such locations. Carefully consider purchases in these venues.

Care should be taken when anyone not well known to you offers you coins at an unusual location. If you travel to meet someone, insist that they meet you in a bank lobby, not at some obscure private address. There have been many instances in which coin buyers seeking bargains and carrying cash have been lured to very unfortunate experiences.

Stop!

Television shopping shows, big spreads of modern coin sets in popular newspapers and magazines, and the like can yield worthwhile coins, but in general the price you will pay for a Morgan silver dollar of 1878, or a Proof set of 1994-S, will be considerably more than your local coin shop will charge or the price you would have to pay at a typical coin show.

An investment salesperson may call and say that he or she has just opened a long-sealed bag of silver dollars, or bought an estate of gold coins, or whatever, and offer you "deals," often emphasizing the gold or silver value and saying what great investments they are. In many instances, these pieces are "certified," but by grading services that are either unknown or disreputable. Be very careful. Insist only on coins certified by leading, reputable grading services, and check the prices carefully. Better yet, make note of the sales pitch, then ask your local coin dealer, or a favorite dealer with whom you've had satisfactory mail transactions, to find you similar pieces— chances are they will be less expensive.

Occasionally, I get such pitches on the telephone, and when I ask the name, business trade style, street address, telephone number, and name of the owner of the company for which the salesman is working, the person usually hangs up!

While traveling, as in South America, Europe, or Asia, never, but *never*, buy "rare coins" from banks, antique dealers, jewelers, or anyone else who is not an established professional. The International Association of Professional Numismatists (IAPN) includes many fine dealers in these areas, and I recommend that you do business *only* with them. You may see many "gold dollars," "three-dollar gold pieces," "trade dollars," or even "1804 silver dollars" offered by nonprofessionals, but 999 out of 1,000 are complete and utter fakes. Although the desire to buy bargains in a distant land is intense, good buys of authentic coins do not happen very often.

Moreover, when traveling, don't tell *anyone* that you collect coins, not even in casual conversation with a newly found friend on a cruise or in a resort. After a couple of retellings over drinks, you may be described as carrying in your luggage a fortune in gold coins! A few years ago at a briefing held for dealers who belonged to the PNG, a prominent dealer from Mexico warned his colleagues not to wear expensive watches, dress nattily, or rent luxury cars when traveling to buy coins in his country.

Full Speed Ahead!

By now, you've probably received enough advice on the techniques of buying coins outright. Utilize what makes sense to you, then go full speed ahead and enjoy the hobby!

CHAPTER FIFTEEN

TECHNIQUES OF SMART BIDDING:
From Auctions to the Internet

If a collector is reasonable and businesslike in his relations with any well-established dealer he will usually be fairly treated and will find it more to his interest in the end to pay a dealer commission for his services and judgment than to enter the lists himself and challenge the jealousy and opposition of the whole trade or profession. Under such circumstances only a collector who has bought literally from many dealers can count upon their consideration as regards the prizes of the sale. It is these that cause the excitement of the occasion.

—Augustus G. Heaton, commenting on having a dealer
as a representative at a sale, November 1894

Auctions: An Inside View

Buying a coin in a private transaction, such as at a coin show, over the counter from a dealer, or through the mail, offers you the opportunity to contemplate, consider, and contemplate some more. You can ask questions, view the coin again after you hear the answers to the questions, and in other ways make a leisurely and informed purchase. Often, you can obtain a specimen on approval and view it over a period of a day or two.

This is not necessarily so when you buy coins at auction. Often, a split-second decision is needed during the heat of competitive bidding. To buy effectively in an auction, you need another set of guidelines—actually, *two* sets: one for sales conducted by professional numismatists (*professional auctions*, to pick a term for illustration) and the other for the proliferation of auctions held on the Internet and elsewhere by people who are not in the trade (*casual auctions*).

Certain practices and procedures apply to both professional and casual auctions, and I discuss them here. Having been in the professional auction business since the 1950s, and having attended countless events held by others, I've seen just about everything! Moreover, as past president of the Professional Numismatists Guild (PNG) and the American Numismatic Association (ANA), I've witnessed many auction problems brought to the attention

of these organizations. I have also been an expert witness in arbitrations and disputes.

Now, I'm going to take you behind the scenes for an inside view.

Before proceeding, I hasten to mention that participating in an auction or a mail-bid sale can be great fun and a very effective way to acquire desirable numismatic items. However, a degree of awareness is called for, and that is what I hope to share with you.

Terms of Sale
Fakes

Just about every seller has terms of sale. In the instance of a printed catalog, they can be multiple pages in length and contain many paragraphs, usually carefully prepared by legal counsel. It is important for you to read the fine print. One auctioneer may permit the return of a coin, if it is found to be fake, within a specified short time, and another might not allow a return at all—selling coins "as-is." In certain sales of confiscated, abandoned, and other coins by the U.S. government (Uncle Sam, guardian of you and me), the items are offered as-is. Buy one and you own it, no matter whether it's phony.

That said, most professional auctions conducted by numismatic firms do permit returns if a coin is proved to be fake. *Proved* is an important word, for your pal Joe Schmo's opinion that it's a fake probably won't mean much when you inform the auction house. Instead, a specified procedure must be followed, or judgment passed by a mutually agreed-upon authority—hopefully, as outlined in the terms of sale.

For many casual sales of coins on the Internet, either no terms are posted, or the website host has general rules not specific to coins. Often, an item is pictured, and if you buy it, you own it. It may be illegal to sell a fake coin, but if you buy one on the Internet from someone a thousand miles away, you are apt to lose everything. Website hosts may allow you to post complaints or "feedback," but if you paid $2,000 for a "rare colonial" that proves to be worthless, there is little actual help to get your money back. You can hire an attorney, but by the time the case is investigated your bill will likely be more than $2,000. If you contact a distant chamber of commerce, or the Better Business Bureau, or a law enforcement agency, the chances are still slight that you will make a significant recovery.

As I have said several times in this text, be sure the seller has good, verifiable credentials.

While your chances of buying an out-and-out fake from an established, professional rare-coin firm are small, it does happen. Usually, if the fake is obvious (which sometimes happens, as large companies run a lot of items through their sales, and many consigned items are cataloged by clerks or other non-experts), a refund is forthcoming—and quickly. If the questioned coin appears to be genuine to the auctioneer and his or her staff, but you and your consultants believe it to be fake, the matter may be arbitrated, or another procedure may be followed. Again, read the terms of sale.

On Internet purchases, you have great exposure if the seller is not a recognized professional with numismatic expertise. Read the terms of sale carefully, but if you have the slightest question about an item offered, or if it seems to be too good to be true, either don't bid or make arrangements to have the coin examined by a professional (if the seller will allow this and if there is time to do so).

Prices and Minimums

Nearly all auction offerings by professionals are subject to minimum bids, usually not disclosed in the catalog or Internet offering. However, the terms of sale usually make note of the practice. On Internet and other offerings by casual sellers, this may not be specified, but minimum bids are still used.

There are several reasons for having minimum bids. A licensed auctioneer, a professional numismatist, or a country seller of antiques is supposed to have a responsibility and obligation to both the owner and the buyer. If Widow Jones consigns a $1,000 bill, Series of 1928, to Auctioneer Smith, the auctioneer cannot, or at least should not, offer it for sale and quickly sell it for $800. There would seem to me to be a responsibility to deliver at least *face value* after charges and commissions! Widow Jones could have spent the bill for face value, so her expectation is to realize more than that.

In such a circumstance, it would be perfectly reasonable for Auctioneer Smith to have a reserve of, say, $1,100, for starters. In this way, if it sells, he makes a few dollars and so does Widow Jones.

In other instances, consignors request or negotiate reserves with the auctioneer. "I have an 1879 Flowing Hair Stella, and you can put it in your next sale, but I want to reserve it at $100,000." The auctioneer contemplates the coin, and if he feels it can sell for an attractive advance over $100,000, will probably accept it. The reserve will likely not be printed in the catalog. The bidding may open at, say, $80,000, to get some "action" going, but until it crosses the $100,000 mark, the house or "book" will also be bidding. In other instances, an agent or representative of the auctioneer (*shill* is the nasty word for this) will be in the audience, unidentified, and will be bidding for the house. In still other instances the auctioneer may make an arrangement with a dealer friend who will run the reserve bids (while giving the appearance that the person is bidding on his or her own account).

Sometimes a sale is advertised as "unreserved" or "absolute." I am not aware that either term has specific legal meaning, at least not universally. I have bid in "unreserved" sales after being told, for example, "Bidding on Lot 335 will commence at $2,000." That, to me, is a reserve!

To summarize, the terms of sale might specify that reserves are on some or all lots. However, if this is not stated, there may be reserves anyway.

The endgame is simple: reserve or no reserve, bid only what a coin is actually worth.

Lot Inspection

Most public sales allow the items to be inspected before the bidding. I say "most," as I have seen a few government and law-authority sales, not auctions conducted by recognized numismatic auctioneers, in which sealed boxes, bags, or tubes of coins are offered sight unseen, in the manner that unclaimed luggage is sometimes sold. However, you are not apt to encounter such a situation.

Most terms of sale in a printed catalog allow for in-person inspection before the sale, usually through a setup in which you can sit down at a table in a firm's home office or in a room near the sale itself, and under security precautions, inspect the lots one at a time. Some professional numismatic firms allow inspection by mail for established clients. Casual auctioneers, such as an auctioneer of antiques who advertises that some coins will be sold at a forthcoming event, usually won't allow mail inspection. In fact, many casual auctioneers consider anyone who asks questions from a distance, instead of simply coming to the sale, to be a pest.

In any event, if you attend a sale in person, regardless of whether you have availed yourself of the opportunity to inspect the items, sales to floor bidders are usually final. The only exception is if a coin is found to

be a fake and rescinding the sale is allowed. If an auction starts at 7:00 in the evening, and you come to the lot-viewing area at 4:00 P.M. and find there is a long wait, or that time for inspection is over, that's your problem, not that of the auction house.

If you attend the sale and buy a coin described as a gorgeous gem and, after you buy it, you find it's ugly as a toad, again, that's your problem.

In short, if you attend a sale, allow sufficient time in advance to inspect each and every lot you bid on.

As to bidding on the Internet, there are few rules. It can be really wild out there! Many if not most casual sellers picture the items, this being the complete situation— no detailed descriptions, no commentary, no anything—just a picture. If a coin is certified by a recognized, leading service of good reputation, this may help. Paper money is even more of a free-for-all. A bill from the First National Bank of Podunk may be pictured, but usually nothing at all is said about its grade. As a professional dealer in paper money, I know that I can't tell from an Internet illustration whether a bill is About Uncirculated, Uncirculated-60, or Uncirculated-63 grade, and I don't imagine you can either.

If you contemplate bidding on the Internet, and the seller is not a recognized professional who describes items with expertise, ask questions (most sites have a method for this) before bidding. In any event, be careful.

Buyer's Fees

Beginning in a strong way in the 1980s and almost universally applied now, numismatic auction houses add a "buyer's fee" to the hammer price or basic sale price of a coin. Some call this a "buyer's *penalty*," and in the numismatic trade, the term *juice* is sometimes used.

In the United States, the typical buyer's fee is 15%. However, higher or lower fees can be charged. Some auctioneers charge no fee at all. The fee procedure will be listed in the terms of sale.

With a 15% buyer's fee, a coin that an auctioneer sells for $1,000—the so-called hammer price—will appear on your bill as $1,150. A coin that is sold for $300 will be billed as $345. A coin that is sold for $100,000 will actually cost you $115,000.

It is not unusual for a newcomer to grouse about the buyer's fee, in absence of understanding it. If a buyer's fee is charged, to me, it makes no difference. I simply figure it in when bidding. If I want to pay no more than the total amount of $1,000 for a coin, I stop bidding around the $875 level. With some experience, it is easy enough to do mental calculations, even if a sale moves quickly.

The hammer price is 86.96% (we'll say 87%) of the total price when 15% is added. You can use a pocket calculator to figure this out at a sale—or at home, if you bid by mail or on the Internet. (Remember always to check the terms of sale, of course—many Internet sales by private individuals do not involve buyer's fees.) If you want to pay $2,000, and no more, for a nice 1955 Doubled-Die Lincoln cent, then bid 87% of this price, or $1,740. If you win it for your full bid, your bill will be at $1,740 plus 15%, or $2,001.

Other Stuff

Read each and every paragraph in the terms of sale. Other text might include information about sales taxes. In some states and cities, taxes are charged against coin auction purchases, possibly for the entire amount, although there may be exceptions. If you are buying for resale and have a valid resale permit, you may be exempt. Sometimes, when lots are shipped out of state, there is an exemption, other times not.

It may be that gold coins are exempt from taxation, but numismatic books might not be. There are hundreds of different twists and turns in sales-tax laws and regulations. If in doubt, ask the auctioneer, who should know.

Are the items illustrated in the catalog or on the Internet the actual items being sold, or are the photographs simply "representa-tive"? The terms of sale should tell you. If not, ask.

Many, if not most, terms of sale state that catalog descriptions notwithstanding, no guarantees, representations, and so on are made concerning the grades of coins, their attributions, their values, their potential for resale, their quality, or their merchantability. So there! Said simply, any coin, token, medal, or piece of currency is what it is—not necessarily conforming to its presale description.

Procedures for bidding by mail, or by telephone, or by Internet, or by in-person attendance may vary. Sometimes mail bids have to be received a day or so before the sale begins, and requirements are in place for e-mail bids as well. In other instances, real-time bidding is allowed by telephone or the Internet. Read such terms carefully.

Some auction houses allow a "maximum expenditure" or "one-lot-only" option, again explained in the terms of sale.

Under a maximum-expenditure arrangement, you can state your budget for the sale (say, $10,000), and the auction house will run your bids until you have spent that much, after which all further bids will be canceled. Remember that the sale is conducted in the order of listing, and if you spend your $10,000 by the time that Lot 600 comes up, and Lot 600 sells for a low price, you won't have the possibility of buying it.

Under a one-lot-only arrangement, if a sale has eight 1881-S dollars in MS-65 grade or three MCMVII (1907) High Relief double eagles in MS-63, and you want just one of each, the auction house may allow you to bid on all of them, but in sequence as they are offered. As soon as you buy one, later bids on similar lots are canceled, even if the later-offered coins are just as nice and sell for cheaper prices.

What if you place a bid by mail or on the Internet, and then want to change or cancel it? What if you want to pay for your lots over a period of time? What about packing and shipping costs? Insurance in transit? Policies vary, and again the terms of sale will provide the answer. On very small purchases, postage and handling can be a large proportion of the transaction. I once bought a $4 postcard on the Internet and was charged an additional $6 postage and handling. On the Internet, it is often the case that such charges are not stated in advance. *Handling* has various meanings when it comes to costs.

Many other opportunities, restrictions, and provisions apply. While printed catalogs and some web sites will list terms of sale in detail, there are other auction venues in which the provisions can be just as strict, or for which there may be interesting opportunities, but they will not be easy to find. In such instances, ask before you bid.

In all instances, when you bid in a sale, be prepared to buy! This might seem obvious, but now and again someone will send in $10,000 in bids on a string of coins, then get an invoice for $9,760, and say, "I was not expecting to actually buy that much." If you bid on $10,000 worth of coins you might not get a thing. On the other hand, you might spend the full amount!

Terms of sale are usually subject to modification at the time of sale, such as by comments of the auctioneer or late postings on the Internet. The right is usually reserved to withdraw any item for sale without notice (the reasons can be many, such as a vague title, insistence by the consignor, changing market conditions, etc.). Entire sales can be canceled without notice—and in today's world of various problems in large cities and elsewhere, this is a real consideration. A few years back, a leading rare coin firm (not active today) offered a collection for auction, then canceled the sale when someone stepped up to buy the entire holding for outright cash. If you plan to travel any distance, verify the sale in advance if you can.

Sometimes an auctioneer will have amenities and services to offer in addition to the sale itself—such as contacts for preferential hotel rates, suggestions for restaurants, or even a presale reception or midsale buffet or dinner.

Auctioneers' Policies: Estimates

Some auction listings have estimates. The terms of sale will probably state that the estimates are just that—*estimates*—and that at the actual sale, higher or lower prices may prevail for a given item. In other instances, the auctioneer will use the estimates for his or her starting bids. In a recent sale of paper money, a well-known auction firm routinely opened every item at 60% of the low estimate figure, unless a higher bid had been received beforehand. Accordingly, a piece of currency estimated at $1,000 to $1,500 opened at $600.

Sometimes states or localities will have rules concerning estimates and opening bids. An example may be that in no instance can a reserve bid be higher than the highest estimate printed for a lot. Under such a rule, a coin with a printed estimate of $2,000 to $3,000 cannot have a reserve bid over $3,000. This means that if someone bids at least $3,000, an actual sale will take place. However, such rules are in place in only a few areas. If you ever want to immerse yourself in almost continuous commentary about auctions and Internet sales (nearly all concerning antiques, art, and non-numismatic material), the monthly *Maine Antique Digest*, published in Waldoboro, Maine (Sam Pennington, editor), is extremely enlightening and informative. I've been a regular reader for years. Don't let the *Maine* part of the title fool you; it covers the entire country.

As a long-time participant in many auction sales, from coins to antiques and beyond, I have concluded that there are at least three different "classes" of estimates. The auctioneer's policy in this regard is not disclosed in the catalog, so you have to figure the situation out for yourself.

To illustrate, I'll use a rare 1877 Indian Head cent, a hypothetical specimen certified by, say, Professional Coin Grading Service (PCGS) in a grade for which, if I were buying it for stock, I would pay $2,500, this being the "bid" price in the *Certified Coin Dealer Newsletter*; if I were offering it for sale I would ask $3,000. The coin is well struck and of nice appearance. So, the real value is $2,500 to $3,000. At a well-conducted auction sale the coin would likely sell for about $3,000. (I'm ignoring the 15% buyer's fee to simplify the illustration.)

The following are some types of estimates, the reasons some auctioneers use them, and what you should do in each case.

Lowball Estimate: $1,000 to $1,500

Reasons for Use. It seems that this will be a grand auction to participate in. Wow! I *might* be able to buy a $3,000 Indian Head cent for just $1,000. It must be so, or it would not be printed as an estimate. At least the *possibility* exists. I'll rearrange my schedule so I can attend.

For the auction house, the lowball estimate makes the firm "look good." Coin papers and advertisements will trumpet: "Coin brings way over estimate! Wow!" An estate attorney or an heir who consigns, but is not conversant with values, will be delighted to see how spectacularly the firm has performed, even if the coin sleeps at $2,000, because hardly anyone participated! If it brings its real value (say, $3,000), he or she will be on cloud nine. In the field of antiques this is the rule, not the exception. Antique music boxes (a passion of mine) are nearly always lowballed.

Strategy for Bidding. Figure what the coin is worth before you submit your bid or make travel plans. Realize that the rarity of the 1877 cent is well known, that the bid price in the *Certified Coin Dealer Newsletter* is $2,500, and the chances the coin will sell at the estimate are like a snowball in you-know-where. If you want the coin, be prepared to pay $2,500 to $3,000 (less an allowance to take care of the buyer's fee).

Negatives. The auction house loses credibility with knowledgeable bidders, even if it makes naïve consignors happy. The auction itself and lot viewing may be congested with bargain hunters who take up time and space, but who don't buy anything when the sale takes place. Those who travel to attend the sale, expecting to gobble up bargains, will be disappointed that everything sold for such "strong prices" that they were not able to buy.

Expert Estimate: $2,500 to $3,200

Reasons for Use. The auction house trades primarily with collectors, dealers, museums, investors, and others who are proven buyers and who have knowledge. Such buyers know that they can rely upon the estimates to be at least in the ballpark. Chances are good that if asked, an auction representative can discuss or defend the estimate.

Strategy for Bidding. The estimate can be relied upon. If you want the coin only if "the price is right" and there is no urgency, bid $2,500 to $2,800 and you might get it. If it is a dandy coin with nice appearance, and it is on your want list, bid $3,000 to $3,500, and you might take it home.

Negatives. If it brings "only" $2,800, a naïve consignor may feel that the coin was sold for too little. If the auction house wants a larger attendance—never mind that some will be bargain hunters who do not buy—there will be fewer on hand when estimates are realistic.

Grandstand Estimate: $5,000 to $7,000

Reasons for Use. This "grandstand" or "come-on" estimate is common in country fairs, huckstering, and the like. "Who'll start this chair at $500? Well, how about $200?" In coins it is less common. The purpose is to put an artificially high price so that those attending the sale will feel they are getting a bargain if they buy it for only $4,000! This often works if there are pigeons or patsies attracted to the sale, but it does not sit well with knowledgeable numismatists. Accordingly, "grandstand estimates" are rare among sales held by professional numismatists. However, they are very common in Internet offerings. Greedy consignors may be delighted that a coin is estimated at $5,000 to $7,000, when other auction houses "appraised" the coin for much less!

Strategy for Bidding. Bid what the coin is really worth.

Negatives. The consignor will be disappointed, even if such a coin brings full market value—say, $3,200. The auction house will not care, as that consignor is history—the estate collection (or whatever) has been sold, and no future business is in the offing. Knowledgeable numismatic buyers may be turned off by the whole thing and not attend or otherwise participate in the sale. They will also think that the firm conducting the sale has a staff with few experts on board, or else that they are a bunch of promoters, or both.

After the Sale: "Prices Realized"

Many numismatic firms publish "prices-realized" lists for their sales. Until a few years ago, such listings included figures for lots that sold as well as those that did not meet their reserve prices, with no identification as to which was which. Today, most professionals list only the prices for items that have actually changed hands.

For an item that sells for $1,500, the price realized is posted on the Internet or in a printed list either as (1) $1,500, with a notation on the list that a buyer's fee of, say, 15% is to be added to each price, or (2) with the fee included, in this case $1,725. Listing with the buyer's fee is the usual practice, and accounts for a lot of odd figures. For example, a coin selling for $820 plus 15% comes to $943.

There can be exceptions, and here are a few hypothetical situations to illustrate:

1. Lot 354 is sold to floor bidder John Doe for $1,500 plus 15%. This is an actual sale, and the figure is listed as the price realized. However, Doe's check bounces a week later, and the auctioneer gets the coin back. It is not usual policy to amend previously issued lists of prices realized to reflect this.

2. Lot 1320 is sold to mail bidder Sam Smith for $200 plus 15%. The coin is sent to the bidder, who has a good

reputation, but is returned to the auctioneer with a note from the Post Office that the bidder moved without leaving a forwarding address, or from a relative saying that Smith died. Still, the list of prices realized reflects that a sale took place.

3. Lot 320 is sold to floor bidder John Q. Public for $75,000, and this is listed as the price. However, Public was also the consignor of the coin; by prearrangement with the auctioneer, Public had the right to buy the coin back at this figure, possibly through a friend (an evasion used if the auction house says a consignor cannot bid on his own material at the sale). Of course, this is tantamount to assigning a reserve bid, but it is not always treated as such.

4. Lot 4560 is sold to Peter Porcupine, a good customer, for $2,000. However, Porcupine does not pay his bill, his credit has turned bad, the coin is returned a month later, and the coin goes back into another auction.

Prices realized can be a good guide to coin values and to future bidding, but should be taken with a grain of salt. However, most posted by recognized numismatic firms are valid.

Enjoy Yourself

Public auctions, mail-bid sales, and Internet sales are meant to be exciting and enjoyable. The preceding comments about terms of sale and the like are necessary to know, but they should be a passport to having a good time rather than an obstacle.

I suppose that if I were going to Muscat, where I've never been, or to Attu in the Aleutians, it would be well for me to read up on the challenges that confront me: travel, the quality and nature of accommodations, what to do about meals, how to spend money or use a credit card, how to contact folks back home, what the sights and attractions are, any medical or health precautions, information about native creatures from insects to sharks, courtesies to be observed, and on and on. Then, properly educated, I would concentrate on having a fine experience!

So it is with auctions. At American Numismatic Rarities (ANR) sales there are quite a few "regulars" I've seen in the salesroom for *decades*. And, at every sale there are newcomers. All are cordially welcome, as are their questions and inquiries. Most other auctioneers would probably say the same.

Bidding is a great way to add to your collection. Now, with some of the technical stuff behind you, let's move on to some strategy.

Smart Bidding Strategies
Public Auctions

Bidding in an auction can be as exciting as playing poker. In your "hand" you have various cards, so to speak—a budget in mind, specific things you are looking for, and an awareness of the game. At the same time, you keep your secrets to yourself, as do others in the same game who want to win the same pot.

The following paragraphs contain some strategies I have used with success in bidding. Others strategies, such as for bidding on the Internet, are from a close friend with extensive Internet experience who has shared her knowledge. She'll remain anonymous (as she also does on the Internet, using a code name there).

For any type of sale venue, start planning as early as you can. Obtain a copy of the catalog as far in advance of the sale as possible. In practice, this will probably be from one to three weeks before the event. Auctioneers like to have their catalogs delivered before the sale, of course, but not so far before that they grow stale or are misplaced. If the listing is on the Internet, tap into it at least a few days before the sale is scheduled to take place.

Just as you do when you play poker (if this is a pastime for you), keep your strategy secret. I cannot emphasize this too strongly. Disclosing what you want to buy

and how much you will pay can result in unfavorable situations, none of which are good for you or your pocketbook.

Now, imagine that a fine sale is about to take place. A well-known auctioneer with good numismatic credentials is to offer a nice collection and other consignments. The auction will be held in Baltimore, New York City, Los Angeles, or another large city, or at a convention somewhere. Participation can be by in-person attendance, mail, Internet, or telephone. The event will be conducted under the aegis of a licensed auctioneer.

Attending a sale in person is very much a part of enjoying numismatics, and I encourage you to go if your time and schedule permit.

Study the catalog carefully, not only for items you specifically need, but also for coins or other things that capture your fancy. Mark in the catalog those of interest. After you do this, spend some time with pricing guides and mark down your bids. Keep the 15% (usual) buyer's fee in mind, and calculate this as part of your bid. Advance thinking is very important, as the sale itself will be conducted at a fast pace, and you will not have the time to do much figuring while the lots are being sold.

For items that you simply must own or cannot live without, figure your bids to be as high as you can. However, do not let "auction fever" cloud your judgment. If a coin has problems, it will remain a "problem coin" while you have it, and when time comes to sell, it will be less attractive to buyers. There are very few coins for which compromise is necessary. Also, if a coin is of nice quality and is not particularly rare, there is no need to pay way over market price to get it. There is something to be said for the opportunity to buy—if you are on the spot and a coin is available—and this opportunity is worth paying a few dollars for. A coin in the hand is worth two in the bush. You then own the coin, one that you have inspected and found to be all that you hoped for in quality, while others still are seeking an example.

Establishing Credit

Before traveling to visit the sale, establish credit. Request an authorization to bid up to a certain amount of your choosing. If you are well known to the auction house, this will be a simple procedure. Based upon your past bidding and credit history, financial documents you may have provided, bank references, or other information, your request will normally be allowed.

If there have been past problems, credit can be denied, or the amount reduced. However, such situations are uncommon.

As you prepare to go to the sale, you will know that the auctioneer is comfortable with your buying coins valued up to a total of $1,000, or $10,000, or $100,000, or whatever your authorization may be. Of course, be prepared to pay for your auction purchases immediately after the sale, unless other arrangements have been made.

Now, on to the sale....

Getting Ready

Before the sale, allow enough time to view all of the lots in which you are interested. This usually means coming at least a day in advance, or even two or three days early. The earlier you arrive, the less crowded the lot viewing is apt to be.

At lot viewing you will be asked to identify yourself. If your credit is not known to the auctioneer, you will be asked to verify this before you will be allowed to bid. As noted, it is good procedure to take care of this at home before you travel to the sale.

Lot viewing is usually conducted in a semi-darkened room with individual attendants showing coins one by one to interested bidders, who fill out sheets of paper giving their names and the lot numbers they wish to see. Security guards are on hand, usually with monitoring cameras as an added precaution.

It is good form to examine the lots as quickly as you can, in keeping with observing whatever details you wish, and not to distract others who are doing the same thing. Often, others are waiting for their turn to see the coins you're looking at.

If you have a technical question, ask the attendant, who will usually call upon one of the firm's experts to assist you. You might ask permission to have your own expert take a look at it, which will probably be fine.

The lot-viewing process may take an hour or two for the viewing of several dozen coins, once you get a seat. If you are going to inspect hundreds of coins, be sure to come a day or two early. As the sale draws nearer, or if lot viewing becomes crowded, there may be a restriction on the number of lots any person can inspect.

As an alternative to the above, many auctioneers can arrange inspection in their home offices long before the sale—a convenience for anyone who intends to make extensive purchases involving many items.

Making Notes in Your Catalog

Most people who view lots make notes beside each catalog listing. Techniques vary. One dealer is fond of using decimal points to indicate what he believes are fine gradations. Thus, a coin certified as MS-65 in the catalog might be annotated by him as 64.8, meaning that in his view it is a tad below full MS-65; or it might be annotated MS-65.8, which means that he thinks it to be a high-end MS-65 and perhaps a candidate for resubmitting to a grading service to be returned as an MS-66.

Another dealer uses pluses and minuses, as MS-65–, meaning that it is slightly below expectations, or MS-65+++, meaning that it is far better. Others simply make notations such as "large nick on chin," "stain at lower obverse," or whatever.

Next comes the calculation of your bids. Do this in a quiet spot where you can concentrate. A good policy is to put down a ballpark figure for a bid (say, $3,000) for a given item, perhaps writing it in a code or in small numerals so it will not be obvious to anyone else who sees your catalog.

The Sale Is About to Start

Chances are good that you can register and sign up for a bidder card or paddle during the lot-viewing process. If you haven't done

Harvey G. Stack, senior member of the firm bearing his name, is the son of Morton Stack, who with J.B. Stack founded Stack's Rare Coins in New York City in 1935. Since that time they have handled many of the finest collections and rarities ever sold.

Larry Stack, son of Harvey, and chief operating officer of the firm, behind the scenes in his office, preparing for a forthcoming sale.

David T. Alexander, a member of the research and cataloging staff at Stack's, examines an Alaska gold token. He is prominent in the Numismatic Literary Guild and the Medal Collectors of America groups.

Ira Goldberg (left) and Larry Goldberg attending to duties during the progress of one of their auction sales.

Auctioneer Herb Kreindler at the podium with staffer Vicken Yegparian to the left, at John J. Ford Collection Sale X, held in Atlanta, May 2005. This particular sale was rich in obsolete currency and Confederate States of America items.

Larry Stack and daughter Rebecca watch the action at an event held in Chicago in 2004 jointly with ANR.

The audience at the Eliasberg Collection sale, New York City, March 2005, being welcomed by Dave Bowers at the podium. (Donn Pearlman photograph)

Chris Karstedt, president of ANR and the first licensed woman auctioneer for any rare coin firm, calls for bids at the Eliasberg Collection sale. (Donn Pearlman photograph)

Consignor Richard A. Eliasberg congratulates the ANR cataloging team after the sale. Left to right: Frank Van Valen, John Pack, Richard Eliasberg, and John Kraljevich. (Donn Pearlman photograph)

Georgie Babalis registering a bidder, dealer Tony Terranova, at the Richard Jewell Collection sale held in 2005.

Frank Van Valen sells lot 2608 at the Medio Collection sale in Chicago.

Chris Karstedt, consignor Richard Jewell, and Dave Bowers after the ANR sale of the Jewell Collection, an incredible cabinet of $3 gold coins.

Professional numismatist Mike Phillips examines auction lots from the Richard C. Jewell Collection. Dealers often spend many hours in this activity, evaluating pieces for their own interest as well as for bids placed by clients.

Melissa Karstedt, Andrew Bowers, and John Kraljevich at the back table at an ANR sale, handling telephone bids for clients at a distance.

Auction-lot viewing at a Heritage sale with the FUN Convention, Fort Lauderdale, Florida, 2005. Prior to each sale, collectors and dealers gather to inspect the coins and other items carefully. (All photographs by Heritage)

Greg Rohan (foreground) and Steve Ivy, principals at Heritage, are busy checking information just prior to an important auction sale.

Auction action at a Heritage sale with the FUN convention in Florida.

Just a few of thousands of lots scheduled to cross the auction block at a Heritage sale.

Bob Merrill sells a coin at a Heritage auction.

Heritage's home facilities are in two high floors in this Dallas office building. In addition to coins, the firm deals in autographs, movie posters, comic books, and other collectibles.

The auction house of R.M. Smythe & Co., founded in the 1880s, is located at 2 Rector Street, New York City, in the financial district. An auction gallery, showroom, conference center, and offices are part of the facilities.

Reception gallery at R.M. Smythe & Co.

Lyn Knight, prominent auctioneer and currency specialist, is shown at work in his new auction gallery / headquarters facility, cataloging notes from the "Permian Basin" collection, an old-time holding of some 500 Texas nationals. On hand are past auction catalogs, paper money references, and three bank directories of the late 19th and early 20th centuries.

All dressed up and ready for an auction sale—the salesroom at R.M. Smythe & Co. The room is also used for visiting lecturers who declaim on paper money, autographs, financial history, and other topics.

On the days his auctioneering services are not required, Eric Knight works on various projects. Here he is scanning notes for an upcoming catalog.

A highly prized $1 note, graded "Extremely Fine plus," 1875 Series, from the First National Bank of Hightstown, New Jersey, pedigreed to the Malcolm A. Trask Collection and sold by Currency Auctions of America. The buyer was dealer Tom Denly, who paid $5,250 plus 15% buyer's fee. This note had been off the market for more than 50 years.

Len Glazer (seated) and Allen Mincho, directors of Currency Auctions of America, in the lot-viewing room prior to a sale.

this, but have looked at lots and have had your credit approved, then check in at the registration table or desk, usually located outside the auction room or gallery.

You will be asked to sign a card or small document stating that you are *personally* responsible for any items you bid upon (even if you have a corporation or trade entity) and will pay for them promptly. Some auction houses will ask for other information, such as about delivery of the lots. Do you want to pick up your lots soon after the sale—such as on the next business day, or at a special pick-up session, or at the auctioneer's bourse table or set-up at a convention being held in another location at the same time? Or do you want them shipped to your home or office?

The typical auction room has rows of chairs, sometimes with working tables or areas in front of some of the chairs. These face the front of the room, where the auctioneer stands at a podium. Open seating is the rule. Early birds who want working tables can usually get them. Seating on an aisle, or in a front row, or in the back is up to you.

Most long-time auction attendees have their favorite spots. Some like to be up front where they can be close to the auctioneer, hear everything clearly, and not be disrupted by the comings and goings of bidders. Also, a person sitting toward the front can bid unobtrusively by holding a bidder paddle in front of his or her chest, so that the movement cannot be seen by those behind.

Other bidders like to sit at the side of the room, or on an aisle. Still others congregate in the back, where they can watch what's going on. Generally, bidders enjoy privacy and do not want to sit next to someone who will glance over their catalogs, ask questions, and so on.

The Auctioneer

As the sale begins, the auctioneer or other auction-house representative will make some opening remarks—perhaps welcoming bidders to the event, reminding them that the sale will be conducted per the terms of sale printed in the catalog (or any revisions announced on the spot), and that all sales are final.

Procedures are then given. The auctioneer states that each lot will start at an opening bid, after which bidders can raise their paddles or cards to participate. The auction proceeds in increments, usually 10% per jump, more or less—for example, $1,000, $1,100, $1,200...$2,000, $2,200, $2,400, and so on. In the case of rarities, you might see a run like this: $80,000, $85,000, $90,000, $95,000, $100,000, $110,000, $120,000....

Depending on the sale and the auction house, there will be rules as to wrong bids and missed bids. Generally, if you were distracted and missed bidding on a lot, and the lot has been sold to someone else, it will not be reopened. However, if you say that you were bidding on the lot and the auctioneer did not see you, and you call out before the next lot is in progress, the auctioneer may at his or her discretion reopen the lot.

If you were bidding on the wrong lot, and bought a lot you did not mean to compete for, if you call this out right away, the auctioneer may at his or her discretion reopen the lot and start the bidding anew.

During the excitement and pace of an auction sale there are many different situations. For most auction houses the decision of the auctioneer is final. Period. He or she is the referee in the game.

Sometimes an auctioneer will allow "cut bids," if used sparingly. If you are bidding on a coin and have a maximum target of $1,050, if the dealer nods to someone else at $1,000, then to you at $1,100, you may be allowed to signal a "cut"—perhaps by moving your hand sideways in the air. Your bid will be accepted at $1,050, or half of the normal advance, but no further bids will be accepted from you on that lot. If someone else bids $1,100, you've lost it. You are no longer in competition.

Often at a sale there will be auction-house employees at the front table or elsewhere, conducting various activities. One will manage the "book," advising the auctioneer for each lot what the opening bid is. The opening bid is either a reserve, a starting bid set by the auction house, a bid on behalf of the consignor below the reserve, or a mail or telephone bid. It is not unusual for bidders in the audience to leave bids on a piece of paper (called *left bids* in the art auction world, though the term is seldom heard in numismatics), as they want to keep their bids private. If they see they are being outbid, they may jump in and bid more from the floor.

As the auction progresses, the person managing the book may keep bidding—either on behalf of the consignor or, often, on behalf of a mail bidder who has posted a higher limit that might not need to be used in its entirety. Additional bidding may come from auction-house employees who are handling real-time bids coming in on the Internet or by telephone.

When a lot appears to be sold, either to a floor bidder or to the book, it often is. However, as noted earlier, it may be bought back by a consignor's reserve. The vast majority of apparent sales conducted by professional rare-coin auctioneers are real sales.

Pace of the Sale

As to the speed of the sale, this depends on the action on the floor, the number of attendees, the spirit of the auctioneer, and the strength of the mail bids already on hand. Unlike country sales of antiques or auctions in some other collectible venue, there is little in the way of huckstering, no comments such as, "*How* can you let such a bargain slip by? Come on, raise your bid!"

A seller of antiques who happens to be offering some coins may operate differently. I recall attending a few sales at the Pennypacker Auction Centre in Pennsylvania. In this venue, usually used to sell antiques, collectibles, and household goods, the auctioneer would size up a coin worth, say, $100, and start: "Who'll give me $300?" If there was no bid, then, "Who'll give me $200?" A few such comments later, "Well, who'll start this coin at $10?" Then the coin would be bid up

and sold for $100. The pace was necessarily slow.

In contrast, the typical professional rare-coin auctioneer moves quickly. The coin (or token, or medal, or piece of paper money) is usually identified only by its lot number: "Lot 652. I have a bid of a thousand dollars." Then the action progresses to $1,100, $1,200, and so on. Finally, when only one bidder paddle remains in the air, "Sold to bidder number 714 for $2,000."

As there are lot numbers, bidder numbers, and prices all in the air, you will need to pay close attention! For a sale with many bids coming from the floor, from the table, and over the telephone and the Internet, the pace might be 75 to 125 lots per hour—quite fast, less than a minute per lot on the average. For a sale with relatively few bidders and not much floor action, or a sale of specialized items, the pace can be faster, perhaps up to 200 or so.

If a popular rarity—say, an 1879 Flowing Hair Stella worth an estimated $100,000—is offered, it can sell quickly or slowly:

Faster scenario: If the auctioneer has two mail bids, one for $85,000 and the other for $100,000, he or she might open the lot up at $90,000 on behalf of the $100,000 high mail-bidder. A floor bidder might signal $95,000, after which the person running the book would now bid $100,000 on the part of the mail bidder, and, absent any other action, the auctioneer would cry, "Sold for $100,000."

Slower scenario: The house has few if any mail bids and decides to open the lot for $40,000. Dealers and collectors know a bargain when they see one. Bidding goes to $45,000, someone cuts the increment to $47,500, then the bid goes to $50,000, to $55,000, on and on, finally to $100,000—taking a significantly longer time.

If a core group of experienced collectors and dealers are bidding on material in a niche category—say, 20 bidders competing for Hard Times tokens or obsolete currency—the bidding will go much faster than if 150 people are in the room, and

Indian Head cents or commemoratives are being auctioned.

Auction Fever in the Salesroom

If a lot opens at $500, then goes rapidly to $550, then to $600, then to $650 and then is sold, this will happen in less than a minute, not giving you much time to figure. The coin may be overpriced even at the opening bid. Or, it might be worth $800, and thus $650 is a bargain. Hopefully, you've planned in advance and have made a notation in your catalog. Otherwise, you might get caught up in auction fever, and afterward realize that you either paid too much or bought a coin you did not want. This happens all the time.

At the same time, many items do not have a specific value. Recently, I competed for a $1 note issued by the Carroll County Bank of Sandwich, New Hampshire. This identical note had crossed the block for nearly $1,500 a few years back, and now was coming on the market through Smythe & Company's offering of the Herb and Martha Schingoethe Collection. Before the sale I figured I would go to $2,000 or so. Then I contemplated the matter further, and wondered where I could possibly find another one if I let this one slip by. James A. Haxby's book on obsolete currency shows a damaged example; my fine friend and fellow paper-money collector John Ferreri, with whom I traded notes in the early 1970s (and he is still at it), does not have one. Here in New Hampshire there is one in the Swasey Collection, but it is not for sale. So, I decided to pay whatever it took—setting a mental limit of $6,000, but allowing myself to change my mind if I had to go higher than that. The sale progressed well, there was a great deal of activity, and when all was said and done I was the winner at $3,500, or twice the last price it sold for. To this I added the 15% buyer's fee and the 5% I paid to my representative at the other end of the telephone, on the sale floor.

I suppose I had a case of auction fever. In any event, I set an all-time record price for this rare variety.

What would *you* have done if you had needed the note? My mindset was and still is that obsolete currency is a niche field, great rarities are apt to sell for low prices, and that for certain rarities the situation is to buy now or forever do without. With some confidence in the future of that niche market, I bravely went ahead.

The point is that I've been around the field for quite a long time, and still the value of this note and what I might do was subject to a last-minute decision.

On the other hand, if for some reason I wanted to buy a 1936 Elgin Centennial commemorative half dollar in MS-65 grade to give to a relative, the situation would have been different. I would have planned in advance, set a price limit, and perhaps allowed myself to succumb to auction fever and pay a bid or two above. However, I would not have paid double the previous sale price or triple.

For standard items that have easily determined values, the decision can be easy. However, even within popular American series there can be a lot of thought involved. Going back to the 1925-S Buffalo nickel I discussed in chapter 2 (and more ahead in chapter 17), if a *needle-sharp* MS-64 specimen came up for sale, I would be perplexed as to what to pay—for this variety is hardly ever found with Full Details (FD). I suppose if I had to play or pass at three times the latest catalog value, I would stay in the game!

One rule does not fit all, and auction fever can lead to mistakes. A coin that seemed like a terrific deal at an auction on Saturday night can give you a headache on Monday morning. It is easy to get carried away.

I recall that in one of my auctions, a rare gold coin I'd figured was worth about $4,000 attracted a lot of attention between two bidders on the sale floor. The price went up and up, and finally the coin was sold for about $20,000. After the sale the winner came up to me and asked, "Do you think this was a good coin to buy?" I said that the coin was great, but the price was a bit strong, and asked him how he figured it.

"I'm new to this, and I simply followed the bidding of another man who knew what he was doing, and paid a bit more to own the coin."

Later, the other bidder came up and asked me if he should have paid more. I asked him how he'd figured his bid, and mentioned that he had been participating at a level far above any record price I was aware of for a similar coin. He said that although he didn't collect gold coins, the description in the catalog was so enticing he wanted to own it. At the sale he watched another bidder, figured that man knew what he was doing, and bid along, before dropping out at $19,000!

The story has a happy ending. Time has a way of fixing things, and if the $20,000 buyer still has the coin, or his heirs do, it is worth about $75,000 today.

Other Ways to Bid and Buy

Most who hold public auctions of rare coins invite bidding by mail for those who cannot attend in person. Specific suggestions and guidelines are printed in the catalog, usually including the deadline for receiving such bids—typically a day before the sale commences. This is because it takes time for auction staff to read the bid sheet and enter the numbers. It is good practice to give one or more telephone numbers in case the auction house has a question and needs to reach you at some odd hour.

The policy for returns, mistakes in bidding, and the like vary from auction house to auction house, so it is best to check the terms of sale carefully.

For buyers of selected significant lots, some of the larger auction companies allow bidding by telephone, by prearrangement with their office at least a few days in advance. As staff time is precious and as telephones may be in short supply, this method is usually employed by established buyers of rarities who have a track record with the auction house.

Using an Agent. Many professional numismatists offer the service of acting as an agent. I often use this method when

buying things of interest, such as tokens, medals, and paper money. The agent, selected for his or her expertise in the field in question, acts as my eyes, examines the lots carefully, and in confidence will bid on my behalf at the sale. I typically pay 5% of the hammer price as a commission to my agents.

Time and again I have had offers from dealer friends to bid for me free of charge. However, I have always insisted on paying a commission, and I recommend that you do as well. The reasons are several. First, your agent has expenses in attending the sale. Second, the agent may pass up the opportunity to buy choice items for his or her own inventory because the bidding is for you. Third, the agent, being a floor bidder, has an absolute responsibility to pay for any and all lots purchased. This means that when the lots are delivered to you, if you find a problem, the obligation still stands. The agent cannot say to the auctioneer, "I'm sorry, I have to return the lot. My customer did not like it."

In order to bid, the agent has to establish credit with the auction house. If the billing is run though the agent, which is what I usually do, the agent must be known to the auctioneer and have an excellent reputation. Alternatively, *you* can contact an auction house directly, establish credit and make other arrangements, and state that at the sale itself John Doe will be bidding on your behalf, but that you will be completely responsible. In such an instance, the billing is directed (and the items are shipped) to you.

Afterglow

With a bit of planning and a knowledge of rarity, availability, and price levels, you will probably do very well in your auction experience. If you get carried away with auction fever and are not too far off the value mark, at least you will have the coin on Monday morning, while all of those bidding against you on Saturday night will still be looking. Most builders of great collections—and, again, such names as Eliasberg, Norweb, and Bass come to mind—set *many* all-time auction records when buying coins! I haven't done the math, but I am fairly sure that each and every "record coin" brought a very handsome profit when their collections were auctioned years later.

In the instance of my earlier-mentioned $3,500 Carroll County Bank note, which actually cost me $4,200 after buyer's fee and commission, I have the note. It is mine. I own it. No longer do I need to hope for one, to wonder when another opportunity will occur. Perhaps one never will. If one does, and supposing Smythe & Company offers it, surely the description will read something like, "In our Schingoethe Sale back in March 2005 a comparable note realized $3,500, plus buyer's fee. It should sell for more now." And it probably will. The $3,500 will be history, and perhaps it will sell for twice the price. Who knows? In the meantime, a bank note actually in my possession is worth more than the hope that another might be coming up for sale someday, but might not be, and in any event the price cannot be predicted.

Later opportunities sometimes occur. If an item did not sell because it did not meet its reserve, it might be available in a private treaty after the sale. This happens often. If you make an offer through the auction house, perhaps the owner will sell it.

Then again, an underbidder against you may decided that, after all, he or she will pay more, and may contact the auction house and authorize them to offer you a profit. Or perhaps an intending bidder was vacationing in Aruba and upon returning home found the auction catalog after the sale had ended. This person, too, may have a great desire to own the coin, yielding a profit to you.

In still other instances—and this is also a common occurrence—you might decide after the sale that you really don't want to own that 1793 copper cent, or a 1915-S Panama-Pacific octagonal $50 gold piece, or other trophy item you acquired in a feverish moment of bidding. The natural thing to do is to consign it back to the auction house. The rates are usually reason-

able, and it will be presented to an audience you already know is enthusiastic.

The Internet

The Internet is a different breed of cat. Basically, if someone is selling coins at auction on the Internet and he or she is a professional numismatist with a good reputation, all will be well. However, the vast majority of people offering numismatic items are apt to be amateur numismatists (not necessarily a problem) or people who have little knowledge about what they are offering.

My first advice is this: know your seller. Ask for identification as to real name, address, and any professional affiliations. If all seems well, fine. However, if the seller is evasive, or is located in some distant place where you or your lawyer may not have effective recourse, forget about bidding. Go to someone else.

Now, on to specifics.

The Customer is King

In recent years, particularly since about 2000, the Internet has become a very dynamic force in the numismatic market. As these words are being written, much is still in a state of flux. Problems are many, and rules are few. Buying or selling on the Internet, particularly buying, must be viewed with a great deal of caution. The future bodes well. In the *Economist*, April 2, 2005, a feature article began: "The claim that 'the customer is king' has always rung hollow. But now the digital marketplace has made it come true, says Paul Markille."

I agree. The Internet beckons with advantages in numismatics that have never existed before. An entire world of information is at your fingertips, as are more buying opportunities than can be found at all coin conventions held this year *combined*.

However, the scenario is just beginning. Rules and regulations, codes and practices, are ever evolving. Perhaps it's like having been involved in railroading in the 1830s— unbridled expansion, accidents aplenty, profit opportunities galore, and saints and sinners all taking part.

Authenticity

Numismatic Items. There are many advantages to the Internet, but some caveats are in order first.

Authenticity can be a huge problem on the Internet, and has been in recent times, as I noted in chapter 14. In 2005 Beth Deisher and the staff of *Coin World* investigated certain Siamese numismatic items offered by a leading Internet auction site, and found that the vast majority of the pieces were out-and-out fakes. United States trade dollars, "1804" silver dollars, and the like are often presented for sale on the Internet, but the majority of these have been forgeries.

The problems are not limited to coins, but extend to tokens, medals, and paper money as well. It is not particularly unusual for someone to make a photocopy of a currency note, usually a colonial or obsolete original in order to avoid federal counterfeiting laws, and to offer it on the Internet—perhaps simply with a picture. Nearly always, the sellers do not identify themselves as being knowledgeable numismatists, nor are they members of the PNG or the Professional Currency Dealers Association. Instead, they are private individuals, antique shops, and others. The usual presentation is to simply picture an item, suggest that it may be of great worth, but position the seller as simply being an antique dealer, or someone handling an estate, or someone who has come across the property of a long-deceased relative, and who is simply presenting a potential treasure for whatever bids may come in.

In early 2005 David M. Sundman saw an Internet offering for a rare colonial note. The picture looked good at first glance, and when he inspected the illustration more closely, it appeared to be genuine. However, Dave found it was a fake. He sent this message: "I am certain you realize this is a modern reproduction. You should describe it as such."

Back came this reply: "I believe I stated I did not know about this, and it would be sold *as is*. I appreciate your information."

The scam continued.

In *Coin World*, Beth Deisher pointed out that hosts of Internet auction sites—including the biggest names in the business—are lax in not eliminating sellers of fakes. I suppose the revenue that certain sellers provide to the Internet hosts supersedes any concern the hosts might have for buyers who are fleeced.

It is very common on the Internet for sellers to post items for sale that are either questionable or are obvious fakes, and hide behind such phrases as "I don't know anything about coins, and I am selling this as-is. I don't know if it is real," or, "This early copper coin came into my antique shop with a bunch of old books. I don't know what it is, but here is a picture."

Dave Sundman persistently tells such people that they are offering fakes, if this can be determined. He has found that sellers continue posting fakes, believing that offering items as-is, or saying that they are not experts, excuses them from any moral or ethical obligations.

With paper money it seems to be popular to make photocopies of real items and offer the copies for sale, without comment. Or, there might be some misleading notation such as "a modern impression," which does not say much—is it a modern reprint from original plates, or is it fresh off a copying machine? The proprietors of *Linn's Stamp Weekly* sent out a mailing some time ago about the dangers of buying stamps on the Internet. It seems that a famous 1918 twenty-four-cent airmail "Jenny" invert was offered, many bids were received, and it sold for just a few thousand dollars—far less than the more than $100,000 that might be normal. However, the "stamp" was a photocopy and worth nothing!

While the desire to buy bargains seems to be ingrained in human beings, the number of true bargains I have ever heard of anyone finding on the Internet is *far* less than the fictitious value of fakes offered or implied as being genuine. Be careful!

As of this writing, it seems to be the practice for Internet auction-site hosts to allow sellers of fakes continue their business merrily, especially if they are big sellers who have racked up a lot of business. This confirms the experiences of David Sundman, Beth Deisher, and others who have taken the time to investigate these frauds. To be sure, a given fake might be removed, but another one is soon offered by the same person.

The presentation of a coin in a slab, even by one of the leading services, is not necessarily an assurance, either. People have made many forgeries of slabs, by constructing the entire holder from scratch—new plastic, new inserts, new everything, but with the addition of coins that are significantly below the values listed on the slabs. In still other instances, photographs of genuine, certified coins posted by legitimate dealers have been copied and offered at auction by people who do not have the coins.

Someday, perhaps an organization of ethical sellers of numismatic items will form a place on the Internet that will serve as a central clearinghouse for fakes and frauds. In the meantime, your best protection is simply to buy coins on the Internet that are offered by established numismatic sellers—members of the Professional Numismatists Guild, the Professional Currency Dealers Association, the International Association of Professional Numismatists, and so on. The PNG and the PCDA would, I am sure, help any motivated Internet host draft a code of ethical conduct. Trouble is, at the moment most hosts don't care!

Meanwhile, a cautionary tale—one of several improbable-but-true stories I could mention, this one being another experience related by David Sundman:

> About a year ago, Littleton Coin VP of Marketing Jeffrey Marsh was contacted by the "buyer" of a specimen of Yap stone money sold on the most familiar site in the Internet auction business. This person had not received the item, for which he'd paid more than $5,000. The "fraudster" had stolen an image from the Littleton Coin Company web site: a photograph of me at our headquarters, standing next to a carved stone I have from the Pacific island of Yap, chosen to be representative of interesting items used as money around the world.

> While the person who stole the image did not mention me or Littleton by name, I am pretty well known, and knowledgeable numismatists who were seeking an example of this rarity could easily assume that this was, indeed, my Yap stone coming up for sale, seemingly with my permission. The Sundman/Littleton connection was a nice pedigree or confirmation of authenticity.

> Later, the FBI contacted us to let us know they were investigating this fraud. I don't know if the hapless Internet buyer has received any of his $5,000 back. Several months later, I saw Ken Hallenbeck, who originally sold me the stone from his collection, and he said, "Did you sell your Yap stone recently?" Ken had seen the Internet listing—with me standing next to my Yap stone!

The lesson to the person who "bought" it on this extremely popular Internet site and to everyone else: make sure the item really exists. These days, with digital images and digital auction sites, not everything is always what it seems—images can be stolen easily. It would be more obvious, but not necessarily different in concept, if someone posted an image of the Brooklyn Bridge and offered it for sale!

To paraphrase John Ruskin, "The bitter taste of buying a fake lasts much longer than the sweet taste of getting a bargain."

It's your money, and you can spend it as you wish. However, I do have a vested interest, in that someone burned badly in an Internet transaction—and there have been *many* victims—is apt to leave numismatics forever. This is a loss for everyone in the hobby.

Vendors. A few more caveats (sorry about that, but these situations on the Internet are real, and they deserve your attention): first of all, most listings consist of illustrations accompanied by a brief description. Sometimes a starting bid is given. However, there seem to be few rules or procedures as to what happens during the bidding process.

Not so long ago, a leading numismatic dealer set up several coded bidder accounts, a couple of which seemed to refer to me, with parts of my name or address in the title, although the individual happened to be located in a distant state. Several people thought that I was bidding eagerly on items posted on the Internet. Doug Plasencia of the ANR staff conducted a private investigation and found out the identity of the person. I protested to that individual, and received a letter of apology. Perhaps I should have taken the matter further.

In another instance, a consignor to an Internet sale posted a reserve of $1,000 on the items sent to the firm conducting the listing. This was a perfectly normal thing to do, as consignors often set reserves.

However, the seller opened the bidding on this coin at a very low price, about $150, after which there was a great flurry of bidding activity—lots of action! Then, at the last minute, a bid of $1,000 was posted. The consignor did not watch the action as it occurred, but checked in toward the end, to find that his piece had attracted many bids and was now standing at $1,000—which, unfortunately, was simply the reserve, dropped in by the seller at the last minute. No real bid for $1,000 had been received.

He asked me to check into it, and I did. I found out that this particular seller's procedure was to lowball the opening bid to attract a great many bidders, so it would look like there was a mad scramble to acquire this piece. True, if the item had been started at $950 to begin with it might have died; starting it at a low figure seemed to indicate there was a lot of interest! This same technique is often used to lowball starting bids in a regular auction salesroom, to stir up excitement and interest. Shill bidding is very common on the Internet, less so in public auction sales held by established numismatic professionals.

First and foremost, a coin, token, medal, or piece of paper money is what it is, noth-

ing more or nothing less. A fake coin is a fake coin, whether it is on the Internet, in a coin shop, in a dealer's stock, or in your own collection. Similarly, a coin is in a particular grade. If an expert would call it MS-60, someone listing it on the Internet as a superb gem MS-67 cannot transmute it into that grade. It is still MS-60. More enticingly, if someone says, "Looks like a superb gem to me," this is probably legal enough to do, as everyone can have an opinion. It could be that some yokel really thinks a coin worn nearly flat is a "superb gem." However, the coin is still low grade.

There are a lot of offers on the Internet for "Rolex" watches for under $100 each, except that they are junk watches that never saw the Rolex factory. So it is with many coin offers, too. They have as much validity as that $1 million lottery prize that is waiting in your name in Europe, or the $5,000,000 waiting to be sent to you when you help bring to the United States the $100,000,000 now held by the third cousin of a deceased African dictator!

What to do? If the seller is not an established professional, the best thing to do is to ask around. In all instances, it is easier not to buy a questionable item than to get your money back once an item is found to be less than satisfactory.

Coins certified by the *leading* grading services can offer an assurance, especially if a sharp photograph gives you other information, such as the color and appearance of the surface, elements of sharp or weak strike, and more. This is probably the most satisfactory way to go. Why doesn't everyone do this? Simply because the lure of finding a bargain is out there—and if someone appears out of nowhere and offers what seems to be a rare coin, that claim will attract a lot of attention.

Bidding Strategies

Assuming you've assured yourself that the Internet auctioneer is knowledgeable and the items are genuine, it's time to think about bidding.

Typically, items are posted in advance on the Internet, with the closing several days ahead or even a week (common on eBay) or more in advance. For a given coin, the seller may start out with a nominal bid, as no mail bids or backup bids are on hand. If the sale closes a week from now, you can watch the bids progress day by day, from a start of, say, $50, jumping to $140 to bidder Z, then to $155 to bidder Q, then a couple of days later to $456 to bidder A.

Unless you cannot be at your computer keyboard in the closing minutes of the sale, I suggest that you not bid in advance. To do so just makes your bid a target. Suppose that the coin mentioned in the above paragraph is worth $800 to you. If you bid $800 right away, someone else might outbid you and get it for $850. Instead, if you let a sleeping dog lie, and quietly watch the action, the coin might creep up to, say, $600 and stay there a while. Then, *at the last instant*, you send in your bid of $800— just a few seconds before the closing (the deadline for which is often stated in hours, minutes, and seconds). This is called "sniping" by those who do it. No one can beat your bid, and if the item is still at $600 when you bid on it, you will get it at a nominal percentage advance.

Another strategy is to keep mum about items of interest. If someone in Boise, Idaho, posts a rare National Bank note for sale, and you want to buy it, keep the matter quiet. Otherwise, you will stir up attention, and others will bid against you—and you'll possibly lose it.

On some sites, the identity of competitors in an auction is listed on the screen. If someone makes up a cute name, say, Frogmoor-Tadpole, and uses it, in some instances other bidders can check on Frogmoor-Tadpole and find that he is a heavy hitter—someone who is willing to spend a lot of money for desired items. The vendor may then engage in shill bidding against you. Ways around this include changing your bidder identification regularly, or having multiple bidder identities, or having a friend bid for you. I see no point at all to cast yourself as a big bidder or well-moneyed buyer when bidding on the Internet.

When searching for items of interest, explore using different keywords. A knowledgeable numismatist might list a piece of currency as "Series of 1880 $10 Silver Certificate, Friedberg-286, crisp Uncirculated-63. Exceedingly rare."

This is fine and proper, and if I searched for "Silver Certificate" I would locate it right away, or would find it among a few dozen other listings for various different Silver Certificate varieties. If I entered "Friedberg" I might also narrow my search and eventually find it. Ditto if I entered in "Series of 1880." A knowledgeable collector might try all of these.

However, on frequent occasions sellers do not identify their items correctly. If a bank cashier in Camp Springs, Kentucky, found such a note in an old safe and decided to offer it, a reasonable description might be "$10 bill with 'Ten Silver Dollars' lettered on the face and a picture of Robert Morris, and with 'Silver' lettered on the back. In very nice shape, a few folds, but bright."

Numismatists might miss such a listing entirely. Hardly anyone would type "Robert Morris" into a search engine, even though his portrait and name are on the face of the note. Probably, a search for "$10" would yield countless results of things priced at $10, but not at all numismatic. "Silver dollars" would also yield so many results as to be a waste of time.

In a situation such as this, for a note worth many thousands of dollars, someone might get lucky, come across the listing by accident, and score a home run. While you may never find anything as valuable as this, by varying the key phrases in your search, you may find things overlooked by mainstream buyers. Another good technique is to alert your friends of your special interests, and they will let you know if they see something while browsing through listings. I've found that nearly all Internet pals/correspondents are very eager to help!

The Internet is growing—and growing fast. We'll all be a part of its development as it revolutionizes the way we do things.

CHAPTER SIXTEEN

COLLECTING COPPER AND BRONZE COINS

A well-conducted hobby is a necessary auxiliary to every man's business or profession. To the businessman, the professional man, the man who does the hardest kind of labor, the possession of a hobby is a safety valve by which he eases the strain and pressure brought to bear upon the various parts of the body. To the man who spends a stated number of hours each day in the pursuit of his profession or trade, a few minutes, or hours, spent in a different line of thought, will rest, as nothing else will, the various nerve centers which are soon run down by long continued use.

—Arthur B. Coover, September 1908

Copper Half Cents (1793–1857)

Copper half cents, minted from 1793 to 1857 (but not continuously), are fascinating to collect. As an investment, they have performed superbly over a long period of years. However, such investment success has gone to collectors who have studied and appreciated the series. Few outside investors have been involved.

Collecting half cents can be done in several ways: by basic type, by date and major variety, and by die variety.

Design Types of Half Cents

1793, Liberty Cap, Head Facing Left— First year of issue. A classic, rare in all grades, the most elusive of the types. When found, examples are usually attractive, although on some the inscription HALF / CENT is weak.

1794, Liberty Cap, Large Head Facing Right—Scarcer than generally appreciated, especially if in VF or better and with good eye appeal. Most are dark and/or on rough planchets.

1795 to 1797, Liberty Cap, Small Head Facing Right—The 1795 half cents are often fairly well struck and on nice planchets, often with rich brown surfaces. The two varieties of 1796 are rarities. Half cents of 1797 are very difficult to find choice.

1800 to 1808, Draped Bust—Usually very attractive, except for the rare 1802, which is typically on a rough planchet. Some of 1807 and 1808 are dark and/or rough. A few hundred 1800 and 1806 half cents exist from old-time hoards. Many die varieties exist for 1804 half cents.

1809 to 1836, Classic Head—Early issues (1809–1811) tend to be weakly struck, while later dates are usually sharp. Some Mint State coins from hoards exist for dates in the 1820s and 1830s, usually with mint orange color and spotted. Half cents of 1831 and 1836 are rarities.

1840 to 1857, Braided Hair—Circulation strikes were made of 1849 Large Date and of 1850, 1851, and 1853 to 1857. Varieties from 1840 to 1848, plus 1849 Small Date and 1852, were made only in Proof finish and are rare. Mint State coins from small hoards exist of 1854 to 1856 and usually have much mint orange with some flecks and spots; these can be very attractive.

Each of these types is readily collectible, although the 1793 is quite rare and expen-

A Mint State half cent of 1793 (die variety Breen-4, Cohen 4). This type, with Miss Liberty facing left and with cap and pole, was made only in 1793. The beaded border is a distinctive touch and was discontinued afterward, possibly because it weakened the dies near the edges. A beaded border was also used on the 1793 Wreath and Liberty Cap cents.

The 1796 is the rarest regular (non-Proof) date in the half cent series. Two varieties were made, one with a pole to the liberty cap (as here) and the other lacking the pole. Note that the coin is struck slightly off center, making the dentils (toothlike projections at the rims) strong on one side and light on the other. (Variety Breen-2, Cohen 2)

The famous (but not rare) 1804 half cent with "Spiked Chin." A bolt or other stray piece of metal fell onto the die, damaging it and causing a thornlike spike to protrude from Miss Liberty's chin (variety Breen-7, Cohen 7). This year saw the production of 1,055,312 half cents, a record quantity up to this point (later exceeded only by the 1,154,172 mintage for 1809). Many different obverse and reverse dies were used. Such varieties are widely collected today.

sive. Not everyone sets aside 1794 as a distinct type, and some group it with the 1795 to 1797 simply to have a Liberty Cap Facing Right style. The other types are collectible easily enough, including in Mint State. Market prices have been steady and stable, immune to price cycles, as half cents have been shunned by most investors. However, for careful *collectors*, half cents of hand-picked quality have done extremely well over the years.

Interesting Dates and Varieties

The dies for early half cents were cut by hand, with the use of individual punches for letters, numerals, and design elements. Accordingly, coins struck from these dies have different features, some of them dramatic. Planchet quality also varies. Half cents of 1793 are apt to be of light brown copper, while those of 1794 are generally dark and rough.

Half cents of 1795 occur in several varieties, including with lettered or plain edge, and with or without pole to the liberty cap. The last was the result of a die's being reground (*relapped* is the numismatic term) to remove surface irregularities, in the process of which the pole was removed.

The 1796 half cents of two varieties are the best-known rarities of the denomination. The first has no pole to the liberty cap, the result of an engraving error—the die maker simply forgot to include it! Only

a few dozen are known. The second, with pole to cap, is also rare, but perhaps 100 to 200 exist. Most 1796 half cents are in low grades. Half cents of 1797, though not rare as a date, might as well have been made on a different planet—generally, the striking is poor, details are lacking, and the planchets are dark and rough. Of course, such rusticity contributes to the charm of these early issues. One variety of this year, quite rare, has a so-called gripped edge, with unusual markings of an unexplained nature. Another has a lettered edge—quite curious, as this style was supposed to have been discontinued in 1795.

If you're new to numismatics, you might think the word *rustic* is merely a euphemism for *poor quality*. However, it isn't—and I leave it up to you, if you care to explore the matter, to interview a few collectors of half cents (or, for that matter, of the "rustic" Vermont copper coins discussed in chapter 4) and see what you learn.

Draped Bust half cents, 1800 to 1808, are readily available, except for 1802. Half cents of that year are all scarce, and the variety with the so-called reverse of 1800 (with just one leaf at each side of the wreath apex) are extremely rare. Most of this date were struck on dark, rough planchets. The Mint obtained its copper from many places, including used roofing, old boilers, and the like, and quality was apt to vary widely. Quite a few die varieties exist for 1804, a common date, and several numismatists have made a specialty of collecting and studying them.

Rarities Among Later Dates

The Classic Head half cent type, designed by John Reich, was made from 1809 to 1811, after which this denomination wasn't coined again until 1825. After then, coinage was intermittent through 1836. The half cent of 1811 is viewed as a scarce issue, a key date, but enough are around that one can be easily acquired.

One easily collected (except in Mint State) variety of 1828 has just 12 stars, the result of an engraver's not paying attention to his work. The 1831 is a rarity. Only 2,200 were made for circulation, and perhaps not even that many ever reached commerce, for examples are exceedingly rare today. Proofs were made, including restrikes (beginning in a significant way in 1859), and these, while rare, exist to the extent of 50 or more pieces and fill the demand. In 1836 Proofs were made, but no circulation strikes. Again, examples were restruck at a later time.

In 1840 the Braided Hair design was introduced, after which it was used continuously through the end of the series in 1857. Half cents were not popular in commerce, and coins of this denomination were hardly ever seen in pocket change. Curiously, at the same time, many prices were expressed with a half-cent ending, such as 12 1/2 and 37 1/2 cents, and payment was made and given out in Spanish-American one-*real* (or "bit") coins worth 12 1/2 cents.

In the Braided Hair series no issues were made for circulation until 1849, and then only 39,864 were struck (all from the Large Date obverse die). Circulation strikes were made in 1850 and 1851, and from 1853 to 1857. In the meantime, Proofs (originals and restrikes) were made of the 1840 through 1848, the 1849 Small Date, and the 1852. Generally, for each of the Proof-only dates, the population is between 50 and 200 pieces. There are die varieties among the Proofs, and some are scarcer than others. Among the 1840 to 1849 issues, the so-called originals made for inclusion in Proof sets of those particular years have large berries on the reverse, while restrikes have tiny berries. However, there are exceptions to this. Probably if just *one* date were made in Proof format and all the others were circulation strikes, that single issue would be worth tens of thousands of dollars. A comparable example would be Morgan silver dollars of 1878 to 1921, in which only one coin, the 1895 Philadelphia, was produced exclusively in Proof format. However, as there are so many, they can be daunting to collectors, and some have simply opted not to include them. This comparison may be of interest:[53]

1840 Original (large berries) Proof half cent (estimated 50 or so known)—Proof-63: $5,000 • Proof-65: $7,500.

1895 Proof Morgan silver dollar (estimated 600 to 700 known)—Proof-63: $35,000 • Proof-65: $65,000.

The engraver must have been daydreaming when making this 1828 die, for one star was omitted, creating the 12-stars variety (Breen-3, Cohen 3). These are not rare today, and thousands exist. However, relatively few are in Mint State grade as shown here.

Proof 1843 half cent, an original striking distinguished by having large berries in the wreath on the reverse (variety Breen-1a). Only a few dozen are known.

These figures are dramatic. While I believe that rare Proof half cents offer a great value for the money, at the same time, their limited popularity can hardly be compared to the widespread popularity of the Morgan silver dollar series—an important factor in the price of the 1895 Morgan dollar.

The Act of February 21, 1857, terminated the half cent. By this time the denomination was redundant, and few people had ever seen one in circulation. Mint director James Ross Snowden later (in 1860) stated that the 35,180 half cents of the last year, 1857, had been held back at the Mint and melted; but this was not true, as a few thousand are known today.

Key to Collecting Half Cents

- **Mint State coins:** Hoard coins of 1800 and 1806, selected issues of the late 1820s and early 1830s, and most varieties of the 1849 Large Date to 1857 appear with regularity on the market. Those of 1849 Large Date, 1853, and 1857 are usually toned brown, while the others can be found with varying degrees of original mint orange color.
- **Circulated coins:** Examples exist in proportion to their mintages. Generally, dates from 1793 to 1811 are seen with extensive wear. Coins of later years are usually at least VF, and for the 1850s, typically at least EF.
- **Strike quality:** Varies widely among issues of 1793 to 1811. Check specialized texts. Later dates are usually well struck with Full Details (FD).
- **Proof coins:** The Proof issues of 1831, 1836, 1840 to 1848, 1849 Small Date, and 1852 are all classic rarities, but not expensive in comparison to many other series. Proofs were made of certain other dates, including all from 1854 to 1857. Many are restrikes.
- **Key issues:** 1793, 1796 Without Pole, 1796 With Pole, 1802 with reverse of 1800, 1831, 1836, 1840 to 1848, 1849 Small Date, 1852.

- **Advice to smart buyers:** Consider starting by buying a type set. Study the series before plunging in deeply. Quality is exceedingly important, and certified holders are often of little help, but therein lies a challenge. Go through steps 1 to 4 (see chapter 2), and if a coin meets this test, be prepared to pay a strong price for it. Join the Early American Coppers Club if you like camaraderie. You'll enjoy the gossip, news, research information, and other items in print in *Penny-Wise*, the journal.
- **Selected bibliography:**

  Breen, Walter. 1983. *Walter Breen's Encyclopedia of United States Half Cents 1793–1857*. South Gate, CA.

  Cohen, Roger S., Jr. 1982. *American Half Cents: The "Little Half Sisters"* (2nd ed.).

  Manley, Ronald. 1998. *The Half Cent Die State Book: 1793–1857*.

Copper Large Cents (1793–1857): Foundation Stones of American Numismatics

Of all early United States coins, the copper cents, minted continuously from 1793 to 1857 (excepting 1815), have been the most steadily collected for the longest time. In the cradle days of the hobby, the 1850s, the disappearance of these from circulation caused many to become interested. Since that time, the passion has never faded. Generation after generation, new collectors discover the pleasures of collecting these pieces.

While few investors have plunged into early copper cents as a speculative medium, legions of dedicated numismatists have caught the fever. So far as I know, each and every dedicated collector who has bought carefully, and over a long period of time, has profited upon the sale of his or her collection. Year in and year out, while the hot coins in the market have had cyclical ups and downs, large copper cents have managed to cross the finish line as winners

The first American cent, the 1793 variety with chain reverse and with the abbreviation AMERI. (variety Sheldon-1). These images are from the *American Journal of Numismatics*, 1869, and are among the first coin photographs ever published in a numismatic periodical.

in the investment category—much like the tortoise beating the hare (the "hot" coins). However, you'd be missing out on a great deal if you bought these coins without a spirit of numismatics and history combined, for these have so much to offer in those areas.

A Type Set of Copper Large Cents

To become acquainted with the series and also to acquire some very nice coins, consider forming a type set—if not complete (for some of the earlier types are rare), then of the issues from the 1796 Draped Bust onward. The designs that a type set would comprise are listed in the next section.

Design Types of Copper Large Cents

1793, Chain AMERI. Reverse—Cents with the abbreviation AMERI. were coined in February 1793 and were the first to reach circulation. Comments were unfavorable; to one writer, Miss Liberty appeared to be "in a fright," and the 15 chain links on the reverse as an "ill omen" for a country that loved liberty. This type is very rare. Usually seen in lower grades.

1793, Chain AMERICA Reverse—As preceding, but with AMERICA spelled out in full. Some collectors of type sets combine this with the preceding and buy just one Chain cent. Rare, but more available than the preceding.

1793, Wreath Reverse—Completely new design, with different portrait of Miss Liberty, in high relief and very detailed.

An artistic triumph. Somewhat scarce, and exceedingly popular.

1793 to 1796, Liberty Cap—Produced in dozens of different dies and combinations, some of which are very interesting.

1796 to 1807, Draped Bust—The first cent type available with frequency and in generally higher grades.

1808 to 1814, Classic Head—This design, by John Reich, lasted for just a short time. Years later, in 1834, chief engraver William Kneass copied it for use on the new $2.50 and $5 gold coins.

1816 to 1835, Matron Head—Beauty is in the eye of the beholder, and Miss Liberty is either homely or else numismatically (at least) attractive. This span of years, sometimes called the middle dates, offers many interesting varieties, generally at low cost.

1836 to 1839, Matron Head Modified—Various portraits were used, the result of experimentation by Mint engraver Christian Gobrecht.

1839 to 1857, Braided Hair—A highly collectible and very popular series. Most are in higher grades, from Fine on up until about 1850, and in VF and better after that.

Forming a basic set of design types is a popular pursuit. Although the two Chain cents and the Wreath cent of 1793 are at once scarce and expensive, all of the others are easily collectible, especially in grades such as Fine to EF. Coinage was continuous from 1793 to 1857, excepting only 1815.

For a bit more challenge, one can collect copper large cents by date and overdate, the *Guide Book* giving some ideas in this regard. Even more challenging is collecting die varieties of 1793 to 1814 identified by Sheldon, or those of 1816 to 1857 identified by Newcomb (see the selected bibliography). The Early American Coppers Club, with its fascinating journal, *Penny-Wise*, has been a favorite for a long time.

1793 Wreath cent with restyled portrait of Miss Liberty. The reverse wreath is curious in that it combines olive leaves with maple leaves and sprays of berries—artistic license (variety Sheldon-11a). The vertical black streak behind the head of Miss Liberty is a planchet flaw, caused when the copper strip was rolled out. Note the beaded border, also used on 1793 half cents.

A beautiful, lustrous cent of 1820, Mint State and possibly from the famous Randall Hoard that came to light in the 1860s (variety Newcomb-2). It is believed that somewhat more than 10,000 coins were in this group, mostly dated from 1817 through 1820.

Die Differences Among Large Cents

Dies of the very early period were cut by hand, with the letters, dates, and motifs added separately. No two are alike. Some vary dramatically, while the differences between others can be subtle. On one variety of 1794 cent, the engraver forgot to put a fraction bar in 1/100, and on another can be found 94 tiny five-pointed stars—for what purpose, no one knows.

In 1869, Dr. Edward Maris created a study, *Varieties of the Copper Issues of the United States Mint in the Year 1794.* This charming work described the dies of cents and half cents, and for the former he assigned names, some of which derived from medicine and mythology: Double Chin, Sans Milling, Tilted 4, Young Head, The Coquette, Crooked 7, Pyramidal Head, Mint Marked Head, Scarred Head, Standless 4, Abrupt Hair, Severed Hairs, The Ornate, Venus Marina, Fallen 4, Short Bust, Patagonian, Nondescript, Amatory Face, Large Planchet, Marred Field, Distant 1, Shielded Hair, The Plicae (for a group of varieties), Roman Plica, and '95 Head.

Such nomenclature adds much to the numismatic interest in these early coins. Aren't you already curious as to how a "Nondescript" head differs from the pleasingly named "Amatory Face"?

In time, production at the Mint became more routine, and varieties of a given date differed less widely. For coins of the early 19th century, through 1814, a good magnifying glass is needed to tell some of the varieties apart. Large cents of later years become increasingly standard in their appearance, although there are many interesting distinctions, including overdates, large/small letters, and so on. The *Guide Book* offers a good, basic overview.

The Appeal of Early Cents

Becoming acquainted with old copper cents is not necessarily easy to do, especially if you have approached numismatics with the thought of collecting gem Mint State and Proof coins of the modern era. Early copper cents are a world apart, and well-struck gems hardly exist anywhere—a new mindset needs to be adopted with regard to these coins.

Worn copper coins have a charm of their own, as discussed in detail in Dr. William H. Sheldon's 1949 book, *Early American Cents,* the basic guide to the series. While silver and gold coins with scuffs, abrasions, and the like are of course collected, at first glance they appear *worn*, not necessarily *charming*. However, most collectors of early copper coins

One of several dozen different die combinations known of the 1794 copper cent (variety Sheldon-43). Over a long period of time the cents of this year have formed a specialty for many numismatists, ranging from Dr. Edward Maris in the early days to John W. Adams and Walter Husak in modern times.

The Lorin G. Parmelee Collection, auctioned in 1890 by the New York Coin & Stamp Company, featured many highly important copper cents, some of which are shown on Plate 6 from the catalog. Lot 671, the sixth coin on the plate, is the finest of four known of the 1793 Strawberry Leaf variety. Also on the plate are two 1787 Fugio cents (lots 663 and 664) and a 1793 half cent (678).

A lightly worn but very attractive specimen of the rare 1804 copper cent (variety Sheldon-266c). Note the die breaks on the obverse and reverse rims. The design is the Draped Bust type used from 1796 to 1807.

One of my "pet" varieties is the 1817 large copper cent, variety Newcomb-16, with 15 obverse stars instead of the correct 13. How the engraver made such a mistake is unknown, but the result was a coin of immense interest to a later generation of numismatists. Today, hundreds of examples exist, nearly all of which are in circulated grades.

The 1823 Newcomb-2 cent, perfect date (not overdate), is one of the more intriguing issues of its era. It was not until the early 21st century that the mintage figure of just 12,500 pieces was located in government financial papers—seemingly a logical explanation why coins of this year are so hard to find. The 1823 is far and away the rarest of the cents of 1816 to 1857, with no close competitor, although an overdate, 1839/6, is more elusive.

The obverse die developed problems at an early time. The illustration shows failure at the dentils at the upper left. Probably, the die was retired quickly, accounting for the low production. As to whether 12,500 represents the total mintage for coins bearing this date, the answer is unknown, as Mint production figures do not necessarily represent coins from dies bearing dates in a given year. However, probably no more than a couple thousand 1823 cents exist today, most of which are well worn, Good-4 to VG-8 or so, and were probably plucked out of circulation in the 1850s. No more than 10 actual Mint State pieces are known, and just a few dozen at the AU level.

would agree that lightly worn cents, half cents, and related items look quite nice with brown patina, and, in fact, many would have them no other way. This is difficult to explain in print, but the appeal is there and has lasted a long time. It would be hard to improve on what Sheldon had to say about this in *Penny Whimsy* in 1958:[54]

> Old copper, like beauty, appears to possess a certain intrinsic quality or charm which for many people is irresistible. An experienced dealer in American numismatic materials recently wrote as follows: "Sooner or later, if a collector stays at the business long enough, it is three to one his interest in all the other series will flag and he will focus his attention on the early cents."
>
> Gold, silver, and even bronze appear to be very much the same wherever you see them. Coins made of these metals become "old money" and "interesting," like the stuff seen in museums, but copper seems to possess an almost living warmth and a personality not encountered in any other metal. The big cent is something more than old money. Look at a handful of the cents dated before 1815, when they contained relatively pure copper. You see rich shades of green, red, brown, yellow, and even deep ebony; together with blending of these not elsewhere matched in nature save perhaps in autumn leaves. If the light is good (direct sunlight is preferable) you will possibly observe that no two of the coins are of quite the same color.

Aspects of Price and Availability

As most large cents were made in quantity, they are quite affordable today. Often collectors will further specialize beyond basic dates and overdates or die varieties, and concentrate on a particular year-segment.

So-called middle-date cents (1816–1835, with an extension to 1839) are generally affordable and widely available, and yet some are elusive enough that it's a great challenge to acquire certain varieties. For my money, a set of basic varieties as listed in the *Guide Book* would do just fine, but if you like to examine tiny differences under high magnification, many other die varieties beckon.

Braided Hair cents of the later years, 1839 through 1857, are also interesting to collect as a separate series, with not a rarity or impossible piece in sight. A nicely matched collection in a given grade, such as VF-20, EF-45, or MS-60 Brown, can be a joy to view. Die varieties for these later cents are sometimes almost impossible to discern, at least for me—with the main differences being in the placement of the date figures. No longer can much be found in the way of large and small date-numerals for the same year, large and small letters, and so on, but there are exceptions. However, some specialists enjoy the series, and as dies are often difficult to tell from each other, many rare or even unlisted varieties can be found for no more than a regular coin would cost. In contrast, a rare die variety of 1794 would no doubt be identified as such by the seller and may cost dozens of times more than a common variety of the same year.

A lot of value for your money can be had if you carefully select coins of the later years, 1816 through 1857, in such grades as EF, AU, and various numbers attached to BN (for brown). Many of these are downright cheap! In contrast, MS-65 RD (for red) coins can be very expensive and also a bit tricky (most are flecked or spotted, and quite a few have been brightened by dipping).

Grading Copper Large Cents

There are quite a few schools of thought concerning the grading of copper cents. So-called EAC grading (from the Early American Coppers Club) tends to be quite tight and conservative in comparison to the typical coin certification. Accordingly, a piece that is not certified, but is graded by an EAC member and specifically stated as EAC graded, might be called AU-55, but the exact same coin, if certified by a popular service, might be MS-63. As might be expected, I have seen quite a few instances in which numismatists would enjoy *buying* coins by EAC grades and then, when they are consigned to auction, having them certified at higher levels! Such is human nature.

In 1839 several different portrait varieties were made by engraver Christian Gobrecht. This one has been designated the Booby Head variety (Newcomb-5), a nickname assigned in the 1850s. Among other varieties of 1839 are the Head of 1838, Silly Head, and Head of 1840 (or Petite Head).

A lustrous Mint State cent of 1848 (variety Newcomb-41). The striking is generally excellent on the obverse and reverse (note the hair details in the portrait and the leaves in the wreath), but there is some lightness at the star centers.

The coins themselves are subject to wide variations in planchet quality, striking, and the like. Accordingly, certification needs to be taken with a grain of salt, as always, but in the instance of copper cents with special care. Use the information on such holders as a starting point, study each piece through magnification, look for eye appeal, and the like. As time goes on, more and more coins will be certified, and this advice will become even more important.

Quite a bit of literature on large copper cents is available, not only in standard books (see the selected bibliography), but in studies from the past (sometimes concentrating on just a few dates), interesting old auction catalogs, 19th-century copies of the *American Journal of Numismatics*, and more. A lot of the fun of collecting is expressed in the pages of *Penny-Wise* by reader articles and contributions.

If intellectual curiosity, an enjoyment of history, the fun of seeking quality coins from among many that are anything but, and the desire for a numismatic challenge all come together in your mind, copper large cents are well worth investigating.

Key to Collecting Copper Large Cents

- **Mint State coins:** A few hundred cents of 1796 are from the Nichols Find (a small hoard), and Mint State pieces of 1816 to 1820, particularly 1818 and 1820, are from the most famous large-cent discovery of all time, the fabulous Randall Hoard, consisting of more than 10,000 pieces (estimated) and marketed to collectors in the late 19th century. Most are widely distributed by now. Beyond that, copper cents of much later years (1850–1856) are often seen with bright mint orange color, some from modest hoards of years ago.

- **Circulated coins:** Most cents can be attractive even if worn considerably, down to Good-4 or VG-8. Surface quality and eye appeal are the key factors no matter what the numerical grade. Cents of the middle and later dates (1816–1857) in EF or AU grade can be very attractive and at the same time quite reasonably priced on the market. I highly recommend a set of basic *Guide Book*–listed varieties of these years, in such grades, as an interesting pursuit.

- **Strike quality:** Striking varies considerably over the entire range of copper large cents. Consult reference books for particulars. Points to check on the obverse include star centers, hair details, and dentils; and, on the reverse, the highest parts of the leaves and the dentils.

- **Proof coins:** Proofs were made of most dates after about 1816, but those from 1854 to 1857 are the only years seen with regularity, and they are rare. Quite a few early "Proofs" are not Proofs, in my opinion. Be careful, and do not buy any Proof without consulting a disinterested expert.

- **Key issues:** The 1793 Chain AMERI., 1793 Chain AMERICA, 1793 Wreath, 1793 Strawberry Leaf (a variety of the 1793 Wreath), 1793 Liberty Cap, 1799/8, 1799, and 1804 are the keys among the earlier dates, although many other die varieties are rare. Among later issues, the rarest by far is 1823, but such dates as 1821 and 1824/2 are elusive. The 1839/6 overdate is rare.

- **Advice to smart buyers:** Same as for collecting copper half cents.

- **Selected bibliography:**

Breen, Walter H. 2001. *Walter Breen's Encyclopedia of Early United States Cents 1793–1814*. Wolfeboro, NH.

Grellman, J.R. 2002. *Attribution Guide for United States Large Cents 1840–1857* (3rd ed.). Bloomington, MN.

Newcomb, Howard R. 1985. *United States Copper Cents 1816–1857* (3rd ed.). New York, NY. (original work published 1944; reprinted 1963, 1985)

Noyes, William C. 1991. *United States Large Cents 1793–1814*. Bloomington, MN.

Noyes, William C. 1991. *United States Large Cents 1816–1839*. Bloomington, MN.

Penny-Wise (official publication of Early American Coppers, Inc.)

Sheldon, William H. 1949. *Early American Cents*.

Sheldon, William H. 1976. *Penny Whimsy*. New York, NY. (original work published 1958; reprinted 1965, 1976)

Wright, John D. 1992. *The Cent Book 1816–1839*. Bloomington, MN.

Copper Small Cents
Flying Eagle Cents (1856–1858)

Flying Eagle cents, minted as patterns in 1856 and as regular issues in 1857 and 1858, are one of the shortest-lived of all American coin designs. These coins have been of enduring popularity ever since May 24, 1857, the first day of release, when hundreds of people stood in line at the Mint to buy these sparkling little pieces.

The Flying Eagle cent series is short and sweet. Generally, one of each major variety is collected, namely the pattern 1856 and the regular 1857, 1858/7 overdate, and two varieties (Large Letters and Small Letters) of 1858. Struck in copper-nickel alloy (88% copper, 12% nickel), these coins have a golden-yellow color and a very hard surface. In fact, the alloy was sufficiently hard that such pieces were difficult to strike.

Somewhat fewer than a thousand 1856 Flying Eagle cents were originally made in that year and in early 1857 to illustrate

The 1856 Flying Eagle cent was made as a pattern in 1856 and early 1857 (from 1856 dies) for distribution to congressmen, newspaper editors, and others, to acquaint them with the new design. Soon, they became popular with numismatists, and in spring 1859 restrikes were first made from Proof dies. Today this is one of the most famous 19th-century rarities.

the new small cent, a great change from the familiar "large" copper cent. They were given to congressmen, sent with an accompanying illustration to newspaper editors, and distributed to others of influence. The Mint sought to avoid any surprise or unfavorable publicity. The coin was successful for all intents and purposes. However, at the Mint there was difficulty in having them strike up properly. When the obverse and reverse dies were in the press, the head and tail of the eagle were opposite heavy areas of the "agricultural wreath," and the metal could not flow effectively in both directions. Many coins showed weak details.

In 1858 the Mint produced patterns for a new cent. Three basic types of obverse were used: the regular Flying Eagle then in service, a new small or "skinny" eagle, and an Indian head. Four basic reverses—the "agricultural wreath," the olive wreath, the oak wreath, and the oak wreath with ornamented shield—were combined with these dies, yielding 12 different varieties total. These proved very popular with collectors, and it's likely that dozens of sets were sold.

In 1859 the Indian Head obverse and laurel wreath reverse were chosen, and the Flying Eagle cent design came to an end.

Collector Interest in Flying Eagle Cents

By early 1859 there was strong collector interest in Flying Eagle cents. In particular, the rare pattern 1856 was in demand, but, seemingly, specimens were few and far between. Director James Ross Snowden soon put in place an extensive but secret program to restrike these and other scarce and rare coins to exchange with collectors for pieces needed in the Mint Cabinet, particularly Washington tokens and medals, which Snowden was collecting with a passion. However, the profit motive arose, and before long these pieces were sold for cash to favored dealers and collectors. No records were kept, but it's likely that about 2,000 of the 1856 Flying Eagle cents were restruck, all with a mirror Proof finish unlike that of the originals, which were circulation strikes. In the same year these had a market value of $1 each—not much by today's terms, but a significant amount at the time (in the late 1850s, a dollar was more or less equivalent to a day's wage).

Today, the demand for 1856 Flying Eagle cents is so fierce and the fame so great that specimens cost thousands of dollars, with a gem Proof crossing the $20,000 line. Choice pieces have always been in the limelight, and if you can afford one, such a piece is well worth owning. Investment-wise, they have performed spectacularly over a long period of time and will probably continue to do so. Most 1856 cents are well struck, but eye appeal can vary widely.

The 1858/7 is rather scarce in all grades, especially in Mint State. This variety was unknown until the late 19th century. Some numismatists opt not to include it in their sets. The regular 1857 cent and those of 1858 are available in most grades, although striking and eye appeal can vary. Most often, Flying Eagle cents are collected in connection with a set of Indian Head cents of 1859 to 1909.

Key to Collecting Flying Eagle Cents

- **Mint State coins:** True Mint State examples are rare for 1856 (most were struck as Proofs, many of which have been incorrectly labeled "Mint State") and seldom seen for 1858/7, but available easily enough for 1857 and both varieties of 1858.

- **Circulated coins:** Available for each of the major varieties.

- **Strike quality:** Varies, especially on cents of 1857 and 1858. Points to check for sharpness include the head and tail of the eagle and the left and right sides of the reverse wreath. Full Details (FD; see chapter 8 for information) coins exist for all—and it is up to you to find them! The 1858/7 occurs with the tip of the 7 visible, and also in a later state with this not visible or very weak; buy one with the feature well defined.

- **Proof coins:** The 1856 is plentiful (rare as a *date* in the context of small cents, but well over 1,000 Proofs exist), the 1857 is exceedingly rare and seems to have been overlooked by collectors in its time, and both varieties of the 1858 are rare.

- **Key issues:** 1856, 1858/7.

- **Advice to smart buyers:** Seek problem-free coins without spots or flecks. Mint State coins should be brilliant or very delicately toned and have deep, rich luster and a lot of "life." Not many do, and you will need to search. Select pieces with sharp details. Eye appeal can vary greatly. Finding truly choice Flying Eagle cents is an art, an aspect of which most buyers are unaware. Certification holders don't help. Be fussy, and when time comes to sell, buyers will beat a path to your door!

- **Selected bibliography:**
  Snow, Richard. 1992. *Flying Eagle and Indian Cents.* Tucson, AZ.

  Steve, Larry, and Kevin Flynn. 1995. *Flying Eagle and Indian Cent Die Varieties.* Jarrettville, MD.

Indian Head Cents (1859–1909): An American Favorite

For a long time, the building of a set of dates of Indian Head cents—1859 to 1909, plus the two mintmarks at the tail end of the series, 1908-S and 1909-S—has been a popular pursuit. All of the basic date and mintmark varieties are collectible, although some are scarcer than others. The most famous coin is the low-mintage 1877. Certain other varieties, such as 1864 with the letter L (for engraver James B. Longacre) on the ribbon, 1871, 1872, and 1909-S, are elusive as well.

The Indian Head motif is unusual in that it features a female face, Miss Liberty, wearing a war bonnet of the type used by *male* Native Americans. Be that as it may, the motif is well done and nearly everyone considers it to be attractive.

The series divides itself neatly into three types, which can be collected separately as part of a type set, or perhaps as a beginning to acquaint yourself with the series, after which you can fill in the others. The types are as follows.

Design Types of Indian Head Cents

1859, Indian Head, Laurel Wreath—Made of the same alloy (88% copper, 12% nickel) as the copper-nickel Flying Eagle cent. The laurel-wreath reverse was used only this year.

1860 to 1864, Indian Head, Oak Wreath (Copper-Nickel)—New Indian Head obverse with a reverse depicting an oak wreath and shield, the design used for the rest of the series.

1864 to 1909, Indian Head, Oak Wreath (Bronze)—Same design as the previous, but struck on a thin bronze planchet.

There are so few types, and these are so easy to find, that I've never met anyone making such a collection a focus. However, if you are new to the field of Indian Head cents, this is a good way to start. Then, you can fill in dates and varieties of interest.

The copper-nickel issues in the early part of the series—the 1859 with laurel wreath reverse and the 1860 through 1864 with oak wreath and shield—are similar to Flying Eagle cents in that many are lightly struck (in this case, the tips of the headdress feathers, the diamonds on the ribbon, and, on the reverse, the central design). More-over, many coins in Mint State (and Proofs as well) are spotted, or are dull from repeated cleaning. Connoisseurship is the order of the day if you want to build a fine collection, and it will take time to do this.

Bronze Indian Head Cents. The Act of April 3, 1864, discontinued the copper-nickel alloy for cents, and authorized mintage of cents and two-cent pieces in "French bronze," an alloy consisting of 95% copper and 5% tin and zinc. Later in 1864, a small modification was made by adding the tiny letter L, for Longacre, to the ribbon, creating a separate variety. The L was continued on all later issues through 1909.

Similar to earlier copper large cents, bronze Indian Head cents can be quite attractive in just about any grade, provided care is given to selecting planchets that are not rough and coins that have nice eye appeal. No doubt had Dr. Sheldon written about Indian Head cents, he could have declaimed eloquently about different shades of toning like autumn leaves. Generally, planchet quality is high, but eye appeal can be another thing entirely. Among higher-grade circulated coins (from Fine to AU and, in the BN category, MS-60 BN and up), *most* have decent eye appeal. However, the going gets treacherous among coins with RB (red and brown) and RD (red) surfaces, and some real dogs are on the market. If I were endeavoring to assemble a set of MS-65 or -66 (or Proof-65 or -66) Indian Head cents, I imagine that I would have to inspect 10 to 20 or more

This 1862 Proof copper-nickel Indian Head cent exhibits sharply struck features. Those made for circulation are usually seen with lightness in some areas. In spring 1864 the copper-nickel alloy was discontinued in favor of the easier-to-strike bronze alloy.

A bronze Indian Head cent of 1864. Made in large quantities, these helped alleviate a coin shortage that had prevailed since 1862.

coins of each date before I found one that I liked. Proofs are especially difficult to find with good eye appeal. If you simply buy 65 holders marked RD, you can complete a full set in a month. If you are fussy and you demand good eye appeal and no spots or staining, get set to spend several years!

Rick Snow, a long-time specialist in Indian Head cents, came up with the idea of taking certified coins, inspecting them, and *only if they passed his approval*, specifically noting them as being desirable for specialists to collect. Of course, beauty is in the eye of the beholder, and no one person can predict what everyone else might like.

To reiterate, as a general rule I suggest that you completely avoid any Indian Head cent that has spotting or staining, or that lacks eye appeal. To me, the color is not as important as the quality (although not everyone would agree).

From an investment viewpoint, such attention will pay rich rewards. A truly superb collection that matches high grading-numbers with the much more difficult aspect of *quality* will create a sensation on the auction market, translating nicely to your bottom line.

Key to Collecting Indian Head Cents

- **Mint State coins:** Generally available for copper-nickel issues from 1859 through 1864, bronze issues of the 1860s, and all dates after 1878, including the mintmarks. *Quality* is a completely separate aspect and must be considered on its own. Generally, the copper-nickel coins have more pleasing surfaces and are easier to obtain than those in bronze, although many are dull or lifeless. As might be expected, throughout the series the issues with higher mintages are generally easier to find than lower-mintage issues.

- **Circulated coins:** Available for all issues, and fairly inexpensively, except for the key dates. Pick and choose, as quality varies widely.

- **Strike quality:** Copper-nickel cents of 1859 to 1864 are apt to be lightly struck in certain areas, most particularly the tips of the feathers on the obverse and certain aspects of the wreath on the reverse. Those of 1862 and 1863 are usually seen with weakness, and the 1864 nearly always is, but few buyers are aware of this (once again, giving you an advantage). Bronze Indian Head cents of 1864 through 1909 are generally better struck, but there are exceptions.

- **Proof coins:** Proofs were made of all dates from 1859 to 1909, and are readily collectible. Those 1864 bronze cents with L on ribbon are very rare in Proof format, and fewer than 20 authentic examples are known to exist. Although many copper-nickel Indian Head cents certified in high Proof grades are quite "nice," the quality and eye appeal of bronze issues of 1864 to 1909 is all over the map, no matter whether the piece is called BN, RB, or RD (although BN pieces seem to have fewer problems). Buy with care and take your time.

- **Key issues:** The 1864 with L on ribbon is considered somewhat scarce, as are 1871 and 1872. The prime rarity in the series is 1877. The 1908-S is somewhat scarce, as is the 1909-S. Some varieties in this series may be of interest and are generally scarce, the best known being the 1873 doubled LIBERTY and the very rare 1888/7.

- **Advice to smart buyers:** There is a little secret with Indian Head cents: most people think collecting a high-quality set is easy to do, as most coins were made in quantity and many are on the market. However, *quality* is an entirely different aspect. Go through steps 1, 2, 3, and 4 in chapter 2, and if a coin survives the gauntlet, don't be afraid to pay a strong price for it!

- **Selected bibliography:** *See the selected bibliography under Flying Eagle cents.*

Lincoln Cents (1909 to Date): A Numismatic Panorama

Lincoln cents, issued since 1909, are the most ubiquitous of American coins. In one particular year (1993), more than 10 *billion* were made at the Philadelphia Mint alone, plus another 6 billion at Denver, or about 30 coins for every man, woman, and child in the United States of America! I am sure if you put this book down and start searching every drawer, purse, piggy bank, and nook in your house, you will not find 30 coins for every person under your roof—say, 90, if three people are in your family. Where are they all? They must be *somewhere*.

From the first Lincoln cent of 1909 down to the latest date, there are hundreds of different varieties to collect, across a handful of different types, these being as follows.

Design Types of Lincoln Cents

1909 V.D.B.—With the initials of Victor David Brenner on the reverse. Complaints arose, and the initials were dropped. The San Francisco Mint version (1909-S V.D.B.) became a popular rarity.

1909 to 1958, Lincoln, Wreath Reverse—Many billions were made across nearly a half-century of the American experience. William Howard Taft was president when the first ones rolled off the presses; in 1958, when the last with this reverse were made, "Ike" was in the White House.

1943 (Zinc-Coated Steel)—Made for just a short time, these cents, in an incredibly hard metal, managed to strike up well on the coining presses, a paradox.

1959 to 1982, Memorial Reverse (Bronze)—Plentiful, and made in enough

During the first decade of the 20th century, coin-operated amusement machines in penny arcades gobbled up millions of Indian Head cents. The typical arcade had an elaborate front with a name such as Automatic Vaudeville, Wonderland, Autorama, Edisonia, or similar. Within were dozens, sometimes hundreds, of devices that displayed comedy or travel filmstrips, dispensed fortune-telling cards, tested strength, played music, and otherwise entertained patrons.

Shown here are the Autorama at the Savin Rock amusement park near Hartford, Connecticut; the Penny Arcade at Canobie Lake near Salem, New Hampshire; and the brilliantly illuminated Automatic Vaudeville on Union Square, New York City.

varieties that a date-and-mintmark set looks impressive.

1982 to date (Copper-Coated Zinc)— Same comment as preceding.

Lincoln cents are hardly ever collected on their own as types, but, of course, they are necessary for a complete type set of United States coins. As types, all are very common.

The Eras of Lincoln Cents

For purposes of availability, I like to divide Lincoln cents into four eras, as follows.

First Era (1909–1933). The First Era is from 1909 to 1933. During this time, cents were made at the Philadelphia, Denver, and San Francisco mints, although not at all mints in all years. It was not until about 1934 and the advent of albums distributed by Wayte Raymond (and later, of "penny boards" by J.K. Post, Whitman Publishing, and others) that the collecting of Lincoln cents by date and mint became wildly pop-

ular. Accordingly, with relatively few exceptions, dealers, collectors, and others did not set aside quantities for resale or investment.

It may come as a surprise that *The Numismatist*, being the only regularly issued periodical in the hobby during this period, took little heed of current Lincoln cents. The advent of the cent in 1909 and the illogical controversy surrounding the V.D.B. initials were covered well enough, including wry observations that lots of other coins had designers' initials, dating back to the times of ancient Greece, and that no one had complained. However, as time went on, there was no interest in current cents, no excitement when the mintage at the Denver Mint dipped to a low level, and no notice that certain 1922-D cents lacked mintmarks. This would all come later, but during the time that such coins were issued, they were ignored.

From the standpoint of preservation of Mint State coins, the first-year-of-issue pieces—the 1909 V.D.B. and 1909-S V.D.B.

Lincoln cent excitement! On August 4, 1909, in the third day of distribution of the new Lincoln cents, lines of people formed at the Sub-Treasury on Wall Street, New York City, hoping to obtain as many as possible for face value. (*Collier's Weekly*)

Everyone's favorite Lincoln cent rarity is the 1909-S V.D.B., with the initials of the engraver, Victor David Brenner, in tiny letters at the bottom of the reverse. Just 484,000 were struck, a small mintage for a one-cent piece of the era. Almost immediately these achieved great popularity. Ever since then, in all coin-market cycles, these have been in great demand.

Sculptor Victor D. Brenner in his studio with a statue of Abraham Lincoln. Brenner, creator of the Lincoln cent, was also involved in the coin hobby and was a member of the American Numismatic Society.

(especially the former)—were saved in quantity. After that, some bank-wrapped rolls of 50 coins each were preserved of Philadelphia dates through about 1911, then little from then until the 1920s, after which a few hundred rolls were probably set aside for dealer stock. Mintmarks were not in demand, and fewer of these were saved. The 1914-D cent, of which 1,193,000 were struck (more than twice the figure of 484,000 for the 1909-S V.D.B.), was ignored in its time. Today, Mint State coins are very rare—and are a key to the series.

When the low-mintage 1931-S cent was publicized, it created attention and became one of the catalysts of the boom in the coin market of the decade. Beginning in 1934, bank-wrapped rolls were saved in large quantities. About this time, some collectors and investors checked with banks and other sources and were able to find some earlier rolls, dating back to 1928 and 1929.

In the meantime, at the several mints, some coins were sharply struck and others had weak features. Generally, all of the 1909 varieties were well struck, as were most of 1910, and a good many others through 1915. In 1916, quality went out the window, and from then until the late 1920s, many if not most branch-mint coins had weakness in one part or another, or were struck from "tired" dies with grainy surfaces. Some at Philadelphia were poorly made as well. To my knowledge, no collectors paid any attention to the striking of these coins, and, for example, a 1917-D cent in brilliant Uncirculated grade filled the 1917-D hole, and that was it, never mind that some features were blurred.

Today, the First Era of Lincoln cents (1909–1933) represents the greatest challenge, especially for *sharply struck* branch-mint coins of 1916 through the late 1920s, with original *fiery orange* mint color.

Matte Proofs were made from 1909 to 1916, but were not popular in their era as they were hard to distinguish from circulation strikes. Today, these are indeed in demand, but when buying be sure to insist on certification by a major service, as there are many traps for the unwary.

Second Era (1934–1958). Each date and mint issue of this era was saved in roll quantities. In the 1950s, when I entered the coin business, it was common to buy and sell roll sets with each date and mint from 1934 onward. In his several dozen leased coin departments in retail stores, Robert Friedberg did a land-office business selling albums filled with sparkling cents, often taken from such roll sets.

The typical numismatist of that era had Uncirculated (Mint State) coins from 1934 to date, plus the earlier issues in such grades as could be afforded. Most coins of the Second Era were well struck, at least at a casual glance, and very lustrous, quite unlike many First-Era coins.

In 1943, to conserve copper for wartime use, the composition of the Lincoln cent was changed to zinc-coated steel, creating an interesting but common type minted in that year only. In 1944 and continuing to 1946, planchets for cents were processed from used cartridge-shell cases, creating an alloy nearly the same as the bronze used earlier.

A lovely and lustrous 1914-D Lincoln cent, a rarity so fine. When this variety was produced there was little collector interest; the age of popular coin albums and folders had not arrived yet, and the survival of Mint State coins was a matter of rare chance.

The 1955 Doubled-Die cent was made to the extent of about 44,000 coins, of which about 24,000 were released. Today, perhaps 5,000 or so exist, mostly in grades of EF and AU. A Mint State coin, as here, is rare.

There were no "key dates," although some rolls were scarcer than others. That ended in 1955, when the Doubled Die was struck. Later, beginning in a significant way with publicity and books published in the 1960s by New Jersey dealer Frank Spadone, interesting die varieties became very popular, with the 1955 Doubled Die leading the way. Still later, Bill Fivaz and J.T. Stanton accelerated the collecting of these and other unusual pieces in various denominations with the publication of their *Cherrypickers' Guide to Rare Die Varieties*.

Third Era (1959–1982). In 1959 the Lincoln Memorial motif was placed on the reverse of the Lincoln cent, although it didn't fit either comfortably or artistically. Numismatic writer Don Taxay remarked that it looked like a trolley car! Never mind, as the wreath reverse was now history (such coins would later be called wheat cents, or *wheaties*), and a new type was born.

Coins of the Third Era were made in large quantities, and basic dates and mintmarks are collected easily enough today—and very cheaply. Some varieties within that span cost more, including the 1960 Small Date and some Doubled Dies.

Fourth Era (1982 to Date). In 1982, in view of the rising cost of copper, the Treasury Department changed the cent composition to copper-coated zinc. Basic date and mintmark varieties made since then are inexpensive. Some interesting die varieties command strong premiums and are in demand by specialists.

Discussion of Quality

Over a long period of years I have handled only a few sets of Lincoln cents for which all pieces were choice or gem Uncirculated, with full *original* mint color. Today, in terms of *original* mint color, the 1926-S might be the rarest of all, but it is difficult to tell. One of my clients, S.B. (a well-known collector of these), told me the story of trying to find a gem 1926-S with red surfaces, locating a number of toned pieces, and keeping notes on their surfaces. Later, these pieces were dipped, certified, and listed as "full red," but he could identify them by tiny marks and other features. Of course, they *were* full red—but not original.

Similar to Indian Head cents, early Lincoln cents should be selected with great patience. Also, high-grade pieces certified as BN and RB can offer tremendous values.

As to later issues, I like such grades as MS-65 and -66 that have been hand selected for quality. Such pieces are rather inexpensive. As to whether they should be certified is up to you, but often the cost of certification is so much that it overwhelms the true value of a modern piece. What I used to do in my set was to take modern issues and coat them on each side with clear fingernail polish, which easily removed if desired, but in the meantime acts as an excellent shield against the pieces' turning color. A commercial product known as the Koin-Tain, a snap-together circular holder, is used by many; it's convenient and inexpensive, and also seems to provide effective protection.

A good way to start a high-quality collection is to build a Mint State set from 1934 to date, adding Proofs as needed (for some later San Francisco varieties were made only in this format). Check each piece for sharpness of strike. Then, gradually fill in the earlier dates, for which the dates and

Gem Proof 1971-S Lincoln cent, common enough (3,220,733 were made), but attractive and interesting to own.

The 1926-S Lincoln cent is fairly scarce in all grades, but in gem Mint State with original red surfaces it is nearly impossible to find. However, many "red" pieces in the marketplace are that color by virtue of having been dipped.

mints of 1909, 1910, and 1928 to 1933 will be no problem, except for striking of the later ones. Then pick and choose the others you need, with patience and care.

In addition to the foregoing, see the notes on striking, below.

Key to Collecting Lincoln Cents

- **Mint State coins:** Common for all issues from 1934 to date, somewhat scarce for certain branch-mint varieties of 1909 to 1933, but with many exceptions. Common surface descriptions are BN, RB, and RD. Those that are BN and RB often sell at deep discounts from full RD. Many coins certified as RD have been dipped or cleaned; for certain dates, full *original* red color is very rare (see my earlier comments on 1926-S!). Quality can be an exceedingly important consideration, and by taking your time you can achieve more value than can your typical competitor in the marketplace.
- **Circulated coins:** Easy enough to find for dates and mints of the 1930s onward, but since Mint State coins are inexpensive, I would opt for those. For earlier dates, plus certain rare varieties (such as 1922 "Plain" and 1955 Doubled Die), circulated coins are often added to sets that otherwise are mostly Mint State.
- **Strike quality:** Generally good for 1909 to 1915, erratic and often poor (especially for Denver Mint coins) from 1916 to the late 1930s, and generally good after that time. Points to check include the hair and beard details of Lincoln and the smoothness and quality of the field on the reverse (which can be wavy, grainy, or otherwise unsatisfactory if struck from an overly used die). In the late 20th century the hub die details became worn and blurred, and later Lincoln cents do not show the delicate features of earlier issues, no matter how well the coins are struck. In 1974 the portrait was modified slightly. The highest area of Lincoln's shoulder is apt to

show minuscule nicks and marks, even on a superb gem coin; this is due to the fact that this part of the coin did not completely fill the die, so that nicks and marks that were on the original planchet were left behind. Very few buyers of Lincoln cents know anything about this!

The quest for Full Details (FD) coins can be very challenging—and really has nothing at all to do with the grades on slabs. As a smart buyer you can gain many advantages simply by being fussy when you add coins to your collection.

- **Proof coins:** Matte Proofs of 1909 to 1916 are usually BN or RB unless dipped. *Original* RD Proofs are exceedingly rare. Mirror-finish Proofs of 1936 to 1942 are often spotted; avoid these. Proofs of 1950 to 1964 are usually found nice, but sometimes not. Some have frosty or cameo surfaces and are in special demand. Proofs from 1968-S to date are generally attractive gems.
- **Key issues:** The most famous issues today are the 1909-S V.D.B., 1914-D, and 1955 Doubled Die, although such issues as 1909-S, 1922 plain (an unusual variety but one that is highly desired), 1924-D, 1926-S, 1931-S are also in the limelight.
- **Advice to smart buyers:** The typical "gem" set of Lincoln cents of the First Era (1909–1933) is apt to be of rag-tag quality if examined closely. However, if you want a quality set, one can be built, with much patience—similar to the task confronting the Indian Head cent specialist, but more difficult. Coins from 1934 and later are easy enough to find, and if you cherrypick for quality, no one will notice, and you'll get nicer pieces. As to die varieties, sometimes newly discovered ones are hot on the market, then fade in popularity. It's best to ask around before spending a lot of money on these. Expert advice is available and worth seeking. If you buy certified coins, be very careful about paying a

The Chapman Brothers: American Legends

The Chapman brothers, S. Hudson (1857–1931) and Henry (1859–1935), began in the coin trade as teenagers in the 1870s, working in the Philadelphia coin shop of J.W. Haseltine. In 1878 they hung out their own shingle. Soon, their catalogs—some with beautiful photographic plates—became the standard of the hobby. Their partnership lasted until the summer of 1906, after which the brothers went their separate ways, with success. S. Hudson Chapman retired in the late 1920s, but Henry remained in the profession for the rest of his life. The elder brother had a particular interest in large copper cents, studied their varieties, and developed photo techniques, including placing the coins underwater in a shallow tray before photographing them. In 1923, he produced a 29-page monograph, *The United States Cents of the Year 1794*. However, an early reading revealed so many mistakes that the edition was not released. In 1926 it was replaced by a revised version.

S. Hudson Chapman, portrait, 1895.

Henry Chapman, portrait, 1895.

Cents of 1794 were a special interest for S. Hudson Chapman.

Audience at Henry Chapman's auction of the Andrew Zabriskie Collection, 1909.

high price for an ultra-grade specimen of a coin made by the millions (or tens of millions) after 1933 that is easily available in MS-65 or -66, as the vast majority of such coins in collectors' and investors' hands have not been considered for certification, but still exist. For a reality check, refer to my analysis of the 1884-CC dollar (chapter 6), of which more than 1,000,000 exist in Mint State today with high enough values to submit to certification services, although just 5% of them have been sent in. In all instances, use the Optimal Collecting Grade philosophy when checking price lists and other offerings.

- **Selected bibliography:**

Fivaz, Bill, and J.T. Stanton. 1994. *The Cherrypickers' Guide to Rare Die Varieties.* Savannah, GA. (This reference is also useful for nearly all other U.S. series.)

Lange, David W. 1996. *The Complete Guide to Lincoln Cents.* Wolfeboro, NH.

Taylor, Sol. 1999. *The Standard Guide to the Lincoln Cent* (4th ed.). Anaheim, CA.

Wexler, John, and Kevin Flynn. 1996. *The Authoritative Reference on Lincoln Cents.* Rancocas, NJ.

Bronze Two-Cent Pieces (1864–1873): A Short-Lived, Challenging Series

Two-cent pieces, designed by Chief Engraver James B. Longacre and made of bronze (95% copper, 5% tin and zinc), were authorized under the Act of April 3, 1864. At the time, there were no silver coins in circulation in the East and Midwest, and the need for small change was filled by federal cents plus Civil War tokens of bronze, Fractional Currency bills, and private scrip. It was felt that the two-cent coin would find a niche in commerce and society.

The obverse design features a shield and inscriptions, including the first use of the motto IN GOD WE TRUST on a circulating coin. For several years prior, back to 1861, patterns had been made with different proposals for a motto reflecting the nation's faith in the Deity. GOD AND COUNTRY and GOD OUR TRUST were among the ideas. Finally, IN GOD WE TRUST was chosen, adapted from a stanza in the *Star Spangled Banner*: "And let this be our motto, in God is our trust." The reverse features a wreath, open at the top, with inscriptions.

During the first year, the mintage was generous: 19,847,500 pieces. After that, production declined to 13,640,000 in 1865, the year that a competitive coin, the nickel three-cent piece, was first used. Later, figures dwindled further, to 1872 when just 65,000 were struck, followed by an estimated 1,500 Proofs for collectors in 1873. The Coinage Act of 1873 abolished the denomination.

Today, most collectors acquire a single two-cent piece for type. Examples are available easily enough, particularly from the first couple of years. The 1864 exists in the scarce Small Motto variety as well as the usually seen Large Motto. The availability of dates in circulated grades as well as Mint State declines as the years progress. Generally, choice and gem pieces are very rare for 1871 and 1872, and especially for 1873.

General guidelines for quality are the same as for bronze Indian Head cents and early Lincoln cents: pieces described as RD, or mint red, can be attractive, but many have problems and others have been recolored. The RB and BN pieces offer excellent values, in my opinion, in both Mint State and Proof formats.

A lustrous Mint State 1865 two-cent piece, the second year of issue of this denomination. Released in 1864, two-cent coins were the first circulating coins to include the motto IN GOD WE TRUST.

Assembling a set of either gem MS-65 or -66 RD, or equivalent Proofs, in the two-cent series is easily done if the holder labels, alone, are inspected. If absence of spots and flecks is desired, and if you want *original* color and, further, good eye appeal, get set to spend several years on this short-lived "easy" series!

Key to Collecting Two-Cent Pieces

- **Mint State coins**: Plentiful for the first two years of issue, scarce thereafter. Quality is hard to find, and assembling a specialized collection of both varieties of 1864 plus others through 1872, in Choice or Gem preservation, could well take several years.
- **Circulated coins**: Plentiful for the first two years, becoming scarcer afterward.
- **Strike quality**: Usually good, but check the shield details on the obverse and the high points of the wreath on the reverse.
- **Proof coins:** Proof mintages are unknown, as no figures have ever been located. Published numbers are estimates. Choice and gem Proofs without spots, staining, or problems are extremely rare, much more so than realized. The 1864 Small Motto Proof is a classic rarity with fewer than two dozen known. The 1873 Proof exists with close 3 and open 3 varieties. Some may have been issued with bronzed (darkened at the mint) surfaces.
- **Key issues:** 1864 Small Motto, 1872 (somewhat scarce), and 1873 (Proofs only).
- **Advice to smart buyers:** Buy a single coin for your type set, and pick out a superb coin with original color and eye appeal. If you go further, such as building a full set, expect a challenge. Use the Optimal Collecting Grade philosophy when checking price lists and other offerings.
- **Selected bibliography:**

  Flynn, Kevin. 1994. *Getting Your Two Cents Worth: A Complete Reference to Two Cent Doubled Dies, Repunched Dates, Clashed Dies, and Overdates*. Rancocas, NJ.

  Kliman, Myron M. 1977. *The Two Cent Piece and Varieties*. South Laguna, CA, 1977.

  Leone, Frank. 1991. *Longacre's Two Cent Piece Die Varieties and Errors*. College Point, NY.

COLLECTING NICKEL COINS

Numismatics is making rapid progress in the country. The *New York Sun* publishes a column article in every Sunday issue, and numerous notes are constantly appearing in the public press. Collectors are increasing, the demand for U.S. cents, half dollars, and gold cannot be supplied except at advancing prices. The buyers of real fine coins have made enormous profits in the past, but we venture to say that the buyers of rare specimens today will realize quadruple their investment inside of 10 years.

—John W. Scott, December 1908

Nickel Three-Cent Pieces (1865–1889): A New Denomination in Nickel

The nickel three-cent piece made its debut in 1865, helping to supply small coins in circulation at a time when silver pieces were nowhere to be seen, having been hoarded since the spring of 1862. Now, small transactions were paid for in cents, two-cent pieces, and Fractional Currency notes. The nickel three-cent piece was expected to become popular as America's highest-denomination circulating coin—certainly a strange circumstance, in retrospect! Although silver three-cent pieces, or trimes, had been minted since 1851, these, too, were squirreled away.

In 1865, 11,382,000 of the new nickel three-cent pieces were made. Soon, these coins largely took the place of two-cent pieces, causing the latter to diminish in importance and eventually to be discontinued. The same thing would happen to the nickel three-cent coins in a year or two, when the new Shield five-cent piece would answer the call for a denomination above the cent, and mintages of the three-cent pieces went into a prolonged decline. In 1866 the mintage was 4,801,000, falling to 3,915,000 in 1867, and sliding all the way to just 390,000 in 1873. Afterward, the figures were up and down, but were mostly low. The Coinage Act of 1889 abolished this denomination, along with the gold $1 and $3 pieces.

Today, nickel three-cent pieces are eminently collectible. A full set can be gathered from 1865 to 1889, one of each year, plus (if you want to include them) two varieties of 1873 (the close 3 and the open 3), and, de rigueur, the 1887/6 overdate. A set of choice and gem Mint State coins is a much greater challenge than a run of Proofs. Among the latter, the 1865, common in Mint State, is the rarest of all Proofs, simply because these coins were not produced until the summer of the year, by which time many collectors had ordered Proof sets lacking this coin. The 1877 and 1878 were

The 1877 nickel three-cent piece is considered by many to be the rarest date in the 1865 to 1889 series. It is estimated that about 1,500 or so were coined, all Proofs. At the time, there was no call for the coinage for general circulation. The denomination is expressed simply with the Roman numeral III, similar to what was done in the silver three-cent series beginning in 1851.

Although the 1877 nickel three-cent piece is the most famous date, in terms of actual rarity the 1887 is probably rarer. Shown here is a Proof, one of an estimated 1,000 struck. Additional coins of this date were made for circulation, but most have disappeared, and today they are far rarer than Proof strikings.

made only in Proof format, but those of 1878 usually are quite lustrous, and if the *Annual Report of the Director of the Mint* did not tell us otherwise, we would think that some circulation strikes were made as well.

As a rule of thumb, both circulation strikes and Proofs of 1865 to 1876 are difficult to find in a combination of gem quality, sharp strike, lack of flecks or spots, and good eye appeal. Those of 1877 to 1889 are much more easily obtained.

Key to Collecting Nickel Three-Cent Pieces

- **Mint State coins:** Coins at this level are generally available for the first several years of the denomination as well as 1879 through 1889, the latter range laden with choice and gem coins. For the years from 1871 to 1876, true gems are rare.
- **Circulated coins:** Common for the earlier dates, elusive for most issues after 1878, except for 1881, 1888, and 1889.
- **Strike quality:** Often with incomplete detail on the tiny ribs that make up the vertical elements in the III denomination on the reverse. Check the head details as well. Generally, those made after 1876 are better strikes than the earlier dates.
- **Proof coins:** The rarest date by far is 1865, with only a few hundred Proofs known (however, circulation strikes of this year are very common). The second rarest Proof is probably 1887, of which only 1,000 are estimated to have been coined. Quality is elusive for Proofs of 1865 to 1876. Later issues are usually choice, but spotting (from moisture drops) can be a problem.
- **Key issues:** 1877, 1878, 1887/6, and 1887 are the keys. Some later dates are rare as circulation strikes, but Proofs abound.
- **Advice to smart buyers:** Check strike, surface quality, and eye appeal. There are enough nice coins in the marketplace that you will not have to stretch to buy what you need. Gem

Mint State coins of the mid-1870s are quite rare if sharply struck, but most people do not know this—giving you the opportunity to pay no more for quality when you find it. Keep Optimal Collecting Grade in mind if there is a big jump in price accompanying a small nudge in grading number.

Nickel Five-Cent Pieces (1866 to Date): A Popular Denomination

Although the Civil War ended in April 1865, silver coins continued to be hoarded, and would be until 1876. The need for circulating small change was filled by the Indian Head cent, then the bronze two-cent piece (1864) and nickel three-cent piece (1865). In 1866 a new denomination, the nickel five-cent piece, made its appearance. In time, the nickel made the two-cent and three-cent pieces redundant. Today, the five-cent piece is one of just a few denominations we still use with regularity in everyday transactions (the others being the cent, dime, and quarter dollar). Made in an alloy of 75% copper and 25% nickel, these might logically be called *coppers*, but to everyone, *nickels* they are.

Although the nickel series includes many dates and, beginning in 1912, mintmarks too, there were just nine different types until 2004, when the Peace Medal and the Keelboat reverse designs appeared, followed in 2005 by a new portrait of Jefferson and two new reverses. Now, nickels have been projected into the limelight as the denomination of choice in the Westward Journey Nickel Series™, a feather in the cap of the U.S. Mint and a delight to the public—just as the statehood quarters have been since 1999.

In the meantime, the nickels of yesteryear furnish a rich opportunity for collecting—a combination of issues common and rare, and widely different in their designs. While there are a few key dates, and the 1913 Liberty Head is a legendary rarity, by and large the series is quite affordable.

The following is a quick guide to the design types.

Design Types of Nickel Five-Cent Pieces

1866 and 1867, Shield, Rays on Reverse—Short-lived design. Not rare, but in the context of the series this is the most elusive type. Strike and eye appeal are important factors.

1867 to 1883, Shield, Without Rays—Second scarcest type.

1883, Liberty, Without CENTS—A great "story coin," common and inexpensive.

1883 to 1913, Liberty, With CENTS—An attractive design. Quality coins are available, especially toward the end of the series.

1913, Buffalo (Indian Head), Raised Mound—Short-lived but very plentiful type. Most are well struck and attractive.

1913 to 1938, Buffalo (Indian Head), Flat Ground—Common, but many are challenging in aspects of sharpness and quality.

1938 to 1965, Jefferson, No Designer's Initials—As a type, common as can be.

1942 to 1945, Jefferson, Wartime Alloy—Plentiful and usually very attractive.

1966 to 2003, Jefferson, With the Designer's Initials FS (for Felix Schlag), Monticello Reverse—A type from our own era.

2004, Jefferson, Peace Medal–Style Reverse—Front row center in the Westward Journey Nickel Series™.

2004, Jefferson, Keelboat Reverse—Ditto.

2005, Revised Jefferson Portrait, Bison Reverse—New kid on the nickel block. Interesting.

2005, Revised Jefferson Portrait, Ocean in View Reverse—Another newcomer.

2006, Coming Attractions—New nickels, including reprise of the Monticello reverse, but with FS (for Felix Schlag) initials to the right of the building (announced in July 2005).

Shield, With Rays (1866–1867)

Introduced in the summer of 1866, the Shield nickel was designed by Chief Engraver James B. Longacre. The shield device on the obverse was largely adapted from his two-cent piece. The reverse depicts a large numeral 5 surrounded by stars and rays, called *stars and bars* at the time, but generally called *with rays* today. Striking difficulties developed, and early in 1867 the rays were dropped, with the result that less metal flow was required. Accordingly, the first type of the Shield nickel is that of 1866 plus early 1867.

Today, the 1866 is plentiful, while the 1867 With Rays is scarce. Most pieces are lightly struck in one area or another. Check the horizontal lines in the shield and, on the reverse, the centers of the stars. Probably not one in 10 coins is sharply struck and with good eye appeal. Opportunities abound for you to cherrypick. Proofs are usually well struck. The 1866 Proof is quite rare, as the denomination was not available until the summer, by which time most collectors had already ordered sets. The 1867 With Rays Proof is a major rarity, with only a few dozen known.

Shield, Without Rays (1867–1883)

Shield nickels without rays were made from 1867 through 1883. These coins were very popular and, for most years through 1876, were made in large quantities. In that

Shield nickel of 1866, type with rays on the reverse, called *stars and bars* at the time. The obverse is similar in motif to that of the bronze two-cent piece of 1864. The nickel five-cent piece proved to be popular with the public, and such pieces have been made ever since, across a wide variety of designs.

year, silver coins reappeared in circulation and the mintage figures dropped, to remain low for the next several years. In 1877 and 1878, only Proofs were made for collectors, while no pieces were made for circulation.

Today, Shield nickels of the With-Rays type can be collected in circulated grades (except for 1877 and 1878) or in a combination of circulated grades, Mint State, and Proof. There are no impossible rarities. Mint State coins of 1879 to 1881 are rare, but the slack is taken up by easily available Proofs for these years. Due to the hardness of the metal, many if not most circulated Shield nickels show interesting die cracks, visible under magnification, resulting from stress and wear. Cracks *do not* detract from a coin's value, but lend interest. There are also a number of interesting repunched dates in the series, as well as the so-called 1879/8 overdate (only in Proof format) and the 1883/2.

Liberty Head, Without CENTS (1883)

Following an extensive series of patterns, in 1883 the Liberty Head nickel by Chief Engraver William Barber made its appearance. The obverse featured Miss Liberty (said to be modeled after the head of the goddess Diana) facing left, surrounded by stars, with the date below. The reverse had the Roman numeral V to represent the denomination, within a wreath, with

inscription surrounding. The Roman numeral was thought to be sufficient as identification, since such had been used on nickel three-cent and silver three-cent pieces for a long time. However, this nickel was the same diameter as the $5 gold piece, and unscrupulous people plated them and attempted to pass them off as $5 coins, as the design gave no indication otherwise. Soon, the Mint changed the reverse, adding CENTS below the wreath.

The 1883 Liberty Head nickel without CENTS created a sensation; newspaper articles stated they were being recalled by the Mint (not true), and that they would soon be of great value (proved to be untrue as well, at least for that era). The public responded as might be expected, and hoarded as many as possible—with the result that today this particular variety is the most plentiful of all Liberty Head nickels, although many others had higher mintages! Still, it is of enduring popularity as the only year of this curious type. This is a nice "story coin," and I suggest you find room in your collection to include one.

Liberty Head, With CENTS (1883–1913)

The modified Liberty Head nickel with CENTS on the reverse was produced continuously for circulation from 1883 through 1912, with Denver and San Francisco mint (D and S) coins for the last year

This Shield nickel of 1869 illustrates the Without-Rays design made from early 1867 through early 1883. The rays or bars had caused problems with metal flow during the striking process, and their elimination resulted in coins with sharper details.

Early in 1883 the Mint released a new nickel five-cent piece. Designed by Chief Engraver William Barber, the obverse featured the head of Miss Liberty while the reverse stated the denomination simply as the Roman numeral V. Many of these were gold plated and passed off as $5 coins of similar diameter. Soon, the word CENTS was added. Word spread that the CENTS-less coins would become very rare and valuable, and millions were hoarded. Today, examples are plentiful.

(the only branch-mint production). In 1913 an estimated five pieces were made privately, possibly by or for William Brown, a Mint employee. Today these are legendary rarities and are highly sought. Over the years I have participated in the sale of three of these and the transfer of another (the gift coin from the Norweb family to the Smithsonian). The finest specimen is the Eliasberg Collection coin, which is also the only one with a Proof surface.

Liberty Head nickels were strictly utilitarian and achieved wide use throughout the time they were issued, although certain dates such as 1885 and 1886 were made in smaller quantities, as was 1912-S.

During the early 20th century a Liberty Head nickel was the passport to many pleasures—ranging from a glass of beer to a cigar, to a two-minute tune on a Regina disc music box, to a fortune card dispensed by a Mills World Horoscope machine. Ornate slot machines made by Mills, Caille, and others invited patrons to drop in nickels and push a crank, causing a colorful wheel to spin; if they were lucky, a cascade of nickels would drop into a cup in the front. All across America thousands of theaters charged five cents admission to watch a series of 12-minute films flicker on a screen, giving rise to the term *nickelodeon*, with *odeon* being a popular word for theater (e.g., the Odeon in Paris). I find this connection with history to be delightful, and in a book, *Adventures With Rare Coins*, devoted a chapter to old-time uses of these coins.

Liberty Head nickels from 1883 through 1912 are readily collectible in Proof format. Mint State pieces can be collected as well, although certain issues of the 1880s and early 1890s are elusive.

To my eyes, the Liberty Head nickel is one of the most attractive and interesting of all American coins from its era. There are ample opportunities for connoisseurship, to avoid coins that are weakly struck (check the obverse star centers and hair details, and the reverse wreath details) and not stained or spotted. Generally, those from the late 1890s to 1912 are easier to find in choice condition. Forming a high-quality set is a challenge and a pleasure, and the resultant collection is beautiful to behold.

Indian Head or Buffalo, Raised Ground (1913)

The Indian Head or Buffalo nickel, the work of artist James E. Fraser, was introduced in 1913. By this time Native Americans had been depicted in fantasy form (females wearing male headdresses) on the Indian

The revised Liberty Head nickel design, with the reverse including CENTS and with a different placement of E PLURIBUS UNUM, was made from spring 1883 through 1912, plus a handful in early 1913.

Much ado about a nickel—a 1913 Liberty Head nickel, that is. In 2003, Ed Lee (left) paid Dwight Manley (center) nearly $3 million for the Eliasberg coin. A gala celebration was hosted in Baltimore, hosted by Steve Geppi (right), at the Diamond International offices, with prominent numismatic, society, and political figures in attendance.

The finest of the five known 1913 Liberty Head nickels and the only one with a full Proof finish. This is the Eliasberg Collection coin, earlier the property of Eric P. Newman and, before that, Colonel E.H.R. Green.

Sculptor James Earle Fraser, designer of the 1913 Indian Head / Buffalo nickel, in his studio. He married one of his students, Laura Gardin, who became well known as a medalist and coin designer.

A 1913-S Buffalo or Indian Head nickel of the Type I style, with the bison standing on a mound inscribed FIVE CENTS. It was believed that the denomination would wear away quickly once such coins were in circulation. Soon, the reverse was modified, creating Type II.

A 1916 Buffalo nickel of the Type II motif, the standard style from spring 1913 to early 1938. While most coins of this type are lightly struck at the obverse center and, on the reverse, the shoulder and front part of the head of the bison, this one shows all details. Struck as a Matte Proof, it was made with special care. Today, the vast majority of buyers pay no attention to whether a Buffalo nickel is sharply struck, nor do certification services take note of what seems to be an important consideration. Accordingly, the alert numismatist can sometimes find sharp coins for little more than weakly struck pieces cost. (Also see chapter 2 for more information on this subject.)

Head cent and the Saint-Gaudens $10 gold, and in true-to-life form on the $5 Silver Certificate of 1899 and the $2.50 and $5 gold coins of 1908. Fraser used three male Native Americans as models for his version. On the reverse the "buffalo," actually a bison, was modeled from life.

The earliest varieties, called Type I by collectors today, show the bison standing on a raised mound and the words FIVE CENTS in raised letters below. It was found that the letters would wear quickly through everyday handling, and soon the mint created the Type II nickel by modifying the ground below the animal. Type I nickels (1913) were made at the Philadelphia, Denver, and San Francisco mints. Examples are commonly seen on the market, and the Philadelphia version is actually plentiful. Most Mint State coins are well struck and have good eye appeal.

Buffalo, Flat Ground (1913–1938)

The Type II Buffalo nickel, introduced in 1913, was minted continuously through early 1938, except for 1922, 1932, and 1933. For most years production took place at the Philadelphia, Denver, and San Francisco mints. All were made in sufficient numbers that a basic set of dates and mintmarks can be collected easily enough today, particularly in lower grades, although the 1913-S Type II and 1926-S are scarce. The 1914/3 overdates, real but not sharply defined, range from scarce to rare. The overdate 1918/7-D nickel is rare in all grades. The 1916 Doubled-Die obverse is a rarity, while the curious 1937-D three-legged variety is somewhat scarce. The interesting 1938-D/S overmintmark is plentiful in all grades.

In Mint State the availability of certain issues dated before 1928 changes dramatically, and a number of the branch-mint issues of the 1920s range from rare to elusive. Striking can be a big problem, particularly with the details of the bison on the reverse, this being especially true of issues of the mid-1920s, with 1926-D often coming flatly struck. Over the years, very few collections have ever been assembled that combine choice Mint State (itself not a great problem) with *sharply struck* details (often a great problem, but not at all recognized on the certification holders).

At a convention not too long ago I had a rather puzzling (to me) conversation with a collector from Maryland. He specialized in Buffalo nickels and was endeavoring to build a registry set (so called) to be listed on the Internet, by which system points are given for combinations of grading numbers and rarity. *Sharpness was not a factor*, which I found to be not only illogical, but downright weird! Anyway, he had a predicament: as a knowledgeable numismatist he had spent years assembling a set of sharply struck nickels, most topping out in grades such as MS-65 and, for a few, MS-66. He was very proud of his accomplishment. Then came the registry concept, and he found that he was losing ground to those who owned weakly struck nickels in grades such as MS-66 and -67. As I bid him adieu he was unsure whether he should cash in his collection and go on to something else, or continue enjoying his superb coins and accept not being a high scorer in the registry sweepstakes.

The following are Mint State listings for two Buffalo nickel varieties, the 1913 Type I, which is usually found very sharp, and the 1926-D, usually seen nearly as flat as a pancake, with fewer than one in 20 being sharp:[55]

1913 Type I Buffalo nickel—MS-60: $35 • MS-63: $50 • MS-64: $75 • MS-65: $150 • MS-66: $350.

1926-D Buffalo nickel—MS-60: $350 • MS-63: $600 • MS-64: $2,000 • MS-65: $6,000 • MS-66: $12,000.

For my money, if I wanted an MS-66 coin, and knowing that the 1913 Type I usually is found sharply struck, I would look in the $350 range. If one were offered at $475, I would reject it, knowing I would have another chance. On the other hand, for the 1926-D in MS-66, if I were offered a weak strike at $12,000 I wouldn't even consider buying it for my collection. However, if a sharply struck MS-65 were offered at the same figure I would be a buyer—for twice catalog—for I would know that I had captured a rarity.

For many years, the collecting of Buffalo nickels has been a popular pastime, indeed ever since convenient albums became available in the 1930s. I have never seen a time in the marketplace when choice pieces were not in demand. For the smart buyer, selected varieties of Buffalo nickels that are usually found weak, but *can* be found sharp if you look long enough, offer acres of diamonds at your feet—just waiting to be picked up. As Dr. Watson might say, "The game is afoot!" Put on your Sherlock Holmes hat and start tracking them down!

As to collecting goals, a nice collection in grades from MS-63 to -65, acquired with care over a long period of time, should be right for most informed buyers. As to MS-66 and higher, keep a weather eye on the Optimal Collecting Grade (OCG). For example, *Coin Values* lists 1934-D in MS-65 at $1,200 and MS-66 for $7,000.[56] For my money, although I could afford the MS-66, the value would not be there. I'd rather spend $1,200 for an MS-65 and take the difference and go to London or Paris!

In the Buffalo nickel series, Proofs of the Matte type were made from 1913 to 1916. These often resemble Mint State coins and are usually needle sharp in their details. These were not popular in their time, but are widely sought today. I recommend that you purchase only pieces certified by a leading service, as there are many deceptions. Proofs of the mirror style were made in 1936 and 1937, although some of

On the popular 1937-D three-legged nickel, the right front leg of the bison is missing. Apparently the die was rough or damaged, and a Denver Mint employee smoothed it by filing away part of the design.

those made early in 1936 have a satin finish (not intentional).

Jefferson (1938 to Date)

Designed by Felix O. Schlag, winner of a nationwide competition, the Jefferson-head nickel made its debut in 1938 and has been minted ever since. Along the way there have been some interesting variations, such as silver-content nickels of 1942 to 1945, during which time a P mintmark (for Philadelphia) was first used, and D and S mintmarks of large size were put over the dome of Monticello on the reverse. Schlag's initials were first added to the coin in 1966 in belated recognition. Beginning in 2004, the Jefferson nickel was selected as the denomination for the Westward Journey Nickel Series™, and in that year two distinctive reverses were made, the Peace Medal and the Keelboat. In 2005 a revised portrait of Jefferson was used in combination with two reverses: the "buffalo" and the "Ocean in View" designs. Nickels were in the forefront of news in the hobby.

All Jefferson nickels are readily collectible, although some are more elusive than others. Years ago the key date was considered to be 1939-D, plus, as a sleeper, the 1942-D. In 1950, 2,630,030 nickels were made at the Denver mint. The 1950-D became a hot item—everyone wanted one, and it's likely that far more than half the mintage was set aside by coin collectors, launching a great interest in investing in coins by acquiring bank-wrapped rolls. Today, the 1950-D nickel is very rare if *worn*, but Mint State pieces are available easily enough due to their being hoarded.

Striking can vary widely among Jefferson nickels, particularly on the details of the steps of the Monticello building on the reverse. If you want to dig into a specialty, just try getting a set with *all six* of the steps on Monticello sharp, including what to the unstudied buyer would seem to be everyday issues of 1938-D, 1939-D, 1952, 1952-D, 1953, 1953-S, 1954-D, 1954-S, 1955-D, 1957, 1958, 1959, 1960, 1960-D, 1961, 1961-D, 1962-D, 1963-D, and many more of the later issues. You might die of old age first!

Not to be an iconoclast or go against my recommendations for being a smart buyer, but in a typical set of dates and mintmarks of lustrous, brilliant Jefferson nickels from 1938 to date, in grades such as MS-63 and MS-64, I see a lot of plain old-fashioned *value* for the money. Just a few hundred dollars will do the trick, including albums for display. If you have children or grandchildren, buy them each one! I feel that as the Westward Journey nickels are created and released, attention will also turn to the Jefferson nickels of yesteryear. In compari-

The award-winning design submitted by Felix O. Schlag for the Jefferson nickel. In final form, modifications were made: the stylistic lettering (notice the E) was changed, and on the reverse a different view of Monticello was used.

A 1938 Jefferson nickel from a Proof set of that year. The design proved to be very popular and since that time has been a familiar sight in pocket change and commerce.

Jefferson nickel of the wartime silver composition type, with the mintmark prominently located over the dome of Monticello. These were made from 1942 through 1945.

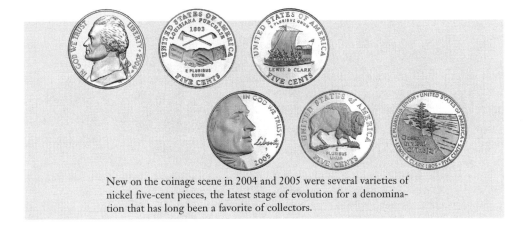

New on the coinage scene in 2004 and 2005 were several varieties of nickel five-cent pieces, the latest stage of evolution for a denomination that has long been a favorite of collectors.

son to the demand for them, some varieties are really scarce.

Afterward, you can become a specialist if you wish, building a set of Jeffersons with full steps, perhaps paying more for a 1954-D MS-66 with six Full Steps (6FS), listed at $2,250 in *Coin Values,* than the total price you paid for all of the sets you bought for your family!

Key to Collecting Nickel Five-Cent Pieces

- **Mint State coins:** Shield nickels are available in Mint State except for the Proof-only 1877 and 1878. Coins of the years 1866 to 1876 are tough to find in a combination of high grade, sharp strike, and good eye appeal. Liberty Head nickels of 1883 without CENTS, and most dates from 1897 to 1912, are plentiful. The 1885 and 1886 are rare, 1912-D is a sleeper (my opinion), and 1912-S is scarce (and is always seen with light striking on parts of the hair).

  Most Buffalo nickels are found in Mint State easily enough, with 1918/7-D and 1926-S being notable exceptions. Most Denver Mint coins of the 1920s and many of the San Francisco Mint are miserably struck. The 1913 nickels and all from 1931 to 1938 are plentiful. I consider 1939 Doubled MONTICELLO (actually a new hub die over an old hub),

1939-D, 1942-D, and 1943/2 to be on the scarce to rare side in relation to the demand for them. Others are available easily enough. The low-mintage 1950-D was mostly saved by investors, so that *circulated* examples are scarce!

- **Circulated coins:** Generally available in proportion to their mintage figures. Lightly worn coins usually have medium-gray surfaces.

- **Strike quality:** The 1866 and 1867 Shield nickels With Rays often have striking problems and are light in one area or another, including the horizontal stripes in the shield, the star centers on the reverse, and elsewhere. It pays to check every feature. Later Shield nickels tend to be better struck, but there are exceptions. Liberty Head nickels are sometimes weak at the star centers and highest hair details on the obverse and on parts of the wreath on the reverse. Buffalo nickels are often weak at the centers, the Denver Mint coins of the 1920s being egregious in this regard. Cherrypicking is essential and also worthwhile, for many buyers are completely clueless about sharp strikes and simply buy based on grading numbers. Aspire to acquire FD (Full Details) coins. On Jefferson nickels, the steps of Monticello are often weak. Seeking out dates that are common if typically struck, but rare if with six Full Steps (6FS), can bring a windfall to you, as such distinctions are not

Liberty Head and early Buffalo nickels served as admission to thousands of theaters across America during the first 15 years of the 20th century. Shown above is Lustig's National Theatre, no location given on the image, which offered Keystone comedies by Roscoe "Fatty" Arbuckle and others. The typical comedy film of the era was one reel in length and ran for about 12 minutes.

The Nickel Theatre, location not known, seems to have been created by conversion of a commercial building to show films. Attractions of the day were advertised by colorful posters. The Nickel seems to have had a good supply.

commonly known at present, although opportunities will fade as information becomes widely published.

- **Proof coins:** Shield nickels of 1866 to 1912 are mirror Proofs. The 1866 is rare, and the 1867 With Rays is extremely rare. Liberty Head nickels are of the mirror type and exist in proportion to their mintages. Buffalo nickels of 1913 to 1916 are of the Matte Proof type, closely resembling circulation strikes; certification is recommended. Proofs of 1936 are either satiny or mirror finish, and those of 1937 are mirrored. Jefferson nickel Proofs from 1938 to date are of the mirror type. Some dated 1950 to 1964 have frosty or cameo designs and are in special demand. From 1968-S to date, most have cameo contrast.
- **Key issues:** 1867 With Rays, 1877, 1878, 1885, 1886, 1912-S, 1913 Liberty Head, and 1918/7-S are the best known of the standard date and mintmark rarities. Some unusual varieties, such as the 1916 Doubled Die, are rare.
- **Advice to smart buyers:** Always seek quality by following steps 1 through 4 (see chapter 2). Keep an eye out for Optimal Collecting Grade for special *value*. While sharpness of strike is important in all nickel series, there is very little about the subject in print for

the Shield and Liberty Head series, and for Buffalo nickels most buyers are blissfully unaware that weak strikes are not as desirable as sharp ones (see chapter 8 for more on Full Details). For my money, an FD 1925-S (as an example) Buffalo nickel in MS-64 grade would be more desirable to own than a weakly struck coin certified MS-66 or -67. This is an iconoclastic view, but one worthy of your consideration. Jefferson nickels offer opportunities for cherrypicking as well. As the Westward Journey Nickel Series™ progresses, I expect that earlier nickels will attract more attention and thus that many pieces will rise in value.

- **Selected bibliography:**

Fletcher, Edward L., Jr. 1994. *The Shield Five Cent Series: A Comprehensive Listing of Known Varieties.* Ormond Beach, FL, 1994.

Lange, David W. 2000. *The Complete Guide to Buffalo Nickels* (2nd ed.). Virginia Beach, VA.

Nagengast, Bernard. 1979. *The Jefferson Nickel Analyst.* Sidney, OH.

Peters, Gloria, and Cynthia Mohon. 1995. *The Complete Guide to Shield and Liberty Head Nickels.* Virginia Beach, VA.

Wescott, Michael. 1991. *The United States Nickel Five-Cent Piece.* Wolfeboro, NH.

CHAPTER EIGHTEEN

COLLECTING SILVER COINS

The true numismatist, while he may specialize in a kind or class of coins, does not do so in his researches concerning those he collects, but strives to acquire a full knowledge of everything pertaining to them. He notes the size, weight, composition, shape and date of issue of each specimen and learns its name and place in the monetary system of the times. He investigates the causes of its rarity, if it is rare—due perhaps to it being one of a small emission or of a recalled issue—and if the latter he tries to learn the cause for the recall....

—Virgil M. Brand, May 1905

Coins struck in silver, alloyed with copper, were first made at the Philadelphia Mint in the 1790s, all according to the standards under the Mint Act of April 2, 1792. The first in this metal were the half dismes of 1792, followed by the 1794-dated half dime, half dollar, and dollar. Dimes made their appearance in 1796, as did quarters. As time went on, designs changed and evolved, as did weights and alloy standards. The silver three-cent piece, or trime, a new denomination, appeared in 1851. In 1873 the silver trade dollar was born, but lasted only until 1878 (plus later Proofs struck for collectors), followed by the even shorter-lived twenty-cent piece of 1875 and 1876 (plus two more years of Proofs for numismatists).

Generally, designs for early silver coins were similar, with most issues of 1794 and 1795 having Flowing Hair (it is usual to capitalize motifs in numismatic text), later denominations having the Draped Bust style, and then the Capped Bust motif, followed by the long-lived Liberty Seated design, then in 1892 the Barber dime, quarter, and half dollar. In the meantime, the twenty-cent piece (1875), the trade dollar (1873), and the new silver dollar (the Morgan dollar of 1878) had their own motifs.

In 1916 artists in the private sector were commissioned to create the "Mercury" dime, Standing Liberty quarter, and Liberty Walking half dollar, each of which went on to become extremely popular with numismatists. In 1921 the Peace silver dollar, also designed by an outside sculptor, joined this illustrious group.

By 1964, silver was becoming expensive on international markets, and after that time the standard alloy of 90% silver and 10% copper was abandoned, although some silver-content half dollars were produced through 1970. Since then, occasional special coins and commemoratives in silver have been made for sale to collectors. Today, for coins used in general circulation, clad alloy replaces silver in such denominations as the dime, quarter, half dollar, and dollar, with the "golden dollar" of 2000 having a distinctive appearance.

Silver Three-Cent Pieces (1851–1873): The Silver Trime

In 1851 there were no silver coins in circulation. In recent times, gold had become more plentiful than ever, due to the vast influx from California and new discoveries in Australia. In comparison, silver metal had become somewhat scarce, and its price rose to the point that it was profitable to melt down old silver coins and illogical to make any new ones.

To provide small silver coins for circulation, the Mint launched the three-cent piece (called the *trime* in certain Treasury Department correspondence), made of a special alloy of 75% silver and 25% copper instead of the normal 90%-10% alloy. As their silver content was less, they presented no attraction to speculators in that metal. The little trimes were well received, circulated widely, and fulfilled their purpose.

Those first made (today called the Type I design) were minted from 1851 through

The Type I silver three-cent piece, or trime (enlarged), style made from 1851 through 1853. These did not strike up well, and on many the shield at the center of the obverse is weak, the present coin being an exception. On the reverse the denomination is expressed as III in Roman numerals. Type I trimes were struck in a special alloy of 75% silver and 25% copper.

On the Type II trime (enlarged), made from 1854 through 1858, the obverse star is in lower relief than on the preceding, and with three frames outlining it. On the reverse an olive branch has been added above the III and a group of arrows below it. This type proved to be very difficult to strike, and on nearly all impressions there is weakness in several areas, in such places as the rim, lettering, frames around the obverse, and the star centers on the reverse. Of all trime types, this is far and away the most difficult to locate in choice preservation.

The Type III design (enlarged), made from 1859 to 1873, featured a shallow-relief obverse star with two outlines, taller letters differently spaced, and a few other subtle changes. Finally, trimes could be struck up properly with most if not all details sharp.

1853. These have no outline around the star on the obverse and no ornaments above or below the Roman numeral III on the reverse. This type included the only branch-mint issue of the entire denomination, the 1851-O. Examples of most Type I trimes are plentiful today.

The Act of February 21, 1853, lowered the authorized weight of Liberty Seated silver coins from the half dime to the half dollar (but not the dollar). Soon, half dimes of the new, lighter weight were made in large quantities and became common in circulation. These were favorites of the public, and the tiny trime became redundant. Mintage quantities for later years fell sharply.

In 1854 the weight of the three-cent piece was lowered (under legislation of 1853), and the normal 90%-10% alloy was used, creating what numismatists call the Type II design. To reflect the change in standard, the Mint modified the design by adding three outlines around the obverse star and ornaments above and below the III. Such pieces were struck from 1854 to 1858. The Mint experienced extreme difficulty in striking this design up properly, with the result that nearly all trimes of 1854 to 1858 are weakly or poorly struck in one area or another. I have never seen a full choice or gem Mint State set of trimes, sharply struck! Regardless of grade, all dates in the Type II category are somewhat scarce, the 1855 being especially so.

As there are no general guidelines in popular use for evaluating the sharpness of trimes, once again you can gain an inside advantage over your competitors in the marketplace. Trimes with Full Details (FD) are apt to cost little more, but are oh-so-much nicer to own! *Some-day*, if the commercial grading services recognize FD (or a similar term), you will be sitting pretty.

In 1858 the design was modified again, creating the Type III, with two outlines around the obverse star and a few other modifications. From that year through 1873 trimes were usually fairly well struck. Demand for the denomination became virtually nonexistent after 1862, when silver coins were hoarded by the public and ceased to circulate. Accordingly, mintages of later years are quite small. Today, while Proofs are available, they are scarce. Choice and gem Mint State trimes are few and far between, particularly for the years after 1865. All three types of the trime were designed by Chief Engraver James B. Longacre.

Design Types of Trimes

1851 to 1853, Type I (No Outline to Star)—The only era in which this denomination was popular. Plentiful as a type, but often lightly struck.

1854 to 1858, Type II (Three Outlines to Star)—Scarcest by far of the three types, and usually very poorly struck. A challenge for the smart buyer.

1859 to 1873, Type III (Two Outlines to Star)—Generally scarce, but when found, apt to be fairly well struck and attractive.

A complete date-and-mintmark (just one branch-mint coin, the 1851-O) set of trimes can be collected easily enough, and in high grades for most dates. However, sharply struck pieces are elusive for some Type I and all Type II coins, and therein lies a challenge for discriminating buyers.

Key to Collecting Silver Three-Cent Pieces

- **Mint State coins:** Most available for the Philadelphia Mint coins of Type I, 1851 through 1853, and 1860 through 1862. Otherwise very elusive, this being particularly true of the Type II (1854–1858) and all dates after 1865.
- **Circulated coins:** Generally available from 1851 through 1862, very scarce to rare after that time.
- **Strike quality:** Type I (1851–1853) usually has some weaknesses, particularly in the shield at the center of the star on the obverse. Check all features carefully. Type II (1854–1858) usually has mushy letters around the obverse and indistinct centers; the star outlines are often irregular, and on the reverse the stars lack detail—a great challenge, and one of the most formidable in the American series of this era. The 1855, the lowest-mintage date, tends to be better struck than the others. Type III (1859–1873) trimes are usually fairly well struck, but all areas should be checked. I have never seen a full set of trimes, 1851 to 1873, with Full Details (FD).

- **Proof coins:** While some earlier Proofs exist, generally such are available only from 1858 onward. Striking is usually quite good. The 1873 is a Proof-only date.
- **Key issues:** 1855, 1863 to 1873.
- **Advice to smart buyers:** Choose with care, especially for aspects of striking and eye appeal. Most high-grade coins on the market are either of the Type I or Type III issues. The true grade of many Proofs is masked by deep or irregular toning; buy only those that are brilliant (with the knowledge that they have been dipped to make them that way) or are lightly and attractively toned.

Half Dimes (1792–1873): An Interesting and Varied Series

Among the denominations of early silver coins, half dimes are among the smallest series in terms of different dates; they are also the most varied. Over the years, several numismatists have fallen in love with these coins, beginning with Harold P. Newlin, who in 1883 wrote a monograph on the series, complete with a good deal of sentiment—especially toward the rare 1802, obviously his pet silver coin of all time.

The first coinage of this denomination was the 1792 half disme, a "story coin" if there ever was one (this was another Newlin favorite in his 1883 text), followed by the 1794 to 1795 Flowing Hair half dimes, the production of which began in 1795 (including those from the 1794-dated dies). In 1796 and 1797 the Draped Bust obverse, Small Eagle reverse half dimes were minted, followed by a gap, then the employment of the new Heraldic Eagle reverse in 1800. This style continued until 1805, after which there was a gap until 1829, from which point Capped Bust half dimes were made through 1837. The Liberty Seated half dimes in various types were coined through 1873, after which the denomination was discontinued.

Design Types of Half Dimes

1792 Half Disme—Struck with Mint equipment, but before the Mint opened. One of America's most historical coins.

1794 and 1795, Flowing Hair—Scarce in all grades, rare in Mint State.

1796 and 1797, Draped Bust, Small Eagle—The most elusive type after 1792.

1800 to 1805, Draped Bust, Heraldic Eagle—Scarce in all grades. Usually weakly struck, except for 1800.

1829 to 1837, Capped Bust—Usually seen well struck and attractive.

1837 and 1838, Liberty Seated, No Stars—A cameo design that was popular when it was released and continues as a collectors' favorite today.

1838 to 1840, Liberty Seated, No Drapery, With Stars—A short-lived type that is usually seen well struck and with good eye appeal.

1840 to 1859, Liberty Seated, With Drapery, With Stars—Available in nearly any grade desired.

1853 to 1855, Arrows at Date—A short-lived but plentiful type.

1860 to 1873, Legend Obverse—Usually seen in higher grades. Proofs are available of all dates.

The first coin of this denomination is the famous 1792 half *disme*, of which 1,500 were coined in the second week of July, 1792, before the foundation to the mint was laid. The operation took place on Mint equipment stored with John Harper, a local mechanic. The term *disme*, while it was used for a long time in government records, seems to have been quickly changed in many places to *dime*, which, of course, is the term we know today.

Today, several hundred 1792 half dismes exist, most of which show extensive circulation, many with planchet damage; but a few Mint State coins are showpieces for their lucky owners. Although some numismatists designate these as patterns, the record shows clearly that they are regular issues.

The Flowing Hair–type half dimes of 1794 and 1795 follow the same motif employed for half dollars and silver dollars of this period, with Miss Liberty facing right, her long hair flowing to the left. On the reverse is a delicate eagle within a wreath. Although dies for 1794 half dimes were made in that year, they were not employed until 1795. Today, half dimes of this type are fairly scarce in higher grades and quite rare in Mint State.

Apparently it was intended that half dimes of the new Draped Bust obverse, Small Eagle reverse were to be coined in 1795, as an obverse die was prepared for that date. However, it appears that it wasn't used at that time, but was later overdated by the punching of a 6 on top of the final figure, yielding the 1796/5—the earliest of all overdates in the American silver series.

Half dimes of this design were made for just two years, with the 1797 existing in three different star counts—15, 16, and 13—for the obverse. It was envisioned that one star would be added for each state in the Union, and in early 1796 there were 15 states. Then Tennessee joined, making 16, at which time it was realized that the idea was unmanageable. The star count was returned to 13, representing the original colonies. Half dimes of this type are elusive in all grades and rare in Mint States.

Half dimes of the type with Draped Bust obverse and Heraldic Eagle reverse, made from 1800 to 1805, except 1804, are scarce as a class. Relatively few were made, and most disappeared. For some reason, the 1800 is far and away the most available issue, and among the Mint State coins that exist, nearly all bear this date. Finding a Mint State 1801, 1803, or 1805 would be a daunting task, and no Mint State examples are known of 1802. The striking of most coins of this type is below average, although, once again, the 1800 emerges as being just about the only date that can be found with most features sharp.

In mid-July 1792, at a private shop not far from where the Mint would be built, 1,500 silver half dismes were struck. The engraver was a Mr. Birch, who also made dies for certain 1792 patterns. For many years numismatists called this the Martha Washington half disme, but the depiction does not resemble any contemporary portrait of her.

Half dimes dated 1794 and 1795 depict the Flowing Hair motif, by Chief Engraver Robert Scot, as also employed on contemporary silver half dollars and dollars. Miss Liberty is artistically depicted, with flowing hair tresses and an amiable countenance. On the reverse, the American eagle has one wing below an olive branch and the other above it, a nice touch. This particular specimen, from the Allison Park Collection (American Numismatic Rarities), is especially well struck, much more detailed than usually seen. (Die variety Logan McCloskey-3)

A rare 1796/5 half dime. However, this particular specimen displays a flat strike and heavy adjustment marks on the reverse. While the coin is desirable and, in fact, has been certified as MS-60, the buyer seeking FD (Full Details) would likely pass this by and continue searching elsewhere.

The FD concept is largely unstudied in the field of late 18th- and early 19th-century coins, and is not reflected on the holders of the popular commercial grading services; most buyers, therefore, are clueless. For you, a smart buyer, this translates into many remarkable opportunities!

This display of 1797-dated half dimes illustrates the star arrangements of this year. The first die had 15 obverse stars, and the next, 16. At the time, it was contemplated to add a star each time a state joined the Union. Artistic considerations intervened: the stars were becoming too crowded, and the last die reverted to 13 stars, representing the number of original colonies.

The 1800 half dime, the first and most plentiful issue of the 1800 to 1805 type, is occasionally found in Mint State. In all grades it is likely to be much better struck than those of later dates.

This 1805 half dime is characteristically weak. Note the lower-left obverse rim, the lack of details at the centers of the stars, and the shallow strike on the bust, not showing any drapery at all. On the reverse is a weak area at the upper right. All half dimes of this date are weak in some areas, a factor taken into consideration by specialists seeking an example of this scarce date.

No half dimes were made for the two decades after 1805, as depositors of silver did not call for them. In the small hours of the morning on July 4, 1829, half dimes were struck in preparation for the laying of the cornerstone for the second Philadelphia Mint building. The design closely follows that of the Capped Bust half dollar, by John Reich, first used in 1807. Half dimes of this type were made in fairly large quantities through 1837, and today are readily collectible by date, although within the dates there are some scarce varieties. A sufficient number of choice and gem pieces exist that acquiring one is not difficult.

The first Liberty Seated half dimes are the 1837 and 1838-O without obverse stars—a miniature representation of the famous 1836 Gobrecht silver dollar. The reverse depicts a wreath and the denomination. For one reason or another, quite a few examples were saved of the 1837, perhaps because of the attractiveness and novelty of the issue. However, those of the New Orleans Mint, 1838-O, are incredible rarities in Mint State.

In 1838, obverse stars were added to the design. In 1840, drapery (extra cloth) was added to the elbow of Miss Liberty, a format continued through 1859, constituting a separate type. Half dimes disappeared from circulation in 1850, when the price of silver made the melting of such pieces profitable. The Act of February 21, 1853, reduced the weight, solving that problem, and pieces circulated effectively thereafter. To signify the lighter weight, most half dimes of 1853 and all of those of 1854 and 1855 have arrowheads at the date.

In 1860, the next and final design change was made in the half dime. UNITED STATES OF AMERICA now appears on the obverse, instead of the reverse, and on the other side is found a wreath of cereal grains enclosing the inscription HALF DIME. Such pieces were produced through 1873, then were discontinued under the Coinage Act of 1873.

Half dimes did not circulate in the East and Midwest after the spring of 1862, due

A lustrous gem Mint State half dime of 1835, the Capped Bust style used from 1829 continuously through 1837. By 1829, this motif, by John Reich, had been used on the dime, quarter dollar, and half dollar for many years.

The Liberty Seated half dime without obverse stars was struck only at the Philadelphia Mint in 1837 and at New Orleans (mintmark O) in 1838. Those of 1837 are known in the Large Date (as here) and Small Date varieties. There is no "drapery," or extra cloth, at Miss Liberty's elbow.

In 1838, stars were added to the obverse of the half dime. This type, continuing the lack of drapery at the elbow, was used into 1840. An 1839-O of this type is shown here.

Half dime of 1844, illustrating the type with obverse stars, now with drapery at the elbow. This motif was used through 1859.

Arrowheads were placed alongside the dates of most 1853 and all the 1854 and 1855 half dimes, to denote a lowering of the authorized weight.

The final type in the half dime series, with UNITED STATES OF AMERICA on the obverse and a "cereal" wreath on the reverse, was made from 1860 to 1873.

to the premium placed on silver coins during the Civil War and afterward. Most struck after this year seem to have been used on the West Coast (where they did circulate) or were later melted.

Notes on Collecting

Today, most numismatists collect half dimes by type, which is easy enough to do, although certain early issues range from scarce to impossible in higher grades. Circulated examples are available for nearly all dates in the half dime series, although the earlier issues are scarce. Later varieties from 1829 onward form a pleasing collecting experience. Of course, in any given instance a Mint State coin is preferable to one showing wear, but few can afford to assemble a full collection at this level.

Liberty Seated half dimes are interesting to collect by date and mint sequence, together with scattered varieties as listed in the *Guide Book* and elsewhere. With the exception of the 1870-S, which is unique, all are readily collectible, although some are rare. Specialists in half dimes of this design often enjoy belonging to the Liberty Seated Collectors Club (LSCC), which publishes an informative magazine, the *Gobrecht Journal*. Emphasis is on interesting die varieties, historical aspects, and the like.

Key to Collecting Half Dimes

- **Mint State coins:** Examples in Mint State are very rare for the 1792 half disme, rare for the 1794 to 1795 Flowing Hair and the 1796 to 1797 types, and very rare for 1800 to 1805 (except for the solitary date 1800; of all other dates of this type *combined*, only about a half dozen true Mint State coins are known). Capped Bust and Liberty Seated half dimes are readily obtainable in Mint State, but certain varieties are scarce, with the 1846 being almost unobtainable.
- **Circulated coins:** The vast majority of later half dimes, 1829 to 1873, are available and inexpensive in such grades as VF and EF, furnishing an interesting opportunity.

- **Strike quality:** Early issues of 1792 to 1805 are apt to be lightly struck in areas, even on pieces of the finest grades. This is to be expected, and a compromise has to be made. Later types are generally available sharp, but not all dates and varieties within those types are. Cherrypicking is the order of the day, with FD pieces being available for many issues.
- **Proof coins:** Although scattered earlier Proofs were made, the first generally available date is 1858, in which year an estimated 210 were made. Proofs from then through 1873 can be acquired with some patience, as hundreds exist of each. Quality tends to be better on the small half dimes than on larger Liberty Seated coins, perhaps as the surface was not as liable to be damaged. Still, care is needed.
- **Key issues:** All issues of 1792 to 1805 range from scarce to rare, with the key issue being 1802. Among later half dimes, all are readily collectible except the 1870-S. Transitional half dimes of 1859 are major rarities, and of the 1860, Director James Ross Snowden stated that just 100 were struck; these delicacies were made for sale to collectors.
- **Advice to smart buyers:** The usual suggestions apply—cherrypick for sharp strike (FD) and eye appeal. If you go beyond collecting a type set, read as much as you can on the series. There are a lot of interesting situations. For example, an MS-63 1865 half dime, mintage just 13,000 pieces, is priced at $1,200 in the *Guide Book*, while in the same grade an 1844-O, mintage 220,000, is valued at $12,000. The answer lies in availability: in 1865, half dimes didn't circulate, and many were saved. In 1844, all were paid out into the channels of commerce, where they became worn.
- **Selected bibliography:**
  Blythe, Al. 1992. *The Complete Guide to Liberty Seated Half Dimes*. Virginia Beach, VA.

Breen, Walter. 1958. *United States Half Dimes: A Supplement*. New York, NY, 1958. (supplement to the Valentine work below)

Logan, Russell J., and John W. McCloskey. 1998. *Federal Half Dimes 1792–1837*. Manchester, MI.

Newlin, Harold P. 1933. *A Classification of the Early Half-Dimes of the United States*. Philadelphia, PA. (original work published 1883; of historical interest only)

Valentine, Daniel W. 1975. *The United States Half Dimes*. New York, NY. (original work published 1931; reprinted 1975)

Dimes (1796 to Date)

Dimes, or ten-cent pieces, have been minted nearly continuously since 1796, with infrequent exceptions. Along the way, many interesting types have been created, all of which are readily collectible today, plus hundreds of dates, mintmarks, and other varieties.

Design Types of Dimes

1796 and 1797, Draped Bust, Small Eagle—Scarce, but not in the rarity category of related quarters and half dollars. Most are in circulated grades. The few choice Mint State coins that exist are mostly dated 1796.

1798 to 1807, Draped Bust, Heraldic Eagle—Not rare as a type, but a great challenge to find sharply struck.

1809 to 1828, Capped Bust, Open Collar—A pleasing era offering a number of interesting varieties. Generally elusive in Mint State.

1828 to 1837, Capped Bust, Closed Collar—Not difficult to find in Mint State. Striking is less of a problem than with earlier types.

1837 and 1838, Liberty Seated, No Stars—The 1837 is the variety usually encountered. The vast majority of Mint State coins are of this date. The 1838-O is quite scarce. Many "Mint State" coins are acid treated or otherwise "improved" AU coins. I've only ever seen a few really choice pieces.

1838 to 1840, Liberty Seated, No Drapery, With Stars—Fairly scarce in comparison to later issues, from the short period they were made.

1840 to 1860, Liberty Seated With Drapery, With Stars—Easily collectible for a type set.

1853 to 1855, Liberty Seated, Arrows at Date—Readily available, although striking can be a problem.

1860 to 1891, Liberty Seated, Legend Obverse—Later dates are usually fairly well struck and have good eye appeal.

1873 and 1874, Liberty Seated, Arrows at Date—Somewhat scarce in higher grades, except for Proof issues.

1892 to 1916, Barber—Common in worn grades and not particularly rare in Mint State, although gems are in a distinct minority.

1916 to 1945, Mercury—Gems are easily available for a type set.

1946 to 1964, Roosevelt (Silver)—This is the date range for regular silver issues. Some silver Proofs were made in later years for collectors. Common in all grades.

1965 to Date, Roosevelt (Clad)—Common in all grades.

Dimes combining the Draped Bust obverse with the Small Eagle reverse were made only in 1796 and 1797. Enough were produced (nearly 50,000 in total) that examples are not prohibitively rare today. However, pieces in EF, AU, or Mint State can be difficult to locate. Most buyers seek a representative example for a type set.

This next type combines the Draped Bust reverse as the preceding with the Heraldic Eagle reverse. Striking these pieces up proved to be extremely difficult, and today nearly all of them are weak in sections, with 1807 being notorious in this regard. Although many interesting die varieties exist, most buyers seek a nice example for a type set.

John Reich's Capped Bust design, first used on half dollars of 1807, made its initial appearance on dimes in 1809. Pieces from that date through 1828 are in the old style, with wider borders and more prominent dentils. In the latter year the dies were modified and the dentils made smaller, and the issues from that point on are more uniform in appearance. Although some dates such as 1822 (in particular) are elusive, all are collectible within this range.

The Liberty Seated dimes closely follow the half dimes in type, except that the dimes extend all the way to 1891. The first issues, the 1837 and 1838-O, are without obverse stars, similar to the illustrious Gobrecht silver dollar of 1836. Stars were added in 1838, and continued through 1860, at which time a modification was made: UNITED STATES OF AMERICA was placed on the obverse, and the reverse was given a cereal wreath. This general style was used through 1891.

Along the way there are other types, including the 1853 to 1855 with arrows at date to signify a reduction in the author-

A dime of 1796, the first year of issue. The Draped Bust obverse is employed with the Small Eagle reverse. Similar to the half dimes and quarter dollars of the same date, there is no mark of denomination on either side of the coin.

In 1798 the reverse of the dime was changed to the Heraldic Eagle motif. Coins of this style were made through 1807, except for 1799. The Mint did not make silver coins on speculation, but coined them only for specific requests made by depositors of bullion, most of whom preferred silver dollars.

Two dimes of 1807 illustrate typical coins of this date, nearly always seen with areas of light striking or other problems.

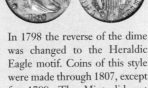

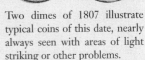

The Capped Bust design was used on dimes from 1809 to 1828, as shown here on a variety of 1814, the older style with larger dentils at the border. In the same year, the dies were modified slightly, making the stars and dentils smaller and more uniform.

Capped Bust dime of 1835, illustrating the modified style used from 1828 to 1837.

Liberty Seated dimes of 1837 and 1838-O (shown here), without obverse stars and without cloth at Miss Liberty's elbow, follow the design used on half dimes of the same dates and mints. These dimes are much scarcer than are half dimes, and the 1838-O dime in Mint State, as here, is a prime rarity. (Koshkarian Collection, ANR)

Liberty Seated dime of 1840, style with obverse stars but without drapery at the elbow, coined from 1838 to 1840.

An 1845 dime with stars around the border and with drapery at Miss Liberty's elbow, the type minted from 1840 to 1859 plus 1860-S, interrupted by the With-Arrows type of 1853 to 1855.

Most dimes of 1853 and all of 1854 and 1855 have arrowheads alongside the date to illustrate the reduction in authorized weight under the Act of February 21, 1853.

Liberty Seated dimes from 1860 to 1891 have UNITED STATES OF AMERICA on the obverse and a cereal wreath on the reverse. Shown here is a gem Mint State 1882.

In early 1873, arrowheads were placed alongside the date of the 1873 dime to denote a slight increase in weight, a style continued in 1874.

Advertisement for *Beadle's Dime Book* series, guides that were popular in their time. (*Frank Leslie's Illustrated Weekly*, March 3, 1860)

A Proof Barber dime of 1896, illustrating the type of 1892 to 1916. The same obverse was used on quarter dollars and half dollars of the era.

Sculptor Adolph A. Weinman in his studio. Weinman created the designs for the 1916 Mercury dime and Liberty Walking half dollar.

The 1916-D dime, produced in the first year of the Mercury design, was struck only to the extent of 264,000 pieces, a small mintage for the series. While disproportionate quantities were saved of many first-year coins, this was not true for the 1916-D. Examples are scarce today, and in choice Mint State, as depicted here, the issue is a rarity.

What do you think? This 1925-D Mercury dime has been certified as MS-67 FB by a leading grading service. Although it may have Full Bands, the date is weak, and the 5 in the date is very shallow. If you have to buy a coin for your collection, would you rather own a certified MS-67 FB with weak date, or a much cheaper MS-64 FB, cherrypicked for Full Details (FD), with full everything?

Or, if you desire an MS-67 FB, do you have the patience to wait for a truly sharp one? When found, it will cost no more than weaker MS-67s! There are many choices of this kind at your fingertips.

ized weight; and 1873 to 1874, again with arrows but for the opposite reason—to signify a slight *increase.*

The entire spectrum of Liberty Seated dimes is extremely interesting, and at any given time several dozen enthusiasts are busy studying die varieties and technical details, while hundreds of others are simply collecting by date and mintmark. Certain issues are elusive, but all are collectible.

Beginning in 1892, the Liberty Head design by Charles Barber, called the *Barber design* today, made its appearance. Coinage became regular, and for a time the Philadelphia, New Orleans, and San Francisco mints all turned out pieces, an output to which the Denver Mint added beginning in 1906. Proofs were struck at Philadelphia. Today, Barber dimes are quite interesting to contemplate. Except for the 1894-S, all are readily collectible, and some of the scarcer rarities do not bring prices commensurate with their elusive quality— always an alluring prospect for the smart buyer. Choice and Gem Mint State coins can be very rare for certain varieties, particularly branch mints, and are generally overlooked in the marketplace. As always, quality is a consideration, and forming a choice set will take some time.

The winged Liberty Head or "Mercury" dime, by noted sculptor Adolph A. Weinman, was first minted in 1916 (Weinman also designed the 1916 Liberty Walking half dollar). The reverse illustrates a fasces and a branch. Coins of this attractive and highly acclaimed motif were minted continuously through 1945, with the exception of 1922, 1932, and 1933.

Although the design was immediately popular, as it is today, it was not until the 1930s that convenient albums became available to store them. At that time, a passion for saving them arose, but most earlier dates were found to be elusive in higher grades, this being particularly true of the mintmarked issues through about 1927. Striking sharpness of Mercury dimes can be erratic, often with light areas on the obverse rim near the date and, on the reverse, on the pairs of horizontal bands crossing the fasces. Specimens with each band distinctly separated in the pair are called Full Bands (FB), and for some issues bring a great premium.

Knowledge is necessary to spend money wisely in this series, and time must be taken. There is *much* you need to know before you can spend your money wisely.

Reality Check Needed!

For Mercury dimes—well, for *any* series if you are a connoisseur and at the same time want good value for your money—a reality check is needed. Below are some actual examples of pricing within the Mercury dime series, for coins without Full Bands (but possibly with all other areas sharp) and for coins with Full Bands (but with no guarantee that the date, rims, etc., will be sharp).

For example, the 1916-S normally comes with split bands, and thus, finding one is desirable but not necessarily unusual. On the opposite end of the spectrum, the otherwise common 1945 Philadelphia issue, one of the most plentiful and inexpensive issues of the series, is scarcely ever seen with Full Bands, and when found is worth many thousands of dollars (more than just a few have been located by collectors who knew what to look for).

Overriding all of this is the curious situation that a Mercury dime can be certified as Full Bands, but have weakness elsewhere! Again, the hobby would benefit from some truly meaningful term such as FD (Full Details). A dime called FD would have full *everything!*

A recent issue of the *Certified Coin Dealer Newsletter* listed these market values for selected grades of certain Mercury dimes, with and without the FB designation:[57]

1916-S (PCGS)—MS-64: $86 • MS-64 FB: $140 • MS-67: $950[58] • MS-67 FB: $6,555.

1916-S (NGC)—MS-64: $54 • MS-64 FB: $127 • MS-67: $1,050 • MS-67 FB: $3,080.

1925-D (PCGS)—MS-64: $795 • MS-64 FB: $1,095 • MS-67: $2,400[59] • MS-67 FB: $21,850.

1925-D (NGC)—MS-64: $865 • MS-64 FB: $978 • MS-67: $2,800[60] • MS-67 FB: $6,700.

1945 (PCGS)—MS-64: $20 • MS-64 FB: $2,400 • MS-67: $57 • MS-67 FB: $18,000.[61]

1945 (NGC)—MS-64: $15 • MS-64 FB: $1,600 • MS-67: $50 • MS-67 FB: $9,750.[62]

A bit of reflection is needed as to what to buy. Let's focus on the 1925-D. (These comments are hypothetical, as the coins themselves must be examined along with the price.)

For the 1925-D we see that an MS-67 FB is said to be worth $21,850 if in a PCGS holder, but just $6,700 if in an NGC holder. Why? I don't know the answer. Perhaps the $21,850 price represents a PCGS coin that had superb eye appeal in addition to Full Bands, while perhaps the NGC coin did not. Or perhaps the PCGS coin was sharp all over (with not only Full Bands, but Full Details), while the NGC coin had weakness in areas other than the bands. Or perhaps the discrepancy is due to something else altogether.

If I were seeking a 1925-D for my collection (again, this is hypothetical, as I do not collect these, but enjoy buying and selling them), I would insist that the coin be completely sharp—with not just Full Bands, but Full Details (i.e., full *everything*). If I were confronted with the choice of buying (a) an MS-64 FB Full Details coin, with Full Details, in the $1,000 range, or (b) for many multiples of that price, an MS-67 FB with weak date and rim, in a heartbeat I would pick the MS-64!

However, if I were building a registry set for competition, my MS-64 would attract no attention, while someone else's MS-67 FB, but with a weak date, would rank high! I wouldn't enter a registry contest with such fuzzy rules! I respectfully suggest that those who pay attention to Full Bands and not to other features might be spending their money unwisely.

As to the whopping price differential among 1945 dimes, even if you owned a

hundred oil wells, you might rather have an MS-64 FD for $20 than an MS-67 FB for $18,000. You could take the $17,980 saved and build a superb numismatic library, with nearly full sets of *The Numismatist*, the *Numismatic Scrapbook Magazine*, and most all leading reference books (see chapter 31). The point is that, with tens of thousands of varieties of coins, tokens, medals, and paper money in the American numismatic spectrum, it would seem to me that the way to go is to get "nice" examples (e.g., a lustrous 1945 Mercury dime for $20). It seems to me that you lose a lot if you buy only a handful of ultra-high-grade certified coins, and ignore the opportunity to build a truly broad collection.

Such situations provide food for thought, and there is no one right answer. However, with such information available, you are in a position to make an educated choice.

You can also see, I hope, that spending a few dollars for subscriptions to current numismatic publications, such as the *Certified Coin Dealer Newsletter*, can be a superb investment in knowledge. However, you must add your own thoughts to the mix before you make purchase decisions.

Other Options

For those who cannot afford or do not desire a full Mint State set of Mercury dimes, it's popular practice to collect the earlier dates (1916–1931) in circulated grades, interspersed with some Mint State pieces, and the later dates (1934–1945) in Mint State.

After Franklin D. Roosevelt died in 1945, thought was given to honoring him on the ten-cent piece, for during his life he had been active in the March of Dimes campaign to raise money to combat the disease of polio. The change was made and in 1946 the Roosevelt dime appeared, and has been made ever since that time. Designed by John Sinnock, the dime features Roosevelt's portrait on the obverse, and a torch and branches on the reverse. Issues from 1946 through 1964 were made in the standard alloy of 90% silver and 10% copper. Later issues have been of clad

Proof 1983-S Roosevelt dime.

metal, punctuated with some silver strikings for collectors.

A quick glance at the *Guide Book* or any other listing will reveal that more than 200 varieties of Roosevelt dimes have been made since 1946. A complete set of choice and gem Mint State and Proof dates and mintmarks can be acquired relatively inexpensively. Again, some judgment is required. A recent issue of *Coin Values* lists prices for a common 1995-D dime as 50¢ in MS-63 grade, $5 in MS-65 grade, and $100 at the MS-67 level. As to the rarity of the 1995-D dime, 1,274,890,000 were made—equal to about four coins for every man, woman, and child in the United States. What grade of 1995-D would you buy? Think about it.

Numismatic Considerations

While early dimes tend to range from scarce to rare, this being true of those from 1796 through the late 1820s, most others are easily collectible in circulated grades, and as the years progress, in Mint State as well. The typical person specializing in Liberty Seated coins and belonging to the Liberty Seated Collectors Club is apt to have a holding ranging from VF through EF and AU, punctuated with occasional Mint State and Proof pieces. On the other hand, investors tend to buy fewer pieces and do not collect systematically, but concentrate on acquiring selected coins that appeal to them.

Barber dimes from 1892 through 1916 are challenging to collect, and except for the 1894-S (of which just 24 were minted and only about 9 are known to exist), all can be obtained in circulated grades as well as low Mint State ranges. Choice and gem Mint State pieces are another thing entirely. These can be difficult, and offer a challenge. Mercury dimes from 1916 to 1945

are generally collected in higher grades, as are Roosevelt dimes from 1946 to date.

In any event, if you form a type set of dimes you'll have the experience of studying the interesting earlier issues, made from hand-cut dies, and see the progression of designs over the years.

Key to Collecting Dimes

- **Mint State coins:** Rare to extremely rare for early issues (1796–1807), quite elusive for later issues through the 1820s, becoming available for selected dates and varieties from 1830 onward. No one rule fits all. Among Liberty Seated dimes, the most often seen in Mint State are Philadelphia issues as well as, generally, pieces dated after 1874. Certain earlier varieties are very elusive, and 1846 and 1859-S are ultra rare in Mint State. Some dimes in the 1880s are very plentiful, but the demand for them is such that the supply is absorbed by investors and others seeking high grades. Mint State Barber dimes are rare for certain mintmark varieties, particularly those before about 1906. Mercury dimes are generally available, although certain issues are rare in relation to the demand for them, most notably the 1916-D, 1942/1, and the 1942/1-D. Roosevelt dimes are all available in Mint State easily enough.

- **Circulated coins:** Pieces in circulated grades exist in approximate proportion to their mintages, except that certain Carson City issues before 1875 seem to have nearly all disappeared and are rarer than even their low mintages indicate. Popular pricing guides are a good key to availability. Barber dimes are all available easily enough well worn, but VF, EF and AU can be scarce, particularly for mintmarks. Mercury dimes exist in all grades, with lower-mintage issues being scarcer. Roosevelt dimes are available in circulated grades, but Mint State pieces are sufficiently inexpensive that most opt for those.

- **Strike quality:** Most early dimes of 1796 to 1828 are lightly struck in one area or another. Usually, some compromise has to be made when buying, and for some dates (e.g., 1807) virtually all are poorly struck. This adds to the lure of tracking down nice pieces. Liberty Seated dimes can be lightly struck on the head of Miss Liberty, on the stars, and on parts of the wreath. On Barber dimes check the wreath. Mercury dimes can be weak at the rims and at the horizontal bands on the reverse. Roosevelt dimes can have lightness noticeable at the torch on the center reverse, and Full Torch (FT) notations are sometimes seen for sharp pieces. As noted in chapter 8, a universally applied term such as FD (Full Details) would be beneficial to the hobby.

- **Proof coins:** Proofs are available for all dates 1858 to 1916 in proportion to their mintages. Those of 1936 to 1942 are from completely polished (including the portrait) dies. Proofs of 1950 to 1964 either can be from polished dies or have cameo frosted contrast, the latter being a collector favorite. Proofs from 1968-S to date are nearly all cameos.

- **Key issues:** 1796 to 1802, 1822, 1871-CC to 1874-CC, 1894-S (trophy coin of the series), 1916-D, 1942/1, and 1942/1-D.

- **Advice to smart buyers:** Although the aspects of sharp striking of Mercury dimes have been discussed and market-valued to a fare-thee-well, very few buyers are informed as to earlier varieties, offering many opportunities, especially for dates prior to 1860. Many branch-mint Barber dimes are rarer in MS-65 or higher grades than their market values suggest; population reports are useful in this analysis. Keep Optimal Collecting Grade (OCG) in mind, and think twice or even three times before paying a stretch price for an ultra-grade coin that is common and inexpensive in MS-65 or -66.

- **Selected bibliography:**

  Ahwash, Kamal M. 1977. *Encyclopedia of United States Liberty Seated Dimes 1837–1891.* Kamal Press. (superseded by the Greer work, below)

  Davis, David, Russell Logan, Allen Lovejoy, John McCloskey, and William Subjack. 1984. *Early United States Dimes 1796–1837.* Ypsilanti, MI. (lists "John Reich [JR] numbers" for varieties)

  Flynn, Kevin. 2001. *The Authoritative Reference on Roosevelt Dimes.* Brooklyn, NY.

  Greer, Brian. 1992. *The Complete Guide to Liberty Seated Dimes.* Virginia Beach, VA.

  Lange, David W. 1993. *The Complete Guide to Mercury Dimes.* Virginia Beach, VA.

  Lawrence, David. 1991. *The Complete Guide to Barber Dimes.* Virginia Beach, VA.

Twenty-Cent Pieces (1875–1878): A Seemingly Good Idea That Wasn't

Silver twenty-cent pieces represent a most unusual denomination—one that probably should not have existed, but did, and hence, everybody wants one!

Senator John P. Jones of Nevada, probably seeking to expand the market for silver mined in that state (for such metal was in a market slump at the time), introduced legislation to create the twenty-cent piece. Already in circulation in the West were dimes and quarter dollars, but Jones suggested that a twenty-cent piece would serve a further purpose in helping buyers and sellers make change. Congress agreed, and under the Act of March 3, 1875, the coin became a reality.

The obverse design, an adaptation of a motif created by Christian Gobrecht, features the familiar Liberty Seated arrangement, with an arc of stars around and date below. Curiously, the word LIBERTY on the shield is *raised*—the twenty-cent piece is the only regular-issue Liberty Seated coin, other than the 1836 Gobrecht silver dollar, with this feature. The reverse of the twenty-cent piece depicts a perched eagle, also similar to the quarter, but in this instance swiped from the motif on the reverse of the trade dollar, and thus with notable differences. The edge is plain rather than reeded. Chief Engraver William Barber created the coin, as he did the trade dollar.

In 1875, silver coins didn't circulate at par in the East or the Midwest, and thus they could be useful only in and around the Pacific Coast. The mintage figures reflect this: 38,910 examples made in Philadelphia, 113,290 in Carson City, and a whopping 1,155,000 in San Francisco. These pieces quickly reached circulation in California and Nevada, and just as quickly the public was confused by them—because they looked like quarters.

The denomination proved useless, and in the second year of its existence, 1876, only 14,640 were produced for circulation in Philadelphia, and 10,000 in Carson City. The San Francisco coining presses turned out none. As there was a glut of them in circulation, nearly all on hand in Carson City went to the melting pot, with perhaps fewer than two dozen escaping into numismatic hands. Today, all but a few of the classic 1876-CC twenty-cent piece rarities are in choice or gem Mint State. My theory is that some of these were kept as curiosities by members of the Assay Commission that met in Philadelphia in early 1877 to review the preceding year's coinage.

The twenty-cent piece, launched in 1875, was soon found to be a failure. Somewhat similar in design and diameter to the quarter dollar, the new denomination was confusing to the public. Following a large mintage in 1875, many fewer were struck in 1876, and in 1877 and 1878 production was limited to Proofs for collectors.

In 1877 and 1878, Proofs were made for collectors, to the extent of 350 and 600 pieces, respectively. Then the denomination was terminated. The public soon forgot the twenty-cent pieces, but numismatists did not. Ever since then examples have been eagerly sought in all grades.

Key to Collecting Twenty-Cent Pieces

- **Mint State coins:** Most often seen are 1875-S, but 1875, 1875-CC, and 1876 come on the market now and then.
- **Circulated coins:** The vast majority are 1875-S, with 1875-CC being several leagues behind, and 1875 and 1876 being also-rans. Generally, the Philadelphia coins are seen in higher average grades.
- **Strike quality:** The 1875-CC is often weak at the top of the eagle's wings, the 1875-S less so. The Philadelphia Mint coins are usually sharply defined.
- **Proof coins:** Available for 1875 to 1878 in proportion to their mintages. Most of 1875 have minute die-finish arc lines near the center.
- **Key issues:** The 1876-CC is a trophy coin, while 1877 and 1878 are rare as Proof-only issues.
- **Advice to smart buyers:** Check for sharpness of strike and eye appeal. The last can be a challenge even for Proofs.

Quarter Dollars (1796 to Date)

The silver quarter dollar, or 25-cent piece, is one of just a few denominations first produced in the early years of the Mint and still made today, although since 1964 silver has been replaced by clad metal for circulating coinage. Since 1999, numismatists have been delighted with the statehood reverse quarters, released at the rate of five different designs each year.

Quarters are fascinating to collect, and many different types invite your interest. With the current 50 State Quarters®

Program (as the Mint designates it), five new types are created each year—a situation without precedent in our hobby. The following are the basic types produced since 1796.

Design Types of Quarter Dollars

1796, Draped Bust, Small Eagle—Design produced only this year. Most Mint State coins are highly prooflike. A rare and highly desired coin at all grade levels.

1804 to 1807, Draped Bust, Heraldic Eagle—Scarce in lower grades, very rare in Mint State. Usually weakly struck in areas, and FD coins are few and far between.

1815 to 1828, Capped Bust, Large Diameter—Produced intermittently during this span, quarters of this design are readily available for a type set, although certain varieties are rare.

1831 to 1838, Capped Bust, Small Diameter—Modified design omitting E PLURIBUS UNUM. Usually seen well struck.

1838 to 1840, Liberty Seated, No Drapery—A scarce, short-lived issue, although not all collectors consider the design to constitute a separate type.

1840 to 1865, Liberty Seated, With Drapery, No Motto—Available in just about any desired grade.

1853, Arrows at Date, Rays on Reverse—Plentiful; however, well-struck pieces can be hard to find.

1854 to 1855, Arrows at Date—Plentiful, and generally seen choicer than the preceding.

1866 to 1891, Liberty Seated, With Motto—Easily available in the context of the series, including in Proof format. In the marketplace, most Mint State coins are dated after 1874.

1873 to 1874, Liberty Seated, Arrows at Date—Somewhat scarce in higher grades.

1892 to 1916, Barber—Easily enough available, although sharply struck gems

are rare. Proofs are available for all years except 1916.

1916 to 1917, Standing Liberty, Bare Breast—A numismatic favorite. Most are Philadelphia Mint issues of 1917.

1917 to 1930, Standing Liberty, Covered Bosom—Plentiful, but pieces with the head and shield-rivet details sharp (FD) are in the minority.

1932 to 1964, Washington, Houdon Portrait (Silver)—Plentiful coins from modern times.

1965 to 1998, Washington, Houdon Portrait (Clad)—Plentiful. Some later-dated silver coins, not regular issues, were made for collectors' sets.

1976 (Dated 1776–1976), Bicentennial, Houdon Portrait (Clad)—Ditto.

1976 (Dated 1776–1976), Bicentennial, Houdon Portrait (Silver Clad)—Plentiful as a numismatic issue.

1999 Onward, Statehood Reverse Series (Clad)—Five different types each year. Plentiful, and well worth owning.

1999 Onward, Statehood Reverse Series (Silver)—Five different types each year, made to be sold at a premium to collectors. Again, plentiful and desirable.

Quarters of the Early Era

Although the silver quarter dollar was authorized by the Mint Act of April 2, 1792, and while certain other silver denominations were made as early as 1794, it was not until 1796 that the dime and the quarter dollar actually made their debuts. The motifs of these two denominations are similar, each with the Draped Bust of Miss Liberty on the obverse, facing right, said to have been from a sketch made by well-known artist Gilbert Stuart (he of the unfinished portrait of Washington so common in schoolrooms). All of the 1796 quarters have 15 stars on the obverse, unlike certain other silver denominations, which can have 13, 15, or even 16. The reverse illustrates an eagle perched or otherwise situated on what seems to be a billowy cloud. A wreath surrounds. Two die varieties were made of the 1796 year; these are known today as Browning-1 and -2, from the descriptive list created by Ard W. Browning and published in 1925.

Every Mint State 1796 quarter I have seen is prooflike to one degree or another, some closely resembling full mirror Proofs—really gorgeous. Most are also nicely framed by long dentils, or projections, on the obverse. The result is a splendid coin. As quarters were produced only to the specific order of bullion depositors, most owners of this metal requested dollars, as they were easier to count. Only 6,146 quarters were made in 1796—a slow start for the denomination, auguring low mintage figures that would be the rule for many years to come.

It was not until 1804 that quarter dollars were again made, this time with the Heraldic Eagle reverse, a motif modeled on

the Great Seal of the United States that had made its debut in federal coinage on the quarter eagle of 1796. Quarter dollars of this style were made through 1807. The combination of relief on the obverse and reverse, plus the striking from hand-powered presses, resulted in coins that today are usually quite weak in one or another areas of the design (this being particularly true of the last year of issue, 1807). Accordingly, a smart buyer can have a field day searching for and occasionally finding a fairly sharp strike of this design type. No information concerning striking is to be found on certified holders—an advantage for you, as a knowledgeable buyer.

The next quarter-dollar coinage took place in 1815 and utilized John Reich's Capped Bust design, a motif first used on the half dollar of 1807. Coins of this style were made through 1828 and are fairly scarce today. Within this range are the 1823/2 overdate rarity, nearly always

Only 6,146 examples were made of the 1796 quarter dollar, the first year of issue and the only year combining the Draped Bust obverse with the Small Eagle reverse. The dies were exceptionally well cut, imparting great beauty to the designs, to which is added the effect of framing by the especially prominent dentils at the border.

No quarter dollars were struck from 1797 to 1803, as depositors of silver bullion did not request them. In 1804 they were again made, now incorporating the Heraldic Eagle reverse. Coins of this type were made through 1807. Of these, the 1804, die variety Browning-1, as shown here, is the scarcest date.

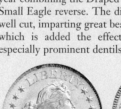 

This lustrous 1806 quarter dollar, die variety Browning-3, has been certified as MS-65. Similar to the majority of quarters of the 1804 to 807 design, it is weakly struck in areas. On this coin the weakness is at the centers. Certain others are very weak at the borders.

Quarter dollars of the Capped Bust design, by John Reich, were made intermittently from 1815 to 1828.

seen in worn condition, plus the classic 1827/3/2, a multiple-digit overdate (the nature of which was first identified by Karl Moulton; struck from the same obverse die, now reworked, used to make the 1823/2). Some of the 1827 Proofs, called *originals*, are distinguished by having a curled base to the 2 in "25 C." on the reverse; while restrikes, coined on least two occasions, are from a different die with the base of the 2 square or straight.

After 1828 no quarter dollars were made until 1831, when the Capped Bust obverse was slightly modified, and the reverse was changed to eliminate the motto E PLURIBUS UNUM. Coins of this design were made through 1838.

As the years progressed, techniques in die-making became more sophisticated, resulting in coins that were more uniform in appearance. Accordingly, quarter dollars of the early years, 1796 through 1828, are apt to show wide differences when studied carefully, but those of the span from 1831 to 1838 are less distinctive.

The Liberty Seated and Later Years

The Liberty Seated motif, created by Christian Gobrecht for use on the 1836 silver dollar, was employed on the quarter dollar beginning in 1838. Early issues lacked extra drapery at the elbow of Miss Liberty, an aspect changed in 1840 (in which year some have drapery and some do not). Miss Liberty in this seated position was employed through and including 1891, but not without some changes along the way. In 1850 the value of silver metal rose on world markets. Profit could be made by taking existing coins and melting them, and this was done. For several years no Liberty Seated coins of any denomination were to be found in general circulation. The Act of

An 1832 quarter dollar illustrating the reduced-diameter type, without motto E PLURIBUS UNUM, minted from 1831 to 1838.

The first Liberty Seated quarter depicts Miss Liberty without drapery at her elbow. The date numerals are arranged in a curve, an elegant touch also seen on certain other Liberty Seated coins, half dimes to silver dollars, of the era from 1836 to 1839. The digits were entered into the die with single-numeral punches. Beginning in 1840, four-digit punches were used, and most later dates are in a straight line.

An 1843-O quarter dollar with drapery at Miss Liberty's elbow.

Following the Act of February 21, 1853, the weight of the quarter dollar was reduced. This was indicated on later coins of this year by the addition of arrowheads at the date and rays around the eagle on the reverse. In 1854 and 1855 the arrowheads were retained, but the rays were dropped. In 1856 the arrowheads were discontinued.

In 1866 the motto IN GOD WE TRUST was added on a long, flowing ribbon above the eagle's head on the reverse. Coins of this type were made through 1891. Many 1873 and all 1874 quarters have arrowheads at the date to signify a slight increase in authorized weight under the Coinage Act of 1873.

An 1897-S quarter dollar illustrating the Barber design used from 1892 to 1916.

February 21, 1853, reduced the authorized weight of the denominations from the half dime to the half dollar, after which the new, lightweight coins circulated effectively. Quarters of the new standard were designated by arrowheads alongside the date and, on the quarter and half dollar only, rays around the eagle. After 1855 the arrowheads were discontinued, but the low weight remained the same.

Beginning in the spring of 1862, silver coins were hoarded by the public as the outcome of the Civil War became increasingly uncertain. Many expected that this squirreling-away of coinage would end when the war did, but the hoarding continued, and it was not until after April 20, 1876, that silver again traded at par with paper money. In the meantime, from 1862 to 1876, it took more than $100 in Uncle Sam's Legal Tender or other currency to buy $100 in quarters (face value), the premium being more than double at one point in 1864.

In 1866 the motto IN GOD WE TRUST was added above the eagle on the reverse, to remain there for the rest of the series. The Coinage Act of February 12, 1873, provided for a slight *increase* in the authorized weight of the dime, quarter, and half dollar, and this was indicated on some later coins of 1873 and all of 1874 by placement of arrowheads alongside the date. Later issues were without arrowheads, but the slightly increased weight remained the same.

After 1876, when quarters were again seen in commerce, citizens recognized the futility of continuing to hold silver coins hoarded in the early 1860s, and tremendous quantities of coins from trimes to dollars were turned loose. This was a numismatic delight, as pieces dating back to the Capped Bust era were available for face value! There was a glut of silver, resulting in sharply lowered mintages of new Liberty Seated coins from 1879 onward, although some years were exceptions. In the meantime, beginning in a significant way in 1858, Proofs of each year were struck for collectors.

The Liberty Head quarter by Chief Engraver Charles E. Barber was introduced in 1892. His initial B was prominent on the neck truncation on the obverse. Mintages in the Barber-quarter series were fairly regular, typically including several different mints (e.g., 1892, 1892-O, and 1892-S) for a given year. Production continued through and including 1916. Along the way, three varieties of exceptionally low mintage were created: 1896-S, of which just 188,039 were minted; 1901-S, with 72,664; and 1913-S, with 40,000. Interestingly, the most available of these three in Mint State is the lowest-mintage 1913-S.

When Barber quarters reached circulation they tended to wear quickly, reducing the high parts of the design and quickly obliterating most of the word LIBERTY. Accordingly, circulated pieces found today in grades such as VF and EF, showing word LIBERTY complete, are very scarce. On the other hand, a Liberty Seated silver half dime of the 1850s, also graded by the completeness of the word LIBERTY (on that coin appearing on the shield) could remain in circulation for *decades* before, at long last, the word disappeared. Such influences are quite interesting to study.

Generally, Barber quarter dollars in Mint State are found with many nicks and bagmarks, and often with areas of light striking (particularly on the eagle's leg on the right). Choice and gem pieces that are well struck and very attractive are extremely hard to find, except in just a few varieties. In the 1950s, Pittsburgh collector Ray Byrne desired to form a full Mint State collection of these, but gave up when most of those he bought, including from leading dealers and important sales, proved to be rubbed or scuffed.

Assembling a really choice set of Barber quarters can be a specialty in itself. Most buyers opt to acquire a single coin for a type set, for which there is no problem. In my entire professional career I have seen only a handful of collections in which all of the Barber quarters were MS-64 or finer and with good eye appeal.

Quarter-Dollar Designs of the 20th Century

Quarters of the Standing Liberty type, created by sculptor Hermon MacNeil, were minted only from 1916 to 1930—a relatively short time. Since then they have captured the imagination and fancy of many numismatists, and today they are favorites for inclusion in both type sets and specialized collections of dates and mints.

The first Standing Liberty quarters of 1916 were produced to the extent of just 52,000 pieces, and apparently were released without much fanfare. Normally, first-year-of-issue coins of any 20th-century design were saved in some quantity by the public, but for the 1916 Standing Liberty quarter this does not seem to be the case. One possibility (not confirmed) is that, when many of the 1917-dated issues—eventually minted to the extent of 8,740,000 in Philadelphia, 1,509,200 in Denver, and 1,952,000 in San Francisco—were released at about the same time, the public snapped those up instead, perhaps seeing them first. Certainly, today the issues of 1917 are plentiful.

The 1916 to 1917 coins, designated Type I by collectors today, feature Miss Liberty standing in an opening or gateway of a parapet, with her right hand holding an olive branch, her left hand holding a shield—symbols of peace and military might (or perhaps protection), and with her right breast exposed. The entire arrangement is quite artistic. The reverse depicts an eagle flying to the right, with stars at the borders to each side and with inscriptions above and below.

MacNeil was dissatisfied with the first design, and suggested modifying Miss Lib-

Sculptor Hermon A. MacNeil in his studio. MacNeil designed the Standing Liberty quarter dollar in 1916, then modified it in 1917.

Only 52,000 were minted of the Standing Liberty quarter in 1916, the first year of issue. Relatively few were saved, and examples are rare today in all grades. Known as the Type I design, it features Miss Liberty with her right breast exposed. On the reverse, there are no stars below the eagle.

erty by encasing her in a coat of armor or mail, perhaps to emphasize the military aspect of the motif. Thus was created Type II, made from partway through 1917 all the way through 1930, except for the year 1922. The reverse was modified as well, and three stars were placed below the eagle, reducing the number to each side. In 1925 a slight modification was made to the obverse, and the date area was slightly recessed, to minimize the effects of wear.

It became numismatic folklore that the Type I design was "naughty," and that the design was changed because of public complaint. *Walter Breen's Complete Encyclopedia of U.S. and Colonial Coins* (1988) amplifies this:

> A feature of the new design, although cherished by the general public, proved to be the downfall of Mac-Neil's own conception. Followers of the unlamented Anthony Comstock, who had waged war on "immorality," noticed that Miss Liberty's drapery exposed her right nipple, including (on the sharpest striking) a realistic aureola. Through their Society for the Suppression of Vice, the guardians of prudery at once began exerting political pressure on the Treasury Department to revoke authorizations for these "immoral coins" and to withdraw them from circulation. By the time they reached Treasury Secretary William G. McAdoo, their success was in sight....
>
> Nevertheless, the Treasury refused to recall the coins already in circulation, and the general public saved enormous quantities of 1917 "Type I" as first of their kind. McAdoo and others falsely claimed that the "Type I" coins would not stack, as an argument for changing their designs...but the real reason for its discontinuance was unquestionably prudery of the kind H.L. Mencken and George Bernard Shaw used to call Comstockery. American official morality was no more ready in 1917 for a semi-nude coin than it had been in 1896–1898

for a semi-nude Miss Electricity on the $5 "educational" note. Whatever we think today of Comstock, his enormous political clout then all too accurately reflected the abysmal state of national consciousness.[63]

As are many of Walter Breen's writings, the preceding is presented in a very authoritative manner, causing little reason for anyone question the text. However, correspondence between MacNeil and Mint personnel reveals without question that it was MacNeil's own idea to change the design, and that prudery, semi-nude exposure, and "Comstockery" were not elements at all.

The Type II design had its own set of problems, real and not imagined. The pieces simply would not strike up properly during normal coinage runs, so the vast majority of pieces made from 1917 to 1930 have weakness in areas, typically in the details of the head of Miss Liberty and on the highest rivets on the shield. For some unusual reason, numismatists have selected *only the head* as an identification spot, and if the details are fairly good (not necessarily needle sharp or completely full), such pieces are called Full Head (FH) and are so described on price lists and holders. A coin can have weak or missing rivets and still be "FH," of course, but as a smart buyer you can avoid such pieces. Accordingly, opportunities abound. Some coins are also weakly struck at the lower part. Pieces of the year 1921 that sometimes have full heads yet also have weakness at the date are still called FH.

This 1919-S quarter illustrates the Type II design minted from 1917 through 1930, except for 1922. Modifications include encasement of Miss Liberty in a jacket of armor and, on the reverse, rearrangement of the stars.

As I've mentioned, a term such as Full Details (FD) or similar should be used to describe a coin that is sharp *everywhere*, including the head, shield rivets, and date. However, I'm afraid that the number of pieces that would qualify would be very small if, indeed, it was required that the head be completely (not partially) full!

All varieties in the Standing Liberty series are collectible, although the 1918/7-S overdate is quite rare, especially in higher grades.

To celebrate the 200th anniversary of George Washington's birth, the Treasury Department decided to change the quarter dollar design. Artists in the private sector were invited to compete. The winner was John Flanagan, a New York sculptor, who utilized the classic bust by Jean Antoine Houdon for the obverse, and on the reverse an eagle that was rather modern but perhaps fit more comfortably on the coin than any national bird before or since.

In the first year, 5,404,000 quarters were struck at the Philadelphia Mint, 436,800 at Denver, and 408,000 at San Francisco. For reasons not known to me, the 1932-D seems to have been saved in much smaller quantities than the lower-mintage 1932-S. Today, in terms of the existence of gem coins, the 1932-D is at least 10 times rarer. Such are the intrigues of numismatics. Another coin later in the series, the 1936-D, has a high mintage, but since collectors were busy with the commemorative-market boom, not many thought to save rolls of this "common" issue, and later they proved to be rare.

From 1932 to date, Washington quarters have been made almost continuously, exceptions being 1933, when none were needed for commerce, and 1975. The latter situation would make a good question for a coin-club quiz: *were any quarters made in 1975?* The answer is yes, but the explanation is that they were all dated 1776–1976, *prestruck* for the forthcoming bicentennial celebration.

Quarters from 1932 through 1964 are struck in 90% silver and 10% copper, while after that time they are of clad composition with an outer layer of copper and nickel (but of silvery appearance) bonded to a core of pure copper.

Among the silver issues, all dates and mintmarks are readily collectible, although the 1932-D and 1932-S are viewed as the keys. In Mint State the 1936-D is a *condition rarity*. Generally, a nice set of coins from MS-63 to -65 or better can be put together easily enough. Clad coins from 1965 to date include the interesting 1776–1976 Bicentennial design, among which are some pieces made in special silver clad metal for collectors. Afterward, from 1977 to 1998, production for circulating coins occurred at the Philadelphia and Denver mints, while San Francisco made those in Proof format for collectors. In addition, some silver Proofs were made in San Francisco.

A Mint State example of the 1932-D Washington quarter dollar (enlarged), the rarest basic date and mintmark variety in the series.

In observance of the bicentennial of American Independence, the quarter dollar (enlarged) was given the double date 1776–1976, and on the reverse a historical design was used in place of the eagle. The motif features a colonial drummer boy, by Jack L. Ahr, and is considered by most numismatists to be the best of the Bicentennial reverses (the others were used on the half dollar and dollar).

Beginning in 1999, the 50 State Quarters® Program commenced. Since that time, five different designs have been introduced each year, in the order in which each of the states joined the Union. As these are regular issues made for circulation, and not commemoratives, each constitutes a *type* in the series. Already, there are more quarter dollar design types than for any other denomination in the federal coinage series. The obverse of the quarter dollar was redesigned in 1999, including the addition of hair squiggles to Washington's portrait, rearrangement of the letters, and elimination of the date by moving it to the reverse.

Under the 50 State Quarters® Program, each U.S. state has charge of selecting a motif that it considers to be historical or representative, but with certain mandated exclusions, such as busts of people. From then until the present time, a virtual panorama of different ideas and depictions has flowed into circulation from the presses at the Philadelphia and Denver mints, plus Proofs for collectors from the San Francisco Mint. The latter include regular clad-metal Proofs as well as silver strikings, both of these versions being sold at premiums. Today, the state-reverse quarters in their entirety form a very dynamic and fascinating series. I collect them myself as each one appears!

Key to Collecting Quarter Dollars

- **Mint State coins:** Quarters of 1796 are available, but are in great demand and expensive. Those of 1804 to 1807 range from scarce to rare, while later issues through 1828 are generally scarce. Dates from 1831 to 1838 are seen more often, including in choice and gem preservation, but are rare in proportion to the demand for them. Liberty Seated quarters of 1838 to 1891 are generally scarcer for the early years and for branch mints prior to 1875, but are seen with some frequency for 1875 to 1891, rarities excepted. Barber quarters are scarcer for the earlier years and for the lower-mintage issues; gems are rare for any

date. Standing Liberty quarters are scarce for certain issues from 1918 to 1924, but eye appeal and strike can be a problem. All dates and mints of Washington quarters from 1932 onward are available, with the least common three being the 1932-D (scarcest), 1932-S, and 1936-D.

- **Circulated coins:** Generally available in proportion to their mintages, with the added factor that pre–Liberty Seated coins had a high attrition factor. Most worn Barber coins are in lower grades; VF and higher coins are rare. Circulated Standing Liberty quarters of the 1916-to-1924 era usually have much of the date worn away. Circulated, early, scarce Washington quarters are collected, but most numismatists desire Mint State coins from the 1940s or 1950s to date.

- **Strike quality:** The 1796 issue is usually weakly struck on the eagle's head. Coins of 1804 to 1807 (especially 1807) are nearly always weak in areas. Striking of coins from 1815 to 1891 varies; check the star centers, eagle details, and other points. Barber quarters are often weak at the eagle's leg at the lower right. Standing Liberty quarters often have weak head and/or weak shield-rivet details. Coins certified as FH (Full Head) often are *almost* FH, and can have weakness elsewhere, particularly on certain rivets on the shield. As mentioned earlier, a term such as FD (Full Details) would be beneficial. Washington quarters are generally well struck.

- **Proof coins:** Collectible for dates 1858 to present, seldom seen for earlier years. The availability is in proportion to mintages. Choice examples are scarce for 1858 to 1915.

- **Key issues:** 1796 (not a great rarity, but in intense demand), 1823/2, 1827, 1842 Small Date, 1870-CC to 1873-CC, 1896-S, 1901-S, 1913-S,

The restyled Washington quarter dollar obverse and a panorama of state-quarter reverse designs, produced at the rate of five each year since 1999.

1916 and 1918/7-S Standing Liberty, 1932-D and -S Washington, and others. In Mint State, 1849-O, 1858-S to 1861-S, and the aforementioned Carson City quarters are extremely rare. As a general rule, quarter dollars from 1796 through the mid-1870s are scarcer than are coins in other silver series, and scarce varieties abound.

- **Advice to smart buyers:** The entire series of quarter dollars from 1796 to the beginning of the Washington design (1932) offers many opportunities for connoisseurship. Sharpness of strike is elusive for many issues, including the entire Barber and Standing Liberty series. As a class, 19th-century quarter dollars are scarcer in the marketplace than are other silver denominations, necessitating a special effort to track down choice pieces. The concept of Optimal Collecting Grade (OCG) will give you more value for your money, in cases in which a small difference in grading numbers means a big difference in price. For modern coins I like MS-65 and -66 coins of hand-picked quality.

- **Selected bibliography:**
Bressett, Kenneth. 2000. *The Official Whitman Statehood Quarters Collector's Handbook.* New York, NY.

Briggs, Larry. 1991. *The Comprehensive Encyclopedia of United States Liberty Seated Quarters.* Lima, OH.

Browning, Ard W. 1992. *The Early Quarter Dollars of the United States 1796–1838.* New York, NY. (original work published 1925)

Cline, J.H. 1996. *Standing Liberty Quarters* (3rd ed.).

Fivaz, Bill, and J.T. Stanton. 1994. *The Cherrypickers' Guide to Rare Die Varieties.* Savannah, GA.

Haseltine, J.W. 1968. *Type Table of United States Dollars, Half Dollars and Quarter Dollars.* Philadelphia, PA. (original work published 1881; rendered obsolete by later works)

Lawrence, David. 1989. *The Complete Guide to Barber Quarters.* Virginia Beach, VA.

Half Dollars (1794 to Date)

The half dollar is one of only a few denominations that have been made more or less continuously since the 1790s and are still in use today. However, "in use today" must be qualified—while in the current era many half dollars have been struck, they are seldom seen in general circulation.

The historic panorama of half dollars is particularly rich, for most were made in fairly large quantities, serving well in trade, and resulting in examples being readily collectible today. Perhaps the most famous instance is the Capped Bust design with lettered edge, designed by John Reich and minted from 1807 to 1836. At the time, no silver dollars were being minted, and for much of that span, from 1821 to August 1834, there were absolutely no U.S. gold coins in domestic commerce. Thus it fell to the half dollar to be the largest and most valuable current American coin of the realm. Many were minted,

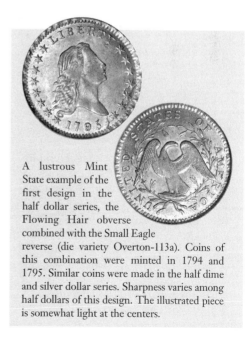

A lustrous Mint State example of the first design in the half dollar series, the Flowing Hair obverse combined with the Small Eagle reverse (die variety Overton-113a). Coins of this combination were minted in 1794 and 1795. Similar coins were made in the half dime and silver dollar series. Sharpness varies among half dollars of this design. The illustrated piece is somewhat light at the centers.

and today these form a dynamic specialty with numismatists.

Half dollars of the later designs, including the 1839 to 1891 Liberty Seated, 1892 to 1915 Barber, and 1916 to 1947 Liberty Walking issues, are enjoyable to collect by date, mintmark, and major variety. Most are very affordable except in higher grades. Each of these types has its own set of challenges. Later types—the Franklin halves of 1948 to 1963, and, especially, the Kennedy halves from 1964 to date—are exceedingly popular.

A collection of the major types of half dollars includes those in the following section, and affords a pleasant exercise to assemble. While the 1794 to 1795 type is scarce and the 1796 to 1797 type falls into the classic-rarity category, all of the others are very affordable—with, of course, higher-grade examples of earlier issues being more expensive. Forming a type set is a great way to collect half dollars. Any one of the coins can then act as a jumping-off spot for a specialized collection, should you develop an interest.

Design Types of Half Dollars

1794 and 1795, Flowing Hair—Scarce in lower grades, rare in Mint State. Coins of this type were made in a wide variety of interesting die combinations.

1796 and 1797, Draped Bust, Small Eagle—The Holy Grail of silver type-coins, rare in all grades. When Mint State coins are seen (which is not often), like as not they are dated 1796.

1801 to 1807, Draped Bust, Heraldic Eagle—Scarcity decreases as the years go on, with 1806 and 1807 being the most available. Striking is a problem.

1807 to 1836, Capped Bust, Lettered Edge—An extensive series of dates, over-dates, and interesting die varieties—a numismatic playground equaled only by copper cents among early 19th-century issues. Find a rare or previously unknown "Overton number" variety, and you'll be sitting pretty.

1836 and 1837, Reeded Edge, 50 CENTS—Short-lived type heralding the use of steam coinage at the Mint. Many are lightly struck.

1838 and 1839, Capped Bust, HALF DOL.—Another brief series. High-grade pieces are scarcer than for the preceding.

1839, Liberty Seated, No Drapery—Coined for just a brief time, the no-drapery half dollar can be considered either a variety or a type. It's a good thing that many opt to view it as a variety, and thus as not necessary for a type set—otherwise there wouldn't be enough to go around!

1839 to 1866, Liberty Seated, With Drapery, No Motto—An extensive and affordable series, with most issues available at least in lower levels of Mint State.

1853, Liberty Seated, Arrows at Date, Rays on Reverse—Not rare, but quality and eye appeal can be a challenge.

1854 and 1855, Liberty Seated, Arrows at Date—Also not rare, and when found in Mint State, usually nicer than the preceding.

1866 to 1891, Liberty Seated, With Motto—Widely available. Most Mint State coins are dated after 1874. Those from 1879 to 1891 have enticingly low mintages, but enough Mint State coins were saved, and Proofs are also available, that this collection-within-a-collection span has been popular for a long time.

1873 and 1874, Liberty Seated, Arrows at Date—Quite scarce in choice or gem Mint State, leading many collectors to opt for Proofs.

1892 to 1915, Barber—A large series with no really key issues. However, choice and gem Mint State coins can be very hard to find, especially if sharply struck.

1916 to 1947, Liberty Walking—A beautiful and popular series that is a delight to collect. However, certain of the issues are so rare with needle-sharp strike that I've never seen a full set formed with them. Few buyers know what to look for, so opportunities beckon!

1948 to 1963, Franklin—Very popular. Easily collectible in choice and gem grades MS-63 to -65, some being rare if you insist on Full Bell Lines (FBL) on the reverse.

1964 and Later, Kennedy (Silver)— Common and popular, as are the rest of the types of this design—some being more plentiful than others, but with enough to go around. Silver issues were made for circulation in 1964. From 1992 to date, silver Proofs have been made for sale to collectors.

1965 to 1970, Kennedy (Silver Clad)— Easily available and very popular.

1971 to Date, Kennedy (Clad)—Same comment.

1976 (Dated 1776–1976), Bicentennial (Clad)—Ditto.

1976 (Dated 1776–1976), Bicentennial (Silver Clad)—Ditto.

Half Dollars of the 1790s

The first type in the series is the Flowing Hair design with Miss Liberty on the obverse facing right, and with a delicate eagle on the reverse, the latter perched upon a rock and surrounded by a wreath. Mint figures suggest that 23,464 were struck in 1794 and 299,680 in 1795. Such numbers are interesting, but bear in mind that the Mint often used perfectly serviceable earlier dies in later years. For example, 1794-dated half dimes were all made in 1795, as Mint records show none produced during the *calendar* year 1794. Similarly, it is quite likely that while 23,464 of the 1794-dated halves were actually made in 1794, it is also likely that of the 299,680 reported for calendar year 1795, some may have been dated 1794.

My reason for mentioning this is that the same philosophy can be extended to all other mintage figures of the era. They are useful, but only up to a point. In some instances they are completely irrelevant (such as the Mint's reporting that no half dimes were coined in 1794—true, but irrelevant, as many with that date were struck in 1795; the mintage figures for sil-ver dollars of 1796 to 1797 are irrelevant for other reasons).

Half dollars of the Flowing Hair type are readily available in worn grades, typically VG through Fine or VF, occasionally EF, but not often AU or higher. Mint State pieces exist, and are very rare. Striking is typically quite casual, and nearly all have weakness of some sort or another. However, the pieces are charming, are fascinating to observe and to collect, and have a strong following. Half dollars of the early years, 1794 and 1795 of this type, but continuing through and including the end of the Capped Bust series in 1836, are often collected by die variety or "Overton number," as described by Al C. Overton (see the selected bibliography).

Interest is so intense that, if a 1795 half dollar in VF-20 grade is worth $750 in the *Guide Book*, and *you* discover a previously unknown die-variety combination, you will own a coin worth a dozen or more times that price! Knowledge is king in such matters, and quite a few people I know have made windfall profits this way. New finds are made regularly across the early American series, and scarcely a year or two will pass without someone's finding a hitherto unrecorded half dollar, half dime, or other issue.

In 1796, continuing in 1797, the Draped Bust obverse was used on the half dollar, creating the rarest type in the American silver series. The motif of Miss Liberty facing to the right is said to have been from a sketch by Gilbert Stuart. The reverse features a rather stocky eagle (in comparison to that used earlier), alighted on a cloud—artistic license. Just 3,918 were made of this design, with three different varieties: 1796 with 15 stars, 1796 with 16 stars, and 1797 with 15 stars. At the time, half dollars were struck only to the specific orders of depositors of bullion; once a large-capacity press was in service at the Mint, by late spring 1795, production of half dollars dropped off almost to the vanishing point, as silver dollars were preferred. In fact, from 1798

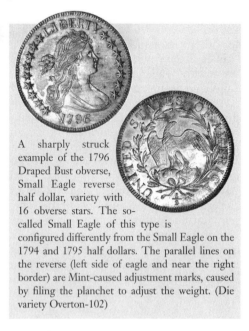

A sharply struck example of the 1796 Draped Bust obverse, Small Eagle reverse half dollar, variety with 16 obverse stars. The so-called Small Eagle of this type is configured differently from the Small Eagle on the 1794 and 1795 half dollars. The parallel lines on the reverse (left side of eagle and near the right border) are Mint-caused adjustment marks, caused by filing the planchet to adjust the weight. (Die variety Overton-102)

through 1800 no half dollars were struck at all. Today, halves of the 1796 to 1797 era are extremely rare and highly admired. The possession of an example in any grade is a badge of accomplishment, and those few who can reflect on the ownership of a Mint State piece are fortunate indeed.

Half Dollars Through 1836

From 1801 through 1807, the Draped Bust obverse was minted in combination with the Heraldic Eagle reverse. As was true in the half dime, dime, and quarter series also using this motif, the Mint experienced great problems in striking the details sharply. As a result, just about every such coin in existence is weak in one place or another—at the star centers on the obverse, or among the stars and clouds on the reverse, or somewhere else. The Mint could have controlled this, but didn't, as evidenced by the fact that those of the earlier dates of the type are generally much better struck than those of the last year, 1807 (some of the latter being downright miserable in terms of detail). Again, certification service grades do not reflect striking, and abundant opportunities exist for smart buyers. No matter how hard you look, perfection in striking is not possible

to find for many of the varieties, and a compromise must be made—by acquiring a better than average strike.

John Reich, hired as an assistant engraver at the Mint in 1807, remained there until 1817. He created the Capped Bust style, first used on the half dollar of 1807, later adapted to other silver series, and, somewhat modified, to gold coins of 1807 and later. In the half dollar denomination this style in combination with lettered edge (FIFTY CENTS OR HALF A DOLLAR) was used continuously through 1836, except for 1816 when none were coined. The engraver's name is memorialized in the John Reich Collectors Society, a special-interest group concentrating on silver coins of 1794 to 1836 and, to a lesser extent, gold of the same era.

Produced in large quantities, many Capped Bust half dollars served as cash reserves in banks, while others were exported. The rarest of those of 1807 to 1836 is the 1815, known only as an overdate, 1815/2. Within the span there is the highly prized 1817/4 overdate, of which just seven are known. Beyond that, there are many rare varieties that have been assigned Overton numbers and are known only to those who follow the descriptions in his book. Some of these can be extremely valuable.

Capped Bust halves are among my favorite series, as they represent the only early silver denomination that can be systematically collected by date (plus a few major varieties as listed in the *Guide Book*), in Mint State, and for reasonably low prices. Over the years I have suggested to many that they form a date run of these, and those who have accepted the challenge have enjoyed the pursuit. Today, costs have risen from what they were several decades ago, and justifiably so in view of the demand—but a collection in, say, MS-63 preservation is still affordable to many advanced collectors. Adding to the thrill of the chase is the search for quality of strike, which often varies. Once again, as a knowledgeable buyer you have the advantage, for most of your competitors in the marketplace consider the grade alone. Eye appeal is usually fairly decent among Mint State coins, but this aspect must be checked as well, this being especially important for the early issues from about 1807 through the early 1820s.

In November 1836 a steam-powered press was used for the first time at the Mint to strike half dollars, these being of the modified design with Capped Bust obverse, but now with a reeded edge, and of a smaller diameter. The reverse was redesigned as well, with the denomination expressed as 50 CENTS A few thousand of these were made in 1836, plus 3,629,820 in 1837. In 1838 the reverse was modified, the eagle and lettering were strengthened, and the denomination was changed to read HALF DOL. Capped Bust half dollars of this style were produced at Philadelphia and also at New Orleans; the 1838-O is a classic rarity, with only 20 believed to have been struck and about 12 to 15 existing today.

Liberty Seated Coinage

In 1839 the Liberty Seated design took its bow in this denomination, the motif having been used earlier on the silver dollar (1836), the half dime and dime (1837), and the quarter dollar (1838; see page 310). The earliest Liberty Seated issues of 1839 lacked extra drapery at the elbow, were made in rather low numbers, and are elusive today, particularly in Mint State. These are sometimes collected as a separate type.

From 1839 through 1891 the Liberty Seated obverse was used continuously, with production in Philadelphia for each of these years and at branch mints for certain of them. New Orleans produced half dollars through 1861, San Francisco from 1855 through 1878, and Carson City from 1870 through 1878.

Several modifications were made to the design within this time span. When the price of silver bullion rose on markets in 1850, coins from the half dime to the dollar disappeared from circulation. The Act

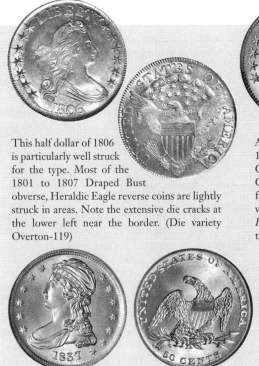

This half dollar of 1806 is particularly well struck for the type. Most of the 1801 to 1807 Draped Bust obverse, Heraldic Eagle reverse coins are lightly struck in areas. Note the extensive die cracks at the lower left near the border. (Die variety Overton-119)

A brilliant, lustrous 1809 half dollar of the Capped Bust type. Coins of this style, made from 1807 to 1836, are avidly collected by varieties described by Al C. Overton in *Early Half Dollar Die Varieties 1794–1836* (the illustrated coin being O-106).

Christian Gobrecht adopted John Reich's Capped Bust design to create the type of 1836 to 1837, smaller diameter, reeded edge, and with slight modification of the details. Coins of this type, with the denomination given as 50 CENTS, were made for only two years, after which the reverse was modified to HALF DOL., the type of 1838 to 1839.

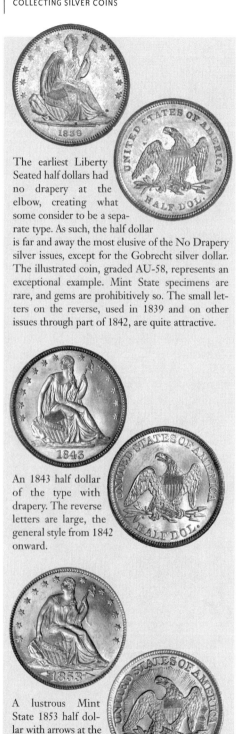

The earliest Liberty Seated half dollars had no drapery at the elbow, creating what some consider to be a separate type. As such, the half dollar is far and away the most elusive of the No Drapery silver issues, except for the Gobrecht silver dollar. The illustrated coin, graded AU-58, represents an exceptional example. Mint State specimens are rare, and gems are prohibitively so. The small letters on the reverse, used in 1839 and on other issues through part of 1842, are quite attractive.

An 1843 half dollar of the type with drapery. The reverse letters are large, the general style from 1842 onward.

A lustrous Mint State 1853 half dollar with arrows at the date and rays around the eagle on the reverse.

of February 21, 1853, lowered the weight of the denominations from the half dime through the half dollar (but not the dollar), after which the lighter coins circulated freely, as it was no longer profitable to melt them down. To reflect this change, most half dollars of 1853 and all of 1854 and 1855 have arrowheads at the date, and most of 1853 have rays around the eagle on the reverse. After 1855 the lighter weight was continued, but the arrows were dropped.

Another change was made in 1866 with the addition of the motto IN GOD WE TRUST to the reverse above the eagle. The Coinage Act of 1873 mandated a slight upward adjustment in the weight of the half dollar, and arrowheads were added to the date for the remainder of this year and in 1874.

Liberty Seated half dollars form an ideal collecting field for the specialist, as all but a handful were made in large quantities and are readily collectible today. Most members of the Liberty Seated Collectors Club have pieces in grades from Fine to EF or AU, sometimes Mint State, but with Mint State and Proof coins being the exception, not the rule.

Buying scattered choice and gem Mint State pieces, but not an entire specialized collection, is also a favorite occupation, particularly for those building type sets and those who simply want to buy nice examples without working on an entire set. Time was when such coins were collected in album pages, and a blank hole beckoned to be filled. Today, with certified coins that are often simply stored in boxes or trays, the hole-filling incentive is lost, and quite a few buyers assemble miscellaneous groups of interesting coins but do not aspire to complete a set. (This is true for all series, not just half dollars.)

Liberty Seated half dollars of the early years through part of 1842 generally have delicate or small letters on the reverse, giving the pieces a particularly attractive aspect. Later, the lettering was larger. The 1844-O Doubled Date shows one date over the other—the result of adding the four-digit date punch to the working die in the wrong position at first, then correcting the problem. A curious 1846 has the final digit of the date over a horizontal 6. While most 1853 half dollars have arrows at the date and rays on the reverse, an exception is provided by certain 1853-O coins with neither, these being quite rare. Only three examples are known, each showing extensive wear.

In 1861 at the New Orleans Mint, 330,000 half dollars were struck under federal auspices, then a further 1,250,000 for the State of Louisiana after it withdrew from the Union, and then 962,633 more under the authority of the Confederate States of America. While those made under Confederate control are not all identifiable, some may be the variety with a die crack from the bridge of Miss Liberty's nose to the border at the left, as this identical obverse die was used to produce *pattern* half dollars intended for the Confederacy, with a specially designed reverse.

There are several overdates in the Liberty Seated series, plus variations in letter and numeral sizes, all of which are delineated in the *Guide Book* and other popular sources. See this section's selected bibliography for specialized texts.

Silver coins were released in quantity into circulation after April 20, 1876, such having been absent from the channels of commerce in the East and Midwest since spring 1862. Many of the long-hoarded pieces were spent by the general public. A tremendous glut of silver coins arose, and there was no need to coin more. From 1879 onward, Liberty Seated half dollar mintages were small. The only reason *any* circulation strikes were made was that the Mint didn't want to create rarities for numismatic speculation and investment profits.

Although production figures were small, the circulation strikes tended to be saved in some quantity, as dealers such as E.B. Mason, Jr., J.W. Haseltine, and J. Colvin Randall, to mention just three, stocked these and sold them to numismatists during the era—this being a time of great growth in the hobby.

Into the 20th Century

In 1892 the Liberty Head motif by Charles E. Barber made its debut, to be continued each year through 1915. Similar to the situation with Barber quarters and dimes, production was accomplished fairly consis-

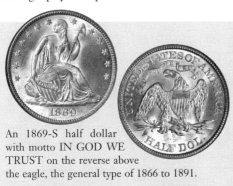

An 1869-S half dollar with motto IN GOD WE TRUST on the reverse above the eagle, the general type of 1866 to 1891.

Some 1873 half dollars and all of 1874 have arrowheads alongside the date to indicate a slight increase in authorized weight. The arrowheads were discontinued in 1875, but the new weight remained the same.

Half dollars of the Barber type, as illustrated by this 1899-S, were made continuously from 1892 through 1915. There are no great rarities in the series, and all can be collected without difficulty. However, for many varieties choice and gem Mint State coins, sharply struck, are elusive.

tently at different mints—Philadelphia, New Orleans, and San Francisco in the early days, joined by Denver in 1906.

The design of the Barber half dollars was such that, when coins reached circulation, the word LIBERTY in the headband was quickly worn; and within several years of circulation, this feature was gone. Half dollars remained in circulation for a long time—indeed, they were seen through the early 1950s, and most were well worn by that time.

Today, there are no classic rarities in the Barber half dollar series, and in worn grades they can all be collected for reasonable prices. Such levels as VF, EF, and AU are *very* rare in comparison to the demand for them, a fact not generally known. Mint State Barber half dollars sometimes can be scruffy or unsatisfactory in appearance in lower grades such as MS-60 to -62, and thus I suggest MS-63 to -65 or -66 as a good goal for the specialist. At the same time, sharpness of strike is a factor, as quite a few have weaknesses in one area or the other, the shield and the leg of the eagle at the lower right of the reverse being key points of observation, for starters. Eye appeal often varies. To form a nicely matched, sharply struck set of MS-65 Barber half dollars, one of each date and mint from 1892 to 1915, will require several years of connoisseurship. Only a few such collections have ever been assembled. If you're collecting U.S. coins by type, the Barber half dollar will be the key issue for you in the 20th-century silver series.

The year 1916 saw the appearance of a new half dollar design: the Liberty Walking type, by sculptor Adolph A. Weinman, whose statuary and other art were widely known at the time. Weinman also created the 1916 "Mercury" dime. On the obverse of the new half dollar, Miss Liberty is portrayed *striding* (nomenclature used by the Mint) with her right hand outstretched, her left hand holding branches of olive, and a star-spangled cape behind her shoulders. At the lower right is a brilliant sun. The reverse depicts an eagle perched on a rocky crag, with a sprig of pine to the left, the latter representing strength (a pine tree, taking root in a rock crevice, can eventually crack or split the rock).

Coins of the Liberty Walking design were minted from 1916 through 1947, except for 1922, 1924 to 1926, and 1930 to 1932. Problems developed in striking the pieces, for if the dies were spaced very closely together, with precision, all of the elements would be sharp, but die breakage would be accelerated. If a slightly overweight planchet were used, the dies might crack. The feasible alternative was to space the dies slightly wider apart than was necessary for optimal clarity, and this was done in nearly all years. Today, sharpness varies from year to year and from mintmark to mintmark. Perhaps the worst struck of all is the 1923-S (a variety that is usually very poorly defined), to which can be added the usually weak 1940-S and 1941-S. Beyond that, other dates and mints have their problems and need to be examined selectively. At present there are no popular guidelines for noting sharpness, but if there ever are, and you have added sharp pieces to your collection, you'll be sitting pretty! Just see what has happened to the prices of some Jefferson nickels, Mercury dimes, and Standing Liberty half dollars that have had such nomenclature as Full Steps, Full Bands, and Full Head added! In a few para-

This 1916-D Liberty Walking half dollar has the D mintmark on the obverse below the R in TRUST. Coins of this design were made intermittently to 1933 and continuously from then through 1947. For many years these have been numismatic favorites. Striking quality can vary widely, and most have some lightness at the center of the obverse and on the highest parts of the eagle on the reverse.

graphs you will encounter the same thing with Full Bell Lines (FBL) Franklin halves. Great opportunities await you.

Franklin Half Dollars

Franklin half dollars appeared in 1948, without much fanfare. The motif was not particularly appreciated by numismatists, as perhaps it was felt to be rather unattractive in comparison to the elegant Liberty Walking design. Whatever the reason, the series was not a favorite for the first decade or so of its existence, and I recall seeing very little demand for them in my business. Later that changed, and today Franklin halves are among the most popular silver series.

Coinage was continuous from 1948 through 1963. In terms of basic scarcity, 1949-S was a traditional key date, and today it remains elusive in Mint State, at least in context of the series—although at one time these actively traded in roll quantities. Today, certain specialists in Franklin half dollars examine the horizontal lines on the Liberty Bell on the reverse, and if they are fully defined, designate them as Full Bell Lines (FBL). For certain varieties these can have great additional values. A recent issue of *Coin Values* includes these prices for a certain issue:[64]

1954-S Franklin half dollar—MS-64: $25 • MS-64 FBL: $100 • MS-65: $60 • MS-65 FBL: $500 • MS-66: $350 • MS-66 FBL: $3,500.

One of the greatest potential areas for profit in American numismatics is the cherrypicking of *sharply struck* coins in series in which certification holders and price catalogs do not notice such things. Time was when FBL characteristics were not important on Franklin halves. Now that they are, consider the profits made by anyone who quietly acquired such pieces years ago. To repeat: many opportunities are at your doorstep!

Kennedy Half Dollars

After the tragic assassination of President John F. Kennedy on November 22, 1963, there was immediate call to depict him on coinage. At the time, dollars weren't being made, and circulating denominations included the cent, nickel, dime, quarter, and half dollar. The image of Lincoln was a sacred cow, so to speak, on the cent. To remove either Jefferson or Roosevelt (both being icons in Kennedy's Democratic party) from the nickel or dime would have been akin to sacrilege, and George Washington was solidly entrenched as the national hero on the quarter dollar. Accordingly, the Franklin half dollar, which most people didn't care for anyway, was the logical choice, even though coins of this design had been minted only since 1948, and current coinage law (sometimes ignored), mandated at least a 25-year usage of a motif.

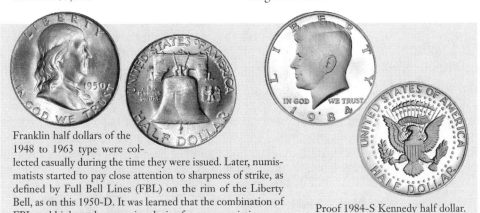

Franklin half dollars of the 1948 to 1963 type were collected casually during the time they were issued. Later, numismatists started to pay close attention to sharpness of strike, as defined by Full Bell Lines (FBL) on the rim of the Liberty Bell, as on this 1950-D. It was learned that the combination of FBL and high grade was quite elusive for many varieties.

Proof 1984-S Kennedy half dollar.

Gilroy Roberts, chief engraver at the Mint, designed the new half dollar's obverse: a profile of Kennedy facing left, perhaps a bit too high on the coin, some said, but no matter—the portrait was enthusiastically appreciated. The reverse, designed by assistant engraver Frank Gasparro, featured a heraldic eagle motif, perhaps a bit mechanical and modernistic, according to some viewers, but again no matter. Made in silver, Kennedy half dollars of the 1964 and 1964-D varieties were released early in that year and created an absolute sensation, trading immediately at a premium. The demand extended all over the world, and for a year or two they retailed for $5 each in Europe.

The price of silver was rising, and in 1965 this metal was dropped from the dime and quarter. For half dollars it was reduced considerably through a silver clad composition from 1965 to 1970, after which it was eliminated entirely, except for some issues made for sale at a premium to collectors. Coinage for circulation was generally accomplished at Philadelphia and Denver. In 1980 the P mintmark, not used earlier in the denomination, was added. From 1968 onward, the San Francisco Mint struck Proofs for collectors.

Similar to the situation with the quarter dollar, no 1975-dated half dollars were struck, although the mints were busy that year—*prestriking* pieces with the 1776–1976 date for the Bicentennial

A 1776–1976 double-dated Bicentennial half dollar, with the regular Kennedy portrait on the obverse and with the special Independence Hall design on the reverse.

observation. The reverse had a modified design depicting a head-on view of Independence Hall in Philadelphia, essentially the same as used on the 1926 commemorative $2.50 piece. Such head-on depictions are seldom successful from an artistic viewpoint, as evidenced by this coin as well as the Lincoln cent with memorial reverse (1959), the Jefferson nickel with Monticello on the reverse (1938), and others. Generally, a view from an angle is better (e.g, as on the 1990 Eisenhower Centennial and 1993 Jefferson commemorative dollars, among others).

Today, more than 130 different dates, mintmarks, and other varieties can be collected for the Kennedy half dollar series— a large panorama of interesting pieces, generally available at low cost in such desirable grades as MS-64 and -65. Most have good eye appeal.

While Liberty Walking and Franklin half dollars were common in pocket change in their time, Kennedy half dollars were hoarded by the public from the outset, and they never did reach circulation in quantity. As a result, by default, the quarter became the coin of choice for a new generation of arcade and vending machines. Today, half dollars are hardly ever seen, but they exist *somewhere*, and more are continually being made, mostly for sale to collectors.

Key to Collecting Half Dollars

- **Mint State coins:** Rare for all years 1794 to 1805, some dates being extremely rare. The 1806 to 1807 Draped Bust, Heraldic Eagle type is scarce, but nearly all are flat strikes. All dates of 1807 to 1836 Capped Bust halves are available, with the earlier years being the most elusive. Later half dollars through the end of the Liberty Seated series are mostly available in Mint State, with low-mintage and branch-mint issues generally being scarcer. Barber half dollars are available in Mint State but are often scruffy in appearance. Barber halves are often lightly struck at the upper right of the shield and nearby wing area. Extreme care is needed to get quality pieces. Liberty Walking halves are scarce for 1916 and 1917, scarce to rare for 1918 through 1929, and fairly plentiful later, especially in the 1940s. Franklin halves are common for all dates, but if you want FBL, a zinger is tossed into the equation, as some are rare and costly. Kennedy halves are easily available and usually have good eye appeal.

- **Circulated coins:** Circulated coins exist in approximate proportion to their original mintage quantities. Most numismatists seek Mint State coins for the 1940s or later.
- **Strike quality:** Finding sharp strikes is a challenge throughout the series, as noted in the text. Cherrypicking is the order of the day.
- **Proof coins:** Proof coins are available for the years 1858 to 1915, with typical grades being Proof-63 or -64. Gems with good eye appeal are in the minority, as most have hairlines. Proofs of 1936 to 1942 and 1950 to 1964 should be selected for eye appeal, but there are many opportunities. Later Proofs are usually found choice.
- **Key issues:** 1794, 1796, 1797, 1801, 1815/2, 1817/4, 1836 Reeded Edge, 1838-O (classic rarity), 1847/6, 1853-O No Arrows or Rays, 1855-S (in Mint State), 1870-CC through 1873-CC (in Mint State), 1878-S, and, among later issues, 1921, 1921-D, and 1921-S.
- **Advice to smart buyers:** Buy slowly and carefully, seeking sharp strikes (FD) and savoring the experience. Consider Optimal Collecting Grade (OCG) carefully. If buying Franklin halves, contemplate whether you simply want a quite nice and inexpensive collection of MS-64 and -65 coins, or you want to make a major investment in FBL pieces. The last would not be my choice, considering the wide cost spreads, but many others feel differently. There is no "right way" as to what you should collect,

and no two people do everything the same way.

- **Selected bibliography:**

Fox, Bruce. 1993. *The Complete Guide to Walking Liberty Half Dollars*, Virginia Beach, VA.

Lawrence, David. 1991. *The Complete Guide to Barber Halves*. Virginia Beach, VA.

Overton, Al C. 1990. *Early Half Dollar Die Varieties 1794–1836* (3rd ed., edited by Donald Parsley). Colorado Springs, CO. (original work published 1967)

Peterson, Glenn R. 2000. *The Ultimate Guide to Attributing Bust Half Dollars*. Rocky River, OH.

Wiley, Randy, and Bill Bugert. 1993. *The Complete Guide to Liberty Seated Half Dollars*. Virginia Beach, VA.

Silver and Clad Dollars (1794 to Date)

The silver dollar represents one of the most historic, interesting, and numismatically popular of all American coin denominations. Today, in the early 21st century, many enthusiasts enjoyably pursue and collect Morgan silver dollars of 1878 to 1921, Peace dollars of 1921 to 1935, and the later, non-silver pieces of clad metal. A significant percentage of all business done by rare coin dealers involves coins of the dollar denomination.

While the series includes the much-discussed "King of American Coins" (the 1804 dollar) and a few other rarities, by and large most dates and mintmarks are readily collectible. Another strategy is to collect by basic design type, as given below. However, there are very few who can resist the temptation of collecting more than one of the Morgan and later dollars! Perhaps a compromise is to collect early coins by type and later ones by date and mint.

Design Types of Silver and Clad Dollars

1794 and 1795, Flowing Hair—Fewer than 150 silver dollars of 1794 exist, to which can be added several thousand or more dated 1795. Many interesting die combinations were made for the latter year.

1795 to 1798, Draped Bust, Small Eagle—This is the scarcest of the early (1794–1804) types and is difficult to find in higher grades. However, enough are around that finding an attractive VF or EF will be no problem.

1798 to 1804, Draped Bust, Heraldic Eagle—Dollars of this design are far and away the most plentiful of the early types, although "plentiful" must be considered in context.

1836, Gobrecht, No Stars on Obverse, Stars on Reverse—Just 1,600 were minted, all in Proof format, most of which went into circulation. A classic rarity since day one.

1839, Gobrecht, Stars on Obverse, No Stars on Reverse—Just 300 originals were made, all in Proof format, most of which were placed into circulation. However, it was not until the late 19th century that this variety was moved from "pattern" status to regular issue. Nearly all in existence today are Proof restrikes, which is probably a good thing, or they would be virtually uncollectible! Of all of the dollar types this is the rarest.

1840 to 1865, Liberty Seated, No Motto—Readily available as a type. Among choice and gem coins Proofs are far more available than are circulation strikes.

1866 to 1873, Liberty Seated, With Motto—Same comment as preceding.

1878 to 1921, Morgan—Abundantly available, with one of the most common of all coins in gem preservation, the 1881-S, readily available with sharply struck details and good eye appeal.

1921, Peace, High Relief—Easily available in Mint State, but I've never seen a circulation strike with needle-sharp details at the obverse center. This is why

the design was soon changed to one with a lower relief.

1922 to 1935, Peace, Low Relief—As common as can be, including choice and gem grades—which is ideal, as lower grades tend to lack eye appeal.

1971 to 1978, Eisenhower (Clad)—Readily available in just about any grade desired.

1971 to 1974, Eisenhower (Silver Clad)—Same comment as above.

1976 (Dated 1776–1976), Bicentennial (Clad)—Common. It's difficult for me to envision why anyone thought the award-winning reverse design was beautiful, but that was how the judges felt.

1976 (Dated 1776–1976), Bicentennial (Silver Clad)—Plentiful, as all were sold to collectors and curio hunters.

1979 to 1999, Susan B. Anthony—The "Susies" were ignored by the public and made fun of by politicians and comedians, but numismatists loved them—and still do.

2000 to Date, Sacagawea—The "golden dollar" was to have replaced the paper bill, but it didn't, and in commerce the idea laid an egg. However, just about every collector I have ever met loves them, as do I. In recent years, production has been for collectors.

Dollars of Our Daddies

The *dollars of our daddies* term is mostly forgotten today. However, in the late 19th century this was what many numismatists and newspaper reporters called the silver dollars of the earlier years, from 1794 to 1804. Later, when Morgan silver dollars were minted (beginning in 1878), the phrase was adopted to refer to Liberty Seated coins as well. These were the remembrance of things past, the large and impressive and valuable silver coins of childhood—when perhaps one or two were tucked away in a drawer, and were not to be spent.

Although the Mint Act of April 2, 1792, specified the dollar as the largest silver denomination, no coins were struck in this metal until 1794, as there were problems in gaining surety bonds for certain Mint officials. In the latter year, silver half dollars and dollars were made (and dies were prepared for the half dime, though they were not used until 1795).

In 1794, the largest press at the Mint was intended for striking coins no larger than a half dollar. Surviving documents indicate that Mint officials lamented the lack of a press suitable for coining silver dollars and medals. It was not until spring 1795 that one of sufficient capacity was installed.

In the meantime, a screw press suitable for coining cents and half dollars was put into service to make silver dollars. The initial coinage of the new denomination was accomplished in the first part of October 1794. The effort was not completely successful, as evidenced by surviving coins, which show areas of weak striking. Apparently, just one blow of the press was used (as evidenced by the lack of double-struck features on all I have seen).

Known silver dollars dated 1794 are from a single pair of dies and are believed to have been made to the extent of perhaps 2,000 coins (Walter H. Breen's estimate), of which 1,758 pieces considered to be more or less satisfactory were delivered by the coiner on October 15, 1794. The remaining impressions, possibly amounting to 242 coins, were rejected as being too weak and probably were kept on hand for later use as planchets. Supporting this theory is the existence of at least one 1795 silver dollar that is plainly overstruck on a 1794 dollar.

The motif of the new dollars was the same as that used on the half dime and half dollar. On the obverse, the head of Miss Liberty faces to the right, with stars to each side, LIBERTY above, and the date below. On the reverse a delicate eagle perched on a rock has been placed within a wreath, with the words UNITED STATES OF AMERICA situated around the border.

There seems to have been no ceremony launching the first American silver dollar, and none are known to have been preserved for collecting purposes. However, a few were preserved by chance, and today a handful exist in Mint State and are at once exceedingly rare and highly prized.

In 1795, coinage of silver dollars was much more extensive, an adequate press having been installed. The mintage was 160,265, across many different die varieties and combinations.

Later in 1795, the Draped Bust motif was said to have been made from a sketch by Gilbert Stuart. The reverse illustrated a revised eagle, somewhat shorter in

Flowing Hair silver dollar of the 1794 to 1795 type. At the bottom border and to the left can be seen many Mint-made adjustment marks, caused by filing the planchet prior to striking, to reduce it to the correct weight. Such adjustment marks are common on silver and gold coins of the decade and are unnoticed on certification holders. This coin was graded MS-65 by NGC.

wingspan and stockier, with clouds below its feet.

In 1798 the reverse was changed to the Heraldic Eagle type, a motif continued in production through 1804. Although 19,570 silver dollars were coined in 1804, these were from earlier-dated dies, probably mostly 1803. Coins of the 1804 date—trophy coins par excellence today—were first minted in 1834 for inclusion in presentation sets. (Others were minted later for collectors, as were so-called Proof "restrikes" dated 1801, 1802, and 1803.)

None of the early dollars bore any mark of denomination on the face, but had lettered edges inscribed HUNDRED CENTS, ONE DOLLAR OR UNIT.

Perhaps as many as several hundred numismatists today collect early dollars by die variety as described by Bolender numbers and also Bowers/Borckardt numbers, these attributions being useful for other issues through 1804 (see the selected bibliography). The number of devotees is but a fraction of those interested in, for example, early copper cents or Capped Bust half dollars. Accordingly, scarce and rare die combinations of early dollars can often be purchased advantageously for little premium over more plentiful varieties.

Gobrecht Dollars of 1836 and 1839

In September 1835, Christian Gobrecht was hired as "second engraver" at the Mint, in effect taking the place of Chief Engraver William Kneass, who had been incapacitated by a stroke. In those times, the chief engravership was a lifetime proposition—a sinecure—and Kneass continued to draw his paycheck until his death on August 27, 1840, although a small part of his salary was transferred to Gobrecht. On December 21 of 1840, Gobrecht was appointed chief engraver, to remain in the post until his passing on June 23, 1844.

The Draped Bust obverse in combination with the Small Eagle reverse (the "small eagle" being different from that on the 1794–1795 dollars) was introduced in 1795 and continued through 1804. The reverse die used on this coin, with small letters and with the words widely spaced, proved to be quite sturdy and was employed with other obverses through early 1798.

This engraving of the 1836 Gobrecht silver dollar appeared in the 1885 edition of A.M. Smith's lengthily titled *Visitor's Guide and History of the United States Mint, Philadelphia, Elaborately Illustrating Each Department, the Business Routine, all Scientific and Mechanical Operations in every Stage of the Work, the Wonderful Machinery and Curios in the Cabinet.*

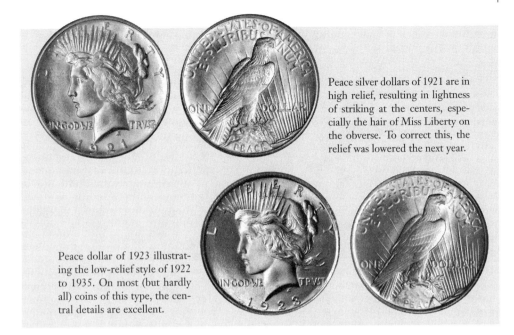

Peace silver dollars of 1921 are in high relief, resulting in lightness of striking at the centers, especially the hair of Miss Liberty on the obverse. To correct this, the relief was lowered the next year.

Peace dollar of 1923 illustrating the low-relief style of 1922 to 1935. On most (but hardly all) coins of this type, the central details are excellent.

after his wife, Teresa Cafarelli. The reverse illustrated an eagle, wings folded, boldly perched on a rock, facing to the right, with the rays of the sun streaming upward, and with letters arranged in two arcs above—another nod to the work of Saint-Gaudens, this arrangement was loosely adapted from the lettering and rays on the reverse of the illustrious MCMVII (1907) double eagle. The relief of the 1921 Peace dollar was too high at the centers, and all pieces showed lightness of detail at that point.

These coins were distributed through banks and other channels, likely putting the entire supply into circulation. In my later studies of silver-dollar distribution, the 1921 Peace silver dollar emerged as the *only* issue of the Peace design for which not even one Mint-sealed bag of 1,000 coins was known to Peace dollar dealers and specialists.

In 1922 the motif was revised to shallow relief on both sides, creating a distinct type that was minted through 1928, and then again in 1934 and 1935.

Peace dollars were made in huge quantities, far more than were needed in commerce, and they, too, piled up in Treasury vaults.

Into the Modern Era

Over the ensuing years, particularly during the holiday seasons, long-stored Morgan and Peace silver dollars were paid out for use as gifts. The denomination circulated to some extent in the Rocky Mountain areas, but not elsewhere. Then, in November 1962, a long-sealed vault was opened at the Philadelphia Mint, bringing to light rare varieties, including hundreds of thousands of the precious 1903-O (see chapter 12, "1962–1964: Treasury Release of Silver Dollars," for details).

Silver dollars of earlier years, dating back to 1878, were available to anyone who wanted one, until the Treasury and bank supplies ran out in March 1964, after which they became somewhat scarce.

These coins, already popular with numismatists, were projected to the front line of importance, and ever since then have been a favorite series. Morgan dollars, of nearly 100 different date and mintmark varieties, and Peace dollars, with 24 varieties, can for the most part be collected in Mint State inexpensively—a powerful attraction.

After silver dollars were no longer available for face value, gambling casinos in Las Vegas and elsewhere used dollar-sized clad metal tokens or chips, made by the Franklin Mint and others, but they were not as popular with patrons as were the old silver dollars. For this and other reasons, in 1971 a new dollar was made, not of silver but of clad metal, and designed by Frank Gasparro. It featured Dwight Eisenhower on the obverse and, on the reverse, an eagle landing on the moon. Eisenhower dollars were produced through 1978 (except in 1975). The 1776–1976 Bicentennial dollar featured a modified reverse with the Liberty Bell and the moon—not particularly attractive to many numismatists, but of course necessary for inclusion in a set. Afterward, the old design was continued for two more years.

In 1979 Frank Gasparro's Susan B. Anthony dollar made its appearance amid fanfare that the new metal dollar would soon replace the paper dollar and would result in a great economy to the Treasury Department. Paper dollars have a very short life, less than two years on the average, whereas it was estimated that an Anthony dollar would be good for nearly 20 years. Later, the Canadian dollar coin featuring a loon (of course, nicknamed the *loonie*) became very popular, as were high-denomination coins in certain other countries. Frank Gasparro had hoped to use a Liberty Cap motif for the dollar, inspired by the copper cent of 1793, and had made up designs of this type. Enthusiasm ran high, and at long last it seemed that collectors could have a truly classic design. However, political correctness intervened, and Susan Anthony, a leader in the suffrage movement, was chosen instead. A rather severe image of her is depicted on the coin.

Gasparro, a fine friend of mine for many years, shared with me his misgivings at the outset. First of all, the coin was too small, nearly the size of a quarter dollar, and could easily be mistaken for it. As if to prove his point, after the first pieces were minted, Gasparro spent one in the cafeteria at the Mint, where it was immediately accepted as a quarter without question. Second, generally in American financial history one type of instrument is preferred for a given denomination in general commerce. As paper dollars were still being made in quantity, the Anthony dollar did not fill a need. Had paper dollars been eliminated, the convenience of the new coins might have been much greater.

A 1972-S Eisenhower dollar, the type of 1971 to 1978, by Chief Engraver Frank Gasparro.

A 1776–1976-S Bicentennial dollar with the Liberty Bell and moon motif, used only on this issue.

The 1999-P Susan B. Anthony dollar, a late-comer to the series, was struck many years after the type was thought to have ended, in 1981.

A 2000-P Sacagawea "golden dollar," a favorite with collectors, but of a type generally ignored by the public. As vending machines were not adapted to take either these or the early Susan B. Anthony dollars, they never replaced the paper dollar.

Third, vending machines, popularly used for high-denomination coins, were not fitted to take the Anthony dollars. These unfortunate factors came together with the result that the public spurned them.

The mintage for the 1979-P issue was 360,222,000, plus 288,015,744 for 1979-D and 109,576,000 for 1979-S. Most of these piled up in vaults. Although they weren't accepted by the public, no one in the government wanted to admit failure. In 1980, additional pieces were made for circulation, including 27,610,000 of 1980-P, 41,628,708 of 1980-D, and 20,422,000 of 1980-S. Several governmental units, regional as well as national, tried to promote their use; methods included signs at toll booths on the way in and out of New York City, stating that Anthony dollars would be accepted, and the paying out of dollars in change in post offices and certain military bases.

However, none of these efforts were to any avail, and in 1981 mintage was limited solely to Proofs for collectors. For reasons not clearly understood by me, in 1999 over 40 million *more* Anthony dollars were struck. Such are the mysteries of government supervision of coinage!

In 2000, not having absorbed the lessons of history, but with new congressmen and others in place, the Mint launched another metal dollar: the Sacagawea "golden dollar," again intended to replace paper bills. This time the coin was minted of a pure copper core with outer surface of manganese brass. The alloy contains 77% copper, 12% zinc, 7% manganese, and 4% nickel, imparting a brassy or golden hue to

the surface that is quite pleasing in appearance. However, paper dollars were not eliminated. The vending-machine industry took a wait-and-see attitude, and the new golden dollars were as useless in these devices as they were in arcade machines. Despite promotions by Mint Director Jay Johnson that bordered on the heroic, including public displays, exhibits, and ceremonies, these dollars also laid an egg. Coinage for circulation the first year amounted to 767,140,000 of the 2000-P and 518,916,000 of the 2000-D. The second year, when no more Sacagawea dollars were needed, the Mint—precisely retracing its own the steps from the Anthony-dollar project—made 62,468,000 more of the 2001-P and 70,939,500 of the 2001-D. Production later slipped to just a few million, which were sold at a premium to collectors.

Key to Collecting Silver and Clad Dollars

- **Mint State coins:** Rare for the early range of the series (1794–1803). Those that do exist tend to be in lower ranges, MS-60 to -63, some having "graduated" from AU due to "grade-flation." Liberty Seated dollars are available in MS-60 to -63 for most dates, including some hoard coins of 1859-O and 1860-O; but in all instances gems are rare. Morgan dollars are generally available in Mint State. Rarities at the gem level include 1879-CC, 1884-S, 1886-O, 1889-CC, 1892-S, 1893-CC, 1893-O, 1893-S, 1894-O, 1895-O, 1896-S, 1896-O,

1897-O, and 1901, among others. All Peace dollars are likewise available in Mint State, with keys at the gem level being 1923-S, 1924-S, 1925-S, 1927-S, and 1928-S. The 1934-S is in demand in all Mint State grades. Eisenhower dollars are plentiful, but gems for certain early issues are rare in the context of the series. Anthony and Sacagawea dollars are plentiful. I suggest that you make good use of the Optimal Collecting Grade (OCG) when contemplating ultra-high-grade examples that are really quite common in lower grades, such as MS-64.

- **Circulated coins:** Examples are the rule, not the exception, for all dollars of 1794 to 1873. Although most varieties of Morgan dollars are common in circulated grades (Carson City coins being notable exceptions), when Mint State coins are available for low prices, most numismatists opt to acquire these.

- **Strike quality:** Early dollars of the 1794 to 1803 era are apt to be weak in areas, such as star centers, the highest areas of the portrait, and the details of the eagle on the reverse. Some, particularly the earlier years, have Mint-caused file or adjustment marks. Gobrecht dollars of 1836 and 1839 are usually well struck. Liberty Seated dollars should be checked for the head of Miss Liberty, the star centers, and details on the eagle, but most are fairly well struck. Morgan and Peace silver dollars vary widely, and cherrypicking is strongly advised for Full Details (FD); this gives you a great advantage, as most of your competitors in the marketplace will look only at the grades on the holders. This, of course, is incredible from a common-sense viewpoint, but that's the way it is!

- **Proof coins:** Gobrecht dollars of 1836 and 1839 are seen only in Proof format. Many are restrikes made at the Mint beginning in spring 1859. Liberty Seated dollars of 1840 to 1873 are all known in Proof format, the 1851 and 1853 being restrikes (no original Proofs were made in those years). Those prior to 1858 are very rare. Proof Morgan dollars were made of all dates, with the 1878 third reverse (slanting top-arrow feather) and 1921 mirror-style Proofs being very rare—although the Proof-only 1895 (880 minted) garners the most publicity. Some Matte-style Proofs were made of Peace dollars in their time, and, later, some others were fabricated to deceive collectors (be careful!). Proofs of Eisenhower, Anthony, and Sacagawea dollars are plentiful and showcase those designs nicely.

- **Key issues:** For the early series—1794, Proof "restrikes" dated 1801 to 1803, 1804 (the "King of American Coins," the most publicized of all rarities, although not the rarest), 1836 Gobrecht, 1839 Gobrecht, 1851, 1852, 1870-S (about 10 known), 1871-CC, and 1873-CC. Morgan dollars—1879-CC, 1889-CC, 1893-S, and 1895 are the key issues, but some that are common in low grades are rarities if choice Mint State. Peace dollars—1934-S.

- **Advice to smart buyers:** If you plan to specialize in a series of dollars, by all means buy specialized texts on that series. For all issues from 1794 to 1935, select coins for sharpness and eye appeal. Investment buying is particularly strong for Peace and Morgan dollars in higher grades, resulting in some huge price jumps for small differences in grade. Seek value for the money paid, perhaps using Optimal Collecting Grade philosophy (in my opinion, this cannot be overemphasized!).

- **Selected bibliography:**
Bolender, M.H. 1988. *The United States Early Silver Dollars From 1794 to 1803* (3rd ed.). Iola, WI. (reprint of 1950 work)
Bowers, Q. David. 1993. *Silver Dollars and Trade Dollars of the United States: A Complete Encyclopedia* (2 vols.). Wolfeboro, NH.

Bowers, Q. David Bowers. 1999. *The Rare Silver Dollars Dated 1804 and the Exciting Adventures of Edmund Roberts.* Wolfeboro, NH.

Bowers, Q. David. 2005. *A Guide Book of Morgan Silver Dollars: A Complete History and Price Guide* (2nd ed.). Atlanta, GA.

Fey, Michael S., and Jeff Oxman. 1998. *The Top 100 Morgan Dollar Varieties: The VAM Keys.* Morris Plains, NJ.

Haseltine, J.W. 1968. *Type Table of United States Dollars, Half Dollars and Quarter Dollars.* Philadelphia, PA. (original work published 1881; rendered obsolete by later works)

Highfill, John W. 1992. *The Comprehensive U.S. Silver Dollar Encyclopedia.* Broken Arrow, OK.

Newman, Eric P., and Kenneth E. Bressett. 1962. *The Fantastic 1804 Dollar.* Racine, WI.

Van Allen, Leroy C., and A. George Mallis. 1997. *Comprehensive Catalogue and Encyclopedia of U.S. Morgan and Peace Silver Dollars.* New York, NY. (the essential text for "VAM" variety attributions)

Wexler, John A., Bill Crawford, and Kevin Flynn. 1998. *The Authoritative Reference on Eisenhower Dollars.* Rancocas, NJ.

Trade Dollars (1873–1885): A Dollar for Foreign Trade

Silver trade dollars were minted for commercial use from 1873 through 1878. After that time, Proofs were coined for collectors until 1883, after which an estimated 10 Proofs of 1884 and five of 1885 were secretly made.

Regular-issue trade dollars of 1873 to 1883 are interesting to collect in a systematic manner. There is only one major design type. While some varieties are scarce, there are no great rarities.

Beginning in 1871 the Treasury Department had an interest in producing what was first called a *commercial dollar,* later a *trade dollar,* to provide a silver coin specifically for use in trade to the Orient and elsewhere, taking the place of Liberty Seated dollars that were used mainly for that purpose. The Coinage Act of 1873, mostly devised by John J. Knox (numismatist and monetary historian), created the trade dollar—a new denomination with 420 grains of silver, 90% pure, the specifications being stated on the reverse.

Chief Engraver William Barber designed the coin, the obverse featuring Miss Liberty seated on bales of merchandise, facing the sea to the viewer's left, looking toward the Orient. Her right hand holds an olive branch aloft, while her left hand holds a ribbon inscribed LIBERTY. The reverse shows a perched eagle holding three arrows and an olive branch, with inscriptions above and below.

Trade dollars were made specifically at the request of depositors of silver bullion

The silver trade dollar, minted in quantity from 1873 to 1878, was made for the export trade with China and served to replace the Liberty Seated dollar for this purpose. Shown is an 1875 Philadelphia Mint variety.

and were mostly exported. Under the Coinage Act of 1873 they were legal tender in the United States. No silver coins were in circulation in the East and Midwest at the time (and would not be until after April 20, 1876), as the public had been hoarding them since the second year of the Civil War. However, in the West, silver coins did circulate, and some of the new trade dollars saw use in commerce, particularly in Nevada.

As noted earlier with regard to Morgan silver dollars, the international market for silver was poor in the 1870s, and prices drifted lower, as large quantities of older European coins were melted into bullion and sold. Increasing production in Nevada and other western states added to an already burgeoning supply. As the price of silver drifted lower, it cost less for the metal needed to make a trade dollar. These figures show the average value of silver in a trade dollar, year by year:

1873: $1.0221 • 1874: $1.0058 • 1875: $0.9814 • 1876: $0.9101 • 1877: $0.9457 • 1878: $0.9070 • 1879: $0.9374 • 1880: $0.9019 • 1881: $0.8969 • 1882: $0.8938 • 1883: $0.8734.

In 1876 a depositor could take 91 cents' worth of silver and receive in exchange a trade dollar that could be spent for the face value of $1. Congress put an end to this unforeseen loophole, and on July 22, 1876, abolished the legal tender status of these coins—a rather unusual move in terms of American numismatic history.

As the price of silver continued to decline, the trade dollars that were already in western commerce, plus some that were now used in the East, were sometimes given in pay envelopes as salary—a cheat on employees, as such pieces traded at banks and with bullion dealers at less than face value. Brokers had a field day and would deduct a further 5¢, 10¢, or more from the silver value. Some banks would not take them at all!

In 1878, when the Morgan silver dollar was first minted, there was a curious situation in American commerce in which a

The works of the Yellow Jacket Silver Mining Company at Gold Hill, Nevada. During the 1870s the mines of Nevada produced far more silver than the market could absorb at then-current prices, and the value of the metal drifted lower during the decade.

The coinage of trade dollars took up some of the supply, but not enough. On February 28, 1878, the Bland-Allison Act eliminated the trade dollar and provided for standard dollars (of the Morgan design) to be minted in large quantities, irrespective of need for them. The government thereafter supported the silver market by purchasing millions of ounces each year.

Morgan silver dollar containing 412 1/2 grains of silver (90% pure) was worth face value (although it contained just 89 cents' worth of silver), but a newly minted 1878 trade dollar, with 420 grains (or 90 cents' worth of silver), was worth only about 80¢ to 85¢ at an exchange office.

Throughout the years of production of circulation strikes (1873–1878), trade dollars were well received in the Orient, their intended destination, where they competed effectively with Spanish-American dollars. Coinage for circulation was accomplished at the Philadelphia, Carson City, and San Francisco mints, with an emphasis on the western mints as most pieces were exported from San Francisco.

In 1875 the obverse of the trade dollar was modified slightly, and the ribbon ends, formerly pointing slightly to the left, now pointed directly down. The new obverse is known today as Type II, but should be called *Variety* II, as it was hardly a change in type. In 1876 the reverse was modified, as there had been problems in striking up the eagle's leg on the right side. The berry below the eagle's claw was eliminated and some other changes were made, creating the misnamed "Type II reverse." Trade dollars of 1875 and 1876 from all mints can be collected in combinations of Type I/I, Type I/II, and Type II/II.

While trade dollars were a great success for exporters, they did little to lift the market for silver bullion. Moreover, coins were made at the request of depositors, so there was no assurance of a continuing volume. The Bland-Allison Act of February 28, 1878, eliminated the trade dollar and put in its place the standard (Morgan) silver dollar, struck to the order of Uncle Sam, who was required to buy millions of ounces of silver each month even though silver dollars were not widely used in circulation. In less than two years, more Morgan silver dollars were struck than during the entire production run of trade dollars!

Proofs of the trade dollar continued to be made for collectors through 1883, including a remarkable 1,541 in 1879 and 1,987 in 1880, due to a speculative bubble at that time. The few Proofs secretly made in 1884 (10 Proofs) and 1885 (5 Proofs) were unknown to the numismatic community until 1907.

Key to Collecting Trade Dollars

- **Mint State coins:** Seen with some frequency in grades of MS-60 to -62, somewhat scarcely at higher grades, and rarely at true MS-65. Most have been dipped to brighten them, as is true of virtually all other "brilliant" silver coins of this era in collections today, except for certain Morgan dollars. Luster is often satiny rather than deeply frosty.

- **Circulated coins:** Available for most dates and mints except 1878-CC (rare in any grade, but when seen, usually Mint State). Many have chopmarks or counterstamps applied by Chinese banks and merchants, signifying their use in the Orient. These add interest, but generally make the values slightly less than for unmarked pieces. Some numismatists collect chopmarked coins as a separate specialty.

- **Strike quality:** Varies. Points to check include the head of Miss Liberty, the star centers, and the eagle's leg at the lower right.

- **Proof coins:** Produced in all years from 1873 to 1885, and readily collectible from 1873 to 1883, with Type I and II issues adding to the interest of the 1875 and 1876 years. Generally, Proofs of 1873 to 1877 are harder to find choice than are later dates. Keep an eye open for Full Details (FD), as some Proofs can have weak stars on the obverse and/or weakness on the eagle's leg on the lower right of the reverse.

- **Key issues:** 1878-CC, 1884 (10 known), 1885 (5 known). In addition, the Proof-only years of 1878 to 1883 have low mintages ranging from 900 (1878) to 1,987 (1880).

- **Advice to smart buyers:** Proceed slowly, for quality can be elusive, especially for circulation strikes. Borrow a copy of *Silver Dollars and Trade Dollars of the United States* (see below) from the ANA Library or elsewhere, and read the extensive section on the history of trade dollars to add to your knowledge and enjoyment.

- **Selected bibliography:**
Bowers, Q. David. 1993. *Silver Dollars and Trade Dollars of the United States: A Complete Encyclopedia* (2 vols.). Wolfeboro, NH.

Willem, John M. 1965. *The United States Trade Dollar* (2nd ed.). Racine, WI.

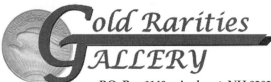

First year of the 1854 to 1889 $3 gold piece.
(Richard C. Jewell Collection)

inscription around. The reverse is an "agricultural" wreath, also used on the 1854 Type II gold dollar (and the 1856 Flying Eagle cent). On the first year of issue, 1854, the word DOLLARS is in very small letters. Later it is significantly larger. However, this does not constitute a major design change.

The logical reason for producing $3 pieces is difficult to ascertain. Some have said that silver three-cent trimes could be bought in groups of 100, as could three-cent postage stamps, but this does not seem to be a good argument for creating a denomination that was so close to the long-established and very successful $2.50 quarter eagle. In the early 1850s the Mint desired to make as many gold coins as possible, what with the tremendous influx of precious metal from California. Perhaps it was thought that a $3 coin would be popular, as $3 bills were a common paper money value. Perhaps this would have worked had there not been a $2.50 denomination already in place in the coinage system. In retrospect, the whole idea seems to have been illogical from the very start, a scenario similar to the later (1875) silver twenty-cent piece production.

In 1854, $3 gold pieces were coined to the extent of 138,618 at the Philadelphia Mint, 1,120 at Dahlonega, and 24,000 at New Orleans, yielding what would prove to be the all-time record figure for a single year. The Dahlonega and New Orleans mints struck no more coins, although beginning in 1855 and continuing intermittently until 1870, a small number were made in San Francisco. The 1870-S, of which only two are believed to have been struck, is unique today, with the only known specimen being part of the

Harry W. Bass, Jr., Collection on loan exhibit at the American Numismatic Association in Colorado Springs. In 1982 I cataloged this as part of the Louis E. Eliasberg, Sr., Collection.

Production for most $3 pieces was small, but even so the collecting of them by date and mint is not as difficult as might be thought, and the vast majority of coins can be purchased in grades such as EF and AU for less than $2,000 each. The key issues, apart from the impossible 1870-S, are the 1854-D, 1873, 1874, and 1875.

Somewhat similar to the situation for gold dollars, $3 pieces of 1879 through 1889 were saved in fairly large quantities in proportion to their mintages. Accordingly, examples are seen with some regularity today.

Key to Collecting $3 Gold Coins

- **Mint State coins:** Readily available for 1854, 1874, and many of the dates from 1878 to 1889, including certain low-mintage years. Later issues are often highly prooflike. For some dates, gem Mint State coins are notably rarer than gem Proofs.

- **Circulated coins:** Generally found for all varieties 1854 through 1878, in proportion to their mintages.

- **Strike quality:** Generally well struck, although details of the feather plumes and, on the reverse, the wreath (the ribbon knot is a key area), should be checked. All but one known (in the Bass Collection) 1854-D is weak in areas.

- **Proof coins:** Exceedingly rare for early years, rare from 1859 to 1878, and scarce to rare after that.

- **Key issues:** 1854-D; 1858 (heralded as a rarity in old-time catalogs, but not in the limelight today); low-mintage issues of the 1860s and 1870s, especially 1873; 1875 (Proofs only); and 1876 (Proofs only). The 1870-S is unique. *Condition* rarities abound, and in Mint State such issues as 1854-D, 1854-O, 1855-S, and 1860-S are seldom seen. In *gem* Mint State, the list can be expanded to include most of the other early issues.

- **Advice to smart buyers:** Quality is not a big problem in this series, but circulated pieces can be extensively bagmarked or lack eye appeal. As usual, follow steps 1 to 4 as outlined in chapter 2.

- **Selected bibliography:**

  Akers, David W. 1979. *U.S. Three Dollar Gold Pieces.* Englewood, OH.

  Bowers, Q. David, and Douglas Winter. 2005. *The United States $3 Gold Pieces 1854–1889.* Wolfeboro, NH.

  Breen, Walter. 1965. *Major Varieties of U.S. Three-Dollar Pieces.* Chicago, IL.

  Taglione, Paul F. 1986. *A Reference to United States Federal Gold Coinage. Volume 3: The Three Dollar Pieces.* Boston, MA.

  Also see the selected bibliography after $20 gold double eagles for general references covering all gold denominations.

$4 Gold Stellas (1879 and 1880): Popular Rarities Par Excellence

In 1879, following the suggestion of John A. Kasson, who served as minister to Austria-Hungary, the Philadelphia Mint struck patterns of the curious $4 denomination. These became known as the *Stella*, from the five-pointed star on the reverse. Kasson thought that a coin of this denomination would be easier to use in international transactions than the current $5 half eagle. However, the logic was flawed, as no foreign coins precisely equaled $4, and if they had, international rates fluctuated so frequently that the parity would not have lasted long.

Design Types of Stellas

1879 and 1880, Flowing Hair—The only readily collectible issue is the 1879 Flowing Hair, of which somewhat more than 700 are estimated to have been made.

The 1880 Flowing Hair is exceedingly rare, with fewer than two dozen known.

1879 and 1880, Coiled Hair—The rarest of the rare. Fewer than two dozen are known of each date.

In 1879, and also from the same dies early in 1880, the Mint produced an estimated 700 or more Stellas designed by Charles E. Barber, son of Chief Engraver William Barber. Miss Liberty is shown facing to the left, her hair streaming down behind her head. Around the border is an inscription, punctuated by stars, including the composition of the alloy and the weight in grams.

Word of the striking of the patterns reached the numismatic community, and there was some stir when examples were not readily available to collectors but could be procured only through dealers with special connections to the Mint. S.K. Harzfeld, for one, inquired, and in early 1880 Stellas from the 1879 Flowing Hair dies became available. The exact minted production is unknown today, but is estimated at somewhat more than 700. In the meantime, many of the 1879 patterns were given to congressmen as souvenirs, to acquaint them with the international coinage concept. A 19th-century commentary suggests that these were sometimes given as gifts to madams in brothels in Washington, DC. (although this sounds like numismatic folklore). Such pieces were crafted into jewelry and may account

Flowing Hair $4 Stella of the 1879 to 1880 type.

Coiled Hair $4 Stella of the 1879 to 1880 type.

today for a fair number of 1879 Flowing Hair Stellas that have been polished or lightly worn.

Somewhat secretly, George T. Morgan also produced a version of the $4 Stella in 1879, a distinctively different obverse motif with coiled hair. Also, without publicity, Flowing Hair and Coiled Hair varieties were made from dies dated 1880. The mintages for the last three varieties are not known, but today there seem to be fewer than two dozen of each. These rarities, seemingly made for the private profit of Mint personnel, were not openly distributed to collectors. Little was known about them until March 1911, when Edgar H. Adams's article "The Stellas of 1879 and 1880," in *The Numismatist*, illustrated and described the varieties.

While the $4 Stella is strictly a pattern, its curious denomination has made it a favorite with collectors for a long time, and it is often sought along with the regular series and so listed, including in the *Standard Catalogue of United States Coins* (in 18 editions from 1934 to 1958) as well as *A Guide Book of United States Coins* (from 1946—1947 cover date—to the present time).

The 1879 Flowing Hair turns up on the market with regularity, and there is always strong competition when such pieces cross the auction block.

Key to Collecting Stellas

- **Mint State coins:** None. All were made in Proof format.

- **Circulated coins:** Lightly worn 1879 Flowing Hair coins are often seen, these being mishandled Proofs.

- **Strike quality:** Nearly always with lightness of details on the highest-relief area of Miss Liberty's hair. Often with parallel planchet-preparation lines (from the drawing-bench process, after the strip-rolling mill procedure). Otherwise sharp.

- **Proof coins:** All were made in this format, from highly polished dies.

- **Key issues:** All, but especially 1879 Coiled Hair and both issues of 1880.

- **Advice to smart buyers:** Eye appeal can vary, but most high-grade pieces are attractive. For years these have been eagerly sought as trophy coins.

- **Selected bibliography:**

  Akers, David W. 1975. *United States Gold Patterns.* Englewood, OH.

  Judd, J. Hewitt. 2005. *United States Pattern Coins* (9th ed.; Q. David Bowers, editor). Atlanta, GA.

  Pollock, Andrew W., III. 1994. *United States Patterns and Related Issues.* Wolfeboro, NH.

  Also see the selected bibliography after $20 gold double eagles for general references covering all gold denominations.

$5 Gold Half Eagles (1795–1929)

Of all denominations of United States gold coins, half eagles were produced the most continuously. For a long period of time after the coinage of the $10 eagle was halted in 1804 (not to resume until 1838), half eagles were made in large quantities and were important in commerce.

The first coins of the $5 denomination were delivered by the coiner on July 31, 1795, and amounted to 744 pieces. By year's end, 8,707 were made. As Spanish-American and other gold coins in commerce were valued by weight, not by any inscriptions on them, the new half eagles bore no inscription relating to value—nor did any other United States gold coins minted in this decade.

Production of $10 gold eagles followed. It soon developed that many, if not most, eagles were exported, rendering them useless to the Treasury Department's desire to develop an extensive supply of U.S. gold coins in general circulation. In 1804, production of eagles was halted, after which the half eagle became dominant in commerce. However, these too were exported in quantity, and from 1821 through the summer of 1834, none were seen in circulation domestically. It cost a depositor more than $5 in gold bullion to have a half eagle struck. Accordingly, they were used for export purposes, where they traded solely on their metal value.

Half eagles continued to be minted for years thereafter, through several changes and modifications in design, until 1916. After that time there was a lapse until the swan-song issue of 1929.

Today, half eagles are interesting to contemplate from a numismatic viewpoint. Most who seek them do so as part of a type set, per the designs delineated below. Collecting by specialized date and major variety is next to impossible, as two issues of 1797 are each unique and are in the Smithsonian Institution. There is only one 1822 in private hands, and only two of the 1854-S are privately held. The Liberty Head series from 1839 to 1908 has been largely neglected by specialists, except for Charlotte and Dahlonega coins, which are popular in their own right.

Design Types of Half Eagles

1795 to 1798, Small Eagle Reverse— The year 1795 in particular offers many different die varieties and combinations, studied by J. Colvin Randall, William H. Woodin, Edgar H. Adams, and others.

1795 to 1807, Heraldic Eagle Reverse— The Heraldic Eagle reverse was first *regularly* used in 1797 on this denomination, but a left-over 1795-dated die was on hand and was used later to strike some pieces of this early date. Half eagles of this design are fairly plentiful in the context of early gold, much more available than are related $2.50 and $10 coins.

1807 to 1812, Capped Draped Bust to Left— Usually seen in grades of AU or lower Mint State.

1813 to 1829, Capped Head to Left, Larger Diameter, Stars Around Head— Many if not most are in Mint State. Issues after 1814 range from rare, to very rare, to extremely rare, to, well, forget it!

1829 to 1834, Capped Head to Left, Smaller Diameter, Stars Around Head— All are rare. For some reason, most of the 1830 to 1834 years (but not 1829) are nicked, marked, and lack eye appeal.

1834 to 1838, Classic Head— Made in large numbers, this type, of reduced weight, was the first half eagle to circulate in many years.

1839 to 1866, Liberty Head— These were widely used in commerce, with little thought to preserving them for numismatic reasons. Although worn and low Mint State coins are available for many issues, gems are unknown for the majority of varieties.

1866 to 1908, Liberty Head, With Motto— Many of the earlier varieties range from scarce to rare, especially in Mint State. After about 1878, Mint State coins of most varieties are readily available.

1908 to 1929, Indian Head— With the exception of the first year of issue, truly choice Mint State coins are scarce and gems are rare. The last year of issue, 1929, is the rarest, with only a few hundred known, nearly all in Mint State with many bagmarks.

Half Eagle Coinage

The first type in the half eagle series displays Miss Liberty on the obverse, with a conical cap (called by the *Guide Book* "Capped Bust to Right"), and on the reverse an eagle perched on a palm branch, holding aloft a wreath. This particular reverse style was also used on the $10 gold piece. The dies are attributed to Chief Engraver Robert Scot. The type was continued through early 1798, in which year just a few of this design were made. Today, only about seven examples of the 1798 Small Eagle $5 gold piece are known.

In the meantime, in 1797 the Heraldic Eagle reverse type came into use, but the obverse style was continued. Coins of this combination were made through 1807. A particularly curious variety is the 1795-dated

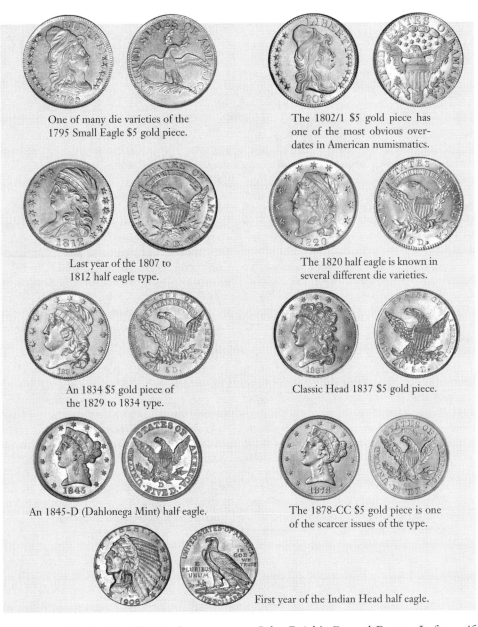

One of many die varieties of the
1795 Small Eagle $5 gold piece.

The 1802/1 $5 gold piece has
one of the most obvious overdates in American numismatics.

Last year of the 1807 to
1812 half eagle type.

The 1820 half eagle is known in
several different die varieties.

An 1834 $5 gold piece of
the 1829 to 1834 type.

Classic Head 1837 $5 gold piece.

An 1845-D (Dahlonega Mint) half eagle.

The 1878-CC $5 gold piece is one
of the scarcer issues of the type.

First year of the Indian Head half eagle.

$5 piece with the Heraldic Eagle reverse, seemingly produced before the design was created—obviously impossible, but neatly explained by the use circa 1798 of an old 1795 obverse die still on hand. Two varieties of 1797 are unique—one with 15 stars on the obverse and the other with 16 stars. Both are in the National Numismatic Collection in the Smithsonian Institution.

John Reich's Capped Bust to Left motif was inaugurated in 1807 and used on half eagles through 1812, such pieces being produced in quantity (in stark contrast to the rarity of same design on the quarter eagle, produced for only a short time in 1808 and to the extent of only 2,710 coins).

In 1813, the design was modified to include stars all around the head of Miss

Liberty, except for the date position, a general motif continued through 1834, but with a reduced diameter and other changes in 1829. The 1815 half eagle is recognized as a rarity today, with only about a dozen known. Among later issues the 1819 is a classic rarity, as are most other dates through 1834. Today, the only generally collectible date in the 1820s is the first year, 1820, which exists in quite a few different obverse and reverse die combinations, suggesting that pieces of this date may have been struck for a number of years afterward and included in *calendar-year* mintages such as 17,796 for 1822 (of which only three are known today).

Although mintages for half eagles of the 1820s and early 1830s were substantial, few of these coins survive today. This is due to the practice of recoinage overseas. When, for example, the Bank of England received American $5 pieces, the bank sent them to the Royal Mint and converted them into British gold sovereigns. Other countries usually did the same. The reason for this was that the treasuries of foreign lands could easily count and keep track of their own gold, but had difficulties with the varying weights and values of foreign gold on deposit. Conversely, when large amounts of French and British gold coins came to the United States, as was often the case, they were quickly converted into United States coins.

The Act of June 28, 1834, reduced the authorized weight of gold coins, after which they circulated effectively once again. To distinguish the new motif, the obverse was redesigned to the Classic Head type, with Chief Engraver Kneass swiping the motif used earlier by John Reich on the copper cent of 1808. The reverse was modified by removal of the motto E PLURIBUS UNUM. At the time, there was a great deal of political adversity in America, generally divided into pro-Jackson and anti-Jackson camps. It was said in a number of metropolitan newspapers that gold coins were produced by the administration of President Andrew Jackson to use as bribes for the 1834 senatorial and congressional elections! Apparently, these pieces appeared in circulation in large quantities beginning in August, but after the November elections they were rather scarce, or at least this is the thread of commentary in such publications as *Niles' Weekly Register.* The truth may never be known. There seems to be no evidence that these coins were struck other than for normal commercial purposes.

In 1838 the Charlotte, Dahlonega, and New Orleans mints went into operation for the first time, and in that year half eagles were struck with C and D mintmarks. (The first New Orleans coins of this denomination were not made until 1840.) In 1839 Christian Gobrecht's Liberty Head half eagle replaced the Classic Head. This style was continued through 1908. In 1866 a change was made to the reverse by addition of the motto IN GOD WE TRUST.

In 1908 Bela Lyon Pratt's Indian Head $5 coin appeared, identical in design to the obverse and reverse of the 1908 quarter eagle, except for the denomination. These pieces featured a realistic portrait of a Native American on the obverse, wearing a war bonnet, and on the reverse a standing eagle facing to the left, adapted from the reverse of the $10 piece of 1907 and, before that, a private inaugural medal made by Augustus Saint-Gaudens for Theodore Roosevelt in 1905.

Numismatic Notes

Today, the usual way to collect half eagles is by design type. All are available, although the modified type from 1829 through 1834 is very rare. Collecting by date and mint has not been as popular as for the $1, $2.50, and $3 gold series, but half eagles have still had many advocates over the years. Forming a complete systematic collection is a dream, not a real-life possibility, but all except about a dozen major varieties can be gathered, given a few years of time and a generous budget.

Among Indian Head half eagles of 1908 to 1929, minted continuously to

1916, then again in 1929, completion is possible. This has been a popular pursuit for many numismatists.

Key to Collecting Half Eagles

- **Mint State coins:** Scarce to rare for the earlier issues. The rare dates of the 1820s are usually Mint State when seen, but this is not often. Those of 1830 to 1834 are very rare. Classic Head half eagles of 1834 are fairly plentiful in the context of that type, while later dates, including mintmarked issues, range from rare to very rare. Liberty Head half eagles range from scarce to rare in lower Mint State ranges through the late 1870s, and in some instances are extremely rare or unknown as gems. Those from the late 1870s through 1908 are mostly available, with many choice and gem pieces dated around the turn of the 20th century. While Mint State Indian Head half eagles are not particularly rare, gems are seldom seen.
- **Circulated coins:** Generally available for all issues, later (1834–1916) in proportion to their mintages.
- **Strike quality:** Varies among earlier issues. Mint-caused adjustment marks are seen on many of the 1790s and some of later years. For Classic Head (1834–1838) issues check the highest areas of the portrait. For Liberty Head coins check the highest portrait areas on the obverse and, on the reverse, around the shield and the lower parts of the eagle. For Indian Head coins check the headdress feathers and the highest part of the eagle. The concept of Full Details (FD) or related terminology is absent from popular guides, giving you a great advantage as a smart buyer.
- **Proof coins:** Proofs before 1859 are exceedingly rare, and those from 1859 to 1878 are very rare. Later Proofs (1879–1907) exist in proportion to

their mintages, but all are elusive. Indian Head half eagles of 1908 and 1912 to 1915 are of the Sand Blast Proof finish, and those of 1910 to 1911 are of Satin Proof finish.

- **Key issues:** For the early issues, a list of dates that are *not* key issues would be shorter! Nearly all from 1795 to 1834 are either scarce or rare, with famous rarities including the 1798 Small Eagle, 1815, and most dates from 1819 through 1834—the Holy Grail being the 1822 (one in private hands, two in the Smithsonian). Among later half eagles, the C and D mints are scarce but collectible, the 1854-S is extremely rare, the 1875 is very elusive, the Carson City issues are mostly rare, and in the context of Indian Head half eagles, the 1909-O and 1929 are the most important.
- **Advice to smart buyers:** Building a type set is always good advice. Beyond that, study the availability and cost of any coins desired. Liberty Head coins are pursued systematically by relatively few collectors, except for C, CC, and D mint issues. Accordingly, many rare Philadelphia, New Orleans, and San Francisco varieties are less expensive than their elusive nature might suggest. This is the only U.S. denomination of which examples can be collected from each of the eight different mints (including West Point, for certain commemorative $5 issues).
- **Selected bibliography:**

Akers, David W. 1979. *U.S. Gold Half Eagles.* Englewood, OH.

Breen, Walter. 1966. *Early United States Half Eagles 1795–1838.* Chicago, IL.

Breen, Walter. 1967. *United States Half Eagles 1839–1929.* Chicago, IL.

Miller, Robert W., Sr. 1997. *U.S. Half Eagle Gold Coins.* Elmwood Park, NJ.

Also see the selected bibliography after $20 gold double eagles for general references covering all gold denominations.

$10 Gold Eagles (1795–1933)

Eagles, or $10 gold pieces, were the largest denomination authorized under the Mint Act of April 2, 1792. The name is derived from the depiction of the national bird on the reverse. (It was therefore logical in 1850, when a denomination of twice that value—the $20 gold coin—became a reality, it would be called a *double* eagle.)

Today, eagles of the early years range from scarce to very rare. Later eagles of the Liberty Head or Coronet type, from 1838 to 1907, and the Saint-Gaudens eagles of 1907 to 1933, are more widely collected, particularly the latter.

Design Types of Eagles

1795 to 1797, Small Eagle Reverse— Produced in small quantities and largely exported, eagles of this design are rare and highly prized today.

1797 to 1804, Heraldic Eagle Reverse— Eagles of this era are collectible, especially for 1799 to 1803, but are generally scarce or rare. Production of this denomination was halted after 1804, at which time the $5 gold half eagle became the dominant coin in this metal.

1838 to 1866, Liberty Head—This marks the first appearance of Christian Gobrecht's Liberty Head motif, soon adapted for use on copper coins and other gold denominations. Produced in large numbers at the Philadelphia, New Orleans, and San Francisco mints, eagles of this era are generally easy to find. However, for some issues, Mint State coins are either extremely rare or unobtainable, as during their era there was no numismatic interest in saving them.

1866 to 1907, Liberty Head, With Motto—Most coins from the early years of the type, up to 1877, range from scarce to rare today. Mint State coins are easy to find for most years after 1877, although for some, gems are elusive.

1907, Indian Head, Periods on Reverse, No Motto—Only about 500 of these exist with wire rim (fewer than 40 with rolled rim), but as they were all distributed as keepsakes and numismatic specimens, nearly all are in choice and gem preservation. None were put into circulation.

1907 to 1908, Indian Head, No Periods, No Motto—The circulating issues of Saint-Gaudens's Indian Head eagle. Many exist, and you have a wide choice.

1908 to 1933, Indian Head, With Motto—Produced continuously through 1916, then intermittently afterward to 1933. Many choice Mint State coins are available.

Early $10 Issues

In their own time, eagles of the 1795 to 1804 era were seldom seen in everyday circulation, as the face value was equivalent to a week or more of wages for the typical person. Instead, these pieces were the coins of choice for large transactions and international commerce.

Government accounts indicate that most were exported and melted, thus being of little value to the intended purpose of establishing a circulating federal coinage. Accordingly, production of this denomination was stopped, and depositors who furnished bullion to the Mint were given $5 half eagles as the largest denomination. In time, the half eagles also were exported. The situation was not remedied until the Act of June 28, 1834, which reduced the authorized weight of gold coins, making them unprofitable to melt down, and thus permitting them to circulate at face value in the United States. Under this legislation, eagles were not produced until 1838. Thus, the entire span of years from 1805 through 1837 does not include any $10 coins.

The first eagle variety of 1795, continued through early 1797, depicted Miss Liberty with a conical cap, facing right, with stars to each side, LIBERTY above, and the date below. The reverse illustrates an eagle perched on a palm leaf, holding aloft a wreath—a classical motif said to have been taken from an ancient cameo. Production

A 1795 eagle, believed to be the first of several die combinations of this year.

The 1801 eagle is one of the more available dates of this scarce type.

An 1844-O eagle of the 1838 to 1866 type.

One of the most plentiful dates of its type, this 1901-S eagle has been graded MS-66.

A 1907 Indian Head $10 gold piece, Wire Rim, Periods on Reverse.

A 1908 $10 gold piece, No Motto.

The 1930-S eagle is one of the rarest coins of the 1908 to 1933 type.

of this design was very small, amounting to just 5,583 in 1795, then 4,146 in 1796, and an estimated 3,615 in 1797.

During this time, the Spanish-American gold doubloon (or eight-escudos piece), valued at about $16, was the mainstay of commerce, along with its fractional coin parts, these keeping good company with the Spanish-American silver 8-*real* or dollar coins and their fractional parts. It was many years—indeed, until the Act of February 21, 1857—before Congress felt that enough federal coins had been produced, and that legislation was passed to eventually discontinue the legal tender status of certain foreign silver and gold issues.

Likely, a well-to-do citizen in New York City in 1797, with $1,000 of current coins on hand, would have few if any U.S. silver or gold pieces—they would all be foreign—but might have a few copper cents plus various state copper coins and tokens.

In 1797 the Heraldic Eagle reverse was combined with the preceding reverse, a type continued through and including 1804. After that time, coinage lapsed.

Liberty Head Eagles

In 1838 Christian Gobrecht's Liberty Head or Coronet Head made its appearance. This was the first depiction of a design that would be modified slightly and eventually used on copper half cents and cents as well as gold $2.50 and $5 coins. Miss Liberty faces to the left, wearing a tiara or coronet inscribed LIBERTY; stars surround, and the date is below. The reverse depicts a perched eagle holding an olive branch and three arrows. Inscriptions surround.

The new Liberty Head eagles were produced in quantity and served well in large transactions, including in domestic commerce. Many were also exported and melted. I have come across numerous accounts of outgoing shipments of vast amounts of these and other gold coins, destined for England, France, and elsewhere.

In 1850 the advent of the new $20 denomination reduced the call for gold eagles, and mintages tended to be low for the next several decades. In 1866 the motto IN GOD WE TRUST was added above the eagle, creating a new type that was produced continuously through 1907.

Branch mints issued eagles at various times, commencing with New Orleans (1841), San Francisco (1854), Carson City (1870), and Denver (1906). From early 1862 through December 17, 1878, gold coins were not used in commerce in the United States, but were hoarded. Their melt-down value was greater than their face value in terms of federal paper money such as Legal Tender notes. In anticipation of gold coins once again returning to circulation and being used widely, large quantities of eagles were made in 1879,

1880, 1881, and 1882. It developed that citizens continued to use paper money, and eagles were not wanted, except for areas in the West. For large international transactions the double eagle remained the coin of choice, and afterward the mintages of eagles generally declined, except for a few years.

The Saint-Gaudens Coinage

From 1905 to 1907 President Theodore Roosevelt was in continuous correspondence with Augustus Saint-Gaudens, America's best-known sculptor, relative to the complete change of American coin designs from the cent to the double eagle. Roosevelt felt the artistry of current coinage was severely lacking. Saint-Gaudens set to work, but he was in declining health, and prior to his death from cancer on August 3, 1907, he had completed basic models for the $10 and $20 values only. An assistant, Henry Hering, finessed the models and made them suitable for coinage production.

Later, artistic coinage of various denominations was continued by other sculptors, including Bela Lyon Pratt for the $2.50 and $5 pieces in 1908, Victor D. Brenner for the Lincoln cent of 1909, James Earle Fraser for the Indian Head or Buffalo nickel of 1913, Adolph Weinman for the "Mercury" dime and Liberty Walking half dollar of 1916, and Hermon MacNeil for the quarter of 1916.

In autumn 1907 the Indian Head design by Augustus Saint-Gaudens made its debut. The obverse featured a female head, modeled by Hettie Anderson, facing left, wearing a feathered Indian war bonnet as typically used by a *male* chief. Thirteen stars were placed along the top border, and the date below. A national brouhaha erupted when the false rumor spread that the portrait was of Mary Cunningham, an Irish waitress. None other than a "pure American" should have been used, it was said. The matter soon passed. For the first time in this denomination there were no dentils or toothlike projections around the rim of the coin. The reverse of the new $10 piece depicted an eagle, standing and facing to the viewer's left, a motif taken from an inaugural medal privately created for President Theodore Roosevelt by Augustus Saint-Gaudens. The edge, as viewed edge-on, had 46 raised stars—one for each state in the Union (a number increased to 48 in 1912 when Arizona and New Mexico became states).

Two rare varieties of Indian Head eagle were made with periods or pellets before and after the words in the reverse motto, creating the "With Periods" issues. One had a regular (sometimes called *rounded*) rim. Although several tens of thousands were minted, nearly all were melted, with the result that only about 30 to 40 are known today. The second With-Periods variety was made with a wire rim, to the extent of about 500 coins, most of which survive today. The With-Periods eagles were distributed through the Treasury Department to friends, certain coin dealers, and others, but were not publicized or generally available to anyone without "connections." Later issues of 1907 and subsequent years lacked periods on the reverse; these were made in quantity and were available to all.

In the summer of 1908 the motto IN GOD WE TRUST, absent from the 1907 and early 1908 Indian Head coins, was added, constituting the final type. Indian Head eagles were produced fairly regularly from 1907 through 1916, then occasionally from 1920 through 1933.

Numismatic Notes

Most often, eagles are collected by type, but basic varieties as listed in the *Guide Book of United States Coins* offer a challenge for anyone with an appropriate budget.

From the viewpoint of numismatic popularity, $10 pieces have had a mixed record. All early American gold coins of the old weight standard from 1795 through 1834 (including the eagle denomination, but only up to 1804) have been avidly collected for a long time. In contrast, Liberty Head eagles, minted from

Head of Victory, second study, was modeled by Hettie Anderson, "a woman supposed to have Negro blood in her veins," according to the artist's son, Homer Saint-Gaudens (*Reminiscences*, Vol. II, p. 332). This was considered for use on the Sherman Victory statuary group (erected at the southeast corner of Central Park, New York City, in 1903), but was not employed for this purpose. Later, it was modified, given an Indian headdress, and used on the 1907 $10 gold coin. (Illustration mirror-image reversed to conform to the profile on the $10 coin)

Saint-Gaudens's plaster models illustrating ideas for the reverse of the double eagle, none of which were adopted on actual coinage. However, a related standing eagle, similar to those at the upper left, was used on the 1907 Indian $10 coin (and was adapted from the reverse of a private inaugural medal the artist had done for Theodore Roosevelt in 1905). According to his son Homer, "All in all he created 70 models of this bird, and often stood 25 of them in a row for visitors to number according to preference" (*Reminiscences*, Vol. II, p. 331).

1838 onward, have always played to a very small audience. There are no impossible rarities among the Liberty Head issues, although certain dates and mintmarks are considered to be scarce.

Carson City eagles, the earlier issues of which are rare, are enthusiastically sought by CC-mint specialists, who also desire $5 and $20 coins. Demand for other Liberty Head eagles is slight. Accordingly, although many Liberty Head eagles from the San Francisco Mint are scarce, collectors for them are scarcer yet, and thus values tend to be low.

In the early years of the Liberty Head series there was virtually no numismatic interest in collecting such pieces, and for many varieties of the 1840s and 1850s, either no Mint State coins are verified at all, or those that have been called Mint State (some by moving up from AU due to "grade-flation") are MS-60 or -61 at best. San Francisco Mint eagles of the early years are likewise very rare. While it could be said that this lackluster (pun) situation offers an opportunity for advantageous numismatic purchases in terms of rarity for the money paid, I do not anticipate that the series will become popular any time soon. Likely, the Liberty Head eagles will remain in the realm of just a few specialists, plus, of course, those desiring single pieces for type sets.

As to rarity versus cost, the 1864-S Liberty Head eagle affords an illustration. Only 2,500 were minted, and of these, only an estimated 20 to 30 exist today, all in circulated grades. The *Guide Book* lists this coin for just $5,000 in VF-20 grade. To be sure, the price jumps up to $35,000 in AU-55 grade (the highest listed).

In sharp contrast to the lack of specialized interest in Liberty Head eagles, the 1907 to 1933 Indian Head eagles have had a strong numismatic following for many years. This demand first arose in the late 1930s after the mintage had concluded; consequently there are many varieties of Indian Head coins that are very rare in gem state, as few were saved at the time of issue.

The design of the Indian Head eagle is such that EF, AU, and low Mint State coins often appear to be rather scruffy and lack eye appeal. Accordingly, if you are seeking a piece for a type set or a specialized collection, it is probably advantageous to begin by examining coins described as MS-63 or finer.

Key to Collecting Eagles

- **Mint State coins:** All early coins (1795–1804) are rare, with 1795 to 1798 and 1804 being especially so. Among Liberty Head eagles, most dates and mintmarks from 1838 to 1878 are rare in Mint State, with some being incredibly so. Except for a few varieties, true gems are unknown. Most pieces graded MS-60 to -63 or so are heavily bagmarked. Liberty Head eagles of 1879 to 1907 are more available, with some dates of the late 1890s to 1907 being very common. Indian Head eagles are readily available in Mint State for 1907 to 1916, 1926, and 1932, but gems are elusive. There are three later rarities—1920-S, 1930-S, and 1933, of which the 1920-S is especially rare in choice or gem preservation; the 1933 is nearly always seen in choice Mint State, with a few gems as well.

- **Circulated coins:** Early issues (1795–1804) range from scarce to rare. Most circulated pieces are in higher grades, EF and AU. Liberty Head and Saint-Gaudens eagles are generally available in proportion to their mintages, except for 1920-S, 1930-S, and 1933, most of which were not distributed and were later melted. In any event, the 1930-S did not circulate to any extent, and the 1933 did not circulate at all; these are not seen in worn grades.

- **Strike quality:** Many early issues (1795–1804) have Mint-caused adjustment marks. Most early issues are weak in one area or another, although there are exceptions. Some of 1795 and 1796 are prooflike. Liberty Head eagles of 1838 to 1907 are sometimes light on the higher parts of the portrait and the lower parts of the eagle. Generally, the later issues are struck more sharply than the early ones. Indian Head eagles are mostly well struck, but check the highest areas of the portrait and the eagle. Once again, the quest for Full Details (FD) coins promises to be rewarding.

- **Proof coins:** Dates before 1860 are exceedingly rare, and those from 1860 through the 1880s are very rare. These were in not in demand by numismatists until the 1930s and 1940s, and absent a strong resale market, many Proof $5, $10, and $20 coins of earlier dates were spent in the era they were issued. Indian Head eagles of 1908 and 1912 to 1915 are of the Sand Blast Proof finish, and those of 1910 to 1911 are Satin Proof finish.

- **Key issues:** All $10 gold coins of 1795 to 1797 with the Small Eagle reverse are rare, 1797 to 1804 Heraldic Eagle varieties are scarce to rare (1798/7 especially), many *condition* rarities from 1838 to 1878, many rarities for worn coins of low-mintage issues (but demand is low as well), Carson City issues of the 1870s, 1879-O, 1907 Indian Head With Periods (two varieties), 1920-S, 1930-S, 1933.

- **Advice to smart buyers:** Quality is elusive among early (1795–1804) eagles, and many have problems of one kind or another. Proceed carefully. It is a buyer's market for scarce and rare Liberty Head eagles, so you can afford to be patient. Avoid coins that are heavily nicked and marked, the nemesis of buyers of Liberty Head coins dated from 1838 through the 1870s (although later dates are hardly exempt). Indian Head eagles often lack eye appeal and must be selected with care. Connoisseurship will reward you in spades when time comes to sell your collection.

- **Selected bibliography:**
Akers, David W. 1980. *U.S. Gold Eagles.* Englewood, OH.

Breen, Walter. 1968. *United States Eagles 1795–1933.* Chicago, IL.

Taraszka, Anthony J. 1999. *United States Ten Dollar Gold Eagles 1795–1804.* Portage, MI.

Also see the selected bibliography after $20 gold double eagles for general references covering all gold denominations.

$20 Gold Double Eagles (1849–1933): The Gold Coins of Choice

The vast influx of precious metal from the California Gold Rush in 1849 prompted Congress to pass the Act of March 3 of that year, creating two new denominations: the gold dollar and the double eagle. As it turned out, Chief Engraver James B. Longacre worked on the gold dollar first, and examples were in circulation within a few months. However, the double eagle was a different story. Some problems developed

A panorama of coins on the sea floor! In 2004 the wreck of the *S.S. Republic*, lost at sea in October 1865, was discovered in the Atlantic Ocean off the coast of Georgia. Thousands of coins were recovered, mainly in the form of half dollars, but including gold $10 and $20 pieces as well. The double eagles included most date and mintmark issues from 1850 onward, including a rare 1854-O. After treatment by the Numismatic Conservation Service (NCS), many of the double eagles were found to be brilliant and lustrous. (Photograph courtesy of the finders, Odyssey Marine Exploration, Inc.)

in creating dies with the proper relief to strike up correctly. Assistance was enlisted from Peter Cross (an outside engraver), and although a unique gold pattern exists with the 1849 date (in the Smithsonian Institution), production for general commerce did not begin until 1850.

The double eagle was an instant success. Depositors of gold preferred the denomination, as it was far easier to count large amounts in double eagles than in smaller coins. At the time, there were no widely circulated federal paper-money notes, and bills in commerce consisted of those issued by state-chartered and private banks. While in many instances they were perfectly fine for local and regional commerce, merchants and banks in England, France, the Netherlands, and elsewhere had no interest in receiving such paper, but demanded gold. Almost immediately, vast quantities were sent overseas, a situation that would endure until the late 1920s. In the meantime, these pieces were so spectacularly successful that more than 75% of the metal value of coins struck under the auspices of the United States of America went into $20 coins!

Today, quite a few collectors aspire to get one of each date and mint—seemingly a daunting challenge, but in reality quite feasible except for just a couple dozen rarities. Mintages of most issues were large, and due to overseas hoards, many coins exist today. Well over 175 varieties can thus be obtained out of slightly more than 200 totally

More popular is the route of collecting by design type, a pleasant pursuit, involving the following.

Design Types of Double Eagles

1850 to 1866, Liberty Head—Coins of this type are readily available in worn grades, but were nearly impossible to find in choice and gem Mint States—until coins from several sunken treasure ships became available in the late 20th and early 21st centuries: double eagles from the *Yankee Blade* (sunk in 1854), *S.S. Central America* (1857), *S.S. Brother Jonathan*

(1865), and *S.S. Republic* (1865). Today, these are highly prized numismatic as well as historical mementoes.

1866 to 1876, Liberty Head, With Motto, TWENTY D.—Readily available in grades through MS-62 and -63, but rare in gem preservation. Carson City coins from this era are highly desired.

1877 to 1907, Liberty Head, With Motto, TWENTY DOLLARS Extremely common as a type, and available in any grade desired, including gem Mint State.

MCMVII (1907), Saint-Gaudens, High Relief—This is considered by many to be America's most beautiful coin. Only 12,867 were struck, but many were saved, and an estimated 6,000 or so exist today, mostly in Mint State. The key issue for a type set.

1907 to 1908, Saint-Gaudens, No Motto—Plentiful in all grades. Gems of 1908 are mostly from the Wells Fargo Hoard of nearly 20,000 pieces.

1908 to 1933, Saint-Gaudens, With Motto—Very common as a type, although the systematic collector will be confronted with more than a dozen rarities.

Liberty Head Double Eagles

The first double eagles of 1850 featured Miss Liberty facing left, wearing a coronet inscribed LIBERTY, with stars surrounding and the date below. The motif was, in effect, a larger version of that on the gold dollar. The reverse of the double eagle depicted an ornate shield, with decorations so prominent at the sides that the shield characteristics took on another aspect when viewed quickly. The denomination was expressed as TWENTY D.

In 1861 a slightly revised die by Anthony C. Paquet, an assistant engraver at the Mint, was used for a brief time. This featured several changes, including the use of taller, heavier letters around the reverse border. It was felt that the dies of the Paquet design would not perform well in service, and its use was negated by the

A splendid 1857-S $20 piece from the *S.S. Central America* treasure.

An 1876-S double eagle.

An 1889-S $20 gold piece, lightly bagmarked, as many such coins are.

The MCMVII double eagle, high on the list of favorites.

Wells-Fargo Hoard 1908 No Motto $20 gold piece.

A 1912 double eagle of the 1908 to 1933 type.

director. Production took place at the Philadelphia and San Francisco mints, with the Philadelphia pieces nearly all destroyed, but with the San Francisco coinage of 19,250 released in its entirety before the director's order was received on the West Coast.

In 1866 the motto IN GOD WE TRUST was added to the reverse of the double eagle, constituting a new variety that endured through 1876. In 1877 the third type was created when the denomination was changed to read TWENTY DOLLARS. Coins of this combination were minted through 1907, including large quantities of some varieties, peaking at more than 11 million in 1904.

The double eagle played a great role in international finance for a long time, but most importantly from about 1873 to the early 20th century. The "silver question" dominated American politics. Many domestic as well as overseas merchants and bankers feared that the government would force the Morgan silver dollar into use in settling international trade balances and other debts, such coins being worth substantially less than face value in terms of silver content. On the other hand, a double eagle contained 20 dollars' worth of gold, a comfort to those who owned them. In *A Guide Book of Double Eagle Gold Coins* (Bowers, 2004), I give many details on this situation—including the near depletion of gold coins in Treasury reserve when these coins were exported in record quantities.

The Saint-Gaudens Coinage

The saga (for that is what is was) of the cooperation between President Theodore Roosevelt and sculptor Augustus Saint-Gaudens is one of the favorite stories in our hobby, a numismatic equivalent of a Hawthorne twice-told tale, involving a sculptor, a saint (sort of), and a scoundrel (in the view of some)—these being the *dramatis personae*—Messrs. Saint-Gaudens, Roosevelt, and Barber. The following appreciation is by John Kraljevich, Jr.:[65]

The MCMII Double Eagle

Although known as the "Rough Rider President," Theodore Roosevelt was perhaps the greatest patron of the arts to occupy the Executive Mansion since Thomas Jefferson. A scholar, adventurer, and winner of the Congressional Medal of Honor, Roosevelt took seriously his opportunity to leave a mark upon the American presidency and the nation in every way, from such grand objects as the military to more ordinary considerations such as the nation's coinage. He famously proclaimed, "We must show, not merely in great crises, but in the everyday affairs of life, the qualities of practical intelligence, of courage, of hardihood, and endurance, and above all the power of devotion to a lofty ideal."

With the "American century" opening before him, Roosevelt enlisted one of the great sculptors of the era to create a coinage for everyday use "worthy of a civilized people," as Roosevelt said, "which is not true of our present coins."

His idealism would be well rewarded with one of the most beloved coin designs ever created, authored by Augustus Saint-Gaudens. Rising to the presidency in 1901 upon the assassination of William McKinley, Roosevelt's first direct involvement with Saint-Gaudens' talent was when he deliberately chose the sculptor to design a private inaugural medal of 1905, as Roosevelt did not like the one provided by the Mint. The privately-produced medal was unlike its predecessors. The delighted Roosevelt identified Saint-Gaudens as the man to redesign the entire realm of American coinage in an effort to replace designs by Charles E. Barber and George T. Morgan, considered to be banal by many, including virtually the entire American artistic community.

President Inspired
by Ancient Coin Art

Roosevelt had a different vision for his nation. "I want to make a suggestion," Roosevelt wrote to Saint-Gaudens in 1905, as the New Hampshire-based artist was employed on new designs.

"I was looking at some gold coins of Alexander the Great today, and I was struck by their high relief. Would not it be well to have our coins in high relief, and also to have the rims raised?" Roosevelt asked earnestly.

Saint-Gaudens knew he had an ally—an especially high ranking ally—for his own vision, and responded to Roosevelt with a tone of friendly approval: "You have hit the nail on the head with regard to the coinage."

Saint-Gaudens continued his encouraging tone, but with a note of caution. "Perhaps an inquiry from you would not receive the antagonistic reply from those who have the say in such matters that would certainly be made to me."

Saint-Gaudens was referring to a 15-year-old rivalry between himself and the insolent Charles Barber, chief engraver at the Mint, whose inflexibility and self-centeredness were well known. In Saint-Gaudens' words, he envisioned "some kind of a (possibly winged) figure of Liberty striding forward as if on a mountain top...in hand perhaps a flaming torch, the drapery would be flowing in the breeze. My idea is to make it a living thing and typical of progress."

His artistic conception of Liberty was ideal to Roosevelt. "It would be beautiful," the President wrote back, and informed the sculptor that he had "summoned all the Mint people, and I am going to see if I cannot persuade them that coins of the Grecian type but with raised rims will meet the commercial needs of the day." He correctly anticipated the opposition that would accompany the designs. Roosevelt met with Leslie Mortier Shaw, the Secretary of the Treasury, in the last days of 1905 to discuss what he called his "pet baby"—the ideas of design change and a high relief gold coin (the $20 denomination was not yet decided upon).

The President recounted the meeting in a January 1906 letter to Saint-Gaudens, saying, "Shaw was really very nice about it. Of course he thinks I am a mere crack-brained lunatic on the subject."

Creating the New Double Eagle

By early 1906, Saint-Gaudens was well into the modeling phase of the new designs, but his health was deteriorating. Roosevelt's enthusiasm for the project continued unabated, but Saint-Gaudens' progress was slow indeed. The sculptor was in and out of a doctor's direct care and had to turn much of the responsibility for the project over to his assistant, Henry Hering. Saint-Gaudens' humor remained though—he told Roosevelt via letter in May 1906 that "if you succeed in getting the best of the polite Mr. Barber down there, you will have done a greater work than putting through your Panama Canal."

Barber had reason to be displeased, of course, as the Mint did not traditionally use outside help. He took Roosevelt's choice of Saint-Gaudens as an affront to his own talents and the grandeur of his position as chief engraver. So he became an obstructionist to the plan, even going so far as to design his own double eagle patterns in 1906, now known as Judd-1773. Henry Hering had the unenviable job of interacting with Barber on the issue, even as Roosevelt and Saint-Gaudens continued their brainstorming and exchange of witticisms.

In early 1907, after Hering's careful shepherding of Saint-Gaudens' models through the reducing and die-sinking phases, a tiny number of what are now called "Extremely [or Ultra] High Relief" MCMVII double eagles were struck. Nine separate impressions were required to raise the designs fully, and the coins were utterly unusable as money. But as art objects they passed with flying colors.

MCMVII Coins for Circulation

Plans were made to reduce the relief somewhat, but to retain the basic sculptured appearance. The result is what is known today as the "High Relief" MCMVII. With the relief reduced somewhat, Hering prepared new models that he believed would satisfy the continuous complaints of Barber that the coins could not be struck under normal conditions, would not stack, and other issues that bespoke small-minded petulance, although he was right about the high relief not being suitable for high-speed production presses.

"It is not in any sense the fault of this department that the dies are not ready," wrote a defensive Barber to the Superintendent of the Mint.

Saint-Gaudens died in New Hampshire on August 3, 1907. He would never see one of the MCMVII double eagles in circulation, but Henry Hering stood by his mission of seeing the design through to completion. The Mint coined 12,867 pieces in high relief even though the detailed dies still required three separate blows on a special hydraulic press to bring up all the intricacies. These pieces were struck, by direct order of the President, even as Barber had his plate full with creating hubs and dies for the lower relief 1907 Arabic date coins.

A November 22 order for 6,000 double eagles struck with high relief was satisfied, and the coins were issued for commerce in December. Immediately, and perhaps predictably, bankers complained about the inability of the wire-rim coins to stack. With slight modification to the design, flat rim pieces were created that stacked better; Barber pompously proclaimed that "they are so well made that I fear the President may demand the continuance of this particular coin, and while the effect of the mill is good it does not increase the output."

An Artistic Treasure

Roosevelt loved the newly created pieces struck in high relief and distributed them with pride to friends. In one letter that accompanied a brand new high relief MCMVII double eagle, the President proclaimed it to be "the best coin that has been struck for 2,000 years." Chief Engraver Barber, of course, disagreed, and laid low the triumphant relief for the regular issues that Hering believed were a disgrace to Saint-Gaudens' memory.

Since their initial coinage the MCMVII (1907) High Relief Saint-Gaudens double eagles have been among the most desirable of United States coins, trading for a premium nearly as soon as they were released to coin collectors, who correctly predicted the classic nature of the designs. Their designs were chosen with deliberation and care, the joint project of an artist and statesmen to produce a majestic piece of gold currency that would say more about the nation that issued them than any coin previously struck at the U.S. Mint. Today the pieces are still scarce and highly desired, with many pieces suffering at the hands of non-collectors who proudly handled, polished, and carried their prized double eagles to the detriment of the coin itself.

But any specimen, whether flawless or a pocket piece can still be an object of pride today—just as they were in 1907 when Roosevelt predicted he would be impeached for his "pet-crime" but called that "a very cheap payment!" for his involvement in the finest design in history of American coining art.

From 1907 through 1929 the Saint-Gaudens double eagle with regular numerals, sometimes called "Arabic" numerals, was the standard. In the summer of 1908 a change was made by addition of the motto IN GOD WE TRUST, creating a new type. In 1912 the number of stars around the obverse border was increased from 46 to 48, reflecting the addition of Arizona and New Mexico to the Union.

These large coins continued to be used primarily for export purposes. In addition, vast quantities were stored in Treasury vaults as backing for paper Gold Certificates. It is likely that certain dates and mints considered to be rare today were released only in small quantities, with the bulk of such coinage melted in the 1930s.

In 1933 President Franklin D. Roosevelt countermanded the further use of gold coins in circulation, and demanded that citizens turn in all they had, except for pieces of recognized numismatic value (not defined at all). Foreign governments, banks, and others holding vast quantities of double eagles had no interest whatsoever of sending them back to the United States and receiving paper money in exchange, so they held onto them more tightly than ever. Years later, in the 1940s, when collecting double eagles became popular, many of these sources were tapped, providing the majority of collectible coins today.

Key to Collecting Double Eagles

- **Mint State coins:** Treasure-ship coins are available for 1854-S (from the *Yankee Blade*; these are lightly etched "seawater Uncirculated"); 1856-S and, in particular, 1857-S, with more than 5,400 of the latter (*S.S. Central America*); 1864-S and 1865-S (*S.S. Brother Jonathan*);

and assorted pieces from the mid-1860s (*S.S. Republic*). These can form a interesting suite in themselves, and, in fact, I have assembled such a set. Most other issues are available in low Mint State grades and are scarce. Double eagles of 1867 to 1878 are generally available in MS-60 to -62 or -63 for most issues, 1870-CC to 1872-CC being notable exceptions. Most high-mintage Liberty Head varieties of 1879 to 1907 are available in choice Mint State, and certain high-mintage issues after 1900 are extremely common in choice and gem Mint State. The MCMVII issue is readily available, as are most other issues to 1916, although for some varieties true gems are elusive. The 1920 to 1933 double eagles are generally found in Mint State, except for 1920-S and 1921; some dates are extremely common, while others are rare.

- **Circulated coins:** Available for most issues of 1850 to 1916 in proportion to the original mintages. Typical preservations are VF to AU, with few known in lesser grades. Circulated 20th-century double eagles of common dates are of little interest to collectors, as Mint State pieces are readily available for prices that are not much higher. Accordingly, the market for worn, common dates is mainly to clueless investors.

- **Strike quality:** Varies and must be checked. On Liberty Head coins check the stars and highest points of the hair on the obverse; the reverse is generally sharp. Type 3 double eagles of 1877 to 1908 are usually sharp. The MCMVII is usually sharp, but the knee can be "shiny" or weak, as this is a high point. Saint-Gaudens coins of 1907 to 1933 can be weak at the center of the obverse (especially 1907–1908 No Motto), around the Capitol building, and at the base of the figure. Sometimes coins from tired or overused dies have arc-like ridges in the fields, particularly on the obverse. Aspire to own FD (Full Details) coins.

- **Proof coins:** Extremely rare to unknown for dates before 1859; 1859 to 1878 are mostly very rare. Later dates are rare and exist in proportion to their mintages.

- **Key issues:** 1854-O, 1856-O, 1861 Paquet (two known), 1861-S Paquet, 1866-S No Motto, 1870-CC, 1879-O, 1881, 1882, 1883 (Proofs only), 1884 (Proofs only), 1885, 1886, 1887 (Proofs only), MCMVII Ultra High Relief (pattern, but listed in the *Guide Book* and other standard references; about 20 known, a trophy coin par excellence), MCMVII High Relief (not a rarity, but in intense demand, dictating a high price), 1920-S, 1921, 1924-D, 1924-S, 1925-D, 1925-S, 1926-D, 1927-S, 1927-D (fewer than 15 known), 1927-S, all 1929 to 1933.

- **Advice to smart buyers:** This is a popular series with many offerings, even of rarities, so you can afford to take your time. Quality can be elusive for the earlier varieties to about 1878, and Mint State coins often lack eye appeal. In contrast, most common issues from the 1890s through 1928 can be found choice and require less effort to find (and not at much of a premium when they are found). Proofs can be marked and extensively hairlined. As always, connoisseurship will pay you dividends when the time comes to sell your coins.

- **Selected bibliography:**

Akers, David W. 1982. *U.S. Gold Double Eagles.* Englewood, OH.

Bowers, Q. David. 2004. *A Guide Book of Double Eagle Gold Coins: A Complete History and Price Guide.* Atlanta, GA, 2004.

Tripp, David E. 2004. *Illegal Tender: Gold, Greed, and the Mystery of the Lost 1933 Double Eagle.* New York, NY.

- **Bibliography for all gold denominations (general references):**

Bowers, Q. David. 1982. *United States Gold Coins: An Illustrated History.* Wolfeboro, NH.

Bowers, Q. David. 2002. *The Harry W. Bass, Jr. Museum Sylloge.* Wolfeboro, NH.

Breen, Walter. 1968. *New Varieties of $1, $2.50, and $5.00 United States Gold.* Chicago, IL.

Breen, Walter. 1988. *Walter Breen's Complete Encyclopedia of U.S. and Colonial Coins.* New York, NY.

Gillilland, Cory. 1992. *Sylloge of the United States Holdings in the National Numismatic Collection of the Smithsonian Institution. Volume 1: Gold Coins, 1785–1834.* Washington, DC.

Goe, Rusty. 2003. *The Mint on Carson Street.* Reno, NV.

Taglione, Paul F. 1986. *A Reference to United States Federal Gold Coinage. Volume 4: An Investment Philosophy for the Prudent Consumer.* Boston, MA.

Winter, Douglas. 1987. *Charlotte Mint Gold Coins: 1838–1861.* Wolfeboro, NH.

Winter, Douglas. 1992. *New Orleans Mint Gold Coins, 1838–1909.* Wolfeboro, NH.

Winter, Douglas. 1997. *Gold Coins of the Dahlonega Mint 1838–1861.* Dallas, TX.

Winter, Douglas, and Lawrence E. Cutler. 1994. *Gold Coins of the Old West: The Carson City Mint 1870–1893.* Wolfeboro, NH.

CHAPTER TWENTY

COLLECTING PROOF COINS

As the hobby or diverting pursuit, the collecting of rare coins affords more pleasure and greater interest than any collectible object.... And it is not necessary to possess all the dates of a given denomination but the various types. The series of dollars, for instance, may be represented by five specimens, representing the different types. The half dollar by seven species and so on, all of which may be obtained at a nominal cost, and yet would make a most interesting collection....

—B. Max Mehl, August 1905

The Panorama of Proof Coinage

While Proof coins are a part of other federal series, they can be interesting to study and collect in their own right. As nearly all were made expressly for numismatists and others, and intended to be saved, the quest for Proofs today is in many ways simpler than for circulation strikes. In this chapter I share facts, thoughts, and ideas about Proofs, here in one place, although scattered references to Proofs are found in earlier chapters.

Proof coins can be loosely defined as pieces struck with a special surface finish or appearance, intended to provide specimens for collectors, display, or presentation. Whereas most other coins were made as *circulation strikes* and turned out on production presses for use in commerce, Proofs are created with special care, slowly, and often from special dies and/or special planchets. Those distributed to collectors were sold at a premium, in the early days called a *proofing charge*.

Walter Breen referred to Proofs as *a coiner's caviar*—coins intended to be the finest examples of their kind, the ultimate products of the Mint. Today, Proofs are widely collected and enjoyed along with circulation strikes. In the 19th century, Proofs were often acquired to the exclusion of regular circulation issues, and a collection of American coins from the late 1850s onward would consist simply of Proof dates and denominations. In fact, the U.S. coins in the Mint Cabinet were gathered in this manner—a Proof for each date and denomination, with no care or

concern for branch-mint issues or other circulation strikes. Today, enlightened numismatists realize that Proofs are one class of coins and circulation strikes are another, and that often their characteristics differ widely. One of the first collectors to realize this was F.C.C. Boyd, who in the 1920s and 1930s endeavored to build sets in each format.

More than just a few numismatists of past generations have made Proof coins the main focus of their attention, even after the collecting of mintmarked varieties became popular. One of the most impressive holdings of Proofs ever to cross the auction block in the modern market since the 1930s was that of Christian A. Allenburger, M.D., an offering sold by B. Max Mehl on March 23, 1948. The offering combined rarity with high quality. Mehl's comment in connection with an 1867 Proof dollar: "Perfect brilliant Proof gem. Dr. Allenburger purchased all these beautiful Proof coins from the Chapmans many years ago. They were all purchased in complete sets and haven't changed hands since the date of issue, probably more than two or three times."

The reference is to S. Hudson Chapman and his brother Henry, important figures in the coin trade from the 1870s until well into the 20th century. John J. Pittman, whose coins were auctioned in the 1990s by David W. Akers, considered Proof coins to be his prime focus. Ed Trompeter concentrated on Proof gold coins and over a period of nearly

An 1864 Liberty Seated dollar of the mirror Proof style, struck from highly polished dies using a specially prepared planchet.

A rare mirror Proof 1831 quarter eagle (enlarged). Proof gold coins are the rarest of the rare of early issues. Only a few were made, and fewer yet survive today. Likely, interested numismatists of the era could obtain individual Proofs or full sets by paying face value plus a small charge.

30 years completed a full set, dollars to double eagles, from 1858 to 1915, save for the solitary exception of the 1858 double eagle.

Just the opposite was the emphasis of Richard C. Jewell, whose collection of $3 gold coins was auctioned in 2005. He endeavored to obtain a choice or gem specimen of each Philadelphia Mint date, bypassing Proofs, which for some dates would have been easier to locate.

As an investment, Proofs of selected quality have performed very well over the years. From a collecting and enjoyment viewpoint, there are many advantages as well. At the end of this chapter I give some ideas for building sets and groups of Proof coins.

Mirror Proofs

The most familiar type is the so-called mirror Proof, years ago called the *brilliant* Proof. As "brilliant Proofs" can become toned and no longer have a bright surface, the latter nomenclature is somewhat confusing. Accordingly, *mirror Proof* serves nicely.

Generally, mirror Proofs were struck from dies given a highly polished or mirrorlike surface in the fields or flat areas. Planchets of high quality were selected and were often cleaned or brightened before use. Proofs were struck at slow speed on a medal press in the early days. In recent decades, old knuckle-action presses have been used, operating at slow speed, with the coins removed individually by hand.

Although there is no general rule, many mirror Proofs were struck twice, to bring up the design detail sharply. Resultant Proofs appeared beautiful to the eye—sharply struck details on the frosty or satiny higher parts set against mirror fields.

Tradition of Early Mirror Proofs

The term *Proof* seems to have been first employed in connection with U.S. federal coins by James Ross Snowden, who served as Mint director from 1853 to 1861. By the late 1850s, the term was in common use with collectors and dealers. Earlier, such terms as *master coin* and *specimen* were used, along with *cabinet coin.* Today *specimen* is still used in Canada for special strikings, including some pieces that United States collectors call Proofs.

As to when the first mirror Proofs were struck at the Philadelphia Mint, opinion of scholars is divided. The late Walter Breen suggested that 1817 was the earliest date, as this was when new equipment was installed. However, as most of that new equipment, set in place after the Mint fire of January 1816, involved metal strip-rolling and planchet preparation in a separate building behind the main Mint structure, rather than die or press devices, this date is questionable.

From at least the 1820s onward, Proofs were specially struck as such, from dies with deliberately polished surfaces. These were used for presentation purposes and were also made available to collectors. The earliest known full Proof set of federal coinage is dated 1821 and is in the National Numismatic Collection at the Smithsonian Institution. This contains the cent, dime, quarter dollar, $2.50 piece, and $5 piece, these being the full range of denominations that were regularly made that year.

In the meantime, true Proof coins had been made for many years at other world mints, public and private. As one of many examples, the privately owned Soho Mint, in Birmingham, England, produced many mirror Proof coins and patterns for collectors in the 1790s. Another example is provided by silver Proof sets of 1746 coinage issued by the Royal Mint, London.

In the 19th century, in the cradle days of the hobby's popularity when there was little information available relating to Proofs, it was not unusual for a cataloger to use the term *Proof* to describe certain coins with "nice" surfaces, such as what today we would call gem Mint State. In such catalogs, one can find just about any series, from 1793 copper cents onward, called "Proof." Accordingly, old-time descriptions are of only limited use to students of the series today.

What Is a Proof?

Contemplate this question: is a Proof a Proof only if it was specifically manufactured as such, or can a coin be a Proof if it looks like one—with full deep mirror fields, sharp striking of design details, and frosty devices and lettering—even though it was not intentionally created as a Proof?

Certain silver coins of 1796, including the *majority* of the quarter dollars struck that year, have mirror surfaces. However, they were made for circulation, not for presentation to collectors. As a hedge or escape from argument, catalogers often call such 1796 quarters *specimens* or *prooflike* today. The *prooflike* term is widely found elsewhere, including obvious circulation-strike coins with some mirror surface, but hardly appearing as Proofs.

Conversely, there are several issues of U.S. coins that we know were struck only in Proof format, but that have every appearance of Mint State coins, with no Proof surface at all. The best known examples are the nickel three-cent pieces and Shield nickels of 1878, of which 2,350 Proofs were made of each, with no circulation strikes at all. If Proofs are to be determined by their appearance alone, these would not qualify! A frosty, lustrous 1878 Shield nickel with no mirror surface is designated as a Proof because the Mint reported that all were made as such. All were sold at a premium as part of minor Proof sets containing the Indian Head cent (which does have a deep mirror surface), the nickel three-cent piece, and the Shield nickel.

A lustrous, frosty 1878 Shield nickel, appearing more like a circulation strike than a Proof. However, as Mint records indicate that just 2,350 nickels were struck this year, and only in Proof format, and as original Proof sets remaining intact from 1878 contain such coins, they are attributed as Proofs today.

A sharply struck Proof silver dollar
of 1865 with deep mirror fields.

There are also some exceptions to the rule that Proofs have sharply struck designs and lettering. In the 1870s and 1880s the Mint became careless, even sloppy, in the making of certain Proofs, particularly in the Liberty Seated dime series, and some seen today are weakly defined in areas. Many Proof quarter dollars of 1858 have lintmarks in the field—curls and lines recessed in the field caused by impressions from threads (from wiping cloths) that adhered to the die surface. Lintmarks are seen on many other Proofs as well, but are not common. Some Proof trade dollars have the eagle's leg (at the lower right of the reverse) weakly struck.

Happily, most mirror Proof coins from the 1850s onward are straightforward in their appearance and are easy to identify as such. However, for Proofs before about 1854 we are entering terra incognita, and in my opinion many circulation strikes have been evaluated or even certified as Proofs. The situation is made no easier by the willingness of the late Walter Breen, who wrote a book on Proof coins in 1977, to sign "papers" attesting to the supposed Proof status of certain early coins, right along with attestations to special "presentations" and "ceremonies" for which no record has been located.

The years 1836, 1837, and 1839 afford an interesting instance in which mirror Proof coins were struck for circulation. These were the 1836-dated Gobrecht silver dollars, produced to the extent of 1,000 pieces in December 1836, and, from the same die pair, a further 600 pieces early in 1837. In 1839, some 300 Proof Gobrecht dollars were struck, most of which were put into circulation.

All of this shows that while there are certain rules for Proofs, there are also quite a few exceptions.

Proofs Become Popular

Beginning in 1854, sets of Proofs attracted significant notice from collectors, and starting in 1858 the Philadelphia Mint made Proofs generally available to all comers. For reasons not known today, it seems that full Proof sets were not made in 1851, 1852, or 1853, but some scattered denominations were made separately with Proof finish. This was just before the great growth era of the hobby that began with the discontinuation of the large copper cent in early 1857. In 1858 an estimated 210 silver Proof sets were sold, each containing a trime, half dime, dime, quarter dollar, half dollar, and dollar. Copper-nickel Flying Eagle cents were sold separately, probably to the extent of several hundred, and gold coins were also sold individually. The denominations of the year were $1, $2.50, $3, $5, $10, and $20.

For many years afterward, continuing to 1915, it was Mint policy to sell silver coins in sets. However, there were occasional exceptions when there was a special demand for a specific denomination, such as for trade dollars in 1879 and 1880 when there was speculation in them, and for Proof gold dollars in the 1880s (also an era of speculation).

Although it is not known when the Mint first offered minor coins (bronze and nickel) separately in Proof sets, by 1878, the first year for which records are available, this was the procedure. In that year a minor Proof set included the Indian Head cent, the nickel three-cent piece, and the Shield nickel (this was the earlier-mentioned group in which the two higher denominations often resembled circulation strikes rather than Proofs). Gold coins continued to be sold individually for most years, although for some years they seem to have been offered only as sets.

Official Mint information pertaining to Proof mintages is sometimes inconsistent or obviously inaccurate. In some instances, such as for the 1889 Proof gold dollar—today the rarest Proof of that decade—the Mint posted a mintage of 1,779, the largest mintage figure to be found for *any* 19th-century Proof gold coin. In 1908 the Mint reported making 236 Proof $2.50 coins, and in 1910, 682 Proofs are said to have been struck of the same denomination. Today, the 1910 is far rarer than the 1908! In these and other instances, some Proofs may have remained unsold and were later melted or spent. More likely, the figures are wrong.

Generally, in the 19th and early 20th centuries the production and distribution of Proofs was under the control of the Medal Department at the Mint, and different accounting procedures were in place. Often, Proofs weren't included in the totals given in the regularly issued *Annual Report of the Director of the Mint.* In some instances Proofs were restruck, but no record was kept of these. Examples of the latter are provided by the Liberty Seated dollars of 1851 and 1853. Apparently, no Proof dollars were originally struck in either of these two years. Later in the decade there was a collector demand for such Proofs, and the Mint struck dollars of these dates either from old dies on hand or from new dies made up for the occasion.

Proofs from the early years through and including 1901 generally have frosted portraits and other areas in relief, set against mirror fields. In recent decades some have called these *cameo Proofs* or *deep cameo Proofs.* However, with few exceptions, all Proof coins of a given year and denomination are the same—either cameo or not. Most are. Beginning in 1902, the first year of full production at the third Philadelphia Mint building, someone in the Medal Department decide to polish the portraits and certain other parts of the dies, in addition to the field. Accordingly, Proofs of 1902 and most of 1903 have "shiny" portraits, as do some of the next several years.

Matte, Sand Blast, and Satin Proofs

In the early 20th century, several other Proof formats were made: Matte (Lincoln cents of 1909–1916 and Buffalo nickels of

A rare Proof 1878 $10 gold eagle, a coin of which only 20 were struck. Typical of 19th-century gold Proofs, this specimen displays frosty cameo portrait and other devices against a deep mirror field.

This gem Proof 1903 $10 gold eagle was struck from dies having the portrait of Miss Liberty polished—a departure from the frosted or cameo style of earlier years. From 1902, continuing for the next several years, Proofs of the different denominations, cents to double eagles, show die polish in the design areas.

1913–1916), Sand Blast (gold coins of 1908 and 1911–1915), and Satin (gold coins of 1909–1910).

Matte Proofs were made by carefully striking coins from dies of which the faces had been given a matte surface by sand-blasting—the directing of a fine stream of sand particles in a high-speed air stream. Coins of the Matte Proof style have surfaces that are minutely grainy, not frosty or lustrous. The edges of the coins—as viewed edge-on—are mirrorlike. Generally, the borders of such coins, where the rim meets the field, are squared off. As the difference between a circulation strike and a Matte Proof can be difficult to discern, I strongly recommend that you buy coins that have been certified by one of the leading services.

Proof gold coins sold to collectors in 1908 and again from 1911 to 1915 are of the Sand Blast type, created by using carefully made coins from regular dies, struck on a medal press to bring up full design detail, and blasting the surfaces with sand particles. Gold Proofs of 1909 and 1910 are of a different style, Satin Finish Proofs, with satiny, bright yellow surfaces. The lat-

ter were made in response to complaints about the 1908 Proofs, such as this barb in *The Numismatist*:

> The types of the gold coins now being issued at the United States Mint do not permit the making of bright finish or brilliant Proof specimens. The face of the die touches almost every part of the planchet, dulling the surface of even a polished blank. Proof coins of the present gold series, so far as issued, have a very dull appearance, the finish being what is known as "sandblast," and are far less pleasing to the eye than the coinage for circulation, which is brighter and of lighter color.[66]

Matte, Sand Blast, and Satin Finish Proofs were intended to make the coins more beautiful by highlighting the design. Some of these processes had been used at the Paris Mint earlier, and at the Philadelphia Mint beginning in the 1890s for use on certain medals.

However, Proof coins with these finishes were very unpopular with American collectors, who preferred the traditional mirror Proof style, and many simply declined to buy them. It was intended that the Satin Finish Proofs of 1909 and 1910 be an improvement over the Sand Blast Proof format, but collectors were not appeased. At its annual convention held in September 1910, the American Numismatic Association passed a resolution against the making of coins of either non-mirror format. Edgar H. Adams, America's foremost numismatic scholar of the era, prepared the wording, which stated that current Proofs are "scarcely distinguishable from those issued for general circulation," while with the old-style mirror Proofs, "a most artistic effect is produced, throwing the design to the eye in a most attractive way, and provides the collector with a superior coin for cabinet purposes and at the same time one which cannot possibly be confused with the coin struck for circulation."

Of the Sand Blast Proofs and Satin Finish Proofs that did find homes in cabinets,

A Sand Blast Proof double eagle of 1912. Such coins were made by blasting the surfaces with a high-speed stream of minute sand particles. Sand Blast Proof was the terminology used in the era in which such coins were made. Later, some catalogers called them Matte Proofs.

many were later spent. Because of this, such Proofs are scarcer today than their mintage figures would suggest.

As complaints were frequent, and even the popularity of silver Proofs (which remained of the mirror Proof style) declined, the Mint terminated the production of silver and gold Proofs after 1915 and the Matte Proof cent and nickel after 1916.

Proofs of Later Years

Beginning in 1936 the Philadelphia Mint resumed making and selling Proof sets to collectors. Such were of the mirror Proof type and contained the Lincoln cent, Buffalo nickel, Mercury dime, Washington quarter, and Liberty Walking half dollar. These were available on a single-coin basis or as a full set. The cents and nickels in the earlier sets of 1936 have a somewhat satiny, rather than mirror, surface. These generated complaints, and later coins of that year, as well as of later years, had mirror surfaces. Nearly all Proofs of the 1936 to 1942 era are from dies that were completely polished—not only the fields of the coins, but the portraits and other design elements as well.

In 1942, two types of Jefferson nickel Proofs were made, one of the regular nickel alloy and the other with silver content. Due to the demands of wartime, Proof production was suspended after that year.

In 1950, Proof coins were again made and sold to collectors, this time only in full sets, each containing the Lincoln cent, Jefferson nickel, Roosevelt dime, Washington quarter, and Franklin half dollar. Some of the earlier 1950 sets were made with semi-mirror, satiny surfaces, until the Mint perfected or re-learned the correct technique. Proofs of this era were sometimes made from completely polished dies (including the designs), and at other times with the higher-relief areas satiny or frosty, in the old style as used in the 19th century. Modern Proofs with frosted surfaces are called *cameo Proofs* today and are especially desired. For some issues of the 1950s and 1960s, cameo Proofs are very rare.

An 1897 Proof Liberty Head nickel with frosted designs set against deep mirror fields.

A 1915 Matte Proof Buffalo nickel with satiny, grainy surfaces somewhat resembling a circulation strike. Such Proofs were not popular with numismatists at the time, but today they are better understood and are highly sought.

A 1937 mirror Proof Buffalo nickel from fully polished dies—the fields as well as the designs.

A gem Proof half dollar from the 1936 set—the first silver Proof set sold to collectors since 1915.

The seeking of cameos is a relatively new discipline and did not gain wide popularity until Rick Jerry Tomaska's book, *Cameo and Brilliant Proof Coinage of the 1950 to 1970 Era*, was published in 1991. I mention this as one of many examples in which a particular aspect of a series can be overlooked or ignored in one era and become the subject of intense interest in another. My earlier discussions concerning great demand for Jefferson nickels with six Full Steps (6FS), Mercury dimes with Full Bands (FB), Standing Liberty quarters with Full Head (FH), and Franklin half dollars with Full Bell Lines (FBL) reflect similar evolutions. Forty years ago, few people paid attention to such things, but those few who did were able to buy sharp pieces for no additional cost.

Similarly, in the years before the 1990s I sold thousands of Proof sets of the 1950s and 1960s without even stopping to notice whether they were cameo or not! Other dealers did the same. Today, there are *many* areas that are not recognized, and offer great potential. Indeed, as mentioned in earlier chapters, very little attention is paid at all to about 90% of American coinage, including such popular series as Buffalo nickels, Liberty Walking half dollars, and Morgan silver dollars! Perhaps someone reading this book 40 years from now will find this to be amazing.

Proof sets were struck through 1964, after which Mint Director Eva Adams mandated that no more be made. There was a nationwide coin shortage; freshly minted coins were hoarded in bags and rolls, and Adams thought that coin collectors were the culprits, although in earlier times she had been warmly greeted at numismatic conventions. She also directed that mintmarks be absent from future Denver Mint coins, to discourage collecting them. (Later, Director Adams "got religion," realizing that collectors were not at fault, but that the general public was responsible. In fact, she developed a strong interest in numismatics, and was elected to a seat on the American Numismatic Association Board of Governors.)

In 1968, Director Adams (who served in the post until 1969) resumed the production of Proof coins, this time at the San Francisco Mint, with each coin bearing an S mintmark. Ever since that time Proofs have been struck continuously at that location. While Proofs were generally sold in sets of five coins, there were special circumstances, including sets with Eisenhower dollars of 1971 to 1978, Susan B. Anthony dollars of 1979 to 1981, and other situations, plus special packaging options.

Most Proofs from 1968 to date are of superb quality, usually with frosty designs set against beautiful mirror surfaces—quality that ranks in the high 60s in grading numbers. It is not unusual for a beginning investor to think a real rarity has been captured by buying a modern Proof-68 or -69 piece, but in actuality such pieces are very common.

Advantages of Collecting Proof Coins
Mintage Figures Are Useful

In many ways, for the collector who has just a casual interest and does not want to expend effort in carefully acquiring coins, buying Proofs from the 1850s to date is much simpler than acquiring circulation strikes. While it can be argued that the unknown is always fascinating, there are those who are more comfortable with facts at hand. Proofs have fewer mysteries surrounding them.

First, estimating the true rarity and availability of Proofs is usually easy to do. Mintage quantities for most copper and nickel Proof coins are known for the years from 1878 to date, for silver coins from about 1858 onward, and for gold from about 1860 onward. As most Proofs were sold to collectors, who paid a premium to get them, their preservation rate was high. Although some high-denomination silver and gold Proofs were spent by collectors who tired of them, probably at least half of the Proofs made from the 1850s onward still exist. Earlier Proofs are scarcer than

A gem Proof $3 gold coin of 1878, of which only 20 specimens are said to have been struck. Such a coin would be a highlight in any advanced collection.

A 1981-S Proof set in the sturdy plastic holder of issue. This set has six coins, from the Lincoln cent to the Susan B. Anthony dollar.

later ones in terms of survival ratios, but many are still around.

Probably 90% of the mintage figures published for Proofs are accurate, although for some years and denominations, an unknown quantity of unsold coins can be deducted. Accordingly, we know that 880 silver Proof sets were made in 1895. Likely, most or all were sold. At some future date we will not be surprised by the appearance of a hoard of 2,000 on the market—the mintage figures indicate that this cannot happen. Instead, we can bank on the 880 figure as being the upper limit. Probably 600 to 700 each of the 1895 dimes, quarters, half dollars, and silver dollars survive today. This is enough that during a typical year a few dozen of each come on the market through private sales and auctions.

Among low-mintage Proof coins, such as gold coins of 1874, 1877, and 1878, of which just 20 sets were made of each, today perhaps 10 to 15 exist of most, with $10 and $20 coins being a bit rarer as they were more likely to be spent. Still, with patience such coins may be found, although several years may elapse between offerings of a specific variety.

In contrast, the survival of circulation-strike coins is often a matter of chance, and there are many such coins with mintages in the thousands, of which few high-quality coins exist today. As an

example, 3,060 were struck of the 1802 half dime, but fewer than 50 are believed to exist today, and none of these is Mint State. Numismatists presume that all of the others became worn and eventually were melted. It is theoretically possible, but not probable, that a hoard of 1,000 Mint State 1802 half dimes might be found. However, for the 1895 Proof dollar, of which 880 were made, there is no such possibility. (By the way, the appearance of an old-time hoard is not much of a "danger," for when this happens—as in the case of hundreds of millions of Morgan and Peace dollars emerging from vaults from November 1962 to March 1964—the availability of specimens increases, but the number of people interested also expands, and, generally, prices *rise!*)

Proofs Are Easier to Find in High Grades

The specialist in Proof coins also has the opportunity of completing sets in high grade, a situation not always true for numismatists who collect circulation strikes. Someone with the money to afford it, who wants to collect Liberty Head $10 coins from 1860 to 1880, from the Philadelphia Mint, will never assemble a set in MS-63 to -65 grade, for some dates do not exist at those levels. On the other

It is likely the case that a gem Mint State 1891 Liberty Head nickel (top pair of photographs) is harder to find than a gem Proof of the same date (bottom pair). In 1891, Proof nickels were made to the extent of 2,350 pieces and were saved by those who purchased them. On the other hand, circulation-strike 1891 nickels, of which 16,832,000 were made, all went into the channels of commerce—and the survival of gems is a matter of rare chance.

hand, Proofs, while rare, do exist and are likely to be found in grades from Proof-63 to -65.

In a less esoteric field, a full set of Proof Liberty Head nickels of 1883 to 1912 in Proof-65 could be completed within a few months by aggressive searching, to which can be added a few more months if the coins are selected one by one for quality. However, to form a set of nickels in MS-65 might well take more than a year. The late Abe Kosoff once told me that one of his clients had completed such a set, except for the 1891, and that he had spent several years looking for a nice example of this particular year. This was in the 1950s. I thought this rather odd at the time, as 1891 is not a rare date. Since then I have owned quite a few choice Mint State 1891 nickels, but I suppose that for any early coin, availability can be erratic.

In the 1950s the rare 1804 silver dollar, called the "King of American Coins," appeared so infrequently that several years would elapse between offerings. However, in the 1990s, there were well over a dozen different opportunities to acquire an example. By 1979, no 1787 gold Brasher doubloon had been auctioned in *decades*, and then in a space of a few months *two*

came on the market (one from the Brand Collection, the other from the Garrett Collection), soon followed by a couple more from the Garrett Collection. Other offerings and re-offerings were made in subsequent years. In 2005, Heritage offered *three* Brasher doubloons (two of 1787 and one of an earlier style) in a single sale.

Proof Barber dimes, quarters, and half dollars were made of each year from 1892 to 1915, and all are available in proportion to their known mintage figures. Assembling a full collection of Proof-65 Barber coins is doable, probably within a year or two (for coins with good eye appeal). On the other hand, a collection of each date and mintmark (not including the super-rare 1894-S dime) in MS-65 grade might well take 10 years or longer to form, if you desire each coin to be sharply struck and with excellent eye appeal.

In summary, high-grade circulation strikes are where you find them, offerings are often erratic, and the acquisition of a desired example is often a matter of chance. In contrast, most Proofs in the copper, nickel, and silver series from 1858 to date come on the market with regularity, as do gold Proofs (especially from the 1880s onward).

Other Advantages of Proofs

Nearly all Proof coins are sharply struck—excellently displaying even the smallest design details. Similarly, nearly all are on excellent planchets, without flakes, laminations, or other problems.

Still another advantage is that the values of Proofs are easier to calculate, as there are fewer variables of striking and planchet quality (although eye appeal remains important and must be considered separately). As outlined in chapter 8, investigation of the 1857-C gold dollar reveals an incredibly fascinating and complex interweaving of the aspects of planchet quality, striking sharpness, availability, and market price. In contrast, there are few variables with Proof coins.

Aspects of Proof Grade and Quality

Handling Proofs in the Early Days

In the 19th century, each Proof coin when first struck was equal to what today we might call Proof-68 to -70, close to perfection or actual perfection itself.

Such coins mostly went to collectors. Relatively few remained pristine and untouched. Happy exceptions included many of the coins gathered by T. Harrison Garrett in the 1870s and 1880s and carefully kept by generations of later owners, and also the Clapp-Eliasberg coins ordered directly from the Mint beginning in the 1890s and carefully kept ever since. Sometimes, long-hidden Proofs come out of the woodwork. A generation ago I visited a family who lived in a mansion on Philadelphia's Main Line. An ancestor had bought Proofs each year from the Philadelphia Mint, from the 1870s through 1915, and simply stored them in a compartment. When I bought the collection I am sure I was the first person to lay eyes on the coins since they were minted! Each coin was absolutely pristine.

In the days before coin albums became popular (beginning in the 1930s), Proofs were usually stored in open trays slid into a wooden cabinet, or in envelopes of coarse paper, and treated casually. It was customary for collectors to pass such coins around for visitors to see, and to otherwise handle them, not often with care. Some advanced collectors didn't even bother to handle coins by their edges—basic etiquette today, but not always so.

During discussions, coins would be held in front of those speaking, or face-up on a table, and drops of moisture, unavoidable when anyone is talking, would fall on the coins. These would be invisible, but later would develop into specks and flecks. Similarly, a tray of coins brought from a heated room into a cold one might develop moisture condensation. More flecks and spots would result.

The preceding methods of storage and handling might seem unusual or even improbable to readers today, but generations ago there was absolutely no emphasis on the *quality* of Proofs, unless they were badly impaired. A Proof was a Proof was a Proof. There were no gradations such as Proof-60 continuing for 10 numbers to Proof-70. If in 1910 you had visited the office of Henry Chapman in Philadelphia and had asked to see some Proof Barber dimes, quarters, and half dollars from 1892 onward, all would be in paper envelopes marked with the date and "Proof," and each variety priced the same—no reduction for coins with a few marks and no premium for superb gems.

If you care to verify this, simply take *any* auction catalog from a reference shelf, and if dated before 1960 it will probably have a listing such as "1904 Liberty nickel. Proof" or "brilliant Proof." My own catalogs of the 1950s were done in this manner, as were those of other dealers of the era—a style that dated back to the previous century.

Carelessness at the Mint

Sometimes in drawers and other containers Proof coins banged against each other. In fact, at the Mint itself Proofs at one time were simply mingled in a box, without protection, causing dealer Harlan P. Smith to register a complaint:

> Harlan P. Smith, being duly sworn, says that he resides in the City of New York and that he called on the U.S. Mint in Philadelphia in June 1886 and went to the Coin and Medal Clerk and requested to be furnished with a Proof gold dollar of the current year. The clerk opened a small writing desk and took out a round paper box which contained numerous gold Proofs. He scraped them over with his fingers and rubbed them together, upon which proceeding deponent looked with utter astonishment as it defaced the coins with pin marks and scratches.

Deponent had always believed and still believes that Proof coins are struck by the government for the benefit of coin collectors who are required to pay a premium for such perfect coins, and that from the improper manner in which they were handled by this clerk they were blemished and therefore collectors ought not to be compelled to pay a premium for such ignorance and incompetence displayed by the clerk in charge of that department.

Deponent further states that the clerk informed him that there were no Proof gold dollars to be had, and that he [deponent] then requested to be furnished with two silver Proof sets and twenty minor Proof sets, and when said request was made the clerk made some remark which left the impression in deponent's mind that the clerk was conferring a great favor upon him and acted as though he owned the entire Mint and the contents thereof. Deponent therefore claims that the government should not employ clerks unless they are fully competent for such position and said clerk, having been shown to be clearly incompetent, should be removed.

6th day of December 1886.
H. P. Smith[67]

In 1979 at the San Francisco Mint I was a guest at a ceremony. Afterward I visited the area in which Proofs were made, and watched an employee carefully take Kennedy halves from the press and stack them in little piles in a tray!

For generations of collectors, a Proof remained simply a Proof, and few buyers cared if it had a bit of friction in the fields or a nick or two. Sometimes these marks were acquired at the Mint, but more often they were from careless handling afterward.

In some instances, Proofs do not have to be *handled* to become damaged. Proofs and other coins stored in trays, museum cases, and other places in which there is atmospheric pollution can be harmed. Such sources as industrial fumes, heating furnaces, or exhaust from nearby traffic can affect coins. When I lived in Beverly Hills, California, my house had bright brass trim on the entry door. It had to be polished regularly, or it would tarnish/corrode to green within a year.

In a related instance, John J. Ford, Jr., told me that when he lived on Long Island, near New York City, he acquired a 1793 cent that had been dipped and cleaned to unnatural brightness. To have it tone brown, he put it on a windowsill. The chemical reaction progressed nicely—until one day the coin disappeared when the house exterior was being painted. He had forgotten about it.

Many of the silver coins in the New York Public Library Collection, which was cataloged and auctioned by my company in 1982, were toned nearly charcoal black on whichever side was face up in the cabinet where they had been stored for over a century. As for copper coins, one client who lived on Florida coast found that his collection of Proof Indian Head cents had acquired microscopic green flecks, from salt particles in the air.

Happily, modern "slabs" are a protection from mishandling and, to a limited extent, from atmospheric conditions as well.

"Brilliant Is Best"

Beginning in the late 19th century a passion arose for *brilliant* Proofs. When a Proof became toned through natural processes, *most* collectors and dealers brightened them by rubbing with silver polish (as the curator of the Mint Collection had done several times by the early 1900s), or by dipping in potassium cyanide (a deadly poison), or by using some other kind of cleaning agent.

In the 1930s Wayte Raymond popularized the "National" line of cardboard coin albums with clear cellulose acetate slides to permit viewing of obverse and reverse. These became the method of choice for storing and displaying collections, rendering obsolete the wooden cabinet with trays. The problem was that when the slides were pulled out and pushed in, they often rubbed across the higher parts of the coin, creating tiny parallel scratches. Many Proof Barber coins (1892–1915) and Morgan silver dollars (1878–1904) show these tiny horizontal scratches on the cheek of Miss Liberty.

For decades, *BU* (for Brilliant Uncirculated) was a very common term in auction catalogs and dealer advertisements. Coins with natural toning were nearly always dipped to make them brilliant and thus salable. While carefully dipping a coin once or twice may not be harmful, repeated dipping over a period of time makes the surface of a Proof coin become cloudy. Deeply toned coins (deep gray or black), if dipped, will often reveal surfaces etched from the toning action, making them dull, grainy, or cloudy.

In the April 1939 issue of *The Numismatist*, ANA president J. Henri Ripstra offered this unfortunate advice:

> There is no use of coin collectors having tarnished silver coins in their collection any longer, as they can

This bright "white" 1894 Barber half dollar has been certified as MS-66. Such coins are in great demand. A careful dipping will remove toning from a silver coin, yielding a brilliant specimen. However, if such a coin is re-dipped, and then dipped some more, it is likely to become lifeless and dull over a period of time.

safely remove the tarnish discoloration from an Uncirculated Proof coin by using the following instructions without any possible danger of injuring the coin whatsoever:

> Lay the coin on a small piece of cotton flannel in a saucer. Squeeze lemon juice on the coin, then apply common baking soda on a wad of cotton batting and gently rub the coin. Add lemon juice and soda until the tarnish is removed. Then dip the coin in boiling water and wipe off with a cotton flannel cloth, and you again have a brilliant coin.

> To properly clean medals of bronze or gold I use common laundry soap and the ordinary household ammonia and scrub well with a bristle brush. Where coins and medals have been lacquered, I remove the lacquer with alcohol. This will not injure the article the least bit.

I am not sure what Ripstra meant by an "Uncirculated Proof" coin, but it is certain that any gem Proof rubbed with baking soda or scrubbed well with a bristle brush gained scratches and hairlines!

Brushes, cleaners, and pastes were widely advertised in *The Numismatist* and elsewhere. Year by year, the number of gem Proofs diminished, sacrificed on the altar of "brilliance"!

"Brilliant is best" remained a catchphrase for many years, well into the 1970s, and it is still heard today, although most numismatists are a bit wiser about the damage caused by cleaning. The widespread search for quality did not occur until the late 20th century. The practice of cleaning and dipping still goes on. It probably will continue so long as certain buyers say they want only "brilliant" or "white" silver dollars and the like.

The cleaning of Proofs adds tiny abrasions, called *hairlines,* to their surfaces. While these lines often remain hidden on the raised parts of the design, they are readily seen in the mirror fields. If a coin has hairlines, it has been cleaned. Moreover, if *any* silver Proof coin from the 19th century is fully brilliant today, without a trace of toning, it has been cleaned or dipped. Sorry about that, but this is reality. Words such as *dipped* and *cleaned* are hardly ever seen in print!

There is a way out, and grading numbers provide a "wholesome" alternative. Any Proof coin described as Proof-60, -61, -62, -63, or any other grade short of near perfection, nearly always has hairlines, nicks, or evidence of cleaning. "Choice Proof-63" does look nice in print, but it may really mean "A Proof that has been cleaned several times, that has many hairlines in the fields, and that is now brilliant because in recent years it has been dipped once again. Accordingly, it is no longer a gem and is graded Proof-63."

The preceding stated, there are many really desirable Proofs out there, although you can see that from generations of exposure and "numismatic improvement" and handling, they are in the minority. Now, here is how to find them.

Being a Smart Buyer of Proof Coins

First and Foremost

When buying Proof coins in *any* grade I recommend that you consider only those coins with good eye appeal—this is the first and foremost commandment.

Such coins can be brilliant or toned, but in every instance a coin should be attractive. If a Proof is very pleasing to your eye, a little numismatic work of art, it will be pleasing to others when the time comes to sell your collection. On the other hand, if it is deeply toned, spotted, or unattractive, it will be shunned in the future. In the entire field of copper, nickel, and silver Proof coins from 1858 (the first year of wide sales to collectors) to date, there are only a few great rarities, so chances are virtually certain that a truly choice specimen of a desired variety will come your way.

If a coin is fully brilliant, you can then consider other aspects, such as the deep-

ness of the mirror field (should be "liquid" and deep mirror, not hazy or cloudy). It should have a minimal number of hairlines and marks. It may be best to use a low-power magnifier when examining coins, to be fully aware of such marks. Brilliant Proofs in the silver and gold series can have good eye appeal in grades from about Proof-63 upward, although many do not.

For toned Proof coins good eye appeal is similarly important. The term *toning* covers a wide range of pleasures as well as problems. A coin with blotchy, stained, or dark toning may be very unattractive. For my money, I would rather have a Proof-63 with good eye appeal than a Proof-66 that had little visual beauty. Sometimes toning so completely masks the true preservation of a coin that a Proof-66 piece; dipping such a coin in the quest for brilliance may reveal a piece that is scuffed and marked. This has happened many times, to the chagrin of the owners of such coins—who are stuck with the problem.

Toning can be very desirable, but it should be light or medium in intensity, not deep or heavy, and it should be nicely blended and have good eye appeal.

Choosing Appropriate Grades

What grades of Proofs should I buy? Is it better to buy 10 different Proof-63 coins for $1,000 each, or would a single superb gem Proof-68 for $10,000 be more desirable?

The answer isn't simple. First and foremost, as stated above, no matter what the grade it should have good eye appeal. Some Proof-63 coins have great eye appeal, while there are some Proof-66 or higher coins that are unattractive.

If a Proof-63 is fairly attractive and is priced at $1,000, while a gem Proof-65 is $3,000, and an ultra-grade Proof-68 is $10,000, it may well be that you would get more pleasure from owning 10 different, carefully selected Proof-63 dates as part of a collection, than you would a single Proof-68 trophy coin. At least, that is what I would do, following the Optimal Collecting Grade (OCG) concept.

This 1883 trade dollar was certified as Proof-62 by a leading service. Upon examination, the writer considered it to be a lot of value for its market price range. In 2005 a Proof-62 trade dollar had a value of $2,750 or so. In the real world, in the marketplace, there were "nice" examples and not-so-nice ones. By searching, you can find quality at the Proof-62 level, perhaps at a premium over the generic value, but still at far less cost than for a gem example.

This 1883 trade dollar was certified as Proof-66 by a leading service. Accordingly, it has a market value in the $10,000 range. Such a superb gem is more desirable, of course, than a Proof-62, but not everyone can afford Proof-66.

Incidentally, coin photographs are not a substitute for in-person inspection of a coin, as sometimes beautiful coins do not photograph well, and at other times unattractive examples can appear to be gorgeous in a photograph.

On the other hand, if you have an unlimited budget, then perhaps Proof-65 would be a good goal, adding occasional higher grades. For some early-date issues, levels of Proof-64 and -65 are about the finest available, and for some really early varieties, Proof-62 or -63 might well be top of the line. It has been my experience that most buyers who concentrate on buying extremely high-grade pre-1916 Proof coins, at levels such as Proof-67 or higher, are buying scattered trophy coins and not forming collections on a systematic basis.

Take as an example the formation of a full date set of Proof Liberty Seated half dollars from 1858 to 1891, followed by a set of Proof Barber half dollars from 1892 to 1915. A reasonable goal for a serious collector or investor is to acquire coins of hand-picked quality in Proof-64 and -65, perhaps with an occasional higher grade. Such a set, with good eye appeal, can be formed in several years. On the other hand,

someone buying only Proof-68 coins, and also insisting on good eye appeal (not all Proof-68 coins are attractive), will be able to obtain only scattered dates, and for very high prices, and will miss completely the satisfaction of building a set.

In the following sections I review U.S. Proof coins of all denominations and share my views on how you can become a smart buyer, gaining an advantage over most others in the marketplace.

Proof Copper Coins
Aspects of Collecting Copper Proofs

Of the various metals used to strike Proof coins, copper and related alloys (including bronze, of 95% copper, 5% tin and zinc) are the most chemically active. Almost from the moment of striking, a fresh copper coin, which might be described as bright orange (the term *red*, in standard use, is a misnomer), begins to acquire natural toning. Carefully kept, such a Proof coin (say, an Indian Head cent) would tone a warm orange with hints of brown—today called *Proof RD*, for "Proof red." As brown becomes more prominent, the designation changes to *Proof RB*, for "red and brown." Fully toned brown, or nearly so, the coin would be designed *Proof BN*, for "brown."

In buying Proof copper coins there are enough caveats to fill a good-size legal brief. First, many coins graded as Proof-65 RD or higher are coins that have been dipped. Sometimes brilliance caused by dipping can be unstable, and within a certified holder blotches can appear. It has happened enough times that just about any dealer can tell you stories.

At the same time there *are* original copper Proofs that are red, but it often takes an expert to tell the difference. Certification is of little help.

Proof RB, or red and brown, covers many possibilities. To my eyes, the only RB coins you should buy are those that have nicely blended colors—no stains, no distracting spots, no blotches.

Proof BN offers many really nice coins if they have toned *naturally* over a period of generations. Such coins should be evenly toned light to medium brown and have full deep mirror surfaces, no blotches.

My advice: do not buy any copper Proofs in any grade until you have familiarized yourself with the territory. After that, you will find that there are many *superb*, indeed *incredible*, opportunities, especially among RB and BN coins—a lot of value for the money spent. Also, while in other metals Proofs in grades below 63 can be attractive, generally Proof-60 to -62 copper coins are not.

Of all coins, copper issues are the most sensitive to moisture, heat, and atmospheric contamination. Be sure to keep your collection in a place away from such possibilities.

Some dealers have said to investors: "Don't buy *any* copper coins." Probably, this is good advice to buyers who simply want to write checks and do little else.

However, for alert, informed buyers, copper coins offer many opportunities. The record clearly shows that choice Proof copper coins have escalated dramatically in value over the years.

An 1847 Proof half cent.

Proof Half Cents (1820s–1857)

Proofs were made for most years that half cents were struck, from the 1820s intermittently through 1857. Dates such as 1836, 1840 to 1849 Small Date, and 1852 are found only in Proof format, originals as well as restrikes, making the acquisition of them a necessity for the systematic collector. Proofs of 1854 through 1857, dates also made as circulation strikes, are rare, but enough were made that acquiring an example of each date will not be difficult. Most Proof half cents have deep mirror fields, sharp details, and wide borders. Nearly all are BN or RB, with few being *original* RD. In my opinion, a number of half cents classified as Proofs, dated in the late 1820s and early 1830s (except 1831), are misattributed prooflike circulation strikes. Most such pieces are very deeply toned, making it difficult to discern the true nature of their surfaces.

Proof half cents are a very interesting, indeed exciting, specialty, and one that requires a good budget in combination with a great deal of patience. However, such a display can be very satisfying to own. Each coin is a rarity.

An 1857 Proof large cent.

Proof Large Cents (1820s–1857)

The only generally available Proof large cents are of the dates from 1854 to 1857, although these are quite rare. The population of 1854 and 1855 cents is in the high dozens, and perhaps a couple hundred or so are known of 1856 and 1857. Most of these have deep mirror fields, sharp details, and wide borders. Nearly all are BN or RB, with few being *original* RD.

Coins from the 1820s to the early 1850s, designated as Proofs, are a mixed bag. Some are unquestioned Proofs, while others are simply prooflike circulation strikes, often very deeply toned, that have been called "Proof" over a long period of time—a situation parallel to that with half cents, discussed earlier. In the 1950s I spent quite a bit of time examining "Proof" large cents in various collections, and concluded that at least half of those dated in the earlier years were not Proofs at all. Today, certification is of no help, as I believe that some certified Proofs are circulation strikes that are so deeply toned that their true nature cannot be easily discerned. My advice concerning these earlier Proofs is not to buy them unless you become a dedicated specialist in large copper cents, at which time you can go ahead with confidence.

An 1856 Proof Flying Eagle cent.

Proof Flying Eagle Cents (1856–1858)

When seen, Proof Flying Eagle cents, struck in copper-nickel, are usually dated 1856, these being the famous *patterns* that have been adopted into the regular series by many collectors. Well over 1,000 of these exist today, mostly in grades from Proof-60 to -63. Proofs of 1857 are exceedingly rare, and only a few dozen exist. Proof cents of 1858 exist in Small Letters and Large Letters varieties, with a total population of a couple hundred or so.

Proofs with good eye appeal are hard to find and are in the distinct minority. To qualify, a coin should have full deep mirror surfaces (or, in the instance of 1856 alone, a mixture of mirror and satin surface); sharp, square rims; and well-struck details (usually not a problem).

A beautiful gem 1856 is at once an American classic rarity and a joy to own, an ideal trophy coin in my opinion.

An 1885 Proof Indian Head cent.

Proof Indian Head Cents (1859–1909)

Indian Head cents from 1859 through the spring of 1864 were struck in copper-nickel alloy. Proofs are available of all dates and are usually fairly well struck (check the feather tips on the obverse and the wreath details on the reverse). Surface quality is another aspect entirely, and many are spotted, stained, or dull in areas. Choose coins that are bright (not deeply toned) and with good eye appeal; these are in the minority of pieces in the marketplace.

Indian Head cents from spring 1864 to 1909 were struck in bronze. Quality varies all over the place, and certification is of little help. Here are some rules to follow when buying:

- Coins described as RD should be completely without stains or spots, and should be orange with some hints of brown. If a coin is fiery brilliant orange, appearing as if it were struck yesterday, it has probably been dipped. Your best bet is to enlist the assistance of a trustworthy dealer or specialist and seek advice.

- Coins offered as RB offer many great opportunities, simply because many buyers prefer RD coins and completely ignore those that are not. In truth, there are many RB coins that are far more appealing than those marked as RD. Choose carefully, and select coins with the red (orange) color nicely blended in with natural brown.

• Indian Head cents described as BN can be very beautiful if with pristine mirror surface and without spots. Cherrypicking is needed to find them, but great treasures await you if you are patient. The beauty part is that most coins, even in higher grades such as Proof-65 BN, are inexpensive. Lots of potential here, in my opinion, simply because these coins are ignored and overlooked by many.

A 1938 Proof Lincoln cent.

Proof Lincoln Cents (1909 to Date)

Lincoln cents from 1909 to 1916 are of the Matte Proof style, with satiny, grainy surfaces caused by striking from dies with sandblasted faces. The rims are square, and the edge is mirrored (when viewed edge-on; not visible if a coin is in a holder). Nearly all *original, uncleaned* Matte Proofs are BN or RB, as the Mint issued these wrapped in tissue that imparted toning to the pieces. Nearly all called RD have been dipped or cleaned. Exceptions, which are few and far between, usually have orange-yellow surfaces with at least some natural brown toning. Buy only those Matte Proofs that have been certified by a leading service, as there are many non-Proofs out there with false credentials.

Lincoln cents from 1936 to 1942 are of the mirror style, with both the fields and the motifs polished in the die. Examples are mostly RB and RD, all undipped pieces having some delicate natural ton-

ing. Spots can be a problem, so examine them under magnification. Even though thousands were made of each date, finding pristine pieces will not be easy.

Lincoln cents from 1950 to 1964 are mostly from fully polished dies per the style of 1936 to 1942, but some have frosted motifs, called *cameo* by the grading services. For some dates, such cameo pieces are rare and command strong premiums. Most Proofs of this era have good eye appeal, and spots are not a problem, but it will pay to check carefully.

Lincoln cents from 1968 onward, struck at the San Francisco Mint, are readily available in gem RD grades, pristine and beautiful. Millions were made of each date, and high-grade coins are common.

An 1873 Proof two-cent piece.

Proof Two-Cent Pieces (1864–1873)

Proof two-cent pieces are easy enough to find in choice and gem certified grades, such as Proof-64 and -65 RD, but pristine coins with superb eye appeal are very rare. In my entire numismatic career I have seen only one or two date sets in Proof-65 RD or finer grade, with the coins being of *original* color!

The rules for buying are similar to those for bronze Indian cents of 1864 to 1909: take your time, search for quality, and be aware that hand-selected RB and BN coins can offer exceptional value for the price paid.

Proof Nickel Coins
Aspects of Collecting Nickel Proofs

When first struck, Proof nickel coins (alloy: 75% copper, 25% nickel) have a bright, silvery surface closely approximating the appearance of a silver coin. As time passes, the alloy naturally tones very slightly to a bluish-gray tint, sometimes with traces of yellow, giving a distinct appearance to the surface.

Today, Proof nickel coins are available in many different grade levels. Shield and Liberty Head nickels that are 100% silvery bright have likely been dipped, which is okay, providing that hairlines are not distracting. My general advice is to select coins that are fairly bright, not necessarily fully brilliant, and with no stains or spots. Take your time.

they were made, and it isn't possible to confuse them with circulation strikes as none of the latter were made.

Proofs from 1879 to 1889 are usually well struck and with good eye appeal. Some are fully mirrorlike and many others have a mixture of mint luster and mirror surfaces.

A fine challenge is to build a Proof-65 or finer set, each coin being of hand-selected quality. Allow a year or two to do this. On the other hand, your competitors in the marketplace, not being aware of the importance of *quality*, but concentrating only on numbers, can do it in a month or two!

An 1883 Proof three-cent piece.

An 1869 Proof Shield nickel.

Proof Nickel Three-Cent Pieces (1865–1889)

Proofs are available of all dates in this range, plus the overdate 1887/6. The rarest Proofs are 1865 and 1887. Proofs of the years 1865 to 1876 are generally less well struck and are not as deeply mirrored as are later ones. Accordingly, great care is needed when buying Proofs of these earlier dates. As always, you have the advantage of knowing what to look for. Most other buyers simply read the label on the holder. It may be the case that for dates in the late 1860s and early 1870s you may have to review 5 or 10 coins before finding a truly choice piece. Points to check include the details on the vertical III denomination and the quality of the mirror fields.

The years 1877 and 1878 were struck only in Proof format, with no related circulation strikes. The 1877 coins exist with finishes ranging from a combination of frost and mirror surface to full mirror. Many of the 1878 coins have *frosty mint luster* and resemble circulation strikes, which is not a problem—this is the way

Proof Shield Nickels (1866–1883)

Proofs were made of each date in the Shield series. Those of 1866 have rays on the reverse, as do the several dozen or so Proofs of the 1867 with rays, the last being a classic rarity. Other issues from 1867 to 1883 do not have rays on the reverse.

Generally, Proofs of the 1866 to 1876 years are hard to find in high quality—with deep mirror fields (no areas of pebbling or irregularity) and good eye appeal. You may have to examine a half dozen or more coins to find a nice one. The year 1866 is in special demand for inclusion in type sets, to illustrate the short-lived With-Rays design.

Shield nickels of 1877 and 1878 were struck only in Proof format, similar to the three-cent pieces of those years. As with three-cent pieces, most 1877 nickels have mirror surfaces, while many of 1878 have frosty mint luster. Nickels of 1879 to 1883 are especially plentiful in the series, and most are of high quality.

A 1900 Proof Liberty Head nickel.

Proof Liberty Head Nickels (1883–1913)

Proofs were struck of each date in the Liberty Head nickel series, with two varieties for 1883 (both with and without CENTS on the reverse). All were made in sufficient quantities that there are no great rarities. Quality can be elusive; this is particularly true for dates from about 1883 to 1900.

Generally, a fine collection can be assembled by reviewing pieces graded Proof-64 or higher, and selecting those of high quality. Avoid obviously hairlined pieces as well as spotted or stained coins.

A 1915 Proof Buffalo nickel.

Proof Buffalo Nickels (1913–1916, 1936–1937)

Buffalo nickels of the 1913 to 1916 years are of the Matte Proof style. Most are of high quality, well struck, and with attractive surfaces ranging from brilliant (with subtle natural toning, unless dipped) to lightly toned. As these are sometimes too difficult to differentiate from Mint State circulation strikes, Matte Proofs are not everyone's cup of tea, but those who seek them will not have great difficulty in finding nice ones. The last year, 1916, is also the most elusive.

Buffalo nickels of 1936 and 1937 are of the mirror field type with polished motifs, but the field area is so small on the coin

that there is not much room for the mirror surface to be displayed. Many of the 1936 coins have satiny rather than mirror-like finish, this being true of the Proof cents of the year as well. Later 1936 and all 1937 coins are deeply mirrored.

A 1939 Proof Jefferson nickel.

Proof Jefferson Nickels (1938 to Date)

Proofs were struck from 1938 to 1942, the last year including the regular nickel alloy as well as the silver-content type. The fields are mirrored and the motifs are polished in the die. Proofs were again struck from 1950 to 1964, most with fully polished dies, but some with cameo contrast to the designs. From 1968 to date Proofs have been made at San Francisco, typically with mirrored fields and cameo devices, and are common in high grades. The revisions to the nickel design, commencing in 2004, lend interest to the series.

Proof Silver Coins
Aspects of Collecting Silver Proofs

Proof silver coins are very popular with collectors and investors alike. When first struck, silver coins are bright. However, the metal is chemically active, and over a period of time silver acquires toning. This can be removed by dipping or cleaning, but each such process takes something away from the surface, and a piece that has been brightened many times will acquire dull or somewhat hazy surfaces.

My rules of engagement when going into the market to buy silver coins of the early era, 1850s to 1916, are these:

- Select coins that range from brilliant to toned. If toned, the intensity should be light or medium, never dark or heavy, and the full depth of the mirror fields should be visible when the coin is held at an angle to the light so as to reflect the surface to the eye. Toning should be attractive and nicely blended, never blotchy, stained, or spotted.

- Brilliant silver coins will show some hairlines except for pieces in very high grades. These hairlines should be subtle, and the fields should be fully and deeply mirrored. As a class, choice silver Proofs are much easier to find than are those of copper, but some effort is still needed to find nice ones.

Forming date sets of Proof silver coins by designs can be a fascinating pursuit.

An 1869 Proof three-cent piece (trime).

Proof Trimes (1851–1873)

Although a few authentic Proofs exist of the Type I silver three-cent pieces, or trimes, 1851 to 1853, most I have seen offered are simply prooflike circulation strikes, often with intense or deep toning that precludes careful examination of the fields. Be careful. The same admonition goes for Proofs of Type II (1854–1858), although authentic Proofs of 1858 occasionally come to market.

Proofs of the Type III style, 1859 to 1873, are readily available. Perhaps one in three or four certified coins is of connoisseur quality, the rest having irregular toning, spots, or other problems. Although their small size makes trimes difficult to appreciate without using a magnifying

glass, choice coins are interesting and enjoyable to own.

An 1872 Proof half dime.

Proof Half Dimes (1820s–1873)

Although some Capped Bust half dimes exist from the 1820s through 1837, and Liberty Seated Proofs of early dates are sometimes seen, the ready availability of Proofs of this denomination begins with 1858. The usual rules apply—seek eye appeal in combination with a sharp strike.

An 1892 Proof dime.

Proof Dimes (1820s to Date)

Similar to the situation with half dimes, although some Proofs exist back to the 1820s, their general availability commences with 1858, in which year an estimated 210 were made. Liberty Seated Proofs were made continuously through 1891, followed by Barber dime Proofs from 1892 to 1915. (Although circulation-strike Barber dimes were made in 1916, no Proofs were struck that year.) Proof Mercury and Roosevelt issues complete the series.

Proofs before 1916 require searching to find, if you desire pieces of high quality. However, the smaller weight and diameter of the dimes seems to have protected them from some of the marks and abrasions sometimes seen on large silver denominations such as half dollars and dollars. Proofs of 1936 and later are generally easy to find well struck and of high quality.

An 1876 Proof twenty-cent piece.

Proof Twenty-Cent Pieces (1875–1878)

There are only four Proofs in this series, and all are readily available over a period of time. The most often seen is 1875, from an obverse die showing a delicate arc-line around the upper part of Miss Liberty— an artifact of the die-finishing process. The 1877 and 1878 dates were made only in Proof format, with no related circulation strikes.

Quality can be elusive, and you may have to examine several coins to find one that is just right. For some reason unknown to me, the 1877 and 1878 Proofs are hardest to find with good eye appeal.

An 1882 Proof quarter dollar.

Proof Quarter Dollars (1820s to Date)

Proofs of the Capped Bust style of the 1820s and 1830s are usually seen only when great collections come on the market. They are so rare that no one has ever formed a complete date run. Liberty Seated Proofs were first made in 1838, but in limited quantities, and not for all dates, until 1858, when an estimated 210 were struck.

Proof Liberty Seated quarters from 1858 to 1891 are easily enough found in average grades, but quality can be elusive. Some are lightly struck. Check the head of Miss Liberty, the star points, and, on the reverse, the lower details of the eagle. Barber Proofs (1892–1915) should also be checked for

sharpness, particularly at the eagle's leg at the lower right. Washington quarters made intermittently from 1936 onward generally present no difficulty, and those from 1968 to present usually have cameo frosted details against mirror surfaces.

An 1873 Proof half dollar.

Proof Half Dollars (1820s to Date)

Although some Proofs were made of Capped Bust half dollars of the 1820s and 1830s, most described as such are simply prooflike circulation strikes. There are some marvelous exceptions, and with care such pieces can be acquired. Proofs are occasionally seen of later issues, but the first readily available date is the Liberty Seated issue of 1858. From then through the end of that design in 1891, examples are readily available, but high-quality specimens are in the minority, except for the later years, 1879 to 1891. Most are well struck, but all features should be checked. Barber halves of 1892 to 1915 are also easily available, but quality coins require effort to find. Check for striking sharpness, particularly at the eagle's leg on the lower right of the reverse.

Proofs of the Liberty Walking, Franklin, and Kennedy series abound in the marketplace, although Franklins with frosty cameo designs are rare and desirable for some years.

Proof Silver and Clad Dollars (1801 to Date)

Proof silver dollars of the Draped Bust obverse, Heraldic Eagle reverse type, of the dates 1801 to 1804, were first made decades after the design had been discon-

An 1882 Proof silver dollar.

An 1874 Proof trade dollar.

tinued. Today these are very rare, with the 1804 being famous in this regard. Gobrecht silver dollars of 1836 (no stars on the obverse, 26 stars on the reverse) and 1839 (13 stars on the obverse, no stars on the reverse) were made as regular issues, although in Proof format. These are rare and desirable today. Many nice pieces exist.

Liberty Seated dollars were struck in Proof format from 1840 to 1873, except for 1851 and 1853. Years later restrikes were made of these two dates. All dates prior to 1858 are very rare today. Most Proof Liberty Seated dollars are well struck, but there are exceptions. Morgan silver dollars were made in Proof format from 1878 to 1921. Striking and contrast varied considerably over this span. Today, collecting a high-quality set of Proof Morgan dollars is a great challenge. Some authentic Matte Proof Peace dollars of 1921 and 1922 exist and are very rare. There are also a number of satiny circulation strikes masquerading as "Proofs" in commercial channels.

Later Proof dollars of the Eisenhower, Anthony, and Sacagawea types, silver as well as clad metal, are readily available and very popular.

Proof Trade Dollars (1873–1885)

Proof trade dollars were made of all dates from 1873 to 1885, but those of 1884 and 1885 were more or less private issues and were unavailable to collectors at the time. Those of the 1873 to 1883 dates were made in sufficient numbers that they are readily available today. The 1879 and 1880 were struck in especially large numbers, as there was a popular investment speculation in them at the time. Generally, those dated 1873 to 1877 are harder to find with good eye appeal than are those of later dates. Striking can be a problem, especially at the lower part of the eagle on the reverse, and it will pay to check carefully.

Proof Gold Coins
Aspects of Collecting Gold Proofs

The collecting of Proof gold coins is a challenging pursuit, for all are rare and many are extremely so. The price of entry for a high-quality example of even one of the higher-mintage dates is in the thousands of dollars.

In modern times only a few numismatists have endeavored to assemble date runs. The most notable in this regard was the late Ed Trompeter, who spent more than 20 years seeking one of each gold coin date and denomination from 1858 to 1915, and upon his passing had acquired all but one: an 1858 double eagle. Several of my friends and clients have aspired to put together Proof sets of gold dollars and $3 pieces.

Most often, today's buyer of Proof gold desires a trophy coin or two, standing alone and not part of a collection of a specific denomination, or else wants to add a few Proof gold coins to a type set of U.S. coins. Still others endeavor to assemble small sets, such as all of the Proof gold coins of a given year, or perhaps a run of Indian Head Proof $2.50 or $5 pieces.

The quality of striking of Proof gold coins varied over a long period of years. Generally, very early Proofs from the 1820s through the 1830s were well struck, with superb details. Mentioning this is more theoretical than practical for use, as such pieces are so rare that they are hardly ever encountered today.

The series of Liberty Head gold coins from the late 1830s to the early 20th century includes denominations from the dollar to the double eagle. Many of the gold Proofs from the 1860s through the 1890s have what are called "orange peel" surfaces in the fields—fully mirrorlike, but somewhat pebbly, in a manner than can be best appreciated by viewing the coins. This orange-peel effect is especially desirable. Most Proof Liberty Head coins have frosted or cameo surfaces until 1902 for the $2.50, $5, $10, and $20 pieces (the only denominations being made at that time), when someone at the Mint decided to polish the portrait of Miss Liberty in the dies. From then through the next several years the coins are of generally low contrast, this being especially true for 1902 and 1903. This polishing of the portraits was also done on lower denominations in other metals, but is not as noticeable. Proofs of 1908 to 1915 are of the Sand Blast and Satin Finish styles discussed earlier in this chapter.

Over a period of years Proof gold coins tone a warm orange color, this from the copper element in the alloy (90% gold, 10% copper). For some early years, silver is an "impurity" in the alloy (part of the 10% reserved for copper), giving the coins a light yellow color.

Planchets used to strike gold coins were generally of high quality. However, for some there was an imperfect mixing of the alloy, yielding tiny flecks of copper. Years later, these flecks often toned to light brown spots. Proof gold coins with such spotting are usually dated from the 1880s to the early 20th century and should be avoided. A few Proofs have tiny black carbon specks, and should be removed from consideration as well.

Although the quest for quality should be everlasting with you, gold coins are somewhat simpler to evaluate than are the other denominations, as spotting, blotching, and deep toning are generally not factors (except for the flecks earlier mentioned). Accordingly, grades such as Proof-60, -61, and so on usually reflect the amount of handling a coin has received. Most coins graded Proof-64 or finer are fairly decent, but there are many exceptions. Cherry-picking is definitely advised.

An 1886 Proof gold dollar.

Proof Gold Dollars

Proofs exist of all dates from 1854 to 1889, and a few dates before then. The earliest year generally available is 1858, itself a rarity. From then through 1878, mintages tended to be small, and survival rates smaller still, with perhaps 50% to 70% remaining for most years. Many of these years are also rare on an absolute basis, as circulation-strike mintages were low.

Beginning in 1879 there was a popular speculation in gold dollars, and many members of the public sought to squirrel away a few, with the thought that they would become rare and valuable. Some of these investors sought Proofs, with the result that mintages jumped sharply during the next decade. Today, these are more available than are the earlier years. The rarest of all in that era is the 1889, which also has the highest mintage figure, for some reason unexplained today.

There are many prooflike circulation strikes that have been attributed as full Proofs. My recommendation is that you buy only coins certified by a leading service. Beyond that, check for quality and eye appeal.

An 1894 Proof $2.50 gold piece.

Proof $2.50 Gold Pieces (Quarter Eagles)

Although Proofs were made of most quarter eagles from 1821 onward, in the marketplace few are available until about the year 1858, and even those are very rare. From then until 1878, mintages tended to be low. The most famous date of this era is the 1863, of which just 30 Proofs were made and no circulation strikes. The 1875 is also remarkable for its rarity.

Liberty Head quarter eagles from 1879 to 1907 come on the market every now and again, and over the period of a year there are apt to be from one to several examples of a given date on the auction block. Proofs of 1902 and the next several years have polished portraits and are not as attractive as are earlier issues. Sand Blast Proofs of 1908 and 1911 to 1915, and Satin Finish Proofs of 1909 and 1910, were not popular in their time, but are in great demand today.

An 1875 Proof $3 gold piece.

Proof $3 Gold Pieces

Although Proof $3 coins of the dates 1854 through 1858 come on the market at widely spaced intervals, true availability does not commence until 1859. Even then, examples are rare, and continue to be until after 1878. Proofs from 1879 onward are the most often seen, but are still rare.

Striking quality is usually good, and the ever-popular orange-peel surface is seen on many, especially of the earlier years. The dates 1873, 1875 (in particular), and 1876 are famous for their absolute rarity and position as keys to the series. Only 20 were reported for 1875, with no related circulation strikes.

An 1879 Proof $4 gold Stella.

Proof $4 Gold Pieces (Stellas)

The four varieties of Stellas—1879 and 1880, each with Flowing Hair or Coiled Hair—were made only in Proof format. The most often encountered is the 1879 Flowing Hair, of which several hundred exist today. The others are great rarities.

The striking of $4 coins usually shows some lightness on the highest area of Miss Liberty's hair. This is normal and is to be expected—and someone demanding otherwise may never acquire a coin. Otherwise, the usual eye appeal should be sought.

An 1865 Proof $5 gold piece.

Proof $5 Gold Pieces (Half Eagles)

Although Proof half eagles exist for most dates back to the early 1820s, realistic availability doesn't commence until the year 1859. As is true of other gold series, half eagles from that point through 1878 are rare and seldom encountered, with some mintages falling as low as 20 pieces. Proof $5 and $10 coins of the late 19th century are rarer than are Proofs of other denominations, as more seem to have been lost or spent. From 1879 to 1907, Proofs are seen with some regularity. Those of 1902 and several later years have polished portraits.

Indian Head half eagles of 1908 and from 1911 to 1915 are available in Sand Blast Proof finish, while those of 1909 and 1910 are encountered as Satin Finish Proofs.

An 1866 Proof $10 gold piece.

Proof $10 Gold Pieces (Eagles)

Although some 1804-dated Proof eagles were struck in 1834 for inclusion in special sets, regular Proof production began with the Liberty Head design in 1838. From then until the late 1850s a few Proofs were made each year. Today, any and all are extreme rarities. Proofs of the 1860s through the 1880s are more available, but are also very rare. Sometimes as much as a decade will pass between auction offerings of a given date. Eagles from the 1890s through 1907 are more available, but still rare. Those of 1902 and several later years have polished portraits.

Indian Head eagles of 1908 and from 1911 to 1915 are of the Sand Blast Proof finish, and those of 1909 and 1910 are Satin Finish Proofs. All are very rare today, but when seen are apt to be in grades of Proof-64 or higher (this being true of other gold Proofs of the same years).

An 1881 Proof $20 gold piece.

Proof $20 Gold Pieces (Double Eagles)

Of all Proof gold denominations, the double eagles are probably the most famous—simply from their large size and impressive appearance, and the inclusion of quite a few key dates. The first generally available date is 1859, a great rarity, after which Proofs of each year remain rare through 1878. From 1879 onward the mintages increased, but *rarity* is still the key word. Such dates as 1883, 1884, and 1887 were struck only in Proof format (no circulation strikes) and are highly important. Proofs of 1902 and several later years have polished portraits. As double eagles are large and heavy, they were more prone to damage, and choice examples are proportionally rarer than for smaller denominations.

Saint-Gaudens $20 gold coins of the MCMVII (1907) High Relief variety are said by some to have been made in Proof finish. Today, the Numismatic Guaranty Corporation (NGC) will certify certain of these as Proofs, but the Professional Coin Grading Service (PCGS) will not. I have been unable to locate any contemporary or early reference to Proofs having been struck. Such seem to have been described in this manner beginning about 1960. Before buying a "Proof," do some investigation and develop an opinion.

Saint-Gaudens $20 coins of the regular dates 1908 and 1911 to 1915 were made with Sand Blast Proof finish, and those of 1909 and 1910 in the Satin Finish Proof style. All are rare, but the 1908 is less so.

Modern Proofs (1936 to Date)
Proofs of 1936 to 1942

In 1936 the Mint resumed making and selling sets of Proof coins to collectors, the first time this had been done since 1915 and 1916. However, in 1936 numismatists were preoccupied with the commemorative coin craze, and not much attention was paid to the new Proofs. The five varieties—the Lincoln cent, Buffalo nickel, Mercury dime, Washington quarter, and Liberty Walking half dollar—were offered singly as well as in sets. The Washington quarter attracted just 3,836 orders, thus defining the number of complete sets made that year. Lincoln cents were the most popular, and 5,569 were sold.

Proof coins of this era were made through 1942, in which year World War II

was raging, and the attention of the Mint turned to producing coins for general commerce. The luxury of making Proofs for collectors was not part of the program. By that time the demand for Proof coins had risen sharply. The number of 1942 Proof sets is once again defined by the lowest-mintage denomination, the quarter dollar, for which 21,123 were struck that year. The highest mintage was for the Lincoln cent, of which 32,600 were made. In this year, two types of Proof Jefferson nickels were made: the style with nickel content, of which 29,600 were struck; and the silver-content 1942-P, of which 27,600 were produced.

Proofs of the years 1936 to 1942 were put up in cellophane sleeves or envelopes with glued seams. After a few years, these seam lines would leave gray or black imprints on some coins. The copper and nickel coins often developed spots, possibly from moisture retained in the envelopes or from careless handling during the packaging process. As the years progressed, the "brilliant is best" philosophy, already entrenched in numismatics, took its toll on Proof coins of this era, and many were dipped and dipped again. The result is that today truly gem pieces can be hard to find, particularly among the Lincoln cents.

Proofs of 1950 to 1964

From 1950 to 1964, Proof sets were routinely produced each year, generally increasing in quantity until a market break in 1956 and 1957. In the early 1950s the Mint rationed the number that could be ordered by a single collector or dealer.

A 1936 Proof quarter dollar.

A 1952 Proof half dollar.

Later, when demand had lessened, they were generally available to all applicants.

In their time, such sets were commonly kept intact—in boxes up to 1955, a transitional year of packaging, and in flat packs afterward. Not much attention was paid to individual coins or varieties, with the dramatic exception of the 1960 sets that contained the Small Date cent, a sensation at the time.

Beginning in a significant way in the 1990s, and increasing due to communications in chat rooms and web sites on the Internet, and to the placement of appropriate markings on holders by certification services, these early sets have been reevaluated. Today, coins are often removed from the sets and graded separately. While most Proofs of this era have polished portraits (such as on Benjamin Franklin), some have frosty cameo motifs. Today, the latter are often seen in certified holders labeled as such. What began as *cameo* nomenclature evolved into *deep cameo*, then *ultra deep cameo*. Whether *super ultra exceptional deep cameo* is coming along in the future, only time will tell. As a general rule, deep cameo Proofs of the 1950 to 1970 era are in the minority, are very beautiful, and in many instances command strong prices. Most later Proofs, including current issues, are made with cameo contrast.

There has also been much activity in seeking very high numerical grades, a delight for the certification services. All of this has been stimulating to thousands of collectors and represents a new era of specialty in our hobby—perhaps necessary, as there are far too few of certain older coins to go around. Considering that only 380 Proof Barber half dollars of 1915 were minted, if all of a sudden thousands of collectors became interested in forming sets of Proof Barber halves from 1892 to 1915, most would be disappointed. Not so for Proofs of the 1950 to 1964 era, as there are many in the marketplace.

My advice is to buy whatever Proofs interest you from these years, and in whatever format you desire (such as cameo), but to be careful when paying high prices for ultra-high grades, as over a period of time the number of coins listed in population reports increases, never decreases. What might be scarce or rare today might be relatively common in some future year.

A 1981-S Proof Susan B. Anthony dollar.

Proofs From 1968 to Date

With the resumption of Proof coinage in 1968, production was shifted from the Philadelphia Mint to the San Francisco Mint, with each Proof coin now bearing an S mintmark. Packaging and quality were improved. As a general rule, Proofs from 1968 to date are of exceptional quality.

Such sets, or the coins individually taken from them, represent a great panorama of coinage of our own era and are delightful to own as part of a general collection.

Suggested Sets and Groups of Proof Coins

While Proofs can be collected randomly across a wide range of series, it is more interesting if you have a *collecting plan*. Most Proofs from the 19th century to date fit nicely into sets or date runs. Here are some that have been especially popular over the years, with my commentary:

- **Indian Head Cents (1859–1909)**— One of each date, including the copper-nickel issues of 1859 to 1864 and the bronze issues of 1864 to 1909. All are available except for the 1864 with L on ribbon, a major rarity in Proof format, with fewer than 20 known to exist. Try to acquire one of each Proof, plus, for completion, the 1864 L and the two mintmarks, 1908-S and 1909-S, in Mint State. Forming a high-quality set will be a great challenge, the numismatic equivalent of descending a nearly vertical ski slope!

- **Lincoln Cents (1909 to Date)**— Matte Proofs from 1909 to 1916 can be collected as a set, with the 1909 V.D.B. being a great rarity. Mirror Proofs of 1936 to 1942, 1950 to 1964, and 1968 to date are all readily available, and when arranged all together show a remarkably large number of coins.

- **Two-Cent Pieces (1864–1873)**— There are two varieties of 1864, the Small Motto (a great rarity, with fewer than 20 Proofs known) and the Large Motto. There are also two varieties of 1873, the Close 3 and Open 3. A typical Proof collection consists of one of each date, plus a Mint State 1864 Small Motto for completion of the set. Although both varieties of the 1873 are listed in the *Guide Book*, not many collectors have aspired to own more than one of this date. Truly choice, pristine coins are few and far between, so patience is required. A great challenge if you are up to it!

- **Nickel Three-Cent Pieces (1865–1889)**—This series offers much— including the opportunity for completion in Proof format. The challenge is medium to difficult, if you concentrate on high quality, the tricky area being the dates 1865 to 1876.

- **Silver Trimes (Three-Cent Pieces; 1851–1873)**—A run of Proofs is a possibility for the years from 1858 to 1873. Earlier dates and the solo mintmark in the series, 1851-O, can be Mint State, for completion of the set. If you insist on sharply struck coins the challenge will be great, for the years 1854 through 1857, for which you will probably seek Mint State coins, are incredibly rare if sharply defined. However, certification holders don't mention this and most of

your competition will be clueless—so if you do find a sharp one, the price will probably be reasonable.

- **Shield Nickels (1866–1883)**—All are available except for the 1867 With Rays rarity, which you can opt to acquire in Mint State. Ditto for the highly interesting 1883/2 overdate, which exists only in circulation-strike format.

- **Liberty Head Nickels (1883–1912)**—This is a popular and very beautiful set. To the Proofs you can add Mint State examples of the 1912-D and 1912-S.

- **Buffalo Nickels (1913–1916)**—A run of Matte Proofs of these years can be assembled, including two varieties of 1913, the Type I and Type II.

- **Jefferson Nickels (1938 to Date)**— An attractive and eminently affordable collection, including the dates 1938 to 1942, 1950 to 1964, and 1968 to the present.

- **Liberty Seated Half Dimes (1858–1873)**—Proofs of these years constitute an attractive set, one that can be assembled without great difficulty, although careful checking for quality is needed. Further, some Proofs of the 1860s have problems with striking sharpness and/or quality of the mirror fields.

- **Liberty Seated Dimes (1858–1891)**—These form a nice date run that is enjoyable to assemble. Quality varies, as always, and some Proofs have problems with striking. However, there are enough around that you can complete a choice set within about a year.

- **Barber Dimes (1892–1915)**—This set of 24 different dates is one of my favorites. All are available, but keep your eyes open in order to get high quality.

- **Mercury Dimes (1936–1942)**—This is a short, sweet, and attractive little set!

- **Roosevelt Dimes (1950 to Date)**—A collection of the Proof dates is easy enough to assemble, and when finished includes quite a few different dates.

- **Twenty-Cent Pieces (1875–1878)**—There are just four coins in this set. All are scarce, but are available with patience.

- **Liberty Seated Quarter Dollars (1858–1891)**—These are harder to find than are the related dimes, but still there are enough around that you can finish a set in a year or two. The result will be a very attractive display.

- **Barber Quarter Dollars (1892–1915)**—This set is more difficult to complete than a set of related dimes, but can be done within, say, a year.

- **Washington Quarter Dollars (1936 to Date)**—The regular years followed by the state-reverse varieties (beginning in 1999) make an interesting and impressive display.

- **Liberty Seated Half Dollars (1858–1891)**—One of my first collections when I was a teenager in the 1950s was a set of Proof Liberty Seated halves. Being optimistic, and living in an era in which hardly anyone collected early-date Proofs (as they were not listed in the *Guide Book*, the arbiter of collecting fashion), I determined to start my collection with the year 1839! Within a few years I had about half of the early years in Proof, and all from 1854 onward. Most of the coins before 1860 were what would be called Proof-63 or -64 today, and later ones were Proof-64 or finer. Today, building a set from 1858 to 1891 is a reasonable goal, and enjoyable to do.

- **Barber Half Dollars (1892–1915)**—This set will be a challenge, more so than the related dimes and quarters.

The years 1914 and 1915 are especially elusive if choice, for in the 1950s a Virginia collector hoarded these two dates, and while in his possession they were all cleaned with an abrasive (he said his secretary did it). A full set of Proof Barber halves is a joy to own.

- **Liberty Walking Half Dollars (1936–1942)**—This is a short but very attractive set, well worth building.

- **Franklin Half Dollars (1950–1964)**—A popular and affordable set, except that some Proofs with frosty or cameo surfaces can be both elusive and expensive if you opt for these.

- **Kennedy Half Dollars (1964 to Date)**—A nice date run of these can be assembled easily enough, includes quite a few different years, and represents one of the most popular designs of our time.

- **Liberty Seated Silver Dollars (1858–1873)**—This is a beautiful series, but one that is difficult to assemble in truly choice quality, and is fairly expensive. The year 1858 is the earliest date seen with some frequency, with an estimated 210 struck. Proofs are available of earlier dates as well, back to 1840, with grades of Proof-63 or finer being reasonable goals. The rarest Proof date is 1853, of which just 12 are said to have been made, all restrikes.

- **Morgan Silver Dollars (1878–1921)**—This is a very challenging set, as most pieces are not of high quality. In addition, the 1878 with seven tail feathers and third reverse (slanting top arrow feather) is very rare, and mirror Proofs of 1921 are rarer yet, with probably fewer than two dozen existing of the latter. The 1895, while not rare as a Proof (880 were made), is famous as a rare date, for no related circulation strikes were made.

- **Later Dollars**—Proof Eisenhower dollars (1971–1978) and the later

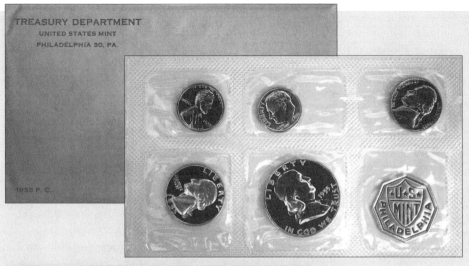

Images are of a 1955 "flat pack" Proof set, inner and outer packaging; 1999 outer packaging for a regular Proof set; and 2005 inner packaging for a special Proof set with certain denominations struck in silver.

Anthony and Sacagawea dollars are interesting and very affordable.

- **Trade Dollars (1873–1883)**—If you select Proofs with excellent eye appeal you will have a very beautiful collection. The hardest dates to find choice are the earlier ones. Proofs of 1884 and 1885 exist as well, to the extent of just 10 and 5 pieces, respectively, and for all practical purposes are unobtainable.

- **Year Sets of Proofs**—Many collectors have picked one or several early years and have endeavored to assemble Proof sets of the same date, with the various denominations. Most often these are sets with copper, nickel, and silver coins, but occasionally gold coins are sought as well. The most extensive early Proof set is 1873, a full set of which includes the Indian Head cent, two-cent piece, nickel three-cent piece, trime, Shield nickel, half dime, dime without arrows at the date, dime with arrows at the date, quarter dollar without arrows, quarter dollar with arrows, half dollar without arrows, half dollar with arrows, Liberty Seated silver dollar, trade dollar, and gold $1, $2.50, $3, $5, $10, and $20 pieces. Proofs from 1936 to date are more often collected as sets, and those from 1950 onward are nearly always kept in this form.

- **Selected bibliography:**

Breen, Walter. 1953. "Proof Coins Struck by the United States Mint." Monograph. *Coin Collectors Journal*, New York, NY.

Breen, Walter. 1977. *Walter Breen's Encyclopedia of United States and Colonial Proof Coins.* New York, NY.

Lange, David W. 2005. *A Guide Book of United States Proof Sets 1936–2004.* Atlanta, GA.

Tomaska, Rick Jerry. 1991. *Cameo and Brilliant Proof Coinage of the 1950 to 1970 Era.* Encinitas, CA.

CHAPTER TWENTY-ONE

COLLECTING COLONIAL AND EARLY AMERICAN COINS

Collect, if possible, coins in the best condition; you then buy but once, and when you want to sell, you have something worth selling.... A library goes hand in hand with the collection of coins. It is better to collect a few series and know your subject than to attempt to collect everything and think you know it all but really know nothing. Every collector should have a Pine Tree shilling, as that is the first question your guests ask if you have.

—Howland Wood, November 1909

Numismatic Aspects of Colonial Coins
Getting Started

Collecting colonial coins is a captivating pursuit, and virtually everyone who takes it up is fascinated by it. Perhaps more than for any other numismatic specialty, a recipe for successful collecting involves two parts reading and investigating to one part buying. Of course, this is very enjoyable to do—and is one of the reasons that the field has so many devotees.

For starters, after you read this chapter, spend an hour with the front section of *A Guide Book of United States Coins*, starting with "Money of the Early Americans." Also review the earlier years described in chapter 10 of the present book. Do this, and when you are finished you will have a basic, casual knowledge of what colonial and early American coins are all about.

In the strictest sense, *colonials* are coins produced before the Confederation and the signing of the Declaration of Independence. In popular practice, colonial coins include coins of the 1780s struck for the states, and even Washington tokens. Regarding *states*, officially the first state was Delaware, which ratified the United States Constitution on December 7, 1787. Accordingly, in the strictest sense, the "state coinages" of Vermont, Connecticut, New Jersey, and Massachusetts, which all commenced before that time, were produced by "states-in-waiting." Vermont did not achieve statehood until 1791. If anything, such nomenclature reflects that definitions for early American issues are often casual.

If your interest in early American coins has been piqued, it's natural to want to get your feet wet right away by buying some colonials. I suggest you do this. However, at the outset, limit yourself to well-struck coins in higher grades (VF or better), without flaws and with good eye appeal. A dealer-specialist in colonials, or at least a professional with a good working knowledge of the series, should be your source—not the Internet and not offerings from sellers who are not knowledgeable. As to certification, it can be a mixed bag. The services attempt to assign a single grading number to each coin, but such numbers give no clues to the many other variables that affect a colonial coin's value.

This 1788 Vermont copper coin, Mailed Bust Right, inscriptions punctuated by stars (die variety Ryder-27), would be a puzzlement to the uninitiated buyer, if he or she were told that this is an exceptionally fine example. Actually it is, but some understanding is necessary. The variety is typically found on a rough, imperfect planchet, as here. Accordingly, the specialist will accept this feature. The sharpness of details at the center of the coin is unusual. All told, this coin deserves a place in a high-level advanced collection.

The 1773 Virginia halfpenny is one of relatively few colonial coins that is readily available in Mint State, due to a hoard of thousands of pieces that was distributed into numismatic circles beginning in the 19th century. Nearly all are well struck and on problem-free planchets—ideal "starter" coins for a collection. (Eliasberg Collection)

Perhaps an easy choice for you would be to buy a 1773 Virginia copper halfpenny in AU or Mint State. There are a lot of these around, and they are usually well struck. If you find one with good eye appeal, it can be bought to advantage—and will not need to be replaced or upgraded later. Once you buy, take an hour to read all about how it was made and distributed, using the Crosby and Breen texts described below. If you *really* want to have a Zen or bonding experience with your newly acquired coin, borrow a copy of Eric P. Newman's 1956 study, *Coinage for Colonial Virginia*, from the ANA Library in Colorado Springs, or track one down from a seller of out-of-print numismatic books.

I do not mean to overemphasize focusing on the histories and backgrounds of the coins you buy. I realize that many readers may simply acquire a piece and then put it into a drawer or safe deposit box. However, a coin can speak to you and tell you a lot if you let it do so. In my All About Coins class at the ANA Summer Seminars a few years ago, I always suggested to my students that they should always carefully examine and appreciate coins themselves, instead of the printed listings about their rarities and values.

There are two books you will need to buy. One is a reprint of Sylvester S. Crosby's 1875 masterwork, *Early Coins of America*. This volume is still the standard source today for historical information! The content of Crosby ranges from dull

(as in the recitation of laws and proclamations) to endlessly fascinating and evocative of mystery (as in the section on Vermont coppers and the curious happenings at Machin's Mills).

The second essential book is *Walter Breen's Complete Encyclopedia of U.S. and Colonial Coins*, published in 1988, for much in-depth commentary about varieties.

If you become serious about this specialty, sign up for membership in the Colonial Coin Collectors Club (C4). Through the American Numismatic Society (New York City), subscribe to the *Colonial Newsletter.*

With the preceding, you will have enough to keep you busy for a month or two in reading and contemplation. If you absorb even half of what you scan, you will be as knowledgeable as most rare-coin dealers are—and by that time, the *colonial* coin bug will have bitten you!

Numismatic Lore and Tradition

The first pieces struck in what is now the United States were those of the Massachusetts Bay Colony, beginning in 1652, and consisting of various denominations in sequence, threepence to shilling (plus a 1662 twopence), and now known as the New England (NE), Willow Tree, Oak Tree, and Pine Tree varieties. These are incredibly historical and interesting, and many of them can be found in the marketplace. It has often been said that the 1652 Pine Tree shilling is the signature or trademark coin of American numismatics—the most storied, the most famous. Ken Bressett has often remarked that these coins represent the first "declaration of independence" for our fledgling nation.

Coins related to the Sommer Islands (Bermuda) are often collected by American specialists, but that location, long ago and today, has nothing to do with the United States except as a modern vacation destination. However, the wild hogs on the obverse and the sailing ships on the reverse of the Sommer Islands denominations are interesting to view—if, indeed, you can discern them, for most remaining pieces are heavily oxidized. However, tradition being what it is, more than just a few other extraneous issues are eagerly sought by American numismatists, including the Voce Populi coppers of 1760 and the Wood's Hibernia coinage of 1722 to 1724. The challenge may be sorting out which coins are truly related to the areas that now comprise the United States, and which pieces are numismatic interlopers that don't belong (but which we might want to let stay anyway).

Time was when collectors aspired to own colonials that were described in Wayte Raymond's *Standard Catalogue of United States Coins*, published in 18 editions from 1934 to 1958. Now, that mantle is upon the *Guide Book of United States Coins*, and if a variety is listed there, it is highly desired. It might be said that the *Guide Book* is the arbiter of fashion throughout the American series, sort of a numismatic equivalent of the *Guide Michelin*. Nowhere is its blessing more evident than listings for early American pieces. There is no logical reason that Voce Populi coppers, made in Ireland in 1760 and used in the British Isles (with no connection at all to the United States), should be desired as part of a collection of American coins; they are among the interlopers I just mentioned. Ditto for the 1722 to 1724 Wood's Hibernia coinage made for Ireland. Significantly, the Lorin G. Parmelee Collection sold in 1890, which included the most impressive holding of American colonials to cross the auction block up to that time, had no Voce Populi or Hibernia coins in it, nor were they delineated by Crosby. If they were to be delisted—poof!—from the *Guide Book*, few Americans would want them. My purpose here is not to dissuade you from collecting these series, but simply to illustrate that listings are sometimes arbitrary or illogical, or both.

More relevant and logical for American numismatists to collect in depth are the many issues produced in England for circulation in America, including silver coins for Maryland—the Rosa Americana issues of 1722 to 1724 (by William Wood, the

same fellow who made the Hibernia coins), and the 1773 Virginia halfpenny, among others.

Coins of the 1780s and Later

Many collectors specialize in the large copper cent–sized coins of the 1780s issued by the various states. These include several dozen varieties of Vermont pieces produced from 1785 to 1788, classified by Ryder numbers as delineated in Henry C. Miller and Hillyer C. Ryder, *The State Coinages of New England*, 1920. Thus, a particular die combination will be designated as Ryder-9. To a specialist, this means "1786 Vermont copper of the Baby Head variety." In chapter 4 I discuss Vermont coppers at some length. The same Miller-Ryder reference is useful for attributing 1785 to 1788 Connecticut coppers (by Miller numbers), of which about 350 different die combinations are known. The copper half cents and cents of 1787 and 1788, struck in Massachusetts, are also attributed by Miller numbers in that book.

New Jersey copper coins, also made in large numbers and existing today in many fascinating varieties, can be attributed to Maris numbers (per Dr. Edward A. Maris, *A Historic Sketch of Coins of New Jersey*, 1881; later reprinted and updated). Fugio coppers, dated 1787 and produced under contract granted by the U.S. government, are described by numbers assigned by Eric P. Newman and later modified by Alan Kessler, the latter under the title of *The Fugio Cents*. Today, these are generally classified under "N" or "NK" designations.

While collecting *counterfeit* coins is anathema to those specializing in the federal series, for coins of the colonial era counterfeits are widely sought, and in many instances they have incredible market values ranging into the thousands of dollars for EF and AU coins. These include pieces listed in the *Guide Book* under the title of "Imitation British Halfpence." Great rarities that have no official status include several coins in the Vermont series (such as the famous 1785 IMMUNE COLUMBIA, the 1787 BRI-

TANNIA, and the 1788 with backward C in AUCTORI, among others), the Nova Constellatio copper dated 1786, many different Connecticut issues (particularly among varieties dated 1788), and more.

To the various issues mentioned can be added the tokens and medals relating to George Washington—not coins in the sense of being used in commerce, but mostly tokens and remembrances, although some of them may have circulated to a small extent. Several pages in the *Guide Book* and Breen texts are devoted to them, as is a dandy 1999 book by Russell Rulau and George Fuld, with contributions from me and others, titled *Medallic Portraits of Washington*—the same title used by W.S. Baker for his important study published in 1885. Washington pieces go far beyond the early American era, and the Rulau-Fuld book will take you well down to the 20th century. However, for "colonial" purposes, such as listings in the early section of the *Guide Book*, the cutoff date is for pieces dated 1795.

Arranging the Early American Series

Coins collected as part of the early American series are wonderfully diverse—so much so that they defy easy classification. Some were made in large quantities and used as money—the 1652-dated Massachusetts Pine Tree shillings and related pieces are examples. Others were produced as medals or souvenirs—the 1776 Pitt token or medalet being one. Likely, in the late 1600s *everyone* in New England was familiar with the Pine Tree coins because they were used everywhere. However, in the 1770s, probably not one citizen in ten thousand ever saw a 1776 Pitt medalet.

Rather than mix these and other issues together in the numismatic equivalent of pick-up sticks, on the following pages I have endeavored to arrange them into categories, giving emphasis to series that were widely used as money in early America. Medalets and tokens, including those made for the numismatic trade but never circulated, are listed apart from basic monetary

issues. At least for me, this helps to understand and appreciate them.

Colonial and Early American Coin Series
Important Coinages of the Colonies

These several series are the heart of early American coinage—pieces struck in large quantities in or for America and intended to provide coins for extensive distribution throughout one of the original 13 colonies or an even larger area.

Massachusetts Silver Coinage (1652–1682)

Massachusetts silver coins, made at a mint set up in Boston under the sponsorship of the General Court of the colony, were ubiquitous in circulation in the Northeast. Although they were struck from 1652 to 1682, most bear the date of their authorization, 1652. *These were the first coins struck in what is now the United States.*

This series includes the New England (NE) coinage, not dated, but struck in 1652. These are simple in nature and consist on one side of the stamp NE, and on the other, the denomination expressed in British pence, as III, IV, and XII, the last equaling 12 pence or a shilling. Today the NE shillings are collectible, but the threepence is unique and the sixpence coins are hardly ever seen.

The simple nature of these coins invited counterfeiting and clipping, the last describing the removal of silver from the edge to make the coins smaller (which, if done on a large scale, yielded a profit to the perpetrators). The solution was to add designs and lettering, so as to fill the faces of the coin. The so-called Willow Tree coins depict an amorphous bush or tree and are lettered around the borders. Dated 1652, these include the threepence (extremely rare), sixpence (very rare), and shilling (very rare), struck from 1653 to 1660. They were crudely struck, yielding doubled impressions in some areas and indistinct features in others. Next came the Oak Tree coinage dated 1652, but struck from 1660 to 1667. These include the threepence, sixpence, and shilling. In addition, a 1662-dated silver twopence was made, the date reflecting the first use of the denomination. Apparently not found to be useful, the twopence was discontinued.

The best-known Massachusetts coins are those of the Pine Tree style: threepence, sixpence, and shilling, made from 1667 to 1682. The shillings come in two formats: large and thin, and small and thick.

Today, the Oak Tree and Pine Tree types are collectible, but are scarce, while the earlier NE and Willow Tree coins range from very rare to unique. As these coins disappeared from circulation, they became the stuff of lore and legend, including a charming tale by Nathaniel Hawthorne.

Maryland Coinage (1659)

Cecil Calvert, the Second Lord Baltimore, desired to set up a mint in the Maryland

Three Massachusetts classics. At the top is a 1652-dated Oak Tree shilling, die variety Noe-5. Below is a 1652-dated large planchet Pine Tree shilling, Noe-10. The lowest coin is a 1652-dated small planchet Pine Tree shilling, Noe-22. (Sundman Collection)

colony, but apparently it was not accomplished. We do know that the Tower Mint in London struck coins to his order, bearing Calvert's portrait on the obverse and various motifs—most notably the arms of Maryland—on the reverse. Denominations include the rare penny or denarium in copper, as well as silver denominations of fourpence (groat), sixpence, and shilling. Made in large quantities, they were quite effective in their time, but seem to have faded away by the advent of the next century.

Maryland coins range from scarce to rare today. Conditions are usually rather low, VG through VF, often with some planchet defects, traces of repair, or other problems that are sometimes necessary to overlook (but nonetheless be aware of). Interestingly, in the past decade a number of choice EF coins have come to light in England. Numismatics is always full of surprises!

Rosa Americana Coinage (1722–1724)

William Wood, an entrepreneur with connections through King George's mistress, the Duchess of Kendal, obtained a patent or franchise from that monarch to strike coins for distribution in the colonies of America. The reverse of most shows a rose and the inscription ROSA AMERICANA, for "American rose," and the inscription UTILE DULCI, "the useful with the sweet."

Made in England in denominations of the halfpenny, penny, and twopence, in a brassy composition (75% copper, 24.7% zinc, and 0.3% silver), they proved difficult to strike up properly. Many of these coins were sent to America, and additional examples seem to have circulated within the British Isles.

A 1722 Rosa Americana halfpenny struck in England by entrepreneur William Wood, and intended for circulation in America.

Rosa Americana pieces are readily collectible today, with the main types being affordable and also available in grades from VF to AU. Interspersed are certain rarities. The typical Rosa Americana coin tends to be yellow-brown in appearance and to have a somewhat rough or "bubbly" surface, due to the nature of the metal when heated during the minting process.

Virginia Coinage (1773–1774)

In 1773, copper halfpennies were struck in England for circulation in the colony of Virginia. Production was delayed, and delivery did not occur until the fires of the Revolution were burning, by which time King George III, depicted on the obverse, was increasingly detested. Nevertheless, these pieces seem to have circulated effectively and widely. Many different die varieties are known. Silver pieces dated 1774, denominated as shillings, seem to have been made as patterns.

Thanks to a hoard of thousands of pieces that came to light in the early 19th century, 1773 Virginia halfpennies are quite available today in Mint State, typically with much of the original orange color faded or mottled to brown. Circulated examples are in the minority. The silver shillings are exceedingly rare and come to market only when major collections are auctioned.

Nova Constellatio Coppers (1783–1786)

Copper coins of halfpenny size (later the size of the American large cent) were made in England and imported in large quantities to the United States as a speculative venture. The "Nova Constellatio" inscription, around an all-seeing eye with a sunburst in stars, refers to the "new constellation" or gathering of 13 colonies to form the United States. The reverse has US and JUSTITIA ET LIBERTAS, or "justice and liberty." These coins were made with dates 1783 and 1785 and imitate the designs used for the American pattern coinage of 1783 (see "Coinages for the American Congress," below).

A 1783 Nova Constellatio copper made in England and imported into the United States for circulation here (die variety 1-A, per the listing in S.S. Crosby, The Early Coins of America, 1875). The obverse design with an all-seeing eye surrounded by rays, and with stars at the border, inspired the reverse of certain Vermont copper coins of 1785 and 1786.

Counterfeits dated 1786 were made in small numbers, probably in the United States, and are extremely rare today.

Today the Nova Constellatio coppers are seen with some frequency. Grades tend to be on the higher side, from VF to EF, occasionally AU, but seldom finer. These can be collected by major type or by die variety, the latter described by Crosby (1875).

Coinages for the American Congress

The following series were made on behalf of the American Congress and constitute a special category—official government coins produced before the federal mint at Philadelphia was a reality (1792).

Continental Currency Dollars (1776)

In 1776, dollars were struck in pewter; on the obverse was a sundial design with the notation FUGIO (meaning "I fly," referring to the rapid passage of time) and the inscriptions MIND YOUR BUSINESS and CONTINENTAL CURRENCY. The reverse displays linked circles, each with the abbreviation of the name of a colony. At the center is AMERICAN CONGRESS and WE ARE ONE. These seem to have been intended to be a substitute for paper dollars. The dies are believed to have been cut by Elisha Gallaudet, whose E.G. initials are seen on some of the coins. Some strikings were made in brass and silver as well and are very rare.

Continental Currency pewter dollars are widely sought by numismatists today. While most show evidence of extensive circulation, some others are AU or even Mint State. Years later, in 1787, the same motif was adopted for use on the 1787 copper Fugio cents.

Nova Constellatio Patterns (1783)

Coins denominated in "units" of 5 to 1,000 were struck as patterns in 1783, as proposals for a federal coinage that never materialized. The designs were created by Benjamin Dudley at the request of Gouverneur Morris—proposals for a decimal-based coinage system intended to be struck at the National Mint. Values include the copper 5 mills, the 100 silver piece, the 500 silver "quint," and 1,000 silver "mark." Several varieties exist, most of which are unique. The National Mint idea lapsed, and years later, on April 2, 1792, the unrelated Mint Act provided for the establishment of the Philadelphia Mint.

A nearly complete set of these patterns appeared in the Garrett Collection sale, 1979, and went into the collection of the late John J. Ford, Jr.

One of several dozen known varieties of the 1787 Fugio copper cent (enlarged), a coin made under contract for the federal government. This coin (die variety Newman 8-X) displays a large die crack on the obverse. FUGIO translates to "I fly," and in combination with the sundial motif refers to the rapid passing of time. Related designs were used on certain varieties of 1776 Continental paper money and the pewter dollars.

Fugio Cents (1787)

On April 21, 1787, the United States Treasury accepted the proposal of James Jarvis to coin 300 tons of copper into cents. The design was to be somewhat similar to those used on the 1776 Continental Currency dollars. The resultant coins had a sundial and FUGIO on the obverse, plus the inscription MIND YOUR BUSINESS. The reverse illustrated interlocked rings, without inscriptions, enclosing UNITED STATES and WE ARE ONE.

Many different die combinations were made during the production of Fugio cents, and complications arose with the contract. The situation is explored at length in *The Colonial Newsletter* and, to a lesser extent, by Breen (1988). Today, several varieties are readily available in Mint State from the Bank of New York hoard of several thousand pieces. Striking is often indistinct in areas.

A 1776 Continental Currency dollar in pewter. The inscriptions were used on certain paper money of the era and were later adapted for the 1787 Fugio copper cents. (Newman die variety 1-C)

American Copper Coins of 1785 to 1788

Copper coinages of the states (or states-to-be) furnish a wonderful playground for numismatic study and acquisition. As such, these have been the focus of attention for several generations of collectors. The combination of interesting die varieties plus fascinating historical and numismatic information can yield a very pleasurable experience.

In particular, some of the varieties of Vermont, Connecticut, and New York (including Machin's Mills issues) are related, as certain of the same diesinkers, including James Atlee, made dies for each; in some instances at Machin's Mills, dies for one state were inadvertently (apparently) combined with those of another.

As a class, state copper coins are scarce. However, as they are off the main path for most numismatists, those who seek them can acquire specimens for very reasonable prices, rare varieties excepted.

Copper Coinage of Vermont (1785–1788)

The series of Vermont coins, the earliest of the state copper coinages, comprises 39 known die varieties. Among these are more distinctive types (see chapter 4) than elsewhere in the state series. The Vermont Legislature granted a contract for coinage to Reuben Harmon, Jr., who set up a mint in a small wooden building in Pawlet. Under circumstances that must have been difficult, coins were struck from 1785 to 1787. Afterward, Harmon became a partner in the Machin's Mills enterprise near Newburgh, New York, and later Vermont coins were struck there, these being official issues (in contrast to the counterfeit coppers that were the main products of that enterprise). Some Vermont-related dies were mixed with dies for counterfeits, creating strange combinations, such as one with the reverse inscribed BRITANNIA.

Vermont coppers are eagerly pursued by numismatists today. A basic set of design types can be gathered without difficulty, although care is urged, as most pieces are either weakly struck or on defective planchets, or both. Sometimes compromises must be made. As to collecting by die varieties, attributed to Ryder numbers, about 20 to 25 different would constitute a fine showing, and 30 or more different would be a great feat.

Copper Coinage of Connecticut (1785–1788)

The state of Connecticut granted a coinage franchise in 1785 to four entrepreneurs—Samuel Bishop, Joseph Hopkins, James Hillhouse, and John Goodrich. A mint was established near New Haven, and coinage commenced. Certain later issues were made elsewhere, most notably the unofficial (counterfeit) pieces struck at Machin's Mills.

Of all the state copper coinages, that of Connecticut is by far the most extensive in terms of die varieties. There is no distinction in desirability between officially authorized issues struck in Connecticut and the numerous unofficial pieces made at Machin's Mills. If anything, the latter are generally more valuable.

From 1785 to 1788 the Connecticut coppers evolved from early issues, generally on heavier planchets and with the designs cut deeply into the dies, to those of 1788, usually lightweight and with shallow features. A fine description of the various main types and their market values can be found in the *Guide Book*.

Copper Coinage of New Jersey (1786–1788)

On July 1, 1786, the legislature of New Jersey granted a franchise to Thomas Goadsby, Albion Cox, and Walter Mould to coin three million coppers (today called *cents* by numismatists), to be completed by June 1788. The state was to receive one-tenth of the coinage as compensation. The coppers were to pass in circulation at the rate of 15 coins to a shilling (a shilling being 12 pence). Problems and differences arose among the franchise holders, who divided the responsibility, and the coins were produced in several different locations.

About 100 different die combinations are known today, with most dated 1787. Most depict a horse's head on the obverse, facing right, with a plow below. A few coins of 1788 have the horse facing to the left. Around the border is NOVA CAESAREA, Latin for New Jersey. The date is near the bottom edge, except for several varieties of 1786 in which it appears in the field at the lower right. The reverse displays a large shield and the inscription E PLURIBUS UNUM, a motto later used on federal coinage. Generally, the coins of 1786 are more sharply struck than are

those of 1787, and 1788 coppers often are weak in areas.

New Jersey copper coins have formed a stimulating specialty for many collectors over a long period of time. The *Guide Book* describes basic types as well as popular varieties. For others, specialists consult the study of series written by Dr. Edward Maris in the 19th century.

Copper Coinage of Massachusetts (1787–1788)

On October 17, 1786, the General Court of Massachusetts passed legislation providing for the establishment of a mint to strike copper, silver, and gold coins, depicting a

A 1786 Vermont copper (die variety Ryder-6) struck in Pawlet, Vermont, in a mint supervised by Reuben Harmon, Jr. The sun-over-mountains or "landscape" type was intended to be representative of Vermont. However, the motif was unfamiliar to users in commerce, and soon the design was altered to feature the portrait of King George II of England, and later that of George III, the latter being especially detested by Americans. The reverse seems to have been inspired by the 1783 Nova Constellatio coppers of 1783.

A 1787 Connecticut copper (die variety Miller 6.1-M), known as the Laughing Head by collectors today. The prominent dentils, or toothlike projections, are similar to those used on certain New Jersey coppers. A study of letter styles indicates that in some instances the same engraver cut dies for Vermont, Connecticut, New Jersey, and other copper issues of the 1880s.

A 1787 New Jersey copper (die variety Maris 43-d, one of the more plentiful die combinations). NOVA CAESAREA is the state name, Latinized. The horse's head is the emblem of the state. On the reverse the E PLURIBUS UNUM motto represents its earliest appearance on an American coin. Such pieces were struck from 1786 to 1788.

The state of Massachusetts operated its own mint to strike copper coins dated 1787 and 1788, the first in the United States to bear the inscriptions HALF CENT and CENT. Dies for the 1787 coinage were cut by Joseph Callender and those for 1788 by Callender and by Jacob Perkins. The mint was closed in 1789 when it was realized that each coin cost about twice face value to produce.

standing Indian (an emblem of the state) in combination with a spread eagle on the reverse. The mint commenced operations in 1787 under the direction of Joshua Witherle. Copper coins were made, each boldly lettered HALF CENT or CENT, the first use of these denominations on American coinage. Most of the dies were cut by Joseph Callender, with a few by Jacob Perkins.

Copper half cents and cents were made with the dates of 1787 and 1788. The die quality and striking procedures were of a high order of excellence, creating the sharpest and finest of the state copper coinages. There was trouble in paradise, however, and when an audit revealed that each coin cost twice face value to produce, the mint was closed.

Today, Massachusetts coppers can be collected easily as to date and type. Die varieties, attributed to Miller numbers, form an interesting pursuit as well.

The following coinages are in many instances closely related, and all have connections to Machin's Mills. Facts are scarce, and these areas furnish an opportunity for further research.

Copper Coinage of New York (1786–1787)

Of all the state coins, those associated with New York (Latinized as NOVA EBORAC and variations, on certain of the coins) are the most enigmatic. Although individuals had petitioned the New York Legislature in 1787 for the franchise to coin coppers, no record has been found of such permission's having been granted. Among those interested were John Bailey, Thomas Machin, and Ephraim Brasher (the last famous today for his 1787 Brasher gold doubloon).

Some pieces identified with New York include the 1786 copper with NON VI VIRTUTE VICI on the obverse and NEO-EBORACENSIS on the reverse, another with a standing Indian, and various die combinations (attributed to Machin's Mills) that likely have no official status. The most extensive production was

of the NOVA EBORAC coppers, dated 1787, known today in several die combinations, attributed to Bailey and Brasher. Certain coppers depicting the State Arms of New York and the motto EXCELSIOR are likewise attributed to these coiners.

Except for the 1787 NOVA EBORAC coppers, pieces related to New York state range from rare to extremely rare. Only a few collections over the years have had a significant number of different varieties. When seen, New York pieces tend to be in grades from Fine to EF.

In addition to contemporary issues, as delineated here, certain struck copies made by James A. Bolen, numismatist and die cutter of Springfield, Massachusetts, are collected in their own right, but are valued far less than originals. Bolen copies, as they are called, were made from expertly crafted dies, close to the originals but differing in tiny details. Bolen also made copies of certain other early issues, including Higley coppers of the 1737 to 1739 era.

Immunis, Confederatio, and Other Coppers (1785–1787)

This series of copper coins consists of about 20 die combinations, some probably produced at Machin's Mills and others at different locations. They are called "experimental or pattern pieces" in the *Guide Book*, but as most known specimens show wear, often extensive, my view is that most were made as circulating issues, but in small quantities. Those with the CONFEDERATIO legend refer to the Confederation, or the group of would-be states, in the early era of the United States government.

Pieces depicting a seated goddess holding a pole with liberty cap, and with the inscription IMMUNE COLUMBIA or IMMUNIS COLUMBIA, were probably mostly struck at Machin's Mills, but evidence is lacking concerning their origin. The obverse wording refers to Columbia (America) as being immune to the problems of the rest of the world.

Of these issues, only a few are collectible, and they are expensive. One of these is the IMMUNE COLUMBIA muling with a

Vermont die, which has the unique distinction of being listed in two separate places in the *Guide Book* (pp. 53 and 67 in the 2006 edition). Most range from extremely rare to impossible to find.

Machin's Mills Counterfeits of British Coppers (1787–1789)

In the annals of American numismatics, the story of Machin's Mills is one of the most curious and mysterious.[68] The Machin's Mills operation was envisioned as a "manufactory of hardware," actually a private mint, and was set up by Captain Thomas Machin, an engineer and prominent figure in the American Revolution, with Samuel Atlee (a brewer of porter), James F. Atlee (a diesinker associated with several state coinages), David Brooks, James Grier, and James Giles (an attorney at law), all of New York City. The agreement, signed on April 18, 1787, provided for a capital of £300, a modest amount, perhaps explained by the partnership's intent to *make* money in the most literal sense. On June 7, four more partners were admitted—Reuben Harmon (holder of the Vermont coinage contract), William Coley (a Vermont jeweler who may have cut some dies for Harmon), Elias Jackson (of Connecticut), and Daniel Van Voorhis (New York City goldsmith and jeweler).

A mint was set up at the outlet of Orange Pond, near Newburgh, New York, and coinage soon commenced. So far as is known, the only official (non-counterfeit) pieces made there were issues of Vermont. The main business of the enterprise seems to have been the making of just about any type of copper coin that would pass in circulation, imitating designs of English halfpence as well as various state coinages; and, along the way, the creation of some designs of their own. The activities of the mint were carried on in secret and make interesting reading in the Crosby text (1875).

The counterfeit British coppers of Machin's Mills are delineated in the *Guide Book* and are collected as a specialty by some numismatists. The key aspect of such coins is that they are *contemporaneous*—struck in the era in which such pieces were used. (In contrast, modern copies or counterfeits have little or no value.)

Early American Coins and Tokens

This category includes coins and tokens made in America, in small numbers or for limited distribution, or for special purposes. Included are some of the most interesting and valuable pieces in the American series, among which are the famous Brasher gold doubloons.

1714–1715: Gloucester (Virginia) Tokens.

These small brass tokens seem to have been used as a check, or perhaps a pattern, denominated XII (one shilling) by Richard Dawson, of Gloucester County, Virginia.

Gloucester tokens are exceedingly rare; only two of 1714 and a possible (under study) 1715 exist. All are in low grades.

1737–1739: Higley or Granby Copper Coinage.

Dr. Samuel Higley and his brother John owned a copper mine near Granby, Connecticut. For amusement or profit they struck many copper coins the size of a halfpenny, but denominated as THREE PENCE. This was viewed as absurd by local merchants, after which the inscriptions were changed to I AM GOOD

Brothers Samuel and John Higley used copper from a local mine, near Granby, Connecticut, to strike their own copper threepence pieces in 1737 and 1739. Numismatic legend has it that local merchants scoffed at the assigned face value, as the coins were about the size and weight of a British halfpenny. On later varieties, as here, the inscription was given, VALUE ME AS YOU PLEASE. All Higley coppers are exceedingly rare today, and most are in very low grades. (Pevehouse and Davis Collections)

COPPER and VALUE ME AS YOU PLEASE. Most pieces are well worn, indicating they must have been popular in commerce at the time, probably trading at the value of a halfpenny.

Higley or Granby coppers were made in several varieties; all range from rare to extremely rare, and are numismatic classics today.

1776: Massachusetts Pattern Coppers.
Three varieties of 1776-dated copper coins are known, each unique and each bearing inscriptions relating to Massachusetts. They were possibly made as patterns for a proposed coinage, or there may be another explanation.

Each is essentially non-collectible.

1776: New Hampshire Pattern Coppers.
The New Hampshire legislature granted William Moulton the right to strike copper coins for the state. Apparently, the project did not advance beyond the striking or casting of a few pieces, possibly as patterns or to acquaint legislators with the pieces.

Little is known about these coins today, and examples are exceedingly rare.

1783: Chalmers Silver Coinage.
Three-pence, sixpence, and shilling coins were struck in several die varieties by John Chalmers, a Maryland silversmith. The most often seen varieties, the silver shillings, show two birds disputing claim to a worm.

Rare, but collectible for the major types. Most are in grades of VF and EF.

Silver shilling dated 1783 (enlarged), struck in Annapolis by silversmith John Chalmers. Many numismatic theories have been advanced as to the significance of the two birds competing for a snake (or worm), with another snake (or worm) in the distance beyond a fence or hedgerow.

(1785): Bar Coppers.
Little is known about these tokens, which are said to have appeared in circulation in New York in 1785. They "may have been made in England," the *Guide Book* suggests. On the other hand, perhaps they were made in America.

Most are in higher grades, EF and AU being typical.

1787: Brasher Gold Doubloons.
These 1787-dated coins, the value of a Spanish doubloon ($16), were struck by Ephraim Brasher, a New York silversmith and goldsmith who at one time was a neighbor of George Washington. A 1747-dated Spanish-style doubloon was also made, probably in 1786 or 1787.

Only about a half dozen exist of the standard 1787 version, the finest of which is the Garrett Collection coin, in Mint State. Among early American coins this is the trophy rarity extraordinaire.

"1789": Mott Tokens.
Bearing the date 1789, this token depicts a version of the American eagle first used by John Reich on the $5 gold coins of 1807. Accordingly, it is presumed that the Mott tokens were issued in the 19th century, with the 1789 date possibly being an anniversary or founding date of this New York City firm of jewelers and clockmakers.

Usually very crudely struck on irregular planchets, thick or thin. Typical grades are VE and EF.

(1790): Albany First Presbyterian Church Pennies.
These issues, the size of a halfpenny or later copper cent, were sold to communicants of the church, who then put them in offering plates.

These church tokens are popular from their *Guide Book* listings. Apart from use by churchgoers in Albany, they had no utility as money.

1790: Standish Barry Threepence.
Standish Barry, a Baltimore silversmith and well-known figure in local politics, struck his own silver threepence bearing the date of "July 4, 90." They seem to have been used as coins, for most show extensive wear.

These pieces are rare and highly desired today.

1818: New Spain (Texas) Jola or Half-Real Coins.
Copper tokens of this denomination were made in 1818 under authority of the military governor of San Antonio; 8,000 were struck by José Antonio de la Garza, whose JAG initials are seen on the coins.

Made in large- and small-planchet varieties, these are relatively new listings for the *Guide Book*, and thus their numismatic tradition is still in the making, in the sense of popular appeal.

European Tokens Relating to America

This category includes tokens and small medals made in Europe, primarily in England, with inscriptions relating to America. If anything, the selection is diverse. British Conder tokens are listed separately in the next section.

1685 (Circa): New Yorke in America Tokens.
These undated tokens, struck in pewter and brass, were probably made in Europe, with inscriptions relating to New York.

They are very rare in any grade.

1688: American Plantations Tokens.
These pieces, once called *Florida tokens*, but now called *American Plantations tokens*, seem to represent the earliest coinage authorized by the British crown to be circulated in America. Struck under a franchise given to Richard Holt, they were made in tin. Several die varieties exist.

An extensive production of restrikes of the American Plantations token were made in England circa 1828 and constitute the majority of those seen today. Tin is a chemically active metal, and when subjected to *low* temperatures develops a black oxidation known as *tinpest*. Most coins, even in higher grades, show some evidence of discoloration. The dies are well made and interesting to contemplate. Varieties range from scarce to rare.

1694: Elephant Tokens for Carolina and New England.
The origin of these is unknown, but they are related to the famous London Elephant tokens (see separate listing below), and bear inscriptions relating to the Carolinas or to New England. These may have been sent to the American colonies for use as promotional or souvenir pieces, less likely as money, for few are known today, indicating a limited production.

Issues referring to CAROLINA AND THE LORD'S PROPRIETORS are very rare today, but are collectible with perseverance and an appropriate budget. Grades tend to be high, VF upward. The 1694 GOD PRESERVE NEW ENGLAND pieces are exceedingly rare, with just three known.

1766: Pitt Tokens.
These medalets, made in two sizes (so-called farthing and halfpenny), depict on the obverse William Pitt, the British parliamentarian who is remembered as a friend to the American colonies. The *Guide Book* states that the halfpenny "served as currency during a shortage of regular coinage" (2006 edition, p. 48), although I am not aware of any documentation to that effect.

The halfpenny-sized token is collectible, but scarce. Some show traces of silvering.

1779: Rhode Island Ship Medals.
These are medals or tokens, not coins, and may have been struck in England circa 1779 or 1780 for the market in the Netherlands. They properly belong to the series of Betts medals delineated in chapter 26. The inscriptions are political and relate to the Treaty of Armed Neutrality (finally signed in December 1780).

Examples are known today in brass (typical), copper (hard to discern from brass), and pewter. When seen they are usually in higher grades, VF to AU or Mint State.

1781: North American Tokens.
Although these tokens are dated 1781, they are believed to have been struck in Dublin, Ireland, at least two decades later. Some

pieces are believed to have circulated in British North America (now Canada).

Examples are plentiful today, usually well worn, Fine to VF, and lacking in detail as the dies themselves were not sharply delineated.

1796: Castorland Medals. Struck in silver and dated 1796, these medals were made for a settlement known as Castorland, at Carthage, New York, to be a refuge for those escaping the French Revolution. Extensive plans were made, and many French settled there. Whether the medals actually circulated at the value of a half dollar is not known, and theories vary. In later years copy dies were made at the Paris Mint, and examples from new dies can be obtained today.

1820: North West Company Tokens. These tokens, dated 1820, are not necessarily "early American"—but because they are listed in the *Guide Book* and elsewhere, they are highly desired. Struck in brass and usually holed at the top, the pieces depict King George IV on the obverse and, on the reverse, a beaver. Distributed to Native Americans in exchange for beaver pelts, these tokens could then be redeemed at a trading post for goods in the district now comprising Washington and Oregon.

Most examples seen today show evidence of burial or of extensive use, making them all the more interesting from a historical viewpoint, as they have a direct connection with their intended purpose. Typical grades range from Fine to VF, often with porous surfaces.

British Conder Tokens Relating to America

Conder tokens are named after James Conder, a British collector who in 1798 created an illustrated listing titled *An Arrangement of Political Coins, Tokens, and Medalets, issued in Great Britain, Ireland, and the Colonies, within the last 20 years, from the Farthing to the Penny Size.*

While some of these tokens, usually the size of an American copper cent, were used in commerce, many others were created in unusual and irrelevant die combinations and were sold to numismatists. Collecting such tokens was a great passion in England in the 1790s. The following bear inscriptions relating to America, and one issue—the Talbot, Allum & Lee cents—was made in quantity and intended for circulation in the United States.

(1792–1795): Kentucky Tokens. These tokens are believed to have been produced sometime between 1792, when Kentucky became the 15th state in the Union, and 1796, when Tennessee became the 16th. The name is derived from the position of the initial K at the top of a pyramid with notations for each of the states. In the 19th century, these were often called *triangle cents.* Kentucky tokens are part of the Conder token series and were struck for numismatists and collectors in England, not for circulation. Varieties exist, mostly with a plain edge.

Plain-edge and certain lettered edge examples are fairly plentiful today and are usually in AU or Mint State, sharply struck, and very attractive.

1794–1795: Talbot, Allum & Lee Cents. Many tens of thousands of these tokens were struck in Birmingham, England, to the order of Talbot, Allum & Lee, India-trade merchants located on Pearl Street in lower New York City. Examples are dated 1794 and 1795 and were made in a number of varieties. In addition, these pieces were popular with British collectors of Conder tokens, and a number of irrelevant dies were muled or combined with Talbot, Allum & Lee dies to create novelties. Distribution of the tokens in the United States was not effective, and large remaining quantities were purchased by the Philadelphia Mint, which struck copper cents from the metal obtained. Planchets were cut out from some of the tokens themselves, and used to coin half cents that today show some of the original Talbot, Allum & Lee legends.

Basic varieties dated 1794 and 1795 are readily collectible today and are usually seen in high grades, EF or finer, often Mint State and usually prooflike.

1794: Franklin Press Tokens. This is another halfpenny in the British Conder tokens series, made for collectors in that country during the passion to collect varieties. The press depicted is associated with Benjamin Franklin, so the piece has been adopted into many American cabinets.

As these pieces never circulated as coins, most seen today are in AU or Mint State, sometimes with traces of original color. Examples are plentiful.

1796: Myddelton Tokens. These beautiful tokens were struck at the Soho Mint, Birmingham, England, from dies cut by Conrad Küchler. These pieces refer to the proposed British settlement in Kentucky, a speculative venture that does not seem to have materialized. Examples were made in copper and silver metals, primarily distributed to numismatists.

All examples today are very rare, with the copper being slightly more so than the silver. These were struck in Proof format.

1797 (Circa): Theatre at New York Tokens. The Theatre at New York token was struck for the numismatic trade, by Skidmore, a London maker of tokens and medals. At the time, there was a passion for collecting copper halfpennies and pennies with interesting inscriptions. This particular variety depicts the front of the Park Theatre, New York, and thus has been collected by many American numismatists, although it never circulated or was used here.

Examples are rare today, with just a few dozen known. They are typically seen in Mint State.

Foreign Coins Mostly Irrelevant to America but Adopted by American Numismatists

This category includes coins made in Europe and intended to be circulated there or, in the instance of the Sommer Islands coinage, made for a British possession in the Atlantic Ocean. For example, St.

Patrick's coinage was not designed and struck for circulation in America, but some were sent there. The others in the list are irrelevant to American money, but are collected by *numismatic tradition*. None of these bear inscriptions relating to the United States.

It is to be remembered that on a much wider scale, silver and gold coins of Spanish America were legal tender in most of the colonies and all of the states, but these are not usually collected as "colonial coins." If the many dozens of Spanish-American coins were to be included, the following list would be vastly longer.

1616 (Circa): Coinage for the Sommer Islands (Bermuda). Made in England for distribution in the Sommer Islands (today called the Bermuda Islands), these pieces were known as *hogge money* in their time, as they depict a wild hog on the obverse, representative of an animal said to have been common in the islands at one time. On the reverse of each is depicted a sailing ship. Denominations included the twopence, threepence, sixpence and shilling. Many if not most were made in brass and lightly silvered.

All Bermuda coins are very rare today, some extremely so. Coins are often oxidized and in rather low grades, which typically range from Good-4 to F-12 or VF-20. Although these have nothing to do with the United States, they have been adopted into the American series for a long time and are widely desired and collected by American numismatists.

1663–1672: St. Patrick (Mark Newby) Coinage. It is said that Mark Newby, who came to New Jersey from Ireland in November 1681, brought some Irish coins with him. In May 1682 the General Assembly of the colony made them worth a halfpenny in trade.

These exist in two different sizes, known today with the unofficial designations of farthing (one fourth of a penny) and halfpenny. Some silver strikings are known as well. Most copper pieces are well worn, and many die varieties exist.

1670–1767: French Colonies Coinage. "None of the coins of the French regime are strictly American," the *Guide Book* (2006, p. 49) observes. "They were all general issues for the French colonies of the New World." These districts included much of what is now eastern Canada and islands in the West Indies. Certain copper coins of 1717 to 1722 were authorized for use in Louisiana, these being pieces that are exceptions to the "not strictly American" rule. All of the French colonies' coins were struck at various mints in France and bear various mint letters. Although there are rarities in the series, most are quite plentiful. For many years the copper sous of 1767 were listed in the *Guide Book* and elsewhere and were widely known, but it has been relatively recent that the extensive silver alloy (billon) and related silver-content coinages have been popularized. Today, interest in these pieces is limited, but those who are involved find the experience to be fascinating.

1694: Elephant Tokens, GOD PRE-SERVE LONDON. These bear on the obverse the depiction of an elephant, and on the reverse, GOD PRESERVE LONDON. It is believed that the inscriptions may refer to the plague that swept London in 1665 or the great fire of 1666. They have no connection with the American series, other than that tokens with similar obverses were made for the Carolinas and New England.

Most examples are in higher grades, EF or finer, and of pleasing appearance. Several varieties exist.

1722–1724: Wood's Hibernia Coinage. These copper coins, of farthing and halfpenny size, were struck by William Wood for circulation in Ireland (*Hibernia* being the ancient name for that land).

Examples are plentiful today, especially of the halfpenny denomination. Most are in higher grades, EF to Mint State.

1760: Voce Populi Coinage. These 1760-dated issues, mostly of halfpenny size, but with some of the farthing denomination,

Copper halfpenny struck by William Wood, a British entrepreneur, for circulation in Ireland. These were produced under license or patent from King George of England, whose portrait is on the obverse. These coins have no special connection to America.

were made in Dublin and used in Ireland. There is no known connection with the American series.

Most are crudely struck, but with bold features and lettering, on irregular planchets. Grades from VF to AU are typical. Many die varieties exist.

1787: Auctori Plebis Tokens. These are British Conder tokens of halfpenny size, made and used in that country. The obverse is copied from a Connecticut copper cent of the 1770s, but these coins have no connection with that state.

Usually seen in grades from VF to AU, and somewhat shallowly struck.

Washington Tokens and Medals

In his lifetime George Washington, the first American president, was widely honored as the subject for coins and tokens. One of the earliest, known as the *Voltaire medal* and said to have been commissioned in the late 1770s by French philosopher and writer Voltaire (1694–1778), bears a fictitious portrait of Washington. Apparently, at this early date there was no likeness available in France, and a generic image was used instead.

Later medals, including many varieties dated 1783 (but produced at a later date) and 1791 to 1793, depicted Washington and were taken from popular portraits and illustrations. As to the 1783 date, this has no particular significance in the biography of Washington, other than its being the year that the peace treaty ending the Revolution was signed. Such pieces can be called antedated coins or *novodels*, these

A 1783 GEORGIVS TRIUMPHO token. This has been collected with the Washington series, although its status is somewhat enigmatic. The 1783 date represents the date of the peace treaty after the Revolution. Our George (Washington) certainly triumphed (TRIUMPHO) in that contest. However, the image is of their George (King George III), and the GEORGIVS spelling is what was found on contemporary British coins, not any made in the United States and relating to George Washington.

This was an era of symbolism, and on the reverse, the seated figure of Britannia, representing England, seems to be trapped behind a grill consisting of 13 bars with French fleur-de-lis decorations, suggesting 13 colonies with the aid of France. As to VOCE POPOLI, or "Voice of the People," perhaps this shows Britannia that the people have spoken.

This token was probably made in Birmingham, quite possibly in or near 1783 (an exception to the novodel rule mentioned in the text), possibly by the same coiner who made Nova Constellatio coppers of this date (and of 1785). Virtually all known examples show extensive wear, indicating that they must have circulated widely at one time—probably more so in England than in America.

A 1791 Washington cent, Small Eagle style. Attributed to the 16-year-old John Gregory Hancock, a teenage engraving prodigy in Birmingham, England (cf. *Breen Encyclopedia*, 137). Made in quantity, these were part of the Conder token series (see chapter 25). Similar to many numismatic items, they are difficult to compartmentalize into a specific category.

Popular numismatic tradition has it that many of these pieces were distributed among members of the American Congress in an effort to secure a contract for coinage. As is so often the case with early issues, facts are scarce.

Copper NON DEPENDENS STATUS coin or token, 1778, from copy dies by George H. Lovett, and so indicated.

being coins struck at a date later than given on the coin, and for which no equivalent original coins of that date were made. Such distinctions have absolutely no effect on the market value of such pieces.

The tokens and medals of concern in this chapter are those included in the *Guide Book*, dated up to and including 1795, and of smaller sizes—most about the diameter of a copper cent. Most were made in England, including as part of the Conder token series. Others were produced in America. None circulated as coins in the United States.

Washington tokens and medals form a special study in themselves. In the early 1860s such pieces were the most sought-after issues in the rare coin market. Today, most varieties listed in the *Guide Book* are readily available and are usually found in higher grades. Washington pieces are often collected separately from early American coinage. (Also see the discussion of Washington medals in chapter 26.)

Curiosa Americana

Mysteries swirl around tokens, and a good example is the NON DEPENDENS STATUS example shown above. It seems that there may or may not be struck pieces dating from 1778, the date shown. *Norton's Literary Letter* No. 2, published in 1858, at the dawn of popular interest in numismatics, included this under "Curiosa Americana":

The next coin is in pure copper, and is truly a well-executed design. On the obverse is a bust facing the right, which resembles that of an Indian chief or warrior; on the shoulder, within a small circle, are to be seen a flag and sword crossed, and the *fleur de lis* of France; on the breast is a small head with wings. Legend—"NON-DEPEN-DENS STATUS." Obverse—Full length figure of an Indian seated on a globe, around the loins is an apron of feathers; in the right hand he holds a branch of tobacco, in the left a shield, with the American flag and sword crossed, and *fleur de lis* the same as on the shoulder-knot of the obverse. Around the whole is the Legend—"AMERICA, 1778."

This piece is without doubt *unique*, and is supposed to be one of the many pattern pieces engraved and designed by Paul Revere.

Although I have seen what seems to be an early hand-engraved item in the form of a token of this design, no coin struck from dies has been located. However, sometime around 1858, New York City diesinker George H. Lovett produced his own version, some marked COPY and others not. The execution of the dies was done in a modern style, and the fields of the coin were smooth and prooflike—not easily mistaken for a coin struck in 1778. These copies found an active market and were probably mainly distributed by Alfred S. Robinson, a Hartford, Connecticut, dealer.

Whimsy and mischief have always been part of the numismatic scene, with games being played. It has often been a sport to look through old directories, or come up with some motto, that *could have been used* at an earlier date, but was not—and to create a modern fantasy along these lines. C. Wyllys Betts, for one, was a master at this, and in our own era there are a few practitioners.

Certainly, "Non Dependens Status" (with Dependens hyphenated on the coin) is a dandy motto evocative of the early

times of the American Revolution, when the colonies no longer had "dependent status" with England.

Key to Collecting

- **Mint State coins:** Early American coins are rarely available in Mint State, as such pieces were not collected in their time. Massachusetts silver coins, copper coins of the states (1785–1788), and other coins *made in America* range from very rare to nonexistent at this grade level. To be sure, there are a few exceptions—such as 1787 Fugio cents. On the other hand, many of the issues made in England can be found in Mint State, these including 1722 to 1724 Rosa Americana and (especially) Hibernia issues, 1773 Virginia halfpennies, tokens of the 1790s (Washington pieces; Myddelton tokens; Talbot, Allum & Lee cents; etc.).

- **Circulated coins:** These are the rule, not the exception, and the finest collections ever formed have included many well-worn examples. Typical issues range from Good-4 to VF-20, with many exceptions, but this is the usual level, such as for specialized collections of state copper coins. Washington tokens and certain issues of the 1790s tend to be in higher grades, such as EF and AU.

- **Strike quality:** Varies widely depending on the issue. Generally, pieces struck in America are more rustic than those struck in Europe and imported to America.

- **Proof coins:** Virtually nonexistent save for certain Washington pieces and tokens made in England.

- **Key issues:** Numerous; see specialized texts on designs and die varieties.

- **Advice to smart buyers:** Proceed in baby steps, learning along the way. Never, but never, buy a colonial coin on the Internet or from a seller who is not knowledgeable, unless you have

The Fascination of Connecticut Die Varieties

Among colonial and early American coins, the characteristics of dies can vary widely. Shown here are several varieties of Connecticut copper coins (enlarged to show details) with attributions to Miller numbers as published in *State Coinages of New England*, 1920.

Miller 1786 2.1-A, with the reverse legend transposed as ET LIB INDE. This is an unauthorized issue struck at Machin's Mills.

Miller 1786 5.3-N, the so-called Hercules Head. The reverse is indistinct, as struck. To the specialist, this crudely made coin is very desirable.

Miller 1787 4-L, known as the *Horned Bust* variety, from the hornlike die break on the obverse. The reverse inscription, INDE ET LIB, represents "independence and liberty."

Miller 1787 37.3-HH, one of many Draped Bust Facing Left varieties, displays planchet rifts or streaks from impurities in the planchet. The rustic nature of nearly all Connecticut coppers adds to their numismatic appeal.

it independently verified first; the *vast majority* of such offerings are fakes! However, authentic coins abound on the *numismatic* market, and are a pleasure to collect. The usual steps 1 through 4 apply (see chapter 2), together with knowledge as to what is reasonable to expect and what exists. Eye appeal never goes out of style and should be a guiding concept unless you are confronted with an incredibly rare variety—and even then, think carefully. Build at least a modest library, including auction catalogs, on various aspects of colonial coins.

• **Selected bibliography:**

American Numismatic Society. 1976. *Studies on Money in Early America*. New York, NY. (collection of monographs)

Breen, Walter. 1988. *Walter Breen's Complete Encyclopedia of U.S. and Colonial Coins*. New York, NY.

Carlotto, Tony. 1998. *The Copper Coins of Vermont*. Chelsea, MI.

The Colonial Newsletter, published by the American Numismatic Society.

Crosby, Sylvester S. 1983. *The Early Coins of America*, Boston, MA. (original work published 1875; reprinted 1945, 1965, 1974, 1983)

Kessler, Alan. 1976. *The Fugio Cents*. Newtonville, MA. (an updating of the 1952 Newman study)

Maris, Edward. 1987. *A Historic Sketch of the Coins of New Jersey*. Philadelphia, PA. (original work published 1881; reprinted 1925, 1974, 1987)

Miller, Henry C., and Hillyer Ryder. 1920. *The State Coinages of New England*. New York, NY. (die-variety information on Vermont [classified by Ryder numbers], Connecticut [Miller numbers], and Massachusetts [Miller numbers] coppers)

Mossman, Philip L. 1993. *Money of the American Colonies and Confederation*. New York, NY. (a worthy extension to the Crosby study)

Nelson, Philip. 1959. *The Coinage of William Wood 1722–1733*. London, UK. (original work published 1903)

Newman, Eric P. 1952. *The 1776 Continental Currency Coinage; Varieties of the Fugio Cent*. New York, NY.

Newman, Eric P. 1956. *Coinage for Colonial Virginia*. New York, NY.

Noe, Sydney P. 1973. *The New England and Willow Tree Coinage of Massachusetts*. New York, NY. (original work published 1943)

Noe, Sydney P. 1973. *The Oak Tree Coinage of Massachusetts*. New York, NY. (original work published 1947)

Noe, Sydney P. 1973. *The Pine Tree Coinage of Massachusetts*. New York, NY. (original work published 1952)

Rulau, Russell, and George Fuld. 1999. *Medallic Portraits of Washington*. Iola, WI.

CHAPTER TWENTY-TWO

COLLECTING COMMEMORATIVE COINS

It is difficult to give any general advice about collecting; it is a matter of taste. If one means to become a collector, and not merely a possessor, it is wisest to choose perhaps a somewhat limited field.... It is in the possession of some special line, after all, that the real joy lies. Numismatics is a broad term. The average dealer in numismatics has a hotchpotch of unrelated specimens on tap. The collector does not want his collection to be like that unless he be the proprietor of a town museum. The average collector should choose some special line in numismatics and follow the same consistently, seeking for the finest examples in season and out. A collection is desirable when it means something.... There is a charm and beauty in it when it is chosen with good judgment, which the devotee can never adequately express nor the Philistine ever understand.

—Waldo C. Moore, December 1918

Collecting Commemoratives

"Real Historical Significance"

The section on commemorative coins in the *Guide Book* includes this:

> The unique position occupied by commemoratives in United States coinage is largely due to the fact that, with few exceptions, all commemorative coins have a real historical significance. The progress and advance of people in the New World are presented in an interesting and instructive manner on the commemorative issues. Such a record of facts artistically presented on U.S. gold and silver memorial issues appeals strongly to the collector who favors the historical side of numismatics. It is the historical features of the commemoratives, in fact, that create interest among many people who would otherwise have little interest in coins.

While in my opinion many other coins have great historical value, there is no doubt that viewing a collection of commemoratives is like going to an art gallery: all sorts of things are represented—the good, bad, and ugly, the talented and the naive, the relevant and the irrelevant. As such, the series is fascinating to contemplate.

I have always enjoyed commemoratives, and in the early days of my collecting activities I built a set of the 48 silver half dollars, plus the 1893 Isabella quarter and

An 1892 Columbian half dollar, America's first silver commemorative coin. The World's Columbian Exposition, held in Chicago, was intended to celebrate the 400th anniversary of Columbus's "discovery" of America. However, projects lagged, and it was not until 1893 that the gates were opened to the general public. An 1893-dated version of this coin was also made. Such coins were sold for $1 each to fairgoers.

The 1893 Isabella quarter was issued for the Board of Lady Managers and offered for $1 each in the Woman's Building. Visitors considered them to be overpriced, as Columbian *half dollars* were available for a like amount, and sales were slow. Most remained unsold and were distributed for years afterward through various coin dealers. Today, choice pieces are highly prized.

The scene at noon, May 1, 1893, when President Grover Cleveland touched a button to close a switch, actuating mechanisms that unfurled flags and set machinery in motion, opening the fair. Notice that *all* men in the crowd were wearing hats—standard custom at the time, but unusual to contemplate today. (*Harper's Weekly*, May 15, 1893)

The gigantic Ferris Wheel was the centerpiece of the exposition. Measuring 250 feet in diameter, and with compartments the size of railroad cars, the wheel made two revolutions in 20 minutes, the duration of a ride. (*Columbian Exposition Album*, 1893)

1900 Lafayette dollar, comprising one each of the different types from the "classic" era. Later, I kept many notes on commemoratives, as I continue to do today, although in modern times it is hard to keep up with all of the new issues. In 1991 my *Commemorative Coins of the United States: A Complete Encyclopedia* was published, the result of digging into just about every nook and cranny I could find to locate information, from obvious to obscure, for each variety up to that time. Much of it had never been published in a single volume before.

Logical and Illogical Designs

Since 1991 many more commemoratives have been produced. Nearly always, in the past as well as in the present time, commemoratives are made on behalf of special-interest groups who lobby their congressional representatives for passage. The motifs can be familiar to just about everyone, as is the 1986 centennial of the dedication of the Statue of Liberty; or they can be obscure or even curious, like the 1991 dollar observing the 38th anniversary of the end of the Korean War—why the 38th? why not the 10th, 25th, or 50th? Actually, in terms of commemorative tradition, Korean War 38th anniversary coin is no weirder than the 1893 World's

Columbian Exposition half dollar, which observed the 401st anniversary of the "discovery" of America (not that it was lost in the first place). Then there is the 1921 Pilgrim Tercentenary half dollar commemorating the landing at Plymouth Rock 301 (not 300) years earlier.

Perhaps beyond ridiculous is the 1921-dated half dollar commemorating the 100th anniversary of the statehood of Alabama, which had taken place *two years earlier*, in 1919! There is a notion that some unwritten rule forbids the depiction of living people on coins. If there is, it has been widely ignored. Governor T.E. Kilby, very much alive in 1921, is seen on the Alabama half dollar of that date. Other living people seen on commemorative halves include Calvin Coolidge on the 1926 Sesquicentennial, Senator Joseph T. Robinson on the 1936 Arkansas, and Senator Carter Glass on the 1936 Lynchburg coins. Eunice Shriver, another living person, can be found on the obverse of a 1995 commemorative dollar, while her deceased relatives, John F. Kennedy and Robert F. Kennedy, are pictured on other commemorative issues—adding up to the most depictions from a single family on such coins.

As to the importance of the events being commemorated, challenging the Korean 38th anniversary issue in terms of irrelevance and obscurity is the 1936 Norfolk half dollar, issued to commemorate the anniversary of the changing of Norfolk, Virginia, from a township in 1682 to a royal borough in 1736! But it is the 1936 Cincinnati that might take the palm: Thomas Melish, a local businessman and numismatist, persuaded Congress to let a group he had formed sell three varieties (one each from the Philadelphia, Denver, and San Francisco mints) of commemorative coin. Seemingly out of nowhere, he came up with the idea of commemorating the 1886 to 1936 anniversary of Cincinnati as, per the inscription, A MUSICAL CENTER OF AMERICA. In doing research for my commemorative *Encyclopedia* I delved into the Cincinnati chronicles for the year 1886 and contacted several historians, but no one could find anything important musically that had its inception in 1886. As if this were not enough to discredit the purpose of this coin, the obverse depicts Stephen Foster, who, per the *Guide Book*, has "no relation" to the supposed event.

George Washington appears on several commemoratives, beginning with the Lafayette-Washington silver dollar of 1900; his portrait was taken from the famous bust by Jean Antoine Houdon (widely used elsewhere, including on the Washington quarter dollars). P.T. Barnum turns up on the obverse of the 1936 Bridgeport, Connecticut, half dollar, and we can find movie actor Errol Flynn on a 1937 Roanoke half dollar (modeling for Sir Walter Raleigh).

In some instances it was desired to depict an individual from history, but there were no reliable paintings or other portraits to copy. The visage of Christopher Columbus on the 1892 and 1893 World's Columbian Exposition halves is an unverified portrait, as no single one of the many depictions of that explorer is known to be authentic. The image of Virginia Dare in a long, flowing skirt that appears on the reverse of the 1937 Roanoke half dollar is also an artist's conception. Perhaps the most far-fetched is that on the 1935 Old

Every commemorative comes with a story, often with a twist. The 1921 Alabama Centennial half dollar was produced two years after the 100th (1819–1919) anniversary had been observed! Featured on the obverse were William Wyatt Bibb and Thomas E. Kilby, Alabama's governors in 1819 and 1919, respectively.

The 1937 Roanoke half dollar commemorates the 350th anniversary of the founding of Sir Walter Raleigh's "Lost Colony," and the birth of Virginia Dare, the first white child to be born in what is now the United States. The portrait of Raleigh is said to have been adapted from a photograph of movie star Errol Flynn, while Ellinor Dare and her child Virginia were conceptions of artist William Marks Simpson, who also designed several other commemoratives of the era.

Spanish Trail half dollar, intended to honor the famous Spanish explorer Cabeza de Vaca. As no likeness could be found, and as his name translates to mean "head of cow," the skull of a steer is shown. Roosevelt can be translated into "field of roses," and it would make just as much sense to have depicted a flower garden, instead of a man's portrait, on the obverse of the Roosevelt dime!

Such things make the contemplating and collecting of commemoratives a fascinating pursuit. *The Commemorative Trail*, published by the Society for U.S. Commemorative Coins, is worth investigating if you have an interest in the historical aspects of these issues. A few years ago the members of the SUSCC were polled as to their favorite design from an artistic viewpoint, and the winner was the Oregon Trail half dollar minted from 1926 to 1939. The U.S. Mint web site (www.usmint.gov) has information on modern and current issues.

Categories of Commemoratives
The History of Commemorative Coins

In American history, the first commemoratives *using* federal coins were the previously issued cents and half dollars that were counterstamped privately in 1824 using dies cut by Joseph Lewis. The occasion was the visit of the Marquis de Lafayette, French hero of the American Revolution, to the United States (noted in the chronicle in chapter 11 under the year 1824), when Congress proclaimed him "the nation's guest." These counterstamps consisted of the portrait of Lafayette on one side and Washington on the other. Seemingly quite popular in their time, perhaps as many as two dozen survive today.

The first commemorative that was actually created at the Mint was the 1848 quarter eagle with CAL. counterstamped on the reverse, signifying that the coin is from a batch of 1,389 pieces produced from a shipment of gold brought from California. It represented the first significant deposit from the Gold Rush era, and its announcement was a catalyst for the Gold Rush. Such coins are rare today, and no more than a few hundred exist.

Classic Silver Commemoratives (1892–1954)

For many years, silver coins of the "classic" era, 1892 to 1954, constituted the primary focus for numismatists interested in commemoratives. The series begins with the World's Columbian Exposition half dollar issues dated 1892 and 1893 and concludes with the Carver-Washington set of Philadelphia, Denver, and San Francisco mint coins of 1951 to 1954. All told, there are 48 basic design types of commemorative half dollars in this span, or, if mintmark and other varieties are counted, 142 of a collection of everything. In addition, the 1893 Isabella quarter and 1900 Lafayette dollar are usually included.

The vista of classic silver commemoratives is a virtual smorgasbord of motifs, events commemorated, and artistic talents. Well-known engravers are represented, including those from the Mint, as well as artists who were little known then and are less known today, except among numismatic specialists. Events commemorated and people and things depicted range from the logical to the improbable, as discussed above.

Although the mintages of certain of these commemoratives are very small, they were sold at a premium and specifically saved, so the survival ratio is fairly high today. The market tends to emphasize MS-65 and higher, which leaves many MS-63 and -64 coins open for serious numismatists who are seeking excellent value for the money paid.

The 1900 Lafayette commemorative dollar is very curious, inasmuch as the dies were made by hand-punching the lettering, rather than using a hub—a reversion to the ways employed at the Mint in the 1830s. Apparently, the project was rush-rush, and this was thought to be the most expeditious procedure. Although not much attention is paid to them, a handful of different die varieties can be collected of this issue.

I have enjoyed these commemoratives for a long time, and I heartily recommend them as an avenue of collecting. Market-wise, they've had their ups and downs over the years, being as subject to cycles as any other series I know. Accordingly, you might want to keep an eye on this aspect of price and value. The best time to buy commemoratives is when the series is quiet, which happens every now and then.

Classic Gold Commemoratives (1903–1926)

My second category contains commemorative coins struck in gold, including nine varieties of gold dollars, two of quarter eagles, and two of $50 pieces. All are readily collectible today, each with its own characteristics. (The $50 coins are, of course, necessarily expensive.)

The first gold dollars are the 1903 Louisiana Purchase issues, made in two varieties, one with a portrait of Thomas Jefferson (president when the Louisiana Purchase took place in 1803), and the other of the recently martyred William McKinley (assassinated in 1901). The sale of these was by numismatic entrepreneur and promoter Farran Zerbe, who had grandiose expectations and persuaded the Mint to strike 250,000 pieces. The hype and promotion at $3 per coin fell flat on its face, and only 17,500 of each were produced. Of course, today these marketplace "failures," which fell sharply in value after they were first issued, are highly desired. Most pieces are seen in Mint State, usually attractive and choice.

Next came the 1904 and 1905 gold dollars made for the Lewis and Clark Centennial Exposition in Portland, Oregon. Just 10,000 were distributed of each. Collector interest was at a minimum, as the sale of the 1903 commemoratives had proved to be a dud, and numismatists did not go back for a second helping. Because of this, most of these coins were distributed to those who actually attended the exposition—members of the general public who handled them carelessly. Today, finding truly choice examples of either issue, particularly the 1905, can be a great challenge.

In 1915 the Panama–Pacific International Exposition opened in San Francisco, and was the largest world's fair since the St. Louis event in 1904 (where the 1903 Louisiana Purchase gold dollars were distributed). No effort was spared to

The round-format commemorative $50 gold coin sold at the Panama–Pacific International Exposition was minted to the extent of 1,500 for sale, but only 483 actually found buyers. The rest were melted, creating the rarest of all regular commemorative issues.

Concessionaire Farran Zerbe's *Money of the World* exhibit within the Palace of Fine Arts at the Panama–Pacific International Exposition, 1915. Among the items for sale were five different commemoratives relating to the event: a silver half dollar, and gold pieces in the denominations of $1, $2.50, and $50 (octagonal and round).

create a virtual "white city," as it was called, of buildings and galleries, complete with statuary, decorations, and other attractions. Farran Zerbe engineered the approval of a special group of commemoratives for the event, including a gold dollar, a quarter eagle, and two varieties of $50 gold pieces, the last made in round and octagonal formats. Once again, his expectations were far too high, and many were returned to the melting pot, this being most relevant in the case of the $50 pieces, of which 1,500 of each were made for sale. Just 483 of the round version actually found buyers, and only 645 of the octagonal. Today, when offered in the marketplace, Panama-Pacific coins are usually in Mint State and are attractive.

The next gold commemoratives from the classic era are the 1916 and 1917 McKinley Memorial gold dollars, the 1917 being particularly scarce. Because they were mainly sold within numismatic circles, including in quantity by B. Max Mehl, most that survive today are in varying degrees of Mint State, sometimes with prooflike surfaces.

In 1922 the Mint issued the final commemorative gold dollars: the Grant Memorial coins, made in two varieties (one with a tiny, incused five-pointed star on the obverse and the other without the star). Nearly all were sold within the numismatic market, though not particularly successfully, as quantities remained for years afterward. Today, both are rather plentiful, and are usually seen in choice or gem Mint State.

The production of the two Grant gold dollar varieties totaled 10,000, the same amount as for the 1905 Lewis and Clark gold dollar. Today, I view the Grant gold dollars as being at least several dozen times more available in gem preservation than the 1905 Lewis and Clark issues! If anything, this illustrates that mintages are one thing, but actual availability can be another. The population reports issued by ANACS, NGC, and PCGS are of assistance in helping to determine survival rates, but, as always, must be used with care and with other knowledge applied. In this instance, a little reading will reveal (as noted above) that the 1905 gold dollars were largely scattered to the wind and sold to the general public, with few being carefully preserved; while nearly all of the Grant coins were sold to collectors, who took better care of them.

The last entry among early commemorative gold coins is the 1926 Sesquicentennial quarter eagle, made for the Sesquicentennial Exhibition held in Philadelphia that year. This was intended to be a grand event, following on such world's fairs as the 1893 Columbian, 1904 St. Louis, and 1915 Panama-Pacific, but it was a flop. Attendance was far below expectations, and the sale of coins was similarly unsatisfactory. However, today many of these quarter eagles survive and are nearly always in Mint State.

Modern Commemoratives (1982 to Date)

After the Carver-Washington half dollars were minted in 1954, the idea of authorizing any more commemoratives had become unpleasant to congressmen and others. The Carver-Washington series commenced in 1951 and continued through 1954, with production at the Philadelphia, Denver, and San Francisco mints, but with very little in the way of public interest. Afterward, petitions for new commemoratives fell upon deaf ears.

From 1954 through the 1970s, the American Numismatic Association, the Professional Numismatists Guild, and other groups often discussed a resumption of commemoratives, and sometimes advanced proposals for such by writing letters to and personally visiting congresspeople. In the related field of stamps, commemoratives proliferated, with many hundreds of varieties issued during this period. However, for numismatists there were no commemoratives at all.

Then in 1982 all of this changed with the George Washington half dollar commemorating the 250th anniversary of his birth. Elizabeth Jones, chief engraver at the Mint, created the motifs, which were

The 1982 Washington half dollar was the first commemorative coin to be made after the Carver-Washington series was discontinued in 1954.

widely acclaimed. Numismatists pursued these pieces with a passion, and a new era of commemorative issuance and enthusiasm was born.

Then followed many other commemoratives, including the 1983 and 1984 issues for the Summer Olympic Games held in Los Angeles the latter year, a 1986 series observing the 100th anniversary of the dedication of the Statue of Liberty, and more. Among these can be found many curious and interesting varieties. The 1990 Eisenhower Centennial dollar, for example, has *two* heads of Ike on the same side of the coin. The 1992 Olympic dollar shows a baseball pitcher about to fire a ball toward home plate; although officially declared to be a "generic" representation, the pitcher was said to have been modeled after real-life baseball hero Nolan Ryan. The 1994 Vietnam Veterans dollar is four times numismatic—as a coin itself and with three medals depicted together on the obverse.

The reverse of the 2002 West Point Bicentennial dollar depicts a snail (well, not really a snail—if examined closely, it's seen to be a helmet that merely looks like a snail). Then there is the 2001 Buffalo/Indian dollar, which is simply an enlarged version of the old-time (1913–1938) Buffalo nickel, but with a few modifications of lettering and so on. The fun continues....

Most modern commemoratives have been made in quantity. Many have been produced in different formats, such as Mint State as well as Proof finishes, and in different types of packaging. The entire spectrum of commemoratives is outlined

in the *Guide Book* and elsewhere, and is worth pursuing.

As to the collecting of modern commemoratives, quite a few people simply endeavor to keep their holdings up to date by ordering new issues as they come out. Others tend to specialize in a particular denomination, with dollar-sized coins being popular. Nearly all are readily available in such grades as MS-/Proof-65 and -66—great for collecting. There has been some interest in pieces in much higher grades, and in recent times increasingly large numbers of these have been certified. It is well to keep in mind that certification-population numbers increase rather than decrease, and that something that's rare in terms of a certified high grade today might not be rare tomorrow. Once again, you are spending your money and I am spending mine, so it's perfectly normal if each of us likes different things!

Commemorative Coin Chronology

The following is a time line of commemorative coins from 1892 onward, a general commentary concerning issues, market conditions, and related aspects. Marketwise, commemoratives have been a world of their own!

1892: First Silver "Souvenir Coins." Amid much fanfare, the 1892 commemorative, called a *souvenir coin* at the time, was launched in connection with the World's Columbian Exposition. Newspapers across America were filled with commentary about the forthcoming exposition and the coins. By year's end, 950,000 had been minted. In the meantime, Charles E. Barber's designs for the regular dime, quarter, and half dollar attracted virtually no attention at all. Following the striking of the first coins, the makers of the Remington typewriter paid $10,000 (as a publicity stunt) for the first coin off the presses—or at least, the one *said* to have been the first (no doubt a few had been made earlier to see what they looked like and to assure all would go well at the ceremony). It is not widely known that on January 1, 1793, Elias Boudinot (who would later become director of the Mint) commented that, because artists differed in their opinions as to how Miss Liberty should appear on a coin (as on the patterns of 1792), the matter could be settled by using the head of Columbus instead. The *Annals of Congress* reported that "Mr. Boudinot supported his motion by some pertinent remarks on the character of Columbus and the obligations the citizens of the United States were under to honor his memory.... On the question being put, the motion was negatived." Years later, Mint Director James Ross Snowden (who served from 1853 to 1861) suggested that the portrait of Columbus would represent an improvement in the designs for high-denomination gold coins.

1893: More of Them. The World's Fair actually opened in 1893, and additional half dollars bearing this date were made, in the enormous amount of 4,052,105 coins. Fairgoers eagerly bought them for $1 apiece. Almost as an afterthought, silver Isabella quarters were made at the request of the Board of Lady Managers, but were not publicized, and were sold only in the Women's Building. After the Exposition closed, 3,600,000 half dollars remained unsold; most of them were dumped into circulation, to the annoyance of everyone who had "invested" $1 in these sure-to-become-valuable coins.

1896: Investment Enticement. In May 1896 *The Numismatist* reprinted an article from the *Philadelphia Times*, commenting on the market for commemoratives, noting that an 1893 Isabella quarter dollar was already worth $1.50, and that

a decade hence a specimen of this coin is likely to fetch $10. These pieces must rise in value because only 40,000 of them were struck. There are not very many to go around among 75 million people. Many of those who possess them will hide them away, lose them, make bangles

of them, and in other ways dispose of them, so that a few years hence only 25,000 of them will be in existence, perhaps. They are interesting for several reasons. For one thing, they are the only coins ever struck or likely to be struck in this country bearing a crowned head. On the obverse is a portrait of Queen Isabella. This, too, is the only distinctively woman's coin ever issued.... The Columbian half dollars will never be rare—they were struck by the millions. The half dollar of 1893 is worth only its face today, for that of 1892 is rare and will fetch 75 cents.

However, although this reads like a market or investment presentation, it would not be until the early 1950s that an Isabella would be worth more than $10!

1900: Lafayette Dollars. In 1900 the next silver commemorative coin—the Lafayette silver dollar, the first of that denomination—appeared. These were to be sold at $2 each, including to schoolchildren across the land, with the proceeds earmarked to erect a statue of Lafayette in Paris. At the time, hardly anyone was concerned with the quality of current coins, and the Lafayette dollars were minted, dumped into bins, and then tossed into cloth bags. Today, a pristine piece might grade MS-63. However, by happenstance a few nicer ones did survive. This point is worth noting, for it was not until the new series of commemoratives decades later (in 1982) that the several mints handled coins with care. Today, in the early 21st century, this need for quality seems obvious, but back then it was not.

1903–1915: Gold Commemoratives. The Louisiana Purchase gold dollars, the Lewis and Clark coins of the same denomination, and the splendid array of Panama-Pacific coins, all discussed above, were made during this period.

1921: What Is Being Commemorated, Anyway? In 1920, the 300th anniversary of the landing at Plymouth Rock was observed by the Pilgrim Tercentenary commemorative half dollar, of which 152,112 were eventually made (net coinage after melting). This was fine and proper in all ways. However, although quantities overhung the market and were still in the hands of the issuing commission, an irrelevant issue dated 1921 was also made, in order to tap the pockets of numismatists! Although commemoratives had been *exploited* to numismatists up to this point (witness the 1903 gold dollars), the 1921 Pilgrim took the situation one step further—the artificial creation of rarities for the numismatic trade. The concept proved successful: additional pieces were sold, and afterward many related "numismatic delicacies" were made, all of which are considered to be very desirable and highly collectible today. The Alabama Centennial commemorative half dollar was also released in 1921, never mind that the centennial itself had taken place in 1919 and was no longer relevant! Two varieties were made, one with a plain field and the other with a small "2x2" (meaning *22*, for the 22nd state) in the field, thus making it necessary for collectors to buy two coins, not one, to have a complete set. The same situation came up this year for the 1921 Missouri centennial half dollar, made with a plain field and also with a 2*4 in the field. Numismatists were identified as the prime target for exploitation and would remain in the crosshairs for years to come.

1922: Grant Commemoratives. The Grant Centennial Commission, observing the 100th anniversary of the birth of that particular president, decided to raise funds by producing commemorative half dollars and gold dollars, each in two varieties: with a plain field and with a star in the field (the star having no significance except to have something else to sell to numismatists).

1923: Market Doldrums. In 1923 the commemorative market was in the doldrums. Dealer Thomas L. Elder commented in *The Numismatist* that

American collectors are, I think, fast awakening to the fact that souvenir gold dollars and half dollars which have been offered to them during the last few years by the hundreds of thousands, at from 100% to 200% premium, are a modernized and systematized sort of a numismatic swindle.... It is my intention to keep hammering against this injustice until these committees get some common sense into their heads. The souvenir coins which have had the greatest demand and which at the present command the very best premiums are those gold dollars which were issued at from $1.65 to $2 apiece, namely those of the Portland Centennial [Lewis and Clark Exposition] and the Panama–Pacific International Exposition. This proves my argument. The McKinley Memorial dollars 1916 and 1917 and the Grant issues seem to have gone dead recently.... The Pilgrim half dollars and those of the Maine Centennial have also gone to seed, and there is little demand for either of them....

The decade of the 1920s saw the production of a number of other commemorative coins, including the meaningless 1923-S Monroe Doctrine Centennial half dollar (issued for an exposition that had no relevance to the event being commemorated) and the unimportant Huguenot-Walloon half dollar, which mainly observed religious history.

1925: Life in the Market. In 1925 the Fort Vancouver half dollar was struck in San Francisco (although someone forgot to put a mintmark on the coin), and the California Diamond Jubilee, Lexington-Concord Sesquicentennial, and Stone Mountain halves were issued. Collectors warmed up to the subject and the market gained strength.

1926: Mixed Messages. The new 1926 Sesquicentennial half dollar was as ugly as sin, and with shallow relief as well. The

Oregon Trail half dollars were a confusing omen: was it necessary to strike the same design at two different mints? The Oregon halves would become another example of the exploitation of collectors—with the series not winding down until 1939!

1928: Hawaii Calls. The 1928 Hawaiian Sesquicentennial half dollar was the first truly *exciting* commemorative issue. Announced as being available for $2 each, most were sold to islanders by the time numismatists on the mainland ordered them—the market rose sharply, and stayed there.

1934: No "Depression" in the Depression. The rare-coin market was gathering strength, due to the release of popular albums, a nationwide focus on hobbies, the advent of the *Standard Catalogue of U.S. Coins,* and other factors. Boone Bicentennial and Maryland Tercentenary half dollars were released and met with a warm reception.

1935: Electricity in the Air. The 1935 Hudson Sesquicentennial halves were sold out (mostly privately to a dealer) before orders from collectors came rolling in. In November, when Frank Dunn of the Boone Bicentennial Commission offered a pair of special Boone halves with a small "1934" date on the reverse (of which only 2,000 each were available), they were a "sellout" at $3.70. They soon rose to $50, then beyond that. The excitement was intense, and the commemorative boom was launched.

In the *Numismatic Scrapbook,* September, editor Lee F. Hewitt commented,

> We cannot understand the attitude of Congress in granting the special privilege of the use of the national coinage for the express purpose of helping to finance some local project. Neither can we understand the purpose and historical significance of some of the local celebrations. The real cause of the president's request that commemorative coinage be discontinued was, no doubt, that the

politics of passing bills of such character was quickly getting beyond control. Using these half dollars as bait, an organization wishing to raise money merely had a congressman introduce a bill authorizing an issue of coins and, when passed, had the various mints issue coins bearing some trifling difference from some other half dollar [a reference to the Oregon Trail halves]. Thus, in taking advantage of a collector's instinct of keeping his collection complete, the organization was able to dispose of four or five half dollars instead of one....

1936, Early in the Year: Market Afire! Prices of older commemoratives continued to rise, while more than a dozen new ones were set to come on the market. In a brochure dated January 20, 1936, dealer B. Max Mehl commented,

> While I do not usually suggest that collectors buy coins for investment, I cannot resist calling your attention to a matter to which I am sure you will agree: In 1929 a share of stock of the American Telephone Co. would have cost you $310. In 1935 you could have bought it for less than $100. A share of U.S. Steel would have cost you in 1929 $261, in 1935 about $50. BUT—in 1928 if you bought a Hawaiian half dollar at its issue price of $2, you would now have a profit of about 500%. The Grant half dollar with star you could have bought at one time for $1, and today it's selling for $20!—more than 2,000% increase in value! The Panama-Pacific half dollar originally sold for $1, and today it retails for up to $15. AND, getting down to recent history, the 10,000 Hudson half dollars were issued about six months ago, selling for $1 each. Now, just a few months later, they bring up to $8.50 each! Just three or four months ago El Paso, Texas issued a half dollar commemorating the Old Spanish Trail.

10,000 coins were minted and sold for $2 each. Today they are quoted at $6 each and will soon advance to about $10 or more.

The race was on!

1936, Year's End: How Could This Happen? The market ran out of buyers. Prices halted their rise. The game was over. Some issuers made false statements that they would soon be sold out; others lowered their prices and dumped quantities in bulk to dealers; and still others held tight, later shipping thousands of coins back to the Mint to be melted.

1939: End of the Trail. By this time, the market for new commemoratives had completely fizzled. In 1939 Congress put an end to their issuance, reacting to complaints received concerning the abuses of selling commemorative coins for private profit. This was the end of the Oregon Trail series as well as the Arkansas Centennial halves, both exploitative beyond belief. However, like most such things, coins unwanted in one era (as in 1939) proved to be very valuable in later years.

1941: Life in the Market. After stewing in the doldrums, the market picked up with the advent of new buyers. Prices began going up, and up some more.

1943: "Growing in Demand." S.J. Kabealo advertised:

> U.S. Commemoratives: This popular series is growing in demand more than ever before. Many new records have been set on a number of coins in this series in recent sales. This is as it should be, for it is the most interesting of any series in the American coinage, offering a variety of designs that attract all classes. It is one of the richest in American history.

1946: New Commemoratives. The Booker T. Washington Birthplace Memorial succeeded in having Congress approve a series-type of coin, which was eventually issued in many repetitive varieties from 1946 to 1951, and then (with a complete design change) in new form as the Carver-Washington half dollar from 1951 through 1954. The designs were uninspiring and collector interest was low. Most later issues went begging. Still, the general market for older commemoratives remained strong. The Iowa Centennial half dollar was produced this year, all at the Philadelphia Mint, and was a success.

1948–1949: Slump. The years 1948 and 1949 were grim, and prices fell in many areas of numismatics, with commemoratives taking their licks. Dealers and investors had a tough time. Of course, this was a good time to *buy* commemoratives!

1950–1959: Revival and Vigor. In 1950 the market for commemoratives and just about everything else began to edge upward. Commemoratives were hot by 1956, then slumped a bit, then resumed their investment popularity.

1960–1964: Good Times. The market was in a boom mode, and Uncirculated and Proof coins led the way, with commemoratives as part of the procession.

1965–1966: Mixed Messages. The investment market for rolls and Proof sets weakened in 1965 and crashed in 1966. Commemoratives cooled off, but prices did not drop precipitously. For the next several years, investment performance was mixed. It was again a good time to buy.

1970s: Up, Up, and Away! Coins became popular as an investment, and commemoratives were again on the fire—just a bit at first, increasing to a glow in 1975, a cherry red in 1976, and white heat from 1977 to 1980 (during the great silver boom). Meanwhile, grading interpretations were all over the map, and one person's gem Uncirculated was another's AU or similar—there were no rules, and all sorts of hyperbole and puffery were seen in print.

1980s, Early: Apathy Abounds. Commemoratives and certain other "investment-grade" coins crashed in April 1980.

Farran Zerbe, Seller of Commemoratives

In the early days of American commemorative coins, no figure loomed larger than that of Farran Zerbe, who promoted the 1903 Louisiana Purchase Exposition, 1904 and 1905 Lewis and Clark, and 1915 Panama–Pacific International Exposition coins. For the best part of three decades, from the early 1900s to the late 1920s, his "Money [or Moneys] of the World" exhibit was displayed at expositions, banks, and other places—accompanied by Zerbe, who had coins and souvenirs for sale and who sought to buy old and rare pieces of interest.

In 1883, as a 12-year-old newsboy in Tyrone, Pennsylvania, Zerbe began examining his pocket change. A "rare" 1883 Liberty Head nickel without CENTS captured his attention, launching his career in numismatics. In 1899 he published a booklet, *Just What You Should Know. Nut Shell Facts on Coins, Stamps, and Paper Money*. At about this time, Zerbe also began in numismatic business, trading as Coin Zerbe from his hometown of Tyrone. Just about anything that was interesting caught his eye. In the meantime, he bought, sold, and traded coins. In May 1901 he stated that he had acquired a hoard of 4,000 Civil War tokens and store cards. During that decade he traveled extensively, visited various mints, wrote stories and travelogues for *The Numismatist*, engaged in research (mostly of a superficial nature), and set up his "Money of the World" exhibit, which grew in size each year.

In 1904, at the Louisiana Purchase Exposition (popularly called the St. Louis World's Fair), Zerbe distributed the 1903-dated commemorative gold dollars with portraits of Jefferson and McKinley, accompanied by puffery and investment claims.

The following year, 1905, he was at the Lewis and Clark Exposition in Portland, Oregon, again setting up a display and again selling commemorative gold dollars. In April the next year, he headed south to San Francisco, where he visited the Mint and stopped by to see collectors, leaving the city just before the earthquake. At the Mint he obtained facts relating to the 1873-S dollar (of which no examples are known today) and the rare 1894-S dime, but never disclosed the information in print. Today, mysteries still surround these two coins.

In September 1907 he was elected president of the ANA at the Columbus (Ohio) convention. After the death on June 16, 1908, of Dr. George F. Heath, founder of *The Numismatist*, Zerbe visited the executor of the Heath estate and made a deal to acquire the magazine for his personal profit—a move that incurred much criticism. By that time, Zerbe had also been scored for his wild claims and hyperbole in selling commemoratives, especially the 1903 gold dollars (at $3 each), which had fallen sharply in value. He was implicated in a few other messy situations in subsequent years, including charges of rigging the ANA election in 1909 to benefit his friend, J.M. Henderson. In 1910, finding the operation of *The Numismatist* not to be what he expected, he sold it to W.W.C. Wilson, who donated it to the ANA.

While enmity toward Zerbe continued, by the early 1920s his reputation had recovered, a new generation of collectors was on hand, and he was recognized as a member of the old guard. During the decade he traveled widely, setting up his display at banks. Then in autumn 1928 his "Money of the World" collection was sold to the Chase National Bank (New York City), which named Zerbe as its curator.

On December 25, 1949, Zerbe died at his home in New York, and was widely mourned. Later, the ANA named its highest honor, the Farran Zerbe Award, after him. His "Money of the World" exhibit was donated by the Chase Manhattan Bank (as it came to be known) to the American Numismatic Society and the Smithsonian Institution.

The publication in 1981 of a fine book by Anthony Swiatek and Walter H. Breen, *The Encyclopedia of United States Silver and Gold Commemorative Coins 1892–1954*, helped a bit, but prices remained in the cellar. Again, it was a good time to *buy*. In 1982 the Mint issued the first new commemoratives since 1954, which were struck to observe the 250th anniversary of the birth of George Washington. These sold moderately well, but not like hotcakes. The seeds for new interest were thus sown, and in ensuing years dozens of new commemoratives would come on the market, with a new generation of buyers. Grading continued to be very erratic.

1980s, Late: At Last, a Sure-Thing Investment! Commemorative coins, especially those certified by PCGS and NGC, were a natural for investors just entering the market. Absolutely and positively nothing could go wrong. The opportunity of opportunities existed to get in on the ground floor. With a precise grade on the holder and with "bid" and "ask" prices, these were blue chips par excellence, it seemed. Merrill Lynch and other stock-market people raced into the field with limited partnerships. With this kind of action, hundreds of millions (or even billions) of dollars of "Wall Street money" would soon be showering down upon those fortunate enough to own coins! Curiously, and, of course, nowhere mentioned in any investment brochures that I have ever seen, *collectors* stopped buying, and many cashed in their collections. The situation was like that in the Netherlands in 1634, when tulip bulbs were hot on the market and were being bought and sold with excitement and ever-escalating prices, but no *gardeners* were among the purchasers (see pages 142–144).

1990s: The Party Ends, the Band Goes Home, and the Lights Are Turned Out. "Investment-grade" coins in many series crashed, often to fractions of their former listings. Collectors didn't mind, for once

again commemoratives were affordable for numismatic purposes. In many instances, new (since 1982) commemoratives slumped to below-issue prices.

2000s: Bifurcation. Commemoratives continue in a slump market, this being especially true for such worthwhile (in my opinion) grades as MS-63 and -64. Higher grades are more active, and "ultra grades" with low populations have a boom of their own, quite separate from what MS-63 coins are doing—a bifurcated market, so to speak. Not that you asked, but I think there are many fine buys in grades among MS-63 and -64 coins and for selected MS-65 pieces. As to higher grades, I'd be careful—*very* careful—and if you have some "rare" MS-68 to -70 issues, consigning them to an auction might be a good idea.

Market Swings and Cycles

The preceding chronology details some of the ups and downs, the passions and lulls, for commemoratives. The following are actual market prices for several commemoratives, including the first issue, the 1892 Columbian half dollar, and how those prices have fared since each was first issued. As there was no price distinction between an extensively bagmarked coin and a gem in the early days, until about the 1970s, the early prices are simply "Mint State." A connoisseur years ago would have acquired a gem, whereas a typical collector may have bought one with many marks. The prices are those I tracked for my 1991 study, *Commemorative Coins of the United States: A Complete Encyclopedia*, plus the latest figures from the 2006 edition of the *Guide Book* (published in 2005).

As to what conclusions to draw, here are some of mine. Years ago, for buyers who selected coins that later were considered gems, connoisseurship paid. Such buyers were in the minority before the advent of certified grading in the late 1980s. I have always encouraged such connoisseurship, and those who followed my advice did well.

After the founding of PCGS in 1986 and NGC in 1987, commemoratives became a very popular investment vehicle. In 1990 they rode a crest, and prices have not recovered since that time. The best time to buy commemoratives is in a quiet market.

These market situations are unique to commemoratives. An analysis of the bellwether 1794 cent would show a steady upward march; bullion gold would reflect different trends; and a key 1909-S V.D.B. cent would be different still.

1892 World's Columbian Exposition Half Dollar

1892, issue price: $1

1895 (things are terrible)—these halves can be found for face value in circulation!)—MS-60 to -65: 55¢

1900 (market asleep)—MS-60 to -65: 60¢ to $1

1905 (market down, commemoratives out of favor)—MS-60 to -65: 60¢ to $1

1910 (market quiet)—MS-60 to -65: 60¢ to $1

1915 (market quiet)—MS-60 to -65: 55¢ to $1

1920 (market lukewarm)—MS-60 to -65: 75¢

1925 (market warming up)—MS-60 to -65: 75¢

1930 (market very quiet)—MS-60 to -65: 75¢

1935 (market at start of boom)—MS-60 to -65: $1

1936 (summer, height of market boom)—MS-60 to -65: $1.25

1940 (bottom of a market cycle)—MS-60 to -65: $1

1945 (market strong)—MS-60 to -65: $1.25

1950 (market beginning to heat up)—MS-60 to -65: $1.25

1955 (market in growth phase)—MS-60 to -65: $2

1960 (market at start of upswing)—MS-60 to -65: $4

1965 (market peak)—MS-60 to -65: $6

1970 (market quiet)—MS-60 to -65: $8

1975 (market quiet)—MS-60 to -65: $25

1980 (height of "silver-market boom," softening setting in)—MS-60 to -65: $160

1985 (grading interpretations vary widely)—MS-63 to -65: $280

1986 (market warming up, PCGS founded)—MS-60: $80; MS-63: $175; MS-64: $380; MS-65: $1,300

1990 (spring, height of "Wall Street money" boom)—MS-60: $75; MS-63: $490; MS-64: $1,500; MS-65: $5,000 (Wow! Can you believe it?)

1990 (December, "Wall Street" boom is fading fast)—MS-60: $55; MS-63: $325; MS-64: $800; MS-65: $3,200

2004 (market rather quiet)—MS-60: $30; MS-63: $75; MS-65: $875

Lewis and Clark $1 gold piece.

1905 Lewis and Clark Gold $1

1905, issue price: $2 and $2.50 (varied)

1910 (market quiet)—MS-60 to -65: $2.25

1915 (market quiet)—MS-60 to -65: $3

1920 (market lukewarm)—MS-60 to -65: $4.50

1925 (market warming up)—MS-60 to -65: $7

1930 (market very quiet)—MS-60 to -65: $12

1935 (market at start of boom)—MS-60 to -65: $12

1936 (summer, height of market boom)—MS-60 to -65: $13

1940 (bottom of a market cycle)—MS-60 to -65: $17

1945 (market strong)—MS-60 to -65: $45

1950 (market beginning to heat up)—MS-60 to -65: $45

1955 (market in growth phase)—MS-60 to -65: $120

1960 (market at start of upswing)—MS-60 to -65: $225

1965 (market peak)—MS-60 to -65: $400

1970 (market quiet)—MS-60 to -65: $320

1975 (market quiet)—MS-60 to -65: $960

1980 (height of "silver market boom," softening setting in)—MS-60 to -65: $5,500

1985 (grading interpretations vary widely)—MS-63 to -65: $2,250

1986 (market warming up, PCGS founded)—MS-60: $1,200; MS-63: $2,375; MS-64: $3,250; MS-65: $6,250

1990 (spring, height of "Wall Street money" boom)—MS-60: $1,400; MS-63: $5,200; MS-64: $14,000; MS-65: $40,000 (Once again, wow!)

1990 (December, "Wall Street" boom is fading fast)—MS-60: $1,600; MS-63: $4,000; MS-64: $9,250; MS-65: $21,000

2004 (market rather quiet)—MS-60: $850; MS-63: $2,500; MS-65: $16,500

1915-S Panama-Pacific Round $50 Gold

1915, issue price: $100

1920 (market lukewarm)—MS-60 to -65: $150

1925 (market warming up)—MS-60 to -65: MS-60 to -65: $450

1930 (market very quiet)—MS-60 to -65: $250

1935 (market at start of boom)—MS-60 to -65: $275

1936 (summer, height of market boom)—MS-60 to -65: $300

1940 (bottom of a market cycle)—MS-60 to -65: $300

1945 (market strong)—MS-60 to -65: $500

1950 (market beginning to heat up)—MS-60 to -65: $600

1955 (market in growth phase)—MS-60 to -65: $6,000

1960 (market at start of upswing)—MS-60 to -65: $2,650

1965 (market peak)—MS-60 to -65: $6,000

1970 (market quiet)—MS-60 to -65: $5,200

1975 (market quiet)—MS-60 to -65: $17,000

1980 (height of "silver market boom," softening setting in)—MS-60 to -65: $70,000

1985 (grading interpretations vary widely)—MS-63 to -65: $33,000

1986 (market warming up, PCGS founded)—MS-60: $30,500; MS-63: $39,000; MS-64: $40,000; MS-65: $44,000

1990 (spring, height of "Wall Street money" boom)—MS-60: $31,500; MS-63: $46,000; MS-64: $68,000; MS-65: $115,000 (Well, this is a high price, but this is one commemorative that held its value, more or less.)

1990 (December, "Wall Street" boom is fading fast)—MS-60: $27,000; MS-63: $38,000; MS-64: $54,000; MS-65: $95,000

2004 (market rather quiet)—MS-60: $33,000; MS-63: $49,000; MS-65: $105,000

1928 Hawaiian Sesquicentennial half dollar.

1928 Hawaiian Sesquicentennial Half Dollar

1928, issue price: $2

1930 (market very quiet)—MS-63: $8

1935 (market at start of boom)—MS-63: $8

1936 (summer, height of market boom)—MS-63: $12

1940 (bottom of a market cycle)—MS-60 to -65: $10

1945 (market strong)—MS-60 to -65: $30

1950 (market beginning to heat up)—MS-60 to -65: $30

1955 (market in growth phase)—MS-60 to -65: $95, 1960; (market at start of upswing)—MS-60 to -65: $480

1965 (market peak)—MS-60 to -65: $575

1970 (market quiet)—MS-60 to -65: $475

1975 (market quiet)—MS-60 to -65: $950

1980 (height of "silver market boom," softening setting in)—MS-60 to -65: $4,500

1985 (grading interpretations vary widely)—MS-63 to -65: $1,750

1986 (market warming up, PCGS founded)—MS-60: $1,100; MS-63: $1,800; MS-64: $3,000; MS-65: $5,750

1990 (spring, height of "Wall Street money" boom)—MS-60: $825; MS-63: $1,800; MS-64: $3,250; MS-65: $10,500

1990 (December, "Wall Street" boom is fading fast)—MS-60: $725; MS-63: $1,600; MS-64: $2,700; MS-65: $6,500

2004 (market rather quiet)—MS-60: $1,400; MS-63: $1,850; MS-65: $5,000

1935 With Small "1934" Boone Pair

1935, November, issue price: $3.70 the pair (one Denver and one San Francisco coin)

1936 (summer, height of market boom)—MS-60 to -65: $80

1940 (bottom of a market cycle)—MS-60 to -65: $30

1945 (market strong)—MS-60 to -65: $65

1950 (market beginning to heat up)—MS-60 to -65: $75

1955 (market in growth phase)—MS-60 to -65: $125, 1960; (market at start of upswing)—MS-63 $285

1965 (market peak)—MS-63 $325

1970 (market quiet)—MS-60 to -65: $275

1975 (market quiet)—MS-60 to -65: $710

1980 (height of "silver market boom," softening setting in)—MS-60 to -65: $2,500

1985 (grading interpretations vary widely)—MS-63 to -65: $1,200

1986 (market warming up, PCGS founded)—MS-60: $900; MS-63: $1,200; MS-64: $1,900; MS-65: $3,500

1990 (spring, height of "Wall Street money" boom)—MS-60: $575; MS-63: $760; MS-64: $1,400; MS-65: $2,300 (To me this was an okay price, as these are rare, but it fell afterward.)

1990 (December, "Wall Street" boom is fading fast)—MS-60: $440; MS-63: $800; MS-64: $1,125; MS-65: $1,900

2004 (market rather quiet)—MS-60: $550; MS-63: $670; MS-65: $1,730

1936 Cleveland Centennial Half Dollar

1936, issue price: $1.50

1936 (summer, height of market boom)—MS-63: $2

1940 (bottom of a market cycle)—MS-60 to -65: 85¢

1945 (market strong)—MS-60 to -65: $1.25

1950 (market beginning to heat up)—MS-60 to -65: $1.75

1955 (market in growth phase)—MS-60 to -65: $3.50

1960 (market at start of upswing)—MS-63: $5

1965 (market peak)—MS-63: $25

1970 (market quiet)—MS-60 to -65: $18

1975 (market quiet)—MS-60 to -65: $40

1980 (height of "silver market boom," softening setting in)—MS-60 to -65: $150

1985 (grading interpretations vary widely)—MS-63 to -65: $120

1986 (market warming up, PCGS founded)—MS-60: $115; MS-63: $225; MS-64: $500; MS-65: $1,000

1990 (spring, height of "Wall Street money" boom)—MS-60: $92; MS-63: $120; MS-64: $220; MS-65: $1,100 (Wow! Can you believe it!)

1990 (December, "Wall Street" boom is fading fast)—MS-60: $77; MS-63: $85; MS-64: $125; MS-65: $580

2004 (market rather quiet)—MS-60: $70; MS-63: $75; MS-65: $210

Summary

Well, you can see by now that commemorative coins are on a different playing field than, say, colonial coins! As I see it, these commemoratives are endlessly fascinating, but they cannot be bought effectively by reading market comments that they are hot and that you should jump in.

Instead, you need to think for yourself. The time to buy is when the market is slow. Then, the next time the market becomes unreal, you might consider selling—with the knowledge that, as there are generous supplies of most commemoratives around, you can buy back in for lower prices. This recommendation goes against my basic "buy carefully and hold for the long term" policy, but, what the heck, we all have a gambling streak, and this may be a good outlet!

In the meantime, as you buy commemoratives, take the time to read and other-

wise learn about the history and significance (if any) of each. In recent years Congress has been inundated with bills proposing such coins, accounts of which are carried regularly in *Coin World* and *Numismatic News*, with many opinions from collectors expressed in the letters-to-the-editor columns of those papers. I wonder what will be next?

Key to Collecting

- **Mint State coins:** The vast majority of commemoratives are found in Mint State today. The availability in different grade categories depends a lot on the original handling and distribution. Generally, the lower-mintage silver varieties from 1892 through 1928 range from scarce to rare in gem preservation, but with exceptions (such as the 1893 Isabella quarter, which is usually choice, and the Oregon Trail issues). Those from 1933 to 1954 vary, with some common as gems (such as 1936 York) and others usually heavily bagmarked (the Booker T. Washington and Carver-Washington issues are examples). Except for the 1904 and 1905 Lewis and Clark gold dollars, all early gold commemoratives (1903–1926) are usually seen in choice to gem Mint State. Modern commemoratives from 1982 to date are usually choice or gem quality, no problem.

- **Circulated coins:** Certain high-mintage early issues are plentiful in worn grades, these including the 1892 and 1893 Columbian issues and the 1923-S Monroe Doctrine. Generally, numismatists prefer Mint State coins, leaving the market for worn pieces to casual buyers.

- **Strike quality:** Varies widely, especially among early issues. The 1923-S Monroe Doctrine and 1926 Sesquicentennial halves, both from shallow-relief dies, are often unsatisfactory in appearance. The 1921 Alabama and

Oregon Trail Memorial commemorative half dollars were produced intermittently from 1926 through 1939, the longest run of any design in the series. A few years ago, members of the Society for U.S. Commemorative Coins voted for their favorite motif among commemorative issues from 1892 to date, and this was the winner. The designs were prepared by James Earle Fraser and his wife, Laura Gardin Fraser.

Missouri halves often have weak areas on the reverse. Nearly all modern (1982 to date) commemoratives are sharply struck. Issues must be studied on an individual basis.

- **Proof coins:** Scattered Proofs were made of certain classic commemoratives, most notably 50 Sand Blast Proofs recorded for the 1928 Hawaiian. Quite a few homemade (outside the Mint) "Matte Proofs" and "Sand Blast Proofs" are around, sometimes with impressive attestations by modern numismatists; in a word, *beware.* Proofs of modern commemoratives 1982 to date are available in choice and gem preservation in proportion to their mintages.

- **Key issues:** Among classic silver issues of 1892 to 1954: 1928 Hawaiian (rarest), 1935 Hudson Sesquicentennial, and 1935 Old Spanish Trail are the rarest *types.* Rare varieties include the 1922 Grant With Star (truly rare if truly gem!) and these, usually seen in high grades: 1935-D and -S Boone pair with small "1934," 1939 Arkansas set, 1938 Boone set, 1939 Oregon Trail set, and other low-mintage issues. Some others are rare only in gem grades. Among classic gold issues, the key gold dollars are 1904 and 1905 Lewis and Clark and the two varieties of 1915-S Panama-Pacific $50 piece.

- **Advice to smart buyers:** Buy carefully, checking for sharpness of strike (usually not a problem) and eye appeal. Use the Optimal Collecting Grade (OCG) concept if a coin in just a slightly higher grade has a much higher price. Commemoratives are especially susceptible to market cycles. Best to buy when the market is quiet, and while it is hot work on other areas of your collection.

- **Selected bibliography:**

Bowers, Q. David. 1991. *Commemorative Coins of the United States: A Complete Encyclopedia.* Wolfeboro, NH.

Bullowa, David M. 1938. *The Commemorative Coinage of the United States 1892–1938.* New York, NY.

Mosher, Stuart. 1940. *United States Commemorative Coins, 1892–1939.* New York, NY.

Slabaugh, Arlie. 1975. *United States Commemorative Coins: The Drama of America as Told by Our Coins.* Racine, WI.

Swiatek, Anthony, and Walter Breen. 1981. *The Encyclopedia of United States Silver and Gold Commemorative Coins 1892–1954.* New York, NY.

Taxay, Don. 1967. *An Illustrated History of U.S. Commemorative Coinage.* New York, NY.

CHAPTER TWENTY-THREE

COLLECTING PATTERN COINS

Collectors and investors alike can profit by investigating the background and history of the coins they buy. Coins are a mirror of history and art, telling the story of mankind over the past 2,600 years and reflecting the economic struggles, wars, prosperity, and creativity of every major nation on earth. We are but the custodians of these historical relics; we must appreciate and care for them while they are in our possession. Those who treat rare coins with the consideration and respect they deserve will profit in many ways, not the least of which can be in the form of a sound financial return on one's investment of time and money.

—Kenneth E. Bressett (*A Guide Book of United States Coins*)

Classes of Pattern Coins

In the American series, pattern coins tell the story of what might have been in coinage, but wasn't. Such coins include ideas that were proposed by congressmen, citizens, or Mint officials, made into coins, examined, considered, and then rejected. In addition, many pieces were produced especially for sale to numismatists.

All told, more than 1,800 different varieties of pattern coins exist from 1792 to date. These are typically classified by Judd numbers, from J. Hewitt Judd, M.D., *United States Pattern Coins: Experimental and Trial Pieces*, published by Whitman. Also popular are Pollock numbers, from Andrew W. Pollock III, *United States Patterns and Related Issues*. Both of these texts are essential for serious collectors— the first giving basic information on history and rarity as well as market prices and certification data, and the second emphasizing history, rarity, and historical appearances, but not current values. The shorthand notation of, say, J-208 (a Judd number) or P-1201 (a Pollock number) is the key to a piece's date, denomination, variety, metal, and other aspects when checked in the appropriate book. Saul Teichman's www.uspatterns.com web site contains many pictures and much useful information.

There is a great deal of camaraderie and sharing of information among collectors of patterns, a nice situation for everyone involved. Although much if not most is already known about technical details and specifications, hardly a month goes by without some new discovery or observation.

Most patterns are rare, and some are extremely so. Interestingly, several of the more plentiful varieties have been adopted into the regular American series and are listed in the *Guide Book* and other standard texts. Due to the increased demand for these particular varieties, they have become much more expensive than the rarer issues found only in the Judd and Pollock books! Examples of patterns that bask in the glow of popular *Guide Book* listings include the 1856 Flying Eagle cent, the 1859 and 1860 transitional half dimes and dimes, the 1838 Gobrecht silver dollar, and the beautiful $4 gold Stellas of 1879 and 1880.

Patterns, first made at the Philadelphia Mint in 1792, were produced intermittently until about 1836, after which time activity increased dramatically, and many different ones were made through 1885. Then followed a period of sparse activity, until 1896, when many patterns were produced for one-cent and five-cent pieces. After that time, and continuing to the present day, patterns have been made occasionally, but most have not been distributed to collectors. In the majority of situations, not even an example was made available to the Smithsonian Institution, repository of the National Coin Collec-

A splendid 1882 pattern Liberty Head nickel, Judd-1690, of the exact type of the famous 1883 without CENTS, but dated a year earlier. Although the rarity at the tail-end of the series, the famous 1913, has been the focus of a lot of attention, relatively few people are aware of the 1882 that precedes the series. Perhaps several dozen exist of J-1690. In the 1960s one of these, all by itself in solitary splendor at the Central States Numismatic Society convention, took the first-prize ribbon!

A trial striking in copper of a 1794 half dime, Judd-15. This was probably made to study the design and die intricacies, or perhaps to adjust the press for striking regular issues. Few records exist relating to early patterns, and today much in print is conjecture.

tion (current name for what used to be called the *Mint Cabinet*, then the *Mint Collection*).

Occasionally, some pieces have sold privately to benefit Mint officials and others (these including gold $20 pieces of 1907), and a few 1916 pattern coins found their way into collectors' hands. However, for all practical purposes, the latest-dated patterns widely available are those of 1896. In addition, in modern times some patterns or test pieces with fantasy designs and inscriptions, made to illustrate concepts such as clad metal, and with no relation to anticipated or current designs, have found their way out of the Mint or private contract firms and into the hands of collectors. Included are a number of pieces with the portrait of Martha Washington.

With relatively few exceptions, from the 19th century up to the present day, very little factual information concerning patterns has been made available by the Mint for the general public. If I were secretary of the Treasury (which, of course, I am not, nor will I ever be), I would direct the Mint to (a) keep a record of models, pattern strikings, and the like for current statehood quarters, new nickels, and other issues, (b) make illustrations and information available to numismatic publications, and (c) place specimens with the Smithsonian, the American Numismatic Society, and the American Numismatic Association—the three leading nonprofit numismatic museums.

Today, the various pieces listed in the Judd and Pollock books are collectively referred to as *patterns*. Let's get technical, at least for a few paragraphs. Patterns can be divided into several categories, some overlapping. Some are not even patterns at all, as the following paragraphs will attest.

Basic Pattern Coins

In its most basic form, a pattern is a coin made to test a proposal or design (or a denomination, format, alloy, etc.) before such is either rejected or officially adopted for regular coinage. Examples include gold $4 Stellas made in 1879 to illustrate this proposed denomination; pattern 1879 dollars made in goloid alloy (a mixture of silver and gold); and pattern 1856 Flying Eagle cents made a year before the design was adopted for regular circulation.

While some patterns of higher-denomination coins were made in copper or aluminum instead of silver and gold, the most highly prized are struck in the standard metals of those denominations. All other things being equal (such as rarity, grade, and

A Gallery of "What Might Have Been"

Many pattern, trial, and experimental pieces are wildly different from the designs that would later be adopted for circulating coins. Others, such as the ones below, are similar enough that—at a quick glance—they appear to be regular issues.

Pattern

Regular issue

With a casual observation, this 1891 half dollar pattern (classified as J-1765 in Judd's *United States Pattern Coins*) might be a common Barber coin—one of millions struck around the turn of the 19th century. Look closer, though: each star on the obverse has five points, rather than six. The differences on the reverse are even more evident: the design is busier, with a wreath of oak surrounding a much smaller eagle, and clouds above. The shield is also smaller, and the stars are tightly spaced stars.

A Barber half dollar of 1892, the first year of issue, will cost you $500 in MS-60. No amount of money will buy you a pattern from the year before: of the type shown here, only two are known—and both reside in the Smithsonian Institution as national treasures.

Pattern

Regular issue

Look at the obverse, and this pattern (J-1565, struck in copper) might appear to be a regular 1878 Morgan dollar, worth $100 or so. Flip to its reverse, however, and the similarity ends: here we have the pattern design of Chief Engraver William Barber, not that of George T. Morgan. Barber's eagle, clutching a bundle of olive branches and arrows, perches with drooped wings. Instead of the words IN GOD WE TRUST appearing in Gothic letters, as on the regular-issue silver dollar of the same year, E PLURIBUS UNUM floats above the eagle. The lettering is different, and there is no wreath; this quite obviously is not a *Morgan* dollar.

The market values of such patterns reflect their rarity: Proof examples of J-1565 are worth between $7,000 (for PF-60) and $22,500 (for PF-65).

quality), a pattern half dollar of 1859, for example, is more valuable if struck in silver than if made in copper.

Trial Pieces

Trial pieces are coins struck from regular dies in metals other than what was intended under the coinage laws. Often, these were created as "fancy pieces" (see below) to provide coins for sale to numismatists. Examples include full Proof sets in aluminum of all denominations in 1868, 1872, 1885, and most other years from the mid-1860s through the mid-1880s. As an example, there was no intention of striking double eagles in aluminum for use in circulation, so such pieces can be described as fancy pieces, numismatic delicacies, or something similar.

On the other hand, in the early years of the Philadelphia Mint, some pieces were struck in lesser metals in order to test the dies or to verify a design. Such include copper strikings of certain 1794 and 1795 silver denominations.

Experimental Pieces

This category overlaps with pattern pieces and includes coins that were intended to test widely differing concepts from those in general use. In this classification are certain pattern cents of 1850 and 1884 with perforated centers, $5 half eagles struck on especially broad planchets (to create thinner coins that could not be hollowed out and filled with base metal—a popular fraud of that era), and an 1863 three-cent piece made in copper and the size of an old "large" cent.

Fancy Pieces

While most early pattern coins were made to test new designs, metals, and other concepts, the majority of those of 1836 to 1885 were made especially for the numismatic trade. After 1859, many dies for earlier patterns were used to make restrikes and novodels, the latter being obverse/reverse combinations that were never struck originally (called *mules* or *mulings* today). In particular, Mint directors James Ross Snowden and Henry R. Linderman, both of whom were numismatists, participated in the creation of curious and illogical pieces. The vast majority of patterns in existence today, and bearing dates from 1836 to 1839, were produced in 1859 or later years, including restrikes from early dies.

Such coins were nearly always made in secrecy, with few if any official records kept, and were quietly distributed through dealers who, like William K. Idler and John W. Haseltine of Philadelphia, had close connections with Mint officials. Much false information was disseminated by Mint officials, including denials of the making certain of these pieces. Every once in a while a concerned collector or dealer would go to the Mint and gain an interview with the superintendent or another staff member (such as W.E. DuBois, in-residence historian), and would be told that restrikes were no longer being made, and so on—this at times when such activity was going full speed ahead! One director even went so far as to say that in the late 1860s, all old dies had been destroyed. Some of these interviews, such as reported by S.K. Harzfeld and others in the early 1880s, are amusing to read today, but in their time the matter was very serious. Research conducted since 1950 has brought to light the truth relating to most of these issues, and they are properly delineated in the Judd and Pollock references. If this scenario is new to you, for an eye-opener, read *The United States Mint and Coinage: An Illustrated History From 1776 to the Present*, by Don Taxay (1966).

The "circumstances of birth" of a pattern are not particularly important to numismatists today, and the majority of the great rarities and expensive pieces fall into this category. We are glad all of them were made—otherwise the Judd and Pollock books would each be less than half their present sizes! Various terms have been devised to describe them in technical listings (rarely in offerings of coins for sale), including *fancy pieces, pièces de caprice,* and, my favorite, *numismatic delicacies.*

Some fancy pieces are later creations of varieties that were never made in original form, such as the combination in 1859 of dies made in the 1830s with other dies created in later times. These are the aforementioned novodels—coins struck at later dates (usually) from dies or in combinations never originally minted.

Market Significance of the Above

As to the financial significance of the above, the answer, in a word, is *nothing.* Today, patterns are collected for what they are—a given variety—and little attention is paid to the preceding classifications.

For a reality check I mention that, similarly, collectors of early American coins are not particularly concerned if a New York or Connecticut copper is an authorized issue of a particular state, or if it was secretly struck at the Machin's Mills private mint. As to novodels, collectors of early American coins know that a 1785 Vermont / IMMUNE COLUMBIA die combination never existed originally, and that examples were struck at Machin's Mills, which was not established until 1787 (but no one cares, so long as it is contemporaneous— that is, made in the general era in which such pieces were used).

I'm not trying to explain away something that is important, but to state how such coins are viewed by numismatists today. If you admire a certain human being, his or her accomplishments and circumstances of birth may be completely unimportant to you. If you have an inquisitive turn of mind, however, such details about an admired person or object may hold great interest for you.

Ways to Collect Pattern Coins

There is no one "right" way to collect pattern coins, and over the years many numismatists have developed their own formulas.[69] While a handful of enthusiasts have had the time, patience, and finances to collect one of every pattern they could find, the most popular discipline over the years has been to acquire pieces that are numismatic favorites, either by design or as part of related series. This is the same method used to collect certain other American series such as colonial coins, paper money of all eras, tokens, and medals.

Collecting With a Regular Series

Off-metal strikes furnish an interesting addition to a collection of regular-series coins. Thus, a specialist in Liberty Head or Coronet $10 gold coins of the late 19th century might well enjoy having a few strikings from Proof dies in aluminum or copper, rather than gold. Similarly, a collector of Indian Head cents might well enjoy owning an 1868 cent struck in aluminum (Judd-612), certainly an item that would bring great attention when shown to others.

For a long time, many specialists in Flying Eagle and Indian Head cents have found it a pleasant exercise to acquire related patterns, of which dozens of varieties exist. Indeed, sets of 12 different 1858 pattern die combinations became early stock-in-trade items for Mint officials. To these can be added pattern cents of 1859, the issues of 1864, and others.

Similarly, specialists in nickel five-cent pieces can find a vast panorama of interesting and often available pattern coins produced from the general era of 1865 to 1896, sometimes incorporating dies used for the Shield series (regularly struck 1866–1883) and the Liberty Head series (1883–1912), but often in combination with strictly pattern reverses never used for circulating coinage. The microcosm of Liberty Head pattern nickels of 1881 to 1883 is a delightful study in themselves.

Collectors of Fractional Currency paper notes, issued by the Treasury Department in the 1860s and 1870s, may find the Postage Currency pattern coins of 1863 (J-325 to -330) to be of interest, as they were intended to be minted for the redemption of the early issues of Fractional Currency (called *Postage Currency*). However, such coins were never adopted for general use.

Numismatists who enjoy regular-issue half dollars have often added a display of patterns to their cabinets, sometimes acquiring dozens of specimens. R.E. Cox, Jr., a Texas numismatist and department-store owner, did precisely that. Similarly, Morgan silver dollar specialists have a wide variety of 1878 and 1879 patterns to choose from. For aficionados of the Morgan head of Miss Liberty, there are also pattern Morgan dimes, quarters, and half dollars with the same portrait. How interesting it is to display a "Morgan dime"!

In at least one series, that of twenty-cent pieces, there are far more varieties of patterns than there are of regular issues!

Trade dollars, first called *commercial dollars*, were made to the extent of dozens of patterns from 1871 to 1873, plus a few scattered later issues, and form a fascinating complement to a regular collection. One client of mine, Harry W. Bass, Jr., loved regular-issue $3 gold coins, and to go with them he endeavored to acquire every pattern coin he could find of the same denomination. Another fine client, Richard Salisbury, focused on $3 patterns as well.

Transitional Patterns

Transitional patterns consist of pieces bearing obverse and reverse designs in the same combination as used for regular coinage, but dated before regular coinage commenced. These pieces are, in essence, the pattern coins from which the designs were adopted.

The most famous of all transitional patterns is the 1856 Flying Eagle cent (Judd-180), struck from the design adopted on February 21, 1857, but dated a year before, and today costing well over $20,000 for a choice Proof example. (By the way, nearly all Proofs of Flying Eagle cents are restrikes made from 1856-dated dies at a later time, after spring 1859, but this has no effect on the market value of such pieces.)

Immediately preceding the regular 1857 Flying Eagle cent is this transitional pattern of 1856, Judd-180. About 2,000 are estimated to exist today. Listed in the Guide Book, this variety is incredibly popular—and has been ever since the cradle days of American numismatics in the late 1850s.

An 1872 commercial dollar pattern, Judd-1212. This was the term for what became known as the trade dollar when this new denomination was authorized by the Coinage Act of 1873. The commercial dollar, which evolved into the trade dollar, was the brainchild of John Jay Knox, comptroller of the currency in the Treasury Department. Knox, an enthusiastic numismatist, was the architect of the far-reaching but later much misunderstood 1873 legislation.

The 1858 Indian Head cent, Judd-208, is another nice and fairly scarce transitional. Most exist in lower Proof levels (Proof-60 to -63). The 1859 Indian Head cent with oak wreath and shield reverse, or type of 1860 (J-228), is another transitional—much rarer than the 1856 Flying Eagle, but a gem costs only a couple thousand dollars or so! The reason is that the 1856 is listed in the *Guide Book* and other references, but the 1858 and 1859 are not. Then there is the 1863 bronze transitional pattern cent (J-299), also inexpensive by comparison to the 1856 Flying Eagle.

In the Shield nickel series there are 1865-dated nickels with the shield obverse and With Rays and Without Rays reverses, plus the 1866 Without Rays, a suite of three coins that make a very nice addition to a regular set of the denomination. The 1882 Liberty Head nickel Without CENTS (J-1690) is similar in design to the famous 1883 issue made for circulation, and is thus is a transitional pattern (see illustration at the beginning of this chapter).

Quarter, half dollar, and dollar patterns of 1863, 1864, and 1865 exist with the motto IN GOD WE TRUST on the reverse, as regularly adopted in 1866 (the 1863 and 1864 issues were not made until the late 1860s, at which time they were struck to provide coins for collectors).[70]

Favorite Pattern Designs

Perusing through the Judd or Pollock pattern texts will acquaint you with many different designs, some of which may be attractive to your eye, some of which may not be.

Among patterns that have been collected simply because they are beautiful and interesting to own are such issues as the 1872 "Amazonian" quarter, half dollar, and dollar; the elegant series of 1877 half dollars; 1879 "Schoolgirl" dollar; and the 1882 "Shield Earring" quarter, half dollar, and dollar, among many others.

At the Eliasberg Collection sale I recall that a bidder set his eye on just one pattern, as it had a story (yet another reason

Immediately preceding the regular 1859 Indian Head cent with laurel wreath reverse is this transitional pattern of 1858, Judd-208. A few hundred pieces are known to exist today. Interestingly, J-208 can be found in several different die varieties, with variations in the placement of the date on the obverse and the number of leaves in the reverse wreath.

Immediately preceding the regular 1860 Indian Head cent with oak wreath and shield reverse is this transitional pattern of 1859, Judd-228. A few hundred pieces are known to exist today, nearly all of which are in Mint State (not Proof format, as might be expected).

An 1865 pattern half dollar, Judd-430, with the motto IN GOD WE TRUST on the reverse, dated one year before the motto was regularly used on this denomination.

Related Designs and Techniques

Pattern half dollar of 1877 by George T. Morgan, Judd-1512. It can be fascinating to trace the inter-relationship of designs across the spectrum of pattern coins and regular issues, identifying motifs that recur here and there, sometimes unexpectedly.

The portrait on this and certain other half dollars of 1877 was used on Morgan's regular-issue silver dollar of 1878. On this pattern note the technique of separating the border lettering by placing it outside of a circular border. On the reverse, note the perched eagle on a cartouche.

In 1878 Mint Director Richard H. Linderman used Morgan's head of Miss Liberty, first employed on pattern half dollars in 1877, to be the motif on the new regular silver dollar.

A 1936 Columbia (SC) Sesquicentennial commemorative half dollar, a regular issue, not a pattern, utilizing a circular border to separate the outermost lettering.

If at first you don't succeed, try, try again! And, that is what Morgan did. Here we see, finally, his perched eagle on a cartouche used on a coin struck in large numbers, having escaped from its status of being only a pattern. The coin is the 1915-S commemorative quarter eagle made for the Panama-Pacific Exposition held in San Francisco that year.

The famous and beautiful "Schoolgirl" pattern silver dollar by George T. Morgan, Judd-1608, utilizes on the reverse a perched eagle on a cartouche, borrowed from his 1877 pattern half dollar.

to acquire a favorite pattern): the "ugly duckling" three-cent piece of 1849 (J-113 and -114), depicting on one side simply a 3 and on the other the Roman numeral III. The "because I like it" incentive to buy a pattern may be one of the best reasons of all!

Other Sets and Specialties

Patterns themselves offer the opportunity to form sets and subsets of pieces of interest. Here are a few suggestions beyond those already mentioned:[71]

Denomination type set—One of each pattern denomination in the *regular denominations* from the half cent to the $20 piece, or, if you are bold, include the pattern-only denominations of the $4 Stella and 1877 $50 piece. Metals of striking can be mixed or matched. A complete denomination set would include the half cent, cent, two-cent piece, nickel three-cent piece, silver trime, half dime, nickel five-cent piece, dime, twenty-cent piece, quarter dollar, half dollar, silver dollar, trade or commercial dollar, and gold dollar, and the $2.50, $3, $4, $5, $10, $20, and $50 pieces.

Year set—Pick a favorite year and endeavor to obtain as many different patterns as possible, in terms of either die combinations or (simpler) an example of each individual die. Two well-known numismatists, Harry X Boosel and Roy Harte, each specialized in patterns of the year 1873. The CEO of the Heath Company, makers of candy, commissioned me to build for him a collection of patterns of 1872, the year his company was founded. The centennial year of 1876 has been a favorite for several others, and the patterns of 1877 have been a specialty for at least two numismatists, possibly three.

Coins from an era—Patterns from the Civil War era (1861–1865) may form a specialty. Or, patterns from the era of the great "silver question" of political importance, the 1870s through the 1890s, when silver (in particular) became a political hot potato, but with gold advocates and paper money

adherents each voicing their own opinions. Or, coins from a particular presidential administration might be a challenge.

Favorite engraver—Concentrate on patterns from the hand of a favorite engraver—Christian Gobrecht, James B. Longacre, George T. Morgan, or another—and collect examples of his work, adding to your enjoyment by learning of his life and background.

Standard Silver set—Review the Standard Silver listings of 1869 and 1870, with a few of 1871. Assembling an example of each die pair can be a fascinating challenge. Or, you can focus upon certain issues and obtain suites of six of the same pair (silver, copper, and aluminum, each with reeded or plain edge).

"Story" coins—Form an exhibit of patterns with emphasis on the odd and curious—design mistakes as on the 1875 twenty-cent piece and trade dollar with the illogical illustration of a ship with its auxiliary sails billowing forward and the smoke from its stack trailing to the rear, or strange situations such as the absence of UNITED STATES OF AMERICA from a coin (or the opposite: its presence on both sides).

You can also simply collect and study. While it always desirable to own pattern coins, a lot of enjoyment can be derived from simply studying them—or studying many patterns while owning relatively few. Among my numismatic acquaintances, Harry W. Bass, Jr., and Rogers M. Fred, Jr., each studied patterns in detail, while owning fine collections of them. In contrast, Saul Teichman and Andrew W. Pollock III have been collectors of *information*, but have not formed extensive cabinets. I can say the same thing for myself—I have a small handful of patterns, nothing particularly rare or valuable, but I love to *study* patterns.

Collecting and Enjoying Patterns

In summary, people collect pattern coins because they enjoy owning them, there

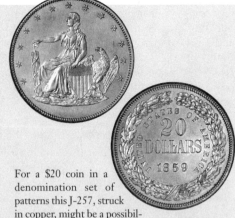

For a denomination type set, to illustrate the one-cent piece this Judd-186 (enlarged) is one of many candidates. Like all patterns, it invites study. The obverse depicts the portrait of Miss Liberty similar to that used on the regular-issue nickel three-cent piece of 1857. The reverse die seems to have been hastily made up, with too much separation between ONE and CENT.

For a $20 coin in a denomination set of patterns this J-257, struck in copper, might be a possibility. The motifs are by Anthony C. Paquet, an assistant engraver on the Mint staff since 1857. No $20 coins of this design, or even close to it, were ever made for general circulation.

A possible candidate for a "favorite engraver" collection is this pattern half dollar of 1838 by Christian Gobrecht, Judd-72. This coin was a favorite with collectors in the 19th century, and many restrikes were made beginning circa 1859. Originals weigh about 208 grains while restrikes, using planchets on hand per the Act of February 21, 1853, used lighter weight planchets of the then-current (1859) standard, 192 grains. Today, students of patterns study weights and other characteristics to try to determine when they were made—often in years other than those marked on the dies.

"Standard Silver" pattern coins, as they were called, were produced in profusion beginning in 1869. Shown here is a half dollar, design by Chief Engraver James B. Longacre, Judd-744. For most die combinations of different denominations, six different varieties were made: copper, aluminum, and silver strikings, each metal with plain edge or reeded edge.

This lovely "Indian Princess" pattern silver dollar, Judd-1010, by Chief Engraver James B. Longacre has interesting aspects. First, there is no name of the issuing country—no UNITED STATES OF AMERICA. Second, it has his surname, LONGACRE, spelled out in full, in the field below the lower right of the seated figure. Third, as Longacre had died on January 1, 1869, he never lived to see this coin.

are no rules as to the best way to form a display. Most series of patterns contain pieces that are readily available as well as others that are unique or will not be found during a collector's lifetime. Thus there is the thrill of the chase for the latter.

No one has ever completed a full set of 1877 pattern half dollars, although a number have tried, and a good "score" is to get at least 10, with 15 or more being truly remarkable. Picking up a familiar analogy, it is like playing a round of golf—no one ever gets a perfect score of 18, but it is fun to try, and a score in the 80s or even the 90s can be a worthy accomplishment.

A comforting aspect of collecting patterns is their inherent value: All patterns are scarce, many are rare, and many others are exceedingly rare. However, as the vast majority of American numismatists do not

Augustus Saint-Gaudens as photographed circa 1905, when he was beginning his planning for what evolved into the MCMVII (1907) High Relief double eagle.

Sketch-model for the obverse of the $20 gold coin, with the artist's notes: "head higher," "shield lower," and so on. The final version omitted the wings on the standing figure and also the shield.

Fame, as she is known, an element of the *Sherman Victory* statuary group, here shown as a small model. This figure formed the basis for the double eagle of 1907. (Courtesy of the Saint-Gaudens National Historic Site, Cornish, NH)

The final version of Saint-Gaudens' masterpiece, the MCMVII High Relief struck for general circulation in December 1907—and today a collectors' favorite.

know of the series, it is possible to obtain coins for which only a half a dozen or a dozen pieces exist, and for prices that are but tiny fractions of the cost of pattern varieties that have been widely popularized by listings in the *Guide Book*.

Key to Collecting

- **Mint State coins:** Although some pattern coins were struck in Mint State (with lustrous rather than mirror surfaces), this being particularly true for those dated before 1836, for the *original* 1856 Flying Eagle cent, the 1859 transitional Indian Head cent, the 1860 transitional half dime, and a few others, most patterns were made in Proof format.

- **Circulated coins:** Not particularly relevant to the field of patterns, as most are of Proof finish and not worn. However, most pre-1836 patterns show light wear. A few stray pieces in the later series—patterns that have been spent—do as well.

- **Strike quality:** Varies considerably over the series. Many have areas of weak striking at the centers or elsewhere. Many Proofs are from incompletely finished dies and show extensive raised striae, or crisscrossed lines (as on many Standard Silver issues of 1868–1870), or are otherwise less than perfect strikes. However, in nearly all instances *this is moot*, for all patterns of a given variety are likely to be that way! Either a variety exists with FD (Full Details) or it doesn't. Accordingly, from the standpoint of striking, you take what you are dealt.

- **Proof coins:** Most patterns are with Proof finish. The degree of die polish varies considerably from issue to issue, but within a given variety all are apt to be the same. Accordingly, all 1838 Gobrecht dollars have highly polished Proof fields, but all 1850

pattern cents have die striae and only partially mirror surfaces. Some copper Proofs were bronzed at the Mint, and were issued with rich chocolate-brown surfaces, this being particularly true of certain varieties of the early 1860s.

- **Key issues:** Just about all are key issues.

- **Advice to smart buyers:** Buy slowly. Be sure coins you consider have excellent eye appeal (you can be forgiven for an ultra rarity that presents a once-in-a-decade opportunity, but otherwise stick to this rule!). Copper coins in particular can be spotted, recolored, or have other problems. Remember, you will never be able to buy one of everything, so make sure that what you do buy is choice. Also, the prices of patterns can vary widely, depending on the seller or the auction sale. The market for patterns is not as deep at the high end, so be careful when considering expensive varieties. In general, popular or famous designs such as Gobrecht dollars, the Amazonian patterns of 1872, the half dollars of 1877, and so on, have more solid values and much greater demand than do off-metal strikings or unusual die combinations of designs that are not artistically pleasing. Auction catalogs of the past decade and their prices realized can be helpful guides. It will pay to consult with trusted dealers and specialists if you are uncertain.

- **Selected bibliography:**
Akers, David W. 1975. *United States Gold Patterns.* Racine, WI.

Judd, J. Hewitt. 2005. *United States Pattern Coins* (9th ed.; Q. David Bowers, editor). Atlanta, GA.

Pollock, Andrew W., III. 1994. *United States Patterns and Related Issues.* Wolfeboro, NH.

CHAPTER TWENTY-FOUR

COLLECTING TERRITORIAL AND PRIVATE GOLD COINS

With the bustling world about us and the ever-changing dire panorama of economic reality, crime, depersonification of the individual, loss of traditional old-time values and so on, it is indeed comforting to know that a hobby such as numismatics provides fellowship, a fascinating challenge, the opportunity for research and new discoveries, and, if investment must be mentioned, a good track record of long-term performance.

—Robert K. Botsford, November 1935

The Story of Territorial and Private Gold

The expansion of American territory was aided and sometimes defined by the discovery of gold. Prominent in the scenario is the California Gold Rush, inaugurated after John Marshall's finding of a nugget at Sutter's Mill on the American River, California, on January 24, 1848. Tens of thousands of adventurers went to the west, and in 1850 California became a state. Now the Union extended from sea to shining sea. Meanwhile, in San Francisco and other cities many different gold coins were struck by minters whose histories today range from well known to obscure.

Earlier, gold discoveries in Georgia and North Carolina in the 1820s onward provided metal in the 1830s for the private coinages of Templeton Reid and, more extensively, Christopher Bechtler and his family. The "Pikes Peak or Bust" gold rush of 1859 spawned the private mint of Clark, Gruber & Co. in Denver. In Salt Lake City the Mormons had their own mint, which turned out gold denominations from $2.50

Miners working in a stream in California. The rush for gold began in spring 1848, attracted thousands from the East and elsewhere in 1849, and expanded until the peak year of production, 1853. At that time, an estimated $60,000,000 in gold was extracted annually. The Gold Rush declined after about 1857, by which time production was mostly in the hands of large companies, not individual miners or groups.

The signature coin of the California Gold Rush is the octagonal $50 gold "slug." This is an 1851 variety bearing the imprint AUGUSTUS HUMBERT UNITED STATES ASSAYER OF GOLD CALIFORNIA around the border. Such coins were made by the thousands and were plentiful in commerce. However, within a decade most had disappeared. Today, such pieces, nearly all of which show evidence of circulation, are highly prized by numismatists.

to $20, the latter preceding the federal coin of the same denomination. In the Pacific Northwest, the Oregon Exchange Company produced coins. Such are variously referred to today as *private, pioneer,* or *territorial* gold issues.

Today all of these coins are scarce, and many are extremely rare. Each has a rich measure of history lending to its appreciation. Over a long period of time I have been involved in the purchase and sale of most of the varieties in the series, in connection with the Garrett (The Johns Hopkins University), Clifford, Norweb, and Eliasberg collections, and other offerings, as well as the distribution of the treasure from the *S.S. Central America.*[72]

Although a basic display of one or two dozen examples of territorial and private gold coins can be assembled for under several thousand dollars per coin, few readers of this text will form definitive collections. Instead, you can appreciate these history-laden issues by reading about them—as you would famous paintings in museums. That is what I do. I may never personally own a gold coin made by J.S. Ormsby, John Parsons, J.J. Conway, or the Pacific Company, but I can enjoy reading their history and, on occasion, cataloging them for auction presentation.

The Necessity for Private Mints

The United States government *eventually* established branch mints in or near gold districts such as Georgia (Dahlonega, 1838), North Carolina (Charlotte, 1838), California (San Francisco, 1854), and Colorado (Denver, 1906). Numismatists can be grateful that congressmen weren't in much of a hurry, for this provided ample opportunity in earlier years for the assaying and refining of gold and the striking of coins by private individuals, banks, and other commercial enterprises.

Such accounts as these (the first two from *Niles' Register* and relating to gold in the south, and the third from *Hunt's Merchant Magazine and Commercial Review* as part of a lengthy article on California)

stirred the imagination of the public and drew many to the gold districts:

August 18, 1827: Gold Mines. The Charleston papers state that a gold mine has been discovered in Union District, S.C. on the waters of Tyger River. The ore is said to be of such extent as to afford employment to 500 hands at good wages. A specimen of the gold has been pronounced by Dr. Cooper, equal in purity to any he ever saw. A company is expected to be formed to work the dust. It is asserted that the members of the company formed to work the gold mines of North Carolina, have divided, each $3,000.

June 5, 1830: Gold. It is said that 4,000 persons are engaged in gathering gold at the Yahoola mines, in the Cherokee country, and that their daily products are worth $10,000!!! At other mines, the daily value, for each hand, is put down at one dollar. The "gold region" appears very extensive—but as yet, notwithstanding, all that has been said of it, we much doubt if gold digging is as profitable as corn planting. Large lumps, worth from one to two hundred dollars, are occasionally met with.

January 1849: The Gold Region of California....One writer only is made eloquent, not so much by his subject, as by the fear of disbelief in the friend to whom he writes. "You are now all incredulous," he says, writing on the 10th September last, "you regard our statements as the dreams of an excited imagination; but what seems to you mere fiction, is stern reality. It is not gold in the clouds, or in the sea, or in the centre of a rock-ribbed mountain, but in the soil of California—sparkling in the sun, and glittering in its streams. It lies on the open plain, in the shadows of the deep ravine, and glows on the summits of the mountains, which have lifted for ages their golden coronets to heaven."...

In these and other districts, gold metal was plentiful in the form of dust and nuggets, but coins were scarce. Individuals and companies used the opportunity to receive precious metal from miners, refine and process it, and deliver stamped coins, taking a small percentage for their own profit.

The circumstances of minting were often primitive. We know that wagon wheels and scrap iron were used to make equipment to strike Oregon Exchange Company $5 and $10 coins in 1849, and that in Sacramento the coiner for J.S. Ormsby whacked the two dies together with a sledgehammer. One can only imagine what it would have been like to have visited the little mint set up by John Parsons in the Tarryall mining district of South Park in the Rocky Mountains.

Only a few of these enterprises seem to have eked out a profit, as it required nearly full bullion value to make a coin, and even then there was the possibility that some newspaper might accuse the proprietors of counterfeiting or fraud. In the face of these and other adversities the private mints did manage turn out a stream of coins for the benefit of miners and townspeople—and to the delight of collectors today.

Numismatic Interest

While the 1787 doubloon produced by Ephraim Brasher in New York City can be considered a private gold coin issue, numismatists and historians today primarily associate the field with the coinage produced from 1830 to 1861, including that by Templeton Reid in Georgia in 1830; the pieces produced by the Bechtlers in North Carolina beginning in the same year; the especially rich array of California gold issues of the period from 1849 to 1855; the 1849 $5 and $10 gold coins of Oregon; the Mormon coinage dated 1849 to 1860; and issues of Colorado from 1860 and 1861.

Jacob R. Eckfeldt and William E. DuBois, assayers and keepers of the Mint Cabinet in Philadelphia, studied and described various California, Mormon, and other gold coins as they were received in deposits for assay and testing, beginning in a significant way in 1849. These two men were probably the first to take a serious numismatic interest in the pieces.

In the general numismatic marketplace, interest in private gold coins was at least slight in the 1850s and 1860s, due in part to the fact that California and related pieces were being bought and sold by bullion exchange houses and listed in coin-value and bullion registers (such as *Thompson's*). However, apart from the Mint Cabinet holdings I am not aware of any systematic collection of them in this early era.

During the 1870s there were scattered offerings in auction sales. By 1877 the Spier Collection, which later passed to the Society of California Pioneers, contained many outstanding private and territorial pieces. Examples were numerous in auction sales of the late 19th century, but the coins were of sufficient scarcity and high value that interest was not widespread. No specialized numismatic reference works on the series were available for consultation or education, and little useful information about them appeared in print.

It was not until Edgar H. Adams delved into the subject in the early 1900s that activity grew apace. Adams's *Official Premium List of the United States, Private, and Territorial Gold Coins* appeared in 1909, to be followed in 1912 and 1913 by the publication in sections of his monumental *Private Gold Coinage of California, 1849–1855*. In more recent times, Walter Breen, Henry Clifford, John J. Ford, Jr., Donald Kagin, Dr. Nolie Mumey, Dan Owens, Dexter C. Seymour, and others have studied and written about the series. My 2002 book *A California Gold Rush History* is another addition to the field.

The close relationship of the privately minted gold coins of Colorado, California, and other areas with the people, economy, and romance of the times has made them favorites with numismatists today.

Private Mints in the South (1830–1852)

Coinage of Templeton Reid

Templeton Reid struck the first private gold coinage in July 1830 in Milledgeville, Georgia, and soon moved to Gainesville (in the same state) to be closer to the mines. His operation seems to have been successful at the outset, and the designs of the $2.50, $5, and $10 denominations consisted of little more than letters and numerals. However, he met an adversary in a local observer who styled himself anonymously as "No Assayer," and who felt that Reid was profiting too greatly by deducting a small amount for his efforts and thereby not delivering coins of full intrinsic value. A "trial by journalism" ensued in the newspapers, forcing Reid to close down. These Georgia issues are exceedingly rare today.

Later he may or may not have gone to California to strike coins, but in any event, dies were made, imprinted CALIFORNIA GOLD, of the $10 denomination of the curious $25. The first is unique and is held by the Smithsonian Institution. The second was unique at one time, but was stolen from the Mint Cabinet in 1858 and never recovered.

Bechtler Coinage

In 1830, Christopher Bechtler, a German immigrant, set up a private mint in Rutherfordton, North Carolina, in conjunction with an assay office. From then through 1852 he and his family, including August Bechtler, produced a wide variety of coins, simple in design, in denominations of $1, $2.50, and $5. Although some complaint was made of this issue by the Mint, no effort was ever made to close down the facility. It seems that Bechtler conducted his business carefully and endeavored to deliver gold coins of full value, less a modest charge for minting.

After the Act of June 28, 1834, which reduced the authorized weights of federal coins, several suggestions were made as to how the new coins could be identified. One of them was to imprint the date

Bechtler $5 gold coin with the imprint AUGUST 1. 1834. Bechtler was careful to have his gold coins be of full weight and value. This date reflects the change in the federal standard as of that date (under provisions of the Coinage Act of June 28, 1834).

August 1, 1834, on the issues. The Mint did not do this, but did use a different head of Miss Liberty and eliminated the motto E PLURIBUS UNUM on the reverse. In the meantime, Bechtler heard of this proposal. Certain of his $5 issues bear the inscription AUGUST 1. 1834, and are of the new authorized weight, reflecting his desire to adhere to current federal standards.

The Bechtler coinage was very successful, and coins from this mint found ready acceptance in commerce. The mint closed down in 1852. Today, the several denominations are readily collectible as types, but certain die combinations are rare. Typical grades are EF and AU, though (less often) low-range Mint State pieces are found. Some are bent or dented, as are many of the gold dollars.

California Gold Coins (1849–1855)

John Marshall's discovery of a gold nugget in the American River at Sutter's Mill on January 24, 1848, ignited the California Gold Rush, which soon changed the boundaries of the United States. The arrival of the Forty-Niners and others brought intense mining and commercial activity to the territory (which in 1850 became a state), but there weren't enough coins to facilitate transactions. The demand was filled by several major private coiners and a handful of lesser ones, who produced different gold coins in denominations from $1 to $50, but mostly of $5, $10, and $20 values.

Bearing such names as Moffat & Co., Miners' Bank, Pacific Co., Dubosq & Co.,

Baldwin & Co., and J.S.O. (for J.S. Ormsby), these coins circulated widely, especially in gambling parlors. After 1849 there was unfavorable publicity concerning certain coiners, and in spring 1851 a newspaper campaign was mounted against such coins (perhaps encouraged by Moffat & Co., dominant in the field at the time), after which time only a few companies engaged in minting.

Beginning in 1851, the facilities of Moffat & Co. were largely devoted to coinage under contract with the federal government, with coins bearing the name of Augustus Humbert, U.S. Assayer of Gold, California, and later (from the same source) the United States Assay Office of Gold. Most impressive were the large, octagonal $50 gold coins produced in 1851 and 1852.

Among later coiners, Wass, Molitor & Co. and Kellogg & Co. minted coins by the thousands, mostly of the large $20 and $50 denominations. Such issues were highly regarded by banks, merchants, and citizens.

The federal San Francisco Mint, successor in 1853 to the building and facilities of Moffat & Co., received its first gold on April 3, 1854, and struck its first coins, $20 pieces, on April 15. However, production did not keep up with demand, and in 1854 and 1855 such private coiners as Wass, Molitor & Co. and Kellogg & Co. continued to strike pieces for general commerce.

Private gold coins remained in general circulation in California through 1857 and 1858, after which time they were seldom seen. By the early 1860s a $50 coin was regarded as a curiosity in commercial channels.

Today, all private California gold coins are scarce, and most are rare. Nearly all show evidence of circulation in the particularly romantic Gold Rush era of American history, and are highly desired by numismatists. In addition, some gold ingots survive from this era and are greatly prized, most notably the pieces recovered from the *S.S. Central America*, sunk in 1857. Other than these treasure pieces, ingots are essentially noncollectible.

The N.G. & N. $5 gold coin of 1849 was produced in Benicia City, on San Francisco Bay, by Norris, Gregg & Norris (operated by representatives of a company that had come to the West from New York City, at which location they'd been prominent in the plumbing supply business). Such coins were in circulation by May 1849 and are considered to be the earliest of the California issues. Presumably, the dies were made in the East.

California Gold Rush Coins and Coiners

Norris, Gregg & Norris (San Francisco and Stockton, 1849–1850)

The leading contender for the title of "first California coiner" is the partnership of Norris, Gregg & Norris, composed of Thomas H. Norris, Charles Gregg, and Hiram A. Norris, New York City plumbing wholesalers and contractors. The entrepreneurs left their business in the hands of others and sailed for California. Presumably, they brought with them coining equipment and dies. In 1849, at a facility (details of which are not known today) at Benicia City, the firm issued $5 coins bearing the imprint of San Francisco. Produced in large quantities, these were highly esteemed in their time. In 1850 a few coins were issued with the imprint of Stockton; only one piece survives today.

Numismatic Notes. Several hundred of the 1849 $5 coins exist. These are usually well struck and very attractive.

Moffat & Co. (San Francisco, 1849–1853)

The firm of Moffat and Company was the most important of the California private coiners in the early period of the Gold Rush. The assay office they conducted became semi-official in character after 1850, when the Treasury Department named it as the facility for Augustus Hum-

Dies for this Moffat & Co. $10 gold coin of 1849 were cut by Albrecht Küner, a German immigrant who came to California in the same year. He went on to engrave dies for many other private gold coins as well as various medals. Moffat & Co. was the most prominent of the early San Francisco coiners.

bert and the U.S. Assay Office of Gold (which began operations in 1851).

The successors to this firm, Curtis, Perry and Ward, later sold their building for use as the San Francisco Mint. In early summer 1849, Moffat & Co. began to issue small, rectangular pieces of gold owing to a lack of coin in the locality, in values from $9.43 to $264, with the $16.00 value being issued in the largest quantity, as this was the trading value in San Francisco of a typical ounce of native gold. The dies for most of the Moffat coins made from 1849 to 1853 are believed to have been cut by a Bavarian immigrant, Albrecht Küner, who also made dies for other firms. The words MOFFAT & CO. appear on the coronet of Liberty instead of the word LIBERTY as in regular U.S. issues.

Numismatic Notes. Most of the Moffat & Co. basic denominations and types are collectible today and are among the more often encountered California Gold Rush coins.

Augustus Humbert, United States Assayer of Gold (San Francisco, 1851–1852)

Augustus Humbert, a New York watchcase maker, was appointed United States Assayer of Gold in San Francisco. Beginning in February 1851, he placed his name on octagonal $50 coins made at the facilities of Moffat & Co., which under Treasury Department auspices became a provisional government mint. The $50 gold piece was

accepted in general commerce (but not for customs duties) at par with standard U.S. gold coins; it was nicknamed variously a *slug* or an *adobe*, but was officially termed an *ingot*. The earliest issues have lettered edges and hand-stamped fineness (880 or 887) and value (50, representing dollars), and involved more than a dozen separate punching operations to create.

The dies were made by Charles Cushing Wright in New York City. By late spring 1851, the process was simplified, and later issues have Humbert's name and other information as part of the dies, these made by Albrecht Küner, and have reeded edges. It is likely that tens of thousands of these $50 coins were made, as evidenced by extensive mention of them in contemporary accounts.

Numismatic Notes. The early $50 "slugs" with lettered edge and hand-stamped notations are great classics and are among the most desired of all California coins. Later, more plentiful issues with reeded edges are desired as well, as are the $10 and $20 denominations.

Moffat and Humbert Issues (1852–1853)

Although most efforts of Augustus Humbert and the facilities of Moffat & Co. were devoted to the making of octagonal $50 coins in 1852, the need for smaller denominations prompted the firm to issue coins of $10 and $20 values. These are of varying designs, but in each instance incorporate the perched-eagle motif used on the $50 coins. In 1853, a $20 coin of the Liberty Head design was issued with the imprint of Moffat & Co. on the obverse coronet.

Numismatic Notes. These types, although rare, are collectible today.

United States Assay Office of Gold (San Francisco, 1852–1853)

Beginning in 1852 and continuing through 1853, most of the coins issued from the mint of Moffat & Co. bore the imprint of

United States Assay Office of Gold 1853 twenty-dollar gold piece, variety with 900 THOUS. Hundreds of thousands of these were produced, and at one time they were common in circulation in California. However, by the late 1850s most had been replaced by double eagles from the San Francisco Mint (which opened in spring 1854). Today, in the context of early California gold issues by private mints, this variety is one of the most frequently encountered, often in Mint State.

the United States Assay Office of Gold, this replacing the Augustus Humbert designation, although Humbert remained with the firm. The principals in the contract coinage were Curtis, Perry & Ward. The U.S. Assay Office of Gold issued denominations of $10, $20, and $50, the last being of the traditional octagonal format. Judging from specimens remaining today, the two most popular issues were the $20 piece of 1853 and the $50 piece of 1852. All denominations used the perched-eagle motif.

Numismatic Notes. Most of the basic types are collectible today, with the $20 piece of 1853 being the most often seen in the marketplace.

Joseph H. Bowie (San Francisco, 1849)

Joseph H. Bowie joined his cousins in San Francisco in 1849 and possibly produced a limited coinage of gold pieces. Little is known about this coining enterprise.

Numismatic Notes. Three hitherto unreported $5 gold coins were discovered by Paul Franklin in a single place in the 1950s and have been publicized in recent years.

An 1849 Cincinnati Mining & Trading Co. $10 gold coin. Only seven of these are known, making them a true rarity.

Cincinnati Mining & Trading Co. (1849)

The name indicates that this firm may have been an Ohio partnership that intended to produce coinage in California. Although few facts have been found concerning the operations of the firm, one of its $10 coins was overstruck on an 1849 J.S. Ormsby $10 piece made in Sacramento, lending credence to the though that the company may have had limited operations in California.

Numismatic Notes. Today, all Cincinnati Mining & Trading Co. coins are extreme rarities.

Massachusetts & California Co. (1849)

The Massachusetts & California Co., organized in Northampton, Massachusetts, in 1848, envisioned producing gold coins once the partners reached California. Whether this was actually accomplished is unknown, but if the venture failed, it was not for lack of paperwork preparation, as lengthy rules and regulations were drawn up to guide dozens of participants.

Numismatic Notes. Today, $5 gold coins bearing the date 1849 are known. It is unclear whether these were produced as samples in the East, or whether coinage was accomplished in California. In addition, a number of restrikes and trial pieces are known, including some from copy dies.

Extreme caution is urged when contemplating the purchase of these pieces.

Miners' Bank $10 gold coin of 1849. Simple in design, such pieces were made in quantity and did much to help assuage a severe shortage of circulating coins. By the mid-1850s most had been melted, to convert into other coins, including by the San Francisco Mint. Today such pieces are rare.

Miners' Bank
(San Francisco, 1849)

The institution of Wright & Co., exchange brokers located in Portsmouth Square, San Francisco, was known as the Miners' Bank. A $10 piece (see p. 460) was issued in the summer of 1849, and may have been struck by the firm of Broderick & Kohler. The Miners' Bank dissolved January 14, 1850, after which time its coins traded at a discount.

Numismatic Notes. Today, fewer than 100 pieces are believed to exist. Nearly all are in high grades, AU being typical.

One of four known examples of the undated $10 gold coin struck by J.S. Ormsby & Co. in 1849.

J.S. Ormsby
(Sacramento, 1849)

The initials J.S.O., which appear on certain issues of California privately coined gold pieces, represent the firm of J.S.

Ormsby & Co., which in 1849 issued $5 and $10 coins of simple design, undated. The firm was of excellent reputation, and its coins were probably readily accepted in regional commerce. However, most were melted later.

Numismatic Notes. All Ormsby coins are extreme rarities.

An example of the 1849 $10 gold coin from the Pacific Company. The reverse shows the recurrence of an old theme, the Liberty Cap on pole.

Pacific Company
(San Francisco, 1849)

Little is known about this firm, whose issues were light in weight. Although such pieces circulated readily in 1849, probably mostly in gambling parlors, later they were criticized and traded only at a discount. Edgar H. Adams wrote that these were probably made by David Broderick and F.D. Kohler, who also operated a jewelry business.

Numismatic Notes. Just two of the $1 coins are known today, and the $5 and $10 coins are extreme rarities.

F.D. Kohler, California
State Assayer (1850)

The State Assay Office was authorized April 12, 1850, as a boon to miners and others who wanted to convert gold dust and nuggets to a more usable form. Governor Burnett appointed Frederick D. Kohler to the post; Kohler thereupon sold his private assaying business to Baldwin & Co. For a short time, offices were maintained in San Francisco and Sacramento. The venture was not a success, due primarily to resistance by banks, exchanges, and gold-dust traders who resented this intrusion into their profitable business. Most banks refused to accept the Kohler ingots, and their manufacture soon ceased. Ingots issued ranged in imprinted value from $36.55 to $150.

Numismatic Notes. These ingots are essentially noncollectible.

Dubosq & Company
(San Francisco, 1850)

Theodore Dubosq, a Philadelphia jeweler, took coining machinery to San Francisco in 1849 and produced many coins there through early 1851, although all known pieces are dated 1850. The obverse die used to strike the 1850 Dubosq $10 piece was later altered extensively, imprinted "W.M. & Co.," redated 1852, and used to strike $10 coins of Wass, Molitor & Co.

Numismatic Notes. Today, all Dubosq coins are very rare.

Baldwin & Company's distinctive horseman design on its $10 gold coin of 1850.

Baldwin & Company
(San Francisco, 1850)

George C. Baldwin and Thomas S. Holman were in the jewelry business in San Francisco and were known as Baldwin & Co. They were the successors to F.D. Kohler & Co., taking over its machinery and other equipment in May 1850. Coins were produced by Baldwin through early 1851. The $10 piece of 1850 has a distinctive vaquero (horseman) design. Due to unfavorable publicity mounted by one of its competitors (Moffat & Co.), Baldwin coins were repudiated by banks and merchants, and coinage was discontinued.

Numismatic Notes. All Baldwin issues are very rare.

Schultz & Company
(San Francisco, 1851)

This firm, located in back of Baldwin's establishment, operated a brass foundry beginning in 1851. Judge G.W. Schultz and William T. Garratt were partners in the enterprise. The coins are imprinted "SHULTS & CO.," a die-cutting error.

Numismatic Notes. Although they were made in large quantities, the $5 coins of this firm are very rare today.

Dunbar & Company
(San Francisco, 1851)

Edward E. Dunbar operated a bank in San Francisco and was involved in many civic and commercial activities. Dunbar later returned to New York and was an officer of the famous Continental Bank Note Co. founded by W.L. Ormsby. The firm struck $5 gold coins.

Numismatic Notes. These coins are very rare today.

Wass, Molitor & Co. $10 gold coin of 1855. This is a very curious variety, from a technical viewpoint. The die was made earlier, and in 1855 the last digit was drilled out and a plug with the numeral 5 was inserted, making it read 1855 as shown here.

Wass, Molitor & Company
(San Francisco, 1852–1855)

The gold-smelting and assaying plant of Wass, Molitor & Co. was operated by two Hungarian patriots, Count S.C. Wass and A.P. Molitor. In 1852 the company issued $5 and $10 coins similar to the federal designs, but with distinctive descriptions, including S.M.V. (Standard Mint Value). Among the several die combinations, a variety of $10 coin was made from a die altered from "1850 Dubosq & Co." No

Wass, Molitor & Co. pieces were coined bearing the dates 1853 or 1854.

In 1855 the company issued $20 coins in an era in which the federal San Francisco Mint was in operation, but lacked the capacity to satisfy the needs of banking and trade. In 1855 a small coinage of $10 ensued, along with an extensive production of $50 pieces, the last being of round shape.

Numismatic Notes. Coins range from scarce to very rare today. The $50 piece of 1855 is in special demand; an estimated 75 to 125 exist today, mostly in VF to AU grades.

This $20 gold coin of 1854, issued by Kellogg & Co., is copied after the federal design, a practice of other private coiners as well.
The portrait is in exceptionally high relief, also a characteristic of the 1855-dated $20 coins. Once common in circulation in California, such pieces are elusive today.

Kellogg & Company
(San Francisco, 1854–1855)

John Glover Kellogg came to San Francisco on October 12, 1849, from Auburn, New York. At first he was employed by Moffat & Co., and remained with that organization when control passed to Curtis, Perry & Ward. When the U.S. Assay Office of Gold was discontinued in 1853, Kellogg became associated with G.F. Richter, who had been an assayer in the government assay office. These two set up business as Kellogg & Richter on December 19, 1853. On Febru-

ary 9 of the following year, Kellogg & Co. placed their first $20 pieces in circulation. The firm dissolved late in 1854 and reorganized as Kellogg & Humbert. The latter partner was Augustus Humbert, for some time identified as U.S. Assayer of Gold in California. Regardless of the fact that the branch mint was then producing coins, Kellogg & Humbert issued $20 coins in 1855 in a quantity greater than before. In 1855 Ferdinand Grüner cut the dies for a round-format $50 gold coin for Kellogg & Co., but coinage seems to have been limited to presentation pieces. Today about 10 to 12 are known.

Numismatic Notes. Years later, in 2001, the California Historical Society, using transfer dies made from the original 1855 round $50 dies, issued 1855 "commemorative restrike" $50 coins using authentic gold taken from Kellogg & Humbert ingots recovered from the *S.S. Central America*. These commemoratives bear the inscription S.S. CENTRAL AMERICA GOLD, C.H.S., on the reverse ribbon, the last reflecting sponsorship of the project by the California Historical Society. Originals of all Kellogg & Co. gold coins range from scarce to rare. The most often seen are the $20 coins of 1854 and 1855, typically in EF and AU grades.

Gold Ingots From the
S.S. Central America

Gold bullion, called *treasure* in newspaper accounts, was regularly shipped from San Francisco to the East, usually by ship to Panama, then connecting overland 50 miles, then by another ship on the Atlantic side, continuing to New York City (usually) or another port. Much of this gold was in the form of rectangular ingots.

On one such run from Panama to New York, the *S.S. Central America* encountered a hurricane, foundered, and sank on September 12, 1857. In the 1980s the Columbus-America Discovery Group, led by Tommy Thompson and Bob Evans, located the long-lost ship in 7,200 feet of water. About 7,500 coins (mostly Mint

State 1857-S double eagles) and more than 500 ingots were recovered.

The ingots furnished a unique opportunity to study specimens that, after conservation, were essentially in the same condition as they were in 1857. These bore the imprints of five different California assayers who operated seven offices. With few exceptions, each ingot bears individual stamps indicating its maker, a serial number, the weight in ounces, the fineness (expressed in thousandths—e.g., .887, indicating 887/1,000 pure gold), and the 1857 value in dollars. The smallest bar found was issued by Blake & Co., weighed 4.95 ounces, was .795 fine, and was stamped with a value of $81.34. The largest ingot, dubbed the *Eureka bar*, bore the imprint of Kellogg & Humbert, and was stamped with a weight of 933.94 ounces, .903 fine, and a value of $17,433.57. Most of these were distributed by the California Gold Marketing Group (Dwight Manley, president). The assayers and ingots:

This Kellogg & Humbert gold ingot from the *S.S. Central America* treasure bears serial number 215, weighs 53.60 ounces, is .944 fine (94.4% pure gold), and in 1857 had a value of $1,045.96. Prior to the discovery of the long-lost ship, such large ingots were not known to exist. Face measurements: 44 mm x 99 mm.

Blake & Co. (Sacramento, California)—34 ingots recovered. • Lowest weight and imprinted value: 4.95 ounces, $81.34. • Highest weight and value: 157.40 ounces, $2,655.05.

Harris, Marchand & Co. (Sacramento and Marysville)—36 ingots attributed to Sacramento were recovered and only one from Marysville. • Lowest weight and value (Sacramento): 9.87 ounces, $158.53. • Highest weight and value (Sacramento): 295.20 ounces, $5,351.73. • Unique Marysville bar: 174.04 ounces, $3,389.06.

Henry Hentsch (San Francisco)—33 ingots recovered. • Lowest weight and value: 12.52 ounces, $251.82. • Highest weight and value: 238.84 ounces, $4,458.35.

Justh & Hunter (San Francisco and Marysville)—60 ingots in the 4,000 serial-number series are tentatively attributed to San Francisco and the 26 ingots in the 9,000 series are attributed to Marysville. • Lowest weight and value (San Francisco): 5.24 ounces, $92.18; Highest weight and value: 866.19 ounces, $15,971.93. • Lowest weight and value (Marysville): 19.34 ounces, $356.21; Highest weight and value: 464.65 ounces, $8,759.90.

Kellogg & Humbert (San Francisco)—346 ingots recovered, constituting the majority of those found. • Lowest weight and value: 5.71 ounces, $101.03. • Highest weight and value: 933.94 ounces, $17,433.57 (the Eureka bar). • A few large

Andrew Bowers views the "Eureka" bar, the largest ingot from the *S.S. Central America* treasure. This impressive, solid gold rectangle weighs 933.94 ounces and bears the imprint of Kellogg & Humbert, Serial No. 1003. Its stamped value in 1857 was $17,433.57 at a time when gold was worth just $20.67 per ounce. It was reported to have sold for a private collector for $8 million, the largest amount ever secured for a numismatic item.

ingots were melted, and the gold was used to produce the 1855 Commemorative Restrike Kellogg & Co. $50 coins discussed above.

California Small-Denomination Gold Coins

Beginning about 1852, gold coins of the denominations of twenty-five cents, fifty cents, and $1 were circulated in California. Made by jewelers and other private interests, these served as small change. Most if not all were worth less in bullion value than the denominations indicated on them.

Generally, these coins can be divided into Liberty Head and Indian Head types, the last being produced later in the series. Other issues, generally scarce to rare, include those with the head of Washington, an eagle, and the State Arms of California. Round and octagonal shapes were used. Coinage continued to about 1882, with issues of the last 20 years mainly serving as souvenirs.

Those with the denomination expressed as CENTS, DOL., DOLL, or DOLLAR are considered by numismatists to be coins. Many of these are very valuable. Representative types are listed in the *Guide Book*. Those with fractions or numerals, such as 1/4, 1/2, or 1, but no letters indicating denomination, are viewed as tokens and have relatively little numismatic value. Restrikes and fantasy issues of the coin, as well as token issues (mostly), were made years later. Today, some tokens are still being produced and occasionally trap the unwary buyer.

Die varieties are usually attributed to Breen-Gillio (BG) numbers as delineated in *California Pioneer Fractional Gold*, by Walter Breen and Ron Gillio, updated and extensively revised in 2003 under the editorial direction of Robert D. Leonard, Jr.

Oregon Gold Coins (1849)
The Need for a Mint

Attracted by exciting news from California, many settlers in the Oregon Territory headed south to the gold fields, where they

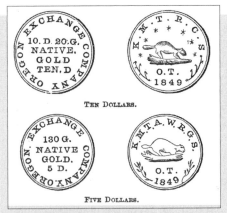

TEN DOLLARS.

FIVE DOLLARS.

Illustrations of the Oregon Exchange Company's $5 and $10 gold coins of 1849. (Hubert H. Bancroft, *History of Oregon*, Vol. 2, 1888)

spent the summer and autumn of 1848. At the time, no mintage or assaying facilities were in operation there, so they had no choice but to return to Oregon with gold dust and nuggets.

In February 1849, petitions were submitted to the legislature of the territory, seeking the establishment of a mint. On February 15, an appropriate act was passed, but on March 3 it was vetoed by Governor Joseph Lane, who felt that this would be in violation of federal laws. As round-trip mail to Washington, DC, took two months or so at the time, there was no way to secure a ruling.

To remedy the situation in a practical way, eight partners formed the Oregon Exchange Company, in Oregon City, and established a private mint. The last initials of the partners were used on the obverse of the coins produced, their names being W.K. Kilborne, Theophilus Magruder, James Taylor, George Abernathy, W.H. Willson, William H. Rector, J.G. Campbell, and Noyes Smith.

$5 and $10 Gold Coins Struck

Hamilton Campbell, a Methodist missionary, cut the dies for a $5 gold coin, and Victor Wallace, a machinist, made the dies for a $10 piece. The obverse of each illustrated a beaver, an open wreath, lettering, and the date 1849. The reverse stated the gold content, denomination, and name of the company.

It is believed that about 6,000 of the $5 coins were made, and 2,850 of the $10 coins. These were used extensively in local commerce. In time, nearly all were melted. Today, somewhat over 100 of the $5 coins and only a handful of the $10 coins exist. Most are in grades from VF to AU, and some show damage. Any Oregon gold coin is considered to be a rare prize. The original dies are preserved by the Oregon Historical Society.[73]

Mormon Gold Coins (1849–1860)

Gold From California

In spring and summer of 1848, Mormon soldiers returning from the war with Mexico to their settlement at Great Salt Lake City, in Utah (known as the State of Deseret), were caught up in the Gold Rush. They set up an encampment on Mormon Island, the name given to a sand-and-gravel bar on the American River downstream from Sutter's Mill, which proved to be one of the richest deposits and yielded millions of dollars in precious metal.

In the autumn most of the Mormons resumed their journey, carrying large amounts of gold with them. Plans were made to establish a mint at Great Salt Lake City. By December, designs had been prepared and dies were ready. Coinage was set to commence on the 10th of that month, from dies believed to have been dated 1849 (as no 1848 coins are known). The standard design depicted a bishop's hat, or mitre, over an all-seeing eye, with HOLINESS TO THE LORD lettered around the border. The reverse of each showed clasped hands at the center, the date below, and the denomination and G.S.L.C.P.G. around the border, the last an abbreviation for Great Salt Lake City Pure Gold. The coins had plain edges.

Mormon Coins Circulate

Coins of the $10 denomination were made first, followed by $2.50, $5, and $20 values, the $20 being the first coin of that denomination to be struck in the United States (antedating the federal double eagle by about a year). Coinage continued through early 1851, from 1849-dated dies plus new $5 dies dated 1850. It is believed that coins totaling a face value of about $75,000 were made during this time. In the meantime, some Mormon adventurers returned to California to continue finding gold.

While at the private mints of Reid and Bechtler in the south and at the various Gold Rush coiners in California, all coins were worth fairly close to face value (typically 95% to 99% intrinsic worth in relation to their stated denominations), the Mormons did not pay attention to such niceties. The Utah coinage was widely condemned outside the Mormon

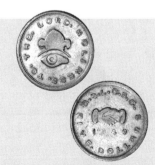

Mormon 1849 $5 coin minted in Salt Lake City, from gold brought from California.

The Mormon mint, near the center of the image, with smoke coming from a chimney. The large structure to the left was known as the Bowery. (Howard Stansbury, *Exploration and Survey of the Valley of the Great Salt Lake of Utah*, 1852)

community when it was learned, for example, that a $10 piece contained only about $8.70 in gold.

On December 1, 1849, this "review" appeared in the *Alta California*, published in San Francisco:

> Mormon Coin—The monetary notions of the Mormons at their Great Salt Lake settlement are no less peculiar it appears than their ideas of society and religion. We have a very curious coin in our possession, which is manufactured and extensively circulated among that remarkable people....
>
> Of all the fanciful forms into which our golden wealth is wrought this sainted shape excels in singularity. Its weight is about 15 pwts. Troy, its current worth among the Mormons, twenty dollars. Its circumference is that of a Spanish half doubloon. One side bears the inscription HOLINESS TO THE LORD, with the All-seeing Eye, surmounted by the prophet's cap; on the reverse appear the initials G.S.L.C.P.G., the grasp of fellowship, with the date (1849) and value of the piece. It is clumsy, and in execution without merit.
>
> Such complaints had no effect in Great Salt Lake City, for the church mandated that they be accepted in trade at face value. And so it was done.

Somewhat more charitable was this exchange item from the *Philadelphia Evening Bulletin*, reprinted in *Banker's Magazine*, February 1850:

> We were shown this morning a twenty dollar gold coin, a number of which have just been received by Messrs. E. W. Clark & Co., brokers, of this city. It is about the diameter of a cent, but much thicker. One side bears the inscription "Holiness of the Lord," with the device of an eye and another figure that we do not understand. On the reverse is a representation of hands clasped in fellowship, with the inscription "1849, Twenty dollars. G.S.L.C.P.G."

The coin is a very fair specimen of the mintage of the City of the Salt Lake. It is represented to be of pure gold, without alloy, and is thus too soft for long use. Those received here are to be sent to the Mint to be recoined according to our standard.

In 1860, the Mormon gold coinage was resumed. Dies for a $5 piece of a different design than used in 1849 and 1850 (now depicting a lion on the obverse and, on the reverse, an eagle, a beehive, and the inscription DESERET ASSAY OFFICE PURE GOLD) were cut by Albrecht Küner, a well-known San Francisco engraver. Lettering around the obverse border was in the Mormon alphabet, a system endorsed by Brigham Young and intended to make spelling simpler, based on phonetics. The concept never caught on, and it was abandoned later in the decade. It is likely that several thousand of the $5 coins of 1860 coins were made. An estimated 100 or so exist today, mostly AU or in the lower ranges of Mint State.

Today, all Mormon coins of 1849, 1850, and 1860 are collectible, the $5 denomination is most often seen. The $10 piece of 1849 is the great rarity of the series, and probably fewer than 20 are known. All of the dies of 1849 and 1850 were cut in low relief with little detail, a factor that must be considered when grading the pieces. The $5 piece of 1860 is from dies with strong relief.

Colorado Gold Coins (1860–1861)

In 1858 and 1859 America had a new gold rush, and covered wagons headed west, some with the rallying cry "Pikes Peak or Bust!" Gold had been found in 1858 in the western reaches of the Kansas Territory around the district that would later become the city of Denver, and in 1859 additional deposits had been located in the Rocky Mountains nearby. The Pikes Peak designation was from the territory's best-known icon. The mountain itself was not near the discoveries. For a time, the area was known as Jefferson Territory, then Colorado Territory.

The opportunity for profit plus the necessity for a regional coinage spawned at least three private mints, one of which— Clark, Gruber & Co.—became prominent.

Clark, Gruber & Company

In 1859, Milton E. Clark, representing the firm of Clark, Gruber & Co. (Leavenworth, Kansas, bankers), traveled to Philadelphia to purchase coining equipment and dies for a private mint. In the spring of 1860, his partners, Austin Clark and Emanuel H. Gruber, went to Denver and acquired land on the corner of McGaa and F streets, where they proceeded to have a two-story brick building erected, later topped with a sign, BANK AND MINT. As it cost 5% expressage and another 5% insurance to send gold east to be coined, and as it took up to three months for a round-trip transaction with coins returned, the utility of a local mint was immediately evident.

By July 1860 all was ready, and the business opened to receive deposits of gold to be assayed and refined. Coins of the $10 denomination were made first. The obverse depicted Pikes Peak in the form of a cone—more like Mount Etna than the real Pikes Peak. No doubt the diesinker, possibly doing his work in Philadelphia, had no idea what the summit looked like. The reverse displayed a wingspread eagle.

On July 25th the *Rocky Mountain News* printed this report of a special preview the editor had witnessed:

> [We visited] the elegant banking house…and were admitted to their coining room in the basement, where we found preparations almost complete for the issue of Pikes Peak coins. A hundred "blanks" had been prepared, weight and fineness tested, and last manipulation gone through with prior to their passage through the stamping press. The little engine that drives the machinery was fired up, belts adjusted, and between 3 and

The Clark, Gruber & Co. bank and mint as it appeared in Denver circa 1860.

The first $10 gold coins issued by Clark, Gruber & Co. in 1860 had a fictitious representation of "Pikes Peak," the name for the gold district in the territory (never mind that the real Pikes Peak was about 75 miles south of Denver and not visible from there, and that in real life Pikes Peak had a completely different appearance from that shown on the coin).

Although circumstances are unknown, it is likely that the change in 1861 to a Liberty Head motif for the $10 and $20 coins, copying the federal design, was made by Clark, Gruber & Co. so that the coins would be more familiar in appearance to those who used them in commerce.

The original press used by Clark, Gruber & Co. to punch planchets (blank discs) from metal strip, as an early stage of the coining process. (On display at the ANA Museum, Colorado Springs, Colorado)

4 o'clock the machinery was put in motion and "mint drops" of the value of $10 each began dropping into a tin pail with the most musical "clink."

About $1,000 were turned out, at the rate of 15 or 20 coins a minute, which was deemed satisfactory for the first equipment. The coins—of which none but $10 pieces are yet coined—are 17 grains heavier than the United States coins of the same denomination. On the face is a representation of the Peak, its base surrounded by a forest of timber, and "Pikes Peak Gold" encircling the summit. Immediately under its base is the word "Denver" and beneath it "Ten D." On the reverse is the American eagle, encircled by the name of the firm "Clark, Gruber & Co.," and beneath it the date, "1860." The coin has a little of the roughness peculiar to newness, but is upon the whole, very credible in appearance, and a vast improvement over "dust" as a circulating medium.

The $10 Pikes Peak coins created a local sensation. The denominations of $2.50 and $5 followed, these of a Liberty Head design quite similar to the federal coinage. On August 28 the *Rocky Mountain News* reported that about $18,000 of these three types had been made. Soon, $20 pieces were struck as well, these being of the Pikes Peak motif.

In 1861, coinage continued, from new dies bearing that date. The same denominations were issued, all of the Liberty Head type. In the summer of that year, Clark, Gruber & Co. issued $5 bills, printed by the American Bank Note Co., redeemable in gold coins. Bills denominated at $1, $2, and $3 were intended to be issued, but it is unknown whether they actually were. These particular $5 bills furnish a curious footnote in American financial history. In the following year, 1862, these notes remained worth a full $5 in gold, whereas Legal Tender bills issued by the federal government could not be exchanged for gold at par, and such paper was heavily discounted.

Coins were last struck in 1861, by which time $594,305 in face value had been made. In 1863 the facility was sold to the Treasury Department and was thereafter designated as the Denver Mint. However, no federal coins were ever struck there, as it functioned only as an assay office, refinery, and storage depot. Years later, in 1906, when Denver Mint coins were first struck, the facilities were in a modern building at a different location.

Today the basic denominations and designs of the 1860 and 1861 Clark, Gruber & Co. gold coins are all collectible, with the 1860 Pikes Peak $20 piece considered the rarest and most valuable, and the $10 piece of 1860 perhaps the most historical. Most coins are EF, AU, or low-range Mint State. Copper patterns or trial pieces of these issues are sometimes encountered, much more often than copper strikings from any other private or territorial coiner.

An undated $2.50 gold coin (enlarged) struck by John Parsons & Company in 1851.

John Parsons & Company

John D. Parsons, or Parson, a medical doctor from Quincy, Illinois, went to Denver in 1858, where for a time he was in the real estate trade. By 1861 he was in the coining business, striking $2.50 and $5 pieces bearing his imprint at Tarryall Mines, midway between Tarryall and Hamilton, near Como, on the way to Breckenridge.

The obverse of each of these coins shows a large, quartz stamping mill, J. PARSON & Co. (on the $2.50) or JNo PARSON & Co. ($5), and the word ORO (Spanish for *gold*). The reverse illustrates an eagle with inscriptions including PIKES PEAK GOLD.

Today, only a few examples are known of each (Breen suggests six of the $2.50 denomination and just three of the $5), making them essentially noncollectible.

An undated $2.50 gold coin (enlarged) struck by J.J. Conway & Company in 1851.

J.J. Conway & Company

In 1861, in a small settlement near Parkville (later to become a ghost town) in the Rocky Mountains at Georgia Gulch (not far from present-day Breckenridge), the jewelry and banking firm of J.J. Conway & Co. struck gold coins of the $2.50, $5, and $10 denominations. Bearing the firm's imprint, the dies may have been ordered through a jewelry supply house, as they closely resemble in style (but not denominations) certain trade tokens of that era, such as those made by John Stanton of Cincinnati.

The pieces were intended to serve local miners, who at the time were receiving just $14 to $15 per ounce for gold dust of high purity, said to be worth $18 per ounce if coined. Conway turned out coins that proved to be debased when they were assayed in Denver. The coins had a fineness of .7725, considerably less than the federal standard of .900. Another assay, this conducted on behalf of Conway, showed a fineness of .882.

As to whether these coins ever achieved utility in and around Parkville is unknown, but the production must have been very small, as fewer than 20 coins are known, in total, of four varieties (one variety of the $2.50 denomination, two of the $5, and one of the $10).

The original dies exist and were used in 1956 to make restrikes in goldine metal. Today they are owned by the Colorado State Historical Society. Impressions of certain dies overstruck on silver coins, and apparently of 19th-century origin, are known.

Key to Collecting

- **Mint State coins:** Across the different coinages, Mint State examples are in the distinct minority. Most likely to be found are those of Moffat & Co. and the United States Assay Office of Gold, San Francisco. Bechtler coins are occasionally encountered in low Mint State grades, often with prooflike surfaces. Gold ingots from the *S.S. Central America* are Mint State.

- **Circulated coins:** Most territorial and private gold coins are found in varying levels of circulated grades, most often EF and AU.

- **Strike quality:** Quality varies widely, but for most issues the coiners paid little or no attention to creating sharply struck coins. Evaluation must be done on an individual basis, to determine what exists sharply struck and what does not. Generally, within a given date, denomination, and type, all are struck the same (weak overall, weak in some areas, sharp, etc.).

- **Proof coins:** Irrelevant to most coins in this specialty. Scattered exceptions include "Chapman restrikes" of Bechtler $5 coins and the 1855 Kellogg & Co. $50 coins (made only in Proof format).

- **Key issues:** Just about everything! Small-denomination California gold is excepted from this rule, but even that series has many rare varieties within it.

- **Advice to smart buyers:** Study each coin carefully. Many have polished, retooled, or repaired surfaces that are not disclosed on holders. Determine your objectives on a coin-by-coin basis. Accordingly, if you can afford it, you may want a choice Mint State 1853 U.S. Assay Office of Gold $20 piece, and you will have multiple opportunities to buy. On the other hand, if an 1849 Oregon Exchange Co. $10 coin comes your way, you cannot be as choosy, for it might be a year, or several years, until you get another chance. Buy as many books of interest as you can from the bibliography below.

- **Selected bibliography:**
Adams, Edgar H. 1913. *Private Gold Coinage of California 1849–55: Its History and Its Issues.* Brooklyn, NY. (Essential.)

Adams, Edgar H. 1909. *Official Premium Lists of Private and Territorial Gold Coins.* Brooklyn, NY. (Of historical interest only.)

Bowers, Q. David. 1979. *The History of United States Coinage as Illustrated by the Garrett Collection.* Los Angeles, CA, 1979.

Bowers, Q. David. 2001. *A California Gold Rush History Featuring the Treasure From the S.S. Central America.* Newport Beach, CA. (Essential. Includes a complete record of all coins and ingots found.)

Breen, Walter. 1988. *Walter Breen's Complete Encyclopedia of U.S. and Colonial Coins.* New York. (Very valuable, possibly essential.)

Breen, Walter, and Ronald Gillio. 2003. *California Pioneer Fractional Gold* (edited by Robert D. Leonard, Jr., et al.). Wolfeboro, NH. (Essential for this specialty.)

Clifford, Henry H. 1961. *Pioneer Gold Coinage in the West—1848–1861.* Reprint from *The Westerners Brand Book—Book Nine.* Los Angeles, CA. (Not essential, but interesting.)

Griffin, Clarence. 1929. *The Bechtlers and Bechtler Coinage and Gold Mining in North Carolina 1814–1830.* Spindale, NC. (Essential for this specialty.)

Kagin, Donald H. 1981. *Private Gold Coins and Patterns of the United States.* New York. (Essential.)

Lee, Kenneth W. 1979. *California Gold Dollars, Half Dollars, Quarter Dollars.* Santa Ana, CA. (Of historical interest only.)

Owens, Dan. 2000. *California Coiners and Assayers.* Wolfeboro, NH. (Essential if you are interested in history.)

Seymour, Dexter C. 1977. *The 1830 Coinage of Templeton Reid.* American Numismatic Society Museum Notes No. 22. New York. (Essential for this specialty.)

CHAPTER TWENTY-FIVE

COLLECTING TOKENS

I have had many active interests in my lifetime. At various times I have made collections of objects nearest to hand. For instance, I made and disposed of several collections of postage stamps, some of them quite extensive; a collection of fossils, acquired when a tutor prescribed for me outdoor activity. And when I was obliged to spend a year in Colorado Springs I made a collection of some hundreds of mineral specimens, chosen chiefly for their beauty. Still later, I collected some thousands of specimens of Indian artifacts, which are now in the Illinois State Collection. I also accumulated some 3,000 books, which were fine as long as they stayed in one place, but several moves found them unwieldy to handle. I also tried to collect etchings. However, of all my interests, I derived the greatest satisfaction from the collecting and studying of coins and medals.

—William G. Jerrems, Jr., October 1941

Collecting Tokens

Seeking Definitions

Tokens are interesting to collect—so much so, that "once a token collector, always a token collector" is a true statement for most numismatists who become involved. The specialty is complex, inasmuch as there are few things standard about it. While some tokens fall into series, the vast majority are different from each other. Accordingly, each piece invites study. This contributes to the charm of the specialty—just as the dozens of different statehood-reverse Washington quarters beckon their owners to take a closer look.

What is a token? As you will see, this is analogous to asking, "What can be found in a zoo?"

Among the more than a half dozen definitions given by *Random House Webster's Unabridged Dictionary* are these:

> Something serving to represent or indicate some fact, event, feeling, etc.; sign. • A memento; souvenir; keepsake. • Something used to indicate authenticity, authority, etc.; emblem; badge. • Also a token coin, a stamped piece of metal, issued as a limited medium of exchange, as for bus fares, at a nominal value much greater than its commodity value. • Anything of only nominal value similarly used, as paper currency.

For numismatic purposes, "a stamped piece of metal, used as a medium of exchange," covers most possibilities, to which can be added "something serving to represent some fact, event, feeling, etc.," as a token from a political campaign. In many instances the distinction between a token and a *medal* can be blurred—perhaps separated, to an extent, by the suggestion that tokens are of small size and intended to be passed from hand to hand, while most medals are larger and intended for display or as mementos.

Most tokens are struck in metals such as copper, brass, white metal (or pewter), and aluminum (beginning in quantity late in the 19th century), except for a few in more unusual materials such as Bakelite, hard rubber, and plastic. Certain tokens made for the numismatic trade have been in silver. Coal-mine tokens, textile-factory tokens, and World War II ration tokens, among others, were made of a fiber composition. Most tokens (and also medals) are round, but some are of other shapes.

Tokens were (and still are) made by private shops and companies, rather than (usually) by government mints or authorities.

Historian and numismatist Katherine Jaeger, who has conducted research on early tokens and medals, has observed:

> This is why tokens appeal so much to me: they were made by hand, one at a time, designed and produced entirely at the whim of their maker and the needs of their customers. They "betoken" the personality not just of their maker, but of their location in geography and time.[74]

471

A Popular Pursuit

Collecting tokens has been a very important specialty in numismatics since the early years of the hobby's popularity. Indeed, in many auction catalogs of the 1860s, such as those prepared by W.E. Woodward and Edward D. Cogan (the two leading figures at the time), tokens often occupied more space per item than did rare federal coins. Much of this was by necessity, as coins could be listed simply by date and grade, but tokens required more detailed descriptions in order to identify them.

Today, tokens play to a wide audience of collectors, many of whom belong to specialized groups such as the Token and Medal Society and the Civil War Token Society.

One of the most used references, and a wonderful guide to the series, is Russell Rulau's *Standard Catalog of United States Tokens, 1700–1900*, which lists and prices thousands of different varieties in these basic categories:

Early American Tokens
Hard Times Tokens
U.S. Merchant Tokens
U.S. Trade Tokens
Civil War Store Cards
Patriotic Civil War Tokens
Civil War Cardboard Chits
Tokens of the Gay Nineties

Early Tokens

Among the earlier tokens used in America are the Talbot, Allum & Lee cents, struck in England and dated 1794 and 1795, issued by a firm located on Pearl Street, New York, and engaged in the import trade. (These are also collected alongside the early American and colonial series [see chapter 21]—one of many examples of a numismatic item's failure to fit neatly into a single category). Another token from the same era served as an admission check to Ricketts's Circus, a traveling show that George Washington attended when it visited Philadelphia.

The tokens of Talbot, Allum & Lee, New York City merchants in the import trade, were produced in England and shipped to America. Bearing the dates 1794 (as here) and 1795, these circulated for the value of one cent. However, the importers found that they had an oversupply, and tens of thousands were sold to the Philadelphia Mint, where they were used (by the removal of planchets from the centers of the tokens) to make copper half cents of 1795 and 1797.

In the meantime, in England there was a great rage for collecting Conder tokens—copper pieces of this size, combining thousands of different dies and edge variations. The designation is taken from a popular guide by James Conder, published in

1798: *An Arrangement of Provincial Coins, Tokens, and Medalets, Issued in Great Britain, Ireland and the Colonies.* Conder tokens with American connections include several varieties of Washington tokens, the 1795 Franklin Press token, and the circa-1792 Kentucky tokens, among others.

Talbot, Allum & Lee dies were muled with irrelevant reverses to create novelties, such as the Fifth Troop, Blofield Cavalry token illustrated above. The cavalry unit had no direct connection with the United States. Such "numismatic delicacies" were avidly collected back then (but in England, not in America, as interest had not developed here). Today, they are still intensely sought by collectors on both sides of the Great Pond.

Above is an engraving of Faneuil Hall (large building in distance to the right) showing Milton's emporium on the ground floor, corner closest to the viewer. (W.H. Bartlett, *American Scenery*, 1840 edition).

Token issued by Wm. H. Milton, proprietor of the Faneuil Hall Clothes Warehouse, listed by Russell Rulau as HTT-163; a rather common issue.

For a long period of time, merchants in leading cities commissioned diesinkers and medalists to create tokens for them, often the size of a large copper cent. These could be paid out in change and would advertise the business. Used locally and regionally, these seem to have been accepted at face value, and could always be taken back to the place of issue for redemption.

Hard Times Tokens

The series of so-called Hard Times tokens covers mostly cent-sized issues of about 1832 to 1844 (extending a bit before the true Hard Times era in U.S. economic history, which commenced in the spring of 1837). Such tokens are divided into two main groups: store cards issued by merchants, and those bearing political messages.

In the 1880s dealer Lyman H. Low took an interest in these tokens and prepared several listings of varieties, utilizing some work done earlier by J.N.T. Levick. In 1899 his book *Hard Times Tokens* was published, followed by a revised edition soon afterward. Eventually, Low listed nearly 200 varieties, these being combinations of dies as well as strikings in different metals. Col-

lecting these became a specialty unto itself, and throughout the 20th century a number of numismatists concentrated in this field, with such names as William Forrester Dunham, Donald Miller, George L. Tilden, F.C.C. Boyd, Robert Schuman, and John J. Ford, Jr., coming to mind. Most have collected these with a veritable passion, giving a proverbial eyetooth to acquire a "Low number" token not already possessed.

In recent years, Russell Rulau has vastly expanded the 1832 to 1844 tokens described by Low, added much historical data and research information, and devised a new series of "HTT numbers." These designations have been coming into use, at first supplanting the Low numbers, and in recent times superseding them.

Representative Examples

The following is a small selection of Hard Times tokens from Rulau's *Standard Catalog*, identified by HTT numbers. The Sheldon Rarity Scale (R-1 to R-9, explained in chapter 6) is used:[75]

HTT-65, Specie Payments Suspended—*Year:* 1837 • *Metal:* Copper • *Rarity:* R-3 • *Diameter:* 28 mm • *Description:* Obverse with Liberty Head and stars in approximation of the then-current federal cent, but with E PLURIBUS UNUM above. Reverse with wreath and inscription: SPECIE PAYMENTS SUSPENDED / MAY TENTH 1837, referring to the day that New York City and many eastern banks stopped exchanging gold and silver coins at par for paper money. • *Market values:* VG, $5; VF, $23; EF, $70; Mint State, $250.

HTT-70, Jackson in safe, jackass with LL.D.—*Year:* 1833 • *Metal:* Copper • *Rarity:* R-1 • *Diameter:* 28 mm • *Description:* Obverse with Jackson in strongbox, holding a bag of money in one hand and a sword in the other, and the inscription I TAKE THE RESPONSIBILITY, a reference to his taking federal funds deposited in the Second Bank of the United States and moving them to other institutions (called *pet banks*). Reverse with a jackass inscribed LL.D., a punning allusion to the doctorate awarded by Harvard to Jackson in June 1833. • *Market values:* VG, $6; VF, $20; EF, $70; Mint State, $275.

Generally, the Hard Times series political and store card issues with lower rarity ratings, R-1 to R-3, are available in higher grades, including Mint State. Strike quality often varies, sometimes widely, with many store cards being weakly struck. However, within a given variety, all usually have the same characteristics of striking. A perusal of illustrations in auction and other listings can be very informative in this regard. Quality never goes out of style, however, and even within some issues that are usually poorly struck (such as Gustin & Blake of Chelsea, Vermont, and Bucklin's Bookkeeping Tables of West Troy, New York) it is possible to acquire pieces with attractive surfaces.

Completion is not a realistic goal in this series. Most collectors review the Rulau catalog and other listings and select pieces of special interest, often ignoring small differences in dies or in metals (e.g., copper vs. brass) for the same die combination. Sometimes there are long periods between market appearances of rarities.

HTT-194 • Nathaniel March and William Simes, Portsmouth, NH • *Year:* 1837 • *Metal:* Copper • *Rarity:* R-1 • *Diameter:* 29.1 mm • *Description:* Jointly issued by two merchants. On one side the inscription refers to the teas, wines, and groceries sold by March, and on the other side, lettering pertaining to Simes' stationery and bookselling business. • *Market values:* VG: $7; VF: $17; EF: $50; Mint State: $170.

HTT-268 (enlarged) • Feuchtwanger Cent, New York, NY • *Year:* 1837 • *Metal:* German silver (Feuchtwanger's Composition) • *Rarity:* R-1 • *Diameter:* 18.5 mm • *Description:* Obverse with an eagle killing a snake, date below. Reverse with wreath, FEUCHTWANGER'S COMPOSITION around border, ONE / CENT within. Issued in quantity by Dr. Lewis Feuchtwanger, a chemist and entrepreneur. Samples were sent to congressmen in an unsuccessful effort to secure use of this alloy for federal coinage. Die varieties exist, some of which are more valuable than the general prices listed here. • *Market values:* VG: $20; VF: $75; EF: $135; Mint State: $300.

Each token offers a generous measure of history, and one of the joys of collecting Hard Times tokens is learning about their background.

Civil War Tokens and Store Cards

During the Civil War, especially in 1862 and 1863, there was a shortage of small circulating change. Diesinkers in Cincinnati (in particular), New York, Chicago, Boston, and elsewhere seized the opportunity to create tokens, mostly the size of a one-cent piece. These are divided into store cards and patriotic pieces (the latter similar to the "political" issues of the Hard Times era).

As years progressed, issues of the *American Journal of Numismatics* (launched in 1866), *The Numismatist*, and other publications ran lists and feature articles on Civil War tokens. In 1925, George Hetrich and Julius Guttag published an impressive book that listed such tokens by HG (Hetrich-Guttag) numbers. These numbers remained in effect until the second half of the second millennium, when the father-and-son team of Melvin and George Fuld jumped into the fray, reorganized the listings completely, and created Fuld numbers for store cards and political tokens.

For the patriotic Civil War tokens, obverse and reverse dies were each given numbers. Letters were given for metals, such as *a* for copper, *b* for brass, and so on, including *f* for silver. By this system, a political token combining dies 360 and 436, struck in copper, is designated as 360/436a. Some patriotic tokens, such as those depicting the four presidential candidates of 1860, could just as well be called *medalets* or small medals. For that matter, these particular pieces were made *before* the Civil War. As with many numismatic categories, the definition of *Civil War token* is flexible.

Civil War store cards, or advertising tokens, were arranged differently: by state, then a number representing the city, followed by a letter representing a merchant

within that city, then a number representing the specific die combination, then a letter for the metal. Accordingly, a copper store card of A.W. Gale, a restaurant operator at the railroad depot in Concord, New Hampshire, is listed as NH-120-A-1a, the 120 representing Concord and the A representing Gale (the only merchant in that city who issued these tokens). In my own files I add the town name after the state, as above, but the Fuld reference uses only the town number.

Merchants who issued tokens secured for themselves a place in numismatic history (see p. 476). Likely, a historian interested in New York City never heard of H.B. Melville (agent and jeweler with premises at 76 Bleecker Street in lower Manhattan), who was one of just a handful of Civil War store card merchants whose portrait appears on his tokens. Most tokens simply give a person's name and trade specialty.

Similarly, a specialist interested in the traditions of Philadelphia probably never heard of H. Mulligan. However, numismatists recognize him as a 19th-century jeweler who advertised on a token that he had THE LARGEST ASSORTMENT & LOWEST PRICES IN THE U.S.—a claim that seems a bit far fetched, but who knows? It has been said that "the coin outlives the throne," in the best tradition of Percy Bysshe Shelley's "Ozymandias," and certainly many artifacts last longer than those who created them. Throughout the Civil War store card series (and, for that matter, store cards from other eras) there are many inscriptions relating to one-time merchant princes who are now forgotten.

The Fuld listings use the following rarity scale, which differs from the Sheldon scale as follows (adapted):

Fuld Civil War Token Rarity Scale

R-1: More than 5,000 estimated to exist

R-2: 2,000 to 4,999

R-3: 500 to 1,999

R-4: 200 to 499

R-5: Scarce: between 75 and 200

Civil War store card (enlarged) issued by H.B. Melville, agent and jeweler, New York City. This is one of relatively few such pieces that bear the portrait of the issuer—an arrangement that must have involved extra expense and, certainly, custom die work. This variety is classified as NY-630-AW-1a in the Fuld text on the series.

Not generally known is the fact that Henry B. Melville was also a numismatist, although little has been learned of him in this regard. No doubt this explains, at least in part, why he desired to create a truly special token. In 1867 he was among the successful bidders in W. Elliot Woodward's sale of the Joseph Mickley Collection.

J. Mahnken, a dealer in liquor and "segars" (preferred spelling of the era) at 19 & 22 West Street, New York City, issued several varieties of Civil War Store cards. Shown here (both enlarged) are Fuld varieties NY-630-AT-2a (19.9 mm) and NY-630-AT-3a (19.9 mm), the first depicting General George B. McClellan and the other an eagle on a globe with UNION FOR EVER.

The dies are the work of William Bridgens of New York City. The address side is the obverse and the pictorial side, from "stock" dies on hand by Bridgens, is known as the reverse, this being the technique used by collectors. Bridgens created three other varieties for Mahnken by employing as many other different reverses.

R.G. Martin, dealer in hardware, stoves, and tin ware, Monroeville, Ohio, issued this Civil War store card, Fuld variety OH-560-A-6a, 19.2 mm (enlarged). These tokens were made by the shop of William K. Lanphear of Cincinnati. The reverse is from a stock die and shows a corner view of a cast-iron kitchen stove with doors at left and front; kettle and pot on top; and reservoir lettered PEACE / MAKER / 1863 at right. This particular die was available to any other customers who wished to use it.

R-6: Very Scarce: between 20 and 75

R-7: Rare: between 10 and 20

R-8: Very Rare: between 5 and 10

R-9: Extremely Rare: between 2 and 5

R-10: Unique: only 1

Examples of Civil War Tokens

The following is a small selection of Civil War tokens attributed by Fuld catalog numbers, with market values from Rulau's *Standard Catalog:*.

Fuld 237/423a, Our Little Monitor— *Year:* 1863 • *Metal:* Copper • *Rarity:* R-1 •

Description: Patriotic token. On the obverse the ironclad *Monitor* is heading to the left; two cannons firing from the turret. Smoke billows from cannons in front of the boat and forms a cloud over the turret. The reverse shows an open wreath, crossed cannons, an anchor at the apex, and the date 1863. • *Market values:* VG, $6; VF, $12; EF, $14; MS-63, $30.

Fuld 0511/514b, WEALTH OF THE SOUTH / NO SUBMISSION TO THE NORTH— *Year:* 1860 • *Metal:* Brass • *Rarity:* R-5 • *Description:* Patriotic token. Obverse with agricultural products and inscription, THE WEALTH OF THE SOUTH, etc. Reverse with palm, cannon, 15 stars, etc., and inscription, NO SUBMISSION TO THE NORTH, 1860. • *Market values:* VG, $100; VF, $300; EF, $400; MS-63, $800.

Fuld NY, New York City-630-J2a, William Bridgens/Washington—*Year:* 1863 • *Metal:* Copper • *Rarity:* R-3 • *Description:* Obverse with advertisement for Bridgens, a die cutter and issuer of store cards. Reverse with portrait of George Washington. • *Market values:* VG, $15; VF, $35; EF, $40; MS-63, $75.

Fuld OH, Cincinnati-165-M-1a, Belknap, the painless dentist—*Year:* 1863 • *Metal:* Copper • *Rarity:* R-6 • *Description:* TEETH EXTRACTED WITHOUT PAIN, BY B.P. BELKNP, the last probably a misspelling of Belknap. Reverse with anchor and rope. • *Market values:* VG, $40; VF, $100; EF, $150; MS-63, $200.

Fuld RI, Providence-700-A-4a, Arcade House / H. Dobson—*Year:* 1864 • *Metal:* Copper • *Rarity:* R-4 • *Description:* Obverse with advertisement for the Arcade House, Providence. Reverse with H. DOBSON, UNION, and 1864. • *Market values:* VG, $8; VF, $15; EF, $25; MS-63, $55.

Collecting Civil War Tokens

The Civil War Token Society devotes its attention to this series, and members enjoy reading the *Civil War Token Journal,* issued four times a year. Although the total number of Civil War token varieties has never been counted, it is probably somewhere around 15,000, including unusual strikings made especially for collectors.

A basic, core collection of copper political and store card issues intended for general circulation would comprise several thousand examples. As with the collecting of other tokens (as well as medals, Currier and Ives prints, obsolete paper money, and other traditional series), and quite unlike the strategy for federal coins, completion

is not possible. Instead, followers in the token series tend to collect pieces that they enjoy owning.

Often, numismatists will specialize, sometimes collecting patriotic tokens to the exclusion of store cards. Among the latter, collecting by states is popular—such as one each from as many merchants as possible from Pennsylvania, Ohio, New Jersey, or another state. Distribution was limited, and, for example, no Civil War tokens were issued in Vermont, only two were distributed in Maine, just one in New Hampshire, and none at all in most Southern and western states. However, varieties abound for New York, New Jersey, Pennsylvania, Ohio (in particular), Indiana, Michigan, Illinois, and Wisconsin, and several others.

The circulating issues of most patriotic and store card Civil War tokens were struck in copper, with a few in brass and fewer still in German silver. Such coins can be collected today in various grades, with VF to AU or Mint State being typical.

In addition, there are many irrelevant die combinations as well as unusual metals such as silver-plated brass or copper, white metal, and silver. Sometimes federal coins were used for planchets, especially copper-nickel Flying Eagle and, most often, Indian Head cents. Some especially rare varieties were struck over silver coins, mostly dimes. These "fancy pieces" were enthusiastically collected at a very early date and were made expressly to the order of numismatists. Tokens in this category are usually seen in Mint State today and are eagerly sought.

Sutlers' Tokens

Related to Civil War tokens are sutlers' tokens, these being issued by the sutlers (or contractors) who operated camp stores in connection with traveling military regiments and companies. Most of these tokens are of rather simple design, although some are pictorial and are from the same dies used to strike Civil War tokens. Most were made in Cincinnati, with John Stanton being the most important supplier. David E. Schenkman wrote the standard refer-

Sutler's token of the 5¢ denomination made by John Stanton, Cincinnati die sinker, for J.H. Alexander, sutler with the 33rd Indiana Regiment. Variety listed as Schenkman IN-F-5C.

In general today, sutlers' tokens range from scarce to rare. Continually being added to the existing numismatic supply are occasional finds by treasure detectors using electronic gear in Civil War battlefield areas. Such recovered tokens are apt to be heavily oxidized.

ence on this series, *Civil War Sutler Tokens and Cardboard Scrip* (1983).

For a soldier in the Union Army, the sutler's tent offered a panorama of delights—comforts and items of pleasure as well as necessities. Products included books, games, stationery, tonics and bitters (the latter heavily laced with alcohol, but sold for alleged medicinal benefits), shirts, and more.

Each sutler was registered with the War Department and had to operate under a set of rules. Unofficially, and not widely recorded in the annals of the Civil War, now and again Union and Confederate soldiers confronting each other in a combat arena would call a cease-fire for an hour or so, and the soldiers would swap souvenirs and other items, mostly bought from sutlers.

Other Token Specialties

While Hard Times tokens and Civil War tokens furnish two major specialties, a dozen or more other niches have attracted collectors over the years. Included are the following, some of which overlap.

Encased Postage Stamps

Encased postage stamps, the concept patented in 1862 by John Gault, consist of a brass frame fronted with clear mica, under which a U.S. postage stamp (of a

value from 1¢ to 90¢) was mounted. These are another entry in the dazzling panorama of numismatic items produced during the Civil War era—a roster that includes Civil War tokens, sutlers' tokens, scrip notes, Postage Currency, Fractional Currency, Confederate States of America paper money, and, if you want to get technical, National Bank Notes as well.

It is indeed curious that while numismatists have studied such tokens closely, and some have made them a specialty, historians of the Civil War are generally clueless about them! It has always amazed me that a historian might know the name of General Meade's horse, or what happened at the Battle of Antietam at 2:12 in the afternoon, but would scratch his head if asked, "What do you know about sutlers' tokens?" Or, even simpler: "What kind of money might a Union soldier with $20 in his pocket be carrying in August 1863?" Chapters 29 and 30 have more on this subject.

The back of the frame of an encased postage stamp is usually imprinted with an advertisement. Such products as Aerated Bread, Drake's Plantation Bitters, and Ayer's Sarsaparilla are among dozens featured. Values for choice pieces can range from a couple hundred dollars or so for a common variety, such as several of the Ayer's issues, to many thousands for rarities such as the encased postage stamps of E.M. Claflin (Hopkinton, Rhode Island) and B.F. Miles (Peoria, Illinois). Useful books on the series have been written by Fred Reed III as well as by the present writer jointly with Michael Hodder.

Political Tokens

Political tokens, medalets, badges, ribbons, and related items form a popular area for collecting. In particular, the quadrennial presidential campaigns have been a focal point for many specialists. The first such contest to generate a large amount of memorabilia, including tokens, was the election of 1840, which pitted William Henry Harrison (the hero of the Battle of Tippecanoe) against incumbent Martin Van Buren. "Tippecanoe and Tyler, too!" was the rally-

Inside a sutler's tent at Harper's Ferry, Virginia, with troops from General Geary's division. (*Frank Leslie's Illustrated Newspaper*, November 29, 1862)

A collage showing the backs of various encased postage stamps. (*A Guide Book of United States Paper Money*, 2005)

Among the more readily available varieties of encased postage stamps are those bearing the imprint of Drake's Plantation Bitters, a tonic and cure-all beverage put out by P.H. Drake and Demas Barnes in New York City. The main ingredient was rum from the Caribbean island of St. Croix. Both men had their fingers in other patent medicines and related products, including Mexican Mustang Liniment and Lyon's Kathairon. The bitters were sold in attractive amber bottles shaped like log cabins, which make nice "go-withs" to a numismatic display of encased postage.

In its day the cabalistic inscription "S.T. 1860. X." caused a lot of talk and speculation. What did it stand for? A popular guess was that it meant, "Started Trade in 1860 with $10."

ing cry of the time, and Harrison and his running mate, John Tyler, trampled the opposition with 234 electoral votes to Van Buren's 64. The four-way contest in 1860, between Lincoln, Douglas, Bell, and Breckenridge, spawned a matching series of tokens sold to the numismatic trade. The hard-fought campaign of 1896, with William Jennings Bryan versus William McKinley, resulted in more tokens and medals—many of them satirical—than any other presidential contest before or since.

Loosely grouped under the heading of political tokens are issues relating to social movements, among them those of abolition (anti-slavery), temperance, and women's suffrage. At one time or another, these were strong influences on presidential campaigns as well as state, local, and regional elections. Tokens relating to contests other than presidential have drawn very little collector interest, except for certain issues that are collected along with other series—such as the tokens of the 1830s depicting New York gubernatorial candidates William Seward and, separately, Gulian C. Verplanck, each of whom used the same portrait! These are also included as part of the Hard Times token series.

Store Cards

Also called *merchants' tokens*, store cards form an integral part of both the Hard Times and Civil War token series noted above. Beyond that, many store cards were produced in other eras, early and late. The Rulau text loosely groups them under these headings: Early American Tokens (1694–1832), U.S. Merchant Tokens (1845–1860), U.S. Trade Tokens (1866–1889), and Tokens of the Gay Nineties (1890–1900).

It has been my experience that these categories are rarely collected by such groupings, although it is a convenient way to list them. Rather, store cards are desired by geographical location or topic. Many specialized books and monographs have been written on tokens from a particular location, such as California, Illinois, Wisconsin, Keokuk (Iowa), Montana,

Cincinnati (Ohio), Nebraska, Massachusetts, and New York City (New York).

Store cards advertising a specialty such as dentistry, saloons, clocks, or hotels can form an interesting collection, the appreciation of which can be enhanced by cross-referencing the pieces to old directories and guides. Many tokens were redeemable in goods or money.

During the 20th century, thousands of different store cards were issued, usually of rather plain design, often in brass or aluminum. While these lack the artistic appeal and the rustic die-cutting of earlier issues, there is compensation in that most are inexpensive—costing just a dollar or two in many instances. These are often available at coin shows, where dealers have albums filled with them, each in a little holder.

In addition to authentic tokens, many fantasy issues are on the market, often marked with the names of "Wild West" saloons, or bordellos, or other popular subjects. As tokens are not subjected to the same counterfeiting laws as legal-tender coins, there is little recourse for those who buy such pieces, which seem to be particularly common in Internet offerings.

Shell Cards

Under the general umbrella of store cards is a niche or specialty, that of shell cards. These are somewhat similar to encased postage stamps in their concept, with embossed brass on one side and advertisements on the other. However, the shell cards, made in the late 1860s and the 1870s, are larger, the size of a contemporary silver dollar or trade dollar. The embossed side bears a design, often a Liberty Head copied from the $20 gold coin, or the Liberty Seated figure from a silver dollar, or the reverse eagle from a trade dollar. The other side consists of a circular disc of hard-faced cardboard, often colored, imprinted with an advertisement.

Several hundred varieties were issued, many of which have been described in the *Token and Medal Society Journal*. If the indefatigable Russell Rulau ever lists these in his heroically-proportioned *Standard*

Brass shell card with one side displaying an eagle (copied from a then-current trade dollar) and the other side with a green-printed cardboard disc advertising the Improved Howe Scales. These tokens were given out as souvenirs to those who called at Howe's display at the Centennial Exhibition in Philadelphia in 1876. The visitor would be weighed on a scale of this make, and his or her weight would be written in pencil on the shell card. This one is inscribed "13 yrs" and "111 lbs."

Catalog of United States Tokens, their popularity will escalate.

Somewhat related to shell cards are "mirror cards," generally of the late 19th and early 20th centuries, with colorful advertisements on celluloid (or a related encasement) on one side and a mirror on the other.

Tickets to See or Ride

Tokens in this category are good for admission to a museum, or a ride on a train, or the right to use a ferry or bridge, or a seat in a theater or circus tent. Among the earliest are tokens issued for admission to Ricketts's Circus, a traveling troupe of the 1790s. An 1825-dated medal served as a pass to ADMIT THE BEARER to Peale's Museum, located in the Parthenon at 252 Broadway, lower New York City. A token of the 1860s bids the bearer to visit the Atlantic Garden, a huge beer garden in the Bowery, New York City, and hear the orchestrion (automatic orchestra) play a concert.

Those involving travel are often referred to as *transportation tokens*, such as one with inscriptions relating to the bridge across the Ohio River, connecting Cincinnati, Ohio, with Covington, Kentucky, on the other side, and another advertising the Roxbury Coaches, a stage line operating near Boston. The American Vecturist

Association, founded on October 31, 1948, by Max M. Schwartz and others, is devoted to transportation tokens and related issues and may be the longest-established special-interest group in American numismatics. The standard reference on the subject is the *Atwood-Coffee Catalogue of United States and Canadian Transportation Tokens*, by John M. Coffee, Jr., and Harold V. Ford (fifth edition), the latest updating and expansion of the classification system developed years ago by Roland C. Atwood.

Tokens for and by Numismatists

Many tokens have been made especially for the numismatic trade. Among the earlier examples are Conder tokens (discussed in chapter 21), such as the Kentucky token, the P.P.P. Myddelton token, and others. Decades later, in the 19th century, several diesinkers produced series of tokens depicting Revolutionary War battles, notable buildings, famous figures in history, and other subjects. Quite a few of these were produced by diesinkers such as George H. Lovett and Robert Lovett, Jr. These can also be called medalets (small medals).

Still other tokens advertised or depicted numismatists. Those in Augustus B. Sage's "Numismatic Gallery" series, which can be called medalets as well, were illustrated with the portraits of collectors of the day, including Charles I. Bushnell and James Chilton. This was intended to be a very impressive series. An advertisement prepared early in 1859 noted:

> *Aug. B. Sage's Numismatic Gallery.* This series will consist of about 30 medalets, having for their obverses the busts of the prominent numismatists of our country. They will also be uniform to the above. A splendid

Aug. B. Sage's Numismatic Series No. 1 token or medalet depicting Charles I. Bushnell, one of the leading numismatists of the era. A grand series of such tokens was planned, but only eight different major varieties are known today.

variety of wreaths and lettering will be introduced in this series.

The dies were cut by George H. Lovett. First produced was No. 1, featuring Charles I. Bushnell. A specimen, possibly hot off the coining press, was presented to the American Numismatic Society on March 23, 1859. Other honorees in this series included Henry Bogert, Jeremiah Colburn, Dr. James R. Chilton, Winslow Lewis, Frank Jaudon, William H. Chesley, Horatio N. Rust, and Robert J. Dodge.

Today all of these are inexpensive, but elusive, an exception being the Chilton token. None of the latter is known to exist, and it may be that the issue was either not created or was suppressed. After Dodge, the series expired, good intentions notwithstanding.

At the turn of the 20th century, many dealers and collectors issued tokens (usually brass) giving their names, addresses, and collecting specialties. Quite a few of these were illustrated and described in the pages of *The Numismatist*. In recent times the Patrick Mint (Jess Patrick, proprietor) has issued hundreds of different tokens for dealers and others, advertising their businesses. Among all numismatics-related tokens, more than 5,000 varieties can be accounted for, most produced in the past 50 years.

Counterstamped Coins

United States and other coins were often counterstamped with advertising, political messages, silversmiths' hallmarks, and other imprints, in effect becoming "little billboards" carried from hand to hand. The slogan VOTE THE LAND FREE, stamped on copper cents of various dates 1844 and earlier, suggested that territories should be free of slavery. DR. G.G. WILKINS stamped thousands of cents and other coins with this inscription, drawing attention to his combined dental practice, saloon, and store in Pittsfield, New Hampshire, complete with a caged bear out front.

Dr. Gregory D. Brunk has compiled listings for hundreds of different issuers of such pieces, delineated in *American and Canadian Countermarked Coins*.

Market values range from a few dollars for coins stamped with stray names or designations that cannot be attributed, to more than $100 for some produced by silversmiths, merchants, and tradesmen whose locations can be identified.

For me, counterstamped copper cents have been a numismatic love since the 1950s. Most exciting is when I decipher or attribute an inscription that appears mysterious on a coin, but that makes sense when combined with an old-time directory listing or advertisement. I wrote a monograph on the aforementioned Dr. G.G. Wilkins

Some interesting counterstamps by Charles H. Goodwin on large copper cents. Although the meaning of the expanded G.G.G.G. letters was not recognized until recently, the other product, G.G.G., was mentioned as early as this listing by W. Elliot Woodward in his sale of May 1, 1863, Lot 1457: "Goodwin's Grand Grease Juice for the Hair, G.G.G., struck over a U.S. cent, very curious."

and a large hardbound book on the Water-ford Water Cure (operated in Waterford, Maine, by Dr. Shattuck, who was fond of advertising his business by counterstamp-ing cents, half dollars, and other coins).

A recent cause of excitement, in cooper-ation with several other researchers and enthusiasts, was learning all about the mys-terious letters G.G.G. and G.G.G.G. fre-quently seen counterstamped on old cents. In a moment of serendipity, in the evening of March 12, 2001, I was curled up in a comfortable chair listening to recorded music and browsing through a large book I had examined many times earlier—inter-esting and important as the very first edi-tion of what became a standard—the 1856 edition of George Adams's *The New Eng-land Business Directory*. I had a four-inch reading glass in one hand and was reading some of the fine print in the advertise-ments. All of a sudden, at 10:03, this popped out at me:

Charles H. Goodwin, Druggist & Manufacturing Chemist. Dealer in Drugs, Medicines, Dye Stuffs, Per-fumery and Fancy Goods. Inventor, Manufacturer and Proprietor of the following preparations:

G.G.G., or Q. of F., GOOD-WIN'S GRAND GREASEJUICE, OR QUINTESSENCE OF FAT, the great American compound for the embellishment, preservation, growth, and beauty of the human hair.

The unrivalled breath perfume, G.G.G.G., GOODWIN'S GRAND GLITTERING GLOBULES, or AMBROSIAL AROMATIC YAN-KEE CACHOUS.

G.G.T., and Q. of Q., Goodwin's Great Tobaccojuice, and Quintes-sence of Quicksilver, the great Amer-ican remedy for the *Cimex Lecularius*, or common bed bug.

Also of Goodwin's Flavoring Extracts, and Madame Delectable's Handkerchief Perfume.

All orders to be addressed to Charles H. Goodwin, Chemist, at

GOODWIN'S GRAND GREASE-JUICE DEPOT, No. 49 Water Street, Exeter, N.H.

Isn't this fun! I used this event as center point to a chapter in a later book, *More Adventures With Rare Coins*. Funny, isn't it, that a "lowly" counterstamped copper cent, such as one of these shown here, most of which are worth less than $100, can be as exciting to me to contemplate as a gem Proof double eagle worth many tens of thousands of dollars!

Later Trade Tokens and "Good-Fors"

After about 1890 there was a great expan-sion in the issuance of small tokens, often of 5¢ value, for use in saloons, restaurants, hotels, and other places of public accom-modation. In the 20th century other issuers of tokens included turnpike and toll-road authorities, streetcar lines, amusement arcades, vending-machine owners and operators, car washes, company stores, and more. Often, suppliers of goods to taverns and hotels, such as the Albert Pick Com-pany, offered tokens made with custom imprints (like as not these were ordered through suppliers in Chicago or Cincin-nati). Most such tokens were of simple design, with numerals and lettering, but rarely with portraits or other motifs. Brass and aluminum were the metals of choice.

Many tokens were meant to be given out as awards in gambling machines or by a class of devices known as *trade stimulators*. Distributors of these devices, including the Mills Novelty Co. (Chicago) and Caille Brothers (Detroit), also offered their cus-tomers the opportunity to order tokens. While many if not most tokens of this type bore the names of merchants, others were stamped with serial numbers pertaining to specific machines—as a control to prevent tokens from one establishment being redeemed in another. Many local and regional ordinances prohibited machines that paid out cash, but those that paid out tokens were allowed to remain in use. Most tokens could be redeemed at the

This impressively named Automatic Cashier & Discount Machine, standing about seven feet high, was manufactured in Burlington, Vermont, by the Yale Wonder Clock Company, about 1905. Upon depositing a nickel, the patron had a chance to win an aluminum token valued at 5¢, 10¢, or 15¢ in trade, to hear a music-box tune, and to watch a changing series of printed advertisements. Tokens used in this particular machine all bore the number 825. What fun! (Preston Evans photograph)

Shown are one each of the three different token denominations made for the Automatic Cashier & Discount Machine, with the denomination at the center of the obverse of each and with a reverse of common style.

counter for cash, perhaps with a wink by the proprietor. Their main use was to buy cigars, candy, beer, or food.

Recently, I had the opportunity to correspond with Preston Evans, who was selling an Automatic Cashier & Discount Machine—a tall, cabinet-style device made circa 1905 by the Yale Wonder Clock Company of Burlington, Vermont. A patron dropped a five-cent coin into the device and was rewarded with changing scenes depicting portraits, landscapes, animals, and other things, while a music box played a short tune. An intricate gambling device built within paid out aluminum tokens valued at 5¢, 10¢, or 15¢, depending on the luck of the patron. These could then be redeemed for merchandise at the counter. Each token was stamped with the number 825, to prevent an outsider with access to similar tokens from switching them around. More than 100 tokens were found inside Evans's machine, and he sent me a set for my collection. I plan to write an article on this machine—which, if anything, illustrates how tokens can lead to interesting research. As to the value of the tokens themselves, it is probably very slight—perhaps a few dollars—simply because hardly anyone knows what they are!

Coin-operated, cylinder-type phonographs, electric pianos, jukeboxes, and penny-arcade amusement devices also had tokens made in connection with them, bearing such inscriptions as EDISONIA, WURLITZER, and COSMORAMA.

Many nickel-sized tokens used in public establishments bear inscriptions including GOOD FOR, followed by a product or service. In collecting parlance these are known, logically enough, as *good-fors*. Most of these were meant for local use, and thus it is not unusual for one to have an inscription reading, for example, PLATTNER'S SALOON, sometimes with a street address, but with no indication of the town where this particular place was located. These are referred to as *mavericks* by collectors, who find it especially satisfying when, through research in old directories and advertising, they can be attributed.

Tokens of the late 19th century and the 20th century may be the most eagerly pursued specialty of all, as recently noted by long-time collector and dealer David Schenkman.[76] Most are inexpensive, from less than a dollar up to several dollars, although those from saloons, or with connections to the "Wild West," or with imprints from territories (before they achieved statehood), can be rare and expensive, into the hundreds of dollars or more. Similar to older tokens, these are popularly collected by category, geographical location, or trade of the proprietor, or some other aspect.

Further Token Series

Often, a particular person or topic can furnish a token-collecting specialty. At least a few dozen tokens are associated with showman P.T. Barnum and his featured attractions, including Jenny Lind (who created a sensation when she came to America in 1850), General Tom Thumb, and Barnum's American Museum. Many different tokens for fairs and expositions are collectible, with issues of the 1876 Centennial Exhibition, 1892 to 1893 World's Columbian Exposition, and 1904 St. Louis World's Fair being particularly numerous. These events also spawned a generous number of large and small medals intended for display, award, or advertising. Masonic chapter pennies have been popular with many collectors, and thousands of varieties exist. Whether some of the smaller pieces should be classified as tokens or as medalets is a matter of opinion.

Pick a topic, and chances are good that tokens can be collected in connection with it.

Collecting and the Marketplace

Market Notes and Observations

The market for most tokens from the early days through the 1860s is very strong, consisting almost entirely of knowledgeable specialists who are willing to pay generous prices for rare material. The price levels are far short of those for the federal coin series, and Civil War tokens of which fewer than a half dozen are known are apt to be priced for a couple hundred dollars or so, this being for very choice examples. Hard Times tokens tend to be priced higher, and early American (pre-1832) issues higher yet. Still, the levels are modest, and even classic rarities tend to be priced in the thousands of dollars—not the tens of thousands. Exceptions to this market activity are tokens of 1845 to 1860, which are often inexpensive in comparison to Hard Times tokens from before that time and Civil War tokens after. Tokens from after the Civil War, continuing to modern times, are generally very inexpensive, one reason being that subjects and issuers are diverse, and they are not often collected as a series. Also, greater quantities of such pieces exist.

While most tokens issued from 1700 to 1900 are delineated in Russell Rulau's *Standard Catalog*, studying issues from 1900 to date can be a challenge. Historical and pricing information is scattered, but much can be found in the pages of the *TAMS Journal*, published by the Token and Medal Society, as well as in dozens of specialized monographs and books.

There are many sources of supply, the most important being dealer specialists. These people know their business and can furnish information concerning rarity and availability. While good buys can sometimes be made on the Internet or in flea markets, many such offerings are fake. My recommendation is either to buy rare pieces from established specialists, or to consult them if you contemplate a purchase. It is not very easy to recoup your money if you buy a fake or fantasy token, and the entire experience may dampen your ardor for collecting. Better to be cautious and safe than sorry.

As to the investment aspects of tokens, in the long term the better-known series—these being early American issues, Hard Times tokens, and Civil War tokens—have done very well. The market is strong, and when choice pieces are offered there is usually a lot of action. However, such concepts as fast movements in the market, "bid" and "ask" prices, and buying for investment's sake are largely unknown. In recent years many of these pieces have been certified by the leading grading services, expanding the market for them and, as a consequence, lifting many prices. Now, dealers who don't know the difference between a Low-54 Hard Times token and a Lord Timothy Dexter warming pan can "expertly" deal in tokens, or so it seems! Still, in my opinion, it is best to deal with a truly knowledgeable seller.

Tokens are best collected for the enjoyment they provide. Buy carefully, and chances are good that you will do well financially. I have collected counterstamped large copper cents for a long time, since 1955, and decade by decade the prices have edged upward. A coin that might have cost $2 in 1955 is worth $25 to $50 now. Civil War tokens that I sold for $3 to $5 each in 1959 are generally worth 10 to 20 times those figures today.

Key to Collecting Tokens

- **Mint State examples:** Among all classes of early tokens, those intended for circulation, political campaigns, or other use are scarce or rare today. Those made for numismatists are usually seen in Mint State. The field is so diverse that no general rules can be made.

- **Circulated examples:** Generally, tokens that were meant to be used in trade, in machines, or for presentation exist today in worn grades.

- **Strike quality:** The striking sharpness of tokens, including those made for collectors, can vary widely.

- **Proof examples:** While some tokens made for collectors were struck with Proof surfaces, the vast majority of pieces were struck with frosty or some other variation of normal surfaces for circulating issues.

- **Key issues:** Each specialty has its rarities and key issues.

- **Advice to smart buyers:** Before buying an expensive token, learn as much as you can about it. Buying from an established dealer-specialist is highly recommended. Insist on a written receipt and guarantee of authenticity. Be especially careful with pieces with "romantic" imprints, such as western stagecoach lines, territorial saloons, and so on, as many fantasies have been made.

- **Selected bibliography:**

Brunk, Gregory G. 1987. *American and Canadian Countermarked Coins*. Rockford, IL.

Coffee, John M., Jr., and Harold V. Ford. 1996. *The Atwood-Coffee Catalogue of United States and Canadian Transportation Tokens* (5th ed.). Boston, MA.

Doty, Richard G. (editor). 1994. *The Token: America's Other Money*. American Numismatic Society, Coinage of the Americas Conference, New York, NY.

DeWitt, J. Doyle. 1859. *A Century of Campaign Buttons 1789–1889*. Hartford, CT.

Fuld, Melvin, and George Fuld. 1975. *U.S. Civil War Store Cards* (2nd ed.). Lawrence, MA.

Fuld, Melvin, and George Fuld. 1982. *Patriotic Civil War Tokens*. Iola, WI.

Low, Lyman Haynes. 1899. *Hard Times Tokens*. New York, NY.

Miller, Donald M. 1962. *A Catalogue of U.S. Store Cards or Merchants' Tokens*. Indiana, PA.

Rulau, Russell. 2004. *Standard Catalog of United States Tokens 1700–1900*. Iola, WI.

Schenkman, David E. 1983. *Civil War Sutler Tokens and Cardboard Scrip*. Bryans Road, MD.

CHAPTER TWENTY-SIX

COLLECTING MEDALS

If you are just beginning to collect and have not yet started to specialize in any country or series, why don't you order a volume or two of the *Coin Collector's Journal*, or the *Numismatic Review*, and just spend several evenings reading the very splendid material on many different coins or types or series? There are conversation topics in every issue of these periodicals, and a wealth of authentic information. It is a pity that the *Numismatic Review* was discontinued, because the type of material included in it was of high caliber and scholarly, timely and easily read.

—D. Dee DeNise, April 1952

The Fascinating Specialty of Medals
Introduction (With a Nod to C. Wyllys Betts)

In the preface to C. Wyllys Betts's study, *American Colonial History Illustrated by Contemporary Medals* (1894), Frederic H. Betts, brother of the deceased author, gave this rationale for the desirability of medals:

> The value of coins and medals, as enduring records of events, has often been emphasized. All original documents and contemporary accounts of occurrences are of peculiar importance to the conscientious historian.
>
> Medals are original documents in metal. In studying them we study history at its source. As contribution to the knowledge of the history of portraiture, dress, and habits, as indices of then existing information in architecture, geography, and the natural sciences, and as means of restoring the knowledge of structures long destroyed, medals are not to be underestimated.
>
> Medals are a body of history, or, perhaps, a collection of pictures in miniature, or so many maps for explaining ancient geography. One is to look upon a cabinet of medals as a treasure, not of money, but of knowledge, and as the means by which a conqueror has sometimes "discharged a debt to posterity, after he has ruined or defaced a strong place, by delivering a model of it, as it stood whole and entire, so as in some measure to repair the mischiefs of his bombs and cannon."[77]

As an intelligent student of history, my late brother was not unconscious, also, of those unintended teachings often to be derived from contemporary medals, which, perhaps, sometimes enable us to realize as vividly the feelings, beliefs, and conditions of the past, also to the purposed labors of chroniclers. "It is safer," it has been said, "to quote a medal than a historian."

C. Wyllys Betts was born on August 13, 1845, the son of Frederic J. Betts, in Newburgh, New York—perhaps propitious of his career, for as a teenager he emulated Captain Thomas Machin, famous Newburgh maker of counterfeit coins. In 1855 the family moved to New Haven to give sons Frederic H. and Wyllys the benefits of the schools in that city. Young Wyllys seems to have been a numismatic rascal, or at least he is sometimes portrayed that way. It is said that at the age of 14 he found in New Haven some old dies for 1787 Fugio coppers. The site was the Broome & Platt store, earlier the site of the mint that had struck these coins.[78] "New Haven restrikes" were coined from these dies. The story fell apart in later years when it was discovered that these dies had been newly made. In 1863, Betts entered Yale College where he gained recognition for literary composition.

Now and then in the annals of numismatics we encounter a brilliant collector or dealer who seeks to improve on the historical record by making fantasy coins. This is usually done by consulting old accounts, business directories, and the like, and creating coins or medals of types that, perhaps, could have been made in the olden times, but were not. Betts, drawing upon his knowledge of history, cut dies for several "colonial" coins, including one dated 1623 and inscribed NOVUM BELGIUM, probably to amuse himself. Apparently tiring of the sport, he consigned or sold some of these creations to W. Elliot Woodward, who included them in a four-page, 45-lot addenda listing to the McCoy Collection sale of May 1864, describing them for what they were.

Years later, dealer Édouard Frossard, who was especially proud of his numismatic knowledge, but quite unaware of the obscure supplement to Woodward's long-ago catalog, grandly announced the "discovery" of a marvelous colonial coin with ties to "New Belgium," a settlement in America. Frossard's competitors found this to be a wonderful comeuppance!

Later, Betts wrote this in a letter, expressing some remorse:

> Unfortunately, someone about 1862 presented me with a set of letters and several engraving tools, and in learning the use of them I made a great number of store cards and medalets, most of which are unique, and all, I think, in the Yale College cabinet. The earlier ones I look upon with some interest because they used to afford me a great deal of amusement, not only in the making, but in the astonishment of collectors when looking over my cabinet.

In 1871, after taking degrees from Columbia and Yale, Wyllys Betts entered the law firm of Whitney and Betts, in which his brother was a partner. This was the beginning of his legal career. In following years he continued in numismatics with a passion, although the period of creating new varieties seems to have passed. In 1886 he was the author of a 17-page

study, *Counterfeit Half Pence Current in the American Colonies, and Their Issue from the Mints of Connecticut and Vermont.* On April 27, 1887, after a week's bout with pneumonia, Betts died at his home in New York City. His masterwork, a study on early medals relating to America, was completed by Lyman H. Low and William T.R. Marvin and published in 1894.

American Medals
Aspects and Appeal of Medals

Medals are closely related to tokens, but were generally issued, not for use in commerce, but to be held and enjoyed, commemorating an accomplishment or individual, or perhaps promoting a cause. While in a broad sense they serve as a mirror of history, as Frederic H. Betts so eloquently stated, the glass can also be clouded. Often, depictions on medals are idealistic, and, other times, if the details of a subject were not known to the engraver, they were simply made up. Admittedly, such situations were in the minority, but they happened often enough that medals must be "interpreted," to use a term popular with historians today.

In this vein, several different medals of George Washington do not depict the American hero at all, but use imaginary portraits—such as the man on the Voltaire medal of Washington and, apparently, the visage of the Duke of Wellington on certain "Washington" medals of 1783. Similarly, a historian, following Betts's suggestion, who sought to determine how Washington dressed, might conclude by looking at medals that he often wore a laurel wreath and occasionally was dressed in a Roman toga!

Hippocampi (mythological creatures similar to sea horses), cornucopias, and other representations on medals can be discarded as being imaginary or symbolic; which other elements *should* be believed, however, is sometimes a matter of study— what with various renderings of fortresses, ships, trees, and exotic animals, along with the fact that most engravers tried to depict their emperors and military heroes in flattering ways.

The preceding is not at all unique to medals. On paper money, too, can be found all sorts of images, from realistic to allegorical, and even the modern Washington quarter dollars with statehood reverses have many imaginary or idealistic features.

Other medals were created for presentation or award purposes—for displaying the finest glassware at an exposition, for membership in the Washington Chowder Club, for good attendance at Sunday school, or for rescuing hapless crewmembers and passengers from a sinking ship such as the *S.S. Somers.*

The Philadelphia Mint produced many different medals, ranging from those for presentation to Indian chiefs, to those remembering military heroes and battles, to mementoes of the annual meetings of the Assay Commission, to commemoratives of the inaugurations of presidents. Dozens of other mints issued medals, ranging from single-proprietor shops to the Medallic Art Company (MACO), the latter being dominant in the field in the 20th century.

During the late 19th and early 20th centuries, fairs and expositions often "awarded" medals to those who set up commercial displays. Sometimes this got a bit expensive. The American Institute, which held annual exhibits in New York City, gave paper certificates in place of medals if an exhibitor gained first place on successive occasions. The Franklin Institute and the Massachusetts Charitable Mechanic Association both bestowed medals from dies cut by Christian Gobrecht (famous in numismatic circles for his dollar design). The Louisiana Purchase Exposition gave medals to those who were patrons, but certain of its awards boldly lettered "Gold Medal" were actually made of copper!

Still other medals were struck for collectors. These range from many different U.S. Mint issues, to those issued by the American Numismatic Society (an early one depicted the martyred Abraham Lincoln),

to several long runs and series made in the early 20th century, to mass-market productions by the Franklin Mint and others.

Unlike the situation for coins, the date on a medal sometimes is different from the year(s) in which it was issued. Further, it was and is common practice to keep medal dies on hand and to strike additional examples on demand. Accordingly, a medal dated, say, 1846 may have been struck in that year, but others like it may have been made for years afterward. Relevant to this, Katherine Jaeger has commented:

> The American Institute was still distributing cheap little medals from Robert Lovett's 1842 28-mm gold medal dies through the 1960s, for their high school science fairs. George H. Lovett's Lifesaving Benevolent Association medals designed in the 19th century are still being struck.[79]

I like to think of a medal as a particularly artistic representation of a person, place, thing, or event, hopefully evocative of reality, but often combined with imagination. Moreover, often a medalist put his or her best foot forward, to create pieces of enduring beauty. In effect, a collection of medals can be like a private art museum.

Selected Medal Series and Specialties

While the subjects covered by medals exceed those on tokens, the following are some specialties that have attracted numismatists over a period of years. These categories often overlap. Thus, a particular medal depicting George Washington can be part of the Washington medal series, but it also might be an award medal or an Assay Commission medal.

Betts Medals

These are medals from the more than 600 varieties specifically listed and described in the 1894 book *American Colonial History Illustrated by Contemporary Medals*, by C. Wyllys Betts, edited by Lyman H. Low and William T.R. Marvin.

Betts-96, one of several Betts-listed medals relating to the stunning British naval victory over the Spanish treasure fleet in the harbor of Vigo, Spain, in 1702. Galleons returning from the New World (hence the Betts connection), laden with silver, were captured and sunk. Much silver and gold was taken by the British. To celebrate their triumph, the British produced silver and gold coins in 1702 and 1703 with VIGO lettered under Queen Anne's portrait. (Thomas Sebring Collection)

Betts-570, the 1780 Happy While United medal, is one of the great rarities in the series. Although its existence was recorded as early as 1781 (by Pierre Eugene Du Simitière), it was not until John W. Adams studied the variety in the 1980s and published "The Virginia Happy While United Medal" (*American Journal of Numismatics*, ANS, 1992) that its history was made fully known. (John W. Adams collection)

The famous Libertas Americana medal, Betts-615, which inspired early American coinage motifs. (Catherine E. Bullowa / John W. Adams; also see description in chapter 5)

Two title words, *American Colonial*, are somewhat misleading, as *American* refers to the entire New World from South America to Canada, and not just the districts that later became the United States of America. The work includes these title-subject areas: Period of Discovery (1556–1631), Period of Colonization (1632–1737), Vernon Medals (1739–1741), American Proclamation Pieces of Ferdinand VI of Spain (1746–1747), From the Peace of Paris to the Revolution (1763–1775), and Independence of America Recognized (1782–1786).

Today, most American numismatists use the Betts book as a guide to what to collect, but usually overlook many of the listings with little direct connection to the 13 original colonies. As examples, the section for Betts-171 through Betts-337 is entirely devoted to cheap, popular medals, mostly sold in England as souvenirs, to honor Admiral Edward Vernon, whose main accomplishment was the capture of the Spanish fort at Porto Bello, Panama, in 1739. Similarly, many will skip the American proclamation pieces of Charles III of Spain, Betts-448 to -506, which deal with Central and South American subjects.

In contrast, the many Betts medals that treat relationships with Indians in North America, voyages to what became the United States, battles of the Revolutionary War, and activities in the 13 colonies are of commanding interest and importance. No doubt, if a modern version of Betts were to be created, it would rearrange its divisions to identify issues specifically addressing the history of the United States, would exclude some that Betts listed in this category, and would add others not treated in the original text.

The Betts text is interspersed with many footnotes describing, often in fascinating detail, the events depicted on the medals. Some not so treated call for description by a new generation of scholars. Further, rarity and condition census information, absent from most Betts listings, would be a welcome addition.

The following is a typical Betts listing, this of a great rarity known today as the "Happy While United" medal (although these words were used on certain other medals of the era as well):

Betts-570: Indian Medal, Virginia. *Obv.* REBELLION TO TYRANTS IS OBEDIENCE TO GOD. On a label in the upper part of the field, VIRGINIA. Arms of Virginia; a woman in armor, with a sword in right hand and a spear in her left, presses her right foot on a man lying prostrate, and with her left foot secures a chain, which he clutches with his left hand; on the ground is a crown.

Rev. HAPPY WHILE UNITED. In exergue, 1780. At the right is a strange sort of tree, under which an Indian at the left and a white officer at the right, are seated; the Indian holds a pipe; at the left is an open sea, on which are three vessels; near them is a rocky point with a house.

Copper, rare (Appleton collection), and pewter, rare. It has a loop, formed of a pipe and eagle's wing. Size 46 [2.78 inches]. *AJN* II, p. 110; VII, 90 (copper); British Museum (pewter).

For many years, the nature of the 1780 Happy While United medal remained a mystery in numismatic circles, with some decrying it as a fake, simply because little could be learned about it. The matter was nicely solved by John W. Adams in his monograph, "The Virginia Happy While United Medal," published by the American Numismatic Society in 1992. A "Eureka!" moment was the finding, in an old magazine on Pennsylvania history, of a May 1781 entry in the notebook of Pierre Eugene Du Simitière, a talented artist of the Revolutionary War era and, possibly, America's first serious numismatist:

A cast copy in copper of a medal made in Virginia last year to be given to the Indians having on one side Liberty trampling down a Tyrant round it.

"Rebellion to Tyrants is Obedience to God." On the top Virginia. On the reverse a white man and an Indian sitting on a bench, under a tree with a pipe in his hand, round "Happy While United," in the exergue 1780, a pipe, an eagle's wing on the top of the medal with an opening to suspend it by, the gift of Isaac Zane. Esq.[80]

While the Happy While United medal is wonderful and rare, not many people are aware of it. Probably, the best known and publicized of the varieties listed in the Betts book is his number 615, the Libertas Americana medal (see p. 490), featuring on the obverse Miss Liberty with cap and pole—the inspiration for the early copper coinage of the Philadelphia Mint.

A Medal of the Post-Revolutionary Era

Among my favorite possessions are two specimens of the issue generally referred to as the Columbia and Washington medal of 1787, the dies for which are believed to have been cut by Paul Revere. Depicted on the obverse are two sailing vessels. The *Columbia Rediviva*, usually referred to as the *Columbia*, as finally constructed was a full-rigged ship, 83 feet long, which displaced 212 tons. The second ship, called here the *Lady Washington* and usually cited simply as the *Washington*, was a sloop of 90 tons. The medals, struck in Boston and sent aboard the ships on their voyage of discovery to the Pacific Northwest, were described in a journal kept by John Hoskins:

1787. That nothing might be wanting to commemorate the voyage and to place a lasting memento in those countries which might be visited or discovered, during its continuance, the owners caused several hundred medals[81] to be struck, and sent to those vessels. On the one side was the Ship and Sloop, encircled with theirs and the commander's name. On the other, the names of the owners, to wit: Joseph Barrell, Samuel Brown, Crowel Hatch, John Derby, Charles

Bulfinch, and John Marsden Pintard, esquires; encircled with, Fitted at Boston, North America, for the Pacific Ocean 1787.

They caused also about a dozen silver ones to be struck, one of which was sent to General Washington, who politely returned his thanks, and paid the owners a very flattering compliment on the occasion; at the same time express'd his best wishes for their success.[82]

I first learned about these medals years ago when John J. Ford, Jr. (who passed away in 2005), expressed to me that this was one of his favorites from that era—perhaps, even his foremost favorite. He urged me to buy a copy of *Voyages of the "Columbia" to the Northwest Coast 1787–1790 and 1790–1793*, edited by F.W. Howay and published by the Massachusetts Historical Society in 1941. This had been out of print for a long time, but through some letter writing (in the quite different days before the Internet!) to leading book dealers, I finally tracked one down. (The price I do not remember, but it was not cheap, perhaps a couple hundred dollars.) I then read it.

In connection with the Garrett Collection consigned to my firm in 1979 and presented in a series of four catalogs, I cataloged the first 1787 Columbia and Washington medal I had ever offered at auction. The buyer at the sale was John W. Adams. A few years later Adams was able to find a better one, and so he sold the Garrett piece to me, and I still have it. Since then I have seen a few others, including at the Massachusetts Historical Society (to which Adams recommended me for membership as a fellow, for which I am grateful) and in the 2004 catalog of the Ford Collection specimens, cataloged by Michael Hodder and sold by Stack's.

In addition to the Howay book I have two dozen or more texts in my library about early sailing expeditions to that area of the Northwest, and about Paul Revere (I have not found any documentation that he cut the dies for this medal, but perhaps he did), as well as related historical volumes. I

Betts-383, the Annapolis Tuesday Club medal, offered as lot 785 in Wayte Raymond's sale of the W.W.C. Wilson Collection, sold in New York City at the Anderson Galleries, November 16 through 18, 1925. The medal brought $80 at the time. Today, the decimal point could be moved over several places! In the same sale, lot 818, a Washington and Columbia medal in silver, well-worn Fine grade, sold for $75. To put values in perspective it is noted that lot 121, a group of three Uncirculated gold dollars (1887, 1888, and 1889) sold for $7, or slightly more than $2 apiece!

Betts-614, the Felicitas Americana medal, from the Betts illustration of 1894. The obverse represents the spirit of America as personified by an Indian, while England is represented by the seated figure of Britannia. The date refers to the peace treaty. The reverse design is styled after the Continental dollar coins of 1776. Betts knew of only two pieces in existence, one with a lettered edge and the other with an ornamented edge.

Perhaps the most historical of all privately issued American medals, the Columbia and Washington medal illustrates on the obverse two exploring ships, the *Columbia* and its escort, the *Lady Washington*. On the reverse, the names of the principals of the voyage are given. The die engraver is unknown and may have been Paul Revere.

also have a handful of numismatic books and catalogs that mention or illustrate the medal. In my book *More Adventures With Rare Coins* (2002), I devoted part of a chapter to it.

My well-worn Columbia and Washington medal speaks to me, in a way. I know that T. Harrison Garrett, the owner of America's most important private collection prior to his death in 1888, once learned of this coin, contemplated buying it, did, and then held it in his hands and studied it in a room in the Evergreen House, his mansion on North Charles Street, Baltimore. As to where it went in acquiring evidence of circulation, the medal keeps its secrets well. I like to think it was traded to a Native American, who cherished it as a keepsake for a long time, after which, somehow, it entered numismatic circles. Or perhaps it was a sailor's pocket piece. Certainly it never circulated as a coin, so the wear must have come from an appreciative owner.

While I've enjoyed owning my well-worn copper version, many years ago I had the chance to view a superb striking in *silver*, perhaps the finest known, owned by a New England collector-friend. Then—lo and behold!—in 2005 the medal became available when the owner wanted to convert its worth into a few rare die varieties of colonial coins he aspired to own. A telephone conversation or two later, it was mine. As to its provenance, he knew little, as do I.

My romance with the 1787 Columbia and Washington medal, then, started with a book. Absent Howay's text, I probably would not own an example now, nor would I know much about it. Curiously, this handsome souvenir from 1787 is "betwixt and between"—too late to be included in C. Wyllys Betts's study of medals illustrating *colonial* history, and not eligible for inclusion in R.W. Julian's study of medals struck at the Philadelphia Mint from 1792 to 1892. Nor is it a *coin*, to merit listing in the *Guide Book*; nor is it a token, although it gained Russell Rulau's notice in the *Standard Catalog of United States Tokens 1700–1900*.

A copper striking in the Massachusetts Historical Society was presented to the society by one of the men named on the back of the medal—this during the early days of the founding of that organization, soon after the Revolutionary War. In another context, Paul Revere contributed a personal reminiscence of his "midnight ride" to the society.

In early 2005, the society featured the aforementioned example on its web site, as "object of the month," noting in part:

> In 1791, acting on behalf of the merchants involved in the voyage, Joseph Barrell presented this copper Columbia and Washington medal to the newly established Massachusetts Historical Society. It has long been treasured as the cornerstone of the Society's numismatic collection.

Think of it, the *cornerstone* of the collection! Some time ago, the society had a Class I 1804 silver dollar, but in 1970 deaccessioned it. I enjoy 1804 silver dollars and have participated in the marketing of several of them. I also enjoy the Columbia and Washington medal, and in my career have sold *one*, the Garrett example. It is interesting to contemplate these two vastly different numismatic items—one designated the "King of American coins" and the other virtually unknown.

Washington Medals

On December 14, 1799, George Washington died at his Virginia home, Mount Vernon (named after Admiral Vernon, of Betts text recognition). Early the following year, eulogies were given, monographs were published, and parades were conducted in Washington's honor (especially on February 22, his birth date). Jacob Perkins, inventor and die cutter of Newburyport, Massachusetts, produced medals early in 1800, inscribed HE IS IN GLORY, THE WORLD IN TEARS. This set the scene for medals (and tokens) memorializing the "Father of Our Country," a recognition that continues to this day.

Washington funeral medal by Jacob Perkins of Newburyport, Massachusetts; variety known as Baker-166, die combination 1-B. Examples were issued with a hole at the top, to permit wearing on a ribbon or cord. Such medals were widely sold in early 1800 and used in memorial parades (especially on February 22, 1800) and services.

A subject of numismatic discussion for a long time is the curious Washington/Lincoln medal, issued in the 1860s during the fever for such items. The flip side depicts Abraham Lincoln and the appropriate designation LINCOLN below, but has REVERSE above. (As to what REVERSE means, my thought is that it was part of the instructions to the die cutter—an intention to order a medal with a "REVERSE depicting LINCOLN," and perhaps given as "REVERSE, LINCOLN." What do you think?)

The Manly medal was produced and sold in 1790, during the lifetime of America's first president. Produced in copper and silver, these enjoyed wide sales in an era in which depictions of Washington were few in books and newspapers. This variety is known as Baker-61B, a copper-alloy striking with a color resembling brass.

In the 1850s there was great popular interest in American history, spurred by several factors. Among the most important was the publication in 1852 of Benson J. Lossing's two-volume octavo work, *Pictorial Field-Book of the Revolution*, which contained many sketches of that conflict and much text about General Washington. There was a also movement to restore and preserve Mount Vernon, with a group that would later be known as the Mount Vernon Ladies Association of the Union (led by Ann Pamela Cunningham) in the forefront. Edward Everett, a famous orator of the era, gave many speeches on the subject (it was Everett who in 1863 gave the "other" address at the dedication of the Gettysburg battlefield). In addition, illustrated weekly magazines were achieving great popularity and contained much information on American history. In 1857, *Historical Magazine* was founded and furthered that interest.

By spring 1859, although dozens of different medals depicting Washington had been issued, the Mint Cabinet had only "four or five" different varieties from among the dozens known to exist.[83] Director James Ross Snowden, an avid numismatist, sought to remedy this, and by exchanging privately made rarities, restrikes, and patterns, he assembled a magnificent display of such medals. The

Peace medal depicting William Penn, variety cataloged as Betts-531. (Illustration from Betts, 1894)

Washington Cabinet was opened at the Mint on Washington's birthday, February 22, 1860. The activities of the 1850s engendered a great passion for Washington tokens and medals, and in the 1860s they were the single most active area in the numismatic market. In 1861 Snowden's handsome, extensively illustrated 203-page book, *A Description of the Medals of Washington*, was published.

In 1885, W.S. Baker's *Medallic Portraits of Washington* described 651 different Washington medals. In the late 20th century the same title was used on a new work, by George Fuld and Russell Rulau, with even more listings. This remains the standard reference today.

The most valuable and rare of the Washington medals are those made during his lifetime, continuing until after his death, and up until the 1832 observation of the centennial of his birth. Later medals include a veritable flood of Washington and related (Revolutionary War events) pieces made from the late 1850s through the 1870s for the numismatic trade. The 1889 centennial of Washington's first inauguration saw many medals produced, as did the bicentennial of his birth in 1932. All of these are described in the Fuld-Rulau text.

Indian Peace Medals

The tradition of presenting medals to Native Americans of importance (usually in silver to the chief, sometimes in copper to others) predated the Revolution. In colonial times, representatives of the governments of England, France, and Spain distributed these, sometimes in large numbers. The typical early medal depicted a monarch on the obverse and, on the reverse, a scene, such as an Indian and a European official together in a tranquil setting. In the late 18th and early 19th centuries, related medals were issued by certain other entities, including the Quakers in Philadelphia (1775) and fur companies trading in the West.

The purpose of the medals was to establish an allegiance and loyalty between the tribal leaders and the distant government authorities. The chiefs wore the medals with pride—a great honor—and were sometimes buried with them.

Beginning with Washington, peace medals were issued for most administrations through the end of the 19th century. The earliest medals given out by emissaries on behalf of President Washington were oval in form and were hand-engraved on each side, depicting a farm scene on the obverse and the Great Seal on the reverse. Next followed the three "Seasons" medals of 1796, struck in England from dies by Conrad Küchler, depicting "The Farmer," "The Shepherd," and "The Home," all evocative of domestic tranquility. These did not arrive in America until the John Adams administration (1797–1801), and were further continued in use during Jefferson's term of office.

New Indian peace-medals designs of the Jefferson administration depicted the president on the obverse and clasped hands with a peace pipe and tomahawk on the reverse. These were produced in small, medium, and large sizes, with the largest being made by fitting together two pieces to form a shell, and filling the interior. No coining press on hand was capable of striking a medal four inches in diameter. As time went on, succeeding administrations issued medals, usually in three sizes. R.W. Julian, in *Medals of the United States Mint: The First Century, 1792–1892*, gives details of the different varieties.

At a later time, great numismatic interest developed, and restrikes were made from original as well as copy dies for most issues of the Jefferson designs onward. Many were struck in copper. These became stock-in-trade items, with many issues still available from the U.S. Mint but with modern matte finishes. Included are some sizes and die combinations never made originally. The Julian text delineates these. On the numismatic market, original medals that were actually used are rare and valuable today. Nearly all are holed at the top for suspension. Mint restrikes and copies in copper and silver are highly collectible today, but at significantly lower price levels. It is a popular caper to take silver restrikes, drill holes in them, toss them around in a tumbler to "antique" them, then offer them for sale to unsuspecting buyers. Probably 90% of such medals sold at firearm, antique, and general history shows are in this category. Never buy an "original" Indian peace medal except from an acknowledged expert.

Military Medals

Medals honoring or depicting military heroes and battles form a large and popular specialty. The R.W. Julian work cited previously describes many different varieties, beginning with the famous Washington Before Boston medal (Julian MI-1), originally made in France from dies by Pierre Simon DuVivier, with an impression in gold presented to General Washington in 1790. Later, restrikes were made at the Paris Mint, and still later many were struck from copy dies at the Philadelphia Mint. "There has been more interest in this medal than perhaps any other struck in this country," Julian noted in his text.[84] This and certain other early medals have the inscription COMITIA

A copper striking, well worn, of the 48 mm Seasons medal, "The Farmer" type. On the obverse a farmer, perhaps George Washington, sows seeds in a field, evocative of domestic tranquility—a philosophy that the American government was endeavoring to instill in the Indians, meanwhile continuing to encroach on their territory.

Such medals, struck in silver and copper, are perhaps the most elegant series in the Indian peace medal specialty. In 1804 to 1806 a supply of these was taken by the Lewis and Clark expedition to give to deserving recipients along the way, on the journey up the Missouri River, across uncharted mountains, descending on the Columbia River to the Pacific.

The story of this particular specimen is unknown. One might imagine that a Native American cherished it for a generation, carrying it in a pouch, showing the medal to others, and occasionally letting it slip to the ground.

Engraving of the medal awarded by Congress to Captain Stephen Decatur, Jr., 65 mm, dies by Moritz Fürst (type known as Julian NA-9). Depicted on the reverse is the encounter between the American warship *United States* and the British *Macedonian*. (Benson J. Lossing, *Pictorial Field-Book of the War of 1812*, 1868)

The War of 1812 furnished the opportunity for an illustrious series of medals authorized by Congress and struck at the Mint. John Reich, who was an assistant engraver at the Mint beginning in 1807 and continuing to 1817, cut some dies for naval medals. Later dies were by Moritz Fürst (born in Hungary in 1782), who had come to Philadelphia in 1807, believing that a position as engraver awaited him at the Mint. This didn't materialize, and he worked in the private sector until 1812, when, at last, he secured work at the Mint as an assistant to Chief Engraver Robert Scot. As viewed today on medals he did for the Mint, including those in the military and Indian peace series, his talents were considerable. Medals for the War of 1812 constitute a popular numismatic specialty today. The War with Mexico in 1846 and 1847 is the theme for another series of military medals made at the Mint, depicting Zachary Taylor, Winfield Scott, loss of the *U.S.S. Somers*, and other themes, including several from dies by Charles Cushing Wright, who today is considered to be the most talented American die engraver of the second quarter of the 19th century. Wright's Erie Canal medal of 1826 (not made at the Mint) is particularly well known.

Most of the military medals struck in Paris and at the Philadelphia Mint are of large diameter, with 65 mm being a popular size. Nearly all were restruck for a long time afterward. In addition to R.W. Julian's study, J.F. Loubat's *The Medallic History of the United States of America, 1776–1876* is an essential text for the study and appreciation of military and other medals, and is particularly rich in historical material.

During the Civil War many medals and medalets were issued, mostly by engravers in the private sector. This field is very diverse and includes items ranging from "dog tags" worn by soldiers (listing their names, towns of enlistment, and military affiliations) to award medals for valor in action. Later wars and military activities are honored or otherwise depicted on

AMERICANA, or "American Congress," reflecting their authorization.

Early medals honoring Horatio Gates, Anthony Wayne, Francois Luis Tessiedre DeFleury, Daniel Morgan, William Washington, John E. Howard, and Nathaniel Greene were struck in France from dies cut by Nicholas Marie Gatteaux and Augustin Dupré. One depicting Henry Lee was to have been made in Paris, but there was a miscommunication, and arrangements were made to have the dies cut in America by Joseph Wright, a well-known artist who is remembered numismatically for the 1792 eagle-on-globe pattern quarter dollar and the 1793 Liberty Cap cent. The dies cracked during the hardening process, and it seems that no examples were struck. Years later, copy dies were made and used at the Mint. Classified separately by Julian are naval medals, the first of which was made in Paris from dies by Dupré, honoring John Paul Jones (Julian NA-1).

many medals too numerous to discuss here, but forming specialties for numismatists. However, it is difficult to resist mentioning this one: in October 1983, reacting to an insurrection, President Ronald Reagan dispatched a military task force to the Caribbean island of Grenada to "rescue" (or at least secure the safety of) 800 Americans attending St. George's School of Medicine. There was no engagement, and soon the troops returned. All involved were awarded medals, causing some consternation among older veterans who were accustomed to receiving medals for

heroic actions, not just for showing up on a vacation isle.

Medals of Presidents and Public Figures

All American presidents have been honored on medals, with the contemporary Mint series commencing with Thomas Jefferson (at a later time, dies were made for Washington and John Adams medals). These include presidential portraits on medals relating to terms of office, inaugurations, the Indian peace series, and other topics. The Mint has continued the series

Medal created to honor the memory of Captain William Lewis Herndon, who went down on the *S.S. Central America* on September 12, 1857. The dies were made by Smith & Hartmann, New York City. Relatively few strikings were made, and today these are extreme rarities. Their elusive nature was recognized in the 19th century, and a search was made to locate the dies in order to provide restrikes for collectors. However, the effort was unavailing.

Assay Commission medal of 1876 depicting George Washington on the obverse and, on the reverse, an inscription relating to the 100th anniversary of American independence. It was originally intended that this reverse design be used on regular-issue silver *trade* dollars, but the idea was scrapped as it was felt that in China, where trade dollars were used, this unfamiliar motif might confuse merchants and bankers.

to the present day. Modern issues as well as restrikes (mostly from copy dies) are readily available. Many original issues of the early 19th century, generally made in copper and silver, are rare.

Apart from Mint medals, far more presidential issues were made by private engravers. Often, these were created in series for sale to numismatists. As might be expected, some presidents offered better sale possibilities than others. Accordingly, varieties depicting Washington (discussed above), Jefferson, and Lincoln are more numerous today than are those featuring, for example, Franklin Pierce, James Buchanan, or Andrew Johnson. In the 20th century, Presidential Art Medals, the Franklin Mint, the Medallic Art Company, and others created many fine pieces with presidential portraits.

Other public figures furnish a rich field for numismatic exploration. The medals of Jenny Lind furnished the subject for a study by Leonidas Westervelt, published by the American Numismatic Society. Phil W. Greenslet's book *The Medals of Franklin: A Catalogue of Medals, Tokens, Medallions and Plaques Issued in Honor of Franklin*, is one of many specialized titles published by the Token and Medal Society. The *TAMS Journal* has featured many articles treating medals that illustrate men and woman of political, commercial, or other importance.

Award, Recognition, and Membership Medals

From the early 19th century, and continuing to modern times, medals have been awarded for exhibits, accomplishments, and participation in sports and other activities. For some categories these are divided into three classes, in ascending order of desirability: copper (or bronze), silver, and gold, the last for winners and first-prize recipients. Trade groups, agricultural societies, Sunday schools, drinking and eating clubs, fraternal organizations, colleges, athenaeums, social clubs, literary societies, institutes, and others have bestowed these.

Generally, award medals for a particular entity are of a standard design, with a portrait or motif on the obverse and, on the reverse, an open space at the center for stamping or engraving information relating to the recipient, date, and product or honor.

A few selected standard obverses: medals of the American Institute, New York City, depict on the obverse a scene of a seated goddess holding a pole with a liberty cap, with her extended right hand bearing a laurel wreath, as if to bestow it upon a worthy recipient. Surrounding are an eagle, shield, spinning wheel, ship, and other symbols of patriotism, industry, and commerce. Franklin Institute award medals have a portrait of Benjamin Franklin (by Gobrecht) on the obverse. Massachusetts Charitable Mechanic Association medals were made in several forms, typically showing a goddess on the obverse. Alcorn University (Mississippi) medals portray Senator James Alcorn on the obverse.

Sometimes, companies that received such medals had reproductions made in quantity, often of a smaller size, and with all inscriptions in the die, to distribute for advertising. Students, musicians, artists, and other individual recipients usually kept their medals. In later years, many such pieces have come into the marketplace, particularly those in copper and silver. Sadly, many if not most gold award medals were melted to realize their metal value. Most medals in copper and silver are inexpensive today.

In a separate class are medals awarded for lifesaving and other heroic accomplishments. Usually made in silver or gold, these are highly valued today, especially if the event, such as the loss of a ship, has a connection with popular history.

Members of the Assay Commission, which met at the Philadelphia Mint early each year to review samples of the preceding year's silver and gold coins and test them for their integrity, received special medals struck at the Mint. In addition, in many instances, particularly from 1860 through the 1890s, additional examples were struck for collectors. Today, these are eagerly collected.

The Mason & Hamlin Organ Company, based in Boston, exhibited its products at many expositions and fairs. In virtually all instances, those conducting such events would "award" exhibitors with medals. Reproductions of these were widely used in advertising. It seems that Mason & Hamlin had enough to start a serious collection! (*Harper's Weekly*, June 5, 1880)

This 1872 advertisement for Marion brand watches, by the United States Watch Company, illustrates two award medals given to it, one by the American Institute and the other by the Chicago Industrial Exposition. Today, actual award medals are readily collectible and are usually inexpensive, especially for copper and silver versions. Gold medals are more rare and often sell for several times their gold-melt value. Medals of the American Institute were of a standard design used for decades.

Medals for Cabinets and Collectors

Over a long period of years, many American medals have been made with the primary purpose of providing specimens for collectors and displays. This built upon a tradition that had been popular in England and France for generations, issues of those nations typically depicting monarchs and other figures in history. Sometimes these long runs of medals included American subjects as well, such as the Series Numismatica, issued in Paris in the early 19th century, which included Washington and Franklin.

Beginning in a significant way in the 1840s, Franklin Peale, chief coiner at the Philadelphia Mint, did an extensive business for his personal profit, by striking military and other medals (discussed above) from old dies on hand, plus new ones created for the purpose.

Beginning in the late 1850s and early 1860s, and continuing into the 1870s, several diesinkers in Philadelphia and New York City created series of medals with scenes from history, important buildings, presidents and politicians, and, often, cur-

rent events. Issuers included Augustus B. Sage, George H. Lovett, Robert Lovett, Jr., Alfred S. Robinson, Isaac F. Wood, and S.K. Harzfeld, among others.

Today, information about these cannot be found in any single place, and the collecting of such medals is often done on a catch-as-catch-can basis. For example, I've collected the medals issued by Robinson, a Connecticut banker and numismatist, but

One of the better-known Mint medals. The first pair of dies was cut by Christian Gobrecht and bore the date of February 22, 1836, the time set for a ceremony to inaugurate the use of a steam-powered coining press at the Mint. However, the equipment was not ready in time, and the ceremony was held on March 23. The date on the medals was altered in the die to read "Mar. 23" as shown here. Examples are still sold by the Mint today and are from copy dies.

Most medals have stories to go with them, but this piece has a longer one than most. On the obverse is a bold portrait of William J. Mullen, "Gold Dial Manufacturer." On the reverse is a scene that a bank-note engraver might have called *furioso*—lots of action, what with angels and cherubs flying around the sky and a corps of youngsters tending a factory below. Struck in copper and measuring 32.6 mm, the medal is listed in two places by Russell Rulau in his *Standard Catalog of United States Tokens* (2004, pp. 213 and 350). He estimates that about 75 to 200 exist today, and that an EF example is worth about $100 or so, and a Mint State in the area of $300.

The medal is one of just two created by Louisa Lander, who went on to become a distinguished sculptor. In 1847, at age 21, she made this medal, a chef d'oeuvre that stands today as one of the most intricate in the American series, what with a virtual paragraph of information strung along the inside reverse border in lettering so small that a magnifying glass is needed to read it. The medals were struck by none other than Charles Cushing Wright, America's most accomplished engraver of that era.

ous medals, not necessarily as part of a series, but on specific topics, such as the Hudson-Fulton Celebration of 1909. The Circle of Friends of the Medallion tapped the talents of well-known artists and sculptors to turn out a fine series of large-diameter medals with widely differing subjects. The development of such series was encouraged by the firms that struck them, including the Medallic Art Company, Whitehead & Hoag, and Joseph K. Davison Company (which evolved to become Joseph K. Davison's Sons). From 1930 to 1995 the Society of Medalists issued two medals per year, except for one in the final year (appropriately titled "The Last Supper"). These 129 different issues are mostly 73 mm, in bronze. Artists represented include many associated with regular and commemorative coinage, including Laura Gardin Fraser, Hermon A. MacNeil, John Flanagan, Anthony de Francisci, Robert I. Aitken, Henry Kreis, Adolph A. Weinman, and Robert Weinman, among others. In modern times the well-known Franklin Mint and other companies, often with "mint" as part of their names, have produced many different issues for collectors.

Silver "rounds" and bars, generally containing an ounce of silver and with a commemorative or commercial imprint, could also be called medals. In the past generation these have been advertised extensively in numismatic periodicals.

Souvenir and Topical Medals

The first large exposition held in the United States was at the Crystal Palace, New York City, in 1853. After that time there were many others, notably including the 1876 Centennial Exhibition in Philadelphia, the 1892 and 1893 World's Columbian Exposition, 1898 Trans-Mississippi Exposition (Omaha), 1904 Louisiana Purchase Exposition (St. Louis World's Fair), 1907 Jamestown Tercentenary Exposition, 1915 Panama–Pacific International Exposition, 1926 Sesquicentennial Exhibition, and 1933 Century of Progress Exposition (Chicago), among

have never encountered a complete listing of all varieties issued. My information has been gathered here and there by consulting old auction catalogs, issues of the *American Journal of Numismatics*, and studies by Richard D. Kenney (published by Wayte Raymond) and J. Doyle DeWitt (Connecticut Historical Society). The plus side of this is that it is fun to track down information, and that rare or possibly even unique pieces can be obtained for nominal prices (typically $50 to $100 or so).

In the early 20th century the American Numismatic Society issued many illustri-

many more, large and small, obscure and memorable. Medals, usually privately struck, were issued for all of these events, including award medals and souvenirs for public sale. These are widely collected today, usually by numismatists who specialize in a single exposition. Often, commemorative stamps, coins, souvenir china, postcards, and other related items are collected along with the medals.

In Victor, Colorado, in 1900 and 1901, Joseph B. Lesher issued souvenir silver "dollar" medals of octagonal shape. These depicted Pikes Peak and were popular in local trade. The series known as *so-called dollars* includes the Lesher pieces and hundreds of others, a classification that loosely groups medals (struck in copper, pewter, and silver) that are more or less the size of a silver dollar, and were issued as souvenirs or, sometimes, for exchange in trade or in political contests.

Many other medals were issued as mementoes of special occasions—the dedication of a building, the opening of a railroad—or to celebrate a wedding or memorialize a life.

Aspects of Collecting
Many Subjects and Possibilities

There seems to be no end of occasions and reasons for the issuance of medals, nor to the subjects depicted on them. The field is so diverse and the issues so numerous that numismatists specialize in areas of particular interest. Medals are also widely sought by historical societies and museums, these being organizations that usually have little or any interest in systematically collecting *coins*.

Medals in popular series such as Washington pieces, the issues of Joseph Lesher, Indian peace medals, and certain Betts and other historical issues are part of an active market. However, even among these, prices can vary widely. A good supply of auction catalogs and price lists is useful to determine values, and dealer-specialists are often willing to help. Over a long period of time the price trend for such medals has been upward.

In contrast, award medals, pieces issued for local and regional fairs, school and college medals, so-called dollars, Mint medal reissues from copy dies, and quite a few others have uncertain values, and even the opinions of dealers can vary widely. I recall being offered a group of so-called dollars issued in California, a quantity of about 200 pieces. After looking around I found one listed for $50. However, as a dealer I couldn't figure out what to do with 200 of them, even at the offered price of $12 each, so I passed.

Unless you are a dealer buying for resale, probably the best reason to acquire medals in an obscure or inactive series is for the enjoyment of owning them, not as an investment on their own. On the other hand, over a period of time most numismatic items tend to increase in value, and all, or nearly all, I have from decades ago are worth more now.

Key to Collecting Medals

- **Mint State examples:** Most medals, regardless of finish, are usually designated as Proof. However, it is also appropriate to classify high-grade pieces with lustrous, frosty, or other non-Proof surface as Mint State.

- **Circulated examples:** Generally, medals that were used for presentation to Indian chiefs exist today in worn grades; examples awarded and used are more valuable than copies made at the Mint for collectors. Some other medals made as souvenirs or for presentation also exist in worn grades, generally from careless handling.

- **Strike quality:** Most medals are very well struck.

- **Proof examples:** Proof finishes for medals range from mirror or brilliant (this being the case for most 19th-century silver and gold issues) to bronzed or matte. Generally, all medals of a given variety and metal were struck with the same type of finish. It is common practice to use the word *Proof* to describe 19th- and 20th-century medals of various finishes, including some with frost or luster. Many 19th-century copper and bronze medals were issued with medium to dark brown surfaces; this is known as a *bronzed finish*. Many 20th-century medals have etched, brushed, "antiqued," and other finishes, considered by the issuers to be artistic.

- **Key issues:** Each specialty has its rarities and key issues.

- **Advice to smart buyers:** Before buying an expensive medal, learn as much as you can about it. Buying from an established dealer-specialist is highly recommended. Insist on a written receipt and guarantee of authenticity, this being especially important for any medal originally issued by the U.S. Mint, as restrikes and copies are often presented as originals. For Betts medals, early American issues, Indian peace medals, and the like, grades such as EF and AU are the norm and are highly desired. For medals from the mid-19th century to date, it is best to acquire choice Proofs, unless the variety is sufficiently rare that another opportunity might not present itself. If a medal is accompanied by an original case or with papers or a certificate, these are worth acquiring as well.

- **Selected bibliography:**

Betts, C. Wyllys. 1894. *American Colonial History Illustrated by Contemporary Medals.* New York, NY.

DeWitt, J. Doyle. 1959. *A Century of Campaign Buttons, 1789–1889.* Hartford, CT.

Hibler, Harold E., and Charles V. Kappen. 1963. *So-Called Dollars: An Illustrated Standard Catalog With Valuations.* New York.

Julian, R.W. 1977. *Medals of the United States Mint: The First Century, 1792–1892* (edited by N. Neil Harris). El Cajon, CA.

Loubat, J.F. 1878. *The Medallic History of the United States of America, 1776–1876* (2 vols.). New York.

Rulau, Russell. 2004. *Standard Catalog of United States Tokens 1700–1900* (4th ed.). Iola, WI. (Also contains listings for many medal series such as those of the 1860s.)

Rulau, Russell, and George Fuld. 1999. *Medallic Portraits of Washington.* Iola, WI.

(In addition to these books, there are hundreds of articles, monographs, and books on certain issues. General texts on history can illuminate the background of most historical medals.)

CHAPTER TWENTY-SEVEN

COLLECTING COLONIAL AND CONTINENTAL PAPER MONEY

Today's collecting is more exciting than at any other point in recent times, as evidenced by member involvement in local club activities and ANA educational programs, seminars and services. Some of the most enthusiastic comments come from collectors who share their hobby with other family members. This common interest has a way of bringing a family together in a wholesome activity that nearly everyone can enjoy, regardless of age or experience.

—Florence M. Schook, July 1986

The field of paper money can be likened to those of tokens and medals—vast, varied, attracting many devotees, and offering great opportunities to combine numismatics and history.[85] Completion is an impossibility, but working toward that goal can be a lot of fun.

As with coin collecting, knowledge is important in acquiring paper money. Market values can vary, sometimes widely. Grading is important, as is knowledge as to whether a note has been "laundered," repaired, or otherwise improved. Certain common but very popular notes can sell for much more than extremely rare or even unique varieties in an obscure series.

An entire subculture of numismatics has arisen for paper money, complete with references to "Haxby," "Newman," and "Friedberg" in conversations at conventions and shows, with many fine dealer specialists, a generous number of students and researchers, and a lot of really nice people.[86]

Grades vs. Values (All Series)

The valuation of currency notes in relation to their grades is very interesting to contemplate. For colonial, Continental Currency, state bank, Confederate, and most other issues prior to about 1865, the situation may seem topsy-turvy until it is explained.

Generally, for these early issues, a bill that is crisp Uncirculated, just like new, not signed, and not used in circulation, is less desirable and valued at a lower price than one that has been signed, placed into circulation, and used for a long time, sometimes even in a low grade! Unused notes are commonly called "remainders." Some of these exist in large quantities.

Overview of Colonial and Early State Currency

In the 17th and 18th centuries, most of the original 13 colonies issued their own paper money, as did Vermont (which hoped to be one of the original ratifying states in the Union, but did not achieve that status until 1791). There being no federal American coinage system in place, these bills were usually denominated in British pounds, shillings, and pence, or, later, in Spanish milled dollars. A basic knowledge of British coin values is useful in understanding the denominations printed on many of the notes. A British pound was equal to slightly less than five Spanish dollars for much of the period, although exchange rates varied, sometimes widely.

British Currency:
- *1 penny* (plural *pence*)—Abbreviation: d.
- *1 shilling*—12 pence. Abbreviation: s.
- *1 crown*—5 shillings. Abbreviation: 5s.
- *1 pound*—20 shillings. Symbol: £

A notation such as 2/6 or 2s/6d means two shillings, six pence. This is also equal to half a crown.

Most early bills were printed from copper plates engraved by hand. Later issues were generally typeset. While the identities

505

W. Hawxhurft,

STILL carries on the Sterling iron works and gives the best encouragement for founders, miners, mine-burners, pounders, and furnace fillers, bank's-men, and flock takers, finers of pig, and drawers of bar; smiths, and anchor smiths, carpenters, colliers, wood cutters, and common labourers: They will be paid ready cash for their labour, and will be supplied with provisions there, upon the best terms.

N. B. Said Hawxhurft continues to sell pig, bar iron, and anchors, which he makes of any weight under 3500, and as he has by him a considerable quantity of anchors, he would sell them by the ton, to retailers or exporters at a lower price than the importers from Europe, or the neighbouring colonies; he has also cart, waggon and chair tire; which he fells on the most reasonable terms, for cash, or Connecticut Proclamation bills. He also will take old and cash by anchors in part of pay for new ones, in proportion as they are in value.

Often, tradesmen would specify payment in certain types of bills, as in this advertisement in *The New York Gazette or Weekly Post-boy* (August 16, 1764). Iron founder W. Hawxhurst solicits "cash, or Connecticut proclamation bills." Cash referred to current silver and gold coins, mostly from Spanish America, while the Connecticut bills are those issued under the act of May 8, 1740, for "new tenor" bills, having an exchange value different from that of earlier notes. Such subtleties were widely understood by merchants and travelers, but not the general public.

In the 18th century most travel from province to province was accomplished by stagecoach, with overnight stops at taverns and hotels. As values of colonial paper money varied widely from place to place, and by some merchants was not accepted at all, most who went a considerable distance were likely to take a purse filled with gold and silver coins.

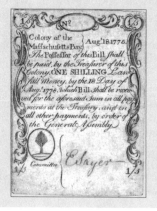

Paul Revere, today remembered as the best-known American engraver of the late 18th century. His work appears on many different bank notes, scenic prints, etc. In numismatics his "Sword in Hand" bills, issued for Massachusetts, are especially popular.

of some engravers are known today, others are not. Workmanship ranged from artistic and elegant to downright crude.

What one man could do another could do also, and parallel to the issuance of early notes a trade in counterfeiting arose. False bills were produced, so many that in the 1940s and 1950s Kenneth Scott was able to create a series of books, state by state, describing activities of these criminals, mostly taken from newspaper articles and court records. Some counterfeiters had large-scale facilities employing printing help, distributors in the field, and more, while others were essentially one-person operations, in which the counterfeiter sometimes carefully copied a genuine note by hand, or made a damp-paper transfer from an original note (creating an inked replica). Such activities were viewed as a great crime against all citizens and a detriment to their financial well-being. The penalty for counterfeiting was often stated as *death*, and this dire warning seems to have been carried out on occasion.

Many if not most bills were issued in order to borrow money—to finance military expeditions, to promote public works, and so on. From time to time the British Parliament sought to regulate or prohibit certain uses of paper money printed in the colonies, such as limiting its use to paying taxes to the province, but such efforts were largely unavailing.

Typical bills were stated to be redeemable at par in gold or silver coins, but such warranties were of little value, as the provincial governments, often in need of money, did not maintain suitable coin reserves for redemption. However, on good faith and credit, most bills circulated at values near their face imprints, at least for a time. The aspect of faith and credit has been widely discussed by economists. Often, in the absence of supplies of gold and silver coins in circulation, the populace had little choice but to accept current paper money. An analogy can be drawn to the Confederate States of America, whose bills readily circulated at a good percentage of their face value early in the Civil War (until the tide turned in 1863), as the citizens of the South had no coins.

In addition to the colonial notes officially issued by provincial authorities, certain merchants, civil projects, and other entities produced paper money. Usually such bills were received at par only in the vicinity of the places they were issued, and usually for just a limited time. Often, older bills would depreciate so as to become worthless. A traveler endeavoring to spend Massachusetts bills in Maryland would find that they would be accepted not at all, or only by a broker or exchange at a deep discount. There was no series of paper money that found acceptance at par over a wide area, no currency equivalent of Spanish-American silver dollars or gold doubloons.

The first colony to issue its own paper money was Massachusetts—a series of bills of 5-, 10-, and 20-shilling and 5-pound denominations, authorized by the General Court on December 10, 1690, to pay expenses for a military action against Canada. This was less than a decade after the final Pine Tree silver coins were made (in 1682, but bearing the date 1652). Each bill depicted an Indian standing and holding a bow and arrow, the emblem of the colony (later used on state copper coinage of 1787 and 1788). The bills feature an Indian calling, "Come over and help us" written in a word balloon. Thus was the stage set for many other issues of the colonies, most of which included emblems, illustrations, and mottoes that are interesting to contemplate today.

Most bills are dated (usually the date of the authorizing act or legislation, not the day, month, and year that a given bill was issued), are numbered serially, and bear signatures of provincial officials, two or three people signing each typical note.

South Carolina was the next issuer of bills, in 1703, followed in 1709 by the currencies of Connecticut, New Hampshire, New Jersey, and New York, then Rhode Island in 1710 and North Carolina in 1712, continuing to include the other original colonies and, later, Vermont.

Massachusetts (1690–1781)

Massachusetts bills[87] were produced through an especially large number of legislative acts, resulting in many varieties. Early issues are from engraved plates. Certain of these were redated multiple times, with a long string of years added, one after the other. This practice allowed serviceable plates to be reused and updated, without the making of new plates. As all such bills are extremely rare today, this does have the numismatic advantage that one later bill with multiple dates can take the place of several!

Early Massachusetts bills range from rare to utterly unobtainable. Fortunate is the collector who is able to obtain a representative note or two. Later issues range from common to rare and are among the most popular series with collectors today.

Time and again, private issues circulated as well.

South Carolina (1703–1788)

Nearly all South Carolina bills were denominated in British currency. The notes are particularly rich in their mottoes and illustrations. Early bills of the colony range from rare to unknown. Many of the issues from the 1770s and 1780s are collectible, but the later era is scattered with rarities as well.

New York (1709–1788)

From May 31, 1709, to February 8, 1788, nearly three dozen series of bills were produced. From the earliest times, the currency was produced using hand-set type in combination with decorative blocks, a departure from the engraved copper plates generally used by other colonies. Most bills from the late 1750s onward are collectible, although some are scarce. Currency of New York has always been especially popular with numismatists.

New Jersey (1709–1786)

Bills of New Jersey were issued under legislation dated from July 1, 1709, to 1786, in many different series and denominations. Early New Jersey bills range from rare to very rare. Those from the late 1750s onward are readily collectible for most varieties.

Connecticut (1709–1780)

The earliest Connecticut issues (July 12, 1709) range from 2 shillings to £5, and were receivable for tax payments, but were not declared legal tender. Now and again, plates of Connecticut bills were redated, simply by the engraving of a later date on a plate with a date used earlier (the same practice was also used elsewhere).

Today, most issues dated prior to the 1770s are very rare. Certain later bills are plentiful in the context of the series.

South Carolina $1 note authorized on December 23, 1776, and printed by Peter Timothy, Charlestown, in 1777. The motto PER ARDUA SURGO translates to "I rise through adversity." The "Death to Counterfeit" warning was common on bills of the various early colonies and states.

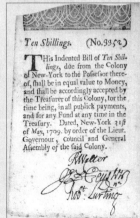

At left, a rare 10-shilling note of New York, May 31, 1709. Notes of this type as well as most other colonial issues of the era became obsolete in their own generation. Relatively few survive today. At right, a promissory note from Boston, dated 1740 and payable by December 31, 1775.

New Hampshire (1709–1780)

The first New Hampshire bills were authorized on December 5, 1709, to the extent of £5,000 total value. Soon after this issue, Massachusetts passed legislation prohibiting their use in that colony. Such was the nature of inter-colony politics and commerce.

Early bills from engraved plates are very rare today, but many were reprinted from the original plates, and each of these provide an affordable alternative—not a substitute, but, to emphasize, an *alternative.* Notes of the 1770s onward are generally collectible, often punch-cancelled, but some varieties are scarce.

Rhode Island (1710–1786)

Bills of Rhode Island, issued under authority from August 16, 1710, to May 1786, were produced in more than 50 series. The final issue amounted to £100,000 worth of bills in denominations from 6 pence to £3. The provincial (later state) emblem of a fouled anchor is a common device.

While most early bills of Rhode Island range from rare to unknown, those from the 1770s onward are readily collectible.

North Carolina (1712–1785)

Bills of North Carolina were issued in more than two dozen series from 1712 to

New Jersey note for 12 shillings, authorization of March 25, 1776. Printed by Isaac Collins in Burlington. The nature-printed leaf on the back was taken from a real-life leaf, a popular technique of the era, a deterrent to easy counterfeiting. A plaster cast taken from a leaf was created to make a transfer in lead, then a transfer to the printing plate element. The process was devised by Benjamin Franklin.

Merchants' note issued in Portsmouth, dated December 25, 1734. Such bills bore interest at 1% per year and were to be payable in silver or gold coins, or in "passable" bills of credit issued by other colonies in New England.

1785. The earliest bills were written out by hand, as no printer was available! The issue of 1734/35 was the first printed series and was made in values from 1 shilling to £10, intended to be exchanged for earlier hand-written bills.

Issues from the 1760s onward are generally available for modest values, although there are some exceptions.

Pennsylvania (1723–1785)

From 1723 through 1785, Pennsylvania issued bills as part of 40 distinct series. From the start they were printed from a combination of set type and inserted illus-

trations. Many varieties of the 1750s and 1760s were printed by Benjamin Franklin.

As Philadelphia was the seat of the Continental Congress for most of the early period, these bills and their printers have an especially close connection to American history. Early notes are rare. Most from the mid-1750s onward exist in fair numbers and are readily collectible.

Delaware (1723–1777)

The first Delaware bills were issued under the authority of legislation dated April 23, 1723, to a total value of £5,000. These got off to an uncertain start when citizens of

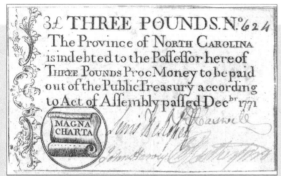

£3 note of North Carolina, issued under the Act of December 1771. The vignette features the Magna Charta, British icon of the independence of the people, perhaps a hint that citizens of North Carolina valued as much independence as they could have.

Pennsylvania note for 10 shillings, October 1, 1773. Depicted on the back is a scene evocative of domestic tranquility—a farm with a rainbow in the offing. Printed in Philadelphia by Hall & Sellers, the partnership that later produced Continental Currency bills.

Delaware bill of 6 shillings, January 1, 1776, authorization date. Although the Revolutionary War was already underway, the emblem on the face is the Royal Arms of England. The sheaf of wheat on the back is reflective of agricultural abundance.

neighboring Pennsylvania would not accept them. Early Delaware notes are very rare today.

The latest bills are dated May 1, 1777, in the early period of the Revolutionary War, and are on the same paper (with mica chips and blue fibers) used for Continental Currency bills. Denominations of the last issue ranged from 3 pence to 20 shillings. While most later bills are collectible, those dated January 1, 1753, and earlier range from rare to unknown.

Maryland (1733–1781)

The earliest bills of Maryland are of 1733, in denominations from 1 to 20 shillings, to the impressive total of £90,000. There was at the time a glut of low-quality tobacco, and in 1734 and 1735 thirty shillings in these bills was given to each taxable person who burned 150 pounds of the commodity.

The issues of 1767 were expressed in *dollars*, this being the first use of that designation on any paper money issue in the world. Elaborately engraved bills produced under authority of the legislative session of July 26, 1775—so-called gunpowder notes—were issued to promote the manufacture of gunpowder in the nascent state.

Most later Maryland bills were issued in large quantities and are readily collectible today.

Georgia (1735–1786)

The earliest currency related to Georgia consists of so-called sola bills, printed in England from 1735 to 1750 and drawn to the order of the Trustees for Establishing the Colony of Georgia. These were later called in and were designated worthless after December 31, 1755.

The first bills issued and printed by the colony were those of February 17, 1755.

The final early bills of the state are dated October 16, 1786, in denominations from 6 pence to 20 shillings. Bills of the Revolutionary and later era are collectible (but are very rare in higher grades), while earlier ones are elusive.

Virginia (1755–1781)

From June 1755 through 1781, Virginia issued currency under more than 30 legislative acts. Beginning with the series of June 8, 1757, most bills were made in large quantities. Most were in British denominations, but some were in dollars.

"Gunpowder note" of Maryland, July 26, 1775, denominated as One Dollar and One Third of a Dollar. This is one of the most "scenic" notes of the Revolutionary War era.

Georgia bill for $5, authorization of September 10, 1777, is redeemable in Continental Currency, the last destined to become worthless. The coiled rattlesnake, with the coils reiterated below the motif for emphasis, is typical of the bold emblems used on bills of this era.

Today, early Virginia notes range from rare to unknown. Most of the later varieties of the 1770s through 1781, including the high-denomination bills, are readily collectible.

Vermont (1781)

The bills of Vermont consisted of £25,155 in total face value issued under the Act of April 14, 1781. The issue included 3,600 each of seven denominations, from 1 shilling through £3.

Most Vermont bills were redeemed and destroyed. Today, *any* Vermont note is viewed with awe, as such are seldom seen. On the rare occasions that a Vermont bill is found in the marketplace, like as not it is damaged, incomplete, repaired, in low grade, or a combination of several of these factors. As Vermont was not one of the 13 colonies that formed the United States, more than just a few numismatists excuse themselves from collecting these! However, Vermont achieved statehood status in 1791. It would have been a part of the Union earlier had it not been for an intense dispute with politically powerful New York regarding the boundary between the two.

Enjoying and Collecting Colonial and Early State Currency

Much more so than for coins, contemporary writers in the colonies often gave details of new paper money issues, counterfeits (a perennial subject for fillers in newspapers), and exchange rates. While it might be said that early copper cents of 1793 to 1814 have been written and talked about to a fare-thee-well, and that a talented newcomer would have difficulty making new discoveries, the opposite is true for currency. Techniques of engraving and printing, details of designs, biographies of printers and signers, and related topics beckon to be analyzed, distilled, and packaged for numismatic consumption. The mottoes on certain early notes are fascinating to contemplate and are often evocative of human emotions, the rights of the colonists, and the spirit of independence.

Bills of the colonies are widely collected, often by series and denominations, hardly ever by signature combinations. However, exploring the biographies of signers can be an interesting pursuit, particularly given the research potential of the Internet. Among the signers of notes of the colonies were certain men who later affixed their names to the Declaration of Independence. Bills with this connection are of special interest.

It is evident from contemporary comments that the circulating life of colonial bills was very short, and that within several years many became tattered. As an example, by 1702 the extensive issue of Massa-

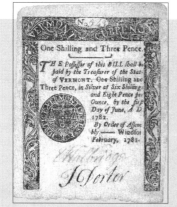

Vermont note, 1781, of 15 pence. All Vermont bills of this issue are great rarities today.

chusetts currency authorized 11 years earlier had suffered such dilapidation that "it became necessary either to abandon bills of credit or emit new bills."[88] Generally, for all currency issues, the higher denominations circulated less extensively and tended to last longer. (The same holds true for today's currency.)

The grades of most early issues range from ragged to Fair or Good. In other words, in many instances you must take what you can find. Auctions regularly feature rare early bills that have parts missing, or are stitched or glued together, or reflect other problems. Still, these attract enthusiastic bids. Probably even a *fragment* of a Vermont note would attract a lot of attention and quickly run up into the hundreds of dollars!

In contrast, currency of the 1770s and 1780s can usually be found in Very Fine and better grades, and, for some states, in AU or finer, sometimes from redeemed bills later deaccessioned by state treasuries and other official entities. Likely, such bills have been canceled by hole-punching, cutting, or other marking.

Nearly all bills, including the later ones, have margins that are wider on one edge than another, or are centered on the face of the note while being off register on the back, or have an edge or two trimmed into the design.

Learning about what is available and what is not is best done by building a file of auction catalogs featuring such notes. A close reading of Eric P. Newman's *Early Paper Money of America* (4th edition, Iola, WI, 1997) is also recommended. Most catalogs published in the past 20 years are extensively illustrated. Early currency catalogs dating back to the 19th century are much less useful, as illustrations range from occasional to nonexistent, and scarcely any useful information is given beyond dates, denominations, and grades.

Counterfeits abound, and in many instances there are no printed references to help you delineate them. Even experts are sometimes confused. Certain bills listed as counterfeit in one place may be called genuine in another, as with certain late-18th-century notes printed by Daniel Fowle of Portsmouth, New Hampshire, who held a contract to print notes for the government, but is alleged to have printed some others on the side for his own account!

While collecting early notes is hardly terra incognita, a degree of expertise is needed to avoid counterfeits and to make intelligent purchases. My recommendations for success are these:

- Learn as much as you can by reading books and catalogs, numismatic and otherwise.

- Browse dealers' stocks, through catalogs or Internet listings. Then make your first purchases carefully, and for inexpensive items. Learn by doing.

- Get to know dealers in the field and ask them for help and advice (along the way doing some business, as a matter of etiquette).

- Look at and study each note as you receive it. Contemplate the engraving work. Consider the mottoes and inscriptions. Likely, it is part of a series of different denominations issued with the same date. Compare it with others, using reference works or, if you have them, specimens in your collection.

- Don't rush. Expect to spend a number of enjoyable years in forming a nice, basic collection. Get to know numismatists who enjoy these early notes. They are a friendly bunch of people!

Overview of Continental Currency
An Extensive Series

The Continental Congress authorized the issuance of paper money on May 10, 1775, to the extent of $3,000,000. Other authorizations followed, through 1779, denominated in "Spanish milled dollars, or the value thereof in gold or silver," although the fledgling American government had no gold or silver coins to fulfill the promise.

Over a period of time, bills in values from one-sixth of a Spanish milled dollar to $80 were produced. Early issues bore the imprint of the United Colonies. Beginning with the authorization of May 20, 1777, the imprint was changed to the United States. The $20 denomination of the first issue was printed on paper ordered in France by Benjamin Franklin and is of unusual dimensions and appearance. All others were on paper made in the United States. The final authorization (January 14, 1779) was for more than $95,000,000.

The bills were printed by Hall and Sellers, of Philadelphia, also well known for producing state currency. Certain of the reverses featured the imprints of leaves from trees, called "nature printing"—a technique also used on certain bills of the colonies. Because the veins and other small features of a given leaf are unique, the notes were not easily copied.

Continental Currency bills were printed in sheets with multiple bills of different denominations. They were signed, and then cut apart for distribution. Each bill with a face value of $1 or more bears two authorized signatures, some of them being made by the signers of the Articles of Confederation, Declaration of Independence (James Wilson), Bill of Rights, and other important early documents. This lends particular interest and value to such bills today.

In addition to regular issues, impressions of certain issues were printed on blue-tinted paper. Unsigned, these were distributed to aid in the detection of counterfeits. Examples are occasionally seen in the marketplace today.

As the financial abilities of the Continental Congress became weaker and weaker, the notes depreciated to the point that they were nearly valueless. By 1781, it took about 75 Continental Currency dollars to buy one Spanish-American silver dollar coin.

Continental Currency notes were printed with a wide variety of fascinating emblems and mottoes. These examples are excerpted from an old almanac published in 1777, when the Revolutionary War was raging:

$3 • On one denomination of the bills there is an eagle on the wing pouncing upon a crane, who turns upon his back and receives the eagle on the point of his long bill, which pierces the eagle's breast; with this motto, EXITUS IN DUBIO EST—"the event is uncertain." The eagle, I suppose, represents Great Britain, the crane America: this device offers an admonition to each of the contending parties. To the crane, not to depend too much upon the success of its endeavors to avoid the contest (by petition, negotiation, &c.) but to prepare for using the means God and nature hath given it; and to the eagle, not to presume on its superiority and strength, since a weaker bird may wound it mortally.

$4 • On another bill is impressed a wild boar of the forest, rushing on the spear on the hunter, with this motto, AUT MORS AUT VITA DECORA; which may be translated—"death or liberty." The wild boar is an animal of great strength and courage, armed with long and sharp tusks, which he well knows how to use in his own defense. He is inoffensive while suffered to enjoy his freedom, but when roused and wounded by the hunter, often turns and makes him pay dearly for his temerity.

Enjoying and Collecting Continental Currency

Although many ragged and incomplete bills exist, most numismatists endeavor to obtain VF or finer issues with clear signatures and serial numbers. Notes of good quality (VF to Uncirculated) can generally be obtained with some patience. Border trimming can be erratic on one side or both. The clarity of signatures can vary—with some faded, some bright.

Continental Currency notes were issued in large quantities. A fine collection of the different series and denominations can be gathered today, an engaging challenge but one that is not particularly expensive, as the series is not widely collected in comparison to federal currency of a century or more later. The majority of the issues are valued from about $100 to $250 each in circulated grades of VF and higher.

Collecting a basic set of issues and denominations is easy enough to do. Beyond that, studying and collecting the signatures of members of the Continental Congress is an intriguing pursuit, as is the relating of these bills to the history of the Revolutionary War. Only one signer of the Declaration of Independence also inked his name on Continental Currency, he being James Wilson. Some Wilson signatures were done by an amanuensis (a ghost-signer),

and authentication is necessary if this aspect is important to you.

Illustrated auction catalogs of the past several decades provide a rich source of images—useful for learning about the clarity of printing, border trimming, and related matters. Counterfeits of Continental Currency bills, described as such, are collected by many numismatists.

Newman's *Early Paper Money of America* provides bibliographies for the notes of each colony as well as for Continental Currency issues. Other recommended reading includes the four-volume *Colonial Currency Reprints* (Prince Society, Inc., Boston, 1910); back issues of *The Numismatist* and *Paper Money*; and various state historical society journals.

The study of Continental Currency mottoes would keep the curious collector/historian busy for some time. These examples were illustrated in *Scott's Standard Catalogue, No. 2, Paper Money*, in 1889.

VIGNETTES ON THE BILLS

ISSUED BY THE

CONTINENTAL CONGRESS.

1 Dollar. Type 1.
"*Depressa Resurgit,*" —Though pressed down it will rise again.

2 Dollars. Type 2.
"*Tribulatio Didat,*" — Affliction enriches.

3 Dollars. Type 3.
"*Exitus in dubio est,*" —The end is in doubt.

4 Dollars. Type 4.
"*Aut mors aut vita decora,*" —Either death or an honorable life.

5 Dollars. Type 5.
"*Sustine vel abstine,*" — Sustain or abstain.

6 Dollars. Type 6.
"*Perseverando,*" — By Persevering.

7 Dollars. Type 7.
"*Serenabit,*" — It will clear up.

8 Dollars. Type 8.
"*Majora minoribus consonant,*" —The greater ones are in harmony with the smaller.

20 Dollars. Type 9.
"*Vi concitatae,*" — Driven by violence.

Mottoes used on early currency can be fascinating, and in the 19th century numismatists began to take a wide interest in them. *Scott's Standard Catalogue, No. 2, Paper Money*, published in 1889, devoted extensive space to the subject, including the page reproduced here.

CHAPTER TWENTY-EIGHT

COLLECTING OBSOLETE BANK NOTES

Once a numismatist, always a numismatist…. Goddess Numisma delights in giving pleasure to all her true devotees.

—Joseph Hooper, October 1891

The term *obsolete bank notes* is generally used to describe bank-issued bills with a stated face value from $1 upward. Many numismatists also include in this category currency issued by insurance companies, towns, and other entities, and intended to be used in commerce. Some of these issuers, though without the word *bank* in their titles, did have banking privileges under various state laws. Examples include the Dayton Manufacturing Company (of Ohio), the Harmony Institute (Pennsylvania), the Washington Social Library Company (Miamisburg, Ohio), and quite a few railroads and canals.

Bills of denominations smaller than $1 were issued as well, but these are generally referred to as *scrip* and are collected as a separate specialty (discussed later in this chapter), save for some issues with specific connections to bank distribution.

Somewhat similar to the situation for tokens and medals, obsolete notes exist in thousands of different varieties. For some issues, information is difficult or impossible to find. This contributes to the fascination many numismatists have for this specialty. Hardly anything is routine!

In the following sections I give a sketch of banking history, then the characteristics of typical bank notes of face values of $1 upward, followed by my thoughts about collecting and enjoying them.

The Early Years

By far, the largest issuers were banks that were chartered under rules of the different states, commencing with the Bank of North America, chartered by Congress on December 31, 1781, and validated by the Pennsylvania State Legislature in 1782.

Although the federal government played an occasional role in banking during the next several decades, nearly all control was by state legislatures. For some states—New York and New Hampshire are examples—the legislatures exercised tight political control over banking privileges, and in early times charters required certain connections. In some other states, banking was essentially a free-for-all.

The first commercial bank in the United States in this category was the aforementioned Bank of North America (established in Philadelphia in 1782), which issued bills at an early date. Basic facts concerning the early notes of this bank are scarce, despite an official history later published by the bank. Even such details as the dates on the bills, who engraved the plates, and whether the notes were accepted in commerce or rejected, are hard to track down.

Banks were soon set up elsewhere. In 1784, the Massachusetts Bank (Boston) was chartered (with authorized capital of $1,600,000); as was the Bank of New York (New York City), with capital set at $950,000. By 1800, there were more than two dozen chartered banks, including the Bank of the United States (of Philadelphia, with national branches), Washington Bank (of Westerly, Rhode Island; capitalized with only $50,000); and others (see page 518).

As you know by reading this far in the present book, I love history. Obsolete bank notes are especially inviting in this regard. Here is what John J. Knox, an accomplished numismatist, high official at the Treasury Department from 1867 to 1884 (deputy comptroller, and later comptroller, of the currency), and architect of the Coinage Act of 1873 (and thus progenitor

Unissued or "remainder" $5 note from the Washington Bank, Westerly, Rhode Island. Engraved by Amos Doolittle of New Haven, Connecticut, this represents the earliest portrait of George Washington on a bank note.

of the silver trade dollar), had to say about an institution that later evolved into the Chase Manhattan Bank:[89]

Manhattan Company

In 1799, when both the branches of the Legislature were in the hands of the Federalists, it was not possible that they would permit their opponents to obtain authority to organize a banking institution. The banking business in New York City was at this time monopolized by the Bank of New York and a branch of the Bank of the United States. There was, therefore, a very profitable field for another institution. The moving spirit of the Bank of New York was Alexander Hamilton. He drafted its constitution and controlled its policy, though holding no other official position than that of a director.

Aaron Burr, his political enemy, was a stockholder in the bank. He had repeatedly made unsuccessful attempts to obtain a charter for a rival institution. The yellow fever had raged in the city with greater virulence in 1798 than in previous years, and this was generally ascribed to unwholesome water. A bill was prepared incorporating a company for the purpose of supplying the city of New York with pure and wholesome water. The capital was to be $2,000,000, but lest it might not be found practicable to employ the whole of it all at once in the water-

works, the company was given the privilege of employing all surplus money in the purchase of public stocks or in any other moneyed transactions and operations not inconsistent with the laws and Constitution of the United States or of the state of New York. The charter was to be a perpetual one. Aaron Burr, who was a member of the Legislature in 1799, drew the bill and secured its passage....

The charter was thus granted on April 2, 1799, and the water-works were begun the same spring. By the close of 1801 twenty miles of wooden pipes had been laid and 1,400 houses supplied.... Notwithstanding the compliance with one part of the charter the principal business of the company was done under the other. In the first year of its existence $1,000,000 was employed in banking. The water-works were dropped when the Croton Aqueduct was completed, and the company became purely a banking institution, although the company still maintains its "water-works," consisting of a well....

While the Manhattan Company is today known wholly as a banking institution, it is required to maintain a water committee, who annually report that no application for a supply of water has been denied. As an assurance of the continued maintenance of its supply, there is always at the annual meeting a pitcher of water drawn freshly from its tank.

Probably not one in a hundred numismatists owning a bill of the Manhattan Company is aware of the described scenario. As if this were not enough history to digest, the firm figured prominently in New York City's first sensational public murder case, involving 17-year-old Guilielma Sands, whose battered body was found in the well on January 2, 1800. The suspect and defendant in the case was Levi Weeks, younger brother of renowned builder Ezra Weeks (who constructed the Tontine Building, City Hotel, Gracie Mansion, and Hamilton Grange). Alexander Hamilton *and* Aaron Burr jointly defended Weeks. The rest of the story is extensive and fascinating, and I refer you to historical sources to learn more.[90] The point here is that, while stray bills of the Manhattan Company are interesting to collect, they become especially fascinating when studied alongside the bank's history.

Into the 19th Century

The early 19th century saw a great increase in the number of banks in the United States. While many if not most in the larger cities operated under the benefit of state charters, quite a few in remote areas simply set up business on their own account. Some of these were legitimate operations in that they made loans, issued and redeemed notes, and were assets to their communities. Others were outright frauds set up to issue bills, but with no banking business. Today, the numismatic history (beyond descriptions of the notes themselves) of this entire field is largely uncharted. Except for cases where bankers were prosecuted and investigations documented, there are few records to reveal which banks were real and which were not.

In the first and second decades of the new century there was a great improvement in the appearance of bank notes. Copper plates, often crudely engraved, gave way to finer work, including the Patent Stereotype Steel Plate, invented by Jacob Perkins, of Newburyport, Massachusetts. Perkins was a multitalented man who is also numismatically remem-

bered for engraving dies for Massachusetts copper half cents and cents of the 1780s, and creating the 1800 Washington funeral medals with HE IS IN GLORY, THE WORLD IN TEARS.

Partnerships of bank-note engravers were formed, with Philadelphia, New York City, and Hartford being centers of activity in the early 19th century. Murray, Draper, Fairman & Co., of Philadelphia, was an especially prominent early firm and had clients extending out to the prairie lands of Ohio. Scenic vignettes, mechanically reproduced or else individually etched or engraved into the plate, became popular on bills and added to their attractiveness.

July 31, 1830, saw the publication of the first issue of *Bicknell's Counterfeit Detector*, listing banks that had failed by that time. The compilation, which reflects extensive study, included state-chartered as well as unofficial banks.

For present-day numismatists Bicknell's listing is significant for reflecting the early era of distressed banks, official and unofficial, in the United States. After this point, and continuing to July 1, 1866 (at which time a federal tax was imposed on such notes, effectively ending their use), a veritable legion of banks failed. The Tombeckbe Bank (Alabama), the Augusta Bridge Company (Georgia), the Farmer's Bank of Belchertown (Massachusetts),

A $5 note of the Penobscot Bank, Buckstown, *Massachusetts*, 1806. In 1820 this section of the country was split off from Massachusetts and became the new state of Maine. Buckstown did a double change, and the town name was changed to Bucksport. Hence, Buckstown, Massachusetts, and Bucksport, Maine, are the same place!

This is a very early-style Patented Stereotype Steel Plate note without tiny letters in the background.

The Owl Creek Bank of Mount Vernon, Ohio, has a very interesting history. The projectors of this bank sought to obtain a state charter as early as December 1814, but were not successful. After this and other pleas failed, they held a public meeting in Mount Vernon on April 10, 1816, and organized the bank on their own account. The capital was set at $250,000, with business to commence as soon as $25,000 had been subscribed for. In this era it was common practice for banks in all states to commence operations without solid cash backing. Often, stock was "paid for" by IOUs given by directors.

Copper plates for printing the Owl Creek Bank's bills were engraved by Richard Harrison, and printed in Pittsburgh by Charles Harrison. Both men had fine reputations. Each note featured a snowy owl perched at the base of a tree, with a mill and dam in the distance. Each was signed by L.S. Silliman as cashier and James Smith as president.

Business was conducted in a small, one-story building, about 14 feet square, constructed of wooden boards, in the Greek Revival style, and painted red. It must have been quite an attrac-

tion! The bank operated successfully for a few months, after which it was widely condemned in the local press—often unfairly—by merchants and others who opposed its operation. Unfavorable news items were soon circulated far and wide, including in the nationally circulated *Niles' Weekly Register*. Things went from bad to worse, and although the bank honored its obligations through the early part of 1819, it was denounced as a fraud. After 1819 it could not meet the demands put upon it.

Claims against the bank dragged on in court for many years, but eventually every bill-holder was paid face value in full, a rare situation for a troubled bank. By that time, "owls" had become a nickname for worthless bank notes!

This $2 note was issued by the Jersey Bank of Jersey City, New Jersey, but was redeemable only at the Ontario Bank in Ontario, New York, hundreds of miles distant, a journey involving at least a week to reach! The plate was engraved by Reed & Bissell, a rare imprint reflecting a partnership between Abner Reed and Edward(?) Bissell.

Hoboken Banking and Grazing Company (New Jersey), the German Bank of Wooster (Ohio), the Virginia Saline Bank (Virginia)—these are just a few of the institutions listed by Bicknell as broken, uncertain, fraudulent, or charter-revoked. The greatest number were in Ohio (then on the leading edge of what was known as the American West) and Pennsylvania, this due to unofficial banking as well as loose state regulations.[91]

Frauds and Other Capers

The Marble Manufacturing Company, a New York City issuer of bank bills listed by Bicknell, was described by the following items, among others, in *Niles' Weekly Register*:

> *April 29, 1826:* The "Marble Manufacturing Company" of New York, which lately commenced the manufacture of something which they passed off as bank notes, has already shut up shop. From what is stated, it appears that the managers of this establishment are rightful candidates for the manufacture of marble—in the penitentiary.

> *July 1, 1826:* Speculation! [Antoine] Malapar, late president of the Marble Manufacturing Company at New

York, who issued a large amount in things like bank notes, has been tried and found guilty of a conspiracy to defraud certain persons named and the public. The development of this affair is said to show as profligate a tissue villainy as ever was exhibited.

> *July 8, 1826:* It is thought that Malapar and his associates—a miserable set of irresponsible and obscure individuals—have defrauded the public of about $500,000. The fellow, a short time before he turned money-manufacturer, kept an oyster cellar. He is a Canadian Frenchman, and especially exerted himself to take-in his Canadian brethren, which he did do, to a large amount.

> *December 2, 1826:* Malapar, the maker of the Marble (paper-money) Manufacturing Company of New York, by which many were swindled, is now at Paris—and has proclaimed his intention of "making a book," to give an account of the business of that rag-shop.

> *July 14, 1827:* Malapar, the fellow who, in New York, by speculation, in a few months, elevated himself from a cleaner of boots or vendor of oysters,

The Marble Manufacturing Company was a fraudulent bank set up in New York City. The engraving and bank-note-printing firm of A.B. & C. Durand & Wright & Co., a partnership that operated in New York City from 1825 to 1827, provided the bills, including the $100 denomination shown here.

Throughout the era of obsolete currency, bank-note firms were willing to provide bills for just about anyone who asked, seemingly not checking their credentials. Today, from a numismatic viewpoint, currency from fraudulent and insolvent banks is generally more available than are bills from sound institutions, which redeemed their bills and destroyed them.

we forget which, to the highest rank among the nobility and gentry of the city, taking the lead in "good society," has been apprehended at Montreal, and there is some prospect that the honorable gentleman will be associated with the "marble company" at present incorporated within the walls of the state prison; and the charter to carry on his operations, may be granted during life!!

Years later, the *New York Daily Times*, October 19, 1852, published a letter from W.L. Ormsby under the title "Startling Revelation in Counterfeiting," which mentioned the Marble Manufacturing Co. plates. Ormsby, a bank note engraver, reported that through the kindness of Mayor Charles Gilpin of Philadelphia, he had visited that city to inspect a large group of counterfeit and discarded genuine bank plates that the city had "accumulated in the course of years past." Excerpt:

> Among the old stock, I found a copper plate, of the denomination $100, on the Union Bank of the City of New-York, an original engraving of Casilear, Durand, Burton, and Edmonds. Also, one copper plate $3, Marble Manufacturers' [*sic*] Company, City of New-York, engraved by A.B. & C. Durand, and Wright. Also, a copper plate $1, same as the last....

Another early account noted that Malapar had been a bartender at Castle Garden in 1825, when, with George I. Pride and associates, he formed the above company. He decked himself out in a suit of rich clothes, sported an expensive gold pencil case, and was seen often at banks and at the Merchants' Exchange. Years later he died a pauper in an almshouse.

There are several instances in banking annals when the president or controlling individual in a fraudulently conducted bank went on to acquire status or even honor in society and politics.

Samuel D. Dakin, a Malapar-like con man, swept through the east (Utica, New York; Wolfeboro, New Hampshire; and Belleville, New Jersey, among other places) and was involved in several frauds. His activities other than banking ranged from newspaper publishing (Utica's *Sentinel and Gazette*), to real estate dealing, to inventing a floating dry-dock circa 1844.

Andrew Dexter, the con man behind the first great American banking scandal—the Farmers Exchange Bank of Gloucester, Rhode Island, in the first decade of the 18th century—masterminded a scheme that floated more than $500,000 in bills. When the state closed down the bank on March 24, 1809, it was found to have just $86.48 in silver and gold coins with which to redeem them! Unprosecuted and undaunted, Dexter went on to run a lavish hotel in Boston, then went to Georgia, where he profited in real estate speculation, after which he was instrumental in establishing the city of Montgomery, Alabama.

One of the most remarkable cases of being transformed from a sinner to a saint, at least in the public eye, is that of Samuel Bell, president of the Hillsborough Bank of Amherst, New Hampshire. This institution entered business in 1806 and failed in 1808, after illegally issuing hundreds of thousands of dollars in worthless bills. Like Dexter in Rhode Island, Bell was not prosecuted. In fact, he went on to become governor of the state from 1819 to 1823, and today is lionized as one of the leading citizens of his time!

Another of many entries in the Banking Hall of Shame is Jacob Barker, a promoter who was best known circa 1819 for operating the Exchange Bank in New York City, but was also involved in capers elsewhere, including the Washington and Warren Bank of Sandy Hill, New York. When questioned as to the worth of Exchange Bank bills, he made a blithe reply to the effect that the bills were indeed good, but at the time he did not have the money to redeem them. As soon as he had ready cash he would publish an advertisement to this effect!

Barker's frauds were successful, and the bills remained utterly worthless. In financial journals of the day his name was anathema, the symbol of banking evil. However, this did not deter the highly respected *Merchants and Bankers Almanac*, 1870, from including this among a short selection of prominent American bankers—a commentary that seems to indicate that he later gained respect (sort of):

Jacob Barker of New Orleans

Jacob Barker is a descendant of the Quakers. He was a resident of New York City 40 years ago, and took up his residence at New Orleans, where he now resides. At the age of 16 years he came to New York, a poor boy, and got employment in the counting room of Isaac Hicks, a merchant of this city. He commenced business for himself before his majority, and was soon in possession of four ships and a brig.

In the year 1801, Aug. 27, he married Elizabeth Hazard, daughter of Thomas Hazard. After the war Mr. Barker engaged as a banker, and unfortunately lost his credit, and was prosecuted for his participation in the affairs of certain insurance companies.

Many years afterwards he removed to New Orleans, and was elected to Congress after the rebellion, but was declared ineligible. During the War of 1812, the credit of Mr. Barker was of the highest. In connection with Mr. Girard, Mr. J.J. Astor, Mr. Parish, and others, he bid for the loans of 1813–1815. He is yet a resident of New Orleans, but failed as a broker since the rebellion.

If there is one thing I've learned in studying the histories of old-time banks and bankers, it is to look in several places to find information. Newspapers, examiners' reports, and court records are best; histories written at a later date, if not the worst, are prime candidates for misleading information.

The 1830s Onward

By the mid-1830s, more than a thousand banks and other currency-issuing entities (canals, factories, railroads, etc.) had been established in the United States. Many of these had failed, or their financial conditions were such that their bills were discredited. However, at the same time, most of the better-capitalized institutions in larger cities remained sound. To help the public differentiate, printed leaflets and bulletins known as *counterfeit detectors* (often spelled *detecters*) were published by

Con artist Samuel D. Dakin was behind the Bank of Central New York (Utica), which somehow got involved with the Oakland County Bank of Pontiac, Michigan, as this bill of 1839 indicates.

A $5 bill of the Exchange Bank, New York City, signed by Jacob Barker as president. The engraving was by Leney & Rollinson, an active firm of the era, but not one of the most important. As to whether Barker was a saint or a scoundrel, this depends on what you read!

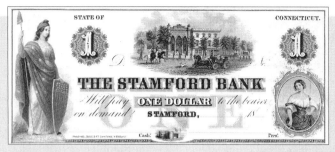

The Stamford Bank of Connecticut was chartered by the state in May 1834 and opened for business on September 10 of the same year. During the Panic of 1837 it engaged in deception by padding its books with fictitious deposits. News of this spread, and by January 30, 1838, bills of this bank were refused at the banks in larger cities. However, the institution continued in business, but with difficulties, into the 1850s.

This proof impression of a $1 bill was engraved by Danforth, Bald & Co., with offices in New York City and Philadelphia, and is from the Schingoethe Collection (sold by Smythe & Co.). While most currency of this era employed stock engravings, this has a custom vignette showing the bank (see enlargement) set amid a scenario of sport and society. Such scenes are often a reflection of life in America at the time.

Numismatists John A. Muscalus and Roger H. Durand, to mention just two prominent figures, have compiled information about vignettes on bank notes to illustrate monographs ranging from Santa Claus (Durand) to depictions of Benjamin Franklin's great-granddaughter-in-law (Muscalus)—a niche subject if ever there were one!

The New England Bank Note Co. used this slug-plate style for many different banks throughout the East and Midwest. The plate had openings into which three slugs could be inserted—one for the bank name, another for the town, and the third, at the bottom, for the state. By use of this system the company could provide ornate bills quickly and inexpensively.

The Farmers Bank of Sandstone, located in Barry, Michigan, was organized on December 30, 1837, with a capital of $50,000. Levi D. Smith was president and Horatio N. Baldwin served as vice president. Apparently, the institution had very little in real assets. According to

historian Harold L. Bowen (*State Bank Notes of Michigan*, 1956), "A sandstone quarry proved to be the only real security, and many notes were redeemed as follows: For every $10 bill a mill stone was offered. For every $5 bill a grind-stone was offered. For every $1 bill a whetstone was offered."

On May 9, 1838, the bank commissioners of Michigan sought an injunction to close the bank. An audit revealed that some $46,933 in bills was in circulation, all of which were completely worthless. The bill shown here bears a date of January 8, 1838, and is signed by both officers. (Ex Don C. Kelly)

entrepreneurs in New York, Philadelphia, Boston, Cincinnati, and elsewhere. By consulting these, a merchant in Pittsburgh could learn that a certain bank in Ohio was defunct and its notes worthless, and that the bills of another bank in Maryland were worth par or perhaps a slight discount.

The Panic of 1837 wrought havoc on the banks in the United States. Hundreds failed, and their bills became worthless. In the same era, even well-managed banks had difficulty and were not paying out specie (gold and silver coins) in exchange for their bills. The monetary system was in disarray.

State legislators in Michigan, New York, and several other states found a solution, or thought they had, in what became known as *free-banking laws*. The theory was that new banks could be established by financially sound entrepreneurs, bringing vigor and prosperity to commerce. Typically, just about any group could get a state charter by agreeing to a capitalization of a given amount, such as $100,000, and posting securities with the state treasurer to guarantee the soundness of the bank. New York required bonds and listed securities for which market values could be established. Michigan had looser arrangements, and IOUs and miscellaneous signed paper of no value were often accepted.

As free banking spread in the late 1830s through the 1850s, hundreds of new banks came into being, with little in the way of government oversight. More than just a few issued paper bills with reckless abandon, often exceeding any limits placed by state regulations. It was popular practice to establish a bank in some remote location, and to ship large quantities of bills to agents in distant cities, at a deep discount from face value, to be circulated in commerce. In other instances, such as in New York State and New Jersey, some banks were established in distant villages, but their currency would be redeemable only at an office in New York City.

In Michigan many banks were established with little or nothing in the way of assets—the Bank of Sandstone in Barry being an example—but issued large quantities of paper. Someone possessing a bill from such a bank would not find it worthwhile to travel a long distance to have it redeemed—and upon doing so, he or she might find that there was no bank at all and that no one locally had ever heard of it. By 1850, more than 90% of the banks in Michigan had failed!

The banking capers continued, as in this account published in *Banker's Monthly* in 1851:

> There is a small locality in New Jersey, under the name of Tom's River, within about a day's journey from New York which has been selected as the nominal place of issue of two Wall Street banks, in addition to one in the immediate neighborhood, at the Bergen Iron Works. From this circumstance, the place derives some interest to us of New York, and it seems desirable to make known that the town or village contains four stores, one public house, and *two banks*, besides the one in the neighborhood.
>
> The landlord of the public house is the president of one of the banks, the Union Bank, Ocean County. The keeper of the dry-goods store, which, like all small country stores, is an *omnium gatherum*, having for sale almost every description of articles, is the president of the other, the Delaware and Hudson Bank, Ocean County. This out-of-the-way place presents several difficulties in the way of the redemption of the bills. The bills are mostly issued in Wall Street, and sold largely to brokers at a discount, to put them in circulation.
>
> Leaving the city at an early hour in the morning, and taking the train by the Amboy Railroad, the locality cannot be reached before six o'clock in the evening—after banking hours. To present them for payment, it is necessary to remain a day there, as the train passes before banking business commences, and a third day must pass

before New York can be again reached....

The bank neighboring those at Tom's River is the Ocean Bank, at Bergen Iron Works. The bills issued are a *fac-simile* of the issues of the bank of the same name in New York City, the names of the officers excepted. This bank has been generally supposed to be located at Bergen in that part of New Jersey neighboring New York, but this is not so....[92]

The Ocean Bank of Bergen Iron Works was capitalized at an impressive half-million dollars, in 20,000 shares of $25 each, 19,993 of which were reserved for Benjamin Snyder, who also had the same interest in the Union Bank at Tom's River, capitalized for a like amount. Neither capital was ever paid in.

Both banks were short-lived and likely did very little real banking business. Their main purpose was to have bills printed in quantity and to distribute them as widely as possible. Apparently, these notes were easily confused at quick glance with the well-known Ocean Bank of New York City, a legitimate concern that had commenced business on December 10, 1849, and also capitalized at $500,000.

What fascinating stuff to read in connection with collecting these bills! Moreover, numismatists can be very grateful for these puffed-up banks of yesteryear, for many of the obsolete notes surviving today are from such enterprises. Also, they are generally among the less expensive items on the market (this being true for well-circulated bills, but not for proof impressions).

The concept of free banking was seriously flawed, and it was not long before a string of banks in New York State failed, wiping out the reserve fund set up to protect the public. Many securities were found to be worth far below their pledged values. In retrospect it seems obvious that to run a *successful* bank it takes more than a group of promoters with $100,000. Banking experience and knowledge are necessary to effectively make and collect loans and to engage in profitable investments.

Diverse Designs

In the meantime, the designs and motifs of bank bills became more ornate and diverse than ever. Most were highly artistic, as bank note companies tried to outdo each other, and their customers—the banks—desired currency that would attract attention.

Normally, designs of bills were not particularly newsworthy, but there were occasional exceptions. The *Portsmouth*

(New Hampshire) *Journal*, April 22, 1854, included this, which must have pleased the directors of the Rockingham Bank, one of several institutions in a highly competitive banking atmosphere:

Rockingham Bank Bills

A complete set of bills from new plates have just been issued by the Rockingham Bank. We have feasted our eyes with the sight of eight denominations ranging from $1 to $100.

The *One* is ornamented by the head of John Jay—the *Twos* by the heads of presidents Taylor and Fillmore—the *Threes* by the heads of Clay, Webster and Calhoun: thus showing the denomination by the number of portraits on each. The *Five* exhibits an original sketch of Portsmouth Navy Yard, taken from Peirce's Island, and the head of Mrs. Crittenden, the belle of Kentucky.

The *Ten* exhibits the blacksmith with his sledge—and the head of a lady. The *Twenty* shows the Capitol with the emblem of Young America in front, and an eagle and the head of Webster. The *Fifty* has a view of the steamer *Pacific* on the ocean. The

Hundred presents the head of Washington and the National Eagle, the proper emblem of the most valuable bills the bank issues.

These are the leading characteristics of the bills, although there are many elegant decorations on each, such as Amphitrite on the *Ones*, the ships of the *Twos*, &c. The whole design is neat and elegant, the engraving is beautiful, and the checks such as will render futile all attempts to alter or counterfeit.[93]

Obsolete bank note vignettes can have their mysteries. Why did the directors of this New Hampshire bank select "Mrs. Crittenden, the belle of Kentucky," to illustrate the popular $5 denomination? As to the view of the Portsmouth Navy Yard, as it is described as "original," was an artist commissioned to travel to Peirce's Island to sketch the facility? The usual method was simply to copy an illustration already published elsewhere. A fascinating sideline in numismatic research is to try to find the *first use* of an image or widely applied design—a nice overlap with another discipline, art history.

Later Years

By 1857, state-chartered banks were widespread in the United States and, for the most part, conducted business successfully, especially in the eastern states where regulations were tighter and often enforced. Most of the poorly managed "free banks" had already failed. Then came a new cloud on the financial horizon. The Panic of 1857 carried away hundreds of banks, and after that time relatively few new ones were chartered. In the meantime there had been a great improvement in the quality of bank bills. Ornate engravings were the rule, and many had colorful overprints.

For a long time, bills had been produced by scattered engraving and printing firms that often prospered for a time, then closed or merged into others. After the Panic of 1857, times were difficult in the industry. On April 29, 1858, the leading firms in the business combined to create the American Bank Note Co. The new company kept the customers of its con-

Impressions of the new bills for the Rockingham Bank, as publicized in 1854. Shown are proof printings of the $1 and $50 bills. An example of the interesting $5 bill has not been located. Representative of ornate work of the era, the bills are from Toppan, Carpenter, Casilear & Co. (Kevin Lafond Collection; Swasey Collection)

stituents, and continued using the old printing plates, now with the addition of the ABNCo monogram.

By this time, most of the promoters of ABNCo could look back upon a long heritage in the business, typically involving partnerships with others. A brief sketch of the life of Charles Toppan illustrates this:

1796: Charles Toppan was born in Newburyport, Massachusetts, on February 10, 1796. The town would soon become very important in the bank note trade with the engraving innovations of Jacob Perkins.

1814: Toppan studied engraving under Gideon Fairman in Philadelphia.

1815–1818: Toppan was on the staff of Murray, Draper, Fairman & Co., 47 Sansom Street, Philadelphia, the most successful bank note engravers in Philadelphia at the time.

1819–1822: In May 1819, Toppan and Jacob Perkins, both living in Philadelphia, journeyed to their hometown of Newburyport to perfect certain business arrangements, then with Asa Spencer they went to London, accompanied by others from Murray, Fairman & Co. In England, Toppan was a partner of Perkins in the firm of Fairman, Perkins & Co., and later with Fairman, Perkins & Heath.

1822–1827: Charles Toppan returned to Philadelphia. In time he joined with John Draper and Thomas Underwood in Fairman, Draper, Underwood & Co., the efforts of which were attended by success.

1829–1830: Toppan was an engraver for his own account at 28 Sansom St., Philadelphia.

1830–1831: Toppan was a partner with Peter Maverick in Toppan, Maverick & Co., Philadelphia. His associate had been in the engraving business in New York City since the early 19th century, including an alliance with Asher B. Durand, a famous engraver, later to become well known as an artist.

1831–1834: Toppan was engaged in the engraving business under the trade style of Charles Toppan & Co., possibly with others.

1833–1835: He was a partner with John Draper, James B. Longacre, and Marcus Bull in the firm of Draper, Toppan, Longacre & Bull, bank note engravers and printers.

1837–1839: Draper, Toppan, Longacre & Co., were in business at the same two addresses. With coins largely absent from circulation due to the Panic of 1837, these were heady times for the bank note trade. Longacre resigned in 1839, and in 1844 he was appointed chief engraver at the Mint.

1839–1844: The firm of Draper, Toppan & Co. was active and over a period of time was listed at several addresses in Philadelphia and New York City.

1843: Draper, Toppan, Carpenter & Co. had an office at 60 State St., Boston. Principals and engravers included John Draper, Charles Toppan, and Samuel H. Carpenter.

1844–1850: Toppan, Carpenter & Co., of Philadelphia and New York City, included as principals and engravers Toppan, Samuel H. Carpenter, Simeon Smith Jocelyn, Nathaniel Jocelyn, Henry E. Saulnier, and William Cumming Smillie. Circa 1849, Charles Toppan was listed as Toppan & Bradford, Boston, although he maintained his residence in Philadelphia.

1850–1855: Toppan, Carpenter, Casilear & Co., Philadelphia and New York, with agencies in other cities, employed a large staff of talented engravers. In 1854 this firm produced the Rockingham (New Hampshire) Bank bills described in the newspaper account quoted above.

1855–1858: Toppan, Carpenter & Co. (a revival of a partnership name used earlier), 111 Broadway, New York City, included as partners and/or engravers, Toppan, Samuel H. Carpenter, Samuel H. Carpenter, Jr., Charles T. Carpenter, James Smillie, William Cumming Smillie, Henry E. Saulnier and Charles Harrison.

1858: On April 29, 1858, Charles Toppan was a signer of the Articles of Association of the newly formed second American Bank Note Co. He became the first president of the new company.

1874: Charles Toppan died at Florence, Italy, on November 20, 1874.

Only a handful of competitors remained in business after the American Bank Note Co. was formed. Perhaps the most important was W.L. Ormsby, who also traded as the New York Bank Note Co., and later founded the Continental Bank Note Company.

Ormsby was a talented artist and engraver, the holder of many patents and innovations, and the originator of the "Unit System" of bank notes. The Unit System, discussed in detail in his impressively illustrated hardbound book *Bank Note Engraving* (1852), held that the face of a bill should be composed of an intricate scene, unique to a given bank and bill denomination. Within this scene the denomination, bank name, and other features would be incorporated. Such a bill would be difficult if not impossible to alter to another bank or value.

The concept was perfect in theory, but flawed in its execution. Such a unique design would take many weeks to prepare for each denomination, involving great cost in addition to delay. In the meantime, under the Patent Stereotype Steel Plate system and related production methods, a standard design, also ornate, could be used for many different banks and denominations, quickly and inexpensively, by the slipping of slug-plates in and out of the master printing plate.

In 1859, the National Bank Note Co. was established in New York City. It is likely that the American Bank Note Co. took 90% or more of the bank note business after 1858, leaving Ormsby, National, and a handful of other engravers with scraps.

Prosperity soon returned to U.S. commerce, and after 1858 relatively few banks failed. However, the era of widespread establishment of new banks had passed, and new charters were few and far between (e.g., in New Hampshire, among the dozens of state-chartered banks in operation in this era, only *one*, the Valley Bank of Hillsborough, was founded after this time).

In 1863, the National Banking Act provided for establishment of federally chartered institutions and, effective July 1, 1866, a tax of 10% on transactions involving notes of state banks. Sometimes local authorities in remote districts winked at the rule, and bills would remain in commercial use for a year or two afterward.

Hundreds of banks converted to become National Banks by dissolving and reforming as new corporations, but with all assets, loans, liabilities, office facilities, and

Ornate $1 bill by W.L. Ormsby for the Morrisania Bank, Morrisania, Westchester County, New York. No records concerning such a bank have been located, and the author surmises that this note may have been made to demonstrate Ormsby's "Unit System" of bank note engraving, a paradigm of elegance in combination with integral mention of the denomination (ONE) in the design.

Such a bill would have been difficult, if not impossible, to have counterfeited or to have changed to another denomination. However, such plates would have been expensive to produce and would have taken a long time, which made them commercially unfeasible. (Formerly in the collection of T.F. Morris, a prominent contributor to the *Essay-Proof Journal*; later in the Schingoethe Collection; to the author, 2004)

personnel remaining in place. So ended the era of currency issued by state-chartered banks. By this time about 2,000 banks, official and otherwise, had issued bills, as did hundreds of railroads, town authorities, manufacturers, and other businesses. Afterward, their currency became *obsolete bank notes*, as they are designated today.

Numismatic Aspects of Obsolete Notes
Main Types of Plates
Engraved Copper Plates (Early)

Most early notes, of the 1780s through the first decade of the 19th century, were made from copper plates. Often, these were engraved entirely by hand, including the lettering or script and, sometimes, small motifs such as animals, ships, or other decorations. Sometimes the work would be done by acid etching—covering the plate with wax or another substance, using a stylus or other tool to add lettering, then bathing it in acid to etch the work into the surface. The wax was then removed, and the plate used for printing.

Such plates were often crude in appearance. Counterfeiting was endemic, as no special apparatus was needed to create them, and there were many engravers who could do such work. Vignettes tended to be small and of simple subjects.

Engraved Copper and Steel Plates (Later)

In the second decade of the 19th century the siderographic (or transfer) process came into use, likely invented by Jacob Perkins. A vignette, an ornate numeral, or sections of text would be hand-engraved into a flat rectangular piece of soft steel, which would then be hardened.

The surface of a roller of soft steel, about the diameter of a small donut, would be impressed into the hardened vignette, transferring the image into *relief* on the roller, which would then be hardened.

The roller was then used to transfer the image into a soft copper plate or into a soft steel plate for the printing of bank notes. The copper plate would then be used as is, and would be good for several thousand impressions. Steel plates would be hardened and used for thousands of impressions. By means of rollers, different elements could be added to a single plate, creating variety. In other instances, some images were transferred in this way, while other parts of the plate were engraved by hand or by acid etching.

After use, a printing plate could be softened, an area of the design hammered flat, and a new inscription, design, or other element *re-entered* (as it was termed) to create a different bill. It was not unusual to change a bank name and/or location this way, so that a plate could be used for more than one customer.

Set Type and Illustrations

By the normal commercial process of setting type a commercial printer would set the required text by using movable type, and then add borders or illustration blocks. The procedure was the same one used to print newspapers, advertising cards, and the like.

This was the standard method for most scrip notes (of fractional denominations, and, earlier, for Continental Currency and other issues), but was not widely used for bank notes, as such bills could be easily counterfeited. The advantage was that such typeset bills could be made quickly, and by just about any local printer.

Slug Plates, Patent Stereotype Steel Plate

Invented by Jacob Perkins of Newburyport, Massachusetts, the Patent Stereotype Steel Plates (PSSPs) were made by using the siderographic process to transfer a complex design to a working plate, including tiny words, such as *Two Dollars*, repeated hundreds of times, with cross-hatched border designs, and other embellishments, most of a geometric nature.

Cut-out spaces were provided in the working plates for the insertion of slugs bearing the name of the bank and, separately, the town and state locations. Some

Typeset obsolete bank notes are elusive today. This one, for the Exchange Bank of Shiawassee, Michigan, was laid out, and not too carefully, by Penniman & Bemis of Cleveland, Ohio. Notice the backward N in MICHIGAN.

of Perkins's plates were made up of six or seven sections, including pieces added to the left and right of the main center portion.

By the slug-plate method, *any* bank could have its own complex, intricate plates for low cost, and quickly. However, there was trouble in this bank note paradise. It was not long before counterfeiters bought up such bills from failed banks, removed the bank names and locations by dissolving the ink, and printed other information in their places. This nefarious practice became widespread.

The PSSPs were technically obsolete by the late 1830s, although a few banks continued to use them. By this time, counterfeits and altered notes were endemic and, besides, the products of other engraving firms were considered to be artistically attractive, often with goddesses, buildings, whaling scenes, and more. During this transition, many plates of the New England Bank Note Co. were a combination of slug-plate engraving with tiny letters, in the Perkins style, with added small, scenic vignettes.

Interestingly, the PSSP received so much publicity as being counterfeit-proof that some economic historians maintained that, at long last, the problem of fake bank notes had ended, these writers having no practical knowledge of numismatics or of the notes themselves. Such accounts are amusing to read today.

Steel Plates

Through the siderographic process, and with the use of a supply of stock lettering and vignettes on rollers, plates would be made up in any way desired, after which the bank name and location would be separately entered.

Bank officers would select from a sample book or sheet any motifs of interest—goddesses, national heroes, rural scenes—creating very attractive bills that reflected credit upon the issuers. The portrait of Washington on a bill was evocative of leadership and integrity—fine attributes for any bank to have. Benjamin Franklin, another popular motif, invoked science, wisdom, and scholarship. A locomotive steaming full speed ahead across the landscape symbolized the latest in innovation and progress.

The full printing plate, often with four bills on it, and with inscriptions and vignettes from a dozen or more transfers by siderography, would be hardened and then used for printing. In many other instances, four separate solid plates, one for each bill, would be locked together in a frame. The latter had the advantage that different denominations such as $1, $2, $3, and $5 could be mixed and matched in groups of four, to create more or fewer of any desired value. The use of solid steel plates (as opposed to slug-plates with movable elements) was the most popular method of bank note printing from the 1820s onward.

Printed Features of Notes
Bank Name

The name of the issuing bank is usually located in the middle, either centered or high. Such inscriptions are usually large and prominent.

Those engaged in the altering of notes found common names (such as "Central Bank") to be a delight. If a Central Bank in one state became defunct, criminals would buy up its worthless notes at cheap prices (typically, exchange brokers charged 1% to 2% of face value for such, and did a lively trade in them), dissolve the black-ink portions showing the state and city names, and print new names in those places. Bills with names such as the Hallowell and Augusta Bank (Maine) and the Erie & Kalamazoo Bank (Adrian, Michigan) were more of a challenge. However, determined counterfeiters could do just about anything.

Town and State

On many obsolete bank notes the town name appears in one place and the state name (which isn't always obvious) in another, not necessarily close to each other. On later bills, of the 1840s onward, the town name is often engraved in script or ornate letters, while the state is apt to be in block letters.

There are many curiosities among the imprints of town and city names. Certain bills of Elizabeth, New Jersey, are imprinted *Elizabeth*, while others have *Elizabeth-Town*. Sometimes banks moved from one village or town to another, and exist today with two different imprints. For example, the Jefferson County Bank was established in Adams, New York, in 1816, but moved to Utica in 1824. The Farmers Bank of Saratoga County was established in Half Moon Village, New York, in 1851— then, without moving, found itself located in Crescent, New York, when the name of the village was changed.

There are some peculiarities with state names as well. Certain bills of the Pocasset Bank of Fall River have no state name at all! The reason is that part of Fall River was once in Rhode Island, but was transferred in jurisdiction to be a part of Massachusetts (as it is today). Prior to 1820, what is now the state of Maine was a district of Massachusetts; thus, without moving, certain banks once located in Massachusetts eventually found themselves in a new state.

A $10 note of the Egg Harbor Bank (Egg Harbor City, New Jersey), skillfully altered to the Valley Bank of Hillsborough, New Hampshire. These alterations were made in large numbers by criminals who bought worthless notes of failed institutions and converted them to appear to be from strong banks. Here, the signatures of the cashier and president closely resemble those on real notes, but are fake.

This $5 note of the John Hancock Bank (Springfield, Massachusetts) would have been difficult to alter, with its bank name depicted as the famous Hancock signature in bold, flowing lines.

Denomination

The value of the note is prominent, usually expressed in some or all corners as a numeral (such as 10), sometimes with lettering (TEN) nearby, and often with the denomination in large letters across the face of the note as well. The dollar sign ($) is rarely used. Many notes also have the denomination in a panel of tiny letters, almost microscopic, with the word repeated many times. Certain of the earlier-mentioned Patent Stereotype Steel Plates depict the denomination hundreds of times in tiny letters.

Among obsolete bank notes the standard denominations are $1, $2, $3, $5, $10, $20, $50, $100, $500, and $1,000. Notes above $20 tend to be rare for most banks, notes of $100 even more so, and notes of $500 and $1,000 seldom offered, except as proofs left over from bank-note company stocks (most particularly the archives, now distributed, of the American Bank Note Co.). In terms of everyday use in circulation, $1 and $5 were probably the most popular denominations.

Many intermediate denominations were also made, such as $4, $6, $7, $8, and $9. Odd denominations are very rare over $10, although a few exist. Now and again a bank would issue fractional values such as $1.25, $1.50, or $2.50. Although for some banks these turn up with frequency, overall, such denominations are scarce (see page 534).

Bills of denominations smaller than $1 were issued by many banks in the early 19th century, particularly circa 1815 and again in the late 1830s, when coins were scarce in circulation. These are usually classified as *scrip* notes, not obsolete bank notes; they are discussed below.

Vignettes and Illustrations

In the panorama of obsolete bank notes from the turn of the 18th century, continuing to 1866, decorations range from scattered small motifs, such as animals, to wonderfully detailed and ornate scenes with goddesses, sailing ships at sea, cityscapes, and more. Smaller illustrations, such as groups of birds, were used for accent.

Often a bill will have a medium-sized vignette at the top center, smaller vignettes at the left and right borders, and a very small vignette centered at the bottom border. The subjects sometimes bear relationship to the bank name or location. Thus, a bill from a bank on the coast may have an ocean scene with sailing vessels, while a bill from the Midwest might show farming scenes or a train. A whaling motif for a New England port, a steamship illustration for a town along an inland waterway, or a farm in a rural area were most appropriate in their time.

Occupations come to the fore in bank note illustrations, and range from glass blowing to shoe cobbling to chicken feeding—reflecting the jobs that people were doing in real life.

Allegorical scenes are available in wonderful profusion. Hebe, cup-bearer to the gods, can be found on many bills, often feeding or nourishing an eagle. Moneta, with a cornucopia of coins, can be seen on various notes. Commerce, agriculture, industry, mechanics, and other lines of endeavor have god and goddess avatars, often accompanied by identifying objects, such as a god of mechanics with a toothed gear.

Sailors are often seen on bank notes, but soldiers are somewhat scarce. War and conflict, popular enough as subjects in decorative prints, were not selected by many bank officers for use on currency. Ships, perhaps reflecting the lure of the outward-bound, adventure, and romance, are seen everywhere—and in many forms, from rowboats to canal boats, fully rigged clippers to side-wheel steamers.

Cherubs playing with Liberty Seated dollars (often dated 1854, with the plate then altered to 1857) are a popular subject, one coin for a $1 bill, up to five for a $5 bill, these by Rawdon, Wright, Hatch & Edson, the preeminent bank note firm of the mid-1850s (see page 535). Gold dollars, early silver dollars of the Draped Bust type (with the Heraldic Eagle reverse shown), Liberty Seated silver coins, and the like can be found. The late George Hatie formed a

Unusual Denominations

A $25 bill from the Bank of Lowville (New York). Produced by Wellstood, Hanks, Hay & Whiting, New York. This denomination is highly unusual.

A $1.25 bill of the Roxbury Bank (Massachusetts), 1838. Years later, Roxbury was incorporated into Boston. Produced by the New England Bank Note Co., Boston.

A $7 bill of the Peoples Bank (Paterson, New Jersey), which produced other unusual denominations. Engraved and printed by Casilear, Durand, Burton & Edmonds, New York City.

A $1.75 bill from the Burlington office of the Vermont State Bank. This, the first of the state-operated banks, was not a success. Patent Stereotype Steel Plate by Jacob Perkins, Newburyport, Massachusetts.

A $1,000 bill of the Manufacturers and Mechanics Bank, Philadelphia. Such high denominations were rare in circulation. Proofs, as here, appear now and then. By Bald, Cousland & Co. Philadelphia / Baldwin, Bald & Cousland, New York.

A $6 bill of the Bank of Bennington (Vermont). The denomination appears boldly in several places. The designation "$ SIX" is an unusual style. By Rawdon, Wright & Hatch, New York.

A $4 bill of the Connecticut River Banking Co. (Hartford, Connecticut). This note was used to illustrate the Haxby text. By Draper, Toppan, Longacre & Co., Philadelphia and New York.

An $8 bill of the Washington County Bank (Calais, Maine). This particular bank also issued $6, $7, and $9 notes in addition to regular denominations, but few were ever made. New England Bank Note Co., Boston.

Various bills issued by the West River Bank (Jamaica, Vermont) featured cupids cavorting with Liberty Seated silver dollars. Such bills are common today, thanks to remainder quantities, but the demand for them is intense. By Rawdon, Wright, Hatch & Edson, New York / New England Bank Note Co., Boston.

collection of bank notes with coin motifs. For the most part such bills are inexpensive, but prices seem to creep up inexorably as more collectors discover the field.

Animals can be found in wide variety. Horses are very common; cows are, as well; sheep less so. Barnyard creatures from pigs to chickens are on some bills. Dogs are very popular, including quite a few images of a dog near a safe, a paw resting on and guarding its key. Cats are rare for some reason. Deer, elk, beavers, grouse, and bears can be found. The national bird predominates; one of these is quite patriotic and wears a pendant with the portrait of George Washington.

Images of Washington, Benjamin Franklin, Lafayette, and other well-known figures are common. Daniel Webster is seen on many notes from the North, while fiery orator John C. Calhoun, foremost Senate exponent of Southern rights, is a familiar figure on bills from that area. Many of these vignettes were "stock" or were bought from bankrupt engravers, and others were widely copied, with the result that the same illustration can be found on bills of different issuers. Occasionally, bank presidents would place their own portraits on notes, not usually captioned, leaving it to the imagination of a later generation of numismatists to guess who they are.

Buildings are a plentiful motif, including quite a few that depict the building of the bank issuing the note. The United States Capitol is another popular illustration, at

first with unfinished details to the dome, later complete. Quite a few "stock" illustrations can be found—reflecting retail commerce, busy city streets, and the like. Factory depictions are sometimes specific, other times generic.

Townscapes and cityscapes are interesting to contemplate. The $1 and $2 bills of the Phenix Village Bank shows what this Rhode Island community must have looked like in the 1850s—with a dam providing water power and with factories and even a mansion in the distance.

A group of obsolete bank notes is often equivalent to a display of fine small prints of life, art, geography, and history.

Imprint of the Printer or Engraver

Various engravers nearly always signed their plates, sometimes simply (e.g., "Reed," for Abner Reed), other times extended (e.g., "New England Bank Note Co. Boston," and its parent company, "Rawdon, Wright, Hatch & Edson, New-York," on the same bill). These serve to identify who made them. After March 1858, when eight firms merged to create the American Bank Note Co., the ABNCo monogram was added to many existing plates when they were used later.

Generally, bills of the very early years, before 1800, carry no imprint. The identities of the engravers are a mystery, unless a connection can be made with another note of similar design and layout that does bear a signature. From 1800 to 1810, imprints

A $3 bill of the Huntingdon (Pennsylvania) Bank, 1815, imprinted, "W. Kneass Philada 125 Market St." In 1824 Kneass was appointed chief engraver at the Philadelphia Mint.

become more frequent on bills, and for those of the next decade, most are identified as to their makers. By the 1830s, imprints were standard, and a bill lacking one is probably counterfeit, although there are a very few exceptions. It was common for an engraver who also printed the notes to add "sc," for *sculpsit*, meaning *engraved it*, after his name, such as "P. Maverick sc.," for Peter Maverick.

Occasionally—very occasionally—individual vignettes are signed, often in microscopic letters in the bottom border of, or immediately below, the illustration. These may or may not relate to the bank-note printing company that used the vignettes.

Plate Letters

Letters identify the position of a note on a four-subject or other plate. If a plate had more than one of the same denomination, sequential letters would be used. Otherwise, A would be used. Usually, a sheet with bills as $1-$1-$2-$3 would have plate letters A-B-A-A, while a sheet with notes as $5-$5-$5-$5 would have letters A-B-C-D. There are many exceptions, such as the use of the letter A for several notes on the same plate, but giving it a different appearance each time, such as capital, lowercase, and script. In some instances a plate letter would be used twice on the same note, such as the letter A at the left and the letter A repeated on the right.

Sometimes, when a plate was strengthened by the reentering of a part of the design, or if the plate was slightly changed in another way, an additional letter would be added, such that a plate formerly marked as, say, A would now appear as aA. On Perkins-style slug-plate notes the term *check letter* was used.

Sometimes, higher denominations such as $100 and up were given letters farther down the alphabet, such as H or J, even though they may have been printed on two-subject or four-subject sheets.

It is not generally known that bills of the same design and denomination can differ from each other slightly. Accordingly a sheet of $5-$5-$5-$5 bills will usually show small variations, such as the distance from a given letter to a nearby vignette. This is because each $5 bill on the plate was made up separately by the entering of the different design elements.

Inscriptions and Obligations

The lettering of each bill typically includes a "promise to pay," or "redeemable in," or some other inscription. Some bills are payable at a later date than the date of issue and are called *post notes*. The typical bill is inscribed, for example, "Will pay TWENTY DOLLARS on demand," with the nature of the $20 not specified. The bank could pay in other currency, or give coins. Certain bills of the Bullion Bank, Washington, DC, issued in the early 1860s, are payable in Demand Notes, with later versions of the bill payable in Treasury Notes. However, such specific inscriptions are rare.

While most bills were redeemable at the office of the issuer, others provided for redemption at a distant city or office and stated such. As an example, certain $5 bills of the Bank of Macomb County (Mount Clemens, Michigan) are payable at the Bank of Tonawanda, New York. Sometimes a bank bills was payable at the bank itself and also at a specific office in New York City.

On many early bills there is a space for a payee, such as "pay to," then a space for an inscription. Often, these were printed by the engraving company, with generic names, such as J. Smith, B. Franklin, H. Clay, and so on.

Seals and Authorizations

Some bills, especially those of the 1840s and later, bear seals or imprints referring to state banking auditors, or stocks deposited as security, and the like. New York state banks are examples. Those with the seals of state offices are official. Other terms such as "Safety Fund," "Real Estate Pledged," or statements that the directors were liable, were apt to have little real meaning.

Color Imprints
and Safety Features

In the late 1850s and early 1860s most bills were overprinted in red (usually), green, or some other color, usually with the denomination, such as FIVE, in large letters, sometimes with panels of repeated tiny letters in color. On most bills the color part was printed first, the sheet was dried, and then black printing was applied. Some numismatic catalogers have called these colored imprints *protectors*.

Several patented anticounterfeiting systems were used, most prominently the "Canada green tint"(consisting of overprinted designs or lettering, patented June 30, 1857). This was the pet innovation promoted by Tracy Edson of Rawdon, Wright, Hatch & Edson, and later by the American Bank Note Co. Dr. Sterry Hunt created the scheme, which was granted Canadian patent 715 and U.S. patent 17,688. Hunt sold it to George Matthews, who sold it to Edson. A few years later Edson convinced the Treasury Department to use a variation of this on the Demand Notes of 1861 and the Legal Tender bills of 1862, although its anticounterfeiting usefulness was never proved.

In other instances, virtually the entire face of the bill was in color, with drop-out white lettering and black vignettes. The Seropyan patent process (1856) to deter counterfeiting was lauded by some and considered a failure by others. Ditto for the Atwater patent and Desopyn's patent red.

Lyman's Protection system came late in the game, and provided for a note to be divided into two main sections, the sizes of which varied with the denomination (see page 538). The $5 Lyman bill printed by the American Bank Note Co. for the State Bank of Michigan, Detroit, includes this inscription in multiple lines: "Lyman's Protection. Bank Note on the right end One Dollar covers one third of the paper. Two Dollars one half. Three Dollars, two thirds. Five dollars, three fourths." It seems to the modern viewer that Lyman's Protection was resistant to alteration or other abuses, but such bills have a rather mechanical appearance, more like checks or documents than paper currency. In any event, the system was never popular.

"Mr. Star's typographical colored printing plan," criticized by W.L. Ormsby in his *Bank Note Engraving* book in 1852, never achieved prominence, nor did Captain Glynn's Anti-Anastatic Bank Note Paper and other such things.

Anticounterfeiting proposals of the 1850s brought together different inventors, some of whose ideas were absurd or impractical, and bank-note printing companies, the latter ever eager to promote their own products while trying to prove that the security processes used by their competitors were worthless.

In an entirely different category, certain bills issued in the 1850s by the Lancaster Bank of Lancaster, Massachusetts, were ordered from the printer with the word MASSACHUSETTS imprinted vertically on the face, with the same paper-

Lyman's Protection system involved dividing the face of a note into blocks, with different proportions depending on the denomination.

tain Patented Stereotype Steel Plate bills had "Check Plate" segments on the back. Many W.L. Ormsby bills had tiny numerals in color repeated hundreds of times. Still other bills had geometric designs.

Certain bills of the late 1850s and 1860s were made with ornate engraving on the back, sometimes including the name of the bank and the denomination. Sometimes the name of a branch would be imprinted on the back.

Information Added to Notes After Delivery
Date of Issue

Each bill has the date, printed either in full or with an 18 or other partial date, with the rest added in ink. Sometimes a partial date would include everything except the completion of the year, as, "January 1, 18," or "January 1, 185," with the last one or two digits to be added. In a few instances, printed dates with day and/or month would be partially inked over with another month or day.

A fully printed date, obviously, is not the precise date that a bill was placed into circulation (which could have been long afterward). Dates that are inked in, such as "Dec. 1, 1856," with the 18 printed and the rest added by hand, are not necessarily reflective of the issue date, either. It was common practice to date large quantities of bills, keep them on hand, and then pass them into circulation as needed.

Serial Numbers

Serial numbers were added in ink, occasionally in two places. A few later varieties had the numbers stamped sequentially. The policy for numbering bills varied, but it is likely that to keep the numbers low

penetrating red ink used for the protector, and printed at the same time. Presumably, this enabled the note to be distinguished at quick glance from a bill of the Lancaster Bank of Lancaster, *New Hampshire*, such being in circulation at the time, but worthless. This Massachusetts variety is exceedingly rare today.

Back Plate

Relatively few bank notes (probably 5% or fewer) were printed on the back. Those that were can be interesting to study. Cer-

and the writing effort minimal, most banks started new sequences for each date on the note, or started numbers anew at the end of a week or month.

Signatures of Cashier and President

Space was provided on bills for the cashier (in the first position) and president to sign their names in ink. Occasionally, someone would sign as assistant cashier or vice president. Bills issued by railroads, merchants, and others often have signatures of treasurers, agents, or clerks.

It is likely that all or nearly all genuine bills issued by sound banks bore the real signatures of their officers, and those of clerks or others. It was common practice for crooks to obtain supplies of unused notes of failed banks, or to alter notes by imprinting other bank names on them, and then adding signatures in ink. Because of this there are many fictitious signatures on bills in numismatic collections today.

Payee

Many bank notes, especially those dated prior to 1850, have space for the name of a payee to be inked in. This seems to have been a nuisance to bank officers, who often made up short names, such as a first initial and a three- or four-letter surname. In other instances, the names of political figures or other luminaries were added.

However, the name of the first recipient of the note was employed as well (which was the intended use). It is likely that the common notes of the Vermont Glass Factory, Salisbury, Vermont, have payee names of employees who received them as wages.

Inking Procedures and Techniques

Often, the date of issue and serial number will be filled in by different hands and, sometimes, different color ink, from the signatures of the officers. It is likely that a clerk, or the cashier in his available time, inked this information in advance. As banks generally avoided the use of high serial numbers, it seems that during an advance

signing, bills dated, say, July 1, 1854, would be given serial numbers from 1 to several thousand; then the next bills would be given the date of July 2, and the sequence would begin over again. Some bills, especially those distributed in the South, were given the same serial number twice on the face of each note.

Separately, the bank president, who was usually not an employee of the bank (and sometimes was located in another town), and whose main duty was presiding at directors' meetings, signed many notes at once, creating a reserve. The cashier might sign in advance and hold the notes until they were issued, or he might wait until they were distributed and sign them at that time. It was thought that until both officers signed, the notes would not be effective as money, and, if they were stolen, the bank would have no obligation to redeem them. However, court decisions sometimes took a different view, stating that the public receiving a note would believe it to be a bank obligation and would not know whether a signature was genuine.

Overprints and Surcharges

On some bills, colored check-letters or numbers were applied, often at the upper right of a note. These are often poorly aligned and were added after the notes were delivered to banks, possibly as control letters for redeeming the notes or to identify areas in which they were placed into circulation. Such items added after a bill was delivered to the customer can be called *overprints* or *surcharges*. Both terms are employed by numismatists.

In other instances, imprints were added by banks when bills were sent to branch offices. Overprints can also identify a place of redemption.

Bills that were judged to be false were sometimes marked COUNTERFEIT, WORTHLESS, or similar. Bills from defunct institutions could be stamped BROKEN BANK. Currency that had been taken back by a bank was sometimes marked REDEEMED. The purpose of

Bank of Louisiana, New Orleans, $10 bill of 1863 with "FORCED ISSUE," and so on, surcharge at the right. This relates to the uncertain monetary conditions in New Orleans after it was recaptured by the Union in 1863, a year after Confederate occupation.

such stamps was to prevent them from being circulated further. Sometimes stamps were applied haphazardly, and it is not unusual to see COUNTERFEIT on a perfectly genuine note of a failed bank.

Sometimes recipients or banks would add information on the back of a note, such as the name of a depositor, or "counterfeit," or "redeemed Jan. 9, 1864," or some other notation—usually by hand in ink, not stamped.

Collecting Obsolete Currency—The Haxby Text

No one has ever chronicled all of the banks and other entities that issued bills during the obsolete-currency period from 1782 to 1866. However, most of the banks (but not canals, railroads, factories, etc.) that had their own currency are described in James A. Haxby's four-volume *Standard Catalog of United States Obsolete Bank Notes 1782–1866* (1988). This text is essential to the appreciation and understanding of the series and, indeed, is one of the most impressive numismatic research efforts of its era.

Haxby lists bills by states, towns, and banks within the towns, in alphabetical order, assigning a number to each bank. The numbers are open, with gaps, making it possible to insert a new listing if information about an unlisted bank is found (as happens now and then). Brief information is given for each bank, as to its period of operation and, often, what happened to it, but there are no bank histories, names of officers, or other background information.

These are sample listings from the Indiana section, from Gosport to Huntington:

Gosport • IN-200 • Citizens Bank of Gosport, circa 1857. A fraudulent bank.

Gosport • IN-205 • Bank of Gosport, 1857–1859. Fate: closed.

Greencastle • IN-210 • Exchange Bank, 1855–1866. Fate: closed.

Harmony • IN-215 • Farmers Bank of Harmony, circa 1820. Fraudulent bank.

Hartford • IN-220 • Hartford Exchange Bank, 1850s. Fraudulent bank.

Hartford • IN-225 • Manufacturers Bank, circa 1858. A fraudulent bank.

Huntington • IN-230 • Huntington County Bank, 1854–1857. Fate: closed.

For each bank, different bills are listed in order by denomination together with a letter designating the nature of the note (G for genuine; C for counterfeit; R for raised from one denomination to another; A for altered; S for spurious; N for unattributed non-genuine).

Under this arrangement, bills from the Exchange Bank of Greencastle, Indiana, are listed as follows in the Haxby text:

IN-201-G-2 • $1 of May 10, 1854 [plus information and value].

IN-201-G-4 • $5 of May 10, 1854 [plus information and the notation SENC, meaning "surviving example not confirmed," noting that neither James A. Haxby nor his contributors knew of a remaining bill].

IN-201-G-4a • $5 of May 10, 1854, as above, but with modified imprint of bank note company [plus information].

These three bills are the only ones Haxby lists for the Exchange Bank. If a $10 bill were to be discovered, it could be assigned a number in the open system, such as IN-201-G-6. If a counterfeit were to be found of the $1 bill, it could be listed as IN-201-C-2.

Valuations are given in two or more grades. The prices are of limited use today, due to the advance of the market. However, in a relative sense they provide information that is valuable. If, in 1988, Haxby listed one note from a given bank at $10 in VF grade and another at $25, the second will likely be the more valuable today, in similar proportion (e.g., $50 and $125).

Books by the Society of Paper Money Collectors

Over a long period of time, more than two dozen specialized books have been produced about the bank notes from particular states. Many of these have the imprint of the Society of Paper Money Collectors, and others have been privately issued. Some treat the issues of state-chartered banks exclusively, while others include bills distributed by factories, railroads, and other businesses. Still others add scrip notes of fractional denominations. These usually include information not found in Haxby (who generally listed only those issuers with the word *bank* in their names).

As many different authors have been involved, there is no consistency in arrangement, although most give basic information as to the denomination, design, and printer or engraver. Only rarely are bank officers (cashier and president) who signed notes mentioned or their terms of service given, information that numismatists would find to be exceedingly useful while examining bills.

Samples from a large shelf of books:

- *State Bank Notes of Michigan* (Harold L. Bowen, 1956). I consider this to be one of the most useful, in that for each bank the bills are listed in denomination order, described as to design and plate letters, and for each bank the names of the cashiers and presidents are given. Moreover, there is a wealth of information on the background of many issuers.

- *Maine Obsolete Paper Money and Scrip* (George W. Wait, Society of Paper Money Collectors [SPMC], 1977). One of an extensive series, with others planned, of red-cloth-covered volumes issued by the society. The Wait study includes a brief overview of banking in the state, then listings by town and issuer. The bills of each issuer are given numbers.

- *Money and Banking in Maryland: A Catalogue of Maryland's Paper Money, 1790–1865* (Denwood N. Kelly,

A $5 note of the Globe Bank, Bangor, Maine, used as an illustration in *Maine Obsolete Paper Money and Scrip.* (Robert A. Vlack Collection)

A $1 note of the Howard Street Savings Bank, Baltimore, used as an illustration in *Money & Banking in Maryland.* Only a few states permitted savings banks to issue currency.

Armand M. Shank, Jr., and Thomas S. Gordon, Maryland Historical Society, 1996). This impressively printed volume illustrates an example of each bill encountered by the authors and gives much historical information, a rarity rating, and cross references to Haxby and selected other guides.

- *South Carolina Obsolete Notes and Scrip* (Austin M. Sheheen, Jr., privately printed, 2003). This book demonstrates what can be done if budget is not a factor. Printed on high-quality paper, the 368-page volume is lavishly illustrated in full color throughout—and so realistically that the notes can almost be picked off the page! Catalog numbers are given for each note. Bank information is brief but essential and includes charter date, officers and terms, and authorized capital. The author has collected paper money for more than 50 years and is one of the best-known and liked figures in the hobby.

Interesting Monographs and Studies

From the 1930s to the 1970s, Dr. John A. Muscalus printed and distributed many small monographs illustrating bills he had collected with certain themes. Text was often minimal, and the contents not comprehensive, but they contributed much interest to the hobby. His output included the following titles (among many, many others), listed here to illustrate the diversity of subjects found on obsolete bank notes: *An Index of State Bank Notes That Illustrate Characters and Events; The Views of Towns, Cities, Falls and Buildings Illustrated on 1800–1866 Bank Paper Money; An Index of State Bank Notes That Illustrate Presidents; State Bank Notes: A Reference List With Identifications of Historic Interest* (published by Wayte Raymond; one of only a few of Muscalus's references to cross the 100-page mark in size); *The Use of Banking Enterprises in the Financing of Public Education, 1796–1866* (202 pages); *Paper Money in Sheets* (probably his most desired publication, and one of those more than 100 pages in length); *The Dismal Swamp Canal and Lake Drummond Hotel on Paper Money, 1838–1865; Landseer's My Horse, Spaniel, and other Paintings on Paper Money; Saint Catherine on Paper Money of the State of Florida and Others; Famous Paintings of God and the Infant Christ on Paper; Lord Byron on Paper Money Issued in the United States; Recycled Southern Paper Money: A Reference List of Southern Paper Money Printed on the Backs of Scarce Unused Notes and Documents; Mississippi Railroad Currency* (coauthored with Byron W. Cook and D.C. Montgomery, Jr.).

In more recent times, Roger H. Durand, a consummate scholar and historian, best known for his excellent 1981 text, *Obsolete Notes and Scrip of Rhode Island and the Providence Plantations*, has created a series of monographs in the *Interesting Notes* series, such as *Interesting Notes About Denominations* (1988); *Interesting Notes About History* (1990); *Interesting Notes About Territories* (1992); and *Interesting Notes About Indians* (1991), to give but a summary of his output. These are well worth adding to a numismatic library.

To these and many other specialized books and numerous monographs can be added issues of *Paper Money*, published by SPMC, and rich with many articles on obsolete currency—so many that a file of these is essential to any advanced library. The same can be said for the excellent *Essay-Proof Journal*, no longer published, but the source of much data on engravers and bank-note printers. The *Bank Note Reporter*, issued monthly, has much information as well as dealer offerings and show-schedules and coverage. Dealer catalogs, usually extensively illustrated, are another essential element of the study and appreciation of this specialty.

Many banks published histories of their operations, usually with only positive information included (scarcely anything about non-redemption of bills, cashiers absconding with a valise filled with bills, etc.), but with listings of bank officers and their terms, illustrations of buildings, and more. These are useful if you have a few "pet banks" of special collecting interest.

Grading of Obsolete Notes

There are no hard-and-fast rules for grading obsolete currency. Interpretations vary all over the place. A "Fine" note to one dealer may be "Extremely Fine" to another. Similar to the situation for coins, grading has become more loose over the years. A bill that I bought from Richard T. Hoober in the 1960s as Fine will easily be Very Fine today. Years ago, a bill with even a slight trace of a fold or crease was automatically excluded from the Uncirculated category. Today, Uncirculated bills can have such traces. And so it goes.

These categories reflect my observation of current grading by many dealers and collectors:

Choice or Gem Uncirculated: A crisp, bright bill with no evidence of creases, folds, or stains. Tom Denly comments: "I consider centering to be a most important part of grade. For instance, a poorly centered note possibly cut into the design can never be called 'gem' or even 'choice,' no matter how nice it is otherwise."[94]

Uncirculated: A new bill, never circulated, but perhaps with slight evidence of a fold, crease, or smudges from handling (presumably by bank officers!). If part of the margin is trimmed away, this should be mentioned, but often is not.

About Uncirculated: A bright, attractive note, with some creases, folds, or light discoloration, but with only slight evidences of use in commerce.

Extremely Fine: A bright and attractive note, with some slight stains or discoloration, perhaps with a pinhole or two, or some small defect, but with overall excellent appearance. A bill that did limited service in circulation.

Very Fine: A well-circulated note, often somewhat faded, but with printing and vignettes clear and with an attractive overall appearance. There may be an edge chip or two, or perhaps a tiny piece off of a corner (but not into the printed part of the note). Much inventiveness is displayed by sellers in the description of missing pieces in the margins of notes, with such terms as *chip*, *pull*, and *nick* employed, among others.

Fine: A note with even more wear, often limp or flimsy from extended use in commerce, but with all printed areas intact and most of them sharply defined. May be stained or discolored in areas.

Very Good: A well-circulated note, usually with some problems or tears, perhaps a small piece missing from the border, and so on. Flimsy and often faded or discolored.

Good: An extensively circulated note, and obviously so, with evidence including small tears, perhaps missing edge pieces, indistinct areas of the printing and vignettes, and, often, old handwriting on the face.

Fair and Poor: Notes that have been in circulation for a very long time, now with ragged edges or pieces missing, and often with significant areas faded or otherwise not discernible.

Two early, rare bills from the Winnipissiogee Bank (Meredith, New Hampshire), 1820s. Both are prizes, but it might take a super-dedicated specialist to appreciate the tattered $2 bill—the only one I have ever been offered.

As noted in the preceding chapter on colonial and other early bills, the significance of high grade for obsolete notes can be just the opposite of what it is for rare coins. An Uncirculated note that was never signed or issued may have a much lower value and interest to a collector than a Good or even Fair circulated bill of a bank of which hardly any are known.

Of course, among notes that actually circulated, it is better to have one in high grade than in low grade. Some exist *only* in low grades, and never is a disparaging glance given to them. The Haxby books show many bills with extensive damage or missing parts.

Aspects of Availability and Value
Classes of Banks

While collecting and studying obsolete paper money over many years, the following observable realities have been of great use to me.

Sound Banks

Fortunately for the financial security of American citizens, the vast majority of large banks were well operated and had responsible officers. Many small, state-chartered banks were also sound, this being especially true for states in which banking laws were enforced. In time, most bills of these banks were redeemed, to be exchanged for later bills or for coins. Nearly all of the hundreds that converted to National Banks in the 1863 to 1866 era redeemed their bills at full par, in exchange for federal Legal Tender or National Bank notes.

Accordingly, a general rule is that today the bills of sound banks are much more rare than those of failed banks of equal capitalization. When found, bills of these banks often show extensive wear. Signed and used bills of these banks, especially those of low capital ($25,000 to $100,000), can be very valuable if in high grades.

However, there are many exceptions—such as when a sound bank redeemed all of its obsolete notes and stored them, and at a later time they became available to the numismatic community.

Failed Banks

Bills from failed banks constitute the vast majority of collectible issues today. Many of these exist in large quantities. Unredeemable in their own time and worthless in commerce, these were kept by unfortunate citizens who received them, or were confiscated and held by state authorities who later disposed of them to numismatic interests. Notes from these banks tend to be in higher grades such as Extremely Fine to Uncirculated, as they were used for only a limited time, if at all.

Because of this, it is easy to assemble a large collection of different bills from, say, Michigan banks—the failure rate in Michigan was greater than 90% in the early 1840s. Compare this to New Hampshire, where only a handful of banks became insolvent; that state's obsolete notes are harder to find in collectible condition today.

Spurious Banks

The term *spurious* is supposed to describe a bank that never existed, but for which bills were issued. An example is provided by the New England Bank of Fairmount, Maine. Bills of $10 and $20 denominations were printed by the highly regarded firm of Rawdon, Wright, Hatch, & Edson (New York City) and delivered to the perpetrators, who inked in the serial numbers and the signatures of cashier A. Martin and president E. Rittenhouse. The bills were superbly printed and very impressive in appearance, and, no doubt "New England Bank" had a ring of solidity to its name. However, no such bank ever existed—yet its notes are highly collectible. Bills of spurious banks tend to be readily available on the numismatic market, as they were never redeemed.

Collectors should note that some banks that have been designated fraudulent or spurious (in the Haxby text and elsewhere) actually operated as private banks—without charter, but still legitimately. As an example, in 1841 the charters of banks operating in Washington, DC, expired. Renewals were not granted on a timely basis and, sometimes, not at all.

A note from a bank that never existed: the spurious New England Bank, supposedly of Fairmount, Maine. Large quantities of such notes were printed by Rawdon, Wright, Hatch & Edson, America's largest bank-note engraving firm. This company aided many criminals in capers, but disclaimed any knowledge of doing so! Denominations of $10 and $20 were printed for the Fairmount Bank and today are highly collectible in their own right.

I enjoy researching the history of such banks, and over a course of years, by digging into obscure documents, newspapers, and such, have found that a number of "fraudulent" or "nonexistent" banks actually did exist and operate, but sometimes for just a short time and without much publicity (or privately and effectively, but without state charters). Also interesting to read are the lofty pronouncements of bank note printers to the effect that they upheld the highest standards of integrity, would not print notes for spurious banks, and so on. Reality, as widely reported in state bank commissioners' reports and in court records, shows that most every firm took whatever business it could get. For an exposé I refer you to W.L. Ormsby's book *Bank Note Engraving* (1852).

Hoards

For some banks, large quantities of bills still survive and can be traced to hoards and old-time accumulations. These include the following categories.

Remainders. For several hundred state-chartered banks and some spurious ones as well, large quantities of unused sheets remained on hand in later years. Usually, these were arranged four notes to a sheet. Sometimes the bills were partially filled in with ink, such as with a serial number and the signature of one of the officers, or both, but they were never cut apart and issued.

After they became worthless, they remained stored in vaults of banks that were successors to the state banks or that had acquired the assets and interests of other banks. In still other instances they remained in the families of bank officers or in storage elsewhere.

Beginning in a significant way in the 1920s and 1930s, when D.C. Wismer produced an extensive serial feature (which ran from 1922 to 1936!) on obsolete currency for *The Numismatist*, a great collector interest developed. Dealers sent mailings to banks and other institutions, offering to buy stocks of old sheets, often enclosing sample bills, such as one of high denomination from the Canal Bank of New Orleans, to emphasize that they were no longer worth face value. Today, many of these remainder notes are on the market, usually cut into separate notes, less often sold in sheets. Nearly all are in crisp Uncirculated condition.

Redeemed and Used Bills. In other instances, banks would keep bundles of redeemed notes on hand, sometimes canceling them with punch holes, cuts, or inked marks. In other instances, bundles of bills from failed banks would be kept by state authorities or by successor banks, later to be distributed into numismatic channels. There is no information in print as to which bank bills fit into this category, but, often, if a common and inexpensive bill is dated from the 1840s to the mid-1860s, and shows extensive circulation, it is one of these.

Gold and Silver vs. Paper

Over the course of American history, *coins* have been saved as souvenirs, gifts, and stores of value. A gold dollar given as a gift in 1851 might survive today as a memento. In great contrast, in their era the bills of state-chartered banks were not considered to be of permanent value; there was always the specter that a note would become worthless, so they would change hands quickly and frequently. For this reason, many bank bills that were common in their era are exceedingly rare today.

In 1857, Aaron White, a Connecticut attorney, observed the panic of that year and the difficulties with paper money. He issued a token inscribed, "Never Keep a Paper Dollar in Your Pocket Till Tomorrow."

Many obsolete currency issues have achieved the ultimate state of rarity: from listings in old references, we know they were made at one time, but not a single example is known today. The Pine River Bank of Ossipee, New Hampshire, once issued thousands of bills, and yet, so far as I know, not a single original note exists today! A $5 gold half eagle of the same era might have been kept as a souvenir, or hoarded in a bank vault. A piece of paper marked "Pine River Bank," on the other hand, would have plummeted in value once the bank closed, and would have been hurriedly redeemed within the allotted period.

Scrip Notes

The term *scrip* generally refers to paper money of small denominations, from a cent up to 50 or 75 cents, issued for a limited time, often during a shortage of regular paper money and coins. Accordingly, many scrip notes were produced during and after the War of 1812, when small-denomination coins were scarce. As an example, in October 1815, when there was a shortage of coins in circulation, the state of Connecticut allowed banks to issue scrip notes of less than a dollar, stating that June 1, 1816, was the latest date these could be issued.

Many more varieties of scrip were produced during the Hard Times era and, in particular, during the Civil War. Indeed, during that conflict, particularly in the years 1862 and 1863, many hundreds of varieties were issued by stores, towns, banks, and others, and are highly collectible today.

Most scrip notes were typeset and produced by local or regional printers, not by bank-note-engraving companies.

Scrip notes also include paper money issued, mostly in the late 19th century, by commercial colleges and training schools to familiarize students with the handling of money. Also classified as scrip are bills (sometimes resembling currency) or tickets entitling the holder to redeem them for bottles of patent medicine or other products or services. On occasion, banks and chambers of commerce issued scrip, as during the Bank Holiday of March 1933.

Information regarding scrip notes is more difficult to find than for the other types discussed here, but generally can be located under specialized references issued by the Society of Paper Money Collectors in connection with obsolete notes of different states. Beyond that, a number of monographs have been produced. However, large geographical areas in which scrip has been issued have not been chronicled at all. Generally, scrip notes are much less expensive than are other types of currency, and great rarities or even hitherto undescribed pieces can often be purchased for a few hundred dollars or less. Many common varieties cost only in the $20 to $40 range.

Proof and Specimen Notes

From the first decade of the 19th century, continuing through the mid-1860s, engravers and bank note printers often made sample impressions from printing

Scrip note issued by the Mt. Pleasant Apothecary Store, Roxbury, Massachusetts, January 1, 1863. The proprietor of this particular establishment was none other than W. Elliott Woodward, then at the beginning of his numismatic career, which would prove to be memorable.

plates. In many instances these were sent to bank officers to suggest designs or to seek approval for motifs already selected. At other times, proofs (usually not capitalized when referring to paper money, unlike for Proof coins) were made to be kept in company files.

Typically, such proofs were made on very thin paper, sometimes called *India paper*, not as durable as that used to print circulating bills. Proofs, if printed singly (rather than as part of a sheet), nearly always had wide margins, again unlike those made for use in commerce. To prevent them from being signed and passed, they were often cancelled with, say, a row of punch holes in the signature area of the bill, or ink marks, or the cutting out of portions of the note.

Some proof impressions, single notes as well as sheets of proofs, were mounted on heavier paper or on cardboard to make them more durable. Proofs can be brittle, and it is not at all unusual for a bright, crisp proof bill to have a piece or two missing from an edge or corner, or to have a slight tear. While it would be nice not to have these, often there is not much choice. Besides, such defects are usually minor and do not noticeably impair the beauty of the note.

Today, buying proofs can be a dangerous game, as many ordinary remainder bills—regular issues that were never signed or issued—are offered as "proofs," sometimes even with rows of punch-cancels emulating proofs. This problem has been around for a long time, and years ago was an occasional topic for discussion in the *Essay-Proof Journal*.

Venture carefully before buying any proofs. This is a very technical area. Here are some guidelines:

Good signs:
- *Wide margins*—Margins that are wide *all around* are a good sign. An ordinary note cut from a remainder sheet might have a wide top margin (if it was the highest note on the sheet), or a wide bottom margin (if it was the lowest note), but not both.

- *Thin paper, crisp details*—It's a good sign when the paper is very thin, almost diaphanous, with the printed impression showing exquisite details.
- *Usual color overprint absent*—When circulated examples of the type were made with red or other color overprints, and the bill in question has none, it's a good sign.
- *Bill is a great rarity*—A listing as "SENC" (Surviving Example Not Confirmed) by Haxby is good; also, a high denomination, such as $50 upward, is usually a positive sign.
- *Seller is an expert*—Many dealers in paper money have a problem distinguishing proofs, and even the most expert of experts sometimes disagree. However, it is always best to buy from an expert. Auction catalog listings by leading firms are usually reliable, but not always.

Bad signs:
- *Note common as a remainder*—If Uncirculated examples of ordinary bills (made for use in commerce) exist, be ultra-aware! Check Haxby or consult a trustworthy dealer if you are not sure.
- *Tight margins*—If margins are close to the printed border, be careful.
- *Seller is not a recognized expert*—Do *not* buy, or even think of buying, a "proof" note offered casually, such as on the Internet, by someone who does not have expertise. Chances of buying a real proof are close to zero.
- *Signatures on the note*—Although real proofs are sometimes (rarely) seen with inked-in serial numbers in low digits, or an inked-in date, they *do not* have signatures of bank officers.
- *Indistinct printing*—If, under a strong magnifying glass, the details of the vignettes are not crisp and distinct, beware. This criterion can also help detect modern copies made on computers or duplicating machines (quite a few such notes are around).
- *Ordinary paper*—If the paper of an offered "proof" matches that used

for circulating notes, beware. This is a difficult concept, as so many different styles of paper were used.

Modern "Proprietary Proofs" and Related

In the late 20th century, many printing plates held by the American Bank Note Co. were dusted off and new impressions taken from them, usually on bright, white paper of medium thickness. Some of these were stamped "SPECIMEN" or had American Bank Note Co. wording on the back, in bright red, but others were unmarked. Those stamped in red were done with an ink that sometimes bled through the paper, making it slightly visible on the face.

Many of these were sold by Christie's in the sales of the American Bank Note Co. archives in the early 1990s. Others filtered out of ABNCo one way or another and came on the market privately. Generally, such bills are designated *proprietary proofs* or *modern proprietary proofs*.

Plates in private hands have been used, and will continue to be used, to make modern proofs. Although these could be called *proprietary*, as the current owner of the plates sponsored their making, it would seem that *modern proof* would be a better notation.

The advantage of modern proofs, proprietary or otherwise, is that impressions of bills not otherwise available are now collectible. In my reference collection I have quite a few such proofs from Vermont, New Hampshire, and Maine, nearly all of which represent bills for which

Original steel plate used by Rawdon, Wright, Hatch & Edson, with ABNCo monogram, to print $1 notes for the Indian Head Bank of Nashua, New Hampshire. (Courtesy of the Bank of America, successor to the Indian Head National Bank and the Indian Head Bank)

originals are either great rarities or completely nonexistent.

Ways to Collect Obsolete Bank Notes
By Location

Obsolete bank bills can be collected in several different ways, the most popular being by state. Accordingly, someone specializing in bills of Ohio might concentrate on issues from the various banks there and have no interest in those from New York or Tennessee. Bills of the southern states have formed the focus for many numismatists, and several books feature them.

Some states offer more diversity than do others. Generally, pickings from states west of the Mississippi are sparse. Bills of states from Georgia north to Maine can be collected in depth, as can those of the District of Columbia.

States in which there were many "wildcat" banks, loosely regulated, offer an easier path than do others with strict regulations. Michigan is the best known of the wild and woolly note-issuing locations, but Indiana and Illinois are fertile fields as well. Again, geography can be interesting. Dubuque, now in Iowa, was once part of Wisconsin, and Toledo, in Ohio, was at one time within the boundaries of Michigan.

As to what is available and what is not, the Haxby texts remain the best overview, although, as mentioned earlier, prices have risen sharply since that series was published.

If a state has a specialized book available (part of the SPMC series), this will be helpful. You will soon discover that most states still have new discoveries and information to yield. I would recommend buying a few history books covering any states of interest, but check the indexes first to be sure there is coverage of early banking and finance.

Collecting currency from a particular town or city can be an interesting subspecialty, but likely not a main thrust, as except for some major municipalities, selections can be

Senator Warren Henderson, a long-time collector and connoisseur of obsolete paper money, with an album of New Hampshire notes.

sparse. In bank notes as in other collecting endeavors, it is essential to be able to make acquisitions regularly in order to sustain your collecting spirit and enthusiasm.

By Topic

Topics can be a fun way to collect currency. Santa Claus is high on the popularity list, and such notes can be quite expensive today, many running into four figures. For rare *coins* this would not mean much, but in the milieu of obsolete bank notes this is at the high end of the scale. Whaling scenes, found on bills from several different banks on the New England coast, are less expensive, but usually command a strong premium.

Railroads are depicted on hundreds of issues, with the locomotives ranging from early wood-fired units pulling cars resembling stagecoaches, to larger, later units in front of long trains. Canals and canal boats

A dramatic whaling scene is featured on this $10 bill of the Stonington Bank of Connecticut. Bills of this particular institution exist in large quantities as remainders. However, widespread demand has made such notes valuable.

are on many vignettes. Horses shown on paper money range from those laboring in farm fields to those carrying soldiers or frisking in pastures. Side-wheel steamships, sometimes identified by name, can be interesting to collect, especially if the histories of the vessels are learned (there is an abundance of literature available on ocean-going steamers as well as inland packets). Sailing ships, sometimes in harbor, other times far out to sea, are plentiful on bank notes. The "Vignettes and Illustrations" section above gives other ideas. The studies by John A. Muscalus and Roger H. Durand offer further food for thought.

Proofs

Until the early 1980s, proofs of obsolete bank notes were considered to range from scarce to rare. The *Essay-Proof Journal* discussed varieties and their characteristics, and dealer Christian Blom, for one, made them a specialty. Relatively few came up for sale, and it was impossible to form a meaningful collection of them. Likely, no more than a few thousand were in the hands of collectors.

Then came a vast quantity into the marketplace, mainly through the Christie's auction house. These included the Alexander Vattemare albums sold in the early 1980s and, much more extensive, the American Bank Note Co. archives auctioned in the early 1990s. In addition to original impressions from the 19th century, modern proprietary proofs, mostly from plates held by the American Bank Note Co., became available, sometimes with red stamping on the back to indicate they were the property of ABNCo, and sometimes not.

"I Like It"

There are many other ways to collect obsolete bills. The "I like it" concept always works. If it's interesting to you, and available, give it a try.

Jim Ruddy liked $3 bills and formed a collection of hundreds of different examples of this once-common, but later curious, denomination. An Ohio client of mine once chased bills depicting George Washington, and found many.

One of my favorite pursuits is to seek notes from banks with interesting histories, regardless of where they are located—examples including the Owl Creek Bank (Mount Vernon, Ohio), with its unofficial status and later trial by newspaper; and the Bank of Central New York (Utica), of which the wily Samuel Dakin was a principal.

A key advantage to collecting obsolete bank notes today is that market prices are generally very modest in comparison to other areas. Great rarities are apt to cost much less than they do in just about any other numismatic specialty. I have seen interest expand greatly, but it is likely that the best is yet to come, especially as more information becomes available to guide buyers into making intelligent purchases.

Selected Bibliography

Haxby, James A. 1988. *Standard Catalog of United States Obsolete Bank Notes 1782–1866* (4 vols.). (This is the essential text. Out of print, and expensive when found, but worth acquiring.)

Specialized books on currency of different states, mostly issued under the imprint of the Society of Paper Money Collectors. Check with the society for titles in print. Others may be available from dealers.

The Bank Note Reporter and *Paper Money* (journal of the SPMC), among other current periodicals.

CHAPTER TWENTY-NINE

COLLECTING UNITED STATES PAPER MONEY

There has been noted in recent months the decidedly increasing interest in the collecting of United States paper money. By this is meant the acquiring and preservation of paper money specimens produced by the government and which were first issued for circulation in 1861.... To one who is interested in this subject, it is an encouraging sign, because the field, which is large and has never been entirely covered, offers many avenues for research and study, and will amply repay anyone who devotes serious attention to it.... Why the subject has not engaged the attention of a larger number of collectors is a matter for conjecture. Possibly the need of a proper catalogue of the various issues has had something to do with it....

—George W. Blake (March 1910)

A Latecomer Among Popular Specialties

Federal paper money from 1861 to date, divided into large size (1861–1929) and small size (1929 to date), is a very dynamic part of American numismatics. In recent decades this specialty, earlier a niche, has come into the spotlight—perhaps not in the center of the beam, but it certainly is gaining attention.

In comparison to the coin market, the market for paper money is in many ways still in a developmental stage, which, as I see it, is a good situation for you! The commercial grading of paper money is a relatively new concept, grading standards and interpretations are still in the process of being developed, and market prices for rare issues are often modest.

Paper money is fun to collect and interesting to contemplate, and the milieu of this branch of the hobby is filled with nice people!

While U.S. coins have been collected with passion for many generations, mainline federal notes have not been. It is perhaps curious, indeed incredible, to relate that in the 19th century, from the 1870s onward, paper money was sought by specialists, but the objects of desire were colonial and Continental Currency notes, Fractional Currency, and even Confederate bills. Scarcely anyone was interested in the main areas of federal paper, such as Legal Tender Notes, Silver Certificates, National Bank Notes, and the like.

A Perplexity, It Seems!

In my view there are several reasons for this lack of mainstream attention in the past. Certainly, at first blush, federal paper money seems to be very complicated.

How should currency be arranged, be listed? *Coins* are simple in comparison. In most instances, denominations are easy to understand. Half cents come before cents, $5 gold coins come before $10 gold coins, and so on. In a coin series, an 1871 Indian cent comes before an 1872, followed by and 1873, then an 1874. Nickel five-cent pieces begin with the Shield type, then go into the Liberty Head series, and so on. However, a few coins are complex. Take dollars. In 1873 the mints were making Liberty Seated silver dollars, silver trade dollars, and gold dollars.

If Morgan silver dollars (1878–1921) appeal to you, at the next coin show or your next visit to your local dealer, you can get started. Of course, some sophistication is needed to be a smart buyer, but, overall, Morgan dollars are easy to understand.

On the other hand, if I were to suggest that you collect $1 bills of the same era, you would be confronted with Legal Tender Notes, Coin or Treasury Notes, National Bank Notes issued by more than 1,000 different banks, Silver Certificates, and Federal Reserve Bank Notes. You would hardly know where to begin! Moreover, if you collect Morgan silver dollars you know that the 1889-CC, 1893-S, 1895, and a few others are rarities, great object of desire. In contrast, if you were to ask 10 dealers the question, "What are the rarest $1 notes of the 1878 to 1921 years?" probably most would have no clue.

Again, I see this as an advantage for you!

Different categories of paper money were produced under different legislation. The congressional bill that created Silver Certificates mandated certain quantities to be made under certain provisions, while in the meantime older legislation set certain rules for Legal Tender bills and National Bank notes. Often, these authorizations overlapped each other. Today, listings of these are always kept separate from each other. Silver Certificates are listed under that category, while Legal Tender Notes have their own section. They are not intermixed or interleaved.

Because of this, you need to learn about each major class of currency. I believe this can be done fairly easily, and in this chapter I have given the matter a "college try"! Hopefully, by the time you finish reading things will be more clear.

Other Complexities

Within the major classes of paper money there are many differences, some obvious and others subtle, that can make a difference in value. These are complex to understand, but, again, I've given it a try. If you find some aspects a bit esoteric, you're in good company—for even leading collectors and dealers often have to look things up in books and catalogs to understand them.

Although each note bore at least two signatures of Treasury officials, and although these terms of office could be looked up in a guide, they had little meaning as to when the bills were actually issued. As an example, although records tell us that S.B. Colby as register of the Treasury and F.E. Spinner as treasurer of the United States were in office together from August 11, 1864, to September 21, 1867, bills with their signatures were still being printed

well into the 1870s! While some of these were printed from plates made from 1864 to 1867, it was also practice to make up new plates with these old signatures. The Gainesville (Alabama) National Bank, charter number 1822, issued plates with the Colby-Spinner signatures, from new plates dated June 15, 1871.

As if this were not enough, only a dedicated paper money collector who gathered information from many sources was likely to know the rarity and desirability differences among styles of the Treasury Seal printed on bills—small red, large brown, blue, or whatever.

Further, until the second half of the 20th century there was no standard way to describe federal notes. Although some listings in auction catalogs might mention signature combinations, or series numbers, or Treasury Seal styles, many did not. As such bills generally had low values, and the Secret Service had strict rules about reproducing illustrations of paper money, it was very difficult for collectors to know even what certain bills looked like!

The Grinnell Collection

It may be relevant for me to mention the greatest collection of U.S. paper money ever auctioned, that formed by Albert A. Grinnell. If you were to acquire a set of catalogs of the offering, you would have great difficulty matching up many of the notes to the Friedberg numbers we all use today (and of which more will be said in this chapter). The bills were not illustrated, and descriptions were sparse. In contrast, if you read the Chapman brothers' catalog of the Bushnell Collection of coins, tokens, and medals, sold in 1882, most everything is completely understandable today.

Grinnell, who was born in New York and became a principal of Grinnell Brothers Music Stores in Detroit—a chain that sold music boxes, phonographs, player pianos, and much more—simply loved paper money, and formed a truly immense collection. He seems to have been particularly active from about 1911 through the

Depression years of the 1930s, when, with virtually no competition, he acquired many National Bank notes and, with only a few other collectors in the field, bought many Legal Tender, National Bank, and Coin Notes, as well as Silver Certificates and other items.

In June 1943, B. Max Mehl sold some coins and other items from the Grinnell cabinet, somewhat misleadingly indicating that this was the most extensive collection of U.S. currency, which it was, but Mehl was *not* the person selling it! There must have been a disagreement between Grinnell and Mehl, for the main paper money collection was consigned to Barney Bluestone, a Syracuse, New York, professional numismatist who had been a coin dealer since about 1926 and a second-tier coin auctioneer since 1931. Bluestone did indeed handle many fine items in his own time, but his catalogs were not particularly memorable, and only the most dedicated scholar is apt to know much about him today. Sold in a series of seven sales from 1944 through 1946, the Grinnell Collection auctions attracted only about a half dozen active bidders at each event. William Donlon later recalled that the only buyers on hand were F.C.C. Boyd, Harley Freeman, James Wade, Richard Saffin, and Herman K. Crofoot, in addition to Donlon himself. Of course, these names were in themselves a formidable line-up.

It is probably correct to say that the Grinnell Collection is more famous in retrospect—it has achieved legendary status among modern scholars—than it was during the time of the sale. Its status in history is certainly justified. Today we can only reflect upon the treasures that were offered, playing to an audience that numbered just a handful of bidders. In the early 21st century we can only read about and, perhaps, weep at what the Grinnell Collection contained, this being but a sample: 35 National Gold Bank notes; one $100 "Watermelon" Coin Note of 1890 and two $1,000 "Grand Watermelon" Coin Notes; 3,300 National Bank Notes

(including 750 from Grinnell's home state of New York and 260 from his adopted state of Michigan); and 43 examples of major currency errors, including two *sheets* of notes with $10 faces and $5 backs, which, offered in the final sale, realized $3,550 each, or probably as much as a 1913 Liberty Head nickel would have been worth at the time!

In the 1940s there was no one source from which to learn about different currency series, signatures, seals, and other aspects. Except to dedicated collector-scholars, the field was terra incognita.

THE Book!

This disarray, this paper money equivalent of the Tower of Babel, changed in 1953 with the publication of *Paper Money of the United States*, by Robert Friedberg (1912–1963). Now, in a single volume, extensively illustrated, all major types and varieties were described. All of a sudden, the obscurity changed to enlightenment.

Still, the very nature of federal paper money mandated arrangement into different categories, such as Silver Certificates, Federal Reserve Notes, and so on. Each of these sections required reading and understanding.

The collecting of federal paper money became a popular specialty, with most popular attention placed on early large-size bills with ornate designs, and, separately, small-size notes from the late 1920s onward. As years passed, *Paper Money of the United States* went through occasional updating. After Robert Friedberg's death in 1963, his two sons, Arthur L. and Ira S., continued updating the book, now in its 17th edition. To this can be added *A Guide Book of United States Paper Money* (Whitman Publishing, 2005), for which I wrote the narrative to accompany listings from the Friedberg text.

Other Market Stimulants

Year by year, interest increased. Dealers who formerly handled only coins now added paper money to their inventories. Such previously arcane terms as *Lazy Two* and *1902 Red Seal* became understood by more and more numismatists.

The Society of Paper Money Collectors (SPMC, formed in 1961), publisher of *Paper Money* magazine, contributed to the growing interest, as did books and studies by several dozen authors, usually on specific topics—although Gene Hessler, for one, cut a wider swath, and in 1974 the first edition of his *Comprehensive Catalog of United States Paper Money* was published. National Bank Notes in particular have been a focus for researchers.

Today, while the specialty is far from mature (which may be a good thing in terms of *opportunity*), there is a lot of useful information available.

Don C. Kelly serves as the collection point for information that from time to time is updated in his book, *National Bank Notes*, building on the work of John Hickman and Dean Oakes. Martin Gengerke has assembled a large database on auction offerings of currency of all issues. Peter Huntoon has explored the recesses of the National Archives and the Smithsonian, seeking information about printing and distribution techniques. A full list of researchers and authors of books and articles would be a lengthy one.

The *Bank Note Reporter*, issued monthly, is filled with advertisements, articles, auction news, and current events. The *Currency Dealer Newsletter*, mailed monthly, addresses market conditions and values. The Professional Currency Dealers Association (PCDA) brings together several dozen dealers across the United States. Lyn F. Knight, Currency Auctions of America (CAA), and R.M. Smythe & Co. each specialize in auctions of paper money; to theirs can be added occasional important offerings by other firms.

All of these factors come together to create a very active interest in paper money. While colonial, obsolete, Confederate, scrip, and other specialties have their advocates, it is federal paper money 1861 to date that commands the most attention and the widest audience. This, perhaps, is as it

should be—for such bills are still being produced, and in quantity.

There's a lot going on!

Understanding U.S. Paper Money
Background to the Federal Issues

After the collapse in value of Continental Currency (produced from 1775 to 1779), the United States did not issue paper money on a widespread basis until 1861. However, the federal government was an important stockholder in the federally chartered Bank of the United States (1791–1811) and its successor, the star-crossed Second Bank of the United States (1816–1836). Both of these banks issued large quantities of paper money, including bills payable at many different branches. All such currency is very rare today, and that identified with certain of the branch offices ranges from extremely rare to unknown.[95] The histories of both banks make fascinating reading. President Jackson's 1830 veto of the charter renewal of Second Bank of the United States was the most controversial political action of that era.

From 1812 to 1815 the Treasury Department issued interest-bearing notes in five different series, to the total face value of $36,000,000, from plates by Murray, Draper, Fairman & Co., Philadelphia bank-note engravers and printers. Denominations ranged from $5 to $1,000. Early issues named a specific payee and place of redemption. Such bills are rare today and, accordingly, are not widely collected.

The standard issues of federal money—the focus of this chapter—commenced with the Interest-Bearing and, separately, the Demand Notes of 1861, the latter issued to help finance the Civil War. In ensuing years many different series of currency were produced, based upon their backing or stated obligation, in values from $1 to $10,000. Legal Tender bills, introduced in 1862, were not specifically redeemable in coin, but later Silver Certificates, Gold Certificates, and Coin Notes

The Bureau of Engraving and Printing, Washington, DC, as it appeared in 1890. By this time the facility had been in use for a decade.

Having operated in the Treasury Building since the days of the National Currency Bureau (established in 1862), the Bureau of Engraving and Printing, as it became known in the 1870s, moved to its own building in July 1880. Now, under one roof there was capacity for all operations of printing, sorting, and storing paper money, bonds, and other security paper.

A room full of spider presses, as they were called. Operated by hand, these were used to print four-subject sheets of paper money. This 1901 view shows piles of Series of 1899 $1 Silver Certificates in the right foreground. These are of the popular "Black Eagle" design. Printing was a slow, messy process. Steam-powered presses were also on hand, but their quality was not as good as that of hand printing, and employees resisted their use on the grounds of unfair labor practices.

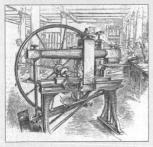

A transfer press permitted different vignettes, ornaments, titles, and other design elements to be added to steel printing plates. Entire plates could also be transferred in this manner. The process of siderography, as it was called, required a high degree of expertise and technical excellence to make minute adjustments in registration and pressure.

Numbering machines in use in 1890. These added serial numbers to bills, usually twice on the face, in any color desired. These machines could also be used to add Treasury Seals, charter numbers (on National Bank Notes), and other imprints.

A 1901 view of a corps of employees using machines to cut four-subject currency sheets into individual notes. When that was done, the bills were arranged in piles, counted, wrapped in paper, and sealed. In earlier times, sheets were cut apart by hand, using large shears, often creating uneven margins on the notes.

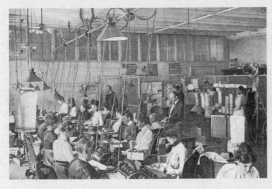

(also called Treasury Notes) were. Large-size bills were issued until 1929, in which year the change was made to the small size still in use today. In the 20th century, Federal Reserve Notes in several variations were introduced. In time, the different classes of currency were terminated, and today just the Federal Reserve Notes remain, made in denominations of $1, $2 (occasionally), $5, $10, $20, $50, and $100. Recently, the designs of bills have undergone changes, with modification of the portraits to larger sizes and with the addition of security features.

Currency was printed by private contractors in New York City in the early years, the most important being the American Bank Note Co. The Continental Bank Note Co. and the National Bank Note Co. also had contracts, and, later, a small amount of work was done by the Columbian Bank Note Co. (Washington, DC).

Whether to call the front and back of a bill the *obverse* and *reverse*, or the *face* and the *back*, is up to you. The Treasury Department used both sets of terms in its correspondence and records, but primarily the latter. Today, *face* is almost always used by numismatists, while both *back* (preferred) and *reverse* are employed. One hardly ever hears *obverse*.

For security purposes, most bills were printed on the face by one firm and the back by another, and the seal and serial numbers were added at the Treasury Department in Washington. Beginning in the mid-1870s, production was transferred to the Bureau of Engraving and Printing, sometimes with the use of older plates. Today, currency is produced in Washington plus a satellite printing facility in Fort Worth, Texas. Bills bear imprints for the 12 Federal Reserve banks, creating many different varieties each time there is a signature combination or design change.

In recent years the Bureau of Engraving and Printing has set up many exhibits at numismatic conventions. By mail, at its Washington headquarters, and at its Fort Worth, facility, the bureau offers an interesting selection of items for sale, including uncut sheets of modern issues.

Classifying Federal Notes

Today, from a collecting viewpoint, certain categories of bills range from rare to nearly impossible to find. Relatively few numismatists will ever own the short-lived Interest Bearing Notes, Demand Notes, Compound Interest Notes, or National Gold Bank Notes, and yet all are important to the history of the specialty. Other series such as Silver Certificates and Legal Tender Notes were produced for decades and include many types that are plentiful on the numismatic market.

I have elected to discuss currency by categories, based on their place in history or their relationship to each other. Then I discuss currency by denominations from $1 to $10,000. Hopefully, this arrangement will be useful to you in understanding a rather complex panorama. Lest you think this was easy for me to do, I hasten to say it was not! I asked several currency specialists to review my commentary, and important changes were made. In the field of paper money I am still learning. Indeed, across this part of the hobby research is ongoing by many people, and surprises pop up with frequency. No doubt if Albert A. Grinnell were to come to life today he would find many of the below-mentioned technicalities to be new information.

The following comments are arranged as follows: large-size notes first, Postage and Fractional Currency next, and small-size notes last.

Road Map to Federal Paper Money Categories
Special Large-Size Currency of the Civil War

Interest-Bearing Notes (Authorized 1861–1865). These early issues—loan certificates, in effect—were authorized shortly before the American Civil War broke out, and served to help finance the war. Ranging from $50 to $1,000 face value (later up to $5,000), nearly all Interest-Bearing Notes were held by banks and investors, rather than used in commerce and circulation. The holders were cognizant of the interest provisions and also of the requirement that no interest accumulate after the expiration date. Accordingly, nearly all were redeemed in due course, with the result that any example is a great rarity today. Certain of the large denominations are not known to exist. Of all major classes of federal paper money, Interest-Bearing Notes are the rarest.

Demand Notes (Authorized 1861). These are also early issues, historically important, but not readily obtained. They were the first of the federal "greenbacks," so called because of the ink used to print their reverses. Demand Notes were part of a $60 million issue of currency intended to finance the war in mid- to late 1861, when it was apparent that victory would not be quick or easy. Today, Demand Notes are quite rare—so much so that they are seldom collected in multiples except by advanced specialists. Among the five branch depositories (in New York City, Philadelphia, Boston, Cincinnati, and St. Louis), no bills with the St. Louis imprint are known today. Lucky is the dedicated numismatist who can obtain a representative example of one each of the $5, $10, and $20 denominations.

The combination of large printing quantities (4,360,000 of the $5; 2,003,000 of the $10; and 910,000 of the $20) and the fact they were mostly held by citizens and were used in commerce resulted in the fact that more were saved of them than of the Interest-Bearing Notes of the same era. Examples of the $5 Demand Note are scarce, and when seen are likely to exhibit extensive circulation. However, enough are around that one can be readily secured to illustrate this historical currency type.

Compound Interest Treasury Notes (Authorized 1863 and 1864). Yet another issue related to financing the Civil War, these too are rarities. Today, Compound Interest Treasury Notes of the $10 and $20 denominations come on the market regularly, but all are scarce. The typical bill shows extensive wear and may have some deterioration of the bronze imprint. The $50 and $100 values are very rare and are trophy notes, especially if found with good eye appeal (not that buyers can be choosy). The $500 and $1,000 values are unknown.

Legal Tender Notes

Legal Tender Notes (Series of 1862–1923). Spawned by the Civil War, these popular "greenbacks" continued to be made into the 20th century in various motifs. The earliest readily obtainable federal bills of the $5 denomination are the Legal Tender Notes of the Series of 1862 and 1863. These notes, with the same general face motifs as the $5 Demand Notes, exist in several varieties, including imprints of the American Bank Note Co. and the National Bank Note Co., both in New York City. Next in the lineup of $5 notes are the Series of 1869 through 1907 featuring Andrew Jackson. Legal Tender Notes of the $10 denomination were made in several different design types and many varieties, the best known of which is the so-called Bison Note, Series of 1901. The $20 notes are generally scarcer than those in lower denominations. Although some varieties are rare, the various types can be collected easily enough. The Series of 1869 $20 bills, part of the "Rainbow Note" lineup of this year, with colorful faces, have a rich geometric design printed in green on the reverse, somewhat Egyptian-esque in aspect. All $50 Legal Tender Notes range from scarce to rare, with some varieties being extremely rare. Then come the $100 issues, inaugurated with the Series of 1862 and 1863, with a particularly bold and imposing American eagle on the face, and with wings outspread. Higher values, $500 to $10,000, are mostly very rare, and some varieties known to have been made are not known to exist today.

Over a long period of time most of the smaller Legal Tender Note denominations were printed in large quantities, making types from $1 through $10 easy to collect today. As denominations increase, rarity increases as well. There are rare signature combinations and seal varieties among the lower denominations, but the premiums charged for them are modest in relation to their elusive nature.

Many of the 19th-century Legal Tender Notes are very artistic, this being true of the issues of the 1860s and the later "Rainbow Notes." Most earlier issues have ornately engraved backs.

Notes Backed by Silver and Gold Coins

Silver Certificates (Series of 1878–1923). First made in 1878 and backed by silver dollars held by the Treasury Department, these bills were made for generations afterward, in a multitude of beautiful designs. Today, large-size Silver Certificates are very popular to collect, particularly by type. We are all fortunate that the artistic highlights in the series are mainly among the lower denominations and exist in significant numbers today.

While most numismatists collect by type, there are many signature combinations and seal varieties that beckon, most of which are affordable. The Holy Grail among the $1 Silver Certificates is Friedberg-229a, a Series of 1899 "Black Eagle" of the Vernon-McClung signature combination and with the date to the right of the Treasury seal, rather than below the serial number. Two gems came on the market in early 2005, one in a CAA sale, the other in a Lyn F. Knight auction, each realizing in the mid-$20,000s, or perhaps about 25 times the price of a comparable note of the regular variety (F-229, date below serial number).

The 1896 "Educational Notes" are of everlasting popularity and are often sought by numismatists who otherwise are not specialists in paper money. The Series of 1886 five-dollar "Silver Dollar Note" is also high on the hit parade. You might think that every collector of Morgan silver dollars would want one of these as a "go-with" item, but that is not the case. Certain of the higher-denomination Silver Certificates with SILVER in large letters across the back are at once rare and impressive. However, offerings are occasional at best, usually only when important collections cross the auction block.

Treasury or Coin Notes (Series of 1890 and 1891). Early varieties of these notes are remarkable for the ornate engraving on their backs. Most Coin Notes are collected by type, with focus on the Series of 1890 issues with their fancy engraving. The $100 "Watermelon Note," which comes on the market with some regularity, but which is very expensive, is a special object of desire. Better yet are the $1,000 "Grand Watermelon Notes," but only a few exist.

The $1, $2, $5, $10, and $20 notes, Series of 1890, are widely collected by type. This leaves the pursuit of signature combinations and seal varieties to the realm of specialists, who can buy rare combinations for just a small premium over more plentiful issues.

I don't expect the fashion for collecting by type to change any time soon, so the availability of rarities for a modest premium above commoner issues is more a point of enjoyment than of great potential profit. However, if I were assembling a type set I would wait and buy an F-348—four times more rare than the related F-347 (going by quantity printed), but valued equally in lower grades, and marked by only a 25% or so premium in Uncirculated. (Gene Hessler's excellent *Comprehensive Catalog of U.S. Paper Money* lists printed quantities, as does the Friedbergs' *Guide Book of United States Paper Money*, for many series.)

The Series of 1891 Coin Notes, lacking the ornate backs of the earlier series, play to a smaller audience but, of course, are necessary for a type collection.

Gold Certificates (Series of 1863–1922). Issued from the Civil War era onward, these notes were backed by gold coins until

President Franklin D. Roosevelt disavowed the obligation printed on them. The notes did not circulate in general commerce, but seem to have been used to settle transactions *payable in gold* among banks and clearinghouses. It was not until 1882 that Gold Certificates were made in quantity, after which they were also produced under series of 1900, 1905, 1906, 1913, and 1922. Later denominations ranged from $10 to $10,000, but not all values were issued in each series. Today, Gold Certificates are mostly collected by type. Most are scarce or rare, but others are very affordable.

Large-Size National Bank Notes

National Bank Notes (Authorized 1863–1902). A veritable playground for collectors, and a wide field for researchers, these bills were issued from the 1860s onward by thousands of different banks. Today, they are dearly loved by many specialists. National Bank Notes can be grouped conveniently into series, as printed on all the bills (except for the Original Series). For many years collectors, dealers, auction-sale catalogers, and authors of important reference books (and less important ones as well) have grouped the large-size bills under names of *First Charter*, *Second Charter*, and *Third Charter* groups. However, as Peter Huntoon has pointed out, this has absolutely no basis in Treasury Department or National Bank legislation, records, or history! He urges, "Rely instead on series; i.e., Original Series, Series of 1875, etc., which says it all without ambiguity."

National Gold Bank Notes (Authorized 1870). Engendered by curious currency provisions, these were issued only in California and only for a short time. In 1862, gold and silver coins had disappeared from circulation in the East and Midwest, with their place taken by Legal Tender Notes. In California, silver and gold coins were still in everyday use, and Legal Tender Notes, brought west by travelers, were accepted only at a deep discount. The solution was a series of National Gold Banks,

established by Congress and authorized to issue bills redeemable at par in gold coins. Among National Gold Bank Notes, Original Series bills were made of all denominations from $5 to $500, while the Series of 1875 bills omitted the $5. As a class the Series of 1875 notes are significantly more rare, but as almost nothing has been said about this in the literature, there is little in the way of price differential! Of course, both types are basically rare. It is thought that of the $50 value, only about six exist of the Original Series and just one of the Series of 1875 (First National Gold Bank of San Francisco). Several other banks are known to have issued $50 notes, but none exist in numismatic collections—the ultimate illustration of rarity. Notes of the $100 denomination are rare, but not in the same category as the $50.

Bills of the $500 value were issued by the First National Gold Bank (300 of the Series of 1875) and the National Gold Bank & Trust Co. (250 of the Original Series), both of San Francisco, and by the National Gold Bank of D.O. Mills & Co. (60 of the Original Series), Sacramento. Treasury records indicate that four such notes are still outstanding, but none are known to numismatists today.

I must not forget to mention that the Kidder National Gold Bank of Boston was authorized under the Act of 1870 and received some National Gold Bank bills, but none were released and none are known today. There are, however, two sets of Kidder proof impressions (faceplates) in existence of the $50 and $100 values, Original Series.

Large-Size Federal Reserve Notes

Federal Reserve Notes (Series of 1914 and 1918). Issued under the auspices of the Federal Reserve banks, such bills were keyed to one or another of the 12 offices. Large-size Federal Reserve Notes were redeemable in dollars, including "in gold on demand at the Treasury Department of the United States in the City of Washington, District of Columbia, or in gold or lawful money at any Federal Reserve

National Bank Byways and Sidelights

The First National Bank of Davenport, Iowa, as it appeared in the late 19th century. Later, the building was doubled in size by the addition of three stories to the top. This was the very first National Bank to open its doors for business.

Austin Corbin, president of the First National Bank of Davenport in 1863, charter number 15. Corbin was president of the bank in Davenport until 1865, when he sold out and moved to New York City, where he settled his family in Brooklyn Heights and, in 1870, opened the Corbin Banking Co., a private institution. Nearby, about two miles of sandy ocean beach beckoned, to Corbin's eyes offering great potential as a popular seaside resort only a few miles from Manhattan, which in summer could be unbearably hot.

He purchased the land, and set about constructing a connection to the newly designated Manhattan Beach, acquiring rolling stock from a rail line used at the 1876 Centennial Exhibition in Philadelphia, now closed. The New York & Manhattan Beach Railway was born, and in due time connected to the immense and impressive 350-room Manhattan Beach Hotel, which opened to the public on July 19, 1877, followed in three years by the Oriental Hotel and two years later by the Argyle (in Babylon). Thus, the resort that the world came to know as Coney Island—with its Luna Park, Dreamland, and other attractions to be built by others of a future generation—came to be established.

Corbin was from Newport, New Hampshire, but was not directly involved in banking there. Corbin lived well; he had a mansion on Fifth Avenue in New York City, and in Babylon, Long Island, not far from his beach properties, a 15-acre estate complete with a fishpond, which President Chester A. Arthur visited in May 1882. Austin Corbin bought a large tract of land north of Newport, eventually comprising 27,000 acres, which became known as Corbin Park. He fenced the perimeter and stocked it with animals not normally encountered—at least not in large numbers—in New Hampshire, including wild boar and buffalo, furnishing a popular subject for postcards. In 1908 the layout was described as "the largest private park in America."

The biography of Corbin, only a small part of which is given here, illustrates how one subject can lead to another when you study the background of National Banks.

A $2 Federal Reserve Bank Note, Boston. F-747. The "Battleship Note." This variety has Treasury signatures of Teehee and Burke in combination with Boston Federal Reserve Bank officers Bullen and Morss.

This note has the tiny plate designation A1 microscopically to the left of the bold A-1 imprint, the latter referring to Boston as branch A, also known as branch 1. That the faceplate number is A1 is a coincidence. On the back the tiny plate number 4 appears in the white space at the inside lower right. While the faceplate was used only to print Boston notes, the back plate could have been used to print bills from other offices as well.

Bank." Accordingly, in a way these can be considered as gold coin notes. Denominations of $5, $10, $20, $50, and $100 (all easily found on the market), and of $500, $1,000, $5,000, and $10,000 (all of which are rare) were produced, in different combinations of bank and treasury officials' signatures and with red or blue seals. The face designs feature portraits of government officials in history, plus lettering and so on, while the reverses have scenic motifs.

The two seal colors, red and blue, are usually collected as separate types or by Federal Reserve Bank locations. The Red Seal notes have the Treasury signatures of Burke and McAdoo, while Blue Seal notes exist in several different combinations. Certain bank and signature combinations are very rare, but there is little interest in systematically collecting them, so premiums for such are not great.

The rare higher denominations are usually collected by one of each value, rather than by bank locations or seal color.

Federal Reserve Bank Notes (Series of 1915 and 1918).

The Federal Reserve *Bank* Notes closely follow the concept of Federal Reserve Notes. They are also inscribed as National Currency, which can be confusing, as National Bank Notes were also inscribed with the same designation.

The Series of 1915 bills include $5, $10, and $20 denominations, and the Series of 1918 include these plus the $1, $2, and $50 (no higher values were made for these notes). The $50 note was made only for the St. Louis Federal Reserve Bank and is a numismatic classic. Treasury records show that only 64 of these are outstanding. In numismatic hands, nearly 50 different specimens have been identified by their serial numbers—seemingly a high survival rate. However, official records of the numbers of bills outstanding are not always reliable, due to the occasional practice of the Treasury to write off certain bills as presumed lost or destroyed. Of nearly $762,000,000 face value in these bills issued, all but about $2,000,000 worth has been redeemed.

At the center of each Federal Reserve Bank Note, the name of the city is boldly displayed. The back designs of the $1 note, with an eagle clutching a flag, and the $2 note, with a dreadnought-type battleship, have been collectors' favorites for a long time. The denominations of $5 to $50 use the same back motifs as on the Federal Reserve Notes.

Federal Reserve Bank Notes were produced with two Treasury signatures and two bank signatures. Sometimes this led to as many as four or five varieties for a single denomination and bank location.

As mentioned, the $1 and $2 bills lead the popularity parade, and most collectors

The National Currency Bureau

The National Currency Bureau, directed by Spencer M. Clark, was established within the Treasury Building in Washington, DC, in the early 1860s. Operations included adding serial numbers and Treasury Seals to paper money, bonds, and other security documents printed elsewhere; adding bronze surcharges to paper money; and printing most of the Fractional Currency issues. Facilities were in the Treasury Department basement and attic. In the 1870s, the NCB evolved into the Bureau of Engraving and Printing, which later occupied its own building.

The United States Treasury Building as it appeared in the 1860s, as illustrated on a vignette distributed by the National Currency Bureau and, later, the Bureau of Engraving and Printing. Printed on cardstock, this vignette was often included in presentation volumes of currency motifs.

Engraving from the 1860s of a row of printing presses at the National Currency Bureau.

Printing sheets of Fractional Currency. The process was labor intensive and involved lightly dampening the paper, then printing one side (generally the back), drying the ink on the sheets, dampening the paper again, and printing the other side. Ink was applied to the printing plates by the use of a roller.

The methods of printing varied over time, and included dry-paper process, different types of paper, and an unsuccessful attempt to use heavy hydrostatic presses (they kept breaking down, due to the pressure of the water in the actuating cylinders).

desire one of each denomination for type. Beyond that, different bank locations provide interesting varieties. Signature combinations are more esoteric, with some being very rare. However, when rarities are found they are often affordable, as the demand is not strong, especially for the $5, $10, and $20 denominations.

Postage and Fractional Currency

On July 14, 1862, Secretary of the Treasury Salmon P. Chase sent a memorial to Congress suggesting that government stamps be made official as legal tender for small transactions. He intended such stamps to fill the need for coins, which were being hoarded due to the Civil War (see pages 20–21). In response to Chase's request, the Act of July 17, 1862, provided for the use of postage stamps for *monetary* transactions, including authority that, by August 1, stamps would be exchangeable for Legal Tender "greenback" notes at all Treasury offices. They were also receivable for government obligations in amounts less than $5, but they were not given official legal tender status, despite the request of Chase.

Postage Currency fractional bills were issued in August 1862. Made in denominations of 5¢, 10¢, and 25¢, and up to 50¢, the notes bore the designs of contemporary stamps printed within a border, and with added inscriptions. Similar to stamps, the Postage Currency notes were issued in perforated sheets, to be torn apart by the recipients. By early 1863 about $100,000 in these notes reached circulation per day, but the demand remained unsatisfied.[96] Later bills were made with straight edges, cut out of sheets instead of torn. A lively trade developed in the making and selling of small cardboard and leather wallets for the storage of these little bills.

The Act of March 3, 1863, provided for a new small-denomination series designated *Fractional Currency*. Distribution of such notes—in 5¢, 10¢, 25¢, and 50¢ denominations—began in October of the same year. In late autumn 1864 a new Fractional Currency denomination, the 3¢ note, reached circulation, but it

never became popular. In summer 1869 another denomination, 15¢, was added to the Fractional Currency lineup, but it was never widely used, either. Face and back colors varied over time, as did the sizes. The Friedberg text gives details.

The Postage Currency and Fractional Currency notes were not without their problems in circulation. For one thing, they tended to become dirty and tattered quickly, and they couldn't be counted easily. The public, although they used them widely, referred to them derisively as *stamps*. On and after April 20, 1876, silver coins returned to circulation, exchangeable at par, and Fractional Currency bills were no longer needed.

The late Matt Rothert, past president of the American Numismatic Association (ANA) and the man who was responsible in 1955 for persuading Congress to add "In God We Trust" to paper money, made Fractional Currency a specialty and wrote several important articles as well as *A Guide Book of United States Fractional Currency* (1963). In 1978, *The Encyclopedia of United States Fractional and Postal Currency*, by Milton Friedberg (no kin to Robert Friedberg) was published, and is essential for anyone desiring to pursue the technicalities of the series.

Today, Postage and Fractional Currency bills are enjoyable to collect. Most seek one each of the different denominations across the five issues. For those who enjoy varieties, there are many curious and sometimes rare variations among letters, surcharges, and the like. The collecting of Specimen bills (face or back designs, printed on one side, in either wide-margin or narrow-margin versions) is popular as well.

Fractional Currency *Shields* are also collectible. These were devised to aid in the identification of counterfeits (which were common) and to provide bills for display to banks and others. They consisted of a shield outline printed in gray (a few in green or pink) surmounted by an eagle and stars. On the shield, 39 specimens of Fractional Currency, consisting of 20 faces and 19 backs, were pasted by hand. These were of the First, Second, and Third issues. Mounted under glass in a wooden frame with a gilt inner strip (though some may have been sold without the frame), and backed by thin wooden slats, these were sold for $4.50 each, beginning in 1867, with prices varying slightly in later times.

As to how many were issued, I am not aware of any specific records. Estimates have ranged from about 200 to 400. However, I believe that more than 200 exist today. Most of these have water stains along the bottom, from slight flooding in the Treasury Department basement where they were stored. Among any and all numismatic items produced in American history, the Fractional Currency Shield is no doubt the most "displayable" in its original form. Indeed, these are one of only a few such 19th-century items originally intended for this purpose. Today, enough exist that one can be found without difficulty.

Postage Currency (First Issue: August 21, 1862–May 27, 1863). The designs copied those of contemporaneous postage stamps. Early printings were issued with perforated edges. Later printings of the series had straight edges (as did all later issues). Denominations consisted of 5¢ (consisting of a single 5¢ stamp), 10¢ (a single 10¢ stamp), 25¢ (five 5¢ stamps in a row), and 50¢ (five 10¢ stamps in a row).

Fractional Currency (Second Issue: October 20, 1863–February 23, 1867). Denominations of 5¢, 10¢, 25¢, and 50¢ were produced for the Second Issue, these inaugurating the Fractional Currency designation. All have the portrait of Washington within an overprinted oval, to which bronzing powder was applied. Although the process was messy and caused many problems, the same bronzing was added to the face of Compound Interest Treasury Notes.

Postage Currency bill, First Issue, 5¢ denomination (Friedberg-1228). Perforated edges. The face design is based on a contemporary stamp. The face was printed by the National Bank Note Co., and bears that firm's imprint. The back was printed by the American Bank Note Co., and bears the ABNCo monogram at the lower right.

Fractional Currency, Second Issue. As the designs were the same, this is the most stereotyped of the Fractional Currency issues.

The 5¢ Fractional Currency bill with the "Clark" portrait is believed to have inspired the Act of April 7, 1866, specifying that "No portrait or likeness of any living person hereafter engraved, shall be placed upon any of the bonds, securities, notes, fractional or postal currency of the United States."

Fractional Currency (Third Issue: December 5, 1864–August 16, 1869). Denominations of 3¢, 5¢, 10¢, 25¢, and 50¢ were made for the Third Issue. The 3¢ denomination was made for just a short time, as the law of March 3, 1865, authorizing the nickel three-cent coin prohibited any further issue of Fractional Currency of this type.

Spencer M. Clark, superintendent of the Currency Bureau, had his own portrait, uncaptioned but referred to as "Clark," placed on the 5¢ note of this issue. Most people thought that *William* Clark, of Lewis and Clark Expedition fame, was the one being honored!

In the Third Issue, the 10¢ note—or at least we suppose it is a 10-*cent* note—simply says 10, with no mention of *cents*, sort of a numismatic precursor to the later famous 1883 CENTS-less Liberty Head nickel.

Fractional Currency (Fourth Issue: July 14, 1869–February 16, 1875). Denominations of 5¢, 10¢, 15¢, 25¢, and 50¢ were made of the Fourth Issue. This series included the 15¢ value, never popular, and was also the first to have the Treasury Seal imprinted. Some were printed on paper with blue tinting, also used on certain National Bank and Legal Tender bills of the era, giving them a special elegance.

Fractional Currency (Fifth Issue: February 26, 1874–February 15, 1876). For the Fifth Issue of Fractional Currency, denominations of 10¢, 25¢, and 50¢ were made. This was in the twilight era of such notes, and many undistributed pieces were sold by banks to dealers, as the collecting of such bills had become popular.

Refunding Certificates (Series of 1879)

Whether these should be included under the category of paper money is a matter for discussion. The answer is probably no. At best, they can be called *miscellany*. However, the Refunding Certificates, of larger size and different proportion than currency, are widely collected as such.

These were issued in the $10 denomination only, under the Act of February 26, 1879, and were loan certificates yielding 4% annual interest, seemingly forever, except that in 1907 Congress changed matters and set a termination date of July 1 of that year.

Refunding Certificates in a total amount of $40,012,750 face value were paid out, including the majority, $39,398,110, in the fourth quarter of 1879. Long lines of people gathered at post office branches and Treasury offices to secure these "baby bonds."

The 1879 $10 Refunding Certificate (Friedberg-214) is collected as part of the paper money series today. However, it is more of a little bond, or certificate. Authorized by the Act of February 26, 1879, each bore on the back this inscription: "Interest on this note will accrue as follows: For each nine days, or one-tenth of a quarter, one cent; for each quarter year, ten cents; for each entire year, forty cents."

Bankers, postmasters, and "other public officers" were enlisted to help sell the certificates. For selling an amount from $1,000 to $100,000 in any given calendar month, a commission of 1/8 of 1% was allowed, plus 1/4 of 1% for any excess. A rule prohibited the sale of more than a hundred dollars' worth to any one investor. Demand was immediate and intense, and in early May the New York City Post Office sold $20,000 to $45,000 per day, as shown in this sketch from *Frank Leslie's Illustrated Newspaper*, May 10, 1879.

Two varieties are known of these certificates—the usual (F-214, of which a few hundred exist), with TEN and other lettering prominent on the reverse; and the rarer (F-213, of which just two can be traced), with the back appearing more as a legal document and printed sideways to the normal viewing position.

Small Size Currency 1929 to Date

Legal Tender Notes (Series of 1928–1966, Red Seal). Small-size Legal Tender Notes, also known as United States Notes, have been made of the Series of 1928 (issued in 1929) to 1966. Printed with a distinctive red Treasury Seal, denominations are $1, $2, $5, and $100, the last being a late-comer produced in the Series of 1966. The designs follow closely those of the small-size Silver Certificates.

Interestingly, the only $1 bills in this class are the Series of 1928. These have the combined signatures of W.O. Woods and W.H. Woodin, the latter being President Franklin D. Roosevelt's first Secretary of the Treasury. Often, collectors simply call these bills *1928 Red Seals*.

The others, including the not-particularly-popular $2 note, were made in larger quantities through the 1960s. Under the Act of May 3, 1878, circulation of Legal Tender Notes was to be maintained at $346,861,016, to which the Treasury adheres today through the use of an adequate remaining supply of Series 1966 and 1966-A $100 bills (a technical

A 1929 Legal Tender Note with red seal. Paper money, especially of older series, can be wonderfully colorful, and black-and-white images don't do justice to the designs. Several such notes are shown in the 16-page color spread, located after page 32.

A $100 Legal Tender Note with red seal, issued in 1966.

and legislative curiosity). No new bills have been printed for many years!

Today, Legal Tender Notes are collected primarily by type. The varieties are not extensive, and forming a set of signature combinations is feasible. The larger denominations are somewhat scarce in Uncirculated grade, as few were saved at the time of issue. As is the case with all small-size notes, those with a star at the serial number, indicating a replacement bill, are avidly sought and sell for significant premiums.

National Bank Notes (Series of 1929 Types 1 and 2, Brown Seal). National Bank Notes in small-size format were distributed in sheets of six notes. These are all Series of 1929, with the Treasury signatures of E.E. Jones and W.O. Woods, who served together from January 22, 1929, to May 31, 1933. However, such bills continued to be issued until May 1935. Each also bore the name and location of each bank and the printed signatures of that bank's cashier and president. These bills were produced in denominations of $5, $10, $20, $50, and $100, with the $50 and $100 values usually in small quantities.

Two "types" were produced, today designated by numismatists as follows:

1929 Type 1—Printed from May 1929 to May 1933. Bank charter number in black,

twice on the face. The six notes on each sheet had the same serial number, six digits, with prefixes A through F, and each with the suffix A. Accordingly, the second sheet printed for a certain bank would have these serials: A000002A, B000002A, C000002A, D000002A, E000002A, and F000002A.

1929 Type 2—Printed from May 1933 to May 1935. Bank charter number in black, twice on the face, and also in brown, twice. The six notes on each sheet had different serial numbers, in sequence, each with the prefix A but with no suffix. Accordingly, the second sheet printed would have these serials: A000007, A000008, A000009, A0000010, A0000011, and A000012.

Today, bills of Type 1 are typically much more plentiful in numismatic hands than are those of Type 2 and therefore are less expensive. However, among certain banks there are exceptions. While most banks issued both types, some used just Type 1 and others just Type 2. Some National Banks that issued large-size notes did not opt to issue those of small size.

As to values, those from more populous states are relatively inexpensive, while those from such states as Arizona and Nevada are considerably more costly. Within any state there can be "rare towns" and "rare banks" for which the bills are very valuable.

A $5 Series of 1929 Type 2 note from the Monadnock National Bank of East Jaffrey, New Hampshire, charter 1242. Faceplate A258, back plate 387. On Type 2 notes the charter number appears four times. The serial numbers, the Treasury Seal, and the two charter numbers near the portrait are in medium brown. (W.M. Clark Collection)

A 1935-A brown-seal Bank Note, with
HAWAII overprints on front and back.

Time was when small-size Nationals were ignored by all but a few specialists. After about 1970 the collecting of these became popular, indeed intense. Today, small-size notes invariably attract a lot of attention when offered at auction or private sale.

Quite a few six-subject sheets exist of these notes, mostly in the lower denominations. Many of these are of the first serial numbers and were saved by bank officers. In the 1930s Colonel E.H.R. Green took an interest in such sheets and acquired hundreds of different ones, accounting for much of the supply available today. The demand for these sheets is intense, and competition is strong when they come on the market.

Silver Certificates (Series of 1928–1957, Blue Seal; plus $1 Hawaii Brown Seal Notes and $1, $5, and $10 WWII Yellow Seal Notes). Silver Certificates of the small size were produced in denominations of $1, $5, and $10. The earliest issues, the $1 bills, were imprinted as the Series of 1928, although the small format was not actually introduced until July 10, 1929. The 1928 Series alone is payable in "one silver dollar." Later $1 bills, as well as all those of the other denominations, are payable "in silver" or in "silver coin" (the rare 1933 ten-dollar bill), but have no mention of silver dollars. Save for certain World War II

issues, all small-size Silver Certificates have the Treasury Seal in blue.

The Series of 1933 ten-dollar notes are rare, as the text of the obligation mentions "payable in silver coin." Many of these were destroyed, to be replaced with the differently worded Series of 1934, "payable in silver" (without mention of coin).

Except for the backs of the $1 bills of Series 1928 through 1934, the small-size bills of these denominations appear quite similar to bills of the same denomination in other series produced through the early years of the 21st century. In the small-size notes, most series were given letter suffixes, changed whenever the signature combination changed. The series *date* was changed only when there was a modification of the design, such modifications typically being of a trivial nature. Thus, for $1 bills the following were made (early changes only): Series 1928, Tate-Mellon signatures; Series 1928-A, Woods-Mellon; Series 1928-B, Woods-Mills; Series 1928-C, Woods-Woodin; Series 1928-D, Julian-Woodin; Series 1928-E, Julian-Morgenthau; Series 1934: Julian-Morgenthau (different arrangement of lettering and seal on face). This sequence was continued through and including Series 1957-B, Granahan-Dillon.

Certain varieties of Series 1935-A were made with a bright red R or S overprint in the field, to the extent of 1,184,000 of each.

These were in connection with printing on two different types of paper. These were placed in circulation and observed for their characteristics of wear. Quite a few were bought up by numismatists, due to publicity they received at the time.

Other collectible varieties in the small-size Silver Certificate series are provided by the overprint HAWAII on the face and back of $1 Series 1934-A. These bills have *brown* seals. These were distributed in the Hawaiian Islands after World War II was declared. If the islands fell into the hands of the Japanese, these bills could be repudiated, preventing the enemy from using them on world markets. Related are those distinguished by *yellow* seals, anomalous in the series. These were for the allied troops in the North African campaign and nearby areas and included $1 Series 1935-A, $5 Series 1934-A, and $10 Series 1934 and 1934-A.

There are no "impossible" rarities among the small-size Silver Certificates, although some are elusive in Uncirculated grade. The best known is the 1928-E one-dollar bill. Some of the $10 bills are rare in Uncirculated grade, but they are not as widely collected as the $1 denomination.

Gold Certificates (Series of 1928–1934, Gold Seal).
Gold Certificates of small size were made for only a short time, in the Series of 1928 and 1928-A and some of 1934, the last mainly not issued. Although the Series of 1928 designation suggests an early printing, small-size bills were not made until 1929. These were made payable in gold coins. After the changes in the use of gold coins and President Roosevelt's restrictive legislation of 1933, the government repudiated this obligation. The later issues of 1934 were used for internal transactions within the Federal Reserve Banks and Treasury system.

Denominations include $10, $20, $50, $100, $500, and $1,000, each with a distinctive yellow seal and serial numbers. The backs were printed in green, unlike the gold used on large-size issues. Examples of the $10 to $100 are readily collectible as types. The $500 and $1,000 denominations are rare, but available.

Gold Certificates of $5,000, $10,000, and $100,000 (Friedberg numbers 2410–2413) were printed with gold backs. These were never released, but were used only for internal transactions of the Treasury Department and Federal Reserve System.

Federal Reserve Bank Notes (Series of 1929, Brown Seal. Emergency Issue of 1933).
Small-size Federal Reserve Bank Notes are among the briefest and most curious major categories of U.S. paper

A 1928 Gold Certificate. The seal and serial numbers are in gold ink, applied in a separate process.

money. Franklin D. Roosevelt was inaugurated as president on March 4, 1933. At the time, the economy was in the depths of the Depression, and prosperity, which President Hoover said was "just around the corner," had not arrived. In fact, the situation had become worse.

In his inaugural address, Roosevelt, paraphrasing the Bible, said he was going to drive the money-changers from the temple. Banks, many of which were in perilous shape, were viewed as part of the problem. He decreed that on Monday, March 6, 1933, all banks were to close their doors, starting what was called the Bank Holiday. Those that met certain tests as to capital and reserves were allowed to reopen later in the week. Others were required to stay closed until they could increase their capital, reorganize, or merge with stronger institutions. Many went into receivership or were merged on sacrifice terms with solid banks.

The Treasury Department envisioned that when banks reopened there would be a great rush by the citizenry to draw down their savings and checking accounts, to take cash in the event that further problems occurred. Cash on hand was viewed as safe, whereas the true condition of any bank seemed to be subject to question, even if it were to reopen. In anticipation, the Treasury desired to print a large quantity of additional paper money.

At the time, it took about eight days to dry the backs of notes, the back being the side printed first. The faces were then printed, and these required about four days to dry. Already on hand were sheets of bills from $5 to $100, printed and dried, intended for use on *National Bank Notes*, and waiting to receive the final imprints of bank name, serial number, Treasury Seal, and other information.

These were quickly overprinted with information for Federal Reserve banks, including the district—Boston, New York, and so on, to San Francisco—12 in all, and the appropriate district letter, A through L. Across the top of the face of each note was the NATIONAL CURRENCY legend used on National Bank Notes. A brown Treasury Seal was applied, slightly larger than that used on National Bank Notes. Printed signatures on these and other notes includes two of Treasury officials (E.E. Jones and W.O. Woods, who served together from January 22, 1929, to May 31, 1933) and two of bank officials. Production was for only a short time. For each district the serial number began with the district letter, such as A for Boston. Denominations produced were $5, $10, $20, $50, and $100. Imprints for each of the 12 districts were made for the $5 to $20 values. However, for the $50 bills none were printed for Boston, Philadelphia, Richmond, Atlanta, or St. Louis, and in the run of the $100 denomination, Boston, Philadelphia, Atlanta, St. Louis, and San Francisco are not represented.

As it turned out, there was no shortage of paper currency following the Bank Holiday, no great "run" on the banks, although many people withdrew funds. Large quantities of certain varieties remained on hand at the Federal Reserve banks and were distributed during World War II, when there was a shortage of new paper money. Some were also distributed in Puerto Rico.

Today, small-size Federal Reserve Bank Notes are mainly collected by design type, not by bank variety. There are many that are scarce or rare in Uncirculated grades, but as customers may be rarer than the notes are, the differentials are not great. Star (replacement) notes are especially rare, and it is estimated that only a few hundred exist across the entire series of districts and denominations.

As the study of paper money becomes increasingly sophisticated, and serial information (combination of a letter and number on the face and a number on the back) on small-size notes comes under study, no doubt some interesting matches will be made between Federal Reserve Bank Notes and National Bank Notes from the same plates. To my knowledge, this is at present unexplored.

Federal Reserve Notes (Series of 1963 to Date, Green Seal; plus $5, $10, and $20 Hawaii Brown Seal Notes). These are the bills of our current era, taking the place of other classes. Each bears a seal with the name, location, and identifying letter of one of the 12 Federal Reserve banks. All standard issues have green seals.

Today, they are printed in denominations of $1, $2 (intermittently and not beginning until the Series of 1976, in connection with the bicentennial), $5, $10, $20, $50, and $100. In the 1930s and 1940s, values of $500, $1,000, $5,000, and $10,000 were made. These higher denominations are all collectors' items, and there is a surprising demand for even the $10,000 due to its novelty. The earliest bills, the Series of 1928 and 1928-A issues, were payable in gold. The government repudiated the obligation for such payment in spring 1933. Later Federal Reserve Notes were not payable in anything in particular, but were (and still are) legal tender.

The designs were more or less similar to other small-size bills until the late 1990s, when significant changes began to be made to the portraits on the faces and the buildings on the backs of each denomination, along with improvements for security, including microscopic printing and anti-copying features. Bills printed before the design revision were with eight-digit serials, prefixed by a letter (A to L) for the bank, the various letter suffixes to expand the number of notes beyond what eight digits allows for. The redesigned bills omit printed mention of specific Federal Reserve Bank branches, but have designations such as G7 (Chicago) or L12 (San Francisco), which numismatists can decipher, but which are not obvious to the general public. In addition, eight-digit serials with double-letter prefixes and single-letter suffixes, not specifically relating to a branch, are used.

Today these bills, especially the smaller denominations, are very popular. The smaller denominations are generally available and quite affordable in Uncirculated grade. They are widely collected on a sys-tematic basis, by bank and by Treasury signature combination (each bill has two printed signatures—that of the secretary of the Treasury, instead of the register, beginning in 1933; and that of the Treasurer). Treasurer Kathryn O'Hay Granahan and Secretary Joseph Barr were in office together only from December 23, 1968, to January 20, 1969. When $1 bills of this combination were released, there was great excitement across America, and the rumor spread that these would become very rare and valuable. Large quantities were hoarded, and dealers were bombarded with calls and visitors seeking to cash in. However, the plates with these signatures were continued in use for a long time afterward; hundreds of millions were printed, and most of the Granahan-Barr bills are very common.

Certain of the Series of 1934 Federal Reserve Notes of $5, $10, and $20 denominations, San Francisco branch, were made with *brown* seals and HAWAII overprints. These were made for distribution in the Hawaiian Islands during World War II, with the thought that if the islands fell into the hands of the Japanese, the bills with these overprints could be invalidated, thus not usable on world markets. Most seen today are in circulated grades.

Beginning with the Series of 1988-A, certain bills were printed in Fort Worth, Texas, at a plant known as the Western Facility, and identified by having a small FW on the face, adding a new element. In theory, for each new signature combination there could be 12 different varieties from the Bureau of Engraving and Printing in Washington, DC, plus 12 star-note varieties, plus the same number of varieties (12 plus 12) from Fort Worth, yielding 48 different in all! Bills from sheet-fed presses have different aspects than those printed on web presses and are collected separately. It is readily appreciated that $1 bills furnish an affordable denomination for such a specialty, but to collect $50 or $100 bills of like varieties would be beyond the reach of most numismatists.

Until recently, this was the design Americans were accustomed to seeing on $20 bills. In 1998 these notes—which are still common in circulation—were supplanted by a newer style (below).

In 1996, the new design for Federal Reserve Notes in the $100 denomination was released, followed by new designs for the $50 (1997), the $20 (1998, pictured here), and the $10 and $5 (2000) bills. The goal of the Bureau of Engraving and Printing is to thwart counterfeiters with high-tech security features.

The year 2005 has seen the release of the most recent updates, the $50 and the $20 Federal Reserve Note denominations (the $100 is due out by the end of 2005). (For a discussion of the latest designs, visit the BEP at http://moneyfactory.com/newmoney/index.cfm.)

Guide to Smart Buying of Federal Paper Money

Some Ways to Collect Federal Notes

Most numismatists specialize in a particular area of paper money, such as National Bank Notes, Silver Certificates, small-size $1 bills by types small-size Federal Reserve Notes by district and signature combination, or something else of interest. The following are some possibilities.

By Type, Large Size, Lower Denominations

A collection of the $1, $2, and $5 values makes a very nice display. A good way to start is with $1 and $2 denominations, for certain of the rare series (Demand Notes, Gold Certificates, etc.) are not represented. Afterward your collection can be expanded to include $5 bills. This is an ideal way to acquaint yourself with the panorama of designs, denominations, and changes over the years.

By Type, Large Size, Expanded

As preceding, but higher denominations such as $10 and $20 can be included, after which point the going becomes difficult, especially for the earlier types. Perhaps just *selected* types of certain $50 and $100 bills can be included. As to $500, $1,000, or even higher values, these are so rare and so expensive that only a few have been fortunate enough to collect them over the years.

By Type, Within Special Series

Looking through popular reference books and auction catalogs will give you some ideas—such as getting one of each major type of Silver Certificate, or one of each Demand Note. It might seem logical that many collectors of Morgan and Peace silver dollars would also desire Silver Certificates, most of which are specifically payable in silver dollars, but this is not the case. The paper and coin specialties seldom meet.

Systematically by Variety, Large Size

Collecting by variety involves going beyond basic types and collecting different signature combinations, Treasury Seal variations, and others listed in the Friedberg text. Not many people do this for large-size bills, with the result that such popular types as the 1890 Coin Notes, 1899 "Indian Chief" $5 bills, and others are more or less priced generically—with little premium added for scarcer signature or seal varieties (although great rarities can be high priced, and justifiably so).

Federal Reserve Bank Notes, Series of 1918, can be collected with different combinations of Federal Reserve banks, each of the two Treasury signatures, and each of two bank signatures, offering many variables.

Across other types of notes, lower denominations, especially the $1 bills, are quite inexpensive and furnish many different varieties. Certain terms of combined service for the register of the Treasury and the treasurer of the United States were very short, the epitome being just 18 days (June 1, 1893, to June 18, for William S. Rosecrans and Daniel N. Morgan). While at first it might seem that short terms together would have created extremely rare and valuable bills, this is not necessarily the case, as printing quantities were sometimes extensive during short terms and sparse during long ones, and in other instances plates with those signatures were used long after one or both persons had left office.

By Type, Small Size

While few people can afford or have the interest in collecting small-size bills from $1 to $100 by all combinations (see below), or, for that matter, the rare $500, $1,000, and $10,000 bills, quite a few numismatists desire to get one each of as many different types as they can. Changes in types were infrequent, and except for the higher values such a display can be acquired in high grades for modest outlay.

Systematically by Variety, Small Size

Small-size bills can be collected by denomination, signature, seal variation, and Federal Reserve Bank district. Lower denominations, especially the $1 bills, are quite inexpensive and furnish many different varieties. Such a collection can be kept current by adding new bills each time there is a signature combination or other change. This field has been the focus of interest for many numismatists.

By Interesting Serial Numbers

This is a particularly popular pursuit, especially for small-size bills of small denominations. The eight serial numbers can yield all sorts of possibilities. The beginning and ending letters are of interest as well, especially if both are A, but most attention is paid to the numerals. Low serials such as 00000001 (especially), 00000092, 00001776, and others sell for premiums. "Lucky" 7s are popular, and 77777777 would be worth passing around at a show for collectors to see, while having a bunch of 7s together, mixed with other numbers, is interesting, too. The digits 83777779, for example, are ideal for "liar's poker," a game played at coin shows in which the winner has the best "poker hand" as reflected in a bill taken from (presumably) random examples in a wallet.

Numbers that are symmetrical (e.g., 12344321 or 44888844) are called *radar* or, more formally, *palindromic* notes. Ascending or descending runs, such as 12345678 or 98765432, are also desirable. Several dealers specialize in interesting serial numbers, and a review of their listings will reveal categories that are popular and valuable.

Large-size notes with low serial numbers always command a premium, with number 1 notes being especially important. Not everyone realizes that on most large-size notes there is more than one number 1 note for a given type. On a four-subject sheet of bills arranged $5-$5-$5-$5, the bills on the first sheet all have the serial number 1 but with different plate letters, such as A, B, C, or D.

Star Notes

Small-size (in particular) notes with a star by the serial number, indicating a replacement note, form an avidly collected series. Values are sometimes dramatically high for with-star varieties that would be inexpensive without this feature.

Currency Errors

All sorts of interesting misprints and errors exist, the most dramatic of which is the double-denomination bill, such as with $5 on one side and $10 on the other, the result of a wrong sheet being fed into the press, or a $10-$10-$10-$20 or other multidenomination sheet being fed upside down (with the first $10 obverse getting a $20 reverse and the $20 getting a $10 reverse). However, the thrust of activity is with more available errors, such as mismatched serial numbers, upside-down serial numbers or seals, missing seals or serials, bold creases showing white areas without ink, and the like.

Beware of phony "errors" created by cutting note-size singles at odd angles, or with part of one note and part of another, from full sheets of bills sold to collectors by the Treasury Department. Sometimes human ingenuity in dreaming up tricks is amazing!

Unlike with coins, the faces and backs of federal notes are oriented in the same direction. Most older sheets of notes were printed on the back first and then dried, after which the front was printed. Notes with one side misaligned are called *inverted backs*, although, technically, it is the face that is inverted.

National Bank Notes

These are collected with wild, unbridled passion, with a checkbook in one hand and a copy of Don Kelly's *National Bank Notes* book in the other (a worthy compilation, now in its fourth edition, built upon many years of effort, most notably the early work of John Hickman and Dean Oakes). The

Kelly tome comes with an optional CD that lists thousands of banks, denominations, and serial numbers of bills reported. Dealers and collectors everywhere contribute to the Kelly listings, quid pro quo, as everyone benefits.

With National Bank bills, as with real estate, the three aspects of value are location, location, and location! A bill from Carson City, Nevada, a "rare town" as well as being a state capital (a specialty for many), is worth an eyetooth, while a common one from the National Park Bank of New York City might merit an unstifled yawn.

Nationals, as they are called, are usually collected by state, in one of several different ways: a note from each town in the state, or from each bank in each town, or of each denomination of each type series of each bank. This can be very serious stuff, and anyone wanting to collect 19th-century notes from rare locations, or rare states, or—the ultimate—rare *territories* (before they achieved statehood), should be prepared to spend a lot of money, but not in a hurry, as many varieties are seldom seen. However, the pursuit is enjoyable, and those who specialize in Nationals are a special breed.

Modifying the location-location-location comment, *denomination* can be important, and, generally, $50 and $100 notes are rare. Condition, while important in Nationals, is sometimes disregarded, as many banks are represented only by low-grade notes. For good measure, the books by Peter Huntoon, about history and technicalities (backed by unstinting research in the National Archives and at the Smithsonian Institution), add much enjoyment.

Sheets

While sheets of large-size bills are sometimes seen, especially for National Banks of the Series of 1902, they are not common and cannot be collected systematically. Sheets of small-size Nationals, six subjects, are more available but are scarce. Many of the latter are from the estate of Colonel E.H.R. Green, who had thousands, acquir-

ing them in the early 1930s via a mail-solicitation campaign to banks.

Sheets for regular bills of the past several decades are plentiful, as the Treasury Department has made them available to collectors, charging a small premium for the service. Sometimes, modern sheets are cut down to a lesser number of bills, but I see no point in paying a premium for such things. Full sheets are interesting, but I find them to be a bit clumsy to store or display.

Other Specialties

Military payment certificates (MPCs) issued to soldiers in the 20th century have been an enthusiastically collected area. Produced in large numbers for use in soldiers' pay, most were quickly redeemed. Today, many varieties are quite scarce.

Notes with so-called courtesy autographs by Treasury officials form an interesting pursuit for many. Among 19th-century bills, those autographed by Daniel N. Morgan (register of the Treasury from June 1, 1893, to June 30, 1897) are particularly numerous. Morgan was an enthusiastic collector and asked visitors to his office to sign an autograph book he kept on hand. Bills created as souvenirs are also popular to collect, with among the best known being the "short snorters" of World War II. These consist of multiple bills taped together end-to-end and signed by soldier or sailor buddies.

Go-Withs

Souvenir banks are collected by many people. Some of these bear National Bank names. Postcards of national and other banks are highly collectible and are inexpensive (I've enjoyed this pursuit for a long time). Bank bags, checks, calendars, blotters, and other items can be interesting to collect.

Grading of U.S. Paper Money

There are no hard-and-fast rules for grading federal notes from 1861 to date, a situation similar to that for obsoletes. The following guidelines are adapted from the 17th (latest) edition of *Paper Money of the United States* and are used by permission from Arthur L. and Ira S. Friedberg. Numerical grades based on the Sheldon scale have been added, reflecting current use in the hobby, including by commercial grading services.

Grade Categories for U.S. Paper Money (Friedberg)

Gem Uncirculated (Unc. 65 or higher). A note that is flawless, with the same freshness, crispness, and bright color as when first printed. It must be perfectly centered, with full margins, and free of any marks, blemishes, or traces of handling.

Choice Uncirculated (Unc. 63). An Uncirculated note that is fresher and brighter than the norm for its particular issue. Almost as nice as gem Uncirculated, but not quite there. Must be reasonably well centered. This is a good all-around grade for many notes and, in fact, is currently used as the Uncirculated category for the Whitman-Bowers *Guide Book of United States Paper Money.*

Uncirculated (Unc. 60). A note that shows no trace of circulation. It may not have perfect centering and may have one or more pinholes, counting smudges, or other evidence of improper handling, while still retaining its original crispness. Sometimes large-size notes will be encountered that are obviously Uncirculated, but that may have some tiny pinholes. (It was customary in the old days to spindle or pin new notes together.) Such imperfections do not generally impair the choice appearance of new notes, and such notes are to be regarded as being in Uncirculated condition, although they generally command slightly lower prices than notes in perfect condition.

About Uncirculated (AU-50, -53, -55, -58). A bright, crisp note that appears new but upon close examination shows a trace of very light use, such as a corner fold or faint crease. About Uncirculated is a borderline condition, applied to a note that may not be quite Uncirculated, but yet

is obviously better than an average Extremely Fine note. Such notes command a price only slightly below that of a new note and are highly desirable.

Extremely Fine (EF-40). A note that shows some faint evidence of circulation, although it will still be bright and retain nearly full crispness. It may have two or three minor folds or creases but no tears or stains and no discolorations.

Very Fine (VF-20). A note that has been in circulation, but not actively or for long. It still retains some crispness and is still choice enough in its condition to be altogether desirable. It may show folds or creases, or some light smudges from the hands of a past generation. Sometimes, Very Fine notes are the best available in certain rare issues, and they should accordingly be cherished just as much as Uncirculated notes.

Fine (F-12). A Fine note shows evidence of much more circulation and has lost its crispness and very fine detail Creases are more pronounced, although the note is still not seriously soiled or stained.

Very Good (VG-8). A note that has had considerable wear or circulation and might be limp, soiled, or dark in appearance and even have a small tear or two on an edge.

Good (G-4). A note that is badly worn, with margin or body tears, frayed margins, and missing corners.

In general, discriminating collectors will not acquire Fine or lower notes because they have lost their aesthetic appeal, but this applies only to common notes. A really rare note has a ready market in even poor condition, because it might not otherwise exist, or if it is choice, will have an extremely high price commensurate with its great rarity.

"Laundering" and "Improving" Currency

Many bills have been improved, some desirably so, by "laundering" to remove dirt and grease, then drying between pieces of tissue paper. Some collectors and dealers have added starch in an effort to restore crispness. Still other bills have had holes or tears repaired. Such improvements are generally accepted and, sometimes, are mentioned in auction listings (if the cataloger can discern them), but rarely in retail offerings. The last is due to a fear that if a bill is described as "lightly cleaned" or, worse, laundered (*laundered* is a bad word!), collectors might not order it.

Reality is reality, and in the marketplace today there are many bills that under careful examination show slight traces of having been folded (such as lightness or microscopic irregularity at the fold marks), but that are as crisp as a new note. Indeed, bills in grades such as VG and Fine, normally quite limp, are often with stiffness. My advice is that if a bill is very rare, this is okay, if you examine and recognize it. For regular low-denomination notes I would prefer bills that have not been treated. The Friedberg-Bowers *Guide Book of United States Paper Money* gives details of this practice over the years, including by the Treasury Department itself, as part of a program to clean soiled bills and render them fit for placing back into circulation.

Aspects of Availability

The following comments reflect my observations of certain United States paper money series 1861 to date.

Denominations Are Important

In any series it is a general rule that the lower denominations are more available than are the higher ones. The lower series are also more often seen in Uncirculated and other high grades, whereas a $50 or $100 bill of a given type might be rare or unknown in such preservation.

Printing Quantities Affect Rarity

Quantities produced can be a guide to availability, but only in part, as such factors as redemption policies, areas of distribution, and the finding of hoards also affect the equation. The Friedberg and Hessler (especially) texts combined will yield printing quantities for most notes.

Hoards

Every once in a while, in an old bank vault or other location, a cache of bills comes to light. Often, these are Uncirculated and have serial numbers in sequence. Although details are rarely announced, for fear of disturbance in the market, the existence of such can be deduced if serial-number clusters of bills in Uncirculated grade are seen.

In addition, nearly all paper money dealers know which notes are available from groups and hoards and which are not, and are often willing to share information. Databases maintained by Don Kelly (Nationals) and Martin Gengerke are very useful. Often, hoard notes are particularly choice and, further, offer the opportunity to acquire examples that might not otherwise be available, at least not easily.

Numismatic Popularity

Certain series have been popular with numismatists for a long time, and in such instances many Uncirculated notes exist from the early days of interest. This is nowhere more true than with Fractional Currency bills, which were avidly collected in the 1860s and 1870s—an era when *no one* collected large-size National Bank bills. Accordingly, most standard varieties, plus Specimens, of Fractional Currency are plentiful today.

Most lower-denomination small-size bills from the Series of 1928 (first issued in 1929) through the 1940s were saved by collectors and dealers, including bundles of popular varieties such as the $1 HAWAII overprints. These used to be common on the market.

After about 1953 (when the Friedberg book made its debut), the collecting of small-size notes became very popular, and quantities of most bills exist for lower denominations since that time. Higher values such as $20, $50, and $100 can be rare for certain small-size varieties.

Souvenirs and Keepsakes

Similar to the situation for obsolete currency, relatively few 19th-century bills of denominations from $1 upward were saved as souvenirs. Recipients preferred gold dollars, quarter eagles, and other coins, which displayed an immediate aspect of permanent value. The worth of paper money remained in serious question for a long time.

Sometimes bank officers would keep a few National Bank Notes with their signatures, accounting for some number 1 bills surviving today. Don Kelly reports in his book that this is especially true for Series of 1902 Nationals with red seals.

Proofs and Vignettes

Proof impressions were printed by the thousands of many Fractional Currency bills. These can be collected as a specialty on their own.

Proofs of regular U.S. bills, often on heavy paper or cardboard and with wide margins, were made in very small quantities and were not widely distributed, but examples become available from time to time. Most are rare and expensive. Many individually printed vignettes from large-size National Bank and other 19th-century bills are on the market, these showing portraits, battle scenes, or other topics, on light cardstock. These are interesting to collect in connection with the bills themselves. Some are from large presentation books of Specimen Notes distributed by the Treasury Department in the 1870s and 1880s with nicely imprinted covers.

Much more rare are specially made books of Fractional Currency with Specimens (not just vignettes) of actual notes.

Selected Bibliography for Federal Bank Notes 1861 to Date

Friedberg, Arthur L., and Ira S. Friedberg. 2004. *Paper Money of the United States* (17th ed.). Clifton, NJ. (standard source for "Friedberg numbers" universally used to describe federal notes)

Friedberg, Arthur L., Ira S. Friedberg, and Q. David Bowers. 2005. *A Guide Book of United States Paper Money*. Atlanta, GA. (includes Friedberg numbers)

Hessler, Gene. 1993. *The Engraver's Line*. Port Clinton, OH. (biographies of engravers)

Hessler, Gene. 1997. *The Comprehensive Catalog of U.S. Paper Money* (6th ed.). Port Clinton, OH.

Hessler, Gene. 2004. *U.S. Essay, Proof, and Specimen Notes* (2nd ed.). Port Clinton, OH.

Huntoon, Peter. 1995. *U.S. Large Size National Bank Notes*. Laramie, WY.

Illustrated auction catalogs of the past 30 years.

Kelly, Don C. 2004. *National Bank Notes* (4th ed.). Oxford, OH. Available with CD. (standard source for populations in this series)

Periodicals: *Bank Note Reporter*, *Paper Money*, and *The Currency Dealer Newsletter*.

CHAPTER THIRTY

COLLECTING CONFEDERATE PAPER MONEY

The difference between the collector and numismatist may be almost precisely likened to that between what is commonly called a builder and an architect. Both represent appreciation, capacity, activity, interest and zeal, both are mutually helpful, but the latter represents just so much more profundity of research, technical ability, scientific attainment and professional training than the former. The main appeals of a coin are its history and artistry.

—Frank C. Higgins, January 1911

Historical Sketch

The Numismatist, March 1919, included this:

> The question has often been asked, "Why did not the Confederate government, having in its possession a well-equipped mint, issue a series of coins?"...
>
> The great need of the Confederate government was money in large quantity, and the smaller the cost of issuing it the more profitable for the government, so the printing presses were called upon to furnish it. Notes of any denomination could be printed at a small cost, and though they depreciated greatly... they were more profitable than issues of coin in the precious metals.

And so it was that the Confederate States of America, which struck some coins early in 1861 from federal dies and bullion on hand at the New Orleans and Dahlonega mints, had no circulating coinage with its own designs. Instead, paper money was issued. Most bills were actually post notes, payable at a future date, such as 12 months or some other time later—as, for example, this on a $10 note of 1863 (known today as Criswell Type 59): "two years after the ratification of a treaty of peace between the Confederate States and the United States."

While the continuing depreciation of Legal Tender and other bills was an annoyance to citizens in the North, the inhabitants of the South had even more difficult

times.[97] Confederate States of America paper money traded (in terms of federal *gold* coins) at a 5% discount when first issued, but soon dropped in value even further. Indeed, depreciated northern greenbacks were very valuable in comparison! The following are a few selected dates and the amount it took in Confederate bills to buy $100 in U.S. gold coins through an exchange broker:

1861: July 1: $110 • January 15: $130

1862: April 1: $175

1863: February 1: $300 • March 1: $500 • July 1: $800 • October 1: $1,300 • December 15: $2,100

1864: October 1: $2,700 • December 21: $5,100

1865: March 1: $10,000 • April 20: $80,000 (the war was over) • May 1: $100,000 (this being the last active day for market trading in these bills)[98]

Some very interesting stories were related about federal paper money being sent by friends and relatives to Union prisoners held in Confederate interment camps. These notes, usually of the $5 denomination, were readily bartered to guards in exchange for goods and favors.

The Union's finances were bolstered by tens of millions of dollars arriving yearly from San Francisco, the entrepôt for gold commerce. The Confederacy had no counterpart, although some small amounts of the precious metal continued to be mined in the hills of Georgia and North Carolina. On international markets, the Union could display at least limited metallic strength, while the Confederacy dealt mainly with hopes and promises. Douglas B. Ball's masterwork, *Financial Failure and Confederate Defeat* (1991), gives much valuable information in this regard.

It is worth mentioning that few if any federal Demand Notes (which did not depreciate) were sent to Europe. The financial interests there were primarily affianced to the Confederate States of America, which was able to float bonds in England and which sent large quantities of paper currency there. The South was a vital supplier of raw cotton to British mills in Lancashire and elsewhere, and it was considered essential to maintain this connection. Nor did government banks in other foreign countries want Union notes or any others of the era, as paper to them was precarious in value. They demanded gold or silver coins (silver being the metal of choice in China, gold mostly elsewhere). In brief, while quantities Confederate bills and even more bonds went to Europe, Union bills did not.

Regarding the situation, Congressman James G. Blaine of Maine included this in his memoirs:

> Confederate bonds were more popular in England than the bonds of the United States. The world's treasuries were closed against us. The banks of Europe, with the Rothschilds in the lead, would not touch our securities. The united clientage included the investors of Great Britain and the Continent, and a popular loan could not be effected without their aid and cooperation. We were engaged, therefore, in a three-fold contest, a military one with the Confederacy, a diplomatic and moral one with the governments of England and France, a financial one with the money power of Europe.

Although neither England nor France became an open military ally of the Confederacy, they provided much help for the "lost cause" (England building and France sheltering the *C.S.S. Alabama*, the most notorious raider of the Civil War, being but one of many examples). The contretemps regarding the Laird "rams"—battleships built in the British Isles for the Confederacy, and outfitted with steel snouts projecting underwater from their bows—filled many columns of newspaper print.

Confederate Paper Money

Early in its existence the Confederate States of America set about issuing its own paper money, $1,000,000 authorized on March 9, 1861, and $20,000,000 on May 16 of the same year. In time, the circulation of these and certain other bills in the South was enforced by the decree that refusing to receive these at par was tantamount to treason.

Paper notes of both sides soon achieved their own market values in terms of silver and gold coins. Brokers and exchange houses did a lively business. It seems that most brokers in the North didn't handle authentic Confederate paper, at least not openly. However, counterfeit Confederate bills were widely advertised for sale in the North, most particularly by S.C. Upham of Philadelphia, and were available at pennies in terms of face-value dollars. Most brokers had a ready stock on hand. Many buyers were northerners who had secured travel passes to the South and hoped to profit by passing them to merchants.

Brokers in the South usually handled Confederate as well as Union bills, in addition to federal coins. Confederate paper money depreciated slowly but inexorably in 1861, but after the unexpected military loss at Fort Donelson in February 1862, the value and reputation of bills and related bonds plummeted. After that time, Confederate paper spiraled downward like a falling autumn leaf. After early 1864 there was no point in issuing any more bills, as their exchange value was so low.

In addition to the C.S.A. government, several Southern states and other entities issued paper money. All told, by the end of the war in 1865, an estimated $1.7 billion in face value had been printed by the Confederacy![99] Seventy-two major types of C.S.A. notes, in denominations up to $1,000 and in hundreds of varieties and signature combinations, were produced. States, railroads, towns, and others issued abut $215,000,000 in additional bills.

The first series of C.S.A. paper was printed by the National Bank Note Co., New York City, and was imprinted "Montgomery," this Alabama city being the first capital of the Confederacy. The so-called

Montgomery notes are very ornate and are in the usual National Bank Note Co. style of the period, used on state-chartered bank bills in the North. Around the denomination (as around the M and the 1000 on the $1,000 bill) are petals or lobes with letters repeating the value. At the center is a green lattice overprint, also used on state bank notes, said to be a deterrent against counterfeiting by photographic means. Montgomery notes were produced in denominations of $50, $100, $500, and

1861 $50 Confederate States of America note, Montgomery, Alabama address—the first capital of the Confederacy. The "Montgomery notes," as they were known today, were printed in New York City by the National Bank Note Company, just before the Civil War was declared. Today these are the best known Confederate bills, "trophy" notes in the series. The vignette of the $50 shows slaves hoeing in a plantation field. (Criswell Type-4)

1861 $100 Confederate States of America "Montgomery note," by the National Bank Note Company. The vignette shows the goddess Columbia, earlier used on various bills of state-chartered banks. The train was also used elsewhere earlier. (Criswell Type-3; Charles A. Hilton Collection)

1861 $500 Confederate States of America "Montgomery note," by the National Bank Note Company. The vignette shows a train crossing a stone bridge while a drover (on horseback in the distance to the right) herds cattle across a stream. (Criswell Type-2)

1861 $1000 Confederate States of America "Montgomery note," by the National Bank Note Company. Depicted are John Calhoun (senator from South Carolina who advocated "states rights" for the South for many years) and Andrew Jackson. (Criswell Type-1; Wayne Hilton Collection)

$1,000. On July 16, 1861, the capital was moved to Richmond, Virginia, and later bills bear that location.

In the North, policies regarding merchants trading with the South were not finalized until the Civil War was well underway. Each of the two major bank note firms, American and National, both in New York, received C.S.A. contracts prior to the commencement of hostilities, and both hoped to continue the relationship afterward. The third significant New York firm, W.L. Ormsby, trading as the New York Bank Note Co., either was unsuccessful in perfecting a contract or may not have been consulted in this regard. Later, Ormsby loudly proclaimed his thus-proven affection for the North and publicized the disloyalty of his competitors.

On April 26, 1861, eleven days after war had been declared against the Confederate States of America, the *New York World* reported that on the 25th of the month, U.S. deputy marshals Bersch and Horton "made an important seizure" at the offices of the American Bank Note Co. of 18 printing plates made for the Confederate bonds. Further:

> The officers of the company state that they ceased printing from them as soon as the President's proclamation was issued. The informer against them asserts that they were being printed as late as four days ago. An hour after the above seizure the United States deputy marshals entered the office of the National Bank Note Company and took into their keeping two plates of cancelled Treasury Notes of the Southern Confederacy, of the denominations of $50, $100, $500, and $1000 [these being the "Montgomery note" plates].
>
> The engraving of the plates is of the best quality, and not unlike the United States Treasury Notes now in circulation. The presidents of both companies are held to await investigation in the matter.

This seems to have ended the direct connection between the North and the South in such printing. However, American Bank Note Co. had a branch in New Orleans, which fell under Confederate control, and several Confederate issues (comprising three different types) were printed there until the city was recaptured by the North on April 24, 1862. Tracy Edson, the wily president of American Bank Note Co. at the time, secured a travel pass to go into the South, to Richmond. One can only speculate whether his unstated mission had to do with printing currency. Edson, an acquaintance of Ormsby since his teenage years, was an opportunist first and foremost. Later, he was implicated in trying to bribe certain government officials with regard to bank note contracts.

Later C.S.A. bills were produced by various printers in the South, most of whom lacked sophisticated equipment such as medallion ruling machines, geometric lathes, siderographic transfer presses, and the like. Instead, they used lithography, often copying portraits and illustrations from the bills of state-chartered banks produced in prewar times by the Northern bank note companies. Grover C. Criswell's *Comprehensive Catalog of Confederate Paper Money* (1996 edition) describes 72 major types, including four Montgomery issues and 68 printed in the South, this listing being the guide for many collectors today.

Most Confederate bills lack detail and sharpness, and some were printed on paper of uncertain quality. However, they have a generous measure of history, and the collecting of them has been pursued with enthusiasm ever since the 1860s. In fact, numismatists widely collected Confederate paper decades before there was a major interest in Legal Tender Notes and related federal issues (except Fractional Currency).

Collecting C.S.A. Currency

"Collecting Confederate paper money is a lot like reliving history," commented Tom Denly, a dealer in these and other notes.[100] "Very few other ways make it possible to

1861 $20 note printed in New Orleans by the Southern Bank Note Company, a branch of the American Bank Note Company (New York City) that had come under control of the Confederacy. In the 1850s this had been an office of Rawdon, Wright, Hatch & Edson. The Southern Bank Note Company printed several varieties, all of which were from high-quality plates. In a way, Confederate paper bills are promissory notes, or post notes, inasmuch as each carried the promise to pay at some future date, in this instance "six months after the ratification of a treaty of peace between the Confederate States and the United States." (Criswell Type-19)

1861 $50 note printed in New Orleans by the Southern Bank Note Company. Payable six months after treaty ratification. Trains were a favorite motif for many Confederate and other Southern notes. (Criswell Type-15)

1861 $100 note printed in New Orleans by the Southern Bank Note Company. This note was payable 12 months after the date on the bill. (Criswell Type-5)

1862 $100 note engraved and printed by J.T. Paterson, Columbia, South Carolina, payable six months after the ratification of a peace treaty. The train on this note is the "straight steam" variety, Criswell Type-39. Another variety, more crudely printed, has "diffuse steam" behind the smokestack and is known as Criswell Type-40. The locomotive motif was copied from a design widely used in the 1850s by W.L. Ormsby and others. In this incarnation the engraver has added a seascape, complete with ship, in the *sky* above the bridge—rather curious!

hold in your hands such solid evidence of the biggest internal struggle in the history of the U.S. Is that brown spot on that $10 Confederate note blood from a fallen or wounded soldier from a famous battle? What a story that note could tell!"

Many Confederate bills still exist, as the Confederacy failed and the notes, never redeemed, became worthless. In fact, in the closing months of the Civil War in early 1865, bills were already so depreciated as to have no practical value. It March it took about $10,000 in CSA bills to buy a federal gold dollar!

Many Southerners are said to have held their currency in hopes that the "South will rise again." After the conflict, they became highly prized as collectibles by numismatists and as souvenirs by the general public. As they were illustrated and often ornate on the face, but blank on the reverse side, they were ideal as a vehicle for advertising, by imprinting the back. Many were overprinted with advertisements and other messages and given out as novelties.

Today, collectors range from those who want to have a few "cheap" notes to be able to hold history in their hands, to those whose collections encompass the 72 major varieties and the many subvarieties. The Criswell text has been in use for many years and draws from earlier research and publications. Most catalog attributions are to Criswell numbers.

Virtually unknown to earlier researchers, but publicized in modern times, is Raphael P. Thian's grand 1880 compilation, *Register of the Issues of Confederate States Treasury Notes Together With Tabular Exhibits of the Debt, Funded and Unfunded of the Confederate States of America*, of which five copies were made. W.W. Bradbeer's 162-page *Confederate and Southern State Currency: Historical and Financial Data, Biographical Sketches, Descriptions with Illustrations* (1915) is useful for its content, as are other books, monographs, and historical studies.

Today, the four varieties of 1861 Montgomery notes remain star attractions, "trophy" notes to some who have acquired

multiple examples. Somewhat more than 100 exist of each denomination. Due to the laws of supply and demand, these routinely bring prices of $15,000 to $100,000 each, the letter for the finest-condition specimens of rarer varieties.

The more than 65 distinct types of bills imprinted "Richmond" (location of the second capital of the C.S.A.), printed at various locations in the South, form the essence of the market today. "One usually starts collecting from that one $10 bill of 1864 that grandma had folded up in her jewelry box or from the tattered $5 bill of 1863 that was bought for $7 on eBay. It many times takes just one note to start a passion for collecting the currency," Denly said. History goes hand in hand with collecting.

As with every other aspect of numismatics, buying and reading the book—in this instance, the Criswell book—is even more important than buying the note. Amanda Sheheen commented:

> How does one get started? Generally, most people have an interest in history and are delighted to learn that Confederate paper money is available and affordable. The first thing that I do as a dealer is to insist that a client buy a Criswell book and start learning. One cannot have the ability to understand why a note is significant or why one note is rare in a certain grade and common in another, until reading this book.
>
> Also, with the Criswell book a "wish list" can be compiled. In my opinion, it is also important to establish contact with one or several reliable dealers. For some varieties known mainly in lower grades, a high-grade example with bright color can be very expensive, and it is important to get some guidance and advice before making a purchase.

The vignettes of the Confederate notes tell the story of the South. Notes that depict President Jefferson Davis, General Stonewall Jackson, slaves hoeing cotton, or the allegorical depiction of the South with sword in hand slaying the North have always been popular.

As might be expected, some of the most enthusiastic collectors of Confederate bills are in the South. However, the specialty knows no boundaries, and they are widely sought by many others as well.

At any given time there are thousands of numismatists who collect Confederate notes as a specialty. Most will buy as many different Criswell types as they can, up to a budget limit—for some, $50 to $100 each; for others, up to a few thousand dollars. Fewer buyers are apt to compete for choice examples of rarities such as the Montgomery notes, or Criswell types 27 (liberty, shield, and eagle vignette) and 35 (Indian princess), due to the cost involved.

It is popular to collect other notes from the Civil War era of the South, such as those issued by railroads, states, banks, and merchants. Most of these are quite inexpensive, and some of them are fascinating to contemplate—such as bills of a new issue printed crosswise on the blank back of an unissued sheet of notes of some other type!

Selected Bibliography for Confederate States of America Currency:

Criswell, Grover C. 1996. *Comprehensive Catalog of Confederate Paper Money*. Port Clinton, OH. (Latest edition with extra material by Douglas Ball and Hugh Shull. The standard reference on the subject.)

Of historical interest (list furnished by Wayne Hilton):

Allen, H.D. The Paper Money of the Confederate States With Historical Data. *The Numismatist* (June 1917–Feb. 1919).

Bradbeer, William W. 1915. *Confederate and Southern States Currency*. Mount Vernon, NY.

Chase, Philip H. 1947. *Confederate Treasury Notes*. Philadelphia, PA.

Fuller, Claud E. 1949. *Confederate Currency and Stamps*. Nashville, TN.

Haseltine, John W. 1876. *Descriptive Catalog of Confederate Notes and Bonds*. Philadelphia, PA.

Lee, William. 1875. *The Currency of the Confederate States of America*. Washington, DC.

Massamore, George W. 1889. *Descriptive and Chronological Catalog of Confederate Currency*. Baltimore, MD.

Slabaugh, Arlie R. 2000. *Confederate States Paper Money* (10th ed.). Iola, WI.

Thian, Raphael P. 1972. *Register of the Confederate Debt*. Boston, MA. (reprint; original work printed 1880)

CHAPTER THIRTY-ONE

YOUR NUMISMATIC LIBRARY

If all new collectors would devote their attention to the information which is available in printed form they could be saved many dollars ultimately squandered upon inferior coins or otherwise not as represented, and which due to their lack of knowledge on the subject has proved to be an expensive lesson.... The collector is not ill-advised who commences by allotting 20% to 25% of his coin budget to his numismatic library.

—David M. Bullowa, November 1949

Reasons to Collect Books

There are many reasons to build a numismatic library. The most obvious is to get information on the items you are currently collecting. The basic reference books are necessities, of course, and I need but mention such key volumes as the *Guide Book of United States Coins* and *Walter Breen's Complete Encyclopedia of U.S. and Colonial Coins* for American numismatics, among perhaps a half dozen other must-have titles. For tokens, an essential volume is Russ Rulau's *Standard Catalog of United States Tokens 1700–1900*; and collectors of federal paper money could hardly live without a copy of Friedberg's *Paper Money of the United States* or the new, related volume, *A Guide Book of United States Paper Money.*

Some such books are also price guides, but even the most carefully compiled listings of market values for a 2005 edition are apt to be out of date by 2006 and, 10 years from now, simply historical curiosities. In my opinion, price guides are useful, but there are so few current ones that much of this information is best obtained outside of mainstream reference books, such as through numismatic periodicals and the Internet.

The collecting and appreciation of numismatic publications has a very rich tradition in America, one that remains dynamic today. In this chapter I explore some of the avenues of this specialty.

For most numismatists in America, basic texts serve as a useful library, perhaps of only a few books. I recall John J. Ford, Jr., commenting to me years ago about a customer who had just spent several thousand dollars in an auction held by the New Netherlands Coin Company. When he picked up his lots after the sale he asked a few questions that, to Ford, seemed elementary. "That guy has a one-volume library, the *Guide Book*," Ford commented. "Now, we have to educate him so he will know what he bought."

Indeed, a one-volume "library" is not all that rare. It is typical—the rule, not the exception—for someone to spend $100,000 on coins, but balk at spending a few hundred dollars on books.

One or two books can provide very useful information on a series, but a true library will enhance the appreciation of coins many times over. This avenue to increased enthusiasm and satisfaction is a very important reason to build a library. There is also something comfy-cozy about a library with unread books beckoning to cheerfully fill idle hours. Books remain a warm and reassuring tradition, even in this fast-paced world of electronic media.

Many Possibilities

There are hundreds of worthwhile numismatic books available, in print as well as out of print, the latter being obtainable from dealer-specialists as well as general vendors on the Internet. Beyond texts that are specifically numismatic, there are thousands of titles addressing state and local histories, operations of the Treasury Department (annual reports of the director of the Mint, annual reports of the comptroller of the currency), congressional documents, biographies and more. Like as not,

Tradition of a Library

The Astor Library in New York City formed the motif for a $1 bill of the Astor Bank, New York City, by the bank-note engraving firm of Baldwin, Adams & Co. Opened to the public on February 1, 1854, it became part of what is today called the New York Public Library. A cabinet of coins was built by the library over the years, augmented by items from the estate of engraver Charles Cushing Wright and donations from dealers J.W. Scott and David U. Proskey.

In the 1850s, Daniel W. Fiske, an assistant librarian at the Astor Library in New York City, and Frank H. Norton, also associated with the library, were a source of information for local collectors. Several shelves were filled with numismatic books, nearly all of which had been published in Europe (in an era

before significant American activity in this area). For many years a special area designated as the Numismatic Alcove, established by early superintendent (and avid numismatist) J. Carson Brevoort, was an attraction.

Charles B. Norton advertisement, 1858: "Have You a Good Library?" This question can still be effectively posed today: Have *you* a good numismatic library? If not, you should have!

HAVE YOU A GOOD LIBRARY?

CHARLES B. NORTON,

Agent for Libraries,

WOULD INFORM

LIBRARY COMMITTEES, LIBRARIANS,

AND BOOKBUYERS GENERALLY,

(THAT HE IS WELL PREPARED TO FURNISH LIBRARIES TO ANY EXTENT.)

With agents in all parts of EUROPE, he is enabled to import on the best terms. OLD LIBRARIES or COLLECTIONS bought and sold. Catalogues prepared and printed. Gentlemen wishing to make DONATIONS OF BOOKS TO COLLEGES, HISTORICAL SOCIETIES, OR PUBLIC LIBRARIES, can have them forwarded to any part of the country by addressing the Subscriber. CATALOGUES sent by mail without charge. Every arrangement made for disposing of Libraries at Auction on the best terms.

☞ On hand, the finest and most extensive

STOCK OF BOOKS RELATIVE TO AMERICA,

ever offered for sale in the United States.

CHARLES B. NORTON,

Agent for Libraries, New York.

Interior view of the bookstore of George G. Evans, Philadelphia, 1859. Several years later, in 1862, he advertised on encased postage stamps. In the 1880s and 1890s he published many editions of the popular *Illustrated History of the United States Mint with a Complete Description of American Coinage.*

Time was when most educated families had libraries in their homes. An 1857 book, *Villas and Cottages*, by architect Calvert Vaux, illustrated many medium-sized and large structures, nearly all of which included a library. The first-floor plan of Design No. 24 featured a large library on the right side, with a bay window permitting a view of the lawn.

A library in New England, 1884.

such volumes either are not of interest to you or can be borrowed if needed, with no need to purchase them. The same goes for related books on history, finance, art, music, geography, literature, and more (the likes of which constitute about 80% of my own library). The range of your numismatic collecting, however, will dictate the range of your library. Having a book or two may be sufficient if you collect only, say, Eisenhower dollars, but it is not if you delve into colonial, pattern, territorial, or other coin byways, or currencies of state-chartered banks, or medals of the War of 1812.

If you want to focus on useful books about American numismatics, not history, economics, and other fields, then probably a core library could be housed in a medium-sized bookcase. If you add old catalogs and periodicals, then another bookcase or two will be needed. I won't even discuss world and ancient coins, for if I did, a much larger vista would be presented.

Books as Collectibles

While creating a *working library* to use in coin buying and selling is eminently practical and ultimately profitable, you can also acquire books, catalogs, and other printed items as *collectibles*. In their own right they can be evaluated for rarity, added as part of a run or sequence, or otherwise systematically collected. The books can be used for research, of course, or they can simply be enjoyed for their ownership. The late Armand Champa formed one of the finest libraries ever, but did not often read his books. Instead, he seemed to view them as rare trophies, which, indeed, they were—including many laid out in a still-memorable display at the 1991 ANA Centennial Convention. The thrill of the hunt was important to him, and he might spend a week trying to negotiate the purchase of a rare Chapman, Woodward, or special-edition catalog, and then, upon getting it, tuck it way on a shelf with no thought of perusing its pages.

Not many numismatists have trophyism as a prime objective, but in the world of collecting rare books in general (especially in the early 20th century), this was the main attraction—witness Henry E. Huntington, young Harry Widener (who went down on the *Titanic*), and dozens of others, delineated in such readable texts as *Books and Bidders* and *Rosenbach*. Not many "books about books," as they are called in the trade, have been written about numismatic texts, but in the wide world of collecting books in general there are many hundreds of titles. The prime objects of desire for great book collectors of the past were such things as first folios of Shakespeare, rare printings of Poe titles, early imprints from colonies and territories, and the like. *Tamerlane* was meant to be collected, not read, and the *Bay Psalm Book* was not to be used as a guide for singing. These were and still are collectible icons.

Some Advice From Colonel Bill Murray

Where to begin? Among writers about and reviewers of books, Colonel William A. ("Bill") Murray is one of the best-known figures of our era. He is a regular columnist for *Coin World* and *COINage*, is prominent in the Numismatic Literary Guild and the Numismatic Bibliomania Society, and is otherwise immersed in books and their lure and lore.

In connection with this book I invited Bill to share his thoughts about building a numismatic library, and he did. The following is his contribution.

Starting a Numismatic Library

Some collectors get their start in numismatics with the gift of a collection already begun by someone else, presumably a friend or relative. Such a collection may already include a modest numismatic library. Lucky collector! For all the others, who start their collections from scratch, I expect that New York City dealer Aaron Feldman's aphorism, "Buy the book before the coin," escapes their attention for some time. Without any guidance, such a collector will no doubt soon find the efficacy of a

The American Numismatic Society and Its Library

Today, the finest numismatic library in America is held by the American Numismatic Society, New York City.

On Tuesday evening, October 6, 1908, the new society building was opened to collectors and others (shown here in an architect's rendering). It was situated on Audubon Terrace, on Broadway between 155th and 156th streets, a district known at the time for its refinement and society. The building was mostly paid for by railroad heir Archer M. Huntington, who dictated much policy for the ANS for years afterward (leading to a diminution of emphasis on American coins and a focus on specialties he liked, mainly ancient issues). On November 13, 1930, the size of the facility was doubled when a large addition, again mostly paid for by Huntington, was opened. It was not until the late 20th century that American coins once again became a main part of the society's activities, mainly under the aegis of president Harry W. Bass, Jr., and, later, by president Don Partrick.

As the years slipped by, the neighborhood of 155th Street and Broadway saw deterioration and increased crime. For this and also the opportunity to be closer to the city's financial center, plans were laid to relocate the organization.

On December 2, 2003, the American Numismatic Society had its first formal event in its new headquarters, the dedication of the Harry W. Bass, Jr. Library. On hand were members of the Bass and Calhoun families, representing the late Harry Bass, ANS president Don Partrick, librarian Frank Campbell, and various numismatic literati and glitterati—a grand occasion. In 2004 the facility was opened for regular activities. Located at 96 Fulton Street not far from Wall Street, the structure was remodeled from its earlier use as a bank and office building, with Don Partrick supervising many of the arrangements.

Doris (Mrs. Harry W.) Bass presents a check to ANS president Don Partrick at the library dedication ceremony held on December 2, 2003. To the left and right are her sons, David and Michael Calhoun.

Harry W. Bass, Jr. (1927–1998), served as president of the American Numismatic Society from 1978 to 1984, and with gifts into the multiple millions of dollars, was one of its greatest benefactors. Harry, a fine friend of mine, formed a great numismatic library, selections from which are now in the Society Library. The main part of the Bass Library, largely redundant to the immense ANS holdings, was auctioned by George Frederick Kolbe. Bass also formed the most extensive collection of 18th and 19th century American gold coins ever assembled, the core of which is on loan display at the American Numismatic Association Headquarters in Colorado Springs, and which is described in a book, *The Harry W. Bass Jr. Museum Sylloge.*

Plaque at the entrance of the Harry W. Bass, Jr. Library.

Seal of the American Numismatic Society, New York City. "Parva ne pereant" translates to "let not the little things perish," appropriate enough to the study of coins. Also, from little acorns might oaks grow—and without doubt the study of numismatics has led to great things for those involved.

numismatic value reference. In most cases it may well be the ubiquitous "Red Book" (*A Guide Book of United States Coins*). It's a good first choice with which to start a numismatic library. However, don't stop there!

Start with conversations with any respected collector or dealer you may know. Among the members of the local coin club (if there is one), some will enjoy a good reputation for their knowledge. Find time to talk to them about a numismatic library. Presumably, they will have good ideas. If they are specialists in some particular facet of the hobby, their libraries will reflect that. Most advanced collectors will gladly recommend some good, basic books on numismatics of the United States to you. Make a list.

Next, take that list with you on a visit to your local coin dealer. Ask if he or she has any of them in stock. If the answer is yes, take a look at them, and do decide to purchase at least one or two. (You're in the process of making a valuable numismatic friend—your dealer.)

Then, making sure that you are not interrupting the dealer's business, find an opportunity to converse about your interests, and ask his or her advice on other books you might add to your library. During this conversation, you might ask if you could peruse *the dealer's* library. Remember, this person is in the business of buying and selling numismatic items, and his or her library will reflect this with its selection of price guides for virtually all such items—U.S. coins and paper money, foreign issues, ancient coins, tokens, medals, and more. Don't ignore those items, but look for what other books the dealer has considered worth putting on the shelves. Owning (and studying) items such as these will enhance your goal of becoming not just a casual collector, but a numismatist.

You've made a start. Now let's take a look at that first expected purchase,

A Guide Book of United States Coins. It is first and foremost a price guide, but in addition to the tables of values it contains other material. Dates of issue of each coin type, its composition, the designer, and some historical background will be found, as will be general grading information. As one dealer told me many years ago, "Use the tables, *but read the reading*."

The sketch or overview of grading presented in the *Guide Book* is simply a beginning. Learning more about grading coins is an imperative, and the *Official A.N.A. Grading Standards for United States Coins* is an essential reference. This book should be an early purchase, before you buy too many coins! The 70-point grading system delineated therein derives from the (not very scientific) system for grading and pricing the large cents of 1793 to 1814 described in William H. Sheldon's *Penny Whimsy*. The Sheldon book, no longer in print, is treasured by many as a valuable addition to their libraries—one of many worthwhile volumes from the past.

As you begin to add to your library, you will find that many of the most valued books (the ones that provide numismatic background, history, and details of the Mint and minting processes) are out of print and, like the Sheldon study, must be sought on the secondary market. Any of several numismatic booksellers may find them for you, or you might track them down in an auction of numismatic books. Auction offerings cover many levels—from inexpensive modern items to rare classics.

Some valued titles by American numismatists, past and present, deserve consideration. A few examples follow.

The Early Coins of America, by Sylvester S. Crosby (1875), covers the myriad of coins and tokens in regular use in the colonies up to and including patterns of the U.S. Mint for the half disme and three different cent patterns. Though new information is available for much of the material covered in this book, it still is considered the basic reference for the colonial and confederation era.

Don Taxay's *The U.S. Mint and Coinage* (1966), starts with a discussion of the Continental Currency paper and the Continental Currency coinage of 1776, continues with early contract coinage, then proceeds to the Act of 1792, which established the U.S. Mint in Philadelphia. Taxay gives excellent information concerning the production of coinage from the 1790s through the advent of the Kennedy half dollar in 1964. This volume is considered essential by most who own a copy.

Walter Breen's Complete Encyclopedia of U.S. and Colonial Coins (1988), deserves to be on the shelf of every American numismatist. Though some corrections and changes have been made by later reviewers and scholars, it still must be considered a very valuable reference.

Much of the history of the development of U.S. coinage has always been available in J. Hewitt Judd's *United States Pattern Coins: Experimental and Trial Pieces*. The ninth edition (2005), edited by Q. David Bowers and simply titled *United States Pattern Coins*, brings the field up to date with modern scholarship.

Another recently published book by Bowers, *A Guide Book of United States Type Coins* (2005), provides valuable guidance to any collector of U S. type coins, whether he or she aims to emulate Louis E. Eliasberg, Sr. (an impossible task), or merely wants to complete a type set of Lincoln cents.

The 100 Greatest U.S. Coins, by Jeff Garrett and Ron Guth, based on a survey of respected dealers, tells the stories of these selected coins. Few of can aspire to own many of these coins, but the beautiful photos and well-written documentation give us the opportunity to enjoy them all through the print medium.

Many more suggestions could be added. As you look, you can expect to find many of particular interest to you. In recent years, dozens of numismatic books serving collectors with various specialties have appeared. They will interest those specializing in—to provide just a few examples—Indian Head cents, Jefferson nickels, the 50 State Quarters® Program, Franklin and Kennedy half dollars, Morgan dollars, varieties and errors of all denominations and eras, or merchant tokens by state. The list goes on.

Be advised: You likely will become addicted to numismatic-book collecting! If so, a special organization awaits you: the Numismatic Bibliomania Society. The group's web site (www.coinbooks.org/club_nbs_member_app.html) has an application.

Areas of Specialty in Numismatic Literature

As in other areas of numismatics, publications (both out-of-print and current) can be grouped into several classifications. I like magazines and periodicals, but these are not a wide favorite with others, save for early issues of *The Numismatist* and the *American Journal of Numismatics*. Auction catalogs, probably the main focus of interest in the collecting field, have been in strong demand for a long time, with classics from the 19th and early 20th centuries commanding a lot of attention when they cross the auction block—especially large-size catalogs by the Chapman brothers, with photographic plates. Reference books are widely collected, sometimes by the subjects they cover, such as large copper cents.

The Numismatic Bibliomania Society, through its journal, *The Asylum*, and its *E-Sylum* (managed by Wayne Homren) on the Internet (https://my.binhost.com/lists/listinfo/esylum), connects hundreds of enthusiasts. I would estimate that several thousand others collect out-of-print numismatic items, but not as a main focus.

A dedicated bibliophile might spend a day trying to find out where Emmanuel Joseph Attinelli, went on vacation in 1874 (if he did), Attinelli being the author of the first book in America on the subject, *Numisgraphics: Or, a List of Catalogues, in Which Occur Coins or Medals, Which Have Been Sold by Auction in the United States, also, A List of Catalogues or Price Lists of Coins, Issued by Dealers, also, a List of Various Publications of More or Less Interest to Numismatologists, Which Have Been Published in the United States* (1876). I suppose that by the time some people finished reading the title, they thought they had read a book! *Numisgraphics*, or simply "Attinelli," is its nickname today, as in "The book is listed in Attinelli." This volume is basic to collecting.

The closest modern equivalent to Attinelli is *American Numismatic Literature:*

Title page of Emmanuel J. Attinelli's *Numisgraphics*, a superb study of American numismatic literature published in 1876 (reprinted in 1976 by Quarterman Publications, Inc.).

An Annotated Survey of Auction Sales 1980–1991, by well-known bookseller Charles E. Davis. The title is a bit misleading; while the *book auctions* occurred in the years indicated, the subject is numismatic literature offered for sale therein, including books, catalogs, and other publications dating back to the early 19th century. I refer to my copy often, and only wish that Davis would update this very useful reference with new information.

Beyond the preceding are several specialized studies, including John W. Adams's two volumes on 19th- and 20th-century auction sales, Remy Bourne's privately printed studies on dealer catalogs and fixed-price lists, and Martin Gengerke's series on auction catalogs, incorporating the holdings of the American Numismatic Society (ANS). This series lists every numismatic auction catalog issued from 1851 through 1990—nearly 15,000 in all!

There would probably be a small but enthusiastic market should Whitman Publishing ever put out *A Guide Book of American Numismatic Literature.* Right now, there is no single place to learn the market value of a given Haseltine, Hesslein, Harzfeld, Hollinbeck, or Heritage auction catalog and what its contents or emphasis might have been. Some books were very common in their time, and turn up with frequency today. However, there is no specific, handy source to turn to for information on the many editions of the *Hub Coin Book, Star Rare Coin Encyclopedia,* or Evans's *History of the United States Mint,* to mention just three ubiquitous titles.

Catalogs with auction and mail-bid offerings of out-of-print books by a generation of dealers form another valuable source of information. The detailed descriptions in the catalog of the John J. Ford, Jr., Library Sale, Part I, conducted by George F. Kolbe in the summer of 2004, provided at least a day's worth of reading, with certain lot descriptions in the form of essays, or almost. Nor should I overlook his catalogs of the past, well over 90 in all, including four sales of the Harry W. Bass, Jr., Library, the Whitman reference library ("A Great

American Numismatic Library"), the Essex Institute, Ted Craige Library, and more.

Certain of the catalogs of Charles E. Davis, not offered frequently, are of fascinating content as well. In the past, Cal Wilson published a newsletter, the *Numismatic Repository*, which made good reading; and *Out on a Limb*, by Myron Xenos and Ken Lowe, included news of publications plus travelogues, convention gossip, and the like. The same duo conducted more than 30 sales under the "Money Tree" trade style. At one time, Frank J. Katen (of Milford, Connecticut, later of Washington, DC) was prominent in the field. Orville Grady held more than 20 sales, but none recently. Today, Fred Lake and a few others issue modest mail-bid catalogs with the advantage that many items are inexpensive, often selling for just a few dollars, and seldom beyond a few hundred dollars. Often, bids can be placed by e-mail in addition to regular letter mail. To learn about the dealers who produce catalogs or have Internet offerings, check a current issue of *The Asylum*.

Periodicals

I find numismatic periodicals to be a particularly great source of information. The possibilities include the *American Journal of Numismatics* from 1866 to about 1914 (after which it turned into a series of monographs on scattered subjects), *The Numismatist* from 1888 to date, *The Numismatic Scrapbook Magazine* from 1935 to 1976, and the *Essay-Proof Journal* in 50 volumes, beginning in 1944. These four form an excellent foundation for research on coins and paper money, collectors, the market, history as it was being made, and more. None of these have been properly indexed and cross-indexed as to *content* (not just by title). Should anyone ever do this, it will be a boon to the hobby.

A full set of the *American Journal of Numismatics*, if in nice bindings, is apt to challenge the $15,000 mark. Also available are facsimile reprints by the Johnson Reprint Corporation. The *AJN* was often printed on brittle paper, and thus original

copies must be handled with care. I love my set and refer to it often. In 1989 the ANS revived the title for a new series.

The Numismatist, brainchild of Monroe, Michigan, medical doctor George F. Heath, first saw the light of day in 1888. From then to the present day it has been issued nearly every month (with some skips and double-dated issues in the early days). Ever since the 1890s it has been the official publication of the American Numismatic Association (ANA). In 2003, "The" was dropped from the title—a move said to be appropriate for a publication that wants to be part of the modern age. Availability of copies ranges from scarce to rare for the early issues, 1888 to 1893, some sets of which have gone far past the $10,000 mark at auction. However, issues from about 1894 onward are fairly inexpensive, and for a few thousand dollars you can get every one from about 1900 to date. This will give you enough reading to last an entire summer or winter, even if you just skim through them!

The *Numismatic Scrapbook Magazine* is a treasure trove in itself, and during the period it was issued, up to the early 1960s, was the most popular of all numismatic periodicals, after which it took a back seat to *Coin World*, *Numismatic News*, and others, finally ceasing publication in 1976. The *Scrapbook*, not known to modern collectors, is often available relatively inexpensively, at around $1,000, give or take, depending on the condition and binding.

I strongly recommend that you acquire as many of the preceding periodicals as you can. Reading them will be interesting and enlightening, a never-ending source of information and enjoyment.

Another favorite of mine, *The Essay-Proof Journal*, is not widely known. This little magazine is remarkable for its scholarly content on the engraving and production of paper money, with much on stamps as well (the vignettes for both fields were often produced by the same people). Full sets of 50 volumes are not offered with regularity, but in 2004 one changed hands for about $2,500, although George Kolbe informs me that this was quite a bit more than the usual going price.[101] The focus of the *Journal* is narrow, and, likely, this will not be on your list of must-have titles unless you enjoy the history of currency.

Numismatic News, first published as a monthly in 1952 and containing mostly classified advertisements, expanded rapidly under the leadership of Chet Krause, later joined by Cliff Mishler and others, to become a very dynamic periodical, with weekly deadlines beginning in the 1960s. Meanwhile in 1960 *Coin World* was launched as the first weekly, and went from one success to another, catching the wave of the coin market at the time, and achieving a peak of more than 150,000 readers! After the coin boom, fueled by the 1960-D Small Date Lincoln cent, the 1950-D Jefferson nickel, and other coins (plus a great deal of enthusiasm), came to an end in 1964, the subscription numbers faded. However, news coverage expanded, and an issue today contains more information than ever. Although I have been a columnist for *Coin World* since the early 1960s, I never seem to have enough time to read through each issue as it arrives.

Coins magazine, issued by Krause Publications, and *COINage*, published in California, appear monthly, are color illustrated, and are mainly sold in newsstands. Each has a fine editorial team and contains many interesting articles. Curiously, relatively few people collect back issues of *Numismatic News*, *Coin World*, *Coins* magazine, or *COINage*, and I must confess that I don't either. However, there is a gold mine of information in them—and anyone with the appropriate storage space would do well to get some. The cost is apt to be minimal.

The Coin Dealer Newsletter (launched in 1963) and *The Certified Coin Dealer Newsletter* contain a tremendous amount of market data. A few years ago, on behalf of the owners of these publications, I compiled a book on their history, illustrating sample prices from each year—a study valuable to anyone interested in market changes and cycles.

Most periodicals from the 1940s to date are very inexpensive, and at coin-club meetings and conventions they are often available for the taking as old-timers empty their shelves. However, few people seriously collect these. For someone to have a full run of *Numismatic News* since 1952 and a set of *Coin World* since 1960 would be very unusual. I do not have such sets myself, but probably should! Although having originals of older publications is desirable, in my opinion, I would be a customer for a searchable file of modern periodicals on CD-ROM, if such is ever published. The ANS recently published a CD-ROM of all back issues of *The Colonial Newsletter*, and I rushed to order one—a fantastic bargain in terms of information.

Special-interest periodicals are generally inexpensive to acquire, and when read will yield much information. Among my favorites are *Paper Money*, *The John Reich Journal*, *The Gobrecht Journal*, *Longacre's Ledger*, *The Token and Medal Society Journal*, *The Journal of the Civil War Token Society*, *Penny-Wise*, *Colonial Coin Collectors Club Newsletter*, *The Bank Note Reporter*, and the aforementioned *Colonial Newsletter* and *The Asylum*. I subscribe to all of these—and more—and enjoy most of them (but not necessarily every issue of each).

Many different general-interest coin clubs and regional societies also produce bulletins and newsletters; *Fun Topics*, issued by the Florida United Numismatists, is just one of many examples. In recent times a number of e-zines have been put on the Internet, following the footsteps of the *E-Sylum* of the Numismatic Bibliomania Society. The main problem with all of these is their ephemeral nature. Even if back "issues" are gathered together in one spot and indexed, to me they lack the permanence of a good old-fashioned paper periodical. However, e-zines have the undeniable advantage of timeliness and instant reporting of the news.

Dealer Magazines and Newspapers

Highly collectible are magazines and house organs published by rare coin dealers. The first to do so in a significant way was Ebenezer Locke Mason, Jr., a Philadelphian who entered the coin trade in the late 1850s. His magazines, issued in several series over a long period of time from the late 1860s, are fascinating to read today.

The 59 issues of Édouard Frossard's *Numisma* make lively reading and imparts a good sense of what the hobby was like in the span during which it was published, January 1877 to December 1891. The Mason and Frossard series are available as reprints (by Charles E. Davis and Remy Bourne).

The Coin Collector's Journal, published from December 1875 until January 1888 by J.W. Scott & Co., was first edited by Édouard Frossard, then for years by David U. Proskey, and comprises 157 issues. In 1892 the title was borrowed or swiped (or just picked up, as it was not being used) by the C.H. Trask Stamp & Publishing Co., in Connecticut, which turned out nine issues of its own *Coin Collector's Journal*, a publication of no account, the last in April 1893. In 1934 the long-unused name was

revivified by Wayte Raymond, who conducted the publication until the late 1950s. In total 160 issues were published—rather boring from an editorial viewpoint in comparison to the lively *Numismatic Scrapbook Magazine*, but containing feature articles and, later, monographs, some of which are highly important sources today.

Now and then, particularly during the great nationwide interest in hobbies in the 1880s, newspapers featuring stamps, coins, birds' eggs, and other collectibles appeared, usually to flourish briefly and then fade away, although *Curiosity World*, issued by John M. Hubbard in Lake Village, New Hampshire, endured for the best part of a decade. Remy Bourne has studied these niche publications and has published his findings on them, these compilations being available on loan from the ANA Library. Although they are not necessarily valuable, some of these ephemeral newspapers are very rare or even one of a kind. When

"Mason's Photographic Gallery of the Coin Collectors of the United States, No. 1," published in the March 1869 issue of *Mason's Coin and Stamp Collectors' Magazine*, illustrates many prominent figures of the day. The two larger photographs at the center are of J.J. Mickley and Montroville W. Dickeson. No. 1 stands as the only one, for No. 2 was never published.

The front page of the first issue of Ed. Frossard's house organ, *Numisma*, January 1877, was composed of advertisements from various dealers. Although news of the hobby and trade was carried, the journal was composed mainly of Frossard's own opinions and observations. Today, a file of these is a fine addition to a numismatic library and provides enjoyable reading.

found, the value of such items is apt to be nominal, on the order of $5 to $10 or so, but there can be exceptions.

In the late 19th and early 20th centuries several dealers turned out magazines, most of which are scarce today. The best of the lot was *Mehl's Numismatic Monthly*; others include *The Coin Journal*, *Steigerwalt's Coin Journal*, *Numismatic News*, *The Curio*, *Elder Monthly*, and the *Numismatic Philistine* (which takes the prize for the most mean-spirited numismatic publication ever printed—perhaps one reason for its short lifespan).

Stack's for a time in the 1940s published the well-regarded *Numismatic Review*, New Netherlands issued the thin but ever-interesting *Numisma*, and beginning in 1958 I edited *Empire Topics*, which led to other magazines over the years, including the *Rare Coin Review* (for a 150-issue run) and

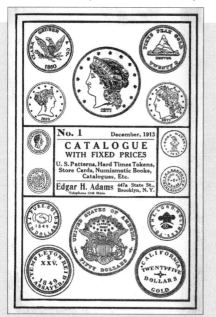

Cover of catalogue no. 1, issued by Edgar H. Adams, December 1913. The interior was primarily devoted to an extensive offering of U.S. pattern coins, each individually priced. Among the offerings, an 1856 Flying Eagle cent was priced at $7.50, and a wide selection of different 1858 pattern cents could be purchased for $3 each.

the current *Numismatic Sun*. Whitman Publishing issued the useful monthly *Whitman Numismatic Journal*, edited by Kenneth Bressett, from 1964 through 1968.

For the most part, these are inexpensive when found. As to which dealer magazines are worth buying to *read*, this is best ascertained by borrowing some from the ANA Library or from a collector, to see what you like. Again, I mention that having a popular and regularly updated guide, with rarity and price information, to the field of out-of-print numismatic literature would be a godsend to all of us.

Fixed-Price Catalogs

Over a long period of years many dealers have issued fixed-price catalogs, not in magazine or house-organ format, but simply as listings of coins with retail prices. In the 19th century J.W. Scott and some others issued lists with just about *everything* included—from common coins to great rarities. Prices were given for each, indicating what would be charged *if* such coins were in stock. Today, such catalogs are of limited interest. More desirable are fixed-price offerings of actual inventory (like those issued by Edgar H. Adams and Elmer S. Sears in the early 20th century), especially if narrative descriptions accompany the basic information.

In later years, many companies issued catalogs. Hundreds of different examples can be collected from the 1940s to date, usually at nominal cost. Of special interest are offerings of notable collections, the Major Lenox R. Lohr Collection of pattern coins (Empire Coin Company), the Wilkison Collection of gold patterns (Paramount International Coin Corporation), the Brobston Collection of half cents (Stack's), the Dr. J. Hewitt Judd Collection (Abe Kosoff), and the John W. Adams Collection of 1794 cents (Bowers and Merena, 1982), to name just a few.

Auction Catalogs

Auction catalogs issued by dealers are very collectible, especially if the person or firm has achieved numismatic recognition.

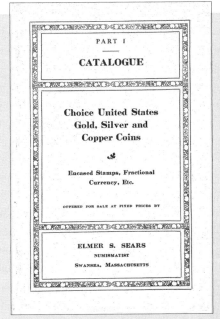

Undated catalog, circa 1918, by Elmer S. Sears of Swansea, Massachusetts, who had recently dissolved his partnership with Wayte Raymond in the United States Coin Co., New York. Page 11 offers a spectacular selection of quarter eagles, including the "finest specimen known" of the 1796 No Stars and other delicacies. Generally, modern-day researchers have pored through most early 20th-century auction catalogs but have overlooked fixed-price lists. Therein can be found many interesting things.

Accordingly, the 19th-century catalogs of W. Elliott Woodward, Edward D. Cogan, the Chapman brothers, the New York Coin & Stamp Company, John W. Haseltine, and several others are eagerly sought. Copies in their original bindings, and those containing photographic plates of the coins being offered, are especially prized by collectors. Some of these were issued for public auctions with in-person attendance by bidders, while others were mail-bid catalogs, with no public participation.

In addition to those offered by "name" issuers of numismatic ability and importance, there are many small catalogs, leaflets, and broadsides produced by auctioneers of general material such as art, books, bric-a-brac, and antiques, who occasionally offered coins. Such names as Bangs, Thomas, Leavitt, McGillvray, Birch, Leonard, and Pennypacker come to mind as I write these words. In many cases there is no identification of the person who did the coin descriptions, which

were usually meager at best. In other instances the same auction houses served as venues for sales cataloged by well-known dealers. No complete catalog of these minor auctioneers of coins is currently available in a single volume, but extensive, indeed exhaustive research has been done by Martin Gengerke for earlier issues and Karl Moulton for later ones.

Among early 20th-century auction catalogs, those by the Chapman brothers, and later (beginning in the summer of 1906) by Henry and S. Hudson Chapman individually, are highly desired by collectors, especially certain editions that have photographic plates. The latter can be very expensive and on occasion run into thousands of dollars. However, normal "paper copies" (as they are called) are apt to be quite affordable. Content is important, and a catalog featuring the holdings of a well-known numismatist is more valuable than one with an obscure offering. Never mind that the obscure presentation might be

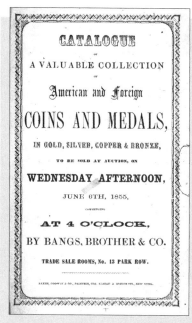

Cover of the Bangs, Brother & Co. offering of the Pierre Flandin Collection, June 6, 1855, one of the more important early auctions of coins to be held in the United States. The offering comprised 230 lots and realized a total of $736.02. Historian Attinelli opined, "This catalogue was, I believe, also issued with date of April 28." The name of Flandin does not appear in the catalog, but was known widely, including to George Parish, Jr., early numismatic bibliophile (cf. *American Journal of Numismatics*, August 1866). The identity of the person writing the catalog remains a mystery to this day.

The Charles White Collection, Part II, sale catalog with paper cover by Harlan P. Smith, New York City, April 15, 1887. Containing 521 numbered lots, the auction realized a grand total of $1,793. According to notes in this copy, carefully annotated by hand by dealer J. Colvin Randall, who was present at the event. Also shown is page 12 from the catalog.

Copies with notations of the prices realized and the names of the buyers are interesting to collect today. Such named-and-priced catalogs were made in several ways: (1) by persons attending the sale or by the dealer who cataloged it; (2) by a clerk in the dealer's office, who often listed just the prices and not the names; or (3) by later collectors who copied the information to make their catalogs more useful.

As is often the case in numismatics, one investigation can lead to another. Concerning White, who built the collection, in the 1850s and 1860s he was cashier of the Northampton Bank in Massachusetts and signed paper money issued by the bank. In 1865 this institution became the Northampton National Bank, charter number 1018. White later moved to New York City. As a numismatist he had many interests, with early quarter dollars being a particular specialty. Part I of his collection was auctioned on March 9, 1886, in a catalog prepared by Harlan P. Smith, and Part II was sold on April 11, 1887, as illustrated here.

Among the buyers noted (with abbreviations, such as "Steig") on page 12 are Charles Steigerwalt, J. Colvin Randall, H.G. Sampson, Ed. Frossard, B.H. Collins, and "Rogers."

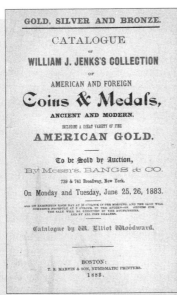

Photographic plate and title page of W. Elliot Woodward's catalog of the William J. Jenks Collection. Comprising 1,407 numbered lots, the sale was conducted in the auction room of Messrs. Bangs & Co., 739 and 741 Broadway, New York City. The plate was photographed on a single negative by placing each coin in position. Relatively few of Woodward's catalogs were illustrated. Of those that were, the coins depicted were not necessarily the most valuable in the sale.

Among the coins depicted are: Lot 109 (1799 $1 Uncirculated), 111 (1800 $1 Uncirculated), 114 (copy of an 1804 dollar, so described, "very desirable for comparison"), 131 (an original 1851 dollar), 845 (reverse of a pattern dollar of 1870, part of a five-coin pattern set offered as one lot), 848 (pattern $1, "Liberty personified as an Indian queen"), and 170 to 172 (rare half dollars of 1796 and 1797, each showing wear).

more rare. There are scattered exceptions, especially among famous numismatists who sometimes issued hard-to-find catalogs. Accordingly, a rare but numismatically meaningless catalog issued by Emmanuel J. Attinelli might bring hundreds of dollars, simply as a collectors' item.

The catalogs of B. Max Mehl from 1906 to 1955 are sometimes collected systematically, but most buyers skip the unimportant sales and concentrate on the highlights such as James Ten Eyck (1922), William Forrester Dunham (1941; Mehl's most important sale), and William Cutler Atwater (1946). *All* of Mehl's auction catalogs were of the mail-bid type.

The 294 auction catalogs of Thomas L. Elder, issued in New York from 1903 to 1940, have been a gold mine of information for me. However, most are rather unprepossessing in appearance, scarcely more than 20 or so have plates, and they are usually available on a catch-as-catch-can basis—individual issues here and there, hardly ever complete runs (although I would love to buy a set, a variation on my usual emphasis of buying selected catalogs of interest).

Elder's catalogs had no indexes, and the title page often gave no clues to important pieces within, so the only solution—a pleasant one—is to look through them all. I have often thought that in today's era of electronic information it would be a worthwhile project for the ANA, the ANS, the Numismatic Bibliomania Society, or some other enlightened organization to create CD-ROM copies of some of these essentially unobtainable references. In that way anyone could sample the contents of these treasures.

There are many other important catalogs from the first half of the 20th century, with the World's Greatest Collection (the name given to the F.C.C. Boyd Collection) by the Numismatic Gallery, 1944 and 1945 being especially important, Stack's sales of the Flanagan and Bell collections (1944), and dozens more. Most of these have skimpy or bare-bones descriptions that offer little in the way of information not found, for example, in the contemporary *Standard Catalog*. Still, as reflections of the art of cataloging of their era they are worth having.

The Adams Study

John W. Adams, builder of a fabulous collection of large copper cents, has emphasized other specialties since then, including numismatic books and early medals. For books he created two impressive studies, published by George F. Kolbe: *United States Numismatic Literature*, Volumes 1 (1982) and 2 (1990). Adams assigned a "quality rating" to each catalog, based on his opinion, reflecting the contents. Catalogs of particular excellence were given the highest rating, A+, while those that deserved no more than passing notice were assigned a "C–."

Among the catalogs of W. Elliot Woodward, the following have A+ ratings: (1) Sale 9, May 17–21, 1864, John F. McCoy Collection; (2) Sale 10, October 18–22, 1864, Levick, Emery, Ilsley & Abbey Collection; (3) Sale 17, October 28, 1867, Jos. J. Mickley Collection; (4) Sale "C," December 5–7, 1871, Dr. Chas. Clay Collection; (5) Sale 62, January 8–10, 1884, Heman Ely Collection; and (6) Sale 77, June 29–July 1, 1885, J.C. Randall Collection.

Jumping ahead to the 20th century, Adams gives these A+ ratings for the catalogs of B. Max Mehl (issued 1905 to 1955): (1) Sale 63, May 2, 1922, James Ten Eyck Collection; (2) Sale 97, June 3, 1941, William Forrester Dunham Collection; (3) Sale 108, June 11, 1946, William C. Atwater Collection; and (4) Sale 110, June 17, 1947, Will W. Neil Collection.

Stack's, for the period studied (up to and including 1975), came in with an A+ listing for Sale 74, December 7–9, 1944, the J.F. Bell Collection.

From the standpoint of readability and numismatic content during the third quarter of the 20th century, the catalogs of New Netherlands Coin Company, New York, take the prize, at least in my opinion. Generally, these were not impressive from a graphics viewpoint, with type crowded together, erratic punctuation and abbreviations, and so on, with scattered plates, but the writing was apt to be fascinating. Only two of them were awarded the coveted A+ by Adams: Sale 38, August 16–21, 1952, 1952 ANA Catalog, Downing, Lathrop, et al. Collections; and Sale 60, December 3–4, 1968, 60th Public Auction, Brand, Lathrop, et al. Collections.

Although New Netherlands had been formed in 1936 by Moritz Wormser, the turning point came in 1950 when John J. Ford, Jr., was hired as a partner by Charles M. Wormser, son of the founder. Beginning in 1952, particularly with the ANA Convention catalog, Ford, with the assistance of staffer Walter Breen, decided that if a word could be used to describe a coin, a sentence was better, and that if someone else was apt to use a sentence, New Netherlands would use a paragraph!

New Netherlands offerings were filled with all sorts of side comments, such as "back room boys" scrubbing and cleaning coins; dealers "touting" bulk coins for investment; other coins (not the ones being offered in the catalog at the moment) being ratty, decrepit, or worse; and so on. All of this was highly entertaining in its time, and attracted a lot of attention.

I recall in the 1950s that the arrival of a New Netherlands catalog would always make me drop everything and start reading, while the catalogs of others could wait until I had leisure time. Ford left New Netherlands about 1970, and although some fine catalogs were issued after that time, this marked the end of the golden era. Today, New Netherlands catalogs are easily enough collected, usually one at a time. Incidentally, my personal favorites include a few not on the A+ list, especially offerings of obscure tokens and medals for which I could not find information easily elsewhere. The Adams study did not go past 1975. Had it done so, no doubt Stack's would have garnered more A+ listings, and there would be accolades for many catalogs of other firms as well.

My advice on buying early auction catalogs is to acquire ones that are either highly acclaimed by Adams (rated, say, B or finer), adding, as appropriate, any others that are of interest to you. As an example, if you are interested in pattern coins, a B catalog with a lot of patterns is a better buy than an A+ catalog filled with rare early U.S. gold, but without a pattern in sight.

Collecting them systematically can be very expensive for Chapman catalogs with photographic plates; but for long series of catalogs by J.W. Haseltine, Édouard Frossard, Lyman Low, and most others of the late 19th century, ordinary copies (not specially bound or with plates) are very affordable. If it comes to a choice, a copy with the prices inked or penciled next to the lots is preferable to one without prices. Better yet, and occasionally found, are copies with prices and also the buyers' registered names. Real names such as Cogan, Woodward, and Chapman will be seen, along with pseudonyms as "North," "Moneta," "Hotchkiss," "Brutus," and more (see below). Such catalogs cost more and are worth it. A degree of flexibility is needed regarding condition, and occasional frayed covers, a tear on a page, or a few stains are best overlooked.

Pseudonyms and Such

In our hobby many people have used pseudonyms, or false names, when bidding in auctions, or noms de plume (pen names) when writing. Collectors of out-of-print publications may find some examples to be of interest.

Charles French, who produced many auction catalogs in the mid-20th century, was born as Charles Lehrenkraus. Richard S. Yeoman, originator of the *Guide Book*, was born with the surname Yeo. T. Harrison Garrett, the famous Baltimore collector, was fond of bidding under pseudonyms, including "South," "Princeton," and "Hotchkiss."

Names, sometimes of dead persons or of living famous persons, have been assigned to titles of auction sales even though the offerings were primarily composed of material from other sources. Examples include the Clarke Gilhousen Collection, Thomas Melish Collection, Adolphe Menjou Collection, and Isaac Edmunds Collection.

Noms de plume have been used many times to sign articles in *The Numismatist*, newspaper articles, publications of whimsy, and the like, examples being "M.N. Dacius," "I. Conoclast," "Matt Nummus," "S.S. Elreep," "Mintmark," "Dahlonega," "Coinetta," "George K. Hickorynuts," "Justitia," "Jonathan Oldbuck," "Gointoem Strong," and "Mark Mintmorgan."

In the 1904 sale by the Chapman brothers of the John G. Mills Collection (April 27–29), pseudonyms used by bidders included "Loop" (Thomas L. Elder) and "Drive" (B. Max Mehl).[102] Further, "Hercules" was the pseudonym used by the buyer of the 1804 silver dollar and 1787 Brasher doubloon in the 1907 sale by Henry Chapman of the Matthew A. Stickney Collection, with Chapman personally representing "Hercules" (J.W. Ellsworth). At sales of the 1860s "Moneta" was a frequent buyer. Farran Zerbe often used the name "Portuguese Joe" as a pseudonym, "joe" being slang for a particular coin of that country.

There are many more examples of false names used in our hobby. A perusal of the literature will uncover a great many of these, much to the delight and entertainment of the reader.

Sales of Our Own Era

Among later catalogs I run the risk of being somewhat biased, for as I write these words I have fond memories of a number of the great cabinets I have described for Bowers and Ruddy Galleries (with Jim Ruddy), Bowers and Merena Galleries (now owned by Spectrum), and my present connection with American Numismatic Rarities (ANR).

The Garrett Collection, sold for The Johns Hopkins University between 1979 and 1981, will forever remain a highlight of my own career and of the numismatic world, as nothing like it had ever been sold before. The Eliasberg Collection, the gold coins of which I cataloged in 1982, and the silver, nickel, and copper coins with staff assistance in 1996 and 1997, are likewise unprecedented, to which can be added the fabulous gold coins of the world from the same cabinet, consigned to ANR in 2004 and sold in 2005 (with cataloging mainly done by John Kraljevich, Frank Van Valen, and John Pack, while I watched with admiration—and contributed a few notes). The Norweb Collection, Childs Collection, Harry W. Bass, Jr., Collection (the most extensive collection of gold coin varieties ever formed), and others come to mind—a long list.

At the same time, Stack's, New England Rare Coin Galleries, Steve Ivy, Mid-American, Paramount, David W. Akers, Rare Coin Company of America (RARCOA), Heritage, Larry and Ira Goldberg, Pacific Coast Auction Galleries, Lyn F. Knight, Sotheby's (occasionally issuing catalogs with notable coin content), Superior, David Lawrence Rare Coins (DLRC), Smythe & Co., and other firms have each had their share of successes, some spectacular.

If I ever write an autobiography I will have to mention that for the art auction house of Christie's, in 2000 I wrote an entire coin catalog (of gold treasure from the *S.S. Central America*), and in 2004 and 2005 I made "guest appearances" in a John J. Ford, Jr., Collection catalog issued by Stack's and a Herb and Martha Schingoethe Collection catalog under the R.M. Smythe & Co. imprint. Great fun!

Most modern auction catalogs issued this side of 1950 are quite inexpensive, and a useful and extensive library can be formed for very little—enough to solidly weight down a well-constructed bookshelf! Don't overlook these treasures, for they are certainly worth having. In fact, in terms of useful content, history, and other information, auction catalogs of the past 50 years handily eclipse those of the previous century! Bookseller Karl Moulton occasionally publishes extensive catalogs of these, and I dare say that for less than $2,000 you can get most of the "name" sales from this later period.

As these words are being written it is common practice for auction houses to post most if not all of their listings on the Internet. To me these are useful and productive, but for permanence and the joy of collecting, I hope that paper catalogs are never rendered obsolete.

Books About U.S. Coins and Paper Money

The collecting of out-of-print books relating to American numismatics is a separate specialty. Some of these, such as John H. Hickcox's 1858 151-page book, *An Historical Account of American Coinage*, printed to the extent of only 200 regular copies plus five on large paper, are very rare today. This particular volume utilizes five separate pages of plates, by J.E. Gavit of Albany, some of them made earlier for the 1850 *Documentary History of the State of New York*, by E.B. O'Callaghan. Gavit was one of the eight engraving firms that combined to form the American Bank Note Co. in 1858, perhaps worth mentioning only if to illustrate that a simple book can have many connections if it is studied carefully.

The *Pledges of History: A Brief Account of the Collection of Coins Belonging to the Mint of the United States, More Particularly of the Antique Specimens*, by William E. Dubois (1846), is likewise rare; and *New Varieties of Gold and Silver Coins, Counterfeit Coins, Bullion with Mint Values*, by William E. Dubois and Jacob Reese Eckfeldt (1850 and other editions), is not rare, but as it contains lots of information on coins made in the California Gold Rush, and as some copies actually contain some authentic gold dust under clear mica affixed to a page, I have seen these run into the thousands of dollars. However, a few years ago $6,000 was paid for a copy by a collector of rocks and minerals, while at the same time I bought one on the numismatic market for $800.

A fine copy of the rare and numismatically significant book *Pledges of History*. (David M. Sundman library)

The *Standard Catalogue of United States Coins & Currency* made its debut in 1934, in a binding and general appearance similar to that used for Scott's *Standard Postage Stamp Catalogue*. The publisher was Scott Stamp & Coin Co., 1 West 47th Street, New York City. The Coin Department was managed by Wayte Raymond. The *Standard Catalogue*, which appeared under several title variations, was published in 18 editions through 1958.

The best way to determine what books you might like to collect is to read texts on American numismatic history, perhaps including my comments here, and to visit a library and examine the copies. If something is rare, but unattractive and not useful, I would not find it particularly interesting to acquire. On the other hand, if it is both scarce and very important—such as W.L. Ormsby's *Bank Note Engraving* (1852), there might be reason to pay several thousand dollars for a copy. The choice is up to you.

Often, numismatic books can be collected within a coin specialty. For a collector of early cents of the year 1794, the 1869 study by Dr. Edward Maris, *Varieties of the Copper Issues of the United States Mint in the Year 1794*, will be a prize acquisition, and, to a lesser extent, the monograph Édouard Frossard and W.W. Hays, *Varieties of United States Cents of the Year 1794, Described and Illustrated*, is worth having.

Someone interested in early half dollars can collect the 1881 *Type Table* by J.W. Haseltine, a rather pithy study written from data swiped from J. Colvin Randall, plus the 1929 book by M.L. Beistle, well

done and handsomely printed, *A Register of Half Dollar Die Varieties and Sub-Varieties. Being a Description of Each Die Variety Used in the Coinage of United States Half Dollars*. The last went on to serve as the standard reference in the series for many years, until in 1967 Al C. Overton published *Early Half Dollar Die Varieties 1794–1836*, since revised.

Copies of price references such as *The Standard Catalogue*, issued in 18 editions from 1934 through 1958, form a very nice section of one's library. *A Guide Book of United States Coins*, first published in 1946 (with a cover date of 1947), can be collected by two varieties of the first issue, and one of many editions since (as of 2005, the 59th edition). The 57th edition included an essay, "The *Guide Book* as a Collectible," which gave interesting information. The first edition, printed in November 1946, consisted of 9,000 copies, followed by 9,000 more in the second run in February 1947. At the bottom of page 135 in the first print run a note reads, "which probably accounts for the scarcity of this date," changed in the second to "…the scarcity of 1903-O." A record was set with the 18th edition, dated 1965, at 1,200,000 copies—this being at the peak of the great coin investment boom that started in 1960.

Values for old copies of the *Guide Book* are listed in grades of Very Good, Fine, Very Fine, and New. In VF grade the most expensive is the first printing of the 1947 edition at $750, followed by $650 for the second printing, then a drop off the cliff to $175 for the second and third editions. Most issues of recent years are listed at a dollar or two, almost pocket change.

Rick Bagg of the ANR staff did some checking, and found that of the present list of contributors to the *Guide Book*, the longest tenures have been those of Gene L. Henry (since 1967) and me (since 1958). In one way, 1958 seems like yesterday. In another way it is positively antediluvian in terms of the changes the hobby has experienced.

Books on Other Subjects

At this point I have touched mainly on references treating U.S. *coins*, but I hasten to note that tokens, medals, and paper money also offer a rich field for collecting out-of-print numismatic publications. Some leaflets by Jacob Perkins, innovator in the bank note field, are worth collecting if you can find them, and the book by Greville and Dorothy Bathe, *Jacob Perkins, His Inventions, His Times, and His Contemporaries* (1943), of which only 200 copies were printed, is a landmark in numismatic literature today. (I do not possess an original, but just a copy.) Ormsby's 1852 book has been mentioned, to which can be added any number of counterfeit detectors (periodicals issued to banks and merchants to help them identify false currency as well as a long series issued by Laban Heath beginning in the 1860s), reports of state banking

Ken Bressett (right) and his son Phil at the Whitman Publishing offices on April 13, 2004, checking on prices and finalizing the 58th edition of *A Guide Book of United States Coins*, which was released in the summer of the same year. Also on hand to help were Jeff Garrett and the present writer.

Sections of Ken Bressett's private library, with thousands of books, catalogs, and other publications on just about every numismatic subject—from primitive and ancient money down to the present day.

commissions, and, for that matter, the annual reports of the Director of the Mint.

The bibliographies given in the chapters above furnish a good place to start a specialized library. A good plan is to start with the most recent or the most comprehensive book first, then fill in others later.

There is no limit to collecting printed items, and tens of thousands of titles beckon. Most likely you will investigate the field and narrow down to things of interest, perhaps a shelf or even a bookcase full. To these can be added other books and magazines on American history, old directories, and more.

In the paper-money section of my library I have a couple hundred books and brochures issued by banks and describing their history, hundreds of old copies of *Hunt's Merchant's Magazine* and *Banker's Magazine*, scattered reports of the Comptroller of the Treasury, a few dozen yearly banking almanacs and directors, and quite a few texts on finance and economics. The Society of Paper Money Collectors (SOPMC) has turned in a brilliant performance in sponsoring the publication of individual histories on obsolete bank notes and scrip from many different states—wonderful resources, and I treasure them all.

Grading and Condition of Publications

There are no universally applied standards for grading books. George F. Kolbe listed these guidelines in a recent catalog:

As New/Mint: No signs of wear or defects.
Very Fine: Near new, minimal signs of use.
Fine: Nice clean copy, slight signs of use.
Very Good: Some wear, no serious defects.
Good: Average used and worn book, complete.
Reading Copy: Poor but readable.
Ex-Library: With library identification marks.

I buy as many books each year as anyone I know. The following section contains some buying guidelines that I have found to be useful.

Tips for Being a Smart Buyer of Books

Be aware. I usually buy most of my books from the same sellers, some of whom I have been doing business with for many years. Virtually every *numismatic* bookseller is fair, describes condition properly, and, if the book is not an auction item, usually grants a return privilege. Most if not all are members of the Numismatic Bibliomania Society.

I also buy a lot of books on the Internet. In that milieu, transactions with established booksellers (such as members of the Antiquarian Booksellers Association of America, or ABAA) who issue catalogs and have expertise are nearly always good, although prices may be higher for choice and rare items (just like with coins!). Mom-and-pop bookstores and casual sellers are a different story completely. Be aware.

Below are some questions I often ask if a listing does not contain details. Some of them are obvious, but each year I get some books that are reprints not described as such, or well-worn copies with no mention of their taped-up bindings or missing pages, and so on. I return them, but there is an annoyance factor, and not everyone allows returns. Some questions you might ask are these:

- Describe the condition of the binding. Is it tight or is it loose?
- Describe the cover and binding imprints—lettered and sharp, faded, or—?
- What does the back of the title page say about the printing date and edition?
- Any water staining?
- If there were maps or plates (often listed in a table in the front of the book) are they all present?
- Are any pages torn or incomplete?
- If there are markings on the book, what are they? (I don't mind library stamps, and to me a nice bookplate or signature of a former owner is fine, but I do not want one with crayon scribbling, etc.)

- Is there a return privilege?

Most casual sellers of books may not want to answer a barrage of questions, so a good first approach is simply to say, "Please tell me all you can about the appearance and condition of the book."

Books as an Investment: George Kolbe's View

Are books a good *financial* investment on their own, without regard to any other consideration? My quick answer is "usually not." I asked dealer George F. Kolbe about this, and here is what he said:

> I have always thought of numismatic literature as an investment in *knowledge* and have never considered it a financial investment vehicle. To my knowledge, Armand Champa is one of the few bibliophiles who, over the years, seemed to be motivated in a meaningful degree by an investment mentality in the formation of his remarkable library. Factoring in binding and travel costs over the years, I would guess that the sale of his landmark library (in a series of very successful landmark auctions by Bowers and Merena Galleries) produced mixed financial results.
>
> The sales of the Harry W. Bass, Jr., and John J. Ford, Jr., libraries are another story. In both cases, the libraries brought far more than the costs involved. But this is due to the era in which they were formed. By the time that Champa began to be active—the beginning of the modern numismatic-literature market in the early 1970s—the Bass library was well along in its formation, and the Ford library had been essentially formed. Item for item, Champa paid far more than did either Bass or Ford.
>
> Some numismatic publications actually sell for less than they did in 1967, when I issued my first price list of rare and out-of-print numismatic literature. Others bring many, many times more. Who knows what the future holds? Are some rare numismatic pub-

lications currently selling for more than they are worth? Perhaps. Others are, no doubt, still quite underappreciated. I am convinced that the person who forms a numismatic library guided by good judgment and taste will be happier when it is dispersed than his or her investor counterpart, regardless of economic return.[103]

The key to investing in books is *knowledge*, which Kolbe gives as his prime reason for buying them. I have thought this for a long time. However, knowledge is also the *key to profit*, and in that way books can be a superb financial investment in the long run—just as going to law school is a good "financial investment" for a lawyer, although it might not be stated that way. To the concepts of knowledge and return on investment can be added *pleasure*, for some books are simply delightful to read.

$5,000 to $10,000 Will Do It!

Probably for less than $10,000 total, you can acquire a good working library of most issues of *The Numismatist* from the early 20th century to date, all issues of *The Numismatic Scrapbook Magazine*, several hundred pounds of modern newspapers and magazines, and hundreds of pounds of modern auction catalogs. Included in the same budget will be standard references (reprints for the rarer ones) in popular American series, including specialties such as tokens, medals, and paper money.

For less than $5,000 you can get most periodicals published since about 1940, most important auction catalogs of the same period, and a basic library on U.S. *coins* (not specialties).

My own experience is that sometimes I do not know if I want an old auction catalog, book, or other publication until I see it, as the contents are important. My shelves constitute a *working library*—publications that are used, at least occasionally. I would never collect anything only because it is *rare*. For me, it must be *useful* and *interesting*. Not so long ago, while moving nearly a thousand old auction catalogs and period-

Books and bidders: Action at George Frederick Kolbe's sale of the John J. Ford, Jr., Library, Part I, at the historic Mission Inn in Riverside, California. This grand event realized $1.6 million, setting a record for any American auction of numismatic books. (Photograph by Timothy Williams)

Book dealer and author Charles Davis at his display of items for sale at a coin show. Due to the logistics involved, not many dealers in out-of-print books set up at coin shows, but those who do are highly appreciated.

When I was president of the American Numismatic Association (1983–1985), I recommended to the ANA board of directors that sellers of old numismatic publications should be given a reduced rate for display space at conventions or, better yet, be given *free* space—as few things can contribute more to education (one of the aims of the ANA). The proposal fell on deaf ears.

A view of part of the library of Wayne Homren, editor of the *E-Sylum*, the weekly email newsletter for numismatic bibliophiles and researchers sponsored by the Numismatic Bibliomania Society. A native of Pittsburgh, Wayne's interests include encased postage stamps and American numismatic literature.

icals from one office to another, I looked at some obscure ones, mainly from the 1930s to date, and asked myself this question of each: will I ever open and use this catalog? If the answer was no, as it was for hundreds, I put the catalog in a big pile, invited American Numismatic Galleries staffers to help themselves, then trashed the remainder. I recommend that you not pay good money for any book, catalog, or other publication that you do not plan to enjoy and use.

You can sample before buying simply by visiting a dealer's setup at a coin show, or seeing a copy owned by a friend or fellow coin-club member, or borrowing one from the ANA Library (rarities excepted). Not that an occasional pearl might not be found among them, but there are some entire *runs* of dealer catalogs that, to me, seem to be boring and essentially useless for research, and I will not give them shelf space.

Most collectors of books, catalogs, and magazines are happy to share their lists of favorites, although such lists will vary. Publications I like might be of no interest to someone else, and vice versa.

Remember, books are meant to be read. Do this now and then!

The American Numismatic Association Headquarters

The second largest numismatic library in the United States is housed in the American Numismatic Association Headquarters building, 818 North Cascade Avenue, Colorado Springs, Colorado, the exterior of which is shown here. Sited on the campus of Colorado College, and adjacent to the Fine Arts Center, it is in a very comfortable and inspiring location.

Within its walls is one of the finest research facilities in our hobby, the Dwight N. Manley Numismatic Library. Named for its major donor, the library is a hands-on resource, and members can borrow most titles by mail. Other attractions at ANA Headquarters include exhibits and a visitors' reception area. (Most photographs courtesy of Barbara Gregory, ANA)

Every now and then, including at the Summer Seminar, the ANA Library holds a book sale for members. Hundreds of books, auction catalogs, and other publications are priced for nominal values—bargains galore! Many if not most have been donated by numismatists who have sold their collections or who are weeding out their libraries.

Such donations benefit everyone, and are far better than having miscellaneous books left to heirs who discard them or otherwise keep them from numismatic hands. The American Numismatic Society, New York City, also gratefully accepts donated books.

A few steps away from the ANA Library in the Headquarters building is the Bass Gallery housing the loan collection of Harry W. Bass, Jr.—not books, but coins. Included is the largest collection of varieties of 1795 to 1834 gold coins ever assembled, a complete collection of $3 coins (including the unique 1870-S), a remarkable display of pattern coins, selected rarities in American currency, and more.

Young visitors to ANA Headquarters admire the displays in one section of the Bass Gallery.

CHAPTER THIRTY-TWO

CONSERVING AND PROTECTING YOUR COLLECTION

The best type of collector is a most valuable member of society. By the best collector I mean one whose pursuit, study and research in connection with his hobby have magnified his imaginative, aesthetic, romantic and intellectual qualities. His wide and varied experiences with various odd and interesting objects, and his painstaking care of them, have given him a remarkable fund of out-of-the-way information, as well as patience, a sense of order and practicality. He is the finest sort of an example of the cultured and refined man.... It emphasizes in no uncertain way that keeping young is largely the result of the mental attitude, for collecting, above all other panaceas, meatless diets, and physical exercise even, keeps people young.

—Thomas L. Elder, December 1916

Cleaning, Dipping, and Conserving Coins

Coins need to be cared for properly. The appearance of rare coins a generation from now will depend on how *you* take care of them. The historical record of numismatic "care" is not pretty.

Today, the vast majority of Proof coins from the 19th century show hairlines and evidence of cleaning, as do many Uncirculated pieces. Moreover, coins that were once toned are now "as you like it," or brilliant. This situation is discussed in chapter 20.

The grade of many if not most Mint State and Proof coins today (excepting hoard coins such as certain gold and silver dollars) is largely influenced by *numismatic handling*. Absent this, every Proof coin minted in the 1880s or 1890s would be a superb gem today, say, Proof-67 or finer. Indeed, on rare occasions when coins untouched since the 19th century (e.g., the Garrett Collection and the Clapp-Eliasberg coins) come on the market, the coins are gems.

Comic-strip character Pogo is often credited with saying, "We have met the enemy, and they are *us*," a parody of Perry's War of 1812 statement. Upon checking, I found that Pogo didn't say this, but close, and anyway, it sounds good. Stated another way, we are our own worst enemy.

Over a very long period of time, collectors have been coached that, given two coins, one toned and one bright, the brilliant one is the better, the most desirable, and the most valuable of the two. Copper, nickel, and silver are chemically active metals, and left to their own account they will naturally acquire a patina, or toning (or, as some say, *tarnish*), over time.

The obvious way to restore toned coins to desirable and valuable brilliance is to clean them. This is the advice given from almost day one in the hobby. However, when this is done, it is usually in secrecy. Somehow, a coin should be presented with the implication that because it is brilliant today, it has always been so, carefully preserved by some magical process. As to the hairlines on a bright, brilliant, dazzling Proof-63 coin? Well, we don't talk about how they got there. The coin is still brilliant.

We all love our 19th-century coins. They are what they are, Proof-63 with artificial toning (not usually mentioned and sometimes a problem with certification services, sometimes not), attractive or unattractive natural toning, or fully brilliant (wonder how they got that way?). All Proof-63 coins are collectible, but to me it is useful to understand why they are Proof-63 and not in gem grades.

In the paragraphs to follow I endeavor to explain how all of this happened, and, afterward, to comment on "good" cleaning and "bad" cleaning. This is often interwoven with how coins are handled and stored. These topics are also included.

To start, the historical record.

Three Scenarios

Scenario 1: In 1861 a book by William C. Prime, *Coins, Medals, and Seals, Ancient and Modern,* was published by Harper Brothers. This 292-page octavo-size volume was the first in America to discuss coin handling, storage, and cleaning in detail, including this:

> Clean your coins very carefully. For brass coins use ammonia two parts, prepared chalk one part, by weight. Place them in a phial together; shake well when used. Wash the coin, rubbing it hard with flannel, and clean off quickly with clear water; then polish with dry flannel.
>
> Clean silver coins with soap and water and a soft brush. Never touch acid to silver or copper coins, unless very cautiously.
>
> Clean copper coins with soap and water, then polish them with powdered soapstone on flannel. Never wash a copper coin to give it a bright copper color. The result will be to show all the scratches and bruises on the coin. It is better to leave the dark color untouched, and the soapstone will almost bronze it. Do not touch ammonia or acid to a copper coin.

Scenario 2: In August 1903, Farran Zerbe gave an account of his visit to Philadelphia to see the Mint Collection:

> I found many of the silver Proof coins of late years partially covered with a white coating. On inquiry I learned that an over zealous attendant during the last vacation months when the numismatic room was closed took it on himself to clean the tarnished coins, purchased some metal polish at a department store, and proceeded with his cleaning operation. Later a coating of white

appeared on the coins, which was now slowly disappearing.

> I expressed my displeasure at this improper treatment of Proof coins, and the custodian explained, "That is nothing. I have been here eight years and they have been cleaned three or four times in my time."

Zerbe wryly commented that should such cleaning continue, future visitors to the Mint Collection would see nothing except badly worn coins or even blank discs!

Scenario 3: Dipping silver coins in acid, sometimes with caution recommended (as per Prime in 1861), remained a common practice for many decades afterward. Often used was potassium cyanide, a deadly poison. The August 1921 issue of *The Numismatist* included this account:

> J. Sanford Saltus, an international figure in the numismatic world, died suddenly at the Hotel Metropole, in London, on June 24. Apparently in the best of health up to the time his body was found in his room, the manner of his death was for a time a mystery until an official investigation revealed that it was due to accidental poisoning. His body was discovered lying on the floor, fully dressed, by one of the hotel maids, and it is believed that death occurred several hours before it became known. A verdict of "death by misadventure" was rendered by the coroner's jury.
>
> The evidence at the inquest disclosed the fact that on the day before his death he had purchased a small quantity of potassium cyanide for the purpose of cleaning some recent purchases of silver coins and retired to his room. Shortly afterward he ordered a bottle of ginger ale. A glass containing the poison and a glass containing the ginger ale were found side by side on the dressing table, and it is believed that while interested in cleaning the coins he took a drink of the poison in

mistake for the ginger ale. Potassium cyanide, although one of the most deadly poisons, is frequently used by collectors in cleaning coins, as it will have the desired effect when other methods fail....

The passing of Saltus did not deter collectors and dealers from the practice. In the 1950s, Dayton, Ohio, dealer Jim Kelly told me that potassium cyanide was the best of all cleaners for silver coins, as it removed rubbing and scuffs from the higher points and made some About Uncirculated coins appear as full Uncirculated. This was particularly effective for Liberty Seated silver, he said. I've never tried the method myself, and do not intend to—nor should you!

If you want a *fourth* scenario, check American Numismatic Association (ANA) president J. Henri Ripstra's poor advice quoted in chapter 20. In fact, space and your indulgence permitting, I could cite dozens of other articles, advisories, and suggestions that, by all means, coins should be kept "bright" and "brilliant" by cleaning them! However, the past is past—on to more positive things.

Good (Really) Advice From Heaton

The August 1894 issue of *The Numismatist* commenced with an article by Augustus G. Heaton on the topic of preserving coins, and is probably the single best commentary I have encountered in 19th-century printed material—a very *rare* perspective. He noted that not only should a collector acquire pieces for his own gratification, but that he "should feel under the obligation of knowing how to keep them that he may bestow as full value upon the future as he has received from the past." He had no regard for those who cleaned coins with acids and other dangerous agents, who brushed and rubbed coins with bristles, skins and powders, and who even re-engraved worn parts of the design, such practices being common at the time. Perpetrators were called "heathen in the world of Numisma."

Heaton suggested that particularly high-grade coins be kept in pasteboard boxes upon beds of fine cotton, not on open trays in wooden cabinets, although the boxes could be stored separately in such an enclosure. Concerning cabinets:

> Wood is rarely perfectly seasoned and the handsome drawers contain in their fiber a quantity of dampness and sap which simple scientific processes will make astonishingly evident. The glue used at the mortises and attaching the division strips in the velvet, and the velvet, is a second peril in the air. The dyes in the velvet itself are a third and always blacken Proof coins displayed upon it. A fourth danger lies in the pasteboard boxes holding the original dampness of the pulp.... A fifth works in the cotton which, unless of the quality prepared for jewelers, always contains here and there minute seeds or fragments which hold oil enough to deface a coin permanently if in contact with it....

As a solution, Heaton proposed that wood used to make cabinets must be taken from old furniture or something old and quite seasoned. Better yet would be the complete abolishment of wood in favor of drawers of metal and trays of glass or porcelain, such trays covered with old white satin or oven-dried silk.

Concerning the viewing of specimens:

> Lustrous coins should of course be handled as little as possible and then after the hands are washed and thoroughly dried. Hands should be clean in more than appearance, for not only invisible staining particles may adhere to them but the natural oil and dampness of the skin are dangerous.
>
> The best plan is to have the thumb and forefinger tips of an old glove cut off, washed clean, and always ready to draw on at need. It is hardly necessary to add that coins should be taken up only by the rim. Inexperienced persons should never be permitted to touch a collector's best pieces....

Further:

> We do not believe in touching fine pieces in any manner except with a view to improving them, but if they are soiled or greasy, they need to be washed carefully with water and Castile soap to avert further injury to them or contamination of the safe atmosphere, and then should be dried near a fire.

What Can You Do?

Probably, any advice I could give about whether to clean coins would not be too important. People make their own decisions, as they do about tobacco, alcohol, and the rituals of courtship.

It seems natural to want to experiment with cleaning coins. Go ahead, but do it with common coins, such as pocket change or paper-wrapped rolls of common coins from the bank. Stay away from numismatic rarities! You do have the option of buying coins that in advance already appear as "brilliant" or as attractively toned as you desire. Just buy those. While expert dipping and conservation (never cleaning with an abrasive) may improve the appearance of a coin, it has been my experience that for 9 out of 10 the value is decreased.

Even careful "good" cleaning (see below) is very bad in the long run. A gem Proof 1901 Barber half dollar with mottled gray toning will, if carefully dipped, become brilliant, perhaps even Proof-67. Then, after a few years, it will naturally tone, perhaps to light gold, perhaps an attractive iridescent hue, perhaps blotchy and spotted. The obvious solution is to dip it again. A bright gem is now at hand, but not quite as brilliant as before, as each dipping has removed some of the metal surface. Finally, 10 dippings later, the Proof is brilliant, but with a dullish, lifeless surface.

Few people will admit that they clean coins, except, perhaps, to a psychiatrist! This is a secret that really isn't secret, something that a lot of people do, but few people are willing to discuss.

Why all the secrecy, I don't know. Certainly in other fields it is customary to clean old master paintings; to clean, replace parts, and varnish a classic 1928 Gar Wood motorboat; to renickel the metal trimmings and shine up the interior parts on an old Mills "Dewey" gambling machine; and, for that matter, to remove foxing and stains and to patch holes in old letters and documents. Such work—and many other examples could be given—often enhances the value of a piece sharply. Specialists in those and other series have no problems with these practices, if properly described.

However, in numismatics *cleaned* is a bad word. Wash your mouth out with soap!

Conserving Coins

Conserving is a nice word, and I like it. Conserving means working with a coin, perhaps with a liquid or chemical, to enhance its appearance *without affecting the integrity of the metal surface*.

Some coins have verdigris or dirt on their surfaces, often in protected areas such as in the letters or between dentils. Careful washing with soap and warm water and patting (not rubbing) dry will often enhance the appearance of such a piece. For deep dirt a jeweler's ultrasonic cleaner can do the trick, but do not add any chemicals that would change the color of a coin's surface or brighten it. Again—and this is important—practice using common coins from the bank or pocket change. In that way, if you make a mistake, no harm is done.

Commercial solvents such as acetone (inflammable, must be used with care, etc.) and alcohol can also remove dirt and verdigris. Soak a coin in the liquid. If there is a stubborn blob of verdigris or dirt, tease it lightly with the end of a Q-tip. Do not rub, or there will be lines left on the coin.

A long time ago—this was in the 1950s—I came across a large batch of state copper coins of 1785 to 1788 that had been unattended for a long time and that had acquired a lot of black grime, green patination, and goo, and looked as ugly as sin. A friend of mine put me on to the idea of buying a small tin container of grease that was available for rubbing on the outside of leather hiking boots. I bought a can of this, and took one of the most severely afflicted copper coins and pushed it edgewise down into the grease. A day later I noticed a little green haze in the grease adjacent to the coin's surface. A week or two later I took the coin out; most of the black and green stuff had been left behind, and the coin was an attractive brown. I viewed this conservation method to be quite effective for copper, and used it for a long time afterward.

There are other ways to conserve coins, and this has been done effectively for gold recovered from the *S.S. Central America* and the *S.S. Republic*. Accumulated rust, scale, and even coral can be removed, if done properly. The Numismatic Conservation Service (NCS) makes a business of this.

Making Coins Brilliant

In the quest for brilliance, there is "good" cleaning and "bad" cleaning.[104] To clean a coin in this sense means to treat its surface so that toning, tarnish, discoloration, or anything else is removed, and the resultant coin is bright copper, silver, nickel, or gold.

In my opinion, if coins must be dipped, they should be in Mint State or Proof, never EF or AU, for bright coins in worn grades are not natural to my eyes, although certification services have no problem with them at all.

Also, I suggest that you stay away from *all* copper coins. Dipping a copper coin is usually just a quick fix, and later it will become blotchy or have other problems. There have been some unfortunate situations in which brightened copper coins have been certified, then became blotchy later, much to the distress of their owners. Some, perhaps all, certification services issue a caveat stating that they will not guarantee copper against such changes.

This leaves nickel, silver, and gold coins to discuss. We can eliminate gold coins, in that if they are dull they are usually *dirty*, not toned, with vault grime or other substances. These should be conserved as per the preceding section, not dipped.

Nickel and silver coins remain for consideration. In my opinion, if a coin has light or medium toning and is attractive, it should be left alone. Candidates for coins to brighten should be those with staining, spotting, blotching, or some other problem. Even so, think twice about doing it. Once again, I suggest you experiment with pocket change, at least for the nickel coins (as silver coins are no longer in the channels of commerce).

Dipping

The substance to use is a liquid silver "dip," never a paste or powder, and never any substance that is abrasive. Add the dip to a shallow plastic dish. Hold the coin by the edges, lower it into the dip, then swirl the dip around the coin. Soon, it will be bright. Take it out and rinse it in a stream of cold running water. Then dip it into another plastic dish containing water and a generous amount of baking soda. Immerse the coin, swirl the water, but do not rub the coin. This will neutralize the dip, or is supposed to. Then rinse it under cold water again, and pat dry (do not rub) with terrycloth or tissue.

Another method is to take an aluminum saucepan, add baking soda sufficient that some remains undissolved at the bottom, and carefully add a coin. Swirl the water, and the reaction will remove toning.

My opinions are just that—opinions. The opinions of others may vary, and widely. Moreover, a coin not cleaned or enhanced, but kept carefully, can always be cleaned or enhanced at a later time, perhaps when better technology is available.

Further, when in doubt about cleaning, don't!

Accordingly, the preceding commentary is not to encourage or recommend that anyone clean anything but, simply, to reflect practices and procedures over the years.

To be avoided at all costs, and not even to be experimented with, are substances that involve any kind of friction or the use of acids, and any devices that do the same. Most efforts at improving coins in the past are viewed as being bad today.

Adding Toning to a Coin

Lightly worn nickel and silver coins are apt to tone to an attractive medium gray—and should be left alone. However, many have been cleaned, giving them the brightness of a freshly minted coin. This is unnatural, and it may be desirable to try to impart toning, although most people don't care. Worn copper coins that have been brightened should be retoned, and some instructions for doing this are included in Dr. William H. Sheldon's *Penny Whimsy*, 1958 (echoing comments made by Sheldon in *Early American Cents*, 1949).

I have no fixed rules for adding nice-appearing toning to artificially brightened coins, except to suggest once again that you experiment first, using coins of low value in case something goes wrong. Methods employed with success in the past have included leaving the coins out on a windowsill, or on a warm (but not hot) top of a central heating furnace for a home, and letting nature take its course, checking the coin at regular intervals. Once, I took a freshly minted silver medal and placed it in the drawer of a recently made oak table. My intent was to take it out soon afterward, but I forgot to do so. A couple months later I looked at it, and the fumes in the oak had given the silver metal some of the most beautiful electric blue and iridescent toning I have ever seen!

Another possibility would be to get some old "National" or other album pages, put your coins in the pages, and subject them to warmth for a period of time— seemingly a popular method for professionals. One well-known dealer told me that putting overly brightened silver coins in a frying pan with vegetable oil and "cooking" them under low heat for a period of time made them turn a lovely gray—but I haven't tried it. Still others have toned the surfaces with fumes from iodine or other substances, which can be a dangerous procedure and, in addition, will usually wash off if the coin is immersed in a solvent. Again, it would be wise to experiment with coins from pocket change.

The careful application of some mineral oil to the surface of a worn copper coin can often enhance its appearance. Neatsfoot oil, used to treat leather, has been used by some, to good effect. For these and other oily (but not acidic) substances, soap and water, carefully applied and without friction, will serve to remove them easily enough.

My advice in a nutshell: At the outset, cherrypick coins that have good eye appeal. Leave the coin brightening, retoning, and other scenarios to "coin doctors," who have been there, done that, and know the tricks. In the meantime, like "Spy vs. Spy" in *Mad* magazine (a favorite read when I was a kid), learn what artificial toning, processing, and such look like, keep a step ahead of the coin doctors, and concentrate on collecting—not on "better coins through chemistry."

Protecting and Storing Coins
Cabinets, Albums, and Envelopes

William C. Prime, in his 1861 *Coins, Medals, and Seals, Ancient and Modern*, gave this advice:

> When your collection justifies it, have a case or cabinet made to hold it. An immense number of coins can be laid in a small space. A case two feet high, two wide, and one deep, with folding doors, filled with drawers each five-eighths of an inch deep, a few being deeper for medals, will hold several thousand coins.
>
> Cover your drawers with cloth or cotton velvet. Let slats be tacked across the drawer from side to side, but do not separate the coins in one row from each other. The only danger of rubbing is in opening and shutting the drawers, and this will be prevented by the slats from side to side.
>
> Arrange...your regular series of United States coins by dates, your tradesmen's cards alphabetically, and your political tokens as best suits your taste.

For many years, until well into the 1930s, wooden cabinets and drawers were the preferred way to store and display coins. This generated the terms *cabinet*, for a collection of coins, and *cabinet friction*, for slight rubbing on the higher surfaces.

In the late 1920s, M.L. Beistle, owner of a cardboard-products company in Ship-pensburg, Pennsylvania, developed a series of album pages. These consisted of a thick cardboard panel with holes for coins, with paper attached to the front and back in a manner so as to hold clear cellulose acetate slides that could be slid in and out over the fronts and backs of the openings. Coins thus stored could be viewed on both sides.

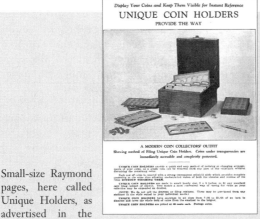

Small-size Raymond pages, here called Unique Holders, as advertised in the 1930s. Storing pages in boxes never became popular, and collectors used small ring-type loose-leaf albums instead.

A collector and his coin cabinet in the early 20th century. (*Mehl's Numismatic Monthly*, September 1908)

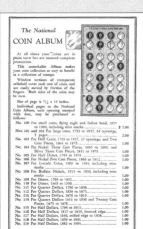

Advertisement for the immensely popular National album pages circa 1940. The filling in of spaces in coin folders, sheets, or albums proved to be a fascinating challenge, similar to working a crossword puzzle. Such albums did much to increase interest in the hobby.

A type set of commemorative half dollars, all issues from the 1892 Columbian to the 1951 Washington-Carver, in two large-size Raymond album pages. This style of album, similar examples of which were made by Meghrig, dominated the hobby until the advent of plastic holders and book-style bound albums.

These seemed to have had a limited sale until they caught the eye of Wayte Raymond, a New York City dealer who operated the Scott Stamp & Coin Company at 1 West 47th Street, and also had his own business. Through an arrangement with Beistle, Raymond expanded the series into two main formats—small, horizontal pages punched on the left edge for insertion in a brown cardboard ring-binder, and a larger version with vertical pages. Pages for popular series such as commemorative coins, Indian cents, large copper cents, and the like were made available with imprints below the openings. For collectors of other series as well as tokens and medals, blank pages were offered. Marketed under the "National" name, the Raymond holders became wildly popular and were one of the great factors affecting the growth of the coin hobby in the 1930s.

Now, at long last, coins could be stored and displayed at the same time, in handy form that could be carried around, such as to a coin-club meeting. Trays and wooden cabinets were soon forgotten.

In the meantime, the 2"x 2" paper envelopes, devised earlier in the century when it was found that such would fit conveniently into player-piano-roll boxes (player pianos being very popular on the American scene and such boxes being easily available), continued to be employed by nearly all dealers for their stocks. Information for each coin was written on the front of the envelope, usually in pen, and often the name of the dealer was imprinted on the envelope. Such could be arranged in logical order in stock boxes and easily mailed to customers.

In 1934, J.K. Post of Neenah, Wisconsin, devised what became known as the *penny board*, a sheet of cardboard with openings for Lincoln cents (later expanded to include Liberty nickels and other coins), backed with a sheet of paper so the coins would not fall out. Each piece was pressed by

hand into the opening. The result made a nice display, suitable for hanging on a wall or framing. Post tapped the resources of the Whitman Publishing Company, then located in Racine, Wisconsin, to make these on order. Whitman realized the potential, acquired the rights, and expanded and marketed the line under its own name, providing its entry into numismatics, dynamic today. Later, Whitman added three-panel folding cardboard albums that became much more popular than the penny boards and that eventually included series through silver dollars.

Later, other albums similar in general concept to Wayte Raymond's "National" holders were marketed by Wynne, Hollander, the Coin and Currency Institute (operated by Robert and Jack Friedberg in New York City), Meghrig & Company, and others. With their empty spaces, such holders invited their owners to fill them, just as a crossword puzzle presents a challenge. Finally, in the case of Lincoln cents, after one had spent many hours looking through coins from circulation, certain holes remained unfilled—typically 1909-S V.D.B., 1914-D, and 1931-S—necessitating a trip to a local coin dealer and possibly launching the buyer to an even greater awareness of numismatics by buying books, learning of obsolete coins, and the like.

An exhibit of coin boards and folders from the collection of David W. Lange won a first-place ribbon at an ANA convention. The "Penny Collector" sheet at the left was made by J.K. Post of Neenah, Wisconsin, in the mid-1930s.

In the meantime, paper envelopes didn't go out of style. Through the early 1990s, until they were edged out by plastic "slabs," paper envelopes were the way to go. They are sometimes used today, especially by dealers in tokens, colonial coins, and other pieces not often "slabbed."

Years ago at Empire Coin Company, when all dealers kept their stocks in 2" x 2" paper envelopes, Jim Ruddy and I used a quick coding system—blue for a Proof coin, yellow for Uncirculated, and white for circulated. In that way we could quickly glance at a box and pick out a Proof 1863 Liberty Seated half dollar, or whatever it was we were looking for. Emery May Holden Norweb used a related system for her collection.

The Plastic Era Begins

Beginning in the early 1950s, plastic holders became popular. Each consisted of three Lucite sheets, a colored (usually) central sheet with circular openings for coins, and then thinner clear sheets on the front and back, secured along the edge with plastic or metal screws. Often the holders bore imprints beneath the openings.

At the same time, Paul Seitz (of Glen Rock, Pennsylvania, and son-in-law of the late dealer Thomas L. Elder) sold a line of two-piece plastic holders with pegs at the centers, spaced to hold coins of different sizes. These were not imprinted and were considerably less expensive, although not as attractive as the three-piece Lucite holders. In time, the Seitz holders disappeared from the market.

Coin dealers, seeking to showcase scarce items such as MCMVII $20 pieces, $4 Stellas, and the like, had such holders custom made, to the delight of their customers. Soon, holders were available for certain popular sets such as a 15-piece collection of Indian Head quarter eagles from 1908 to 1929, a type set of 20th-century gold coins, a five-piece modern Proof set, and more. As a youngster just entering numismatics I visited Edmund Karmilowicz, a collector in my home town of Forty Fort, Pennsylvania, and was treated to seeing his Mercury dimes, commemoratives, Peace silver dollars, and other series, all in beautiful plastic holders—as pretty as a museum exhibit. At the time, such holders were unusual. Most important collections were stored in Raymond "National" albums.

When I first began collecting Lincoln cents as a teenager in 1952, I used the three-panel Whitman holders. I wanted my Uncirculated coins to stay "bright," so I came up with the simple expedient of coating them with clear fingernail polish, then pushing them into the openings. This did quite well. Such polish could be removed easily enough with either commercial fingernail-polish remover or acetone. Since then I have used the same method on several occasions on tokens and other items in my collection, with excellent results. In this way the coins can be stored in old-time albums and remain as attractive as ever.

Plastic holders became increasingly popular, and by the 1960s a number of companies were actively engaged in their manufacture, including George Leffler (Temple City, California), Leroy Kurtzeborn (Wisconsin), and, seemingly dominating the trade, the Capital Plastics Company (Massillon, Ohio). Beautiful holders were available for just about any series, complete with imprints. A plastic holder shaped in the outline of Nevada, with spaces for each of the Carson City Morgan dollars, seemed to sell well, as I saw quite a few of them at conventions.

Clear Envelopes Containing PVC

In the 1970s, clear envelopes of heavy plastic became popular, as the coins could be clearly seen. Such envelopes could be labeled by the placement of a tag inside or the attachment of a sticker. However, it soon developed that many of these contained polyvinyl chloride (PVC), which leached out of the plastic and formed a deposit or goo on the surface of the coins. PVC is chemically active, and tends to attack and damage the surfaces of copper and (especially) nickel coins. Silver coins do not seem to be particularly affected, other than by acquiring greenish goo or beads on the surface, which can be removed by acetone without apparent harm. Gold coins are not affected at all.

Although not much was said publicly about PVC, its use diminished, and today PVC envelopes are used only for *temporary* storage, such as for viewing auction lots, and are not recommended for long-term use. Most auction houses include a warning to this effect. In the meantime, Mylar, a clear plastic, is considered to be inert and has been adapted for coin holders.

Aspects of Toning

In the 1990s the Bell Laboratories in New Jersey developed a chemical process to retard the toning on coins. This came to market under the name of Intercept Shield and was endorsed by various hobby leaders, including Ken Bressett, editor of the *Guide Book*. Cardboard holders so treated were stated to last for many years without the coins' becoming toned.

Meanwhile, silver coins that had been stored in cardboard "National" albums developed halo-like toning, most intense at the rims of the coins where they contacted the cardboard holder, and changing through various iridescent colors to light silver at the centers. This peripheral toning was viewed as being exceedingly desirable, and for many coins sharply increased their value. Although such instances were perfectly fine, and, indeed, desirable, most numismatists today prefer that their stored or displayed coins remain constant in their appearance and gain no *new* toning.

Today, millions of coins are encapsulated in plastic holders or "slabs" certified by one or another of the services. These are not airtight and they can trap moisture, but they seem to be quite good for normal storage—in the same manner that three-piece Lucite holders are. Plastic is not a protection against heat, moisture, or industrial fumes. However, the slabs do protect coins from handling and make them easy to see (except for rim details and the edges). Certified holders are rather clumsy, in my opinion, and take up a lot of space. I see much opportunity for innovation in such holders as well as panels or some other way to attractively hold and display a half dozen or more certified coins at once.

Possible Improvements in Holders

Alternatively, the certifiers themselves might do well to devise holders with an artistic appearance, just as a maker of fine Swiss watches might spend some time in creating a box or background for watches offered for sale. No doubt a Rolex watch in a rectangular plastic box would not be as attractive as it would in one of the beautiful containers that are now used.

Still another idea, one that has appealed to me for some time, would be for the certifiers of coins to come up with a small *circular* sealed holder, slightly larger in diameter than the coin itself, with informa-

A dealer looks through a box filled with "slabs," and studies a nicely toned Morgan silver dollar.

A veritable sea of slabs containing coins that will soon be owned by various collectors and dealers around the country. (Heritage photos)

tion imprinted on the plastic rim. Accordingly, a circular certified holder for a Jefferson nickel might have the total size of a quarter dollar. These round, certified holders could then be put in album pages or larger display holders, just as coins were placed in albums and Lucite holders years ago. Collectors could then add their own lettering and such. When time comes to sell the coins, they could be removed from the holders and the certification information would remain intact.

Coin stores and convention exhibitors offer for sale numerous varieties of coin albums, cases, single plastic holders, and other supplies. Many are very attractive.

For paper money, plastic envelopes of Mylar or another inert substance are recommended. Quality and protection vary, and some old types of transparent holders can make notes brittle. It is wise to consult a currency expert for a line of holders that is satisfactory. Several varieties of display albums are available, typically holding several bills per page, the bills themselves being stored within Mylar envelopes.

Hiding and Safekeeping Places

A bank safe-deposit box provides a safe and convenient place to store coins. However, they are accessible only during banking hours. When seeking such a facility, be sure the safe deposit vault or room is dry (some basement locations can be damp). The Eliasberg, Garrett, and Norweb collections were kept in such vaults, with no problems.

Banks do not take responsibility for, nor do they insure the contents of, safe-deposit boxes. Buy private insurance in this regard. A typical policy will provide for a certain amount of coverage while the coins are in the bank, and will allow a lesser number of coins to be taken from the bank, such as to your home or office, and still be covered.

Coin insurance policies are best obtained from an underwriter who has a good business in this field. All policies have rules and exceptions, and these should be read carefully. It is likely that your coins will not be covered if, say, they're unattended in an automobile.

Some numismatists store their coins at home, in safes or in rooms with electronic protection. Others keep their collections in their business offices, typically under some type of security. A good rule is not to discuss where you keep your collection, as it should be no one's business but your own.

Take Possession of Your Coins

Every once in a while an investment-oriented seller of coins will propose to sell coins to customers and then store them as an accommodation. The customer is given a document stating that such-and-such double eagles and so-and-so Morgan dollars are "in our vault" safely kept. Then, when the same salesperson sells them for a great profit, all the customer has to do is cash a check.

Good idea, except that over the years this has been a popular game with con artists. The trick is that a few hundred or a few thousand different rare coins are in the vault. That splendid MCMVII (1907) High Relief $20 piece that you bought is plainly listed on an invoice, and you can come to see it any time. Trouble is that exactly the same MCMVII is also on the account documents of John Doe, of Fresno, who bought it, and of Sam Schmo of Peoria, who put it in his "portfolio." Of course, John and Sam can also come to see their MCMVII, so long as they don't visit at the same time. No problem there, as visits are by appointment, to go into the safe and security area.

In October 1982 the collapse of such a company made headlines. I found the news reports to be amusing (probably not the right word choice!), for we had lost some business to this company, whose prices were lower than ours. Now, it had filed for bankruptcy and was not answering its telephone calls. It apparently had several thousand investors, holding certificates and statements listing rare coins, now all clamoring to obtain coins that had been paid for but were being stored by the seller.

Such scams and variations thereof have been going on for a long time. A generation ago the International Gold Bullion

Exchange (sounds impressive, doesn't it?) was a heavy advertiser in leading financial papers. The firm illustrated its advertisements with pictures of a skyscraper in which it had its headquarters. They offered to sell gold for *below market price*, under certain conditions. Sounds too good to be true, but millions of dollars poured into the company. Then the outfit collapsed, and investors lost their shirts.

A variation on this theme was a creative enterprise that offered private vaults to people who wanted to store coins and other precious items without using the facilities of a bank. The only trouble was that some burglars broke in one weekend, emptied the vaults, and fled undetected. "So sorry," said the president of the vault company.

Here is another piece of advice: *Always take physical possession of any rare coins you purchase.*

Keeping Track of Things
Records of Your Collection
It is a good idea to keep a record book or inventory of what you have. Several computer programs are available and can be of help, even keeping a running tab on total costs and market values. Some have room for extensive comments, but this is usually sacrificed to give more fields for data. The Excel spreadsheet marketed by Microsoft seems to be especially popular.

If you keep information in a record book and want to carry it around, you might devise a 10-letter substitution code for the prices, to keep them confidential (except to puzzle solvers!). TRADE QUICK, BLACKSTONE, and CHARLESTON are three such codes used by well-known dealers in the past.

With CHARLESTON, where C = 1, H = 2, and so on, a cost of $735 would be encrypted as SAL. Some red herrings or nulls could be added, these being letters that have no meaning, such as B, W, and X. Under that arrangement, instead of SAL you could have WSBAL for one coin that

cost $735 and XSXABL for another at the same price. However, such things can get confusing if taken too far.

Years ago, pocket-sized inventory books for coins caught on in a big way, among the first being Ben G. Green's *The Numismatists' Reference and Check Book; Being a List of Coins Issued by the U. S. Mint and Branches*, published in 1902. In the 1930s, Charles Green (no kin to Ben, so far as I am aware) issued *Mint Records of U.S. Coins 1793–1931, Inclusive*, and *Mint Record and Type Table of United States Coins*, which included mintage figures and scattered facts. Lee F. Hewitt, of the *Numismatic Scrapbook Magazine*, continued the Green series. These were used widely, including by Louis E. Eliasberg, Sr.

Taxes, Accounting, Etc.
If your coins are bought primarily as investments it might be possible to deduct as expenses your costs of travel to conventions, subscriptions to magazines and societies, and other things. I do not practice accounting, and rules often change, but you may wish to contact a competent professional to determine your options.

There are other possibilities that require professional guidance, such as including coins in retirement plans, determining tax liability and possible favorable options when selling, and other aspects.

The accounting for sales taxes will require study as well. In some states there is no tax at all on coin purchases; in others, coins have a special treatment (e.g., no tax on any purchase amount exceeding $1,000); and in others a full retail tax is due. There are also practices and requirements involving buying coins out-of-state to avoid or reduce tax, the use of dealer and resale permits, and more. Tax added to a coin increases its cost, although some buyers overlook this. A $105 coin bought tax-free is cheaper than a $100 coin bought if an 8% sales tax has to be paid. Again, seek a professional for advice.

CHAPTER THIRTY-THREE

ENJOYING AND SHARING YOUR COLLECTION

500 ANA members were sent an extensive readership survey.... Tops on your list of preferred reading were articles focusing on the care and preservation of collections (56.9%); brief articles detailing events in U.S. numismatic history (50.4%); instructional articles about basic grading techniques (49%); and in-depth historical studies of specific U.S. coins (44.6%).

[Then followed] personal observations about the hobby by average collectors (39.7%); reminiscences of well-known collectors (35%); and technical or scientific approaches to numismatics in general (31.8%). Articles about ancient coinage and history, and U.S. paper money interested 25.1% of our readers, while 27.4% said they'd like to see more articles about exhibiting or displaying their collections.

—The Numismatist, January 1988

For the Fun of It

Enjoying Your Collection

The preceding chapter was about taking care of business, keeping records, protecting coins, and other procedural stuff. The present chapter is a bit more fun. Coins and other numismatic items are meant to be *enjoyed*.

How can you enjoy a coin? a token? a medal? a currency note?

There are many ways.

The Hunt and Capture

First, you can enjoy a coin even before you own it—this being the thrill of the hunt, the interest and excitement of tracking it down.

A 1955 Doubled-Die cent is coming up for auction. Described as AU-55 (by Professional Coin Grading Service, or PCGS), it looks nice in the picture, and seems to fill the bill for this "story coin," a key to the series. What should you bid? Think about it, send in an offer by mail or email, or give your commission to a dealer—or, you can attend the sale in person (in which instance you must examine the coin before bidding), or telephone an agent while the sale is in progress, or bid "live" on the Internet.

Then see what happens. *Aha! I own it!* Already, the coin has been enjoyed—the story of "how you two first met."

Once it is home, examine it under a 4x to 8x pocket magnifier. Study not only the dramatic date numerals, but see what other features are doubled on the coin, and by what degree. For good measure, look at the other aspects of the coin—the portrait of Lincoln, the modernistic wheat sheaves on the reverse, the style of the lettering.

You will have enjoyed locating the 1955 Doubled-Die cent, considering it for inclusion in your collection, and laying plans to make it your very own. Afterward, you will have enjoyed it more by examining it closely.

In another scenario, you have decided to collect as many National Bank bills as you can find from your home state—say, New York—but it could be anywhere. At a convention you approach a dealer in currency and see a bunch of bills marked "New York." Riffling through them, each in a plastic envelope, you pick out one from New York City, because it is in high grade and is inexpensive; another from Amenia, because the town name sounds interesting and you've never heard of it, although the note is not cheap; and a third from Syracuse, because that is where you grew up.

You then discuss each note with the dealer by simply asking: "Tell me as much as you can about each of these three. I'm new to this specialty." He speaks, and you listen. Before you leave the show you buy a copy of Don Kelly's *National Bank Notes* book.

623

At home you look at each of the bills. The New York City note is a 1902 Plain Back, inexpensive. The signatures are rubber-stamped. The bill isn't rare, you find out from the Kelly book, but it will serve as a nice example of the type. The Amenia bill is an 1882 Brown Back, quite picturesque; maybe you can buy a few other Brown Backs to go with it. As to the Syracuse note, in the Kelly book you learn that your hometown had quite a few banks that issued currency—perhaps you can see how many different ones you can get.

Buying something in a *new* specialty is always enjoyable. At the outset, you have everything ahead of you to learn and experience. Of course, you shouldn't plunge too deeply before learning more and also determining whether the new specialty has staying power—that your interest will be maintained.

Enjoy What You Own

Coins you already have can furnish continuing enjoyment. As an example, find a common-date Morgan dollar in high grade. Run it through this little process:

- *Time allotted: 3 minutes.* Look at the obverse and reverse and make a mental note of what you see—the date, the stars, the "stuff" at the front in Miss Liberty's hair, and, on the reverse, the eagle and its feathers, the lettering, and anything else you can find. Spend a full three minutes. If you finish early, then look at the obverse again.
- *Time allotted: 10 minutes.* In *Walter Breen's Complete Encyclopedia of U.S. and Colonial Coins,* read about how the Morgan silver dollar was designed and distributed.
- *Time allotted: 10 minutes.* Return to the coin and *really* look at the details. Notice that the obverse stars are very peculiar—they are only geometric figures, flat on top, with no ribs or center high points, quite unlike those on Barber or Liberty Seated coins (if you have one to compare, do so). Look at the date numerals—study how each

digit is formed, how close they are to each other, which parts of each digit are bold and which are weak. While you are in that area of the coin, find the M initial of the engraver (reminding yourself that this coin was signed on both sides, and in due course, check the other M, too). Look at the face of Miss Liberty, its outline, her cheek, her ear, details of her hair. What's that stuff above the word LIBERTY?

On the reverse, study the national bird, its wings and breast, its feathers, its head and beak, its feet. Look at the wreath and contemplate its details. Then examine the lettering. Is it not weird that In God We Trust is in Old English upper- and lowercase letters—not matching the rest of the coin?

When you are finished with all of this, if someone were to ask, "Can you tell me about the Morgan silver dollar?" chances are good that you could give an authoritative impromptu talk.

As time passes, your 1955 Doubled-Die cent, Morgan dollar, $10 bill from Amenia, New York, and other items should be examined from time to time, just to re-appreciate what you have.

The Magic of Electronics

Today, through the magic of digital imaging, you can also enjoy your collection from a distance. In some ways this is not as good as having your coins, tokens, medals, and paper money at hand, but in other ways it can be better.

Among the things I enjoy collecting are obsolete and federal bank notes. I have captured images of each of these on an inexpensive flatbed scanner. The pictures are in color and of high definition. While the bills themselves remain securely stored in a bank vault, I can pop a picture of any bill onto the screen of my laptop computer, and enjoy studying it. In fact, by means of the zoom button I don't need a magnifying glass to study details of an engraver's signature or the vignette of a side-wheel steamer.

This can also be done with coins, tokens, and medals. As time permits, I hope to do this with other things I have stored in the bank, and then I can enjoy and study them at home, too.

For many of my items, in addition to scanning them I record their details in separate paragraphs in Microsoft Word files, enabling me to add historical information, and to key the first words or numerals so that the whole file sorts automatically. This information, plus a scanned image of the note, gives me a record almost as good as carrying the note and a handful of reference books around with me!

All around the country, museums are setting up "virtual" exhibits of everything from wagon trains to dinosaurs to politicians. By means of the computer age you can have a virtual numismatic museum in your laptop computer. For me, this is very enjoyable.

Social Aspects of Numismatics
The Internet

The Internet offers another electronic way to appreciate and enjoy numismatics. Earlier, I discussed some ways to buy and bid

The author on a visit with a New England collector, to scan currency notes for use in a future book. Modern scanners and cameras make it easy to capture images of your own collection and items shared by others.

effectively. Beyond the ability to acquire items for your collection, you will find chat rooms and message boards filled with news, advice, gossip, and just about anything and everything else—a social aspect of this medium. Dealer web sites, necessarily self-serving, are also interesting to read and contemplate, and they often have editorial features. Blogs (web logs) are other sources of information.

As the Internet is a low-cost way of disseminating information, dealers who would never issue printed catalogs can turn out full-color offerings of coins, paper money, and everything else.

Watching auctions in progress can be absorbing—where does the time go? A relatively new *entertainment* medium is eBay, something no one would have dreamed of a generation ago.

On the Internet, "show and tell" takes on a new dimension with the postings of registry sets, sometimes under fictitious names. For many, this has been a game—keeping score as in an arcade test of skill or the statistics on the back of a baseball card. Many people are fiercely proud of their positions on these lists, and the concept itself has brought much money into the market.

On a more personal level, Internet communications are a great way to share information, discoveries, opinions, and more. Most of my interface with Peter Huntoon, well-known paper money researcher, has been by the Internet, including his contributions to this book. David Sundman, my co-researcher in the field of New Hampshire paper money, and I probably email each other 20 times for each single time we talk on the telephone.

The Internet is a time-sink. Time flies. Often, I've spent a few hours poking around here and there on the Internet, not doing business, but simply seeing what's going on.

As for buying on the Internet, see my comments in chapters 14 and 15.

Coin Clubs

If there is a coin club in your area, check it out. Typically, a group meets once a month, in the evening, in some public hall. The quality and interest level are apt to vary, but most I have attended have been worthwhile.

In the early 1950s I learned a lot by going to the Wilkes-Barre (Pennsylvania) Coin Club. Those who wanted to get in some chatting or trade a coin or two often came early. Then the meeting began, with a brief reading of the minutes from the last one, then 5 to 10 minutes of coin talk by the president of the club (about stuff read in the latest *Numismatic Scrapbook*, or a report of a New York auction sale, or news that a member had found a 1914-D cent in circulation), followed by a program.

The talks varied, and like as not were about some obscure branch of numismatics unknown to just about everyone present. This was for the good, as we all learned about German notgeld, or Capped Bust half dollars (no one called them by that name then, and no one had heard of John Reich), or emergency paper money of World War II. A coin quiz might be next, or the 20-questions game.

Sometimes a member would bring an album of coins and pass it around, telling stories about the different pieces. When Dr. Albert Thomas brought his large "National" pages filled with cents, I saw my first 1799 and my first 1856 Flying Eagle. He pushed the 1856 out of its slot and let me hold it. What a thrill! Other times a slide show, with illustrations sent by mail from the American Numismatic Association (ANA), would be shown. (I remember one on commemorative coins.)

Then came the club auction in which members put things up for sale, with starting bids. It was proper etiquette for dealers (such as me) not to bid unless there was no collector interest. One evening a

gem prooflike 1879 half dollar came up, I thought it was wonderful, but it caused no interest at all, and I bought it for the starting bid of $5 (today it would be worth $1,000+ had I kept it!).

Afterward there was general milling around the room, and some buying and selling by vest-pocket (part-time) dealers who had brought boxes of coins. Just about every club member would buy *something* at a meeting—to add to the interest. It was always worth going.

Coin clubs have faded from the scene in recent decades, as has attendance at lodge and evening club meetings. A lot of this is due to television, now added to by the Internet. People can be entertained without leaving home. Still, there are some fine clubs in existence, and I enjoy reading the reports that some of them mail to me.

Special Interest Groups

Special-interest or niche groups have proliferated since about 1960, although a few were formed earlier. One of the first was the American Vecturist Association, founded in 1948.

Birds of a numismatic feather like to flock together, and, accordingly, collectors of Flying Eagle and Indian Head cents (both showing feathers!) have their own group, the Flying Eagle and Indian Cent Collectors Society, nicknamed the Fly-In Club. Devotees of large copper cents are attracted to the Early American Coppers Club, which for some reason uses just one C in its abbreviation, EAC. Its journal, *Penny-Wise*, edited by Harry Salyards, is one of the best periodicals in our hobby.

The Colonial Coin Collectors Club ("C-4"), formed a few years ago by Mike Hodder, has grown considerably and has its own newsletter. After hearing about C-4 I suggested that there were other possibilities, such as the Cos Cob, Connecticut, Copper Colonial Coin Collectors Club (C-8), but I never received an answer when I wrote about it!

Liberty Seated aficionados can join the Liberty Seated Collectors Club and receive the *Gobrecht Journal*, while devotees of

Seal of the New York Numismatic Club. Organized on the evening of December 11th at Keen's Old English Chop House at 36th Street and Sixth Avenue, New York City, the group was to go on to many years of brilliant successes and was to include in its membership over a period of time many of the most prominent numismatists in the greater New York area.

Annual breakfast meeting of the Rittenhouse Society, this one in Philadelphia in 2000. The first four people on the left are Ed Reiter, P. Scott Rubin, R.W. Julian, and David T. Alexander. The first four on the right are Eric P. Newman, John Kraljevich, Denis Loring, and Dick Johnson. The group was formed in 1957 and had its first formal meeting (if they can be called that) in 1960. (Mark Borckardt photograph)

Annual breakfast meeting of the Rittenhouse Society, this one in Pittsburgh in 2004. First four on left: Hank Spangenberger, P. Scott Rubin, Joel Orosz, and R.W. Julian. First four on right: Rick Bagg, John Kraljevich, Ken Bressett (standing), and Denis Loring. Mark Borckardt is at the end of the table, figuring out the check (?). Dave Bowers and Bill Fivaz are standing against the wall.

early silver coins may find it worthwhile to investigate the John Reich Collectors Society, publisher of the *John Reich Journal*. The Civil War Token Society, the Token and Medal Society, the Medal Collectors of America, and the Society of Paper Money Collectors are on the roster of special interest groups, along with the Society for U.S. Commemoratives, the Numismatic Bibliomania Society, and the Rittenhouse Society.

Publications of these groups can be valuable reference sources. A partial listing of articles published in the *Gobrecht Journal*, 2002 to early 2004, indicates the diversity of that magazine's contents: "A Detailed Study of the 1842-O Half Dime," "An Incredible Hoard of 1844 Dimes," "Toning: Tarnish That Masks Reality," "Comments on the Book, *100 Greatest U.S. Coins*," "The Mint on Carson Street," "Triple Protection for a Brilliant Uncirculated 1877-CC Quarter," "Assessing the Completeness and Quality of a Seated Dollar Collection," "Counterfeit Seated Dollars and Trade Dollars on eBay," "Of Coins Like This are Dreams Made."

Some special-interest groups have gone, such as the one devoted to collecting 1976 Bicentennial $2 bills bearing postmarks from around the country. There once was a Standing Liberty Quarter Club (SLQC), but I don't believe it's active now. I've given lots of talks and presentations over the years, but an especially memorable one was to the SLQC, as featured speaker. The time was set at 10 in the morning, and I arrived a few minutes early to be greeted by the club president and secretary. Ten o'clock came and went, but no one else walked through the door. That was it! (I later found out that the show's opening or something else of wider interest had been set for the same hour.)

Special-interest groups are worth investigating if there is one devoted to some area you collect or anticipate doing.

Telling About and Exhibiting Your Coins
Show and Tell

Exhibiting treasures from your collection can be interesting and enjoyable. The easiest and most informal way is to bring selected coins or currency to a club meeting and hold court while others view them. Your listeners will enjoy knowing about your favorite specimens and how you acquired them.

Sometimes a club will have topic of the day. The New York Numismatic Club, years ago (and perhaps still today), would state in advance that the next meeting would be about Hard Times tokens, or Proof coins, or something else. The New England Currency Club picks topics on paper money—perhaps animals for one meeting, ships for another. For such meetings you can bring what you have in these categories—an adult version of "show and tell."

The more obscure the exhibit or talk at a club meeting, the better. Recently Dave Sundman and I went to Newton, Massachusetts, to attend the 145th anniversary meeting of the Boston Numismatic Society (founded in 1860) in combination with a meeting of the New England Currency Club. Keynote speaker was Anne Bentley, curator of the Massachusetts Historical Society. Her topic was rare scrip notes issued in Massachusetts during the Civil War—little notes with values of 5¢, 10¢, or whatever, circulated at a time when coins were scarce. Along the way she said that of all the things she took care of at the society, numismatic items were the most interesting. I thought that was a fine tribute to our hobby.

Bentley told of digging into old directories to find out about the people who issued these scrip notes. One was a certain Atwood, proprietor of an oyster house. She found that there were more than a dozen different Atwoods in the oyster trade, one of them a 13-year-old boy. The audience was spellbound by the hour-long talk, and everyone learned something new. At the end of her presentation she exhibited many different bills from the society's collection.

Sharing your experiences at an auction sale, or on a trip to a coin show, or with a lucky find can be interesting to do and enjoyable for your audience. A general rule is the more casual, the better. Human interest always trumps a recitation of dry facts and numbers.

Making a Display

Coin-club chat or no, you might find it interesting to set up a formal display at a coin show or convention. Not all have these, but many do.

Contrary to the views of some, coins, tokens, medals, and paper money do not necessarily have to be valuable or great rarities to attract attention or even to win prizes. In fact, such is the exception, not the rule. Generally, first-, second-, and third-place awards in different categories go to exhibits that are the most attractively and informatively arranged.

At the 2004 ANA convention, held in Pittsburgh, I made the rounds of the exhibits, several dozen in all. To be sure, there were some breathtaking rarities (such as a gorgeous set of $3 pieces by date and mint, complete except for the 1870-S), but most featured pieces of average value and quality. I lingered for quite a while on an exhibit of state quarters, with accompanying information as to the designers, motifs, and even an opinion of the quality of the art. Another exhibit showed paper money from in and around the Pittsburgh area, with currency ranging from common to rare, but quite interesting when displayed in connection with historical information. One exhibit featured encased postage stamps, popular numismatic items from 1862 and 1863 featuring real postage stamps mounted behind mica in a brass frame, with advertisements in the back.

The collection was not complete, but it didn't matter. Reflective of this, the numismatist setting it up showed six empty holders reflecting the types that he still lacked. Still another, and one of the most interesting, was a display of coin holders and albums from the 1930s onward.

Exhibit Suggestions

As a viewer of many exhibits and a judge of quite a few, I have found many ideas to be effective.

First, it's important to create a theme. This can take the simple form of a numismatic set, such as a complete collection of Peace silver dollars from 1921 to 1935, a run of Flying Eagle and Indian cents from 1856 to 1909, an arrangement of medals issued for the World's Columbian Exhibition held in Chicago in 1892 and 1893, or different signature-combinations on small-sized $1 bills from the late 1920s to date.

Generally, simple displays showing only the dates and mints of coins without much else are not apt to attract much attention. However, with some spicing, such a display can be of great interest. For example, a set of 24 dates and mintmarks of Peace silver dollars could be accompanied by a page or two of narrative stating how the coins were designed, when they were released, and their different characteristics (such as the 1921 being in high relief, the 1934-S being rare, and so on). Some biographical information concerning the designer, Anthony deFrancisci, would also be interesting, as would, perhaps, some picture postcards or magazine illustrations from the 1921 to 1935 era, or photographs of the three mints used to strike the pieces. Add these things, and what started out as a set of 24 dates and mintmarks becomes a museum-quality array enticing the visitor to spend several minutes or more learning all of the details.

Similarly, a set of Flying Eagle Indian cents could discuss the engraver (James B. Longacre),

how the designs were created, perhaps some illustrations of patterns before the regular types were adopted (or patterns themselves if they are on hand), and illustrations of the era. Most of us know that the 1877 Indian cent is indeed a rarity, but what happened in American history in 1877 is less known—and perhaps a description of the life and times of that year would be a worthwhile addition.

A set of Columbian Exposition medals could be enhanced with all sorts of guidebooks, cards, ribbons, and other memorabilia from the same event, made in large quantities at the time and readily available today. As to small-sized $1 bills, the Hawaii overprint and Yellow Seal varieties have great histories, the R and S red surcharges invite explanation—and then there is the story of the "Barr notes," thought to be rare, but actually very common.

Exhibits should be arranged in logical order, and if in more than one case, the cases might be numbered, beginning with the leftmost and continuing to the right. By use of a home computer and printer, effective titles and headlines can be made. All text should be large enough to be easily read at a distance.

All elements of the exhibit should be explained, as many visitors will not be familiar with Flying Eagle cents, Peace dollars, Columbian Exposition medals, early varieties of $1 bills, or whatever else

At a recent Florida United Numismatists (FUN) convention, Nancy Wilson (standing) and Gene Hynds (seated to her left) brief the exhibit judges. Such aspects as originality, attractiveness of presentation, information imparted to the viewer, and the importance of the items shown all contribute to determining who gets ribbons at the show. (Fred Lake photograph)

you decide to show. When writing your descriptions be sure to be accurate. Given a choice, a viewer would probably prefer to see one medal with a couple of paragraphs of interesting history accompanying it, than to see a half dozen medals with no explanations.

When I have been an exhibit judge, if the accompanying text showed blatant errors or contained gross misinformation, I would not consider it eligible for an award. Similarly, if there copies or forgeries were included without being identified as such, the exhibit would be disqualified. However, no one rule fits all.

Exhibits can cover just about any subject under the numismatic sun—the more obscure the better, this being the key to the earlier-mentioned Civil War scrip shown by Anne Bentley.

On the other hand, the commonplace can be interesting, too. I recall one exhibit showing simply some pocket change, explaining what had been found, and the grades of the various pieces. I eagerly absorbed all the details. At a show held in Portland, Oregon, a number of years ago, someone put up a case with the "history of slabs," or certified coins, showing plastic holders of various types, with different labels and imprints, made from the 1980s to date—a simple exhibit, to be sure, and one that was not of particularly great value, but it became the talk of the show.

Often, dedicated numismatists will gain ideas for new specialties by seeing what's on exhibit at a convention. One effort encourages another.

Exhibit Security and Arrangements

Generally, major conventions have exhibit areas that are under guard, and that feature flat glass-topped cases laid on tables, the cases measuring about 32 inches wide by 20 inches front to back and 2 or more inches deep. Each is fastened with a lock in the front. Security, of course, is a concern, and it is worthwhile to obtain insurance for your pieces unless the show itself provides

insurance. Your insurance company may issue a rider for your personal policy.

Although rules vary, generally exhibits are to be set up early in the first day of the show and taken down late in the last day, which will have an impact on your travel schedule, especially if the convention runs for the best part of a week, as the ANA show does. Other conventions are apt to last for just a day or two.

Were it not for the aspects of security and the need to come early and leave late, no doubt there would be many more exhibits than at present.

Display Practices and Prizes

It is an unwritten rule that items in numismatic exhibits are not assigned market values, any more than coins, paintings, or statues in a museum would bear price tags. This also has the benefit of not attracting the wrong type of person. A casual viewer from the general public, if presented with a coin bearing a $10,000 price tag, might contemplate stealing it. However, the same coin without a price tag would be recognized by a numismatist, and we all know that coin collectors are in general nice people who don't do such things!

Another unwritten rule is that the owner of the exhibit is not identified, except in instances in which a noncompetitive or institutional display is arranged.

Larger conventions such as the ANA show often have many prizes to be awarded, sometimes in special categories such as tokens, commemoratives, ancient coins, paper money, medals, or whatever. Sometimes the categories are so specialized that there might not be even a single entry, or as happens often, just one entry resulting in a rather mediocre exhibit's winning first prize. Competition or no, taking home a ribbon is always a matter of pride.

Smaller shows tend to be a bit simpler in categories and may have "best in show," then second place and third place, or something similar. Quite popular in recent years has been a ballot box for the "people's choice award"—where those seeing the exhibits can write down their favorites, the

This competitive exhibit, "The Two Faces of Liberty: A Study of Six Half-Cent Errors" earned a prize ribbon at an ANA convention. Above each coin is an enlarged photograph and an explanation of its characteristics.

This convention display of a collection of $3 gold coins is accompanied by descriptive material and, at the bottom, an illustrated time line of events during the 1854-1889 three-dollar gold coin era. Each coin is mounted in a certified holder or "slab."

Two encased postage stamps issued in 1862 by J.C. Ayer & Co., Lowell (MA) seller of patent medicines and beauty preparations, form the focal point for this show exhibit. Associated items, sometimes called "go-withs," set the theme of the products and era—including trade cards and several almanacs issued by Ayer.

Paper money issued by the First National Bank of Vanderbilt, PA, is accompanied by a photograph of the old bank building as it appeared years later, converted to an auto repair shop. Other notes from the western part of Pennsylvania are also shown together with related material.

results often being quite different from what the judges decide.

If you are considering making an exhibit, give the idea a try. Start with one or two cases—something small—perhaps at a local coin club meeting or regional show. Then finesse it and go to something larger. In today's computer age it is possible to download images from history to accompany whatever you want to exhibit. I have exhibited quite a few times over the years and have always enjoyed it. You will also.

Suggestions by Walter Breen

For good measure, here is what Walter Breen said on the subject, under title of "Forming an Effective Exhibit," in May 1958. This was before the era of personal computers and advances in graphics, but many of the points are still relevant:

> Most would-be exhibitors are (or should become) familiar with the ANA point-value criteria for awarding prizes, so I won't go into them here. What follows goes beyond that. In preparing his assembly, the exhibitor ought always to remember that both the judges and the viewing public appreciate unusual and aesthetically pleasing arrangements of material together with legible explanatory notes. The eye becomes fatigued with crowded rows and columns of unlabeled or scantily labeled coins of series unfamiliar or commonplace. Handwritten material is frequently almost unreadable by viewers who aren't used to the exhibitor's script—or when the lighting is none too adequate, a frequent complaint. Elite typewritten work is not too good, particularly if it is single spaced. Material clipped or copied from the *Guide Book* is not worth the effort; be original! IBM typewritten, or outsize (1/4 inch or more) lettering, or the like, will be far better for display purposes than is ordinary typing. White on black background is particularly eye-catching. Different backgrounds for gold, silver

> and bronze coins would help too. Paper money, whether in cases or on easels, becomes dull if merely exhibited with Friedberg numbers and no explanations. Give it some historical dressing up. One of the best such displays I have seen showed original vignettes and Proofs side by side with the finished notes.

> If you must exhibit commemoratives, find some "gimmick" to induce the viewer to stay more than a few seconds at your case. One particularly effective device of this kind was an enlarged map; others might include old engravings of the people and scenes depicted or memorialized. Proof sets, regardless of arrangement or holders used, have a certain sameness about them; the only exhibitors who have broken through this barrier to interest have been Harry Boosel and John Pittman, the former with his trial pieces in other metals, the latter with his pre-1858 coins.

> Colonial coppers, even in choice condition, would greatly benefit from special lighting. I recall one particularly impressive display whose owner had the good sense to attach a universal-joint lamp to the case so that the viewer could illuminate each coin in turn; this idea deserves wider circulation.

> Exhibits dressed up with appropriate photographic enlargements, etchings, drawings, related non-numismatic articles, etc., are also attention-getting. A display of Washington medals, for instance, might include the old engraved portraits copied by the designers of the medals, as in the Paul Magriel exhibit some years back. Obsolete paper money might be accompanied with one of those banknote engraving firms' specimen sheets illustrating the various vignettes; Confederate currency, with old portraits (and biographical sketches) of the Southern statesmen whose faces were shown on the notes.

Pioneer gold might well be shown beside old San Francisco directories which included advertisements by the firms who made the coins....

"Collecting Collectors"
Numismatists of Generations Past

Another way to enjoy numismatics is to read about collectors, dealers, and others of the past. "Collecting collectors" can be a fascinating pursuit—and one that costs very little.

Sometimes this can be done in conjunction with acquiring coins. In 1982, assisted by Dr. Richard A. ("Rick") Bagg, I had the opportunity to describe and list in a special fixed-price catalog the collection of 1794-dated large copper cents formed over a long period of time by John W. Adams. To him, a cent was all the more interesting if he knew its provenance—sometimes dating back a century or more, through a string of former owners and dealers. For each, he sought a biography. In the catalog, each coin was illustrated, provided with details, and priced, accompanied by a biographical sketch of every collector known to have owned it in the past.

In the Eliasberg Collection Sale, 1996, Lot 510, a lovely and rare 1799 copper coin known as the Abbey Cent was accompanied by a provenance listing of about two dozen former owners! The roster, compiled by John J. Ford, Jr., and later added and corrected by Del Bland, began:

1. Purchased by a dealer named Rogers (Fulton St., N.Y.) from a yokel for $2.
2. Sold by said dealer circa 1844–46 to Lorenzo H. Abbey for $25.
3. Abbey Collection, 1856, private sale.

It might be great fun to explore the names on the entire list and learn as much about them as possible. Later catalogers and owners of the coin included W. Elliot Woodward (one of the most important figures in numismatics from the 1860s to the early 1890s, although no extensive biography has ever been written about him), Joseph J. Mickley (another numismatist of legendary renown), Edward Betts, the Chapman brothers, B. Max Mehl, and many more.

The biography of Abbey himself beckons. Here is what Emmanuel J. Attinelli said about him in *Numisgraphics* (1876) in connection with the auction sale of his coins on September 8, 1863, by Henry H. Leeds & Co., New York City:

This was a coin sale, succeeding one of furniture, etc. The owner of the coins was the gentleman whose name is perpetuated in the celebrated "Abbey Cent" of 1799, which, notwithstanding so many years have elapsed, since it was brought to the notice of the numismatic public, still maintains its position as one of the finest known.

Mr. Abbey is a native of this state [New York], having been born in Herkimer County, on the 14th of January, 1823. He has long been a resident of the city, carrying on an extensive business in needles, fishing-hooks, and tackle. His introduction to numismatology occurred through the following incident:

Mr. John Martense, a friend of his and a numismatist, having a duplicate Uncirculated cent of 1826, presented it to Mr. Abbey, stating that it was worth about $5. Being somewhat incredulous, he took it to Mr. [Augustus B.] Sage, who at once offered Mr. Abbey $7 for the cent.

Somewhat astonished by finding fine coins to have such a value, he at once applied himself in diligent search for others, and with some considerable success. The very next day he procured from a grocer's till the rare "large head" Nova Eborac. The 1799 cent above alluded to, he bought for $25 from Mr. Rogers in Fulton St., who had bought it from a countryman for $2. Among other pieces he

William Sumner Appleton, Numismatist

William Sumner Appleton was one of the most prominent collectors of the past. Today, his legacy can be "collected" in a way: various coins he once owned occasionally reappear on the market.

Born in Boston on January 11, 1840, Appleton began collecting coins as a youth. He was sufficiently advanced in his interest to join such veteran collectors such as Winslow Lewis, William Eliot Lamb, and George Williams Pratt in the formation of the Boston Numismatic Society on March 3, 1860. That same year, Appleton graduated from Harvard College, but he never engaged in business or a profession. His family was well to do, which permitted him the leisure of engaging in his hobbies on a full-time basis. He studied coins intently, and soon was recognized as one of America's most knowledgeable authorities.

At the October 4, 1866, meeting of the Boston Numismatic Society he reported on his recent trip to Europe, noting that in London he bought a 1793 Wreath cent in "perfectly brilliant condition," a silver Voltaire medal of Washington, and a bronze medal of Washington with "an old and ugly head, but an exquisite reverse."

In 1867, Appleton scored a coup by buying *en bloc* from dealer W. E. Woodward the collection of American gold coins assembled by Joseph J. Mickley, prompting mention in the *American Journal of Numismatics*. Most of the rest of Mickley's coins were auctioned by Woodward, including an 1804 silver dollar, which Appleton snapped up amid great bidding interest.

Ever the traveler, on September 14, 1871, Appleton, then in Interlaken, Switzerland, wrote a letter to the Boston Numismatic Society stating that in a London sale he had obtained United States half dollars of 1796 and 1797, a Washington half dollar in copper, a British Settlement in Kentucky token with a Copper Company of Upper Canada reverse, and other delicacies. In 1873, *Description of Medals of Washington in the Collection of W.S. Appleton, Secretary of the Boston Numismatic Society*, was published, to add to the knowledge in print. In 1875–1876 he published a checklist of known dates of United States coins that had been minted. The survey did not include mintmarks, which were not widely noted at the time. However, after completing the series, in July 1876 he published a list of New Orleans issues known to him, quite possibly the first such checklist ever to reach print. It was not completely accurate (for example, it listed an 1861-O silver dollar, a variety never confirmed elsewhere).

William Sumner Appleton died on April 27, 1903, following a long illness. Most of his American numismatic cabinet went to the Massachusetts Historical Society in 1905, although some items were auctioned by Charles Steigerwalt and in two sales held by Thomas L. Elder (the first featuring numismatic literature and the second, world coins). In 1970, the Massachusetts Historical Society consigned many of Appleton's United States coins, including the 1804 dollar, to Stack's. Since that time coins with this illustrious pedigree have reappeared now and then.

Appleton collected many rarities over the years,
including one of the 15 known 1804 silver dollars.

I've been associated with him since 1972, in the sale of the Armand Champa Collection of U.S. pattern coins and rarities.

Since that time, in a span of more than three decades, he has worked with more than 10,000 consignors with more than $500 million in coins who have selected my auction firms to sell their collections. That includes the majority of the greatest and most valuable and famous collections ever to cross the auction block: Garrett, Norweb, Eliasberg, Bass, and others, including, in recent times, the Koshkarian, Jung, Jewell, Logies, and other important holdings. In fact, Rick has probably handled (processed) more coins and negotiated with more consignors than any other auction director in the business today.

I also asked John Pack, who works as a team with Rick, to share his thoughts. I requested to both of them that they do this from a seller's point of view.

Here are the steps they recommend for someone with desirable numismatic properties to sell, to which I have added my own thoughts.

Dr. Richard A. ("Rick") Bagg, shown here in the back row of a recent auction sale, has worked with collectors, dealers, museums, and institutions for decades, and in the process has participated in the sale of some of the finest collections and rarities in numismatics.

Reputation Is Most Important

Reputation is not only important, it is absolutely vital. Go with the acknowledged auction leaders and the numismatists whose names you recognize. Watch the news in the numismatic trade publications such as *Coin World* or *Numismatic News* and read about the firms you are thinking of calling who will sell your collection. Examine their sale results. See how the press treats their auctions. Are the results extraordinary? Is the firm in the news for reasons other than auctioning coins? Do the staff numismatists discover new coin varieties? Do they write scholarly articles for various trade publications?

Look at the auction-house advertisements very carefully. Is the firm promoting itself, or the collections? An auction's reputation is partly based on the number of sophisticated numismatists' collections that have gone through it. Make sure the firm is not trying to build a reputation at your expense.

Investigate the auction house to learn which ones photograph, market, and provide the most informative and authoritative descriptions about collections to collectors, investors, dealers and institutions. The efforts on the part of the auction firm to properly market your collection will increase your bottom line and theirs. Auctions are the perfect sales vehicle to properly sell your important coins. Both parties benefit, since the auction house works on a commission basis. Choose an auction house that you want to have on your side.

Read letters of recommendation about past results. These letters are often very thought provoking. Ask your favorite dealer, or speak to other collectors at your local coin club or conventions about what they have done when selling their coins. This is very vital information that will reveal the thoughts of others, many of whom have had auction consignment experience. Now you are almost ready to make your call to an auction firm.

Plan Your Conversation

Ask yourself some questions first. Is sale-by-auction the route you have determined, or are you just mulling the possibility? Is your collection memorable? Do you want your name on the catalog? Do you have duplicates that you want marketed? Are you liquidating as an investor? Are you switching coin series? Are you upgrading pieces from your collection? Have your coins been inherited? Are your coins certified, or raw? Are there things you would like the auction house to do for you, such as create specialized advertisements or hard-bound catalogs, or take you on a trip to the auction site?

State your purpose in calling the auction house. Ask to speak to someone authoritative, a person in charge of consignments or a principal of the company. Yours is not a casual inquiry! Ask the auction house lots of questions.

Explain your collection briefly, but with much information. Discuss your collecting theme, approximate value of the collection, number of pieces, time frame you desire for the sale, and so on. Do you want to contribute to the catalog as it is being created, or do you want the auction house staff to do it completely?

If you inherited the collection, gather as much information as you can locate. Look for inventories and invoices and have a few examples of coins that look interesting in front of you before you make your call. It will be expected that you might not be able to converse in numismatic jargon.

After you obtain general answers to your questions, ask about the terms of sale. One of the most common inquiries is, "What is the commission rate?"

This is an important question, but is one that cannot be answered until more information is at hand. If your consignment is a mint-sealed bag of 1,000 1885-CC silver dollars, is valuable, and does not require much effort to catalog, the rate is apt to be nominal. On the other hand, if it is a collection of 1785 to 1788 Connecticut copper coins by die variety, and it is desired that each one be attributed, a discussion of the rarity and characteristics of each be included, and that there be a numismatic preface and history, the rate will be significantly higher.

Also important is how the collection is to be presented. If you are bottom-fishing for the lowest possible rate, and if you shop around various auction houses, you will find the lowest rate but, quite possibly, the poorest-quality catalog and the worst results.

When asking about rates, first say what you expect or hope to receive, and discuss the coins in your collection. In that way the auctioneer can quote a rate that will fill your needs. Come to think of it, how could a lawyer, doctor, or any other professional quote a rate before he or she heard your story?

Inquire about the schedule of the auction house. Does the auction happen around an important coin convention? What times during the day are the coins sold? Request a sample catalog and auction consignment contract and study the auction house's Internet site carefully.

Details Are Important

How are the coins to be transported to the auction house? Does the company provide adequate insurance? Ask for evidence. Are your coins secured throughout the whole transaction, that is, until you are paid? Will the auction payment be timely? Is the contract clear and easy to understand? Ask the auction house if you have left out an important question that you should have the answer to. Questions are best asked first.

Examine the Catalog

Do their catalogs have sharp and beautiful photos? Does the firm win awards for their catalogs? Are the descriptions educational, interesting, and compelling to prospective buyers, or are they mostly filled with population reports and figures easily obtained elsewhere (what we like to call "empty descriptions," although they can occupy paragraphs of space!).

Does the catalog offer large *quantities*, including many multiples, of less impor-

Armand, who was quite up to date on the coin market, felt that, somehow, these great offers were not so great, so he consigned the coins to my partner at that time (Jim Ruddy) and me. We cataloged his coins and offered them for sale. He was so delighted that afterward on his own volition he took out advertisements in the leading coin magazines to say what a good job we had done, and that his collection had brought nearly double the highest "great offer" he had received privately.

On the other hand, it can be advantageous to try to place rare items privately. Recently I purchased a specialized collection as a single lot in an auction, paying a record price for it. After I owned it for a while, the novelty passed and I decided to let it go. If I reconsigned it to the auction house, I would probably lose money. As the collection was a fine one, I placed it in the hands of a dealer-specialist to see if it could be sold privately, offering to split any profit with him.

Sometimes a rarity that has been offered several times at auction, but has not found a buyer, is best sold privately. Another beneficial circumstance develops if a private buyer is willing to pay a generous price, and you have done some research to be sure that it is not worth far more. However, while I have witnessed many dealers' setting record prices in the auction room, it is only occasionally that anyone will set a record price in a private transaction.

All dealers I have ever met are in business to earn a profit, and in most instances, the profit spread on direct sales is higher than the commission at auction.

The Internet

Selling through an Internet auction can be fun if you have the time to do it. Quite a few collectors have used such sales as an effective way to sell lower-value items, including tokens, medals, error coins, and more. It is not particularly effective for important rarities, simply because many of the people who have the most money to spend—professionals in their 50s and 60s—are not Internet users and will miss the offerings.

There are a lot of shenanigans going on on the Internet, including fake offerings and nonexistent bidders. Some time ago, a leading dealer in paper money decided to devise multiple "identities" on eBay, creating people who ostensibly were bidding against each other, including one that had "qdb" in the bidder name and another whose name suggested a Wolfeboro, New Hampshire, origin. After being asked why I was bidding record prices for currency specialties I was not known to collect, I expressed surprise. A staff member contacted eBay, the identity of the perpetrator was learned, and the false identities and sham sales were ended (I presume).

In another instance (in October 2004) I started bidding on a rare $1 note, at about $400, went up to close to $1,000, then dropped out, but then other bidders carried it far past there. Perhaps it was a surprise when I stopped participating. In any event, the eBay seller contacted me and said that the other bidders had not been "qualified," and that the item was once again available, and did I want it for a lower price?

Internet facilitators such as eBay have their own sets of rules, and these should be checked. My advice would be to insist on full, guaranteed payment before you deliver anything to anyone, unless the individual has impeccable *numismatic* credentials.

Many numismatic firms have regular auctions on the Internet, and these can be an effective way to sell for a cheap commission rate. However, some well-financed buyers may not be in the offing, for reasons given above.

POSTSCRIPT—
ACTUALLY,
TWO OF THEM

How're you gonna keep them down on the farm after they've seen Paree?

—Popular song. Lyrics by Sam M. Lewis and Joe Young,
music by Walter Donaldson, 1919

Perhaps, after reading this book, you will have "seen Paree," and will no longer remain down on the farm of ordinary collecting. The vistas are exciting and many, and it is my hope that in the preceding pages your interest has been piqued to investigate a bit further.

As it is the commendation of a good Huntsman to find game in a wide wood, so it is no imputation if he hath not caught all, and likewise to me, some things are to be left to the inquisitive diligence of others.

—William Camden, 1610

Numismatics is indeed a "wide wood," and no collector or dealer has ever captured all of the game in it. The lure of the unknown, the undiscovered, beckons and provides one of the great lures of what many have called the world's greatest hobby.

Enjoy.

The author in 1960, by which time he had been a dealer for all of seven years.

Notes

Chapter 1

1. Much of the rest of the 1975 talk is given in chapter 7, "In the Words of Louis E. Eliasberg, Sr.," of my 1996 book, *Louis E. Eliasberg, Sr., King of Coins*. The "King of Coins" book title was taken from a comment in a large, full-color spread, "Gems From the Greatest Collection of U.S. Coins," in *Life* magazine, April 27, 1953.
2. The stock market versus the coin market was the subject of several of my "Joys of Collecting" columns in *Coin World*, autumn 1998.
3. *Wall Street Journal*, March 7, 2005, p. C1.
4. Russell Rulau, *Standard Catalog of United States Tokens, 1700–1900*, 4th edition, 2004, p. 172. Of course, this is hypothetical, and an infusion into the market all at once might cause the price per unit to drop. On the other hand, in many instances the availability of hoard coins has caused prices to *rise*, as it did in the 1962 to 1964 Treasury distribution of silver dollars.
5. "Under the Glass," *Numismatic News*, August 17, 2004.
6. Here slightly edited by the author, also drawing on David L. Ganz, "Under the Glass," *Numismatic News*, August 17, 2004, to clarify grading and certain nomenclature.

Chapter 2

7. From the Argus, published in Boston on March 26, 1793, quoting an account from Newark, New Jersey. Reprinted in *Historical Magazine*, February 1859.

Chapter 3

8. *Coin World*, "Numbers Confirm Coin Hobby Core," November 18, 2002.
9. Citation suggested by John Kraljevich.
10. Issue of December 14, 2004.

Chapter 4

11. November 15, 2004, p. 3: "'Penny Frenzy' attracts children to art institute; kids fill coin boards from 45,000 cents."
12. Anthony Swiatek, "How Can a $40,000 Slabbed Coin Lose Four of Its Zeroes and Become a $4 Coin?" *Commemorative Trail*, 2004, Vol. 22, No. 2, p. 19.
13. *Coin Values*, March 7, 2005.
14. *The Numismatist*, April 1914.

Chapter 5

15. Price illustrations for coins in this chapter are mostly from *A Guide Book of United States Coins*, 59th edition. Prices for other items are mostly the author's estimates as of 2005.
16. Provenance adapted from Bowers, *The Rare Silver Dollars Dated 1804* (1999, with a 2004 correction furnished by P. Scott Rubin). More details concerning this specimen can be found in that text.
17. Newman and Bressett, *The Fantastic 1804 Dollar*, p. 130.
18. See communication between Scirpo and Bowers, 1999.

Chapter 6

19. Example suggested by Kenneth E. Bressett.
20. Certain information is from Sheridan Downey, P. Scott Rubin, and the late Stewart Witham, provided to the author in connection with describing this same coin as Lot 1735 in the Louis E. Eliasberg, Sr., Collection, 1997.
21. Letter to the author, April 3, 1992.
22. Studied in March 2005. ANACS does not include any grades below MS-60; accordingly, populations for VG-8 to AU-58 are for NGC and PCGS only.
23. As adapted from my 1993 study, *Silver Dollars and Trade Dollars of the United States: A Complete Encyclopedia*, plus new information. These estimates have been used by numismatists for more than a decade now, and to date no one has questioned them.

Chapter 7

24. Sheldon's coin thefts, as well as misrepresentations and pseudo-science in his widely publicized and (at one time) much admired medical research (the subject of an exposé by the Sunday *New York Times Magazine*) came to light after his 1977 death. Through diligent effort, many of the ANS coins were recovered in the 1990s.
25. *Coin World*, February 28, 2005: "Editorial Opinion—Fakes Online Auction Site Problem," by Beth Deisher.
26. Here slightly edited and adapted. Selected illustrations are from Littleton Coin Company and are not from the ANA book.

27. "Sight unseen" is an oxymoron if there ever was one! Wynn Bowers suggests that it is derived or (mal)adapted from "site unseen" a description of real estate at a distant location.
28. Advertisement in the *The Numismatist*, April 1986.
29. Advertisement in the *The Numismatist*, March 1988.
30. I was a stockholder in the short-lived Hallmark, but was not involved in its management or operations.
31. An excerpt from "Coin Values," *Coin World*, July 19, 2004.

Chapter 8
32. *Certified Coin Dealer Newsletter*, standard caveat. Emphasis mine.
33. Some account of this is in JJF correspondence quoted by George F. Kolbe in his Ford Library Sale II, 2005.
34. Adapted from Clair M. Birdsall, *The United States Branch Mint at Dahlonega, Georgia*, Table VI, from R.W. Julian's research in the National Archives.
35. Communication, JK to QDB, October 11, 2004.
36. Issue of August 27, 2004.

Chapter 9
37. *Banker's Magazine*, September 1847, text adapted from the *Westminster Review*, July 1847. Subtitles added.

Chapter 10
38. His biography is detailed in *The Eagle That Is Forgotten: Pierre Eugène Du Simitière, Founding Father of American Numismatics*, by Joel J. Orosz, 1988. Certain information about early collectors is adapted from my book, *American Numismatics Before the Civil War, 1760–1860*, published in 1998.
39. Orosz, pp. 64–65, adapted from correspondence between Dr. Orosz and Eric P. Newman, and mention of Eliot in Newman's *The Secret of the Good Samaritan Shilling*, American Numismatic Society, 1959.
40. Bentley's diary entries were quoted in *The Numismatist*, January 1907 and June 1945.
41. Other related terms used in the early days to describe spurious copper coins include *brummagem* and *bungtowns*.
42. Judge James Winthrop (1752–1821).
43. *American Journal of Numismatics*, April 1874.

44. George Parish, Jr., *American Journal of Numismatics*, August 1866; also, Attinelli, *Numisgraphics*, 1876, pp. 5, 85. In 1876, when he compiled his work, this was the earliest American coin sale Attinelli could find.
45. Per a comment from Edward D. Cogan in the *American Journal of Numismatics*, March 1868. Cogan had no firsthand knowledge of the activities of the Mint in the 1820s and 1830s, for he did not become involved in numismatics until the late 1850s.
46. *Norton's Literary Letter* No. 3, 1859, p. 67. Mease, a prominent Philadelphian and member of the Academy of Natural Sciences, prepared a catalog of Peale's Philadelphia Museum and was an acquaintance of naturalist John James Audubon, introducing him to scientists in the city at the start of the latter's career. Joshua Francis Fisher (1808–1873) was from Philadelphia, not Baltimore.
47. No doubt Mexican dollars, for U.S. dollars had not been coined since 1804 and were not in general circulation at the time.
48. Alpheus Felch, "Early Banks and Banking in Michigan," 1878.

Chapter 11
49. Excerpt from *The Bankers' Magazine and Statistical Register*, August 1857, from *The Philadelphia Bulletin*.
50. The $285 figure is from R.W. Julian (letter, December 27, 1998); another source states $290. No doubt, exchange rates varied from city to city and from broker to broker.

Chapter 14
51. Based upon a commentary sent by Kenneth Bressett after a reading of the draft of this chapter.
52. Comment to the author, April 7, 2005.

Chapter 16
53. Prices from the 58th edition of *A Guide Book of U.S. Coins*, except for the Proof-65 1895, not listed at that level, and here taken from *Coin Values*, published by *Coin World*, September 6, 2004.
54. *Penny Whimsy* is the revised version of *Early American Cents*, 1949. The quotation appears on pages 6 and 7.

Chapter 17
55. From *Coin Values*, published by *Coin World*, September 6, 2004.
56. Issue of March 7, 2005.

Chapter 18
57. February 25, 2005.
58. "Bid" price for MS-67; no "market" price listed for PCGS.
59. "Bid" price for MS-67; no "market" price listed for PCGS.
60. "Bid" price for MS-67; no "market" price listed for NGC.
61. "Bid" price for MS-67; no "market" price listed for PCGS.
62. "Bid" price for MS-67; no "market" price listed for NGC.
63. Breen, p. 361.
64. March 7, 2005.

Chapter 19
65. Courtesy of an American Numismatic Rarities catalog, 2004, here slightly adapted. I've written about the scenario often enough, and it is a pleasure to share the words of someone else.

Chapter 20
66. April 1908 commentary discussing Proofs of the preceding year.
67. *Walter Breen's Encyclopedia of U.S. and Colonial Proof Coins, 1722–1977*, p. 182.

Chapter 21
68. In the 1950s, when I first studied colonial and state coins, I had an active correspondence with Eric P. Newman, Kenneth E. Bressett, and Walter Breen. All four of us found Machin's Mills to be incredibly interesting. Today, I still feel the same.

Chapter 23
69. Certain text under this heading is from, or adapted from, a piece I did for the *Coin Dealer Newsletter* in 2003, in response to an invitation to share my ideas with readers of that weekly periodical.
70. Saul Teichman's estimate of the time of striking; communication to the author, October 15, 2004.
71. Certain ideas were supplied by Robert L. Hughes in 2003.

Chapter 24
72. Many of my comments on territorial gold coins for the Eliasberg sale catalogs of 1996 and 1997 are used in this chapter, as are notes compiled for possible future use by Kenneth E. Bressett in the *Guide Book*.

73. "A Gnawing Mystery," by George Fuld (*Coin World*, December 2, 1996), noted that at least one gold restrike has been made of the $10, and that at one time certain of the dies could not be accounted for, but were later found.

Chapter 25
74. Comment to the author, April 21, 2005, after reading a draft copy of this chapter.
75. Used by permission of Russell Rulau, Krause Publications. Adapted.
76. Communication to the author, October 13, 2004.

Chapter 26
77. Quoted by Betts and credited to Joseph Addison (1762–1719), "Dialogues on Medals."
78. Bowers, *American Coin Treasures and Hoards*, 1996, chapter 1, gives an expanded account.
79. Letter, April 21, 2005.
80. William John Potts, "Du Simitière, Artist, Antiquary and Naturalist" (*Pennsylvania Magazine for History*, October 1889, p. 375, cited by Adams, 1992). His life is the subject of Dr. Joel J. Orosz's 1988 book, *The Eagle That Is Forgotten*.

Katherine Jaeger (letter, April 21, 2005) commented about the obverse motif: "This image is derived from the State Seal of Virginia, approved at Virginia's 1776 Constitutional Convention. The design is attributed to George Wythe. The seal bears the motto 'Sic Semper Tyrannis.' After the state seceded from the Union in the eve of the Civil War, George H. Lovett cut a new seal for the state, as it was desired to alter slightly the position of the crown falling off of the tyrant's head."
81. Original footnote in Howay's text: "John Henry Cox found some of these medals at Hawaii in September 1789, and gave a description of them; see George Mortimer, *Observations and Remarks Made during a Voyage in the Brig Mercury* (Dublin, 1791), p. 88. Martinez reports in his ms. diary, under date May 8, 1789, that two of them were found that day on his vessel. A reproduction of the medal will be found in this volume."
82. Howay, p. 162, from pp. 2 and 3 of Hoskins's journal; here edited for punctuation.

83. James Ross Snowden, *The Medallic Memorials of Washington*, page v (part of an account of how the Washington Cabinet was formed).

84. Julian, p. 114.

Chapter 27

85. Much of the content of this chapter is new, but certain commentaries and observations have been drawn from my articles in *Paper Money*, my work with the currency of Harry W. Bass, Jr., and data collected as part of an ongoing research project on currency with David M. Sundman.

86. The following organizations and publications cover all areas of paper money collecting, from colonial to federal issues. The Society of Paper Money Collectors comprises several thousand members. Its publication, *Paper Money*, furnishes a useful key to research, discoveries, history, and general appreciation of the title subject. The monthly *Bank Note Reporter* features coverage of current events, auctions, and more. The Professional Currency Dealers of America (PCDA) group includes specialists in the commercial end of the field.

87. The first book on American numismatics ever printed in this country is *An Historical Account of Massachusetts Currency*, by Joseph B. Felt, 1839. Remarkably, nearly all of the information on bills and coins is still relevant. Today, Massachusetts offers several marvelous archives for scholars and devotees of early paper money, including the Massachusetts Historical Society (Boston) and the American Antiquarian Society (Springfield).

88. *Colonial Currency Reprints*, vol. 1, p. 27.

Chapter 28

89. *A History of Banking*, Bradford Rhodes & Company, New York, 1909. Essays and comments by Knox (1828–1891) published posthumously. Knox joined the American Numismatic and Archaeological Society on November 8, 1879.

90. Excerpt from an account furnished by Katherine Jaeger. Popular histories and Internet sources can be consulted for more about the "Manhattan Well Murder," the first case in the city to be spread extensively across newspapers—prompting publishers to realize that such accounts are exciting to readers.

91. Obvious errors in spelling in the original have been corrected here. States are listed here in alphabetical order for easy reference; in the original they were in random order.

92. As quoted in William H. Dillistin, *Bank Note Reporters and Counterfeit Detectors 1826–1866*, 1949.

93. Citation provided by Richard Winslow III.

94. Communication to the author, October 19, 2004.

Chapter 29

95. *The Standard Catalog of United States Obsolete Bank Notes 1782–1866*, by James A. Haxby, 1988, includes listings of these.

96. Neil Carothers, *Fractional Money*, 1930, pp. 177–178.

Chapter 30

97. Certain historical commentary and information relating to monetary conditions during the Civil War are adapted from my writing in connection with the treasure ship *S.S. Brother Jonathan* (lost at sea in 1865) and from my work with paper money in the description and sale of items from the Harry W. Bass, Jr., collection. Thomas M. Denly furnished market information relating to Confederate paper, and Amanda Sheheen added comments.

98. "Price of Gold for Confederate Currency During the War," *The Numismatist*, September 1917.

99. Grover C. Criswell, *Comprehensive Catalog of Confederate Paper Money*, 1996, p. 38.

100. Communication to the author, October 15, 2004.

Chapter 31

101. Communication to the author, March 28, 2005.

102. Charles Davis, Henry Chapman, and Numismatic and Antiquarian Society of Philadelphia sale, March 22, 1997.

103. Letter, September 29, 2004.

Chapter 32

104. In 1970 I wrote about this subject for James F. Ruddy's *Photograde* book, including some of the concepts I mention here. Consult *Photograde* for an expanded view.

Chapter 33

105. Attinelli, *Numisgraphics*, 1876, p. 30.

Index